WEST'S LAW SCHOOL ADVISORY BOARD

SECURITIES LITIGATION AND ENFORCEMENT

CASES AND MATERIALS

Third Edition

■ ■ ■

By

Donna M. Nagy
C. Ben Dutton Professor of Law
Indiana University Maurer School of Law

Richard W. Painter
C. Walter Richey Professor of Corporate Law
University of Minnesota Law School

Margaret V. Sachs
Robert Cotten Alston Professor of Law
University of Georgia School of Law

AMERICAN CASEBOOK SERIES®

WEST®
A Thomson Reuters business

Mat #41186344

610 Opperman Drive
St. Paul, MN 55123
1–800–313–9378

Printed in the United States of America

ISBN: 978–0–314–27781–7

To Brian and Caitlin
D.M.N.

To William H. Painter
R.W.P.

To the memory of my mother and father
M.V.S.

Preface

This casebook fills a gap in currently available materials for securities law courses: the absence of materials designed specifically to acquaint students with the theoretical as well as practical aspects of federal securities litigation and enforcement. Important actions and issues are presented in the clusters in which they arise in actual securities litigation, thereby maximizing student preparedness to represent clients in private litigation, in enforcement actions by the Securities and Exchange Commission, and in criminal prosecutions. Even before the corporate governance and accounting scandals at Enron, WorldCom and numerous other companies, the need for such a casebook was great. But the scandals – and their fallout – have generated considerably more student interest in securities litigation and enforcement, in part because students (rightly) recognize its growing importance as an area of practice. Student interest has been piqued still further by the subsequent round of scandals culminating in the mortgage meltdown, the Lehman Brothers bankruptcy, and the financial crisis of 2008.

The third edition incorporates developments since 2007. These developments include, in addition to the 2008 financial crisis, the massive Ponzi scheme perpetrated by Bernard Madoff, the Dodd-Frank Wall Street Reform and Consumer Protection Act of 2010, and a number of major Supreme Court decisions. Two of these decisions in particular have literally transformed the legal landscape – *Janus Capital Group, Inc. v. First Derivative Traders* and *Morrison v. National Australia Bank, Ltd.* We enjoy the intellectual challenges that such developments provide and hope that your students do, too.

We have designed this casebook for use in a variety of two or three credit courses or seminars. These include (i) a "securities litigation" course examining litigation topics under the Securities Exchange Act (e.g., Rule 10b-5, proxy fraud, tender offer fraud, class actions, and international securities fraud) as well as Securities Act liability for material misstatements and omissions, and securities arbitration; (ii) a course in "securities litigation and enforcement" that covers some of the just-mentioned topics but also encompasses SEC enforcement issues (including the conduct of SEC investigations and the professional responsibilities of lawyers and accountants), insider trading, market manipulation, and criminal enforcement; or (iii) more specialized courses or seminars that focus on such areas as enforcement, insider trading, or market manipulation, or that build around the theme of "current topics in securities litigation."

A course or seminar in securities litigation and enforcement need not come after a course in securities regulation. We do not presuppose familiarity with the contents of the securities regulation course, and students who have not taken that course are at no disadvantage. But in order to challenge and stimulate more experienced students, we have included materials and problems that allow such students to explore doctrinal nuances and practical issues that they are unlikely to have encountered previously.

We have edited most of the cases and materials to keep each chapter a manageable length. Asterisks (***) indicate substantive omissions, but citations, footnotes, and concurring and dissenting opinions may have also been omitted without a specific notation that such an omission has been made. Footnotes included in cases and materials retain their number from the original source.

Throughout our work on this casebook, we have been encouraged and informed by our many friends and colleagues in law schools and in the practicing bar. We hope that they—as well as others who use our casebook—will share their comments and suggestions for future editions.

DONNA M. NAGY
RICHARD W. PAINTER
MARGARET V. SACHS

October, 2011

Acknowledgments

Donna M. Nagy wishes to express thanks and appreciation to the many individuals who have contributed to this casebook. Dean Lauren Robel and faculty, staff, and students at Indiana University Maurer School of Law provided substantial encouragement and support during the preparation of the third and second editions. Dean Emeritus Joseph P. Tomain and faculty, staff, and students at the University of Cincinnati College of Law supported and encouraged the work on the first edition. Dean Stephen Todd and the faculty and staff of the University of Canterbury School of Law in Christchurch, New Zealand provided a warm welcome and generous resources during a sabbatical semester. Ralph C. Ferrara and other talented securities litigators at the law firm of Debevoise & Plimpton served as excellent mentors.

Richard W. Painter is grateful to the University of Illinois and the University of Minnesota for supporting his past and future work on this casebook.

Margaret V. Sachs is very grateful for the steadfast support she received from numerous friends and colleagues in connection with this casebook, especially Alexander M. Meiklejohn, Charles R.T. O'Kelley, and Camilla E. Watson. She also appreciates very much the invaluable technological assistance of the University of Georgia School of Law Library, especially that of Anne E. Burnett, Maureen A. Cahill, and Carol A. Watson.

All three of us owe a huge debt of gratitude to Leslie Coss and Jane Decker at Indiana University Maurer School of Law and Connie Miller at the University of Cincinnati College of Law for their stellar word processing skills and dedication to this project. Many law students at the University of Georgia School of Law worked diligently on cite-checking the manuscript, and Eric Garber is deserving of special thanks for his work on the third edition.

Finally, we acknowledge with appreciation the following authors, publishers, and journals who have graciously granted permission to reprint excerpts from their publications.

ABA Section of Business Law, Committee on the Law of Cyberspace, Achieving Legal and Business Order in Cyberspace: A Report on Global Jurisdiction Issues Created by the Internet, 55 Bus. Law 1801, 1932 (2000). Copyright ©2000 by the American Bar Association. Reprinted with permission.

ABA Committee on Federal Regulation of Securities, Report of the Task Force on SEC Settlements, 47 Bus. Law. 1083, 1091-94 (1992). Copyright ©1992 by the American Bar Association. Reprinted with permission.

American Law Institute, Restatement (Second) of Torts §551(2)(a)-(e). Copyright ©1976 by the American Law Institute. Reprinted with permission. All rights reserved.

John W. Avery, Securities Litigation Reform: The Long and Winding Road to the Private Securities Litigation Reform Act of 1995, 51 Bus. Law. 335, 362 (1996). Copyright ©1996 by the American Bar Association. Reprinted with permission.

Janet Cooper Alexander, Rethinking Damages in Securities Class Actions, 48 Stan. L. Rev. 1487, 1491-93 (1996). Reprinted with permission of the Stanford Law Review.

Stephen M. Bainbridge, Insider Trading Regulation: The Path Dependent Choice Between Property Rights and Securities Fraud, 52 SMU L. Rev. 1589, 1606-08 (1999). Reprinted with permission from the SMU Law Review, the Southern Methodist University School of Law, and the author.

Dennis M. Carlton and Daniel R. Fischel, The Regulation of Insider Trading, 35 Stan. L. Rev. 857, 866-68 (1983). Reprinted with permission of the Stanford Law Review.

John C. Coffee, Jr., Reforming the Securities Class Action: An Essay on Deterrence and Its Implementation, 106 Colum. L. Rev. 1534 (2006). Reprinted with permission of the Columbia Law Review and the author.

James D. Cox, Making Securities Fraud Class Actions Virtuous, 39 Ariz. L. Rev. 497 (1997). Reprinted with permission of the Arizona Law Review and the author.

James D. Cox & Randall S. Thomas, SEC Enforcement Heuristics: An Empirical Inquiry, 53 Duke L. J. 737, 743-44 (2003). Reprinted with permission of the authors.

Jessica Erickson, Corporate Governance in the Courtroom: An Empirical Analysis, 51 Wm. & Mary L. Rev. 1749, 1754 (2010). Reprinted with permission of the William and Mary Law Review and the author.

Ralph C. Ferrara and Philip S. Khinda, SEC Enforcement Proceedings: Strategic Considerations for When the Agency Comes Calling, 51 Admin. L. Rev. 1143, 1148-1166 (1999). Copyright ©1999 by the American Bar Association. Reprinted with permission.

Financial Industry Regulatory Authority, Inc. (FINRA, Inc.), Dispute Resolution Statistics ©2011, and Arbitration Procedures ©2011. Reprinted with permission of FINRA, Inc.

Daniel R. Fischel and David J. Ross, Should the Law Prohibit "Manipulation" in Financial Markets?, 105 Harv. L. Rev. 503, 508-10 (1991). Copyright ©1991 by the Harvard Law Review Association. Reprinted with permission of the Harvard Law Review and the authors.

Jill I. Gross & Barbara Black, When Perception Changes Reality: An Empirical Study of Investors' Views of the Fairness of Securities Arbitration, 2008 J. Disp. Resol. 349 (2008). Reprinted with permission of the authors and the Journal of Dispute Resolution, University of Missouri, Center for the Study of Dispute Resolution, 206 Hulston Hall, Columbia, MO 65211.

Roberta S. Karmel, Outsider Trading on Confidential Information—A Breach in Search of A Duty, 20 Cardozo L. Rev. 83, 112-113 (1998). Reprinted with permission of the Cardozo Law Review and the author.

Henry G. Manne, In Defense of Insider Trading, Harvard Bus. Rev., Nov.-Dec., 1966 at 113-19. Reprinted with permission of Harvard Business School Publishing.

William R. McLucas, J. Lynn Taylor, Susan A. Mathews, A Practitioner's Guide to the SEC's Investigative and Enforcement Process, 70 Temple L. Rev. 53, 111-16 (1997). Reprinted with permission of the Temple Law Review and the authors.

Pace Law School Investor Rights Clinic, Investor's Guide to Securities Industry Disputes Resolving Disputes: The Arbitration Process. Reprinted with permission of Professor Jill I. Gross (on behalf of the Clinic) and FINRA, Inc.

Richard W. Painter, Kimberly D. Krawiec, Cynthia A. Williams, Don't Ask, Just Tell: Insider Trading After *United States v. O'Hagan*, 84 Va. L. Rev. 153, 211-12, 219-28 (1998). Copyright ©1998 by Virginia Law Review. Reprinted with the permission of the Virginia Law Review and the authors.

Richard M. Phillips, Glenn R. Reichardt, Michael J. Missal, and Robyn J. Lipton, SEC Investigations: The Heart of SEC Enforcement Practice in Kirkpatrick & Lockhart LLP, The Securities Enforcement Manual: Tactics and Strategies (Richard M. Phillips, ed. 1997). Copyright ©1997 by the American Bar Association. Reprinted with permission of the American Bar Association.

Kim Lane Scheppele, "It's Just Not Right:" The Ethics of Insider Trading, 56 Law & Contemp. Probs. 123, 162-63 (1993). Reprinted with permission.

Andrew M. Smith, SEC Cease-and-Desist Orders, 51 Admin. L. Rev. 1197, 1217-1225 (1999). Copyright ©1999 by the American Bar Association. Reprinted with permission.

Lynn A. Stout, Type I Error, Type II Error, and the Private Securities Litigation Reform Act, 38 Ariz. L. Rev. 711, 713-14 (1996). Copyright ©1996 by the Arizona Board of Regents. Reprinted by permission of the Arizona Board of Regents and the author.

William J. Stuntz, The Pathological Politics of Criminal Law, 100 Mich. L. Rev. 505 (Dec. 2001). Copyright ©2001 by the Michigan Law Review Association. Reprinted by permission of the Michigan Law Review and the author.

William K.S. Wang, Stock Market Insider Trading: Victims, Violators and Remedies—Including an Analogy to Fraud in the Sale of a Used Car with a Generic Defect, 45 Vill. L. Rev. 27, 28-38 (2000). Reprinted by permission of the Villanova Law Review and the author.

Summary of Contents

Table of Contents

Table of Cases

The principal cases are in bold type. Cases cited or discussed in the text are roman type. References are to pages. Cases cited in principal cases and within other quoted materials are not included.

SECURITIES LITIGATION AND ENFORCEMENT

CASES AND MATERIALS

Third Edition

Chapter 1

AN OVERVIEW OF SECURITIES LITIGATION AND ENFORCEMENT

Securities litigation and enforcement is a dynamic area of legal practice with important developments occurring on a number of fronts. Many of these developments have been fueled by the massive financial frauds at Enron, WorldCom, and other large companies that occurred as the twenty-first century dawned. These scandals prompted Congress to enact the Sarbanes-Oxley Act of 2002 (the SOX). A further round of scandals, culminating in the mortgage meltdown, the Lehman Brothers bankruptcy, and the financial crisis of 2008, precipitated Congress's enactment of the Dodd-Frank Wall Street Reform and Consumer Protection Act of 2010 (the Dodd-Frank Act).

The SOX and the Dodd-Frank Act are each multi-pronged legislation. The SOX heightened corporate disclosure obligations, enhanced federal regulation of attorneys and accountants, established new securities crimes, and lengthened the limitations period for private securities fraud actions. The Dodd-Frank Act, on the other hand, targeted the stability and risk management practices of commercial banks, investment banks, and other financial institutions as well as the mortgage and consumer lending market.

The scandals that gave rise to these two statutes have had other significant consequences as well. Thus, the Enron, Worldcom and other scandals that led to the SOX gave rise to class action settlements of unprecedented size that broke new ground by being funded partly from the pockets of individual defendants. In addition, these scandals prompted the Securities and Exchange Commission (SEC) and the Department of Justice (DOJ) to engage in intensified enforcement activity extending beyond the scandals themselves to matters such as Internet fraud, the backdating of stock options, insider trading (including at hedge funds), and international securities fraud. Moreover, the scandals that prompted the Dodd-Frank Act have likewise culminated in numerous government and private fraud actions.

Securities litigation and enforcement involve businesses and transactions of all sizes. Indeed, small—even one on one—securities transactions can (and do) precipitate complex litigation. Thus, lawyers in small firms and solo practitioners who represent family businesses or individual investors are almost as likely to become involved in securities litigation as are lawyers who represent parties to the transactions that make front page news.

Representing clients in all these situations requires familiarity with more than substantive securities law. It also requires knowledge of the relevant procedural rules as well as the strategies employed by plaintiffs (be they investors or the government) and by defendants (be they individuals or corporations). Likewise important to successful advocacy is awareness of the politics underlying recent legislation and case law developments.

This casebook is intended to provide a grounding in both the theoretical and practical aspects of securities litigation and enforcement. Throughout, the intention is to address important causes of action and issues in the clusters in which they are likely to arise in actual cases. This overview is followed by twelve additional chapters: Section 10(b) of the Exchange Act and Rule 10b-5 (Chapter 2); Securities Act Liability for Material Misstatements, Omissions, and Fraudulent Conduct (Chapter 3); Proxy Fraud (Chapter 4); Tender Offer Fraud (Chapter 5); Securities Class Actions (Chapter 6); Insider Trading (Chapter 7); Market Manipulation (Chapter 8); SEC Enforcement (Chapter 9); Enforcement Issues Involving Attorneys and Accountants (Chapter 10); Criminal Enforcement (Chapter 11); International Securities Fraud (Chapter 12); and Securities Arbitration (Chapter 13).

The present Chapter provides background and perspectives that will enhance your understanding of later chapters. After a canvass of the federal securities statutes (Section A), it examines the roles played in securities litigation and enforcement by the courts (Section B), the SEC (Section C), the DOJ (Section D), state law (Section E), and social and economic forces (Section F). Section G presents the efficient capital markets hypothesis, an economic theory underlying many of the important case law and legislative developments appearing throughout the casebook. Section H concludes with some themes and questions to keep in mind in connection with the chapters that follow.

A. THE FEDERAL SECURITIES STATUTES

The principal federal securities statutes are the Securities Act of 1933 (the Securities Act) and the Securities Exchange Act of 1934 (the Exchange Act). These two statutes were among the first laws enacted by an overwhelmingly Democratic Congress after President Franklin D. Roosevelt took office. The statutes responded to public outrage at widespread failures in American financial markets. Indeed, by 1932, the stock market had lost almost 90% of the value that it had prior to the "Great Crash" of 1929. Many Americans lost their life savings that they had either invested in stocks or placed in deposits with uninsured banks that collapsed when the market did.

The necessity of federal regulation seemed apparent given the inadequacy of state securities statutes, the so-called "blue sky" laws enacted in the early 1900s to protect investors from promoters selling stock worth only "so many feet of blue sky." *Hall v. Geiger-Jones Co.*, 242 U.S. 539, 550 (1917). State regulators had done little to halt manipulation of stock prices or other deceptive practices that had run rampant prior to the Crash, despite the fact that much of the malfeasance violated blue sky laws as well as state criminal fraud statutes.

Many of the statutory provisions that you will encounter in this casebook were part of the Securities Act and the Exchange Act as originally enacted (although some were added later). You will understand these provisions better if you bear in mind the unique historical situation from which they sprang.

In addition to the Securities Act and the Exchange Act, Congress enacted a number of specialized securities statutes during the 1930s that target specific abuses in the securities markets: the Public Utility Holding Company Act of 1935 (directed at complex and often fraudulent holding company structures used by public utility companies, but repealed by Congress in 2005), the Trust Indenture Act of 1939 (regulation of the contracts between issuers of debt securities and the bank trustees retained to enforce those contracts on behalf of investors, as well as of the conflicts of interest that arise in this situation), the Investment Company Act of 1940 (regulation of mutual funds and other companies with assets consisting primarily of securities of other issuers), and the Investment Advisers Act of 1940 (regulation of conflicts of interest and other problems affecting investment advisers). For a variety of views concerning the federal securities legislation enacted in the 1930s, see Joel Seligman, The Transformation of Wall Street (3d ed. 2003); William O. Douglas, Protecting the Investor, 23 Yale Rev. 521 (1934); James M. Landis, The Legislative History of the Securities Act of 1933, 28 Geo. Wash. L. Rev. 29 (1959); Paul G. Mahoney, The Stock Pools and the Securities Exchange Act, 5 J. Fin. Econ. 343 (1999); A.C. Pritchard & Robert B. Thompson, Securities Law and the New Deal Justices, 95 Va. L. Rev. 841 (2009); Steve Thel, The Original Conception of Section 10(b) of the Securities Exchange Act, 42 Stan. L. Rev. 385 (1990).

Following a sketch of the Securities Act and the Exchange Act that highlights provisions of especial importance to litigators, we survey three major congressional enactments—the Private Securities Litigation Reform Act of 1995 (the PSLRA), the SOX, and the Dodd-Frank Act. Another such enactment, the Securities Litigation Uniform Standards Act of 1998 (the SLUSA), is discussed later in this Chapter in connection with state law.

1. *The Securities Act of 1933*

To combat the market abuses that led to the 1929 Crash, the Securities Act emphasizes both the disclosure of information and the prevention of fraud. The emphasis on disclosure reflects the influence of Justice Brandeis, who wrote: "Publicity is justly commended as a remedy for social and industrial diseases. Sunlight is said to be the best of disinfectants; electric light the most efficient policeman." Louis D. Brandeis, Other People's Money and How the Bankers Use It 62 (2d. ed. 1933). In embracing a disclosure approach, Congress rejected the so-called merit approach, which, philosophical considerations aside, would have been considerably more expensive. Under the merit approach, currently in place in various states, regulators prohibit public sales of securities by companies that they conclude are financially troubled, regardless of whether those financial troubles are publicly disclosed.

The Securities Act is primarily concerned with securities offerings by issuers and those who control them (in contrast to the Exchange Act, which focuses on the secondary trading markets). The Securities Act applies both to initial public offerings (IPOs) as well as to subsequent offerings by seasoned issuers that have long been publicly held. Section 5 of the Act requires that all offerings of securities be registered, unless an exemption from registration applies. The Act places enforcement in the hands of the SEC and the DOJ as well as investors (who have at their disposal several express private actions).

a. The Registration Requirement

An issuer wishing to make an offering of securities for which no registration exemption is available must file a registration statement with the SEC. The registration statement—the centerpiece disclosure document of the Securities Act—provides detailed information about the company's business and management along with the terms of the offering and certified financial statements. The preparation of the registration statement is less onerous for the largest companies, which are entitled to incorporate into their registration statements the annual and quarterly reports (described below) that the Exchange Act requires them to file regularly with the SEC. This fusion of Securities Act and Exchange Act disclosure requirements is known as "integrated disclosure."

An issuer can begin selling the securities covered by a registration statement only when the SEC allows the registration statement to become effective. The wait averages four to six weeks in the case of an IPO and substantially less time in the case of an offering by a seasoned issuer. A prospectus containing substantially the same information as the registration statement must be provided to dealers selling the securities in the registered offering as well as to those who purchase in the offering.

In reviewing a registration statement, the SEC makes no affirmative investigation of the facts that the issuer sets forth. Therefore, unless there are obvious red flags, the SEC is unlikely to question the accuracy of the company's representations. Misleading disclosures thus usually do not come to light until after the sale of the securities to the public. Hence the principal deterrent against fraud or negligence consists of *ex post* enforcement actions by investors, the SEC, and the DOJ.

b. Exemptions from Registration

The Securities Act provides numerous exemptions from the registration requirements. Litigators need to be familiar with these exemptions for two reasons. First, suppose an issuer offers securities pursuant to an exemption without satisfying the exemption's requirements. Under these circumstances, the purchasers have a right to rescission under Section 12(a)(1) of the Act, even if no misleading statement was made to them. Second, the availability of Section 12(a)(2), a private action for material misstatements and omissions, may turn on which exemption the offering of securities was based.

The exemptions from registration rest on a variety of rationales. These include the nature of the issuer or of the investors, the size of the offering, or the fact that some other regulatory authority is in the picture.

The exemptions from registration include securities issued by the United States and by state or local governments as well as by banks and non-profit institutions. See Sections 3(a)(2) and 3(a)(4). Also exempt are intrastate offerings, which are offerings of securities sold to residents of a single state by an issuer both incorporated and doing most of its business within that state. See Section 3(a)(11) and Rule 147. The traditional rationale for the intrastate exemption is two-fold: the ability of states to regulate offerings within their borders coupled with the ability of investors to discover information about companies located in the state in which they live.

Exemptions based at least partly on the size of the offering include those provided by Rules 504 and 505 of Regulation D as well as by Regulation A. The statutory basis for each of these is Section 3(b), which authorizes the SEC to adopt exemptions for offerings not exceeding $5 million where registration is "not necessary in the public interest and for the protection of investors." A Rule 504 offering cannot exceed $1 million, can be made only by issuers not subject to the Exchange Act's reporting requirements (described infra), and does not require disclosure of information to investors. A Rule 505 offering, available to reporting companies and non-reporting companies alike, cannot exceed $5 million. Disclosure of specified information must be made to investors who are not "accredited investors" (a category which includes certain institutions, certain insiders of the issuer, and individuals with a net worth exceeding $1 million – excluding, pursuant to a provision of the Dodd-Frank Act, the value of the investor's primary residence– or a yearly income exceeding $200,000). A Rule 505 offering is limited to 35 purchasers, not including accredited investors. A Regulation A offering cannot exceed $5 million and can be made only by issuers not subject to the Exchange Act's reporting requirements. Often referred to as "mini-registration" or "junior registration," Regulation A requires the issuer to file with the SEC an abbreviated registration statement (that need not include audited financials) and to distribute an abbreviated prospectus to investors.

A very important exemption is the private offering exemption, set forth in Section 4(2). This exemption from the Securities Act's registration requirements encompasses "transactions by an issuer not involving any public offering." According to the Supreme Court, the private offering exemption applies only to those offerings made to persons with "access to the kind of information which registration would disclose" and with the capacity to "fend for themselves." *SEC v. Ralston Purina Co.*, 346 U.S. 119, 125-27 (1953). A quintessential private offering would be an offering to ten banks, but private offerings can also be made to sophisticated individuals. Far from clear, however, is the precise nature of the attributes that these individuals must have. Thus, the SEC has adopted a "safe harbor" rule under Section 4(2) that provides issuers with an alternative to Section 4(2) itself. The safe harbor is Rule 506, which, like Rules 504 and 505 described earlier, is part of Regulation D. Rule 506 provides an exemption for offerings of any dollar amount, to an unlimited number of accredited investors (see Rule 505 supra) and up to 35 additional investors who must each be sophisticated—that is, have "such knowledge and experience in financial and business matters that he is capable of evaluating the merits and risks of the *** investment." Rule 506(b)(2)(ii). As with Rule 505 discussed supra, disclosure of specified information must be made to investors who are not accredited investors.

Additional exemptions from registration are set forth in Regulation S, which encompasses offerings made outside the United States by either domestic or foreign issuers. Regulation S draws distinctions based on the probability that the securities in question will find their way to the United States. The greater the probability, the more restrictions the issuer must satisfy in order to obtain an exemption from registration.

c. *Liability Provisions*

The Securities Act contains several liability provisions. First, recall that we have already mentioned Section 12(a)(1), which confers a right of rescission on private plaintiffs who can establish a violation of Section 5 of the Securities Act.

The Securities Act also includes two express private actions for material omissions and misstatements. Under Section 11, purchasers in registered offerings may sue the issuer and numerous other specified defendants (including underwriters, accountants, directors, and certain corporate officers) for material omissions and misstatements in the registration statement. Under Section 12(a)(2), those who purchase in registered offerings as well as in some exempt offerings may sue their "sellers" (a category that the Act does not define) for material omissions and misstatements made "by means of a prospectus" or, in some instances, orally. Sections 11 and 12(a)(2) impose fewer demands on plaintiffs than would a traditional common law fraud action. For example, neither Section requires proof that the defendant acted with scienter (i.e., an intent to deceive) and, under Section 11, an issuer is strictly liable for any material misrepresentations or omissions in the registration statement.

In designing Sections 11 and 12(a)(2), Congress thought much about the "gatekeeping" functions performed by those who assist issuers with securities offerings. Indeed, the so-called "due diligence defenses" available to non-issuer Section 11 defendants such as accountants and underwriters, along with the "reasonable care" defense available to Section 12(a)(2) defendants, provide substantial incentives to make the issuer's disclosures accurate and complete.

Another significant fraud provision is Section 17(a), which prohibits three sets of fraudulent acts "in the offer or sale of a security." The Supreme Court has held that subsection 17(a)(1) requires proof of scienter but that subsections 17(a)(2) and (3) do not. See *Aaron v. SEC*, 446 U.S. 680 (1980). Section 17(a) is an important enforcement tool of the SEC and the DOJ. Section 17(a) does not contain an express private action and courts have declined to recognize an implied private action.

2. *The Securities Exchange Act of 1934*

As noted earlier, the Exchange Act focuses mainly on the secondary trading markets. Its wide-ranging regulation of these markets includes the following aspects of particular significance to securities litigators.

a. *Section 10(b) and Rule 10b-5*

From the standpoint of securities litigation and enforcement, by far the most important provision in the Exchange Act (as well as in the federal securities laws generally) is Section 10(b). That Section makes it "unlawful *** [t]o use or employ, in connection with the purchase or sale of any security ***, any manipulative or deceptive device or contrivance" in contravention of SEC rules. In 1942, the SEC adopted Rule 10b-5, which proscribes fraud in a manner virtually as wide-ranging as Section 10(b) itself. The Rule, applicable regardless of the size of the transaction or the securities issuer, serves not only as a general prohibition against fraud "in connection with the purchase or sale of any security" but also as a prohibition against insider trading (a subject addressed by Section 16(b) as well).

As originally contemplated by their drafters, Section 10(b) and Rule 10b-5 were to be enforced only by the SEC and the DOJ. Beginning in 1946, however, courts recognized an implied private action that is now established "beyond peradventure." *Herman & MacLean v. Huddleston,* 459 U.S. 375, 380 (1983). The importance of the implied private action has undoubtedly been enhanced by the limited scope and onerous burdens imposed by the Exchange Act's two express private fraud actions: an action under Section 9(e) for market manipulation and an action under Section 18(a) for material misstatements in reports filed with the SEC.

b. Market Manipulation

The Exchange Act contains numerous provisions that specifically target market manipulation. These include—in addition to Section 10(b) and Rule 10b-5—Section 9, which bars various types of manipulative practices involving securities (other than government securities); Section 10(a), which authorizes the SEC to adopt rules regulating short sales and stop-loss orders involving securities (other than government securities); Section 14(e), which prohibits "fraudulent, deceptive, or manipulative acts or practices, in connection with any tender offer;" and Section 15(c), which prohibits "any fraudulent, deceptive, or manipulative act or practice" by brokers and dealers. The Exchange Act does not define manipulation, however, and the precise meaning of the term is by no means self-evident.

c. Disclosure Obligations: Reporting Companies

To reduce the frequency of fraud and manipulation in public markets, the Exchange Act requires certain companies—known as reporting companies—to file reports on a regular basis with the SEC. A number of provisions important to litigators—not only in the Exchange Act but also in the PSLRA and the SOX—are applicable only to reporting companies (or only to Section 12 companies, which comprise the first and second reporting company categories listed below).

Reporting companies are companies that fall into any of the following three categories:

- Companies which, as provided by Section 12(b), have a class of securities (equity or debt) listed on a national securities exchange (including the NASDAQ Stock Market, which began operation in August 2006). These companies must comply with the reporting requirements set forth in Section 13(a).
- Companies which, as provided by Section 12(g) and Rule 12g-1, have total assets exceeding $10 million and a class of equity securities held by at least 500 shareholders. These companies must comply with the reporting requirements set forth in Section 13(a).
- Companies that do not fit either of the above two categories must nonetheless satisfy the Exchange Act's reporting

requirements if, as provided by Section 15(d), they have filed a registration statement under the Securities Act that has become effective.

The vast majority of publicly traded companies (also known as public companies or publicly held companies) are reporting companies. In recognition of this fact and for reasons of convenience, Congress and the SEC sometimes refer to reporting companies as "publicly traded companies." See, e.g., Section 807 of the SOX (entitled "criminal penalties for defrauding shareholders of publicly traded companies" but applicable to companies that either have securities registered pursuant to Section 12 or that are required to file reports pursuant to Section 15(d)). Likewise for reasons of convenience, we also occasionally employ the same shorthand throughout this casebook.

The most significant report that reporting companies must file is the annual report (the 10-K). The 10-K includes, among other things, management's discussion and analysis of the company's performance as well as audited financial statements. Reporting companies must also file quarterly reports (the 10-Q) as well as reports (the 8-K) for special occurrences, such as the dismissal of the company's accounting firm. The substance of these reports, as well the frequency with which they must be filed, stand on the verge of substantial change. Indeed, Section 13(*l*) of the Exchange Act, added in 2002 by the SOX, empowers the SEC to adopt rules requiring reporting companies to disclose "on a rapid and current basis such additional information concerning material changes in the financial condition or operations of the issuer."

d. *Proxy Regulation*

By enacting Section 14(a) of the Exchange Act, Congress sought to combat abuses prevalent in the 1920s involving the solicitation of proxies from a corporation's shareholders. These abuses flowed from inadequacies in state law which, while allowing shareholders to vote to elect directors and to approve mergers and other corporate transactions, did not require that they be given information relevant to deciding how to vote. Nor did state law do much to address deceitful proxy solicitations by the company's managers. Indeed, while proxy fraud was, at least theoretically, a breach of state law fiduciary duties, a state court was in fact unlikely to enter an order invalidating a shareholder vote that fraud had tainted.

Section 14(a) gives the SEC a broad mandate to adopt rules governing the solicitation of proxies in Section 12 companies—that is, companies that fit either the first or second of the reporting company categories described above. Pursuant to Section 14(a), the SEC has adopted numerous proxy rules. The proxy rules mandate that shareholders receive information on the matters as to which their votes are sought (although state law continues to control what those matters are). In addition, the proxy rules regulate such things as the form and content of proxy solicitation materials as well as the communications, both written and oral, that are used in connection with the proxy solicitation process.

Especially important is Rule 14a-9, which prohibits material omissions or misrepresentations in proxy solicitations. The Rule is enforceable not only by the SEC and the DOJ, but also by investors. To be sure, Rule 14a-9 says nothing about private enforcement. But the Supreme Court has recognized an implied private action under the Rule. See *J. I. Case Co. v. Borak*, 377 U.S. 426 (1964).

e. *Tender Offer Regulation*

The Exchange Act has regulated tender offers since 1968, when Congress amended the Exchange Act for this purpose. These amendments, now embodied in Sections 13(d), 13(e), and 14(d)-(f) of the Exchange Act and known as the Williams Act, were precipitated by the growing number of tender offers in the 1960s. While the Williams Act does not define a "tender offer," the phrase typically refers to a publicized offer, sometimes by a hostile bidder, to buy shares of a publicly owned company at an advertised price within a confined time period. The regulation established by the Williams Act has three principal aspects.

The first aspect involves disclosure of information. Under Section 13(d), an acquiror (whether pursuant to tender offer or otherwise) of more than 5% of a class of equity security of a Section 12 company (that is, a company that fits either the first or second of the reporting company categories described supra) must, within ten days of making the acquisition, provide a report (the Schedule 13D) to the SEC, the target company, and any exchanges on which the security is traded. Disclosures required by Schedule 13D include, among other things, the acquiror's identity, background, and source of financing as well as his purpose in making the acquisition. Section 14(d) requires similar disclosure (the Schedule TO) by anyone who makes a tender offer for more than 5% of a class of equity security of a Section 12 company.

The second aspect involves regulating the process of tender offers so as to reduce shareholder coercion. Thus, the offer must remain open for twenty business days (Rule 14e-1), the tendered shares must be accepted by the bidder on a pro rata rather than on a "first-come-first-served" basis (Section 14(d)(6) and Rule 14d-8), tendered shares may be withdrawn by the shareholders during the period that the tender offer remains open (Section 14(d)(5) and Rule 14d-7) and all tendering shareholders must be paid the same price (Section 14(d)(7) and Rule 14d-10).

Finally, and of greatest importance to securities litigators, the Williams Act prohibits fraud in connection with any tender offer. This prohibition is contained in Section 14(e), a provision modeled on Rule 10b-5 and applicable to tender offers in all companies (whether they are Section 12 companies or not). Section 14(e) is enforceable by the SEC and the DOJ as well as by private parties. While Section 14(e) does not create an express private action, courts have recognized such an action by implication.

f. *Self-Regulatory Organizations*

Self-regulatory organizations (SROs) are industry groups with a distinctive status under the Exchange Act: they are regulated by the SEC but exercise considerable regulatory authority themselves. The most important SROs are the stock exchanges and the Financial Industry Regulatory Authority (FINRA), the product of the 2007 consolidation of the National Association of Securities Dealers with the member regulation, enforcement, and arbitration functions of the New York Stock Exchange. The FINRA is also the forum for almost all securities arbitrations.

3. *The Private Securities Litigation Reform Act* of 1995

The PSLRA imposes numerous restrictions on private securities actions. Enacted in the wake of the 1994 Republican landslide, the PSLRA took aim at purportedly frivolous securities class actions which, in the view of Congress, were filed by lawyers desirous of simply reaching a settlement and collecting a fee. Some PSLRA restrictions apply to class actions specifically, whereas others apply more broadly. Moreover, while some restrictions are substantive, others are procedural.

On the substantive side, the PSLRA gives certain issuers a "safe harbor" which, when satisfied, shields them from claims that they made fraudulent forward-looking statements (that is, predictions of earnings or of other matters). See Securities Act Section 27A and Exchange Act Section 21E. The safe harbor represented Congress's response to complaints by issuers, particularly Silicon Valley high-technology companies whose share prices depend heavily on estimated future earnings, that the threat of litigation inhibited them from making forecasts that the market needed in order to place a value on their stock. Other substantive changes wrought by the PSLRA include requirements that plaintiffs prove loss causation (Securities Act Section 12(b); Exchange Act Section 21D(b)(4)); an adjustment to the calculation of damages (Exchange Act Section 21D(e)); and a system of proportionate liability that in most circumstances replaces joint and several liability (Exchange Act Section 21D(f); see also Securities Act Section 11(f)(2)).

Probably the two most important procedural hurdles that the PSLRA imposes on plaintiffs are (i) heightened pleading requirements mandating the setting forth of specific facts (Exchange Act Section 21D(b)(1)-(2)) and (ii) a stay on discovery pending resolution of a defendant's motion to dismiss on the pleadings (Exchange Act Section 21D(b)(3); Securities Act Section 27(b)). The combined effect of these two provisions is that a plaintiff who files a lawsuit without the facts necessary to show a strong likelihood of prevailing on the merits is likely to have his lawsuit dismissed before he has had the opportunity to acquire additional facts through discovery.

The PSLRA also contains numerous provisions directed at class actions specifically, including those requiring the court to appoint a "lead plaintiff," presumptively the largest shareholder willing to serve, as well as a "lead counsel;" restricting "professional plaintiffs" from serving as lead plaintiffs; and prohibiting class representatives from receiving greater awards than other class members. For discussion of the PSLRA's impact, see Stephen J. Choi, Do the Merits Matter Less After the Private Securities Litigation Reform Act?, 23 J. L. Econ. & Org. 598 (2007); Marilyn F. Johnson, et al., Do the Merits Matter More? The Impact of the Private Securities Litigation Reform Act, 23 J. L. Econ. & Org. 627 (2007); Michael A. Perino, Did the Private Securities Litigation Reform Act Work?, 2003 U. Ill. L. Rev. 913.

4. *The Sarbanes-Oxley Act of 2002*

In the wake of the massive accounting frauds at Enron,WorldCom, and other large publicly traded companies, Congress enacted the SOX. Among other things, the Act heightens corporate disclosure obligations (Section 409); places the accounting industry under the oversight of a Board appointed by and under the supervision of the SEC (Sections 101-109); requires the SEC to adopt professional responsibility rules for securities lawyers, including a rule that compels a lawyer to report evidence of securities violations up-the-ladder to her client's board of directors (Section 307 and Rule 205); establishes several new securities crimes (e.g., Sections 807 and 906(c)); toughens the penalties for some already existing securities crimes; and extends the statute of limitations for private actions for securities fraud (Section 804).

Whether the changes wrought by the SOX will reduce the incidence of corporate fraud remains an unsettled question. In the opinion of some observers, the 2008 financial crisis was fueled in part by the SOX's emphasis on disclosure unaccompanied by substantive regulation of risk in the financial industry. It is also instructive to consider what the SOX did not do, namely, repeal even one of the many restrictions on private securities actions established by the PSLRA. For discussion of the SOX's impact, see Henry N. Butler & Larry E. Ribstein, The Sarbanes-Oxley Debacle: What We've Learned; How to Fix It (2006); Roberta Romano, Sarbanes-Oxley and the Making of Quack Corporate Governance, 114 Yale L. J. 1521 (2005); Robert A. Prentice, Sarbanes-Oxley As Quack Corporate Governance: How Wise is the Received Wisdom?, 95 Geo. L. J. 1843 (2007).

5. *The Dodd-Frank Wall Street Reform and Consumer Protection Act of 2010*

President Barack Obama signed the Dodd-Frank Act into law on July 21, 2010. In direct response to the 2008 financial crisis (precipitating what has been the worst economic recession in the U.S. since the Great Depression), the Act dramatically increases the degree of government supervision over large financial institutions and establishes new consumer financial protections. Enormous and far reaching, the Act spans more than a thousand pages, with thousands of additional pages in rules anticipated. We point out here only a few of its most notable features.

The Financial Stability Oversight Council. The Act creates a new "super regulator," the Financial Stability Oversight Council, to oversee the financial industry and address future financial crises. The Council has the power to identify firms that threaten stability and subject them to stricter oversight by the Federal Reserve. The Council and the Federal Reserve can break up firms that have not responded to stricter oversight measures and continue to pose a threat.

The Council consists of ten voting members and five nonvoting members. The voting members are the Secretary of the Treasury (who serves as the Chair); the heads of the Federal Reserve, SEC, Commodities Futures Trading Commission (CFTC), Federal Deposit Insurance Corporation (FDIC), Comptroller of the Currency (OCC), Federal Housing Finance Agency (FHFA), National Credit Union Administration (NCUA), the newly created Bureau of

Consumer Protection (discussed below); and an independent member with insurance expertise appointed by the President with the advice and consent of the Senate. The nonvoting members include a state insurance commissioner, a state banking supervisor, and a state securities commissioner as well as the Directors of the new Office of Financial Research (the information-gathering arm of the Council) and the Federal Insurance Office (a new unit within the Treasury Department responsible for monitoring the insurance industry).

Enhanced Authority for the FDIC. The Act establishes for the FDIC a new "resolution," or orderly liquidation, authority, pursuant to which that agency has broad discretion to intervene between a financial institution and its creditors. Critics of the Act say that this authority institutionalizes the bailout of large investment banks, insurance companies, investment funds and other firms that the government undertook in response to the 2008 financial crisis. The Act's supporters, however, see it as a long overdue acknowledgment that some financial institutions are "too big to fail" and that government oversight and windup authority cannot be limited to commercial banks. These supporters commend the Act for increasing the predictability and orderliness of the bailout process.

The Consumer Financial Protection Bureau. The Act creates a new independent executive agency within the Federal Reserve, the Consumer Financial Protection Bureau, with a Director appointed by the President and confirmed by the Senate. The Bureau has very broad rulemaking, supervisory, and enforcement authority over persons and entities offering or providing "consumer financial products or services." Much of this new power will involve the regulation of consumer lending, which was the origination point for much of the financial risk-taking that precipitated the financial crisis. The Bureau assumes most of the consumer protection functions that had previously been exercised by other federal regulators such as the Federal Reserve, FDIC, OCC, and Federal Trade Commission (FTC). The Bureau's jurisdiction does not, however, encompass persons and entities subject to SEC or CFTC regulation or insurance activities.

Enhanced SEC and CFTC Authority Over Derivatives Trading. The Act gives the SEC and CFTC new and broad regulatory authority over the trading of over-the-counter derivative securities, including credit default swaps, and other financial instruments linked to the financial crisis. The Act also requires bank holding companies to spin off riskier derivatives trading into separate affiliates. Earlier drafts of the legislation had curtailed even more sharply the ability of financial institutions to trade in derivative securities for their own account, but these provisions were scaled back after intensive lobbying by the banking industry.

Regulation of Private Equity and Hedge Funds. The Act requires private equity and hedge funds with assets of $150 million or more to register with the SEC, although venture capital funds enjoy an exemption from full registration. Moreover, banks are prohibited from owning or sponsoring a private equity or hedge fund if the investment exceeds three percent of the bank's Tier 1 (core) capital or three percent of the total ownership of the fund.

Credit Rating Agencies. The Act makes the specific finding that inaccurate ratings on structured financial products "contributed significantly to the mismanagement of risks by financial institutions and investors, which in turn adversely impacted the health of the economy in the United States and around the world." It then addresses credit rating agencies by enhancing the SEC's enforcement and examination authority over nationally recognized statistical rating organizations (NRSROs); by imposing on NRSROs greater transparency, internal control, reporting, and board independence requirements; by subjecting statements by credit rating agencies to the same enforcement and penalty provisions that govern statements by registered public accounting firms or securities analysts;" by facilitating private actions against credit rating agencies through the relaxation of the pleading requirements that must be met by plaintiffs seeking damages under Rule 10b-5; and by directing the SEC to establish a new Office of Credit Ratings.

Corporate Governance. The Act expands the federal government's involvement in corporate governance in several respects. It requires a broad range of financial institutions to have a risk committee responsible for overseeing the firm's risk management practices, which committee must include at least one risk management expert with experience with similar firms. The Federal Reserve is assigned the task of determining the requisite number of independent directors that the committee must have.

A number of provisions involve executive compensation, some of which reach beyond financial institutions in particular. These provisions include: a requirement that U.S. public companies provide shareholders with a non-binding say-on-pay vote; a directive to the SEC to instruct the stock exchanges to adopt new listing standards imposing enhanced independence requirements for board compensation committees; and a grant of authority to the SEC to promulgate rules requiring U.S. public companies to provide "proxy access" to certain shareholders who wish to include director nominees in a company's proxy solicitation materials. In addition, specified federal regulators (including the SEC and the Federal Reserve) must "jointly prescribe regulations or guidelines" for large financial institutions that will prohibit incentive-based executive compensation arrangements that encourage inappropriate risks or that have the potential to lead to material financial loss.

Investor Protection. The Act contains a host of provisions aimed at "Investor Protection and Improvements to the Regulation of Securities," the name given to Title IX of the Act. These provisions include: monetary incentives and protections for whistleblowers who provide the SEC with "original information" about possible securities law violations; new authority for the SEC to impose civil monetary penalties in administrative proceedings; clarification that the SEC may pursue actions against aiders and abetters who recklessly provide substantial assistance to a primary violator of the federal securities laws; and specific authority for the SEC and DOJ to engage in extraterritorial fraud enforcement.

Rules, Studies, and Offices. The Act requires the SEC to promulgate numerous new rules and to conduct many special studies – 95 rules and 17 studies, by the count of the law firm of Davis, Polk & Wardwell. Various new rules must likewise be promulgated by, among others, the CFTC and federal bank regulators. Moreover, the Act directs the SEC to create five new offices: an Office of the Investor Advocate; an Office of Credit Ratings; an Office of Municipal Securities; an Office of Minority and Women Inclusion; and an Office to administer and enforce the new whistleblower incentives and protections described above. For commentary on the Dodd-Frank Act, see Stephen M Bainbridge, Dodd-Frank: Quack Corporate Governance Round II, 95 Minn. L. Rev. 1779 (2011); Jeffrey N. Gordon & Christopher Muller, Confronting Financial Crisis: Dodd-Frank's Dangers and the Case for a Systemic Emergency Insurance Fund, 28 Yale J. on Reg. 151 (2011).

The week after the Act was enacted, SEC Chairman Mary Schapiro shared with Congress the Commission's plan to add 800 new staff members – a sure sign that securities litigation and enforcement will be a booming area of legal practice for many years to come.

B. THE COURTS

Besides providing a forum for securities actions, the federal courts play a substantial role in shaping the substantive law of securities litigation. This is so mainly for two reasons.

The first reason has to do with the federal securities laws themselves. As you will see throughout this casebook, the federal securities laws are written in broad language. For example, Section 10(b) of the Exchange Act prohibits "any manipulative or deceptive device or contrivance" and Rule 10b-5 prohibits "any device, scheme, or artifice to defraud." Moreover, definitions of critical terms are frequently lacking, such as what makes misstatements or omissions "material" (as they must be under Rule 10b-5, Rule14a-9, and Section 14(e) of the Exchange Act as well as under Sections 11 and 12(a)(2) of the Securities Act); what it means for a defendant to commit his violation "willfully" (a prerequisite for criminal conviction under the Securities Act and the Exchange Act); and what qualifies as a "tender offer" (the focus of regulation under the Williams Act). As Congress undoubtedly expected, courts step in to supply the missing content.

The second reason involves a happenstance of timing. Many questions of foundational importance for securities litigation reached the courts in the 1960s and 1970s, an era of judicial activism across the legal landscape. Thus, in the 1960s and 1970s, a period when the Supreme Court recognized constitution entitlements to privacy and abortion and issued other expansive rulings in the areas of civil liberties and criminal defense, it also upheld implied private actions under Rule 10b-5 and Rule 14a-9 and established presumptions of reliance or causation on behalf of investors who sued under those provisions. See *Affiliated Ute Citizens v. United States,* 406 U.S. 128, 152-54 (1972) (upholding presumption of reliance under Rule 10b-5); *Superintendent of Ins. v. Bankers Life & Cas. Co.,* 404 U.S. 6, 13 n. 9 (1971) (upholding implied private action under Rule 10b-5); *Mills v. Elec. Auto-Lite Co.,* 396 U.S. 375, 384-85 (1970) (upholding presumption of causation under Rule 14a-9); *J. I. Case Co. v. Borak,* 377 U.S. 426 (1964) (upholding implied private action under Rule 14a-9). Likewise during this period, the lower federal courts recognized an implied private action under Section 14(e) of the Exchange Act, read Rule 10b-5 to prohibit insider trading (a subject to which the Rule does not refer), and accorded Rule 10b-5 a substantial international reach (despite the absence of virtually any guidance on this matter from Congress).

These decisions from the 1960s and 1970s had the effect of further expanding judicial power. Indeed, having recognized implied private actions, the courts could not avoid shaping their elements. Similarly, having concluded that Rule 10-5 encompasses insider trading and international transactions, the courts could not avoid plumbing the meaning of insider trading and the reach of extraterritoriality.

To be sure, judicial activism in securities law subsided and some of the expansive interpretations from the 1960s and 1970s were cut back by later decisions and legislative developments. But the rights and duties that courts recognized in the 1960s and 1970s have largely remained in place. The private actions under Rule 10b-5, Rule 14a-9, and Section 14(e) continue to be highly important enforcement tools. Moreover, Rule 10b-5's applicability to insider trading and to international transactions appears rock solid.

As the above discussion demonstrates, the lower federal courts play a pivotal role in developing securities law. Although all federal appellate and district courts contribute in this regard, the appellate courts of the Second Circuit and the Ninth Circuit are widely regarded as the most important. The reason ultimately involves geography. The Second Circuit, known as the "Mother Court" of securities law, *Blue Chip Stamps v. Manor Drug Stores,* 421 U.S. 723, 762 (1975) (Blackmun, J., dissenting), hears appeals from the federal district court in New York City, not only an international commercial center but also the home of the securities industry and most of its law firms. The Ninth Circuit hears appeals involving the numerous class actions brought against high-technology companies located in the Silicon Valley and elsewhere in the western United States.

The Supreme Court has an impact by virtue of not only what it decides but also what it fails to decide (and thereby leaves to the lower courts for resolution). Important issues, such as the viability of the misappropriation theory of insider trading or the existence of aiding and abetting liability under Rule 10b-5, remained unresolved for years after first being raised, and then left open, by Supreme Court decisions decided on other grounds. Compare *Chiarella v. United States,* 445 U.S. 222, 235-37 (1980) (acknowledging, but not addressing, the misappropriation theory) with *United States v. O'Hagan*, 521 U.S. 642, 665 (1997) (upholding the misappropriation theory); compare *Ernst & Ernst v. Hochfelder*, 425 U.S. 185, 191 n. 7 (1976) (reserving the question of aiding and abetting liability under Rule 10b-5) with *Central Bank, N.A. v. First Interstate Bank, N.A.*, 511 U.S. 164 (1994) (rejecting aiding and abetting liability in private actions under Rule 10b-5). Moreover, the Court has yet to say whether recklessness satisfies Rule 10b-5's scienter requirement, even though more than thirty years have elapsed since the Court posed but declined to answer that question. See *Ernst v. Ernst v. Hochfelder*, supra, 425 U.S. at 193 n. 12. Cf. *Tellabs, Inc. v. Makor Issues & Rights, Ltd.*, 551 U.S. 308, 319 n.3 (2007) (again reserving the question).

As you proceed through this casebook, notice the many Supreme Court decisions in which the Court splits 5-4. This suggests that many of the same political and jurisprudential divisions operative in the Court's decisions in other substantive areas affect its securities decisions as well.

Congress has only occasionally overridden the courts. While the most striking example is probably the wide range of procedural and substantive changes brought about by the PSLRA, other instances include three amendments to the Exchange Act. The first, enacted in 1988 in the wake of a surge of insider trading scandals, overrode a Second Circuit decision barring private actions based on the misappropriation theory of insider trading. See Exchange Act Section 20A. The second, enacted in 1995, clarified the SEC's right to sue aiders and abetters following a 1994 Supreme Court decision that called the agency's right to do so into question. See Exchange Act Section 20(e). The third, enacted in 2010 as part of the Dodd-Frank Act, reinstated the extraterritorial anti-fraud authority of the SEC and DOJ as it existed prior to a Supreme Court decision issued earlier that year. See Exchange Act Section 27(b); Securities Act Section 22 (c).

C. THE SECURITIES AND EXCHANGE COMMISSION

A major accomplishment of the Exchange Act was the establishment of the SEC (also known as the Commission), an independent agency charged with enforcing the federal securities laws. The SEC is composed of five commissioners appointed by the President and confirmed by the Senate for five year terms, no more than three of whom can come from the same political party. Since its founding, the SEC has played a formidable and multi-faceted role in the development of the federal securities laws.

First, the SEC is empowered to adopt rules that implement those laws. Among the most important rules ever adopted by the SEC are Rules 10b-5 and 14a-9.

Second, the SEC has the power both to initiate administrative actions against securities law violators as well as to adjudicate those actions. In this capacity, the SEC may from time to time issue important rulings on statutory questions as to which the courts have not yet had the opportunity to speak.

Third, the SEC frequently brings enforcement actions in the federal courts. It thus shapes the law through its decisions regarding which cases to prosecute. See generally James D. Cox & Randall S. Thomas, Public and Private Enforcement of the Securities Laws: Have Things Changed Since Enron?, 80 Notre Dame L. Rev. 893 (2005).

Fourth, the SEC often files amicus briefs on federal securities issues in private actions in which it is not a party. The courts are at least attentive to the SEC's positions although they do not by any means always follow them.

Finally, the SEC's Chairperson and sometimes other Commissioners or staff testify before Congress, as well as provide informal input, when Congress considers legislation amending the securities laws. In this instance as well, the SEC does not by any means always get its way.

The SEC consists of five principal divisions, the most important of which from the standpoint of securities litigators is the Enforcement Division. That Division conducts investigations and, where appropriate, files administrative or court actions against securities law violators. Where criminal prosecution appears warranted, the matter is referred to the DOJ.

D. THE DEPARTMENT OF JUSTICE

The DOJ has exclusive authority over criminal enforcement of the federal securities laws. While (as previously noted) the SEC sometimes refers cases to the DOJ, it is the DOJ (and not the SEC) that makes the final decision as to whether to bring criminal charges. Moreover, the DOJ prosecutes numerous securities cases that did not originate with the SEC.

The Securities Act and the Exchange Act are "hybrid civil-criminal statutes." That is, they are statutes which, in general, bottom criminal and civil actions on the same violations. Criminal actions are nonetheless distinctive in two respects. First, they have a special state of mind requirement, pursuant to which the defendant must have committed the violation "willfully," or, in some instances "knowingly" (the difference between "willfully" and "knowingly," if any, being a matter that remains unsettled). Second, they have a unique burden of proof – namely,"proof beyond a reasonable doubt" rather than the preponderance standard applicable to civil actions.

The SEC and the DOJ from time to time prosecute the same offenses simultaneously. These parallel SEC civil actions and DOJ criminal actions may engender procedural conflicts as well as the application of inconsistent substantive legal standards to the same facts.

The consequences of prosecuting corporate defendants can be substantial, as the saga of accounting giant Arthur Andersen amply shows. See generally *Arthur Andersen, LLP v. United States*, 544 U.S. 696 (2005). Convicted of obstructing an SEC proceeding, the firm lost, as the result of the conviction, the right to practice before the SEC. That loss in turn led to Andersen's terminating thousands of employees and going out of business. In the wake of these developments, the DOJ has tended to avoid corporate indictments.

E. STATE LAW

Although this casebook focuses on the federal securities laws, state law constitutes a significant aspect of securities litigation. Sometimes the state law at issue is that of the state of incorporation; at other times it is the law of the state where the securities were sold. Each state continues to have its own blue sky laws and state officials may bring both civil and criminal actions under those statutes. See generally Mark A. Sargent, A Future for Blue Sky Laws, 62 U. Cin. L. Rev. 471 (1993).

As originally enacted, the Securities Act and the Exchange Act preserved state law actions brought by private parties as well as by state governments. In the years that followed, courts assumed that this preservation extended to class actions filed in state court under state law. Nonetheless, after the enactment of the PSLRA in 1995, its supporters complained that plaintiffs' lawyers were avoiding its restrictions, including the bar on discovery pending resolution of motions to dismiss, by filing class actions in state court (mostly in California). Preemption of these state class actions was supported by the high-technology companies of Silicon Valley, who were often defendants in securities class actions, as well as by the major accounting firms.

In 1998 Congress enacted the Securities Litigation Uniform Standards Act (SLUSA), which preempted class actions for securities fraud under the common law and statutes of all fifty states. Investors, with the exception of state and local governments and their pension funds, are now barred from bringing in state court or under state law a class action alleging fraud in connection with the purchase or sale of a "nationally traded security" (encompassing those listed on the New York Stock Exchange, the American Stock Exchange, or the NASDAQ). SLUSA also authorizes federal courts to stay discovery in state court of any private action (whether or not a class action) while a federal action is pending. The Act does, however, preserve state jurisdiction over certain types of corporate law claims.

Congress has also received complaints from Wall Street firms of excessive prosecutorial zeal by state attorneys general, most notably the New York Attorney General (later Governor) Eliot Spitzer, who in 2002 led an investigation that culminated in a $100 million settlement with Merrill Lynch & Co., Inc. involving overly optimistic recommendations by securities analysts who allegedly sought to win lucrative investment banking business for their firm. Although bills were introduced in Congress that would have preempted such state enforcement activities, the SEC's well-publicized agreement to join forces with Spitzer and other state attorneys general tempered these calls for legislative action. The financial crisis of 2008 led to another round of enforcement proceedings by state attorneys general, as well as the federal government, against some of the country's largest banks. Many of these proceedings have appeared to receive strong political support.

F. SOCIAL AND ECONOMIC FORCES

Social and economic forces have always had a substantial impact on securities litigation and enforcement. Blue sky laws were enacted in response to widespread financial scandals of the 1890s and the crash of 1907. Moreover, as noted previously, the crash of 1929 and the disastrous bear market of 1929-1932 led to the enactment of the Securities Act, the Exchange Act, and other federal securities statutes. Nor has the impact of social and economic forces on securities law abated since.

Beginning in the 1970s, widespread concern developed in American society, and particularly in the business community, over the extent of government regulation, the volume of litigation, and the prevalence of judicial activism. Responding to these concerns from the mid-1970s through the mid-1990s, the Supreme Court restricted the scope of the implied private actions previously recognized under the federal securities laws as well as of certain express private actions under those laws. This period is often referred to as one of "retrenchment."

In adopting at least some of these restrictions, the Supreme Court may well have been influenced by the fact that the stock market was rising. Indeed, when the economy is booming, concern about protecting investors can take a back seat to other priorities, such as curtailing what was perceived to be excessive litigation. Similarly, the rising stock market no doubt likewise made possible Congress's restraints on private securities actions in the PSLRA.

The Internet brings huge consequences as well. Consider its two-fold impact. First, the Internet creates new opportunities for deception, since vast audiences can now be reached by tricksters who operate anonymously. Second, the Internet's global reach generates substantial jurisdictional questions. For example, suppose a foreign national, operating in a foreign country, posts on the Internet fraudulent corporate information that affects the investment decisions of United States residents. Do the federal securities fraud provisions reach this far? What about personal jurisdiction over the foreign national? See generally John C. Coffee, Jr., Brave New World? The Impact(s) of the Internet on Modern Securities Regulation, 52 Bus. Law. 1195, 1223 (1997) (identifying the Internet's two-fold impact).

Indeed, even putting the Internet to the side, the internationalization of the securities markets that began in the 1960s has had—and continues to have—significant ramifications for securities litigation and enforcement. United States investors now trade vast quantities of foreign securities, and foreign investors trade vast quantities of United States securities as well. As a result, federal securities fraud litigation often involves foreign plaintiffs, foreign defendants, and foreign securities in various permutations as well as fraud that occurred in whole or in part on foreign soil. The Supreme Court and Congress have both recently weighed in on the extraterritorial reach of the federal securities antifraud provisions, while lower courts have been engaged in an ongoing struggle to determine which such cases they are entitled to hear and which lie beyond the scope of their authority. See *Morrison v. National Australia Bank Ltd.*, 130 S. Ct. 2869 (2010) (reading Section 10(b) and Rule 10b-5 to encompass securities transactions occurring on U.S. exchanges or otherwise in the U.S.) and Section 929P(b) of the Dodd-Frank Act (explicitly authorizing the SEC and the DOJ, but not private parties, to bring extraterritorial securities fraud prosecutions that involve domestic conduct or domestic effects)

Next, revelations of large-scale accounting frauds at a number of the country's largest companies—including Enron, Global Crossings, Sunbeam, Waste Management, and WorldCom— have had and will continue to have consequences for years to come. These revelations also led to Congress's enactment of the SOX (which has numerous ramifications of its own).

Only a few years later, the SEC and the DOJ began exposing a series of high profile frauds involving investment advisors, whose purported successes appeared to be – and were in fact – too good to be true. Many of these frauds were Ponzi schemes – frauds that deceive new investors about nonexistent investment returns that encourage them to invest money, which is then used to pay earlier investors. Those prosecuted included high tech fund managers Alberto Vilar and Gary Tanaka, who stole millions of dollars from investors, followed by Tom Petters , who stole more than $3.65 billion dollars. These were relatively modest amounts compared with what soon followed – the revelation of the Ponzi scheme operated by former NASDAQ Chairman and renowned fund manager Bernard L. Madoff. Losses in the Madoff scheme totaled over $65 billion (by some calculations), and his victims included prominent financiers, foundations and charitable organizations. Afterwards, another prominent financier and philanthropist, Allen Stanford of Texas, was charged with masterminding a Ponzi scheme involving approximately $8 billion in certificates of deposit.

Many of these money managers used philanthropic commitments (which they did not always pay) to gain the confidence of well-to-do investors. Some, such as Madoff, took advantage of investors who saw themselves as belonging to the same religious, racial, or other group as the money manager – a phenomenon known as "affinity fraud."

Finally, and most devastating for investor confidence and for the economy, came the mortgage meltdown, the Lehman Brothers bankruptcy, and the federally-orchestrated bailouts of AIG, Bear Stearns, Merrill Lynch, and other large financial firms. Some of these firms were merged into existing banks, making the "too big to fail" problem even more difficult to resolve. Much like the 1929 crisis, the 2008 crisis resulted in the deepest and longest recession in seventy years. As in the 1930s, the public became skeptical about the integrity and risk management practices of the financial services industry. The Dodd-Frank Act allayed some of these concerns, but the government's bailout of Wall Street has continued to be very unpopular. Moreover, the Dodd-Frank Act has been criticized for failing to adopt more far reaching solutions such as the reimposition of the separation of commercial and investment banking that existed in the United States until 1999. Exacerbating the public perception of bankers has been the fact that some of the bailed-out firms paid extremely large bonuses within months of receiving federal bailout funds.

G. THE EFFICIENT CAPITAL MARKETS HYPOTHESIS

The Efficient Capital Market Hypothesis (ECMH) has been a highly influential economic theory that has had (and in some respects continues to have) a substantial impact on both securities law in general and securities litigation and enforcement in particular. For example, the fraud-on-the-market doctrine and the puffery doctrine that you will encounter in later chapters are based on the ECMH, as is the statutory safe harbor for forward-looking statements that Congress enacted as part of the PSLRA. While the fraud-on-the-market doctrine is a boon to plaintiffs (because it gives them a presumption of reliance), most of the doctrines and legislation predicated on the ECMH benefit defendants instead.

3 variations

The ECMH comes in three versions: weak, semi-strong, and strong. The weak version, which commands virtual universal acceptance, posits only that security prices are determined by currently available information rather than historical market trends. The widely accepted semi-strong version, on which the doctrines and legislation draw, posits that once information becomes public, it is quickly impounded into securities prices. The highly controversial strong version posits that even nonpublic information is routinely impounded into security prices through leaks and insider trading.

A distinction is sometimes made between informational efficiency and fundamental efficiency. For a market to be informationally efficient, it is necessary only for prices to react quickly to new public information. For a market to be fundamentally efficient, however, it is necessary in addition for prices to reflect the true value of the shares. Thus, a market can be informationally efficient and not be fundamentally efficient.

Markets become efficient as the result of heavy trading by sophisticated investors, many of them institutions, based on what they and their advisers cull from available public sources about the securities and the companies that issue them. Not all public markets are efficient markets by any means. Public markets that are thinly traded or have few or no institutional investors are unlikely to be efficient because they lack the ingredients of market efficiency. The IPO market is prototypically inefficient, whereas the market for New York Stock Exchange-traded securities is prototypically efficient. See generally Lawrence A. Cunningham, From Random Walks to Chaotic Crashes: The Linear Geneology of the Efficient Capital Market Hypothesis, 62 Geo. Wash. L. Rev. 546 (1994); Ronald J. Gilson & Reinier H. Kraakman, The Mechanisms of Market Efficiency, 70 Va. L. Rev. 549 (1984).

Yet recent events have generated considerable skepticism about the efficiency of the markets for even the largest companies. Consider the fact that prior to the collapse of Enron and Worldcom, the stock prices of those companies failed to reflect negative information about those companies that was then publicly available. The same holds true for most of the leading financial firms that imploded in 2008 – namely, Lehman Brothers, Bear Stearns, Merrill Lynch and AIG. Many of these firms had robust stock prices and considerable market capitalization only months before they failed, even though these firms were know to have substantial exposure to mortgage-backed securities of dubious value.

Indeed, debates swirl over whether and to what extent markets are inefficient because of trading driven by psychological factors such as faddishness, overestimation or underestimation of risk, loss aversion (placing greater value on avoiding loss than in making a gain of equivalent size), and anchoring (allowing sometimes arbitrary numbers to exert a gravitational pull on estimations of value). See, e.g., Brad M. Barber & Terrance Odean, Boys Will Be Boys: Gender, Overconfidence, and Common Stock Investment, 116 Q. J. Econ. 261 (2001); Donald C. Langevoort, Taming the Animal Spirits of the Stock Markets: A Behavioral Approach to Securities Regulation, 97 Nw. L. Rev. 135 (2002); Lynn A. Stout, The Mechanisms of Market Inefficiency: An Introduction to the New Finance, 28 J. Corp. L. 635 (2003).

H. LOOKING AHEAD

As with any area of the law, securities litigation and enforcement involves a number of recurrent themes. Some of those themes are reflected in the following questions, which you should ponder in connection with the chapters that lie ahead:

- **Congress vs. the Courts.** What accounts for Congress's tendency to defer to the courts on matters of securities litigation and enforcement? Under what circumstances has Congress been unwilling to defer?

- **The Many Roles of the SEC.** What types of issues are raised by the fact that the SEC – as a single administrative body—has the power to make law (through rulemaking), to enforce the law (through prosecutorial decisions), and to interpret the law (through adjudicating administrative proceedings)?

- **SEC Actions vs. Private Actions.** What are the respective advantages and disadvantages of relying on SEC actions rather than private actions to deter violations of the federal securities laws? Why have both Congress and the courts been more hospitable to SEC actions than to private actions for the past 25 years?

- **Implied Private Actions.** What difficulties are confronted by courts in interpreting, and by parties in litigating, implied private actions, such as those under Section 10(b) and Rule 10b-5, Section 14(a) and Rule 14a-9, and Section 14(e) of the Exchange Act?

- **Civil vs. Criminal.** When interpreting a securities provision in a civil action, must the court take account of the fact that the provision is also enforceable in a criminal action? If so, what should be the impact upon interpretation?

- **The Scope of Judicial Power.** Do courts exceed their authority when they "update" the federal securities laws to accommodate changes that have occurred since the 1930s, such as the greater ease of detecting insider trading or the increased internationalization of the securities markets? Why don't courts leave such updating to Congress?

- **Federal Law vs. State Law.** When interpreting the federal securities laws, how do courts distinguish between the competency of federal law and state corporate law? Does it make sense to distinguish between disclosure issues (covered by federal securities law) and fiduciary duty issues (covered by the law of the issuer's state of incorporation), particularly in view of the fact that disclosure is often an element of fiduciary duty and the additional fact that most breaches of fiduciary duty are concealed by the perpetrator? What are the implications for courts, and for counsel, of having numerous cases heard simultaneously in both state court (where fiduciary duty issues are resolved) and federal court (where disclosure issues under the federal securities laws are resolved)? What are the implications of introducing, on top of this dual forum litigation, the possibility of litigation under the blue sky laws of states where the issuer's securities are sold?

- **United States Law vs. Law of other Nations.** As the Supreme Court emphasized in *Morrison v. National Australia Bank, Ltd.,* 130 S. Ct. 2869 (2010), the United States is not the only country that endeavors to regulate securities markets. Seeking to avoid stepping on the toes of other such countries, the *Morrison* Court confined the reach of the anti-fraud provisions to transactions occurring domestically, whether on exchanges or otherwise. This territorial approach – subsequently rejected by the Dodd-Frank Act for purposes of SEC and DOJ enforcement but left standing for purposes of private enforcement – may be unworkable for a marketplace in which global exchanges are widely perceived to be just around the corner.

Chapter 2

SECTION 10(b) OF THE EXCHANGE ACT AND RULE 10b-5

Rule 10b-5 is the leading anti-fraud weapon in the federal securities laws. Its reach is vast, embracing fraud in the context of large publicly traded corporations as well as tiny close corporations. Likewise varied are its forms of enforcement: individual and class actions by investors, civil and administrative actions by the Securities and Exchange Commission (SEC or Commission), and criminal actions by the Department of Justice (DOJ).

The Commission adopted Rule 10b-5 in 1942 pursuant to Section 10(b) of the Exchange Act. Section 10 reads in pertinent part:

> It shall be unlawful for any person, directly or indirectly, by the use of any means or instrumentality of interstate commerce or of the mails, or of any facility of any national securities exchange— ***
>
> (b) To use or employ, in connection with the purchase or sale of any security registered on a national securities exchange or any security not so registered, *** any manipulative or deceptive device or contrivance in contravention of such rules and regulations as the Commission may prescribe as necessary or appropriate in the public interest or for the protection of investors.

Rule 10b-5 (which largely mirrors the language of Section 17(a) of the Securities Act) encompasses virtually as much as Section 10(b) itself:

> It shall be unlawful for any person, directly or indirectly, by the use of any means or instrumentality of interstate commerce, or of the mails or of any facility of any national securities exchange,
>
> (a) to employ any device, scheme, or artifice to defraud,
>
> (b) to make any untrue statement of a material fact or to omit to state a material fact necessary in order to make the statements made, in the light of the circumstances under which they were made, not misleading, or
>
> (c) to engage in any act, practice, or course of business which operates or would operate as a fraud or deceit upon any person,
>
> in connection with the purchase or sale of any security.

As is apparent, Rule 10b-5 and Section 10(b) say nothing about private enforcement. Beginning with *Kardon v. Nat'l Gypsum Co.*, 69 F. Supp. 512 (E.D. Pa. 1946), however, lower federal courts recognized an implied private action for violations of the Rule. The Supreme Court upheld the implied private action in a footnote in *Superintendent of Ins. v. Bankers Life & Cas. Co.,* 404 U.S. 6, 13 n. 9 (1971). See *Janus Capital Group, Inc. v. First Derivative Traders,* 131 S.Ct. 2296, 2303 (2011) (describing the action as "settled"); *Herman & MacLean v. Huddleston,* 459 U.S. 375, 380 (1983) (describing the action as "beyond peradventure"). While initially offering no rationale, the Court later observed that "the theory *** [was] to supplement" actions by the SEC and the DOJ. See *Musick, Peeler & Garrett v. Employers Ins.,* 508 U.S. 286, 291 (1993). See also *Tellabs, Inc. v. Makor Issues & Rights, Ltd.,* 551 U.S. 308, 313 (2007) (collecting cases acknowledging this theory).

Indeed, the courts (rather than the Commission) have been the principal interpreters of Rule 10b-5. Recognizing the implied private action has been only one aspect of this interpretative project (albeit an important one). Another aspect has been identifying the elements of the implied private action as well as those of SEC and criminal actions and giving the elements substantive content. Courts construing Rule 10b-5 have faced (and continue to face) formidable challenges given the confluence of the following:

• *Broad Language.* Section 10(b) and Rule 10b-5 are broadly worded, offering few bright lines as to how far the Rule's prohibition extends. Moreover, the language of the Section and the Rule is especially uninstructive with respect to matters that bear exclusively on the implied private action (such as standing or reliance), since neither provision was written with private actions in mind.

• *Limited History.* In the course of enacting the Exchange Act in 1934, Congress made only scant references to Section 10(b) in the floor debates and official reports. Moreover, when the SEC commissioners approved Rule 10b-5, the only comment made was "we are against fraud, aren't we?" Conference on Codification of the Federal Securities Laws, 22 Bus. Law. 793, 921-22 (1967) (comments of Milton Freeman).

• *Multiple Enforcement Contexts.* As mentioned, Rule 10b-5 is enforceable in criminal actions as well as in various types of civil actions. Interpretations of the Rule in one context may have undesirable ramifications when applied in other contexts.

• *Shifting Policies.* Until the mid-1970s, the Supreme Court gave Section 10(b) and Rule 10b-5 a relatively liberal reading in order to protect gullible investors from exploitation. See, e.g., *Affiliated Ute v. United States,* 406 U.S. 128, 151-54 (1972). Thereafter, the Court came to see at least some investors as essentially puppets of lawyers who filed securities actions irrespective of their merit simply to reach a settlement and collect a fee. Curtailing frivolous private actions thus became an important judicial policy. See, e,g., *Blue Chip Stamps v. Manor Drug Stores,* 421 U.S. 723, 739-47 (1975); *Stoneridge Inv. Partners, LLC v. Scientific-Atlanta, Inc.,* 552 U.S. 148, 163-64 (2008). But (perhaps not surprisingly) that policy has not invariably determined the result in specific cases. See, e.g., *Herman & MacLean v. Huddleston,* 459 U.S. 375, 387 (1983) (allowing Rule 10b-5 to reach conduct falling within the purview of Section 11 of the Securities Act).

The vastly diminished status of investor protection as a policy animating the interpretation of Rule 10b-5 emerges from *Morrison v. National Australia Bank, Ltd.*, 130 S.Ct. 2869 (2010), a decision addressing the Rule's extraterritorial reach. See generally Chapter 12. Taking up that reach for the first time, the Court read it narrowly without confronting the impact of its reading on investor protection.

In addition, beginning in the 1970s, the Court adopted approaches to statutory interpretation that have carried significant consequences for the interpretation of Section 10(b) and Rule 10b-5. Those approaches consist of strict construction, constriction of implied private actions, and disregard for legislative history.

• *The Influence of the Efficient Capital Markets Hypothesis.* Recall from Chapter 1.G the efficient capital markets hypothesis (ECMH), which posits that the price of a security traded in an efficient market reflects all publicly available information. Courts have developed various Rule 10b-5 doctrines based on the ECMH. One such doctrine is that of "fraud-on-the-market," which may undermine the policy of curtailing frivolous private actions mentioned above. Indeed, the fraud-on-the-market doctrine (where applicable) spares the plaintiffs the necessity of proving their individual reliance on the defendant's fraud by giving them a presumption of reliance on the integrity of the market price. Other Rule 10b-5 doctrines based on the ECMH include the "truth-on-the-market" defense (relevant when the information the defendant failed to disclose reaches the market through another source, such as a trade magazine) and the "puffery" defense (relevant when the alleged fraud amounts to overheated rhetoric lacking the specificity necessary to impact the market).

• *The Absence of Dependable Analogies.* Because Section 10(b) and Rule 10b-5 prohibit fraud, they virtually invite judicial analogies to common law deceit. See, e.g., *Dura Pharm., Inc. v. Broudo*, 533 U.S. 336, 341 (2005) (noting that the private Rule 10b-5 action "resembles, but is not identical to," a common law deceit action). But cf. *Stoneridge Inv. Partners, LLC v. Scientific-Atlanta, Inc.*, 552 U.S. 148, 162 (2008) (asserting that "Section 10(b) does not incorporate common law fraud into federal law"). The deceit analogy is far from perfect, however, since Congress intended the federal securities laws to "rectify perceived deficiencies in the available common-law protections." *Herman & MacLean v. Huddleston*, 459 U.S. 375, 389 (1983).

Another obvious potential analogy is Rule 14a-9, which you will study in Chapter 4. Adopted by the Commission pursuant to Section 14(a) of the Exchange Act, Rule 14a-9 prohibits material misstatements and omissions in proxy solicitations and, like Rule 10b-5, is enforceable in implied private actions as well as in SEC and criminal actions. Yet the proxy voting context involves distinctive considerations that may render Rule 14a-9 (at least some of the time) a less than reliable benchmark for interpreting Rule 10b-5.

• *Subsequent Congressional Enactments.* Congress has not ceded control of Section 10(b) and Rule 10b-5 entirely to the courts. Its most significant contribution in this regard has been the Private Securities Litigation Reform Act of 1995 (PSLRA), which makes maintenance of private securities actions more difficult by stiffening the pleading requirements, providing a safe harbor for fraud involving forward-looking statements, establishing an affirmative requirement of loss causation, adjusting the calculation of damages, and creating a scheme of proportionate liability. This Chapter addresses these matters, while Chapter 6 considers additional aspects of the PSLRA applicable exclusively to class actions.

Likewise important for Rule 10b-5 purposes is the Sarbanes-Oxley Act of 2002 (the "SOX"). Not only did that Act lengthen the statute of limitations for private actions under the Rule. In addition, it empowered the SEC to expand the scope of the "duty to disclose" upon which Rule 10b-5 liability often turns by authorizing the agency to adopt "real time" disclosure rules for reporting companies. (For a discussion of reporting companies see Chapter 1.A.2.c.) This Chapter addresses the new statute of limitations and "real time" disclosure. Other aspects of the SOX are considered in connection with SEC enforcement (Chapter 9) and SEC regulation of accountants and attorneys (Chapter 10).

Finally, the Dodd-Frank Act of 2010 has made significant contributions to the Rule 10b-5 landscape. Those addressed in this Chapter include expanded SEC authority to sue aiders and abettors and controlling persons. Other Rule 10b-5-related aspects of the Dodd-Frank Act are covered in Chapter 9 (SEC enforcement), Chapter 12 (international securities fraud), and Chapter 13 (arbitration).

This Chapter examines the elements of Rule 10b-5, with emphasis upon the Rule's private enforcement. It is divided into ten sections: the requirement of manipulation or deception; the materiality requirement; the "in connection with" requirement; the scienter requirement; the purchaser-seller requirement; causation (encompassing both reliance and loss causation); damages; primary and secondary liability; the statute of limitations; and the overlap between Rule 10b-5 and the express private actions for material misstatements and omissions. Later chapters draw upon the elements of Rule 10b-5 in connection with securities class actions (Chapter 6); insider trading (Chapter 7); market manipulation (Chapter 8); SEC enforcement (Chapter 9); criminal enforcement (Chapter 11); and international securities fraud (Chapter 12).

As you proceed through the present Chapter, consider the following. Would Section 10(b) and Rule 10b-5 benefit from greater congressional involvement? Why have Congress's interventions (thus far at least) been largely marginal? Why do courts pay so little attention to the language of Rule 10b-5 and fixate instead on that of Section 10(b)? To what extent does the policy of curbing frivolous private actions influence the outcome of decisions even when it is not mentioned explicitly? How (if at all) have the scandals at companies such as Enron and WorldCom impacted the interpretation of Section 10(b)? Have courts done enough to make the implied private action live up to the ostensible purpose for which it was created—to serve as a viable supplement to SEC and criminal actions?

In considering Rule 10b-5, it is important to keep in mind certain critical procedural matters. These involve pleading, dismissal of actions, discovery stays, and the burden of proof.

Pleading. The Federal Rules of Civil Procedure apply to all civil complaints filed in federal court. Rule 8 provides that plaintiffs need only plead "a short and plain statement of the claim showing that [they are] entitled to relief." The Supreme Court has extracted an additional unstated requirement from Rule 8 – that the allegations in the complaint qualify as "plausible." *Ashcroft v. Iqbal,* 556 U.S. 662 (2009).

Rule 9 sets the standard for "Pleading Special Matters," with Rule 9(b) providing that in "all averments of fraud or mistake, the circumstances constituting fraud or mistake shall be stated with particularity." Courts generally construe Rule 9(b) to require particularity in the pleading of what material misstatements or omissions were made, who made them, and where and when they were made.

The pleading burdens on private plaintiffs grew even greater with the enactment of the PSLRA, which added Section 21D(b)(1) to the Exchange Act:

Section 21D(b)(1)—Misleading Statements and Omissions

> In any private action arising under [the Exchange Act] in which the plaintiff alleges that the defendant—
>
> (A) made an untrue statement of a material fact; or
>
> (B) omitted to state a material fact necessary in order to make the statements made, in the light of the circumstances in which they were made, not misleading;
>
> the complaint shall specify each statement alleged to have been misleading, the reason or reasons why the statement is misleading, and, if an allegation regarding the statement or omission is made on information and belief, the complaint shall state with particularity all facts on which that belief is formed.

While at first blush this Section appears to pertain only to the pleading of material omissions and misstatements, its reach is actually broader. For example, the requirement to plead "the reason or reasons why the statement is misleading" bears on materiality and reliance. (The PSLRA also substantially raised a private plaintiff's burden of pleading scienter by adding Section 21D(b)(2) to the Exchange Act. We address this provision in connection with the scienter requirement in Section D of this Chapter).

Dismissal of Actions and Discovery Stays. The above-mentioned heightened pleading requirements for private plaintiffs must be considered in light of two other provisions added to the Exchange Act by the PSLRA. One is Section 21D(b)(3)(A), which states that in any private action arising under the Exchange Act, "the court shall, on the motion of any defendant, dismiss the complaint" if the heightened requirements in Section 21D(b) are not met. The other equally significant addition is Section 21D(b)(3)(B), which requires a court to stay discovery during the pendency of any such motion to dismiss. This mandatory stay of discovery while a dismissal motion is pending permits only a limited exception when a "court finds upon motion of any party that particularized discovery is necessary to preserve evidence or to prevent undue prejudice to that party." As you read this Chapter, consider how Fed. R. Civ. P. 9(b) and the PSLRA's requirements for heightened pleading and mandatory discovery stays interact with a plaintiff's ability to state a claim under Rule 10b-5.

Mandatory Sanctions. A final noteworthy provision that the PSLRA added to the Exchange Act is Section 21D(c). That provision requires the court to review every private action at the time of final adjudication to determine whether a party or attorney has committed a violation of Rule 11(b) of the Federal Rules of Civil Procedure – for example, filing a motion for purposes of delay, making a frivolous legal argument, or offering a factual contention that lacks evidentiary support. In the event a violation is found, Section 21D(c) makes sanctions mandatory and establishes as the presumptive sanction an award of the opposing party's attorney's fees and expenses. See Section 21D(c)(2)-(3). As you continue to read about Rule 10b-5 actions, think about what the impact of Section 21D(c) is likely to be.

Burden of Proof. For the small percentage of Rule 10b-5 civil actions that reach the trial stage, the burden of proof is a "preponderance-of-the-evidence" – that is, "more likely than not." *Herman & MacLean v. Huddleston*, 459 U.S. 375, 390 (1983).

A. THE REQUIREMENT OF MANIPULATION OR DECEPTION

Section 10(b) of the Exchange Act prohibits, in connection with the purchase or sale of a security, "any manipulative or deceptive device or contrivance" in contravention of rules promulgated by the SEC for the protection of investors. Therefore, the scope of Section 10(b)—and hence also of Rule 10b-5—turns on the meaning of the phrase "manipulative or deceptive," regardless of whether the action is brought by a private party, the SEC, or the DOJ. The term "manipulative" has a specialized meaning (as the following materials show) and is explored thoroughly in Chapter 8. The meaning of the term "deceptive"—traditionally the more nettlesome problem for the securities litigator—is our focal point here.

The term deception includes outright misrepresentations as well as statements that mislead by omission. Both types of deception fall within the explicit text of Rule 10b-5(b):

> It shall be unlawful for any person *** [t]o make any untrue statement of a material fact or to omit to state a material fact necessary in order to make the statements made, in the light of the circumstances under which they were made, not misleading *** in connection with the purchase or sale of a security.

Statements that mislead by omission include half-truths. See *SEC v. Gabelli*, __ F.3d __, 2011 WL 3250556 (2d Cir. 2011) (observing that "[t]he law is well settled [ ] that so-called "half-truths" — literally true statements that create a materially misleading impression — will support claims for securities fraud"). Likewise, a defendant's secret intention not to honor a promise may render other statements made by him materially misleading. The Court made this clear in *Wharf (Holdings) Ltd. v. United Int'l Holdings, Inc.*, 532 U.S. 588 (2001), when it held that:

> To sell an option while secretly intending not to permit the option's exercise is misleading, because a buyer normally presumes good faith. Cf., e.g., Restatement (Second) of Torts § 530, Comment *c* (1976) ("Since a promise necessarily carries with it the implied assertion

> of an intention to perform[,] it follows that a promise made without such an intention is fraudulent"). For similar reasons, the secret reservation misled United about the option's value. Since Wharf did not intend to honor the option, the option was, unbeknownst to United, valueless.

Id. at 596.

Deception may occur, however, even when no statements of any kind are made. Reflecting this, subsections (a) and (c) of Rule 10b-5 are phrased in very broad terms, prohibiting both "schemes to defraud" as well as acts which "operate as a fraud." These prohibitions may extend to so-called pure silence cases, see *Chiarella v. United States*, 445 U.S. 222, 228 (1980) ("one who fails to disclose material information prior to the consummation of a transaction commits fraud [ ] when he is under a duty to do so"), as well as cases involving deceptive conduct, see *Stoneridge Inv. Partners, LLC v. Scientific–Atlanta, Inc.*, 552 U.S. 148, 158 (2008) ("Conduct itself can be deceptive;" there need not be "a specific oral or written statement before there could be liability under § 10(b) or Rule 10b–5"). However, "broad as the concept of 'deception' may be, it irreducibly entails some act that gives the victim a false impression." *United States v. Finnerty*, 533 F.3d 143, 148 (2d Cir.2008).

Much of the litigation generated by the high-profile accounting scandals at WorldCom, Xerox, Rite Aid, Enron, and other industry giants focused on material misstatements and omissions in the companies' annual and quarterly SEC filings and, more specifically, in their audited financial statements. The dollar amounts of those misstatements were staggering: WorldCom (alleged to have inflated revenues by over $11 billion); Xerox ($1.9 billion); Rite Aid ($1.6 billion); and Enron ($1.2 billion). And while those scandals raised a host of interesting and complex doctrinal questions, it would (to say the least) be exceedingly difficult to argue that deception was not present.

This section of the Chapter addresses aspects of the deception element that are far less settled. The first part explores issues involving material misstatements and omissions in general, whereas the second part focuses on issues involving material omissions in particular.

1. Material Misstatements or Omissions in General

We begin in subsection *a* with *Santa Fe Industries, Inc. v. Green*, 430 U.S. 462 (1977), a critical starting point for understanding the meaning of the term "deceptive" in Section 10(b). That decision also allows us to examine the circumstances capable of transforming a breach of fiduciary duty or other acts of corporate mismanagement into deception that is actionable under Section 10(b) and Rule 10b-5. As subsection *b* makes clear, such a transformation requires, among other things, that the aggrieved investors show that the deception resulted in the loss of a state remedy.

a. *"Mere" Breaches of Fiduciary Duty*

SANTA FE INDUSTRIES, INC. v. GREEN

430 U.S. 462 (1977)

JUSTICE BRYON WHITE:

The issue in this case involves the reach and coverage of §10(b) of the Securities Exchange Act of 1934 and Rule 10b-5 thereunder in the context of a Delaware short-form merger transaction used by the majority stockholder of a corporation to eliminate the minority interest.

I

In 1936, petitioner Santa Fe Industries, Inc. (Santa Fe), acquired control of 60% of the stock of Kirby Lumber Corp. (Kirby), a Delaware corporation. Through a series of purchases over the succeeding years, Santa Fe increased its control of Kirby's stock to 95%; the purchase prices during the period 1968- 1973 ranged from $65 to $92.50 per share. In 1974, wishing to acquire 100% ownership of Kirby, Santa Fe availed itself of § 253 of the Delaware Corporation Law, known as the "short-form merger" statute. Section 253 permits a parent corporation owning at least 90% of the stock of a subsidiary to merge with that subsidiary, upon approval by the parent's board of directors, and to make payment in cash for the shares of the minority stockholders. The statute does not require the consent of, or advance notice to, the minority stockholders. However, notice of the merger must be given within 10 days after its effective date, and any stockholder who is dissatisfied with the terms of the merger may petition the Delaware Court of Chancery for a decree ordering the surviving corporation to pay him the fair value of his shares, as determined by a court-appointed appraiser subject to review by the court. Del. Code Ann., Tit. 8, §§ 253, 262 (1975 ed. and Supp.1976).

Santa Fe obtained independent appraisals of the physical assets of Kirby land, timber, buildings, and machinery and of Kirby's oil, gas, and mineral interests. These appraisals, together with other financial information, were submitted to Morgan Stanley & Co. (Morgan Stanley), an investment banking firm retained to appraise the fair market value of Kirby stock. Kirby's physical assets were appraised at $320 million (amounting to $640 for each of the 500,000 shares); Kirby's stock was valued by Morgan Stanley at $125 per share. Under the terms of the merger, minority stockholders were offered $150 per share.

The provisions of the short-form merger statute were fully complied with. The minority stockholders of Kirby were notified the day after the merger became effective and were advised of their right to obtain an appraisal in Delaware court if dissatisfied with the offer of $150 per share. They also received an information statement containing, in addition to the relevant financial data about Kirby, the appraisals of the value of Kirby's assets and the Morgan Stanley appraisal concluding that the fair market value of the stock was $125 per share.

Respondents, minority stockholders of Kirby, objected to the terms of the merger, but did not pursue their appraisal remedy in the Delaware Court of Chancery. Instead, they brought this action in federal court on behalf of the corporation and other minority stockholders, seeking to set aside the merger or to recover what they claimed to be the fair value of their shares. The amended complaint asserted that, based on the fair market value of Kirby's physical assets as revealed by the appraisal included in the information statement sent to minority shareholders, Kirby's stock was worth at least $772 per share. The complaint alleged further that the merger took place without prior notice to minority stockholders; that the purpose of the merger was to appropriate the difference between the "conceded pro rata value of the physical assets," and the offer of $150 per share to "freez[e] out the minority stockholders at a wholly inadequate price;" and that Santa Fe, knowing the appraised value of the physical assets, obtained a "fraudulent appraisal" of the stock from Morgan Stanley and offered $25 above that appraisal "in order to lull the minority stockholders into erroneously believing that [Santa Fe was] generous." This course of conduct was alleged to be "a violation of Rule 10b-5 because defendants employed a 'device, scheme, or artifice to defraud' and engaged in an 'act, practice or course of business which operates or would operate as a fraud or deceit upon any person, in connection with the purchase or sale of any security.'" Morgan Stanley assertedly participated in the fraud as an accessory by submitting its appraisal of $125 per share although knowing the appraised value of the physical assets.

The District Court dismissed the complaint for failure to state a claim upon which relief could be granted. As the District Court understood the complaint, respondents' case rested on two distinct grounds. First, federal law was assertedly violated because the merger was for the sole purpose of eliminating the minority from the company, therefore lacking any justifiable business purpose, and because the merger was undertaken without prior notice to the minority shareholders. Second, the low valuation placed on the shares in the cash-exchange offer was itself said to be a fraud actionable under Rule 10b-5. ***

A divided Court of Appeals for the Second Circuit reversed. *** As to the first aspect of the case, the Court of Appeals did not disturb the District Court's conclusion that the complaint did not allege a material misrepresentation or nondisclosure with respect to the value of the stock; and the court declined to rule that a claim of gross undervaluation itself would suffice to make out a Rule 10b-5 case. With respect to the second aspect of the case, however, the court fundamentally disagreed with the District Court as to the reach and coverage of Rule 10b-5. The Court of Appeals' view was that, although the Rule plainly reached material misrepresentations and nondisclosures in connection with the purchase or sale of securities, neither misrepresentation nor nondisclosure was a necessary element of a Rule 10b-5 action; the Rule reached "breaches of fiduciary duty by a majority against minority shareholders without any charge of misrepresentation or lack of disclosure." The court went on to hold that the complaint, taken as a whole, stated a cause of action under the Rule:

> We hold that a complaint alleges a claim under Rule 10b-5 when it charges, in connection with a Delaware short-form merger, that the majority has committed a breach of its fiduciary duty to deal fairly with minority shareholders by effecting the merger without any justifiable business purpose. The minority shareholders are given no prior notice of the merger, thus having no opportunity

to apply for injunctive relief, and the proposed price to be paid is substantially lower than the appraised value reflected in the Information Statement.

We granted the petition for certiorari challenging this holding because of the importance of the issue involved to the administration of the federal securities laws. We reverse.

II

Section 10(b) of the 1934 Act makes it "unlawful for any person ... to use or employ ... any manipulative or deceptive device or contrivance in contravention of [Securities and Exchange Commission rules]"; Rule 10b-5, promulgated by the SEC under § 10(b), prohibits, in addition to nondisclosure and misrepresentation, any "artifice to defraud" or any act "which operates or would operate as a fraud or deceit." The court below construed the term "fraud" in Rule 10b-5 by adverting to the use of the term in several of this Court's decisions in contexts other than the 1934 Act and the related Securities Act of 1933. The Court of Appeals' approach to the interpretation of Rule 10b-5 is inconsistent with that taken by the Court last Term in *Ernst & Ernst v. Hochfelder*, 425 U.S. 185 (1976).

Ernst & Ernst makes clear that in deciding whether a complaint states a cause of action for "fraud" under Rule 10b-5, "we turn first to the language of § 10(b), for '[t]he starting point in every case involving construction of a statute is the language itself.'" Id., at 197, quoting *Blue Chip Stamps v. Manor Drug Stores*, 421 U.S. 723, 756 (1975) (Powell, J., concurring). In holding that a cause of action under Rule 10b-5 does not lie for mere negligence, the Court began with the principle that "[a]scertainment of congressional intent with respect to the standard of liability created by a particular section of the [1933 and 1934] Acts must ... rest primarily on the language of that section," 425 U.S. at 200, and then focused on the statutory language of § 10(b) "[t]he words 'manipulative or deceptive' used in conjunction with 'device or contrivance.' " Id., at 197. The same language and the same principle apply to this case.

To the extent that the Court of Appeals would rely on the use of the term "fraud" in Rule 10b-5 to bring within the ambit of the Rule all breaches of fiduciary duty in connection with a securities transaction, its interpretation would, like the interpretation rejected by the Court in *Ernst & Ernst*, "add a gloss to the operative language of the statute quite different from its commonly accepted meaning." Id., at 199. But, as the Court there held, the language of the statute must control the interpretation of the Rule:

> "Rule 10b-5 was adopted pursuant to authority granted the [Securities and Exchange] Commission under § 10(b). The rulemaking power granted to an administrative agency charged with the administration of a federal statute is not the power to make law. Rather, it is " 'the power to adopt regulations to carry into effect the will of Congress as expressed by the statute' " [The scope of the Rule] cannot exceed the power granted the Commission by Congress under § 10(b)." Id., at 212-214.

The language of § 10(b) gives no indication that Congress meant to prohibit any conduct not involving manipulation or deception. Nor have we been cited to any evidence in the legislative history that would support a departure from the language of the statute. "When a statute speaks so specifically in terms of manipulation and deception, ... and when its history reflects no more expansive intent, we are quite unwilling to extend the scope of the statute...." Id., at 214. Thus the claim of fraud and fiduciary breach in this complaint states a cause of action under any part of Rule 10b-5 only if the conduct alleged can be fairly viewed as 'manipulative or deceptive' within the meaning of the statute.

III

It is our judgment that the transaction, if carried out as alleged in the complaint, was neither deceptive nor manipulative and therefore did not violate either § 10(b) of the Act or Rule 10b-5.

As we have indicated, the case comes to us on the premise that the complaint failed to allege a material misrepresentation or material failure to disclose. The finding of the District Court, undisturbed by the Court of Appeals, was that there was no "omission" or "misstatement" in the information statement accompanying the notice of merger. On the basis of the information provided, minority shareholders could either accept the price offered or reject it and seek an appraisal in the Delaware Court of Chancery. Their choice was fairly presented, and they were furnished with all relevant information on which to base their decision.[14]

We therefore find inapposite the cases relied upon by respondents and the court below, in which the breaches of fiduciary duty held violative of Rule 10b-5 included some element of deception. Those cases forcefully reflect the principle that "[§] 10(b) must be read flexibly, not technically and restrictively" and that the statute provides a cause of action for any plaintiff who "suffer[s] an injury as a result of deceptive practices touching its sale [or purchase] of securities. ..." *Superintendent of Insurance v. Bankers Life & Cas. Co.*, 404 U.S. 6, 12-13 (1971). But the cases do not support the proposition, adopted by the Court of Appeals below and urged by respondents here, that a breach of fiduciary duty by majority stockholders, without any deception, misrepresentation, or nondisclosure, violates the statute and the Rule.

It is also readily apparent that the conduct alleged in the complaint was not 'manipulative' within the meaning of the statute. "Manipulation" is "virtually a term of art when used in connection with securities markets." *Ernst & Ernst*,

---

14. In addition to their principal argument that the complaint alleges a fraud under clauses (a) and (c) of Rule 10b-5, respondents also argue that the complaint alleges nondisclosure and misrepresentation in violation of clause (b) of the Rule. Their major contention in this respect is that the majority stockholder's failure to give the minority advance notice of the merger was a material nondisclosure, even though the Delaware short-form merger statute does not require such notice. Brief for Respondents 27. But respondents do not indicate how they might have acted differently had they had prior notice of the merger. Indeed, they accept the conclusion of both courts below that under Delaware law they could not have enjoined the merger because an appraisal proceeding is their sole remedy in the Delaware courts for any alleged unfairness in the terms of the merger. Thus, the failure to give advance notice was not a material nondisclosure within the meaning of the statute or the Rule. Cf. *TSC Industries, Inc. v. Northway, Inc.*, 426 U.S. 438 (1976).

425 U.S., at 199. The term refers generally to practices, such as wash sales, matched orders, or rigged prices, that are intended to mislead investors by artificially affecting market activity. See, e. g., § 9 of the 1934 Act (prohibiting specific manipulative practices). Section 10(b)'s general prohibition of practices deemed by the SEC to be "manipulative"—in this technical sense of artificially affecting market activity in order to mislead investors—is fully consistent with the fundamental purpose of the 1934 Act " 'to substitute a philosophy of full disclosure for the philosophy of *caveat emptor*....' " *Affiliated Ute Citizens v. United States*, 406 U.S. 128, 151 (1972), quoting *SEC v. Capital Gains Research Bureau*, 375 U.S. 180, 186 (1963). Indeed, nondisclosure is usually essential to the success of a manipulative scheme. No doubt Congress meant to prohibit the full range of ingenious devices that might be used to manipulate securities prices. But we do not think it would have chosen this "term of art" if it had meant to bring within the scope of § 10(b) instances of corporate mismanagement such as this, in which the essence of the complaint is that shareholders were treated unfairly by a fiduciary.

IV

The language of the statute is, we think, "sufficiently clear in its context" to be dispositive here, *Ernst & Ernst*, supra, at 201; but even if it were not, there are additional considerations that weigh heavily against permitting a cause of action under Rule 10b-5 for the breach of corporate fiduciary duty alleged in this complaint. Congress did not expressly provide a private cause of action for violations of §10(b). Although we have recognized an implied cause of action under that section in some circumstances, *Superintendent of Insurance v. Bankers Life & Cas. Co.*, supra, [404 U.S.] at 13 n. 9, we have also recognized that a private cause of action under the antifraud provisions of the Securities Exchange Act should not be implied where it is "unnecessary to ensure the fulfillment of Congress' purposes" in adopting the Act. *Piper v. Chris-Craft Industries*, 430 U.S., at 41, 97. Cf. *J. I. Case Co. v. Borak*, 377 U.S. 426, 431-433 (1964). As we noted earlier, the Court repeatedly has described the "fundamental purpose" of the Act as implementing a "philosophy of full disclosure"; once full and fair disclosure has occurred, the fairness of the terms of the transaction is at most a tangential concern of the statute. Cf. *Mills v. Electric Auto-Lite Co.*, 396 U.S. 375, 381-385 (1970). As in *Cort v. Ash*, 422 U.S. 66, 80 (1975), we are reluctant to recognize a cause of action here to serve what is "at best a subsidiary purpose" of the federal legislation.

A second factor in determining whether Congress intended to create a federal cause of action in these circumstances is "whether 'the cause of action [is] one traditionally relegated to state law. ...'" *Piper v. Chris-Craft Industries, Inc.*, 430 U.S., at 40, quoting *Cort v. Ash*, supra, at 78. The Delaware Legislature has supplied minority shareholders with a cause of action in the Delaware Court of Chancery to recover the fair value of shares allegedly undervalued in a short-form merger. Of course, the existence of a particular state-law remedy is not dispositive of the question whether Congress meant to provide a similar federal remedy, but as in *Cort* and *Piper*, we conclude that "it is entirely appropriate in this instance to relegate respondent and others in his situation to whatever remedy is created by state law." 422 U.S., at 84; 430 U.S., at 41.

The reasoning behind a holding that the complaint in this case alleged fraud under Rule 10b-5 could not be easily contained. It is difficult to imagine how a court could distinguish, for purposes of Rule 10b-5 fraud, between a majority stockholder's use of a short-form merger to eliminate the minority at an unfair price and the use of some other device, such as a long-form merger, tender offer, or liquidation, to achieve the same result; or indeed how a court could distinguish the alleged abuses in these going private transactions from other types of fiduciary self-dealing involving transactions in securities. The result would be to bring within the Rule a wide variety of corporate conduct traditionally left to state regulation. In addition to posing a "danger of vexatious litigation which could result from a widely expanded class of plaintiffs under Rule 10b-5," *Blue Chip Stamps v. Manor Drug Stores*, 421 U.S., at 740, this extension of the federal securities laws would overlap and quite possibly interfere with state corporate law. Federal courts applying a "federal fiduciary principle" under Rule 10b-5 could be expected to depart from state fiduciary standards at least to the extent necessary to ensure uniformity within the federal system. Absent a clear indication of congressional intent, we are reluctant to federalize the substantial portion of the law of corporations that deals with transactions in securities, particularly where established state policies of corporate regulation would be overridden. As the Court stated in *Cort v. Ash*, supra: "Corporations are creatures of state law, and investors commit their funds to corporate directors on the understanding that, except where federal law *expressly* requires certain responsibilities of directors with respect to stockholders, state law will govern the internal affairs of the corporation." 422 U.S., at 84 (emphasis added).

We thus adhere to the position that "Congress by § 10(b) did not seek to regulate transactions which constitute no more than internal corporate mismanagement." *Superintendent of Insurance v. Bankers Life & Cas. Co.*, 404 U.S., at 12. There may well be a need for uniform federal fiduciary standards to govern mergers such as that challenged in this complaint. But those standards should not be supplied by judicial extension of § 10(b) and Rule 10b-5 to "cover the corporate universe."[17]

The judgment of the Court of Appeals is reversed, and the case is remanded for further proceedings consistent with this opinion. ***

NOTES AND QUESTIONS

1. Federal vs. State Law. The Court distinguished between a breach of fiduciary duty (governed by the corporate governance law of the issuer's state of incorporation) and conduct involving deception in connection with the purchase or sale of a security (governed by the federal securities laws as well as

---

17. Cary, Federalism and Corporate Law: Reflections Upon Delaware, 83 Yale L.J. 663, 700 (1974) (footnote omitted). Professor Cary argues vigorously for comprehensive federal fiduciary standards, but urges a "frontal" attack by a new federal statute rather than an extension of Rule 10b-5. He writes: "It seems anomalous to jig-saw every kind of corporate dispute into the federal courts through the securities acts as they are presently written." Ibid.

by state blue sky laws). The United States is unique among major industrialized countries in drawing a jurisdictional as well as doctrinal distinction between "corporate law" and "securities law." Do these distinctions make sense? Are the distinctions as sharp as they may have been prior to the SOX? Can you point to specific provisions in which Congress legislated corporate governance? For articles anticipating an even greater role for Congress in the area of corporate governance, see Mark J. Roe, Delaware and Washington as Corporate Lawmakers, 34 Del. J. of Corp. L. 1 (2009); Renee M. Jones, Rethinking Corporate Federalism in the Era of Corporate Reform, 29 J. Corp. L. 625 (2004); Mark J. Roe, Delaware's Competition, 117 Harv. L. Rev. 588 (2003).

Consider also whether the distinction between conduct involving deception and conduct "merely" involving a breach of fiduciary duty is as obvious as the Court makes it seem. See Donald C. Langevoort, Seeking Sunlight in *Santa Fe*'s Shadow: The SEC's Pursuit of Managerial Accountability, 79 Wash. U. L. Q. 449, 451 (2001) (emphasizing that "[t]here are not many instances of governance abuse that are disclosed with complete candor" and that "[h]idden breaches of fiduciary obligation can almost always be characterized in terms of fraud or misrepresentation"). See also Robert B. Thompson & Hillary A. Sale, Securities Fraud as Corporate Governance: Reflections Upon Federalism, 56 Vand. L. Rev. 859 (2003); Jennifer O'Hare, Director Communications and the Uneasy Relationship Between the Fiduciary Duty of Disclosure and the Anti-Fraud Provisions of the Federal Securities Laws, 70 U. Cin. L. Rev. 475 (2002); Faith Stevelman Kahn, Transparency and Accountability: Rethinking Corporate Fiduciary Law's Relevance to Corporate Disclosure, 34 Ga. L. Rev. 505 (2000).

2. ***Judicial Economy.*** Was the *Santa Fe* decision justified by considerations of judicial economy? Consider the ramifications if the Court had held breach of fiduciary duty claims to be actionable under Section 10(b) and Rule 10b-5. Under these circumstances, would federal courts have generated a federal common law of fiduciary duties or would they have endeavored to follow state corporate law? If the latter, what would have happened if federal and state courts arrived at different interpretations of state law? What consequences would have ensued if the same fiduciary duty issue arose in federal and state courts simultaneously?

3. ***An Eventual Victory From the Jaws of Defeat?*** Consider how the Court's decision in *Santa Fe* may have affected the development of both federal and state law with respect to going-private transactions. As Professor Roberta Karmel has observed:

> As the preeminent authority on state corporate law, the Delaware courts have frequently reacted to federal securities law developments by changing interpretations of Delaware law. The SEC on the other hand often reacts to Delaware case law developments through rulemaking to overcome or clarify doctrines that the SEC believes do not provide investors adequate protection ***. A good example of this dialogue between the Delaware courts and the SEC occurred after the U.S. Supreme Court decided *Santa Fe*. After the Court rejected the plaintiff's claims that breaches of fiduciary duty could be a federal action and that a freezeout merger without a corporate business purpose was fraudulent under Rule 10b-5, the Delaware courts were challenged to express greater concern for minority shareholder interests in going-private transactions.

> The Delaware Supreme Court, in response, held that a long-form merger made for the sole purpose of freezing out minority shareholders was an abuse of the corporate process and a breach of duty. Then, in 1979, the SEC passed Rule 13e-3, which requires the issuer in a going-private transaction to disclose the true purpose of the transaction and alternative ways of achieving that purpose, the probable detriments and benefits to the issuer and minority shareholders, and whether the issuer believes the transaction is fair to unaffiliated holders. A few years later, in *Weinberger v. UOP, Inc.*, [457 A.2d 701 (Del. 1983)] the Delaware Supreme Court held that a parent tender offer for shares of a 50.5% owned subsidiary had to be entirely fair to the minority; this meant fair dealing and fair price. In view of this holding and an expanded appraisal remedy, however, the court abandoned the [ ] business purpose test.

Roberta S. Karmel, Realizing the Dream of William O. Douglas – The Securities and Exchange Commission Takes Charge of Corporate Governance, 30 Del. J. Corp. L. 79, 96-97 (2005).

Minority shareholders in going-private transactions therefore stand in far better stead today, in part because of enhanced federal disclosures, and in part because Delaware law now recognizes that such shareholders are entitled to their pro rata share of the value of the entire firm, without a discount taken simply because the minority lacks control. See *Paskill Corp. v. Alcoma Corp.*, 747 A.2d 549, 553 (Del. 2000) (stating that the "task in an appraisal proceeding is to value what has been taken from the shareholder, *i.e.,* the proportionate interest in the going concern"). Can you point to specific language in *Santa Fe* which may have prompted Delaware to enhance the protections available to minority shareholders in such transactions?

4. ***Reconsidering Fairness.*** As part of its sweeping legislation precipitated by the corporate and accounting scandals that rocked the securities markets in 2001-02, Congress required, and the SEC subsequently adopted, broad new rules mandating the certification of the annual and quarterly filings that must be made by reporting companies under the Exchange Act. Under these new rules, the issuer's chief executive officer and chief financial officer (or persons performing similar functions) must make a number of certifications, including that:

> (1) He or she has reviewed the report being filed; [and]
>
> (2) Based on his or her knowledge, the report does not contain any untrue statement of a material fact or omit to state a material fact necessary to make the statements made, in light of the circumstances under which such statements were made, not misleading with respect to the period covered by the report; [and]
>
> (3) Based on his or her knowledge, the financial statements, and other financial information included in the report, fairly present in all material respects the financial condition, results of operations and cash flows of the issuer as of, and for, the periods presented in the report.

Exchange Act Rules 13a-14 and 15d-14. See also Section 302 of the Sarbanes-Oxley Act.

Consider how (or whether) a report that satisfies the truthfulness condition in subsection (2) could nonetheless violate the fairness condition in subsection (3). Ascertaining the meaning of this fairness requirement will clearly be a top corporate priority, particularly because another provision of the Sarbanes-Oxley Act imposes similar certification requirements upon CEOs and CFOs and authorizes stiff criminal fines and prison terms for a "knowing" certification of a noncomplying report. See Section 906 of the Sarbanes-Oxley Act (codified at 18 U.S.C. § 1350 and providing for fines of up to $1 million and prison terms of not more than 10 years, or both, when the certification is "knowing" and fines up to $5 million and prison terms of not more than 20 years, or both, when the certification is not only "knowing" but done "willfully"). Note also that in its release adopting Rules 13a-14 and 15d-14, the SEC specifically stated that "an officer providing a false certification potentially could be subject to *** both Commission and private actions for violating Section 10(b) of the Exchange Act and Exchange Act Rule 10b-5." Final Rules: Certification of Disclosure in Companies' Quarterly and Annual Reports, Exchange Act Release No. 46427 (Aug. 29, 2002).

What is the difference between the fairness representation now required by CEOs and CFOs and the fairness issue that arose in *Santa Fe*?

---

b. Corporate Mismanagement and Lost State Remedies

In its landmark decision in *Goldberg v. Meridor*, 567 F.2d 209 (2d Cir. 1977), the Second Circuit built on footnote 14 in *Santa Fe* to hold that Section 10(b)'s deception requirement encompasses a breach by directors of their fiduciary duty to minority shareholders regarding an impending corporate transaction in the situation where the directors misstated or omitted certain material information and because of that deception, the minority shareholders lost the opportunity to have the transaction enjoined under state law. The following decision by the Third Circuit in an analogous case discusses *Goldberg*. Which opinion do you find more persuasive—that of the majority or the dissent?

HEALEY v. CATALYST RECOVERY OF PENNSYLVANIA, INC.

616 F.2d 641 (3rd Cir. 1980)

COLLINS J. SEITZ, CHIEF JUDGE:

Five individual and three corporate defendants appeal from a judgment entered against them on a jury verdict awarding the plaintiff damages for violation of §10(b) of the Securities Exchange Act of 1934 and rule 10b-5. ***

II. Existence of a Cause of Action

The major contention of the defendants concerns a recurring problem of recent years: the role of rule 10b-5 in the context of mergers effected under state law. At trial, the plaintiff argued that if he had been given the information he requested, he would have tried to enjoin the merger in state court. He relied on *Goldberg v. Meridor*, 567 F.2d 209 (2d Cir. 1977), which held that such a theory states a basis for a cause of action under rule 10b-5. ***

Initially, we must determine whether this circuit should adopt the reasoning of *Goldberg*. Some have argued that *Goldberg* is inconsistent with the Supreme Court's opinion in *Santa Fe Industries, Inc. v. Green*, 430 U.S. 462

(1977). ***

In *Santa Fe*, the minority's only possible state law remedy was appraisal. See id. at 474 n.14. The United States Court of Appeals for the Second Circuit distinguished the case in part on this ground in *Goldberg v. Meridor*, 567 F.2d 209 (2d Cir. 1977). In that case, under New York law the plaintiffs could seek an injunction against the merger in addition to their appraisal rights. Thus the information in the case was material to a reasonable investor because he could have used it to attempt to obtain an injunction.

It is important to note at the outset the difference between *Goldberg* and *Santa Fe*. The mere existence of a state injunctive remedy would be insufficient, by itself, to distinguish *Santa Fe*. The crucial difference is whether there was misrepresentation or omission in the flow of information between the majority and minority shareholders. In *Santa Fe*, the Supreme Court expressly noted that there had been no misinformation connected with the merger. By contrast, in *Goldberg*, the plaintiffs claimed that a parent corporation had either not disclosed or misleadingly disclosed information concerning its sale of the overvalued assets of its controlled subsidiary, some of the shares of which were held by the public.

We believe that this distinction concerning the flow of information between the majority and minority shareholders is persuasive. There is a strong federal interest, evidenced by the entire field of federal securities regulation, in ensuring a proper flow of information between the parties to a securities transaction. The Supreme Court has sanctioned a private cause of action under rule 10b-5 on behalf of sellers to enforce that federal interest. See *Santa Fe*, supra, 430 U.S. at 477, citing *Superintendent of Insurance v. Bankers Life & Casualty Co.*, 404 U.S. 6, 13 n.9 (1971). All that *Goldberg* holds is that if some misrepresentation or omission by the defendant prevents the plaintiff from stopping the merger through a state injunction, then there is a cause of action under rule 10b-5. Because this result flows from misinformation that harms the plaintiff, it is precisely the type of situation to which rule 10b-5 is addressed.

Nor do we perceive an inconsistency between this result and Part IV of *Santa Fe*. Part IV should not be read out of context. What was objectionable in *Santa Fe* was use of rule 10b-5 by the federal courts to override traditional areas of state law "[a]bsent a clear indication of congressional intent." 430 U.S. at 479. Thus the problem in *Santa Fe* was not merely federal judicial intrusion into areas of state law, but rather federal judicial invasion of areas of state law without explicit federal statutory authority.

Here, by contrast, the plaintiff alleges that the defendants engaged in conduct expressly forbidden by the statute and the rule: an omission of certain information claimed to be material. That the harm to the plaintiff from the omission was deprivation of a state remedy in no sense diminishes the federal interest in preventing the omission and thereby ensuring full disclosure of all material information in securities transactions. Indeed, deprivation of state rights and remedies often forms the basis for federal claims. See, e. g., Hart & Wechsler's The Federal Courts and the Federal System 500-06 (2d ed. 1973).

Moreover, the federal courts have a duty under the supremacy clause of the Constitution to ensure that federal interests are vindicated. The Supreme Court has permitted use of the securities laws in the merger context where there has been misinformation that violates a specific federal provision. See, e.g., *TSC Industries, Inc. v. Northway, Inc.*, 426 U.S. 438 (1976) (proxy rules). Thus we do not feel that *Santa Fe* can be read to force us to stay our hand from remedying the harm that flows from the very type of conduct to which specific federal statutory and regulatory provisions are addressed.

Accordingly, we hold that where a misrepresentation or omission of material information deprives a proper plaintiff minority shareholder of an opportunity under state law to enjoin a merger, there is a cause of action under rule 10b-5. ***

Having determined that the plaintiff has a cause of action, we now consider the defendants' [contention] *** that a plaintiff must make some type of showing on the question of whether he would have actually been granted the injunction had he been given the information in question.

*** Seen as a question of materiality, the issue of the plaintiff's ability to secure an injunction is easily resolved. Unless there is a reasonable probability that a shareholder could have used the information to obtain an injunction, then the information would not be important to the decisionmaking process of a reasonable investor. We therefore hold that in a case such as this, the plaintiff must demonstrate that at the time of the misrepresentation or omission, there was a reasonable probability of ultimate success in securing an injunction had there been no misrepresentation or omission. ***[W]e frame the test in terms of a reasonable probability for two reasons. First, we believe absolute certainty to be both an impossible goal as well as an impracticable standard for a jury to implement. Second, in most cases the state remedy will be a preliminary injunction, which looks to the likelihood of ultimate success.

It is important to stress here the relationship of the information to the injunction. As already noted, the mere existence of an injunctive remedy is not enough; the information must be of a type that if the plaintiff had the information not supplied, he could use it to seek an injunction. For example, in a case of omitted information, the question is whether, if the plaintiff had received the information, it would have been significant to the determination of the reasonable probability of ultimate success. ***

RUGGERO J. ALDISERT, CIRCUIT JUDGE, DISSENTING:

*** Healey's private action does not further the policies embodied in the securities laws. As the Court noted in *Santa Fe*, "the 'fundamental purpose' of the Act [is to implement] a 'philosophy of full disclosure'; once full and fair disclosure has occurred, the fairness of the terms of the transaction is at most a tangential concern of the statute." 430 U.S. at 477-78 (citation omitted). Although Healey does allege nondisclosure, the entire thrust of his state claim for injunctive relief would have been that the terms of the merger were unfair to him. By requiring him to demonstrate a reasonable probability of success in the state action, the majority require him to demonstrate unfairness to prevail on his federal claim. The majority thus deem concern for fairness, under the guise of nondisclosure, sufficient under the federal statutory schema to serve as a passport into a federal courtroom. Apart from its unjustified assumption that the concern for fairness cannot be vindicated in the state court system, the failure of this approach is dramatically demonstrated by the effect of the federal action. Healey's action serves only to protect his state breach of fiduciary duty action, which deals with a concern—fairness—that is "'at best a subsidiary purpose' of the federal legislation." 430 U.S. at 478. Thus, Healey has succeeded in slipping through the back door what federal courts are loathe to let him do directly: He challenges the fairness of a state corporate transaction, using the majority's test of "a reasonable probability of ultimate success" in the state action, by asserting his claim under the federal securities laws. ***

*** Healey's action also enters an area traditionally relegated to state law, *** [and a] clearer instance of a plaintiff asking federal courts to usurp state functions is difficult to imagine. The allegation is that the defendants violated federal law by withholding information critical to Healey's state claim. Not only does Healey's claim present an unpersuasive case for a federal remedy, it creates a startling irony. Under the majority's formulation, only if a plaintiff has a state claim for an injunction can he recover under federal rule 10b-5 for breach of fiduciary duty. If state injunctive relief is unavailable, as in *Santa Fe*, the plaintiff also has no federal remedy. Thus, rather than aiding plaintiffs under federal law who have no state remedy, the majority's formulation provides federal relief to plaintiffs who have state remedies, but denies federal relief to plaintiffs who have no state remedy! See Note, *Goldberg v. Meridor*: The Second Circuit's Resurrection of Rule 10b-5 Liability for Breaches of Corporate Fiduciary Duties to Minority Shareholders, 64 Va.L.Rev. 765, 776 (1978).

In *Santa Fe* the Court admonished against "extension of the federal securities laws" to the extent that they "overlap and quite possibly interfere with state corporate law." 430 U.S. at 479. By recognizing a federal action for the mere failure to release information relevant to a state action, the majority risk interference with state corporate law. ***

Most bothersome, however, is the implicit assumption by the majority that only federal courts can grant proper relief to an injured party whenever transactions in securities are involved. Traditional state remedies guarantee the plaintiff an appraisal procedure through which he can obtain the fair value of his stock. An action under rule 10b-5 guarantees him no more. Because it assures the plaintiff of no greater recovery than he could obtain in his state action, I cannot see how it promotes greater disclosure than the state action. Absent explicit legislative sanction, therefore, federal encroachment into this area is justified only if the federal courts do a superior job of administering the remedy. *** Because I cannot begin to accept the notion that federal judges have better expertise in state corporate law than state judges, I have no qualms about deferring to the state judiciaries and legislatures. Deference is supported by the admonitions of the Supreme Court regarding the breadth of the securities laws and its statements regarding the relationship of federal and state judiciaries.

Accordingly, because I cannot justify the majority's bold action in "federaliz[ing a] substantial portion of the law of corporations that deals with transactions in securities," *Santa Fe Industries, Inc. v. Green*, 430 U.S. at 479, I dissent. I would vacate the judgment of the district court and remand these proceedings with a direction to dismiss the action for lack of federal subject matter jurisdiction.

NOTES AND QUESTIONS

*1. **A Back Door Through*** **Santa Fe.** The dissenting opinion asserts that the majority effectively gives plaintiffs a means of overcoming the Supreme Court's *Santa Fe* decision. Is it correct in so asserting? For a federal court following the *Goldberg / Healey* line of cases, what types of state law issues might it have to decide in order to determine the existence of an actionable deception under Rule 10b-5?

*2. **Demonstrating the Loss of a State Remedy***. Under what circumstances is a plaintiff most likely to succeed in showing that he lost a state remedy? Is a plaintiff in a stronger position if he shows an undisclosed breach of fiduciary duty coupled with (i) a lost opportunity to seek an appraisal, (ii) a lost opportunity to seek an injunction against a transaction, and/or (iii) a lost opportunity to sue for damages? Is the appropriate standard *Healey*'s "reasonable probability of ultimate success" in the state action? Would a higher standard be better? A lower one?

*3. **Pleading and Preparing a Lost-State-Remedy Case.*** In *Goldberg/Healey*-type cases, the complaint will typically include: (i) a specific description of the shareholders' lost-state-law remedy and an explanation of why it would have been available to them under state procedural and substantive law; (ii) an explanation of how the undisclosed information related to the availability of the state remedy; (iii) an explanation of how the undisclosed information would have affected a reasonable shareholder's decision about whether to seek a state remedy; and (iv) the shareholders' likelihood of prevailing in state court had they sought the state remedy in question. How much emphasis would you give to each of these factors? In determining your strategy, be sure to consider the heightened pleading requirements in Section 21D(b)(1) of the Exchange Act (set forth at the beginning of this Chapter).

*4. **State vs. Federal Court.*** The dissent in *Healey* emphasized that the federal Rule 10b-5 remedy for the alleged deception was essentially the same as the state court remedy for the alleged breach of fiduciary duty: either action would have required the defendants to pay a successful plaintiff the fair value of his stock. Why nonetheless might the plaintiffs in *Healey* and *Goldberg* have favored litigation in federal court over state court? Would you expect a plaintiff in a similar situation to make the same decision today? What factors may account for this newfound fondness for state court litigation?

*5. **Litigation Decisions vs. Investment Decisions.*** *Goldberg* and *Healey* present one approach to whether undisclosed breaches of fiduciary duty are actionable under Rule 10b-5. The Seventh Circuit has rejected that approach in favor of an alternative which looks to whether the alleged misstatements or omissions affect "an investment decision." Consider Judge Easterbrook's analysis:

> ***What should happen when the missing information affected a decision not to file a lawsuit about the securities, as in *Goldberg v. Meridor*?

> We have suggested in recent years that the appropriate inquiry is whether the information disclosed or withheld affected an investment decision. E.g., *Harris Trust & Savings Bank v. Ellis,* 810 F.2d 700, 704 (7th Cir.1987). See also *Rand v. Anaconda-Ericsson, Inc.*, 794 F.2d 843, 847-48 (2d Cir.1986). The securities laws single out investment decisions concerning financial instruments from among the many decisions people must make. Whether to buy a house or go to school or take a job or file a suit may be important, but the securities laws do not apply to these decisions. The securities laws deal with instruments that have at least the potential to be traded in liquid markets, see *Marine Bank v. Weaver,* 455 U.S. 551, 560 (1982). Information about these instruments should be compiled and released by a single source, usually the issuer, to facilitate both trading among passive investors and the ability to compare the prospects of one firm against the prospects of others—a comparison essential if capital is to flow to its most valuable uses. If a person is locked into possession of a security, however, disclosure serves neither of these functions. Capital has been committed, and trading will not occur. Decisions concerning the securities then are not fundamentally different from decisions concerning works of art. The buyer of a purported Rembrandt who learns that the painting was only by "the studio of" the artist faces a tough decision, but not an investment decision.

LHLC Corp. v. Cluett, Peabody & Co., 842 F.2d 928, 931-32 (7th Cir. 1988). Is the Seventh Circuit's approach preferable?

At issue in *LHLC* was a misrepresentation involving a valuation of inventory that was made in connection with the sale of securities. Judge Easterbrook concluded that "[t]he [misrepresented] information, even if conventionally 'material,' did not affect the investment decision." Id. at 931. When the focus is on the "investment decision," what other elements of a Rule 10b-5 action are implicated? Does the following Note suggest at least a partial answer?

6. A Possible Proxy Fraud Analogy. A problem analogous to that in *Healey* arose in *Virginia Bankshares, Inc. v. Sandberg,* 501 U.S. 1083 (1991), an action under Section 14(a) of the Exchange Act and Rule 14a-9. In *Virginia Bankshares* (which is a principal case in Chapter 4), the plaintiff challenged a material misstatement in a proxy statement urging approval of a merger. That approval was assured based on the shares controlled by management, regardless of how the minority shareholders voted. Id. at 1099. At issue was whether the plaintiff could show, notwithstanding the superfluousness of the minority shareholders' vote, a causal connection between the fraudulent proxy statement and her injury. See id. The plaintiff attempted to establish this connection by arguing that the fraudulent proxy statement insulated management from a state law proceeding that the minority shareholders would have initiated in order to void the merger on conflict of interest grounds. See id. at 1101. The Court concluded that "[t]his case does not *** require us to decide whether § 14(a) provides a cause of action for lost state remedies, since there is no indication in the law or facts before us that the proxy solicitation resulted in any such loss." Id. at 1107. Does the Court's reservation of this question involving Rule 14a-9 causation undercut *Goldberg* and *Healey*?

Following *Virginia Bankshares,* lower federal courts have allowed causation to be established in Rule 14a-9 cases based on the loss of a state remedy. See, e.g., *Wilson v. Great Am. Indus., Inc.*, 979 F.2d 924 (2d Cir. 1992).

See also *Howing Co. v. Nationwide Corp.*, 972 F.2d 700, 709-710 (6th Cir. 1992) (accepting a lost state remedy argument in connection with claim made under Section § 13(e) of the Exchange Act). Do such lower court rulings bolster *Goldberg* and *Healey*?

7. Deceptive Opinions. The *Virginia Bankshares* decision described in the preceding note bears on Section 10(b)'s deception element in yet another respect. The challenged misrepresentation in *Virginia Bankshares* consisted of the directors' opinion as to what would be a fair price for the shares, thereby raising the question whether an opinion is a "fact" the misrepresentation of which can be actionable under Rule 14a-9. Id. at 1091. The Court concluded that while an opinion constitutes a "fact," it is not actionable simply because it is material and "misstate[s] the speaker's reasons." Id. at 1095. It must also be "false or misleading about its subject." Id. at 1095-96. Thus, the directors' assertion that $42 per share was a "fair price" for the stock would be actionable under Rule 14a-9 only so long as (i) the directors did not believe that $42 was a fair price and (ii) the price was not fair in fact. Cf. id. at 1109 (Scalia, J., concurring in part and concurring in the judgment).

These requirements from *Virginia Bankshares* are routinely imported into Rule 10b-5 decisions involving deceptive opinions. See, e.g., *Mayer v. Mylod,* 988 F.2d 635, 639 (6th Cir. 1993) (emphasizing that "[m]aterial statements which contain the speaker's opinion are actionable under Section 10(b) *** if the speaker does not believe the opinion and the opinion is not factually well-grounded"); *Elliott Assocs., L.P. v. Covance, Inc.*, 2000 WL 1752848 at *9 (S.D.N.Y. 2000) (stating that "unless plaintiffs can sufficiently plead that the speakers were aware of contrary information at the time they expressed their opinions regarding the status of the merger, such statements are not actionable under section 10(b) or Rule 10b-5"). Is it appropriate to import these requirements from Rule 14a-9 into Rule 10b-5? Are these requirements apt to be difficult to satisfy? In thinking about this question, consider the effect of the heightened pleading requirements in Section 21D(b)(1) of the Exchange Act (set forth at the beginning of this Chapter).

PROBLEM 2-1

Susan and Tim Anderson are minority shareholders of Apex, Inc., a closely held corporation with ten shareholders. Apex's board has three directors, elected annually. In February 2011, Susan and Tim learned of the board's unanimous decision to sell all of Apex's stock in XYZ, Inc., a wholly-owned subsidiary, to the Betta Group for $1 million. Four months later (after the sale had closed), the couple was stunned to discover that the Betta Group is owned by two of Apex's three directors. Susan then did additional research revealing that the fair market value of the former subsidiary was more than $3 million. Are the Andersons able to state a Rule 10b-5 claim against the directors for deception? Even if so, would you expect them to look toward a federal court for their remedy?

2. *Material Omissions in Particular*

We now focus specifically on material omissions as a category distinct from misleading statements, including half-truths. Here, the principal question is: when does a person's "pure" silence about material facts in a securities transaction satisfy Section 10(b)'s deception element?

a. The General Rule—Silence is Not Deceptive Absent a Duty to Speak

GALLAGHER v. ABBOTT LABORATORIES

269 F.3d 806 (7th Cir. 2001)

FRANK H. EASTERBROOK, CIRCUIT JUDGE:

Year after year the Food and Drug Administration inspected the Diagnostic Division of Abbott Laboratories, found deficiencies in manufacturing quality control, and issued warnings. The Division made efforts to do better, never to the FDA's satisfaction, but until 1999 the FDA was willing to accept Abbott's promises and remedial steps. On March 17, 1999, the FDA sent Abbott another letter demanding compliance with all regulatory requirements and threatening severe consequences. This could have been read as more saber rattling—Bloomberg News revealed the letter to the financial world in June, and Abbott's stock price did not even quiver—but later developments show that it was more ominous. By September 1999 the FDA was insisting on substantial penalties plus changes in Abbott's methods of doing business. On September 29, 1999, after the markets had closed, Abbott issued a press release describing the FDA's position, asserting that Abbott was in "substantial" compliance with federal regulations, and revealing that the parties were engaged in settlement talks. Abbott's stock fell more than 6%, from $40 to $37.50, the next business day. On November 2, 1999, Abbott and the FDA resolved their differences, and a court entered a consent decree requiring Abbott to remove 125 diagnostic products from the market until it had improved its quality control and to pay a $100 million civil fine. Abbott took an accounting charge of $168 million to cover the fine and worthless inventory. The next business day Abbott's stock slumped $3.50, which together with the earlier drop implied that shareholders saw the episode as costing Abbott (in cash plus future compliance costs and lost sales) more than $5 billion. ***

Plaintiffs in these class actions under § 10(b) of the Securities Exchange Act of 1934 and the SEC's Rule 10b-5 contend that Abbott committed fraud by deferring public revelation. The classes comprise all buyers of Abbott's securities between March 17 and November 2. (One class consists of persons who bought securities in ALZA, a firm that Abbott proposed to acquire through an exchange of securities and whose market price thus tracked Abbott's. For simplicity we treat these plaintiffs as purchasers of Abbott stock.) The district judge dismissed the complaints under Fed.R.Civ.P. 12(b)(6) for failure to state a claim on which relief may be granted *** [though] the judge's reasons seem more akin to an invocation of Fed.R.Civ.P. 9(b), which requires fraud to be pleaded with particularity, or the extra pleading requirements for securities cases created by the Private Securities Litigation Reform Act of 1995. But it is not necessary to decide whether Rule 12(b)(6), Rule 12(c), Rule 9(b), or the Reform Act supplies the best basis of decision. Nor is it necessary to decide whether the news was "material" before the FDA's negotiating position stiffened, to decide whether Abbott acted with the state of mind necessary to support liability under Rule 10b-5, or to address other potential stumbling blocks. What sinks plaintiffs' position is their inability to identify any false statement—or for that matter any truthful statement made misleading by the omission of news about the FDA's demands.

Much of plaintiffs' argument reads as if firms have an absolute duty to disclose all information material to stock prices as soon as news comes into their possession. Yet that is not the way the securities laws work. We do not have a system of continuous disclosure. Instead firms are entitled to keep silent (about good news as well as bad news) unless positive law creates a duty to disclose. See, e.g., *Basic, Inc. v. Levinson*, 485 U.S. 224, 239 n. 17 (1988); *Dirks v. SEC*, 463 U.S. 646, 653-54 (1983); *Chiarella v. United States*, 445 U.S. 222, 227-35 (1980); *Stransky v. Cummins Engine Co.*, 51 F.3d 1329, 1331 (7th Cir.1995); *Backman v. Polaroid Corp.*, 910 F.2d 10, 16 (1st Cir.1990) (en banc). Until the Securities Act of 1933 there was no federal regulation of corporate disclosure. The 1933 Act requires firms to reveal information only when they issue securities, and the duty is owed only to persons who buy from the issuer or an underwriter distributing on its behalf; every other transaction is exempt under § 4. (No member of either class contends that he purchased securities from Abbott, or an underwriter on Abbott's behalf, between March 17 and November 2.) Section 13 of the Securities Exchange Act of 1934 adds that the SEC may require issuers to file annual and other periodic reports—with the emphasis on *periodic* rather than continuous. Section 13 and the implementing regulations contemplate that these reports will be snapshots of the corporation's status on or near the filing date, with updates due not when something "material" happens, but on the next prescribed filing date.

Regulations implementing §13 require a comprehensive annual filing, the Form 10-K report, and less extensive quarterly supplements on Form 10-Q. The supplements need not bring up to date everything contained in the annual 10-K report; counsel for the plaintiff classes conceded at oral argument that nothing in Regulation S-K (the SEC's list of required disclosures) requires either an updating of Form 10-K reports more often than annually, or a disclosure in a quarterly Form 10-Q report of information about the firm's regulatory problems. The regulations that provide for disclosures on Form 10-Q tell us which items in the annual report must be updated (a subset of the full list), and how often (quarterly).

Many proposals have been made to do things differently—to junk this combination of sale-based disclosure with periodic follow-up and replace it with a system under which *issuers* rather than *securities* are registered and disclosure must be continuous. E.g., American Law Institute, Federal Securities Code xxvii-xxviii, § 602 & commentary (1978); Securities and Exchange Commission,

Report of the Advisory Committee on the Capital Formation and Regulatory Process 9-14, 36-38 (1996). Regulation S-K goes some distance in this direction by defining identical items of disclosure for registration of stock and issuers' subsequent reports, and by authorizing the largest issuers to use their annual 10-K reports as the kernels of registration statements for new securities. But Regulation S-K does not replace periodic with continuous disclosure, and the more ambitious proposals to do this have not been adopted.

The ALI's proposal, for example, was embraced by the SEC, see 1933 Act Release No. 6242 (Sept. 18, 1980); 1933 Act Release No. 6377 (Jan. 31, 1982), but never seriously pursued, and revisions of Regulation S-K satisfied many of the original supporters of the ALI's proposal. The advisory committee report, prepared by a distinguished group of scholars and practitioners under the leadership of Commissioner Steven M.H. Wallman, did not persuade the SEC's other members and was not taken up by the agency as a legislative plan or even as the basis of a demonstration project. Whatever may be said for and against these proposals, they must be understood as projects for legislation (and to a limited extent for the use of the SEC's rulemaking powers); judges have no authority to scoop the political branches and adopt continuous disclosure under the banner of Rule 10b-5. *Especially* not under that banner, for Rule 10b-5 condemns only fraud, and a corporation does not commit fraud by standing on its rights under a periodic-disclosure system. The Supreme Court has insisted that this judicially created right of action be used only to implement, and not to alter, the rules found in the text of the 1933 and 1934 Acts. See *Central Bank of Denver, N.A. v. First Interstate Bank of Denver, N.A.*, 511 U.S. 164, 173 (1994) ("We have refused to allow [private] 10b-5 challenges to conduct not prohibited by the text of the statute.").

Trying to locate some statement that was either false or materially misleading because it did not mention the FDA's position, plaintiffs pointed in the district court to several reports filed or statements made by Abbott before November 2, 1999. All but two of these have fallen by the wayside on appeal. What remain are Abbott's Form 10-K annual report for 1998 filed in March 1999 and an oral statement that Miles White, Abbott's CEO, made at the annual shareholders' meeting the next month.

Plaintiffs rely principally on Item 303(a)(3)(ii) of Regulation S-K, which provides that registration statements and annual 10-K reports must reveal

> any known trends or uncertainties that have had or that the registrant reasonably expects will have a material favorable or unfavorable impact on net sales or revenues or income from continuing operations.

The FDA's letter, and its negotiating demands, are within this description, according to the plaintiff classes. We shall assume that this is so. The 10-K report did state that Abbott is "subject to comprehensive government regulation" and that "[g]overnment regulatory actions can result in ... sanctions." Plaintiffs say that this is too general in light of the FDA's letter and Abbott's continuing inability to satisfy the FDA's demands. Again we shall assume that plaintiffs are right. But there is a fundamental problem: The 10-K report was filed on March 9, 1999, and the FDA's letter is dated March 17, eight days later. Unless Abbott had a time machine, it could not have described on March 9 a letter that had yet to be written.

Attempting to surmount this temporal problem, plaintiffs insist that Abbott had a "duty to correct" the 10-K report. Yet a statement may be "corrected" only if it was *in*correct when made, and nothing said as of March 9 was incorrect. In order to maintain the difference between periodic-disclosure and continuous-disclosure systems, it is essential to draw a sharp line between duties to correct and duties to update. We drew just this line in *Stransky* and adhere to it now. If, for example, the 10-K report had said that Abbott's net income for 1998 was $500 million, and the actual income was $400 million, Abbott would have had to fix the error. But if the 10-K report had projected a net income of $125 million for the first quarter of 1999, and accountants determined in May that the actual profit was only $100 million, there would have been nothing to correct; a projection is not rendered false when the world turns out otherwise. See *Wielgos v. Commonwealth Edison Co.*, 892 F.2d 509 (7th Cir.1989). Amending the 10-K report to show the results for 1999 as they came in—or to supply a running narrative of the dispute between Abbott and the FDA—would *update* the report, not *correct* it to show Abbott's actual condition as of March 9.

Updating documents has its place in securities law. A registration statement and prospectus for a new issue of securities must be accurate when it is used to sell stock, and not just when it is filed. Section 12(a)(2) of the '33 Act; Regulation S-K, Item 512(a). Material changes in a company's position thus must be reflected in a registration statement promptly. But this does not imply changes in a 10-K annual report, even when that report is used (as it can be with securities registered on Form S-3, or for a shelf offering under Rule 415) as the principal disclosure document. Instead of changing the 10-K report weekly or monthly, the issuer must file and distribute an addendum to that document bringing matters up to date. See Form S-3, Item 11. Anyway, as we've already mentioned, Abbott did not sell any stock to the class members during the period from March 17 to November 2, 1999.

As for White's statements at the annual meeting: he said very little that was concrete (as opposed to puffery), and everything concrete was true. White said, for example:

> The outcome [of our efforts] has been growth more than five times faster than the diagnostics market. We expect this trend to continue for the foreseeable future, due to the unprecedented state of our new product cycle. By supplementing our internal investment with opportunistic technology acquisitions, Abbott's diagnostics pipeline is fuller than ever before.

The statement about past performance was accurate, and the plaintiffs have not given us any reason to doubt that White honestly believed that similar growth would continue, or that White honestly believed "Abbott's diagnostics pipeline [to be] fuller than ever before." Even with the benefit of hindsight these statements cannot be gainsaid. Here is where Rule 9(b) pinches: Plaintiffs have done nothing to meet the requirements for pleading fraud with respect to the annual meeting, even if it were possible (which we doubt) to treat as "fraud" the predictive components in White's boosterism. See *DiLeo v. Ernst & Young*, 901 F.2d 624 (7th Cir.1990). ***

NOTES AND QUESTIONS

*1. **The Right to Remain Silent.*** In *Abbott*, the Seventh Circuit joined a long line of other courts, including the Supreme Court, in emphasizing that remaining silent about both good news and bad is a right that a securities issuer may exercise in the absence of a positive duty to disclose that information. See, e.g., *Basic Inc. v. Levinson*, 485 U.S. 224, 239 n.17 (1988) ("[s]ilence, absent a duty to disclose, is not misleading under Rule 10b-5"); *In re Time Warner Sec. Litig.*, 9 F.3d 259, 267 (2d Cir. 1993) ("a corporation is not required to disclose a fact merely because a reasonable investor would very much like to know that fact"); *In re Burlington Coat Factory Sec. Litig.*, 114 F.3d 1410, 1432 (3d Cir. 1997) ("there is no general duty on the part of a company to provide the public with all material information"). Note that this general rule in Rule 10b-5 cases is consistent with the common law, where the principle of caveat emptor generally governs in the absence of some affirmative duty giving rise to an obligation of disclosure. See, e.g., Restatement (Second) of Torts § 551(1) (emphasizing that liability for fraudulent nondisclosure attaches "if, but only if, [one party to a transaction] is under a duty to the other to exercise reasonable care to disclose the matter in question").

*2. **Silence as Deception in Insider Trading Cases.*** The Supreme Court's discussion of silence as deception has occurred largely in insider trading cases. But cf. *Basic Inc. v. Levinson,* 485 U.S. 224, 239 n. 17 (1988) (noting in the context of a fraud-on-the-market action that "[s]ilence, absent a duty to disclose, is not misleading under Rule 10b-5"). The Court's most important discussion of silence as deception occurred in *Chiarella v. United States*, 445 U.S. 222 (1980). As we shall see in Chapter 7 (which is devoted exclusively to insider trading), Chiarella was a financial printer who bought stock in target companies prior to the public announcement of the tender offers, based on information he had learned from confidential documentation supplied to his employer by the acquiring companies. In deciding whether Chiarella could legally trade target company securities without disclosing the material nonpublic information in his possession, the Court emphasized the following:

> At common law, misrepresentation made for the purpose of inducing reliance upon the false statement is fraudulent. But one who fails to disclose material information prior to the consummation of a transaction commits fraud only when he is under a duty to do so.

Id. at 227-28. The Court eventually concluded that Chiarella did not in fact deceive the target company shareholders because "the element required to make [his] silence fraudulent—a duty to disclose—is absent in this case." Id. at 232. The Court explained:

> Section 10(b) is aptly described as a catchall provision, but what it catches must be fraud. When an allegation of fraud is based on a nondisclosure, there can be

> no fraud absent a duty to speak. We hold that a duty to disclose under § 10(b) does not arise from the mere possession of nonpublic market information. The contrary result is without support in the legislative history of § 10(b) and would be inconsistent with the careful plan that Congress has enacted for regulation of the securities markets. Cf. *Santa Fe Industries, Inc. v. Green*, 430 U.S., at 479.

Chiarella, 445 U.S. at 234-35. In extensive dicta, the Court observed that Chiarella's silence would have constituted deception had he been an officer or director of one of the target companies in which he bought shares. See id. at 228-29 (noting that the relationship between corporate insiders and shareholders "gives rise to a duty to disclose because of the 'necessity of preventing a corporate insider from ... tak[ing] unfair advantage of the uninformed minority stockholders' "). See also *Dirks v. SEC*, 463 U.S. 646, 656 n. 14 (1983) (extending the duty to disclose to corporate "outsiders" such as lawyers or accountants who "have entered into a special confidential relationship in the conduct of the business of the enterprise and are given access to information solely for corporate purposes"). The *Chiarella* Court declined to rule on whether the defendant could be held liable based on his misappropriation of the information from his employer and his employer's client. In the Court's view, the government had not adequately presented the misappropriation theory to the jury. See *Chiarella*, supra, 445 U.S. at 235-37. The Court thereafter upheld the misappropriation theory in *United States v. O'Hagan*, 521 U.S. 642, 665 (1997) (applying the theory to an attorney who worked in the law firm retained by the tender offeror and who traded in the target company's securities).

Note that *Abbott* cited *Chiarella* and *Dirks* in support of its statement that "firms are entitled to keep silent (about good news as well as bad news) unless positive law creates a duty to disclose." For the argument that insider trading cases are unique and thus "unlikely to be helpful in solving different 10b-5 problems, such as the issuer's duty to disclose," see Donald C. Langevoort & G. Mitu Gulati, The Muddled Duty to Disclose Under Rule 10b-5, 57 Vand. L. Rev. 1639, 1675 (2004).

b. The Duty to Disclose

The general rule that silence under Rule 10b-5 does not constitute deception without a duty to disclose is merely an empty vessel absent analysis of the numerous ways in which a duty to disclose can arise. The *Chiarella* Court began to fill this vessel by focusing on the fiduciary relationship between corporate insiders and shareholders, and in *Abbott* Judge Easterbrook added further substance by focusing on the disclosure requirements of the Securities Act and the Exchange Act and the so-called duties to update and correct. The balance of the material in this subpart explores these and other sources of disclosure duties.

i. Line-Item and Real Time Disclosure Requirements

As noted in *Abbott*, the Securities Act's registration requirement as well as the Exchange Act's periodic reporting requirements impose on securities issuers an affirmative duty to disclose information about a wide range of matters including results of business operations, financial position, transactions involving directors and other related persons, and known trends or uncertainties (including pending litigation) that the issuer expects will have a favorable or unfavorable impact on net sales or revenues. Most of these disclosures take the form of "line-items" in Regulations S-X (for accounting-related information) and S-K (for all other information), and these line-items must be included in any registration statements filed with the SEC (on a Form S-1, for example) as well as in a reporting company's annual report (Form 10-K) and quarterly reports (Form 10-Qs). Particularly sweeping are the disclosure requirements set out in Item 303(a) of Regulation S-K, which is often referred to as MD & A disclosures ("Management's Discussion and Analysis").

Additional disclosure obligations under the Exchange Act are imposed for specific transactions or events. For example, Section 14(a) imposes disclosure requirements in connection with proxy solicitations in connection with a security registered under Section 12. Section 13(d) requires disclosure in connection with the acquisition of more than 5% of a class of equity security of a Section 12 company; Section 14(d) requires disclosure when a tender offer is the means of accomplishing the acquisition of more than 5% of a class of equity security of a Section 12 company; and Section 14(e) prohibits fraud in connection with tender offers in all companies. The schedules that must be filed with the SEC on the occurrence of these transactions or events (i.e., Schedule 14A, Schedule 13D, or a Schedule TO) contain highly detailed line-item requirements, many of which simply draw upon the line-items set out in Regulations S-X and S-K.

To be sure, when *Abbott* was decided in 2001, reporting companies were under only a minimal obligation to update information previously disclosed in annual and quarterly reports because only six "momentous" events had to be reported on a Form 8-K: changes in control of the issuer; acquisition or disposition of significant assets not in the ordinary course of business; bankruptcy or receivership; changes in accountants; resignation of directors; and change in fiscal year. Although such companies were entitled to utilize Form 8-K to report the occurrence of any other event deemed "of importance to securities holders," such reporting was voluntary rather than mandatory

But the continued vitality of *Abbott's* blanket statement that "[w]e do not have a system of continuous disclosure" now turns on what the SEC decides to do with its rulemaking power under SOX Section 409, which added a new Section 13(*l*) to the Exchange Act.

> **Section 13(*l*) REAL TIME ISSUER DISCLOSURES**—Each issuer reporting under section 13(a) or 15(d) shall disclose to the public on a rapid and current basis such additional information concerning material changes in the financial condition or operations of the issuer, in plain English, which may include trend and qualitative information and graphic presentations, as the Commission determines, by rule, is necessary or useful for the protection of investors and in the public interest.

Even before Congress provided this specific statutory authorization for a system of real time disclosure, the SEC had been contemplating for some time an overhaul of the periodic disclosure system. Specifically, a little more than a month before SOX's enactment, the SEC had proposed significant revisions to the types of disclosures required of reporting companies on Form 8-K and a shortening of the time period for such reporting.

In March 2004, after a period of notice and comment, the SEC announced significant new amendments to Form 8-K. See Final Rule: Additional Form 8-K Disclosure Requirements and Acceleration of Filing Date, Release No. 34-49424 (March 16, 2004). The final rule modified some of the SEC's original proposals, but responded to the congressional mandate for "real time disclosure" by adding eight new items to Form 8-K, transferring two items from periodic reports, and expanding disclosures under two existing Form 8-K items. The items subject to mandatory Form 8-K reporting now include:

Item 1.01 – Entry into a Material Definitive Agreement

Item 1.02 – Termination of a Material Definitive Agreement

> *[Adopting Release specifies that Items 1.01 & 1.02 are intended to apply to contracts and other agreements "that are not made in the ordinary course of business." The Release also makes clear that letters of intent for mergers and acquisitions need only be disclosed if they impose "enforceable obligations" by or against the registrant.]*

Item 1.03 – Bankruptcy or Receivership

Item 2.01 – Completion of Acquisition or Disposition of Assets

> *[Adopting Release refers to a "significant asset test" – generally met if the acquisition or disposition exceeds 10% of the registrant's total assets]*

Item 2.02 – Results of Operations and Financial Condition

Item 2.03 – Creation of a Direct Financial Obligation or an Obligation Under an Off-Balance Sheet Arrangement of a Registrant

Item 2.04 – Triggering Events That Accelerate or Increase a Direct Financial Obligation or an Obligation under an Off-Balance Sheet Arrangement

Item 2.05 – Costs Associated with Exit or Disposal Activities

Item 2.06 – Material Impairments

Item 3.01 – Notice of Delisting or Failure to Satisfy a Continued Listing Rule or Standard; Transfer of Listing

Item 3.02 – Unregistered Sales of Equity Securities

Item 3.03 – Material Modifications to Rights of Security Holders

Item 4.01 – Changes in Registrant's Certifying Accountant

Item 4.02 – Non-Reliance on Previously Issued Financial Statements or a Related Audit Report or Completed Interim Review

Item 5.01 – Changes in Control of Registrant

Item 5.02 – Departure of Directors or Principal Officers; Election of Directors; Appointment of Principal Officers

Item 5.03 – Amendments to Articles of Incorporation or Bylaws; Change in Fiscal Year

Item 5.04 – Temporary Suspension of Trading Under Registrant's Employee Benefit Plans

Item 5.05 – Amendments to the Registrant's Code of Ethics, or Waiver of a Provision of the Code of Ethics

The Form 8-K amendments also shorten an issuer's filing deadline for most items to four business days after the triggering event.

In addition to expanding significantly the type of information that issuers must report on Form 8-K and shortening the time period for such reporting, the SEC adopted a limited safe harbor from public and private claims under Exchange Act Section 10(b) and Rule 10b-5 for an issuer's failure to timely file a Form 8-K with respect to the following items:

Item 1.01 – Entry into a Material Definitive Agreement

Item 1.02 – Termination of a Material Definitive Agreement

Item 2.03 – Creation of a Direct Financial Obligation or an Obligation under an Off-Balance Sheet Arrangement of a Registrant

Item 2.04 – Triggering Events that Accelerate or Increase a Direct Financial Obligation under an Off-Balance Sheet Arrangement

Item 2.05 – Costs Associated with Exit or Disposal Activities

Item 2.06 – Material Impairments

Item 4.02(a) – Non-Reliance on Previously Issued Financial Statements or a Related Audit Report or Completed Interim Review (in the case where a company makes the determination and does not receive a notice described in Item 4.02(b) from its accountant)

The safe harbor for these items provides that "[n]o failure to file a report on Form 8-K that is required solely pursuant to [the above items] shall be deemed to be a violation" of Section 10(b) and Rule 10b-5. What policy justifications support the adoption of this Rule 10b-5 safe harbor? Why did the SEC limit this safe harbor to the seven items specified above?

PROBLEM 2-2

Reconsider the facts of *Gallagher v. Abbott Laboratories*. If the new revisions to Form 8-K had been effective at the time that Abbott received the FDA's March 17, 1999 letter demanding compliance and threatening severe consequences, would Abbott have owed its shareholders a duty to disclose this information? If so, is it now correct to say that we have a system of continuous disclosure for reporting companies? If not, do you think that result would be consistent with the congressional intentions behind Section 13(*l*)'s real time disclosure directive? In other words, does the SEC have an obligation to build on the Form 8-K amendments adopted in March 2004?

Note that even if the SEC adopts rules requiring a company to disclose information such as the FDA letter in *Abbott*, rules of this sort will produce a system of "real time" disclosure only to the extent that they are rigorously enforced. Instructive on this point are the experiences of the New York Stock Exchange, the American Stock Exchange, and the National Association of Securities Dealers Automated Quotation System (NASDAQ) which, for decades, have required listed companies to comply with what was, in effect, a continuous disclosure requirement. Consider, for example, Section 202.05 in the NYSE Listed Company Manual:

> A listed company is expected to release quickly to the public any news or information which might reasonably be expected to materially affect the market for its securities. This is one of the most important and fundamental purposes of the listing agreement which the company enters into with the Exchange.

Listed companies that violate the exchanges or the NASDAQ's disclosure requirements risk the imposition of sanctions by the exchange or NASDAQ including an order to halt trading in the company's securities. Yet it is widely believed that a listed company's risk of sanction is minimal, given the negligible enforcement efforts made by the exchanges and the NASDAQ. One particularly staunch critic of this practice is Professor Dale Oesterle, who has stated:

> [O]ur most important market, the NYSE, has a continuous disclosure requirement that is extraordinary in its breadth, its lack of any exception for sensitive information, and its imprecision. However, the sloppiness is revealing. An exchange that does not specifically enforce the language of its rules can afford to be imprecise and over-broad because no-one cares. It is a classic bargain of mutual convenience: lawyers advise firms that the language is not enforced, and firms safely ignore it. The exchanges enjoy whatever positive public relations come from having the language in their listing manuals.

Dale Arthur Oesterle, The Inexorable March Toward a Continuous Disclosure Requirement for Publicly Traded Corporations: "Are We There Yet?" 20 Cardozo L. Rev. 135, 163 (1998). And while the shareholders of these listed companies would no doubt be ready and willing to pursue such enforcement efforts through private litigation, courts have generally been consistent in holding that Rule 10b-5 does not provide a private right of action for violating the continuous disclosure provisions of the exchanges and the NASDAQ. See *Freedman v. Louisiana-Pacific Corp.*, 922 F. Supp. 377, 390 (D. Or. 1996) ("[p]laintiffs' citations to the NYSE Manual *** are irrelevant with respect to establishing [defendant's] duty to disclose under § 10(b) and Rule 10b-5"). See also *State Teachers Retirement Bd. v. Fluor Corp.*, 654 F.2d 843, 852-53 (2d Cir. 1981).

ii. A Brief Word About Regulation FD

Another important issue relating to the duty to disclose under the federal securities laws involves Regulation FD (for "Fair Disclosure"), adopted by the SEC in August 2000 and applicable to companies required to file reports under Sections 13(a) and 15(d) of the Exchange Act. See Regulation FD, Rules 100-03. To be sure, Regulation FD does not compel these companies to make public disclosure of information. But it does prohibit them from engaging in selective disclosure of information to securities analysts or to other favored constituencies by requiring any such disclosure to be shared with the general public. The Regulation is, however, enforceable only in an action brought by the SEC, and by its specific terms "[n]o failure to make a public disclosure required solely by [Regulation FD] shall be deemed to be a violation of Rule 10b-5 under the Securities Exchange Act." Id., Rule 102. Why was the Regulation drafted so as to sever any connection to Rule 10b-5? We will consider Regulation FD again in connection with insider trading in Chapter 7.

iii. The Duty to Update

For years prior to Congress's recent embrace of "real time" disclosure, a number of federal appeals courts had recognized a so-called "duty to update" as an exception to a securities issuer's general right to remain silent about new material information. See, e.g, *Weiner v. Quaker Oats Co.*, 129 F.3d 310, 318 (3d Cir. 1997). The case law on the duty to update remains important even now that SOX is on the books. First, because any real time disclosure rules will apply only to reporting companies, the duty continues to be relevant as a source of obligation for non-reporting companies as well as for individuals. Second, even for reporting companies, the SEC's "real time" rulemaking is apt to leave uncertain the necessity of disclosing many types of information. The duty to update may therefore continue to function as an additional source of disclosure obligation.

In the federal circuits in which it is recognized, the duty to update imposes a duty, typically on a securities issuer, to modify or supplement a prior statement that, although accurate when made, has since become inaccurate or misleading in light of subsequent developments. Such past disclosures, however, need be updated only to the extent that they remain "alive" in the minds of reasonable investors. See *Weiner v. Quaker Oats Co.*, supra, 129 F.3d at 318 (concluding that "[t]he complaint alleges facts on the basis of which a reasonable factfinder could determine that Quaker's statements regarding its total debt-to-total-capitalization ratio guideline would have been material to a reasonable investor, and hence that Quaker had a duty to update such statements when they became unreliable").

One of the most notable cases recognizing a securities issuer's duty to update is *In re Time Warner Sec. Litig.*, 9 F.3d 259 (2d Cir. 1993). In that case, Time Warner had voluntarily disclosed to its shareholders that it was negotiating with unnamed "strategic partners," mostly in Europe, who would provide Time Warner with cash flow needed to pay off debt from its recent highly leveraged merger (consummated, among other reasons, in order to fend off a hostile takeover bid for Time from Paramount Communications). When negotiations with these "strategic partners" failed, Time Warner had to raise the necessary cash with a rights offering, which diluted the value of the shares held by the company's existing stockholders. Some of these stockholders alleged that Time Warner's failure to disclose that it had been considering the rights offering as an alternative to the strategic partnerships made the prior public disclosures about negotiations for these partnerships materially misleading. Although the district court dismissed this claim, the Second Circuit reversed, holding that "when a corporation is pursuing a specific business goal and announces that goal as well as an intended approach for reaching it, it may come under an obligation to disclose other approaches to reaching the goal when those approaches are under active and serious consideration." Id. at 268. In effect, the Second Circuit found that an issuer's public statement about a specific plan can trigger a duty to update when the issuer begins seriously to consider an alternative plan to achieve the same goal in a different way. But a subsequent Second Circuit decision cautioned against construing the duty to update in a manner that amounts to a requirement of continuous disclosure. See *San Leandro Emergency Med. Group Profit Sharing Plan v. Philip Morris Cos.*, 75 F.3d 801, 810 (2d Cir. 1996) (noting that *Time Warner* "went nearly to the outer limit of the line that separates disclosable plans from plans that need not be disclosed," and concluding that Philip Morris did not have a duty to disclose its alternative plan for marketing cigarettes, even though the new plan constituted a radical change from its previously announced pricing strategy that would reduce the company's profits for the upcoming year by more than $2 million dollars).

Rather than attempting to distinguish between which subsequent plans or events require disclosure and which do not, the Seventh Circuit has rejected outright the existence of a duty to update. In *Stransky v. Cummins Engine Co.*, 51 F.3d 1329 (7th Cir. 1995), the Seventh Circuit refused to impose on an issuer a duty to update its projections merely because subsequent events showed them to be inaccurate. The court based its refusal on Rule 10b-5(b)'s language prohibiting "any untrue statement of material fact or [omitting] to state a material fact necessary in order to make the statements made, *in the light of the circumstances under which they were made*, not misleading" (emphasis added). Id. at 1332. In the court's opinion, this language "implicitly precludes basing liability on circumstances that arise after the speaker makes the statements." Id. The court therefore concluded that a "projection can lead to liability under Rule 10b-5 only if it was not made in good faith or was made without a reasonable basis." Id. at 1333. The court found that such an approach "remains true" to Rule 10b-5's text and restricts the imposition of liability "to the small number of statements that are most harmful in the marketplace." Id. Significantly, *Stransky* did not confine its rejection of the duty to update to prior statements involving projections or other soft information (subjects covered in connection with the materiality requirement in Section B of this Chapter). Indeed, recall that *Abbott* cited *Stransky* to buttress its conclusion that there was no obligation to disclose the existence of the FDA letter threatening sanctions.

Does recognition of a duty to update inevitably emasculate the general rule that silence is not actionable absent a duty to speak? Can a valid line be drawn between subsequent plans or events as to which updating is necessary and those as to which disclosure should be voluntary? It appears that the court in *San Leandro* drew a distinction between financing strategy that had been the subject of much corporate "hype" (*Time Warner*) and more ordinary business decisions such as Philip Morris's plans to change its marketing. Is this distinction a workable one? Finally, consider the First Circuit's policy argument that "[f]ear that statements of historical fact might be claimed to fall within [the duty to update], could inhibit disclosures altogether." See *Backman v. Polaroid Corp.*, 910 F.2d 10, 17 (1st Cir. 1990). Is this a valid concern?

iv. The Duty to Correct

The duty to correct arises when a statement already made is later discovered to have been false when made. The duty to correct thus requires a company to redress intentional or negligent misrepresentations as well as statements that it believed to be true when made but subsequently learned were materially false, incomplete, or misleading.

Most courts recognize some form of a duty to correct when the prior false statements were made by the issuer or one of its officials. See *Abbott*, supra. See also *Stransky v. Cummins Engine Co.*, 51 F.3d 1329, 1331 (7th Cir. 1995) (stating that the duty to correct arises "when a company makes a historical statement that, at the time made, the company believed to be true, but as revealed by subsequently discovered information actually was not"); *In re MobileMedia Sec. Litig.*, 28 F. Supp.2d 901 (D.N.J. 1998) (finding that MobileMedia's discovery of past instances of noncompliance with FCC regulation placed the company under a duty to correct prior statements made in FCC filings as to the company's full compliance). An accountant who fails to correct a certified opinion may also incur liability under Rule 10b-5 as a primary violator, when that accountant "1) makes a statement in its certified opinion that is false or misleading when made; (2) subsequently learns or was reckless in not learning that the earlier statement was false or misleading; (3) knows or should know that potential investors are relying on the opinion and financial statements; yet (4) fails to take reasonable steps to correct or withdraw its opinion and/or the financial statements." *Overton v. Todman & Co.*, 478 F.3d 479, 486-87 (2d Cir. 2007).

There is substantially more doubt, however, as to whether (and when) issuers may be under a duty to correct false statements made by third parties. Virtually all courts agree that issuers are not under a duty to correct third party statements (including inaccurate rumors) when such statements cannot be attributed to the issuer or its officials. See *State Teachers Retirement Bd. v. Fluor Corp.*, 654 F.2d 843, 850 (2d Cir.1981) ("[a] company has no duty to correct or verify rumors in the marketplace unless those rumors can be attributed to the company"). See also *Eisenstadt v. Centel Corp.*, 113 F.3d 738, 744 (7th Cir. 1997) (stating that "[o]bviously a corporation has no duty to correct rumors planted by third parties" and speculating that "[t]he rumor might be planted by the target of a hostile takeover and be designed to elicit, if there is a legal duty to correct inaccurate rumors, a premature disclosure of the takeover firm's intentions").

An issuer may, however, assume an obligation to correct a third party's misstatement of material facts where the issuer had become "entangled" with the third party statement. Typically this situation arises in connection with material misstatements or omissions in an analyst's report as to which the issuer provided extensive assistance. One of the more notable decisions on the so-called entanglement theory is *Elkind v. Liggett & Myers, Inc.*, 635 F.2d 156 (2d Cir. 1980). In that decision, the Second Circuit made the following statement:

> We have no doubt that a company may so involve itself in the preparation of reports and projections by outsiders as to assume a duty to correct material errors in those projections. This may occur when officials of the company have, by their activity, made an implied representation that the information they have reviewed is true or at least in accordance with the company's views.

Id. at 163. See also *Raab v. General Physics Corp.*, 4 F.3d 286, 289 (4th Cir. 1993) (in order to be liable for statements in an analyst's report, a company must "sufficiently entangle[ ] itself with the analyst['s] forecasts to render those predictions attributable to it," quoting *Elkind,* supra); *Cooper v. Pickett*, 122 F.3d

1186, 1193-94 (9th Cir. 1997) (holding plaintiffs' allegations regarding entanglement sufficient to survive motion to dismiss).

A duty to correct may be based not only on an entanglement theory but also on the theory that the issuer "adopted" the third-party statement after its publication. Similar to the entanglement theory, this so-called "adoption" theory is premised on an issuer's implied representation to the market that the statement published by the securities analyst is accurate. See *In re Presstek, Inc.*, Exchange Act Release No. 39472, 66 SEC Docket 328 (Dec. 22, 1997) (cease-and-desist order stating that "[s]uch adoption occurs 'when a company conveys the suggestion that the analyst's forecasts are accurate or at least in accordance with its views,' " quoting *In re Cypress Semiconductor Sec. Litig.*, 891 F. Supp. 1369, 1377 (N.D. Cal. 1995), aff'd mem. sub nom. *Eisenstadt v. Allen*, 113 F.3d 1240 (9th Cir. 1997)). See also *Schaffer v. Timberland Co.*, 924 F. Supp. 1298, 1310 (D.N.H. 1996) (liability may attach to an analyst's statements where the defendants "have expressly or impliedly adopted the statements, placed their imprimatur on the statements, or have otherwise entangled themselves with the analysts to a significant degree").

Not surprisingly, cases involving theories of "entanglement" or "adoption" have presented a continuing source of frustration for courts, issuers, and attorneys. See generally D. Joseph Meister, Note, Securities Issuer Liability for Third Party Misstatements: Refining the Entanglement Standard, 53 Vand. L. Rev. 947 (2000). Cf. *SEC v. Bausch & Lomb, Inc.*, 565 F.2d 8, 9 (2d Cir. 1977) (stating that "[m]any a corporate executive, conscious of the antifraud provisions of the Securities Acts, may analogize an encounter with a financial analyst to a fencing match conducted on a tightrope").

v. Fiduciary Relationships and Other Duties at Common Law

Any discussion of duties to disclose under Rule 10b-5 must include the disclosure duties imposed by the common law on the parties to a business transaction. Courts frequently draw on these common law duties when interpreting Rule 10b-5. Thus, in *Chiarella v. United States*, 445 U.S. 222 (1980), the Supreme Court observed that officers and directors who trade in their company's securities while failing to disclose material information are liable under Rule 10b-5 because their fiduciary obligations to shareholders under the common law include a disclosure duty:

> [O]ne who fails to disclose material information prior to the consummation of a transaction commits fraud only when he is under a duty to do so. And the duty to disclose arises when one party has information "that the other [party] is entitled to know because of a fiduciary or other similar relation of trust and confidence between them."

Id. at 228, quoting Restatement (Second) of Torts § 551(2)(a) (1976). Cf. *Basic Inc. v. Levinson*, 485 U.S. 224, 253 (1988) (White, J., concurring in part and dissenting in part) (emphasizing that "[i]n general, the case law developed in this Court with respect to § 10(b) and Rule 10b-5 has been based on doctrines with which we, as judges, are familiar: common-law doctrines of fraud and deceit"); *Blue Chip Stamps v. Manor Drug Stores*, 421 U.S. 723, 744 (1975) (stating that "it is not inappropriate to advert briefly to the tort of misrepresentation and deceit, to which a claim under Rule 10b-5 certainly has some relationship").

In relying on Section 551(2)(a) of the Restatement (Second) of Torts, the *Chiarella* Court focused on one of five situations set forth in Section 551(2) in which one party to a business transaction has a common law duty to disclose to the other party. The five situations consist of the following:

> (a) matters known to him that the other is entitled to know because of a fiduciary or other similar relation of trust and confidence between them; and
>
> (b) matters known to him that he knows to be necessary to prevent his partial or ambiguous statement of the facts from being misleading; and
>
> (c) subsequently acquired information that he knows will make untrue or misleading a previous representation that when made was true or believed to be so; and
>
> (d) the falsity of a representation not made with the expectation that it would be acted upon, if he subsequently learns that the other is about to act in reliance upon it in a transaction with him; and
>
> (e) facts basic to the transaction, if he knows that the other is about to enter into it under a mistake as to them, and that the other, because of the relationship between them, the customs of the trade or other objective circumstances, would reasonably expect a disclosure of those facts.

Restatement of Torts (Second) §551(2)(a)-(e). Reconsider the duties to disclose that we have seen thus far under Rule 10b-5. Which of these duties receives additional support from the common law? Note also that Rule 10b-5's prohibition against half-truths is reflected in Section 551(2)(b).

Moreover, courts rely on common law disclosure duties to impose Rule 10b-5 liability not only on officers and directors but also on securities issuers who buy or sell their own securities while withholding material information from the public. See *Castellano v. Young & Rubicam, Inc.*, 257 F.3d 171, 179 (2d Cir. 2001) (maintaining that "under §10(b) and Rule 10b-5, closed corporations that purchase their own stock have a special obligation to disclose to sellers all material information"); *Shaw v. Digital Equip. Corp.*, 82 F.3d 1194 (1st Cir. 1996) (maintaining that issuer engaged in a stock offering may not sell stock if it is in possession of undisclosed information); *Jordan v. Duff & Phelps, Inc.*, 815 F.2d 429, 435-39 (7th Cir. 1987) (maintaining that issuer may not purchase employee's securities without disclosing material information in its possession); *McCormick v. Fund Am. Cos.*, 26 F.3d 869, 875-876 (9th Cir. 1994) (maintaining that issuer's purchases triggered a duty to disclose all material information, but concluding that alleged omissions were not material). But see Deborah A. DeMott, Beyond Metaphor: An Analysis of Fiduciary Obligation, 1988 Duke L.J. 879, 916-921 (1988) (contending that issuers do not owe "fiduciary duties" to their shareholders, but acknowledging that the insiders in control of the issuer owe such duties and the corporation may be vicariously liable for their breaches).

vi. The Relation Between the Duty to Disclose and Materiality

To be actionable under Rule 10b-5, omitted information must be material as well as be subject to a disclosure duty. It is important to keep the materiality question and the duty question distinct. Consider Professor Langevoort's observations:

> Courts sometimes confuse materiality and duty issues, sometimes in the direction of declaring something immaterial—even though shareholders would

> find it important—on grounds that it is not the sort of thing the issuer should have to disclose. That should be the work of the "duty" analysis. Materiality should be the question of what the reasonable investor would likely find significant, nothing more, nothing less. However, it is also important to avoid the converse error: assuming a duty simply because materiality is present.

Donald C. Langevoort, Seeking Sunlight in *Santa Fe*'s Shadow: The SEC's Pursuit of Managerial Accountability, 79 Wash. U. L.Q. 449, 458 (2001).

We examine materiality (which is applicable to misstatements as well) in the very next section of this Chapter. But because we have yet to do so, you should focus as much as possible on the duty question rather than on the materiality question in the problems that follow.

PROBLEM 2-3

General Physics Corporation, a company whose shares are listed on the NYSE, provides technical services to the nuclear power industry as well as to the U.S. Department of Energy (DOE) and to contractors who assist DOE with production and maintenance of nuclear weapons and disposal of waste from nuclear weapons. A portion of General Physics's DOE contracts involve peaceful use of nuclear energy, but a significant number of its contracts are tied to DOE expenditures on nuclear weapons programs. After the end of the Cold War in the early 1990s, General Physics's management believes that there will likely be a significant slowdown in nuclear weapons contracts from DOE.

General Physics has made the following public statements in its Annual Report to shareholders about its peacetime nuclear energy contracts with DOE:

> (1) "Regulatory changes resulting from [nuclear power accidents at Three Mile Island and Chernobyl] combined with the rising importance of environmental restoration and waste management, have created a marketplace for the DOE Services Group with an expected annual growth rate of 10% to 30% over the next several years;"
>
> (2) "Helping the DOE prime contractors respond to these directives is expected to be an increasing segment of General Physics' business in 1992;" and
>
> (3) "With experienced management, engineers, scientists and technicians in place, the DOE Services Group is poised to carry the growth and success of 1991 well into the future."

On the same day this Annual Report was issued, General Physics also released a statement to its shareholders stating that the first quarter earnings were likely to be half of analysts' estimates and that "the lower than anticipated earnings resulted primarily from administrative delays in contract awards by [DOE] and the resultant increased overhead costs associated with retaining professional staff pending contract awards by the DOE," but that General Physics believed that "conditions in the 1st quarter are temporary and that results during the remainder of 1992 should be in line with analysts' current projections."

About a month earlier, a Goldman Sachs research report recommended purchase of shares in the company, stating "General Physics has indicated that the pace of contract awards has increased significantly in recent weeks." The report, however, did not specify a source for this comment.

a) Was General Physics's Annual Report materially misleading under Rule 10b-5? Were the Annual Report and the statement to shareholders, taken together, materially misleading?

b) Is General Physics's required to disclose management's concern that DOE contracts would decline for nuclear weapons related projects?

c) Was it materially misleading for the company to report its belief that the slowdown in DOE contracts was temporary?

d) Is General Physics under a duty to correct the statement in the Goldman Sachs report that was attributed to a company official?

e) If General Physics's company web site had provided a hyperlink to the Goldman Sachs report, and General Physics's general counsel later learns of the hyperlink and removes it from the company's web site, must General Physics do anything more to comply with its obligations under Rule 10b-5.?

See *Raab v. General Physics Corp.*, 4 F.3d 286 (4th Cir. 1993).

PROBLEM 2-4

Fluor Corporation, whose common shares are listed on the NYSE, receives a $1 billion contract for engineering work from a South African utility company, SASOL. The contact is contingent on SASOL's ability to secure adequate financing. To that end, SASOL requests that Fluor delay announcing the contract until SASOL has had an opportunity to meet with investment bankers in France. In the meantime, rumors start to circulate that Fluor has entered into a contract with SASOL and there is a significant upswing in Fluor's stock price.

a) Is Fluor under a duty to disclose the existence of the SASOL contract? Can Fluor's officials deny these rumors in a press conference if SASOL officials specifically request that they do so?

b) If Fluor responds "no comment" to the rumors, is Fluor still liable under Rule 10b-5 to investors who sold Fluor stock if Fluor, a NYSE listed company, violated NYSE rules that require listed companies to either disclose significant developments such as the SASOL contract or request suspension of trading in their shares?

c) How should a company in Fluor's position reconcile the business reasons for confidentiality with the regulatory demands of a system of "real time" disclosure? Should the SEC promulgate a rule that allows a company in Fluor's situation to delay disclosure of such material developments for a reasonable period of time? How would you draft such a rule?

See *State Teachers Retirement Bd. v. Fluor Corp.*, 654 F.2d 843 (2d Cir. 1981).

PROBLEM 2-5

David Davis began working for Hammerville Furniture Company, a closely held corporation, in 1990. He worked diligently at the company's Chicago office for a number of years, and in 1993, Hammerville's management offered David the opportunity to buy 200 shares of Hammerville common stock. (The company had 39 other shareholders with 20,000 shares of stock outstanding.) David was delighted with the opportunity and agreed to purchase his 200 shares at "book value" (the accounting net worth of Hammerville divided by the number of shares outstanding), resulting in a price of $40 per share. Prior to the purchase, David signed a contract with Hammerville committing him to sell back his shares to the company upon termination of his employment with Hammerville, for any reason, including resignation, discharge, retirement, or death (thereby committing his estate to the resale). The contract provided that David would receive for the resale of his 200 shares the adjusted book value of the shares on December 31 of the year preceding when the termination took place.

In May 2011, David decided to resign his position with Hammerville to move his family to Houston because David's wife did not get along with David's mother in Chicago. On May 15, pursuant to his contract with Hammerville, David resold his shares to the company, and received $23,225 for his 200 shares (approximately $116 a share).

Less than a week later, David was stunned by Hammerville's announcement to the media of a merger between Hammerville and one of the country's largest furniture manufacturers. Under the terms of the merger, which was agreed to in principle at a meeting between the companies on May 12, Hammerville was valued at $25 million, such that the acquiring company was willing to pay $1,250 per outstanding share.

Did Hammerville violate Rule 10b-5 by re-purchasing David's shares while remaining silent about the merger negotiations?

Cf. *Jordan v. Duff & Phelps, Inc.*, 815 F.2d 429 (7th Cir. 1987).

B. THE MATERIALITY REQUIREMENT

To be actionable under Section 10(b) and Rule 10b-5, the omitted or misstated information must be "material" in nature. The materiality requirement has its origins in common law deceit and appears explicitly in Rule 10b-5(b).

Our examination of materiality begins with the basic definition and proceeds to the complexities that arise when the information at issue is "soft" rather than "hard." We then give special attention to an important subcategory of soft information—forward-looking statements—and the administrative, judicial, and statutory approaches that surround them.

1. Materiality Defined

The definition of materiality applicable to Rule 10b-5 comes from *TSC Indus., Inc. v. Northway, Inc.*, 426 U.S. 438 (1976). In *Northway*, an action under Section 14(a) of the Exchange Act and Rule 14a-9, the plaintiff alleged that a proxy statement seeking shareholder approval of a merger contained material omissions (involving control of the acquired corporation and the advantageousness of the deal). Regarding the materiality of those omissions, the Supreme Court had this to say:

> The question of materiality, it is universally agreed, is an objective one, involving the significance of an omitted or misrepresented fact to a reasonable investor. Variations in the formulation of a general test of materiality occur in the articulation of just how significant a fact must be or, put another way, how certain it must be that the fact would affect a reasonable investor's judgment.
>
> The Court of Appeals in this case concluded that material facts include "all facts which a reasonable shareholder *might* consider important." (emphasis added). This formulation of the test of materiality has been explicitly rejected by at least two courts as setting too low a threshold for the imposition of liability under Rule 14a-9. *Gerstle v. Gamble-Skogmo, Inc.*, 478 F.2d 1281, 1301-1302 (C.A.2 1973); *Smallwood v. Pearl Brewing Co.*, 489 F.2d 579, 603-604 (C.A.5 1974). In these cases, panels of the Second and Fifth Circuits opted for the conventional tort test of materiality—whether a reasonable man *would* attach importance to the fact misrepresented or omitted in determining his course of action. See Restatement (Second) of Torts § 538(2) (a) (Tent.Draft No. 10, Apr. 20, 1964). ***
>
> The general standard of materiality that we think best comports with the policies of Rule 14a-9 is as follows: An omitted fact is material if there is a substantial likelihood that a reasonable shareholder would consider it important in deciding how to vote. *** It does not require proof of a substantial likelihood that disclosure of the omitted fact would have caused the reasonable investor to change his vote. What the standard does contemplate is a showing of a substantial likelihood that, under all the circumstances, the omitted fact would have assumed actual significance in the deliberations of the reasonable shareholder. Put another way, there must be a substantial likelihood that the disclosure of the omitted fact would have been viewed by the reasonable investor as having significantly altered the "total mix" of information made available. ***

Id. at 445-49. See *Basic Inc. v. Levinson*, 485 U.S. 224, 232 (1988) (adopting *Northway* standard of materiality for purposes of Rule 10b-5). See also *Matrixx Initiatives, Inc. v. Siracusano*, 131 S.Ct. 1309 (2011) (reaffirming applicability of *Northway* standard to Rule 10b-5).

NOTES AND QUESTIONS

1. ***Might vs. Would.*** As *Northway* acknowledged, the lower courts had been divided over whether to define materiality in terms of facts the reasonable investor "would consider important" in making her decision and facts she "might consider important." Which position carried the day in *Northway*?

2. ***Puffery.*** A misstatement is immaterial if it constitutes "puffery"—that is, if it is so vague as to be meaningless. The puffery doctrine (sometimes called the puffery defense) arose initially in securities cases involving brokers. See, e.g., *Zerman v. Ball*, 735 F.2d 15, 21 (2d Cir. 1984) (characterizing as puffery the statement "when E.F. Hutton Talks, People Listen"); *Rotstein v. Reynolds & Co.*, 359 F. Supp. 109, 113 (N.D. Ill. 1973) (characterizing as puffery the statement that a stock was "red-hot"). Now expanded in scope, the puffery doctrine is today frequently invoked by corporations and their managers in connection with statements about the operation of their firms. See, e.g., *In re Ford Motor Co. Sec. Litig.*, 381 F.3d 563, 570-71 (6th Cir. 2004) (characterizing as puffery the statements "Ford has made quality a top priority" and "Ford wants to make customers lives safer"); *Nathenson v. Zonagen, Inc.*, 267 F.3d 400, 419 (5th Cir. 2001) (characterizing as puffery the description of a drug as a "fast-acting, improved formulation").

Judge Posner has offered the following rationale for the puffery doctrine:

> *Everybody* knows that someone trying to sell something is going to look and talk on the bright side. You don't sell a product by bad mouthing it. *** The heart of a reasonable investor does not begin to flutter when a firm announces that some project or process is proceeding smoothly, and so the announcement will not drive up the price of the firm's shares to an unsustainable level – Unless *** the announcement is concealing a disaster. *** "Going smoothly" may mean nothing more than – going; but it means at least that; if the process has been stopped, a representation that it is continuing may well induce purchases of the stock at a price that reflects the prospect that the process will continue to its end.

Eisenstadt v. Centel Corp., 113 F.3d 738, 745 (7th Cir. 1997). Notice that an otherwise puffing statement may be actionable if it is "concealing" something negative. Thus, a statement describing the project as being "on schedule" was held not to be puffery because the plaintiff produced evidence that the defendant knew otherwise. See *In re Cigna Corp. Sec. Litig.*, 2006 WL 782431 at *3-4 (E.D. Pa. 2006). See also *Zaluski v. United Am. Healthcare Corp.*, 527 F.3d 564, 574-75 (6th Cir. 2008) (finding of puffery based in part on the defendant's lack of knowledge of falsity). What does this suggest about the relationship between puffery and scienter?

Eisenstadt (as well as *Cigna* and *Zaluski*) show that determining whether a statement constitutes puffery may entail examining the context in which the statement appears. See, e.g.,*Glassman v. Computervision Corp.*, 90 F.3d 617, 635-36 (1st Cir. 1996) (holding statement to be puffery in light of other statements made by the company). But cf. *Malone v. Microdyne Corp.*, 26 F.3d 471, 479-80 (4th Cir. 1994) (holding statement to be puffery based on the statement itself). Professors Bainbridge and Gulati maintain that courts often ignore the context of alleged puffery in order to "make[] dismissal more plausible." See Stephen M. Bainbridge & G. Mitu Gulati, How Do Judges Maximize? (The Same Way Everybody Else Does – Boundedly): Rules of Thumb in Securities Fraud Opinions, 51 Emory L. J. 83, 123 (2002). For other discussions of puffery, see Jennifer O'Hare, The Resurrection of the Dodo: The Unfortunate Re-emergence of the Puffery Defense in Private Securities Fraud Actions, 59 Ohio St. L. J. 1697 (1998).

3. ***The (In)significance of Statistical Significance.*** Does materiality sometimes turn on statistical significance (or the lack thereof)? This question arose in *Matrixx Initiatives, Inc. v. Siracusano*, 131 S.Ct. 1309 (2011). There the plaintiffs sued a pharmaceutical company and three of its officers for failing to disclose reports that the company's cold remedy led some users to lose their sense of smell. The defendants argued that the reports were not material because the number of such reports lacked statistical significance. Rejecting this argument, the Court explained:

> Given that medical professionals and regulators act on the basis of evidence of causation that is not statistically significant, it stands to reason that in certain cases reasonable investors would as well. As Matrixx acknowledges, adverse event reports "appear in many forms, including direct complaints by users to manufacturers, reports by doctors about reported or observed patient reactions, more detailed case reports published by doctors in medical journals, or larger scale published clinical studies." Brief for Petitioners 17. As a result, assessing the materiality of adverse event reports is a "fact-specific" inquiry, *Basic*, 485 U.S., at 236, that requires consideration of the source, content, and context of the reports. This is not to say that statistical significance (or the lack thereof) is irrelevant—only that it is not dispositive of every case.

Id. at 1321. Are you persuaded? What if a statistically insignificant number of reports showed that use of the cold remedy was fatal?

4. Materiality and Efficient Markets. When a Rule 10b-5 action involves securities traded in an efficient market (see Chapter 1.G), the market itself serves as the stand-in for the reasonable investor. Thus, when the company publicly corrects the alleged omission or misrepresentation, the movement – or the lack of movement – in the security's market price is regarded as "at least telling of what a reasonable investor would consider significant." *No. 84 Employer-Teamster JT Council Pension Trust Fund v. Am. West Holding Co.*, 320 F.3d 920, 950 (9th Cir. 2003). But cf. *In re Merck & Co., Inc. Sec. Litig.*, 432 F.3d 261, 274 (3rd Cir. 2005) (in an efficient market, material information is information that *changes* the market price). To what extent (if at all) is there tension between the *Merck* view of materiality and the view that emerges from *Matrixx*, described in the preceding Note?

Moreover, in an efficient market, the "the total mix of information" is the total mix *available to the market*. See, e.g., *In re Burlington Coat Factory Sec. Litig.*, 114 F.3d 1410, 1425 (3rd Cir. 1997) (availability to the market of information concerning increase in sales during 53rd week in fiscal year); *In re Convergent Techs. Sec. Litig.*, 948 F.2d 507, 513 (9th Cir. 1991) (availability to the market of information concerning knowledge of likely lessening of demand for computer work stations); *In re Pfizer, Inc. Sec. Litig.*, 538 F. Supp. 2d 621, 632 (S.D.N.Y. 2008) (availability to the market of contradictory evidence regarding drug's effectiveness).

5. Materiality and Inefficient Markets. Suppose that unsophisticated investors trading in an inefficient market succumb to fraud that the reasonable investor would dismiss as absurd. See e.g., *SEC v. Roor*, 2004 WL 1933578 at *1 (S.D.N.Y. 2004) (promise of greater than 200% annual returns made on Internet web site). Should the court dismiss the case? See generally Margaret V. Sachs, Materiality and Social Change: The Case for Replacing "the Reasonable Investor" with "the Least Sophisticated Investor" in Inefficient Markets, 81 Tul. L. Rev. 473 (2006).

PROBLEM 2-6

Playday, Inc., a toy manufacturer and reporting company under the Exchange Act, was in the midst of making a private offering of securities to raise money for a new plant. Mary was contemplating buying shares in the offering upon the advice of her broker. Mary is strongly committed to equal rights for women and seeks to invest only in those companies that make use of women's talents. Accordingly, she asked Joe, a Playday vice president and a neighbor, whether the Playday board had any female members. Sensing that Mary would purchase securities in the offering only if she found his answer satisfactory, Joe told her that 30% of the board was female. In fact, the board was entirely male. Did Joe make a material misrepresentation to Mary?

PROBLEM 2-7

Are the following statements puffery? Why or why not?

a. A stock broker, who knows the issuer of a stock has severe liquidity problems that are not yet publicly known, tells one of his customers: "This stock is one of the best buys out there right now."

b. The same broker describes the same company to his customer as "a sound company that is rolling in cash."

c. An issuer's CEO says to a group of analysts, "our earnings are poised for growth," a day before the issuer announces that earnings are 50% below that of the previous year.

d. The same CEO says "our market share is likely to increase dramatically in the next few years." All the internal projections the CEO has received from his marketing officers suggest that the company's market share is likely to remain flat for the next five years, and at several board meetings the directors have based strategic planning on the assumption that the company's market share will remain flat for the foreseeable future.

2. *The Materiality of Soft Information*

Materiality is typically easier to assess when the information at issue is "hard" rather than "soft." Hard information is information rooted in historical or objective fact (e.g., the plant burned to the ground yesterday). Soft information, on the other hand, is information with a subjective or futurist aspect (e.g., the corporation is considering a merger; a competitor's new product may soon put the corporation out of business). The Supreme Court addressed the materiality of soft information in the following decision, which also explicitly adopted the *Northway* definition of materiality for purposes of Rule 10b-5.

BASIC INC. v. LEVINSON

485 U.S. 224 (1988)

JUSTICE HAROLD A. BLACKMUN:

This case requires us to apply the materiality requirement of § 10(b) of the Securities Exchange Act of 1934 (1934 Act) and the Securities and Exchange Commission's Rule 10b-5, promulgated thereunder, in the context of preliminary corporate merger discussions. We must also determine whether a person who traded a corporation's shares on a securities exchange after the issuance of a materially misleading statement by the corporation may invoke a rebuttable presumption that, in trading, he relied on the integrity of the price set by the market. [*The Court's treatment of this presumption is set forth in Section F.1.b of this Chapter, which addresses the reliance requirement*].

I

Prior to December 20, 1978, Basic Incorporated was a publicly traded company primarily engaged in the business of manufacturing chemical refractories for the steel industry. As early as 1965 or 1966, Combustion Engineering, Inc., a company producing mostly alumina-based refractories, expressed some interest in acquiring Basic, but was deterred from pursuing this inclination seriously because of antitrust concerns it then entertained. In 1976, however, regulatory action opened the way to a renewal of Combustion's interest. The "Strategic Plan," dated October 25, 1976, for Combustion's Industrial Products Group included the objective: "Acquire Basic Inc. $30 million."

Beginning in September 1976, Combustion representatives had meetings and telephone conversations with Basic officers and directors, including petitioners here, concerning the possibility of a merger. During 1977 and 1978, Basic made three public statements denying that it was engaged in merger negotiations.[4] On December 18, 1978, Basic asked the New York Stock Exchange to suspend trading in its shares and issued a release stating that it had been "approached" by another company concerning a merger. On December 19, Basic's board endorsed Combustion's offer of $46 per share for its common stock, and on the following day publicly announced its approval of Combustion's tender offer for all outstanding shares.

Respondents are former Basic shareholders who sold their stock after Basic's first public statement of October 21, 1977, and before the suspension of trading in December 1978. Respondents brought a class action against Basic and its directors, asserting that the defendants issued three false or misleading public statements and thereby were in violation of § 10(b) of the 1934 Act and of Rule 10b-5. Respondents alleged that they were injured by selling Basic shares at artificially depressed prices in a market affected by petitioners' misleading statements and in reliance thereon.

The District Court *** granted summary judgment for the defendants. It held that, as a matter of law, any misstatements were immaterial: there were no negotiations ongoing at the time of the first statement, and although negotiations were taking place when the second and third statements were

---

4. On October 21, 1977, after heavy trading and a new high in Basic stock, the following news item appeared in the Cleveland Plain Dealer:

> [Basic] President Max Muller said the company knew no reason for the stock's activity and that no negotiations were under way with any company for a merger. He said Flintkote recently denied Wall Street rumors that it would make a tender offer of $25 a share for control of the Cleveland- based maker of refractories for the steel industry.

On September 25, 1978, in reply to an inquiry from the New York Stock Exchange, Basic issued a release concerning increased activity in its stock and stated that "management is unaware of any present or pending company development that would result in the abnormally heavy trading activity and price fluctuation in company shares that have been experienced in the past few days."

On November 6, 1978, Basic issued to its shareholders a "Nine Months Report 1978." This Report stated: "With regard to the stock market activity in the Company's shares we remain unaware of any present or pending developments which would account for the high volume of trading and price fluctuations in recent months."

issued, those negotiations were not "destined, with reasonable certainty, to become a merger agreement in principle."

The United States Court of Appeals for the Sixth Circuit *** reversed the District Court's summary judgment, and remanded the case. *** In the Court of Appeals' view, Basic's statements that no negotiations were taking place, and that it knew of no corporate developments to account for the heavy trading activity, were misleading. With respect to materiality, the court rejected the argument that preliminary merger discussions are immaterial as a matter of law, and held that "once a statement is made denying the existence of any discussions, even discussions that might not have been material in absence of the denial are material because they make the statement made untrue." ***

We granted certiorari to resolve the split among the Courts of Appeals as to the standard of materiality applicable to preliminary merger discussions ***

II

*** The Court previously has addressed various positive and common-law requirements for a violation of § 10(b) or of Rule 10b-5. The Court also explicitly has defined a standard of materiality under the securities laws, see *TSC Industries, Inc. v. Northway, Inc.*, 426 U.S. 438 (1976), concluding in the proxy-solicitation context that "[a]n omitted fact is material if there is a substantial likelihood that a reasonable shareholder would consider it important in deciding how to vote." Id., at 449. Acknowledging that certain information concerning corporate developments could well be of "dubious significance," id., at 448, the Court was careful not to set too low a standard of materiality; it was concerned that a minimal standard might bring an overabundance of information within its reach, and lead management "simply to bury the shareholders in an avalanche of trivial information—a result that is hardly conducive to informed decisionmaking." Id., at 448-449. It further explained that to fulfill the materiality requirement "there must be a substantial likelihood that the disclosure of the omitted fact would have been viewed by the reasonable investor as having significantly altered the 'total mix' of information made available." Id., at 449. We now expressly adopt the *TSC Industries* standard of materiality for the § 10(b) and Rule 10b-5 context.

III

The application of this materiality standard to preliminary merger discussions is not self-evident. Where the impact of the corporate development on the target's fortune is certain and clear, the *TSC Industries* materiality definition admits straightforward application. Where, on the other hand, the event is contingent or speculative in nature, it is difficult to ascertain whether the "reasonable investor" would have considered the omitted information significant at the time. Merger negotiations, because of the ever-present possibility that the contemplated transaction will not be effectuated, fall into the latter category.[9]

A

Petitioners urge upon us a Third Circuit test for resolving this difficulty. Under this approach, preliminary merger discussions do not become material until "agreement-in-principle" as to the price and structure of the transaction has been reached between the would-be merger partners. See *Greenfield v. Heublein, Inc.*, 742 F.2d 751, 757 (CA3 1984). By definition, then, information concerning any negotiations not yet at the agreement-in-principle stage could be withheld or even misrepresented without a violation of Rule 10b-5.

Three rationales have been offered in support of the "agreement-in-principle" test. The first derives from the concern expressed in *TSC Industries* that an investor not be overwhelmed by excessively detailed and trivial information, and focuses on the substantial risk that preliminary merger discussions may collapse: because such discussions are inherently tentative, disclosure of their existence itself could mislead investors and foster false optimism. The other two justifications for the agreement-in-principle standard are based on management concerns: because the requirement of "agreement-in-principle" limits the scope of disclosure obligations, it helps preserve the confidentiality of merger discussions where earlier disclosure might prejudice the negotiations; and the test also provides a usable, bright-line rule for determining when disclosure must be made. See *Greenfield v. Heublein, Inc.*, 742 F.2d, at 757; *Flamm v. Eberstadt*, 814 F.2d 1169, 1176-1178 (CA7 1987).

None of these policy-based rationales, however, purports to explain why drawing the line at agreement-in-principle reflects the significance of the information upon the investor's decision. The first rationale, and the only one connected to the concerns expressed in *TSC Industries,* stands soundly rejected, even by a Court of Appeals that otherwise has accepted the wisdom of the agreement-in-principle test. "It assumes that investors are nitwits, unable to appreciate—even when told—that mergers are risky propositions up until the closing." *Flamm v. Eberstadt*, 814 F.2d, at 1175. Disclosure, and not paternalistic withholding of accurate information, is the policy chosen and expressed by Congress. We have recognized time and again, a "fundamental purpose" of the various Securities Acts, "was to substitute a philosophy of full disclosure for the philosophy of *caveat emptor* and thus to achieve a high standard of business ethics in the securities industry." *SEC v. Capital Gains Research Bureau, Inc.*, 375 U.S. 180, 186 (1963). The role of the materiality requirement is not to "attribute to investors a child-like simplicity, an inability to grasp the probabilistic significance of negotiations," *Flamm v. Eberstadt*, 814 F.2d, at 1175, but to filter out essentially useless information that a reasonable investor would not consider significant, even as part of a larger "mix" of factors to consider in making his investment decision.

The second rationale, the importance of secrecy during the early stages

9. We do not address here any other kinds of contingent or speculative information, such as earnings forecasts or projections. See generally Hiler, The SEC and the Courts' Approach to Disclosure of Earnings Projections, Asset Appraisals, and Other Soft Information: Old Problems, Changing Views, 46 Md.L.Rev. 1114 (1987).

of merger discussions, also seems irrelevant to an assessment whether their existence is significant to the trading decision of a reasonable investor. To avoid a "bidding war" over its target, an acquiring firm often will insist that negotiations remain confidential, see, e.g., *In re Carnation Co.,* Exchange Act Release No. 22214 (1985), and at least one Court of Appeals has stated that "silence pending settlement of the price and structure of a deal is beneficial to most investors, most of the time." *Flamm v. Eberstadt,* 814 F.2d, at 1177.

We need not ascertain, however, whether secrecy necessarily maximizes shareholder wealth—although we note that the proposition is at least disputed as a matter of theory and empirical research—for this case does not concern the *timing* of a disclosure; it concerns only its accuracy and completeness. We face here the narrow question whether information concerning the existence and status of preliminary merger discussions is significant to the reasonable investor's trading decision. Arguments based on the premise that some disclosure would be "premature" in a sense are more properly considered under the rubric of an issuer's duty to disclose. The "secrecy" rationale is simply inapposite to the definition of materiality.

The final justification offered in support of the agreement- in-principle test seems to be directed solely at the comfort of corporate managers. A bright-line rule indeed is easier to follow than a standard that requires the exercise of judgment in the light of all the circumstances. But ease of application alone is not an excuse for ignoring the purposes of the Securities Acts and Congress' policy decisions. Any approach that designates a single fact or occurrence as always determinative of an inherently fact- specific finding such as materiality, must necessarily be overinclusive or underinclusive. In *TSC Industries* this Court explained: "The determination [of materiality] requires delicate assessments of the inferences a 'reasonable shareholder' would draw from a given set of facts and the significance of those inferences to him...." 426 U.S., at 450. After much study, the Advisory Committee on Corporate Disclosure cautioned the SEC against administratively confining materiality to a rigid formula. Courts also would do well to heed this advice.

We therefore find no valid justification for artificially excluding from the definition of materiality information concerning merger discussions, which would otherwise be considered significant to the trading decision of a reasonable investor, merely because agreement-in-principle as to price and structure has not yet been reached by the parties or their representatives.***

C

Even before this Court's decision in *TSC Industries*, the Second Circuit had explained the role of the materiality requirement of Rule 10b-5, with respect to contingent or speculative information or events, in a manner that gave that term meaning that is independent of the other provisions of the Rule. Under such circumstances, materiality "will depend at any given time upon a balancing of both the indicated probability that the event will occur and the anticipated magnitude of the event in light of the totality of the company activity." *SEC v. Texas Gulf Sulphur Co.*, 401 F.2d [833, 849 (CA2 1968)]. Interestingly, neither the Third Circuit decision adopting the agreement-in-principle test nor petitioners here take issue with this general standard. Rather, they suggest that with respect to preliminary merger discussions, there are good reasons to draw a line at agreement on price and structure.

In a subsequent decision, the late Judge Friendly, writing for a Second Circuit panel, applied the *Texas Gulf Sulphur* probability/magnitude approach in the specific context of preliminary merger negotiations. After acknowledging that materiality is something to be determined on the basis of the particular facts of each case, he stated:

> Since a merger in which it is bought out is the most important event that can occur in a small corporation's life, to wit, its death, we think that inside information, as regards a merger of this sort, can become material at an earlier stage than would be the case as regards lesser transactions—and this even though the mortality rate of mergers in such formative stages is doubtless high.

SEC v. Geon Industries, Inc., 531 F.2d 39, 47-48 (1976). We agree with that analysis.

Whether merger discussions in any particular case are material therefore depends on the facts. Generally, in order to assess the probability that the event will occur, a factfinder will need to look to indicia of interest in the transaction at the highest corporate levels. Without attempting to catalog all such possible factors, we note by way of example that board resolutions, instructions to investment bankers, and actual negotiations between principals or their intermediaries may serve as indicia of interest. To assess the magnitude of the transaction to the issuer of the securities allegedly manipulated, a factfinder will need to consider such facts as the size of the two corporate entities and of the potential premiums over market value. No particular event or factor short of closing the transaction need be either necessary or sufficient by itself to render merger discussions material.[17]

As we clarify today, materiality depends on the significance the reasonable investor would place on the withheld or misrepresented

---

17. To be actionable, of course, a statement must also be misleading. Silence, absent a duty to disclose, is not misleading under Rule 10b-5. "No comment" statements are generally the functional equivalent of silence. See *In re Carnation Co.*, supra. See also New York Stock Exchange Listed Company Manual § 202.01 (premature public announcement may properly be delayed for valid business purpose and where adequate security can be maintained).

It has been suggested that given current market practices, a "no comment" statement is tantamount to an admission that merger discussions are underway. See *Flamm v. Eberstadt*, 814 F.2d, at 1178. That may well hold true to the extent that issuers adopt a policy of truthfully denying merger rumors when no discussions are underway, and of issuing "no comment" statements when they are in the midst of negotiations. There are, of course, other statement policies firms could adopt; we need not now advise issuers as to what kind of practice to follow, within the range permitted by law. Perhaps more importantly, we think that creating an exception to a regulatory scheme founded on a prodisclosure legislative philosophy, because complying with the regulation might be "bad for business," is a role for Congress, not this Court.

information.[18] The fact-specific inquiry we endorse here is consistent with the approach a number of courts have taken in assessing the materiality of merger negotiations. Because the standard of materiality we have adopted differs from that used by both courts below, we remand the case for reconsideration of the question whether a grant of summary judgment is appropriate on this record. ***

NOTES AND QUESTIONS

*1. **Assessing Magnitude and Probability.*** Assessments of magnitude are sometimes relatively easy, since corporate events such as mergers are frequently of clearcut importance. Assessments of probability, however, are often considerably more challenging. Transactions such as mergers, leveraged buyouts, or initial public offerings are often conditioned on numerous factors that cannot be predicted (e.g., market conditions, availability of financing, resolution of antitrust and other regulatory issues). How can such uncertainties be overcome when applying the probability/magnitude test?

*2. **The Problem of Hindsight Bias.*** Further confounding assessments of probability is the fact that these assessments are typically made after the merger or other event in question has occurred (or failed to occur). The event's occurrence contributes to the perception that the probability at the relevant earlier point was higher than it may actually have been, just as the event's non-occurrence has the opposite effect. This phenomenon—known as hindsight bias—can impact the fact-finding of a judge or jury (or even the SEC or the DOJ). An empirical study of securities opinions showed that judges are quick to dismiss complaints as amounting to mere "fraud by hindsight" with scant appreciation for how the fraud-by-hindsight phenomenon impacts their own judgments. Mitu Gulati, et al., Fraud By Hindsight, 98 Nw.U. L. Rev. 773 (2004). Should a plaintiff's lawyer flag this study for the judge when opposing a motion to dismiss?

*3. **Reaching Beyond Merger Negotiations.*** Prior to *Basic,* lower federal courts applied the probability/magnitude test not only to merger negotiations but also to other contingent events. See, e.g., *Harkavy v. Apparel Indus., Inc.,* 571 F.2d 737, 740-42 (2d Cir. 1978) (application to a clothing manufacturer's plan to introduce a new line of sportswear). Following *Basic,* that pattern has continued. See, e.g., *United States v. Smith,* 155 F.3d 1051, 1065 (9th Cir. 1998) (application to forecasts tipped in insider trading); *meVC Draper Fisher Jurvetson Fund I, Inc. v. Millenium Partners, LP,* 260 F. Supp. 2d 616, 636 n.31 (S.D.N.Y. 2003) (application to prospect of choosing a certain investment adviser). But see *Garcia v. Cordova,* 930 F.2d 826, 829 n.1 (10th Cir. 1991) (rejecting application to land appraisals and stock valuation). Are there

---

18. We find no authority in the statute, the legislative history, or our previous decisions for varying the standard of materiality depending on who brings the action or whether insiders are alleged to have profited. See, e.g., *Pavlidis v. New England Patriots Football Club, Inc.,* 737 F.2d 1227, 1231 (CA1 1984) ("A fact does not become more material to the shareholder's decision because it is withheld by an insider, or because the insider might profit by withholding it"); cf. *Aaron v. SEC,* 446 U.S. 680, 691 (1980) ("[S]cienter is an element of a violation of § 10(b) and Rule 10b-5, regardless of the identity of the plaintiff or the nature of the relief sought"). ***

reasons to restrict the probability/magnitude test to merger negotiations?

PROBLEM 2-8

Vroom Corporation is a drug company with an aggressive research and marketing agenda developed by its president (Marvin). This agenda (and the crucial role of Marvin in its fulfillment) was extensively described in the company's SEC's filings as well as in press releases throughout the past year. None of those documents, however, revealed a matter known to the board and top officers—that Marvin (who until recently had 20/20 vision) was contemplating resigning because of a degenerative eye disease. Indeed, for some months he had been able to function professionally only by wearing unusually thick glasses. By year's end, Marvin submitted his resignation, effective immediately. Would Vroom's failure to disclose Marvin's situation be regarded as material in a Rule 10b-5 action against the company? Is there additional information that would be useful to have in answering this question?

3. Forward-Looking Statements

Until the 1970s, the Commission generally barred the inclusion of earnings projections, statements of future plans and other forward-looking statements from documents required to be filed under the Securities Act or the Exchange Act. Forward-looking information could, however, be disseminated in other ways, such as in speeches or press releases. Cf. *Marx v. Computer Sciences Corp.,* 507 F.2d 485, 488 (9th Cir. 1974) (Rule 10b-5 action challenging a forecast contained in vice president's speech). The Commission's rationale—that forward-looking statements were unreliable and likely to mislead gullible investors—received blistering criticism. See, e.g., Homer Kripke, The SEC, the Accountants, Some Myths and Some Realities, 45 N.Y.U. L. Rev. 1151, 1197-99 (1970).

In an about-face in 1973, the Commission announced that it would "take the first steps toward integrating projections into the disclosure system." Securities Act Release No. 5362, 1 SEC Docket 4 (Feb. 2, 1973). In 1978, it issued a release urging companies to provide projections both in filed documents and otherwise. See Securities Act Release No. 5992, 16 SEC Docket 112 (Nov. 7, 1978). Moreover, beginning in 1980, it required companies complying with certain Securities Act and Exchange Act disclosure requirements to set forth "any known trends or uncertainties" likely to impact their performance. See Item 303 of Regulation S-K. It simultaneously distinguished such "presently known data which will impact upon future operating results" from "forward-looking information," which companies were "encouraged, but not required, to supply." Instruction 7 to ¶ 303(a), Regulation S-K. See also Item10(b), Regulation S-K.

But companies worried that by disclosing forward-looking information, they would make themselves vulnerable to fraud actions when their predictions failed to materialize. We consider the solutions provided by the SEC, the courts, and Congress to address this concern: (i) SEC Rules 175 and 3b-6; (ii) the judicial bespeaks caution doctrine; and (iii) the statutory safe harbor for forward-looking statements.

a. Rules 175 and 3b-6

Adopted by the Commission in 1979, Rule 175 (under the Securities Act) and Rule 3b-6 (under the Exchange Act) do little to allay companies' anxieties about releasing forward-looking information. First, the rules do not provide insulation from fraud liability when a forward-looking statement "was made or reaffirmed without a reasonable basis or was disclosed other than in good faith." Because the existence of bad faith and a reasonable basis are generally questions of fact for which a hearing is necessary, these rules do not ordinarily enable defendants to obtain a dismissal at an early stage of the proceedings. Second, the rules apply only to forward-looking statements that appear in SEC filings.

b. The Bespeaks Caution Doctrine

Courts developed the bespeaks caution doctrine partly as a response to the limitations inherent in Rules 175 and 3b-6. Consider the following decision.

IN RE DONALD J. TRUMP CASINO SEC. LITIG.

7 F.3d 357 (3rd Cir. 1993)

EDWARD R. BECKER, CIRCUIT JUDGE:

*** In November, 1988 the Trump defendants offered to the public $675 million in first mortgage investment bonds (the "bonds") with Merrill Lynch acting as the sole underwriter. The interest rate on the bonds was 14%, a high rate in comparison to the 9% yield offered on quality corporate bonds at the time. The Trump defendants issued the bonds to raise capital to: (1) purchase the Taj Mahal, a partially-completed casino/hotel located on the boardwalk, from Resorts International, Inc. (which had already invested substantial amounts in its construction); (2) complete construction of the Taj Mahal; and (3) open the Taj Mahal for business.

As is well-known, the Taj Mahal was widely touted as Atlantic City's largest and most lavish casino resort. When ultimately opened in April, 1990 it was at least twice the size of any other casino in Atlantic City. It consisted of a 42-story hotel tower that contained approximately 1,250 guest rooms and an adjacent low-rise building encompassing roughly 155,000 square feet of meeting, ballroom and convention space, a 120,000 square foot casino, and numerous restaurants, lounges and stores. The entire structure occupied approximately seventeen acres of land.

The prospectus accompanying the bonds estimated the completion cost of the Taj Mahal, including the payment of interest on the bonds for the first fifteen months of operation, at $805 million. It explained that, to obtain that amount, the Trump defendants were relying on the $675 million in bond proceeds, a $75 million capital contribution by Donald Trump, investment income derived from those sums, a contingent additional loan of $25 million from the Trump Line of Credit, and loans from other sources.

Plaintiffs ground their lawsuits in the text of the prospectus. ***

The defendants moved to dismiss the complaints pursuant to Rule 12(b)(6), asserting that the plaintiffs had failed to state actionable securities fraud claims ***. The district court granted the defendants' motion ***.

*** The plaintiffs allege that the prospectus contained material misrepresentations. Their principal claim is that the defendants had neither an honest belief in nor a reasonable basis for one statement in the MD & A section of the prospectus: "The Partnership believes that funds generated from the operation of the Taj Mahal will be sufficient to cover all of its debt service (interest and principal)." Before the district court and again before us, the plaintiffs concentrate on this statement and its allegedly misleading character. ***

The statement the plaintiffs assail as misleading is contained in the MD & A section of the prospectus, which follows the sizable "Special Considerations" section, a section notable for its extensive and detailed disclaimers and cautionary statements. More precisely, the prospectus explained that, because of its status as a new venture of unprecedented size and scale, a variety of risks inhered in the Taj Mahal which could affect the Partnership's ability to repay the bondholders. For example, it stated:

> The casino business in Atlantic City, New Jersey has a seasonal nature of which summer is the peak season.... Since the third interest payment date on the Bonds [(which constitutes the first interest payment not paid out of the initial financing)] occurs before the summer season, the Partnership will not have the benefit of receiving peak season cash flow prior to the third interest payment date, which could adversely affect its ability to pay interest on the Bonds.
>
> ... The Taj Mahal has not been completed and, accordingly, has no operating history. The Partnership, therefore, has no history of earnings and its operations will be subject to all of the risks inherent in the establishment of a new business enterprise. Accordingly, the ability of the Partnership to service its debt to [Taj Mahal Funding Inc., which issued the bonds,] is completely dependent upon the success of that operation and such success will depend upon financial, business, competitive, regulatory and other factors affecting the Taj Mahal and the casino industry in general as well as prevailing economic conditions....
>
> The Taj Mahal will be the largest casino/hotel complex in Atlantic City, with approximately twice the room capacity and casino space of many of the existing casino/hotels in Atlantic City. [No] other casino/hotel operator has had experience operating a complex the size of the Taj Mahal in Atlantic City. Consequently, no assurance can be given that, once opened, the Taj Mahal will be profitable or that it will generate cash flow sufficient to provide for the payment of the debt service....

Prospectus at 8.

The prospectus went on to relate, as part of its "Security for the Bonds" subsection, the potential effect of the Partnership's default on its mortgage payments. For example, this subsection unreservedly explained that if a default occurred prior to completion of the Taj Mahal, "there would not be sufficient proceeds [from a foreclosure sale of the Taj Mahal] to pay the principal of, and accrued interest on, the Bonds." Prospectus at 9.

The "Special Considerations" section also detailed the high level of competition for customers the completed Taj Mahal would face once opened to the public:

> Competition in the Atlantic City casino/hotel market is intense. At present, there are twelve casino/hotels in Atlantic City.... Some Atlantic City casino/hotels recently have completed renovations or are in the process of expanding and improving their facilities.... *The Partnership believes* that, based upon historical trends, *casino win per square foot of casino space will decline in 1990* as a result of a projected increase in casino floor space, including the opening of the Taj Mahal.

Prospectus at 14 (emphasis added). In a section following the MD & A section, the prospectus reiterated its reference to the intense competition in the Atlantic City casino industry:

> Growth in Atlantic City casino win is expected to be restrained until further improvements to the City's transportation system and infrastructure are undertaken and completed and the number of non-casino hotel rooms and existing convention space are increased. No assurance can be given with respect to either the future growth of the Atlantic City gaming market or the ability of the Taj Mahal to attract a representative share of that market.

Prospectus at 33. The prospectus additionally reported that there were risks of delay in the construction of the Taj Mahal and a risk that the casino might not receive the numerous essential licenses and permits from the state regulatory authorities.

In this case the Partnership did not bury the warnings about risks amidst the bulk of the prospectus. Indeed, it was the allegedly misleading statement which was buried amidst the cautionary language. At all events, in addition to reading the allegedly misleading statement setting forth the Partnership's belief that it could repay the principal and interest on the bonds, a prospective investor would have also read the dire warnings and cautionary statements a sampling of which we have just outlined. Moreover, an investor would have read the sentence immediately following the challenged statement, which cautioned: "[n]o assurance can be given, however, that actual operating results will meet the Partnership's expectations."

*** [W]e must consider an alleged misrepresentation within the context in which the speaker communicated it. Here the context clearly and precisely relayed to the bondholders the substantial uncertainties inherent in the completion and operation of the Taj Mahal. The prospectus contained both general warnings that the Partnership could not assure the repayment of the bonds as well as specific discussions detailing a variety of risk factors that rendered the completion and profitable operation of the Taj Mahal highly uncertain. Within this broad context the statement at issue was, at worst, harmless.

C. The Bespeaks Caution Doctrine

The district court applied what has come to be known as the "bespeaks caution" doctrine. In so doing it followed the lead of a number of courts of appeals which have dismissed securities fraud claims under Rule 12(b)(6) because cautionary language in the offering document negated the materiality of an alleged misrepresentation or omission. See *Sinay v. Lamson & Sessions Co.*, 948 F.2d 1037, 1040 (6th Cir. 1991); *I. Meyer Pincus & Assocs. v. Oppenheimer & Co.*, 936 F.2d 759, 763 (2d Cir. 1991); *Romani v. Shearson Lehman Hutton*, 929 F.2d 875, 879 (1st Cir. 1991); *Polin v. Conductron Corp.*,

552 F.2d 797, 806 n.28 (8th Cir. 1977). We are persuaded by the *ratio decidendi* of these cases and will apply bespeaks caution to the facts before us.

The application of bespeaks caution depends on the specific text of the offering document or other communication at issue ***. Nevertheless, we can state as a general matter that when an offering document's forecasts, opinions or projections are accompanied by meaningful cautionary statements, the forward-looking statements will not form the basis for a securities fraud claim if those statements did not affect the "total mix" of information the document provided investors. In other words, cautionary language, if sufficient, renders the alleged omissions or misrepresentations immaterial as a matter of law.

The bespeaks caution doctrine is, as an analytical matter, equally applicable to allegations of both affirmative misrepresentations and omissions concerning soft information. Whether the plaintiffs allege a document contains an affirmative prediction/opinion which is misleading or fails to include a forecast or prediction which failure is misleading, the cautionary statements included in the document may render the challenged predictive statements or opinions immaterial as a matter of law. Of course, a vague or blanket (boilerplate) disclaimer which merely warns the reader that the investment has risks will ordinarily be inadequate to prevent misinformation. To suffice, the cautionary statements must be substantive and tailored to the specific future projections, estimates or opinions in the prospectus which the plaintiffs challenge.

Because of the abundant and meaningful cautionary language contained in the prospectus, we hold that the plaintiffs have failed to state an actionable claim regarding the statement that the Partnership believed it could repay the bonds. We can say that the prospectus here truly bespeaks caution because, not only does the prospectus generally convey the riskiness of the investment, but its warnings and cautionary language directly address the substance of the statement the plaintiffs challenge. That is to say, the cautionary statements were tailored precisely to address the uncertainty concerning the Partnership's prospective ability to repay the bondholders. ***

D. Conclusion

*** [W]e think it clear that the accompanying warnings and cautionary language served to negate any potentially misleading effect that the prospectus' statement about the Partnership's belief in its ability to repay the bonds would have on a reasonable investor. The prospectus clearly and precisely cautioned that the bonds represented an exceptionally risky, perhaps even speculative, venture and that the Partnership's ability to repay the bonds was uncertain. Given this context, we believe that no reasonable jury could conclude that the subject projection materially influenced a reasonable investor.***

For the foregoing reasons we will affirm the orders of the district court dismissing the plaintiffs' complaints under Rule 12(b)(6). ***

NOTES AND QUESTIONS

1. ***Reaching Efficient Markets.*** The *Trump* court applied the bespeaks caution doctrine to an IPO, which (as you will recall from Chapter 1.G) is ordinarily not sold in an efficient market. Should the doctrine apply in the efficient market context as well?

2. ***The Relevance of the Defendant's Bad Faith.*** Does the bespeaks caution doctrine provide the basis for dismissal where the plaintiff can show that the defendant did not believe the forecast when he made it? Consider the following argument against applying the doctrine in such circumstances:

> [O]ne could construct a completely inaccurate and fraudulent offering memorandum, yet be shielded from a fraud claim as long as there was language in the document cautioning investors of the specific risks. To the extent that such a rule would allow, if not encourage, fraud and non-disclosure on the part of corporate actors, it clearly is not a viable application of the "bespeaks caution" doctrine.

Gurfein v. Sovereign Group, 826 F. Supp. 890, 908 n. 20 (E.D. Pa. 1993). Are you persuaded? What (if anything) does *Trump* suggest about the relevance of the defendant's bad faith to the application of "bespeaks caution"?

3. ***Omitted Forecasts.*** The *Trump* court maintained that the bespeaks caution doctrine applies when forecasts are omitted as well as misrepresented. A claim involving an omitted forecast is subject to dismissal based not only on the bespeaks caution doctrine but also on the absence of a duty to disclose. See, e.g., *In re VeriFone Sec. Litig.*, 11 F.3d 865, 869 (9th Cir. 1993) (omitted sales forecasts not actionable under Rule 10b-5 because no duty to disclose existed). But cf. *Provenz v. Miller*, 102 F.3d 1478, 1488-89 (9th Cir. 1996) (trial necessary to determine whether omitted forecast rendered disclosed forecast false and misleading).

4. ***The Psychological Dimension.*** Consider the following critique of the *Trump* decision in particular and the bespeaks caution doctrine in general: "This court's reasoning that optimistic forward-looking statements are offset by 'meaningful cautionary language' because the 'total mix' of information is unaffected ignores the powerful affect of such optimistic forward-looking statements." Peter H. Huang, Moody Investing and the Supreme Court: Rethinking the Materiality of Information and the Reasonableness of Investors, 13 S. Ct. Econ. Rev. 99, 124 (2005). Do you agree? Would a similar critique apply to puffery as well? See id.

5. ***Justifications.*** While the bespeaks caution doctrine may increase companies' willingness to make forward-looking statements, it may do something else as well—eliminate weak actions prior to the discovery phase of the litigation and thereby spare the defendants the time and expense that discovery entails. Are you comfortable with this justification? Are there other Rule 10b-5 doctrines that emerge from a desire to weed out tenuous actions rather than from substantive considerations?

c. *The Statutory Safe Harbor for Forward-Looking Statements*

In 1995, a newly elected Republican majority in Congress enacted the Private Securities Litigation Reform Act (PSLRA) over President Clinton's veto. The override received significant support from Democrats as well, without whom it would not have been possible.

The PSLRA added a safe harbor for forward-looking statements to the Exchange Act (Section 21E) as well as to the Securities Act (Section 27A). Other changes wrought by the PSLRA are addressed later in this Chapter as well as in subsequent Chapters (especially Chapter 6 on class actions).

The statutory safe harbor is explicitly limited to private actions (and thus does not come into play in actions brought by the SEC or the DOJ). Moreover, it applies only when the firm that issued the securities is a reporting company under the Exchange Act (see Chapter 1.A.2.c). It is not available to certain types of firms (for example, partnerships and limited liability companies) or transactions (for example, initial public offerings and tender offers). But cf. *In re Merck & Co. Sec. Litig.*, 432 F.3d 261, 273 (3d Cir. 2005) (holding safe harbor applicable to statement in press release issued "several months before a planned IPO that never subsequently happened;" affirmatively not addressing safe harbor's application to "statements made in registration statements and prospectuses *** if an IPO does not occur").

The statutory safe harbor authorizes three independent bases for dismissal of a fraud action involving a forward-looking statement. The first ground, modeled on the judicial bespeaks caution doctrine, requires that the forward-looking statement be "identified as a forward-looking statement, and [be] accompanied by meaningful cautionary statements identifying important factors that could cause actual results to differ materially from those in the forward-looking statement." Section 21E(c)(1)(A)(i). The second ground requires that the forward-looking statement be "immaterial." Section 21E(c)(1)(A)(ii). The third ground authorizes dismissal when the plaintiff fails to show that the defendant made the forward-looking statement "with actual knowledge" of its falsity. Section 21E(c)(1)(B). The third ground has the effect of making "actual knowledge" the requisite state of mind in private Rule 10b-5 actions involving forward-looking statements. Note also that dismissals based on the third ground are proper regardless of whether the fraud is material.

Two other points merit mention. First, a special subsection of the statutory safe harbor specifically addresses oral forward-looking statements. See Section 21E(c)(2). Second, during the pendency of a motion to dismiss, discovery is stayed. See Section 21E(f).

Courts struggle with numerous aspects of the statutory safe harbor. Consider the following case.

ASHER v. BAXTER INTERNATIONAL, INC.

377 F.3d 727 (7th Cir. 2004)

FRANK H. EASTERBROOK, CIRCUIT JUDGE:

Baxter International, a manufacturer of medical products, released its second-quarter financial results for 2002 on July 18 of that year. Sales and profits did not match analysts' expectations. Shares swiftly fell from $43 to $32. This litigation followed; plaintiffs contend that the $43 price was the result of materially misleading projections on November 5, 2001, projections that Baxter reiterated until the bad news came out on July 18, 2002. Plaintiffs want to represent a class of all investors who purchased during that time either in the open market or by exchanging their shares of Fusion Medical Technologies. (Baxter acquired Fusion in a stock-for-stock transaction; plaintiffs think that Baxter juiced up the market price so that it could secure Fusion in exchange for fewer of its own shares.). *** [T]he district court dismissed the complaint for failure to state a claim on which relief may be granted. The court did not doubt that the allegations ordinarily would defeat a motion under Fed.R.Civ.P. 12(b)(6). Still, it held, Baxter's forecasts come within the safe harbor created by the Private Securities Litigation Reform Act of 1995. The PSLRA creates rules that judges must enforce at the outset of the litigation; plaintiffs do not question the statute's application before discovery but do dispute the district court's substantive decision.

Baxter's projection, repeated many times (sometimes in documents filed with the SEC, sometimes in press releases, sometimes in executives' oral statements), was that during 2002 the business would yield revenue growth in the "low teens" compared with the prior year, earnings-per- share growth in the "mid teens," and "operational cash flow of at least $500 million." Baxter often referred to these forecasts as "our 2002 full-year commitments," which is a strange locution. No firm can make "commitments" about the future-Baxter can't compel its customers to buy more of its products-unless it plans to engage in accounting shenanigans to make the numbers come out right no matter what happens to the business. But nothing turns on the word; the district court took these "commitments" as "forward-looking statements," and plaintiffs do not quarrel with that understanding. What they do say is that the projections were too rosy, and that Baxter knew it. That charges the defendants with stupidity as much as with knavery, for the truth was bound to come out quickly, but the securities laws forbid foolish frauds along with clever ones.

According to the complaint, Baxter's projections were materially false because (1) its Renal Division had not met its internal budgets in years; (2) economic instability in Latin America adversely affected Baxter's sales in that part of the world; (3) Baxter closed plants in Ronneby, Sweden, and Miami Lakes, Florida, that had been its principal source of low-cost dialysis products; (4) the market for albumin (blood-plasma) products was "over-saturated," resulting in lower prices and revenue for the BioSciences Division; (5) sales of that division's IGIV immunoglobin products had fallen short of internal predictions; and (6) in March 2002 the BioScience Division had experienced a sterility failure in the manufacture of a major product, resulting in the destruction of multiple lots and a loss exceeding $10 million. The district court assumed, as shall we, that failure to disclose these facts would create problems but for the statutory safe harbor-though items (2) and (4) at least are general business matters rather than Baxter's secrets, and the securities laws do not require issuers to disclose the state of the world, as opposed to facts about the firm. See *Wielgos v. Commonwealth Edison Co.*, 892 F.2d 509 (7th Cir.1989). Item (3) also was public knowledge (Baxter issued a press release announcing the closings and a substantial charge against earnings)-though the cost of products that had been made at these plants may have been secret. Whether all firm- specific non-disclosures add up to a material non-disclosure-and whether Baxter had some non- public information about those matters that seem to be general information-are topics we need not tackle.

Section 77z-2, which deals with statements covered by the Securities Act of 1933 (here, those in the registration statement and prospectus for the stock that Baxter exchanged for Fusion's shares) and § 78u-5, which deals with statements covered by the Securities Exchange Act of 1934 (here, the statements in Baxter's press releases, press conferences, and periodic filings) are identical in all significant respects, so from now on we mention only the former statute. The statutory safe harbor forecloses liability if a forward-looking statement "is accompanied by meaningful cautionary statements identifying important factors that could cause actual results to differ materially from those in the forward-looking statement." The fundamental problem is that the statutory requirement of "meaningful cautionary statements" is not itself meaningful. What must the firm say? Unless it is possible to give a concrete and reliable answer, the harbor is not "safe"; yet a word such as "meaningful" resists a concrete rendition and thus makes administration of the safe harbor difficult if not impossible. It rules out a caution such as: "This is a forward-looking statement: caveat emptor." But it does not rule in any particular caution, which always may be challenged as not sufficiently "meaningful" or not pinning down the "important factors that could cause actual results to differ materially"-for if it had identified all of those factors, it would not be possible to describe the forward-looking statement itself as materially misleading. A safe harbor matters only when the firm's disclosures (including the accompanying cautionary statements) are false or misleadingly incomplete; yet whenever that condition is satisfied, one can complain that the cautionary statement must have been inadequate. The safe harbor loses its function. Yet it would be unsound to read the statute so that the safe harbor never works ***.

Baxter provided a number of cautionary statements throughout the class period. This one, from its 2001 Form 10-K filing-a document to which many of the firm's press releases and other statements referred-is the best illustration:

> Statements throughout this report that are not historical facts are forward-looking statements. These statements are based on the company's current expectations and involve numerous risks and uncertainties. Some of these risks and uncertainties are factors that affect all international businesses, while some are specific to the company and the health care arenas in which it operates.
>
> Many factors could affect the company's actual results, causing results to differ materially, from those expressed in any such forward-looking statements. These factors include, but are not limited to, interest rates; technological advances in the medical field; economic conditions; demand and market acceptance risks for new and existing products, technologies and health care services; the impact of competitive products and pricing; manufacturing

> capacity; new plant start-ups; global regulatory, trade and tax policies; regulatory, legal or other developments relating to the company's Series A, AF, and AX dialyzers; continued price competition; product development risks, including technological difficulties; ability to enforce patents; actions of regulatory bodies and other government authorities; reimbursement policies of government agencies; commercialization factors; results of product testing; and other factors described elsewhere in this report or in the company's other filings with the Securities and Exchange Commission. Additionally, as discussed in Item 3-"Legal Proceedings," upon the resolution of certain legal matters, the company may incur charges in excess of presently established reserves. Any such change could have a material adverse effect on the company's results of operations or cash flows in the period in which it is recorded.
>
> Currency fluctuations are also a significant variable for global companies, especially fluctuations in local currencies where hedging opportunities are unreasonably expensive or unavailable. If the United States dollar strengthens significantly against mist foreign currencies, the company's ability to realize projected growth rates in its sales and net earnings outside the United States could be negatively impacted.
>
> The company believes that its expectations with respect to forward-looking statements are based upon reasonable assumptions within the bounds of its knowledge of its business operations, but there can be no assurance that the actual results or performance of the company will conform to any future results or performance expressed or implied by such forward-looking statements.

The district court concluded that these are "meaningful cautionary statements identifying important factors that could cause actual results to differ materially from those in the forward-looking statement". They deal with Baxter's business specifically, mentioning risks and product lines. Plaintiffs offer two responses. First they contend that the cautionary statements did not cover any of the six matters that (in plaintiffs' view) Baxter had withheld. That can't be dispositive; otherwise the statute would demand prescience. As long as the firm reveals the principal risks, the fact that some other event caused problems cannot be dispositive. Indeed, an unexpected turn of events cannot demonstrate a securities problem at all, as there cannot be "fraud by hindsight." *Denny v. Barber*, 576 F.2d 465, 470 (2d Cir.1978) (Friendly, J.). The other response is that the cautionary statement did not follow the firm's fortunes: plants closed but the cautionary statement remained the same; sterilization failures occurred but the cautionary statement remained the same; and bad news that (plaintiffs contend) Baxter well knew in November 2001 did not cast even a shadow in the cautionary statement.

Before considering whether plaintiffs' objections defeat the safe harbor, we ask whether the cautionary statements have any bearing on Baxter's potential liability for statements in its press releases, and those its managers made orally. The press releases referred to, but did not repeat verbatim, the cautionary statements in the Form 10-K and other documents filed with the Securities and Exchange Commission. The oral statements did not do even that much. Plaintiffs say that this is fatal, because § 77z-2(c)(1)(A)(i) provides a safe harbor only if a written statement is "accompanied by" the meaningful caution; a statement published elsewhere differs from one that accompanies the press release. As for the oral statements: § 77z-2(c)(2)(A)(ii), a special rule for oral statements, provides a safe harbor only if the statement includes "that the actual results could differ materially from those projected in the forward-looking statement" and in addition:

(i) the oral forward-looking statement is accompanied by an oral statement that additional information concerning factors that could cause actual results to differ materially from those in the forward-looking statement is contained in a readily available written document, or portion thereof;

(ii) the accompanying oral statement referred to in clause (i) identifies the document, or portion thereof, that contains the additional information about those factors relating to the forward-looking statement; and

(iii) the information contained in that written document is a cautionary statement that satisfies the standard established in paragraph (1)(A).

15 U.S.C. § 77z-2(c)(2)(B). When speaking with analysts Baxter's executives did not provide them with all of this information, such as directions to look in the 10-K report for the full cautionary statement. It follows, plaintiffs maintain, that this suit must proceed with respect to the press releases and oral statements even if the cautionary language filed with the SEC in registration statements and other documents meets the statutory standard.

If this were a traditional securities suit-if, in other words, an investor claimed to have read or heard the statement and, not having access to the truth, relied to his detriment on the falsehood-then plaintiffs' argument would be correct. But this is not a traditional securities claim. It is a fraud-on-the-market claim. None of the plaintiffs asserts that he read any of Baxter's press releases or listened to an executive's oral statement. Instead the theory is that other people (professional traders, mutual fund managers, securities analysts) did the reading, and that they made trades or recommendations that influenced the price. In an efficient capital market, all information known to the public affects the price and thus affects every investor. *Basic Inc. v. Levinson*, 485 U.S. 224, 241-47 (1988), holds that reliance on the accuracy of the price can substitute for reliance on the accuracy of particular written or oral statements, when the statements affect the price-as they do for large and well-followed firms such as Baxter, for which there is a liquid public market. This works only to the extent that markets efficiently reflect (and thus convey to investors the economic equivalent of) all public information. See Daniel R. Fischel, Efficient Capital Markets, the Crash, and the Fraud on the Market Theory, 74 Cornell L.Rev. 907, 917-22 (1989); Jonathan R. Macey & Geoffrey P. Miller, Good Finance, Bad Economics: An Analysis of the Fraud-on-the-Market Theory, 42 Stan. L.Rev. 1059 (1990).

When markets are informationally efficient, it is impossible to segment information as plaintiffs propose. They ask us to say that they received (through the price) the false oral statements but not the cautionary disclosures. That can't be; only if the market is inefficient is partial transmission likely, and if the market for Baxter's stock is inefficient then this suit collapses because a fraud-on-the-market claim won't fly. An investor who invokes the fraud-on-the-market theory must acknowledge that all public information is reflected in the price, just as the Supreme Court said in *Basic*. See 485 U.S. at 246. Thus if the truth or the nature of a business risk is widely known, an incorrect statement can have no deleterious effect, and if a cautionary statement has been widely disseminated, that news too affects the price just as if that statement had been handed to each investor. If the executives' oral statements came to plaintiffs through professional traders (or analysts) and hence the price, then the cautions reached plaintiffs via the same route; market professionals are savvy enough to discount projections appropriately. Then § 77z-2(c)(2)(B) has been satisfied for the oral statements (and so too § 77z-2(c)(1)(A)(i) for the press releases). And if the cautions did not affect the price, then the market must be inefficient and the suit fails for that reason. So we take the claim as the pleadings framed it: the market for Baxter's stock is efficient, which means that Baxter's cautionary language must be treated as if attached to every one of its oral and written statements. That leaves the question whether these statements satisfy the statutory requirement that they adequately "identify [ ] important factors that could cause actual results to differ materially from those in the forward-looking statement."

The parties agree on two propositions, each with support in decisions of other circuits. First, "boilerplate" warnings won't do; cautions must be tailored to the risks that accompany the particular projections. Second, the cautions need not identify what actually goes wrong and causes the projections to be inaccurate; prevision is not required. See *Halperin v. eBanker USA.COM, Inc.*, 295 F.3d 352, 359 (2d Cir.2002); *Ehlert v. Singer*, 245 F.3d 1313, 1320 (11th Cir.2001) (discussing a judicially developed defense, the bespeaks-caution doctrine, that applies to statements such as those made in tender offers to which the statutory safe harbor does not apply). Unfortunately, these principles don't decide any concrete case-for that matter, the statutory language itself does not decide any concrete case. It is the result of a compromise between legislators who did not want any safe harbor *** and those who wanted a safe harbor along the lines of the old Rule 175 *** that did not require any cautionary statements but just required the projection to have a reasonable basis. As is often the situation, a compromise enabled the bill to pass but lacks much content; it does not encode a principle on which political forces agreed as much as it signifies conflict about both the scope and the wisdom of the safe harbor. Compromises of this kind lack spirit. Still, the language was enacted, and we must make something of it.

Plaintiffs say that Baxter's cautions were boilerplate, but they aren't. Statements along the lines of "all businesses are risky" or "the future lies ahead" come to nothing other than caveat emptor (which isn't enough); these statements, by contrast, at least included Baxter-specific information and highlighted some parts of the business that might cause problems. For its part, Baxter says that mentioning these business segments demonstrates that the caution is sufficient; but this also is wrong, because then any issuer could list its lines of business, say "we could have problems in any of these," and avoid liability for statements implying that no such problems were on the horizon even if a precipice was in sight.

What investors would like to have is a full disclosure of the assumptions and calculations behind the projections; then they could apply their own discount factors. For reasons covered at length in *Wielgos*, however, this is not a sensible requirement. Many of the assumptions and calculations would be more useful to a firm's rivals than to its investors. Suppose, for example, that Baxter had revealed its sterility failure in the BioSciences Division, the steps it had taken to restore production, and the costs and prospects of each. Rivals could have used that information to avoid costs and hazards that had befallen Baxter, or to find solutions more quickly, and as Baxter could not have charged the rivals for this information they would have been able to undercut Baxter's price in future transactions. Baxter's shareholders would have been worse off. Similarly Baxter might have added verisimilitude to its projections by describing its sales policies and the lowest prices it would accept from major customers, but disclosing reservation prices would do more to help the customers than to assist the investors.

Another form a helpful caution might take would be the disclosure of confidence intervals. After saying that it expected growth in the low teens, Baxter might have added that events could deviate 5% in either direction (so the real projection was that growth would fall someplace between 8% and 18%); disclosure of the probability that growth will be under 10% (or over 16%) would have done much to avoid the hit stock prices took when the results for the first half of 2002 proved to be unexpectedly low. Baxter surely had developed internally some estimate of likely variance. Revealing the mean, median, and standard deviation of these internal estimates, and pinpointing the principal matters that could cause results to differ from the more likely outcome, could help to generate an accurate price for the stock. Knowledge that the mean is above the median, or that the standard deviation is substantial, would be particularly helpful to those professional investors whose trades determine the market price. (It might imply, for example, that as in *Wielgos* the firm was projecting what would happen if nothing unexpected happened; because some things always go wrong, investors could apply discounts.) Perhaps, however, a firm's data do not permit estimates to be stated in probabilities. If, for example, a major source of uncertainty for Baxter's business was how Congress would resolve the debate about Medicare coverage for prescription drugs, or whether a rival would manage to win the FDA's approval for a product that would compete with one of Baxter's most profitable items, it would be hard to reduce these chances to probabilities. Events such as these are discrete rather than continuous variables, so standard confidence intervals would be meaningless even if probabilities could be attached to the likely outcomes.

Whether or not Baxter could have made the cautions more helpful by disclosing assumptions, methods, or confidence intervals, none of these is required. The PSLRA does not require the most helpful caution; it is enough to "identify[ ] important factors that could cause actual results to differ materially from those in the forward-looking statement". This means that it is enough to point to the principal contingencies that could cause actual results to depart from the projection. The statute calls for issuers to reveal the "important factors" but not to attach probabilities to each potential bad outcome, or to reveal in detail what could go wrong; as we have said, that level of detail might hurt investors (by helping rivals) even as it improved the accuracy of stock prices. (Requiring cautions to contain elaborate detail also would defeat the goal of facilitating projections, by turning each into a form of registration statement. Undue complexity would lead issuers to shut up, and stock prices could become even less accurate. Incomplete information usually is better than none, because market professionals know other tidbits that put the news in context.) Moreover, "[i]f enterprises cannot make predictions about themselves, then securities analysts, newspaper columnists, and charlatans have protected turf. There will be predictions aplenty outside the domain of the securities acts, predictions by persons whose access to information is not as good as the issuer's. When the issuer adds its information and analysis to that assembled by outsiders, the *collective* assessment will be more accurate even though a given projection will be off the mark." *Wielgos*, 892 F.2d at 514 (emphasis in original).

Yet Baxter's chosen language may fall short. There is no reason to think-at least, no reason that a court can accept at the pleading stage, before plaintiffs have access to discovery-that the items mentioned in Baxter's cautionary language were those that at the time were the (or any of the) "important" sources of variance. The problem is not that what actually happened went unmentioned; issuers need not anticipate all sources of deviations from expectations. Rather, the problem is that there is no reason (on this record) to conclude that Baxter mentioned those sources of variance that (at the time of the projection) were the principal or important risks. For all we can tell, the major risks Baxter objectively faced when it made its forecasts were exactly those that, according to the complaint, came to pass, yet the cautionary statement mentioned none of them. Moreover, the cautionary language remained fixed even as the risks changed. When the sterility failure occurred in spring 2002, Baxter left both its forecasts and cautions as is. When Baxter closed the plants that (according to the complaint) were its least-cost sources of production, the forecasts and cautions continued without amendment. This raises the possibility-no greater confidence is possible before discovery-that Baxter omitted important variables from the cautionary language and so made projections more certain than its internal estimates at the time warranted. Thus this complaint could not be dismissed under the safe harbor, though we cannot exclude the possibility that if after discovery Baxter establishes that the cautions did reveal what were, ex ante, the major risks, the safe harbor may yet carry the day.

Baxter urges us to affirm the judgment immediately, contending that the full truth had reached the market despite any shortcomings in its cautionary statements. If this is so, however, it is hard to understand the sharp drop in the price of its stock. A "truth-on-the-market" defense is available in principle, *** but not at the pleading stage. Likewise one must consider the possibility that investors looked at all of the projections as fluff and responded only to the hard numbers; on this view it was a reduction in Baxter's growth rate, not the embarrassment of a projection, that caused the price decline in July 2002; again it is too early in the litigation to reach such a conclusion. It would be necessary to ask, for example, whether the price rose relative to the rest of the market when Baxter made its projections; if not, that might support an inference that the projections were so much noise.

Nor has the time arrived to evaluate Baxter's contention that its projections panned out, so there was no material error. Baxter insists that all of the projections dealt with the entire calendar year 2002, and that by year-end performance was up to snuff-close enough to the projections that any difference was immaterial. Once again, it is inappropriate to entertain such an argument at the pleading stage. The district court will need to determine whether all of the forward-looking statements referenced calendar 2002 as a whole, rather than anticipated improvements quarter-by- quarter over the preceding year. It will be necessary to evaluate whether differences between the projections and the outcome were material under the standard of *Basic*. Finally it may be necessary to explore what Baxter's full-year results actually were; plaintiffs' reply brief accuses Baxter of using gimmicks to report extra revenue in 2002 at the expense of later years. The implication is that Baxter may have overstated its 2002 results. Whether that is so cannot be determined on the pleadings, even when supplemented with the documents that Baxter has filed with the SEC.

Reversed and Remanded.

NOTES AND QUESTIONS

1. ***Seeking a Limiting Principle.*** Does *Asher* give the plaintiff an automatic entitlement to discovery prior to a ruling on a dismissal motion based on the safe harbor? If so, does that fly in the face of the safe harbor itself? If not, what made the *Asher* case special?

2. ***Incorporation By Reference.*** The court held that in an efficient market, cautions contained in SEC filings "must be treated as if attached to every one of [the company's] oral and written statements." See also *Yellen v. Hake*, 437 F. Supp. 2d 941, 963-64 (S.D. Iowa 2006) (collecting cases to the same effect). Do you agree? Suppose that the plaintiff does not plead fraud-on-the-market (or otherwise allege an efficient market). Under these circumstances, should cautions in SEC filings attach to the company's other statements?

3. ***Omitting the Factor that "Dwarfs" the Others.*** According to *Asher*, the safe harbor "does not require the most helpful caution" but merely "the principal contingencies that could cause actual results to depart from the projections." Yet there remains the question whether the safe harbor applies when the defendant knowingly excludes the one contingency that is "such a market-driver that it dwarfs" the others in importance. See *Harris v. Ivax Corp.*, 209 F.3d 1275, 1276 (11th Cir. 2000) (decision on petition for rehearing). In an amicus brief in partial support of a rehearing, the SEC argued that the answer was no. See id. The court denied the petition with the observation that the "argument [made by the Commission] had not been made to the panel, and *** we have therefore not considered it." Id. What do you think that the answer should be?

4. ***The Present vs. The Future.*** Although the safe harbor applies only to *forward- looking* statements, a given statement may refer to the future as well as to the present (or the past), thereby making categorization difficult. As the Second Circuit has observed:

> A forward-looking statement (accompanied by cautionary language) expresses the issuer's inherently contingent prediction of risk or future cash flow; a non-forward-looking statement provides an ascertainable or verifiable basis for the investor to make his own prediction.
>
> The line can be hard to draw, and we do not now undertake to draw one. However, a statement specifying the risk of default is distinct from a statement of present or historical financial instability, even though they both bear upon the same risk. And a statement of confidence in a firm's operations may be forward-looking ***-- even while statements or omissions as to the operations in place (and present intentions as to future operations) are not.

Iowa Pub. Emps.' Ret. Sys. v. M.F. Global, Ltd., 620 F.3d 137, 143-44 (2d Cir. 2010) (bespeaks caution doctrine case).

Consider also the analysis in *In re Stone & Webster Inc. Sec. Litig.*, 414 F.3d 187 (1st Cir. 2005). At issue was the following sentence in a registration statement: The company "has on hand and has access to sufficient sources of funds to meet its anticipated *** needs." Id. at 211. The First Circuit held the sentence to be not forward-looking:

> Essentially the statement asserts that the Company has *present* access to funds sufficient to meet anticipated *future* needs. The part of the statement that speaks of the quantity of cash on hand speaks of a present fact. The part that speaks of the amount of "anticipated operating, dividend and capital expenditure needs" speaks of a projection of future economic performance. The claim of fraud, however, does not involve a contention that the defendants were underestimating the amount of their future cash needs. The claim is rather that the defendants were lying about the Company's present access to funds. The Company was, according to the allegations of the Complaint, in an extreme liquidity crunch.
>
> We believe that in order to determine whether a statement falls within the safe harbor, a court must examine which aspects of the statement are alleged to be false. The mere fact that a statement contains some reference to a projection of future events cannot sensibly bring the statement within the safe harbor if the allegation of falsehood relates to non-forward-looking aspects of the statement. The safe harbor, we believe, is intended to apply only to allegations of falsehood as to the forward-looking aspects of the statement.
>
> *** In our view, the safe harbor *** does not confer a *carte blanche* to lie in such representations of current fact. We reject the district court's conclusion that the statements assuring that the Company had access to sufficient cash to cover anticipated needs were within the safe harbor.

Id. 212-213.

Consider finally the challenged statement in *Harris v. Ivax Corp.*, 182 F.3d 799 (11th Cir. 1999), which appeared in a press release: "The challenges unique to this period are now behind us." Id. at 805. Rejecting the significance of the present-tense verb, the court deemed the statement forward-looking because "whether the worst of Ivax's challenges were behind it was a matter verifiable only after the chairman so declared." Id.

Which of these approaches do you regard as the most useful? Is it possible that they all have their uses? Is it relevant that *Stone & Webster* involved a registration statement whereas *Ivax* involved a press release?

5. *The Problem of Mixed Lists.* The *Ivax* decision described in the preceding Note also addressed a different issue – how to categorize an entire list of factors (only some of which involved the future) that were expected to impact the company's business in the third quarter. The court concluded that the entire list was forward-looking:

> The *** press release *** contained a list of factors "relating to [Ivax's] generic drug business [that] will influence [Ivax's] third quarter results." Those five factors included high customer inventory levels and low orders; declining prices; "shelf stock adjustments" for existing customers; higher reserves for returns; and the bankruptcy of a major customer who owed Ivax $16 million. The list is a mixed bag, with some sentences that are forward-looking and some that are not. The statement's choice of language suggests that three of the factors had already been observed: "customer re-orders remain depressed";

> "prices have continued to decline"; and "a wholesaler customer who owed us approximately $16 million filed a Chapter 11 bankruptcy petition." Observed facts of this kind are not "assumptions," and they are not any kind of prediction, either, that would put them within the definition of a forward-looking statement. These sentences are not, therefore, forward-looking. Two other factors, however, are worded as assumptions about future events: "we expect reserves for returns and inventory writeoffs to be well above typical quarters" and "lower prices ... will increase shelf stock adjustments." As "assumptions underlying" the predictions elsewhere in the press release, these sentences are forward-looking. 15 U.S.C. § 78u-5(i)(l)(D).
>
> The mixed nature of this statement raises the question whether the safe harbor benefits the entire statement or only parts of it. Of course, if any of the individual sentences describing known facts (such as the customer's bankruptcy) were allegedly false, we could easily conclude that that smaller, non-forward-looking statement falls outside the safe harbor. But the allegation here is that the list *as a whole* misleads anyone reading it for an explanation of Ivax's projections, because the list omits the expectation of a goodwill write-down. If the allegation is that the whole list is misleading, then it makes no sense to slice the list into separate sentences. ***
>
> We conclude that the entire list is due forward-looking treatment. *** Congress enacted the safe-harbor provision in order to loosen the "muzzling effect" of potential liability for forward-looking statements, which often kept investors in the dark about what management foresaw for the company. See H.R. Conf. Rep. 104-369, at 42 (1995). Forward-looking conclusions often rest both on historical observations and assumptions about future events. Thus, were we to banish from the safe harbor lists that contain both factual and forward-looking factors, we would inhibit corporate officers from fully explaining their outlooks. Indeed, liability-conscious officers would be relegated to citing only the factors that could individually be called forward-looking. That would hamper the communication that Congress sought to foster.
>
> Treating mixed lists as forward-looking may open a loophole for misleading omissions, but there are two circumstances that should put investors on guard, anyway. First, a list or explanation will only qualify for this treatment if it contains assumptions underlying a forward-looking statement. Investors should know, under the current statutory scheme, that relying on assumptions is dangerous; there will often be no legal recourse even if the assumption is false. Second, a defendant can fully benefit from the safe harbor's shelter only when it has disclosed risk factors in a warning accompanying the forward- looking statement. This disclosure as well should warn investors against blind reliance on mixed lists.

Ivax, supra, 182 F.3d at 805-07. Did the the court give the "loophole" its due? Cf. *In re BankAtlantic Bancorp, Inc. Sec. Litig.*, 2011 WL 1585605 at *35 (S.D. Fla. 2011) (finding *Ivax*'s "mixed list" analysis inapplicable when the allegations target discrete statements rather than the defendant's statements as a whole).

6. The Meaning of "Or." The safe harbor consists of alterative prongs connected by the word "or." Thus, it would seem clear that liability cannot attach to a forward-looking statement made with knowledge of its falsity when the statement is accompanied by cautions satisfying the "bespeaks caution" prong. See, e.g., *Edward J. Goodman Life Income Trust v. Jabil Circuit, Inc.*, 594 F.3d 783, 795 (11th Cir. 2010). Why would Congress authorize dismissal of actions that involve deliberate defrauding of investors? Cf. *In re Stone &*

Webster Inc. Sec. Litig., 414 F.3d 187, 212 (1st Cir. 2005) (describing the safe harbor as "surprising," "curious," and "a license to defraud").

The Second Circuit has nonetheless called the independence of the prongs into question:

> We find Congress's directions difficult to apply in this case. ***[T]he Conference Report requires cautionary statements to convey substantive information about factors that realistically could cause results to differ materially from projections. In order to assess whether an issuer has identified the factors that realistically could cause results to differ, we must have some reference by which to judge what the realistic factors were at the time the statement was made. We think that the most sensible reference is the major factors that the defendants faced at the time the statement was made. But this requires an inquiry into what the defendants knew because in order to determine what risks the defendants faced, we must ask of what risks were they aware.
>
> Congress may wish to give further direction on how to resolve this tension, and in particular, the reference point by which we should judge whether an issuer has identified the factors that realistically could cause results to differ from projections. May an issuer be protected by the meaningful cautionary language prong of the safe harbor even where his cautionary statement omitted a major risk that he knew about at the time he made the statement? In this case, however, we need not decide that thorny issue because we conclude that at any rate the cautionary statement the defendants point to here was vague.

Slayton v. American Express Co., 604 F.3d 758, 771-72 (2d Cir. 2010). Do you agree that Congress should act? If so, what should it do? To what extent (if at all) does *Asher* reflect the tension described in *Slayton*? For further discussion of these issues, see Allan Horwich, Cleaning the Murky Safe Harbor for Forward-Looking Statements: An Inquiry Into Whether Actual Knowledge of Falsity Precludes the Meaningful Cautionary Statement Defense, 35 J. Corp. L. 519 (2010); Anne Morales Olazabal, False Forward-Looking Statements and the PSLRA's Safe Harbor, 86 Ind. L. J. 595 (2011).

7. ***The Impact of the Safe Harbor.*** The enactment of the safe harbor has not led to the dissemination of more forward-looking statements, according to all but one of the empirical studies of this question. See Hugh C. Beck, The Substantive Limits of Liability for Inaccurate Predictions, 44 Am. Bus. L. J. 161, 164 n.12 (2007) (collecting the studies). Why might this be? An equally important question has as yet no definitive answer: Has the statutory safe harbor precipitated the release of more forward-looking statements that are materially misleading?

8. ***Bespeaks Caution Revisited.*** Given the statutory safe harbor, in what respects does the bespeaks caution doctrine continue to be relevant?

PROBLEM 2-9

Decide whether the following statements are forward-looking:

a. Our new shampoo is in the process of becoming an industry benchmark.

b. Our loan loss reserves are adequate.

c. We expect that Phase 2 of our building plan will begin in 5 months.

d. The misrepresentation at issue in *Basic Inc. v. Levinson,* 485 U.S. 224 (1988), which you read earlier in this section of the Chapter.

PROBLEM 2-10

Luna, Inc. is an electronics parts manufacturer whose stock is listed on the New York Stock Exchange. Needing capital to expand its production capacity, Luna decided to make a registered stock offering. This offering began on December 15, 2011 and concluded on January 15, 2012.

The registration statement for the offering described the planned capacity expansion in its "Use of the Proceeds" section. The registration statement also stated the following in a section entitled "Description of Business": "Management plans to complete its expansion of current production facilities by the end of March 2012, and expects both an increase in manufacturing orders from its existing customers and an influx of manufacturing orders from new customers. See 'Risk Factors.'" In a "Risk Factors" section, the registration statement stated only that "all statements regarding completion of our new production facilities and our increase in revenue from additional manufacturing orders are merely projections and may not be realized."

The expansion project was completed on schedule, but shortly thereafter, Luna's largest customer (Alva) announced that it was planning to relocate almost all of its manufacturing offshore, and would therefore be placing no future orders with the company. Luna issued a press release announcing its cessation of business with Alva and adding that the competition it now faced from electronics parts manufacturers outside the continental United States might significantly impact the projected revenue from its capacity expansion.

As a result of the press release, the price of Luna stock fell significantly, and shareholders who purchased in the registered offering instituted a class action lawsuit against Luna under Rule 10b-5 based on alleged material misstatements in the registration statement's "Description of Business" section.

On plaintiff's motion to a very sympathetic judge, the trial court allowed a limited amount of pre-trial discovery to prevent "undue prejudice." This limited pre-trial discovery revealed that, prior to the filing of the registration statement as well as during the entire period of the offering, Luna's management assumed without any investigation that its existing customers would renew their short-term contracts and had no plans to move offshore. Had Luna's management investigated, they would have learned that Alva had been placing at least some new orders with offshore electronics parts manufacturers beginning at least two months before the public offering.

At the conclusion of this phase of limited discovery, Luna made a motion for summary judgment, claiming that it was not liable as a matter of law under the statutory safe harbor for forward-looking statements. Discuss the likely outcome of this motion. How (if at all) would your answer differ if the motion had been based on the bespeaks caution doctrine?

C. THE "IN CONNECTION WITH" REQUIREMENT

The "in connection with" requirement emerges from the language of Section 10(b) and Rule 10b-5, which prohibits fraud "in connection with" the purchase or sale of any security. The language is silent, however, about what the nature of that connection must be, as is the legislative history. Consider the Supreme Court's interpretation in the decision that follows.

SEC v. ZANDFORD

535 U.S. 813 (2002)

JUSTICE JOHN PAUL STEVENS:

The Securities and Exchange Commission (SEC) filed a civil complaint alleging that a stockbroker violated both § 10(b) of the Securities Exchange Act of 1934 and the SEC's Rule 10b-5, by selling his customer's securities and using the proceeds for his own benefit without the customer's knowledge or consent. The question presented is whether the alleged fraudulent conduct was "in connection with the purchase or sale of any security" within the meaning of the statute and the rule.

I

Between 1987 and 1991, respondent was employed as a securities broker in the Maryland branch of a New York brokerage firm. In 1987, he persuaded William Wood, an elderly man in poor health, to open a joint investment account for himself and his mentally retarded daughter. According to the SEC's complaint, the "stated investment objectives for the account were 'safety of principal and income.' " The Woods granted respondent discretion to manage their account and a general power of attorney to engage in securities transactions for their benefit without prior approval. Relying on respondent's promise to "conservatively invest" their money, the Woods entrusted him with $419,255. Before Mr. Wood's death in 1991, all of that money was gone.

In 1991, the National Association of Securities Dealers (NASD) conducted a routine examination of respondent's firm and discovered that on over 25 separate occasions, money had been transferred from the Woods' account to accounts controlled by respondent. In due course, respondent was indicted in the United States District Court for the District of Maryland on 13 counts of wire fraud in violation of 18 U.S.C. § 1343. The first count alleged that respondent sold securities in the Woods' account and then made personal use of the proceeds. Each of the other counts alleged that he made wire transfers between Maryland and New York that enabled him to withdraw specified sums from the Woods' accounts. Some of those transfers involved respondent writing checks to himself from a mutual fund account held by the Woods, which required liquidating securities in order to redeem the checks. Respondent was convicted on all counts, sentenced to prison for 52 months, and ordered to pay $10,800 in restitution.

After respondent was indicted, the SEC filed a civil complaint in the same District Court alleging that respondent violated § 10(b) and Rule 10b-5 by engaging in a scheme to defraud the Woods and by misappropriating approximately $343,000 of the Woods' securities without their knowledge or consent. The SEC moved for partial summary judgment after respondent's criminal conviction, arguing that the judgment in the criminal case estopped respondent from contesting facts that established a violation of § 10(b).[1] Respondent filed a motion seeking discovery on the question whether his fraud had the requisite "connection with" the purchase or sale of a security. The District Court refused to allow discovery and entered summary judgment against respondent. It enjoined him from engaging in future violations of the securities laws and ordered him to disgorge $343,000 in ill-gotten gains.

The Court of Appeals for the Fourth Circuit reversed the summary judgment and remanded with directions for the District Court to dismiss the complaint. It first held that the wire fraud conviction, which only required two findings—(1) that respondent engaged in a scheme to defraud and (2) that he used interstate wire communications in executing the scheme—did not establish all the elements of a § 10(b) violation. Specifically, the conviction did not necessarily establish that his fraud was "in connection with" the sale of a security. Id., at 562.

The court then held that the civil complaint did not sufficiently allege the necessary connection because the sales of the Woods' securities were merely incidental to a fraud that "lay in absconding with the proceeds" of sales that were conducted in "a routine and customary fashion." Respondent's "scheme was simply to steal the Woods' assets" rather than to engage "in manipulation of a particular security." Ultimately, the court refused "to stretch the language of the securities fraud provisions to encompass every conversion or theft that happens to involve securities." Adopting what amounts to a "fraud-on-the-market" theory of the statute's coverage, the court held that without some "relationship to market integrity or investor understanding," there is no violation of § 10(b).

We granted the SEC's petition for a writ of certiorari to review the Court of Appeals' construction of the phrase "in connection with the purchase or sale of any security." Because the Court of Appeals ordered the complaint dismissed rather than remanding for reconsideration, we assume the allegations contained therein are true and affirm that disposition only if no set of facts would entitle petitioner to relief. We do not reach the question whether the record supports the District Court's grant of summary judgment in the SEC's favor—a question that requires all potential factual disputes to be resolved in respondent's favor. We merely hold that the allegations of the complaint, if true, entitle the SEC to relief; therefore, the Court of Appeals should not have directed that the complaint be dismissed.

II

Section 10(b) of the Securities Exchange Act makes it "unlawful for any person ... [t]o use or employ, in connection with the purchase or sale of any security ..., any manipulative or deceptive device or contrivance in contravention of such rules and regulations as the [SEC] may prescribe." Rule 10b-5, which implements this provision, forbids the use, "in connection with the purchase or

---

1. The scope of Rule 10b-5 is coextensive with the coverage of § 10(b), see *United States v. O'Hagan,* 521 U.S. 642, 651 (1997); *Ernst & Ernst v. Hochfelder,* 425 U.S. 185, 214 (1976); therefore, we use § 10(b) to refer to both the statutory provision and the Rule. ***

sale of any security," of "any device, scheme, or artifice to defraud" or any other "act, practice, or course of business" that "operates ... as a fraud or deceit." Among Congress' objectives in passing the Act was "to insure honest securities markets and thereby promote investor confidence" after the market crash of 1929. *United States v. O'Hagan,* 521 U.S. 642, 658 (1997). More generally, Congress sought "'to substitute a philosophy of full disclosure for the philosophy of *caveat emptor* and thus to achieve a high standard of business ethics in the securities industry.' " *Affiliated Ute Citizens of Utah v. United States,* 406 U.S. 128, 151 (1972) (quoting *SEC v. Capital Gains Research Bureau, Inc.,* 375 U.S. 180, 186 (1963)).

Consequently, we have explained that the statute should be "construed 'not technically and restrictively, but flexibly to effectuate its remedial purposes.' " 406 U.S., at 151 (quoting *Capital Gains Research Bureau, Inc.,* 375 U.S., at 195). In its role enforcing the Act, the SEC has consistently adopted a broad reading of the phrase "in connection with the purchase or sale of any security." It has maintained that a broker who accepts payment for securities that he never intends to deliver, or who sells customer securities with intent to misappropriate the proceeds, violates § 10(b) and Rule 10b-5. See, e.g., *In re Bauer,* 26 S.E.C. 770 (1947); *In re Southeastern Securities Corp.,* 29 S.E.C. 609 (1949). This interpretation of the ambiguous text of § 10(b), in the context of formal adjudication, is entitled to deference if it is reasonable, see *United States v. Mead Corp.,* 533 U.S. 218, 229-230, and n. 12 (2001). For the reasons set forth below, we think it is. While the statute must not be construed so broadly as to convert every common-law fraud that happens to involve securities into a violation of § 10(b), *Marine Bank v. Weaver,* 455 U.S. 551, 556 (1982) ("Congress, in enacting the securities laws, did not intend to provide a broad federal remedy for all fraud"), neither the SEC nor this Court has ever held that there must be a misrepresentation about the value of a particular security in order to run afoul of the Act.

The SEC claims respondent engaged in a fraudulent scheme in which he made sales of his customer's securities for his own benefit. Respondent submits that the sales themselves were perfectly lawful and that the subsequent misappropriation of the proceeds, though fraudulent, is not properly viewed as having the requisite connection with the sales; in his view, the alleged scheme is not materially different from a simple theft of cash or securities in an investment account. We disagree.

According to the complaint, respondent "engaged in a scheme to defraud" the Woods beginning in 1988, shortly after they opened their account, and that scheme continued throughout the 2-year period during which respondent made a series of transactions that enabled him to convert the proceeds of the sales of the Woods' securities to his own use. The securities sales and respondent's fraudulent practices were not independent events. This is not a case in which, after a lawful transaction had been consummated, a broker decided to steal the proceeds and did so. Nor is it a case in which a thief simply invested the proceeds of a routine conversion in the stock market. Rather, respondent's fraud coincided with the sales themselves.

Taking the allegations in the complaint as true, each sale was made to further respondent's fraudulent scheme; each was deceptive because it was neither authorized by, nor disclosed to, the Woods. With regard to the sales of shares in the Woods' mutual fund, respondent initiated these transactions by writing a check to himself from that account, knowing that redeeming the check would require the sale of securities. Indeed, each time respondent "exercised his power of disposition for his own benefit," that conduct, "without more," was a fraud. *United States v. Dunn,* 268 U.S. 121, 131 (1925). In the aggregate, the sales are properly viewed as a "course of business" that operated as a fraud or deceit on a stockbroker's customer.

Insofar as the connection between respondent's deceptive practices and his sale of the Woods' securities is concerned, the case is remarkably similar to *Superintendent of Ins. of N.Y. v. Bankers Life & Casualty Co.,* 404 U.S. 6 (1971). In that case the directors of Manhattan Casualty Company authorized the sale of the company's portfolio of treasury bonds because they had been "duped" into believing that the company would receive the proceeds of the sale. Id., at 9. We held that "Manhattan was injured as an investor through a deceptive device which deprived it of any compensation for the sale of its valuable block of securities." Id., at 10. In reaching this conclusion, we did not ask, as the Fourth Circuit did in this case, whether the directors were misled about the value of a security or whether the fraud involved "manipulation of a particular security." In fact, we rejected the Second Circuit's position in *Superintendent of Ins. of N.Y. v. Bankers Life & Casualty Co.* that because the fraud against Manhattan did not take place within the context of a securities exchange it was not prohibited by § 10(b). 404 U.S., at 10. We refused to read the statute so narrowly, noting that it "must be read flexibly, not technically and restrictively." Id., at 12. Although we recognized that the interest in "'preserving the integrity of the securities markets,'" was one of the purposes animating the statute, we rejected the notion that § 10(b) is limited to serving that objective alone. Ibid.

Like the company directors in *Bankers Life,* the Woods were injured as investors through respondent's deceptions, which deprived them of any compensation for the sale of their valuable securities. They were duped into believing respondent would "conservatively invest" their assets in the stock market and that any transactions made on their behalf would be for their benefit for the "'safety of principal and income.'" The fact that respondent misappropriated the proceeds of the sales provides persuasive evidence that he had violated § 10(b) when he made the sales, but misappropriation is not an essential element of the offense. Indeed, in *Bankers Life,* we flatly stated that it was "irrelevant" that "the proceeds of the sale that were due the seller were misappropriated." It is enough that the scheme to defraud and the sale of securities coincide.

The Court of Appeals below distinguished *Bankers Life* on the ground that it involved an affirmative misrepresentation, whereas respondent simply failed to inform the Woods of his intent to misappropriate their securities. We are not persuaded by this distinction. Respondent was only able to carry out his fraudulent scheme without making an affirmative misrepresentation because the Woods had trusted him to make transactions in their best interest without prior approval. Under these circumstances, respondent's fraud represents an even greater threat to investor confidence in the securities industry than the misrepresentation in *Bankers Life.* Not only does such a fraud prevent investors from trusting that their brokers are executing transactions for their benefit, but it undermines the value of a discretionary account like that held by the Woods. The benefit of a discretionary account is that it enables individuals, like the Woods, who lack the time, capacity, or know-how to supervise investment decisions, to delegate authority to a broker who will make decisions in their best interests without prior approval. If such individuals cannot rely on a broker to exercise that discretion for their benefit, then the account loses its added value. Moreover, any distinction between omissions and misrepresentations is illusory in the context of a broker who has a fiduciary duty to her clients. See *Chiarella v. United States,* 445 U.S. 222, 230 (1980) (noting that "silence in connection with the purchase or sale of securities may operate as a fraud actionable under § 10(b)" when there is "a duty to disclose arising from a relationship of trust and confidence between parties to a transaction"); *Affiliated Ute Citizens of Utah v. United States,* 406 U.S., at 153.

More recently, in *Wharf (Holdings) Ltd. v. United Int'l Holdings, Inc.,* 532 U.S. 588 (2001), our decision that the seller of a security had violated § 10(b) focused on the secret intent of the seller when the sale occurred. The purchaser claimed "that Wharf sold it a security (the option) while secretly intending from the very beginning not to honor the option." Although Wharf did not specifically argue that the breach of contract underlying the complaint lacked the requisite connection with a sale of securities, it did assert that the case was merely a dispute over ownership of the option, and that interpreting § 10(b) to include such a claim would convert every breach of contract that happened to involve a security into a violation of the federal securities laws. We rejected that argument because the purchaser's claim was not that the defendant failed to carry out a promise to sell securities; rather, the claim was that the defendant sold a security while never intending to honor its agreement in the first place. Similarly, in this case the SEC claims respondent sold the Woods' securities while secretly intending from the very beginning to keep the proceeds. In *Wharf,* the fraudulent intent deprived the purchaser of the benefit of the sale whereas here the fraudulent intent deprived the seller of that benefit, but the connection between the deception and the sale in each case is identical.

In *United States v. O'Hagan,* 521 U.S. 642 (1997), we held that the defendant had committed fraud "in connection with" a securities transaction when he used misappropriated confidential information for trading purposes. We reasoned that "the fiduciary's fraud is consummated, not when the fiduciary gains the confidential information, but when, without disclosure to his principal, he uses the information to purchase or sell securities. The securities transaction and the breach of duty thus coincide. This is so even though the person or entity defrauded is not the other party to the trade, but is, instead, the source of the nonpublic information." Id., at 655-656. The Court of Appeals distinguished *O'Hagan* by reading it to require that the misappropriated information or assets not have independent value to the client outside the securities market. We do not read *O'Hagan* as so limited. In the chief passage cited by the Court of Appeals for this proposition, we discussed the Government's position that "[t]he misappropriation theory would not ... apply to a case in which a person defrauded a bank into giving him a loan or embezzled cash from another, and then used the proceeds of the misdeed to purchase securities," because in that situation "the proceeds would have value to the malefactor apart from their use in a securities transaction, and the fraud would be complete as soon as the money was obtained." 521 U.S., at 656. Even if this passage could be read to introduce a new requirement into § 10(b), it would not affect our analysis of this case, because the Woods' securities did not have value for respondent apart from their use in a securities transaction and the fraud was not complete before the sale of securities occurred.

As in *Bankers Life, Wharf,* and *O'Hagan,* the SEC complaint describes a fraudulent scheme in which the securities transactions and breaches of fiduciary duty coincide. Those breaches were therefore "in connection with" securities sales within the meaning of § 10(b).[4] Accordingly, the judgment of the Court of Appeals is reversed, and the case is remanded for further proceedings consistent with this opinion. ***

NOTES AND QUESTIONS

1. ***Exclusive or Not.*** The Court tells us that the SEC satisfied the "in connection with" requirement because the fraud and the sale "coincided." Does the Court suggest that establishing a coincidence is the only way to satisfy the "in connection with" requirement?

2. ***The Potential for Differentiating Private Actions.*** Prior to *Zandford,* some courts took the position that in order to discourage vexatious private litigation, the "in connection with" requirement should be made more difficult for private plaintiffs than for government plaintiffs. See, e.g., *SEC v. Clark,* 915 F.2d 439, 449 n. 18 (9th Cir. 1990). What impact (if any) does *Zandford* have in this regard?

3. ***Coextensive Statute and Rule.*** *Zandford* asserts that "[t]he scope of Rule 10b-5 is co-extensive with the coverage of § 10(b)" and cites as support *United States v. O'Hagan,* 521 U.S. 642 (1997), and *Ernst & Ernst v. Hochfelder,* 425 U.S. 185 (1976). But do those decisions actually go that far? See *O'Hagan,* supra, 521 U.S. at 651 ("Liability under Rule 10b-5 *** does not extend beyond conduct encompassed by § 10(b)'s prohibition"); *Hochfelder,* supra, 425 U.S., at 214 (the Rule's "scope cannot exceed the power granted the Commission by Congress under § 10(b)"). Does *Zandford's* assertion render Rule 10b-5 an irrelevant benchmark for shaping the elements of the Rule 10b-5 action?

In the following decision, the court interprets the "in connection with" requirement in a factual situation quite different from that of *Zandford.*

---

4. Contrary to the Court of Appeals' prediction, our analysis does not transform every breach of fiduciary duty into a federal securities violation. If, for example, a broker embezzles cash from a client's account or takes advantage of the fiduciary relationship to induce his client into a fraudulent real estate transaction, then the fraud would not include the requisite connection to a purchase or sale of securities. Likewise if the broker told his client he was stealing the client's assets, that breach of fiduciary duty might be in connection with a sale of securities, but it would not involve a deceptive device or fraud. Cf. *Santa Fe Industries, Inc. v. Green,* 430 U.S. 462 (1977).

SEC v. PIRATE INVESTOR LLC

580 F.3d 233 (4th Cir. 2009)

PER CURIAM:

Frank Porter Stansberry and Pirate Investor LLC (collectively, "Appellants") offered and sold an e-mail stock tip. The offer and the tip contained representations that information in both documents was the product of conversations with a senior executive inside the company that was the focus of the tip. After conducting a bench trial, the district court concluded that the representations concerning the source of information in the e-mail stock tip were false, and it determined that Appellants had violated Section 10(b) of the Securities Exchange Act of 1934, and Rule 10b-5 promulgated thereunder, by offering and selling the stock tip. The district court ordered disgorgement of Appellants' profits from the sales of the stock tip, imposed civil penalties, and issued an injunction against future violations of Section 10(b) and Rule l0b-5. *** For the following reasons, we affirm.

I

Pirate Investor LLC is a Maryland limited liability company that publishes investment newsletters. Pirate also provides an e-mail service to its subscribers called the "Blast." Pirate is wholly owned by Agora, Inc., a Maryland corporation that publishes books, magazines, and newsletters covering a wide range of topics. Stansberry is the editor--in-chief of Pirate, and in this capacity he writes and publishes investment newsletters.

Sometime in April 2002, Stansberry became aware of a company called USEC, Inc. USEC is a provider of uranium-enrichment services that began as an arm of the United States government.[4] The company currently is the executive agent of the United States government under a disarmament pact that was signed between the United States and Russia in 1993. Under the pact, known as "Megatons to Megawatts," Russia sells uranium that was formerly used in Soviet nuclear warheads to the United States for use as fuel in nuclear power plants. The pact further requires USEC and OAO Techsnabexport ("Tenex"), its Russian counterpart, to periodically renegotiate the price of the uranium. Any new pricing agreement is subject to approval by both the United States and Russian governments. The pricing agreement between USEC and Tenex expired at the end of 2001, and the two companies negotiated a new agreement in February of 2002. Neither the Russian nor the United States governments had approved this new agreement as of May 2002, however, and USEC requested that the United States government place the pricing agreement on the agenda for a summit between President George W. Bush and Russian President Vladimir Putin that was planned for that month.

After becoming aware of the circumstances surrounding USEC's pricing agreement, Stansberry contacted Steven Wingfield, USEC's Director of Investor Relations, and on May 2, 2002, conducted a telephone interview with Wingfield. This case revolves around two communications – a special report on USEC

---

4. USEC was privatized in July of 1998.

("USEC Special Report") and a solicitation hawking that report ("Super Insider Tip E-mail")-that Stansberry prepared following that telephone conversation.

The Super Insider Tip E-mail was a promotional document calling on investors to "DOUBLE YOUR MONEY ON MAY 22ND WITH THIS 'SUPER INSIDER' TIP." Specifically, the document purported to contain information obtained from "a senior company executive" that would allow investors to know exactly when "a major international agreement between the United States and Russia" would be concluded, resulting in substantial profits for a particular U.S. company. The document identified May 22 as the day the deal would close and inveigled investors with assurances that "[t]his is the kind of insider information that could make you a lot of money."

The Super Insider Tip E-mail also included some back ground on the company, as well as details of how the upcoming deal would benefit the company. The document did not provide the name of the company. For that nugget of information, investors were told that they would have to pay $1,000. Stansberry signed the e-mail under the pseudonym "Jay McDaniel."

Those who responded to the Super Insider Tip E-mail and paid $1,000 would receive the USEC Special Report. This communication identified USEC as the company referenced in the Super Insider Tip E-mail. The USEC Special Report engaged in a financial analysis of USEC's fundamentals and discussed its role as the United States' agent under the 1993 disarmament pact. It observed that USEC had reached an agreement with its Russian partner regarding a market-based pricing agreement for nuclear fuel, but cautioned that "implementation of the agreement is subject to review and approval by the U.S. and Russian governments." The USEC Special Report then repeated the claim made in the Super Insider Tip E-mail that: "A USEC senior executive has assured me that the new Russian agreement will be approved prior to the upcoming Bush-Putin summit. In fact, he said 'watch the stock on May 22nd.' "

On May 13, 2002, Stansberry sent the Super Insider Tip E-mail to the Pirate Investor Blast Database, a list of e-mail addresses of subscribers to Pirate products. After an initial favorable response, Stansberry caused the Super Insider Tip E-mail to be sent to numerous other electronic databases associated with Agora products, as well as at least one database that had no affiliation with Agora. Ultimately, over 800,000 individuals received the Super Insider Tip E-mail. Investors purchased 1,217 copies of the USEC Special Report, resulting in net proceeds of $1,005,000. Pirate received $626,500 of that sum.

Of course, what investors did not know, and what became the focus of the SEC's case against Stansberry and Pirate, was that Wingfield had never told Stansberry that approval of the USEC-Tenex pricing agreement would be announced on May 22. Indeed, nothing was announced on May 22, and the pricing agreement was ultimately announced on June 19, 2002. On April 18, 2003, the United States Securities and Exchange Commission ("SEC") filed a civil complaint charging Agora, Pirate, and Stansberry with securities fraud under § 10(b) of the Securities Exchange Act of 1934. Following a bench trial, the district court concluded that Appellants violated § 10(b) by falsely claiming that a company insider provided the information in the Super Insider Tip E-mail and the USEC Special Report. ***

II.

We begin with Appellants' claim that their conduct did not constitute a violation of § 10(b). In a civil enforcement action under § 10(b), the SEC must establish that the defendant "(1) made a false statement or omission (2) of material fact (3) with scienter (4) in connection with the purchase or sale of securities."[10] *McConville v. SEC*, 465 F.3d 780, 786 (7th Cir.2006). The SEC bears the burden of establishing each element by a preponderance of the evidence. *Herman & MacLean v. Huddleston*, 459 U.S. 375, 387-91 (1983). We address each element in turn.

A.

Section 10(b) requires that a defendant act deceptively in order to fall within the coverage of the statute. *Santa Fe Indus., Inc. v. Green*, 430 U.S. 462, 473 (1977). *** Appellants' representations that they based their predictions on information obtained from a source within USEC were misstatements of fact.

B.

It is not enough, however, for the SEC to point to a false statement -- the misrepresentation must concern a material fact. See *Basic Inc. v. Levinson*, 485 U.S. 224, 238, (1988). ***

***Appellants promised investors that the information they were receiving was the product of a conversation with a company insider. The materiality determination thus turns on whether the reasonable investor would treat a particular stock recommendation differently depending on whether or not the recommender was acting on inside information. We fail to see any clear error in the district court's determination that an investor would consider this question important in deciding whether to purchase the recommended security. ***

C.

Next, we consider whether Appellants acted with the requisite intent, or scienter. "[T]he term 'scienter' refers to a mental state embracing intent to deceive, manipulate, or defraud." *Ernst & Ernst v. Hochfelder*, 425 U.S. 185, 193 n. 12 (1976). ***Here, the district court determined that the SEC met its burden of proving that Stansberry acted with the requisite intent, and the court imputed Stansberry's scienter to Pirate. ***

D.

Finally, we turn to § 10(b)'s fourth requirement, the "in connection with" requirement. Appellants claim that the fraud in this case did not make the necessary connection to securities transactions because Appellants did not trade in USEC stock or breach any fiduciary duties. We disagree, and for the reasons discussed below we find no error in the district court's determination that Appellants committed fraud "in connection with" the purchase or sale of

---

10. Unlike private litigants, the SEC need not prove the additional elements of reliance or loss causation. *See SEC v. Rana Research, Inc.*, 8 F.3d 1358, 1364 (9th Cir.1993).

securities. *** We construe the statute "not technically and restrictively, but flexibly to effectuate its remedial purposes." *[SEC v.] Zandford*, 535 U.S. [813], 819 [(2002)]. Under Supreme Court case law, fraudulent activity meets the "in connection with" requirement of § 10(b) whenever it "touches" or "coincides" with a securities transaction. *Merrill Lynch, Pierce, Fenner & Smith, Inc. v. Dabit*, 547 U.S. 71, 85 (2006). *Superintendent of Ins. of N.Y. v. Bankers Life & Cas. Co.*, 404 U.S. 6, 12-13 (1971).

Of course, to say that a fraud is "in connection with" a securities transaction whenever it "coincides" with that transaction hardly clarifies the matter. We find direction in several factors that other courts have considered relevant when determining whether the "in connection with" requirement has been satisfied in a particular case. These factors include, but are not limited to: (1) whether a securities sale was necessary to the completion of the fraudulent scheme, *Zandford*, 535 U.S. at 820-21; (2) whether the parties' relationship was such that it would necessarily involve trading in securities, *Rowinski v. Salomon Smith Barney Inc.*, 398 F.3d 294, 302-03 (3d Cir.2005); (3) whether the defendant intended to induce a securities transaction, *United Int'l Holdings, Inc. v. Wharf (Holdings) Ltd.*, 210 F.3d 1207, 1221 (10th Cir.2000), aff'd, 532 U.S. 588 (2001); and (4) whether material misrepresentations were "disseminated to the public in a medium upon which a reasonable investor would rely," *Semerenko v. Cendant Corp.*, 223 F.3d 165, 176 (3d Cir.2000). Importantly, these factors are not mandatory requirements that a fraud must satisfy in order to meet § 10(b)'s "in connection with" requirement. They exist merely to guide the inquiry, and we do not presume to exclude other factors that could help distinguish between fraud in the securities industry and common law fraud that happens to involve securities. See *Zandford*, 535 U.S at 820. Moreover, a fraud need not satisfy all of the factors to be "in connection with" a securities transaction; a close fit with one factor may well be enough for a fraud to result in § 10(b) liability. The application of the factors should be rooted in the understanding that the "in connection with" requirement is a flexible one and that questions concerning its scope are best examined on a case-by-case basis. See *Semerenko*, 223 F.3d at 175; *Chem. Bank v. Arthur Andersen & Co.*, 726 F.2d 930, 942 (2d Cir.1984).

i.

We first consider whether a securities transaction was necessary to the completion of the fraudulent scheme. In *Zandford*, for example, the Supreme Court noted that the stock sales in that case were a fundamental component of the defendant's fraudulent scheme:

> [E]ach sale was made to further respondent's fraudulent scheme; each was deceptive because it was neither authorized by, nor disclosed to, the Woods. With regard to the sales of shares in the Woods' mutual fund, respondent initiated these transactions by writing a check to himself from that account, knowing that redeeming the check would require the sale of securities.

Zandford, 535 U.S. at 820-21.

Appellants argue that the fraud in this case was complete when investors purchased the USEC Special Report because the $1,000 purchase price was the only material benefit that Appellants received. Under this theory of the case, Appellants derived no benefit from the purchasers' securities trading. They claim:

> [T]he alleged fraud was consummated and concluded when the Report was sold and the reader paid $1000. If there was a fraudulent scheme, no subsequent securities transactions were necessary to it, as neither the Publisher nor the Author derived any benefit from such trading. Indeed, the defendants would have committed fraud if not a single purchaser of the Report bought USEC shares, or if the Report named a fictitious company with a fictitious ticker symbol, because they still would have 'defrauded' readers of the cost of the publication.

(Reply Br. at 9.) We believe that this is a rather short-sighted view of the fraudulent scheme and, taking the facts in the light most favorable to the SEC, we conclude that Appellants did benefit from securities trading by purchasers of the USEC Special Report.

First, Appellants' characterization of the fraud fails to recognize that Appellants used stock purchases by early purchasers of the USEC Special Report as a way of enhancing the credibility of the report. Over 800,000 investors received the Super Insider Tip E-mail that offered the USEC Special Report for sale, but they did not receive the solicitation at the same time. Rather, Appellants sent out the solicitation in waves to various groups of investors. And, later versions of the solicitation pointed to a rise in USEC's stock price-which the district court determined was the result of purchases by early recipients of the solicitation and special report-as supporting the trustworthiness of the tip.

When Stansberry first circulated the solicitation to the Pirate Investor Blast Database, on May 13, the solicitation noted that the stock was "only a $7.00 stock." On May 17, however, Stansberry edited the solicitation e-mail to reflect a change in the stock's price. Future versions of the e-mail reflected the stock's updated price of $9.00 a share. Moreover, and most importantly, future versions of the solicitation e-mail used this jump in price as a selling point. The e-mail pointed out that the stock in question "has jumped this week and looks poised to go much higher," and quickly followed with an offer to sell the identity of the company for $1,000. Thus, the rising stock was important to the success of the scheme because it served to motivate later purchasers to part with their requisite $1,000 payment. The fraud was not complete when investors paid $1,000 to learn the identity of the company in question; Appellants also needed those investors to purchase the stock thereby increasing the stock price so as to boost the credibility of the solicitation e-mail to obtain more $1,000 payments. ***

In addition, the record shows that Appellants were not only relying on the rise in USEC's stock price to boost the credibility of this particular stock recommendation. They expected that the rise in USEC's price would lead to a general increase in Appellants' reputation as trusted purveyors of internet investment advice. The fraud's ultimate success involved not only the $1,000 purchase price, but also the boost in reputation that would accrue with those who purchased stock in reliance on the report-a reputational gain that would lead to future purchases of future reports on different companies. As Stansberry noted in an e-mail, "[i]f we're able to sell this to 250 people *and it works*, we'll be able to charge almost whatever we want next time."(emphasis added). In effect,

Appellants' own definition of success depended on people purchasing securities in reliance on the report.

ii.

The next factor that we consider-whether the parties' relationship was such that it would necessarily involve trading in securities-weighs in favor of Appellants. Appellants sold investment advice; ultimately, the decision to purchase securities rested squarely with those who received the solicitation and USEC Special Report. In this respect, Appellants differ from the defendant in *Zandford*. In that case the defendant, a broker, possessed a general power of attorney-granted by his victims-allowing him to engage in securities transactions on their behalf. 535 U.S. at 815. The very purpose of the broker/investor relationship is trading in securities. *Rowinski*, 398 F.3d at 303. No such relationship existed in this case. ***

iii.

The third factor we consider is whether Appellants made their misrepresentations with the intent to induce a securities transaction. On this point we find no error in the district court's conclusion that "[t]he very essence of the fraudulent scheme was to induce its victims to purchase USEC stock prior to May 22, 2002...." *** If, as Appellants claim, the misrepresentations were only intended to induce investors to purchase the USEC Special Report, why were they repeated in the report itself, which directly called investors to action? The record evidence compels the conclusion that Appellants intended the recipients of the solicitation and the USEC Special Report to trade in securities.

iv.

Finally, we turn to the factor that the district court primarily relied on in making its determination that the fraud satisfied the "in connection with" requirement-whether Appellants utilized a device "that would cause reasonable investors to rely thereon" and "so relying, cause them to purchase or sell a corporation's securities." *In re Carter-Wallace, Inc. Sec. Litig.*, 150 F.3d 153, 156 (2d Cir.1998). This standard is derived from a Second Circuit opinion, *SEC v. Texas Gulf Sulphur Co.*, 401 F.2d 833 (2d Cir.1968) (en banc). In *Texas Gulf*, the Second Circuit held that "Rule 10b-5 is violated whenever assertions are made ... in a manner reasonably calculated to influence the investing public ..." Id. at 862. Subsequent decisions have refined *Texas Gulf*, and several circuits now agree that:

> Where the fraud alleged involves public dissemination in a document such as a press release, annual report, investment prospectus or other such document on which an investor would presumably rely, the "in connection with" requirement is generally met by proof of the means of dissemination and the materiality of the misrepresentation or omission.

Rana Research, Inc., 8 F.3d at 1362.

Under the *Texas Gulf* standard, the SEC must establish two distinct elements: (1) the misrepresentations in question were disseminated to the public in a medium upon which a reasonable investor would rely and (2) they were material when disseminated. *Semerenko*, 223 F.3d at 176. We have already considered whether the misrepresentations in this case were material. Here, we focus our attention on the first element of *Texas Gulf*. The SEC must show that reasonable investors would base their investment decisions on the types of communications at issue in this case-mass e-mails from a purveyor of internet investment advice.

At first glance, we question whether any reasonable investor would rely on the Super Insider Tip E-mail.[18] As we noted above, the *Texas Gulf* standard encompasses "press release[s], annual report[s], investment prospectus[es] or other such document[s]." *Rana Research, Inc.*, 8 F.3d at 1362. Courts have applied this standard, for example, when misrepresentations are disseminated in investment research reports from a reputable broker, see *Rowinski*, 398 F.3d at 302; prospectuses, see *In re Lord Abbett Mut. Funds Fee Litig.*, 407 F.Supp.2d 616, 628 (D.N.J.2005); the sales and marketing materials at brokerage houses and other points of sale, *In re Dreyfus Mut. Funds Fee Litig.*, 428 F.Supp.2d 342, 355 (W.D.Pa.2005); SEC filings, *In re Tyco Int'l, Ltd. Multidistrict Litig.*, 2004 WL 2348315, at *4-5 (D.N.H.2004); and detailed drug advertisements published in sophisticated medical journals, *In re Carter-Wallace, Inc. Sec. Litig.*, 150 F.3d at 156. Clearly, the communications at issue in the present case have little in common with the types of communications that have heretofore led to liability under the *Texas Gulf* standard. In fact, we feel confident that a reasonable investor would not base investment decisions on mass e-mail communications such as these-which the SEC's attorney characterized as SPAM during oral argument-that purport to offer a stock tip based on insider information.

Thus, at first blush, it would appear that this factor weighs in favor of Appellants' arguments. We fear, however, that applying the *Texas Gulf* standard to remove Appellants' fraud from coverage under § 10(b) would neglect the reasoning behind the *Texas Gulf* standard. At its core, the *Texas Gulf* standard is about notice-attaching liability under the securities laws for statements made in any medium, no matter how tangentially related to the securities markets, would run the risk of roping in speakers who had no idea that their conduct might implicate Section 10(b). Thus, by requiring that misstatements be communicated in a medium upon which a reasonable investor would rely, the *Texas Gulf* standard protects these unknowing speakers from liability and ensures that there is a sufficient nexus between the misrepresentations and the securities sales that they induce to satisfy the Supreme Court's command that the fraud and securities sales "coincide."

---

18. The record contains scant evidence on this point, but what little information is in the record suggests that reasonable investors would not rely on the communication at issue. For example, the SEC cross-examined one of Stansberry's experts, David Nelson, regarding one of the texts that Nelson relied on when preparing his report. The SEC presented the following excerpt:

> Essentially critics of the investment letters have argued that the advisers are ignorant, they may have no formal experience or education in investment, incompetent, their investment record can be bad, dishonest, they can lie about their records, jerks, all of which can be true.

Other statements from the text that the SEC pointed to include "Investors newsletters accurate as a coin flip" and "Their advice was no better than throwing a dart at the stock quotes page of the Wall Street Journal and buying whatever it hits."

This case simply does not implicate the notice concerns that animate the *Texas Gulf* standard. To the contrary, Appellants knew that recipients of the solicitation and USEC Special Report would rely on them when making their investment decisions. After all, Appellants did not target the public at large when they circulated the solicitation e-mail. Rather, Appellants circulated the e-mail solicitation to investors on the specific subscriber lists of internet investment newsletters. These were investors who trusted internet investment advice.

Appellants certainly should not have been shocked to learn that their fraudulent statements induced securities transactions. Under these circumstances, an application of the *Texas Gulf* standard to exclude the communications would run contrary to § 10(b)'s core purpose-"to protect investors, to prevent inequitable and unfair practices and to insure fairness in securities transactions generally." 3 Fletcher Cyc. Corp. § 900.65 (perm. ed.2002). Although ordinary reasonable investors might well have taken one look at Appellants' solicitation and marked it for the SPAM box, Appellants knew that they were directing their misstatements to particular investors who did rely on internet investment advice. We believe that this knowledge supports finding that the misstatements occurred "in connection with" securities transactions.[19] See *SEC v. Park*, 99 F.Supp.2d 889, 900 (N.D.Ill.2000) ("[F]raud in the sale of investment advice may qualify as 'in connection' with the sale of securities when it is expected that the advisees will act on the advice.")[20] ***

[Parts III and IV of the opinion, which discuss and reject the appellants' constitutional challenges under the First Amendment, are omitted]

V.

In conclusion, for the reasons stated above, the judgment of the district court is affirmed.

---

19. On this point we take direction from the common law's treatment of the materiality standard. Under the common law, a representation may be material, even if a reasonable man would disregard it, if "the maker of the representation knows or has reason to know that its recipient regards or is likely to regard the matter as important in determining his choice of action." Restatement (Second) of Torts § 538(2)(b) (1977). ***While we do not suggest that the Restatement's treatment of materiality controls our analysis of § 10(b)'s "in connection with" requirement, we do note that the Supreme Court often turns to the Restatement to inform its jurisprudence on these issues. *See Dura Pharms., Inc. v. Broudo,* 544 U.S. 336, 344 (2005); *Wharf (Holdings) Ltd.,* 532 U.S. at 596. Moreover, and more importantly, we believe the above principle to be a sound one-Appellants have little room to complain that their conduct has implicated § 10(b) when they knew that readers would rely on the communications and they actively encouraged them to do so.

20. Our conclusion here does not imply that an individual investor in this case would be able to demonstrate that he "justifiably relied" on the Super Insider Tip E-mail as required to establish a securities violation in a private suit. *See Miller v. Asensio & Co., Inc.,* 364 F.3d 223, 227 (4th Cir.2004). Although the two types of reliance may share some similarities, it would not be appropriate to import wholesale our "reasonable reliance" analysis into a "justifiable reliance" analysis required in a private suit.

NOTES AND QUESTIONS

1. ***Whither the Coincidence.*** If the court had applied *Zandford*'s "coincidence" approach to the "in connection with" requirement, what would have been the result? Was the court justified in reading "coincidence" as a sufficient -- but not a necessary – test for determining whether the "in connection with" element has been satisfied? Is it possible to have a single approach to the "in connection with" requirement that would apply in all circumstances?

2. ***The Multi-Factoral Approach.*** The court identified four non-exclusive factors for us as a "guide" to the "in connection with" inquiry. Should we cheer the flexibility of this approach or bemoan its (likely) lack of predictability?

3. ***Materiality Revisited.*** Notice the court's assertion that "[t]he materiality determination *** turns on whether the reasonable investor would treat a particular stock recommendation differently depending on whether or not the recommender was acting on inside information." Should it have been relevant for materiality purposes that the information was communicated through a mass email? In thinking about this question, recall that when addressing the "in connection with" requirement, the court maintained that a reasonable investor would not make an investment decision on the basis of such an email.

4. ***Non-Trading Defendants.*** Under the Second Circuit's seminal holding in *Texas Gulf Sulphur,* the "in connection with" requirement can be satisfied regardless of whether the defendant traded the security in question, the defendants assertions were made "in a manner reasonably calculated to influence the investment public." But as we shall see, *Blue Chip Stamps v. Manor Drug Stores,* 421 U.S. 723 (1975), imposes a purchaser-seller requirement for private plaintiffs at least partly on the basis of the "in connection with" language. Is requiring plaintiffs but not defendants to be buyers or sellers troublesome as a matter of either policy or statutory construction?

PROBLEM 2-11

Maddax told his customers that he would buy blue-chip stocks on their behalf. In reality, he made no trades with their money. Instead, he used it to live a lavish lifestyle as well as to fund pay-outs to those few investors who elected to withdraw their money.

Maddax mailed his customers monthly statements of their trades based on prices drawn from the public markets. The percentage of growth reflected in these statements held steady, month after month, regardless of what else was happening in the market.

In a Rule 10b-5 action against Maddax, will the "in connection with" requirement be satisfied?

Cf. *In re J.P. Jeanneret Assocs., Inc.*, 769 F. Supp. 2d 340 (S.D.N.Y. 2011).

PROBLEM 2-12

George is the lawyer for Martha, who was dismissed from her position as senior vice president of Designer Dresses, Inc., a large company whose shares are listed on the New York Stock Exchange. George's negotiations with the company on Martha's behalf have not been going well. George told a reporter for a national newspaper that Martha would soon file a class action charging the company with gender discrimination. George's assertion appeared in the newspaper and caused the price of the company's stock to drop. In fact, George (and Martha) have no intention of filing a class action. If George is named as a defendant in a Rule 10b-5 action, will the "in connection with" requirement be satisfied?

D. THE SCIENTER REQUIREMENT

Scienter, a Latin word for "knowingly," is a term used to describe a person's state of mind at the time he or she took action or failed to take action. An action taken with scienter is taken intentionally, or at least recklessly. On the other hand, an action taken negligently, or even grossly negligently, is said to lack scienter.

The first part of this section explores *Ernst & Ernst v. Hochfelder*, 425 U.S. 185 (1976), which held that scienter is necessary to establish liability under Section 10(b) and Rule 10b-5. The second part focuses on the requirements for pleading scienter that apply to all plaintiffs in Rule 10b-5 cases, as well as on the heightened pleading requirements for private plaintiffs enacted as part of the Private Securities Litigation Reform Act of 1995 (PSLRA).

1. The Substantive Standard

ERNST & ERNST v. HOCHFELDER

425 U.S. 185 (1976)

JUSTICE LEWIS F. POWELL:

The issue in this case is whether an action for civil damages may lie under § 10(b) of the Securities Exchange Act of 1934 and Securities and Exchange Commission Rule 10b-5 in the absence of an allegation of intent to deceive, manipulate, or defraud on the part of the defendant.

I

Petitioner, Ernst & Ernst, is an accounting firm. From 1946 through 1967 it was retained by First Securities Company of Chicago (First Securities), a small brokerage firm and member of the Midwest Stock Exchange and of the National Association of Securities Dealers, to perform periodic audits of the firm's books and records. In connection with these audits Ernst & Ernst prepared for filing with the Securities and Exchange Commission (Commission) the annual reports required of First Securities under § 17(a) of the 1934 Act. It also prepared for First Securities responses to the financial questionnaires of the Midwest Stock Exchange (Exchange).

Respondents were customers of First Securities who invested in a fraudulent securities scheme perpetrated by Leston B. Nay, president of the firm and owner of 92% of its stock. Nay induced the respondents to invest funds in "escrow" accounts that he represented would yield a high rate of return. Respondents did so from 1942 through 1966, with the majority of the transactions occurring in the 1950's. In fact, there were no escrow accounts as Nay converted respondents' funds to his own use immediately upon receipt. These transactions were not in the customary form of dealings between First Securities and its customers. The respondents drew their personal checks payable to Nay or a designated bank for his account. No such escrow accounts were reflected on the books and records of First Securities, and none was shown on its periodic accounting to respondents in connection with their other investments. Nor were they included in First Securities' filings with the Commission or the Exchange.

This fraud came to light in 1968 when Nay committed suicide, leaving a note that described First Securities as bankrupt and the escrow accounts as "spurious." Respondents subsequently filed this action for damages against Ernst & Ernst in the United States District Court for the Northern District of Illinois under § 10(b) of the 1934 Act. The complaint charged that Nay's escrow scheme violated § 10(b) and Commission Rule 10b-5, and that Ernst & Ernst had "aided and abetted" Nay's violations by its "failure" to conduct proper audits of First Securities. As revealed through discovery, respondents' cause of action rested on a theory of negligent nonfeasance. The premise was that Ernst & Ernst had failed to utilize "appropriate auditing procedures" in its audits of First Securities, thereby failing to discover internal practices of the firm said to prevent an effective audit. The practice principally relied on was Nay's rule that only he could open mail addressed to him at First Securities or addressed to First Securities to his attention, even if it arrived in his absence. Respondents contended that if Ernst & Ernst had conducted a proper audit, it would have discovered this "mail rule." The existence of the rule then would have been disclosed in reports to the Exchange and to the Commission by Ernst & Ernst as an irregular procedure that prevented an effective audit. This would have led to an investigation of Nay that would have revealed the fraudulent scheme. Respondents specifically disclaimed the existence of fraud or intentional misconduct on the part of Ernst & Ernst.

After extensive discovery the District Court granted Ernst & Ernst's motion for summary judgment and dismissed the action. The court rejected Ernst & Ernst's contention that a cause of action for aiding and abetting a securities fraud could not be maintained under § 10(b) and Rule 10b-5 merely on allegations of negligence. It concluded, however, that there was no genuine issue of material fact with respect to whether Ernst & Ernst had conducted its audits in accordance with generally accepted auditing standards.

The Court of Appeals for the Seventh Circuit reversed and remanded, holding that one who breaches a duty of inquiry and disclosure owed another is liable in damages for aiding and abetting a third party's violation of Rule 10b-5 if the fraud would have been discovered or prevented but for the breach.[7] The court reasoned that Ernst & Ernst had a common-law and statutory duty of inquiry into the adequacy of First Securities' internal control system because it had contracted to audit First Securities and to prepare for filing with the Commission the annual report of First Securities' financial condition required under § 17 of the 1934 Act and Rule 17a-5. The court further reasoned that respondents were beneficiaries of the statutory duty to inquire and the related duty to disclose any material irregularities that were discovered. The court concluded that there were genuine issues of fact as to whether Ernst & Ernst's failure to discover and comment upon Nay's mail rule constituted a breach of its duties of inquiry and disclosure and whether inquiry and disclosure would have led to the discovery or prevention of Nay's fraud.

We granted certiorari to resolve the question whether a private cause of action for damages will lie under § 10(b) and Rule 10b-5 in the absence of any allegation of "scienter"—intent to deceive, manipulate, or defraud.[12] We conclude that it will not and therefore we reverse.

II

*** Although § 10(b) does not by its terms create an express civil remedy for its violation, and there is no indication that Congress, or the Commission when adopting Rule 10b-5, contemplated such a remedy, the existence of a private cause of action for violations of the statute and the Rule is now well established. *Blue Chip Stamps v. Manor Drug Stores*, 421 U.S. 723, 730 (1975); *Affiliated Ute Citizens v. United States*, 406 U.S. 128, 150-154 (1972); *Superintendent of Insurance v. Bankers Life & Cas. Co.*, 404 U.S. 6, 13, n. 9 (1971). During the 30-year period since a private cause of action was first implied under § 10(b) and Rule 10b-5, a substantial body of case law and commentary has developed as to its elements. Courts and commentators long have differed with

---

7. *** In view of our holding that an intent to deceive, manipulate, or defraud is required for civil liability under § 10(b) and Rule 10b-5, we need not consider whether civil liability for aiding and abetting is appropriate under the section and the Rule, nor the elements necessary to establish such a cause of action. [Editor's Note: Almost two decades later, the Supreme Court held that Section 10(b) and Rule 10b-5 do not encompass aiding and abetting liability. See *Central Bank, N.A. v. First Interstate Bank, N.A.*, 511 U.S. 164 (1994), a principal case in Section H of this Chapter.]

12. Although the verbal formulations of the standard to be applied have varied, several Courts of Appeals have held in substance that negligence alone is sufficient for civil liability under § 10(b) and Rule 10b. *** But few of the decisions announcing that some form of negligence suffices for civil liability under § 10(b) and Rule 10b-5 actually have involved only negligent conduct.

In this opinion the term "scienter" refers to a mental state embracing intent to deceive, manipulate, or defraud. In certain areas of the law recklessness is considered to be a form of intentional conduct for purposes of imposing liability for some act. We need not address here the question whether, in some circumstances, reckless behavior is sufficient for civil liability under § 10(b) and Rule 10b-5.

Since this case concerns an action for damages we also need not consider the question whether scienter is a necessary element in an action for injunctive relief under § 10(b) and Rule 10b-5.

regard to whether scienter is a necessary element of such a cause of action, or whether negligent conduct alone is sufficient. In addressing this question, we turn first to the language of § 10(b), for "(t)he starting point in every case involving construction of a statute is the language itself." *Blue Chip Stamps*, supra, at 756 (Powell, J., concurring).

A

Section 10(b) makes unlawful the use or employment of "any manipulative or deceptive device or contrivance" in contravention of Commission rules. The words "manipulative or deceptive" used in conjunction with "device or contrivance" strongly suggest that § 10(b) was intended to proscribe knowing or intentional misconduct. See *SEC v. Texas Gulf Sulphur Co.*, 401 F.2d 833, 868 (CA2 1968) (Friendly, J., concurring); Loss, Summary Remarks, 30 Bus. Law. 163, 165 (Special Issue 1975).

In its *amicus curiae* brief, however, the Commission contends that nothing in the language "manipulative or deceptive device or contrivance" limits its operation to knowing or intentional practices. In support of its view, the Commission cites the overall congressional purpose in the 1933 and 1934 Acts to protect investors against false and deceptive practices that might injure them. See *Affiliated Ute Citizens v. United States*, supra, at 151; *Superintendent of Insurance v. Bankers Life & Cas. Co.*, supra, 404 U.S., at 11-12; *J. I. Case Co. v. Borak*, 377 U.S. 426, 432-433 (1964). The Commission then reasons that since the "effect" upon investors of given conduct is the same regardless of whether the conduct is negligent or intentional, Congress must have intended to bar all such practices and not just those done knowingly or intentionally. The logic of this effect-oriented approach would impose liability for wholly faultless conduct where such conduct results in harm to investors, a result the Commission would be unlikely to support. But apart from where its logic might lead, the Commission would add a gloss to the operative language of the statute quite different from its commonly accepted meaning. The argument simply ignores the use of the words "manipulative," "device," and "contrivance" terms that make unmistakable a congressional intent to proscribe a type of conduct quite different from negligence.[20] Use of the word "manipulative" is especially significant. It is and was virtually a term of art when used in connection with securities markets. It connotes intentional or willful conduct designed to deceive or defraud investors by controlling or artificially affecting the price of securities.[21]

---

20. Webster's International Dictionary (2d ed. 1934) defines "device" as "(t)hat which is devised, or formed by design; a contrivance; an invention; project; scheme; often, a scheme to deceive; a stratagem; an artifice," and "contrivance" in pertinent part as "(a) thing contrived or used in contriving; a scheme, plan, or artifice." In turn, "contrive" in pertinent part is defined as "(t)o devise; to plan; to plot ... (t)o fabricate ... design; invent ... to scheme...." The Commission also ignores the use of the terms "(t)o use or employ," language that is supportive of the view that Congress did not intend § 10(b) to embrace negligent conduct.

21. Webster's International Dictionary, supra, defines "manipulate" as "to manage or treat artfully of fraudulently; as to manipulate accounts.... 4. *Exchanges.* To force (prices) up or down, as by matched orders, wash sales, fictitious reports ...; to rig."

In addition to relying upon the Commission's argument with respect to the operative language of the statute, respondents contend that since we are dealing with "remedial legislation," *Tcherepnin v. Knight,* 389 U.S. 332, 336 (1967), it must be construed "'not technically and restrictively, but flexibly to effectuate its remedial purposes.'" *Affiliated Ute Citizens v. United States,* 406 U.S., at 151, quoting *SEC v. Capital Gains Research Bureau,* supra, 375 U.S., at 195. They argue that the "remedial purposes" of the Acts demand a construction of § 10(b) that embraces negligence as a standard of liability. But in seeking to accomplish its broad remedial goals, Congress did not adopt uniformly a negligence standard even as to express civil remedies. In some circumstances and with respect to certain classes of defendants, Congress did create express liability predicated upon a failure to exercise reasonable care. E. g., 1933 Act § 11(b)(3)(B) (liability of "experts," such as accountants for misleading statements in portions of registration statements for which they are responsible). But in other situations good faith is an absolute defense. 1934 Act § 18 (misleading statements in any document filed pursuant to the 1934 Act). And in still other circumstances Congress created express liability regardless of the defendant's fault, 1933 Act § 11(a) (issuer liability for misleading statements in the registration statement).

It is thus evident that Congress fashioned standards of fault in the express civil remedies in the 1933 and 1934 Acts on a particularized basis. Ascertainment of congressional intent with respect to the standard of liability created by a particular section of the Acts must therefore rest primarily on the language of that section. Where, as here, we deal with a judicially implied liability, the statutory language certainly is no less important. In view of the language of § 10(b), which so clearly connotes intentional misconduct, and mindful that the language of a statute controls when sufficiently clear in its context, further inquiry may be unnecessary. We turn now, nevertheless, to the legislative history of the 1934 Act to ascertain whether there is support for the meaning attributed to § 10(b) by the Commission and respondents.

B

Although the extensive legislative history of the 1934 Act is bereft of any explicit explanation of Congress' intent, we think the relevant portions of that history support our conclusion that § 10(b) was addressed to practices that involve some element of scienter and cannot be read to impose liability for negligent conduct alone. ***

The most relevant exposition of the provision that was to become § 10(b) was by Thomas G. Corcoran, a spokesman for the drafters. Corcoran indicated:

> Subsection (c) (§ 9(c) of H.R. 7852 later § 10(b)) says, 'Thou shalt not devise any other cunning devices.'
>
> Of course subsection (c) is a catch-all clause to prevent manipulative devices. I do not think there is any objection to that kind of clause. The Commission should have the authority to deal with new manipulative devices.

Hearings on H.R. 7852 and H.R. 8720 before the House Committee on Interstate and Foreign Commerce, 73d Cong., 2d Sess., 115 (1934). This brief explanation of § 10(b) by a spokesman for its drafters is significant. The section was described rightly as a "catchall" clause to enable the Commission "to deal with new manipulative (or cunning) devices." It is difficult to believe that any lawyer, legislative draftsman, or legislator would use these words if the intent was to create liability for merely negligent acts or omissions.***

C

The 1933 and 1934 Acts constitute interrelated components of the federal regulatory scheme governing transactions in securities. See *Blue Chip Stamps*, 421 U.S., at 727-730. As the Court indicated in *SEC v. National Securities, Inc.*, 393 U.S. 453, 466 (1969), "the interdependence of the various sections of the securities laws is certainly a relevant factor in any interpretation of the language Congress has chosen...." Recognizing this, respondents and the Commission contrast § 10(b) with other sections of the Acts to support their contention that civil liability may be imposed upon proof of negligent conduct. We think they misconceive the significance of the other provisions of the Acts.

The Commission argues that Congress has been explicit in requiring willful conduct when that was the standard of fault intended, citing § 9 of the 1934 Act which generally proscribes manipulation of securities prices. Sections 9(a)(1) and (a)(2), for example, respectively prohibit manipulation of security prices "(f)or the purpose of creating a false or misleading appearance of active trading in any security ... or ... with respect to the market for any such security," and "for the purpose of inducing the purchase or sale of such security by others." See also § 9(a)(4). Section 9(e) then imposes upon "(a)ny person who willfully participates in any act or transaction in violation of" other provisions of § 9 civil liability to anyone who purchased or sold a security at a price affected by the manipulative activities. From this the Commission concludes that since § 10(b) is not by its terms explicitly restricted to willful, knowing, or purposeful conduct, it should not be construed in all cases to require more than negligent action or inaction as a precondition for civil liability.

The structure of the Acts does not support the Commission's argument. In each instance that Congress created express civil liability in favor of purchasers or sellers of securities it clearly specified whether recovery was to be premised on knowing or intentional conduct, negligence, or entirely innocent mistake. See 1933 Act §§ 11, 12, 15; 1934 Act §§ 9, 18, 20. For example, § 11 of the 1933 Act unambiguously creates a private action for damages when a registration statement includes untrue statements of material facts or fails to state material facts necessary to make the statements therein not misleading. Within the limits specified by § 11(e), the issuer of the securities is held absolutely liable for any damages resulting from such misstatement or omission. But experts such as accountants who have prepared portions of the registration statement are accorded a "due diligence" defense. In effect, this is a negligence standard. An expert may avoid civil liability with respect to the portions of the registration statement for which he was responsible by showing that "after reasonable investigation" he had "reasonable ground(s) to believe" that the statements for which he was responsible were true and there was no omission of a material fact. § 11(b)(3)(B)(i). The express recognition of a cause of action premised on negligent behavior in § 11 stands in sharp contrast to the language of § 10(b), and significantly undercuts the Commission's argument.

We also consider it significant that each of the express civil remedies in the 1933 Act allowing recovery for negligent conduct, see §§ 11, 12(2), 15, is subject to significant procedural restrictions not applicable under § 10(b). Section 11(e) of the 1933 Act, for example, authorizes the court to require a plaintiff bringing a suit under §11, § 12(2), or § 15 thereof to post a bond for costs, including attorneys' fees, and in specified circumstances to assess costs at the conclusion of the litigation. Section 13 specifies a statute of limitations of one year from the time the violation was or should have been discovered, in no event to exceed three years from the time of offer or sale, applicable to actions brought under §11, § 12(2), or § 15. These restrictions, significantly, were imposed by amendments to the 1933 Act adopted as part of the 1934 Act. *** We think these procedural limitations indicate that the judicially created private damages remedy under § 10(b)—which has no comparable restrictions—cannot be extended, consistently with the intent of Congress, to actions premised on negligent wrongdoing. Such extension would allow causes of action covered by §§ 11, 12(2), and 15 to be brought instead under § 10(b) and thereby nullify the effectiveness of the carefully drawn procedural restrictions on these express actions. We would be unwilling to bring about this result absent substantial support in the legislative history, and there is none.

D

We have addressed, to this point, primarily the language and history of § 10(b). The Commission contends, however, that subsections (b) and (c) of Rule 10b-5 are cast in language which—if standing alone—could encompass both intentional and negligent behavior. These subsections respectively provide that it is unlawful "(t)o make any untrue statement of a material fact or to omit to state a material fact necessary in order to make the statements made, in the light of the circumstances under which they were made, not misleading...." and "(t)o engage in any act, practice, or course of business which operates or would operate as a fraud or deceit upon any person.... " Viewed in isolation the language of subsection (b), and arguably that of subsection (c), could be read as proscribing, respectively, any type of material misstatement or omission, and any course of conduct, that has the effect of defrauding investors, whether the wrongdoing was intentional or not.

We note first that such a reading cannot be harmonized with the administrative history of the Rule, a history making clear that when the Commission adopted the Rule it was intended to apply only to activities that involved scienter. More importantly, Rule 10b-5 was adopted pursuant to authority granted the Commission under § 10(b). The rulemaking power granted to an administrative agency charged with the administration of a federal statute is not the power to make law. Rather, it is "'the power to adopt regulations to carry into effect the will of Congress as expressed by the statute.'" *Dixon v. United States*, 381 U.S. 68, 74 (1965), quoting *Manhattan General Equipment Co. v. Commissioner*, 297 U.S. 129, 134 (1936). Thus, despite the broad view of the Rule advanced by the Commission in this case, its scope cannot exceed the power granted the Commission by Congress under § 10(b). *** When a statute speaks so specifically in terms of manipulation and deception, and of implementing devices and contrivances—the commonly understood terminology of intentional wrongdoing—and when its history reflects no more expansive intent, we are quite unwilling to extend the scope of the statute to negligent conduct.

III

Recognizing that § 10(b) and Rule 10b-5 might be held to require proof of more than negligent nonfeasance by Ernst & Ernst as a precondition to the imposition of civil liability, respondents further contend that the case should be remanded for trial under whatever standard is adopted. Throughout the lengthy history of this case respondents have proceeded on a theory of liability premised on negligence, specifically disclaiming that Ernst & Ernst had engaged in fraud or intentional misconduct. In these circumstances, we think it inappropriate to remand the action for further proceedings. ***

JUSTICE HAROLD A. BLACKMUN, WITH WHOM JUSTICE BRENNAN JOINS, DISSENTING:

Once again—see *Blue Chip Stamps v. Manor Drug Stores*, 421 U.S. 723, 730 (1975)—the Court interprets § 10(b) of the Securities Exchange Act of 1934 and the Securities and Exchange Commission's Rule 10b-5 restrictively and narrowly and thereby stultifies recovery for the victim. This time the Court does so by confining the statute and the Rule to situations where the defendant has "scienter," that is, the "intent to deceive, manipulate, or defraud." Sheer negligence, the Court says, is not within the reach of the statute and the Rule, and was not contemplated when the great reforms of 1933, 1934, and 1942 were effectuated by Congress and the Commission.

Perhaps the Court is right, but I doubt it. The Government and the Commission doubt it too, as is evidenced by the thrust of the brief filed by the Solicitor General on behalf of the Commission as *amicus curiae*. The Court's opinion, to be sure, has a certain technical consistency about it. It seems to me, however, that an investor can be victimized just as much by negligent conduct as by positive deception, and that it is not logical to drive a wedge between the two, saying that Congress clearly intended the one but certainly not the other.***

NOTES AND QUESTIONS

1. Driving Wedges. Do you agree with the majority that in drafting Section 10(b), Congress intended to "drive a wedge" (to borrow Justice Blackmun's phrase) between conduct that is intentional and conduct that is merely negligent or even grossly negligent? Is Justice Blackmun correct in focusing on the ultimate effect of a material misrepresentation on investors? In pondering this question, consider the observation of Professors Loss and Seligman that "[a] pedestrian fatally hit by a negligent driver is just as dead as if the driver had been roaring drunk, but that does not convict the negligent driver of manslaughter." 8 Louis Loss and Joel Seligman, Securities Regulation 3684 (3d ed. revised 2004). How would Justice Blackmun likely respond to this analogy? To what extent was the majority's allegiance to intent apt to have been influenced by the critical role played by Rule 10b-5 in private securities litigation?

2. Don't Close That Dictionary! Note that in footnotes 20 and 21, the Court draws on Webster's International Dictionary for definitions of the terms "device," "contrivance" and "manipulative." Note particularly the lack of definition for the term "deceptive." Had the Court continued its march through the dictionary, would it have made a difference to the outcome of the case?

Professor James Cox's analysis of this question suggests that this is a distinct possibility. See James D. Cox, *Ernst & Ernst v. Hochfelder*: A Critique and an Evaluation of Its Impact upon the Scheme of the Federal Securities Laws, 28 Hastings L. J. 569 (1977). In that article, Professor Cox contended that the word deceptive "suggests no established state of mind. It instead describes the potential impact of conduct upon a person's perception, regardless of the actor's mental state." Id. at 575. As authority, he cited to the dictionary definition of deceptive: "[t]ending to deceive; having the power to mislead." Id. at 575 n. 30. He also noted that "[a]lthough the common meaning of 'device' or 'contrivance' suggests deliberate conduct by the participants, in the context of section 10(b) both nouns definitively exclude only transactions or conduct initiated solely by accident or inadvertence." Id. at 574. He therefore concluded:

> The broader meaning of "deceptive" has obvious significance for the purpose of determining whether congressional intent was clear; the enabling statute used the disjunctive, not the conjunctive, thereby leaving open the possibility of a much broader scope than that attributed to the statute in *Ernst & Ernst*.

Id. at 575.

3. The Element of Scienter in Government-Initiated Rule 10b-5 Cases. Does the scienter requirement upheld in *Ernst & Ernst* in the context of a Rule 10b-5 private action apply as well to actions under the Rule initiated by the SEC or the DOJ? When faced with this question in *Aaron v. SEC*, 446 U.S. 680 (1980), a six member majority of the Supreme Court stated:

> In our view, the rationale of *Hockfelder* [sic] ineluctably leads to the conclusion that scienter is an element of a violation of § 10(b) and Rule 10b-5, regardless of the identity of the plaintiff or the nature of the relief sought. ***

Id. at 691. In what had become a predictable pattern in federal securities decisions, Justice Blackmun, joined by Justices Brennan and Marshall, dissented from the majority's holding, emphasizing again the effect on investors:

> If the Commission is denied the ability effectively to nip in the bud the misrepresentations and deceptions that its investigations have revealed, honest investors will be the ones who suffer. Often they may find themselves stripped of their investments through reliance on information that the Commission knew was misleading but lacked the power to stop or contain.

Id. at 704 (Blackmun, J., concurring in part and dissenting in part). Is there an effective response to Justice Blackmun's concerns? Consider this question again in the Chapter 3, particularly when you study Sections 17(a)(2) and (3) of the Securities Act.

4. Recklessness as a Form of Scienter. The Supreme Court has declined on five occasions to address whether reckless conduct establishes scienter under Section 10(b) and Rule 10b-5. See *Ernst & Ernst*, supra, at n. 12; *Aaron v. SEC*, 446 U.S. 680, 686 n. 5 (1980); *Herman & MacLean v. Huddleston*,

459 U.S. 375, 378 n. 4 (1983); *Tellabs, Inc. v. Makor Issues & Rights, Ltd.*, 551 U.S. 308, 319 n.3 (2007); *Matrixx Initiatives, Inc. v. Siracusano* 131 S.Ct. 1309 (2011). Yet as the Court explicitly acknowledged in *Tellabs*: "Every Court of Appeals that has considered the issue has held that a plaintiff may meet the scienter requirement by showing that the defendant acted intentionally or recklessly, though the Circuits differ on the degree of recklessness required." Among the many definitions of recklessness, the following is cited frequently:

> [R]eckless conduct may be defined as ... highly unreasonable [conduct], involving not merely simple, or even inexcusable negligence, but an extreme departure from the standards of ordinary care, and which presents a danger of misleading buyers or sellers that is either known to the defendant or is so obvious that the actor must have been aware of it.

Sunstrand Corp. v. Sun Chem. Corp., 553 F.2d 1033, 1045 (7th Cir. 1977). Courts have both ratcheted up and ratcheted down from this basic definition. Compare *Nathenson v. Zonagen Inc.*, 267 F.3d 400, 408 (5th Cir. 2001) (plaintiffs must prove the defendant's "severe recklessness," which is "limited to those highly unreasonable omissions or misrepresentations that involve not merely simple or even inexcusable negligence, but an extreme departure from the standard of ordinary care, and that present a danger of misleading buyers or sellers which is either known to the defendant or is so obvious that the defendant must have been aware of it") (quoting *Broad v. Rockwell Int'l Corp.*, 642 F.2d 929, 961-62 (5th Cir. 1981)) with *Keirnan v. Homeland, Inc.*, 611 F.2d 785, 788 (9th Cir. 1980) (stating that recklessness exists when defendants "had reasonable grounds to believe material facts existed that were misstated or omitted, but nonetheless failed to obtain and disclose such facts although they could have done so without extraordinary effort"). Note also that in response to Congress's decision to heighten the pleading requirements for private plaintiffs in federal securities fraud cases (a subject that is addressed in detail in the next part of this section of the Chapter), the Ninth Circuit adopted a standard for recklessness that is arguably the most restrictive in the country. See *In re Silicon Graphics Inc. Sec. Litig.*, 183 F.3d 970, 985 (9th Cir. 1999) (requiring plaintiffs to plead with particularity "facts giving rise to a strong inference of the required state of mind, i.e., at least deliberate recklessness"). See also id. at 977 (stating that "recklessness only satisfies scienter under § 10(b) to the extent that it reflects some degree of intentional or conscious misconduct").

All that being said, businesses that are frequently named in Rule 10b-5 actions, such as high-technology companies and accounting firms, have long insisted that a showing of recklessness does not satisfy Section 10(b)'s requirement of scienter. On several occasions, most notably in 1995 and 1998, lobbyists supporting defendants' interests sought to persuade Congress that Rule 10b-5 liability should not attach absent proof of a defendant's actual intent to deceive. From your study of the PSLRA thus far, what evidence can you identify that Congress recognizes—and implicitly approves of—recklessness as a mental state sufficient to establish liability under Rule 10b-5? Consider this question again in Section G of this Chapter when you study the scheme for proportionate liability now set forth in Section 21D(f) of the Exchange Act.

5. Circumstantial Evidence as Proof of Scienter. As the Supreme Court recognized in *Herman & MacLean v. Huddleston*, 459 U.S. 375 (1983), proof of scienter in Rule 10b-5 cases "is often a matter of inference from circumstantial evidence." Id. at 390 n. 30. In *Greebel v. FTP Software, Inc.*, 194 F.3d 185 (1st Cir. 1999), the First Circuit compiled the following list of factors that could evidence scienter in a Rule 10b-5 case alleging material misstatements or omissions:

- insider trading [at suspicious times or in suspicious amounts];
- divergence between internal reports and external statements on the same subject;
- closeness in time of an allegedly fraudulent statement or omission and the later disclosure of inconsistent information;
- evidence of bribery by a top company official;
- existence of an ancillary lawsuit charging fraud by a company and the company's quick settlement of that suit;
- disregard of the most current factual information before making statements;
- disclosure of accrual basis information in a way which could only be understood by someone with a high degree of accounting skill;
- the personal interest of certain directors in not informing disinterested directors of an impending sale of stock; and
- the self-interested motivation of defendants in the form of saving their salaries or jobs.

Id. at 196-97. Consider the actual showing that a plaintiff would need to make to establish one or more of these factors. Which factors can be proven based on evidence that is publicly available to a shareholder-plaintiff? Which factors can be proven based on evidence that is likely to be found in internal corporate documents? Which factors can be proven based on evidence most apt to be obtainable from civil interrogatories or depositions?

In addition to the factors listed by the *Greebel* court, what other types of evidence might support a circumstantial case that the defendant acted with scienter, i.e., with recklessness or intent to deceive ? Are there ways of proving scienter other than by using circumstantial evidence?

6. Seeking State Law Alternatives. Some state courts have held that plaintiffs suing under anti-fraud provisions contained in blue sky laws must prove only that the defendant acted negligently. See e.g. *Kittilson v. Ford*, 93 Wash. 2d 223, 226, 608 P.2d 264, 265 (1980) ("We believe the holding in *Ernst & Ernst v. Hochfelder* [is] inapplicable to our Securities Act."). For this reason, blue sky laws may sometimes provide a more attractive vehicle for securities plaintiffs than does federal litigation under Rule 10b-5. Note, however, that in 1998, Congress constricted this state law option by preempting securities class actions brought under state law counterparts to Rule 10b-5 where the action involves a security listed on a stock exchange or traded on the NASDAQ. See discussion of the Securities Litigation Uniform Standards Act of 1998 (SLUSA), infra, Chapter 6.D.

7. The Problem of Corporate Scienter. A plaintiff can establish the scienter of a corporate defendant by showing the individual scienter of the corporation's directors or high ranking officers. See *Teamsters Local 445 Freight Div. Pension Fund v. Dynex Capital Inc.*, 531 F.3d 190, 195 (2d Cir. 2008) (observing that "the most straightforward way to raise such an inference [of scienter] for a corporate defendant will be to plead it for an individual defendant"). Should a plaintiff also be able to show a corporation's scienter based upon "the piecemeal knowledge of various actors," even without any single individual's having the requisite scienter? See Donald C. Langevoort, The Epistemology of Corporate-Securities Lawyering: Beliefs, Biases and Organizational Behavior, 63 Brook. L. Rev. 629, 660-61 (1997). See generally, Patricia S. Abril & Ann Morales Olazabal, The Locus of Corporate Scienter, 2006 Colum. Bus. L. Rev. 81 (analyzing and applying principles of criminal law to the problem of corporate scienter in Rule 10b-5 cases).

To be sure, most courts have concluded that corporate liability for Rule 10b-5 follows only if the individual(s) who made the statement had the requisite scienter. See, e.g., *Mizzaro v. Home Depot, Inc.*, 544 F.3d 1230, 1254 (11th Cir. 2008) (stating that "[b]ecause the allegations in this case relate to allegedly fraudulent public statements, we 'look to the state of mind of the individual corporate official or officials who make or issue the statement (or order or approve it or its making or issuance, or who furnish information or language for inclusion therein, or the like)'" quoting *Southland Securities Corp. v. INSpire Ins. Solutions, Inc.*, 365 F.3d 353, 366 (5th Cir. 2004)). See also Bradley J. Bondi, Dangerous Liaisons: Collective Scienter in SEC Enforcement Actions: 6 N.Y.U. J.L. & Bus. 1 (2009) (observing that while the SEC has not had occasion to litigate the theory, in the context of private litigation, most courts have rejected collective scienter). But a few courts have allowed plaintiffs to (or at least suggest that they may) establish corporate scienter by aggregating the knowledge of several individuals in that corporation. See, e.g., *Dynex Capital*, supra, 531 F.3d at 195 (observing that "it is possible to raise the required inference with regard to a corporate defendant without doing so with regard to a specific individual defendant"); *Glazer Capital Mgmt LP. v. Magistri*, 549 F.3d 736, 744 (9th Cir. 2008) (leaving open the "possibility that, in certain circumstances, some form of collective scienter pleading might be appropriate"); *In re WorldCom, Inc. Sec. Litig.*, 352 F.Supp.2d 472, 497 (S.D.N.Y. 2005) (stating that "plaintiffs in securities fraud cases need not prove that any one individual employee of a corporate defendant also acted with scienter. Proof of a corporation's collective knowledge and intent is sufficient"). What benefits and/or drawbacks would come about from allowing an aggregation approach to a corporation's scienter?

8. Good Motives vs. Bad. Does a person act with scienter if he or she intentionally misrepresents (or omits) a material fact with an arguably laudable motive? Consider, for example, the CEO of a potential takeover target who denies to a reporter the existence of merger negotiations to prevent a run-up in the stock price (which would make the transaction substantially less attractive to a potential bidder).

Securities fraud cases generally draw the same distinction between motive and intent that is common in the criminal law. That is, proof of motive often evidences an intent to deceive, but such intent does not require a nefarious motive. Recall that in *Basic Inc. v. Levinson*, 485 U.S. 224 (1988), the Supreme

Court expressed a clear unwillingness to insulate "white lies" from Rule 10b-5 liability, stating "we think that creating an exception to a regulatory scheme founded on a prodisclosure legislative philosophy, because complying with the regulation might be 'bad for business,' is a role for Congress, not this Court." Id. at 240, n. 17. See also *SEC v. Falstaff Brewing Corp.*, 629 F.2d 62, 77 (D.C. Cir. 1980) (when a defendant "[knows] the nature and consequences of his actions, he act[s] with scienter"); Restatement (Second) of Torts § 8A (1965) ("If the actor knows that the consequences are certain, or substantially certain, to result from his act, and still goes ahead, he is treated by the law as if he had in fact desired to produce the result"); *AUSA Life Ins., Co. v. Ernst & Young*, 206 F.3d 202, 221 (2nd Cir. 2000) (citing Restatement, supra, and concluding that the district had "inappropriately ma[de] the scienter issue one of 'what did the defendant *want* to happen' as opposed to 'what could the defendant reasonably foresee as a potential result of his action'"). See generally Donald C. Langevoort, Reflections on Scienter (and the Securities Fraud Case Against Martha Stewart that Never Happened), 10 Lewis & Clark L. Rev. 1, 8 (2006) (contending that cognitive research "strengthens the preference for an 'awareness' standard rather than one based on motivation or purpose").

The normative question of whether the lie told with "good motives" should be insulated from liability under the federal securities laws has provoked interesting commentary. See, e.g., Ian Ayres, Back to *Basics*: Regulating How Corporations Speak to the Market, 77 Va. L. Rev. 945, 946 (1991) (arguing that "corporations should be given the option of lying [to the market] but that corporations that contemplate lying should be forced to disclose that they do not warrant the truth of their statements"); Marcel Kahan, Games, Lies and Securities Fraud, 67 N.Y.U. L. Rev. 750 (1992) (using game theory to suggest that some lies told in the context of corporate negotiations should not trigger liability); Jonathan R. Macey & Geoffrey P. Miller, Good Finance, Bad Economics: An Analysis of the Fraud-on-the-Market Theory, 42 Stan. L. Rev. 1059, 1091 (1990) (arguing that "valuable corporate information should not be disclosed if, in the business judgment of the officers and directors involved, such disclosure would jeopardize the aggregate value of the firm's shares"). Should Congress act on any of these suggestions?

PROBLEM 2-13

Reconsider the facts of Problem 2-5 in Section A of this Chapter. What difficulties, if any, will the plaintiff encounter in establishing scienter? If the corporation in Problem 2-4 had denied the existence of the contract in accordance with the foreign government's request, would the plaintiffs be able to establish scienter?

PROBLEM 2-14

Orange, Inc. designs, manufactures, and markets personal computers, mobile communication and media devices, and portable digital music players. At a major press conference, Orange's CEO, Henry Hobbs, made several favorable statements about one of Orange's newest computers. At the time he made those statements, Hobbs held a non-reckless belief in their truth and accuracy. However, several other high-ranking officials in the company knew that Orange was experiencing significant problems with the design and production of that new computer.

One month later, Orange held a follow-up press conference where Hobbs acknowledged that some new models had an overly-sensitive power switch that could result in an abrupt power cut-off and loss of data. Within minutes of that announcement, Orange's stock price dropped significantly.

A securities fraud class action lawsuit has been filed on behalf of investors who purchased Orange shares during the period between the two press conferences. Assume that plaintiffs cannot state a claim against Hobbs because he lacked the necessary scienter. Is it likely that plaintiffs will be able to establish scienter on the part of Orange?

Cf. *In re Apple Computer, Inc.*, 127 F. App'x 296 (9th Cir. 2005).

2. *Requirements for Pleading Scienter*

As noted at the beginning of this Chapter, all complaints alleging violations of Rule 10b-5 must satisfy the pleading requirements of Rule 9(b) of the Federal Rules of Civil Procedure:

> In all averments of fraud or mistake, the circumstances constituting fraud or mistake shall be stated with particularity. Malice, intent, knowledge, and other condition of mind of a person may be averred generally.

By allowing general allegation regarding a "condition of mind," Rule 9(b) may at first blush seem to set a rather low hurdle for pleading scienter in Rule 10b-5 cases. But in cases involving claims of securities fraud, many courts – most particularly the Second Circuit – put additional teeth into Rule 9(b), requiring plaintiffs (including the SEC) to allege in their complaints specific facts giving rise to a strong inference of scienter. The Second Circuit also developed the so-called "motive and opportunity" test, under which plaintiffs could satisfy the requirement of pleading a "strong inference" of scienter by alleging facts "establishing a motive to commit fraud and an opportunity to do so." See, e.g., *In re Time Warner, Inc. Sec. Litig.*, 9 F.3d 259, 269 (2d Cir. 1993). Alternatively, plaintiffs could satisfy the "strong inference" standard by alleging "facts constituting circumstantial evidence of either reckless or conscious behavior." Id.

In 1995, Congress established a uniform standard for the pleading of state of mind in complaints filed in federal court under the Exchange Act by private plaintiffs seeking money damages. Specifically, the PSLRA added a new Section 21D(b)(2) to the Exchange Act:

> **Section 21D(b)(2)**—*Required State of Mind*.—In any private action arising under [the Exchange Act] in which the plaintiff may recover money damages only on proof that the defendant acted with a particular state of mind, the complaint shall, with respect to each act or omission alleged to violate [the Exchange Act], state with particularity facts giving rise to a strong inference that the defendant acted with the required state of mind.

Congress also added to the Exchange Act a new Section 21D(b)(3)(A), which requires a court, on the motion of any defendant, to dismiss a complaint for failure to meet Section 21D(b)'s pleading requirements, and a new Section

21D(b)(3)(B), which imposes an automatic stay on discovery during the pendency of dismissal motions, unless the court finds that "particularized discovery is necessary to preserve evidence or to prevent undue prejudice to that party." Courts vary considerably as to the meaning of "undue prejudice." Compare *Medical Imaging Ctrs. of Am., Inc. v. Lichtenstein*, 917 F. Supp. 717, 721 n.3 (S.D. Cal. 1996) (maintaining that a stay of discovery can result in undue prejudice when it effectively "shield[s] *** [defendants] from eventual liability for any material violations of the securities laws") with *SG Cowen Sec. Corp. v. United States Dist. Court for the N. Dist. of Cal.*, 189 F.3d 909, 913 (9th Cir. 1999) (holding "as a matter of law, failure to muster facts sufficient to meet the [PSLRA's] pleading requirements cannot constitute the requisite 'undue prejudice' to the plaintiff justifying a lift of the discovery stay under [Section 21D(b)(3)(B)]").

Did Congress swing the pendulum too far in a pro-defendant direction when it coupled the heightened pleading requirements in Section 21D(b)(1) and (2) with the automatic stay of discovery in Section 21D(b)(3)(B)? Prior to the passage of the PSLRA, district courts in Rule 10b-5 cases typically allowed the civil discovery process to continue while the defendant's motion to dismiss was pending. And the process of discovery generally allowed the plaintiffs to garner additional evidence which they added to their cases in the form of amended complaints. See Hillary A. Sale, Heightened Pleading and Discovery Stays: An Analysis of the Effect of the PSLRA's Internal-Information Standard on '33 Act and '34 Act Claims, 76 Wash. U. L.Q. 537, 562 (1998) (emphasizing that prior to the PSLRA, plaintiffs routinely "amended their complaints while the discovery process progressed, resulting in several amended and consolidated complaints and concomitant motions to dismiss"). Many of the PSLRA's strongest proponents argued that allowing discovery to be utilized in this way promoted frivolous litigation by encouraging plaintiffs to "file-first-and-research-the-complaint-later." Id. at 553.

As you read the decision that follows, consider the extent to which disagreements about the meaning of "strong inference" relate to disagreements about when defendants should be subjected to the burdens of civil discovery.

TELLABS, INC. v. MAKOR ISSUES & RIGHTS, LTD.

551 U.S. 308 (2007)

JUSTICE RUTH BADER GINSBURG:

This Court has long recognized that meritorious private actions to enforce federal antifraud securities laws are an essential supplement to criminal prosecutions and civil enforcement actions brought, respectively, by the Department of Justice and the Securities and Exchange Commission (SEC). See, e.g., *Dura Pharmaceuticals, Inc. v. Broudo*, 544 U.S. 336, 345 (2005); *J.I. Case Co. v. Borak*, 377 U.S. 426, 432 (1964). Private securities fraud actions, however, if not adequately contained, can be employed abusively to impose substantial costs on companies and individuals whose conduct conforms to the law. See *Merrill Lynch, Pierce, Fenner & Smith Inc. v. Dabit*, 547 U.S. 71, 81 (2006). As a check against abusive litigation by private parties, Congress enacted the Private Securities Litigation Reform Act of 1995 (PSLRA).

Exacting pleading requirements are among the control measures Congress included in the PSLRA. The Act requires plaintiffs to state with particularity both the facts constituting the alleged violation, and the facts evidencing scienter, i.e., the defendant's intention "to deceive, manipulate, or defraud." *Ernst & Ernst v. Hochfelder*, 425 U.S. 185, 194, & n. 12 (1976). This case concerns the latter requirement. As set out in § 21D(b)(2) of the PSLRA, plaintiffs must "state with particularity facts giving rise to a strong inference that the defendant acted with the required state of mind."

Congress left the key term "strong inference" undefined, and Courts of Appeals have divided on its meaning. In the case before us, the Court of Appeals for the Seventh Circuit held that the "strong inference" standard would be met if the complaint "allege[d] facts from which, if true, a reasonable person could infer that the defendant acted with the required intent." That formulation, we conclude, does not capture the stricter demand Congress sought to convey in § 21D(b)(2). It does not suffice that a reasonable factfinder plausibly could infer from the complaint's allegations the requisite state of mind. ***

I.

Petitioner Tellabs, Inc., manufactures specialized equipment used in fiber optic networks. During the time period relevant to this case, petitioner Richard Notebaert was Tellabs' chief executive officer and president. Respondents (Shareholders) are persons who purchased Tellabs stock between December 11, 2000, and June 19, 2001. They accuse Tellabs and Notebaert (as well as several other Tellabs executives) of engaging in a scheme to deceive the investing public about the true value of Tellabs' stock.

Beginning on December 11, 2000, the Shareholders allege, Notebaert (and by imputation Tellabs) "falsely reassured public investors, in a series of statements ... that Tellabs was continuing to enjoy strong demand for its products and earning record revenues," when, in fact, Notebaert knew the opposite was true. From December 2000 until the spring of 2001, the Shareholders claim, Notebaert knowingly misled the public in four ways. First, he made statements indicating that demand for Tellabs' flagship networking device, the TITAN 5500, was continuing to grow, when in fact demand for that product was waning. Second, Notebaert made statements indicating that the TITAN 6500, Tellabs' next-generation networking device, was available for delivery, and that demand for that product was strong and growing, when in truth the product was not ready for delivery and demand was weak. Third, he falsely represented Tellabs' financial results for the fourth quarter of 2000 (and, in connection with those results, condoned the practice of "channel stuffing," under which Tellabs flooded its customers with unwanted products). Fourth, Notebaert made a series of overstated revenue projections, when demand for the TITAN 5500 was drying up and production of the TITAN 6500 was behind schedule.. Based on Notebaert's sunny assessments, the Shareholders contend, market analysts recommended that investors buy Tellabs' stock.

The first public glimmer that business was not so healthy came in March 2001 when Tellabs modestly reduced its first quarter sales projections. In the next months, Tellabs made progressively more cautious statements about its projected sales. On June 19, 2001, the last day of the class period, Tellabs disclosed that demand for the TITAN 5500 had significantly dropped. Simultaneously, the company substantially lowered its revenue projections for the second quarter of 2001. The next day, the price of Tellabs stock, which had reached a high of $67 during the period, plunged to a low of $15.87. ***

II

***Section 10(b), this Court has implied from the statute's text and purpose, affords a right of action to purchasers or sellers of securities injured by its violation. See, e.g., *Dura Pharmaceuticals*, 544 U.S., at 341. See also id., at 345, ("The securities statutes seek to maintain public confidence in the marketplace .... by deterring fraud, in part, through the availability of private securities fraud actions."); *Borak*, 377 U.S., at 432 (private securities fraud actions provide "a most effective weapon in the enforcement" of securities laws and are "a necessary supplement to Commission action"). To establish liability under § 10(b) and Rule 10b-5, a private plaintiff must prove that the defendant acted with scienter, "a mental state embracing intent to deceive, manipulate, or defraud." *Ernst & Ernst*, 425 U.S., at 193-194, and n. 12.[3]

In an ordinary civil action, the Federal Rules of Civil Procedure require only "a short and plain statement of the claim showing that the pleader is entitled to relief." Fed. Rule Civ. Proc. 8(a)(2). Although the rule encourages brevity, the complaint must say enough to give the defendant "fair notice of what the plaintiff's claim is and the grounds upon which it rests." *Dura Pharmaceuticals*, 544 U.S., at 346. Prior to the enactment of the PSLRA, the sufficiency of a complaint for securities fraud was governed not by Rule 8, but by the heightened pleading standard set forth in Rule 9(b). Rule 9(b) applies to "all averments of fraud or mistake"; it requires that "the circumstances constituting fraud ... be stated with particularity" but provides that "[m]alice, intent, knowledge, and other condition of mind of a person, may be averred generally."

Courts of Appeals diverged on the character of the Rule 9(b) inquiry in § 10(b) cases: Could securities fraud plaintiffs allege the requisite mental state "simply by stating that scienter existed," or were they required to allege with particularity facts giving rise to an inference of scienter? Circuits requiring plaintiffs to allege specific facts indicating scienter expressed that requirement variously. The Second Circuit's formulation was the most stringent. Securities fraud plaintiffs in that Circuit were required to "specifically plead those [facts] which they assert give rise to a *strong inference* that the defendants had" the requisite state of mind. *Ross v. A.H. Robins Co.*, 607 F.2d 545, 558 (1979) (emphasis added). The "strong inference" formulation was appropriate, the Second Circuit said, to ward off allegations of "fraud by hindsight." See, e.g.,

---

3. We have previously reserved the question whether reckless behavior is sufficient for civil liability under § 10(b) and Rule 10b-5. See *Ernst & Ernst v. Hochfelder*, 425 U.S. 185, 194, n. 12 (1976). Every Court of Appeals that has considered the issue has held that a plaintiff may meet the scienter requirement by showing that the defendant acted intentionally or recklessly, though the Circuits differ on the degree of recklessness required. The question whether and when recklessness satisfies the scienter requirement is not presented in this case.

Shields v. Citytrust Bancorp, Inc., 25 F.3d 1124, 1129 (1994) (quoting *Denny v. Barber*, 576 F.2d 465, 470 (C.A.2 1978) (Friendly, J.)).

Setting a uniform pleading standard for § 10(b) actions was among Congress' objectives when it enacted the PSLRA. Designed to curb perceived abuses of the § 10(b) private action – "nuisance filings, targeting of deep-pocket defendants, vexatious discovery requests and manipulation by class action lawyers," *Dabit*, 547 U.S., at 81 (quoting H.R. Conf. Rep. No. 104-369, p. 31 (1995)) – the PSLRA installed both substantive and procedural controls.[4] Notably, Congress prescribed new procedures for the appointment of lead plaintiffs and lead counsel. This innovation aimed to increase the likelihood that institutional investors – parties more likely to balance the interests of the class with the long-term interests of the company – would serve as lead plaintiffs. See id., at 33-34. Congress also "limit[ed] recoverable damages and attorney's fees, provide[d] a "safe harbor" for forward-looking statements, ... mandate[d] imposition of sanctions for frivolous litigation, and authorize[d] a stay of discovery pending resolution of any motion to dismiss." *Dabit*, 547 U.S., at 81. And in § 21D(b) of the PSLRA, Congress "impose[d] heightened pleading requirements in actions brought pursuant to § 10(b) and Rule 10b-5."

Under the PSLRA's heightened pleading instructions, any private securities complaint alleging that the defendant made a false or misleading statement must: (1) "specify each statement alleged to have been misleading [and] the reason or reasons why the statement is misleading;" and (2) "state with particularity facts giving rise to a strong inference that the defendant acted with the required state of mind." In the instant case, as earlier stated, the District Court and the Seventh Circuit agreed that the Shareholders met the first of the two requirements: The complaint sufficiently specified Notebaert's alleged misleading statements and the reasons why the statements were misleading. But those courts disagreed on whether the Shareholders, as required by § 21D(b)(2), "state[d] with particularity facts giving rise to a strong inference that [Notebaert] acted with [scienter]."

The "strong inference" standard "unequivocally raise[d] the bar for pleading scienter," 437 F.3d, at 601, and signaled Congress' purpose to promote greater uniformity among the Circuits, see H.R. Conf. Rep., p. 41. But "Congress did not ... throw much light on what facts ... suffice to create [a strong] inference," or on what "degree of imagination courts can use in divining whether" the requisite inference exists. 437 F.3d, at 601. While adopting the Second Circuit's "strong inference" standard, Congress did not codify that Circuit's case law interpreting the standard. With no clear guide from Congress other than its "inten[tion] to strengthen existing pleading requirements," H.R. Conf. Rep., p. 41, Courts of Appeals have diverged again, this time in construing the term "strong inference." Among the uncertainties, should courts consider competing inferences in determining whether an inference of scienter is "strong?" Our task

---

4. Nothing in the Act, we have previously noted, casts doubt on the conclusion "that private securities litigation [i]s an indispensable tool with which defrauded investors can recover their losses"-a matter crucial to the integrity of domestic capital markets. See *Merrill Lynch, Pierce, Fenner & Smith Inc. v. Dabit*, 547 U.S. 71 (2006) .

is to prescribe a workable construction of the "strong inference" standard, a reading geared to the PSLRA's twin goals: to curb frivolous, lawyer-driven litigation, while preserving investors' ability to recover on meritorious claims.

III

A

We establish the following prescriptions: First, faced with a Rule 12(b)(6) motion to dismiss a §10(b) action, courts must, as with any motion to dismiss for failure to plead a claim on which relief can be granted, accept all factual allegations in the complaint as true. See *Leatherman v. Tarrant County Narcotics Intelligence and Coordination Unit*, 507 U.S. 163, 164 (1993). On this point, the parties agree.

Second, courts must consider the complaint in its entirety, as well as other sources courts ordinarily examine when ruling on Rule 12(b)(6) motions to dismiss, in particular, documents incorporated into the complaint by reference, and matters of which a court may take judicial notice. See 5B Wright & Miller § 1357 (3d ed.2004 and Supp.2007). The inquiry, as several Courts of Appeals have recognized, is whether all of the facts alleged, taken collectively, give rise to a strong inference of scienter, not whether any individual allegation, scrutinized in isolation, meets that standard.

Third, in determining whether the pleaded facts give rise to a "strong" inference of scienter, the court must take into account plausible opposing inferences. The Seventh Circuit expressly declined to engage in such a comparative inquiry. A complaint could survive, that court said, as long as it "alleges facts from which, if true, a reasonable person could infer that the defendant acted with the required intent"; in other words, only "[i]f a reasonable person could not draw such an inference from the alleged facts" would the defendant prevail on a motion to dismiss. But in § 21D(b)(2), Congress did not merely require plaintiffs to "provide a factual basis for [their] scienter allegations,", i.e., to allege facts from which an inference of scienter rationally could be drawn. Instead, Congress required plaintiffs to plead with particularity facts that give rise to a "strong" – i.e., a powerful or cogent-inference. See American Heritage Dictionary 1717 (4th ed.2000) (defining "strong" as "[p]ersuasive, effective, and cogent"); 16 Oxford English Dictionary 949 (2d ed.1989) (defining "strong" as "[p]owerful to demonstrate or convince" (definition 16b)); cf. 7 id., at 924 (defining "inference" as "a conclusion [drawn] from known or assumed facts or statements"; "reasoning from something known or assumed to something else which follows from it").

The strength of an inference cannot be decided in a vacuum. The inquiry is inherently comparative: How likely is it that one conclusion, as compared to others, follows from the underlying facts? To determine whether the plaintiff has alleged facts that give rise to the requisite "strong inference" of scienter, a court must consider plausible nonculpable explanations for the defendant's conduct, as well as inferences favoring the plaintiff. The inference that the defendant acted with scienter need not be irrefutable, i.e., of the "smoking-gun" genre, or even the "most plausible of competing inferences." Recall in this regard that § 21D(b)'s pleading requirements are but one constraint among many the PSLRA installed to screen out frivolous suits, while allowing meritorious actions to move forward. Yet the inference of scienter must be more than merely "reasonable" or "permissible"-it must be cogent and compelling, thus strong in light of other explanations. A complaint will survive, we hold, only if a reasonable person would deem the inference of scienter cogent and at least as compelling as any opposing inference one could draw from the facts alleged.

Justice Alito agrees with Justice Scalia, and would transpose to the pleading stage "the test that is used at the summary-judgment and judgment-as-a-matter-of-law stages." But the test at each stage is measured against a different backdrop. It is improbable that Congress, without so stating, intended courts to test pleadings, unaided by discovery, to determine whether there is "no genuine issue as to any material fact." See Fed. Rule Civ. Proc. 56(c). And judgment as a matter of law is a post-trial device, turning on the question whether a party has produced evidence "legally sufficient" to warrant a jury determination in that party's favor. See Rule 50(a)(1).

B

Tellabs contends that when competing inferences are considered, Notebaert's evident lack of pecuniary motive will be dispositive. The Shareholders, Tellabs stresses, did not allege that Notebaert sold any shares during the class period. While it is true that motive can be a relevant consideration, and personal financial gain may weigh heavily in favor of a scienter inference, we agree with the Seventh Circuit that the absence of a motive allegation is not fatal. As earlier stated, allegations must be considered collectively; the significance that can be ascribed to an allegation of motive, or lack thereof, depends on the entirety of the complaint.

Tellabs also maintains that several of the Shareholders' allegations are too vague or ambiguous to contribute to a strong inference of scienter. For example, the Shareholders alleged that Tellabs flooded its customers with unwanted products, a practice known as "channel stuffing." But they failed, Tellabs argues, to specify whether the channel stuffing allegedly known to Notebaert was the illegitimate kind (e.g., writing orders for products customers had not requested) or the legitimate kind (e.g., offering customers discounts as an incentive to buy). We agree that omissions and ambiguities count against inferring scienter, for plaintiffs must "state with particularity facts giving rise to a strong inference that the defendant acted with the required state of mind." We reiterate, however, that the court's job is not to scrutinize each allegation in isolation but to assess all the allegations holistically. In sum, the reviewing court must ask: When the allegations are accepted as true and taken collectively, would a reasonable person deem the inference of scienter at least as strong as any opposing inference?

IV

Accounting for its construction of § 21D(b)(2), the Seventh Circuit explained that the court "th[ought] it wis[e] to adopt an approach that [could not] be misunderstood as a usurpation of the jury's role." In our view, the Seventh Circuit's concern was undue. A court's comparative assessment of plausible inferences, while constantly assuming the plaintiff's allegations to be true, we think it plain, does not impinge upon the Seventh Amendment right to jury trial.

Congress, as creator of federal statutory claims, has power to prescribe what must be pleaded to state the claim, just as it has power to determine what must be proved to prevail on the merits. It is the federal lawmaker's prerogative, therefore, to allow, disallow, or shape the contours of – including the pleading and proof requirements for – § 10(b) private actions. No decision of this Court questions that authority in general, or suggests, in particular, that the Seventh Amendment inhibits Congress from establishing whatever pleading requirements it finds appropriate for federal statutory claims. Cf. *Swierkiewicz v. Sorema N. A.*, 534 U.S. 506, 512-513 (2002); *Leatherman*, 507 U.S., at 168 (both recognizing that heightened pleading requirements can be established by Federal Rule, citing Fed. Rule Civ. Proc. 9(b), which requires that fraud or mistake be pleaded with particularity). ***

While we reject the Seventh Circuit's approach to § 21D(b)(2), we do not decide whether, under the standard we have described, the Shareholders' allegations warrant "a strong inference that [Notebaert and Tellabs] acted with the required state of mind." Neither the District Court nor the Court of Appeals had the opportunity to consider the matter in light of the prescriptions we announce today. We therefore vacate the Seventh Circuit's judgment so that the case may be reexamined in accord with our construction of § 21D(b)(2).

The judgment of the Court of Appeals is vacated, and the case is remanded for further proceedings consistent with this opinion. ***

JUSTICE ANTONIN G. SCALIA, CONCURRING IN THE JUDGMENT:

I fail to see how an inference that is merely "at least as compelling as any opposing inference," can conceivably be called what the statute here at issue requires: a "strong inference." If a jade falcon were stolen from a room to which only A and B had access, could it possibly be said there was a "strong inference" that B was the thief? I think not, and I therefore think that the Court's test must fail. In my view, the test should be whether the inference of scienter (if any) is more plausible than the inference of innocence.

The Court's explicit rejection of this reading rests on two assertions. The first (doubtless true) is that the statute does not require that "[t]he inference that the defendant acted with scienter ... be irrefutable, i.e., of the "smoking-gun" genre." It is up to Congress, however, and not to us, to determine what pleading standard would avoid those extremities while yet effectively deterring baseless actions. Congress has expressed its determination in the phrase "strong inference;" it is our job to give that phrase its normal meaning. And if we are to abandon text in favor of unexpressed purpose, as the Court does, it is inconceivable that Congress's enactment of stringent pleading requirements in the Private Securities Litigation Reform Act of 1995 somehow manifests the purpose of giving plaintiffs the edge in close cases.

The Court's second assertion (also true) is that "an inference at least as likely as competing inferences can, in some cases, warrant recovery." *** [The *Summers* case cited by the majority] represented "a relaxation" of "such proof as is ordinarily required" to succeed in a negligence action. There is no indication that the statute at issue here was meant to relax the ordinary rule under which a tie goes to the defendant. To the contrary, it explicitly strengthens that rule by extending it to the pleading stage of a case.

We must be content to give "strong inference" its normal meaning. I hasten to add that, while precision of interpretation should always be pursued for its own sake, I doubt that in this instance what I deem to be the correct test will produce results much different from the Court's. How often is it that inferences are precisely in equipoise? All the more reason, I think, to read the language for what it says.

JUSTICE SAMUEL A. ALITO, JR., CONCURRING IN THE JUDGMENT.

I agree with the Court that the Seventh Circuit used an erroneously low standard for determining whether the plaintiffs in this case satisfied their burden of pleading "with particularity facts giving rise to a strong inference that the defendant acted with the required state of mind." I further agree that the case should be remanded to allow the lower courts to decide in the first instance whether the allegations survive under the correct standard. In two respects, however, I disagree with the opinion of the Court. First, the best interpretation of the statute is that only those facts that are alleged "with particularity" may properly be considered in determining whether the allegations of scienter are sufficient. Second, I agree with Justice Scalia that a "strong inference" of scienter, in the present context, means an inference that is more likely than not correct. ***

JUSTICE JOHN PAUL STEVENS, DISSENTING.

***The basic purpose of the heightened pleading requirement in the context of securities fraud litigation is to protect defendants from the costs of discovery and trial in unmeritorious cases. Because of its intrusive nature, discovery may also invade the privacy interests of the defendants and their executives. Like citizens suspected of having engaged in criminal activity, those defendants should not be required to produce their private effects unless there is probable cause to believe them guilty of misconduct. Admittedly, the probable-cause standard is not capable of precise measurement, but it is a concept that is familiar to judges. As a matter of normal English usage, its meaning is roughly the same as "strong inference." Moreover, it is most unlikely that Congress intended us to adopt a standard that makes it more difficult to commence a civil case than a criminal case.

In addition to the benefit of its grounding in an already familiar legal concept, using a probable-cause standard would avoid the unnecessary conclusion that "in determining whether the pleaded facts give rise to a "strong" inference of scienter, the court *must* take into account plausible opposing inferences." There are times when an inference can easily be deemed strong without any need to weigh competing inferences. For example, if a known drug dealer exits a building immediately after a confirmed drug transaction, carrying a suspicious looking package, a judge could draw a strong inference that the individual was involved in the aforementioned drug transaction without debating whether the suspect might have been leaving the building at that exact time for another unrelated reason.

If, using that same methodology, we assume (as we must) the truth of the detailed factual allegations attributed to 27 different confidential informants described in the complaint and view those allegations collectively, I think it clear that they establish probable cause to believe that Tellabs' chief executive officer "acted with the required intent," as the Seventh Circuit held. ***

NOTES AND QUESTIONS

*1. **The Reasonable Person Standard.*** The Court in *Tellabs* cited the Seventh Circuit's acknowledgment "that the PSLRA 'unequivocally raise[d] the bar for pleading scienter.'" Yet the Seventh Circuit had concluded that the requirement of a "strong inference" could be met by alleging facts from which, if true, "a reasonable person could infer that the defendant acted with the required intent." Was there any way in which the Seventh Circuit's standard could have been read to "capture the stricter demand that Congress sought to convey in § 21D(b)(2)"?

*2. **The Government's Suggested Standard.*** In an amicus brief, the Government urged the Court to define the term "strong inference" as "a high likelihood that the conclusion that the defendant possessed scienter follows from the facts alleged with particularity." Brief for the U.S. as Amicus Curiae Supporting Petitioners at 10. As noted in the introduction to this Chapter, Rule 10b-5 cases rarely reach the trial stage, but when they do, the standard of proof that the plaintiffs must meet is "preponderance of the evidence" (taken to mean "more likely than not"). Was the Government urging the Court to adopt a pleading standard that required a quantum of evidence even greater than that necessary for a plaintiff to prove scienter at trial? Could Congress have intended that result?

*3. **Choosing Among Standards.*** Consider the standard adopted by the majority and the many proposed alternatives. Which standard is the easiest for a court to apply? Which standard is most consistent with the text of Section 21D(b)(2)? Which standard is most aligned with the "PSLRA's twin goals: to curb frivolous, lawyer-driven litigation, while preserving investors' ability to recover on meritorious claims"? How would you have defined the term "strong inference?" For an argument that the post-*Tellabs* application of Section 21D(b)(2) has made the motion to dismiss in securities fraud cases a hybrid falling somewhere between Rule 12(b)(6) and a Rule 56 motion for summary judgment, see Geoffrey P. Miller, Pleading After *Tellabs*, 2009 Wis. L. Rev. 507, 532.

*4. **A Blow to Investors?*** Many commentators were quick to describe the *Tellabs* decision as anti-investor. See Stephen Labaton, Investors' Suits Face Higher Bar, Justices Rule, N.Y. Times (June 22, 2007) at A1 (stating that the Court "dealt a blow to investors who want to sue companies and executives because of suspected fraud"). Is this a fair reading of the majority's opinion? In what ways could the *Tellabs* opinion be characterized as "pro-private plaintiff?"

Consider also how the *Tellabs* plaintiffs actually faired when the case was remanded to the Seventh Circuit. In finding that the plaintiffs met their heightened burden of pleading scienter under Section 21D(b)(2), the court reasoned that:

The critical question [ ] is how likely it is that the allegedly false statements ***were the result of merely careless mistakes at the management level based on false information fed it from below, rather than of an intent to deceive or a reckless indifference to whether the statements were misleading. It is exceedingly unlikely. The 5500 and the 6500 were Tellabs's most important products. The 5500 was described by the company as its "flagship" product and the 6500 was the 5500's heralded successor. They were to Tellabs as Windows XP and Vista are to Microsoft. That no member of the company's senior management who was involved in authorizing or making public statements about the demand for the 5500 and 6500 knew that they were false is very hard to credit, and no plausible story has yet been told by the defendants that might dispel our incredulity. ***

All this is not to say that the plaintiffs could name "management" as a defendant or, less absurdly, name each corporate officer. That would be an example of the group pleading doctrine [which] *** is inconsistent with the "strong inference" requirement. But it is possible to draw a strong inference of corporate scienter without being able to name the individuals who concocted and disseminated the fraud. Suppose General Motors announced that it had sold one million SUVs in 2006, and the actual number was zero. There would be a strong inference of corporate scienter, since so dramatic an announcement would have been approved by corporate officials sufficiently knowledgeable about the company to know that the announcement was false.

Against all this the defendants argue that they could have had no motive to paint the prospects for the 5500 and 6500 systems in rosy hues because within months they acknowledged their mistakes and disclosed the true situation of the two products, and because there is no indication that Notebaert or anyone else who may have been in on the fraud profited from it financially. The argument confuses expected with realized benefits. Notebaert may have thought that there was a chance that the situation regarding the two key products would right itself. If so, the benefits of concealment might exceed the costs. *** The fact that a gamble — concealing bad news in the hope that it will be overtaken by good news — fails is not inconsistent with its having been a considered, though because of the risk a reckless, gamble. It is like embezzling in the hope that winning at the track will enable the embezzled funds to be replaced before they are discovered to be missing.

So the inference of corporate scienter is not only as likely as its opposite, but more likely. And is it cogent? Well, if there are only two possible inferences, and one is much more likely than the other, it must be cogent. Suppose a person woke up one morning with a sharp pain in his abdomen. He thought it was due to a recent operation to remove his gall bladder, but realized it could equally well have been due to any number of other things. The inference that it was due to the operation could not be thought cogent. But suppose he went to a doctor who performed tests that ruled out any cause other than the operation or a duodenal ulcer and told the patient that he was 99 percent certain that it was the operation. The plausibility of an explanation depends on the plausibility of the alternative explanations. As more and more alternatives to a given explanation are ruled out, the probability of that explanation's being the correct one rises. *** Because in our abdominal-pain example all other inferences had been ruled out except the 1 percent one, the inference that the pain was due to the operation would be cogent. This case is similar. Because the alternative hypotheses — either a cascade of innocent mistakes, or acts of subordinate employees, either or both resulting in a series of false statements — are far less likely than the hypothesis of scienter at the corporate level at which the statements were approved, the latter hypothesis must be considered cogent.

> And at the top of the corporate pyramid sat Notebaert, the CEO. The 5500 and the 6500 were his company's key products. Almost all the false statements that we quoted emanated directly from him. Is it conceivable that he was unaware of the problems of his company's two major products and merely repeating lies fed to him by other executives of the company? It is conceivable, yes, but it is exceedingly unlikely.

Makor Issues & Rights, Ltd. v. Tellabs Inc. (Tellabs II), 513 F.3d 702, 709-11 (7th Cir. 2008).

For another example of investors who succeeded in pleading a strong inference of scienter in the wake of *Tellabs,* see *Matrixx Initiatives, Inc. v. Siracusano,* 131 S.Ct. 1309, 1324-25 (2011) (finding that "Matrixx's proposed bright-line rule requiring an allegation of statistical significance to establish a strong inference of scienter is just as flawed as its approach to materiality" and concluding that the complaint's allegations "'taken collectively' give rise to a 'cogent and compelling' inference that Matrixx elected not to disclose the reports of adverse events not because it believed they were meaningless but because it understood their likely effect on the market," quoting *Tellabs,* 551 U.S., at 323).

5. Heightened Pleading Standards and the Constitution. The Seventh Amendment provides that in suits at common law, "the right to a jury trial shall be preserved." In light of the nexus between Rule 10b-5 and common law fraud, courts have long held that this right to a jury trial applies to private actions for damages under Rule 10b-5. See *In re U.S. Fin. Sec. Litig.*, 609 F. 2d 411, 428 n.38 (9th Cir. 1979) (citing cases). In *Tellabs,* the majority concluded that a judge's "weighing" of competing inferences at the motion to dismiss stage does not violate the Seventh Amendment. For analysis and critique, see Suja A. Thomas, Why the Motion to Dismiss Is Now Unconstitutional, 92 Minn. L. Rev. 1851, 1882 (2008) (contending that under the common law, courts were not permitted "to assess the plausibility of the inferences that arise from the facts alleged by the plaintiff," nor were they permitted to "review plausible inferences that favor the defendant and weigh those against plausible inferences that favor the plaintiff"). See also Allan Horwich & Sean Siekkinen, Pleading Reform or Unconstitutional Encroachment? An Analysis of the Seventh Amendment Implications of the Private Securities Litigation Reform Act, 35 Sec. Reg. L. J. 4, 16 (2007) (arguing that, "if the court engages in drawing inferences at the pleading stage, it can usurp questions from the jury because the jury's role as a fact finder often extends beyond pure questions of fact to mixed questions of fact and law"). What if, rather than a "strong inference," Congress had required private plaintiffs to plead particularized facts demonstrating scienter "beyond a reasonable doubt?'" Would a pleading standard that was higher than the standard of proof at trial usurp the jury's prerogative to resolve disputed questions of fact? Might Seventh Amendment considerations explain why Justices Scalia and Alito advocated a preponderance standard rather than the presumably higher standard of pleading urged by the Government?

6. Group Pleading. Prior to the enactment of the PSLRA, the majority of courts had recognized the so-called "group pleading" doctrine:

> In cases of corporate fraud where the false or misleading information is conveyed in prospectuses, registration statements, annual reports, press releases, or other "group-published information," it is reasonable to presume that these are the collective actions of the officers. Under such circumstances, a plaintiff fulfills the particularity requirement of Rule 9(b) by pleading the misrepresentations with particularity and where possible the roles of the individual defendants in the misrepresentations.

Wool v. Tandem Computers, Inc., 818 F.2d 1433, 1440 (9th Cir.1987). Does the group pleading doctrine survive the enactment of the PSLRA's heightened requirement for pleading scienter? Compare *Winer Family Trust v. Queen*, 503 F.3d 319, 337 (3d Cir. 2007) (holding that "the group pleading doctrine is no longer viable in private securities actions after the enactment of the PSLRA") with *In re Pfizer Inc. Sec. Litig.*, 584 F. Supp. 2d 621, 638 (S.D.N.Y. 2008) (stating that "this [c]ourt joins the others in this district that have held the group pleading doctrine is 'alive and well' following the passage of the PSLRA") (quoting *In re BISYS Sec. Litig.*, 397 F. Supp. 2d 430, 439 (S.D.N.Y. 2005)). In *Tellabs*, the Seventh Circuit's initial decision rejected the group pleading doctrine as it pertained to scienter, holding that "allegations of scienter made against one defendant cannot be imputed to all other defendants" – a holding that the Supreme Court did not disturb on appeal. *Tellabs*, 551 U.S. at 327 n.6 (2007) (citing 437 F.3d 588, 602-03 (7th Cir. 2006)). On remand, the Seventh Circuit reiterated its view that group pleading was inconsistent with Section 21D(b)(2)'s requirements. See Note 4 above (discussing *Tellabs II*). Assuming that the Seventh Circuit is correct that a strong inference of scienter must be created "with respect to each individual defendant in multiple defendant cases," might group pleading continue to satisfy the heightened pleading standard in §21D(b)(1) (see page 27 of the casebook)?

7. ***Anonymous Sources.*** Another contentious issue concerns the PSLRA's impact on the fairly common practice of citing unnamed or confidential sources in a securities fraud complaint. Just four weeks after the Supreme Court decided *Tellabs*, the Seventh Circuit concluded in *Higginbotham v. Baxter Int'l, Inc.*, 495 F.3d 753, 757 (7th Cir. 2007) that "anonymity frustrates" the Court's mandate that competing inferences must be weighed. In dismissing the action, the panel "discounted" the allegations that the complaint attributed to five confidential sources, reasoning that "[i]t is hard to see how information from anonymous sources could be deemed compelling or how we could take account of plausible opposing inferences." Id. The court elaborated that "confidential witness must be discounted rather than ignored. Usually that discount will be steep." Id.

Recall, however, that the complaint at issue in *Tellabs* included facts conveyed by 27 confidential sources. The Court remanded the case without addressing the question of how those confidential sources should be treated. Here is what the Seventh Circuit had to say in *Tellabs II*:

> ****Higginbotham v. Baxter International, Inc.* *** was a very different case from this one. The misconduct alleged consisted of frauds committed by Baxter's Brazilian subsidiary, but because the suit was against the parent, the plaintiffs had to show that the parent knew about the Brazilian fraud. The subsidiary had tried to conceal it from its parent as well as from the Brazilian government. There was no basis other than the confidential sources, described merely as three ex-employees of Baxter and two consultants, for a strong inference that

the subsidiary had failed to conceal the fraud from its parent and thus that the management of the parent had been aware of the fraud during the period covered by the complaint.

The confidential sources listed in the complaint in this case, in contrast, are numerous and consist of persons who from the description of their jobs were in a position to know at first hand the facts to which they are prepared to testify, such as the returns of the 5500s, that sales of the 5500 were dropping off a cliff while the company pretended that demand was strong, that the 6500 was not approved by Regional Bell Operating Companies, that it was still in the beta stage and failing performance tests conducted by prospective customers, and that it was too bulky for customers' premises. The information that the confidential informants are reported to have obtained is set forth in convincing detail, with some of the information, moreover, corroborated by multiple sources. It would be better were the informants named in the complaint, because it would be easier to determine whether they had been in a good position to know the facts that the complaint says they learned. But the absence of proper names does not invalidate the drawing of a strong inference from informants' assertions. See *In re Daou Systems, Inc.*, 411 F.3d 1006, 1015–16 (9th Cir.2005); *California Public Employees' Retirement System v. Chubb Corp.*, 394 F.3d 126, 146–47 (3d Cir.2004); *ABC Arbitrage Plaintiffs Group v. Tchuruk*, 291 F.3d 336, 353–54 (5th Cir.2002); *Novak v. Kasaks,* 216 F.3d 300, 312–14 (2d Cir.2000).

Makor Issues & Rights, Ltd. v. Tellabs Inc., (Tellabs II) 513 F.3d 702, 711-12 (7th Cir. 2008).

Was *Higginbotham* correct in its reading of the Court's decision in *Tellabs* to require an automatic "steep" discounting of information provided by confidential witnesses? Did *Tellabs II* apply this steep discount notwithstanding its decision to allow the complaint to go forward? See generally Gideon Mark, Confidential Witnesses in Securities Litigation, 36 J. Corp. L. 551, 565 (2011) (observing that "[w]hile *Tellabs II* can be and has been read to represent a retreat from *Higginbotham*, the earlier case is alive and well").

*8. **Insider Trading as a "Motive and Opportunity" For Fraud.*** Corporate insiders who are themselves trading in an issuer's securities presumably have a motive to conceal bad news from other investors until they have executed their own trades, and their control over an issuer's disclosure policies provides them with a clear opportunity to deceive shareholders. Thus, both before and after the PSLRA, many plaintiffs in Rule 10b-5 cases have sought to satisfy the requirements for pleading scienter by providing evidence that corporate officials were trading in the issuer's stock at the time of the material misstatement or omission alleged in the complaint. But the PSLRA seems to have precipitated a stark increase in the number of securities fraud complaints containing claims of insider trading. See Hillary A. Sale, Judging Heuristics, 35 U.C. Davis L. Rev. 903, 924 (2002) (noting that in 1996 there were two judicial opinions on motions to dismiss securities suits with insider trading allegations, but 12 in 1997, 23 in 1998, 28 in 1999, and 44 in 2000).

Courts, however, are quite clear in holding that mere allegations of insider trading are insufficient to meet the "strong inference" pleading requirement. Rather, the complaint must include specific facts demonstrating that the insider trading is "unusual" and "suspicious." See, e.g., *In re Silicon Graphics Sec. Litig.*, 183 F.3d 970, 986 (9th Cir. 1999) (stating that "[a]lthough

mere allegations of insider trading fail strong inference standard 'unusual' or 'suspicious' stock sales by corporate insiders may constitute circumstantial evidence of scienter, insider trading is suspicious only when it is 'dramatically out of line with prior trading practices at times calculated to maximize the personal benefit from undisclosed inside information' "); *In re Scholastic Corp. Sec. Litig.*, 252 F.3d 63, 74-75 (2d Cir. 2001) (noting that "[f]actors considered in determining whether insider trading activity is unusual include the amount of profit from the sales, the portion of stockholdings sold, the change in volume of insider sales, and the number of insiders selling"). The problem that follows provides an opportunity to explore these factors.

PROBLEM 2-15

Shareholders of Katteller Corporation have filed a class action lawsuit against the company and four of its current or former officers and directors, alleging violations of Rule 10b-5 through the numerous intentional or reckless omissions of material adverse information and through the intentional or reckless dissemination of false and misleading statements over a period of time from March through August 2002. Plaintiffs seek to satisfy Section 21D(b)(2)'s heightened pleading requirement through the allegation of specific facts demonstrating insider trading on the part of three of the named officials. That is, plaintiffs claim that "massive insider selling on the part of the company's three principal officers is evidence of the defendants' motive to commit fraud through inflating the stock price of company shares."

The plaintiff's complaint includes the following allegations:

1. Officer A, the company's president until May 31, 2002 and a current director, sold 390,000 shares of Katteller stock between April and May 2002 for approximately $11.7 million dollars. These stock sales constituted more than 60% of the president's holdings in the company. Previously, the president had never sold more than 10% of his Katteller holdings in any given year.

2. Officer B, the company's chief executive officer and chairman of its board of directors, sold 1.2 million shares of Katteller stock between April and August 2002, for over $30 million dollars. This constituted more than 39% of his holdings in the company. Previously, the CEO had never sold more than 5% of his Katteller holdings in any given year.

3. Officer C, the company's chief financial officer and director of the company, sold 7,000 shares of Katteller stock on April 20, 2002, for approximately $220,000. This constituted 10% of the CFO's holdings in Katteller, and he had made no other Katteller stock sales in the previous five years.

4. During the class period, the price of Katteller's stock ranged from $22 to $32 per share. On September 1, 2002, when all of defendants' material omissions and misrepresentations came to light, Katteller's stock price fell to approximately $10 a share, and currently trades in the range of $12-15.

5. When combined, the sales of officers A, B, and C amounted to approximately 12% of all outstanding shares of Katteller's stock.

In their memorandum supporting their motion to dismiss under Section 21D(b)(3)(a) of the Exchange Act, defendants emphasize the following facts:

1. Officer A's stock sales immediately preceded his retirement from the company on May 31, 2002, and individuals leaving employment with a company frequently sell a large percentage of their shares.

2. Officer B purchased 10,000 shares of Katteller stock on April 1, 2002.

3. Officer C sold his Katteller stock in order to free up cash to assist his daughter and her new husband with a down payment for the purchase of their first home. During the period of the alleged fraud, Officer C continued to hold more than 60,000 shares of common stock in the company.

4. Officer D, the company's president as of June 1, 2002 and previously on the board of directors, sold no shares of Katteller stock during the class period, though he owned more than 500,000 shares in the company.

If you were the district judge ruling on defendants' motion to dismiss plaintiffs' complaint under Section 21D(b)(3)(A), would you find that the plaintiffs had satisfied their pleading burden under Section 21D(b)(2)?

E. THE PURCHASER-SELLER REQUIREMENT

Private plaintiffs suing for damages under Rule 10b-5 must satisfy the purchaser-seller requirement. This requirement need not be satisfied, however, in actions under the Rule brought by the SEC or by the DOJ.

The Supreme Court upheld the purchaser-seller requirement in the following landmark decision. The decision is noteworthy also for articulating a policy that has played a critical role in the interpretation of Rule 10b-5—the necessity of curbing vexatious private actions.

BLUE CHIP STAMPS v. MANOR DRUG STORES

421 U.S. 723 (1975)

JUSTICE WILLIAM H. REHNQUIST:

This case requires us to consider whether the offerees of a stock offering, made pursuant to an antitrust consent decree and registered under the Securities Act of 1933 (1933 Act) may maintain a private cause of action for money damages where they allege that the offeror has violated the provisions of Rule 10b-5 ***, but where they have neither purchased nor sold any of the offered shares.

I

In 1963 the United States filed a civil antitrust action against Blue Chip Stamp Co. (Old Blue Chip), a company in the business of providing trading stamps to retailers, and nine retailers who owned 90% of its shares. In 1967 the action was terminated by the entry of a consent decree. The decree contemplated a plan of reorganization whereby Old Blue Chip was to be merged into a newly formed corporation, Blue Chip Stamps (New Blue Chip). The holdings of the majority shareholders of Old Blue Chip were to be reduced, and New Blue Chip, one of the petitioners here, was required under the plan to offer a substantial number of its shares of common stock to retailers who had used the stamp service in the past but who were not shareholders in the old company. ***

The reorganization plan was carried out, the offering was registered with the SEC as required by the 1933 Act, and a prospectus was distributed to all offerees as required by § 5 of that Act. Somewhat more than 50% of the offered units were actually purchased. In 1970, two years after the offering, respondent, a former user of the stamp service and therefore an offeree of the 1968 offering, filed this suit ***. Defendants below and petitioners here are Old and New Blue Chip, eight of the nine majority shareholders of Old Blue Chip, and the directors of New Blue Chip (collectively called Blue Chip).

Respondent's complaint alleged *** that the prospectus prepared and distributed by Blue Chip in connection with the offering was materially misleading in its overly pessimistic appraisal of Blue Chip's status and future prospects. It alleged that Blue Chip intentionally made the prospectus overly pessimistic in order to discourage respondent and other members of the allegedly large class whom it represents from accepting what was intended to be a bargain offer, so that the rejected shares might later be offered to the public at a higher price. The complaint alleged that class members because of and in reliance on the false and misleading prospectus failed to purchase the offered units. Respondent therefore sought on behalf of the alleged class some $21,400,000 in damages representing the lost opportunity to purchase the units; the right to purchase the previously rejected units at the 1968 price; and in addition, it sought some $25,000,000 in exemplary damages.

The only portion of the litigation thus initiated which is before us is whether respondent may base its action on Rule 10b-5 *** without having either bought or sold the securities described in the allegedly misleading prospectus. ***

II

*** Section 10(b) does not by its terms provide an express civil remedy for its violation. Nor does the history of this provision provide any indication that Congress considered the problem of private suits under it at the time of its passage. See, e.g., Note, Implied Liability Under the Securities Exchange Act 61 Harv. L. Rev. 858, 861 (1948); A. Bromberg, Securities Law: Fraud—SEC Rule 10b-5 § 2.2(300)-(340) (1968)(hereinafter Bromberg); S. Rep. No.792, 73d Cong., 2d Sess., 5-6 (1934). Similarly there is no indication that the Commission in adopting Rule 10b-5 considered the question of private civil remedies under this provision. SEC Securities Exchange Act Release No. 3230 (1942).

Despite the contrast between the provisions of Rule 10b-5 and the numerous carefully drawn express civil remedies provided in the Acts of both 1933 and 1934,[4] it was held in 1946 by the United States District Court for the Eastern District of Pennsylvania that there was an implied private right of action under the Rule. *Kardon v. National Gypsum Co.*, 69 F. Supp. 512. This Court had no occasion to deal with the subject until 25 years later, and at that time we confirmed with virtually no discussion the overwhelming consensus of the District Courts and Courts of Appeals that such a cause of action did exist. *Superintendent of Insurance v. Bankers Life & Cas. Co.*, 404 U.S. 6, 13 n. 9

---

4. See, e.g., §§ 11, 12, 15 of the 1933 Act; §§ 9, 16, 18, 20 of the 1934 Act.

(1971); *Affiliated Ute Citizens v. United States*, 406 U.S. 128, 150-154 (1972). Such a conclusion was, of course, entirely consistent with the Court's recognition in *J. I. Case Co. v. Borak*, 377 U.S. 426, 432 (1964), that private enforcement of Commission rules may "[provide] a necessary supplement to Commission action."

Within a few years after the seminal *Kardon* decision the Court of Appeals for the Second Circuit concluded that the plaintiff class for purposes of a private damage action under § 10(b) and Rule 10b-5 was limited to actual purchasers and sellers of securities. *Birnbaum v. Newport Steel Corp.*, [193 F.2d 461 (2d Cir. 1952)].

*** But in this case a majority of the Court of Appeals found that the facts warranted an exception to the *Birnbaum* rule. For the reasons hereinafter stated, we are of the opinion that Birnbaum was rightly decided, and that it bars respondent from maintaining this suit under Rule 10b-5. ***

III

*** Just as this Court had no occasion to consider the validity of the *Kardon* holding that there was a private cause of action under Rule 10b-5 until 20-odd years later, nearly the same period of time has gone by between the *Birnbaum* decision and our consideration of the case now before us. As with *Kardon*, virtually all lower federal courts facing the issue in the hundreds of reported cases presenting this question over the past quarter century have reaffirmed *Birnbaum's* conclusion that the plaintiff class for purposes of § 10(b) and Rule 10b-5 private damage actions is limited to purchasers and sellers of securities.

In 1957 and again in 1959, the Securities and Exchange Commission sought from Congress amendment of § 10(b) to change its wording from "in connection with the purchase or sale of any security" to "in connection with the purchase or sale of, *or any attempt to purchase or sell*, any security." 103 Cong.Rec. 11636 (1957) (emphasis added); SEC Legislation, Hearings on S. 1178-1182 before a Subcommittee of the Senate Committee on Banking & Currency, 86th Cong., 1st Sess., 367-368 (1959); S. 2545, 85th Cong., 1st Sess. (1957); S. 1179, 86th Cong., 1st Sess. (1959). In the words of a memorandum submitted by the Commission to a congressional committee, the purpose of the proposed change was "to make section 10(b) also applicable to manipulative activities in connection with any attempt to purchase or sell any security." Hearings on S. 1178-1182, supra, at 331. Opposition to the amendment was based on fears of the extension of civil liability under § 10(b) that it would cause. Id. at 368. Neither change was adopted by Congress.

The longstanding acceptance by the courts, coupled with Congress' failure to reject *Birnbaum's* reasonable interpretation of the wording of § 10(b), wording which is directed toward injury suffered "in connection with the purchase or sale" of securities, argues significantly in favor of acceptance of the *Birnbaum* rule by this Court.

Available evidence from the texts of the 1933 and 1934 Acts as to the congressional scheme in this regard, though not conclusive, supports the result reached by the *Birnbaum* court. The wording of § 10(b) directed at fraud "in connection with the purchase or sale" of securities stands in contrast with the parallel antifraud provision of the 1933 Act, § 17(a) reaching fraud "in the offer of sale" of securities. Cf. § 5 of the 1933 Act. When Congress wished to provide a remedy to those who neither purchase nor sell securities, it had little trouble in doing so expressly. Cf. § 16(b) of the 1934 Act. ***

The principal express nonderivative private civil remedies, created by Congress contemporaneously with the passage of § 10(b), for violations of various provisions of the 1933 and 1934 Acts, are by their terms expressly limited to purchasers or sellers of securities. Thus § 11(a) of the 1933 Act confines the cause of action it grants to "any person acquiring such security" while the remedy granted by § 12 of that Act is limited to the "person purchasing such security." Section 9 of the 1934 Act, prohibiting a variety of fraudulent and manipulative devices, limits the express civil remedy provided for its violation to "any person who shall purchase or sell any security" in a transaction affected by a violation of the provision. Section 18 of the 1934 Act, prohibiting false or misleading statements in reports or other documents required to be filed by the 1934 Act, limits the express remedy provided for its violation to "any person . . . who . . . shall have purchased or sold a security at a price which was affected by such statement . . ." It would indeed be anomalous to impute to Congress an intention to expand the plaintiff class for a judicially implied cause of action beyond the bounds it delineated for comparable express causes of action.

Having said all this, we would by no means be understood as suggesting that we are able to divine from the language of § 10(b) the express "intent of Congress" as to the contours of a private cause of action under Rule 10b-5. When we deal with private actions under Rule 10b-5, we deal with a judicial oak which has grown from little more than a legislative acorn. Such growth may be quite consistent with the congressional enactment and with the role of the federal judiciary in interpreting it, see *J. I. Case Co. v. Borak*, supra, but it would be disingenuous to suggest that either Congress in 1934 or the Securities and Exchange Commission in 1942 foreordained the present state of the law with respect to Rule 10b-5. It is therefore proper that we consider, in addition to the factors already discussed, what may be described as policy considerations when we come to flesh out the portions of the law with respect to which neither the congressional enactment nor the administrative regulations offer conclusive guidance.

Three principal classes of potential plaintiffs are presently barred by the *Birnbaum* rule. First are potential purchasers of shares, either in a new offering or on the Nation's post-distribution trading markets, who allege that they decided not to purchase because of an unduly gloomy representation or the omission of favorable material which made the issuer appear to be a less favorable investment vehicle than it actually was. Second are actual shareholders in the issuer who allege that they decided not to sell their shares because of an unduly rosy representation or a failure to disclose unfavorable material. Third are shareholders, creditors, and perhaps others related to an issuer who suffered loss in the value of their investment due to corporate or insider activities in connection with the purchase or sale of securities which violate Rule 10b-5. It has been held that shareholder members of the second and third of these classes may frequently be able to circumvent the *Birnbaum* limitation through bringing a derivative action on behalf of the corporate issuer if the latter is itself a purchaser or seller of securities. See, e.g., *Schoenbaum v. Firstbrook*, 405 F.2d 215, 219 (CA2 1968). But the first of these classes, of which respondent is a member, cannot claim the benefit of such a rule.

A great majority of the many commentators on the issue before us have taken the view that the *Birnbaum* limitation on the plaintiff class in a Rule 10b-5 action for damages is an arbitrary restriction which unreasonably prevents some deserving plaintiffs from recovering damages which have in fact been caused by violations of Rule 10b-5. See, e.g., Lowenfels, The Demise of the *Birnbaum* Doctrine: A New Era for Rule 10b-5, 54 Va. L. Rev. 268 (1968). The Securities and Exchange Commission has filed an *amicus* brief in this case espousing that same view. We have no doubt that this is indeed a disadvantage of the *Birnbaum* rule, and if it had no countervailing advantages it would be undesirable as a matter of policy, however much it might be supported by precedent and legislative history. But we are of the opinion that there are countervailing advantages to the *Birnbaum* rule, purely as a matter of policy, although those advantages are more difficult to articulate than is the disadvantage.

There has been widespread recognition that litigation under Rule 10b-5 presents a danger of vexatiousness different in degree and in kind from that which accompanies litigation in general. This fact was recognized by Judge Browning in his opinion for the majority of the Court of Appeals in this case, 492 F.2d at 141, and by Judge Hufstedler in her dissenting opinion when she said:

> The purchaser-seller rule has maintained the balances built into the congressional scheme by permitting damage actions to be brought only by those persons whose active participation in the marketing transaction promises enforcement of the statute without undue risk of abuse of the litigation process and without distorting the securities market. Id. at 147.

Judge Friendly in commenting on another aspect of Rule 10b-5 litigation has referred to the possibility that unduly expansive imposition of civil liability "will lead to large judgments, payable in the last analysis by innocent investors, for the benefit of speculators and their lawyers...." *SEC v. Texas Gulf Sulphur Co.*, 401 F.2d 833, 867 (CA2 1968) (concurring opinion).

We believe that the concern expressed for the danger of vexatious litigation which could result from a widely expanded class of plaintiffs under Rule 10b-5 is founded in something more substantial than the common complaint of the many defendants who would prefer avoiding lawsuits entirely to either settling them or trying them. These concerns have two largely separate grounds.

The first of these concerns is that in the field of federal securities laws governing disclosure of information even a complaint which by objective standards may have very little chance of success at trial has a settlement value to the plaintiff out of any proportion to its prospect of success at trial so long as he may prevent the suit from being resolved against him by dismissal or summary judgment. The very pendency of the lawsuit may frustrate or delay normal business activity of the defendant which is totally unrelated to the lawsuit. See, e.g., Sargent, The SEC and the Individual Investor: Restoring His Confidence in the Market, 60 Va. L. Rev. 553, 562-572 (1974); Dooley, The

Effects of Civil Liability on Investment Banking and the New Issues Market, 58 Va. L. Rev. 776, 822-843 (1972).

Congress itself recognized the potential for nuisance or "strike" suits in this type of litigation, and in Title II of the 1934 Act amended § 11 of the 1933 Act to provide that:

> In any suit under this or any other section of this title the court may, in its discretion, require an undertaking for the payment of the costs of such suit, including reasonable attorney's fees.... § 206(d).

Senator Fletcher, Chairman of the Senate Banking and Finance Committee, in introducing Title II of the 1934 Act on the floor of the Senate, stated in explaining the amendment to § 11(e): "This amendment is the most important of all." 78 Cong. Rec. 8669. Among its purposes was to provide "a defense against blackmail suits." Ibid.

Where Congress in those sections of the 1933 Act which expressly conferred a private cause of action for damages, adopted a provision uniformly regarded as designed to deter "strike" or nuisance actions, that fact alone justifies our consideration of such potential in determining the limits of the class of plaintiffs who may sue in an action wholly implied from the language of the 1934 Act.

The potential for possible abuse of the liberal discovery provisions of the Federal Rules of Civil Procedure may likewise exist in this type of case to a greater extent than they do in other litigation. The prospect of extensive deposition of the defendant's officers and associates and the concomitant opportunity for extensive discovery of business documents, is a common occurrence in this and similar types of litigation. To the extent that this process *** permits a plaintiff with a largely groundless claim to simply take up the time of a number of other people, with the right to do so representing an *in terrorem* increment of the settlement value, rather than a reasonably founded hope that the process will reveal relevant evidence, it is a social cost rather than a benefit. ***

Without the *Birnbaum* rule, an action under Rule 10b-5 will turn largely on which oral version of a series of occurrences the jury may decide to credit, and therefore no matter how improbable the allegations of the plaintiff, the case will be virtually impossible to dispose of prior to trial other than by settlement. ***

The *Birnbaum* rule, on the other hand, permits exclusion prior to trial of those plaintiffs who were not themselves purchasers or sellers of the stock in question. The fact of purchase of stock and the fact of sale of stock are generally matters which are verifiable by documentation, and do not depend upon oral recollection, so that failure to qualify under the *Birnbaum* rule is a matter that can normally be established by the defendant either on a motion to dismiss or on a motion for summary judgment. ***

*** The *Birnbaum* rule undoubtedly excludes plaintiffs who have in fact been damaged by violations of Rule 10b-5, and to that extent it is undesirable. But it also separates in a readily demonstrable manner the group of plaintiffs who actually purchased or actually sold, and whose version of the facts is therefore more likely to be believed by the trier of fact, from the vastly larger world of potential plaintiffs who might successfully allege a claim but could seldom succeed in proving it. And this fact is one of its advantages.

The second ground for fear of vexatious litigation is based on the concern that, given the generalized contours of liability, the abolition of the *Birnbaum* rule would throw open to the trier of fact many rather hazy issues of historical fact the proof of which depended almost entirely on oral testimony. We in no way disparage the worth and frequent high value of oral testimony when we say that dangers of its abuse appear to exist in this type of action to a peculiarly high degree. ***

But in the absence of the *Birnbaum* rule, it would be sufficient for a plaintiff to prove that he had failed to purchase or sell stock by reason of a defendant's violation of Rule 10b-5. *** Plaintiff's proof would not be that he purchased or sold stock, a fact which would be capable of documentary verification in most situations, but instead that he decided not to purchase or sell stock. Plaintiff's entire testimony could be dependent upon uncorroborated oral evidence of many of the crucial elements of his claim, and still be sufficient to go to the jury. The jury would not even have the benefit of weighing the plaintiff's version against the defendant's version, since the elements to which the plaintiff would testify would be in many cases totally unknown and unknowable to the defendant. The very real risk in permitting those in respondent's position to sue under Rule 10b-5 is that the door will be open to recovery of substantial damages on the part of one who offers only his own testimony to prove that he ever consulted a prospectus of the issuer, that he paid any attention to it, or that the representations contained in it damaged him. The virtue of the *Birnbaum* rule, simply stated, in this situation, is that it limits the class of plaintiffs to those who have at least dealt in the security to which the prospectus, representation, or omission relates. And their dealing in the security, whether by way of purchase or sale, will generally be an objectively demonstrable fact in an area of the law otherwise very much dependent upon oral testimony. In the absence of the *Birnbaum* doctrine, bystanders to the securities marketing process could await developments on the sidelines without risk, claiming that inaccuracies in disclosure caused nonselling in a falling market and that unduly pessimistic predictions by the issuer followed by a rising market caused them to allow retrospectively golden opportunities to pass. ***

Thus we conclude that what may be called considerations of policy, which we are free to weigh in deciding this case, are by no means entirely on one side of the scale. Taken together with the precedential support for the *Birnbaum* rule over a period of more than 20 years, and the consistency of that rule with what we can glean from the intent of Congress, they lead us to conclude that it is a sound rule and should be followed.

IV

The majority of the Court of Appeals in this case *** noted that prior cases have held that persons owning contractual rights to buy or sell securities are not excluded by the *Birnbaum* rule. Relying on these cases, it concluded that respondent's status as an offeree pursuant to the terms of the consent decree served the same function, for purposes of delimiting the class of plaintiffs, as is normally performed by the requirement of a contractual relationship.

The Court of Appeals recognized, and respondent concedes here, that a well-settled line of authority from this Court establishes that a consent decree is not enforceable directly or in collateral proceedings by those who are not parties to it even though they were intended to be benefited by it. *United States v. Armour & Co.*, 402 U.S. 673 (1971); *Buckeye Coal & R. Co. v. Hocking Valley Co.*, 269 U.S. 42 (1925).

A contract to purchase or sell securities is expressly defined by § 3(a) of the 1934 Act, as a purchase or sale of securities for the purposes of that Act. Unlike respondent, which had no contractual right or duty to purchase Blue Chip's securities, the holders of puts, calls, options, and other contractual rights or duties to purchase or sell securities have been recognized as "purchasers" or "sellers" of securities for purposes of Rule 10b-5, not because of a judicial conclusion that they were similarly situated to "purchasers" or "sellers," but because the definitional provisions of the 1934 Act themselves grant them such a status.

holders of options are purchasers b/c definitions include them

Even if we were to accept the notion that the *Birnbaum* rule could be circumvented on a case-by-case basis through particularized judicial inquiry into the facts surrounding a complaint, this respondent and the members of its alleged class would be unlikely candidates for such a judicially created exception. While the Birnbaum rule has been flexibly interpreted by lower federal courts,[14] we have been unable to locate a single decided case from any court in the 20-odd years of litigation since the *Birnbaum* decision which would support the right of persons who were in the position of respondent here to bring a private suit under Rule 10b-5. Respondent was not only not a buyer or seller of any security but it was not even a shareholder of the corporate petitioners. ***

*** As a purely practical matter, it is doubtless true that respondent and the members of its class, as offerees and recipients of the prospectus of New Blue Chip, are a smaller class of potential plaintiffs than would be all those who might conceivably assert that they obtained information violative of Rule 10b-5 and attributable to the issuer in the financial pages of their local newspaper. And since respondent likewise had a prior connection with some of petitioners as a result of using the trading stamps marketed by Old Blue Chip, and was intended to benefit from the provisions of the consent decree, there is doubtless more likelihood that its managers read and were damaged by the allegedly misleading statements in the prospectus than there would be in a case filed by a complete stranger to the corporation.

But respondent and the members of its class are neither "purchasers" nor "sellers," as those terms are defined in the 1934 Act, and therefore to the extent that their claim of standing to sue were recognized, it would mean that the lesser practical difficulties of corroborating at least some elements of their proof would be regarded as sufficient to avoid the *Birnbaum* rule. While we have noted that these practical difficulties, particularly in the case of a complete

---

14. Our decision in *SEC v. National Securities, Inc.*, 393 U.S. 453 (1969), established that the purchaser-seller rule imposes no limitation on the standing of the SEC to bring actions for injunctive relief under § 10(b) and Rule 10b-5.

stranger to the corporation, support the retention of that rule, they are by no means the only factor which does so.

*** Were we to agree with the Court of Appeals in this case, we would leave the *Birnbaum* rule open to endless case-by-case erosion depending on whether a particular group of plaintiffs was thought by the court in which the issue was being litigated to be sufficiently more discrete than the world of potential purchasers at large to justify an exception. We do not believe that such a shifting and highly fact-oriented disposition of the issue of who may bring a damages claim for violation of Rule 10b-5 is a satisfactory basis for a rule of liability imposed on the conduct of business transactions. Nor is it as consistent as a straightforward application of the *Birnbaum* rule with the other factors which support the retention of that rule. ***

NOTES AND QUESTIONS

*1. **Pretenses Abandoned.*** The Supreme Court has recently disavowed any statutory language underpinning for its *Blue Chip Stamps* holding:

> This Court in *Blue Chip Stamps* relied chiefly and candidly on policy considerations in adopting the [purchaser-seller] limitation. The *Blue Chip Stamps* Court purported to define the scope of a private right of action under Rule 10b-5 – not to define the words "in connection with the purchase or sale."

Merrill Lynch Pierce Fenner & Smith, Inc. v. Dabit, 547 U.S. 71, 84 (2006). The *Dabit* decision addressed the Securities Litigation Uniform Standards Act (the SLUSA), which also contains "in connection with" language. You will encounter *Dabit* (and the SLUSA) in Chapter 6 (Class Actions).

*2. **Curbing Vexatious Private Litigation Then and Now.*** How does the purchaser-seller requirement curb vexatious litigation? At what price? To what extent did the Court act like a legislature in taking this policy consideration into account? Did the Court suggest that policy considerations are always relevant when construing Rule 10b-5?

The *Blue Chip Stamps* Court chose to curb vexatious private litigation twenty years before the enactment of the PSLRA. With the PSLRA on the books, should the Court revisit the question whether the purchaser-seller requirement still has more benefits than costs? What would be your answer to this question?

*3. **Standing to Sue For Contract Holders.*** The Court upheld standing to sue for those holding a contract to buy or sell securities based on the Exchange Act's definitions of "purchase" and "sale." See Exchange Act Section 3(a)(13) - (14) (defining "purchase" to include "a contract to purchase" and "sale" to include "a contract to sell"). Is this conclusion unavoidable as a matter of statutory construction? Does it follow from the Court's policy analysis?

*4. **Oral Contracts.*** In *Wharf (Holdings) Ltd. v. United Int'l Holdings, Inc.*, 532 U.S. 588 (2001), the Supreme Court held that a contract to buy or sell securities provides standing to sue under Rule 10b-5 even if it is oral:

> *Blue Chip Stamps* said nothing to suggest that oral purchases or sales fall outside the scope of the Act. Rather, the Court's concern was about "the abuse potential and proof problems inherent in suits by investors who neither bought nor sold, but asserted they would have traded absent fraudulent conduct by

> others." *United States v. O'Hagan*, 521 U.S. 642, 664 (1997). Such a "potential purchase" claim would rest on facts, including the plaintiff's state of mind, that might be "totally unknown and unknowable to the defendant," depriving the jury of "the benefit of weighing the plaintiff's version against the defendant's version." *Blue Chip Stamps*, supra, at 746. An actual sale, even if oral, would not create this problem, because both parties would be able to testify as to whether the relevant events had occurred.
>
> Neither is there any other convincing reason to interpret the Act to exclude oral contracts as a class. The Act itself says that it applies to "any contract" for the purchase or sale of a security. [Exchange Act §§ 3(a)(13),(14)]. Oral contracts for the sale of securities are sufficiently common that the Uniform Commercial Code and statutes of frauds in every State now consider them enforceable. Any exception for oral sales of securities would significantly limit the Act's coverage, thereby undermining its basic purposes.
>
> Wharf makes a related but narrower argument that the Act does not encompass oral contracts of sale that are unenforceable under state law. But we do not reach that issue. The Court of Appeals held that Wharf's sale *** was not covered by the then-applicable Colorado statute of frauds, and hence was enforceable under state law. Though Wharf disputes the correctness of that holding, we ordinarily will not consider such a state-law issue, and we decline to do so here.

532 U.S. at 594-96. By allowing an oral contract to give rise to standing to sue, has the *Wharf* Court undermined the policy of curbing vexatious litigation articulated in *Blue Chip Stamps*?

*5. **Exceptions?*** Does the Court in *Blue Chip Stamps* shut the door on all exceptions to the purchaser-seller requirement? In thinking about this question, revisit Part IV of the opinion, which acknowledges that there are at least plausible arguments for creating an exception on behalf of the plaintiffs in this case. Is it significant that the Court chose as its vehicle for upholding the purchaser-seller requirement a case in which such arguments could be made? You will have the opportunity to consider these matters further in connection with the next case.

COWIN v. BRESLER

741 F.2d 410 (D.C. Cir. 1984)

ROBERT H. BORK, CIRCUIT JUDGE:

Bresler & Reiner, Inc. is a publicly-owned company incorporated in the State of Delaware and engaged in the development and management of residential and commercial properties in the District of Columbia. In late 1980, Daniel Cowin, a Bresler & Reiner shareholder, sued the company and its directors on his own behalf. Cowin has a minority interest in the company. The individual directors-appellees, with their families, own in excess of 79% of the company's stock. Appellees Bresler and Reiner together hold more than 70% of the company's outstanding shares, and their control of the corporation is undisputed.

The thrust of Cowin's charges is that the appellees have manipulated the business for their personal profit at the expense of the minority shareholders.

P says Ds manipulated business for their personal profit at expense of minority S/Hs

The complaint alleges numerous instances of corporate mismanagement, fraud, and self-dealing, all in breach of the common law fiduciary duty owed by the directors of the company to the appellant as a shareholder. ***

The remainder of the complaint charges appellees with violations of the federal securities laws ***. Specifically, Cowin claims that Bresler and Reiner caused the company to "disseminate reports to the public shareholders which were materially deceptive" and concealed material information in violation of Rule 10b-5 and section 10(b) ***

Appellant's federal claims raise novel questions under the Securities Exchange Act of 1934. Although Cowin did not buy or sell his stock in connection with the allegedly misleading reports issued by the company, he relies upon section 10(b) of the Act and Rule 10b-5 in seeking to prevent appellees from "depress[ing] the value of [his] stock and ... eliminat[ing] the public market in that stock through dissemination of deceptive statements." In short, appellant claims not that he was wrongfully induced to buy or sell stock by appellees' misrepresentations but rather that his stock was made less valuable by appellees' misrepresentations to the investing public generally. He does not seek damages but an injunction requiring an end to the alleged misrepresentations and disclosure of past misrepresentations. It is clear from *Blue Chip Stamps v. Manor Drug Stores,* 421 U.S. 723 (1975), that appellant could not maintain an action for damages under section 10(b) or Rule 10b-5. The question before us is whether he may bring suit for an injunction. ***

Cowin argues that the purchaser-seller limitation does not apply to actions seeking equitable relief. He points to a pre-*Blue Chip* line of cases holding that a private party who seeks only injunctive relief need not have bought or sold securities to sue under Rule 10b-5, see, e.g., *Kahan v. Rosenstiel,* 424 F.2d 161 (3d Cir.1970); *Mutual Shares Corp. v. Genesco, Inc.,* 384 F.2d 540 (2d Cir.1967), and contends that the "exception" to the purchaser-seller rule in those cases survives *Blue Chip* because the Supreme Court limited its holding in that case to private damage actions. We appear to be the first court of appeals squarely to address this issue, and we think *Blue Chip* cannot be so limited. ***

The relaxed standing requirement urged on us by appellant would be contrary to the rationale of section 10(b) and Rule 10b-5 as perceived by the Supreme Court in *Blue Chip.* While it may be possible to discern differences between an action for damages and a suit for an injunction, most of the Supreme Court's argument in *Blue Chip* applies quite as much to the latter as to the former. The scope of section 10(b) and Rule 10b-5 is limited to fraud "in connection with the purchase or sale of a security." Congress was asked on two different occasions to expand the jurisdictional reach of those provisions but chose not to. In contrast, Congress did choose to define the scope of other provisions in the 1933 and 1934 Acts in terms that clearly reflected a broader jurisdictional reach. Congress also limited standing in those instances where it did create express remedies under the Act to a class of persons including only purchasers or sellers. Thus, the purchaser-seller limitation is "sufficiently supported by the statutory structure of the Securities Act." The Supreme Court, 1974 Term, supra, 89 Harv. L. Rev. at 269. These features also constrain us to accept, in the context of an injunctive suit, the common meaning of the terms "purchase or sale" and reject an expansive construction of the Rule, as *Blue Chip* did for damage actions.

Attempting to fashion a different concept of standing for cases like this would involve us in distinctions altogether too awkward to be persuasive. As *Blue Chip* noted, the "wording of § 10(b) ... is surely badly strained when construed to provide a cause of action, not to purchasers and sellers of securities, but to the world at large." 421 U.S. at 733 n. 5. The Court also stated that it "would indeed be anomalous to impute to Congress an intention to expand the plaintiff class for a judicially implied cause of action beyond the bounds it delineated for comparable express causes of action." Id. at 737.

Our analysis might well end here. However, because *Blue Chip* went beyond statutory analysis to examine certain "policy considerations," 421 U.S. at 737, Cowin argues that relaxing the purchaser-seller requirement in his case is proper because that would not contradict the several policies relied upon by *Blue Chip*. Several lower courts, including the lower court in this case, have distinguished the Supreme Court's opinion in this fashion. See, e.g., *Fuchs v. Swanton Corp.*, 482 F.Supp. 83, 89-90 (S.D.N.Y.1979); *Hundahl v. United Benefit Life Insurance Co.,* 465 F.Supp. 1349, 1357-59 (N.D.Tex.1979).

If we thought this question open, we might conclude that injunctive suits present many of the same problems of vexatiousness, "strike" suits, abuse of discovery, and the like that damage actions do. We need not decide that, however, for we think the approach appellant suggests is foreclosed by *Blue Chip* itself. There, the plaintiff had contended that two policies articulated by the Court—the difficulties in corroborating the elements of Rule 10b-5 proof and the potential for an unlimited class of plaintiffs—were simply not raised on the facts of the case. If plaintiffs were allowed to sue, the Court said, "it would mean that the lesser practical difficulties of corroborating at least some elements of their proof would be regarded as sufficient to avoid the *Birnbaum* rule." 421 U.S. at 754-55. The Court rejected this result stating that while its decision to affirm *Birnbaum* was in part based on these "practical difficulties," the consistency of the rule with "the statutes involved and their legislative history [were] likewise bases for retaining the rule." Id. at 755. To take such arguments into account "would leave the *Birnbaum* rule open to endless case-by-case erosion." Id. Thus, while "policy considerations" did play a role in the *Blue Chip* decision, when those policy considerations were inconsistent with the retention of a flat rule and with the other grounds on which the decision rested—the statute and its history—they were not strong enough to create an exception. ***

NOTES AND QUESTIONS

1. Unlikely Vehicle? Was there anything about *Cowin* that made it an unlikely vehicle for establishing an injunction exception to the purchaser-seller requirement?

injunction exception is open for question in other circuits

2. Open Question. *Cowin* notwithstanding, the viability of the injunction exception remains an open question in other circuits. See, e.g., *Trump Hotels & Casino Resorts, Inc. v. Mirage Resorts, Inc.,* 140 F.3d 478, 486 (3d Cir. 1998); *Advanced Resources Int'l, Inc. v. Tri-Star Petroleum Co.,* 4 F.3d 327, 332 (4th Cir. 1993). What are the arguments for retaining this exception in the wake of *Blue Chip Stamps*? What are the arguments against retention? See generally

Trustcash Holdings, Inc. v. Moss, 668 F. Supp. 2d 650, 658-59 (D.N. J. 2009) (identifying arguments for and against the injunction exception and then concluding that the arguments against are "stronger").

3. Forced Seller Exception. Another exception to the purchaser-seller requirement that was on the books prior to *Blue Chip Stamps* involved forced sellers. Consider *Vine v. Beneficial Fin. Co.*, 374 F.2d 627 (2d Cir. 1967), which involved an alleged multi-part scheme consisting of a deceptive tender offer followed by a short form merger that squeezed out those who had not previously tendered their shares. The plaintiff had not, however, tendered his own shares. Nor had he, at the time of the lawsuit, exchanged his shares for cash pursuant to the short form merger. The court nonetheless held that he had standing to sue under Rule 10b-5:

> [O]nce the conditions for a short form merger had been achieved, appellant's rights in his own stock were frozen. He had and still has only the options of exchanging his stock *** pursuant to appellee's offer, or pursuing his right of appraisal, which would result in cash from appellee. *** Since, in order to realize any value for his stock, appellant must exchange the shares for money from appellee, as a practical matter appellant must eventually become a party to a "sale" *** [R]equiring him to do so as a condition to suit seems a needless formality.

Id. at 634. Lower courts are currently divided about whether the "forced seller" exception survives *Blue Chip Stamps.* Compare *7547 Corp. v. Parker & Parsley Dev. Partners, L.P.*, 38 F.3d 211, 229 (5th Cir. 1994) (exception survives) with *Isquith v. Caremark Int'l, Inc.*, 136 F.3d 531, 536 (7th Cir. 1998) (exception unlikely to have survived). What arguments support its survival? What arguments support its elimination? See generally Eric C. Chaffee, Standing Under Section 10(b) and Rule 10b-5: The Continued Validity of the Forced Seller Exception to the Purchaser-Seller Requirement, 11 U. Pa. J. Bus. L. 843 (2009).

4. De Facto Seller Exception. Likewise granted standing to sue under Rule 10b-5 prior to *Blue Chip Stamps* were "de facto sellers"—trust beneficiaries who alleged fraud in connection with trades made by their trustees. See, e.g., *James v. Gerber Prods. Co.*, 483 F.2d 944, 948-50 (6th Cir. 1973); *Heyman v. Heyman*, 356 F. Supp. 958, 965 (S.D.N.Y. 1973).

Does the de facto seller exception survive *Blue Chip Stamps*? Does the answer turn on whether the beneficiary participates in the investment decisions in question? Compare *Wendt v. Handler, Thayer & Duggan, LLC*, 613 F. Supp. 2d 1021, 1028-29 (N.D. Ill. 2009) (participation essential to survival of exception) with *Ross v. Abercrombie & Fitch Co.*, 257 F.R.D. 435, 148-50 (S.D. Ohio 2009) (participation not essential).

5. The Section 29(b) Alternative. At least some plaintiffs who are unable to satisfy the purchaser-seller requirement may nonetheless have an action under Section 29(b) of the Exchange Act, which reads in pertinent part:

> Every contract made in violation of any provision of this Act or rule or regulation thereunder, and every contract *** the performance of which involves the violation of *** any provision of this Act or rule or regulation thereunder, shall be void ***.

According to the Supreme Court, Section 29(b) "confers a 'right to rescind' a contract void under the criteria of the statute." *Transam. Mortgage Advisors, Inc. v. Lewis*, 444 U.S. 11, 19 (1979) (quoting *Mills v. Electric Auto-Lite Co.*, 396 U.S. 375, 388 (1970)).

To obtain this right, the plaintiff must show that "(1) the contract involved a 'prohibited transaction,' (2) he is in contractual privity with the defendant, and (3) he is 'in the class of persons the Act was designed to protect.' " *Reg'l Props., Inc. v. Fin. & Real Estate Consulting Co.*, 678 F.2d 552, 559 (5th Cir. 1982). See *Berkeley Inv. Group, Ltd. v. Colkitt*, 455 F.3d 195, 205 (3d Cir. 2006) (upholding these elements and remanding for determination as to whether they were satisfied); *Frati v. Saltzstein*, 2011 WL 1002417 at *5-*6 (S.D.N. Y. 2011) (upholding these elements and concluding that the plaintiff had failed to state a claim). See generally Samuel H. Gruenbaum & Marc I. Steinberg, Section 29(b) of the Securities Exchange Act of 1934: A Viable Remedy Awakened, 48 Geo. Wash. L. Rev. 1 (1979).

In *Regional*, the court found these elements satisfied by a real estate developer which wished to rescind its contracts with a securities broker for the marketing of limited partnerships. Because the broker had not complied with the Exchange Act's broker registration requirement, performance of the contracts constituted a "prohibited transaction." *Reg'l Props., Inc.*, 678 F. 2d at 561. The court held that the developer was within the class of people the Act was designed to protect even though he was not an investor:

> The statute does not in terms limit the class of persons who may invoke its contractual voidness provisions to investors. *** If a party to these contracts could not attack them, it would be yet more difficult to find reason to permit assault by the nonparty issuers and investors whom, according to *** [the defendant], the Act was designed to protect.

Id. at 561. Why couldn't the plaintiff in *Regional* have invoked his status as a contract holder and sued under Rule 10b-5?

PROBLEM 2-16

Endring Corporation was a large publicly traded company with 3,000 employees and a longstanding track record of profitability. In 1990, the company's board of directors established the Endring Retirement Stock Fund. Employees were entitled to contribute a portion of their salaries to the Fund (which was invested exclusively in Endring stock) and they retained the right to liquidate their contributions in whole or in part whenever they chose to do so.

Last year, Endring assured the world in general and their employees in particular that the company was strong, its future bright. In reality, a small circle of senior executives were cooking the books to hide the fact that the company was in dire straits. Early this year, the truth about Endring emerged, and the market price of Endring stock plummeted to near zero. The numerous employees who had made contributions to the Fund were aghast that important information had been withheld from them. They have said that if they had known the company's actual situation, they would have liquidated their Fund accounts. Do they have standing to sue under Rule 10b-5?

PROBLEM 2-17

Amy sent Dewey, her broker, a check to cover the cost of stock in several companies, all of which Dewey had told her were great investments. Amy's monthly statement from Dewey itemized these purchases, but the companies were in fact altogether fictitious. Amy has now discovered the fraud. Does she have standing to sue under Rule 10b-5? What about an action under Section 29(b)?

F. CAUSATION

Rule 10b-5 has two causation requirements: reliance (also known as transaction causation) and loss causation. Both causation requirements apply only to the implied private action and do not come into play when the plaintiff is either the SEC or the DOJ.

1. The Reliance Requirement

The reliance requirement focuses on whether the plaintiff relied on the defendant's fraud when buying or selling the securities in question. Courts imported this requirement from tort law in order to restrict the implied private action:

> [T]he aim of *** rule [10b-5] *** is to qualify *** the doctrine of caveat emptor—not to establish a scheme of investors' insurance. Assuredly, to abandon the requirement of reliance would be to facilitate *** proof of *** fraud ***. But this strikes us as an inadequate reason for reading out of the rule so basic an element of tort law as the principle of causation in fact.

List v. Fashion Park, Inc., 340 F.2d 457, 463 (2d Cir. 1965). See, e.g., *Wilson v. Comtech Telecomm. Corp.*, 648 F.2d 88, 94 (2d Cir. 1981) (denying recovery to a plaintiff who relied on his broker's advice in making his purchases rather than on the defendant's fraud).

To ease the burden on plaintiffs, courts presume reliance under various circumstances. The presumptions facilitate class actions by eliminating the need for mini-trials on the reliance of each plaintiff. The presumptions are, however, applicable to individual actions as well.

We examine (i) the *Affiliated Ute* presumption; (ii) the fraud-on-the-market presumption; and (iii) the fraud-created-the-market presumption. We conclude our study of reliance by considering when the plaintiff must also show that her reliance was justifiable.

a. The Affiliated Ute *Presumption*

This presumption originated in the Supreme Court's decision in *Affiliated Ute Citizens v. United States*, 406 U.S. 128 (1972). In that case the plaintiffs, Native Americans of the Ute tribe, brought a Rule 10b-5 action against a bank and two bank employees. The bank served as the transfer agent for the stock of the corporation established to allocate tribal assets. The plaintiffs alleged that the defendants had purchased their shares without disclosing that they had established a secondary market in which the stock traded at a higher price. The Court held that the plaintiffs could maintain their action without having to prove that they sold their shares in reliance on what the defendants had failed to tell them:

> The defendants may not stand mute while they facilitate the mixed-bloods' sales to those seeking to profit in the non-Indian market the defendants had developed and encouraged ***. The sellers had the right to know that the defendants were in a position to gain financially from their sales and that their shares were selling for a higher price in that market.
>
> Under the circumstances of this case, involving primarily a failure to disclose, positive proof of reliance is not a prerequisite to recovery. All that is necessary is that the facts withheld be material ***. This obligation to disclose and this withholding of a material fact establish the requisite element of causation in fact.

Id. at 153-54.

NOTES AND QUESTIONS

1. ***A Presumption is Born.*** The well-established consensus is that *Affiliated Ute* creates a rebuttable presumption of reliance. See, e.g., *Stoneridge Inv. Partners, LLC v. Scientific-Atlanta, Inc.*, 552 U.S. 148, 159 (2008). It is of course true that *Affiliated Ute* itself did not make explicit the existence of a presumption. Cf. *Chris-Craft Indus., Inc. v. Piper Aircraft Corp.*, 480 F.2d 341, 400 (2d Cir. 1973) (Mansfield, J., concurring and dissenting) (maintaining that by failing to "expressly or impliedly speak in terms of a 'presumption,'" *Affiliated Ute* indicated that reliance had been established as a matter of law).

2. ***The "[C]ircumstances" to Which the Presumption Applies.*** What were the "circumstances" in *Affiliated Ute* that prompted the Court to spare the plaintiffs the need to prove reliance? According to one view, the circumstances were that "the parties had dealt directly with each other and there clearly was a duty of disclosure owed." *Laventhall v. Gen. Dynamics Corp.*, 704 F.2d 407, 413 n. 4 (8th Cir. 1983).

The most widely articulated view of the circumstances, however, is that the fraud in question involves an omission, rather than a misrepresentation. Although unstated by *Affiliated Ute,* the rationale for presuming reliance in an omissions case is the "unique difficulty of proving reliance on a failure to disclose material information of which the plaintiff did not know." *Grubb v. FDIC*, 868 F.2d 1151, 1163 (10th Cir. 1989).

Is it truly so much easier to prove reliance on a misrepresentation? Does the presumption apply in cases in which omissions and misrepresentations are both present? Consider these questions in connection with the next case.

BINDER v. GILLESPIE

184 F.3d 1059 (9th Cir. 1999)

OTTO R. SKOPIL, JR., CIRCUIT JUDGE:

Albert Binder brought this action against Aqua Vie Beverage Corporation (AVBC), various AVBC officers and directors, and the accounting firm of Deloitte & Touche (Deloitte), asserting, on his own behalf and as a representative for a class of investors, that defendants violated federal and state securities laws. The district court decertified the class and declined to exercise supplemental jurisdiction over the related state law class claims. *** Final judgments were entered pursuant to Federal Rule of Civil Procedure 54(b). We affirm.

Tom Gillespie and Marie Mullen Gillespie formed AVBC in 1991 by purchasing a publicly owned shell corporation and merging it with their Hawaii-based beverage company, KWC, Inc. They moved their operations to Sun Valley, Idaho. Shortly thereafter, Diane Karban joined the company as Chief Financial Officer and Deloitte was hired as the company's accounting firm. AVBC stock soon began trading publicly on the over-the-counter (OTC) market.

In the summer of 1991, Cottell Bottling agreed to manufacture, and Golden Brands agreed to distribute, AVBC's product—"lightly flavored," noncarbonated spring water. Industry publications touted AVBC as a promising, if speculative, investment, and AVBC stock sold for $2.75 per share by August. On September 24, 1991, Binder purchased 3000 shares at $4.00 per share. A month later, AVBC's bid price reached its peak at $4.50 per share.

AVBC began production in 1992. Chief of quality control John Good, however, warned CEO Tom Gillespie and consultant Gordon Sim that there was instability in the product formula. Sixty days after it was bottled, the water turned brown. AVBC adjusted the formula but continued to experience problems with the product's shelf life. By the end of the year, AVBC was forced to repurchase the defective water from Golden Brands, which eventually resigned as AVBC's distributor and sued for past-due debts.

In 1993, AVBC struggled to raise funds and to establish a distribution network for its product. On December 29, 1993, Binder sold his 3000 shares at less than one dollar per share. In 1994, AVBC suspended operations, and Binder filed this action. *** In February 1995, the action against AVBC was stayed pending Chapter 11 bankruptcy proceedings. ***

The district court reasoned that the class would have to satisfy the reliance element through a presumption; otherwise individual questions of reliance would predominate over questions common to the class. See Fed. R. Civ. P. 23(b)(3); *Basic Inc. v. Levinson,* 485 U.S. 224, 242 (1988) (noting that individualized proof of reliance by each class member would preclude a class action). The court concluded that no presumption was available under the facts of the case, and, accordingly, decertified the class[.] ***

Binder argues that the class is eligible for a presumption of reliance pursuant to *Affiliated Ute Citizens v. United States,* 406 U.S. 128, 153-54 (1972). Such a presumption is generally available to plaintiffs alleging violations of section 10(b) based on omissions of material fact. The district court, however, characterized Binder's action as "not primarily an omissions case" and held that the *Affiliated Ute* presumption was unavailable. We agree with the district court's characterization of Binder's action. Binder's complaint contains both allegations of omissions and misrepresentations, and at the very least, must be characterized, as the district court noted, as "a mixed case of misstatements and omissions."

We have applied the *Affiliated Ute* presumption to cases that "are, or can be, cast in omission or non-disclosure terms." *Blackie v. Barrack,* 524 F.2d 891, 905 (9th Cir.1975). We have not squarely decided, however, whether the presumption may be invoked in a case involving misrepresentations or both omissions and misrepresentations. Nevertheless, in *Blackie,* we embraced the presumption because of the difficulty of proving "a speculative negative"—that the plaintiff relied on what was not said. *Blackie,* 524 F.2d at 908. This suggests to us that *Affiliated Ute* should be confined to cases that primarily allege omissions.

Most circuits have limited the presumption accordingly. A handful of circuits have addressed mixed cases, concluding that the preferred approach is to do as the magistrate judge did here and "analytically characterize [the] action as either primarily a nondisclosure case (which would make the presumption applicable), or a positive misrepresentation case." *Finkel v. Docutel/Olivetti Corp.,* 817 F.2d 356, 359 (5th Cir.1987); see also *Austin v. Loftsgaarden,* 675 F.2d 168, 178 n. 21 (8th Cir.1982).

We agree with these circuits that the *Affiliated Ute* presumption should not be applied to cases that allege both misstatements and omissions unless the case can be characterized as one that primarily alleges omissions. *** Accordingly, we agree with the district court that Binder's plaintiff class is not entitled to the *Affiliated Ute* presumption of reliance. ***

STEPHEN R. REINHARDT, CIRCUIT JUDGE, DISSENTING IN PART:

Because the plaintiffs are entitled to a presumption of reliance under the doctrine of *Affiliated Ute Citizens v. United States,* 406 U.S. 128, 153-54 (1972), I would reverse the district court's decision to decertify the class of investors represented by Binder. I therefore respectfully dissent.

In today's decision, the majority decides that the *Affiliated Ute* presumption does not apply to cases involving both material misrepresentations and material omissions, "unless the case can be characterized as one that primarily alleges omissions." In so holding, the majority resolves a question that we have previously, and explicitly, reserved: "whether *Affiliated Ute Citizens* applies equally to misrepresentations." *Kramas v. Security Gas & Oil, Inc.,* 672 F.2d 766, 769 n. 2 (9th Cir.1982). To reach this conclusion, the majority simply adopts the procedure followed by two other circuits. See *Finkel v. Docutel/Olivetti Corp.,* 817 F.2d 356, 359 (5th Cir.1987); *Cavalier Carpets, Inc. v. Caylor,* 746 F.2d 749, 756 (11th Cir.1984). Those circuits have determined that, in mixed cases, it is necessary to "analytically characterize [the] action as either primarily a nondisclosure case ... or a positive misrepresentation case." *Finkel,* 817 F.2d at 359. I believe, however, that the logic behind the *Affiliated Ute* decision and the reasoning contained in our decisions implementing *Affiliated Ute* make it clear that the presumption applies equally to misrepresentations, and that it is irrelevant whether the case is primarily a misrepresentations case or primarily an omissions case. In either event, the plaintiff is entitled to a presumption of reliance.

In *Blackie v. Barrack,* 524 F.2d 891, 908 (9th Cir.1975), on which the majority relies, we examined a material omissions case in which the plaintiff bought stock based in part on material omissions made by the defendant. We examined the *Affiliated Ute* rule and concluded that the *Blackie* plaintiffs did not need to prove reliance. We explained that such proof would require "proof of a speculative negative." Id. In other words, to establish reliance, the plaintiff would have to prove the following proposition: "I would not have bought had I known." Id. We rejected such a requirement because:

> Direct proof would inevitably be somewhat pro-forma, and impose a difficult evidentiary burden, because addressed to a speculative possibility in an area where motivations are complex and difficult to determine.... Here, the requirement [of proving reliance] is redundant—the same causal nexus can be adequately established indirectly, by proof of materiality coupled with the common sense that a stock purchaser does not ordinarily seek to purchase a loss in the form of artificially inflated stock.

Id. Because *Blackie* was a pure omissions case, we did not have occasion to determine whether the same reasoning would apply to material misrepresentations.

One year later, however, in *Little v. First California Co.,* 532 F.2d 1302, 1305 n. 4 (9th Cir.1976), we stated the rather obvious proposition that "[t]he categories of 'omission' and 'misrepresentation' are not mutually exclusive." As we wrote:

> All misrepresentations are also nondisclosures, at least to the extent that there is a failure to disclose which facts in the representation are not true. Thus, the failure to report an expense item on an income statement, when such a failure is material in the *Affiliated Ute* sense, can be characterized as (a) an omission of a material expense item, (b) a misrepresentation of income, or (c) both.

Id. This observation, besides being binding upon us as a matter of law, is clearly correct as a matter of logic. Omissions and misrepresentations both deprive the investor of truthful information relevant to the investment decision, and both result in the artificial pricing of a stock.

Most important for our purposes here, it is *equally* difficult to establish reliance on a misrepresentation and on an omission. While a plaintiff in an omissions case—absent the *Affiliated Ute* presumption—would bear the daunting task of proving 'I would not have bought/sold had I known what you failed to tell me' see *Blackie,* 524 F.2d at 908, the plaintiff in a misrepresentation case bears the equally daunting burden of proving 'I would not have bought/sold had I known what you failed to tell me; namely, the truth.' In either case, the plaintiff must prove that he would have acted differently if he had known something that he did not actually know, i.e., the full truth.

In an omissions case, the plaintiff does not know the truth because the defendant said nothing; in a misrepresentations case the plaintiff does not know the truth because the defendant lied. But as far as the plaintiff's ability to demonstrate reliance, this is a distinction without a difference. In either case, the plaintiff must attempt to prove that he would have acted differently had he known the truth. The evidentiary burden is therefore equally difficult in either case, and there is no logical reason to afford the presumption of reliance to plaintiffs in omissions cases but not in misrepresentations cases. The rule we announced in *Blackie,* that the "causal nexus can be adequately established indirectly, by proof of materiality coupled with the common sense that a stock purchaser does not ordinarily seek to purchase a loss in the form of artificially inflated stock," id., applies with equal force of logic to misrepresentations. ***

*** I would therefore hold that plaintiffs in mixed cases are entitled to the *Affiliated Ute* presumption of reliance whether the case is primarily an omissions case or primarily a misrepresentations case. Accordingly, whether this case is properly classified simply as a mixed omissions and misrepresentations case, or as "primarily" a misrepresentations case, I would hold that the Binder class was entitled to a presumption of reliance, and would therefore reverse the decertification of the class.[3]

NOTES AND QUESTIONS

1. ***Taking the Complaint At Face Value.*** According to *Binder*, the trial judge must ascertain whether the complaint alleges "primarily" omissions instead of a combination of omissions and misrepresentations (or misrepresentations alone). In deciding upon the correct characterization, must the court take the complaint at face value? Cf. *Cavalier Carpets, Inc. v. Caylor*, 746 F.2d 749, 757 (11th Cir. 1984) (noting that the complaint alleged three omissions and three misrepresentations and therefore was "not primarily an omission case"); *In re Enron Corp. Sec. Deriv. & ERISA Litig.*, 2006 WL 4381143 at *26 & n.53 (S.D.Tex. 2006) (observing that because many of the alleged misrepresentations did not state a cause of action, "this case is primarily one of omissions"). If so, what impact is such an approach likely to have on the drafting of complaints?

2. ***An Alternative Approach.*** Rather than taking the complaint at face value, other courts attempt to dig deeper to discover the true essence of the fraud allegations. Consider *Sharp v. Coopers & Lybrand*, 649 F.2d 175 (3d Cir. 1981). There the plaintiffs alleged fraud in an accounting firm's tax opinion letter issued in connection with the sale of limited partnerships by Westmoreland Minerals Corp. (WMC). Acknowledging that the letter contained both omissions and misrepresentations, the court found the *Affiliated Ute* presumption applicable based on the following reasoning:

> We conclude that the proper approach *** is to analyze the plaintiff's allegations, in light of the likely proof at trial, and determine the most reasonable placement of the burden of proof of reliance. ***
>
> We agree with the district court that the burden in this case should fall on Coopers & Lybrand. The opinion letter issued by Coopers & Lybrand was intended to influence the investment decisions of persons interested in WMC partnerships. *** [Coopers & Lybrand] undoubtedly foresaw that it would have that effect. As in *Affiliated Ute,* Coopers & Lybrand by its action facilitated the transactions at issue but failed to disclose certain facts. Its misrepresentation of other facts should not alleviate its burden of proving nonreliance.

---

3. A different question, one not presented here, is whether plaintiffs are entitled to a presumption of reliance in pure misrepresentation cases. *** In light of the logic of *Affiliated Ute,* and for the reasons I have outlined above, I would hold (were I called upon to reach the question) that plaintiffs are entitled to a presumption of reliance even in pure misrepresentation cases.

Id. at 188-89. See *Starr v. Georgeson Shareholder, Inc.*, 412 F.3d 103, 109 n.5 (2d Cir. 2005) (concluding that omissions did not predominate because the plaintiff "focuses most heavily on the allegedly misleading misstatements" and because his "principal objection to the omissions *** is that the omissions exacerbated the misleading nature of the affirmative statements"). What are the advantages and disadvantages of this approach?

3. Misrepresentations Alone. The dissenting opinion in *Binder* endorsed a presumption of reliance even in pure misrepresentation cases, a position that has attracted scant support. See *In re Interbank Funding Corp. Sec. Litig.*, 629 F.3d 213, 219-20 (D.C. Cir. 2010) (noting that "[n]o court of appeals has applied the *Affiliated Ute* presumption in a case involving a claim that primarily alleges affirmative misrepresentations"). Does the dissent's position nonetheless have some merit?

How likely is it that the stated disagreements between the dissenting and the majority opinions mask unstated disagreements about the value of private securities actions?

PROBLEM 2-18

Healthy Foods, Inc. produces frozen vegetarian entrees for sale in grocery stores. Its brochures seek to lure new investors with the statement that "our research department is always in the process of developing multiple new entrees." In fact, its research "department" consists of one person who focuses on one new entree project at a time, while simultaneously considering which of many other new projects he will move to next. Kim received a Healthy Foods brochure in the mail and thereafter bought stock in the company. She now wishes to bring a Rule 10b-5 action that challenges the brochure as fraudulent. Would she be entitled to a presumption of reliance based on *Affiliated Ute*?

b. The Fraud-on-the-Market Presumption

The following decision provides an alternative presumption available regardless of whether the alleged fraud involves omissions, misrepresentations, or a combination. The engine for the vast majority of Rule 10b-5 class actions, it arguably ranks as the most important securities decision of our time.

BASIC INC. v. LEVINSON

485 U.S. 224 (1988)

JUSTICE HAROLD A. BLACKMUN:

[*The facts of this case were set out supra in Section B.2 of this Chapter in the discussion of materiality. In brief, the plaintiffs brought a class action against Basic Inc., the shares of which were listed on the New York Stock Exchange. At issue were Basic's three public statements denying that it was involved in merger negotiations. After holding those denials to have been material misstatements, the Court turned to reliance and fraud-on-the-market.*]

IV

A

We turn to the question of reliance and the fraud-on-the-market theory. Succinctly put:

> The fraud-on-the-market theory is based on the hypothesis that, in an open and developed securities market, the price of a company's stock is determined by the available material information regarding the company and its business.... Misleading statements will therefore defraud purchasers of stock even if the purchasers do not directly rely on the misstatements.... The causal connection between the defendants' fraud and the plaintiffs' purchase of stock in such a case is no less significant than in a case of direct reliance on misrepresentations."

Peil v. Speiser, 806 F.2d 1154, 1160-1161 (CA3 1986). Our task, of course, is not to assess the general validity of the theory, but to consider whether it was proper for the courts below to apply a rebuttable presumption of reliance, supported in part by the fraud-on-the-market theory.

This case required resolution of several common questions of law and fact concerning the falsity or misleading nature of the three public statements made by Basic, the presence or absence of scienter, and the materiality of the misrepresentations, if any. In their amended complaint, the named plaintiffs alleged that in reliance on Basic's statements they sold their shares of Basic stock in the depressed market created by petitioners. *** Requiring proof of individualized reliance from each member of the proposed plaintiff class effectively would have prevented respondents from proceeding with a class action, since individual issues then would have overwhelmed the common ones. The District Court found that the presumption of reliance created by the fraud-on-the-market theory provided "a practical resolution to the problem of balancing the substantive requirement of proof of reliance in securities cases against the procedural requisites of [Federal Rule of Civil Procedure] 23." The District Court thus concluded that with reference to each public statement and its impact upon the open market for Basic shares, common questions predominated over individual questions, as required by Federal Rules of Civil Procedure 23(a)(2) and (b)(3).

Petitioners and their *amici* complain that the fraud-on-the-market theory effectively eliminates the requirement that a plaintiff asserting a claim under Rule 10b-5 prove reliance. They note that reliance is and long has been an element of common-law fraud, see, e.g., Restatement (Second) of Torts § 525 (1977); Prosser and Keeton on Law of Torts § 108 (5th ed. 1984), and argue that because the analogous express right of action includes a reliance requirement, see, e.g., § 18(a) of the 1934 Act, so too must an action implied under § 10(b).

We agree that reliance is an element of a Rule 10b-5 cause of action. See *Ernst & Ernst v. Hochfelder,* 425 U.S. [196, 206 (1976)] (quoting Senate Report). Reliance provides the requisite causal connection between a defendant's misrepresentation and a plaintiff's injury. See, e.g., *Wilson v. Comtech Telecommunications Corp.,* 648 F.2d 88, 92 (CA2 1981); *List v. Fashion Park, Inc.,* 340 F.2d 457, 462 (CA2 1965). There is, however, more than one way to demonstrate the causal connection. Indeed, we previously have dispensed with a requirement of positive proof of reliance, where a duty to disclose material information had been breached, concluding that the necessary nexus between the plaintiffs' injury and the defendant's wrongful conduct had been established. See *Affiliated Ute Citizens v. United States,* 406 U.S. [128, 153-154 (1972)]. Similarly, we did not require proof that material omissions or misstatements in a proxy statement decisively affected voting, because the proxy solicitation itself, rather than the defect in the solicitation materials, served as an essential link in the transaction. See *Mills v. Electric Auto-Lite Co.,* 396 U.S. 375, 384-385 (1970).

The modern securities markets, literally involving millions of shares changing hands daily, differ from the face-to-face transactions contemplated by early fraud cases,[21] and our understanding of Rule 10b-5's reliance requirement must encompass these differences.[22]

> In face-to-face transactions, the inquiry into an investor's reliance upon information is into the subjective pricing of that information by that investor. With the presence of a market, the market is interposed between seller and buyer and, ideally, transmits information to the investor in the processed form of a market price. Thus the market is performing a substantial part of the valuation process performed by the investor in a face-to-face transaction. The market is acting as the unpaid agent of the investor, informing him that given all the information available to it, the value of the stock is worth the market price.

In re LTV Securities Litigation, 88 F.R.D. 134, 143 (ND Tex.1980).

B

Presumptions typically serve to assist courts in managing circumstances in which direct proof, for one reason or another, is rendered difficult. The courts below accepted a presumption, created by the fraud-on-the-market theory and subject to rebuttal by petitioners, that persons who had traded Basic shares had done so in reliance on the integrity of the price set by the market, but because of petitioners' material misrepresentations that price had been fraudulently depressed. Requiring a plaintiff to show a speculative state of facts, i.e., how he would have acted if omitted material information had been disclosed, see *Affiliated Ute Citizens v. United States,* 406 U.S., at 153-154, or if the misrepre-

---

21. Prosser and Keeton on Law of Torts 726 (5th ed. 1984) ("The reasons for the separate development of [the tort action for misrepresentation and nondisclosure], and for its peculiar limitations, are in part historical, and in part connected with the fact that in the great majority of the cases which have come before the courts the misrepresentations have been made in the course of a bargaining transaction between the parties. Consequently the action has been colored to a considerable extent by the ethics of bargaining between distrustful adversaries") (footnote omitted).

22. Actions under Rule 10b-5 are distinct from common-law deceit and misrepresentation claims, see *Blue Chip Stamps v. Manor Drug Stores,* 421 U.S. 723, 744-745 (1975), and are in part designed to add to the protections provided investors by the common law, see *Herman & MacLean v. Huddleston,* 459 U.S. 375, 388-389 (1983).

sentation had not been made, see *Sharp v. Coopers & Lybrand,* 649 F.2d 175, 188 (CA3 1981), would place an unnecessarily unrealistic evidentiary burden on the Rule 10b-5 plaintiff who has traded on an impersonal market. Cf. *Mills v. Electric Auto-Lite Co.,* 396 U.S., at 385.

Arising out of considerations of fairness, public policy, and probability, as well as judicial economy, presumptions are also useful devices for allocating the burdens of proof between parties. The presumption of reliance employed in this case is consistent with, and, by facilitating Rule 10b-5 litigation, supports, the congressional policy embodied in the 1934 Act. In drafting that Act, Congress expressly relied on the premise that securities markets are affected by information, and enacted legislation to facilitate an investor's reliance on the integrity of those markets:

> No investor, no speculator, can safely buy and sell securities upon the exchanges without having an intelligent basis for forming his judgment as to the value of the securities he buys or sells. The idea of a free and open public market is built upon the theory that competing judgments of buyers and sellers as to the fair price of a security brings *[sic]* about a situation where the market price reflects as nearly as possible a just price. Just as artificial manipulation tends to upset the true function of an open market, so the hiding and secreting of important information obstructs the operation of the markets as indices of real value. H.R.Rep. No. 1383, at 11.

The presumption is also supported by common sense and probability. Recent empirical studies have tended to confirm Congress' premise that the market price of shares traded on well-developed markets reflects all publicly available information, and, hence, any material misrepresentations.[24] It has been noted that "it is hard to imagine that there ever is a buyer or seller who does not rely on market integrity. Who would knowingly roll the dice in a crooked crap game?" *Schlanger v. Four-Phase Systems Inc.,* 555 F.Supp. 535, 538 (SDNY 1982). Indeed, nearly every court that has considered the proposition has concluded that where materially misleading statements have been disseminated into an impersonal, well-developed market for securities, the reliance of individual plaintiffs on the integrity of the market price may be presumed.[25] Commentators generally have applauded the adoption of one

---

24. See *In re LTV Securities Litigation,* 88 F.R.D. 134, 144 (ND Tex.1980) (citing studies); Fischel, Use of Modern Finance Theory in Securities Fraud Cases Involving Actively Traded Securities, 38 Bus. Law. 1, 4, n. 9 (1982) (citing literature on efficient-capital-market theory); Dennis, Materiality and the Efficient Capital Market Model: A Recipe for the Total Mix, 25 Wm. & Mary L. Rev. 373, 374-381, and n. 1 (1984). We need not determine by adjudication what economists and social scientists have debated through the use of sophisticated statistical analysis and the application of economic theory. For purposes of accepting the presumption of reliance in this case, we need only believe that market professionals generally consider most publicly announced material statements about companies, thereby affecting stock market prices.

25. See, e.g. *Peil v. Speiser,* 806 F.2d 1154, 1161 (CA3 1986); *Blackie v. Barrack,* 524 F.2d 891, 905-908 (CA9 1975).

variation or another of the fraud-on-the-market theory.[26] An investor who buys or sells stock at the price set by the market does so in reliance on the integrity of that price. Because most publicly available information is reflected in market price, an investor's reliance on any public material misrepresentations, therefore, may be presumed for purposes of a Rule 10b-5 action.

C

The Court of Appeals found that petitioners "made public, material misrepresentations and [respondents] sold Basic stock in an impersonal, efficient market. Thus the class, as defined by the district court, has established the threshold facts for proving their loss."[27] The court acknowledged that petitioners may rebut proof of the elements giving rise to the presumption, or show that the misrepresentation in fact did not lead to a distortion of price or that an individual plaintiff traded or would have traded despite his knowing the statement was false.

Any showing that severs the link between the alleged misrepresentation and either the price received (or paid) by the plaintiff, or his decision to trade at a fair market price, will be sufficient to rebut the presumption of reliance. For example, if petitioners could show that the "market makers" were privy to the truth about the merger discussions here with Combustion, and thus that the market price would not have been affected by their misrepresentations, the causal connection could be broken: the basis for finding that the fraud had been transmitted through market price would be gone.[28] Similarly, if, despite petitioners' allegedly fraudulent attempt to manipulate market price, news of the merger discussions credibly entered the market and dissipated the effects of the misstatements, those who traded Basic shares after the corrective statements

---

26. See, e.g., Black, Fraud on the Market: A Criticism of Dispensing with Reliance Requirements in Certain Open Market Transactions, 62 N.C. L. Rev. 435 (1984); Note, The Fraud-on-the-Market Theory, 95 Harv. L. Rev. 1143 (1982); Note, Fraud on the Market: An Emerging Theory of Recovery Under SEC Rule 10b-5, 50 Geo. Wash. L. Rev. 627 (1982).

27. The Court of Appeals held that in order to invoke the presumption, a plaintiff must allege and prove: (1) that the defendant made public misrepresentations; (2) that the misrepresentations were material; (3) that the shares were traded on an efficient market; (4) that the misrepresentations would induce a reasonable, relying investor to misjudge the value of the shares; and (5) that the plaintiff traded the shares between the time the misrepresentations were made and the time the truth was revealed.

Given today's decision regarding the definition of materiality as to preliminary merger discussions, elements (2) and (4) may collapse into one.

28. By accepting this rebuttable presumption, we do not intend conclusively to adopt any particular theory of how quickly and completely publicly available information is reflected in market price. Furthermore, our decision today is not to be interpreted as addressing the proper measure of damages in litigation of this kind.

would have no direct or indirect connection with the fraud.[29] Petitioners also could rebut the presumption of reliance as to plaintiffs who would have divested themselves of their Basic shares without relying on the integrity of the market. For example, a plaintiff who believed that Basic's statements were false and that Basic was indeed engaged in merger discussions, and who consequently believed that Basic stock was artificially underpriced, but sold his shares nevertheless because of other unrelated concerns, e.g., potential antitrust problems, or political pressures to divest from shares of certain businesses, could not be said to have relied on the integrity of a price he knew had been manipulated. ***

JUSTICE BYRON R. WHITE, WITH WHOM JUSTICE O'CONNOR JOINS, CONCURRING IN PART AND DISSENTING IN PART:

*** I dissent *** because I do not agree that the "fraud-on-the-market" theory should be applied in this case. ***

Even when compared to the relatively youthful private cause-of-action under § 10(b), see *Kardon v. National Gypsum Co.*, 69 F.Supp. 512 (E.D. Pa. 1946), the fraud-on-the-market theory is a mere babe. Yet today, the Court embraces this theory with the sweeping confidence usually reserved for more mature legal doctrines. In so doing, I fear that the Court's decision may have many adverse, unintended effects as it is applied and interpreted in the years to come. ***

*** Even if I agreed with the Court that "modern securities markets ... involving millions of shares changing hands daily" require that the "understanding of Rule 10b-5's reliance requirement" be changed, I prefer that such changes come from Congress in amending § 10(b). The Congress, with its superior resources and expertise, is far better equipped than the federal courts for the task of determining how modern economic theory and global financial markets require that established legal notions of fraud be modified. In choosing to make these decisions itself, the Court, I fear, embarks on a course that it does not genuinely understand, giving rise to consequences it cannot foresee. ***

At the bottom of the Court's conclusion that the fraud-on-the-market theory sustains a presumption of reliance is the assumption that individuals rely "on the integrity of the market price" when buying or selling stock in "impersonal, well-developed market[s] for securities." Even if I was prepared to accept (as a matter of common sense or general understanding) the assumption that most persons buying or selling stock do so in response to the market price, the fraud-on-the-market theory goes further. For in adopting a "presumption of reliance," the Court *also* assumes that buyers and sellers rely—not just on the

---

29. We note there may be a certain incongruity between the assumption that Basic shares are traded on a well-developed, efficient, and information-hungry market, and the allegation that such a market could remain misinformed, and its valuation of Basic shares depressed, for 14 months, on the basis of the three public statements. Proof of that sort is a matter for trial, throughout which the District Court retains the authority to amend the certification order as may be appropriate. ***

market price—but on the "*integrity* " of that price. It is this aspect of the fraud-on-the-market hypothesis which most mystifies me.

To define the term "integrity of the market price," the majority quotes approvingly from cases which suggest that investors are entitled to "'rely on the price of a stock as a reflection of its value.'" Ante (quoting *Peil v. Speiser,* 806 F.2d 1154, 1161 (CA3 1986)). But the meaning of this phrase eludes me, for it implicitly suggests that stocks have some "true value" that is measurable by a standard other than their market price. While the scholastics of medieval times professed a means to make such a valuation of a commodity's "worth," I doubt that the federal courts of our day are similarly equipped.

Even if securities had some "value"—knowable and distinct from the market price of a stock—investors do not always share the Court's presumption that a stock's price is a "reflection of [this] value." Indeed, "many investors purchase or sell stock because they believe the price *inaccurately* reflects the corporation's worth." See Black, Fraud on the Market: A Criticism of Dispensing with Reliance Requirements in Certain Open Market Transactions, 62 N.C.L.Rev. 435, 455 (1984) (emphasis added). If investors really believed that stock prices reflected a stock's "value," many sellers would never sell, and many buyers never buy (given the time and cost associated with executing a stock transaction). As we recognized just a few years ago: "[I]nvestors act on inevitably incomplete or inaccurate information, [consequently] there are always winners and losers; but those who have 'lost' have not necessarily been defrauded." *Dirks v. SEC,* 463 U.S. 646, 667, n. 27 (1983). Yet today, the Court allows investors to recover who can show little more than that they sold stock at a lower price than what might have been.[7]

I do not propose that the law retreat from the many protections that § 10(b) and Rule 10b-5, as interpreted in our prior cases, provide to investors. But any extension of these laws, to approach something closer to an investor insurance scheme, should come from Congress, and not from the courts. ***

And who will pay the judgments won in such actions? I suspect that all too often the majority's rule will "lead to large judgments, payable in the last analysis by innocent investors, for the benefit of speculators and their lawyers." Cf. *SEC v. Texas Gulf Sulphur Co.,* 401 F.2d 833, 867 (CA2 1968) (en banc) (Friendly, J., concurring). This Court and others have previously recognized that

---

7. This is what the Court's rule boils down to in practical terms. For while, in theory, the Court allows for rebuttal of its "presumption of reliance"—a proviso with which I agree, in practice the Court must realize, as other courts applying the fraud-on-the-market theory have, that such rebuttal is virtually impossible in all but the most extraordinary case. See *Blackie v. Barrack,* 524 F.2d, at 906-907, n. 22; *In re LTV Securities Litigation,* 88 F.R.D. 134, 143, n. 4 (ND Tex.1980).

Consequently, while the Court considers it significant that the fraud-on-the-market presumption it endorses is a rebuttable one, the majority's implicit rejection of the "pure causation" fraud-on-the-market theory rings hollow. In most cases, the Court's theory will operate just as the causation theory would, creating a nonrebuttable presumption of "reliance" in future Rule 10b-5 actions.

"inexorably broadening ... the class of plaintiff[s] who may sue in this area of the law will ultimately result in more harm than good." *Blue Chip Stamps v. Manor Drug Stores,* supra, at 747-748. See also *Ernst & Ernst v. Hochfelder,* 425 U.S., at 214. Yet such a bitter harvest is likely to be reaped from the seeds sewn by the Court's decision today. ***

NOTES AND QUESTIONS

*1. **The Presumption's Prerequisites.*** What are the prerequisites needed to invoke the presumption? This question presents a puzzle. In footnote 27, *Basic* identifies, and arguably endorses, the prerequisites used by the court below, including in particular an efficient market and public, material fraud. Cf. *In re Salomon Analyst Metromedia Litig.*, 544 F.3d 474, 481 (2d Cir. 2008) (adopting the prerequisites from footnote 27); *In re PolyMedica Corp. Sec. Litig.*, 432 F.3d 1, 7-8 n. 11 (1st Cir.2005) (same). These prerequisites are seemingly captured as well by the following statement from the *Basic* text: "Because most publicly available information is reflected in market price, an investor's reliance on any public material misrepresentation, therefore, may be presumed ***."

Yet when the Supreme Court addressed the prerequisites for the fraud-on-the market presumption in *Erica P. John Fund, Inc. v. Halliburton Co.*, 131 S.Ct. 2179 (2011), it omitted the materiality prerequisite:

> It is undisputed that securities fraud plaintiffs must prove certain things in order to invoke *Basic* 's rebuttable presumption of reliance. It is common ground, for example, that plaintiffs must demonstrate that the alleged misrepresentations were publicly known (else how would the market take them into account?), that the stock traded in an efficient market, and that the relevant transaction took place "between the time the misrepresentations were made and the time the truth was revealed." *Basic*, 485 U.S., at 248, n. 27; id., at 241–247.

Id. at 2185. Was the omission of the materiality prerequisite deliberate? If so, what would be the reason? Cf. *Schleicher v. Wendt*, 618 F.3d 679, 687 (7th Cir. 2010) (Easterbrook, J.) (rejecting materiality prerequisite and arguing that footnote 27 of *Basic* does not actually endorse it).

At issue in *Halliburton* was whether "loss causation" qualifies as yet another prerequisite. Giving a negative answer, the Supreme Court held that the imposition of such a prerequisite – adopted only by the Fifth Circuit – was incompatible with *Basic.* You will encounter the loss causation element of Rule 10b-5 later in this Chapter. See infra F.2.

*2. **Identifying An Efficient Market.*** Consider what *Basic* suggests about the appropriate benchmark for measuring market efficiency. Is that benchmark the academic economic literature or can it be something at least somewhat kinder and gentler?

The principal post-*Basic* judicial touchstone has been the following set of five factors originating in a 1989 federal district court case:

> (1) the average weekly trading volume; (2) the number of security analysts following and reporting on the security; (3) the extent to which market makers traded the security; (4) the issuer's eligibility to file an SEC registration Form S–3; and (5) the cause-and-effect relationship between material disclosures and

factors in determining an efficient market

changes in the security's price.

In re DVI, Inc. Sec. Litig., 639 F.3d 623, 633 n.14 (3d Cir. 2011) (citing *Cammer v. Bloom*, 711 F.Supp. 1264, 1286–87 (D.N.J.1989)). See id. at n. 16 (collecting federal appellate cases adopting the so-called "the *Cammer* factors"). But cf. *In re Merrill Lynch Auction Rate Sec. Litig.*, 704 F. Supp. 2d 378, 395 n.9 (S.D.N.Y. 2010) (noting that the *Cammer* factors do not apply to debt securities, as to which no methodology for measuring efficiency has yet been developed).

Especially since 2003, the inquiry into efficiency has tended towards the zealous. See, e.g., *Bell v. Ascendant Solutions, Inc.*, 422 F.3d 307 (5th Cir. 2005) (remanding efficiency question with respect to a stock traded on the NASDAQ); *Unger v. Amedisys, Inc.*, 401 F.3d 316 (5th Cir. 2005); *In re PolyMedica Corp. Sec. Litig.*, 432 F.3d 1 (1st Cir. 2005); *In re Xcelera.com Sec. Litig.*, 430 F.3d 503 (1st Cir. 2005); *Gariety v. Grant Thornton, LLP*, 368 F.3d 356 (4th Cir. 2004). Thus, the *Cammer* factors "must be weighed analytically, not merely counted" and "do[] not represent an exhaustive list." *Unger*, supra, 401 F.3d at 323. To this end, recourse to expert witnesses has become commonplace. See, e.g., *PolyMedica*, supra, 432 F.3d at 18, n.21; *Xcelera.com*, supra, 430 F.3d at 506. See generally Patricia Groot, Note, Fraud on the Market Gets A Mini-Trial: *Eisen* through *In re IPO*, 58 Duke L. J. 1143 (2009).

There are two explanations for the zealousness. One is that until 2003, courts were entitled to certify a class "conditionally" pursuant to the then existing version of Rule 23 of the Federal Rules of Civil Procedure.

The other explanation emerges from the growing doubts among economists as to whether truly efficient markets exist in the first place. See *Bell*, supra, 422 F.3d at 314-15 (citing scholarship criticizing efficient market theory). See generally Paul A. Ferrillo, et al., The "Less than" Efficient Capital Markets Hypothesis: Requiring More Proof from Plaintiffs in Fraud-on-the-Market Cases, 78 St. John's L. Rev. 81, 107-116 (2004); William O. Fisher, Does the Efficient Market Theory Help Us do Justice in a Time of Madness?, 54 Emory L. J. 843, 898-921 (2005). Some courts have using these doubts as a club with which to bludgeon would-be securities class actions. Should doubts among economists control the availability of the fraud-on-the-market presumption? Does *Basic* itself suggest an answer?

As you contemplate these questions, consider the following view about the form the efficient market standard should take:

> ***[I]n the reliance context, *** the standard for efficiency should be relatively low and tied to the fundamental reliance question. This question is whether but for the defendant's statements the plaintiff would have purchased the security at the price at which the plaintiff did purchase it. In the reliance context, *** a market should be deemed ""efficient"" if an investor would be justified in relying on the integrity of the market price, i.e., if an investor knowing full well that the market cannot be perfectly efficient and that, accordingly, the market price may not reflect the true value of the stock, nevertheless would be justified in treating the market price as if it reflected true value. Reliance on the integrity of the market price invariably will result in reliance on a defendant's statements because *** even grossly inefficient securities markets incorporate information to some degree such that, but for the

> fraud, the plaintiff would not have purchased the stock at the price at which the plaintiff did purchase it. The precise extent to which the price was affected by the fraud is irrelevant to the reliance question. *** Reliance on the integrity of the market price is sensibly presumed *** if the market bears enough hallmarks of efficiency that investors, mindful of the costs they would incur if they went out and conducted their own research into stock values, reasonably could decide instead to treat the market's prices as indicative of fair value.

Bradford Cornell & James C. Rutten, Market Efficiency, Crashes, and Securities Litigation, 81 Tul. L. Rev. 443, 448-49 (2006).

*3. **The Truth-on-the-Market Defense.*** *Basic* allows the defendant to rebut the presumption by showing that the market was not in fact defrauded. This form of rebuttal – known as the truth on the market defense – can be established in one or the other of two (closely related) ways: by proving either "that the 'market makers' were privy to the truth" and "thus that the market price would not have been affected by their misrepresentations;" or, that truthful information on the matter in question "credibly entered the market and dissipated the effects of the misstatements."

For an example, consider *In re Apple Computer Sec. Litig.*, 886 F.2d 1109 (9th Cir. 1989). There Apple Computer obtained summary judgment on the claim that it had defrauded the market regarding its Lisa computer:

> The press portrayed Lisa as a gamble, with the potential for either enormous success or enormous failure. At least twenty articles stressed the risks Apple was taking, and detailed the underlying problems producing those risks. Many of the optimistic statements challenged by plaintiffs appeared in those same articles, essentially bracketed by the facts which plaintiffs claim Apple wrongfully failed to disclose. The market could not have been made more aware of Lisa's risks.

Id. at 1116. See *In re Boston Scientific Corp Sec. Litig*, 708 F. Supp. 2d 110, 128 -29 (D. Mass. 2010) (summary judgment granted based in part on successful truth on the market defense), aff'd on other grounds, 649 F.3d 5 (1st Cir. 2011).

As a general matter, however, truth on the market defenses tend typically to fail. See, e.g., *Kaplan v. Rose,* 49 F.3d 1363, 1377 (9th Cir. 1995) (summary judgment denied where the news articles submitted by the defendant "came from obscure sources, and only a few mention any specific problems"); *Jaffe Pension Plan v. Household Int'l, Inc.*, 756 F. Supp. 2d 928, 933 (N.D. Ill. 2010) (defense rejected by jury); *Freeland v. Iridium World Commc'ns, Ltd.*, 545 F. Supp. 2d 59, 79 (D.D.C. 2008) (defense rejected on summary judgment). See generally Elliott J. Weiss & John S. Beckerman, Let the Money Do the Monitoring: How Institutional Investors Can Reduce Agency Costs in Securities Class Actions, 104 Yale L. J. 2053, 2076 (1995).

But the terrain appears to be changing to some extent. Truth on the market defenses are now sometimes succeeding at the motion to dismiss stage. The rationale for considering the defense so early in the litigation is that if the market knew the truth, the misrepresentation or omission lacks materiality. See, e.g., *In re Merrill Lynch Auction Rate Sec. Litig.*, 704 F. Supp. 2d 378, 394-97 (S.D.N.Y. 2010); *In re Discovery Labs. Sec. Litig.*, 2006 WL 3227767 at *11 (E.D. Pa. 2006). Is it appropriate to recast rebuttal of the presumption as a materiality issue?

Can a defendant defeat a motion for certification with a truth on the market defense? Compare *In re Salomon Analyst Metromedia Litig.*, 544 F.3d 474, 485 (2d Cir. 2008) (giving affirmative answer) with *Erica P. John Fund, Inc. v. Halliburton Co.*, 131 S.Ct. 2179, 2187 (2011) (declining to address when rebuttal can occur). We will explore this question further in connection with class actions in Chapter 6.

*4. **Rebuttals as to Specific Plaintiffs.*** *Basic* also allows defendants to rebut the presumption as to those plaintiffs who did not rely on the market price in making their trades. See, e.g., *In re DVI, Inc. Sec. Litig.*, 639 F.3d 623, 641 (3d Cir. 2011) (presumption available to plaintiff who believed that "successful arbitrage is possible"); *Gurary v. Winehouse*, 1998 WL 54641 (S.DN.Y. 1998) (presumption not available to plaintiff who had received from a corporate insider information unknown to the market), aff'd in part, vac. on other grounds, 190 F.3d 37, 44 (2d Cir. 1999). See generally *Jaffe Pension Plan v. Household Int'l, Inc.*, 756 F. Supp. 2d 928, 933-34 (N.D. Ill. 2010) (describing method for inquiring into individual reliance questions after trial at which truth-on-the-market defense failed).

Can a defendant rebut by showing that the plaintiff sold her stock because she was desperate for money? See generally Barbara Black, The Strange Case of Fraud on the Market: A Label in Search of a Theory, 52 Alb. L. Rev. 923 (1988).

*5. **Extending the Presumption to Securities Analysts.*** The *Basic* plaintiffs received a presumption of reliance when suing an issuer. Is the presumption also available when the defendant is a securities analyst? The Second Circuit has given an affirmative answer:

> Defendants argue that the *Basic* presumption should be limited to suits involving misrepresentations made by issuers, because misrepresentations by third parties are less likely to materially effect market prices. But they cite no case, and we have found none, that supports such a rule. Moreover, the *Basic* Court did not so limit its holding and its logic counsels against doing so. The reason is simple: the premise of *Basic* is that, in an efficient market, share prices reflect "all publicly available information, and, hence, *any* material misrepresentations." Id. at 246 (emphases added). It thus does not matter, for purposes of establishing entitlement to the presumption, whether the misinformation was transmitted by an issuer, an analyst, or anyone else.

In re Salomon Analyst Metromedia Litig., 544 F.3d 474, 481(2d Cir. 2008). See *In re HealthSouth Corp. Sec. Litig*, 257 F. R.D. 260, 279 n.20 (N.D. Ala. 2009) (same); *In re Credit Suisse -AOL Sec. Litig.*, 253 F.R.D. 17, 28 (D. Mass. 2008) (same).

Prior to *Salomon*, dicta in two Second Circuit decisions took a dim view of extending the presumption of reliance to lawsuits against analysts. See, e.g., *In re Initial Public Offering Sec. Litig.*, 471 F.3d 24, 43 (2d Cir. 2006) (describing it as "doubtful whether the *Basic* presumption can be extended beyond its original context, to tie-in grading, underwriter compensation, and analyst reports"); *Hevesi v. Citigroup, Inc.*, 366 F.3d 70, 80 (2d Cir. 2004) (noting that"the application of the fraud-on-the-market doctrine to opinions expressed by research analysts would extend the potentially coercive effect of securities class actions to a new group of corporate and individual defendants-namely, to research analysts and their employers"). What do you think?

*6. **The Reasonableness of Relying on Market Price Integrity.*** Is it reasonable for investors to presume that a security's market price is untainted by fraud? See generally Donald C. Langevoort, *Basic* at Twenty: Rethinking Fraud on the Market, 2009 Wis. L. Rev. 151.

*7. **Vexatious Litigation.*** Recall that in *Blue Chip Stamps v. Manor Drug Stores*, 421 U.S. 723 (1975), the Court upheld the purchaser-seller requirement in order to curb the vexatiousness of private Rule 10b-5 litigation. See supra Section E of this Chapter. Does *Basic*'s fraud-on-the-market presumption tend to promote vexatious litigation? If so, what accounts for the *Basic* Court's seeming indifference to this matter?

*8. **Inattentive Investors.*** One of the main goals of the federal securities laws is to compel disclosure of information and thereby to equip investors to make well-grounded decisions. Yet plaintiffs can invoke the fraud-on-the-market presumption regardless of whether they have read the documents they challenge as fraudulent. Would it be better to limit use of the presumption to those who have done the reading?

*9. **Limiting the Presumption to Efficient Markets.*** The Court limited the fraud-on-the-market presumption to efficient markets. Is it good policy to withhold the presumption from investors who purchased securities traded in inefficient markets and thereby impede the ability of these investors to bring class actions?

10. **Basic *and Congress.*** In the course of enacting the PSLRA, Congress at least contemplated overturning *Basic*. What about *Basic* do you think generated congressional concern? Why do you suppose that Congress decided against overturning it?

PROBLEM 2-19

After scrutinizing all available public information regarding Spotlight, Inc., which trades in an efficient market, investor Boris Box decided that the company's stock was overvalued. He based this decision on the company's earnings coupled with the threat posed by the competition. He became a short seller—selling shares of Spotlight he did not own (borrowed from a broker) and gambling that he would make money on his eventual obligatory purchase when the price went down. Prior to Box's short sale, Spotlight issued a fraudulent press release that misrepresented the company's earnings and competitive situation. The effect was to artificially inflate the stock price. After a number of months, the price climbed higher than ever.

Seeking to cut his losses, Box made the purchase required by his short position and in so doing lost $50,000. Thereafter, as the result of more accurate information distributed by Spotlight, the stock price tumbled. If Box sued Spotlight under Rule 10b-5, is he entitled to the fraud-on-the-market presumption?

Cf. *Zlotnick v. TIE Communications, Inc.*, 836 F.2d 818 (3d Cir. 1988).

PROBLEM 2-20

Allied Artists, Inc., a pioneer in the manufacture of video tapes, was a large company whose shares traded in an efficient market. The following two paragraphs on Allied appeared in a Wall Street Journal article on the video cassette market:

> Several analysts contend that Allied Artists is in a good position to take advantage of the growing demand for video tapes, having pioneered the development of pre-recorded cassettes.
>
> Andrew G. Racz of Philips, Appel & Walden, Inc. says Allied Artists, besides having a head start in video tapes and cassettes, is negotiating with TV networks, other film producers and makers of educational films to put their films on video cassettes. "The educational and informational area constitutes a tremendous market for video cassettes," says Mr. Racz, adding: "We continue to be bullish on Allied Artists. It's an attractive turn-around situation."

Zelda, a retired school teacher, read the article and was intrigued by the reference to the educational use of video cassettes. After checking the price of Allied stock (for the sole purpose of ascertaining whether the price was within her budget), she telephoned her broker and asked if there was any negative news about the company. After consulting the Standard & Poor's tear sheet on Allied (which contained an extensive abstract of the company's most recent annual report), her broker told her that there was no negative news. Zelda thereupon purchased 500 shares of Allied. Seven months later, Allied filed for bankruptcy.

Zelda responded by filing a Rule 10b-5 action against Allied's officers and its accountants for various alleged material omissions and misrepresentations in the company's most recent annual report. The principal misrepresentation involved an inflation of profits. The principal omission was the failure on the part of the accountants to mention doubts that the company could continue as a going concern. All of the alleged omissions and misrepresentations appeared in the abstract of the annual report included in the Standard and Poor's tear sheet on which Zelda's broker had relied. Zelda did not claim to have read the annual report herself.

Zelda argued that if Allied's annual report had been truthful, the company would not have been touted by the analysts to whom the Wall Street Journal spoke, the above-quoted paragraphs on the company's prospects would not have appeared in the Journal article, and she would not have bought the stock. She claimed that she relied on the integrity of the market in producing the information reported. Should she receive a presumption of reliance? Why or why not?

See *Panzirer v. Wolf*, 663 F.2d 365 (2d Cir. 1981), vac. as moot, 459 U.S. 1027 (1982).

c. *The Fraud-Created-the-Market Presumption*

The presumption upheld in the next decision applies only to primary securities offerings.

SHORES v. SKLAR

647 F.2d 462 (5th Cir. 1981) (en banc)

CHARLES CLARK, CIRCUIT JUDGE:

Clarence E. Bishop, Jr., was one of a number of purchasers of First Mortgage Revenue Bonds of the Industrial Development Board of Frisco City, Alabama [Bonds"] The lessee of the industrial business premises, the sole source of the income necessary to amortize the revenue Bonds, almost immediately defaulted in the payment of rent, causing the value of the Bonds to drop precipitously.[1] Bishop sued most of those involved with the issuance of the Bonds, alleging that he was the victim of a pervasive scheme to defraud members of the investing public in violation of the securities laws. In essence, the complaint alleged that the defendants had fabricated a materially misleading Offering Circular in order to induce the Industrial Development Board ("Board") to issue, and the public to buy, fraudulently marketed bonds.[2] ***

The bond issue in question had its genesis in 1972 when J. C. Harrelson, president and chief shareholder of Alabama Supply and Equipment Company (ASECo), and Clarence Hamilton, president of Investors Associates of America, Inc., a Tennessee underwriter, decided to seek industrial development financing to construct and equip a facility for the construction of mobile homes in Frisco City, Alabama. Alabama law provides for such financing pursuant to the Wallace-Cater Act, which authorizes the incorporation of an Industrial Development Board in a municipality in order to induce industry to locate in Alabama. Such a board has the authority to issue tax-exempt bonds. With the proceeds of such an issue, a board can build an industrial facility, which it may then lease to a manufacturing, industrial, or commercial enterprise. The amount of rental payments is calculated to amortize the interest and principal of the bonds and is ostensibly lower than that which could be obtained without

---

1. After the sale of the lessee's plant, the identifiable Bond holders received $373.33 per $1000 bond.

2. Throughout the opinion we refer to these Bonds as being "fraudulently marketed." This means the fraudulent scheme alleged by Bishop was so pervasive that without it the issuer would not have issued, the dealer could not have dealt in, and the buyer could not have bought these Bonds, because they would not have been offered on the market at any price.

tax-free financing. ***

Neither Harrelson nor ASECo was a paragon of financial integrity or industrial ability. Harrelson had been only moderately successful in previous business ventures and had little experience in the development of plants for the construction of modular or mobile homes. ASECo's management was inept and unsophisticated, its projections for the sales of mobile homes were mere marketing assumptions, and its financial condition was weak. Indeed, Harrelson and Hamilton both knew that ASECo did not have the financial capability to engage in the manufacture of mobile homes and related products or to pay the rent necessary to amortize the principal and interest on the Bonds. Nevertheless, they determined to induce the Town of Frisco City to create an Industrial Development Board to finance ASECo's facility as a scheme to defraud the investing public.

Hamilton retained defendant Jerald H. Sklar, a Tennessee attorney, as bond counsel. ***

Sklar also drafted the Offering Circular, based on material furnished to him by the underwriter, the lessee company, and those associated with them, but he intentionally or recklessly disregarded other facts of which he was aware. Sklar omitted from the Offering Circular, for example, that the Securities and Exchange Commission had investigated and commenced a civil action against Hamilton and Investors Associates (and against Jackson Municipals, Inc., the assignee who ultimately underwrote the issue) for violations of the securities laws; he even failed to name the underwriter in the Offering Circular. He misleadingly portrayed ASECo as the owner of 519 acres of Florida real estate valued at $2,284,000, already approved for development, recklessly disregarding not only that ASECo had filed no development plans but also that it had no ownership or equity interest in the property. Although Sklar knew that Harrelson had been only moderately successful at past efforts, he falsely represented Harrelson in the Offering Circular as a successful and experienced developer of modular home manufacturing plans with well-established mobile home sales. Furthermore, Sklar relied on an opinion letter that no actions were pending against or threatening ASECo, even though the opinion letter was obviously deficient and was prepared by a lawyer other than the one originally selected to give an opinion, as Sklar knew. In fact, an action affecting the Florida investment real estate listed on ASECo's balance sheet was pending at the time of the opinion letter.

Part of the information Sklar incorporated into the Offering Circular was a financial statement prepared by George C. Rakard, a certified public accountant from Salem, Illinois. Rakard's financial statement was materially false and misleading because of numerous misrepresentations and omissions. It included as assets of ASECo a number of items of doubtful worth. Open notes and capital stock subscriptions from Harrelson and his wife were valued at $376,000, in reckless disregard of their true value and without taking into account the Harrelsons' probable inability to satisfy these obligations. Three-quarters of the assets were investment properties, including the Florida real estate in which ASECo in fact had no interest. Moreover, although Rakard's forwarding letter accompanying the financial statement stated that the audit fairly presented the financial condition of ASECo, Rakard knew or recklessly disregarded the fact that the financial statement constituted mere "window dressing" that did not fairly present ASECo's financial condition.

By the time Sklar incorporated Rakard's financial statement into the Offering Circular, he knew or recklessly disregarded the fact that Harrelson was already in default on at least one of the notes listed as an asset of ASECo and that ASECo was in default on its obligation in the lease to maintain at least $400,000 in working capital.

Meanwhile, Investors Associates had determined that it did not possess sufficient capital to underwrite the proposed issue and assigned the right to underwrite the issue to Jackson Municipals, Inc., a Tennessee underwriting firm headed by Cecil Lamberson. Jackson Municipals and Lamberson proceeded to offer the Bonds for sale to the public on the basis of the Offering Circular, even though they knew it contained materially false misrepresentations and omissions. They knew Harrelson was inexperienced and unsophisticated, contrary to the Offering Circular's representation. They purported to rely on Hamilton and Investors Associates, but because they were all defendants in the same SEC action (which the Offering Circular failed to disclose) they knew that Investors Associates needed to induce another firm to underwrite the bond issue or it would lose the value of all the time and effort it had put into the issue thus far.

Lamberson and Jackson Municipals knew that while Harrelson was not as financially secure as represented, 95% of ASECo's current assets consisted of open notes from Harrelson and over 75% of ASECo's listed assets was the Florida real estate, but failed to investigate the true value of either of these assets. They knew that the financial statement did not reflect ASECo's true assets. They even failed to inquire whether Harrelson had paid $200,000 due ASECo on a stock subscription, knowing that ASECo would be in default if Harrelson had not. In spite of this knowledge, Jackson Municipals bought the bond issue from the Board in three increments, commencing on December 14, 1972, and resold the Bonds to securities dealers.

The Phenix National Bank *** had been chosen to act as trustee of the Bond proceeds. The Bank's responsibility was to ensure that the lessee complied with the terms and conditions of the lease, one of which was that ASECo at all times have working capital in the amount of $400,000.00 or more. The Bank had the duty to determine the existence of any default in the lease requirements by the lessee, and to demand a cure of the default or else declare the Bonds due and payable upon failure to cure. *** The Bank knew or recklessly disregarded *** that ASECo was in breach of the lease requirement that it maintain $400,000.00 in working capital. ***

Bishop purchased three of the Bonds in January, paying $3,052.67, and one more in February, for $1,043.37. *** The district court found Bishop purchased as part of the primary offering. ***

Bishop never saw the Offering Circular nor knew one existed. He bought the Bonds based solely on his broker's oral representations. ***

After the ASECo plant had been constructed, the lessee ceased all operations at the plant and, on April 15, 1974, defaulted in payment of rent under the lease. Although Harrelson had unconditionally guaranteed the performance of the lease by ASECo, he did not have sufficient assets to back up his guarantee. The Trustee Bank declared the lease in default. ***

Bishop's original complaint sought relief for himself and for the class of all purchasers of the Bonds under *** the Securities Exchange Act of 1934, rule 10b-5, and an unspecified Alabama law. The court *** permitted Bishop to amend his complaint twice in order to allege that he relied on the Offering Circular. Bishop's inability to make such an allegation resulted in the dismissal here on appeal. ***

Bishop alleged that the Offering Circular contained material misrepresentations and failed to state material facts necessary to make the statements made not misleading. At the same time, he admitted that he never read or otherwise relied on the Offering Circular. If the *Ute* presumption applies to these nondisclosures, Bishop's admission rebuts it. Bishop's claim that he was deceived by the misrepresentations and omissions of the Offering Circular was correctly dismissed by the district court because of his failure to read or even seek to read the Offering Circular. ***

The district court erred, however, in construing the remainder of Bishop's complaint as narrowly confined to charges of misrepresentations and omissions in the Offering Circular that would have defrauded investors who did rely. It would permit proof that the defendants engaged in an elaborate scheme to create a bond issue that would appear genuine but was so lacking in basic requirements that the Bonds would never have been approved by the Board nor presented by the underwriters had any one of the participants in the scheme not acted with intent to defraud or in reckless disregard of whether the other defendants were perpetrating a fraud. Rather than containing the entire fraud, the Offering Circular was assertedly only one step in the course of an elaborate scheme.

*** Bishop's 10b-5(2) claim *** cannot withstand his admitted lack of reliance on the Offering Circular. However, his 10b-5(1) and (3) claims *** assert something more that prevents dismissal at this preliminary stage.

*** His pleadings would permit him to show that he was willing to accept any marketable risk. If a municipal authority was willing to authorize the issuance of the Bond, and the underwriters were willing to present the issue to the market, that was sufficient for Bishop's purposes. His pleadings allow him to show that he sought to make investments in securities which were entitled to be marketed.

*** The requisite element of causation in fact would be established if Bishop proved the scheme was intended to and did bring the Bonds onto the market fraudulently and proved he relied on the integrity of the offerings of the securities market. His lack of reliance on the Offering Circular, only one component of the overall scheme, is not determinative. *Blackie v. Barrack*, 524 F.2d 891, 906 (9th Cir. 1975).

Bishop has alleged the necessary elements of an action under 10b-5(1) or (3). In the literal words of rule 10b-5, he must be able to show a "scheme ... to defraud ... or ... [an] act, practice or course of business which operates as a fraud or deceit upon [him] ... in connection with the sale of [the Bonds]...." Bishop's burden of proof will be to show that (1) the defendants knowingly conspired to bring securities onto the market which were not entitled to be marketed, intending to defraud purchasers, (2) Bishop reasonably relied on the Bonds' availability on the market as an indication of their apparent genuineness, and (3) as a result of the scheme to defraud, he suffered a loss. ***

The thrust of the arguments against our holding is that a recovery in this circumstance is not consonant with the central purpose of the securities laws, which, it is argued, is to provide full disclosure so that investors may make informed investment decisions. It is asserted that allowing recovery to one who has never read the Offering Circular minimizes the importance of such documents and discourages investors from reading them.

We disagree. First, the purpose of the securities acts and rule 10b-5 are far broader than merely providing full disclosure or fostering informed investment decisions. The Supreme Court has held that the acts were designed "to protect investors against fraud ... and to promote ethical standards of honesty and fair dealing. See H.R. Rep. No. 85, 73d Cong., 1st Sess., 1-5 (1933)." *Ernst & Ernst v. Hochfelder*, 425 U.S. 185, 195 (1976). *** Full disclosure is only one means, albeit a central one, of enhancing our goals.

Second, the role of the Offering Circular will continue undiminished even if Bishop proves his allegations and recovers. He has alleged that the fraud caused the Bonds to be offered for sale on the market. If Bishop proves no more than that the bonds would have been offered at a lower price or a higher rate, rather than that they would never have been issued or marketed, he cannot recover. Thus, a purchaser of securities will still have the strongest incentive to read the disclosure statement if he wants to ensure he gets full value for his securities purchases.

Under Bishop's broader theory, it would have availed him nothing to have read the Offering Circular. This theory is not that he bought inferior bonds, but that the Bonds he bought were fraudulently marketed. The securities laws allow an investor to rely on the integrity of the market to the extent that the securities it offers to him for purchase are entitled to be in the market place.

Finally, we reject the contention that our holding imposes new burdens on defendants or enhances their liability. Lawyers, underwriters, and accountants who participate in bond issues in good faith are unaffected by our decision. Liability results only if they act with intent to deceive or defraud. ***

The dissent asserts that we adopt a "new theory" because we separate Bishop's claim under 10b-5(2) that the Offering Circular was misleading from his claim under 10b-5(1) and (3) that defendants' fraudulently marketed Bonds caused his loss. It is not our "theory" but the words of rule 10b-5 which confer the right of action we hold Bishop is entitled to try to prove. ***

*** Whenever the rule 10b-5 issue shifts from misrepresentation or omission in a document to fraud on a broader scale, the search for causation must shift also. The "reliance" that produces causation in the latter type of case cannot come from reading a document. *** The rule is recognized also to provide the basis for a federal cause of action for more elaborate, intentional schemes which deceive or defraud purchasers of securities. ***

The judgment dismissing plaintiff's complaint is vacated and the cause remanded for further proceedings not inconsistent with this opinion. The district court also ruled that this action could not be maintained as a class action because of lack of typicality, lack of adequate representation, and lack of a showing that common questions of fact would predominate. All three of these determinations, however, were premised on the belief that reliance on the Offering Circular was crucial to Bishop's claim. On remand, the court must reconsider the maintainability of this action as a class action as to members of a properly defined class of Bond purchasers who did not so rely. ***

Carolyn Dineen Randall, Circuit Judge, with whom Brown, Roney, Gee, Tjoflat, Hill, Fay, Rubin, Reavley, and Hatchett, Circuit Judges, join, dissenting:

The majority opinion today adopts a new theory of recovery in federal court under Rule 10b-5. It holds that a purchaser of securities offered to the public by means of a misleading offering circular, who has heretofore been foreclosed from recovering in federal court under Rule 10b-5 because of his admitted lack of reliance on the offering circular, will not henceforth be foreclosed from recovering under the Rule if he is able to prove that the defendants knowingly conspired to bring securities onto the market which were not "entitled to be marketed" and that he reasonably relied on the availability of the securities on the market as an indication of their entitlement to be marketed.

This newly-devised route to recovery under Rule 10b-5 is completely without supporting precedent; indeed, it conflicts with the prior decisions of this and every other circuit and with the clear implication of recent Supreme Court decisions in the securities field. But even if the majority were writing on a blank slate, its novel holding would be profoundly unwise for several reasons. First, it introduces into the law under Rule 10b-5 a distinction between securities that are "entitled to be marketed," *i e.*, securities that may be the subject of a fraudulent marketing scheme, but which, absent the fraud, could be sold at *some* price, and securities that are not "entitled to be marketed," *i.e.*, securities that are the subject of a fraudulent marketing scheme and that, absent the fraud, could not be sold at *any* price. The requirements for recovery under Rule 10b-5 in any case hinge upon which category of securities the defrauded plaintiff purchased. If he purchased a security that was entitled to be marketed, he must have relied on the defendants' misrepresentations or omissions in order to recover. If, however, he can show that he purchased a security which was not entitled to be marketed, he can recover in spite of his nonreliance on the defendants' misrepresentations or omissions if he can show that he reasonably relied on the integrity of the marketplace to offer him securities that were entitled to be marketed. This novel theory permits recovery under the Rule to one who has elected not even to seek to read what the seller is obligated by the Rule to disclose, thereby defeating the primary objective of the Rule—the making of an informed investment decision. Second, the majority opinion has great potential for increasing the volume of litigation under Rule 10b-5 by providing a federal forum to those plaintiffs who by their own actions would otherwise have forfeited the protection of the Rule and have relegated themselves to state court actions for conversion. Finally, the majority opinion also has great potential for protracting much Rule 10b-5 litigation that would heretofore have terminated at the summary judgment stage. For these reasons, I respectfully dissent. ***

NOTES AND QUESTIONS

1. ***The Meaning of "Unmarketable."*** To obtain a presumption based on fraud-created-the-market, plaintiffs must show that the securities in question were "unmarketable." Courts have defined that term in the following ways.

(a) *Economic Unmarketability.* This definition requires that the securities in question "could 'not have been offered on the market at any price' absent the fraudulent scheme." *Ross v. Bank South, N.A.*, 885 F.2d 723, 729 (11th Cir. 1989), quoting *Shores v. Sklar* at n. 2.

(b) *"Patently Worthless" Enterprise.* This definition requires that the enterprise offering the securities be a "sham" or a "hoax." *Abell v. Potomac Ins. Co.*, 858 F.2d 1104, 1122 (5th Cir. 1988) (arguing that in *Shores,* the defendants "never intended to start a legitimate" business), judgment vac. on other grounds sub nom. *Fryar v. Abell*, 492 U.S. 914 (1989).

(c) *Legal Unmarketability.* This definition requires the existence of a legal bar to the marketing of the securities in question. *T.J. Raney & Sons, Inc. v. Fort Cobb, Oklahoma Irrigation Fuel Auth.*, 717 F.2d 1330, 1333 (10th Cir. 1983) (finding that the municipal authority that issued the bonds was barred by state law from doing so).

Which of these definition(s) are consistent with *Shores*? What are the advantages and disadvantages of each? To what extent are the definitions conceptually distinct? Compare *Malack v. BDO Seidman, LLP*, 617 F.3d 743, 748 (3d Cir. 2010) (calling the distinctions "hazy") with *In re Interbank Funding Corp. Sec. Litig*, 668 F. Supp. 2d 44, 52 (D.D.C. 2009) (combining the first and second of the above definitions into a single one), aff'd on other grounds, 629 F.3d 213 (D.C. Cir. 2010).

2. ***The Reasonableness of Relying on the Market to Prevent the Offering of Unmarketable Bonds.*** What mechanisms (if any) ordinarily operate to prevent the offering of unmarketable bonds? Compare *In re HealthSouth Corp. Sec. Litig.*, 261 F.R. D. 616, 644 (N.D. Ala. 2009) (identifying the mechanisms as "SEC review and reasonable investigation by a reputable underwriter and accountant, as well as civil and criminal penalties for willful violations") with *Malack v. BDO Seidman, LLP*, 617 F.3d 743, 749 (3d Cir. 2010) (arguing that "[t]he security's promoter and other entities involved in the issuance, such as the underwriter, the auditor, and legal counsel – the very entities often charged with fraud – cannot be reasonably relied upon to prevent

fraud"). What do you think? Is relying on the market to prevent the offering of unmarketable bonds appreciably less reasonable than relying on the integrity of the market price?

*3. **"Fraud on a Broader Scale."*** The *Shores* court justified its presumption partly on the ground that the allegations involved not merely a "misrepresentation or omission in a document" but rather "fraud on a broader scale." Are you comfortable with this justification?

*4. **Rebuttal.*** How can a defendant rebut a presumption of fraud-created-the-market?

*5 **Vexatious Litigation.*** According to the dissenting opinion in *Shores*, the presumption recognized by the majority encourages vexatious litigation. Do you agree?

*6. **Contentious Issue.*** Support for the fraud-created-the-market presumption extends well beyond the Fifth Circuit. The Tenth and Eleventh Circuits have likewise given the presumption their imprimatur. See, e.g., *Ross v. Bank South*, 885 F.2d 723 (11th Cir. 1989) (en banc); *T. J. Raney & Sons, Inc. v. Fort Cobb, Okla. Irrigation Fuel Auth.*, 717 F.2d 1330 (10th Cir. 1983). See also *Regents of Univ. of Cal. v. Credit Suisse First Boston (USA), Inc.*, 482 F.3d 372, 391-92 (5th Cir. 2007) (reaffirming *Shores* while finding it inapplicable under the circumstances).

On the other hand, the Seventh Circuit has rejected the presumption, at least where marketability is defined in economic (rather than legal) terms:

> The *existence* of a security does not depend on, or warrant, the adequacy of disclosure. Many a security is on the market even though the issuer or some third party made incomplete disclosures. Federal securities law does not include "merit regulation." Full disclosure of adverse information may lower the price, but it does not exclude the security from the market. Securities of bankrupt corporations trade freely; some markets specialize in penny stocks.

Eckstein v. Balcor Film Investors, 8 F.3d 1121, 1130-31 (7th Cir. 1993). Going even further, the Third Circuit has rejected the presumption in all of its varieties. *Malack v. BDO Seidman, LLP*, 617 F.3d 743, 749 (3d Cir. 2010) .

How would the Supreme Court be likely to respond to this circuit split? Consider this question further in connection with the Supreme Court cases that you encounter later in this Chapter.

7. Tweaking Fraud-Created-the-Market. The Fifth Circuit has recently tweaked the fraud-created-the-market-doctrine in the course of finding it inapplicable under the circumstances:

> *Shores* does not preclude the decision we reach in this case. The basis of the fraud-created-the-market theory is that the fraudster directly interfered with the market by introducing something that is not like the others: an objectively unmarketable security that has no business being there. This is qualitatively different from what the banks are alleged to have done, namely engage in transactions elsewhere that gave a misleading impression of the value of Enron securities that were already on the market. Moreover, in *Shores* the manipulation happened when the bogus security was introduced into the market; lawyers

> and other secondary actors were rendered liable for having conspired to achieve that end. In the wake of *Central Bank [N.A., v. Interstate Bank, N.A.*, 511 U.S. 164 (1994)], however, conspiracy is no longer a viable theory of § 10(b) liability, so that aspect of Shores has been overruled.

Regents of Univ. of Cal. v. Credit Suisse First Boston (USA), Inc., 482 F.3d 372, 391-92 (5th Cir. 2007). Did *Shores* characterize the violation at issue as "manipulation"? Does that characterization give the fraud- created-the-market presumption a firmer foundation? We examine *Central Bank* and conspiracy liability under Rule 10b-5 later in this Chapter. See infra Section H. Manipulation is the subject of Chapter 8.

PROBLEM 2-21

By means of the Internet and the telephone, Dwayne persuaded numerous investors to buy shares of Spring Cure Company. According to Dwayne, Spring Cure has developed a treatment for pollen allergies that is far superior to any treatment currently available. In fact, both the cure and the company are a complete fiction. Investors whom Dwayne has defrauded have brought an action against him under Rule 10b-5. Can these investors satisfy the reliance requirement?

d. The Justifiableness of the Reliance

In private Rule 10b-5 actions, courts imported from tort law not only the reliance requirement but in addition the requirement of justifiable reliance (also known as "reasonable reliance" or "due diligence" or "the duty of care"). Consider the following decision.

BROWN v. EARTHBOARD SPORTS USA, INC.

481 F.3d 901 (6th Cir. 2007)

DANNY J. BOGGS, CHIEF JUDGE:

Plaintiff-Appellant Clinton Brown, a wealthy businessman, made a risky investment in the securities of a small privately-held California company called Earthboard Sports USA ("Earthboard"). He was induced to embark on such a course of action by the "tip" he had received from Defendant-Appellee Jeffrey Vaughn, an acquaintance and financial advisor who considered Brown to be a prospective client, that a large public company was about to acquire Earthboard on extremely, even ridiculously, favorable terms. However, the promised acquisition turned out to be an entirely fictitious creation of Earthboard's president, one Hugh Jeffreys, a felon. When the truth was finally revealed, Brown and many others lost their investments. Brown then sued Earthboard, Jeffreys, Vaughn, and Vaughn's employer Lincoln Financial Advisors Corp. ("Lincoln") in federal court, claiming a variety of federal and state securities violations. The district court entered default judgment against Earthboard and Jeffreys.

Subsequently, the district court granted summary judgment in favor of Vaughn and Lincoln. *** For the reasons stated below, we reverse the district court with respect to the claims against Vaughn, but affirm summary judgment in favor of Lincoln. ***

As Brown appeals from summary judgment, we review the adduced evidence in the light most favorable to him. Earthboard is a privately-held Cosa Mesa, California corporation that designs and manufactures all-terrain "extreme" skateboards and related equipment. In 1999, it offered subscriptions in certain of its securities and filed for an exemption from federal registration requirements *** pursuant to Rule 506 of Regulation D, a safe harbor provision authorized by Section 4(2) of the 1933 Securities Act, for limited private placements. ***

Brown ran his own marketing firm from 1988 until 1999. In 1998, Brown's accountant, Gene Schindler, introduced him to Vaughn, a financial advisor and registered representative employed by Lincoln. Vaughn solicited 401(k) business from Brown's marketing firm, "ask[ing] to be one of [Brown's] investment advisors." Vaughn viewed Brown as a prospective client, and knew that Brown would received a large sum of money if he sold his firm. When Brown finally sold his company in 1999, Vaughn "wanted to know what [Brown's] plans were for the earn-out money." Thereafter, Vaughn contacted Brown periodically. During that time, it seems that Brown and Vaughn met on social occasions, playing golf occasionally, taking a golf vacation together at Brown's Arizona home, and enjoying Brown's time-share jet. They were both fans of Indiana University's basketball team, and they attended an Indiana/Kentucky game together. Brown dined at Vaughn's home at least once, Vaughn attended a Christmas party at Brown's home, and they attended a few charity-benefit dinners together.

Apparently, in August 2001, Vaughn first heard about Earthboard from his builder, who told him that the company was raising capital for expansion and put him in contact with the company's president, Jeffreys. Vaughn spoke with Jeffreys by telephone in August 2001, and again in late September 2001. They apparently did not meet each other in person until March 2002. According to Brown, Jeffreys told Vaughn on the telephone that Earthboard was involved in acquisition negotiations with VANS, a publicly-traded footwear company, and that, according to the terms of the deal, one share of Earthboard's securities would be exchanged for one share of VANS when the transaction finally closed. At that time, VANS shares were trading at about $12, but Jeffreys offered his company's shares to Vaughn for just $1 apiece. Thus, Vaughn stood to realize a 1100% capital gain when and if the promised transaction was closed. It was almost too good to be true.

Armed with what he probably took to be illicit or illegal "insider information," Vaughn allegedly decided to reap the rewards. Of course, the essential value of such an illicit "tip" lies in its concealment from the public eye, so it was probably impossible for Vaughn or anyone else to conduct any proper investigation of the transaction. But Vaughn allegedly did not allow his fundamental ignorance about Jeffreys, a felon previously convicted of fraud, or about the supposed Earthboard-VANS transaction, to govern his decisions. Of course, there was apparently not an ounce of truth to Jeffreys's "tips."[3]

According to the evidence adduced by Brown, Vaughn started by investing his own money in this scheme, and he ultimately purchased about $228,000 worth of Earthboard shares. He signed a subscription agreement on September 25, 2001, and purchased 100,000 shares for $1 per share. *** After introducing investors such as Brown to the "opportunity," he purchased another 99,000 shares on his own account for $99,000 on March 3, 2002, and the company gave him an additional 7,000 shares for free at that time "in lieu of [paying] me a commission," presumably to thank him for advising investors like Brown about the opportunity. He purchased another 29,000 shares on his own account in December 2002 for $1 per share.

After deciding to invest for himself, Vaughn began to solicit friends and acquaintances to participate in this "opportunity." Taking the evidence in the light most favorable to Brown, Vaughn contacted Brown in late November or early December 2001 to tell him that he "wanted the opportunity to prove to ... [Brown] how valuable he could be as a financial advisor and that he had an investment opportunity." Vaughn "wanted to meet [Brown] to discuss it." Due to "a sense of urgency in the phone call," Brown agreed to meet Vaughn for lunch about two days later. At that meeting, Vaughn "shared with ... [Brown] the details of this privately held enterprise called Earthboard, [and] its imminent sale to a publicly traded firm called VANS." To bolster the story's veracity, Vaughn allegedly lied to Brown by claiming that Earthboard's president, Jeffreys, was "a personal friend or acquaintance of his, that they had done business before in some way, shape or form and that [Jeffreys] owed him a favor." Vaughn then explained that subscriptions in Earthboard stock were available to a limited group of investors at $6 per share, and that the purported one-for-one stock swap upon the transaction's closing offered Brown the prospect of doubling his investment overnight. But Vaughn warned that time was pressing, for the VANS transaction was "imminent and ... [Brown] needed to move quickly if [he] wanted to be a part of it."

Brown said he was interested, and Vaughn replied "I need to get you a subscription agreement." Vaughn made arrangements to have a subscription agreement sent to Brown by fax. Earthboard sent the subscription agreement to Brown on December 5, 2001. Brown consulted his financial advisors, two of whom specifically questioned how Vaughn could have access to such inside information about an unannounced transaction involving a public company, but Brown would not be deterred. Relying entirely on Vaughn's "tip," Brown saw this as an opportunity to invest in VANS, a company he found to be "solid," though he did not independently investigate Earthboard.

P relied on the tip, didn't do any independent investigation

3. Jeffreys recently pleaded guilty to violating federal securities fraud laws, and has been sentenced to 41 months in federal prison. United States v. Jeffreys, 8:05-cr-00184-DOC (C.D.Cal.2006). The SEC has also filed a still-pending civil securities suit against Jeffreys and Earthboard, seeking recovery of some of the illicit gains. *SEC v. Jeffreys*, 1:05-cv-00372-WR-DAR (D.D.C.).

Brown received his subscription agreement and wire transfer instructions directly from Earthboard. Brown claims that Vaughn assisted him in completing the form. He clearly saw "$1" listed as the original share price, and it had been marked out and replaced by "$6." Brown assumed the stock price had risen because of the imminent transaction. He neither saw nor asked for a Private Placement Memorandum ("PPM"), though it was referenced in the subscription agreement he had signed. He faxed the completed subscription form directly to Earthboard on December 13, 2001, requesting 100,000 shares. Vaughn then faxed wire instructions to Brown from Lincoln's fax machine, and Brown finally wired $600,000 to Earthboard.

After completing this transaction, Vaughn and Brown engaged in numerous conversations regarding their investments in Earthboard, and both spoke about the fluctuating price of VANS stock. Brown asked Vaughn to "[s]end me whatever you get" from Earthboard, and Vaughn sent press releases and announcements from Earthboard to Brown, who apparently did not receive them directly from Earthboard. On January 9, 2002, Vaughn faxed an Earthboard press release to Brown from Lincoln's fax machine, wherein Earthboard announced a "definitive agreement" to have "its stock acquired by a publicly traded major footwear company." According to this "press release," Earthboard stock would be exchanged on a "one for one basis," apparently confirming the lies told to Brown. Brown continued to follow VANS stock, assuming that the transaction was complete and awaiting only public announcement. Brown and Vaughn even discussed whether to sell or hold the VANS stock after the merger. Vaughn kept assuring Brown that the transaction with VANS was "imminent," and so Brown continued to believe that Vaughn remained in constant contact with Earthboard's management. In fact, however, as of January 2002, Vaughn had allegedly not yet even met with Earthboard's president in person, and there is a genuine issue of material fact with respect to the question of whether had he conducted any due diligence about Earthboard or the rumored transaction prior to soliciting Brown: in his deposition, Vaughn at first claims that he personally met Jeffreys and toured Earthboard's factory in early 2001, but almost immediately he seems to have corrected himself by admitting that the meeting and tour did not occur until March 2002.

VANS shares having risen to $14, Brown decided to purchase an additional 40,000 shares of Earthboard at $6 per share on February 28, 2002. For this investment, he signed a new subscription agreement for his entire purchase of 140,000 shares (for a total investment of $840,000), which contained more complete and legible disclosures than the subscription agreement that he had received in December 2001. This agreement warned that the securities "have not been registered" and that the securities were offered pursuant to Section 4(2) of the 1933 Securities Act. To make this purchase, Brown again acknowledged that *** he had relied solely on his own independent investigation in making the investment decision. Brown claims that he asked for, but never received, Earthboard's financial statements, the offering circular, the PPM, and any other disclosures about the company. ***

Time passed, but the fictitious transaction never closed, and it was finally revealed that the whole scheme was fraudulent. Brown filed a complaint against all defendants in September 2003 ***. On May 27, 2005, the district court entered default judgment against Earthboard and Jeffreys, holding them jointly and severally liable for $840,000 plus pre- and post-judgment interest (representing Brown's entire investment) even though those parties are almost certainly judgment-proof. On August 2, 2005, the district court entered summary judgment in favor of Vaughn and Lincoln. *** The claim against Lincoln was dismissed because it depended entirely on the claim against Vaughn. Brown filed a timely appeal.***

*** Brown filed this action pursuant to Section 10(b) of the 1934 Securities Exchange Act, Rule 10b-5 promulgated thereunder and a virtually identical state statute. Vaughn and Lincoln both dispute that Brown has created a genuine issue of material fact with respect to three elements of securities fraud: scienter, reliance, and loss causation. * **

1

*** We think that Brown has successfully alleged Vaughn's scienter and has adduced sufficient evidence to withstand summary judgment. Vaughn is a licensed securities professional who, by his trade, is fully cognizant of the prohibitions contained in federal securities laws, and *** should be aware of fraudulent schemes such as this one.*** It is inherently reckless for a securities professional to attempt to violate the law, and it is no defense to suggest that he actually believed the tip to be true as that simply further demonstrates his foiled intent to circumvent the law. ***

2

*** Brown has adduced evidence sufficient to withstand summary judgment that he was induced to invest in Earthboard as a result of Vaughn's reckless misrepresentations, and that the revelation of the truth about the purported VANS merger proximately caused his economic loss.

3

Alternatively, the appellees claim that the context of the purchase indicates that Brown could not, as a matter of law, have reasonably or justifiably relied on the information that Vaughn allegedly provided. To support their contention, appellees especially note that the subscription agreement that Brown signed contained an integration clause in which Brown waived any claim that he relied on third party advice in making his purchase. Appellees point to certain decisions by several of our sister circuits for the proposition that non-reliance clauses in sales contracts absolutely foreclose later suits for deceit by prior representation. *Emergent Capital Inv. Mgmt., LLC v. Stonepath Group, Inc.*, 343 F.3d 189, 195 (2d Cir.2003); *Rissman v. Rissman*, 213 F.3d 381, 383-84 (7th Cir.2000); *Jackvony v. RIHT Financial Corp.*, 873 F.2d 411 (1st Cir.1989).

The appellees overstate their case. In the first place, the law of our circuit requires us to engage in a contextual analysis in order to ascertain whether, as a matter of law, a party has introduced sufficient evidence of reasonable reliance to withstand summary judgment. In assessing reasonable or justifiable reliance on summary judgment, we apply a recklessness standard in looking at the context of the asserted reliance. *Wright v. National Warranty*

Co., L.P., 953 F.2d 256, 261 (6th Cir.1992). Among the factors that we have employed in the past to ascertain reasonable reliance "in a non-insider context" are

> (1) The sophistication of expertise of the plaintiff in financial and securities matters; (2) the existence of long standing business or personal relationships; (3) access to the relevant information; (4) the existence of a fiduciary relationship; (5) concealment of the fraud; (6) the opportunity to detect the fraud; (7) whether the plaintiff initiated the stock transaction or sought to expedite the transaction; and (8) the generality or specificity of the misrepresentations.

Ibid. To erect a *per se* rule with respect to non-reliance clauses would undermine the essential point of undertaking a contextual analysis, and we do not choose to adopt such a blanket rule now.

Moreover, we do not read the opinions of our sister circuits in the appellees' preferred manner: far from erecting a *per se* rule foreclosing the possibility of recovery for deceit in all situations where an allegedly injured party has signed a non-reliance clause, these opinions simply accord an appropriate weight to evidence of the signing of such a clause in the entire context of the alleged fraud. *AES Corp. v. The Dow Chemical Co.*, 325 F.3d 174, 181 (3d Cir.2003); *Rogen v. Ilikon Corp.*, 361 F.2d 260, 267-68 (1st Cir.1966). Finally, it is noteworthy that the appellees were not themselves parties to the subscription agreement containing the non-reliance clause.

Under the unusual factual circumstances of this suit, including the non-reliance clause in the subscription agreement, we do not think that Brown acted unreasonably, as an unavoidable matter of law, in relying on the alleged tip of a securities broker who so obviously wanted to impress a prospective client. Instead, Brown has introduced enough evidence of reasonable reliance to withstand summary judgment at this stage. Based on the evidence before us, therefore, we leave the final determination of reliance to the trier of fact. ***

GERALD E. ROSEN, DISTRICT JUDGE, CONCURRING, IN PART, AND DISSENTING, IN PART.

*** Although I agree with the majority that Brown has introduced sufficient evidence of scienter and loss causation-two of the three requisite elements of a securities fraud claim at issue in this case-I do not believe that Brown has introduced sufficient evidence to establish reasonable reliance, and this failure is fatal to his securities fraud case.[1]

By way of preface to my analysis of Brown's arguments supporting his purported reasonable reliance, I am reminded of a verse from Simon and Garfunkel's 1969 classic song, "The Boxer":

I have squandered my resistance

---

1. Although the district court did not address the reliance issue, the issue was fully briefed and argued before both the district court and this court. In ruling on a district court's grant of summary judgment, an appellate court does not have to rely on the same reasons that persuaded the lower court. See *City Mgmt. Corp. v. U.S. Chem. Co.*, 43 F.3d 244, 251 (6th Cir.1994).

For a pocketful of mumbles
Such are promises
All lies and jests.
Still a man hears what he wants to hear
And disregards the rest.[2]

Such is the nature of Mr. Brown's reliance, in my view. But beyond Paul Simon's insights into human failings, I also rely upon well-established precedent. In assessing whether a plaintiff's alleged reliance was reasonable, "the entire context of the transaction, including factors such as its complexity and magnitude, the sophistication of the parties, and the content of any agreements between them" must be considered. *Emergent Capital Inv. v. Stonepath Group, Inc.*, 343 F.3d 189, 195 (2nd Cir.2003). Although the majority enumerates the various factors for consideration which we delineated in *Wright v. National Warranty Co., L.P.*, 953 F.2d 256, 261 (6th Cir.1992), it neglects to discuss *any* of these factors, and instead, finds only that the non-reliance clause in the subscription agreement executed by Plaintiff was insufficient in and of itself to show non-reliance.

In my view, applying the factors set forth in *Emergent Capital* and *Wright*, Brown's "reliance" is not only not reasonable, it is virtually non-existent beyond the fact that Vaughn made the representations to him-a fact which by itself is simply not sufficient as a matter of law.

The record here demonstrates that Brown, by his own statement, was a sophisticated businessman who founded a marketing research firm that he sold for $22 million. He had a great deal of prior investment experience, multiple brokerage accounts, and the ability to assess risk. Importantly, he had substantial prior experience with private placement investments which demonstrated his knowledge of their high risk profile. He testified that before making private placement investments he consulted with both his attorney and his accountant. He also testified that before investing in Earthboard he consulted with two of his financial advisors. He had no prior business relationship with Defendant Vaughn; the two had only a friendly relationship based on Indiana basketball and occasional golf outings, and the few times they dined together with their families.

Brown admitted in his deposition that he knew that none of Vaughn's information about Earthboard was firsthand, that Vaughn was not personally involved in any merger negotiations, and that Vaughn was simply reporting what Jeffreys had told him. Brown further admitted that he had access to any information about Earthboard that he wanted and that neither Vaughn nor anybody else prevented him from investigating Earthboard. Where a plaintiff has equal access to information but simply fails to inquire for himself, his claimed reliance is not reasonable or justifiable. See *Aschinger v. Columbus Showcase Co.*, 934 F.2d 1402, 1410-11 (6th Cir.1991). This should certainly be

2. "The Boxer", ©1968 Paul Simon.

even more true for a sophisticated investor such as Brown.

Brown's deposition testimony, however, is not the only evidence that belies his claim of reasonable reliance; he also signed an Earthboard Subscription Agreement that warned him that the investment involved a "high degree of risk" and he categorically acknowledged that in making the investment, he "relied solely upon independent investigations made by [himself] and by no other third party." He also checked the box on the Subscription Agreement indicating that he had knowledge and experience in financial and business matters and in private placement investments and that he was capable of evaluating the merits and risks of an investment in the shares. We held in *Wright v. National Warranty Co.*, supra, 953 F.2d at 260, that a securities fraud plaintiff is bound by statements made in a subscription agreement. See also *Rissman v. Rissman*, 213 F.3d 381, 383 (7th Cir.2000) ("Securities law does not permit a party to a stock transaction to disavow such representations-to say, in effect, 'I lied when I told you I wasn't relying on your prior statements' and then to seek damages for their contents.").

For the foregoing reasons, I believe the record here amply supports a determination that Plaintiff failed to establish reasonable reliance and, therefore, I would affirm the district court's grant of summary judgment on the securities fraud claim on this alternative basis.

NOTES AND QUESTIONS

1. To Each His Own Context. The *Earthboard* majority concluded that the plaintiff did not act unreasonably, given "the unusual factual circumstances of this suit." What are those circumstances? How do they contrast with the circumstances found salient by the dissent?

2. Merger Clauses and Justifiable Reliance. Both the majority and dissent adopt the view that a merger clause bears on justifiable reliance but is not dispositive. See also *AES Corp. v. Dow Chemical Co.*, 325 F.3d 174, 180 (3d Cir. 2003) (same). This view is not universally shared, however.

Another view is that a merger clause by itself "precludes any claim of deceit by prior representations." *Rissman v. Rissman,* 213 F.3d 381, 383-84 (7th Cir. 2000) (collecting cases).

Still another view holds that a merger clause has no relevance for the justifiable reliance question as the result of Exchange Act Section 29(a), which reads:

> Any condition, stipulation, or provision binding any person to waive compliance with any provision of this chapter or any rule or regulation thereunder, or of any rule of an exchange required thereby, shall be void.

The impact of Section 29(a) has been explained thus:

> At its core, section 29 seeks to prevent parties from contractually avoiding the requirements of Rule 10b-5. If the void stipulation may be evidence in a later Rule 10b-5 claim, how likely is it that the seller of securities will lose the 10b-5 claim? Imagine the mountains of evidence the 10b-5 plaintiff will need to compete with the evidence of the stipulation. Realistically, how will a plaintiff convince a reasonable juror that he reasonably relied on a representation when

> he signed a provision that stated otherwise? To permit the void stipulation to serve as evidence of a lack of reasonable reliance would be to take the teeth out of section 29. It would make a 10b-5 claim logically possible, but essentially hopeless. Congress meant more when it enacted section 29(a).

AES Corp., supra, 325 F.3d at 184 (Wallace, J., concurring and dissenting). Of the three views on the merger clause- justifiable reliance relationship, which do you find the most persuasive?

Does the philosophy underlying Section 29(a) clash with the justifiable reliance requirement in general (quite apart from any arguable clash between the text of Section 29(a) and merger clauses in particular)?

3. Burden-Shifting: Misrepresentations vs. Omissions. Assume an omissions case in which the *Affiliated Ute* presumption of reliance attaches. Should that presumption carry with it a presumption of justifiable reliance as well? Compare *Starr v. Georgeson Shareholder, Inc.*, 412 F.3d 103, 109 & n. 5 (2d Cir. 2005) (suggesting that if the plaintiff had alleged an omission, he would not have to plead justifiable reliance) with *Emergent Capital Inv. Mgt., LLC v. Stonepath Group, Inc.*, 343 F.3d 189, 195 (2d Cir. 2003) (requiring the plaintiff to establish reasonable reliance as to both omissions and misrepresentations)

4. Burden- Shifting: Fraud-on-the-Market. Ordinarily, justifiable reliance issues outside the fraud- on- the-market context, such as in *Brown*. But those issues can on occasion arise within the fraud-on-the-market context as well. For example, assume a fraud-on-the-market action by Jane, who through encounters with a corporate insider gleaned information that arguably qualifies as a "red flag" that the company's public statements at issue in her litigation contain fraud. Should Jane have to plead and prove her justifiable reliance or should the defendant have to prove that she lacked it? Cf. *Harsco Corp. v. Segui*, 91 F.3d 337, 342 n. 5 (2d Cir. 1996) (maintaining that the burden is on the defendant).

Is there any philosophical tension between the fraud-on-the-market presumption and the justifiable reliance requirement?

5. Element or Defense. Like virtually all courts, the *Earthboard* majority treats justifiable reliance as an element of the plaintiff's prima facie case rather than as a defense. Which makes more sense – requiring the plaintiff to establish her justifiable reliance or instead requiring the defendant to establish the plaintiff's lack of justifiable reliance?

6. Justifying Justifiable Reliance. Courts have offered each of the following as rationales for the justifiable reliance requirement. Which (if any) do you find persuasive?

(a) Causation. The justifiable reliance requirement "insures that there is a causal connection between the misrepresentation and the plaintiff's harm." *Zobrist v. Coal-X, Inc.,* 708 F.2d 1511 (10th Cir. 1983).

(b) Protecting Defendants. Without a justifiable reliance requirement, "even the most careful seller is at risk, for it is easy to claim: 'Despite what the written documents say, one of your agents told me something else.' " *Acme Propane, Inc. v. Tenexco, Inc.*, 844 F.2d 1317, 1322 (7th Cir. 1988).

(c) Anti-Fraud. Justifiable reliance "'requir[es] plaintiffs to invest carefully" and thereby "'promotes the anti-fraud policies' of the securities acts by making fraud more readily discoverable." *Banca Cremi, S.A. v. Alex. Brown & Sons, Inc.*, 132 F.3d 1017, 1028 (4th Cir. 1997) (quoting *Dupuy v. Dupuy*, 551 F.2d 1005, 1014 (5th Cir. 1977)).

7. ***Conflict?*** Consider whether the justifiable reliance requirement can be reconciled with *Bateman Eichler, Hill Richards, Inc. v. Berner*, 472 U.S. 299 (1985). In *Bateman*, the plaintiffs brought a Rule 10b-5 action against a corporate insider and a broker for allegedly providing them with fraudulent nonpublic information. The defendants invoked the defense of *in pari delicto* (Latin for "equal fault"): their argument was that by trading on the information in question, the plaintiffs had themselves violated the securities laws and thus should be barred from recovery. The Supreme Court held that an *in pari delicto* defense to a federal securities action can succeed only when two conditions are satisfied: "(1) as a direct result of his own actions, the plaintiff bears at least substantially equal responsibility for the violation he seeks to redress and (2) preclusion of suit would not significantly interfere with the effective enforcement of the securities laws and protection of the investing public." Id. at 310-311.

Examining the first condition, the Court held that at least as a general rule, an insider and a broker bear greater responsibility than do their tippees. The Court acknowledged that the plaintiffs "may well have violated the securities laws." Id. at 314. But it observed that "there are important distinctions between the relative culpabilities of tippers, securities professionals, and tippees in these circumstances." Id. at 312-313. First, the Court noted that the tippee is apt to be less culpable because his liability is "solely derivative" from the tipper. Id. at 313. Second, the Court observed that insiders and brokers who tip may commit additional offenses in which their tippees are not involved, such as violating fiduciary duties owed the issuer. Id. at 313. The Court termed these offenses "particularly egregious when committed by a securities professional." Id. at 314.

Examining the second condition, the Court held that barring the lawsuit would undermine enforcement of Rule 10b-5. The Court observed that given the Commission's limited resources, disallowance of private actions by tippees against tippers would mean that many tippers would escape prosecution altogether. Lawsuits against tippers are a vital weapon against insider trading, the Court asserted, because they target the "sources" of inside information. Id. at 315-16.

One of your casebook authors has argued that the justifiable reliance requirement cannot be reconciled with *Bateman*:

> Although *Bateman* addressed only the *in pari delicto* defense, the decision applies equally to other common law doctrines. If this defense is subordinate to enforcement considerations, there is no principled basis for preventing subordination of other common law doctrines that are antithetical to enforcement.
>
> ***The duty of care requires that courts dismiss the claims of careless plaintiffs who have not themselves violated Rule 10b-5. Defendants in these actions, however, have violated Rule 10b-5. Dismissing suits against violators

in pari delicto defense

2 reqs for the defense

> in order to penalize nonviolators undermines the enforcement of section 10(b) in direct violation of *Bateman* ***.

Margaret V. Sachs, The Relevance of Tort Law Doctrines to Rule 10b-5: Should Careless Plaintiffs Be Denied Recovery?, 71 Cornell L. Rev. 96, 135, 137 (1985). On the other hand, the Fifth Circuit has expressed a very different view:

> The due diligence standard *** ultimately foster[s] the same law enforcement goal as *Bateman* Eichler[.] *** These standards relating to a plaintiff's conduct encourage an investor to complain promptly about violations of his or her rights and, in so doing, to enable those with authority to control wrongdoing before additional investors are injured.

Stephenson v. Paine Webber, Jackson & Curtis, 839 F.2d 1095, 1099 (5th Cir. 1988).

PROBLEM 2-22

Ralph made a number of stock purchases over the years, all of which lost money. Recently he purchased an interest in West-X, a limited partnership involved in oil drilling. None of Ralph's previous investments involved oil drilling.

West-X's general partner is Dewey, as to whom Ralph had no previous personal knowledge. If Ralph had searched the Internet, he would have learned that Dewey had a lengthy criminal record. Ralph did not conduct such a search, largely as the result of Dewey's winning personality.

In conversations with Ralph, Dewey spoke glowingly about West-X's favorable tax situation. In fact, West-X's tax situation was anything but favorable, as the private placement memorandum made clear.

Ralph did not read the private placement memorandum. He did, however, tell Dewey to remove any merger clause (if there was one) because he would not invest if the memorandum contained such a clause.

Dewey later told Ralph that he had removed the merger clause. Taking Dewey at his word, Ralph signed the contract to purchase. In fact, the merger clause remained in the contract.

Not long afterwards, West-X imploded due largely to tax-related problems. Ralph has filed a Rule 10b-5 action based on Dewey's oral statements about West-X's tax situation. Will Ralph succeed in meeting the justifiable reliance requirement? Why or why not?

2. The Loss Causation Requirement

The loss causation requirement has become one of the most contentious aspects of Rule 10b-5. The requirement focuses on whether the plaintiff's loss can be attributed in significant measure to the defendant's fraud rather than to market or industry conditions or other factors extraneous to the fraud. The rationale for the requirement has been articulated as follows:

> No social purpose would be served by encouraging everyone who suffers an investment loss because of an unanticipated change in market conditions to pick through offering memoranda with a fine-tooth comb in the hope of uncovering

a misrepresentation. Defrauders are a bad lot and should be punished, but Rule 10b-5 does not make them insurers against national economic calamities.

Bastian v. Petren Res. Corp., 892 F.2d 680, 685 (7th Cir. 1990) (Posner, J.).

The loss causation requirement originated under Rule 10b-5 as a judicial construct, imported from tort law. But in 1995 Congress codified the requirement as part of the PSLRA:

> In any private action arising under this Act, the plaintiff shall have the burden of proving that the act or omission of the defendant alleged to violate this Act caused the loss for which the plaintiff seeks to receive damages.

Section 21D(b)(4) of the Exchange Act.

The Supreme Court has made two excursions into loss causation territory: the decision set out below as well as *Erica P. John Fund, Inc. v. Halliburton Co.*, 131 S.Ct. 2179 (2011), discussed in the Notes and Questions following *Dura*.

DURA PHARMACEUTICALS, INC. v. BROUDO

544 U.S. 336 (2005)

JUSTICE STEPHEN G. BREYER:

A private plaintiff who claims securities fraud must prove that the defendant's fraud caused an economic loss. 15 U.S.C. § 78u-4(b)(4). We consider a Ninth Circuit holding that a plaintiff can satisfy this requirement – a requirement that courts call "loss causation" – simply by alleging in the complaint and subsequently establishing that "the price" of the security "*on the date of purchase* was inflated because of the misrepresentation." In our view, the Ninth Circuit is wrong, both in respect to what a plaintiff must prove and in respect to what the plaintiffs' complaint here must allege.

I

Respondents are individuals who bought stock in Dura Pharmaceuticals, Inc., on the public securities market between April 15, 1997, and February 24, 1998. They have brought this securities fraud class action against Dura and some of its managers and directors (hereinafter Dura) in federal court. In respect to the question before us, their detailed amended (181 paragraph) complaint makes substantially the following allegations:

(1) Before and during the purchase period, Dura (or its officials) made false statements concerning both Dura's drug profits and future Food and Drug Administration (FDA) approval of a new asthmatic spray device.

(2) In respect to drug profits, Dura falsely claimed that it expected that its drug sales would prove profitable.

(3) In respect to the asthmatic spray device, Dura falsely claimed that it expected the FDA would soon grant its approval.

(4) On the last day of the purchase period, February 24, 1998, Dura announced that its earnings would be lower than expected, principally due to slow drug sales.

(5) The next day Dura's shares lost almost half their value (falling from about $39 per share to about $21).

(6) About eight months later (in November 1998), Dura announced that the FDA would not approve Dura's new asthmatic spray device.

(7) The next day Dura's share price temporarily fell but almost fully recovered within one week.

Most importantly, the complaint says the following (and nothing significantly more than the following) about economic losses attributable to the spray device misstatement: *"In reliance on the integrity of the market, [the plaintiffs] ... paid artificially inflated prices for Dura securities" and the plaintiffs suffered "damage[s]" thereby*. (emphasis added).

The District Court dismissed the complaint. In respect to the plaintiffs' drug-profitability claim, it held that the complaint failed adequately to allege an appropriate state of mind, *i.e.*, that defendants had acted knowingly, or the like. In respect to the plaintiffs' spray device claim, it held that the complaint failed adequately to allege "loss causation."

The Court of Appeals for the Ninth Circuit reversed. In the portion of the court's decision now before us – the portion that concerns the spray device claim – the Circuit held that the complaint adequately alleged "loss causation." The Circuit wrote that "plaintiffs establish loss causation if they have shown that the price *on the date of purchase* was inflated because of the misrepresentation." (emphasis in original). It added that "the injury occurs at the time of the transaction." Since the complaint pleaded "that the price at the time of purchase was overstated," and it sufficiently identified the cause, its allegations were legally sufficient.

Because the Ninth Circuit's views about loss causation differ from those of other Circuits that have considered this issue, we granted Dura's petition for certiorari. Compare ibid. with, e.g., *Emergent Capital Investment Management, LLC v. Stonepath Group, Inc.*, 343 F.3d 189, 198 (C.A.2 2003); *Semerenko v. Cendant Corp.*, 223 F.3d 165, 185 (C.A.3 2000); *Robbins v. Koger Properties, Inc.*, 116 F.3d 1441, 1447-1448 (C.A.11 1997). We now reverse.

II

Private federal securities fraud actions are based upon federal securities statutes and their implementing regulations. Section 10(b) of the Securities Exchange Act of 1934 forbids (1) the "use or employ[ment] ... of any ...deceptive device," (2) "in connection with the purchase or sale of any security," and (3) "in contravention of" Securities and Exchange Commission "rules and regulations." Commission Rule 10b-5 forbids, among other things, the making of any "untrue statement of material fact" or the omission of any material fact "necessary in order to make the statements made ... not misleading."

The courts have implied from these statutes and Rule a private damages action, which resembles, but is not identical to, common-law tort actions for deceit and misrepresentation. See, e.g., *Blue Chip Stamps v. Manor Drug Stores*, 421 U.S. 723, 730, 744 (1975); *Ernst & Ernst v. Hochfelder*, 425 U.S. 185, 196

(1976). And Congress has imposed statutory requirements on that private action. E.g., 15 U.S.C. § 78u-4(b)(4).

In cases involving publicly traded securities and purchases or sales in public securities markets, the action's basic elements include:

(1) *a material misrepresentation (or omission),* see *Basic Inc. v. Levinson*, 485 U.S. 224, 231-232(1988);

(2) *scienter, i.e.*, a wrongful state of mind, see *Ernst & Ernst*, supra, at 197, 199;

(3) *a connection with the purchase or sale of a security,* see *Blue Chip Stamps*, supra, at 730-731;

(4) *reliance*, often referred to in cases involving public securities markets (fraud-on-the-market cases) as transaction causation," see *Basic*, supra, at 248-249 (nonconclusively presuming that the price of a publicly traded share reflects a material misrepresentation and that plaintiffs have relied upon that misrepresentation as long as they would not have bought the share in its absence);

(5) *economic loss*, 15 U.S.C. § 78u-4(b)(4); and

(6) *"loss causation," i.e.*, a causal connection between the material misrepresentation and the loss, ibid.; cf. T. Hazen, Law of Securities Regulation, §§12.11[1], [3] (5th ed.2002).

Dura argues that the complaint's allegations are inadequate in respect to these last two elements.

A

We begin with the Ninth Circuit's basic reason for finding the complaint adequate, namely, that at the end of the day plaintiffs need only "establish," *i.e.*, prove, that "the price *on the date of purchase* was inflated because of the misrepresentation." In our view, this statement of the law is wrong. Normally, in cases such as this one (*i.e.*, fraud-on-the-market cases), an inflated purchase price will not itself constitute or proximately cause the relevant economic loss.

For one thing, as a matter of pure logic, at the moment the transaction takes place, the plaintiff has suffered no loss; the inflated purchase payment is offset by ownership of a share that *at that instant* possesses equivalent value. Moreover, the logical link between the inflated share purchase price and any later economic loss is not invariably strong. Shares are normally purchased with an eye toward a later sale. But if, say, the purchaser sells the shares quickly before the relevant truth begins to leak out, the misrepresentation will not have led to any loss. If the purchaser sells later after the truth makes its way into the market place, an initially inflated purchase price *might* mean a later loss. But that is far from inevitably so. When the purchaser subsequently resells such shares, even at a lower price, that lower price may reflect, not the earlier misrepresentation, but changed economic circumstances, changed investor expectations, new industry-specific or firm-specific facts, conditions, or other events, which taken separately or together account for some or all of that lower price. (The same is true in respect to a claim that a share's higher price is lower than it would otherwise have been – a claim we do not consider here.) Other things being equal, the longer the time between purchase and sale, the more likely that this is so, *i.e.*, the more likely that other factors caused the loss.

Given the tangle of factors affecting price, the most logic alone permits us to say is that the higher purchase price will *sometimes* play a role in bringing about a future loss. It may prove to be a necessary condition of any such loss, and in that sense one might say that the inflated purchase price suggests that the misrepresentation (using language the Ninth Circuit used) "touches upon" a later economic loss. But, even if that is so, it is insufficient. To "touch upon" a loss is not to *cause* a loss, and it is the latter that the law requires. 15 U.S.C. § 78u-4(b)(4).

For another thing, the Ninth Circuit's holding lacks support in precedent. Judicially implied private securities-fraud actions resemble in many (but not all) respects common-law deceit and misrepresentation actions. See *Blue Chip Stamps*, supra, at 744; see also L. Loss & J. Seligman, Fundamentals of Securities Regulation, 910-918 (5th ed.2004) (describing relationship to common-law deceit). The common law of deceit subjects a person who "fraudulently" makes a "misrepresentation" to liability "for pecuniary loss caused" to one who justifiably relies upon that misrepresentation. Restatement (Second) of Torts § 525, p. 55 (1977) (hereinafter Restatement of Torts); see also *Southern Development Co. v. Silva*, 125 U.S. 247, 250 (1888) (setting forth elements of fraudulent misrepresentation). And the common law has long insisted that a plaintiff in such a case show not only that had he known the truth he would not have acted but also that he suffered actual economic loss. See, e.g., *Pasley v. Freeman*, 3 T.R. 5:1, 100 Eng. Rep. 450, 457 (1789); *Freeman v. Venner*, 120 Mass. 424, 426 (1876); see also M. Bigelow, Law of Torts 101 (8th ed.1907); 2 T. Cooley, Law of Torts section 348, p. 551 (4th ed.1932); W. Keeton, D. Dobbs, R. Keeton, & D. Owen, Prosser and Keeton on Law of Torts § 110, p. 765 (5th ed.1984).

Given the common-law roots of the securities fraud action (and the common-law requirement that a plaintiff show actual damages), it is not surprising that other courts of appeal have rejected the Ninth Circuit's "inflated purchase price" approach to proving causation and loss. See, e.g., *Emergent Capital*, 343 F.3d, at 198 (inflation of purchase price alone cannot satisfy loss causation); *Semerenko*, 223 F.3d, at 185 (same); *Robbins*, 116 F.3d, at 1448 (same). Indeed, the Restatement of Torts, in setting forth the judicial consensus, says that a person who "misrepresents the financial condition of a corporation in order to sell its stock" becomes liable to a relying purchaser "for the loss" the purchaser sustains "when the facts ... become generally known" and "as a result" share value "depreciate[s]." § 548A, Comment *b*, at 107. Treatise writers, too, have emphasized the need to prove proximate causation. Prosser and Keeton § 110, at 767 (losses do "not afford any basis for recovery" if "brought about by business conditions or other factors").

We cannot reconcile the Ninth Circuit's "inflated purchase price" approach with these views of other courts. And the uniqueness of its perspective argues against the validity of its approach in a case like this one where we consider the contours of a judicially implied cause of action with roots in the common law.

Finally, the Ninth Circuit's approach overlooks an important securities law objective. The securities statutes seek to maintain public confidence in the marketplace. See *United States v. O'Hagan*, 521 U.S. 642, 658 (1997). They do so by deterring fraud, in part, through the availability of private securities fraud actions. *Randall v. Loftsgaarden*, 478 U.S. 647, 664 (1986). But the statutes make these latter actions available, not to provide investors with broad insurance against market losses, but to protect them against those economic losses that misrepresentations actually cause. Cf. *Basic*, 485 U.S., at 252 (White, J., joined by O'Connor, J., concurring in part and dissenting in part) ("[A]llowing recovery in the face of affirmative evidence of nonreliance – would effectively convert Rule 10b-5 into a scheme of investor's insurance. There is no support in the Securities Exchange Act, the Rule, or our cases for such a result"). The statutory provision at issue here and the paragraphs that precede it emphasize this last mentioned objective. Private Securities Litigation Reform Act of 1995, 109 Stat. 737. The statute insists that securities fraud complaints "specify" each misleading statement; that they set forth the facts "on which [a] belief" that a statement is misleading was "formed"; and that they "state with particularity facts giving rise to a strong inference that the defendant acted with the required state of mind." 15 U.S.C. §§ 78u-4(b)(1), (2). And the statute expressly imposes on plaintiffs "the burden of proving" that the defendant's misrepresentations "caused the loss for which the plaintiff seeks to recover." § 78u-4(b)(4).

The statute thereby makes clear Congress' intent to permit private securities fraud actions for recovery where, but only where, plaintiffs adequately allege and prove the traditional elements of causation and loss. By way of contrast, the Ninth Circuit's approach would allow recovery where a misrepresentation leads to an inflated purchase price but nonetheless does not *proximately cause* any economic loss. That is to say, it would permit recovery where these two traditional elements in fact are missing.

In sum, we find the Ninth Circuit's approach inconsistent with the law's requirement that a plaintiff prove that the defendant's misrepresentation (or other fraudulent conduct) *proximately caused* the plaintiff's economic loss. We need not, and do not, consider other proximate cause or loss-related questions.

B

Our holding about plaintiffs' need to *prove* proximate causation and economic loss leads us also to conclude that the plaintiffs' complaint here failed adequately to *allege* these requirements. We concede that the Federal Rules of Civil Procedure require only "a short and plain statement of the claim showing that the pleader is entitled to relief." Fed. Rule Civ. Proc. 8(a)(2). And we assume, at least for argument's sake, that neither the Rules nor the securities statutes impose any special further requirement in respect to the pleading of proximate causation or economic loss. But, even so, the "short and plain statement" must provide the defendant with "fair notice of what the plaintiff's claim is and the grounds upon which it rests." *Conley v. Gibson*, 355 U.S. 41, 47, (1957). The complaint before us fails this simple test.

As we have pointed out, the plaintiffs' lengthy complaint contains only one statement that we can fairly read as describing the loss caused by the defendants' "spray device" misrepresentations. That statement says that the plaintiffs "paid artificially inflated prices for Dura's securities" and suffered "damage[s]." The statement implies that the plaintiffs' loss consisted of the "artificially inflated" purchase "prices." The complaint's failure to claim that Dura's share price fell significantly after the truth became known suggests that the plaintiffs considered the allegation of purchase price inflation alone sufficient. The complaint contains nothing that suggests otherwise.

For reasons set forth in Part II-A, supra, however, the "artificially inflated purchase price" is not itself a relevant economic loss. And the complaint nowhere else provides the defendants with notice of what the relevant economic loss might be or of what the causal connection might be between that loss and the misrepresentation concerning Dura's "spray device."

We concede that ordinary pleading rules are not meant to impose a great burden upon a plaintiff. *Swierkiewicz v. Sorema, N. A.*, 534 U.S. 506, 513-515 (2002). But it should not prove burdensome for a plaintiff who has suffered an economic loss to provide a defendant with some indication of the loss and the causal connection that the plaintiff has in mind. At the same time, allowing a plaintiff to forgo giving any indication of the economic loss and proximate cause that the plaintiff has in mind would bring about harm of the very sort the statutes seek to avoid. Cf. H.R. Conf. Rep. No. 104-369, p. 31 (1995) (criticizing "abusive" practices including "the routine filing of lawsuits ...with only a faint hope that the discovery process might lead eventually to some plausible cause of action"). It would permit a plaintiff "with a largely groundless claim to simply take up the time of a number of other people, with the right to do so representing an *in terrorem* increment of the settlement value, rather than a reasonably founded hope that the [discovery] process will reveal relevant evidence." *Blue Chip Stamps*, 421 U.S., at 741. Such a rule would tend to transform a private securities action into a partial downside insurance policy. See H.R. Conf. Rep. No. 104-369, at 31.

For these reasons, we find the plaintiffs' complaint legally insufficient. We reverse the judgment of the Ninth Circuit, and we remand the case for further proceedings consistent with this opinion. ***

NOTES AND QUESTIONS

1. ***Inevitable or Not.*** The Supreme Court held the plaintiffs' allegations of loss causation insufficient. Could the Court plausibly have held otherwise? To what extent could the plaintiffs have improved their prospects by pleading differently?

2. ***The Threat of Vexatious Private Litigation.*** To justify its holding, the Court invoked the threat of vexatious private litigation – lawsuits consisting of "largely groundless claim[s]" that are filed solely for their settlement value. Is there a basis for supposing that *Dura* itself presented such a threat?

3. ***The Tort Law Analogy.*** The Court twice referred to the resemblance between the Rule 10b-5 private damages action and the common law deceit action and devoted a fair amount of space to the particulars of common law deceit. Is tort law an appropriate reference point for determining the parameters of Rule 10b-5? See generally Robert B. Thompson, Federal Corporate Law: Torts and Fiduciary Duty, 31 J. Corp. L. 877 (2006). What result if tort law principles shaped the contours of loss causation? See Jill E. Fisch, Cause for Concern: Causation and Federal Securities Fraud, 94 Iowa L. Rev. 811 (2009).

4. ***Reasons for Plaintiffs to Worry.*** The Court said little about what plaintiffs must allege in order to plead loss causation sufficiently. For example, it did not address whether the allegations must include "a corrective disclosure followed by a stock price drop," requirements which, according to the appeals court below, the district court had imposed by implication. 339 F.3d 933, 938. Does *Dura* contain anything that ought to worry Rule 10b-5 plaintiffs (and their lawyers)?

5. ***Making Fraud Attractive.*** Does *Dura* encourage companies to engage in fraud? Consider the following:

> *Dura Pharmaceuticals, Inc. v. Broudo* makes lying optimal for firms with multiple business projects or multiple periods of reporting. All in all, the *Dura* rule fails to adequately internalize the costs of fraud onto the firm, making fraud profitable.***
>
> ***[T]he *Dura* decision moves securities fraud jurisprudence toward an ex post loss rule that requires an ex post decline in share value, and away from the ex ante loss rule that allowed a plaintiff to recover for inflated share price at the time of transacting. The implications of the move are several. First, the ex post loss rule does not adequately internalize fraud losses when firms can bundle projects, when firms can wait before disclosing bad news, or when other factors may overlap with the fraud in causing a plaintiff's loss. Fraud now becomes an optimal strategy for many or most firms, and can increase the cost of funding good projects because investors tend to discount firms' disclosures. Second, the impact of *Dura* depends on the extent to which firms can disaggregate themselves or their disclosures in order to retain credibility and transparency: a firm that becomes a single project or discrete disclosure firm is perfectly deterred by an ex post rule. ***

James C. Spindler, Why Shareholders Want Their CEOs to Lie More after *Dura Pharmaceuticals*, 95 Geo. L. J. 653, 657, 691 (2007).

6. ***Whither the PSLRA's Pleading Requirements.*** Why did the Court "assume, at least for argument's sake" that the heightened pleading standard in Exchange Act Section 21D(b)(1) is inapplicable to loss causation? This PSLRA-imposed requirement is set out on page 27 of the Casebook.

7. ***Loss Causation and Class Certification.*** Alone among the circuits, the Fifth Circuit conditioned certification of a fraud-on-the-market action on proof of loss causation. See *Archdiocese of Milwaukee Supporting Fund, Inc. v. Halliburton Co.*, 597 F.3d 330 (5th Cir. 2010); *Oscar Private Equity Invs. v. Allegiance Telecom, Inc.*, 487 F.3d 261 (5th Cir. 2008). As its rationale

for doing so, the Fifth Circuit claimed that loss causation provides additional assurance of market efficiency. See *Oscar*, supra, 487 F.3d at 269-70.

Overriding these decisions, the Supreme Court held that a loss causation prerequisite could not be reconciled with *Basic, Inc. v. Levinson*, 485 U.S. 224 (1988):

> Such a rule contravenes *Basic*'s fundamental premise—that an investor presumptively relies on a misrepresentation so long as it was reflected in the market price at the time of his transaction. The fact that a subsequent loss may have been caused by factors other than the revelation of a misrepresentation has nothing to do with whether an investor relied on the misrepresentation in the first place, either directly or presumptively through the fraud-on-the-market theory. Loss causation has no logical connection to the facts necessary to establish the efficient market predicate to the fraud-on-the-market theory.

Erica P. John Fund, Inc. v. Halliburton Co., 131 S.Ct. 2179, 2187 (2011). Do you agree? We will return to certification of fraud-on-the-market cases in Chapter 6 (Class Actions).

The following post-*Dura* decision probes the nature of the required connection between the fraud and the loss.

IN RE OMNICOM GROUP, INC. SEC. LITIG.

597 F.3d 501 (2d Cir. 2010)

RALPH K. WINTER, CIRCUIT JUDGE:

The New Orleans Employees' Retirement System, the lead plaintiff in this class action, appeals from Judge Pauley's grant of summary judgment dismissing its complaint alleging securities fraud in violation of Section 10(b) against Omnicom Group, Inc. and its managers. The district court held that appellant proffered no evidence sufficient to support a finding of loss causation. For the reasons set forth below, we affirm.

BACKGROUND

Given the procedural posture of this matter, an appeal from a grant of summary judgment dismissing a complaint, "we construe the evidence in the light most favorable to the plaintiff, drawing all reasonable inferences and resolving all ambiguities in [its] favor." *Colavito v. N.Y. Organ Donor Network, Inc.*, 438 F.3d 214, 217 (2d Cir.2006).

a) *The Seneca Transaction*

Omnicom is a large global marketing and advertising holding company. Around 1996, Omnicom began using its subsidiary, Communicade, to invest in internet marketing and advertising companies. The value of the internet companies began to decline in 2000. Omnicom determined that these losses were not "other-than-temporary impairment[s]," and thus non-reportable, a position that was reviewed without exception by Arthur Andersen.

During the first quarter of 2001, Omnicom entered into a transaction with Pegasus Partners II, L.P., a Delaware private equity firm, that created a new company, Seneca, owned by both Omnicom and Pegasus. In a press release, Omnicom and Pegasus stated that the objective of the Seneca transaction was to "maximize consolidation and other strategic opportunities among companies in the currently depressed e-services consulting and professional services marketplace." The Seneca transaction involved Omnicom's transfer to Seneca of $47.5 million in cash and its Communicade subsidiary, whose sole assets were the internet companies, and Pegasus's promise to transfer a total of $25 million in cash, $12.5 million up front and $12.5 million when Seneca requested it. Omnicom received $325 million in Seneca's non-voting preferred stock, while Pegasus received all of Seneca's common stock. Omnicom reported that it would incur no gain or loss from this transaction because it was exchanging the internet companies, purported to be worth $277.5 million, and $47.5 million in cash for preferred stock of equivalent value.

Appellant alleges that the accounting for the Seneca transaction was fraudulent, a claim we assume to be true, albeit one that is disputed. While Omnicom's auditors, it is claimed, viewed Pegasus's willingness to invest $25 million in Seneca as support for Omnicom's valuation of the internet companies at $277.5 million, there is evidence that, despite the representations that Pegasus would immediately transfer $12.5 million to Seneca, it instead transferred only $100 to Seneca, while transferring the $12.5 million to a Pegasus holding company. Appellant argues that this fact, which was not disclosed to the market in any of the news articles that appellant relies on, raises doubts about Omnicom's valuation of the assets transferred to Seneca.

Appellant also claims that Omnicom misrepresented the value of its Seneca stock to its auditors at the end of 2001. To conceal the decline in the value of Seneca's assets, Omnicom is said to have arranged for Seneca, rather than Omnicom, to buy a technology license from Live Technology Holdings, Inc., one of Seneca's investee companies. Seneca would then sell the license to Omnicom for $75 million. The $75 million would nearly offset Seneca's yearly losses.

b) *Publicly Available Information About the Seneca Transaction*

Several news articles at or near the time reported the Seneca transaction and suggested that it was an attempt to move the internet companies, whose value was deteriorating, off Omnicom's books. Indeed, observers expressed these views well into 2002. However, Omnicom's stock never experienced any statistically significant drop in value at or near the time of these news reports.

On June 5, 2002, Omnicom filed a Form 8–K disclosing that Robert Callander, an outside director and Chair of Omnicom's Audit Committee, had resigned from its board of directors on May 22, 2002. Although the Form 8–K did not disclose the reason for Callander's resignation, appellant argues that it was because of Callander's concern over the accounting of the Seneca transaction. Appellant relies on Callander's request for a review of the Seneca transaction by a separate accounting firm, his handwritten notes on a copy of Omnicom's 2001 Form 10–K, his request for Seneca's financial statements, questions he asked during audit committee meetings, and his request for advice regarding his responsibilities from a Columbia Business School professor.

Appellant also relies on the fact that Callander resigned the same day that the board rejected his suggestion that the audit committee review Omnicom's proposal to reacquire two of the internet companies recently transferred to Seneca.

On June 6, 2002, Omnicom's stock price declined as rumors circulated that *The Wall Street Journal* would be publishing a negative article about accounting issues at Omnicom. That same day, Salomon Smith Barney issued a report noting "an article circulated on Briefing.com which speculated that The Wall Street Journal was set to break a potentially negative story about accounting issues at Omnicom." However, the report also expressed the belief that Callander resigned because his "relationship with other board members had become increasingly strained and counter-productive," noting that "[h]ad Mr. Callander complained about or disagreed with something in particular, Omnicom would have had to disclose it." Id. ***

On June 10, 2002, *The Wall Street Journal* published a short article in which it stated that Callander "quit the board after expressing concerns about the creation of an entity that houses Omnicom's Internet assets," and, in particular, his "unhapp[iness] with Omnicom management's limited disclosure to the audit committee about the entity that holds many of Omnicom's former Internet assets." Vanessa O'Connell & Jesse Eisinger, *Leading the News: Omnicom Director Quits Due to Entity Concerns,* Wall St. J., June 10, 2002, at B4. ***

Late on June 11, 2002, the *Financial Times* published an article describing Omnicom's investors' "post-Enron concerns about disclosure." Richard Tomkins & Christopher Grimes, *Omnicom Shares Wobble Amid Disclosure Fears,* Fin. Times, June 11, 2002. It acknowledged that "there is no suggestion of impropriety, still less any breaking of the rules," but noted that, nonetheless, industry executives and analysts were still concerned with Omnicom's methods of calculating organic growth. ***

On June 12, 2002, *The Wall Street Journal* published the rumored article on Omnicom that discussed Callander's resignation and the Seneca transaction. Vanessa O'Connell & Jesse Eisinger, *Unadvertised Deals: At an Ad Giant, Nimble Financing Fuels Rapid Gth — But Omnicom's Web Stakes Spark Board Controversy; A Question of Disclosure —The Impact of Acquisitions,* Wall St. J., June 12, 2002, at A1. The article stated that Callander had "resigned amid questions about how the company handled a series of soured Internet investments," that "[h]e questioned whether something wasn't being disclosed to the board about the initial off-loading of the problematic investments and the proposal to buy two Internet firms," that "he had voiced doubts about Seneca's purpose for months," and that he had concerns that management "had engaged in transactions without running it through the board." ***

The June 12 article also raised questions about Omnicom's general accounting practices. For example, the article stated that "[i]n the wake of the collapse of Enron Corp., investors are demanding clearer and simpler financial statements from big companies, putting particular pressure on serial acquirers with tangled webs of deals." It noted that Omnicom "uses a more aggressive means than its competitors to calculate the critical statistic of how much of its gth it generates from existing operations." The article also claimed that "[t]he clash over Seneca [between Callander and management] signals new concern about the financial side of the Omnicom juggernaut." ***.

Later that day, Omnicom held a telephone conference to reassure investors. During the conference, Omnicom's CEO stated that there was no dissent among the board members, but acknowledged that "Mr. Callander's reasons [for resigning from the board] were presented accurately as in 'The Journal' this morning."

A number of articles and analyst reports also responded to the June 12 article, some of which suggested that the article raised questions about Omnicom's accounting practices. For example, a *Reuters* article that day stated that Omnicom "was forced to play defense on Wednesday amid questions about its accounting," and suggested that Omnicom's management's credibility was harmed by the June 12 article. Adam Pasick, *UPDATE 1–Omnicom Defends Accounting as Stock Plunges,* Reuters, June 12, 2002. Nonetheless, the article also noted that "Omnicom said Callander's resignation was the result of a misunderstanding: that he was told, erroneously, that the board had not approved the creation of Seneca when it [sic] fact it had." A *New York Times* article on June 13 also suggested that Omnicom "scrambled yesterday to repair damage caused by a newspaper article critical of its accounting practices." Stuart Elliott, *Omnicom Shares Tumble 20%,* N.Y. Times, June 13, 2002, at C11. ***

However, some analyst reports and news articles also indicated that the June 12 article did not raise any new factual issues and suggested that the market's negative reaction was due to the article's negative tone and innuendo in the Enron market. See, e.g., Merrill Lynch, FlashNote, *Omnicom Group Inc.: Good News: No New News in WSJ Article,* June 12, 2002; Richard Morgan, *Hatchet Job,* TheDeal.com, June 14, 2002; Bear Stearns, Omnicom Group (OMC–62.30)—*Buy: Follow Up On WSJ Article,* June 13, 2002; SalomonSmithBarney, *Omnicom Group Inc. (OMC): Comments on Management Meeting,* June 13, 2002; SalomonSmithBarney, *Omnicom Group Inc. (OMC): Comments on WSJ Article,* June 12, 2002; Richard Tomkins, *Omnicom Slides on S & P's Move to Cut Outlook,* Fin. Times, June 13, 2002; UBS Warburg, *Global Equity Research: Omnicom Group (OMC),* June 13, 2002.

In the two days following the June 12 article, Omnicom's stock dropped over twenty-five percent relative to trading prices and activity in the market and the industry. However, after Omnicom announced that its new auditor, KPMG, reviewed the accounting for the Seneca transaction and had not recommended any changes, Omnicom's stock increased substantially relative to the industry and the market.

c) *The Present Action*

On June 13, 2002, as Omnicom's closing price fell, appellant and other plaintiffs filed this action. On May 19, 2003, appellant filed an amended complaint, which appellees moved to dismiss. The district court granted appellees' motion in part, dismissing claims involving Omnicom's organic growth calculations and its earn-out and put-out liabilities, but denied the motion with regard to the Seneca transaction. The complaint made three allegations of fraud concerning the Seneca transaction. First, it alleged that Omnicom should have written down the value of the internet companies before engaging in the Seneca transaction. Second, it alleged that the accounting of the Seneca transaction was fraudulent because Omnicom failed to appropriately value the internet companies. Third, it alleged that Omnicom should have accounted for Seneca's losses after the Seneca transaction occurred because Omnicom controlled Seneca. Each allegation, therefore, focused on the loss in value of the internet companies and the failure to reflect that loss on Omnicom's books.

The class action complaint invoked the rebuttable presumption of shareholder reliance established in *Basic, Inc. v. Levinson,* 485 U.S. 224, 241–42 (1988). It alleged that Omnicom was an actively traded company and that the market for its shares promptly reflected public information about the company.

In July 2005, appellant moved to certify a class "consisting of all persons and entities who purchased or otherwise acquired the securities of Omnicom from February 20, 2001 through June 11, 2002 and who were damaged thereby." Appellant's Br. at 24. The district court certified the class on April 30, 2007.

After extensive discovery and in response to appellees' motion for summary judgment, appellant proffered, *inter alia,* a report of its expert witness, Dr. Scott D. Hakala. Dr. Hakala prepared an event study analysis and was prepared to testify that "the investing public's initial reactions to the partially corrective disclosures in June 2002 were tied to the news of Omnicom's inappropriate accounting for investments in Internet-related entities and not to other news during that time period." He claimed that "[i]nvestors legitimately feared that Omnicom's transfers of its Internet investments created the potential for losses and hidden liabilities and/or had allowed Omnicom to hide losses in the past." Dr. Hakala also stated that:

> [T]he declines from June 5 to June 13, 2002, would not have occurred on those dates had Defendants not previously engaged in the fraudulent scheme alleged by Plaintiffs. The information revealed in that time period constituted a partial revelation of information about this scheme.

On January 29, 2008, the district court granted appellees' motion for summary judgment. The district court, in a thorough and well-reasoned opinion, held that appellant had failed to proffer sufficient evidence that the fraud alleged—the Seneca transaction—caused the drop in stock price that damaged the class. We agree.

DISCUSSION

a) *Standard of Review*

*** Summary judgment is only appropriate if the record shows "that there is no genuine issue as to any material fact and that the movant is entitled to judgment as a matter of law." Fed.R.Civ.P. 56. An issue of fact is genuine "if the evidence is such that a reasonable jury could return a verdict for the nonmoving party." *Anderson v. Liberty Lobby, Inc.,* 477 U.S. 242, 248 (1986). In looking at the record, we "constru[e] the evidence in the light most favorable to the nonmoving party and draw[ ] all inferences and resolv[e] all ambiguities in favor of the nonmoving party." *Doro v. Sheet Metal Workers' Int'l Ass'n,* 498 F.3d 152, 155 (2d Cir.2007). ***

b) *The Section 10(b) Claims*

*** The district court granted summary judgment on the ground that appellant failed to proffer sufficient evidence to show loss causation. ***

Having sought to establish investor reliance by the fraud-on-the-market theory, appellant faces a difficult task. The fraud alleged — the Seneca transaction and failure to write down the value of the internet companies — was the subject of continuing media reports beginning in May 2001. The stock price decline, which is the basis for the damages claim, occurred in June 2002. In short, appellant must concede that the numerous public reports on the Seneca transaction were "promptly digested" by the market and "reflected ... in Omnicom's stock price" in 2001 while seeking to recover for a stock price decline a year later in 2002.

Appellant seeks to do so through two means: first, by claiming the existence of cause-in-fact on the ground that the market reacted negatively to a corrective disclosure of the fraud, and, second, by arguing the existence of proximate cause on the ground that negative investor inferences drawn from Callander's resignation and from the news stories in June 2002 caused the loss and were a foreseeable materialization of the risk concealed by the fraudulent statement. Establishing either theory as applicable would suffice to show loss causation.

1) Corrective Disclosure

A fraud regarding a company's financial condition in May 2001, if concealed, may cause investors' losses in June 2002 when disclosure of the fraud is made and the available public information regarding the company's financial condition is corrected. *See Lentell,* 396 F.3d at 175 n. 4. Appellant argues that information disclosed to the market in June 2002, particularly by the June 12 article, constituted a partial corrective disclosure of the fraud and that the disclosure caused the market to respond negatively.

To reiterate, the June 12 article reported that Callander, a director and Chair of Omnicom's Audit Committee, had resigned amid questions he had raised for months regarding the purpose of the Seneca transaction. Callander was also reported to have questioned whether the board had received full information about the initial Seneca transaction and about the new proposal to buy back two of the internet companies. The article also noted concerns, including those of accounting professors, about Omnicom's aggressive accounting strategy and about Omnicom's cash flow and increased borrowing. In opposing the motion for summary judgment, appellant offered the expert testimony of Dr. Hakala regarding causation issues.

However, none of these matters even purported to reveal some then-undisclosed fact with regard to the specific misrepresentations alleged in the complaint concerning the Seneca transaction. The use of the Seneca transaction as an accounting method to remove losses from Omnicom's books was known to the market a year before Callander's resignation. There was no ambiguity in that regard in these articles.

All that the June 12 article stated was that Callander's resignation was due to general concerns over an aggressive accounting strategy, including perhaps Omnicom's year-old failure to write-down the value of the internet companies, and other matters concerning governance, in particular management's keeping the board informed. At best, from appellant's viewpoint, it has shown that the market may have reacted as it did because of concerns that Callander's resignation and the negative tone of the June 12 article implied accounting or other problems in addition to the known Seneca transaction.

Appellant also relies on comments in the June 12 article by the two accounting professors to support a nexus between the fraud alleged and the June 2002 decline in share price. They argue that "a reasonable jury could conclude that the professor found Omnicom's accounting suspicious in light of Callander's resignation and Omnicom's decision to unwind Seneca, which were newly disclosed facts." However, the conclusory suspicions of the accounting professors and the unwinding of the Seneca transaction added nothing to the public's knowledge that the Seneca transaction was designed to remove losses from Omnicom's books.[4]

P has only shown a negative characterization of already public info and that is not a corrective disclosure

What appellant has shown is a negative characterization of already-public information. See *Teacher's Ret. Sys. of La. v. Hunter,* 477 F.3d 162, 187–88 (4th Cir.2007) (negative characterization of previously known information cannot constitute a corrective disclosure); *In re Merck & Co. Sec. Litig.,* 432 F.3d 261, 269–70 (3d Cir.2005) (same). A negative journalistic characterization of previously disclosed facts does not constitute a corrective disclosure of anything but the journalists' opinions. After all, no hard fact in the June 12 article suggested that the avoidance of the write-down was improper.

Dr. Hakala's study does not alter our conclusion. It is true that "[w]here, as here, there are conflicting expert reports presented, courts are wary of granting summary judgment." *Harris v. Provident Life & Accident Ins. Co.,* 310 F.3d 73, 79 (2d Cir.2002). However, summary judgment is not *per se* precluded because there are conflicting experts. See *Raskin v. Wyatt Co.,* 125 F.3d 55, 65 (2d Cir.1997). Although the reports must be construed in the non-moving party's favor, "if the admissible evidence is insufficient to permit a rational juror to find in favor of the plaintiff, the court remains free to direct a verdict or grant summary judgment for defendant." *Amorgianos v. Nat'l R.R. Passenger Corp.,* 303 F.3d 256, 267 (2d Cir.2002).

Summary judgment is appropriate here because Dr. Hakala's testimony does not suffice to draw the requisite causal connection between the information in the June 12 article and the fraud alleged in the complaint. ***

---

4. Appellant also relies on the fact that Omnicom's stock price recovered after Omnicom announced that KPMG had reviewed its accounting of the Seneca transaction and did not recommend any changes. Appellant's Br. at 52–53. However, KPMG's conclusion that there was no fraud in the Seneca transaction hardly supports a finding that fraud in the Seneca transaction caused a loss.

If Dr. Hakala is opining that Omnicom's stock dropped because investors first became aware in June 2002 of the fraud alleged in the complaint, that opinion is, as a matter of law, unsustainable on this record. It runs squarely into the undisputed fact that the internet company losses and the failure to write them down was known in May 2001 and into appellant's allegation that the market for Omnicom's securities at all times promptly digested and reflected in its share price all public information. If he is opining that Omnicom's stock dropped because the fraud in May 2001 caused the negative press of June 2002 attending Callander's resignation, then his testimony is irrelevant because these events were not proximately caused by the fraud alleged, for reasons discussed immediately below. The remainder of his report establishes only that, as previously noted, the June 12 article raised questions about potential accounting concerns, including the Seneca transaction.

Because appellant failed to demonstrate any new information in the June 12 article regarding Omnicom's alleged fraud, appellant has failed to show a price decline due to a corrective disclosure.

2) The Materialization of the Risk Theory

Appellant argues that, even if no new financial facts were revealed in June 2002, Callander's resignation and the ensuing negative media attention were foreseeable risks of the fraudulent Seneca transaction and caused the temporary share price decline in June 2002. The losses suffered by the class are, the argument goes, due to the materialization of that risk.

As noted, plaintiffs can prove loss causation by showing "that the loss was foreseeable and caused by the materialization of the risk concealed by the fraudulent statement." *ATSI,* 493 F.3d at 107. A misrepresentation is "the 'proximate cause' of an investment loss if the risk that caused the loss was within the zone of risk *concealed* by the misrepresentations...." *Lentell,* 396 F.3d at 173. Because Omnicom's internet company losses were publicly known, the matter concealed must be the invalidity of Omnicom's accounting for those losses in the Seneca transaction.

The zone of risk is determined by the purposes of the securities laws, *i.e.,* "to make sure that buyers of securities get what they think they are getting." *Chem. Bank v. Arthur Andersen & Co.,* 726 F.2d 930, 943 (2d Cir.1984). In this context, therefore, recovery is limited to only the foreseeable losses "for which the intent of the laws is served by recovery." *AUSA,* 206 F.3d at 234 (Winter, J., dissenting).

Fraud may lead to a director's resignation—to escape personal liability, if for no other reason, see, e.g., 15 U.S.C. § 77k(b)(1) (providing exemption from civil liability for director who resigns before effective date of fraudulent registration statement) — and to negative stories by the media. In such circumstances, it is generally the facts underlying the fraud and resignation that causes a compensable investor's loss. In the present case, as noted, the facts were known a year before the resignation, and the resignation did not add to the public knowledge any new material fact about the Seneca transaction. The essence of the claim is that Callander's resignation concerned the Seneca transaction and that the resultant negative publicity suggesting possible accounting malfeasance may lead to recovery for a temporary drop in share price.

To be sure, the record shows that Callander was concerned over general accounting practices and governance problems. In that regard, he was concerned about the Seneca transaction, but he had also been mistakenly informed that the Board had never approved it. On the present record, appellant has at best shown that Callander's resignation and resulting negative press stirred investors' concerns that other unknown problems were lurking in Omnicom's past. Indeed, there is no allegation that investors were ever told that improper accounting had in fact occurred with regard to the Seneca transaction, either in the June 2002 stories or later.

The generalized investor reaction of concern causing a temporary share price decline in June 2002, is far too tenuously connected — indeed, by a metaphoric thread — to the Seneca transaction to support liability. The securities laws require disclosure that is adequate to allow investors to make judgments about a company's intrinsic value. Firms are not required by the securities laws to speculate about distant, ambiguous, and perhaps idiosyncratic reactions by the press or even by directors. To hold otherwise would expose companies and their shareholders to potentially expansive liabilities for events later alleged to be frauds, the facts of which were known to the investing public at the time but did not affect share price, and thus did no damage at that time to investors. A rule of liability leading to such losses would undermine the very investor confidence that the securities laws were intended to support.

CONCLUSION

Appellant has failed to raise a material issue of fact that would support a finding of loss causation, and, as a result, the district court properly granted defendants' summary judgment motion. For the foregoing reasons, we affirm.

NOTES AND QUESTIONS

*1. **Why So Strict.*** Was the court's strict approach to loss causation necessitated either by *Dura* or by the PSLRA's loss causation requirement (Section 21D(b)(4), set forth at the beginning of this subsection)? Was a strict approach more likely because this case involved fraud- on-the-market?

*2. **The Corrective Disclosure Theory.*** The court held that the June 12, 2002 Wall Street Journal article merely spun old facts in a new way and thus did not constitute a "corrective disclosure." Do you agree?

The court's holding in this regard illustrates the difficulties that can arise in identifying what constitutes a "corrective disclosure." For example, suppose a company revises downward a misleading earnings prediction in its financial statement and later announces that it will have to restate the financial statement. Which disclosure corrected the misleading earnings prediction – the downward revision or the announcement of the necessity to restate? For discussion of this question, see Allen Ferrell & Atanu Saha, The Loss Causation Requirement for the Rule 10b-5 Cause of Action: The Implications of *Dura Pharmaceuticals, Inc. v. Broudo*, 63 Bus. Law. 163, 172-74 (2007).

*3. **Psyching Out the Market.*** What might explain the market's non-reaction to the news reports concerning the Seneca transaction at the time that the transaction occurred? What might account for the market's strong reaction in the wake of the June 12, 2002 Wall Street Journal article?

*4. **The Materialization of the Risk Theory.*** Must the plaintiff show a corrective disclosure when invoking the materialization of the risk theory? Consider the view that the answer is no "because the news of the materialized risk would itself be the revelation of the fraud that caused the plaintiffs' loss." *Teachers' Ret. Sys. of La. v. Hunter*, 477 F.3d 162, 187-88 n.3 (4th Cir. 2007). Do you agree?

Is the materialization of the risk theory consistent with the Supreme Court's *Dura* decision? Why or why not?

*5. **Damages Contrasted.*** You will study Rule 10b-5 damages in the next section, but the following distinction between damages and loss causation may nonetheless be helpful now:

> To satisfy the loss causation requirement, a plaintiff need not show that a misrepresentation was the sole reason for the investment's decline in value. Ultimately, however, a plaintiff will be allowed to recover only damages actually caused by the misrepresentation. *** Consequently, as long as the misrepresentation is one substantial cause of the investment's decline in value, other contributing forces will not bar recovery under the loss causation requirement. But in determining recoverable damages, these contributing forces must be isolated and removed.

Robbins v. Kroger Properties, Inc., 116 F.3d 1441, 1447 n. 5 (11th Cir. 1997).

PROBLEM 2-23

Frank Scrubman, a star analyst at Meritt Smitt Blarney (MSB), authored more than 40 glowing research reports on InterMedia Corp., a company that provided marketing solutions to the digital advertising industry. InterMedia was trading at $15 when MSB initiated coverage in February 1999, rose to a high of $55 in January 2000, and then plummeted to $2 in February 2001. During this time period, MSB's investment-banking arm had assisted InterMedia in its acquisition of 18 companies, and underwrote a $100 million convertible bond offering in March 2000.

Plaintiffs, who were not clients of MSB, have filed a class action lawsuit alleging violations of Rule 10b-5 by MSB, Scrubman, and other MSB analysts from February 20, 1999 through February 20, 2001 (the "class period"). Plaintiffs allege that MSB, through Scrubman and other research analysts, issued false and misleading reports recommending that investors purchase shares of InterMedia, even though the analysts did not believe that the company was a sound investment. To support this allegation, Plaintiffs cite to specific internal e-mails in which Scrubman and other MSB analysts privately characterized InterMedia stock as "junk" and a "dog." Plaintiffs further allege that MSB held out Scrubman and the other analysts to the public as independent assessors of business prospects, while simultaneously encouraging these analysts to issue the falsely optimistic reports in order to cultivate investment banking business from InterMedia. Plaintiffs contend that the fraudulent hype about the company substantially inflated and maintained InterMedia's market price at an artificially high level until the internet stock market bubble burst in February 2001, and that Plaintiffs lost millions of dollars when InterMedia's stock price plummeted.

Defendants have filed a motion to dismiss on the ground that Plaintiffs cannot establish loss causation under Rule 10b-5, even if their claims of material misrepresentation and omission are assumed to be true.

a. In view of the allegations described above, would a district judge likely grant that motion?

b. What if Plaintiffs' complaint contained specific allegations that Frank Scrubman had failed to disclose material nonpublic information in his possession about InterMedia's volatility risks and/or that he concealed the company's true financial condition by employing a valuation model not used for any other company. How would those allegations change the loss causation analysis?

Cf. *Lentell v. Merrill Lynch & Co.*, 396 F.3d 161 (2d Cir. 2005).

G. DAMAGES

To recover damages under Rule 10b-5, a private plaintiff is obliged to prove them. Cf. *Miller v. Asensio & Co.*, 364 F.3d 223 (4th Cir. 2004) (finding that damages were not proven, although liability had been). The law of damages is relatively undeveloped, owing to the small number of judicial opinions addressing the subject. What accounts for the small number?

We examine three aspects of damages: their measurement; the system of proportionate liability established by the PSLRA; and the question of who supplies the money that plaintiffs recover. These issues apply to private actions only, since actions brought by the SEC or the DOJ do not require proof of damages.

1. *The Measurement of Damages*

Section 10(b) and Rule 10b-5 say nothing about how to measure damages. Given that the drafters of those provisions did not anticipate private enforcement, this silence is not surprising. Lower federal courts must therefore look elsewhere for guidance.

One benchmark is Section 28(a) of the Exchange Act, which provides that "no person permitted to maintain a suit for damages under the provisions of this Act shall recover, through satisfaction of judgment in one or more actions, a total amount in excess of his actual damages on account of the act complained of." As its language suggests, Section 28(a) precludes multiple recoveries for the same wrong. It has also been routinely held to prohibit punitive damages. See, e.g., *Pelletier v. Stuart-James Co.*, 863 F.2d 1550, 1557 (11th Cir. 1989) (Rule 10b-5 action); *CSI Inv. Partners II, LP v. Cendant Corp.*, 507 F. Supp. 2d 384, 427 n.37 (S.D.N.Y. 2007) (same) (collecting cases), aff'd, 328 F. App'x 56 (2d Cir. 2009).

Other benchmarks consist of two Supreme Court decisions that specifically reference methods of measuring damages. The first such decision is

Affiliated Ute v. United States, 406 U.S. 128 (1972), which you will recall from your study of the reliance requirement in Section F.1.a of this Chapter. In *Affiliated Ute*, the Court designated as the default measure for Rule 10b-5 actions the "out of pocket rule" from common law deceit, with disgorgement (originating in contract law) as an alternative measure:

> In our view, the correct measure of damages under § 28 of the Act, is the difference between the fair value of all that the [plaintiff] received and the fair value of what he would have received had there been no fraudulent conduct, except for the situation where the defendant received more than the [plaintiff's] actual loss. In the latter case damages are the amount of the defendant's profit.

Affiliated Ute, supra, 406 U.S. at 155.

Later, in *Randall v. Loftsgaarden*, 478 U.S. 647 (1986), the Court opened up the possibilities still further by assuming (but not actually upholding) the at least occasional appropriateness of rescission—the unwinding of the transaction (or the monetary equivalent). See id. at 662. See also id. at 666 (reserving the question of "whether, assuming that a rescissory recovery may sometimes be proper under § 10(b), plaintiffs in such cases should invariably be free to elect a rescissory measure of damages rather than out-of-pocket damages"); Moreover, according to the Court, the a rescissionary recovery does not have to be reduced by the amount of tax benefits received. See id. at 663. See also *Lewin v. Lipper Convertibles, LP*, 756 F. Supp. 2d 432, 440 (S.D.N.Y. 2010) (noting that the rescission remedy is rarely granted in Rule 10b-5 cases) (collecting cases).

Given these minimalist constraints, lower federal courts exercise enormous discretion in deciding how to measure Rule 10b-5 damages. Consider the consequences of this discretion as we focus first, on the measurement of Rule 10b-5 damages generally, and, second, on the special complexities raised by class actions.

a. In General

As you read the following decision, ask yourself whether the court reached a just result.

ROWE v. MAREMONT CORPORATION

850 F.2d 1226 (7th Cir. 1988)

DANIEL A. MANION, CIRCUIT JUDGE:

Herbert J. Rowe, his wife, Ann M. Rowe, and the Continental Illinois National Bank sued Maremont Corporation for securities fraud under Section 10(b) of the Securities and Exchange Act of 1934 and SEC Rule 10b-5. The suit arose from a face-to-face transaction in July, 1977 in which Maremont purchased 225,986 shares of stock in Pemcor, Inc. from the Rowes. After a bench trial, the district court entered judgment for the Rowes for $745,423.80 plus prejudgment interest and costs. Maremont appeals the district court's judgment. The Rowes cross-appeal, claiming that the district court awarded inadequate damages. We reject the contentions made in both the appeal and cross-appeal, and affirm.

I.

*** In early 1977, Herbert and Ann Rowe owned 8,921 shares of stock in

Pemcor, Inc. The Rowes were also co-trustees, with Continental Illinois Bank, of a trust Mrs. Rowe's father had established in his will. The trust owned 216,965 shares of Pemcor stock. Together, the Rowes' and the trust's shares comprised 11 1/2 percent of Pemcor's outstanding stock. (We will refer to the shares collectively as the "Rowe shares" or "Rowe block," as did the district court.)

Although Pemcor was listed on the New York Stock Exchange, the Rowes could not sell their shares on the open market because the shares were not registered. The Rowe shares were also subject to an agreement between the Rowes and Potter-Englewood Corporation (the corporate predecessor to Pemcor) providing that the Rowes would not sell the shares before notifying Pemcor and receiving an opinion from Pemcor's counsel that the sale would not violate the 1933 Securities Act.

By early 1977, the Rowes had decided to sell their Pemcor shares. The Rowes explored selling the shares both by private placement and by a secondary public offering. In a secondary offering, the Rowe shares would have fetched between $5 and $6 1/2 per share. At that time, Pemcor's market price was around $12-$13 per share.

The investment bankers whom the Rowes had contacted concerning a private placement were having no luck finding a buyer. However, at around the same time the Rowes became interested in selling their shares, Maremont had become interested in expanding its operations by acquiring new companies. As part of this expansion program, Maremont retained Skadden, Arps, Slate, Meagher & Flom, a New York law firm active in mergers and acquisitions. In January, 1977, Maremont executed a commission agreement with The Illinois Company, a Chicago brokerage firm. The Illinois Company recommended Pemcor to Maremont as a potential acquisition and arranged meetings between Pemcor's and Maremont's executives. Although the meetings were cordial, Pemcor was not interested in a merger or affiliation at that time.

Around July 13, 1977, The Illinois Company informed Richard Black, Maremont's president, that the Rowe shares might be available. On July 18, pursuant to Black's instructions, Gordon Teach of The Illinois Company offered, on behalf of an undisclosed principal, to purchase the Rowe shares for that day's closing market price, $13 per share. Although Mrs. Rowe agreed the price was good (it was, in fact, an all-time high), she refused to sell the shares without knowing the purchaser's name. Therefore, Mrs. Rowe arranged to fly from her home in Virginia to Chicago the next day to meet Teach.

Over the next three days, the Rowes and their representatives met with Maremont representatives to negotiate the stock sale. On July 19, Mrs. Rowe, the Rowes' attorney, Robert Fuchs, and two Continental Illinois trust department officers, Darryl Hoovel and Gordon Martin, met with Teach in Chicago. After Mrs. Rowe insisted on knowing the purchaser's name, Teach told her that Maremont was the purchaser. Teach asked the Rowes not to disclose Maremont's name to anybody until twenty-four hours after the sale. Teach also told the Rowes that Maremont had recently sold a division, that it wanted the Rowe shares as an investment, that it wanted to protect its investment by electing a director, and that it wanted to purchase up to 20 percent of Pemcor's stock. At the close of the meeting, Mrs. Rowe agreed to sell the Rowes' Pemcor shares to Maremont for $13 per share. Before the Rowes and Maremont could close the deal, however, they needed to agree to and prepare written documents. Therefore, further meetings were necessary. ***

During the afternoon of July 20, Robert Pirie and Milton Strom, two Skadden Arps lawyers, arrived to handle the transaction for Maremont. Although Maremont had specifically retained Skadden Arps to work on a possible Pemcor acquisition, Shapiro [, Maremont's Treasurer,] introduced Pirie and Strom as two New York lawyers in Chicago on other business who were "stopping by" to help Maremont with the Rowe transaction.

Sometime during one of the meetings, on July 20 or 21, Marvin Temple, Fuchs' law partner, asked Shapiro whether Maremont was going to make a tender offer for Pemcor. Shapiro replied, "No." ***

By the end of the afternoon on July 21, the Rowes and Maremont had agreed on the final form of the documents necessary to complete the sale. *** Maremont and the Rowes subsequently executed all the documents.

During the days immediately following the execution of the Rowe contract, Maremont took steps to acquire the rest of Pemcor's stock. Black contacted Edward Anixter, Pemcor's president, to discuss a friendly takeover. Anixter was not receptive to the idea; a hostile tender offer thus seemed the most likely course. Skadden Arps' attorneys drafted "anticipatory tender offer documents" so that Maremont could move quickly. Maremont also arranged financing for its offer. On Friday, July 29, Black sent Anixter a "bear hug" letter advising Anixter that Maremont intended to offer $16.75 per share for all Pemcor shares. Pemcor did not respond to the letter. On August 1, Maremont publicly announced that it intended to make a tender offer. Pemcor opposed the tender offer. *** On August 3, Pemcor sued both Maremont and the Rowes to prevent the Rowes from transferring the shares to Maremont. Pemcor's complaint sought $30 million in damages and injunctive relief.

In the meantime, the Rowes *** went about the business of trying to complete the sale of their Pemcor stock. Immediately after the documents were signed, Fuchs phoned Chuck Kaufman, Pemcor's outside counsel, to ask Kaufman to cooperate in obtaining the necessary opinion letter. During that conversation, Kaufman asked Fuchs whether Maremont would make a tender offer. Fuchs replied that Maremont had advised him there would be no tender offer. ***

Fuchs and the Rowes learned about Maremont's tender offer on August 2. The Rowes were angry, and told Fuchs they wanted their stock back. Gordon Martin of Continental Illinois complained to Fuchs that the Rowes and the trust had been "taken." Fuchs, however, decided to move cautiously and to keep the Rowes' options open. The Rowes thus moved on a dual track, taking the necessary steps to complete the transaction while at the same time exploring the possibility of rescission.

*** On August 15, Fuchs spoke by phone with Pirie. *** At trial, Fuchs testified that he *** told Pirie that it was "incredible" that Maremont had not disclosed that it was going to make a tender offer, and that the Rowes were entitled to rescission. Fuchs did not, however, formally request rescission at that time. On August 23, Fuchs sent Maremont a letter formally requesting rescission. Although the rescission letter mentioned several alleged misstatements and omissions by Maremont (e.g., the representation that Maremont planned to obtain only up to 20 percent of Pemcor's stock), the letter did not mention Shapiro's statement that Maremont would not make a tender offer.

On August 30, the Rowes filed a counterclaim against Pemcor. Part of the relief the Rowes requested was an order directing Pemcor to transfer the Rowe shares to Maremont. On October 27, 1977, the Rowes filed a cross-claim against Maremont, alleging securities fraud (among other things). The cross-claim, like the rescission letter, did not mention the "No" tender offer representation.

*** On April 8, 1978, the escrow agent (over the Rowes' objections) delivered the Rowe shares to Maremont. Pemcor successfully rebuffed all merger attempts by Maremont until a white knight, Esmark, came to Pemcor's rescue. Pemcor merged into Esmark, and Maremont exchanged the Rowe shares for a block of Esmark shares. In August, 1979, Maremont sold the Esmark shares for $7,039,439. Thus, Maremont made a total profit of $4,056,834 from purchasing the Rowe shares.

II.

[*The Court of Appeals affirmed the district court's determination that Rule 10b-5 had been violated.*]

III.

The district court awarded the Rowes $745,423.80 in damages. Both the Rowes and Maremont challenge the district court's damage award. The Rowes complain that the district court did not award enough damages; Maremont contends that the district court should not have awarded any damages. ***

The district court made several key findings regarding damages. The court found that the Rowes were eager to sell, and that they would not have held onto their Pemcor stock even had Maremont not come along. The court also found that had the Rowes known the truth, they would have negotiated for a 25 percent premium from Maremont. The court found no evidence that Maremont would have rejected a demand for a premium, and noted that "Maremont had been willing to pay [the Rowes] market price for their [restricted] stock ... and might have been willing to pay more had plaintiffs negotiated for the same." Implicit in the above findings is a finding that Maremont would have paid a premium over market price for the Rowe shares had the Rowes asked for it. In fact, the court noted that the price per share it awarded as damages was close to the 25 percent premium Fuchs testified he would have sought had he known the truth.

The Supreme Court has broadly stated that in Rule 10b-5 cases involving defrauded sellers, "the correct measure of damages ... is the difference between the fair value of all the ... seller received and the fair value of what he would have received had there been no fraudulent conduct, except for the situation where the defendant received more than the seller's actual loss. In the latter case damages are the amount of the defendant's profit." *Affiliated Ute Citizens of Utah v. United States,* 406 U.S. 128, 155 (1972). Based on this statement in *Affiliated Ute,* the Rowes argue that the district court should have ordered Maremont to pay them the over $4,000,000 profit it eventually made from purchasing the Rowe shares.

Despite its broad language in *Affiliated Ute,* the Court has not set any hard and fast rule concerning disgorgement of profits. Cf. *Randall v. Loftsgaarden,* 478 U.S. 647 (1986) (leaving open the question whether plaintiffs in Rule 10b-5 actions are "invariably" free to elect disgorgement). It is within the district court's discretion to determine whether disgorgement or some other damage measure is appropriate. *Arrington v. Merrill Lynch, Pierce, Fenner, & Smith,* 651 F.2d 615, 621 (9th Cir.1981). "The court's function is to fashion the remedy best suited to the harm." Id.*; Nye v. Blyth Eastman Dillon & Co.,* 588 F.2d 1189, 1198 (8th Cir.1978).

The district court properly rejected the Rowes' disgorgement request. Being a rescissionary measure of damages, disgorgement is meant to place a defrauded seller in the same position he would have occupied had the buyer's fraud not induced him to enter the transaction. See *Nelson v. Serwold,* 576 F.2d 1332, 1339 (9th Cir.1978). Disgorgement also prevents a defendant from being unjustly enriched by his fraud. *Randall,* 106 S.Ct. at 3153*; Hackbart,* [*v. Holmes,* 675 F.2d at 1114, 1122 (10th Cir. 1982)]. Making Maremont disgorge all its profit from purchasing the Rowe shares would accomplish neither of these purposes. Since the Rowes would have sold their Pemcor stock absent Maremont's fraud none of the profit Maremont made from the Rowe shares (besides that representing the higher purchase price the Rowes would have received from Maremont had the Rowes known the truth) would have accrued to the Rowes; thus, disgorgement is not necessary to place the Rowes in the same position they would have occupied but for the fraud. See *Capital Investments, Inc. v. Bank of Sturgeon Bay,* 430 F.Supp. 534, 537 (E.D.Wis.1977) ("[W]here it is shown that the seller would not have retained the securities had full disclosure been made, there is no reason to allow the plaintiff accrued profits as damages"), aff'd, 577 F.2d 745 (7th Cir.1978). And since Maremont would have obtained the stock from the Rowes even absent its fraud, any profit it earned above the premium it would have paid the Rowes absent the fraud is not unjust enrichment.

The Rowes argue that what would have happened if they had not sold to Maremont is speculative and in such a case courts should give plaintiffs—the defrauded parties—the benefit of the doubt and require defendants to disgorge their profits. We have no quarrel with this general principle—after all, "[i]t is more appropriate to give the defrauded party the benefit even of windfalls than to let the fraudulent party keep them." *Janigan v. Taylor,* 344 F.2d 781, 786 (1st Cir.1965). The problem here is that the district court did not have to "speculate"—in the legal sense—about the Rowes' course of conduct absent the fraud. There was more than sufficient evidence to support the court's finding that the Rowes would have sold their stock even absent Maremont's fraud.

The Rowes also argue that what they would have done absent the fraud is irrelevant because disgorgement is based on "simple equity" and on deterring fraudulent conduct. Deterrence is an important consideration in allowing disgorgement, see *Randall,* 106 S.Ct. at 3154, but "[d]isgorgement is remedial and not punitive." [*SEC v. MacDonald,* 699 F.2d at 47, 54 (1st Cir. 1983) (en banc)]. To make Maremont pay back profits that it would have made even if it told the truth is harsh and punitive. Equity requires only that a defendant give up its *unjust* enrichment. The district court did not err in rejecting full disgorgement as a measure of damages.

Maremont argues that the district court erred in awarding the Rowes any damages at all. The district court found that if Maremont had not come along, the Rowes would have sold their stock at a secondary offering for much less than the $13 per share they received from Maremont. Since the Rowes received more by selling their shares to Maremont than they would have if they had not sold to Maremont, Maremont contends that its fraud did not damage the Rowes. The problem with this argument is that Maremont *did* come along, and *did* induce the Rowes to sell their stock for $13 per share by lying about its intent to acquire Pemcor. Therefore, the district court correctly determined that it could base a damage award on the difference between what the Rowes actually received and what the Rowes would have received had Maremont not committed fraud. See *Affiliated Ute,* 406 U.S. at 155.

Maremont also argues that no evidence supports the district court's damage award. In determining how much the Rowes would have received if they had known the truth, the district court examined evidence of Pemcor's performance in the market to determine the value the market placed on the tender offer information. The district court found that

> Maremont's purchase of the Rowe shares was publicly announced the same day that Pemcor announced a substantial improvement in earnings: the stock (which had been inching up the entire period of the Rowe-Maremont negotiations) jumped over one point the next trading day to a high of 16.5. The stock then dropped to around 15, but climbed up again to 16.3 shortly after Maremont announced its tender offer. The stock price thereafter fluctuated and dropped below 16 until mid-November. Not until November 22, 1977 did the stock price again exceed 16.3.

650 F.Supp. at 1114-15. From this market evidence, the court concluded that by the market's evaluation of the information 16.3 represented a likely negotiated price between the Rowes and Maremont, and that the difference between 16.3 and the $13 per share Maremont paid the Rowes was the proper damage amount.

Maremont argues that the district court could not rely on the market information because the Rowes offered no expert testimony to demonstrate how much of the rise in Pemcor's stock price was caused by the tender offer information. While it is true that Pemcor's stock price rose to 16.5 after it announced substantial increases in dividends and earnings, the price fell to 15 during the next week and did not rise again until after Maremont announced its intention to make a tender offer. This raises the inference that the tender offer was a substantial factor in Pemcor's increased price. Even if other factors caused part of the price increase, it was Maremont's burden to present evidence to segregate those factors. See *Daniels Towing Service, Inc. v. Nat Harrison*

Associates, 432 F.2d 103, 106 (5th Cir.1970) ("once illicit damage of consequence is established, the burden of segregating damages should be on the [defendant]"); *Meyers v. Moody,* 475 F.Supp. 232, 248 (N.D.Tex.1979), aff'd, 693 F.2d 1196 (5th Cir.1982) (applying *Daniels* in a Rule 10b-5 action). Maremont did not meet this burden.

Moreover, Maremont's attack on the district court's use of the market evidence misses the mark because the market evidence was not the only evidence the district court relied on in determining damages. The district court also relied on evidence that the Rowes would have received a 25 percent (or $3.25 per share) premium from Maremont had Maremont disclosed its intent to make a tender offer. This evidence reinforces the inference raised by the market evidence that the Rowes would have been able to negotiate for a price near $16.30 per share had they known the truth.

Maremont protests that there was no evidence that the Rowes would have received, or that Maremont would have paid, more than $13 per share. However, several of the Rowes' witnesses, including Fuchs, testified that they would have negotiated for a premium had they known the truth. Jerry Williams, who headed Maremont's corporate planning department, testified by deposition that Maremont normally paid a 25 percent premium for control stock. There was no evidence that Maremont would not have paid a premium if the Rowes had asked for one.

Maremont points out that the Rowes' stock was unregistered and restricted, and therefore incapable of being sold on the market. But Maremont did not want the stock for resale; it wanted the stock for control. Maremont could vote the stock like any other stock, and the Rowe shares represented the largest single bloc of Pemcor stock. Maremont had been pursuing Pemcor for some time, so it seems unlikely that Maremont would have simply given up and walked away from the bargaining table had the Rowes asked for more money. Given Maremont's control intentions, it was reasonable to conclude that the Rowe shares were just as (or almost as) valuable to Maremont as any other Pemcor stock (for which Maremont was willing to pay $16.75 per share); therefore, the district court could conclude that Maremont would have paid a premium over market to get the Rowe shares, even though the stock was not marketable.

Taken together, the market evidence and the evidence that Maremont likely would have paid a premium if it had told the truth support the district court's damage award. Although a damages award based on a purchase price of $16.30 per share is slightly higher than the 25 percent premium the Rowes testified they would have asked for, this difference does not require us to reduce the damages. A district court need not calculate damages with mathematical precision; it is enough that the evidence be sufficient to allow the district court to intelligently estimate damages. See *Feldman v. Pioneer Petroleum, Inc.,* 813 F.2d 296, 301 (10th Cir. 1987); *Freight Terminals, Inc. v. Ryder System, Inc.,* 461 F.2d 1046, 1053 (5th Cir.1972). ***

NOTES AND QUESTIONS

*1. **Overlapping Measures?*** What measure did the court apply—out of pocket, disgorgement, rescission, or perhaps a blend?

*2. **The Role of Deterrence.*** Did the court give appropriate weight to deterrence? Judge Easterbrook and Professor Fischel have argued that from a deterrence standpoint, "the optimal sanction is the net harm that activity imposes on other people divided by the probability that the activity will be detected and prosecuted successfully." Frank H. Easterbrook & Daniel R. Fischel, Optimal Damages in Securities Cases, 52 U. Chi. L. Rev. 611, 618 (1985). Application of this formula is likely to be difficult. What is the net social harm, say, of the fraud attributed to Enron Corporation? Even more challenging, at the time of the commission of such fraud, what was the probability that it would eventually be discovered?

*3. **Loss Causation Revisited.*** Recall that as part of the PSLRA, Congress codified a loss causation requirement by adding Section 21D(b)(4) to the Exchange Act. See supra Section F.2. Would the *Rowe* plaintiffs have satisfied this requirement had it been on the books at the time of their lawsuit? To what extent would their proof of loss causation have overlapped their proof of damages?

PROBLEM 2-24

Fred is the president of Bosley, Inc., a closely held corporation and a widget manufacturer. Fred developed a plan for producing more and better widgets that he believed would double the company's profits. Not wanting to share these profits with anyone else, Fred asked the other shareholders to sell him their stock. At a shareholders' meeting called to discuss the matter, one of the other shareholders (Carl) asked Fred whether anything had recently occurred or was about to occur that should cause them to adopt a different view of the company. Fred replied that there was none. Shortly thereafter, Fred purchased the stock of the other shareholders for $100,000, a price determined in an appraisal commissioned for this purpose. Immediately after becoming the sole owner, Fred began putting into place his plan for more and better widgets. Execution of the plan required enormous effort and imagination on his part. As the result of the plan, the company's profits quadrupled. Shortly thereafter, he sold Bosley for $10 million.

Upon learning what Fred had done, Carl and the other shareholders sued Fred under Rule 10b-5. They allege that his denial to them concerning any impending changes constituted fraud. Assuming that they satisfy the other elements of Rule 10b-5, how should their damages be measured?

Cf. *Janigan v. Taylor*, 344 F.2d 781 (1st Cir. 1965).

b. Damages in the Class Action Context

In the context of a class action, the measurement of damages becomes especially complex. Consider Professor Alexander's description of those complexities:

> The class damages are supposed to consist of the sum of the individual damages of each member of the class. Calculating the total class damages is a two-step process. The first step is to determine the "per-share damages," the amount of

the actual market price attributable to the nondisclosure on each day of the class period. The second step is to determine the aggregate damages of the class. To determine per-share damages, an expert economic witness constructs a "value line" which represents the "true value" of the stock—what purchasers would have been willing to pay if they had known the undisclosed information—on each day of the class period. The damages sustained by any particular member of the class can then, in theory, be determined by comparing the price actually paid with the value line for the date of the transaction.

The value line is a hypothetical construct. The most common method of estimating per-share damages is to start with the share price after disclosure of the relevant information, and then, through an event study,[5] to isolate the effects of the withheld information from other factors, unrelated to the litigation, that may have affected the stock price between the time of the purchase and the time of the disclosure. Determining the value line is the least problematic aspect of the class action damages calculation, but it is subject to serious difficulties. The event study methodology depends on various debatable factual assumptions. As a result, the value line calculations of the experts for the two sides can differ greatly, even when they are using the same methodology. Moreover, even at its best the event study methodology can only calculate the price effect of the disclosure, which is not necessarily the same as the price effect of the information that was withheld.

From the value line, one can determine each class member's damages. A member of the class who bought shares during the class period and held them until the close of the class period (typically the date when the bad news was finally disclosed) suffered damages of the difference between the price paid and the value line, multiplied by the number of shares purchased. If a plaintiff resold the shares during the class period, however, both the purchase price and the selling price were inflated by the nondisclosure. The windfall the plaintiff received on the sale must therefore be offset against the loss incurred on the purchase. If the value of the undisclosed information remained constant during the class period, these amounts would cancel each other out, and those who bought and sold during the class period ("in-and-out traders") would have no damages. If the value of the information fluctuated during the class period, in-and-out investors' damages would depend on the dates of their transactions.

Related to this issue is the question of the number of shares in the class. Because some shares are bought and sold, often repeatedly, within the class period, the number of shares in the class is not simply the sum of the daily volume of trading during the class period. Indeed, the total daily trading volume may exceed the total number of shares outstanding. The methodology for calculating aggregate class damages must therefore include a procedure to account for in-and-out traders and to net out their windfalls against their losses. This step, however, introduces a fatal amount of uncertainty. The parties cannot reconstruct a share-by-share trading history of the shares traded during the class period, because most shares are held by brokers in street name. Individual buyers are not in fact matched to individual sellers, and

---

5. Event studies begin with the change in the share price on the day of disclosure. Using regression analysis, the study eliminates events that are not firm specific (for example, an across the board fall in market prices) and isolates the extent to which the price change can be attributed to the disclosure. Working backwards, the study then establishes a hypothetical price for each day from the date of actual disclosure to the date that the information should have been disclosed. Ronald J. Gilson & Bernard S. Black, The Law and Finance of Corporate Acquisitions 185-228 (2d ed. 1995).

individualized records of such transactions are not kept. Therefore, the parties cannot determine directly either the number of shares in the class or the precise damages attributable to each share in the class. Adjusting for in-and-out traders requires the use of a statistical model which estimates how many of the shares that traded on a given day had traded before during the class period, and on what days. The results of such models depend critically on empirical assumptions about trading patterns. Those assumptions, in turn, are subject to considerable doubt. It is possible that the most widely used model overstates actual aggregate class damages by 100 percent or more, even in a relatively short class period.

Thus, while the doctrinal statement of the measure of damages is relatively straightforward, the practical and methodological difficulties of calculating aggregate class damages make the damages inquiry in class actions complex and the ultimate outcome at trial uncertain. ***

Janet Cooper Alexander, Rethinking Damages in Securities Class Actions, 48 Stan. L. Rev. 1487, 1491-93 (1996). What is the likely impact of these uncertainties on the filing of class actions? What might explain Congress's failure to tackle the problem of class action damages in the PSLRA?

NOTES AND QUESTIONS

1. Holes in the Out of Pocket Measure. The out of pocket measure seeks to ascertain what the fraud cost the plaintiff on the date he bought or sold the security in question. But the fraud's impact as of that date is not easy to pinpoint.

Why, as Professor Alexander put it, is the "price effect of the [corrective] disclosure *** not necessarily the same as the price effect of the information withheld?" The market price on the announcement date (invariably after the plaintiff's trade date) likely reflects not only the market's response to the fraud but also to numerous extraneous factors unrelated to the fraud. See generally Robert B. Thompson, "Simplicity and Certainty" in the Measure of Recovery Under Rule 10b-5, 51 Bus. Law. 1177, 1181 (1996). Indeed, the corrective disclosure itself may compound the array of factors by

> convey[ing] more information than the original disclosure misstated and, accordingly, ha[ving] a greater impact on the stock price than an initial truthful disclosure would have had. The facts in *Basic* are frequently used to illustrate over-disclosure. In that case, management's misstatements were denials about the existence of merger talks; the corrective disclosure was the corporation's announcement of a merger agreement. ***

Barbara Black, Reputational Damages in Securities Litigation, 35 J. Corp. L. 169, 173 (2009).

To be sure, courts can and do hear testimony from experts about how to discount the extraneous factors, but the invariable disagreement among the experts makes the scope (if not also the existence) of plaintiff's recovery impossible to ascertain in advance. How do you suppose this lack of predictability affects Rule 10b-5 litigation?

There may even be a more fundamental problem with the out of pocket measure. That measure assumes that without the misrepresentation, the market would have known the truth. But "[i]f the more likely alternative to a defendant's misrepresentation would have been to say nothing at all, or to engage in lawful "puffery" rather than tell the truth, then damages based on the standard assumption overcompensate." Donald C. Langevoort, Reading *Stoneridge* Carefully: A Duty-Based Approach to Reliance and Third Party Liability under Rule 10b-5, 158 U. Pa. L. Rev. 2125, 2143 (2010).

2. Market Overreactions. Conceivably an announcement acknowledging fraud may cause the market to overreact temporarily. The PSLRA attempted to address this concern by adding the so-called "the 90 day bounce-back provision" to the Exchange Act:

> *** [I]n any private action arising under this title in which the plaintiff seeks to establish damages by reference to the market price of a security, the award of damages to the plaintiff shall not exceed the difference between the purchase price or sale price paid or received, as appropriate, by the plaintiff for the subject security and the mean trading price of that security during the 90-day period beginning on the date on which the information correcting the misstatement or omission that is the basis for the action is disseminated to the market.

Section 21D(e)(1). See *Jaffe Pension Plan v. Household Int'l, Inc.*, 756 F. Supp. 2d 928, 936 (N.D. Ill. 2010) (applying the 90 day bounce-back provision in a fraud-on-the-market case). See also Section 21D(e)(2) (providing cap on damages for those selling or repurchasing before the end of the 90 day period).

The 90 day bounce-back provision has received considerable criticism. Consider the following view:

> There are at least three fundamental flaws in the PSLRA formula. First, if the problem is that independent factors may have caused stock price to fall between the time of purchase and corrective disclosure, it makes no sense to look to the ninety days *following* the corrective disclosure to filter them out. Second, independent factors may also affect the price of the stock during the ninety days following corrective disclosure. The company may release further bad news or the market as a whole may fall. Third, if indeed the market as a whole falls during the ninety-day period, the stock in question may be more affected or less affected by the market-wide drop in prices if the stock is more risky or less risky than the market as a whole.

Richard A. Booth, Windfall Awards Under the PSLRA, 59 Bus. Law. 1043, 1046 (2004). See also Jonathan C. Dickey & Marcia Kramer Mayer, Effect on Rule 10b-5 Damages of the 1995 Private Securities Litigation Reform Act: A Forward-Looking Assessment, 51 Bus. Law. 1203, 1209 (1996) (maintaining that section 21D(e) suffers from "asymmetry" because "[i]ncreases in share price during the ninety-day post curative period limit damages, but decreases in price do not necessarily expand damages"). What do you think?

Consider also the question of to which actions the 90 day bounce-back provision applies. Is it limited to actions based on the fraud-on-the-market theory? Does it apply to all actions that look to the market price (whether exclusively or partly) to set damages? Had it been on the books at the time, would it have applied in *Rowe*?

3. Reputational Damages. Can Rule 10b-5 plaintiffs receive damages from declines in the market price resulting from a revised judgment of the caliber of the management that perpetuated the fraud? Compare Barbara Black,

Reputational Damages in Securities Litigation, 35 J. Corp. L. 169 (2009) (giving affirmative answer) with Bradford Cornell & James C. Rutten, Collateral Damage and Securities Litigation, 2009 Utah L. Rev. 717 (2009) (giving negative answer) and Allen Ferrell & Atanu Saha, The Loss Causation Requirement for Rule 10b-5 Causes of Action: The Implications of *Dura Pharmaceuticals, Inc. v. Broudo*, 63 Bus. Law. 163, 180-81 (2007) (same).

---

2. *Proportionate Liability*

Prior to the PSLRA, courts maintained that defendants were jointly and severally liable for damages under Rule 10b-5. See, e.g., *TBG, Inc. v. Bendis,* 36 F.3d 916, 927 (10th Cir. 1994). Consequently, the plaintiff was entitled to recoup the entire amount of the damages from any defendant (who in turn could bring contribution actions against the others). See id. See also *Musick Peeler & Garrett v. Employers Ins.,* 508 U.S. 286 (1993) (recognizing an implied right to contribution among those who violate Rule 10b-5).

The PSLRA radically upended this state of affairs with its addition of Section 21D(f) to the Exchange Act. That Section establishes a scheme of proportionate liability under which a defendant (with limited exceptions) is liable exclusively for the fraction of the judgment for which she bears responsibility. Joint and several liability remains for those defendants who commit their violations "knowingly" (and who may seek contribution from each other pursuant to an express action enacted for this purpose). Whether each defendant acted knowingly as well as how much responsibility he bears for the total wrong are jury questions that must be answered pursuant to special interrogatories. In deciding upon each defendant's respective share, the jury is to take account of "each of the other persons claimed by any of the parties to have caused or contributed to the loss incurred by the plaintiff, including persons who have entered into settlements with the plaintiff." Section 21D(f)(3). There is an explicit prohibition against disclosing to the jury how their decisions will affect the award of damages. See Section 21D(f)(6).

The PSLRA's proportionate liability scheme has been highly controversial. One commentator has summarized the debate as follows:

> Advocates of proportionate liability argued that joint and several liability is inequitable because it forces parties who are only partially responsible for the harm to bear more than their proportionate share of the damages. The accounting profession, in particular, argued that the current system provides plaintiffs with an incentive to join as many "deep pocket" defendants as possible, and compels defendants to settle weak claims in order to avoid disproportionate liability.
>
> The response to this argument is that, although the traditional doctrine of joint and several liability may cause accountants and others to bear more than their proportional share of liability in particular cases, this is because the system is based on equitable principles that operate to protect innocent investors. As between defrauded investors and defendants who are found knowingly or recklessly to have participated in a fraud, the risk of loss should fall on the latter. Proportionate liability would inevitably have the greatest effect on investors in the most serious cases, such as those in which the issuer becomes bankrupt after a fraud is exposed.

John W. Avery, Securities Litigation Reform: The Long and Winding Road to the Private Securities Litigation Reform Act of 1995, 51 Bus. Law. 335, 362 (1996).

Congress enacted the PSLRA's proportionate liability scheme largely in response to lobbying from accounting firms. In a *quid pro quo*, the accounting firms endorsed an amendment to the Exchange Act requiring them to report illegal conduct to the issuer's directors and to the SEC. See Section 10A of that Act.

The pivotal role played by accountants in the Enron scandal has led some to argue that Congress should repeal Section 21D(f). Does proportionate liability make sense or does it encourage auditors and other collateral participants to be more reckless in the face of client fraud? To what extent is it necessary to abolish joint and several liability in order to protect defendants from having to pay more of the judgment than is just? On the latter question, see Donald C. Langevoort, The Reform of Joint and Several Liability Under the Private Securities Litigation Reform Act of 1995: Proportionate Liability, Contribution Rights, and Settlement Effects, 51 Bus. Law. 1157, 1158-59 (1996).

The question of repeal aside, Section 21D(f) might benefit from reform. Would it be a good idea to limit joint and several liability to those who not only knew about the fraud but also played a major role in its commission? See Donald C. Langevoort, Reading *Stoneridge* Carefully: A Duty-Based Approach to Reliance and Third Party Liability under Rule 10b-5, 158 U. Pa. L. Rev. 2125, 2168-69 (2010).

PROBLEM 2-25

The president of Worldwide Corporation perpetrated a massive fraud which was facilitated by the company's outside law and accounting firms. The company is now bankrupt, as is the president. As the attorney for the shareholders, you have brought a Rule 10b-5 action against the law and accounting firms. You worry, however, that a jury will hold these firms responsible for only a small fraction of the harm done to your clients. What are your alternatives?

3. Who Pays for Recoveries?

When plaintiffs recover damages under Rule 10b-5, from where does the money come? Can corporations indemnify their officers and directors? The answers turn largely on whether the litigation ends in a judgment of liability (relatively rare) or in a settlement without a judgment of liability (far more common).

When a court finds a defendant liable for intentional violations of the federal securities laws, courts have long prohibited indemnification on public policy grounds. See *In re Enron Corp. Sec., Deriv., & ERISA Litig.*, 2008 WL 2566867 at *10 (S.D.N.Y. 2008); *McLean v. Alexander*, 449 F. Supp. 1251, 1266 (D. Del. 1978) (collecting cases). Such a defendant may nonetheless be protected by insurance. See id. at 1266 n. 51 (noting that exclusionary clauses notwithstanding, "some policies may be more expansive than the courts would permit through indemnification"), rev'd on other grounds, 599 F.2d 1190 (3rd Cir. 1979). In the case of a corporate defendant, recovery may come either from insurance or from the corporate treasury (and therefore ultimately from the shareholders themselves).

Where the litigation is settled without a finding of wrongdoing, the situation changes in several respects. Corporations are entitled to indemnify their officers and directors. See, e.g., *Raychem Corp. v. Fed. Ins. Co.,* 853 F. Supp. 1170, 1176-77 (N.D. Cal. 1994) (collecting cases). In addition, insurance coverage is more likely to be applicable. For decades, the availability of indemnification and insurance spared individual defendants from having to fund settlements from their own pockets. But some individual defendants have recently been obliged to do precisely that. See, e.g., Judge Approves Settlement for WorldCom Investors, N.Y. Times at C6 (Sept. 22, 2005) (noting that former directors contributed $55 million to the settlement).

NOTES AND QUESTIONS

1. ***Public Policy.*** If indemnification is objectionable on public policy grounds, what makes insurance any different?

2. ***Deciding Whether to Settle.*** Do the rules regarding indemnification and insurance make settlement more or less likely?

3. ***Tinkering at the Margins.*** As part of the PSLRA, Congress codified a right to recover attorneys' fees and costs on behalf of a defendant "that prevails in any private action" insofar as "a contractual relation permits." See Section 21D(f)(2)(B)(ii) of the Exchange Act. Does this small change signify that Congress otherwise approves of the indemnification/insurance schema as it currently operates?

H. PRIMARY AND SECONDARY LIABILITY

A Rule 10b-5 violation typically involves a number of participants, be they individuals, business entities, or a combination. Which of them can be held liable for the violation? This important question has been rocking the courts for some time.

1. Primary Liability

In the 5-4 decision that follows, the Supreme Court addressed the fundamental question of primary liability: who can be said to "make" a materially misleading statement.

JANUS CAPITAL GROUP, INC. v. FIRST DERIVATIVE TRADERS

131 S.Ct. 2296 (2011)

JUSTICE CLARENCE THOMAS:

This case requires us to determine whether Janus Capital Management, LLC (JCM), a mutual fund investment adviser, can be held liable in a private action under Securities and Exchange Commission (SEC) Rule 10b–5 for false statements included in its client mutual funds' prospectuses. Rule 10b–5 prohibits "mak[ing] any untrue statement of a material fact" in connection with

can an investment advisor be held liable under 10b-5 for statements in clients' prospectuses?
- No, b/c they didn't make the statements

the purchase or sale of securities. We conclude that JCM cannot be held liable because it did not make the statements in the prospectuses.

I

Janus Capital Group, Inc. (JCG), is a publicly traded company that created the Janus family of mutual funds. These mutual funds are organized in a Massachusetts business trust, the Janus Investment Fund. Janus Investment Fund retained JCG's wholly owned subsidiary, JCM, to be its investment adviser and administrator. JCG and JCM are the petitioners here.

Although JCG created Janus Investment Fund, Janus Investment Fund is a separate legal entity owned entirely by mutual fund investors. Janus Investment Fund has no assets apart from those owned by the investors. JCM provides Janus Investment Fund with investment advisory services, which include "the management and administrative services necessary for the operation of [Janus] Fun[d]," but the two entities maintain legal independence. At all times relevant to this case, all of the officers of Janus Investment Fund were also officers of JCM, but only one member of Janus Investment Fund's board of trustees was associated with JCM. This is more independence than is required: By statute, up to 60 percent of the board of a mutual fund may be composed of "interested persons." [See Investment Company Act §10(a); see also id. at § 2(a)(19) (defining "interested person")].

As the securities laws require, Janus Investment Fund issued prospectuses describing the investment strategy and operations of its mutual funds to investors. The prospectuses for several funds represented that the funds were not suitable for market timing and can be read to suggest that JCM would implement policies to curb the practice.[1] For example, the Janus Mercury Fund prospectus dated February 25, 2002, stated that the fund was "not intended for market timing or excessive trading" and represented that it "may reject any purchase request ... if it believes that any combination of trading activity is attributable to market timing or is otherwise excessive or potentially disruptive to the Fund." Although market timing is legal, it harms other investors in the mutual fund.

---

1. Market timing is a trading strategy that exploits time delay in mutual funds' daily valuation system. The price for buying or selling shares of a mutual fund is ordinarily determined by the next net asset value (NAV) calculation after the order is placed. The NAV calculation usually happens once a day, at the close of the major U.S. markets. Because of certain time delays, however, the values used in these calculations do not always accurately reflect the true value of the underlying assets. For example, a fund may value its foreign securities based on the price at the close of the foreign market, which may have occurred several hours before the calculation. But events might have taken place after the close of the foreign market that could be expected to affect their price. If the event were expected to increase the price of the foreign securities, a market-timing investor could buy shares of a mutual fund at the artificially low NAV and sell the next day when the NAV corrects itself upward. See Disclosure Regarding Market Timing and Selective Disclosure of Portfolio Holdings, 68 Fed.Reg. 70402 (proposed Dec. 17, 2003).

In September 2003, the Attorney General of the State of New York filed a complaint against JCG and JCM alleging that JCG entered into secret arrangements to permit market timing in several funds run by JCM. After the complaint's allegations became public, investors withdrew significant amounts of money from the Janus Investment Fund mutual funds.[2] Because Janus Investment Fund compensated JCM based on the total value of the funds and JCM's management fees comprised a significant percentage of JCG's income, Janus Investment Fund's loss of value affected JCG's value as well. JCG's stock price fell nearly 25 percent, from $17.68 on September 2 to $13.50 on September 26.

Respondent First Derivative Traders (First Derivative) represents a class of plaintiffs who owned JCG stock as of September 3, 2003. Its complaint asserts claims against JCG and JCM for violations of Rule 10b–5 and § 10(b) of the Securities Exchange Act of 1934. First Derivative alleges [in its petition for certiorari] that JCG and JCM "caused mutual fund prospectuses to be issued for Janus mutual funds and made them available to the investing public, which created the misleading impression that [JCG and JCM] would implement measures to curb market timing in the Janus [mutual funds]. Had the truth been known, Janus [mutual funds] would have been less attractive to investors, and consequently, [JCG] would have realized lower revenues, so [JCG's] stock would have traded at lower prices." First Derivative contends that JCG and JCM "materially misled the investing public" and that class members relied "upon the integrity of the market price of [JCG] securities and market information relating to [JCG and JCM]." The complaint also alleges that JCG should be held liable for the acts of JCM as a "controlling person" under [Exchange Act § 20(a)].

The District Court dismissed the complaint for failure to state a claim. The Court of Appeals for the Fourth Circuit reversed, holding that First Derivative had sufficiently alleged that "JCG and JCM, by participating in the writing and dissemination of the prospectuses, *made* the misleading statements contained in the documents." With respect to the element of reliance, the court found that investors would infer that JCM "played a role in preparing or approving the content of the Janus fund prospectuses," but that investors would not infer the same about JCG, which could be liable only as a "control person" of JCM under § 20(a).

II

We granted certiorari to address whether JCM can be held liable in a private action under Rule 10b–5 for false statements included in Janus Investment Fund's prospectuses. Under Rule 10b–5, it is unlawful for "any person, directly or indirectly, ... [t]o make any untrue statement of a material fact" in connection with the purchase or sale of securities. To be liable, therefore, JCM must have "made" the material misstatements in the

---

2. In 2004, JCG and JCM settled these allegations and agreed to reduce their fees by $125 million and pay $50 million in civil penalties and $50 million in disgorgement to the mutual fund investors.

prospectuses. We hold that it did not.[5]

A

The SEC promulgated Rule 10b–5 pursuant to authority granted under § 10(b) of the Securities Exchange Act of 1934. Although neither Rule 10b–5 nor § 10(b) expressly creates a private right of action, this Court has held that "a private right of action is implied under § 10(b)." *Superintendent of Ins. of N.Y. v. Bankers Life & Casualty Co.,* 404 U.S. 6, 13, n. 9 (1971). That holding "remains the law," *Stoneridge Investment Partners, LLC v. Scientific–Atlanta, Inc.,* 552 U.S. 148, 165 (2008), but "[c]oncerns with the judicial creation of a private cause of action caution against its expansion," ibid. Thus, in analyzing whether JCM "made" the statements for purposes of Rule 10b–5, we are mindful that we must give "narrow dimensions ... to a right of action Congress did not authorize when it first enacted the statute and did not expand when it revisited the law." Id., at 167.

1

One "makes" a statement by stating it. When "make" is paired with a noun expressing the action of a verb, the resulting phrase is "approximately equivalent in sense" to that verb. 6 Oxford English Dictionary 66 (def.59) (1933) (hereinafter OED); accord, Webster's New International Dictionary 1485 (def.43) (2d ed. 1934) ("*Make* followed by a noun with the indefinite article is often nearly equivalent to the verb intransitive corresponding to that noun"). For instance, "to make a proclamation" is the approximate equivalent of "to proclaim," and "to make a promise" approximates "to promise." See 6 OED 66 (def.59). The phrase at issue in Rule 10b–5, "[t]o make any ... statement," is thus the approximate equivalent of "to state."

For purposes of Rule 10b–5, the maker of a statement is the person or entity with ultimate authority over the statement, including its content and whether and how to communicate it. Without control, a person or entity can merely suggest what to say, not "make" a statement in its own right. One who prepares or publishes a statement on behalf of another is not its maker. And in the ordinary case, attribution within a statement or implicit from surrounding circumstances is strong evidence that a statement was made by — and only by — the party to whom it is attributed. This rule might best be exemplified by the relationship between a speechwriter and a speaker. Even when a speechwriter drafts a speech, the content is entirely within the control of the person who delivers it. And it is the speaker who takes credit — or blame — for what is ultimately said.

This rule follows from *Central Bank of Denver, N.A. v. First Interstate Bank of Denver, N. A.,* 511 U.S. 164 (1994), in which we held that Rule 10b–5's private right of action does not include suits against aiders and abettors. Such

---

5. Although First Derivative argued below that JCG violated Rule 10b–5 by making the statements in the prospectuses, it now seeks to hold JCG liable solely as a control person of JCM under § 20(a). The only question we must answer, therefore, is whether JCM made the misstatements. Whether First Derivative has stated a claim against JCG as a control person depends on whether it has stated a claim against JCM.

suits — against entities that contribute "substantial assistance" to the making of a statement but do not actually make it — may be brought by the SEC, see [Exchange Act § 20(e)], but not by private parties. A broader reading of "make," including persons or entities without ultimate control over the content of a statement, would substantially undermine *Central Bank*. If persons or entities without control over the content of a statement could be considered primary violators who "made" the statement, then aiders and abettors would be almost nonexistent.[6]

This interpretation is further supported by our recent decision in *Stoneridge*. There, investors sued "entities who, acting both as customers and suppliers, agreed to arrangements that allowed the investors' company to mislead its auditor and issue a misleading financial statement." 552 U.S., at 152–153. We held that dismissal of the complaint was proper because the public could not have relied on the entities' undisclosed deceptive acts. Significantly, in reaching that conclusion we emphasized that "nothing [the defendants] did made it necessary or inevitable for [the company] to record the transactions as it did." Id., at 161. This emphasis suggests the rule we adopt today: that the maker of a statement is the entity with authority over the content of the statement and whether and how to communicate it. Without such authority, it is not "necessary or inevitable" that any falsehood will be contained in the statement. Our holding also accords with the narrow scope that we must give the implied private right of action. Although the existence of the private right is now settled, we will not expand liability beyond the person or entity that ultimately has authority over a false statement.

2

The Government contends that "make" should be defined as "create." Brief for United States as *Amicus Curiae* 14–15 (citing Webster's New International Dictionary 1485 (2d ed.1958) (defining "make" as "[t]o cause to exist, appear, or occur")). This definition, although perhaps appropriate when "make" is directed at an object unassociated with a verb (*e.g.,* "to make a chair"), fails to capture its meaning when directed at an object expressing the action of a verb.

Adopting the Government's definition of "make" would also lead to results inconsistent with our precedent. The Government's definition would permit private plaintiffs to sue a person who "provides the false or misleading information that another person then puts into the statement." Brief for United

---

6. The dissent correctly notes that *Central Bank* involved secondary, not primary, liability. But for *Central Bank* to have any meaning, there must be some distinction between those who are primarily liable (and thus may be pursued in private suits) and those who are secondarily liable (and thus may not be pursued in private suits).

We draw a clean line between the two — the maker is the person or entity with ultimate authority over a statement and others are not. In contrast, the dissent's only limit on primary liability is not much of a limit at all. It would allow for primary liability whenever "[t]he specific relationships alleged ... warrant [that] conclusion" — whatever that may mean.

States as *Amicus Curiae* 13.[8] But in *Stoneridge,* we rejected a private Rule 10b–5 suit against companies involved in deceptive transactions, even when information about those transactions was later incorporated into false public statements. 552 U.S., at 161. We see no reason to treat participating in the drafting of a false statement differently from engaging in deceptive transactions, when each is merely an undisclosed act preceding the decision of an independent entity to make a public statement.

For its part, First Derivative suggests that the "well-recognized and uniquely close relationship between a mutual fund and its investment adviser" should inform our decision. It suggests that an investment adviser should generally be understood to be the "maker" of statements by its client mutual fund, like a playwright whose lines are delivered by an actor. We decline this invitation to disregard the corporate form. Although First Derivative and its *amici* persuasively argue that investment advisers exercise significant influence over their client funds, see *Jones v. Harris Associates L. P.,* 130 S.Ct. 1418, 1422–1423 (2010), it is undisputed that the corporate formalities were observed here. JCM and Janus Investment Fund remain legally separate entities, and Janus Investment Fund's board of trustees was more independent than the statute requires.[9] Any reapportionment of liability in the securities industry in light of the close relationship between investment advisers and mutual funds is properly the responsibility of Congress and not the courts. Moreover, just as with the Government's theory, First Derivative's rule would create the broad liability that we rejected in *Stoneridge.*

Congress also has established liability in § 20(a) for "[e]very person who, directly or indirectly, controls any person liable" for violations of the securities laws. First Derivative's theory of liability based on a relationship of influence resembles the liability imposed by Congress for control. To adopt First Derivative's theory would read into Rule 10b–5 a theory of liability similar to — but broader in application than — what Congress has already created expressly elsewhere.[10] We decline to do so.

---

8. Because we do not find the meaning of "make" in Rule 10b–5 to be ambiguous, we need not consider the Government's assertion that we should defer to the SEC's interpretation of the word elsewhere. We note, however, that we have previously expressed skepticism over the degree to which the SEC should receive deference regarding the private right of action. See *Piper v. Chris–Craft Industries, Inc.,* 430 U.S. 1, 41, n. 27 (1977) (noting that the SEC's presumed expertise "is of limited value" when analyzing "whether a cause of action should be implied by judicial interpretation in favor of a particular class of litigants"). This also is not the first time this Court has disagreed with the SEC's broad view of § 10(b) or Rule 10b–5. [citing *Central Bank, Dirks v. SEC; Ernst & Ernst v. Hochfelder,* and *Blue Chip Stamps*].

9. Nor does First Derivative contend that any statements made by JCM to Janus Investment Fund were "public statements" for the purposes of *Basic Inc. v. Levinson,* 485 U.S. 224, 227–228 (1988). We do not address whether and in what circumstances statements would qualify as "public."

10. We do not address whether Congress created liability for entities that act through innocent intermediaries in [Exchange Act § 20(b)]. See Tr. of Oral Arg. 6, 61.

B

Under this rule, JCM did not "make" any of the statements in the Janus Investment Fund prospectuses; Janus Investment Fund did. Only Janus Investment Fund — not JCM — bears the statutory obligation to file the prospectuses with the SEC. The SEC has recorded that Janus Investment Fund filed the prospectuses. There is no allegation that JCM in fact filed the prospectuses and falsely attributed them to Janus Investment Fund. Nor did anything on the face of the prospectuses indicate that any statements therein came from JCM rather than Janus Investment Fund — a legally independent entity with its own board of trustees.[11]

First Derivative suggests that both JCM and Janus Investment Fund might have "made" the misleading statements within the meaning of Rule 10b–5 because JCM was significantly involved in preparing the prospectuses. But this assistance, subject to the ultimate control of Janus Investment Fund, does not mean that JCM "made" any statements in the prospectuses. Although JCM, like a speechwriter, may have assisted Janus Investment Fund with crafting what Janus Investment Fund said in the prospectuses, JCM itself did not "make" those statements for purposes of Rule 10b–5.

*** The statements in the Janus Investment Fund prospectuses were made by Janus Investment Fund, not by JCM. Accordingly, First Derivative has not stated a claim against JCM under Rule 10b–5. The judgment of the United States Court of Appeals for the Fourth Circuit is reversed.***

JUSTICE STEPHEN G. BREYER, WITH WHOM JUSTICE GINSBERG, JUSTICE SOTOMAYOR, AND JUSTICE KAGAN JOIN, DISSENTING.

***The specific legal question before us is whether Janus Management can be held responsible under the Rule for having "ma[d]e" certain false statements about the Janus Fund's activities. The statements in question appear in the Janus Fund's prospectuses. The Court holds that only the Janus Fund, not Janus Management, could have "ma[d]e" those statements. The majority points out that the Janus Fund's board of trustees has "ultimate

---

11. First Derivative suggests that "indirectly" in Rule 10b–5 may broaden the meaning of "make." We disagree. The phrase "directly or indirectly" is set off by itself in Rule 10b–5 and modifies not just "to make," but also "to employ" and "to engage." We think the phrase merely clarifies that as long as a statement is made, it does not matter whether the statement was communicated directly or indirectly to the recipient. A different understanding of "indirectly" would, like a broad definition of "make," threaten to erase the line between primary violators and aiders and abettors established by *Central Bank*.

In this case, we need not define precisely what it means to communicate a "made" statement indirectly because none of the statements in the prospectuses were attributed, explicitly or implicitly, to JCM. Without attribution, there is no indication that Janus Investment Fund was quoting or otherwise repeating a statement originally "made" by JCM. Cf. *Anixter v. Home–Stake Production Co.,* 77 F.3d 1215, 1220, and n. 4 (C.A.10 1996) (quoting a signed " 'Auditor's Report' " included in a prospectus); *Basic,* supra, at 227, n. 4 (quoting a news item reporting a statement by Basic's president). More may be required to find that a person or entity made a statement indirectly, but attribution is necessary.

authority" over the content of the statements in a Fund prospectus. And in the majority's view, only "the person or entity with ultimate authority over the statement, including its content and whether and how to communicate it" can "make" a statement within the terms of Rule 10b–5. In my view, however, the majority has incorrectly interpreted the Rule's word "make." Neither common English nor this Court's earlier cases limit the scope of that word to those with "ultimate authority" over a statement's content. To the contrary, both language and case law indicate that, depending upon the circumstances, a management company, a board of trustees, individual company officers, or others, separately or together, might "make" statements contained in a firm's prospectus — even if a board of directors has ultimate content-related responsibility. And the circumstances here are such that a court could find that Janus Management made the statements in question.

I

Respondent's complaint sets forth the basic elements of a typical Rule 10b–5 "fraud on the market" claim. It alleges that Janus Management made statements that "created the misleading impression that" it "would implement measures to curb" a trading strategy called "market timing." The complaint adds that Janus Management knew that these "market timing" statements were false; that the statements were material; that the market, in pricing securities (including related securities) relied upon the statements; that as a result, when the truth came out (that Janus Management indeed permitted "market timing" in the Janus Fund), the price of relevant shares fell; and the false statements thereby caused respondent significant economic losses.

The majority finds the complaint fatally flawed, however, because (1) Rule 10b–5 says that no "person" shall "directly or indirectly ... *make* any untrue statement of a material fact," (2) the statements at issue appeared in the *Janus Fund's* prospectuses, and (3) only "the person or entity with ultimate authority over the statement, including its content and whether and how to communicate it" can "make" a false statement.

But where can the majority find legal support for the rule that it enunciates? The English language does not impose upon the word "make" boundaries of the kind the majority finds determinative. Every day, hosts of corporate officials make statements with content that more senior officials or the board of directors have "ultimate authority" to control. So do cabinet officials make statements about matters that the Constitution places within the ultimate authority of the President. So do thousands, perhaps millions, of other employees make statements that, as to content, form, or timing, are subject to the control of another.

Nothing in the English language prevents one from saying that several different individuals, separately or together, "make" a statement that each has a hand in producing. For example, as a matter of English, one can say that a national political party has made a statement even if the only written communication consists of uniform press releases issued in the name of local party branches; one can say that one foreign nation has made a statement even when the officials of a different nation (subject to its influence) speak about the matter; and one can say that the President has made a statement even if his press officer issues a communication, sometimes in the press officer's own name. Practical matters related to context, including control, participation, and relevant audience, help determine who "makes" a statement and to whom that statement may properly be "attributed" — at least as far as ordinary English is concerned.

Neither can the majority find support in any relevant precedent. The majority says that its rule "follows from *Central Bank of Denver, N.A. v. First Interstate Bank of Denver, N. A.*, 511 U.S. 164, (1994)," in which the Court "held that Rule 10b–5's private right of action does not include suits against aiders and abettors." But *Central Bank* concerns a different matter. And it no more requires the majority's rule than free air travel for small children requires free air travel for adults.

Central Bank is a case about *secondary* liability, liability attaching, not to an individual making a false statement, but to an individual helping *someone else* do so. ***

By way of contrast, the present case is about *primary* liability — about individuals who allegedly themselves "make" materially false statements, not about those who help *others* to do so. The question is whether Janus Management is *primarily* liable for violating the Act, not whether it simply helped others violate the Act. The *Central Bank* defendant concededly did *not* make the false statements in question (others did), while here the defendants allegedly *did* make those statements. And a rule (the majority's rule) absolving those who allegedly *did* make false statements does not "follow from" a rule (*Central Bank* 's rule) absolving those who concededly did *not* do so. ***

The majority also refers to *Stoneridge,* but that case offers it no help. In *Stoneridge,* firms that supplied electronic equipment to a cable television company agreed with the cable television company to enter into a series of fraudulent sales and purchases, for example, a sale at an unusually high price, thereby providing funds which the suppliers would use to buy advertising from the cable television company. These arrangements enabled the cable television company to fool its accountants (and ultimately the public) into believing that it had more revenue (for example, advertising revenue) than it really had. As part of the agreement, the companies exchanged letters and backdated contracts to conceal the fraud. Investors subsequently sued the cable television company, some of its officers, its auditors, and the equipment suppliers, as well, claiming that all of them had engaged in a scheme to defraud securities purchasers. In respect to most of the defendants, investors identified allegedly materially false statements contained in the cable television company's financial statements or similar documents. But in respect to the equipment suppliers, investors claimed that the relevant deceptive conduct was in the letters, backdated contracts, and related oral conversations about the scheme. The investors argued that the equipment suppliers, "by participating in the transactions," violated § 10(b) and Rule 10b–5.

The Court held that the equipment suppliers could not be found liable for securities fraud in a private suit under § 10(b). But in doing so, it did not deny that the equipment suppliers *had made* the false statements contained in the letters, contracts, and conversations. Rather, the Court said the issue in the case was whether "any deceptive statement or act respondents made was not actionable because it did not have the requisite *proximate relation* to the investors' harm." And it held that these deceptive statements or actions could not provide a basis for liability because the investors could not prove sufficient *reliance* upon the particular false statements that the equipment suppliers had made.

The Court pointed out that the equipment suppliers "had no duty to disclose; and their deceptive acts were not communicated to the public." And the Court went on to say that "as a result," the investors "cannot show reliance upon any" of the equipment suppliers' actions, "except in an indirect chain that we find too remote for liability." The Court concluded,

> [the equipment suppliers'] deceptive acts, which were not disclosed to the investing public, are too remote to satisfy the requirement of reliance. It was [the cable company], not [the equipment suppliers], that misled its auditor and filed fraudulent financial statements; nothing [the equipment suppliers] did made it necessary or inevitable for [the cable company] to record the transactions as it did.

Insofar as the equipment suppliers' conduct was at issue, the fraudulent "arrangement ... took place in the marketplace for goods and services, not in the investment sphere."

It is difficult for me to see how *Stoneridge* "support[s]" the majority's rule. No one in *Stoneridge* disputed the *making* of the relevant statements, the fraudulent contracts and the like. And no one in *Stoneridge* contended that the equipment suppliers were, in fact, the *makers* of the cable company's misstatements. Rather, *Stoneridge* was concerned with whether the equipment suppliers' *separate* statements were sufficiently disclosed in the securities marketplace so as to be the basis for investor reliance. They were not. But this is a different inquiry than whether statements acknowledged to have been disclosed in the securities marketplace and ripe for reliance can be said to have been "ma[d]e" by one or another actor. How then does *Stoneridge* support the majority's new rule?

The majority adds that its rule is necessary to avoid "a theory of liability similar to — but broader in application than" — § 20(a)'s liability, for " '[e]very person who, directly or indirectly, controls any person liable' " for violations of the securities laws. But that is not so. This Court has explained that the possibility of an express remedy under the securities laws does not preclude a claim under § 10(b). *Herman & MacLean v. Huddleston,* 459 U.S. 375, 388 (1983).

More importantly, a person who is liable under § 20(a) controls another *"person" who is "liable"* for a securities violation. *Morrison v. National Australia Bank Ltd.,* 130 S.Ct. 2869, 2876, n. 2 (2010) ("Liability under § 20(a) is obviously derivative of liability under some other provision of the Exchange Act"). We here examine whether a person is primarily liable whether they do, or they do not, control another person *who is liable.* That is to say, here, the liability of some "other person" is not at issue.

And there is at least one significant category of cases that § 10(b) may address that derivative forms of liability, such as under § 20(a), cannot, namely, cases in which one actor exploits another as an innocent intermediary for its misstatements. Here, it may well be that the Fund's board of trustees knew nothing about the falsity of the prospectuses. See, e.g., *In re Lammert,* Release No. 348, 93 S.E.C. Docket 5676, 5700 (2008) (Janus Management was aware of market timing in the Janus Fund no later than 2002, but "[t]his knowledge was never shared with the Board"). And if so, § 20(a) would not apply.

The possibility of guilty management and innocent board is the 13th stroke of the new rule's clock. What is to happen when guilty management writes a prospectus (for the board) containing materially false statements and fools both board and public into believing they are true? Apparently under the majority's rule, in such circumstances *no one* could be found to have "ma[d]e" a materially false statement — even though under the common law the managers would likely have been guilty or liable (in analogous circumstances) for doing so as *principals* (and not as aiders and abettors). See, e.g., 2 W. LaFave, Substantive Criminal Law § 13.1(a) (2d ed.2003); 1 M. Hale, Pleas of the Crown 617 (1736); Perkins, Parties to Crime, 89 U. Pa. L.Rev. 581, 583 (1941) (one is guilty as a principal when one uses an innocent third party to commit a crime); Restatement (Second) of Torts § 533 (1976).

apparent absurd consequences from majority's rule

Indeed, under the majority's rule it seems unlikely that the SEC itself in such circumstances could exercise the authority Congress has granted it to pursue primary violators who "make" false statements or the authority that Congress has specifically provided to prosecute aiders and abettors to securities violations. See [Exchange Act § 20(e) (granting SEC authority to prosecute aiders and abettors). That is because the managers, not having "ma[d]e" the statement, would not be liable as principals and there would be no other primary violator they might have tried to "aid" or "abet." *SEC v. DiBella,* 587 F.3d 553, 566 (C.A.2 2009) (prosecution for aiding and abetting requires primary violation to which offender gave "substantial assistance").

If the majority believes, as its footnote hints, that § 20(b) could provide a basis for liability in this case, ante, n. 10, then it should remand the case for possible amendment of the complaint. "There is a dearth of authority construing Section 20(b)," which has been thought largely "superfluous in 10b–5 cases." 5B A. Jacobs, Disclosure and Remedies Under the Securities Law § 11–8, p. 11–72 (2011). Hence respondent, who reasonably thought that it referred to the proper securities law provision, is faultless for failing to mention § 20(b) as well.

In sum, I can find nothing in § 10(b) or in Rule 10b–5, its language, its history, or in precedent suggesting that Congress, in enacting the securities laws, intended a loophole of the kind that the majority's rule may well create.

II

Rejecting the majority's rule, of course, does not decide the question before us. We must still determine whether, in light of the complaint's allegations, Janus Management could have "ma[d]e" the false statements in the prospectuses at issue. In my view, the answer to this question is "Yes." The specific relationships alleged among Janus Management, the Janus Fund, and the prospectus statements warrant the conclusion that Janus Management did "make" those statements.

In part, my conclusion reflects the fact that this Court and lower courts have made clear that at least *sometimes* corporate officials and others can be held liable under Rule 10b–5 for having "ma[d]e" a materially false statement even when that statement appears in a document (or is made by a third person) that the officials do not legally control. In *Herman & MacLean,* for example, this Court pointed out that "certain individuals who play a part in preparing the registration statement," including corporate officers, lawyers, and accountants, may be primarily liable even where "they are not named as having prepared or certified" the registration statement. And *** this Court wrote in *Central Bank* that a "lawyer, accountant, or bank, who ... makes a material misstatement (or omission) on which a purchaser or seller of securities relies *may be liable as a primary violator under 10b–5,* assuming *all* of the requirements for primary liability under Rule 10b–5 are met."

Given the statements in our opinions, it is not surprising that lower courts have found primary liability for actors without "ultimate authority" over issued statements. One court, for example, concluded that an accountant could be primarily liable for having "ma[d]e" false statements, where he issued fraudulent opinion and certification letters reproduced in prospectuses, annual reports, and other corporate materials for which he was not ultimately responsible. *Anixter v. Home–Stake Production Co.,* 77 F.3d 1215, 1225–1227 (C.A.10 1996). In a later case postdating *Stoneridge,* that court reaffirmed that an outside consultant could be primarily liable for having "ma[d]e" false statements, where he drafted fraudulent quarterly and annual filing statements later reviewed and certified by the firm's auditor, officers, and counsel. *SEC v. Wolfson,* 539 F.3d 1249, 1261 (C.A.10 2008). And another court found that a corporation's chief financial officer could be held primarily liable as having "ma[d]e" misstatements that appeared in a form 10–K that she prepared but did not sign or file. *McConville v. SEC,* 465 F.3d 780, 787 (C.A.7 2006). One can also easily find lower court cases explaining that corporate officials may be liable for having "ma[d]e" false statements where those officials use innocent persons as conduits through which the false statements reach the public (without necessarily attributing the false statements to the officials). See, e.g., *In re Navarre Corp. Securities Litigation,* 299 F.3d 735, 743 (C.A.8 2002) (liability may be premised on use of analysts as a conduit to communicate false statements to market); *In re Cabletron Systems, Inc.,* 311 F.3d 11, 38 (C.A.1 2002) (rejecting a test requiring legal "control" over third parties making statements as giving "company officials too much leeway to commit fraud on the market by using analysts as their mouthpieces"); *Novak v. Kasaks,* 216 F.3d 300, 314–315 (C.A.2 2000).

My conclusion also reflects the particular circumstances that the complaint alleges. The complaint states that "Janus Management, as investment advisor to the funds, is responsible for the day-to-day management of its investment portfolio and other business affairs of the funds. Janus Management furnishes advice and recommendations concerning the funds' investments, as well as administrative, compliance and accounting services for the funds." Each of the Fund's 17 officers was a vice president of Janus Management. The Fund has "no assets separate and apart from those they hold for shareholders." Janus Management disseminated the fund prospectuses through its parent company's

Web site. Janus Management employees drafted and reviewed the Fund prospectuses, including language about "market timing." And Janus Management may well have kept the trustees in the dark about the true "market timing" facts. *In re Lammert,* 93 S.E.C. Docket, at 5700.

Given these circumstances, as long as some managers, sometimes, can be held to have "ma[d]e" a materially false statement, Janus Management can be held to have done so on the facts alleged here. The relationship between Janus Management and the Fund could hardly have been closer. Janus Management's involvement in preparing and writing the relevant statements could hardly have been greater. And there is a serious suggestion that the board itself knew little or nothing about the falsity of what was said. Unless we adopt a formal rule (as the majority here has done) that would arbitrarily exclude from the scope of the word "make" those who manage a firm — even when those managers perpetrate a fraud through an unknowing intermediary — the management company at issue here falls within that scope. We should hold the allegations in the complaint in this respect legally sufficient.

With respect, I dissent.

NOTES AND QUESTIONS

1. ***Cutting to the Chase.*** Applying the "ultimate authority" test, the Court found that the Fund, not JCM, made the statements in question. Its "ultimate authority" notwithstanding, the Fund was apparently at most negligent, and thereby incapable of incurring primary liability under Rule 10b-5. After *Janus,* can *any* entity or person be held accountable under Rule 10-5 for intentionally or recklessly including material misstatements and omissions in the Fund's prospectus – whether in the context of an implied private action for damages or in an SEC (or DOJ) enforcement action? Consider this question again after you have read Note 5 below on scheme liability as well as the materials on secondary liability in the sections that follow.

2. ***Ultimate Authority, Attribution, and Reliance.*** To conclude that JCM lacked "ultimate authority" over the Fund's statements, the Court in footnote 11 flagged the failure of the prospectus to "attribute" those statements to JCM. In the very next sentence of that footnote, however, the Court seemed dubious that attribution alone would suffice to show "ultimate authority." On the other hand, the Court observed in the text that attribution provides "strong evidence that a statement was made by – and only by – the party to whom it is attributed." To what extent are these assertions in tension?

Consider also the interrelationship between attribution and Rule 10b-5's element of reliance (which private plaintiffs must plead and prove). Many courts have been willing to infer reliance so long as the (mis)statement in question was publicly attributed to the defendant at the time of its release. See, e.g., *Pacific Inv. Mgmt Co., LLC v. Mayer Brown, LLP,* 603 F.3d 144 (2d Cir. 2010). Is such attribution-based liability compromised after *Janus*?

3. **Janus *vs.* Central Bank .** The Court claimed fidelity to its decision in *Central Bank, N.A. v. Interstate Bank, N.A.,* 511 U.S. 164 (1994), famous for its elimination of aiding and abetting liability in implied private actions under

Rule 10b-5. Seeking to downplay the significance of the demise of aiding and abetting, *Central Bank* heralded primary liability's continued potential:

> The absence of § 10(b) aiding and abetting liability does not mean that secondary actors in the securities markets are always free from liability under the securities Acts. Any person or entity, including a lawyer, accountant, or bank, who employs a manipulative device or makes a material misstatement (or omission) on which a purchaser or seller of securities relies may be liable as a primary violator under 10b–5, assuming *all* of the requirements for primary liability under Rule 10b–5 are met. In any complex securities fraud, moreover, there are likely to be multiple violators; in this case, for example, respondents named four defendants as primary violators.

Id. at 191. Is the prospect of "multiple" primary violators at odds with *Janus*? Consider what the *Janus* dissenters had to say with respect to this aspect of *Central Bank*:

> [A]s far as *Central Bank* is concerned, depending upon the circumstances, board members, senior firm officials, officials tasked to develop a marketing document, large investors, or others (taken together or separately) all might "make" materially false statements subjecting themselves to primary liability. The majority's rule does not protect, it *extends, Central Bank*'s holding of no-liability into new territory that *Central Bank* explicitly placed outside that holding. And by ignoring the language in which *Central Bank* did so, the majority's rule itself undermines *Central Bank*. Where is the legal support for the majority's "draw[ing] a clean line," that so seriously conflicts with *Central Bank?* Indeed, where is the legal support for the majority's suggestion that plaintiffs must show some kind of "attribution" of a statement to a defendant, ante, n. 11 — if it means plaintiffs must show, not only that the defendant "ma[d]e" the statement, but something more?

Janus, 131 S.Ct. at 2308 (Breyer, J., dissenting). Do you agree that the majority's ruling in *Janus* "undermines" *Central Bank*'s view of primary liability? Assuming that *Janus* does undermine *Central Bank*, is this a positive or negative normative development?

4. Janus *vs. the PSLRA*. As we saw in the previous section on damages, the PSLRA established a scheme of proportionate liability under which, with limited exceptions, co-defendants in private actions will be liable only for the fraction of the judgment for which they bear responsibility. See Exchange Act Section 21D(f). Does the concept of proportionate liability presuppose that multiple persons and entities can "make" a false statement, even if those persons lack "ultimate authority over the statement"? Is it likely that Congress would have amended the Exchange Act to provide for proportionate liability if it regarded the "maker" of a material misstatement or omission to be only "the person or entity with ultimate authority over the statement"?

5.* Janus *vs.* Stoneridge *(and Scheme Liability). The *Janus* majority also claimed fidelity to the decision in *Stoneridge Inv. Partners, LLC v. Scientific-Atlanta, Inc.*, 552 U.S. 148 (2008). There the plaintiffs argued that the defendants were primarily liable for participating in a scheme to create misleading financial statements. Their theory of liability – known as "scheme liability" – proceeded from the assumption that *Central Bank* implicated only the prohibition in Rule 10b-5(b) ("to make any untrue statement of a material fact or *** to omit to state a material fact") and said nothing about those in either Rule 10b-5(a) ("to employ any device, scheme, or artifice to defraud") or Rule 10b-5 (c) ("to engage in any act, practice, or course of business which operates *** as a fraud or deceit upon any person"). As the *Janus* dissent emphasizes, the facts of *Stoneridge* centered on the defendants' alleged willingness to enter into sham transactions which allowed the issuer to trick its auditor into certifying financial statements that included materially inflated revenues and operating cash flow.

The *Stoneridge* Court did not reject the theory of scheme liability as such. Indeed, in an otherwise fractured 5-3 decision (Justice Breyer took no part in its consideration), the Court was unanimous on one important issue: Section 10(b) extends to all forms of deceptive conduct. *Stoneridge,* 552 U.S. at 158 ("Conduct itself can be deceptive;" there need not be "a specific oral or written statement before there could be liability under § 10(b) or Rule 10b–5"). The majority, however, prevailed on its view that Rule 10b-5 liability was inappropriate because of the investors' failure to establish their reliance on the defendant's alleged misconduct. Accordingly, after *Stoneridge,* a scheme liability theory has at least in principle been available to private plaintiffs who were able to establish reliance. See, e.g., *Pac. Inv. Mgmt Co, LLC,* supra, at 159 (dismissing the plaintiffs' scheme liability allegations for failing to address reliance); Robert A. Prentice, Scheme Liability: Does It Have A Future After *Stoneridge*?, 2009 Wis. L. Rev. 351. Moreover, Rule 10b-5 scheme liability has also been available to the SEC, which is not encumbered by a reliance requirement. See, e.g., *SEC v. Brown,* 740 F. Supp. 2d 148, 171-72 (D.D. C. 2010); *SEC v. Battenberg,* 2010 WL 1416981 at *4 (E.D. Mich. 2010). Notably, the *Stoneridge* Court itself preserved the SEC's ability to pursue "schemers" as Rule 10b-5 primary violators when it observed that "if business operations are used, as alleged here, to affect securities markets, the SEC enforcement power may reach the culpable actors." *Stoneridge*, 552 U.S. at 161.

What is the status of scheme liability in the wake of *Janus*? Would *Janus* allow either the SEC or investors to argue that an investment advisor employs a "scheme" to defraud or engages in a fraudulent "course of business" when it knowingly drafted materially false or misleading statements that appear in a prospectus issued by a mutual fund? If so, could such investors establish that they relied on those misstatements to their detriment? In answering the latter question, consider the following passage from the majority opinion in *Stoneridge*:

> [R]espondents were acting in concert with [the securities issuer] in the ordinary course as suppliers and, as matters then evolved in the not so ordinary course, as customers. Unconventional as the arrangement was, it took place in the marketplace for goods and services, not in the investment sphere. [The issuer] Charter was free to do as it chose in preparing its books, conferring with its auditor, and preparing and then issuing its financial statements. In these circumstances the investors cannot be said to have relied upon any of respondents' deceptive acts in the decision to purchase or sell securities; and as the requisite reliance cannot be shown, respondents have no liability to petitioner under the implied right of action. This conclusion is consistent with the narrow dimensions we must give to a right of action Congress did not authorize when it first enacted the statute and did not expand when it revisited the law. ***

Stoneridge, 552 U.S. at 166-67.

6. Ultimate Authority and Corporate Insiders. At issue in *Janus* was the liability of JCM for the misleading statements published by a separate legal entity, namely, the Fund. Does the ultimate authority test apply as well to corporate insiders, that is, directors, officers, and other corporate officials? If so, does the ultimate authority test effectively eliminate the possibility that individuals can be held primarily liable under Rule 10b-5(b) for material misstatements and omissions contained in SEC reports, press releases, and other documents filed or disseminated by a securities issuer?

What if the material misstatement or omission occurred in the context of an insider's speech or other statement to the public? Is it arguable that the company had ultimate authority even if the board of directors did not approve the statement? What if the board had approved the statement? Would that mean that the insider lacked ultimate authority?

7. Delayed But Not Denied. The Court acknowledged that the plaintiffs might be able to state a claim under Exchange Act Section 20(b) – a provision which, the dissent noted, has rarely been construed. We will return to Section 20(b) in connection with controlling person liability and respondeat superior liability infra.

PROBLEM 2-26

Big-Box, Inc., is an exchange-traded company facing stiff competition and a declining customer base. Big-Box's president (Jed) granted an interview to a major financial newspaper, during which he made various material misrepresentations regarding the company's competitive situation and future prospects. Unaware of Jed's fraud but convinced of the interview's newsworthiness, the newspaper published a lengthy article reporting on what Jed had said about Big-Box. In response to the publication of this article, the market price of Big-Box rose, only to tumble later when the truth emerged.

Investors who relied on the integrity of the market price would like to bring a Rule 10b-5 action. Whom can they hope to hold primarily liable? Would it make any difference if the newspaper had published a verbatim transcript of Jed's interview?

PROBLEM 2-27

To satisfy the statutory requirement that a registered public accounting firm certify the Form 10-K financial statements, Albemarle Co. retained the services of PrideWaterton. After several weeks of work, PrideWaterton issued a "clean" audit report stating that in its professional opinion, Albemarle's financial statements passed muster without any qualifications or exceptions. However, in performing its audit, PrideWaterton recklessly failed to detect several material misrepresentations in the financial statements relating to the company's earned revenues. Albemarle's CEO and CFO had actual knowledge of those misstatements, and two of Albemarle's outside directors had harbored suspicions about the accuracy of the financial statements but recklessly remained silent. Albemarle's six other outside directors may have been negligent in failing to detect the misstatements, but their conduct could not be deemed reckless.

Eliza claims to have purchased Albemarle stock only after reviewing the financial statement certified by PrideWaterton. In a Rule 10b-5 action by Eliza, who can be primarily liable?

2. *Secondary Liability*

The concept of secondary liability allows plaintiffs to sue more defendants than otherwise would be possible were liability restricted to primary actors. While secondary liability has increased in importance in the wake of the contraction of primary liability, it is no panacea. The reason is that it is available only if the plaintiff can establish that another person or entity committed a primary violation.

a. *Aiding and Abetting Liability*

In *Central Bank, N.A. v. Interstate Bank, N.A.*, 511 U.S. 164, 167 (1994), the question presented was "whether private civil liability under § 10(b) extends *** to those who do not engage in the manipulative or deceptive practice, but who aid and abet the violation." That is, as the Court itself emphasized, "aiding and abetting liability reaches persons who do not engage in the proscribed activities at all, but who give a degree of aid to those who do." Id., at 176. The particular facts of *Central Bank* were recounted as follows by the dissenters in *Janus*:

> *Central Bank* involved a bond issuer accused of having made materially false statements, which overstated the values of property that backed the bonds. *Central Bank* also involved a defendant that was a bank, serving as indenture trustee, which was supposed to check the bond issuer's valuations. The plaintiffs claimed that the bank delayed its valuation checks and thereby *helped* the issuer make its false statements credible. The question before the Court concerned the bank's liability — a *secondary* liability for "aiding and abetting" the bond issuer, who (on the theory set forth) was primarily liable.
>
> The Court reviewed a Court of Appeals decision that had defined the elements of aiding and abetting as "(1) *a primary violation* of § 10(b); (2) recklessness by the aider and abettor as to the existence of the primary violation; and (3) *substantial assistance given to the primary violator* by the aider and abettor." *Central Bank,* 511 U.S., at 168 (emphasis added).

Janus, 131 S.Ct. at 2307 (Breyer, J., dissenting).

In a 5-4 opinion, *Central Bank* overturned the Tenth Circuit's decision – as well as other decisions from each and every federal circuit – holding that liability under Section 10(b) and Rule 10b-5 extends to aiding and abetting. In applying a death knell to aiding and abetting liability under Rule 10b-5, the Court stated that:

> Congress knew how to impose aiding and abetting liability when it chose to do so. See, e.g., 18 U.S.C. § 2 (general criminal aiding and abetting statute); Packers and Stockyards Act, 7 U.S.C. § 192(g) (civil aiding and abetting provision). If, as respondents seem to say, Congress intended to impose aiding and abetting liability, we presume it would have used the words "aid" and "abet" in the statutory text. But it did not.

We reach the uncontroversial conclusion, accepted even by those courts recognizing a § 10(b) aiding and abetting cause of action, that the text of the 1934 Act does not itself reach those who aid and abet a § 10(b) violation. Unlike those courts, however, we think that conclusion resolves the case. It is inconsistent with settled methodology in § 10(b) cases to extend liability beyond the scope of conduct prohibited by the statutory text. To be sure, aiding and abetting a wrongdoer ought to be actionable in certain instances. The issue, however, is not whether imposing private civil liability on aiders and abettors is good policy but whether aiding and abetting is covered by the statute. ***

Because this case concerns the conduct prohibited by § 10(b), the statute itself resolves the case, but even if it did not, we would reach the same result. When the text of § 10(b) does not resolve a particular issue, we attempt to infer "how the 1934 Congress would have addressed the issue had the 10b-5 action been included as an express provision in the 1934 Act." *Musick, Peeler,* 508 U.S., at 294. For that inquiry, we use the express causes of action in the securities Acts as the primary model for the § 10(b) action. The reason is evident: Had the 73d Congress enacted a private § 10(b) right of action, it likely would have designed it in a manner similar to the other private rights of action in the securities Acts. See id., at 294-297. ***

Following that analysis here, we look to the express private causes of action in the 1933 and 1934 Acts. ***

From the fact that Congress did not attach private aiding and abetting liability to any of the express causes of action in the securities Acts, we can infer that Congress likely would not have attached aiding and abetting liability to § 10(b) had it provided a private § 10(b) cause of action. There is no reason to think that Congress would have attached aiding and abetting liability only to § 10(b) and not to any of the express private rights of action in the Act. ***

Our reasoning is confirmed by the fact that respondents' argument would impose 10b-5 aiding and abetting liability when at least one element critical for recovery under 10b-5 is absent: reliance. A plaintiff must show reliance on the defendant's misstatement or omission to recover under 10b-5. *Basic Inc. v. Levinson,* 485 U.S., at 243. Were we to allow the aiding and abetting action proposed in this case, the defendant could be liable without any showing that the plaintiff relied upon the aider and abettor's statements or actions. Allowing plaintiffs to circumvent the reliance requirement would disregard the careful limits on 10b-5 recovery mandated by our earlier cases.

Central Bank, 511 U.S. at 176-80.

NOTES AND QUESTIONS

1. ***Two Interpretative Approaches.*** The Court maintained that the interpretation of Section 10(b) turns on the underlying substantive issue. If that issue involves the scope of the prohibited conduct, the focus should be on the statutory text. If, on the other hand, the issue involves a matter unique to the implied private action, the focus should be on identifying Congress's hypothetical intent – what Congress would have done had it created an express private action under Section 10(b). Do the decisions that you have read so far in this Chapter comport with this distinction? See generally Jill E. Fisch, The Scope of Private Securities Litigation: In Search of Liability Standards for Secondary Defendants, 99 Colum. L. Rev. 1293 (1999).

2. The Text of Section 10(b). Is it arguable that Section 10(b)'s text does encompass aiding and abetting liability, the Court's insistence to the contrary notwithstanding? See Donald C. Langevoort, Words From On High About Rule 10b-5: *Chiarella*'s History, *Central Bank*'s Future, 20 Del. J. Corp. L. 865, 886-87 (1995) (focusing on the language "us[ing] or employ[ing] *** a manipulative or deceptive device or contrivance").

3. Aiding and Abetting and the SEC. The Court's analysis called into question the SEC's authority to sue for aiding and abetting. *SEC v. Fehn*, 97 F.3d 1276, 1282 (9th Cir. 1996); Lewis D. Loewenfels & Alan R. Bromberg, A New Standard for Aiding and Abetting Under the PSLRA of 1995, 52 Bus. Law. 1, 2 (1996). See *Central Bank, N.A. v. Interstate Bank, N.A.*, 511 U.S. 164, 200 (1994) (Steven, J. dissenting) (noting that "[t]he majority leaves little doubt that the Exchange Act does not even permit the SEC to pursue aiders and abettors"). To safeguard the SEC's authority in this regard, Congress enacted Exchange Act Section 20(e) as part of the PSLRA. As originally enacted, Section 20(e) allowed the SEC to sue anyone who "knowingly provides substantial assistance to another person" in violating an Exchange Act provision or rule. Interpreting this language, courts divided over whether "knowingly" encompassed "recklessly." Compare *Fehn*, supra, 97 F.3d at 1294 (requiring actual knowledge) with *SEC v. Pimco Advisors Fund Mgmt, LLC,* 341 F. Supp. 2d 454, 468 (S.D.N.Y. 2004) (not requiring actual knowledge).

Responding to this division, Congress, as part of the Dodd-Frank Act, amended Section 20(e) to embrace anyone who provides substantial assistance "knowingly or recklessly." Accordingly, Exchange Act Section 20(e) now reads as follows:

> For purposes of any action brought by the Commission under paragraph (1) or (3) of section 21(d) [authorizing injunctions and civil monetary penalties], any person that knowingly or recklessly provides substantial assistance to another person in violation of a provision of this Act, or any rule or regulation issued under this Act, shall be deemed to be in violation of such provision to the same extent as the person to whom such assistance is provided.

The Dodd-Frank Act also added new, similarly worded aiding and abetting provisions to Section 15(b) of the Securities Act, Section 48(b) of the Investment Company Act, and Section 209(f) of the Investment Advisers Act.

Note that there was no need to safeguard the DOJ's authority to proceed on an aiding and abetting theory, given the separate criminal aiding and abetting provision, 18 U.S.C. § 2.

4. A Private Action For Aiding and Abetting? In the Dodd-Frank Act, Congress instructed the Government Accounting Office to conduct a study of the advisability of creating a private action for aiding and abetting. The GAO report contains an exhaustive survey of the development of the law in the area along with the arguments for and against the creation of such an action. It concludes with the observation that "[d]ebate continues over whether a private cause of action for aiding and abetting securities fraud should be created." Government Accounting Office, B-321063, 11-664, Securities Fraud Liability of Secondary Actors 45 (July 21, 2011).

Do you think that private plaintiffs should be able to sue for aiding and abetting? Why or why not?

5. ***Conspiracy Liability.*** Before *Central Bank,* a claim that the defendants conspired to violate Rule 10b-5 was viable. See, e.g., *Brown v. Hutton Group,* 795 F. Supp. 1317, 1324 (S.D.N.Y. 1992); *Kronfeld v. First Jersey Nat'l Bank,* 638 F. Supp. 1454, 1468 (D.N.J. 1986). Establishing a conspiracy required proof of "(i) an agreement between the conspirator and the wrongdoer and (ii) a wrongful act committed in furtherance of the conspiracy." *Brown,* supra, 795 F. Supp. at 1324.

In the wake of *Central Bank,* however, Rule 10b-5 conspiracy claims have been repeatedly rejected. See *Dinsmore v. Squadron, Ellenoff, Plesent, Sheinfeld & Sorkin,* 135 F.3d 837, 841 (2d Cir. 1998) (collecting cases); *Burnett v. Rowzee,* 561 F. Supp. 2d 1120, 1125 (C.D. Cal. 2008). Is this rejection warranted? Can conspiracy claims be premised on the language of Rule 10b-5(a), which prohibits any person from "employ[ing] any device, *scheme,* or artifice to defraud" (emphasis added)?

Suppose that a conspiracy is alleged by the SEC rather than by a private party. Does the SEC's allegation stand on a different footing due to Section 20(e)? Note that the DOJ has the authority to allege criminal conspiracies based on provisions that you will study in Chapter 11.

6. State Law Alternatives. Aiding and abetting liability remains an option under the blue sky laws of many states as well as under common law fraud. Moreover, collateral participants in securities fraud (such as lawyers) are sometimes sued for malpractice or breach of fiduciary duty by the client/primary violator after the latter becomes insolvent and enters receivership. See *O'Melveny & Myers v. FDIC,* 512 U.S. 79 (1994). Money recovered in such litigation is then passed on to the investors, who are claimants of the insolvent entity's estate.

b. Controlling Person Liability

Controlling person liability is the only form of secondary liability explicitly authorized by the Exchange Act (excepting SEC actions under Section 20(e) for aiding and abetting). The authorization is set forth in Section 20(a), which reads as follows:

> Every person who, directly or indirectly, controls any person liable under any provision of this Act or any rule or regulation thereunder shall also be liable jointly and severally with and to the same extent as such controlled person to any person to whom such controlled person is liable *(including to the Commission***),* unless the controlling person acted in good faith and did not directly or indirectly induce the act or acts constituting the violation or cause of action.

The language authorizing lawsuits by the SEC came by way of an amendment to Section 20(a) that was enacted as part of the Dodd-Frank Act. The amendment resolved a circuit split over whether the SEC was entitled to utilize Section 20(a). Compare *SEC v. J.W. Barclay & Co.,* 442 F.3d 834, 842-43 (3d Cir.

2006) (giving affirmative answer) with *SEC v. Coffey*, 493 F.2d 1304, 1318 (6th Cir. 1974) (giving negative answer).

As Section 20(a) indicates, controlling person liability requires (i) a primary violation of the Exchange Act committed by the controlled person and (ii) the defendant's control over a primary violator. See, e.g., *SEC v. Todd*, 642 F.3d 1207, 1223 (9th Cir. 2011); *Adams v. Kinder-Morgan, Inc.*, 340 F.3d 1083, 1107 (10th Cir. 2003). The controlled person need not, however, be joined as a defendant. See, e.g., *In re Suprema Specialties, Inc. Sec. Litig.*, 438 F.3d 256, 285 (3d Cir. 2006).

Note that Section 20(a) does not provide a definition of control. As you read the following case, ask yourself why the court found the defendant to have control as well as how the defendant might establish his good faith defense at trial.

ARTHUR CHILDREN'S TRUST v. KEIM

994 F.2d 1390 (9th Cir. 1993)

JOHN T. NOONAN, JR., CIRCUIT JUDGE:

*** The underlying action against Keim is for securities fraud in violation of *** Rule 10b-5. He is alleged to have been a control person *** of an issuer of fraudulent securities. *** We reverse the summary judgment in favor of Keim ***.

FACTS

In January 1985 an agreement for a joint venture called Los Caballos Development Associates (the Venture) was entered into by Los Caballos de Santa Fe, Inc., a New Mexico corporation (the Santa Fe Company) and Parkland Development Corporation, an Arizona corporation (Parkland). The agreement provided that the Santa Fe Company would "initially contribute" certain real estate and services to the Venture "in the form of administrative and development expertise" and that Parkland would "initially contribute" certain real estate and services "in the form of administrative, and financing and development expertise." A Management Committee was created whose duties were stated in the agreement as follows:

> Except as expressly provided herein, neither of the Venturers shall have the authority to act for the other Venturer, but instead the management of the business affairs of the Venture shall be vested in a Management Committee ... Any major or significant business decisions affecting the Venture shall be made by the Management Committee, including, but not limited to ... incurring of any obligation on behalf of the Venture in excess of Twenty Thousand Dollars ($20,000), the employment of professionals and other employees, and any other decision which may materially affect the Venture.

A special section of the agreement, entitled "Additional Funds," provided:

> If in the judgment of the Management Committee additional funds are required for the Venture's operations and purposes from time to time, and if the Management Committee determines that the funds are not to be borrowed, then the additional funds required shall be contributed by the Venturers fifty percent (50%) each upon ten (10) days' advanced notice, and shall be treated as additional capital contributions to the Venture.

The Management Committee was to consist of eight members, with each venturer nominating four and Parkland having the right to designate the chairman, whose vote in case of a tie would be decisive and who was to be responsible for "the day-to-day business decisions and operations." Parkland nominated John Hill, Michael Smith, Timothy Sprague and Larry LaPrade, with LaPrade designated as chairman. The Santa Fe company nominated its chairman, Burton Melton; its president, Don Burt; and two of its directors, Mark Conkling and Keim.

The purpose of the Venture was a real estate development south of Santa Fe which, when completed, would include private residences, retail shops, a hotel and—as a centerpiece—a stadium and accompanying facilities to constitute a major equestrian convention center—hence the project's appealing name, "The Horses," in Spanish.

LaPrade and Smith began the task of money-raising, using as a vehicle Incor, a corporation controlled by them. As a result of Incor's solicitation the Investors, mostly pension plans for doctors, were led to purchase the Venture's notes. All the representations made to the Investors were made by Incor, LaPrade or Smith. The Venture put no restrictions on their methods. No representations to the Investors were made by Keim.

On March 1, 1985 the Venture issued a promissory note for $3,760,000 *** The interest was 16 percent on the unpaid principal balance beginning April 1, 1985, with a balloon payment of the entire unpaid principal balance plus all unpaid interest due 12 months from the date of the note. The note was secured by a second mortgage by the Venture on its real estate in Santa Fe. The mortgage and the note were executed by the Venture with the signatures of Los Caballos de Santa Fe, Inc., joint venturer, by Peter C. Webb, its secretary-treasurer, and Parkland Development Corporation, joint venturer, by Michael Smith, its treasurer.

Soon after this financing had been accomplished, the Venture was in difficult straits. According to a memorandum of July 3, 1985 from Peter Webb, controller of the Santa Fe company, to the members of the Management Committee of the Venture, including Keim, the committee on June 17, 1985 discussed the "precarious situation regarding our financial capabilities to meet our obligations to the Incor investors and our other contractual obligations." The Venture's current deposits were "adequate to cover our Incor interest obligations," but if "we continue to pay our development obligations we could be out of money as soon as October." Michael Smith had stated that if construction financing were not in place by October he "would address the problem." In light of this statement, "it was agreed" that Webb "should continue to pay our obligations as they are incurred or due using all available funds including those previously earmarked for interest payments to Incor's investors."

According to the minutes of the Management Committee for July 10, 1985, at which Keim was present, a large number of topics were discussed. Among other things:

> Larry LaPrade emphasized the profit portion of Sheet 16 [of the Financial Package]. The lenders are interested in hard numbers, and the profit that will be generated.

> Financing package was discussed. Sprague stated that we had to raise from three to five million dollars worth of equity. He suggested to the Management Committee that they should begin putting names, addresses of potential investors. He said that there were tax considerations to think of, perhaps potential pension fund money. Three and one half million dollars raised by ourselves, the rest banks. Great tax shelters for prospective investors. Keim felt tax benefits would be there. Pension Plan money is easier to tap.

Following a discussion of "the appraisal," Larry LaPrade raised the possibility of a bridge loan, "starting in August." Keim said "he was prepared to give all out whatever it takes. Pension Plan 15%."

In addition to being a member of the Management Committee of the Venture, Keim was chairman of its Development Committee. He had a 10 percent equity interest in the enterprise. He was also owed a $100,000 "development fee" by the Santa Fe company, a fee which he asserted in a letter to Larry LaPrade of November 27, 1985 had been assumed by LaPrade, apparently meaning that the Venture had assumed it. A budget of the Venture reflects only one fee for development—$100,000 owed Keim.

According to the affidavit of Timothy Sprague:

> [V]arious discussions were had between members of the management committee, including Howard Keim, with respect to the raising of seed capital for the project. As time progressed throughout 1985, the project having continued to incur significant development expenses and no construction or permanent financing having been obtained for the project, these discussions among the members of the management committee included "rolling over" previous loans secured for the project by Michael Smith and Larry LaPrade, together with the raising of new monies through additional loans.
>
> Mr. Keim—who was constantly pressing the venture for payment of his own fees—was generally an advocate of Smith and LaPrade's lending activities, his comments essentially being to get it done.

Sprague further swore that at the July 1985 meeting or prior thereto, Smith advised the members of the Management Committee that "he was borrowing monies for the project from doctor pension plans by offering to secure their loans by the project's real property, on a 50% loan to value ratio. Previously, at the time of the original loan, it was discussed that it would also be secured by the personal guarantees of all the Los Caballos venturers, excluding defendant Keim, who I understand refused to provide one." On a flight from Albuquerque to Phoenix in July 1985 Sprague also described to Keim "Smith and LaPrade's manner of raising funds."

On March 1, 1986 the Venture again executed a promissory note, secured by a mortgage on its real estate, in the amount of $5,400,000. *** The interest was 16 percent on the unpaid principal balance, due beginning April 1, 1986, "with a balloon payment of the entire unpaid principal plus all unpaid interest due and payable six months from the date of receipt of invested funds." The note and mortgage were executed by the same entities and persons as the note and mortgage of March 1, 1985. The proceeds of this issue were used to repay the 1985 note.

All of the foregoing facts are not disputed, with one large exception. According to Keim's deposition, he had no knowledge of how LaPrade and Smith were raising the money and no knowledge of who was providing it.

The Venture was a financial disaster. LaPrade and Smith entered bankruptcy. The Investors lost their money.

PROCEEDINGS

On December 21, 1988 the Investors filed suit under the Securities Exchange Act of 1934 against six of the members of the Management Committee, including Keim, and against several others associated with the enterprise. *** The third claim for relief asserted that the defendants who had been members of the Management Committee of the Venture were controlling persons in the sense that section 20(a) *** defines "controlling persons." They were alleged to have known the dire financial straits of the Venture and, knowing it, to have also known that no one would have invested in it unless provided incentives which no defendant had reason to believe were being promised or unless there were false representations. In this situation, knowing that millions of dollars were being raised for their project from private investors, the control persons allegedly undertook no action to implement controls on LaPrade, Smith and Sprague; they allegedly exercised no "internal control or supervision" to prevent violation of the securities law; they allegedly either did not inquire as to the representations made to induce the loans or knew that the loans were induced by fraudulent representations. ***

On May 30, 1991, the district court found that Keim had no control over the financing and was therefore not a control person. Moreover, the court found "nothing to indicate that Keim knew anything about 'false representations.' Therefore, he is not liable as a controlling person." *** The court granted Keim's motion for summary judgment ***.

ANALYSIS

The Case Against Keim

The Issuer. The notes and mortgages given to the Investors by the Venture in 1985 and 1986 were investment contracts constituting securities under the Securities Act of 1933. *SEC v. Howey Co.,* 328 U.S. 293, 301 (1946). Accordingly, the Venture was an issuer under the statute.

The Issuer's Scienter. If the representations made by LaPrade were false, the issuer had the scienter that *Ernst & Ernst v. Hochfelder,* 425 U.S. 185 (1976) requires for Rule 10b-5 liability. Id. at 212-14. The issuer is chargeable with the knowledge of LaPrade, the head of its Management Committee, acting to market the issuer's securities. That LaPrade acted through Incor cannot insulate the issuer from his knowledge. The issuer is equally possessed of scienter if the providing of the appraisal reports to Incor for fund-raising is found to have been the providing of information not fraudulently but recklessly. *Hollinger v. Titan Capital Corp.,* 914 F.2d 1564, 1568-69 (9th Cir.1990). ***

The Controlling Persons of the Issuer. In general, the determination of who is a controlling person for purposes of liability under [Section 20] is an intensely factual question. See 4 Louis Loss & Joel Seligman, Securities

Regulation 1724 (1990). A director is not automatically liable as a controlling person. *Burgess v. Premier Corp.,* 727 F.2d 826, 832 (9th Cir.1984) (a director who was uninvolved in the company's day-to-day cattle business and was without experience in the business and had nothing to do with the prospectuses issued to the doctor investors was not a controlling person, nor was a director who had minimal interaction with the company, due partly to ill health). Citing *Burgess,* Loss and Seligman observe: "Accordingly, although a person's being an officer or director does not create any *presumption* of control, it is a sort of red light." 4 Loss & Seligman, supra, at 1724 (emphasis in original). It is not uncommon for control "to rest with a group of persons, such as the members of the corporation's management." Id. at 1722.

Here the persons controlling the issuer in every material respect were the Management Committee, whose decisions, as the Joint Venture Agreement specifies, were "binding on the Venturers." The "major or significant business decisions affecting the Venture" were to be made by the Management Committee. Every decision which might "materially affect the Venture" was the Management Committee's to make. A line was drawn by the agreement between decisions of this kind which were confided to the committee and "day-to-day business decisions and operations."

The terms and representations on which the Venture's financing were obtained were not a day-to-day affair. They were "major" or "significant." They materially affected the Venture. They had to be determined by the Management Committee.

In the words of the agreement, Parkland was "initially" to contribute "administrative, and financing and development expertise." The agreement did not specify that this obligation of Parkland was to continue beyond the beginning of the Venture. In particular, the raising of additional funds was expressly left to "the judgment of the Management Committee" which was to determine whether "additional funds are required for the Venture's operations and purposes from time to time." It was further expressly provided in the agreement that neither of the Venturers had "the authority to act for the other Venturer," so Parkland had no authority to raise money by itself. As the agreement puts it, "instead the management of the business affairs of the Venture shall be vested in a Management Committee." The members of this committee were "a narrowly defined group" charged with the task of making these decisions, hence "it is reasonable to presume that [they] had the power to control." *Wool v. Tandem Computers Inc.,* 818 F.2d 1433, 1441 (9th Cir.1987).

Webb's memorandum of July 3, 1985 shows that the Management Committee on June 17, 1985 specifically discussed the "precarious situation regarding our financial capabilities to meet our obligations to the Incor investors." According to that memorandum, the members of the Management Committee, including Keim, were informed that the Venture would run out of money as soon as October 1985. The Management Committee then decided to use for current obligations funds "previously earmarked for interest payments to Incor's investors."

According to the minutes of the Management Committee for July 10, 1985, which Keim attended, there was explicit discussion of the "financing package"—necessarily a reference to the package to be put together by Incor, the company doing the financing. Sheet 16 of that package, dealing with the residential property of the project, was discussed in terms of expected profits. The amount to be raised was discussed. Keim specifically addressed the tapping of pension plan money. Keim also took the lead in stating what rate of interest should be paid.

Webb's memorandum of the June 17, 1985 meeting and the minutes of the meeting of July 10, 1985 show the Management Committee acting by consensus, not by vote. The committee does not appear to have been dominated by LaPrade or by the Parkland members as a whole. Keim appears as a vocal and active participant in the management of the Venture.

Keim states that in fact he had no control over LaPrade, Smith and Incor and argues that this undisputed fact should relieve him of liability as a controlling person. Keim misunderstands the basis on which his liability is alleged. He is sued not because he controlled those marketing the investment contracts but because he was one of the persons controlling the issuer of the investment contracts.

The Controlling Person's Scienter. To establish the liability of a controlling person, the plaintiff does not have the burden of establishing that person's scienter distinct from the controlled corporation's scienter. If the plaintiff had this obligation, the controlling person provision "would hardly make anyone liable who would not be so otherwise." *G.A. Thompson & Co. v. Partridge,* 636 F.2d 945, 960 (5th Cir.1981). But a defendant who is a controlling person of an issuer with scienter has the burden of proving his absence of scienter. *Hollinger,* 914 F.2d at 1575; *Partridge,* 636 F.2d at 960. Under the controlling person statute that means that Keim, as a person controlling the issuer, was subject to liability unless he establishes that he "acted in good faith and did not directly or indirectly induce the act or acts constituting the violation or cause of action."

Some of our earlier cases took the position that in proving the liability of a controlling person, the plaintiff has the burden of showing that the defendant does not come within the good faith exception. E.g., *Christoffel v. E.F. Hutton & Co.,* 588 F.2d 665, 668-69 (9th Cir.1978). But it has now been established that this burden falls upon the controlling person. *Hollinger,* 914 F.2d at 1575. Although *Hollinger* is specifically directed to a broker-dealer in relation to its registered securities salesman, id. at 1575 n. 24, we have extended the holding beyond this context. See *San Mateo County Transit Dist. v. DeArman, Fitzgerald and Roberts, Inc.,* 979 F.2d 1356 (9th Cir.1992). There is no reason to construe the statute as though it were restricted only to broker-dealers and their salespersons. Congress was well aware of the special duties owed by a broker-dealer and could have put the rules on control person liability solely in that context if it so desired. Congress did not act in this restricted way. Those controlling an issuer of securities are liable for the conduct of the issuer and so are liable if an issuer intentionally or recklessly permitted the fraudulent marketing of its securities.

Consequently, Keim has the burden of proving his good faith. His own declaration of innocence does not meet that burden when the Investors have offered evidence disputing his ignorance of the financing; when Webb's memo of July 3, 1985 shows Keim was aware that Incor had recruited the Investors and that the interest payments to them were in jeopardy; when the minutes of the Management Committee for July 10, 1985 show him as a participant in the discussion of financing; when his letter to LaPrade of November 27, 1985 and the affidavit of Sprague show him pressing for his $100,000 developer's fee; when Sprague's affidavit shows him influential enough to avoid giving the personal guarantee extracted from the others; when Sprague has deposed that Keim was told that the loans from the Investors were to be secured on the basis that they would be half the value of the property; and when his responsibilities as a member of the Management Committee necessarily made him familiar with the cash needs and cash resources of the Venture. In the face of these proffered facts, Keim's alleged good faith and his not having directly or indirectly induced the allegedly fraudulent marketing of the Venture's notes could not be determined by summary judgment. Accordingly, summary judgment in his favor is reversed. ***

NOTES AND QUESTIONS

*1. **The Meaning of Control.*** Most courts assess control by looking at whether the defendant (i) exercised control over the primary violator's operations and (ii) had the power to control the specific activity at issue in the litigation. See, e.g., *Maher v. Durango Metals, Inc.*, 144 F.3d 1302, 1305 (10th Cir. 1998) (collecting cases); *Donohoe v. Consol. Operating & Prod. Corp.*, 30 F.3d 907, 911-12 (7th Cir. 1994). See *Maher*, supra, 144 F.3d at 1305-06 n.8 (noting "potential circuit split" as to the sufficiency of the mere power to control the primary violator's operations). Does this two-pronged definition comport with the result reached in *Keim*?

An SEC rule defines control as "the possession, direct or indirect, of the power to direct or cause the direction of the management and policies of a person, whether through ownership of voting securities, by contract, or otherwise." Rule 12b-2 of the Exchange Act. While some decisions acknowledge this rule when addressing controlling person liability under Rule 10b-5, they do not typically apply it. See, e.g., *Howard v. Everex Sys., Inc.*, 228 F.3d 1057, 1065 n. 9 (9th Cir. 2000). Why do you suppose that is so?

*2. **The Significance of Status.*** The *Keim* court noted that "'although a person's being an officer or director does not create any *presumption* of control, it is a sort of red light.'" (quoting Professors Loss & Seligman). The red light shines most brightly at the motion to dismiss stage. See, e.g., *Adams v. Kinder-Morgan, Inc.*, 340 F.3d 1083, 1108-09 (10th Cir. 2003) (denying dismissal motions by CEO and CFO in action involving financial reporting); *In re Miller Indus. Inc. Sec. Litig.*, 12 F. Supp. 2d 1323, 1333 (N.D. Ga. 1998) (denying dismissal motion by officers and directors). Suppose that the motion to dismiss is made by an outside director. Should such a motion be treated differently than one by an officer or inside director? Why or why not? Cf. *Adams*, supra, 340 F.3d at 1108 (granting motion to dismiss by outside director as to whom no additional facts were pled).

3. Culpable Participation. The circuits are divided over whether the plaintiff must also show that the controlling person was a "culpable participant" in the controlled person's fraud. Compare *ATSI Commc'ns, Inc. v. Shaar Fund,* Ltd., 493 F.3d 87 (2d Cir. 2007) (endorsing culpable participation); *In re Suprema Specialties Inc. Sec. Litig.*, 438 F.3d 256, 284 n.16 (3d Cir. 2006) (same) with *Lustgraaf v. Behrens.*, 619 F.3d 867, 877 (8th Cir. 2010) (rejecting culpable participation); *Howard v. Everex Sys., Inc.,* 228 F.3d 1057 (9th Cir. 2000) (same) and with *In re Stone & Webster, Inc. Sec. Litig.*, 414 F.3d 187, 194 n. 4 (1st Cir. 2005) (leaving question open). Consider whether you are persuaded by the following justification for requiring culpable participation:

> Judge Adams *** reviewed the legislative history of Rule 10b-5 and concluded that Congress, through the use of words such as " 'cunning,' 'manipulative,' 'deceptive,' 'fraudulent,' 'illicit,' 'fraud,' and lack of 'good faith' " intended that liability would not attach unless the element of culpability was present. Since the standard of culpability is ever-present in the securities laws, it is reasonable that the same standard should be included in Section 20(a).

Rochez Bros. v. Rhoades, 527 F.2d 880, 885 (3d Cir. 1975). Can you identify additional justifications for the culpable participation requirement? Is the requirement consistent with the language of Section 20(a)? What is the likely impact of the requirement on the behavior of those who otherwise possess "control"? Would Keim qualify as a "culpable participant"?

In circuits requiring culpable participation, district courts divide over whether the plaintiff must *plead* culpable participation in order to survive a motion to dismiss. See, e.g., *Lautenberg Found. v. Madoff,* 2009 WL 2928913 at *14 (D.N.J. 2009) (identifying split within Third Circuit); *In re MBIA, Inc., Sec. Litig.,* 700 F. Supp. 2d 566, 598 (S.D.N.Y. 2010) (identifying split within Second Circuit). What factors fuel the controversy surrounding the pleading issue?

4. The Statutory Defense. To determine whether the defendants have established the statutory defense, courts typically "examine what the defendants could have done under the circumstances to prevent the violation, and then to ask whether the defendants—aware that they could take such measures—decided not to." *Donohoe v. Consol. Operating & Prod. Corp.,* 30 F.3d 907, 912 (7th Cir. 1994). As *Keim* illustrates, such an inquiry is heavily fact-specific. Cf. *Brown v. Earthboard Sports USA, Inc.*, 481 F.3d 901 (6th Cir. 2007) (panel divided over whether facts suffice to satisfy defense).

The defense must meet a higher standard when the defendant is a broker-dealer firm sued in connection with an employee's primary violation. In this instance, the defendant must show that "its supervisory system was adequate and that it reasonably discharged its responsibilities under the system." *Hollinger v. Titan Capital Group,* 914 F.2d 1564, 1576 (9th Cir. 1990) (en banc). Why is the bar raised for broker-dealer firms? Should other defendants likewise be required to have supervisory systems in place? One court has said that the answer should turn on the following considerations:

> a) whether the controlling person derives direct financial gain from the activity of the controlled person, b) the extent to which the controlled person is tempted to act unlawfully because of the controlling person's policies (e.g., compensation system), c) the extent to which statutory or regulatory law or the defendant's own policies require supervision, d) the relationship between the plaintiff and

> the controlling person, and e) the demonstration of some public policy need to impose such a requirement.

Kersh v. Gen. Council of Assemblies of God, 804 F.2d 546, 550 (9th Cir. 1986). Cf. *Dellastratious v. Williams,* 242 F.3d 191, 195-96 (4th Cir. 2001) (evaluating whether directors established their defense by looking at directors' obligations under state law). If the *Kersh* factors had been applied to *Keim,* would the defendant have had to establish maintenance of an adequate supervisory system?

*5. **Proportionate Liability Revisited.*** Recall that earlier in this Chapter, we saw the scheme of proportionate liability, enacted as part of the PSLRA, which is set forth in Exchange Act Section 21D(f). See supra Section G.2. Pursuant to that scheme, a defendant (with limited exceptions) is liable exclusively for the fraction of the judgment for which she bears responsibility. How (if at all) does this proportionate liability system interface with the joint and several liability regime of Section 20(a)? Consider whether you agree with the Eleventh Circuit, which gave the following answer:

> [F]or the purpose of determining whether the controlling person is responsible for the entire amount of damages or only its proportionate share, we look to the proportionate liability provisions of the PSLRA, as we do for all "covered persons." Under these provisions joint and several liability for all the damages exists only if the fact finder specifically determines that the controlling person knowingly committed the violation. 15 U.S.C. § 78u–4(f)(2)(A). Where a controlling person fails to affirmatively establish good faith and lack of inducement under section 20(a) but the fact finder does not specifically find a knowing violation, there is liability for the violation but responsibility for the damages is only proportionate, not joint and several. 15 U.S.C. § 78u–4(f)(2)(B)(i).

Laperriere v. Vesta Ins. Group, Inc., 526 F. 3d 715, 727-28 (11th Cir. 2008).

*6. **The Infrequently Considered Potential of Section 20(b).*** Recall that the *Janus* Court acknowledged that the plaintiffs might have a claim under Section 20(b), which reads as follows:

> **Section 20. Liability of Controlling Persons and Persons Who Aid and Abet Violations**
>
> *** (b) It shall be unlawful for any person, directly or indirectly, to do any act or thing which it would be unlawful for such person to do under the provisions of this title or any rule or regulation thereunder through or by means of any other person.

Consider the following observation from one of the few courts to construe Section 20(b):

> Under section 20(b), there must be shown to have been knowing use of a controlled person by a controlling person before a controlling person comes within its ambit. Without such a restriction, every link in a chain of command would be personally criminally and civilly liable for the violations of inferior corporate agents.

SEC v. Coffey, 493 F.2d 1304, 1318 (6th Cir. 1974). See *Cohen v. Citibank*, 954 F. Supp. 621, 630 (S.D.N.Y. 1996) (adopting *Coffey*'s interpretation and dismissing the Section 20(b) claim for failing to allege control as well as knowing use). Think about Section 20(b)'s utility to a plaintiff's lawyer. Is it an important string to her bow? We will return once more to Section 20(b) in connection with respondeat superior liability infra.

PROBLEM 2-28

Inkwell, Inc. is a publicly traded company that manufactures pens and pencils. Forty percent of its shares are owned by George (the son of the company's founder), who has not involved himself with the company's operation. In a recent press release, Inkwell claimed that a new product had caught on well with consumers, whereas in fact the opposite was the case. In a Rule 10b-5 action against Inkwell challenging the fraudulent press release, would George qualify as a controlling person?

See *Aldridge v. A.T. Cross Corp.*, 284 F.3d 72 (1st Cir. 2002).

PROBLEM 2-29

Sam Sivard has been employed for a year as a financial reporter for a major daily newspaper owned by Quibble, Inc. In March 2000, Sam wrote a column praising the management and potential of Vroom, Inc., a company he claimed to have stumbled on during the previous week. In fact, Sam had been a Vroom shareholder for five years. The newspaper knew nothing about Sam's investment portfolio (or that of the other reporters). Nor did the newspaper attempt to confirm the accuracy of the facts stated in Sam's column (or the columns of other reporters).

In the wake of Sam's column, the price of Vroom shares rose drastically. Sam sold most of his shares at a substantial profit. Assume that Sam's conduct violates Rule 10b-5 and that an action has been brought against Quibble as a controlling person. Can Quibble avoid liability on the basis of the statutory defense?

Cf. *Zweig v. Hearst Corp.*, 521 F.2d 1129 (9th Cir. 1975).

---

c. *Respondeat Superior Liability*

For many years, courts imported into Rule 10b-5 the tort law doctrine of respondeat superior, which renders an employer vicariously liable for the primary violation of an employee committed within the scope of employment or pursuant to apparent authority. See, e.g., *Hollinger v. Titan Capital Corp.*, 914 F.2d 1564, 1577-78 (9th Cir. 1990); *In re Citisource, Inc. Sec. Litig.*, 694 F. Supp. 1069, 1078 (S.D.N.Y. 1988). Such courts regarded respondeat superior liability and controlling person liability as complementary:

> When both remedies are available, then the agent who personally committed the wrong is primarily liable *** ; the principal who acts through the agent (assuming the agent is acting within the scope of his employment) is secondarily liable; and other persons who are not subject to respondeat superior but who nevertheless control the wrongdoer can be held liable under § 20(a).

Hollinger, supra, 914 F.2d at 1577-78. But can respondeat superior liability continue in the wake of the Supreme Court's decision in *Central Bank, N.A. v. Interstate Bank, N.A.*, 511 U.S. 164 (1994)? The dissent in *Central Bank* was dubious. See 511 U.S. at 200 n.12 (Stevens, J. dissenting) (describing respondeat superior liability as "unlikely to survive").

But the obituary may have been unwarranted. See, e.g., *Southland Sec. Corp. v. INSpire Ins. Solutions, Inc.*, 365 F.3d 353, 384 (5th Cir. 2004) (finding respondeat superior claim to withstand motion to dismiss); *In re Parmalat Sec. Litig.*, 474 F. Supp. 2d 547, 551 (S.D.N.Y. 2007) (upholding respondeat superior claim and stating that *Central Bank* "left respondeat superior untouched"); *In re Blech Sec. Litig.*, 2002 WL 31356498 at *22 (S.D.N.Y. 2002) (denying summary judgment partly because fact question remained as to respondeat superior claim); *Seolas v. Bilzerian*, 951 F. Supp. 978, 983 (D. Utah 1997). But see *In re Fidelity/Micron Sec. Litig.*, 964 F. Supp. 539, 544 (D. Mass. 1997) (concluding that respondeat superior does not survive). The commentary is divided. Compare Robert A. Prentice, Conceiving the Inconceivable and Judicially Implementing the Preposterous: the Premature Demise of Repondeat Superior Liability Under Section 10(b), 58 Ohio St. L. J. 1325 (1997) (doctrine survives) with Joel Seligman, The Implications of *Central Bank*, 49 Bus. Law. 1429, 1430 (1994) (doctrine does not survive).

NOTES AND QUESTIONS

1. ***Viability.*** Do you think that respondeat superior liability survives *Central Bank*? Is the answer the same for private actions and SEC actions? Putting *Central Bank* aside, to what extent does respondeat superior liability undermine Section 20(a)?

On the other hand, respondeat superior liability may have a firmer foundation than is generally recognized. Such a foundation might come from Section 20(b), the text of which appears supra in Note 6 after the *Keim* case. In this connection Professor Prentice has observed: "[S]ection 20(b) can plausibly be read to authorize imposition of respondeat superior liability, although no court has so held." Robert A. Prentice, Conceiving the Inconceivable and Judicially Implementing the Preposterous: The Premature Demise of Respondeat Superior Liability Under Section 10(b), 58 Ohio St. L. J. 1325, 1408 (1997). Do you agree?

2. ***The Relevance of the Statutory Definition of "Person."*** Also arguably relevant to the viability of respondeat superior liability is the fact that Section 10(b) and Rule 10b-5 apply to "any person," a term defined by the Exchange Act to include "a corporation." See Exchange Act Section 3(a)(9). The Second Circuit has made this observation:

> Congress evidently intended that a corporation might be liable in some instances as a "person"; and this can only be by virtue of agency principles, since a corporation can act only through its agents. Were §§ 15 [of the Securities Act] and 20(a) the sole measures of corporate liability *** the inclusion of corporations under the definitions of "person" would be not only unnecessary but also misleading.

SEC v. Mgmt. Dynamics, Inc., 515 F.2d 801, 812 (2d Cir. 1975). See *Adams v. Kinder-Morgan, Inc.*, 340 F.3d 1083, 1106-07 (10th Cir. 2003) (holding corporation liable for securities violations based on agency principles and collecting cases doing the same). Thus, one commentator has predicted that "if the courts reject respondeat superior as such, we will soon see a blossoming of the law of what constitutes primary wrongdoing by organizational entities." Donald C. Langevoort, Words From On High About Rule 10b-5: *Chiarella's* History, *Central Bank's* Future, 20 Del. J. Corp. L. 865, 894 (1995).

PROBLEM 2-30

Reconsider Problem 2-29. Would Quibble be liable on a respondeat superior theory in a jurisdiction in which that form of liability is still viable?

I. STATUTE OF LIMITATIONS

This section addresses the statute of limitations for Rule 10b-5 private actions only. The limitations periods for SEC and criminal actions under the Rule will be considered in Chapters 9 and 11 respectively.

As originally enacted, the Exchange Act did not contain a limitations period applicable to private Rule 10b-5 actions. This omission was to be expected, since Congress did not have private actions in mind when it enacted Section 10(b).

To supply the limitations period, lower courts for years borrowed the most analogous statute of limitations period from the common law or blue sky law of the relevant state. See *Ernst & Ernst v. Hochfelder,* 425 U.S. 185, 210 n. 29 (1976) (acknowledging practice of state law borrowing and observing that "it is not always certain which state statute of limitations should be followed").

The practice of state-law borrowing came to a halt with the Supreme Court's decision in *Lampf, Pleva, Lipkind, Prupis & Petigrow v. Gilbertson,* 501 U.S. 350 (1991). There the Court adopted for Rule 10b-5 purposes the limitations period from Exchange Act Section 9(e), which reads as follows:

> No action shall be maintained to enforce any liability created under this section, unless brought within one year after the discovery of the facts constituting the violation and within three years after such violation.

See *Lampf*, supra, at 364 n.9

The ground shifted again with the enactment of the Sarbanes-Oxley Act of 2002 (the "SOX"). Section 804 of the SOX replaced *Lampf*'s one year/three year structure with a two year/five year structure:

> *** [A] private right of action that involves a claim of fraud, deceit, manipulation, or contrivance in contravention of a regulatory requirement concerning the securities laws, as defined in section 3(a)(47) of the Securities Exchange Act of 1934, may be brought not later than the earlier of—
>
> (1) 2 years after the discovery of the facts constituting the violation; or
>
> (2) 5 years after such violation.

(enacted as 28 U.S.C. 1658(b)). The term "securities laws" is defined in Exchange Act Section 3(a)(47) to include, among other statutes, the Securities Act, the Exchange Act , and the Sarbanes-Oxley Act.

What is meant by the phrase "after the discovery of the facts constituting the violation"? According to the circuit courts addressing this question after *Lampf*, the phrase encompassed not only "actual notice" but also "inquiry notice" – that is, the appearance of indicators (sometimes known as "storm signals") indicating that fraud might exist. See, e.g., *Shah v. Meeker*, 435 F.3d 244, 249 (2d Cir. 2006); *In re NAHC Inc. Sec. Litig.,* 306 F.3d 1314, 1325 (3d Cir. 2002).

The Supreme Court upended the circuit courts' post-*Lampf* perspective in the decision that follows.

MERCK & CO., INC. v. REYNOLDS

130 S. Ct. 1784 (2010)

JUSTICE STEPHEN G. BREYER:

This case concerns the timeliness of a complaint filed in a private securities fraud action. The complaint was timely if filed no more than two years after the plaintiffs "discover[ed] the facts constituting the violation." 28 U. S. C. §1658(b)(1). Construing this limitations statute for the first time, we hold that a cause of action accrues (1) when the plaintiff did in fact discover, or (2) when a reasonably diligent plaintiff would have discovered, "the facts constituting the violation"— whichever comes first. We also hold that the "facts constituting the violation" include the fact of scienter, "a mental state embracing intent to deceive, manipulate, or defraud," *Ernst & Ernst v. Hochfelder*, 425 U. S. 185, 194, n. 12 (1976). Applying this standard, we affirm the Court of Appeals' determination that the complaint filed here was timely.

I

The action before us involves a claim by a group of investors (the plaintiffs, respondents here) that Merck & Co. and others (the petitioners here, hereinafter Merck) knowingly misrepresented the risks of heart attacks accompanying the use of Merck's pain-killing drug, Vioxx (leading to economic losses when the risks later became apparent). The plaintiffs brought an action for securities fraud under §10(b) of the Securities Exchange Act of 1934.

The applicable statute of limitations provides that a "private right of action" that, like the present action, "involves a claim of fraud, deceit, manipulation, or contrivance in contravention of a regulatory requirement concerning the securities laws . . . may be brought not later than the earlier of—

> (1) 2 years after the discovery of the facts constituting the violation; or
>
> (2) 5 years after such violation. 28 U. S. C. §1658(b).

The complaint in this case was filed on November 6, 2003, and no one doubts that it was filed within five years of the alleged violation. Therefore, the critical date for timeliness purposes is November 6, 2001—two years before this complaint was filed. Merck claims that before this date the plaintiffs had (or should have) discovered the "facts constituting the violation." If so, by the time the plaintiffs filed their complaint, the 2-year statutory period in §1658(b)(1) had run. The plaintiffs reply that they had not, and could not have, discovered by the critical date those "facts," particularly not the facts related to scienter, and that their complaint was therefore timely.

A

We first set out the relevant pre-November 2001 facts, as we have gleaned them from the briefs, the record, and the opinions below.

1. 1990's. In the mid-1990's Merck developed Vioxx. In 1999 the Food and Drug Administration (FDA) approved it for prescription use. Vioxx suppresses pain by inhibiting the body's production of an enzyme called COX–2 (cyclooxy- genase-2). COX–2 is associated with pain and inflammation. Unlike some other anti-inflammatory drugs in its class like aspirin, ibuprofen, and naproxen, Vioxx does not inhibit production of a second enzyme called COX–1 (cyclooxygenase-1). COX–1 plays a part in the functioning of the gastrointestinal tract and also in platelet aggregation (associated with blood clots).

2. March 2000. Merck announced the results of a study, called the "VIGOR" study. The study compared Vioxx with another painkiller, naproxen. The study *** revealed that approximately 4 out of every 1,000 participants who took Vioxx suffered heart attacks, compared to only 1 per 1,000 participants who took naproxen.

Merck's press release acknowledged VIGOR's adverse cardiovascular data. But Merck said that these data were "consistent with naproxen's ability to block platelet aggregation." *** And Merck added that "safety data from all other completed and ongoing clinical trials . . . . showed no indication of a difference in the incidence of thromboembolic events between Vioxx" and either a placebo or comparable drugs.

This theory—that VIGOR's troubling cardiovascular findings might be due to the absence of a benefit conferred by naproxen rather than due to a harm caused by Vioxx— later became known as the "naproxen hypothesis." In advancing that hypothesis, Merck acknowledged that the naproxen benefit "had not been observed previously." Journalists and stock market analysts reported all of the above—the positive gastrointestinal results, the troubling cardiovascular finding, the naproxen hypothesis, and the fact that the naproxen hypothesis was unproved.

3. February 2001 to August 2001. Public debate about the naproxen hypothesis continued. In February 2001, the FDA's Arthritis Advisory Committee convened to consider Merck's request that the Vioxx label be changed to reflect VIGOR's positive gastrointestinal findings. The VIGOR cardiovascular findings were also discussed. In May 2001, a group of plaintiffs filed a products-liability lawsuit against Merck, claiming that "Merck's own research" had demonstrated that "users of Vioxx were four times as likely to suffer heart attacks as compared to other less expensive, medications." In August 2001, the Journal of the American Medical Association wrote that the available data raised a "cautionary flag" and strongly urged that "a trial specifically assessing cardiovascular risk" be done. At about the same time, Bloomberg News quoted a Merck scientist who claimed that Merck had "additional data" that were "very, very reassuring," and Merck issued a press release stating that it stood "behind the overall and cardiovascular safety profile . . . of Vioxx."

4. September and October 2001. The FDA sent Merck a warning letter released to the public on September 21, 2001. It said that, in respect to cardiovascular risks, Merck's Vioxx marketing was "false, lacking in fair balance, or otherwise misleading." At the same time, the FDA acknowledged that the naproxen hypothesis was a "possible explanation" of the VIGOR results. But it found that Merck's "promotional campaign selectively present[ed]" that hypothesis without adequately acknowledging "another reasonable explanation," namely, "that Vioxx may have pro-thrombotic [i.e., adverse cardiovascular] properties." The FDA ordered Merck to send healthcare providers a corrective letter.

After the FDA letter was released, more products liability lawsuits were filed. Merck's share price fell by 6.6% over several days. By October 1, the price rebounded. On October 9, 2001, the New York Times said that Merck had reexamined its own data and "found no evidence that Vioxx increased the risk of heart attacks." It quoted the president of Merck Research Laboratories as positing "'two possible interpretations'": "'Naproxen lowers the heart attack rate, or Vioxx raises it.'" Stock analysts, while reporting the warning letter, also noted that the FDA had not denied that the naproxen hypothesis remained an unproven but possible explanation.

B

We next set forth three important events that occurred after the critical date.

1. October 2003. The Wall Street Journal published the results of a Merck-funded Vioxx study conducted at Boston's Brigham and Women's Hospital. After examining the medical records of more than 50,000 Medicare patients, researchers found that those given Vioxx for 30-to 90 days were 37% more likely to have suffered a heart attack than those given either a different painkiller or no painkiller at all. *** Merck defended Vioxx and pointed to the study's limitations.

2. September 30, 2004. Merck withdrew Vioxx from the market. It said that a new study had found "an increased risk of confirmed cardiovascular events beginning after 18months of continuous therapy." A Merck representative publicly described the results as "totally unexpected." Merck's shares fell by 27% the same day.

3. November 1, 2004. The Wall Street Journal published an article stating that "internal Merck e-mails and marketing materials as well as interviews with outside scientists show that the company fought forcefully for years to keep safety concerns from destroying the drug's commercial prospects." The article said that an early e-mail from Merck's head of research had said that the VIGOR "results showed that the cardiovascular events 'are clearly there,'" that it was "'a shame but . . . a low incidence,'" and that it "'is mechanism based as we worried it was.'" It also said that Merck had given its salespeople instructions to "'DODGE'" questions about Vioxx's cardiovascular effects.

C

The plaintiffs filed their complaint on November 6, 2003. As subsequently amended, the complaint alleged that Merck had defrauded investors by promoting the naproxen hypothesis, knowing the hypothesis was false. It said, for example, that Merck "knew, at least as early as 1996, of the serious safety issues with Vioxx," and that a "1998 internal Merck clinical trial . . . revealed that . . . serious cardiovascular events . . . occurred six times more frequently in patients given Vioxx than in patients given a different arthritis drug or placebo."

Merck, believing that the plaintiffs knew or should have known the "facts constituting the violation" at least two years earlier, moved to dismiss the complaint, saying it was filed too late. The District Court granted the motion. The court held that the (March 2001) VIGOR study, the (September 2001) FDA warning letter, and Merck's (October 2001) response should have alerted the plaintiffs to a "*possibility* that Merck had knowingly misrepresented material facts" no later than October 9, 2001, thus placing the plaintiffs on "inquiry notice" to look further. (emphasis added). Finding that the plaintiffs had failed to "show that they exercised reasonable due diligence but nevertheless were unable to discover their injuries," the court took October 9, 2001, as the date that the limitations period began to run and therefore found the complaint untimely.

The Court of Appeals for the Third Circuit reversed. A majority held that the pre-November 2001 events, while constituting "storm warnings," did not suggest much by way of scienter, and consequently did not put the plaintiffs on "inquiry notice," requiring them to investigate further. ***

Merck sought review in this Court, pointing to disagreements among the Courts of Appeals. Compare *Theoharous v. Fong*, 256 F. 3d 1219, 1228 (CA11 2001) (limitations period begins to run when information puts plaintiffs on "inquiry notice" of the need for investigation), with *Shah v. Meeker*, 435 F. 3d 244, 249 (CA2 2006) (same; but if plaintiff does investigate, period runs "from the date such inquiry should have revealed the fraud"), and *New England Health Care Employees Pension Fund v. Ernst & Young, LLP*, 336 F. 3d 495, 501 (CA6 2003) (limitations period *always* begins to run only when a reasonably diligent plaintiff, after being put on "inquiry notice," should have discovered facts constituting violation).We granted Merck's petition.

II

Before turning to Merck's arguments, we consider a more basic matter. The parties and the Solicitor General agree that §1658(b)(1)'s word "discovery" refers not only to a plaintiff's *actual* discovery of certain facts, but also to the facts that a reasonably diligent plaintiff would have discovered. We agree. But because the statute's language does not make this interpretation obvious, and because we cannot answer the question presented without considering whether the parties are right about this matter, we set forth the reasons for our agreement in some detail.

We recognize that one might read the statutory words "after the discovery of the facts constituting the violation" as referring to the time a plaintiff *actually* discovered the relevant facts. But in the statute of limitations context, the word "discovery" is often used as a term of art in connection with the "discovery rule," a doctrine that delays accrual of a cause of action until the plaintiff has "discovered" it. The rule arose in fraud cases as an exception to the general limitations rule that a cause of action accrues once a plaintiff has a "complete and present cause of action," *Bay Area Laundry and Dry Cleaning Pension Trust Fund v. Ferbar Corp. of Cal.*, 522 U.S. 192, 201 (1997). This Court long ago recognized that something different was needed in the case of fraud, where a defendant's deceptive conduct may prevent a plaintiff from even *knowing* that he or she has been defrauded. *** Accordingly, "where a plaintiff has been injured by fraud and remains in ignorance of it without any fault or want of diligence or care on his part, the bar of the statute does not begin to run until the fraud is *discovered*." *Holmberg v. Armbrecht*, 327 U. S. 392, 397 (1946) (emphasis added). And for more than a century, courts have understood that "[f]raud is deemed to be discovered . . . when, in the exercise of reasonable diligence, it could have been discovered." 2 H. Wood, Limitations of Actions § 276b(11) p. 1402 (4th ed. 1916).

More recently, both state and federal courts have applied forms of the "discovery rule" to claims other than fraud. Legislatures have codified the discovery rule in various contexts. In doing so, legislators have written the word "discovery" directly into the statute. And when they have done so, state and federal courts have typically interpreted the word to refer not only to actual discovery, but also to the hypothetical discovery of facts a reasonably diligent plaintiff would know. See, e.g., *Mobley v. Hall*, 202 Mont. 227, 232, 657 P.2d 604, 606 (1983); *Tregenza v. Great American Communications Co.*, 12 F.3d 717, 721-722 (C.A.7 1993).

Thus, treatise writers now describe "the discovery rule" as allowing a claim "to accrue when the litigant first knows *or with due diligence should know* facts that will form the basis for an action." 2 Corman § 11.1.1, at 134 (emphasis added).

Like the parties, we believe that Congress intended courts to interpret the word "discovery" in §1658(b)(1) similarly. Before Congress enacted that statute, this Court, having found in the federal securities laws the existence of an implied private §10(b) action, determined its governing limitations period by looking to other limitations periods in the federal securities laws. *Lampf, Pleva, Lipkind, Prupis & Petigrow v. Gilbertson*, 501 U. S. 350 (1991). Noting the existence of various formulations "differ[ing] slightly in terminology," the Court chose the language in 15 U. S. C. §78i(e), the statutory provision that governs securities price manipulation claims. 501 U. S., at 364, n. 9. And in doing so, the Court said that private §10(b) actions "must be commenced within one year *after the discovery of the facts constituting the violation* and within three years after such violation." Id. at 364 (emphasis added). ***

Subsequently, every Court of Appeals to decide the matter held that "discovery of the facts constituting the violation" occurs not only once a plaintiff *actually* discovers the facts, but also when a hypothetical reasonably diligent plaintiff would have discovered them. See, e.g., *Law v. Medco Research, Inc.*, 113 F.3d 781, 785-786 (C.A.7 1997); *Dodds v. Cigna Securities, Inc.*, 12 F.3d 346, 350, 353 (C.A.2 1993). Some of those courts noted that other limitations provisions in the federal securities laws explicitly provide that the period begins to run " 'after the discovery of the untrue statement ... or after such discovery should have been made by [the] exercise of reasonable diligence,' " whereas the formulation adopted by the Court in *Lampf* from 15 U.S.C. § 78i(e) does not. *Tregenza*, supra, at 721 (quoting § 77m; emphasis added in *Tregenza*). But, courts reasoned, because the term "discovery" in respect to statutes of limitations for fraud has long been understood to include discoveries a reasonably diligent plaintiff would make, the omission of an explicit provision to that effect did not matter. *Tregenza*, supra, at 721; accord, *New England Health*

Care, 336 F.3d, at 499-500.

In 2002, when Congress enacted the present limitations statute, it repeated *Lampf's* critical language. The statute says that an action based on fraud "may be brought not later than the earlier of . . . 2 years *after the discovery of the facts constituting the violation*" (or "5 years after such violation"). §804 of the Sarbanes-Oxley Act, codified at 28 U. S. C. §1658(b) (emphasis added). *** Not surprisingly, the Courts of Appeals unanimously have continued to interpret the word "discovery" in this statute as including not only facts a particular plaintiff knows, but also the facts any reasonably diligent plaintiff would know. See, e.g., *Staehr v. Hartford Financial Servs. Group, Inc.*, 547 F.3d 406, 411 (C.A.2 2008); *Sudo Properties, Inc. v. Terrebonne Parish Consolidated Govt.*, 503 F.3d 371, 376 (C.A.5 2007).

We normally assume that, when Congress enacts statutes, it is aware of relevant judicial precedent. See, e.g., *Edelman v. Lynchburg College*, 535 U.S. 106, 116-117, and n. 13 (2002). Given the history and precedent surrounding the use of the word "discovery" in the limitations context generally as well as in this provision in particular, the reasons for making this assumption are particularly strong here. We consequently hold that "discovery" as used in this statute encompasses not only those facts the plaintiff actually knew, but also those facts a reasonably diligent plaintiff would have known. And we evaluate Merck's claims accordingly.

III

We turn now to Merck's arguments in favor of holding that petitioners' claims accrued before November 6, 2001. First, Merck argues that the statute does not require "discovery" of scienter-related "facts." We cannot agree, however, that facts about scienter are unnecessary.

The statute says that the limitations period does not begin to run until "discovery of the *facts constituting the violation*." 28 U. S. C. §1658(b)(1) (emphasis added). Scienter is assuredly a "fact." In a §10(b) action, scienter refers to "a mental state embracing intent to deceive, manipulate, or defraud." *Ernst & Ernst*, 425 U. S., at 194, n. 12. And the "'state of a man's mind is as much a fact as the state of his digestion.'" *Postal Service Bd. of Governors v. Aikens*, 460 U. S. 711, 716 (1983) (quoting *Edgington v. Fitzmaurice*, [1885] 29 Ch. Div. 459, 483).

And this "fact" of scienter "constitut[es]" an important and necessary element of a §10(b) "violation." A plaintiff cannot recover without proving that a defendant made a material misstatement *with an intent to deceive*—not merely innocently or negligently. See *Tellabs, Inc. v. Makor Issues & Rights, Ltd.*, 551 U. S. 308, 319 (2007); *Ernst & Ernst*, supra. Indeed, Congress has enacted special heightened pleading requirements for the scienter element of §10(b) fraud cases. See 15 U. S. C. §78u–4(b)(2) (requiring plaintiffs to "state with particularity *facts* giving rise to a strong inference that the defendant acted with the required state of mind" (emphasis added)). As a result, unless a §10(b) plaintiff can set forth facts in the complaint showing that it is "at least as likely as" not that the defendant acted with the relevant knowledge or intent, the claim will fail. *Tellabs*, supra, at 328 (emphasis deleted). It would therefore frustrate the very purpose of the discovery rule in this provision—which, after all, specifically applies only in cases "involv[ing] a claim of fraud, deceit, manipulation, or contrivance," §1658(b)—if the limitations period began to run regardless of whether a plaintiff had discovered any facts suggesting scienter. So long as a defendant concealed for two years that he made a misstatement with an intent to deceive, the limitations period would expire before the plaintiff had actually "discover[ed]" the fraud.

We consequently hold that facts showing scienter are among those that "constitut[e] the violation." In so holding, we say nothing about other facts necessary to support a private §10(b) action. Cf. Brief for United States as Amicus Curiae 12, n. 1 (suggesting that facts concerning a plaintiff's reliance, loss, and loss causation are not among those that constitute "the violation" and therefore need not be "discover[ed]" for a claim to accrue).

Second, Merck argues that, even if "discovery" requires facts related to scienter, facts that tend to show a materially false or misleading statement (or material omission) are ordinarily sufficient to show scienter as well. But we do not see how that is so. We recognize that certain statements are such that, to show them false is normally to show scienter as well. It is unlikely, for example, that someone would falsely say "I am not married" without being aware of the fact that his statement is false. Where §10(b) is at issue, however, the relation of factual falsity and state of mind is more context specific. An incorrect prediction about a firm's future earnings, by itself, does not automatically tell us whether the speaker deliberately lied or just made an innocent (and therefore nonactionable) error. Hence, the statute may require "discovery" of scienter-related facts beyond the facts that show a statement (or omission) to be materially false or misleading. Merck fears that this requirement will give life to stale claims or subject defendants to liability for acts taken long ago. But Congress' inclusion in the statute of an unqualified bar on actions instituted "5 years after such violation," §1658(b)(2), giving defendants total repose after five years, should diminish that fear. Cf. *Lampf*, 501 U. S., at 363 (holding comparable bar not subject to equitable tolling).

Third, Merck says that the limitations period began to run prior to November 2001 because by that point the plaintiffs were on "inquiry notice." Merck uses the term "inquiry notice" to refer to the point "at which a plaintiff possesses a quantum of information sufficiently suggestive of wrongdoing that he should conduct a further inquiry." Brief for Petitioners 20. And some, but not all, Courts of Appeals have used the term in roughly similar ways. See, e.g., *Franze v. Equitable Assurance*, 296 F.3d 1250, 1254 (C.A.11 2002) ("[I]nquiry notice [is] 'the term used for knowledge of facts that would lead a reasonable person to begin investigating the possibility that his legal rights had been infringed' "). Cf. *Dodds*, 12 F.3d, at 350 ("duty of inquiry" arises once "circumstances would suggest to an investor of ordinary intelligence the probability that she had been defrauded").

If the term "inquiry notice" refers to the point where the facts would lead a reasonably diligent plaintiff to investigate further, that point is not necessarily the point at which the plaintiff would already have discovered facts showing scienter or other "facts constituting the violation." But the statute says that the plaintiff's claim accrues only after the "discovery" of those latter facts. Nothing in the text suggests that the limitations period can sometimes begin *before* "discovery" can take place. Merck points out that, as we have discussed, the court-created "discovery rule" exception to ordinary statutes of limitations is not generally available to plaintiffs who fail to pursue their claims with reasonable diligence. But we are dealing herewith a statute, not a court-created exception to a statute. Because the statute contains no indication that the limitations period should occur at some earlier moment before when a plaintiff would have begun investigating, we cannot accept Merck's argument.

As a fallback, Merck argues that even if the limitations period does generally begin at "discovery," it should nonetheless run from the point of "inquiry notice" in one particular situation, namely, where the actual plaintiff fails to undertake an investigation once placed on "inquiry notice." In such circumstances, Merck contends, the actual plaintiff is not diligent, and the law should not "effectively excuse a plaintiff's failure to conduct a further investigation" by placing that nondiligent plaintiff and a reasonably diligent plaintiff "in the same position." Brief for Petitioner 48.

We cannot accept this argument for essentially the same reason we reject "inquiry notice" as the standard generally: We cannot reconcile it with the statute, which simply provides that "discovery" is the event that triggers the 2 year limitations period—for all plaintiffs. Furthermore, the statute does *not* place all plaintiffs "in the same position" no matter whether they investigate when investigation is warranted. The limitations period puts plaintiffs who fail to investigate once on "inquiry notice" at a disadvantage because it lapses two years after a reasonably diligent plaintiff would have discovered the necessary facts. A plaintiff who fails entirely to investigate or delays investigating may well not have discovered those facts by that time or, at least, may not have found sufficient facts by that time to be able to file a §10(b) complaint that satisfies the applicable heightened pleading standards.

Merck further contends that its proposed "inquiry notice" standard is superior, because determining when a hypothetical reasonably diligent plaintiff would have "discover[ed]" the necessary facts is too complicated for judges to undertake. But courts applying the traditional discovery rule have long had to ask what a reasonably diligent plaintiff would have known and done in myriad circumstances. And courts in at least five Circuits already ask this kind of question in securities fraud cases. See, e.g., *Rothman v. Gregor*, 220 F.3d 81, 97 (C.A.2 2000); *New England Health Care*, 336 F.3d, at 501; *Young*, supra, at 1, 9-10; *Marks v. CDW Computer Centers, Inc.*, 122 F.3d 363, 367-368 (C.A.7 1997). Merck has not shown this precedent to be unworkable. We consequently find that the "discovery" of facts that put a plaintiff on "inquiry notice" does not automatically begin the running of the limitations period.

We conclude that the limitations period in §1658(b)(1) begins to run once the plaintiff did discover or a reasonably diligent plaintiff would have "discover[ed] the facts constituting the violation"—whichever comes first. In determining the time at which "discovery" of those "facts" occurred, terms such as "inquiry notice" and "storm warnings" may be useful to the extent that they identify a time when the facts would have prompted a reasonably diligent plaintiff to begin investigating. But the limitations period does not begin to run until the plaintiff thereafter discovers or a reasonably diligent plaintiff would have discovered "the facts constituting the violation," including scienter—irrespective of whether the actual plaintiff undertook a reasonably diligent investigation.

IV

Finally, Merck argues that, even if all its other legal arguments fail, the record still shows that, before November 6, 2001, the plaintiffs had discovered or should have discovered "the facts constituting the violation." In respect to scienter Merck primarily relies upon (1) the FDA's September 2001 warning letter, which said that Merck had "'minimized'" the VIGOR study's "'potentially serious cardiovascular findings'" and (2) pleadings filed in products-liability actions in September and October 2001alleging that Merck had "'omitted, suppressed, or concealed material facts concerning the dangers and risks associated with Vioxx'" and "*purposefully* downplayed and/or understated the serious nature of the risks associated with Vioxx." Brief for Petitioners at 36-37.

The FDA's warning letter, however, shows little or nothing about the here-relevant scienter, i.e., whether Merck advanced the naproxen hypothesis with fraudulent intent. The FDA itself described the pro-Vioxx naproxen hypothesis as a "possible explanation" for the VIGOR results, faulting Merck only for failing sufficiently to publicize the alternative less favorable to Merck, that Vioxx might be harmful. App. 340.

The products-liability complaints' statements about Merck's knowledge show little more. Merck does not claim that these complaints contained any specific information suggesting the fraud alleged here, i.e., that Merck knew the naproxen hypothesis was false even as it promoted it. And, without providing any reason to believe that the plaintiffs had special access to information about Merck's state of mind, the complaints alleged only in general terms that Merck had concealed information about Vioxx and "purposefully downplayed and/or understated" the risks associated with Vioxx—the same charge made in the FDA warning letter. App. 393.

In our view, neither these two circumstances nor any of the other pre-November 2001 circumstances that we have set forth in Part I–A, supra, whether viewed separately or together, reveal "facts" indicating scienter. Regardless of which, if any, of the events following November 6, 2001, constituted "discovery," we need only conclude that prior to November 6, 2001, the plaintiffs did not discover, and Merck has not shown that a reasonably diligent plaintiff would have discovered, "the facts constituting the violation." In light of our interpretation of the statute, our holdings in respect to scienter, and our application of those holdings to the circumstances of this case, we must, and we do, reach that conclusion. Thus, the plaintiffs' suit is timely. We need not—and do not—pass upon the Court of Appeals' suggestion that the November 2003 Brigham and Women's study might have triggered the statute of limitations. The judgment of the Court of Appeals is affirmed.

JUSTICE JOHN PAUL STEVENS, CONCURRING IN PART AND CONCURRING IN THE JUDGMENT.

In my opinion the Court's explanation of why the complaint was timely filed is convincing and correct. In this case there is no difference between the time when the plaintiffs actually discovered the factual basis for their claim and the time when reasonably diligent plaintiffs should have discovered those facts. For that reason, much of the discussion in Part II of the Court's opinion, is not necessary to support the Court's judgment. Until a case arises in which the difference between an actual discovery rule and a constructive discovery rule would affect the outcome, I would reserve decision on the merits of Justice Scalia's argument (opinion concurring in part and concurring in judgment). With this reservation, I join the Court's excellent opinion.

JUSTICE ANTONIN G. SCALIA, WITH WHOM JUSTICE THOMAS JOINS, CONCURRING IN PART AND CONCURRING IN THE JUDGMENT.

Private suits under §10(b) of the Securities Exchange Act of 1934 must be brought within "(1) 2 years after the discovery of the facts constituting the violation" or "(2) 5 years after such violation," whichever comes first. 28 U. S. C. §1658(b)(1). I agree with the Court that scienter is among the "facts constituting the violation" that a plaintiff must "discove[r]" for the limitations period to begin. I also agree that respondents' suit is timely, but for a reason different from the Court's: Merck has not shown that respondents actually "discover[ed]" scienter more than two years before bringing suit.

In ordinary usage, "discovery" occurs when one actually learns something new. See Webster's New International Dictionary of the English Language 745 (2d ed. 1957) (defining "discovery" as "[f]inding out or ascertaining something previously unknown or unrecognized"). As the Court notes, however, in the context of statutes of limitations "discovery" has long carried an additional meaning: It also occurs when a plaintiff, exercising reasonable diligence, *should have* discovered the facts giving rise to his claim. See, e.g., *Wood v. Carpenter*, 101 U.S. 135, 140-142 (1879). Read in isolation, "discovery" in §1658(b)(1) might mean constructive discovery.

In context, however, I do not believe it can. Section 13 of the Securities Act of 1933, explicitly established a constructive-discovery rule for claims under §§11and 12 of that Act:

> No action shall be maintained to enforce any liability created under section 77k or 77l(a)(2) of this title unless brought within one year after the discovery of the untrue statement or the omission, or after such discovery should have been made by the exercise of reasonable diligence . . . ." 15 U. S. C. §77m.

"[D]iscovery" in §77m obviously cannot mean constructive discovery, since that would render superfluous the phrase "or after such discovery should have been made by the exercise of reasonable diligence." Ibid. With §77m already on the books, Congress added limitations periods in the 1934 Act, 15 U. S. C. §§78i(e), 78r(c), that did not contain similar qualifying language; instead, each established a time bar that runs from "discovery" *simpliciter*. When Congress enacted §1658(b)(1) in 2002, establishing a limitations period for private actions for "fraud, deceit, manipulation, or contrivance in contravention of a regulatory requirement concerning the securities laws," specifically including the 1933 and 1934 Acts, see 15 U. S. C. §78c(a)(47), it likewise included no constructive-discovery caveat. To interpret §1658(b)(1) as imposing a constructive-discovery standard, one must therefore assume, contrary to common sense, that the same word means two very different things in the same statutory context of limitations periods for securities-fraud actions under the 1933 and 1934 Acts. ***

*** There is good reason, moreover, for providing an actual-discovery rule for private §10(b) claims but providing (explicitly) a constructive discovery rule for claims governed by §77m: The elements of §10(b) claims, which include scienter, are likely more difficult to discover than the elements of claims under §77k or §77l(a)(2), which do not. And a constructive-discovery standard may be easier to apply to the claims covered by §77m. Determining when the plaintiff should have uncovered an untrue assertion in a registration statement or prospectus is much simpler than assessing when a plaintiff should have learned that the defendant deliberately misled him using a deceptive device covered by §10(b).

Unable to identify anything in the statutory context that warrants giving "discovery" two meanings, the Court relies on the historical treatment of "discovery" in limitations periods (particularly for fraud claims) as incorporating a constructive-discovery rule. But that history proves only that "discovery" *can* carry that technical meaning, and that without §77m it would be reasonable (other things equal) to read it that way here. It does not show what "discovery" means in §1658(b)(1) *in light of* §77m's codification of a constructive-discovery rule. In my view, the meaning of "discovery" in the broader context of limitations provisions is overcome by its meaning in the more specific context of the federal securities laws. ***

*** I would hold that only actual discovery suffices to start the limitations period for §10(b) claims. Since Merck points to no evidence showing respondents actually discovered scienter more than two years before bringing this suit, I agree with the Court that the suit was not time barred. ***

NOTES AND QUESTIONS

***1. Assessing the Impact of* Merck.** The impact of *Merck* turns in significant measure on something that decision left unstated – what quantum of information renders a fact discoverable? According to the Second Circuit, a fact becomes discoverable when "a reasonably diligent plaintiff would have sufficient information about that fact to adequately plead it in a complaint." *City of Pontiac Gen'l Emps.' Ret. Sys. v. MBIA, Inc.*, 637 F.3d 169, 175 (2d Cir. 2011). Does that conclusion follow from *Merck*? Are there other justifications for the conclusion? See *Pontiac*, supra, 537 F.3d at 174-75.

Bearing in mind the demanding requirements for pleading scienter that a Rule 10b-5 plaintiff must satisfy, is it arguable that *Merck* effectively establishes a five year statute of limitations? Does the Court anywhere suggest that this might be the case? Ponder the impact of *Merck* again in connection with Note 2 below.

2. Between A Rock and A Hard Place? Consider the following assessment of the interplay between the limitations period and scienter:

> When a defendant raises the statute of limitations defense, it is a lose-lose situation for plaintiffs: either defeat the statute of limitations defense by conceding that previous events did not establish the defendant's culpable state of mind and thus expose the case to ready dismissal; or lose on the statute of limitations defense and be forever barred from suit.

Michael J. Kaufman & John M. Wunderlich, Towards a Just Measure of Repose: The Statute of Limitations for Securities Fraud, 52 Wm. & Mary L. Rev. 1547, 1585 (2011). Do you agree?

3. False Claims of Being Married. The Court cited the statement 'I am not married' as an example of a statement which, if false, is virtually certain to have been made with scienter: "It is unlikely *** that someone would [make that statement] without being aware of the fact that the statement is false." Can you think of examples of this type of misstatement that are apt to occur in the corporate context?

4. Elements Other Than Scienter. The Court did not address whether facts evidencing elements aside from scienter must also be discovered (or be discoverable) in order for the cause of action to accrue. The Court did, however, note that, in the view of the Solicitor General, facts evidencing reliance, loss, and loss causation need not be discovered (or be discoverable) for limitations purposes. But cf. *In re Merrill Lynch Auction Rate Sec. Litig.*, 758 F. Supp. 2d 264, 275 (S.D.N.Y. 2010) (holding that facts bearing on loss causation must be discovered). Do you agree with the Solicitor General? Why or why not?

5. The Future of Inquiry Notice and Storm Warnings. Rather than completely rejecting the terms "inquiry notice" and "storm warnings," the Court observed that such "terms *** may be useful to the extent that they identify a time when the facts would have prompted a reasonably diligent plaintiff to begin investigating." What is the significance of the continued potential relevance of these terms? Is it more a boon for plaintiffs or defendants? Or does it simply enhance judicial discretion?

6. Policy-Free Zone? The Court does not expressly invoke policy considerations to support its conclusions about the statute of limitations. Do such considerations nonetheless lurk below the surface?

7. Bleeding Elements. Which (if any) of the facts set forth in *Merck* would, in your view, provide a predicate for:

a. a "truth on the market" rebuttal to the materiality element, thereby providing a rationale for excluding from the class those plaintiffs who purchased Merck shares after a certain date?

b. the argument that those plaintiffs who purchased Merck shares after a certain date did not reasonably rely on Merck's alleged misrepresentations?

c. the argument that those plaintiffs who purchased Merck shares after a certain date did not incur damages caused by the defendants' alleged fraud because the price they paid for their shares that already reflected the truth about Vioxx?

In light of your answers to these questions, consider whether (and to what extent) the dispute over the meaning of "discovery" in the statute of limitations is merely another version of the argument over when the plaintiffs – or the market -- knew or should have known about the falsity of the alleged misrepresentations.

*8. **Justice Scalia's Concurrence.*** Justice Scalia focuses on the statutory text, as he is wont to do. Does his reading of the text tend to favor the plaintiffs? Can you identify circumstances in which his reading would favor the defendants?

PROBLEM 2-31

Daniel owned the Stars Casino, Inc., where Martin frequently gambled. Martin, a truck driver with considerable sophistication about the gambling business, recently inherited a sizable amount of money upon the death of his father. Having heard about Martin's inheritance, Daniel invited Martin to become an "owner" of Stars.

According to Martin, Daniel promised him that he would receive $90 thousand yearly within two years of investing $150 thousand. This alleged promise was not memorialized in writing.

Under the terms of the agreement, Stars would have to make a yearly profit of $750 thousand for Martin to receive a $90 thousand payment. Prior to signing, Martin received documentation indicating that Stars had sustained a $400 thousand loss one year earlier. After signing, Daniel provided Martin with (accurate) financial data about Stars upon Martin's request.

Martin signed the agreement in 2006. Two years later, Martin had received no money from Stars. Six months after that, Martin filed a Rule 10b-5 lawsuit against Stars and Daniel. Stars has filed a motion to dismiss based on Section 1658(b). What is the likely result?

Cf. *Neale v. Suarez*, 2011 WL 677420 (W.D. Wash. 2011).

J. THE OVERLAP BETWEEN RULE 10b-5 AND THE EXPRESS ACTIONS FOR MATERIAL MISSTATEMENTS AND OMISSIONS

Sometimes the conduct at issue in an implied private action under Rule 10b-5 also supplies the predicate for invoking an express private action that provides liability for material misstatements and omissions—Sections 11 or 12(a)(2) of the Securities Act or Sections 9(e) or 18(a) of the Exchange Act. Under these circumstances, should the implied action be barred?

In the decision that follows, the Supreme Court addressed a private plaintiff's use of Rule 10b-5 to challenge conduct actionable under Section 11. Ask yourself what guidance this decision gives us when the overlap is between Rule 10b-5 and an express action other than Section 11.

HERMAN & MACLEAN v. HUDDLESTON

459 U.S. 375 (1983)

JUSTICE THURGOOD MARSHALL:

*** In 1969 Texas International Speedway, Inc. ("TIS"), filed a registration statement and prospectus with the Securities and Exchange Commission offering a total of $4,398,900 in securities to the public. The proceeds of the sale were to be used to finance the construction of an automobile speedway. The entire issue was sold on the offering date, October 30, 1969. TIS did not meet with success, however, and the corporation filed a petition for bankruptcy on November 30, 1970.

In 1972 plaintiffs Huddleston and Bradley instituted a class action in the United States District Court for the Southern District of Texas on behalf of themselves and other purchasers of TIS securities. The complaint alleged violations of Section 10(b) of the 1934 Act and SEC Rule 10b-5 promulgated thereunder. Plaintiffs sued most of the participants in the offering, including the accounting firm, Herman & MacLean, which had issued an opinion concerning certain financial statements and a pro forma balance sheet that were contained in the registration statement and prospectus. Plaintiffs claimed that the defendants had engaged in a fraudulent scheme to misrepresent or conceal material facts regarding the financial condition of TIS, including the costs incurred in building the speedway.

After a 3-week trial, the District Judge submitted the case to the jury on special interrogatories relating to liability. The judge instructed the jury that liability could be found only if the defendants acted with scienter. *** After the jury rendered a verdict in favor of the plaintiffs on the submitted issues, the judge concluded that Herman & MacLean and others had violated § 10(b) and Rule 10b-5 by making fraudulent misrepresentations in the TIS registration statement. The court then determined the amount of damages and entered judgment for the plaintiffs.

On appeal, the United States Court of Appeals for the Fifth Circuit held that a cause of action may be maintained under § 10(b) of the 1934 Act for fraudulent misrepresentations and omissions even when that conduct might also be actionable under § 11 of the 1933 Act. ***

We granted certiorari to consider whether an implied cause of action under § 10(b) of the 1934 Act will lie for conduct subject to an express civil remedy under the 1933 Act, an issue we have previously reserved ***. We now affirm the Court of Appeals' holding that plaintiffs could maintain an action under § 10(b) of the 1934 Act ***.

II.

The Securities Act of 1933 and the 1934 Act "constitute interrelated components of the federal regulatory scheme governing transactions in securities." *Ernst & Ernst v. Hochfelder,* 425 U.S. 185, 206 (1976). The Acts created several express private rights of action, one of which is contained in § 11 of the 1933 Act. In addition to the private actions created explicitly by the 1933 and 1934 Acts, federal courts have implied private remedies under other provisions of the two laws. Most significantly for present purposes, a private right of action under § 10(b) of the 1934 Act and Rule 10b-5 has been consistently recognized for more than 35 years. The existence of this implied remedy is simply beyond peradventure.

The issue in this case is whether a party should be barred from invoking this established remedy for fraud because the allegedly fraudulent conduct would apparently also provide the basis for a damage action under § 11 of the 1933 Act. The resolution of this issue turns on the fact that the two provisions involve distinct causes of action and were intended to address different types of wrongdoing.

Section 11 of the 1933 Act allows purchasers of a registered security to sue certain enumerated parties in a registered offering when false or misleading information is included in a registration statement. The section was designed to assure compliance with the disclosure provisions of the Act by imposing a stringent standard of liability on the parties who play a direct role in a registered offering. If a plaintiff purchased a security issued pursuant to a registration statement, he need only show a material misstatement or omission to establish his prima facie case. Liability against the issuer of a security is virtually absolute, even for innocent misstatements. Other defendants bear the burden of demonstrating due diligence.

Although limited in scope, § 11 places a relatively minimal burden on a plaintiff. In contrast, § 10(b) is a "catchall" antifraud provision, but it requires a plaintiff to carry a heavier burden to establish a cause of action. While a § 11 action must be brought by a purchaser of a registered security, must be based on misstatements or omissions in a registration statement, and can only be brought against certain parties, a § 10(b) action can be brought by a purchaser or seller of "*any* security" against "*any* person" who has used "*any* manipulative or deceptive device or contrivance" in connection with the purchase or sale of a security. However, a § 10(b) plaintiff carries a heavier burden than a § 11 plaintiff. Most significantly, he must prove that the defendant acted with scienter, *i.e.*, with intent to deceive, manipulate, or defraud.

Since § 11 and § 10(b) address different types of wrongdoing, we see no reason to carve out an exception to § 10(b) for fraud occurring in a registration statement just because the same conduct may also be actionable under § 11. Exempting such conduct from liability under § 10(b) would conflict with the basic purpose of the 1933 Act: to provide greater protection to purchasers of registered securities. It would be anomalous indeed if the special protection afforded to purchasers in a registered offering by the 1933 Act were deemed to deprive such purchasers of the protections against manipulation and deception that § 10(b) makes available to all persons who deal in securities.

While some conduct actionable under § 11 may also be actionable under § 10(b), it is hardly a novel proposition that the 1934 Act and the 1933 Act "prohibit some of the same conduct." *United States v. Naftalin,* 441 U.S. 768, 778 (1979) (applying § 17(a) of the 1933 Act to conduct also prohibited by § 10(b) of the 1934 Act in an action by the SEC). " 'The fact that there may well be some overlap is neither unusual nor unfortunate.' " Ibid, quoting *SEC v. National*

Securities., Inc., 393 U.S. 453, 468 (1969). In savings clauses included in the 1933 and 1934 Acts, Congress rejected the notion that the express remedies of the securities laws would preempt all other rights of action. Section 16 of the 1933 Act states unequivocally that "[t]he rights and remedies provided by this title shall be in addition to any and all other rights and remedies that may exist at law or in equity." Section 28(a) of the 1934 Act contains a parallel provision. These provisions confirm that the remedies in each Act were to be supplemented by "any and all" additional remedies.

This conclusion is reinforced by our reasoning in *Ernst & Ernst v. Hochfelder,* which held that actions under § 10(b) require proof of scienter and do not encompass negligent conduct. In so holding, we noted that each of the express civil remedies in the 1933 Act allowing recovery for negligent conduct is subject to procedural restrictions not applicable to a § 10(b) action.[18] We emphasized that extension of § 10(b) to negligent conduct would have allowed causes of action for negligence under the express remedies to be brought instead under § 10(b), "thereby nullify[ing] the effectiveness of the carefully drawn procedural restrictions on these express actions." In reasoning that scienter should be required in § 10(b) actions in order to avoid circumvention of the procedural restrictions surrounding the express remedies, we necessarily assumed that the express remedies were not exclusive. Otherwise there would have been no danger of nullification. Conversely, because the added burden of proving scienter attaches to suits under § 10(b), invocation of the § 10(b) remedy will not "nullify" the procedural restrictions that apply to the express remedies.

This cumulative construction of the remedies under the 1933 and 1934 Acts is also supported by the fact that, when Congress comprehensively revised the securities laws in 1975, a consistent line of judicial decisions had permitted plaintiffs to sue under § 10(b) regardless of the availability of express remedies. In 1975 Congress enacted the "most substantial and significant revision of this country's Federal securities laws since the passage of the Securities Exchange Act in 1934." See Securities Acts Amendments of 1975, 89 Stat. 97. When Congress acted, federal courts had consistently and routinely permitted a plaintiff to proceed under § 10(b) even where express remedies under § 11 or other provisions were available. In light of this well-established judicial interpretation, Congress' decision to leave § 10(b) intact suggests that Congress ratified the cumulative nature of the § 10(b) action.

A cumulative construction of the securities laws also furthers their broad remedial purposes. In enacting the 1934 Act, Congress stated that its purpose was "to impose requirements necessary to make [securities] regulation and control reasonably complete and effective." 15 U.S.C. § 78b. In furtherance of that objective, § 10(b) makes it unlawful to use "*any* manipulative or deceptive device or contrivance" in connection with the purchase or sale of any security. The effectiveness of the broad proscription against fraud in § 10(b) would be undermined if its scope were restricted by the existence of an express remedy

---

18. For example, a plaintiff in a § 11 action may be required to post a bond for costs ***. In contrast, § 10(b) contains no provision requiring plaintiffs to post security for costs. ***

under § 11. Yet we have repeatedly recognized that securities laws combating fraud should be construed "not technically and restrictively, but flexibly to effectuate [their] remedial purposes." *SEC v. Capital Gains Research Bureau, Inc.*, 375 U.S. 180, 195 (1963). We therefore reject an interpretation of the securities laws that displaces an action under § 10(b).

Accordingly, we hold that the availability of an express remedy under § 11 of the 1933 Act does not preclude defrauded purchasers of registered securities from maintaining an action under § 10(b) of the 1934 Act. ***

NOTES AND QUESTIONS

1. ***Cumulativeness Across the Board?*** Does the Court in effect call for adoption of a cumulative approach whenever the implied private action under Rule 10b-5 overlaps with an express private action under the federal securities laws? If not, what circumstances must be present in order to render the express action exclusive?

The answers may have become somewhat more elusive with the Supreme Court's 5-4 decision in *Janus Capital Group, Inc. v. First Derivative Traders*, 131 S.Ct. 2296 (2011), which you read earlier in Section H of this Chapter. There the Court rejected the plaintiff's argument partly on the ground that it "would read into Rule 10b-5 a theory of liability similar to – but broader in application than" – the control person liability provision (Section 20(a)). Id. at 2304. The dissent countered this assertion by noting that it contravened *Huddleston*. Id. at 2310 (Breyer, J., dissenting).

2. ***The Case for Codification.*** The Court acknowledged that the existence of an implied private action under Rule 10b-5 was "beyond peradventure." Cf. *Janus Capital Group, Inc. v. First Derivative Traders*, 131 S.Ct. 2296, 2303 (2011) (describing that existence as "settled"). Should Congress codify the action and thereby eliminate any remaining uncertainties over cumulativeness?

3. ***Rule 10b-5 and Section 12(a)(2).*** Section 12(a)(2) of the Securities Act, a principal subject of Chapter 3, allows purchasers in a public offering to sue their sellers when a prospectus or oral communication contains a material misstatement or omission. Like Section 11, Section 12(a)(2) does not require scienter. Largely for this reason, courts have taken a cumulative approach to Rule 10b-5 and Section 12(a)(2). See, e.g., *Berger v. Bishop Inv. Corp.*, 695 F.2d 302, 308 (8th Cir. 1982). Does *Huddleston* counsel otherwise?

4. ***Rule 10b-5 and Section 18(a).*** Section 18(a) of the Exchange Act provides an action for anyone who buys or sells a security in reliance on a material misstatement in an SEC filing "at a price affected by such misstatement." While a plaintiff need not establish scienter, she must nonetheless satisfy several other demanding requirements: actual reliance on the document in question, a causal relationship between reliance and damages, and a causal relationship between the misstatement and the price paid. Courts have taken a cumulative approach to Section 18(a) and Rule 10b-5 on the ground that Rule 10b-5 requires scienter but Section 18(a) does not. See, e.g., *Wachovia Bank & Trust Co. v. Nat'l Student Mktg. Corp.*, 650 F.2d 342, 356-58 (D.C. Cir.

1980); *Ross v. A. H. Robins Co.*, 607 F.2d 545, 556 (2d Cir. 1979). Is the likely result the nullification of Section 18(a) and thereby the contravention of *Huddleston*?

As you contemplate the appropriate relationship between Section 18(a) and Rule 10b-5, consider what would happen if Section 18(a) stood as the exclusive remedy for material misstatements in documents filed with the SEC. According to Professor Aldave, the consequences would be anomalous:

> [P]ersons deceived by misstatements in documents that were not filed with the SEC would have a more effective remedy than persons deceived by misstatements in documents filed with the SEC, even though Congress enacted Section 18 as part of its effort to ensure that filed documents would be accurate and complete.

Barbara Bader Aldave, "Neither Unusual Nor Unfortunate": The Overlap of Rule 10b-5 With the Express Liability Sections of the Securities Acts, 60 Tex. L. Rev. 719, 749 (1982).

5. Rule 10b-5 and Section 9(e). Section 9(e) of the Exchange Act, a principal subject of Chapter 8, provides a remedy to purchasers and sellers of securities who are injured by specified forms of market manipulation. The plaintiff must meet a demanding two-pronged causation requirement: the manipulation must not only cause the plaintiff's damages but also affect the price at which he bought or sold. Moreover, unlike any other private federal securities remedy, the plaintiff must show that the defendant acted "willfully."

Does *Huddleston* support a cumulative approach to Rule 10b-5 and Section 9(e)? The majority of a Fifth Circuit panel gave an affirmative answer. See *Chemetron Corp. v. Business Funds, Inc.,* 718 F.2d 725 (5th Cir. 1983). The active judges voted for a rehearing en banc. See id. at 730. The case was settled, however, and thus the rehearing en banc did not occur. For analysis of whether a cumulative approach to Rule 10b-5 and Section 9(e) is warranted, see Marc I. Steinberg, The Propriety and Scope of Cumulative Remedies Under the Federal Securities Laws, 67 Cornell L. Rev. 557, 588-94 (1982).

6. The Savings Clauses. To support its cumulative approach to Section 11 and Rule 10b-5, the *Huddleston* Court referred to the language in Section 16 of the Securities Act and Section 28(a) of the Exchange Act stating that the statutory "rights and remedies" are "in addition to any and all other rights and remedies that may exist at law and equity." While this language may or may not have been designed to insure cumulation of express and implied remedies, it was clearly designed to insure cumulation of federal and state remedies. Cf. *Credit Suisse Sec. (USA) LLC v. Billing*, 551 U.S. 264, 275 (2007) (savings clauses do not safeguard every federal antitrust remedy). Why would Congress have taken this approach in the 1930s? The approach remained in place until 1998, when the Securities Litigation Uniform Standards Act amended Sections 16 and 28(a) to preempt state law class actions involving nationally traded securities. See infra Chapter 6.D.

7. The More the Merrier? Section 28(a) of the Exchange Act provides that "no person permitted to maintain a suit for damages under the provisions of [the Exchange Act] shall recover, through satisfaction of judgment in one or more actions, a total amount in excess of his actual damages on account of the act complained of." Thus, even if a plaintiff establishes the requisite elements of multiple provisions (be they state and federal securities provisions or federal securities provisions exclusively), his recovery cannot exceed his "actual damages." Are there nonetheless strategic advantages to suing under multiple provisions?

Chapter 3

LIABILITY UNDER THE SECURITIES ACT FOR MATERIAL MISSTATEMENTS, OMISSIONS, AND FRAUDULENT CONDUCT

This Chapter examines provisions of the Securities Act that authorize liability for material misstatements, omissions, and fraudulent conduct. Two of these provisions — Sections 11 and 12(a)(2) — create express private actions. The third — Section 17(a) — is enforceable by the government only.

To be sure, the Securities Act also contains a provision — Section 12(a)(1) — that creates an express private action for violations of Section 5 of the Securities Act. But because this Chapter does not focus principally on registration, Section 12(a)(1) is considered only insofar as it sheds light on its statutory sibling, Section 12(a)(2).

A. SECTIONS 11 AND 12(a)(2): EXPRESS PRIVATE ACTIONS FOR MATERIAL MISSTATEMENTS AND OMISSIONS

Sections 11 and 12(a)(2) both authorize express private actions to challenge material misstatements and omissions. We examine these actions separately and then consider briefly certain features that they share.

Sections 11 and 12(a)(2) both apply to offerings registered under Section 5 of the Securities Act (although, as we will see, the reach of Section 12(a)(2) is broader than this). Therefore, before turning to these Sections specifically, we identify the persons responsible for the accuracy of the registration statement — the document filed with the SEC in a registered offering (part one of which is the prospectus distributed to investors):

The Issuer. This is the company whose securities are sold to the public pursuant to the registration statement. The issuer's officers and directors are responsible for the content of the registration statement and for cooperating with the auditor and underwriters in their efforts to confirm the truthfulness of the registration statement.

The Auditor. This is the accounting firm that must conduct a detailed audit of the issuer and certify that the issuer's financial statements have been prepared in accordance with Generally Accepted Accounting Principles (GAAP).

The Underwriters. Occasionally, a small offering (known as a direct public offering) will be sold directly to investors without an underwriter. More commonly, however, the issuer retains one or more investment banks as underwriters. The investment bank leading the effort to sell the securities is known as the managing underwriter (or lead underwriter), and the other underwriters are "major bracket" or "minor bracket" underwriters, depending on the amount of securities for which they agree to be responsible.

The issuer and the underwriters sometimes agree to a "firm commitment" underwriting, pursuant to which the underwriters buy the securities from the issuer and resell them. In so doing, the underwriters assume the market risk prior to resale as well as the risk of being unable to resell. Firm commitment underwriting is typically utilized when the issuer is well-established.

Alternatively, the issuer and the underwriter may agree to a "best efforts" underwriting, pursuant to which the underwriters do not purchase the securities from the issuer but instead utilize their "best efforts" in helping the issuer sell the securities. A "best efforts" underwriting may be canceled, and the money returned to investors, if a predetermined amount of the securities are not sold.

Regardless of whether the underwriting is of the "firm commitment" or "best efforts" variety, the underwriters are compensated with a "spread" — the percentage difference (often about 5% for an equity offering, but less for a debt offering) between the consideration paid by investors for the securities and the proceeds from the offering received by the issuer. One problem with this compensation system is that underwriters, unlike auditors and for the most part unlike lawyers, are paid only if the offering is consummated or "closed," thereby giving the underwriters an incentive to close an offering even if they know that the registration statement is misleading. One way in which the Securities Act addresses this problem is to subject underwriters to substantial liability under Section 11 if securities are sold pursuant to a misleading registration statement.

The brokers who distribute the securities to investors comprise the "selling group." In contrast to the underwriters, the brokers are not in privity of contract with the issuer.

The Lawyers. The issuer as well as the managing underwriter typically retain lawyers to assist with the preparation of the registration statement and related duties. The issuer's lawyer usually takes the principal role in drafting the registration statement, although the underwriters' lawyer usually also has a significant involvement. As we will see, neither Section 11 nor Section 12(a)(2) imposes liability on lawyers based on their drafting of the registration statement or their investigation of its accuracy.

As you examine Sections 11 and 12(a)(2), ask yourself the following. Why did Congress enact these private actions in the first place? How do they complement each other? What advantages and disadvantages do they offer investors as compared with the implied private action under Section 10(b) and Rule 10b-5?

1. *Section 11*

Section 11(a) is undoubtedly one of the longest single sentences in the federal securities laws. An examination of that sentence, however, reveals a straightforward cause of action: a purchaser of a security sold pursuant to a registration statement may sue any enumerated defendant if the registration statement contained a material misstatement or omission on the date it became effective. The enumerated defendants include the following:

- Signers of the registration statement. (Note that Section 6(a) of the Securities Act lists those who must sign the registration statement, and that the required signers include the issuer);
- Every person who was a director of the issuer at the time of registration;
- Every future director who, with his or her consent, was named in the registration statement;
- Any accountant who certified any financial statement contained in the registration statement, where at least one of the material misstatements or omissions at issue appears in the statement that he certified;
- Any other person who certified a part of the registration statement (say, an attorney who attested to the validity of patents or, as discussed below, a bond rating agency that consented to the inclusion of its ratings in the registration statement), where at least one of the material misstatements or omissions at issue appears in the statement that he certified; and
- Every underwriter involved in the offering.

Why did Congress cast the net of liability so widely? To what extent was it seeking to ensure that the issuer's officers and directors took seriously the disclosure obligations of a registered offering? To what extent was it prodding the underwriters and accountants to fulfill their roles as gatekeepers?

In 2010, as part of the Dodd-Frank Act, Congress expanded this liability net even further with its repeal of SEC Rule 436(g). That Rule created an exemption from expert liability under Section 11 for references to ratings by nationally recognized statistical rating organizations (NRSROs). Henceforth, issuers of debt or preferred stock must either omit references to such ratings in the registration statement or else obtain the consent of the NRSRO (many of which have indicated their refusal to give it). For discussion of the ramifications of Rule 436(g)'s repeal, see Andrew F. Tuch, Multiple Gatekeepers, 96 Va. L. Rev. 1558, 1568-70 (2010).

For the issuer, liability under Section 11 is strict. That is, unless the issuer proves that the plaintiff knew of the misstatement or omission at issue at the time of purchasing the security (see Section 11(a)) or unless the statute of limitations has run (see Section 13), the issuer has no defenses. To be sure, an issuer may be able to reduce (or even eliminate) damages by showing negative causation — sometimes known as the negative causation defense (see Section

11(e)).

Defendants other than the issuer have "due diligence" defenses. In accordance with Section 11(b), these defendants can avoid liability by establishing that they acted diligently in investigating the facts set forth in the registration statement. Such defendants may also avoid liability based on the plaintiff's knowledge of the misstatement or omission, the statute of limitations, or negative causation.

Contrast the elements of a Section 11 action and the implied private action under Section 10(b) and Rule 10b-5. Unlike Rule 10b-5, Section 11 does not require the plaintiff to prove scienter or causation. Moreover, Section 11 requires the plaintiff to establish reliance on the material misstatement or omission only in rare circumstances – namely, where she bought the securities after the issuer distributed audited financial statements covering the 12 month period after the effective date of the registration statement (see Section 11(a)).

To be sure, there appears to be a fledgling trend towards expanding the role played by reliance under Section 11. The seminal decision is *APA Excelsior III LP v. Premiere Techs., Inc.*, 476 F.3d 1261 (11th Cir. 2007), which involved a registration statement issued in connection with an arms-length merger. The Eleventh Circuit held that Section 11 creates a "presumption of reliance" that fails to attach when the plaintiffs made a "binding pre-registration commitment" to purchase the shares. Id. at 1273. Thereafter, albeit in dictum, several trial courts have arguably extended the reach of *Excelsior* beyond a commitment of that sort. See, e.g. *In re HealthSouth Corp. Sec. Litig.*, 261 F.R.D. 616, 647 (N.D. Ala. 2009) (observing that Section 11 liability does not attach "'where it is certain that a purchase of the securities was motivated by factors other than the registration statement,'" quoting *Excelsior*, supra, at 1275-76, and noting that *Excelsior*'s progeny have "recognized the obvious [point that] a registration statement cannot be the basis for an investment decision where an investor made its investment decision *before* the registration statement has been filed"); *In re Countrywide Fin. Corp. Sec. Litig.*, 588 F. Supp. 2d 1132, 1162 n. 34 (C.D. Cal. 2008) (reading *Excelsior* to make reliance under Section 11 applicable "in the unusual case where it appears from the face of the complaint that a plaintiff cannot have actually relied on the registration statement"). For discussion of this development, see Marc I. Steinberg & Brent A. Kirby, The Assault on Section 11 of the Securities Act: A Study in Judicial Activism, 63 Rutgers L. Rev. 1, 12-26 (2010). Do you agree that Section 11 creates a "presumption of reliance"?

A Section 11 plaintiff does not establish a prima facie case merely by showing that the registration statement contains one or more material misstatements or omissions. In addition, she must demonstrate her standing to sue, which, as we will see, constitutes a significant hurdle. We begin with standing to sue and then consider the defenses of due diligence and negative causation.

a. Standing to Sue

In the following decision, the court confronted the question whether Section 11 provides a cause of action only for the original purchasers in a registered offering, or whether those who thereafter purchase such shares may tracing req / for secondary purchasers

sue as well. While the court did give subsequent purchasers the right to sue, it required that they "trace" their shares back to the registration statement in question.

Notice that in reaching its conclusions, the court contrasted Section 11 with Section 12(a)(2) and drew upon *Gustafson v. Alloyd Co.,* 513 U.S. 561 (1995), a Supreme Court decision involving Section 12(a)(2) that we will examine later in this Chapter. In making the contrast, the court demonstrated that Sections 11 and 12(a)(2) have important similarities and differences.

LEE v. ERNST & YOUNG, LLP

294 F.3d 969 (8th Cir. 2002)

THEODORE MCMILLIAN, CIRCUIT JUDGE:

This appeal arises from consolidated securities fraud lawsuits filed against Summit Medical Systems, Inc. ("Summit"), Summit's officers and directors, and Summit's public accountant- independent auditor, Ernst & Young ("E & Y") (collectively "defendants") by Summit shareholders ("plaintiffs") in the United States District Court for the District of Minnesota. Following the entry of final judgment, plaintiffs appeal from orders of the district court resulting in the dismissal, pursuant to Fed.R.Civ.P. 12(b)(6), of their claim against E & Y for allegedly violating § 11 of the Securities Act of 1933 ("the 1933 Act") by making materially false and misleading statements and omissions in Summit's registration statement filed with the Securities and Exchange Commission ("SEC") in connection with Summit's initial public offering in August 1995. For reversal, plaintiffs argue that the district court *** erred in holding as a matter of law that standing to bring the § 11 claim exists only for those plaintiffs who acquired their stock in the initial public offering. *** For the reasons discussed below, we reverse the district court's holding on the § 11 standing issue *** and remand the case to the district court for further proceedings consistent with this opinion. ***

Background

Summit is a corporation headquartered in Minneapolis, Minnesota, which provides "clinical outcomes" medical database software and related products and services. According to the first amended complaint, 2.5 million shares of Summit common stock began trading publicly on August 4, 1995, at $9.00 per share. Following the initial public offering, the Summit stock price increased even though no profit was shown by Summit. A secondary public offering was made in June 1996. At the end of 1996, the Summit stock price began to decline, and it eventually fell below the price at which the stock was initially offered to the public. On March 3, 1997, Summit publicly disclosed that it had been improperly recognizing revenues. Following an investigation, Summit announced that it planned to restate its financial results dating back to 1994. On April 4, 1997, Summit filed revised statements with the SEC showing the total revenues for the years 1994 and 1995, and the first nine months of 1996, to be $5.6 million less than originally reported, representing an 11% cumulative shortfall.

corrective / disclosure in 1997

Following Summit's public disclosures, numerous lawsuits were brought against defendants, resulting in the present consolidated action. *** According to the first amended complaint, the registration statement identified E & Y as an "expert" which had audited and certified Summit's financial statements, and it set forth E & Y's opinion that Summit's consolidated financial statements "presented fairly, in all material respects, the consolidated financial position of [Summit] for the 1993 and 1994 fiscal years, and the results of [Summit's] consolidated operations and its consolidated cash flows for 1992, 1993, and 1994, 'in conformity with generally accepted accounting principles [("GAAP")].'" In Count III of the first amended complaint, plaintiffs asserted that, because of Summit's premature recognition of revenue in violation of GAAP and Summit's own publicly-stated revenue recognition policies, the registration statement contained materially false and misleading statements and omissions regarding Summit's actual financial status and accounting practices from as early as 1994. ***

Defendants, including E & Y, moved to dismiss the first amended complaint on several grounds. The district court granted in part and denied in part defendants' motion to dismiss. As to the § 11 claim against E & Y, the district court held, as a matter of law, that only those plaintiffs who purchased their stock in the Summit initial public offering had standing to sue. In support of this holding, the district court relied upon *Gustafson v. Alloyd Co.*, 513 U.S. 561 (1995) (holding that aftermarket purchasers of securities did not have a claim under § 12(2) of the 1933 Act). The district court explained that the 1933 Act must be read as a whole and that, based upon the shared legislative history and legislative intent behind § 11 and § 12(2) of the 1933 Act, "the standing principles announced in *Gustafson* apply equally to Section 11 and 12 claims." ***

Following an agreement by the parties to settle the remaining claims against Summit and its officers and directors, the district court entered an order approving the terms of the settlement and entering final judgment. This appeal [on the § 11 claims against E & Y] followed.

Discussion

*** We review the district court's interpretation of a federal statute *de novo*. Plaintiffs, with the support of the SEC as an amicus curiae, argue that the district court erroneously interpreted § 11 of the 1933 Act when it held that only those plaintiffs who acquired stock in the Summit August 1995 initial public offering have standing to sue under § 11. Plaintiffs argue that aftermarket purchasers may bring a claim under § 11 so long as they can "trace" their securities to the public offering under the registration statement alleged to be false and misleading. See, e.g., *Kirkwood v. Taylor*, 590 F.Supp. 1375 (D. Minn. 1984) (allowing an aftermarket purchaser to establish standing by "direct tracing" — that is, by showing that the security was issued under the registration statement alleged to be defective, and not under a different registration statement), aff'd, 760 F.2d 272 (8th Cir.1985) (unpublished table decision). Plaintiffs maintain that the district court erroneously relied on the Supreme Court's decision in *Gustafson* in rendering its decision. Plaintiffs contend that, because *Gustafson* involved § 12(2) of the 1933 Act, not § 11, its holding is limited to the question of what constitutes a "prospectus" under § 12. Plaintiffs note that the majority of federal courts that have addressed this issue, including the only two circuit courts of appeals to have ruled on it since

Gustafson was decided, have concluded that the *Gustafson* holding does not extend to § 11 claims. See Brief for Appellants at 14-16 (citing, e.g., *Joseph v. Wiles*, 223 F.3d 1155, 1159-61 (10th Cir. 2000); *Hertzberg v. Dignity Partners, Inc.*, 191 F.3d 1076, 1080-82 (9th Cir. 1999)). ***

*** This court has yet to rule upon the § 11 standing issue in a published opinion. By affirming the district court's pre-*Gustafson* decision in *Kirkwood v. Taylor*, we have, however, upheld an interpretation of § 11 which allows aftermarket stock purchasers to establish standing by tracing their securities to the registration statement alleged to be defective.

*** Prior to *Gustafson*, the First and Second Circuits had indicated a similar view. See *Versyss Inc. v. Coopers & Lybrand*, 982 F.2d 653, 657-58 (1st Cir.1992); *Barnes v. Osofsky*, 373 F.2d 269, 271-72 (2d Cir.1967) (assuming that § 11 allows claims based upon tracing to the registration statement in question, but rejecting the even broader interpretation urged by the appellant, which would provide a cause of action for purchasers of securities "of the same nature" as those issued pursuant to the registration statement in question). ***

Section 11(a) provides in relevant part:

> In case any part of the registration statement, when such part became effective, contained an untrue statement of a material fact or omitted to state a material fact required to be stated therein or necessary to make statements therein not misleading, *any person acquiring such security* (unless it is proved that at the time of such acquisition he knew of such untruth or omission) may, either at law or in equity, in any court of competent jurisdiction, sue .... (emphasis added)

The phrase "any person acquiring such security" is not only broad on its face but, more importantly, is broad when compared to the language of § 12(2), the provision at issue in the *Gustafson* decision. Section 12(2) provides that any person who "offers or sells a security" by means of a "prospectus or oral communication" containing a materially false or misleading statement or omission shall be liable "to the person purchasing such security from him" (subject to exceptions not pertinent herein). Section 12(2), therefore, expressly requires privity between the issuer and the purchaser of the security at issue. Section 11, by contrast, has no comparable language—it simply refers to "any person acquiring such security," with "such security" referring to a security registered under the registration statement alleged to be defective. We perceive the absence in § 11 of limiting language similar to that found in § 12(2) to indicate Congress's intent to convey a relatively broader meaning. In other words, we read § 11's plain language to state unambiguously that a cause of action exists for any person who purchased a security that was originally registered under the allegedly defective registration statement — so long as the security was indeed issued under *that* registration statement and not another. Therefore, even in light of *Gustafson*, § 11 is broad enough to encompass some aftermarket purchasers, subject, of course, to the long-recognized requirement that the plaintiff must directly trace his or her security to the allegedly defective registration statement at issue in the case, as was required in *Kirkwood v. Taylor*. In addition, we note that, under § 11(e), damages are generally calculated as the difference between the amount paid for the security, *not exceeding the price at which the security was offered to the public*, and the price of the security at the time the lawsuit was filed or the security was disposed of in the market. It would be unnecessary to limit the price to no more than the price offered to the public if the cause of action were limited to participants in the initial public offering. Similarly, § 11(g) — which expressly caps the maximum amount recoverable to the price offered to the public — would likewise be superfluous if only those who participated in the initial public stock offering could bring a § 11 claim.

We next consider whether there is clear legislative intent contrary to our interpretation of § 11. The purpose and scope of the 1933 Act was to regulate the initial distribution of securities. Central to the regulatory scheme was the requirement that publicly-offered securities be registered with the SEC. The importance of the registration statement to Congress's regulatory and enforcement framework is indicated by the standard imposing liability for materially false and misleading misstatements or omissions, without a scienter requirement. By making the cause of action available to anyone who purchased stock that was originally issued under the registration statement in question, not just those who actually participated in the initial public offering, Congress enhanced the incentive for compliance and bolstered the mechanism for enforcing § 11. Our interpretation of § 11 is also consistent with the recognition that a material misstatement or omission in connection with an initial public offering can adversely affect aftermarket purchasers. However, to protect issuers of publicly- traded securities against abuses of the process, Congress additionally incorporated a requirement for certain aftermarket purchasers to prove that they *relied* on the registration statement in question. See [Section 11(a)] ("If such person acquired the security after the issuer has made generally available to its security holders an earning statement covering a period of at least twelve months beginning after the effective date of the registration statement, then the right of recovery under this subsection shall be conditioned on proof that such person acquired the security relying upon the such untrue statement in the registration statement or relying upon such registration statement and not knowing of such omission, but such reliance may be established without proof of the reading of the registration statement by such person.") Finally, requiring aftermarket purchasers to show that their securities can be traced to the allegedly defective registration statement further ensures fidelity to the statutory purpose, and we again emphasize that tracing is a requirement of aftermarket purchaser standing under § 11 in this circuit. See, e.g., *Kirkwood v. Taylor*, 590 F.Supp. at 1378-79.

Conclusion

We hold in the present case that standing to pursue a claim against E & Y pursuant to § 11 of the 1933 Act exists for aftermarket purchasers of Summit stock who can make a prima facie showing that the Summit shares they purchased can be traced to the registration statement alleged to be false and misleading. Accordingly, we reverse the district court's holding to the contrary. In light of our holding on the § 11 standing issue, we reverse the dismissal of plaintiff's § 11 claim *** The case is remanded to the district court for further proceedings consistent with this opinion.

Section 11's tracing requirement can itself be traced to *Barnes v. Osofsky*, 373 F.2d 269 (2d Cir. 1967). In *Barnes,* Judge Friendly interpreted the language of Section 11 to limit standing to those shareholders who had acquired securities "issued pursuant to the registration statement" in question. Consider his reasons for so doing as well as his reasons for rejecting the plaintiff's broader reading of the statutory language:

> The key phrase [in Section 11(a)] is "any person acquiring such security"; the difficulty, presented when as here the registration is of shares in addition to those already being traded, is that "such" has no referent. Although the narrower reading — "acquiring a security issued pursuant to the registration statement" — would be the more natural, a broader one — "acquiring a security of the same nature as that issued pursuant to the registration statement" — would not be such a violent departure from the words that a court could not properly adopt it if there were good reason for doing so. Appellants claim there is. Starting from the seemingly correct premise that an unduly optimistic prospectus will affect the price of shares already issued to almost the same extent as those of the same class about to be issued, they say it would therefore be unreasonable to distinguish newly registered shares from those previously traded. In addition, they contend that once it is agreed that § 11 is not limited to the original purchasers, to read that section as applying only to purchasers who can trace the lineage of their shares to the new offering makes the result turn on mere accident since most trading is done through brokers who neither know nor care whether they are getting newly registered or old shares. Finally, appellants argue that it is often impossible to determine whether previously traded shares are old or new, and that tracing is further complicated when stock is held in margin accounts in street names since many brokerage houses do not identify specific shares with particular accounts but instead treat the account as having an undivided interest in the house's position. Therefore, they urge that the narrower construction offends the cardinal principle of equal treatment for persons whose entitlement is not significantly different ***.
>
> Appellants' broader reading would be inconsistent with the over-all statutory scheme. The Securities Act of 1933 had two major purposes, "[t]o provide full and fair disclosure of the character of securities sold in interstate and foreign commerce and through the mails, and to prevent frauds in the sale thereof, *** " 48 Stat. 74 (1933). These aims were "to be achieved by a general antifraud provision and by a registration provision." 1 Loss, Securities Regulation 178-79 (1961). Section 11 deals with civil liability for untrue or misleading statements or omissions in the registration statement; its stringent penalties are to insure full and accurate disclosure through registration. Since, under §§ 2(1) and 6, only individual shares are registered, it seems unlikely that the section developed to insure proper disclosure in the registration statement was meant to provide a remedy for other than the particular shares registered. *** Beyond this, the over-all limitation of § 11(g) that "In no case shall the amount recoverable under this section exceed the price at which the security was offered to the public," and the provision of § 11(e) whereby, with qualifications not here material, an underwriter's liability shall not exceed "the total price at which the securities underwritten by him and distributed to the public were offered to the public," point in the direction of limiting § 11 to purchasers of the registered shares, since otherwise their recovery would be greatly diluted when the new issue was small in relation to the trading in previously outstanding shares.

Id. at 271-72.

NOTES AND QUESTIONS

1. ***A Substantial Hurdle.*** Often, an issuer will have sold fungible securities pursuant to multiple registration statements. If so, investors are likely to have a difficult — if not impossible — time tracing their securities to the registration statement at issue in their lawsuits. The reason is that today investors typically own their shares in "street" name, that is, in the name of their brokerage firm, but brokers ordinarily do not segregate newly-issued shares from previously-issued shares of the same issuer or assign particular shares to particular investors. Street name ownership was not the norm, however, at the time of Section 11's original enactment. See *Krim v. PCOrder.com, Inc.*, 402 F.3d 489, 498 & n.42 (5th Cir. 2005).

The tracing requirement is relatively easy to meet when the securities sold pursuant to the registration statement are the only securities that the issuer ever sold to the public. See *Hertzberg v. Dignity Partners, Inc.*, 191 F.3d 1076, 1080 (9th Cir. 1999). But it does not follow that tracing is invariably easy in every IPO. Indeed, even in an IPO, there may be secondary market trading in securities of the issuer, fungible with those sold in the IPO, that were previously sold pursuant to offerings exempt from the registration requirement.

If a plaintiff cannot meet the tracing requirement, what remedies might be available to her in place of Section 11?

2. ***Judicial Creation?*** Judge Friendly sought to anchor the tracing requirement in the language of Section 11(a), but he nonetheless acknowledged that the language would also support a broader reading. Does it follow that the tracing requirement was a judicial creation?

3. ***The Roads Not Taken.*** Would it have been better if Judge Friendly had adopted the broader reading of Section 11(a)? What would have been the drawbacks of the broader reading? Assuming that the narrower reading was preferable, does it necessarily follow that the plaintiff should have the burden of proof on the tracing issue?

4. ***Methods of Tracing.*** In *Kirkwood v. Taylor*, 590 F. Supp. 1375 (D. Minn. 1984), aff'd mem., 760 F.2d 272 (8th Cir. 1985), the court discussed four methods of tracing the plaintiff's securities to the registered offering. It approved "direct tracing," but rejected three other methods: "fungible-mass tracing," "contrabroker tracing," and "heritage tracing." Fungible-mass tracing, also known as "statistical tracing," uses statistics to demonstrate the likelihood that the plaintiff's shares were acquired pursuant to the registration statement. In the court's view, proof of a mere likelihood is insufficient for Section 11 purposes. Contrabroker tracing links the plaintiffs' shares to an underwriter involved in the registered offering. According to the court, acceptance of this method would mean that "anyone who ever purchased from a participant in the underwriting after the offering date could claim he or she bought 'new' stock." Id. at 1381. Heritage tracing establishes a match between code numbers of stock certificates registered in the plaintiffs' names and those issued in the registered offering. The *Kirkwood* plaintiffs had trouble with the matching, however, and thus the court's rejection of this form of tracing may have been limited to the facts of this particular case. Id. at 1378-83. See also *Krim v. PCOrder.com, Inc.*, 402 F.3d 489, 502 (5th Cir. 2005) (rejecting statistical tracing).

Several scholars endorse abandoning the direct tracing requirement. Professor Sale supports a statistical approach similar to that rejected by the *Kirkwood* and *Krim* decisions. See Hillary A. Sale, Disappearing Without a Trace: Sections 11 and 12(a)(2) of the 1933 Securities Act, 75 Wash. L. Rev. 429, 484-94 (2000). In contrast, Professor Oh favors requiring investors to "designate an offering" at the time of purchase:

> That designation would be recorded by the central depository or issuer, contemporaneous with the purchase. The total number of designations possible would be tied to the number of securities offered. *** [D]esignations would operate on a "First-Come, First-In" basis; once all securities in a particular offering are designated, that option would disappear and the process would continue until all such designations of offerings were complete. Security holders would be permitted only to trace, and then claim value for designated offerings.

Peter B. Oh, Tracing, 80 Tul. L. Rev. 849, 894 (2006). Do you think that one (or both) of these alternatives is preferable to direct tracing?

5. The Relevance of Timing. A few courts have found the tracing requirement satisfied where the plaintiff purchased her shares within days of the registered offering at issue. See, e.g., *Wade v. Indus. Funding Corp.*, 1993 WL 650837 (N.D. Cal. 1993). Is this approach sound?

6. Tracing and the Preponderance Standard. A plaintiff must prove her securities case by a preponderance of the evidence. See *Herman & MacLean v. Huddleston,* 459 U.S. 375, 390 (1983). Does judicial insistence on direct tracing in effect exceed that standard? See *Krim v. PCOrder.com, Inc.*, 402 F.3d 489, 494 n.21 (5th Cir. 2005) (rejecting argument to this effect). But cf. Sale, supra, 75 Wash. L. Rev. at 484 n. 351.

PROBLEM 3-1

Garrett, a securities broker, met with his clients Molly and Polly, identical twins, and recommended that they purchase stock in the upcoming registered offering by Peacock, Inc. Garrett showed them the Peacock preliminary prospectus, which captured their fancy. When the offering occurred, Molly and Polly purchased 1000 Peacock shares each, obtaining stock certificates in their own names (rather than in "street" name).

Thereafter, it became apparent that the Peacock registration statement was fraudulent. Molly and Polly consulted with Garrett, who ascertained that Molly had received newly registered shares, whereas Polly had received shares that had been issued pursuant to a registered offering that Peacock had made six months earlier.

Does Molly have standing to bring a Section 11 action? What about Polly?

b. The Due Diligence Defenses

As mentioned previously, Section 11 imposes strict liability on the issuer. Often, however, the issuer has become bankrupt, and therefore judgment proof, prior to the time the Section 11 action is filed. Under these circumstances, the plaintiff's ability to recover may turn on whether the non-issuer defendants can establish their due diligence defenses under Section 11(b).

Section 11(b) distinguishes between the expertised and non-expertised portions of the registration statement. The expertised portions are portions to which an expert (such as an accountant) has expressly certified. The non-expertised portions (the bulk of the registration statement) has no such certification attached.

Consider a director who wishes to establish his due diligence defenses. With respect to the non-expertised portions, the director must show that:

> he had, after reasonable investigation, reasonable ground to believe and did believe, at the time such part of the registration statement became effective, that the statements therein were true and that there was no omission to state a material fact required to be stated therein or necessary to make the statements therein not misleading.

Section 11(b)(3)(A). With respect to the expertised portions, the director has a lesser showing, namely that:

> he had no reasonable ground to believe and did not believe, at the time such part of the registration statement became effective, that the statements therein were untrue or that there was an omission to state a material fact required to be stated therein or necessary to make the statements therein not misleading, or that such part of the registration statement did not fairly represent the statement of the expert or was not a fair copy of or extract from the report or valuation of the expert.

Section 11(b)(3)(C).

An expert can be liable only in connection with those portions of the registration statement that he has certified. For example, an accountant who wishes to establish his due diligence defense with respect to the financial statements that he has certified must show that:

> (i) he had, after reasonable investigation, reasonable ground to believe and did believe, at the time such part of the registration statement became effective, that the statements therein were true and that there was no omission to state a material fact required to be stated therein or necessary to make the statements therein not misleading, or (ii) such part of the registration statement did not fairly represent his statement as an expert or was not a fair copy of or extract from his report or valuation as an expert.

Section 11(b)(3)(B).

The following landmark decision, familiar to all securities litigators, contains a comprehensive discussion of the due diligence defenses.

ESCOTT v. BARCHRIS CONSTRUCTION CORPORATION

283 F.Supp. 643 (S.D.N.Y. 1968)

EDWARD C. MCLEAN, DISTRICT JUDGE:

This is an action by purchasers of 5 1/2 per cent convertible subordinated fifteen year debentures of BarChris Construction Corporation (BarChris). ***

The action is brought under Section 11 of the Securities Act of 1933. Plaintiffs allege that the registration statement with respect to these debentures *** contained material false statements and material omissions. ***

*** At the time relevant here, BarChris was engaged primarily in the construction of bowling alleys, somewhat euphemistically referred to as "bowling centers." ***

BarChris was an outgrowth of a business started as a partnership by Vitolo and Pugliese in 1946.***

The introduction of automatic pin setting machines in 1952 gave a marked stimulus to bowling. It rapidly became a popular sport, with the result that "bowling centers" began to appear throughout the country in rapidly increasing numbers. BarChris benefitted from this increased interest in bowling. Its construction operations expanded rapidly. It is estimated that in 1960 BarChris installed approximately three per cent of all lanes built in the United States. ***

In general, BarChris's method of operation was to enter into a contract with a customer, receive from him at that time a comparatively small down payment on the purchase price, and proceed to construct and equip the bowling alley. When the work was finished and the building delivered, the customer paid the balance of the contract price in notes, payable in installments over a period of years. BarChris discounted these notes with a factor and received part of their face amount in cash. The factor held back part as a reserve.

*** BarChris was compelled to expend considerable sums in defraying the cost of construction before it received reimbursement. As a consequence, BarChris was in constant need of cash to finance its operations, a need which grew more pressing as operations expanded.

In December 1959, BarChris sold 560,000 shares of common stock to the public at $3.00 per share. ***

By early 1961, BarChris needed additional working capital. The proceeds of the sale of the debentures involved in this action were to be devoted, in part at least, to fill that need.

The registration statement of the debentures, in preliminary form, was filed with the Securities and Exchange Commission on March 30, 1961. A first amendment was filed on May 11 and a second on May 16. The registration statement became effective on May 16. The closing of the financing took place on May 24. On that day BarChris received the net proceeds of the financing.

By that time BarChris was experiencing difficulties in collecting amounts due from some of its customers. Some of them were in arrears in payments due to factors on their discounted notes. As time went on those difficulties increased. Although BarChris continued to build alleys in 1961 and 1962, it became increasingly apparent that the industry was overbuilt. Operators of alleys, often inadequately financed, began to fail. Precisely when the tide turned is a matter of dispute, but at any rate, it was painfully apparent in 1962.

In May of that year BarChris made an abortive attempt to raise more money by the sale of common stock. It filed with the Securities and Exchange Commission a registration statement for the stock issue which it later withdrew. In October 1962 BarChris came to the end of the road. On October 29, 1962, it filed in this court a petition for an arrangement under Chapter XI of the Bankruptcy Act. BarChris defaulted in the payment of the interest due on November 1, 1962 on the debentures.

The Debenture Registration Statement

In preparing the registration statement for the debentures, [director and outside counsel] Grant acted for BarChris. He had previously represented BarChris in preparing the registration statement for the common stock issue. In connection with the sale of common stock, BarChris had issued purchase warrants. In January 1961 a second registration statement was filed in order to update the information pertaining to these warrants. Grant had prepared that statement as well.

Some of the basic information needed for the debenture registration statement was contained in the registration statements previously filed with respect to the common stock and warrants. Grant used these old registration statements as a model in preparing the new one, making the changes which he considered necessary in order to meet the new situation.

The underwriters were represented by the Philadelphia law firm of Drinker, Biddle & Reath. John A. Ballard, a member of that firm, was in charge of that work, assisted by a young associate named Stanton.

Peat, Marwick, BarChris's auditors, who had previously audited BarChris's annual balance sheet and earnings figures for 1958 and 1959, did the same for 1960. These figures were set forth in the registration statement. In addition, Peat, Marwick undertook a so-called "S-1 review," the proper scope of which is one of the matters debated here.

*** The prospectus [included in the registration statement] contained, among other things, a description of BarChris's business, a description of its real property, some material pertaining to certain of its subsidiaries, and remarks about various other aspects of its affairs. It also contained financial information. It included a consolidated balance sheet as of December 31, 1960, with elaborate explanatory notes. These figures had been audited by Peat, Marwick. It also contained unaudited figures as to net sales, gross profit and net earnings for the first quarter ended March 31, 1961, as compared with the similar quarter for 1960. In addition, it set forth figures as to the company's backlog of unfilled orders as of March 31, 1961, as compared with March 31, 1960, and figures as to BarChris's contingent liability, as of April 30, 1961, on customers' notes discounted and its contingent liability under the so-called alternative method of financing.

Plaintiffs challenge the accuracy of a number of these figures. They also charge that the text of the prospectus, apart from the figures, was false in a number of respects, and that material information was omitted. ***

[*The court found that the registration statement, including the financial statements attached thereto, did contain material false statements of fact and omitted to state material facts which should have been stated in order to prevent it from being misleading.*]

The "Due Diligence" Defenses

*** Before considering the evidence, a preliminary matter should be disposed of. The defendants do not agree among themselves as to who the "experts" were or as to the parts of the registration statement which were expertised. ***

*** To say that the entire registration statement is expertised because some lawyer prepared it would be an unreasonable construction of the statute. Neither the lawyer for the company nor the lawyer for the underwriters is an expert within the meaning of Section 11. The only expert, in the statutory sense, was Peat, Marwick, and the only parts of the registration statement which purported to be made upon the authority of an expert were the portions which purported to be made on Peat, Marwick's authority.

*** I turn now to the question of whether defendants have proved their due diligence defenses. The position of each defendant will be separately considered.

Russo

Russo was, to all intents and purposes, the chief executive officer of BarChris. He was a member of the executive committee. He was familiar with all aspects of the business. He was personally in charge of dealings with the factors. He acted on BarChris's behalf in making the financing agreements with Talcott and he handled the negotiations with Talcott in the spring of 1961. He talked with customers about their delinquencies.

Russo prepared the list of jobs which went into the backlog figure. He knew the status of those jobs. ***

It was Russo who arranged for the temporary increase in BarChris's cash in banks on December 31, 1960, a transaction which borders on the fraudulent. He was thoroughly aware of BarChris's stringent financial condition in May 1961. He had personally advanced large sums to BarChris of which $175,000 remained unpaid as of May 16.

In short, Russo knew all the relevant facts. He could not have believed that there were no untrue statements or material omissions in the prospectus. Russo has no due diligence defenses. ***

Kircher

Kircher was treasurer of BarChris and its chief financial officer. He is a certified public accountant and an intelligent man. He was thoroughly familiar with BarChris's financial affairs. He knew the terms of BarChris's agreements with Talcott. He knew of the customers' delinquency problem. He participated actively with Russo in May 1961 in the successful effort to hold Talcott off until the financing proceeds came in. He knew how the financing proceeds were to be applied and he saw to it that they were so applied. ***

Moreover, as a member of the executive committee, Kircher was kept informed as to those branches of the business of which he did not have direct charge. *** In brief, Kircher knew all the relevant facts.

Kircher worked on the preparation of the registration statement. He conferred with Grant and on occasion with Ballard. He supplied information to them about the company's business. He read the prospectus and understood it. He knew what it said and what it did not say.

Kircher's contention is that he had never before dealt with a registration statement, that he did not know what it should contain, and that he relied wholly on Grant, Ballard and Peat, Marwick to guide him. He claims that it was their fault, not his, if there was anything wrong with it. He says that all the facts were recorded in BarChris's books where these "experts" could have seen them if they had looked. He says that he truthfully answered all their questions. In effect, he says that if they did not know enough to ask the right questions and to give him the proper instructions, that is not his responsibility.

There is an issue of credibility here. In fact, Kircher was not frank in dealing with Grant and Ballard. He withheld information from them. But even if he had told them all the facts, this would not have constituted the due diligence contemplated by the statute. Knowing the facts, Kircher had reason to believe that the expertised portion of the prospectus, i.e., the 1960 figures, was in part incorrect. He could not shut his eyes to the facts and rely on Peat, Marwick for that portion.

As to the rest of the prospectus, knowing the facts, he did not have a reasonable ground to believe it to be true. On the contrary, he must have known that in part it was untrue. Under these circumstances, he was not entitled to sit back and place the blame on the lawyers for not advising him about it.

Kircher has not proved his due diligence defenses. ***

Birnbaum

Birnbaum was a young lawyer, admitted to the bar in 1957, who, after brief periods of employment by two different law firms and an equally brief period of practicing in his own firm, was employed by BarChris as house counsel and assistant secretary in October 1960. Unfortunately for him, he became secretary and a director of BarChris on April 17, 1961, after the first version of the registration statement had been filed with the Securities and Exchange Commission. He signed the later amendments, thereby becoming responsible for the accuracy of the prospectus in its final form.

Although the prospectus, in its description of "management," lists Birnbaum among the "executive officers" *** the fact seems to be that he was not an executive officer in any real sense. He did not participate in the management of the company. As house counsel, he attended to legal matters of a routine nature. ***

Birnbaum examined contracts. In that connection he advised BarChris that the T-Bowl contracts were not legally enforceable. He was thus aware of that fact.

One of Birnbaum's more important duties, first as assistant secretary and later as full-fledged secretary, was to keep the corporate minutes of BarChris and its subsidiaries. This necessarily informed him to a considerable extent about the company's affairs. ***

It seems probable that Birnbaum did not know of many of the inaccuracies in the prospectus. He must, however, have appreciated some of them. In any case, he made no investigation and relied on the others to get it right. *** [H]e was entitled to rely upon Peat, Marwick for the 1960 figures, for as far as appears, he had no personal knowledge of the company's books of account or financial transactions. But he was not entitled to rely upon Kircher, Grant and Ballard for the other portions of the prospectus. As a lawyer, he should have known his obligations under the statute. He should have known that he was required to make a reasonable investigation of the truth of all the statements in the unexpertised portion of the document which he signed. Having failed to make such an investigation, he did not have reasonable ground to believe that all these statements were true. Birnbaum has not established his due diligence defenses except as to the audited 1960 figures.

Auslander

Auslander was an "outside" director, i.e., one who was not an officer of BarChris. He was chairman of the board of Valley Stream National Bank in Valley Stream, Long Island. In February 1961 Vitolo asked him to become a director of BarChris. Vitolo gave him an enthusiastic account of BarChris's progress and prospects. As an inducement, Vitolo said that when BarChris received the proceeds of a forthcoming issue of securities, it would deposit $1,000,000 in Auslander's bank.

In February and early March 1961, before accepting Vitolo's invitation, Auslander made some investigation of BarChris. He obtained Dun & Bradstreet reports which contained sales and earnings figures for periods earlier than December 31, 1960. He caused inquiry to be made of certain of BarChris's banks and was advised that they regarded BarChris favorably. He was informed that inquiry of Talcott had also produced a favorable response.

On March 3, 1961, Auslander indicated his willingness to accept a place on the board. *** Auslander observed that BarChris's auditors were Peat, Marwick. They were also the auditors for the Valley Stream National Bank. He thought well of them.

Auslander was elected a director on April 17, 1961. The registration statement in its original form had already been filed, of course without his signature. On May 10, 1961, he signed a signature page for the first amendment to the registration statement which was filed on May 11, 1961. This was a separate sheet without any document attached. Auslander did not know that it was a signature page for a registration statement. He vaguely understood that it was something "for the SEC."

Auslander attended a meeting of BarChris's directors on May 15, 1961. At that meeting he, along with the other directors, signed the signature sheet for the second amendment which constituted the registration statement in its final form. Again, this was only a separate sheet without any document attached. Auslander never saw a copy of the registration statement in its final form.

At the May 15 directors' meeting, however, Auslander did realize that what he was signing was a signature sheet to a registration statement. This was the first time that he had appreciated that fact. A copy of the registration statement in its earlier form as amended on May 11, 1961 was passed around at the meeting. Auslander glanced at it briefly. He did not read it thoroughly.

At the May 15 meeting, Russo and Vitolo stated that everything was in order and that the prospectus was correct. Auslander believed this statement.

In considering Auslander's due diligence defenses, a distinction is to be drawn between the expertised and non-expertised portions of the prospectus. As to the former, Auslander knew that Peat, Marwick had audited the 1960 figures. He believed them to be correct because he had confidence in Peat, Marwick. He had no reasonable ground to believe otherwise.

As to the non-expertised portions, however, Auslander is in a different position. He seems to have been under the impression that Peat, Marwick was responsible for all the figures. This impression was not correct, as he would have realized if he had read the prospectus carefully. Auslander made no investigation of the accuracy of the prospectus. He relied on the assurance of Vitolo and Russo, and upon the information he had received in answer to his inquiries back in February and early March. These inquiries were general ones, in the nature of a credit check. The information which he received in answer to them was also general, without specific reference to the statements in the prospectus, which was not prepared until some time thereafter.

It is true that Auslander became a director on the eve of the financing. He had little opportunity to familiarize himself with the company's affairs. The question is whether, under such circumstances, Auslander did enough to establish his due diligence defense with respect to the non-expertised portions of the prospectus.

*** Section 11 imposes liability in the first instance upon a director, no matter how new he is. He is presumed to know his responsibility when he becomes a director. He can escape liability only by using that reasonable care to investigate the facts which a prudent man would employ in the management of his own property. In my opinion, a prudent man would not act in an important matter without any knowledge of the relevant facts, in sole reliance upon representations of persons who are comparative strangers and upon general information which does not purport to cover the particular case. To say that such minimal conduct measures up to the statutory standard would, to all intents and purposes, absolve new directors from responsibility merely because they are new. This is not a sensible construction of Section 11, when one bears in mind its fundamental purpose of requiring full and truthful disclosure for the protection of investors.

I find and conclude that Auslander has not established his due diligence defense with respect to the misstatements and omissions in those portions of the prospectus other than the audited 1960 figures. ***

Grant

Grant became a director of BarChris in October 1960. His law firm was counsel to BarChris in matters pertaining to the registration of securities. Grant drafted the registration statement for the stock issue in 1959 and for the warrants in January 1961. He also drafted the registration statement for the debentures. ***

Grant is sued as a director and as a signer of the registration statement. This is not an action against him for malpractice in his capacity as a lawyer. Nevertheless, in considering Grant's due diligence defenses, the unique position which he occupied cannot be disregarded. As the director most directly concerned with writing the registration statement and assuring its accuracy, more was required of him in the way of reasonable investigation than could fairly be expected of a director who had no connection with this work.

*** Having seen [Grant] testify at length, I am satisfied as to his integrity. I find that Grant honestly believed that the registration statement was true and that no material facts had been omitted from it.

In this belief he was mistaken, and the fact is that for all his work, he never discovered any of the errors or omissions which have been recounted at length in this opinion, with the single exception of Capitol Lanes. He knew that BarChris had not sold this alley and intended to operate it, but he appears to have been under the erroneous impression that Peat, Marwick had knowingly sanctioned its inclusion in sales because of the allegedly temporary nature of the operation.

Grant contends that a finding that he did not make a reasonable investigation would be equivalent to a holding that a lawyer for an issuing company, in order to show due diligence, must make an independent audit of the figures supplied to him by his client. I do not consider this to be a realistic statement of the issue. There were errors and omissions here which could have been detected without an audit. The question is whether, despite his failure to detect them, Grant made a reasonable effort to that end.

Much of this registration statement is a scissors and paste-pot job. Grant lifted large portions from the earlier prospectuses, modifying them in some instances to the extent that he considered necessary. But BarChris's affairs had changed for the worse by May 1961. Statements that were accurate in January were no longer accurate in May. Grant never discovered this. He accepted the assurances of Kircher and Russo that any change which might have occurred had been for the better, rather than the contrary.

It is claimed that a lawyer is entitled to rely on the statements of his client and that to require him to verify their accuracy would set an unreasonably high standard. This is too broad a generalization. It is all a matter of degree. To require an audit would obviously be unreasonable. On the other hand, to require a check of matters easily verifiable is not unreasonable. Even honest clients can make mistakes. The statute imposes liability for untrue statements regardless of whether they are intentionally untrue. The way to prevent mistakes is to test oral information by examining the original written record.

There were things which Grant could readily have checked which he did not check. For example, he was unaware of the provisions of the agreements between BarChris and Talcott. He never read them. Thus, he did not know, although he readily could have ascertained, that BarChris's contingent liability on Type B leaseback arrangements was 100 per cent, not 25 per cent. He did not appreciate that if BarChris defaulted in repurchasing delinquent customers' notes upon Talcott's demand, Talcott could accelerate all the customer paper in its hands, which amounted to over $3,000,000.

As to the backlog figure, Grant appreciated that scheduled unfilled orders on the company's books meant firm commitments, but he never asked to see the contracts which, according to the prospectus, added up to $6,905,000. Thus, he did not know that this figure was overstated by some $4,490,000. ***

The application of proceeds language in the prospectus was drafted by Kircher back in January. It may well have expressed his intent at that time, but his intent, and that of the other principal officers of BarChris, was very different in May. Grant did not appreciate that the earlier language was no longer appropriate. He never learned of the situation which the company faced in May. He knew that BarChris was short of cash, but he had no idea how short. He did not know that BarChris was withholding delivery of checks already drawn and signed because there was not enough money in the bank to pay them. He did not know that the officers of the company intended to use immediately approximately one-third of the financing proceeds in a manner not disclosed in the prospectus, including approximately $1,000,000 in paying old debts. ***

As far as customers' delinquencies is concerned, although Grant discussed this with Kircher, he again accepted the assurances of Kircher and Russo that no serious problem existed. He did not examine the records as to delinquencies, although BarChris maintained such a record. Any inquiry on his part of Talcott or an examination of BarChris's correspondence with Talcott in April and May 1961 would have apprised him of the true facts. ***

Grant was entitled to rely on Peat, Marwick for the 1960 figures. He had no reasonable ground to believe them to be inaccurate. But the matters which I have mentioned were not within the expertised portion of the prospectus. As to this, Grant, was obliged to make a reasonable investigation. I am forced to find that he did not make one. After making all due allowances for the fact that Bar Chris's officers misled him, there are too many instances in which Grant failed to make an inquiry which he could easily have made which, if pursued, would have put him on his guard. *** Each case must rest on its own facts. I conclude that Grant has not established his due diligence defenses except as to the audited 1960 figures.

The Underwriters and Coleman

The underwriters other than Drexel made no investigation of the accuracy of the prospectus. *** They all relied upon Drexel as the "lead" underwriter.

Drexel did make an investigation. The work was in charge of Coleman, a partner the firm, assisted by Casperson, an associate. Drexel's attorneys acted as attorneys for the entire group of underwriters. Ballard did the work, assisted by Stanton.

On April 17, 1961 Coleman became a director of BarChris. He signed the first amendment to the registration statement filed on May 11 and the second amendment, constituting the registration statement in its final form, filed on May 16. He thereby assumed a responsibility as a director and signer in addition to his responsibility as an underwriter. ***

*** [Coleman] was first introduced to BarChris on September 15, 1960. Thereafter he familiarized himself with general conditions in the industry ***.

Coleman continued his general investigation. He obtained a Dun & Bradstreet report on BarChris on March 16, 1961. He read BarChris's annual report for 1960 which was available in March. ***

After Coleman was elected a director on April 17, 1961, he made no further independent investigation of the accuracy of the prospectus. He assumed that Ballard was taking care of this on his behalf as well as on behalf of the underwriters. ***

Like Grant, Ballard, without checking, relied on the information which he got from Kircher. He also relied on Grant who, as company counsel, presumably was familiar with its affairs. ***

*** [I]t is clear that no effectual attempt at verification was made. The question is whether due diligence required that it be made. Stated another way, is it sufficient to ask questions, to obtain answers which, if true, would be thought satisfactory, and to let it go at that, without seeking to ascertain from the records whether the answers in fact are true and complete?

I have already held that this procedure is not sufficient in Grant's case. Are underwriters in a different position, as far as due diligence is concerned?

The underwriters say that the prospectus is the company's prospectus, not theirs. Doubtless this is the way they customarily regard it. But the Securities Act makes no such distinction. The underwriters are just as responsible as the company if the prospectus is false. And prospective investors rely upon the reputation of the underwriters in deciding whether to purchase the securities.

There is no direct authority on this question, no judicial decision defining the degree of diligence which underwriters must exercise to establish their defense under Section 11.

There is some authority in New York for the proposition that a director of a corporation may rely upon information furnished him by the officers without independently verifying it. See *Litwin v. Allen*, 25 N.Y.S.2d 667 (Sup.Ct.1940).

In support of that principle, the court in *Litwin* (25 N.Y.S.2d at 719) quoted from the opinion of Lord Halsbury in *Dovey v. Cory*, (1901) App.Cas. 477, 486, in which he said:

> "The business of life could not go on if people could not trust those who are put into a position of trust for the express purpose of attending to details of management."

Of course, New York law does not govern this case. The construction of the Securities Act is a matter of federal law. But the underwriters argue that *Litwin* is still in point, for they say that it establishes a standard of reasonableness for the reasonably prudent director which should be the same as the standard for the reasonably prudent underwriter under the Securities Act.

In my opinion the two situations are not analogous. An underwriter has not put the company's officers "into a position of trust for the express purpose of attending to details of management." The underwriters did not select them. In a sense, the positions of the underwriter and the company's officers are adverse. It is not unlikely that statements made by company officers to an underwriter to induce him to underwrite may be self-serving. They may be unduly enthusiastic. As in this case, they may, on occasion, be deliberately false.

The purpose of Section 11 is to protect investors. To that end the underwriters are made responsible for the truth of the prospectus. If they may escape that responsibility by taking at face value representations made to them by the company's management, then the inclusion of underwriters among those liable under Section 11 affords the investors no additional protection. To effectuate the statute's purpose, the phrase "reasonable investigation" must be construed to require more effort on the part of the underwriters than the mere accurate reporting in the prospectus of "date presented" to them by the company. It should make no difference that this data is elicited by questions addressed to the company officers by the underwriters, or that the underwriters at the time believe that the company's officers are truthful and reliable. In order to make the underwriters' participation in this enterprise of any value to the investors, the underwriters must make some reasonable attempt to verify the data submitted to them. They may not rely solely on the company's officers or on the company's counsel. A prudent man in the management of his own property would not rely on them.

It is impossible to lay down a rigid rule suitable for every case defining the extent to which such verification must go. It is a question of degree, a matter of judgment in each case. In the present case, the underwriters' counsel made almost no attempt to verify management's representations. I hold that that was insufficient.

On the evidence in this case, I find that the underwriters' counsel did not make a reasonable investigation of the truth of those portions of the prospectus which were not made on the authority of Peat, Marwick as an expert. Drexel is bound by their failure. It is not a matter of relying upon counsel for legal advice. Here the attorneys were dealing with matters of fact. Drexel delegated to them, as its agent, the business of examining the corporate minutes and contracts. It must bear the consequences of their failure to make an adequate examination.

The other underwriters, who did nothing and relied solely on Drexel and on the lawyers, are also bound by it. It follows that although Drexel and the other underwriters believed that those portions of the prospectus were true, they had no reasonable ground for that belief, within the meaning of the statute. Hence, they have not established their due diligence defense, except as to the 1960 audited figures.

The same conclusions must apply to Coleman. Although he participated quite actively in the earlier stages of the preparation of the prospectus, and contributed questions and warnings of his own, in addition to the questions of counsel, the fact is that he stopped his participation toward the end of March 1961. He made no investigation after he became a director. When it came to verification, he relied upon his counsel to do it for him. Since counsel failed to do it, Coleman is bound by that failure. Consequently, in his case also, he has not established his due diligence defense except as to the audited 1960 figures.

Peat, Marwick

*** The part of the registration statement purporting to be made upon the authority of Peat, Marwick as an expert was, as we have seen, the 1960 figures. But because the statute requires the court to determine Peat, Marwick's belief, and the grounds thereof, "at the time such part of the registration statement became effective," for the purposes of this affirmative defense, the matter must be viewed as of May 16, 1961, and the question is whether at that time Peat, Marwick, after reasonable investigation, had reasonable ground to believe and did believe that the 1960 figures were true and that no material fact had been omitted from the registration statement which should have been included in order to make the 1960 figures not misleading. In deciding this issue, the court must consider not only what Peat, Marwick did in its 1960 audit, but also what it did in its subsequent "S- 1 review." The proper scope of that review must also be determined. ***

Peat, Marwick's work was in general charge of a member of the firm, Cummings, and more immediately in charge of Peat, Marwick's manager, Logan. Most of the actual work was performed by a senior accountant, Berardi, who had junior assistants, one of whom was Kennedy.

Berardi was then about thirty years old. He was not yet a C.P.A. He had had no previous experience with the bowling industry. This was his first job as a senior accountant. He could hardly have been given a more difficult assignment.

After obtaining a little background information on BarChris by talking to Logan and reviewing Peat, Marwick's work papers on its 1959 audit, Berardi examined the results of test checks of BarChris's accounting procedures which one of the junior accountants had made, and he prepared an "internal control questionnaire" and an "audit program." Thereafter, for a few days subsequent to December 30, 1960, he inspected BarChris's inventories and examined certain alley construction. Finally, on January 13, 1961, he began his auditing work which he carried on substantially continuously until it was completed on February 24, 1961. Toward the close of the work, Logan reviewed it and made various comments and suggestions to Berardi. ***

Berardi made the S-1 review in May 1961. He devoted a little over two days to it, a total of 20 1/2 hours. He did not discover any of the errors or omissions pertaining to the state of affairs in 1961 which I have previously discussed at length, all of which were material. The question is whether, despite his failure to find out anything, his investigation was reasonable within the meaning of the statute.

What Berardi did was to look at a consolidating trial balance as of March 31, 1961 which had been prepared by BarChris, compare it with the audited December 31, 1960 figures, discuss with Trilling certain unfavorable developments which the comparison disclosed, and read certain minutes. He did not examine any "important financial records" other than the trial balance. As to minutes, he read only what minutes Birnbaum gave him, which consisted only of the board of directors' minutes of BarChris. He did not read such minutes as there were of the executive committee. He did not know that there was an executive committee, hence he did not discover that Kircher had notes of executive committee minutes which had not been written up. He did not read the minutes of any subsidiary.

In substance, what Berardi did is similar to what Grant and Ballard did. He asked questions, he got answers which he considered satisfactory, and he did nothing to verify them. ***

Accountants should not be held to a standard higher than that recognized in their profession. I do not do so here. Berardi's review did not come up to that standard. *** Most important of all, he was too easily satisfied with glib answers to his inquiries.

This is not to say that he should have made a complete audit. But there were enough danger signals in the materials which he did examine to require some further investigation on his part. Generally accepted accounting standards required such further investigation under these circumstances. It is not always sufficient merely to ask questions.

*** I conclude that Peat, Marwick has not established its due diligence defense. ***

NOTES AND QUESTIONS

1. ***Due Diligence and the*** **Barchris** ***Defendants.*** In applying Section 11 to the defendants, the court may (or may not) have made various distinctions. Consider the following.

(a) Outside vs. Inside Directors. To what extent did the court draw a distinction between the duties of inside and outside directors?

(b) Attorney Directors. Were directors who were also attorneys held to a higher standard? Did the court apply the same standard to Grant and Birnbaum? Should it have?

(c) Outside Directors vs. Outside Directors. Were Grant and Auslander held to the same standard? Should they have been?

(d) Underwriter Directors. Would Coleman have established his due diligence defense as to the non-expertised portion of the registration statement had he not been an underwriter?

(e) Underwriters. According to the court, to what extent are underwriters entitled to rely on management's representations? Should there be a distinction between underwriters and directors in this regard?

(f) Accountants. The court maintained that "accountants should not be held to a standard higher than that recognized in their profession." Is this a sound approach?

2. ***Piling It On?*** Note that once the court determined that a particular (non-expert) defendant had failed to satisfy his due diligence defense as to the non-expertised portion of the registration statement, it did not stop there. Instead, it went on to consider the defendant's liability as to the expertised

portion. If a defendant is already liable as to the non-expertised portion, why bother ascertaining his liability as to the expertised portion as well?

3. ***The Role of Rule 176.*** In 1982, the SEC adopted Rule 176 as an aid to determining whether a Section 11 defendant has satisfied his due diligence defenses:

> In determining whether or not the conduct of a person constitutes a reasonable investigation or a reasonable ground for belief meeting the standard set forth in section 11(c), relevant circumstances include, with respect to a person other than the issuer:
>
> (a) The type of issuer;
>
> (b) The type of security;
>
> (c) The type of person;
>
> (d) The office held when the person is an officer;
>
> (e) The presence or absence of another relationship to the issuer when the person is a director or proposed director;
>
> (f) Reasonable reliance on officers, employees, and others whose duties should have given them knowledge of the particular facts (in the light of the functions and responsibilities of the particular person with respect to the issuer and the filing);
>
> (g) When the person is an underwriter, the type of underwriting arrangement, the role of the particular person as an underwriter and the availability of information with respect to the registrant; and
>
> (h) Whether, with respect to a fact or document incorporated by reference, the particular person had any responsibility for the fact or document at the time of the filing from which it was incorporated.

Would it be a good idea for the SEC to adopt a rule providing defendants with more definitive protection? Consider that question again in connection with the next decision.

The following important decision on the due diligence defenses has sparked controversy.

IN RE WORLDCOM, INC. SEC. LITIG.

346 F.Supp.2d 628 (S.D.N.Y. 2004)

DENISE COTE, DISTRICT JUDGE:

This Opinion addresses issues related to an underwriter's due diligence obligations. Following the conclusion of fact discovery, several of the parties in this consolidated securities class action arising from the collapse of WorldCom, Inc. ("WorldCom") have filed for summary judgment.***

It is undisputed that at least as of early 2001 WorldCom executives engaged in a secretive scheme to manipulate WorldCom's public filings concerning WorldCom's financial condition. Because those public filings were incorporated into the registration statements for the two bond offerings, the underwriters are liable for those false statements unless they can show that they were sufficiently diligent in their investigation of WorldCom in connection with the bond offerings. Through these motions, the Lead Plaintiff emphasizes that the underwriters did almost no investigation of WorldCom in connection with their underwriting of the bond offerings for the company, and because they did essentially no investigation, will be unable to succeed with their defense that they were diligent. The Lead Plaintiff contends moreover that there were "red flags" that should have led the underwriters to question even the audited financials filed by WorldCom.

For their part, the underwriters emphasize that WorldCom management concealed the fraud from almost everyone within WorldCom, from WorldCom's outside auditor, and from the underwriters themselves. They assert that they were entitled to rely on WorldCom's audited financial statements as accurately describing the company's financial condition, and also on the comfort letters that WorldCom's outside auditor provided for the unaudited financial statements.***

*** Beginning in the late 1960s, the SEC embarked on a "program to integrate the disclosure requirements of the Securities Act and the Securities Exchange Act of 1934." See Circumstances Affecting the Determination of What Constitutes Reasonable Investigation and Reasonable Grounds for Belief Under Section 11 of the Securities Act, SEC Release No. 6335 (Aug. 6, 1981) ("SEC Rel. 6335"). The chief purpose of the integrated disclosure system was to furnish investors with "meaningful, nonduplicative information both periodically and when securities distributions are made to the public," while decreasing "costs of compliance for public companies." Reproposal of Comprehensive Revision to System for Registration of Securities Offerings, SEC Release No. 6331 (Aug. 6, 1981) ("SEC Rel. 6331").

*** [T]he SEC aimed in the early 1980s to integrate the two acts, "primarily by incorporating by reference Exchange Act reports into Securities Act registration statements." SEC Rel. 6335. The push to incorporate by reference was motivated by the growing recognition that "for companies in the top tier, there is a steady stream of high quality corporate information continually furnished to the market and broadly digested, synthesized and disseminated." Shelf Registration, SEC Release No. 6499 (Nov. 17, 1983) ("SEC Rel. 6499"). The SEC reasoned that top-tier companies should be able to incorporate their Exchange Act filing by reference, since these disclosures, along with "other communications by the registrant, such as press releases, ha [ve] already been disseminated and accounted for by the market place." SEC Rel. 6331. ***

Short-form registration was accompanied by related changes in shelf registration, the process by which securities are registered to be offered or sold on a delayed or continuous basis. The purpose of shelf registration is to allow a single registration statement to be filed for a series of offerings. SEC Rel. 6499. Shelf registration aims to afford the issuer the "procedural flexibility" to vary "the structure and terms of securities on short notice" and "time its offering to avail itself of the most advantageous market conditions." Id. ***

Together, the mechanism of incorporation by reference and the expansion of shelf registration significantly reduced the time and expense necessary to prepare public offerings, thus enabling more "rapid access to today's capital markets." SEC Rel. 6335. As the SEC recognized, these changes affected the time in which underwriters could perform their investigations of an issuer. Underwriters had weeks to perform due diligence for traditional registration statements. By contrast, under a short-form registration regime, "[p]reparation time is reduced sharply" thanks to the ability to incorporate by reference prior disclosures. Id.

These two innovations triggered concern among underwriters. Members of the financial community worried about their ability "to undertake a reasonable investigation with respect to the adequacy of the information incorporated by reference from periodic reports filed under the Exchange Act into the short form registration statements utilized in an integrated disclosure system." Id. *** Because an underwriter could select among competing underwriters when offering securities through a shelf registration, some questioned whether an underwriter could "afford to devote the time and expense necessary to conduct a due diligence review before knowing whether it will handle an offering and that there may not be sufficient time to do so once it is selected." SEC Rel. 6499. Others doubted whether they would have the chance "to apply their independent scrutiny and judgment to documents prepared by registrants many months before an offering." Id.

Because of concerns like those described here, the SEC introduced Rule 176 in 1981 "to make explicit what circumstances may bear upon the determination of what constitutes a reasonable investigation and reasonable ground for belief as these terms are used in Section 11(b)." SEC Rel. 6335. ***.

Although "[n]o court has ever been called upon to interpret Rule 176," the SEC's own commentary on the rule makes clear that Rule 176 did not alter the fundamental nature of underwriters' due diligence obligations. Langevoort, 63 Law & Contemp. Probs. at 65; Task Force Report, 48 Bus. Law. at 1210. *** Instead, emphasizing that "nothing in the Commission's integrated disclosure system precludes conducting adequate due diligence," the SEC advised underwriters concerned about the time pressures created by integrated disclosure to "arrange [their] due diligence procedures over time for the purpose of avoiding last minute delays in an offering environment characterized by rapid market changes." Id. *** As recently as December 1998, the SEC recalled that it "expressly rejected the consideration of competitive timing and pressures when evaluating the reasonableness of an underwriter's investigation." 63 Fed.Reg. at 67231.

The SEC's intent to maintain high standards for underwriter due diligence is confirmed by its many discussions of appropriate due diligence techniques in the integrated disclosure system. In proposing Rule 176, the SEC acknowledged that different investigatory methods would be needed "in view of the compressed preparation time and the volatile nature of the capital markets." SEC Rel. 6335. Nonetheless, it emphasized that such techniques must be "equally thorough." Id. (emphasis supplied). Among the strategies recommended by the SEC were the development of a "reservoir of knowledge about the companies that may select the underwriter to distribute their securities registered on short form registration statements" through a "careful review of [periodic Exchange Act] filings on an ongoing basis," consultation of analysts' reports, and active participation in the issuer's investor relations program, especially analysts and brokers meetings. Id.

At the time the SEC finalized the shelf registration rule two years later, it again recognized that "the techniques of conducting due diligence investigations of registrants qualified to use short form registration ... would differ from due diligence investigations under other circumstances." SEC Rel. 6499. Nonetheless, it stressed the use of "anticipatory and continuous due diligence programs" to augment underwriters' fulfillment of their due diligence obligations. Id. Among other practices, the SEC approvingly noted the increased designation of one law firm to act as underwriters' counsel, which "facilitates continuous due diligence by ensuring on-going access to the registrant on the underwriters' behalf"; the holding of "Exchange Act report 'drafting sessions,' " which allow underwriters "to participate in the drafting and review of periodic disclosure documents before they are filed"; and "periodic due diligence sessions," such as meetings between prospective underwriters, their counsel, and management shortly after the release of quarterly earnings. Id. ***

It must be noted that academics and practitioners alike have asserted that the current regime for underwriter liability under Section 11 no longer makes sense. Professor Coffee, for one, has observed that "it is not clear that the underwriter today still performs the classic gatekeeping function.... Many argue that serious due diligence efforts are simply not feasible within the time constraints of shelf registration. Given these constraints, they claim that the solution lies in downsizing the threat under section 11." John C. Coffee, Jr., Brave New World?: The Impact(s) of the Internet on Modern Securities Regulation, 52 Bus. Law. 1195, 1211 (1997). Another professor has remarked that "there is a strong practical case to be made for absolving underwriters of all inquiry obligations short of recklessness.... As underwriter involvement diminishes in significance relative to the deal as a whole, it becomes that much more problematic to apply a negligence-based standard in the first place." Langevoort, 63 Law & Contemp. Probs. at 67. A third asserts that in today's capital markets, "it is reasonable to question whether the underwriter's 'due diligence' role is justified at all.... [F]or shelf registrations, disinterested advance due diligence is the exception not the rule." Frank Partnoy, Barbarians at the Gatekeepers?: A Proposal for a Modified Strict Liability Regime, 79 Wash. U.L.Q. 491, 522 (2001) ("Barbarians at the Gatekeepers").

In a related vein, a Task Force of experienced counsel to underwriters concludes that the "'integrated disclosure system' and the expansion of shelf registration statements have called into question whether underwriters any longer 'sponsor' an issue in a meaningful way, as opposed to delivering advice and distribution services." Task Force Report, 48 Bus. Law. at 1239. ***

Thus, academics and practitioners have called for a reexamination of underwriters' liability under Sections 11 and 12(a)(2) on the grounds that "Congress's assumptions in 1933 and 1934 about registrants working with individual underwriters in a relatively leisurely atmosphere are at odds with today's competition by multiple underwriters for high-speed transactions." Id. Implicit in these calls for a legislative change is the recognition that current law continues to place a burden upon an underwriter to conduct a reasonable investigation of non-expertised statements in a registration statement, including an issuer's interim financial statements. ***

Section 11(b) plainly commands that underwriters conduct an investigation as to portions of a registration statement not made on the authority of an expert. "When a word is not defined by statute, we normally construe it in accord with its ordinary or natural meaning." *Smith v. United States*, 508 U.S. 223, 228 (1993). Today, as in 1933 when Section 11 became law, the word "investigation" connotes a "thorough" or "searching inquiry." Compare Webster's New International Dictionary of the English Language 1306 (2d ed. 1934) ("Webster's 1934") with Webster's Third New International Dictionary of the English Language 1189 (1993) ("Webster's 1993"). Then and now, it can also mean the process of investigating. See Webster's 1934 at 1306; Webster's 1993 at 1189. Under this latter definition, an investigation is no less demanding, as the word "investigate" is defined as "to inquire and examine into with systematic attention to detail and relationship." Webster's 1934 at 1306; see also Webster's 1993 at 1189 ("to inquire into systematically.")***

The Lead Plaintiff points to one issue that it contends gave the Underwriter Defendants a reasonable ground to question the reliability of WorldCom's 1999 Form 10-K. According to the computations presented by the Lead Plaintiff, WorldCom's reported E/R ratio was significantly lower than that of the equivalent numbers of its two closest competitors, Sprint and AT & T. The Lead Plaintiff argues that, in the extremely competitive market in which WorldCom operated, that discrepancy triggered a duty to investigate such a crucial measurement of the company's health. The Lead Plaintiff has shown that there are issues of fact as to whether the Underwriter Defendants had reasonable grounds to believe that the 1999 Form 10-K was inaccurate in the lines related to the E/R ratio reflected in that filing.

The Underwriter Defendants argue that the difference in the E/R ratios was insufficient as a matter of law to put the Underwriter Defendants on notice of any accounting irregularity. In support of this, they point to the fact that this difference was publicly available information and no one else announced a belief that it suggested the existence of an accounting fraud at WorldCom.

The fact that the difference was publicly available information does not absolve the Underwriter Defendants of their duty to bring their expertise to bear on the issue. The Underwriter Defendants do not dispute that they were required to be familiar with the Exchange Act filings that were incorporated by reference into the Registration Statement. If a "prudent man in the management of his own property," 15 U.S.C. § 77k(c), upon reading the 1999 Form 10-K and being familiar with the other relevant information about the issuer's competitors would have questioned the accuracy of the figures, then those figures constituted a red flag and imposed a duty of investigation on the Underwriter Defendants. A jury would be entitled to find that this difference was of sufficient importance to have triggered a duty to investigate the reliability of the figures on which the ratio was based even though the figures had been audited.

The Underwriter Defendants contend that an audited figure can never constitute a red flag and impose a duty of investigation. This argument mischaracterizes the Lead Plaintiff's position. The Lead Plaintiff has pointed to facts extraneous to WorldCom's audited figures to argue that a reasonable person would have inquired further about the discrepancy between the audited figures and the comparable information from competitors. *** [T]he existence of red flags can create a duty to investigate even audited financial statements. ***

In their analysis of the E/R ratio discrepancy itself, the Underwriter Defendants contend that a difference in ratios is not necessarily suspicious in a competitive industry and that the Lead Plaintiff's expert has incorrectly calculated the comparable ratios for AT & T and Sprint. Each of these arguments raises questions of fact that must be resolved at trial. ***

The Underwriter Defendants make several arguments concerning the issue of goodwill and asset impairment. They contend that it was public knowledge that AT & T and Sprint took asset impairment charges to their core networks in 2000 while WorldCom did not, that the telecommunications sector was in decline, and that analysts had described the equity value of the MCI tracking stock as close to zero. To the extent that these arguments are meant to suggest that bondholders cannot show that they relied on any misstatement in the WorldCom financials, there is no requirement of such a showing under either Section 11 or Section 12(a)(2). Furthermore, the issue in connection with the reliance defense is not whether the red flag information was well known, but whether the red flags existed and imposed a duty upon the Underwriter Defendants under the "prudent man" standard to inquire of WorldCom and/or Andersen about the reporting of WorldCom's assets because the Underwriter Defendants had a reasonable ground to believe that the reporting of assets may have been inaccurate.

The Underwriter Defendants next contend that WorldCom's treatment of the accounting issue was defensible. The Underwriter Defendants may be able to establish at trial that there was no misrepresentation of WorldCom's assets, but they have not moved for summary judgment on that ground. Instead, they have moved for summary judgment on their reliance defense by arguing that they had no duty to make any inquiry regarding the accuracy of WorldCom's statement of its assets. The Lead Plaintiff has shown that there are issues of fact regarding WorldCom's statement of its assets that a jury may find raised a red flag and imposed upon the Underwriter Defendants the obligation to inquire. ***

The Lead Plaintiff has shown that there are questions of fact *** as to whether the Underwriter Defendants conducted a reasonable investigation in either 2000 or 2001. It points to what it contends is evidence of the limited number of conversations with the issuer or its auditor, the cursory nature of the inquiries, the failure to go behind any of the almost formulaic answers given to questions, and the failure to inquire into issues of particular prominence in the Underwriter Defendants' own internal evaluations of the financial condition of the issuer or in the financial press. It argues in particular with respect to 2001, that having internally downgraded WorldCom's credit rating and having taken steps to limit their exposure as WorldCom creditors, the Underwriter Defendants were well aware that WorldCom was in a deteriorating financial position in a troubled industry, and that a reasonable investigation would have entailed a more searching inquiry than that undertaken by the Underwriter Defendants. Given the enormity of these two bond offerings, and the general deterioration in WorldCom's financial situation, at least as of the time of the 2001 Offering, they argue that a particularly probing inquiry by a prudent underwriter was warranted. These issues of fact require a jury trial.

The Underwriter Defendants have framed their summary judgment motion in a way that is incompatible with their burden of proving their due diligence defense under Section 11. They seek to restrict the inquiry on their due diligence solely to the work undertaken with respect to the interim financial statements and therefore to restrict it to a determination of whether any red flags existed that would put them on notice of a duty to make an inquiry of the interim financial statements. This formulation converts the due diligence defense into the reliance defense and balkanizes the task of due diligence.

In order to succeed with a due diligence defense, the Underwriter Defendants will have to show that they conducted a reasonable investigation of the non-expertised portions of the Registration Statements and thereafter had reasonable ground to believe that the interim financial statements were true. In assessing the reasonableness of the investigation, their receipt of the comfort letters will be important evidence, but it is insufficient by itself to establish the defense.

It is important to note that even if no reasonable investigation would have uncovered a fraud, an underwriter will prevail on its defense if can show it did conduct a reasonable investigation. Conversely, an underwriter must conduct a reasonable investigation to prevail on the due diligence defense, even if it appears that such an investigation would have proven futile in uncovering the fraud. Without a reasonable investigation, of course, it can never be known what would have been uncovered or what additional disclosures would have been demanded.

The Underwriter Defendants argue that if they are not entitled to rely on a comfort letter, the costs of capital formation in the United States will be substantially increased since underwriters will have to hire their own accounting firms to rehash the work of the issuer's auditor. Nothing in this Opinion should be read as imposing that obligation on underwriters or the underwriting process. The term "reasonable investigation" encompasses many modes of inquiry between obtaining comfort letters from an auditor and doing little more, on one hand, and having to re-audit a company's books on the other. Nonetheless, if aggressive or unusual accounting strategies regarding significant issues come to light in the course of a reasonable investigation, a prudent underwriter may choose to consult with accounting experts to confirm that the accounting treatment is appropriate and that additional disclosure is unnecessary.

Underwriters perform a different function from auditors. They have special access to information about an issuer at a critical time in the issuer's corporate life, at a time it is seeking to raise capital. The public relies on the underwriter to obtain and verify relevant information and then make sure that essential facts are disclosed. Acting with the degree of diligence that applies to a prudent man when managing his own property, underwriters should ask those questions and seek those answers that are appropriate in the circumstances. They are not being asked to duplicate the work of auditors, but to conduct a reasonable investigation. If their initial investigation leads them to question the accuracy of financial reporting, then the existence of an audit or a comfort letter will not excuse the failure to follow through with a subsequent investigation of the matter. If red flags arise from a reasonable investigation, underwriters will have to make sufficient inquiry to satisfy themselves as to the accuracy of the financial statements, and if unsatisfied, they must demand disclosure, withdraw from the underwriting process, or bear the risk of liability. ***

The Underwriter Defendants contend that they will be able to show at trial that the continuous due diligence that they performed with respect to WorldCom amounted to a reasonable investigation for both Offerings. This Opinion does not address the likelihood of that showing because the Underwriter Defendants have not moved for summary judgement on that ground. For that reason, it is also unnecessary to address their arguments about the difficulty of meeting the traditional standard for due diligence in the context of integrated disclosure and shelf registrations. In any event, the Underwriter Defendants have not shown that the prudent man standard in Section 11 has been diluted by any regulatory changes. The processes through which and the timing in which due diligence is performed have changed, but the ultimate test of reasonable conduct in the specific circumstances of an offering remains unchanged.

NOTES AND QUESTIONS

*1. **Alarm Bells?*** How worrisome is the *WorldCom* decision for underwriters sued under Section 11? What significance (if any) does the decision carry for other Section 11 defendants?

*2. **But the Information was "Publicly Available."*** The defendants argued that their inattention to the discrepancy between *WorldCom*'s E/R ratio and those of its competitors was irrelevant, since the information was "publicly available" and "no one else [had] announced a belief that it suggested the existence of an accounting fraud at WorldCom." Was the court right to reject this argument? Consider the following view, which draws upon the Efficient Capital Markets Hypothesis (ECMH) that you have encountered in previous Chapters:

> [T]he ECMH could certainly inform an analysis of whether publicly available information constituted a red flag. Is there a better epitome of a "prudent man in the management of his own property" than the consensus of market professionals reflected in the price of a stock traded in a well-developed market?***
>
> *** Certainly the court should at least have explained why it believes applying the ECMH in the context of the reasonable reliance standard is inappropriate instead of just dismissing it out of hand.

William K. Sjostrom, Jr., The Due Diligence Defense Under Section 11 of the Securities Act of 1933, 44 Brandeis L. J. 549, 606-07 (2006). Do you agree?

*3. **The Costs of Due Diligence.*** Who bears the costs of the simultaneous due diligence required of issuers, underwriters and auditors under Section 11? Do recent accounting scandals suggest that the gatekeepers are not taking their responsibilities seriously enough?

*4. **Due Diligence for Asset-Backed Securities.*** One cause of the 2008 financial crisis was inadequate due diligence undertaken in connection with offerings of mortgage-backed and other asset-backed securities (ABS). Congress responded with Section 945 of the Dodd-Frank Act, which directs the SEC to promulgate rules requiring issuers making registered offerings of ABS "to perform a review of the assets underlying" the ABS and "to disclose the nature of the review."

Complying with that directive, the SEC adopted Rule 193, which states that the review "must be designed to provide reasonable assurance that the disclosure *** is accurate in all material respects." Consider how to integrate Rule 193 with Section 11. That is, how (if at all) does the Rule's "reasonable assurance" phraseology affect the showing that non-issuer defendants must make to establish their due diligence?

In addition, Rule 193 gives issuers the choice of performing the review itself or retaining a third party to do it. A third party to whom the "findings and conclusions of the review are attributed *** must be named in the registration statement and consent to be named as an expert ***."

5. ***Rating Agencies as Underwriters in ABS Offerings?*** Normally one does not conceive of rating agencies as underwriters of the debt securities or preferred stock for which they provide a passive evaluation of credit risk. In the ABS market, however, rating agencies sometimes play a more active role. Thus, in *In re Lehman Bros. Mortgage-Backed Sec. Litig.*, __ F.3d __, 2011 WL 1778726 (2d Cir. 2011), the plaintiffs argued that the ratings agencies should be classified as underwriters because they helped to structure the mortgage pass through certificates in question. The Second Circuit rejected the argument:

> The plain language of the statute limits liability to persons who participate in the purchase, offer, or sale of securities for distribution. While such participation may be indirect as well as direct, the statute does not reach further to identify as underwriters persons who provide services that facilitate a securities offering, but who do not themselves participate in the statutorily specified distribution-related activities. ***
>
> Furthermore, expanding § 11 to cover the conduct of the Rating Agencies would contradict that section's specific enumeration of liable parties, which does not include a number of persons necessary to the creation of securities, such as banks that originated the underlying loans, traders who structured the transactions, or experts who did not consent to being named. See 15 U.S.C. § 77k(a). Because plaintiffs' theory would render these narrowly drawn categories meaningless and contradict well-settled canons of statutory construction, we decline to adopt it. Rather, we conclude that the mere structuring or creation of securities does not constitute participation in statutory underwriting.

Id. at *5, *13. Recall also from this Chapter's introductory material that ratings agencies are no longer exempt from expert liability under Section 11 in the wake of Congress's repeal of Rule 436(g).

PROBLEM 3-2

SEC reforms adopted in 2005 designate the largest securities issuers as "well-known seasoned issuers" (WKSIs) and give them various privileges, including the right to file a registration statement and sell the securities on the same day. Taking advantage of this particular privilege, of course, makes due diligence even more difficult to fulfill.

Mega Corporation is a WKSI. On July 7, 2010, it not only filed a registration statement but also sold the shares, as the recent SEC reforms allow. Not long afterwards, a Section 11 action was begun in connection with that offering, with Mega, its underwriters, and a number of its officers and directors named as defendants. The action was brought in a jurisdiction different from the one that heard *WorldCom* and alleged misrepresentations involving Mega's competitive situation.

Several of the individual Mega defendants have consulted you. They admitted that the offering process had been a mad scramble against time but claimed that they did the best they could under the circumstances of an exceedingly tight time-frame. Only in retrospect, they told you, did it occur to them that the description of Mega's competitive situation, accurate as of several weeks earlier, was actually out of date.

They have asked you two questions. One is whether the fact that SEC now allows WKSIs to file and sell on the very same day will help them establish the reasonableness of their conduct and hence their due diligence defenses. The other is what the implications for them of the *WorldCom* decision are likely to be. What will you tell them?

c. *Damages and Negative Causation*

Section 11(e) provides a formula for the calculation of damages that allows the plaintiff to recover:

> the difference between the amount paid for the security (not exceeding the price at which the security was offered to the public) and (1) the value thereof as of the time such suit was brought, or (2) the price at which such security shall have been disposed of in the market before suit, or (3) the price at which such security shall have been disposed of after suit but before judgment if such damages shall be less than [the damages specified in (1) above].

See *McMahan & Co. v. Wherehouse Entertainment, Inc.*, 65 F.3d 1044, 1048 (2d Cir. 1995) (noting that courts must "apply the prescribed formula in every section 11 case"). This formula must be read together with Section 11(g): "In no case shall the amount recoverable under this section exceed the price at which the security was offered to the public." See *Initial Public Offering Sec. Litig.*, 241 F. Supp. 2d 281, 347-51 (S.D.N.Y. 2003) (holding that plaintiffs who sold securities above the offering price lack right to sue under Section 11).

11(g) caps damages price at public offering price

So Ps who sell above IPO price have no Sec 11 standing

Section 11(e) also contains a so-called "negative causation" defense pursuant to which a defendant can reduce — or even eliminate entirely — the amount of damages he might otherwise owe:

> [I]f the defendant proves that any portion or all of such damages represents other than the depreciation in value of such security resulting from such part of the registration statement, with respect to which his liability is asserted, not being true or omitting to state a material fact required to be stated therein or necessary to make the statements therein not misleading, such portion of or all such damages shall not be recoverable.

Cf. *McMahon & Co.*, supra, 65 F.3d at 1048 (reversing the district court because it had not permitted the defendant to establish negative causation).

Consider the court's application of these provisions in the following decision.

AKERMAN v. ORYX COMMUNICATIONS, INC.

810 F.2d 336 (2d Cir. 1987)

THOMAS J. MESKILL, CIRCUIT JUDGE:

*** This case arises out of a June 30, 1981, initial public offering of securities by Oryx, a company planning to enter the business of manufacturing and marketing abroad video cassettes and video discs of feature films for home entertainment. Oryx filed a registration statement and an accompanying prospectus dated June 30, 1981 *** for a firm commitment offering of 700,000 units. Each unit sold for $4.75 and consisted of one share of common stock and one warrant to purchase an additional share of stock for $5.75 at a later date.

The prospectus contained an erroneous *pro forma* unaudited financial statement relating to the eight month period ending March 31, 1981. It reported net sales of $931,301, net income of $211,815, and earnings of seven cents per share. Oryx, however, had incorrectly posted a substantial transaction by its subsidiary to March instead of April when Oryx actually received the subject sale's revenues. The prospectus, therefore, overstated earnings for the eight month period. Net sales in that period actually totaled $766,301, net income $94,529, and earnings per share three cents.

Oryx's price had declined to four dollars per unit by October 12, 1981, the day before Oryx revealed the prospectus misstatement to the SEC. The unit price had further declined to $3.25 by November 9, 1981, the day before Oryx disclosed the misstatement to the public. After public disclosure, the price of Oryx rose and reached $3.50 by November 25, 1981, the day this suit commenced. ***

Section 11(a) of the 1933 Act imposes civil liability on the signatories of a registration statement if the registration statement contains a material untruth or omission of which a "person acquiring [the registered] security" had no knowledge at the time of the purchase. Plaintiffs in the Akermans' situation, if successful, would be entitled to recover the difference between the original purchase price and the value of the stock at the time of suit. A defendant may, under section 11(e), reduce his liability by proving that the depreciation in value resulted from factors other than the material misstatement in the registration statement. A defendant's burden in attempting to reduce his liability has been characterized as the burden of "negative causation." *Beecher v. Able,* 435 F. Supp. 397, 409 (S.D.N.Y. 1975).

The district court determined that plaintiffs established a prima facie case under section 11(a) by demonstrating that the prospectus error was material "as a theoretical matter." The court, however, granted defendants' motion for summary judgment on damages under section 11(e), stating: "[Defendants] have carried their heavy burden of proving that the [Oryx stock price] decline was caused by factors other than the matters misstated in the registration statement." The precise issue on appeal, therefore, is whether defendants carried their burden of negative causation under section 11(e).

Defendants' heavy burden reflects Congress' desire to allocate the risk of uncertainty to the defendants in these cases. Defendants' burden, however, is not insurmountable; section 11(e) expressly creates an affirmative defense of disproving causation. ***

The misstatement resulted from an innocent bookkeeping error whereby Oryx misposted a sale by its subsidiary to March instead of April. Oryx received the sale's proceeds less than one month after the reported date. The prospectus, moreover, expressly stated that Oryx "expect[ed] that [the subsidiary's] sales will decline." Indeed, Morris Akerman conceded that he understood this disclaimer to warn that Oryx expected the subsidiary's business to decline.

Thus, although the misstatement may have been "theoretically material," when it is considered in the context of the prospectus' pessimistic forecast of the performance of Oryx's subsidiary, the misstatement was not likely to cause a stock price decline. Compare *Escott v. BarChris Construction Corp.*, 283 F.Supp. 643 (S.D.N.Y. 1968) (failure to disclose facts clearly indicating impending financial demise). Indeed, the public not only did not react adversely to disclosure of the misstatement, Oryx's price actually *rose* somewhat after public disclosure of the error.

The applicable section 11(e) formula for calculating damages is "the difference between the amount paid for the security (not exceeding the price at which the security was offered to the public) and ... the value thereof as of the time such suit was brought." The relevant events and stock prices are:

Date	*Event*	*Orynx Stock Price*
June 30, 1981	Initial public offering	$4.75
October 15, 1981	Disclosure of error to SEC	$4.00
November 10, 1981	Disclosure of error to public	$3.25
November 25, 1981	Date of suit	$3.50

The price decline before disclosure may not be charged to defendants. See *Beecher v. Able*, 435 F. Supp. 397, 407 (S.D.N.Y.1975) (price decline before misstatement revealed not attributable to defendants under section 11(e)); *Fox v. Glickman Corp.*, 253 F. Supp. 1005, 1010 (S.D.N.Y.1966) (same). At first blush, damages would appear to be zero because there was no depreciation in Oryx's value between the time of public disclosure and the time of suit.

The Akermans contended at trial, however, that the relevant disclosure date was the date of disclosure to the SEC and not to the public. Under plaintiffs' theory, damages would equal the price decline subsequent to October 15, 1981, which amount to fifty cents per share. Plaintiffs attempted to support this theory by alleging that insiders privy to the SEC disclosure — Oryx's officers, attorneys and accountants, and underwriters and SEC officials — sold Oryx shares and thereby deflated its price before public disclosure. *** After extensive discovery, however, plaintiffs produced absolutely no evidence of insider trading. Plaintiffs' submissions and oral argument before us do not press this theory. ***

The district court invited statistical studies from both sides to clarify the causation issue. Defendants produced a statistical analysis of the stocks of the one hundred companies that went public contemporaneously with Oryx. The study tracked the stocks' performances for the period between June 30, 1981 (initial public offering date) and November 25, 1981 (date of suit). The study indicated that Oryx performed at the exact statistical median of these stocks and that several issues suffered equal or greater losses than did Oryx during this period. Defendants produced an additional study which indicated that Oryx stock "behaved over the entire period ... consistent[ly] with its own inherent variation."

Plaintiffs offered the following rebuttal evidence. During the period between SEC disclosure and public disclosure, Oryx stock decreased nineteen percent while the over-the-counter (OTC) composite index rose five percent (the first study). During this period, therefore, the OTC composite index outperformed Oryx by twenty-four percentage points. Plaintiffs also produced a study indicating that for the time period between SEC disclosure and one week after public disclosure, eighty-two of the one hundred new issues analyzed in the defendants' study outperformed Oryx's stock.

Plaintiffs' first study compared Oryx's performance to the performance of the OTC index in order to rebut a comparison offered by defendants to prove that Oryx's price decline resulted not from the misstatement but rather from an overall market decline. As previously stated, defendants' comparison indicated that the OTC index generally declined for the period between Oryx's offering date and the date of suit. The parties' conflicting comparisons, however, lack credibility because they fail to reflect any of the countless variables that might affect the stock price performance of a single company. ***

The studies comparing Oryx's performance to the other one hundred companies that went public in May and June of 1981 are similarly flawed. The studies do not evaluate the performance of Oryx stock in relation to the stock of companies possessing any characteristic in common with Oryx, e.g., product, technology, profitability, assets or countless other variables which influence stock prices, except the contemporaneous initial offering dates.

Perhaps more important, the Akermans' study of the one hundred new issues focuses on a time frame which controverts one of their own theories explaining the public's failure to react adversely to disclosure. The Akermans argue that the thin market in Oryx stock prevented immediate public reaction to disclosure of the prospectus error. Their study, however, measures Oryx's performance from SEC disclosure to *one week* after public disclosure. A thin market, according to the Akermans' own explanation, would not reflect the impact of bad news in such a short time period (one week). This internal inconsistency seriously undercuts the probative value of the Akermans' study.

Finally, we note that this time period drew its relevance from the Akermans' theory that insider trading deflated Oryx's price during this period. As previously stated, this theory has no support even after extensive discovery and is not pressed on appeal.

Granting the Akermans every reasonable, favorable inference, the battle of the studies is at best equivocal; the studies do not meaningfully point in one direction or the other. ***

Defendants met their burden, as set forth in section 11(e), by establishing that the misstatement was barely material and that the public failed to react adversely to its disclosure. With the case in this posture, the plaintiffs had to come forward with "specific facts showing that there is a genuine issue for trial." *Anderson* [*v. Liberty Lobby, Inc.*, 106 S. Ct. 2505, 2511 (1986]). Despite extensive discovery, plaintiffs completely failed to produce any evidence, other than unreliable and sometimes inconsistent statistical studies and theories, suggesting that Oryx's price decline actually resulted from the misstatement. Summary judgment was properly granted. ***

NOTES AND QUESTIONS

1. ***Allocating the Burden of Proving Negative Causation.*** Section 11(e) places the burden of proving negative causation on the defendant. Did the *Ackerman* court comply? If not, why not? Did the court's allocation of the burden of proof on this issue affect the result?

2. ***Negative Causation vs. Loss Causation Under Rule 10b-5.*** Recall that Rule 10b-5 plaintiffs must satisfy the loss causation requirement set forth in Exchange Act Section 21D(b)(4). See supra Chapter 2.F.2. What are the differences between Rule 10b-5's loss causation requirement and Section 11's negative causation defense?

3. ***Theoretical Materiality.*** In *Akerman*, the court described the misstatement at issue as "theoretically material" but nonetheless as "not likely to cause a stock price decline." Can information be material on the one hand but have no impact on the market price on the other hand? Cf. supra Chapter 2.B.1 (discussing the definition of materiality).

4. ***To Sell or Not to Sell.*** Look again at Section 11(e)'s formula for calculating damages. Once a plaintiff files her Section 11 action, is she best advised to sell or retain her shares?

5. ***Focusing on "Value."*** Note that Section 11(e) looks to "the difference between the amount paid for the security" and "the *value* thereof at the time such suit was brought." (emphasis added). Congress's use of the word "value" is significant:

> Congress' [s] use of the term "value," as distinguished from the terms "amount paid" and "price" indicates that, under certain circumstances, the market price may not adequately reflect the security's value. See *Beecher v. Able*, 435 F.Supp. 397, 404-05 (S.D.N.Y 1977) (adjusting the market price to account for panic selling in the market that was unrelated to the misrepresentations in the registration statements); *Grossman v. Waste Management, Inc.*, 589 F.Supp. 395, 415-16 (N.D.Ill.1984) (holding that subsequent fraud on the market may make market price an unreliable indication of the security's value). However, instances where the market price of a security will be different from its value are "unusual and rare" situations. *** Moreover, even where market price is not completely reliable, it serves as a good starting point in determining value. See *Beecher*, 435 F.Supp. at 406.

McMahan & Co. v. Wherehouse Entertainment, Inc., 65 F.3d 1044, 1048-49 (2d Cir. 1995).

6. Joint and Several Liability and Contribution. Most Section 11 defendants are jointly and severally liable for the damages that may be awarded. See Section 11(f)(1). Under this arrangement, any defendant may be liable for all the damages, but may thereafter obtain contribution from anyone who, "if sued separately, would have been liable to make the same payment, unless the person who has become liable was, and the other was not, guilty of fraudulent misrepresentation." Id. Two categories of defendants, however, are treated differently: underwriters and outside directors.

The exception for underwriters is set forth in Section 11(e). That provision states that unless an underwriter received a benefit from the issuer not received by the other underwriters, his liability under Section 11 is capped at "the total price at which the securities underwritten by him and distributed to the public were offered to the public." Thus, in a $300 million offering, an underwriter who sold $50 million in securities would be liable only for $50 million.

The exception for outside directors — set forth in Section 11(f)(2)(A) — was added by the Private Securities Litigation Reform Act of 1995 (PSLRA). Pursuant to this provision, a Section 11 defendant who is an outside director is subject to proportionate (rather than joint and several) liability so long as he did not act "knowingly." See generally Chapter 2.G.2 (discussing proportionate liability in the context of Rule 10b-5).

Professor Horwich has questioned the wisdom of giving outside directors special treatment:

> [I]f the original intent of imposing full joint and several liability was to induce persons who are exposed under section 11 to conduct sufficient due diligence, there is insufficient reason to grant to outside directors – persons with independence who may be seen as more likely to serve as guardians of the public – a dispensation that could have the effect of imposing a disproportionate burden on all other (non-expert) individuals.

Allan Horwich, Section 11 of the Securities Act: The Cornerstone Needs Some Tuckpointing, 58 Bus. Law. 1, 30 (2002). Do you agree?

---

2. *Section 12(a)(2)*

Section 12(a)(2) creates an express private action for securities purchasers against their sellers for material misstatements and omissions made "by means of a prospectus" or, in some instances, orally. It reads as follows:

> Any person who — ***
>
> (2) offers or sells a security (whether or not exempted by the provisions of section 3, other than paragraphs (2) and (14) of subsection (a) thereof), by the use of any means or instruments of transportation or communication in interstate commerce or of the mails, by means of a prospectus or oral communication, which includes an untrue statement of a material fact or omits to state a material fact necessary in order to make the statements, in the light of the circumstances under which they were made, not misleading (the

purchaser not knowing of such untruth or omission), and who shall not sustain the burden of proof that he did not know, and in the exercise of reasonable care could not have known, of such untruth or omission, shall be liable *** to the person purchasing such security from him, who may sue either at law or in equity in any court of competent jurisdiction, to recover the consideration paid for such security with interest thereon, less the amount of any income received thereon, upon the tender of such security, or for damages if he no longer owns the security.

Prior to 1995, Section 12(a)(2) was codified as Section 12(2) and some courts continue to refer to it in that fashion.

Like Section 11, Section 12(a)(2) waters down the traditional elements of common law fraud. Thus, under Section 12(a)(2), the plaintiff does not have to prove scienter or causation. Nor does she have to prove reliance (similar to Section 11, except that Section 11 does require the plaintiff to prove reliance in the rare circumstance noted earlier).

Section 12(a)(2) provides the defendant with a defense of reasonable care (which we will contrast with the due diligence defenses under Section 11). The defendant may also reduce, or conceivably avoid, liability based on negative causation (see Section 12(b)).

Sections 12(a)(2) and 11 overlap only in part. To be sure, both apply to registered offerings (although the misleading statement must appear in "a prospectus or oral communication" under Section 12(a)(2) but in the registration statement under Section 11). Unlike Section 11, however, Section12(a)(2) also applies to certain exempt offerings as well as to offerings in violation of Section 5 (i.e., offerings that were neither exempted nor registered). In addition, Sections 12(a)(2) and 11 involve different defendants. Indeed, some Section 11 defendants cannot be sued under Section 12(a)(2), just as some Section 12(a)(2) defendants cannot be sued under Section 11.

We begin with two Supreme Court decisions. The first restricts the transactional reach of Section 12(a)(2) based on its interpretation of the statutory phrase "by means of a prospectus or oral communication." The second addresses who may be sued. We then consider the reasonable care defense, damages, and negative causation.

a. "By Means of a Prospectus or Oral Communication"

The following controversial decision, which split the Supreme Court 5-4, held Section 12(a)(2) inapplicable to private offerings as well as to secondary market trading. Prior to this decision, Section 12(a)(2) had been widely regarded as applicable to both.

GUSTAFSON v. ALLOYD CORPORATON

513 U.S. 561 (1995)

JUSTICE ANTHONY M. KENNEDY:

Under § 12(2) of the Securities Act of 1933 buyers have an express cause of action for rescission against sellers who make material misstatements or omissions "by means of a prospectus." The question presented is whether this right of rescission extends to a private, secondary transaction, on the theory that recitations in the purchase agreement are part of a "prospectus."

I

Petitioners Gustafson, McLean, and Butler (collectively Gustafson) were in 1989 the sole shareholders of Alloyd, Inc., a manufacturer of plastic packaging and automatic heat sealing equipment. Alloyd was formed, and its stock was issued, in 1961. In 1989, Gustafson decided to sell Alloyd and engaged KPMG Peat Marwick to find a buyer. In response to information distributed by KPMG, Wind Point Partners II, L. P., agreed to buy substantially all of the issued and outstanding stock through Alloyd Holdings, Inc., a new corporation formed to effect the sale of Alloyd's stock. The shareholders of Alloyd Holdings were Wind Point and a number of individual investors.

In preparation for negotiating the contract with Gustafson, Wind Point undertook an extensive analysis of the company, relying in part on a formal business review prepared by KPMG. Alloyd's practice was to take inventory at year's end, so Wind Point and KPMG considered taking an earlier inventory to use in determining the purchase price. In the end they did not do so, relying instead on certain estimates and including provisions for adjustments after the transaction closed.

On December 20, 1989, Gustafson and Alloyd Holdings executed a contract of sale. Alloyd Holdings agreed to pay Gustafson and his coshareholders $18,709,000 for the sale of the stock plus a payment of $2,122,219, which reflected the estimated increase in Alloyd's net worth from the end of the previous year, the last period for which hard financial data were available. Article IV of the purchase agreement, entitled "Representations and Warranties of the Sellers," included assurances that the company's financial statements "present fairly ... the Company's financial condition" and that between the date of the latest balance sheet and the date the agreement was executed "there ha[d] been no material adverse change in ... [Alloyd's] financial condition." The contract also provided that if the year-end audit and financial statements revealed a variance between estimated and actual increased value, the disappointed party would receive an adjustment.

The year-end audit of Alloyd revealed that Alloyd's actual earnings for 1989 were lower than the estimates relied upon by the parties in negotiating the adjustment amount of $2,122,219. Under the contract, the buyers had a right to recover an adjustment amount of $815,000 from the sellers. Nevertheless, on February 11, 1991, the newly formed company (now called Alloyd Co., the same as the original company) and Wind Point brought suit in the United States District Court for the Northern District of Illinois, seeking outright rescission of the contract under § 12(2) of the Securities Act of 1933 (1933 Act or Act). Alloyd (the new company) claimed that statements made by Gustafson and his coshareholders regarding the financial data of their company were inaccurate, rendering untrue the representations and warranties contained in the contract. The buyers further alleged that the contract of sale was a "prospectus," so that any misstatements contained in the agreement gave rise to liability under § 12(2) of the 1933 Act. Pursuant to the adjustment clause, the defendants remitted to the purchasers $815,000 plus interest, but the adjustment did not cause the purchasers to drop the lawsuit.

Relying on the decision of the Court of Appeals for the Third Circuit in *Ballay v. Legg Mason Wood Walker, Inc.*, 925 F.2d 682 (1991), the District Court granted Gustafson's motion for summary judgment, holding "that section 12(2) claims can only arise out of the initial stock offerings." Although the sellers were the controlling shareholders of the original company, the District Court concluded that the private sale agreement "cannot be compared to an initial offering" because "the purchasers in this case had direct access to financial and other company documents, and had the opportunity to inspect the seller's property."

On review, the Court of Appeals for the Seventh Circuit vacated the District Court's judgment and remanded for further consideration in light of that court's intervening decision in *Pacific Dunlop Holdings Inc. v. Allen & Co. Inc.*, 993 F.2d 578 (1993). In *Pacific Dunlop* the court reasoned that the inclusion of the term "communication" in the Act's definition of prospectus meant that the term "prospectus" was defined "very broadly" to include all written communications that offered the sale of a security. Id., at 582. Rejecting the view of the Court of Appeals for the Third Circuit in *Ballay*, the Court of Appeals decided that § 12(2)'s right of action for rescission "applies to any communication which offers any security for sale ... including the stock purchase agreement in the present case." 993 F.2d, at 595. We granted certiorari to resolve this Circuit conflict, and we now reverse.

II

*** As this case reaches us, we must assume that the stock purchase agreement contained material misstatements of fact made by the sellers and that Gustafson would not sustain its burden of proving due care. On these assumptions, Alloyd would have a right to obtain rescission if those misstatements were made "by means of a prospectus or oral communication." The Courts of Appeals agree that the phrase "oral communication" is restricted to oral communications that relate to a prospectus. See *Pacific Dunlop*, supra, at 588; *Ballay*, supra, at 688. The determinative question, then, is whether the contract between Alloyd and Gustafson is a "prospectus" as the term is used in the 1933 Act.

Alloyd argues that "prospectus" is defined in a broad manner, broad enough to encompass the contract between the parties. This argument is echoed by the dissents. Gustafson, by contrast, maintains that prospectus in the 1933 Act means a communication soliciting the public to purchase securities from the issuer.

Three sections of the 1933 Act are critical in resolving the definitional question on which the case turns: § 2(10), which defines a prospectus; § 10, which sets forth the information that must be contained in a prospectus; and § 12, which imposes liability based on misstatements in a prospectus. In seeking to interpret the term "prospectus," we adopt the premise that the term should be construed, if possible, to give it a consistent meaning throughout the Act. That principle follows from our duty to construe statutes, not isolated provisions.

A

We begin with § 10. It provides, in relevant part:

> Except to the extent otherwise permitted or required pursuant to this subsection or subsections (c), (d), or (e) of this section —
>
> (1) a prospectus relating to a security other than a security issued by a foreign government or political subdivision thereof, shall contain the information contained in the registration statement ...;
>
> (2) a prospectus relating to a security issued by a foreign government or political subdivision thereof shall contain the information contained in the registration statement...

Section 10 does not provide that some prospectuses must contain the information contained in the registration statement. Save for the explicit and well-defined exemptions for securities listed under § 3 (exempting certain classes of securities from the coverage of the Act), its mandate is unqualified: "[A] prospectus ... shall contain the information contained in the registration statement."

Although § 10 does not define what a prospectus is, it does instruct us what a prospectus cannot be if the Act is to be interpreted as a symmetrical and coherent regulatory scheme, one in which the operative words have a consistent meaning throughout. There is no dispute that the contract in this case was not required to contain the information contained in a registration statement and that no statutory exemption was required to take the document out of § 10's coverage. It follows that the contract is not a prospectus under § 10. That does not mean that a document ceases to be a prospectus whenever it omits a required piece of information. It does mean that a document is not a prospectus within the meaning of that section if, absent an exemption, it need not comply with § 10's requirements in the first place.

An examination of § 10 reveals that, whatever else "prospectus" may mean, the term is confined to a document that, absent an overriding exemption, must include the "information contained in the registration statement." By and large, only public offerings by an issuer of a security, or by controlling shareholders of an issuer, require the preparation and filing of registration statements. It follows, we conclude, that a prospectus under § 10 is confined to documents related to public offerings by an issuer or its controlling shareholders.

This much (the meaning of prospectus in § 10) seems not to be in dispute. Where the courts are in disagreement is with the implications of this proposition for the entirety of the Act, and for § 12 in particular. We conclude that the term "prospectus" must have the same meaning under §§ 10 and 12. In so holding, we do not, as the dissent by Justice Ginsburg suggests, make the mistake of treating § 10 as a definitional section. Instead, we find in § 10 guidance and instruction for giving the term a consistent meaning throughout the Act. ***

The conclusion that prospectus has the same meaning, and refers to the same types of communications (public offers by an issuer or its controlling shareholders), in both §§ 10 and 12 is reinforced by an examination of the structure of the 1933 Act. Sections 4 and 5 of the Act together require a seller to file a registration statement and to issue a prospectus for certain defined types of sales (public offerings by an issuer, through an underwriter). Sections 7 and 10 of the Act set forth the information required in the registration statement and the prospectus. Section 11 provides for liability on account of false registration statements; § 12(2) for liability based on misstatements in prospectuses. Following the most natural and symmetrical reading, just as the liability imposed by § 11 flows from the requirements imposed by §§ 5 and 7 providing for the filing and content of registration statements, the liability imposed by § 12(2) cannot attach unless there is an obligation to distribute the prospectus in the first place (or unless there is an exemption). ***

The primary innovation of the 1933 Act was the creation of federal duties — for the most part, registration and disclosure obligations — in connection with public offerings. We are reluctant to conclude that § 12(2) creates vast additional liabilities that are quite independent of the new substantive obligations the Act imposes. It is more reasonable to interpret the liability provisions of the 1933 Act as designed for the primary purpose of providing remedies for violations of the obligations it had created. Indeed, §§ 11 and 12(1) — the statutory neighbors of § 12(2) — afford remedies for violations of those obligations. ***

On the other hand, accepting Alloyd's argument that any written offer is a prospectus under § 12 would require us to hold that the word "prospectus" in § 12 refers to a broader set of communications than the same term in § 10. *** Nowhere in the statute, however, do the terms "formal prospectus" or "informal prospectus" appear. Instead, the Act uses one term — "prospectus" — throughout. In disagreement with the Court of Appeals and the dissenting opinions, we cannot accept the conclusion that this single operative word means one thing in one section of the Act and something quite different in another. The dissenting opinions' resort to terms not found in the Act belies the claim of fidelity to the text of the statute.

Alloyd, as well as Justice Thomas in his dissent, respond that if Congress had intended § 12(2) to govern only initial public offerings, it would have been simple for Congress to have referred to the § 4 exemptions in § 12(2). The argument gets the presumption backwards. Had Congress meant the term "prospectus" in § 12(2) to have a different meaning than the same term in § 10, that is when one would have expected Congress to have been explicit. Congressional silence cuts against, not in favor of, Alloyd's argument. The burden should be on the proponents of the view that the term "prospectus" means one thing in § 12 and another in § 10 to adduce strong textual support for that conclusion. And Alloyd adduces none.

B

Alloyd's contrary argument rests to a significant extent on § 2(10), or, to be more precise, on one word of that section. Section 2(10) provides that "[t]he term 'prospectus' means any prospectus, notice, circular, advertisement, letter, or communication, written or by radio or television, which offers any security for sale or confirms the sale of any security." Concentrating on the word "communication," Alloyd argues that any written communication that offers a security for sale is a "prospectus." Inserting its definition into § 12(2), Alloyd insists that a material misstatement in any communication offering a security for sale gives rise to an action for rescission, without proof of fraud by the seller or reliance by the purchaser. In Alloyd's view, § 2(10) gives the term "prospectus" a capacious definition that, although incompatible with § 10, nevertheless governs in § 12.

The flaw in Alloyd's argument, echoed in the dissenting opinions, is its reliance on one word of the definitional section in isolation. To be sure, § 2(10) defines a prospectus as, *inter alia,* a "communication, written or by radio or television, which offers any security for sale or confirms the sale of any security." The word "communication," however, on which Alloyd's entire argument rests, is but one word in a list, a word Alloyd reads altogether out of context. ***

There is a better reading. From the terms "prospectus, notice, circular, advertisement, [or] letter," it is apparent that the list refers to documents of wide dissemination. In a similar manner, the list includes communications "by radio or television," but not face-to-face or telephonic conversations. Inclusion of the term "communication" in that list suggests that it too refers to a public communication.

When the 1933 Act was drawn and adopted, the term "prospectus" was well understood to refer to a document soliciting the public to acquire securities from the issuer. See Black's Law Dictionary 959 (2d ed. 1910) (defining "prospectus" as a "document published by a company ... or by persons acting as its agents or assignees, setting forth the nature and objects of an issue of shares ... and inviting the public to subscribe to the issue"). In this respect, the word "prospectus" is a term of art, which accounts for congressional confidence in employing what might otherwise be regarded as a partial circularity in the formal, statutory definition. See [Section 2 (10)] ("The term 'prospectus' means any prospectus ..."). The use of the term "prospectus" to refer to public solicitations explains as well Congress' decision in § 12(2) to grant buyers a right to rescind without proof of reliance.

The list of terms in § 2(10) prevents a seller of stock from avoiding liability by calling a soliciting document something other than a prospectus, but it does not compel the conclusion that Alloyd urges us to reach and that the dissenting opinions adopt. Instead, the term "written communication" must be read in context to refer to writings that, from a functional standpoint, are similar to the terms "notice, circular, [and] advertisement." The term includes communications held out to the public at large but that might have been thought to be outside the other words in the definitional section. ***

D

It is understandable that Congress would provide buyers with a right to rescind, without proof of fraud or reliance, as to misstatements contained in a document prepared with care, following well-established procedures relating to investigations with due diligence and in the context of a public offering by an issuer or its controlling shareholders. It is not plausible to infer that Congress created this extensive liability for every casual communication between buyer and seller in the secondary market. It is often difficult, if not altogether impractical, for those engaged in casual communications not to omit some fact that would, if included, qualify the accuracy of a statement. Under Alloyd's view any casual communication between buyer and seller in the aftermarket could give rise to an action for rescission, with no evidence of fraud on the part of the seller or reliance on the part of the buyer. In many instances buyers in practical effect would have an option to rescind, impairing the stability of past transactions where neither fraud nor detrimental reliance on misstatements or omissions occurred. We find no basis for interpreting the statute to reach so far. ***

In sum, the word "prospectus" is a term of art referring to a document that describes a public offering of securities by an issuer or controlling shareholder. The contract of sale, and its recitations, were not held out to the public and were not a prospectus as the term is used in the 1933 Act.

The judgment of the Court of Appeals is reversed, and the case is remanded for further proceedings consistent with this opinion.

JUSTICE CLARENCE THOMAS, WITH WHOM JUSTICE SCALIA, JUSTICE GINSBURG, AND JUSTICE BREYER JOIN, DISSENTING:

From the majority's opinion, one would not realize that § 12(2) *** was involved in this case until one had read more than halfway through. In contrast to the majority's approach of interpreting the statute, I believe the proper method is to begin with the provision actually involved in this case, § 12(2), and then turn to the 1933 Act's definitional section, § 2(10), before consulting the structure of the Act as a whole. Because the result of this textual analysis shows that § 12(2) applies to secondary or private sales of a security as well as to initial public offerings, I dissent. ***

There is no reason to seek the meaning of "prospectus" outside of the 1933 Act, because Congress has supplied just such a definition in § 2(10). That definition is extraordinarily broad:

> When used in this subchapter, unless the context otherwise requires —
>
> . . . (10) The term 'prospectus' means any prospectus, notice, circular, advertisement, letter, or communication, written or by radio or television, which offers any security for sale or confirms the sale of any security.

For me, the breadth of these terms forecloses the majority's position that "prospectus" applies only in the context of initial distributions of securities. Indeed, § 2(10)'s inclusion of a prospectus as only one of the many different documents that qualify as a "prospectus" for statutory purposes indicates that Congress intended "prospectus" to be more than a mere "term of art." Likewise, Congress' extension of prospectus to include documents that merely *confirm* the sale of a security underscores Congress' intent to depart from the term's ordinary meaning. Section 2(10)'s definition obviously concerns different types of communications rather than different types of transactions. Congress left the job of exempting certain classes of transactions to §§ 3 and 4, not to § 2(10). We should use § 2(10) to define "prospectus" for the 1933 Act, rather than, as the majority does, use the 1933 Act to define "prospectus" for § 2(10). ***

The majority's analysis of § 12(2) is motivated by its policy preferences. Underlying its reasoning is the assumption that Congress could never have intended to impose liability on sellers engaged in secondary transactions. Adopting a chiding tone, the majority states that "[w]e are reluctant to conclude that § 12(2) creates vast additional liabilities that are quite independent of the new substantive obligations that the Act imposes." Yet, this is exactly what Congress did in § 17(a) of the 1933 Act as well as in § 10(b) of the 1934 Act. Later, the majority says: "It is not plausible to infer that Congress created this extensive liability for every casual communication between buyer and seller in the secondary market." It is not the usual practice of this Court to require Congress to explain why it has chosen to pursue a certain policy. Our job simply is to apply the policy, not to question it.

*** The majority is concerned that a contrary reading would have a drastic impact on the thousands of private and secondary transactions by imposing new liabilities and new transaction costs. But the majority forgets that we are only enforcing *Congress'* decision to impose such standards of conduct and remedies upon sellers. If the majority believes that § 12(2)'s requirements are too burdensome for the securities markets, it must rely upon the other branches of Government to limit the 1933 Act.

Unfortunately, the majority's decision to pursue its policy preferences comes at the price of disrupting the process of statutory interpretation. *** I doubt that the majority would read in so narrow and peculiar a fashion most other statutes, particularly one intended to restrict causes of action in securities cases. ***

JUSTICE RUTH BADER GINSBURG, WITH WHOM JUSTICE BREYER JOINS, DISSENTING:

A seller's misrepresentation made "by means of a prospectus or oral communication" is actionable under § 12(2) of the Securities Act of 1933. To limit the scope of this civil liability provision, the Court maintains that a communication qualifies as a prospectus only if made during a public offering.[1] Communications during either secondary trading or a private placement are not "prospectuses," the Court declares, and thus are not covered by § 12(2). ***

To construe a legislatively defined term, courts usually start with the defining section. Section 2(10) defines prospectus capaciously as "any prospectus, notice, circular, advertisement, letter, or communication, written or by radio or television, which offers any security for sale or confirms the sale of any security." The items listed in the defining provision, notably "letters" and "communications," are common in private and secondary sales, as well as in public offerings. The § 2(10) definition thus does not confine the § 12(2) term "prospectus" to public offerings.

The Court bypasses § 2(10), and the solid support it gives the Court of Appeals' disposition. Instead of beginning at the beginning, by first attending to the definition section, the Court starts with § 10, a substantive provision. The Court correctly observes that the term "prospectus" has a circumscribed meaning in that context. A prospectus within the contemplation of § 10 is a formal document, typically a document composing part of a registration statement; a § 10 prospectus, all agree, appears only in public offerings. The Court then

1. I understand the Court's definition of a public offering to encompass both transactions that must be registered under § 5, and transactions that would have been registered had the securities involved not qualified for exemption under § 3.

proceeds backward; it reads into the literally and logically prior definition section, § 2(10), the meaning "prospectus" has in § 10.

To justify its backward reading — proceeding from § 10 to § 2(10) and not the other way round — the Court states that it "cannot accept the conclusion that [the operative word 'prospectus'] means one thing in one section of the Act and something quite different in another." Our decisions, however, constantly recognize that "a characterization fitting in certain contexts may be unsuitable in others." *NationsBank of N.C., N.A. v. Variable Annuity Life Ins. Co.*, [513 U.S. 251, 262 (1995)]. ***

According "prospectus" discrete meanings in § 10 and § 12(2) is consistent with Congress' specific instruction in § 2 that definitions apply "unless the context otherwise requires." As the Court of Appeals construed the Act, § 2(10)'s definition of "prospectus" governs § 12(2), which accommodates without strain the definition's broad reach; by contrast, the specific context of § 10 requires a correspondingly specific reading of "prospectus." ***

Most provisions of the Securities Act govern only public offerings, and the legislative history pertaining to the Act as a whole shares this orientation. Section 17(a) of the Act, however, is not limited to public offerings; that enforcement provision, this Court has recognized, also covers secondary trading. See *United States v. Naftalin*, 441 U.S. 768 (1979). The drafting history is at least consistent with the conclusion that § 12(2), like § 17(a), is not limited to public offerings. ***

In light of the text, drafting history, and longstanding scholarly and judicial understanding of § 12(2), I conclude that § 12(2) applies to a private resale of securities. If adjustment is in order, as the Court's opinion powerfully suggests it is, Congress is equipped to undertake the alteration. Accordingly, I dissent from the Court's opinion and judgment.

NOTES AND QUESTIONS

1. ***A Failing Grade in Statutory Construction?*** To ascertain the meaning of "prospectus," the Court focused its attention on the use of that term in Section 10 rather than on the statutory definition in Section 2(a)(10). Commentators have been thunderously critical. See, e.g., Stephen M. Bainbridge, Securities Act Section 12(2) After the *Gustafson* Debacle, 50 Bus. Law. 1231, 1231-32 (1995) (describing *Gustafson* as "the most poorly-reasoned, blatantly results-driven, securities opinion in recent memory"); Ted J. Fiflis, *Gustafson v. Alloyd Co., Inc.*: Judicial vs. Legislative Power, 23 Sec. Reg. L. J. 423, 425 (1996) (observing that "[t]he reasoning used by the majority *** is so flawed that its full implications will not be known for some time"); Kimberly D. Krawiec, *Gustafson v. Alloyd Co.*: The Wrong Decision, But It Is Still Business as Usual in the Securities Markets, 31 Tulsa L.J. 509, 514 (1996) (maintaining that *Gustafson* "violates nearly every rule of statutory construction"). Are the commentators correct in their assertions? Or is the Court's methodology defensible?

2. ***Section 12(a)(2) and "Public Offerings."*** *Gustafson* tells us that Section 12(a)(2) applies to "public offerings," but does not define the boundaries of that category. Certainly, it includes registered offerings as well as illegal offerings that were neither registered nor exempt from registration. But what about exempt offerings? (In thinking about this question, you may wish to reread the overview of registration exemptions in Chapter 1.A.1.b).

Two points are relevant at the outset. First, offerings are presumably not "public" if they qualify as a so-called "private offering" under Securities Act Section 4(2) (exempting from registration "transactions by an issuer not involving any public offering"). Cf. *Yung v. Lee*, 432 F.3d 142, 148 (2d Cir. 2005) (collecting cases to this effect). Due to a landmark Supreme Court decision, Section 4(2) is available only when the offerees have "access to the kind of information which registration would disclose" as well as the capacity "to fend for themselves." *SEC v. Ralston Purina Co.*, 346 U.S. 119, 125-27 (1953). Second, it is important to notice that *Gustafson*'s majority and dissenting opinions both suggest that the "public offering" category includes at least some offerings made pursuant to the Section 3 exemptions. Where in the opinions do these suggestions appear?

These preliminary points give rise to two alternative approaches – a "bright line" approach and a "functional" approach. As you examine these approaches, ask yourself which seems more consistent with *Gustafson*. Likewise consider which makes more sense from a policy standpoint.

Bright Line Approach. Under the "bright line" approach, Section 12(a)(2) embraces offerings exempt under Section 3 (except for subsections (2) and (14) thereof, excluded on the face of Section 12(a)(2)) but not those exempt under Section 4. Offerings exempt under Section 3 would include Section 3's progeny, such as Rule 147, Regulation A, and Rules 504 and 505 of Regulation D. Similarly, offerings exempt under Section 4 would include Section 4's progeny, such as Rule 506 of Regulation D.

Functional Approach. Under the "functional" approach, the statutory source of the exemption does not necessarily carry the day. The key is instead whether the offering satisfies the Section 4(2) exemption, even if it also satisfies a Section 3 exemption. Thus, Section 12(a)(2) would not apply to an offering exempted by Section 3 if the offering simultaneously satisfied Section 4(2). On the other hand, the functional approach may conceivably enable Section 12(a)(2) to reach a Rule 506 offering if the offering did not satisfy Section 4(2) absent the Rule 506 safe harbor. Such a situation might arise, for example, when a purchaser was an accredited investor based on net worth but failed to meet the *Ralston Purina* criteria.

3. ***Private Offerings Marketed Pursuant to A Registration Statement.*** Suppose that an issuer markets a private offering by using a prospectus from a recent registered offering. Would the use of such prospectus in the private offering enable the purchasers in that offering to sue under Section 12(a)(2)? The Second Circuit has said no:

> The defendants were under no "obligation to distribute" the June 29, 1998 prospectus or any other prospectus to the plaintiffs in connection with the challenged private transactions. *Gustafson* indicates that without such an obligation, a securities transaction cannot reasonably be deemed to have occurred "by means of a prospectus." *Gustafson v. Alloyd Co.*, 513 U.S. at 571 ("[T]he liability imposed by § 12[(a)](2) cannot attach unless there is an obligation to distribute the prospectus in the first place (or unless there is an

> exemption).").
>
> In any event, under the express terms of the subscription and letter agreements, the parties agreed that the ITNG securities at issue "were not offered ... by means of publicly disseminated advertisements or sales literature." See, e.g., Subscription Agreement dated Dec. 23, 1998, § 2.01(c). Where, as in this case, plaintiffs were aware at the time they signed this disclaimer that they had reviewed a prospectus disseminated in connection with a separate public offering, they will not be permitted to disavow this contract term to claim that the challenged offering was "by means of" the prospectus. See *Grumman Allied Indus. v. Rohr Indus.*, 748 F.2d 729, 734-35 (2d Cir. 1984) (citing *Danann Realty Corp. v. Harris*, 5 N.Y.2d 317, 319 (1959)).

Yung v. Lee, 432 F.3d 142, 149 (2d Cir. 2005). Do you agree? What (if anything) does the court's reasoning imply for Section 12(a)(2)'s embrace of offerings based on the Section 3 exemptions? Is the court's contract law discussion essential to the result reached? In this regard, consider the possible relevance of Section 14 of the Securities Act which provides that "[a]ny condition, stipulation, or provision binding any person acquiring any security to waive compliance with any provision of this title or of the rules and regulations of the Commission shall be void."

4. ***Section 12(a)(2) and Registered Offerings.*** While those who purchase securities in registered offerings are entitled to utilize Section 12(a)(2), recall that they may also utilize Section 11. Under what circumstances would such purchasers utilize Section 12(a)(2) rather than (or in addition to) Section 11?

5. ***Section 12(a)(2) and Oral Communications.*** Section 12(a)(2) refers not only to a "prospectus" but also to an "oral communication." The *Gustafson* Court endorsed lower court decisions holding that an "oral communication" is actionable under Section 12(a)(2) only where it "relate[s] to a prospectus." Is this limitation significant? Is it likely to require difficult line-drawing? Is it sound from the standpoint of statutory construction? From the standpoint of policy?

6. ***Section 12(a)(2) and the Free Writing Prospectus.*** Prior to reforms made by the SEC in 2005, participants in the registration process faced sharp restrictions regarding their use of materials that supplemented the registration statement. The 2005 reforms loosened those restrictions by creating the concept of the "free writing prospectus" – written (or electronic) material allowed to supplement the registration statement so long as certain conditions are satisfied. See Securities Act Rules 164 and 433. The free writing prospectus is "public, without regard to its method of distribution" because it is "related to the public offering of securities that are the subject of a filed registration statement." Rule 433(a), supra.

In its release accompanying the 2005 reforms, the SEC stated that "any seller offering or selling securities by means of the free writing prospectus will be subject to disclosure liability under Securities Act Section 12(a)(2)." Securities Offering Reform, Securities Act Release No. 33-8591,70 Fed. Reg. 44722, 44759 (Aug. 3, 2005). Liability under Section 11, on the other hand, would ordinarily not be available: "A free writing prospectus will not be part of a registration statement subject to liability under Securities Act § 11, unless the issuer elects to file it as part of the registration statement." Id.

7. ***Section 12(a)(2) and the Aftermarket.*** If, as *Gustafson* held, Congress did not intend Section 12(a)(2) to reach secondary market trading, it would seem to follow that Congress did not intend investors in the aftermarket to have any fraud cause of action at all. Indeed, recall that Section 11 has only a highly limited application to the aftermarket (and in any event applies only to misstatements and omissions in the registration statement). And while it is true that Section 17(a) of the Securities Act prohibits fraud in the aftermarket, that Section does not authorize an express private action and is widely thought not to give rise to an implied private action. See infra Section 2.B. Nor did Congress assume that aftermarket purchasers would be able to invoke Rule 10b-5: "No one could have anticipated in 1934 that rule 10b-5 would be adopted eight years later, let alone that the courts would imply a private right of action for its violation ***." Louis Loss, The Assault on Securities Act Section 12(2), 105 Harv. L. Rev. 908, 915-16 (1992). Did Congress in the early 1930s actually intend to relegate aftermarket investors to state law private actions? Or is *Gustafson* mistaken in its conclusion?

8. ***Does* Gustafson *Matter?*** To what extent should it matter to securities litigators that *Gustafson* narrowed the scope of Section 12(a)(2)? Cf. Kimberly D. Krawiec, *Gustafson v. Alloyd Co.*: The Wrong Decision, But It is Still Business as Usual in the Securities Markets, 31 Tulsa L.J. 509, 518-19 (1996) (maintaining that *Gustafson* does not alter the advice that a transactional attorney should give to a client regarding the importance of full disclosure). After all, Rule 10b-5 remains available to address fraud in private placements and secondary market transactions. But is Rule 10b-5 as attractive as Section 12(a)(2)? Why might a plaintiff prefer Section 12(a)(2) to Rule 10b-5 (or to blue sky law)?

PROBLEM 3-3

Decide whether Section 12(a)(2) is available to the following after *Gustafson*:

a. An issuer sold interests in a cooperative agricultural venture to a large number of investors in a single state. Cf. *SEC v. Howey Co.*, 328 U.S. 293 (1946) (holding an offering of interests in cultivated orange groves to be an offering of securities under the Securities Act). The offering is exempt from the Securities Act's registration requirements pursuant to the intrastate offering exemption set forth in Securities Act Section 3(a)(11). There are no written offering materials other than the subscription agreement and a single page newspaper advertisement, each of which contains (the same) material misstatement. Both state in bold letters at the top of the page as follows: "This intrastate sale of securities is exempt from registration under federal securities laws and this document is not a prospectus."

b. An issuer made a $5 million Regulation A offering but failed to attract any individual investors. All of the purchasers were large institutions.

c. Shortly after the completion of an IPO by Box, Inc., a purchaser (Mary) learned not only that the prospectus was materially misleading but also that Box stood on the brink of bankruptcy. Mary thereupon decided to sell the

Box stock that she had just purchased. Rather than selling the stock on the open market, she negotiated a private sale to an institutional investor to whom she sent a copy of the Box prospectus, accompanied by a cover letter stating as follows: "Enclosed is the Box prospectus for the sale of the stock that I purchased, which is to the best of my knowledge true and accurate." The institutional investor bought Mary's stock, relying on the prospectus that she had sent.

d. Assume in (c) that Mary instead sold her Box stock on the open market to someone who had read the Box prospectus after downloading it from the Internet.

---

b. Who is a Seller?

Section 12(a)(2) imposes liability on the person who sold the securities in question, but does not tell us who qualifies as a "seller." In the decision that follows, the Supreme Court answered this question in the context of Section 12(a)(1). Ask yourself whether the Court's answer is equally applicable to Section 12(a)(2).

PINTER v. DAHL

486 U.S. 622 (1988)

JUSTICE HAROLD A. BLACKMUN:

*** Th[is] controversy arises out of the sale prior to 1982 of unregistered securities (fractional undivided interests in oil and gas leases) by petitioner Billy J. "B.J." Pinter to respondents Maurice Dahl and Dahl's friends, family, and business associates. Pinter is an oil and gas producer in Texas and Oklahoma, and a registered securities dealer in Texas. Dahl is a California real estate broker and investor, who, at the time of his dealings with Pinter, was a veteran of two unsuccessful oil and gas ventures. In pursuit of further investment opportunities, Dahl employed an oil field expert to locate and acquire oil and gas leases. This expert introduced Dahl to Pinter. Dahl advanced $20,000 to Pinter to acquire leases, with the understanding that they would be held in the name of Pinter's Black Gold Oil Company and that Dahl would have a right of first refusal to drill certain wells on the leasehold properties. Pinter located leases in Oklahoma, and Dahl toured the properties, often without Pinter, in order to talk to others and "get a feel for the properties." Upon examining the geology, drilling logs, and production history assembled by Pinter, Dahl concluded, in the words of the District Court, that "there was no way to lose."

After investing approximately $310,000 in the properties, Dahl told the other respondents about the venture. Except for Dahl and respondent Grantham, none of the respondents spoke to or met Pinter or toured the properties. Because of Dahl's involvement in the venture, each of the other respondents decided to invest about $7,500.

Dahl assisted his fellow investors in completing the subscription-agreement form prepared by Pinter. Each letter-contract signed by the purchaser stated that the participating interests were being sold without the benefit of registration under the Securities Act, in reliance on Securities and

Exchange Commission (SEC or Commission) Rule 146. In fact, the oil and gas interests involved in this suit were never registered with the Commission. Respondents' investment checks were made payable to Black Gold Oil Company. Dahl received no commission from Pinter in connection with the other respondents' purchases.

When the venture failed and their interests proved to be worthless, respondents brought suit against Pinter in the United States District Court for the Northern District of Texas, seeking rescission under § 12(1) of the Securities Act, for the unlawful sale of unregistered securities.

In a counterclaim, Pinter alleged that Dahl, by means of fraudulent misrepresentations and concealment of facts, induced Pinter to sell and deliver the securities. Pinter averred that Dahl falsely assured Pinter that he would provide other qualified, sophisticated, and knowledgeable investors with all the information necessary for evaluation of the investment. Dahl allegedly agreed to raise the funds for the venture from those investors, with the understanding that Pinter would simply be the "operator" of the wells. ***

The District Court, after a bench trial, granted judgment for respondent-investors. The court concluded that Pinter had not proved that the oil and gas interests were entitled to the private-offering exemption from registration. Accordingly, the court ruled that, because the securities were unregistered, respondents were entitled to rescission pursuant to § 12(1). The court also concluded that the evidence was insufficient to sustain Pinter's counterclaim against Dahl. ***

A divided panel of the Court of Appeals for the Fifth Circuit affirmed. ***

The Court of Appeals *** considered whether Dahl was himself a "seller" of the oil and gas interests within the meaning of § 12(1), for if he was, the court assumed, he could be held liable in contribution for the other plaintiffs' claims against Pinter.[9] Citing Fifth Circuit precedent, the court described a statutory seller as "(1) one who parts with title to securities in exchange for consideration or (2) one whose participation in the buy-sell transaction is a substantial factor in causing the transaction to take place." While acknowledging that Dahl's conduct was a "substantial factor" in causing the other plaintiffs to purchase securities from Pinter, the court declined to hold that Dahl was a "seller" for purposes of § 12(1). Instead, the court went on to refine its test to include a threshold requirement that one who acts as a "promoter" be "motivated by a desire to confer a direct or indirect benefit on someone other than the person he has advised to purchase." The court reasoned that "a rule imposing liability (without fault or knowledge) on friends and family members who give one another gratuitous advice on investment matters unreasonably interferes with

---

9. *** Unlike § 11 of the Securities Act, § 12 does not expressly provide for contribution. The Court of Appeals did not reach the question whether Pinter is entitled to contribution under § 12(1) because it found that Dahl was not a seller for purposes of § 12(1), and therefore would not be the proper subject of a contribution claim. The parties have not raised or addressed the contribution issue before this Court, and we express no view as to whether a right of contribution exists under § 12(1).

well-established patterns of social discourse." Accordingly, since the court found no evidence that Dahl sought or received any financial benefit in return for his advice, it declined to impose liability on Dahl for "mere gregariousness." ***

III

*** In determining whether Dahl may be deemed a "seller" for purposes of § 12(1), such that he may be held liable for the sale of unregistered securities to the other investor-respondents, we look first at the language of § 12(1). That statute provides, in pertinent part: "Any person who ... offers or sells a security" in violation of the registration requirement of the Securities Act "shall be liable to the person purchasing such security from him." This provision defines the class of defendants who may be subject to liability as those who offer or sell unregistered securities. But the Securities Act nowhere delineates who may be regarded as a statutory seller, and the sparse legislative history sheds no light on the issue. The courts, on their part, have not defined the term uniformly.

At the very least, however, the language of § 12(1) contemplates a buyer-seller relationship not unlike traditional contractual privity. Thus, it is settled that § 12(1) imposes liability on the owner who passed title, or other interest in the security, to the buyer for value. Dahl, of course, was not a seller in this conventional sense, and therefore may be held liable only if § 12(1) liability extends to persons other than the person who passes title.[20]

A

In common parlance, a person may offer or sell property without necessarily being the person who transfers title to, or other interest in, that property. We need not rely entirely on ordinary understanding of the statutory language, however, for the Securities Act defines the operative terms of § 12(1). Section 2(3) defines "sale" or "sell" to include "every contract of sale or disposition of a security or interest in a security, for value," and the terms "offer to sell," "offer for sale," or "offer" to include "every attempt or offer to dispose of, or solicitation of an offer to buy, a security or interest in a security, for value." Under these definitions, the range of persons potentially liable under § 12(1) is not limited to persons who pass title. The inclusion of the phrase "solicitation of an offer to buy" within the definition of "offer" brings an individual who engages in solicitation, an activity not inherently confined to the actual owner, within the scope of § 12. ***

---

20. The "offers or sells" and the "purchasing such security from him" language that governs § 12(1) also governs § 12(2), which provides a securities purchaser with a similar rescissionary cause of action for misrepresentation. Most courts and commentators have not defined the defendant class differently for purposes of the two provisions.

The question whether anyone beyond the transferor of title, or immediate vendor, may be deemed a seller for purposes of § 12 has been litigated in actions under both § 12(1) and § 12(2). Decisions under § 12(2) addressing the "seller" question are thus relevant to the issue presented to us in this case, and, to that extent, we discuss them here. Nevertheless, this case does not present, nor do we take a position on, the scope of a statutory seller for purposes of § 12(2).

An interpretation of statutory seller that includes brokers and others who solicit offers to purchase securities furthers the purposes of the Securities Act — to promote full and fair disclosure of information to the public in the sales of securities. In order to effectuate Congress' intent that § 12(1) civil liability be *in terrorem,* the risk of its invocation should be felt by solicitors of purchases. The solicitation of a buyer is perhaps the most critical stage of the selling transaction. It is the first stage of a traditional securities sale to involve the buyer, and it is directed at producing the sale. In addition, brokers and other solicitors are well positioned to control the flow of information to a potential purchaser, and, in fact, such persons are the participants in the selling transaction who most often disseminate material information to investors. Thus, solicitation is the stage at which an investor is most likely to be injured, that is, by being persuaded to purchase securities without full and fair information. Given Congress' overriding goal of preventing this injury, we may infer that Congress intended solicitation to fall under the mantle of § 12(1).

Although we conclude that Congress intended § 12(1) liability to extend to those who solicit securities purchases, we share the Court of Appeals' conclusion that Congress did not intend to impose rescission based on strict liability on a person who urges the purchase but whose motivation is solely to benefit the buyer. When a person who urges another to make a securities purchase acts merely to assist the buyer, not only is it uncommon to say that the buyer "purchased" from him, but it is also strained to describe the giving of gratuitous advice, even strongly or enthusiastically, as "soliciting." Section 2(3) defines an offer as a "solicitation of an offer to buy ... for value." The person who gratuitously urges another to make a particular investment decision is not, in any meaningful sense, requesting value in exchange for his suggestion or seeking the value the titleholder will obtain in exchange for the ultimate sale. The language and purpose of § 12(1) suggest that liability extends only to the person who successfully solicits the purchase, motivated at least in part by a desire to serve his own financial interests or those of the securities owner. If he had such a motivation, it is fair to say that the buyer "purchased" the security from him and to align him with the owner in a rescission action.[23]

B

Petitioner is not satisfied with extending § 12(1) primary liability to one who solicits securities sales for financial gain. Pinter assumes, without explication, that liability is not limited to the person who actually parts title with the securities, and urges us to validate, as the standard by which additional defendant-sellers are identified, that version of the "substantial factor" test utilized by the Fifth Circuit before the refinement espoused in this case. Under that approach, grounded in tort doctrine, a nontransferor § 12(1) seller is defined

---

23. *** [T]here is no reason to think that Congress wanted to bind itself to the common-law notion of the circumstances in which rescission is an appropriate remedy. *** [W]e may infer that Congress, in order to effectuate its goals, chose to impose this relief on any defendant it classified as a statutory seller, regardless of the fact that such imposition was somewhat inconsistent with the use of rescission at common law. Congress chose rescission for its effects; there is no indication that Congress employed the remedy for its delineation of potential defendants.

as one "whose participation in the buy-sell transaction is a substantial factor in causing the transaction to take place." *Pharo v. Smith*, 621 F.2d 656, 667 (CA5 1980). The Court of Appeals acknowledged that Dahl would be liable as a statutory seller under this test.

We do not agree that Congress contemplated imposing § 12(1) liability under the broad terms petitioners advocate. There is no support in the statutory language or legislative history for expansion of § 12(1) primary liability beyond persons who pass title and persons who "offer," including those who "solicit" offers. Indeed, § 12's failure to impose express liability for mere participation in unlawful sales transactions suggests that Congress did not intend that the section impose liability on participants collateral to the offer or sale. When Congress wished to create such liability, it had little trouble doing so.[26] ***

The substantial-factor test reaches participants in sales transactions who do not even arguably fit within the definitions set out in § 2(3); it "would add a gloss to the operative language of [§ 12(1)] quite different from its commonly accepted meaning." *Ernst & Ernst v. Hochfelder*, 425 U.S., at 199. We conclude that Congress did not intend such a gross departure from the statutory language. Accordingly, we need not entertain Pinter's policy arguments. Being merely a "substantial factor" in causing the sale of unregistered securities is not sufficient in itself to render a defendant liable under § 12(1).

C

We are unable to determine whether Dahl may be held liable as a statutory seller under § 12(1). The District Court explicitly found that "Dahl solicited each of the other plaintiffs (save perhaps Grantham) in connection with the offer, purchase, and receipt of their oil and gas interests." We cannot conclude that this finding was clearly erroneous. It is not clear, however, that Dahl had the kind of interest in the sales that make him liable as a statutory seller. We do know that he received no commission from Pinter in connection with the other sales, but this is not conclusive. Typically, a person who solicits the purchase will have sought or received a personal financial benefit from the sale, such as where he "anticipat[es] a share of the profits," *Lawler v. Gilliam*,

---

26. Congress knew of the collateral participation concept and employed it in the Securities Act and throughout its unified program of securities regulation. Liabilities and obligations expressly grounded in participation are found elsewhere in the Act, see, e.g., [Section 2(11)] (defining "underwriter," who is liable under § 5, as including direct and indirect participants), and in the later Roosevelt administration securities Acts. For example, § 9 of the 1934 Act, passed by the same Congress that enacted the Securities Act, creates a private right of action that expressly imposes liability on participants.

Section 11 of the Securities Act lends strong support to the conclusion that Congress did not intend to extend § 12 primary liability to collateral participants in the unlawful securities sales transaction. That section provides an express cause of action for damages to a person acquiring securities pursuant to a registration statement that misstates or omits a material fact. Section 11(a) explicitly enumerates the various categories of persons involved in the registration process who are subject to suit under that section, including many who are participants in the activities leading up to the sale. There are no similar provisions in § 12, and therefore we may conclude that Congress did not intend such persons to be defendants in § 12 actions.

569 F.2d, at 1288, or receives a brokerage commission, *Cady v. Murphy*, 113 F.2d, at 990. But a person who solicits the buyer's purchase in order to serve the financial interests of the owner may properly be liable under § 12(1) without showing that he expects to participate in the benefits the owner enjoys.

The Court of Appeals apparently concluded that Dahl was motivated entirely by a gratuitous desire to share an attractive investment opportunity with his friends and associates. This conclusion, in our view, was premature. The District Court made no findings that focused on whether Dahl urged the other purchases in order to further some financial interest of his own or of Pinter. Accordingly, further findings are necessary to assess Dahl's liability. ***

The judgment of the Court of Appeals is vacated, and the case is remanded for further proceedings consistent with this opinion.

JUSTICE JOHN PAUL STEVENS, DISSENTING:

*** I am unable to join Part III because I am persuaded that the discussion of the § 12(1) term "seller" in the context of a contribution suit is both advisory, because no such suit was brought in this case, and misleading, because it assumes that the class of persons who sell securities to purchasers (i.e., § 12(1) "sellers") is coextensive with the class of potential defendants in claims for contribution, not brought directly under § 12(1), asserted by § 12(1) sellers. ***

NOTES AND QUESTIONS

*1. **Not Only Title Passers.*** The Court held that "seller" status extends beyond the person who passed title. Look again at the language of Section 12(a)(2) and compare it with that of Section 11. Is there reason to suppose, *Pinter* notwithstanding, that Congress intended to limit "seller" status under Section 12(a)(2) to the person who passed title?

*2. **The Meaning of Solicitation.*** The Court held that a seller must "successfully solicit the purchase," but it did not define solicitation. What light does *Pinter* shed regarding the meaning of solicitation? Does someone who solicits have to intend to do so?

*3. **The Meaning of Financial Interests.*** According to *Pinter,* a seller must engage in solicitation "motivated at least in part by a desire to serve his own financial interests or those of the securities owner." What sorts of financial interests would qualify in this regard? On remand, what showing might Pinter make in order to establish Dahl's requisite financial interests?

*4. **Firm Commitment vs. Best Efforts Underwriting.*** Return to the beginning of this Chapter and the discussion of the role of underwriters in preparing the registration statement. Note the distinction between "firm commitment" underwriting (where the underwriters buy the securities from the issuer and resell them) and "best efforts" underwriting (where the underwriters do not buy the securities but instead use their best efforts to effectuate the distribution).

Consider first a "best efforts" underwriting. Title to the securities remains with the issuer, who is thus the passer of title and hence a "seller" for purposes of Section 12(a)(2). The underwriter may also be a seller, so long as it engages in "solicitation," since its activities on behalf of the issuer's sale are motivated by the underwriting commission it will receive if the offering is successful.

Next consider "firm commitment" underwriting. Various pre-2005 decisions held that the issuer in this situation – not being the title passer – qualified as a Section 12(a)(2) seller only if it solicited in the *Pinter* sense. See, e.g., *Lone Star Ladies Inv. Club v. Schlosky's, Inc.*, 238 F.3d 363, 370 (5th Cir. 2001) (noting the relative rarity of an issuer's engaging in *Pinter*-type solicitation); *Shaw v. Digital Equip. Corp.*, 82 F.3d 1194, 1215-16 (1st Cir. 1996). These holdings did not sit well with the SEC, which made the following statement in its release accompanying the 2005 reforms: "We believe that an issuer offering or selling its securities in a registered offering pursuant to a registration statement containing a prospectus that it has prepared and filed *** can be viewed as soliciting purchases of the issuer's registered securities." SEC, Securities Offering Reform, Release 33-8591, 70 Fed. Reg. 44722, 44769 (Aug. 3, 2005). Accordingly, the reforms included a new rule that deems an issuer a "seller" under Section 12(a)(2) "regardless of the underwriting method used to sell the issuer's securities." Rule 159A(a). Did the SEC do the right thing?

*5. **Suing the Right Underwriter.*** Recall that Section 11 allows the plaintiff to sue all the underwriters in the registered offering. Section 12(a)(2) is different in this regard. Under Section 12(a)(2), the plaintiff may sue only the underwriter or underwriters who were his sellers, that is, who passed him title or solicited his purchase for financial gain. Consider *Griffin v. PaineWebber, Inc.*, 2001 WL 740764 (S.D.N.Y. 2001), a Section 12(a)(2) class action against, among others, an underwriter (CIBC) who had neither transferred title to the named plaintiff nor solicited his purchase. The court dismissed the action:

> [B]ecause Griffin's complaint makes clear that he does not have an individual claim against CIBC that would allow him to represent the class of plaintiff who may have such a claim, his standing to maintain the action cannot be established. Accordingly, the claim against CIBC is dismissed on the basis of Griffin's lack of standing to bring the claim. Plaintiffs will be granted leave to amend the complaint *** to identify, in connection with the Offering, a named plaintiff who actually purchased Livent securities from, or was solicited directly by, CIBC.

Id. at *2. What steps might a plaintiff's lawyer in a class action take in advance in order to avoid the problem that arose in *Griffin*? If a Section 12(a)(2) class action alleges sales by more than one underwriter to more than one named plaintiff, are there likely to be sufficient questions of law and fact common to the class to allow certification of the class?

6. **Gustafson *Revisited.*** Reconsider the Supreme Court's decision in *Gustafson v. Alloyd, Inc.*, 513 U.S. 561 (1995). Is it arguable that *Gustafson* has the effect of qualifying who is a seller for purposes of Section 12(a)(2)?

*7. **The Question of Contribution.*** Unlike Section 11, Section 12(a)(2) makes no mention of contribution. Note, however, that *Pinter* left the question open in a footnote. See generally Mark I. Steinberg & Christopher D. Olive, Contribution and Proportionate Liability Under the Federal Securities Laws in Multidefendant Securities Litigation After the Private Securities Litigation Reform Act of 1995, 50 SMU L. Rev. 337, 352 n. 76 (1996) (discussing the possible right of contribution under Section 12(a)(2) and noting that the case law following *Pinter* has declined to recognize such a right).

Assume that you represent a defendant in a Section 12(a)(2) action in a jurisdiction that has not yet decided whether a defendant in such an action is entitled to obtain contribution from others who meet the *Pinter* "seller" criteria. What arguments could you make in support of your client's right to do so?

8. ***Rationalizing Restrictiveness.*** The Supreme Court's decisions in *Pinter* and *Gustafson* restricted the reach of Section 12(a)(2), just as Supreme Court decisions such as *Blue Chip Stamps, Hochfelder,* and *Central Bank* that you read in Chapter 2 restricted the reach of the implied private action under Rule 10b-5. Compare the reasons given by the Court for imposing restrictions in these two sets of decisions. Are they similar or different? Consistent or inconsistent?

9. ***Section 12(a)(2) vs. Rule 10b-5.*** Why do you suppose that Rule 10b-5, and not Section 12(a)(2), is the centerpiece of most large securities fraud class actions?

10. ***Using Section 12(a)(2) as a Litigation Strategy.*** While plaintiffs suing under Section 12(a)(2) do not have to plead or prove scienter, plaintiffs suing under Rule 10b-5 face dismissal if they fail to plead scienter with adequate specificity. See supra Chapter 2.D.2. Thus, a Section 12(a)(2) action, if it survives a motion to dismiss, may be useful for obtaining discovery as to scienter that can facilitate the amendment of the complaint, or a new complaint, that alleges Rule 10b-5 claims against a broader class of defendants (including persons who would not meet the *Pinter* definition of "seller") on behalf of a broader class of plaintiffs (including persons who purchased shares on the secondary market and thus under *Gustafson* would be ineligible to sue under Section 12(a)(2)).

Should courts allow plaintiffs to use Section 12(a)(2) to make an end-run around the stay on discovery in private Rule 10b-5 actions that becomes operative upon the filing of a motion to dismiss? See Exchange Act Section 21D(b)(3)(B), discussed supra Chapter 2.D.2. Is there language in either the Securities Act or the Exchange Act, or in the PSLRA, pursuant to which the discovery stay provision was added to the Exchange Act, suggesting that such a tactic should be disallowed?

PROBLEM 3-4

Determine which of the following meets the *Pinter* definition of "seller" for purposes of Section 12(a)(2):

a. A lawyer who prepared the prospectus on behalf of the issuer in a registered offering.

b. A lawyer who prepared the prospectus on behalf of the issuer in a registered offering and who was compensated for his work on the prospectus with shares of the issuer's stock, the value of which will substantially increase if the offering is successful.

c. A lawyer who prepared the prospectus on behalf of the issuer in a registered offering and who also made telephone calls to several institutional investors in which he encouraged them to buy the issuer's stock.

d. A broker who, as a member of the selling group in a registered offering, solicited a plaintiff's purchase of the securities from one of the underwriters. The broker was paid a commission for soliciting the purchase.

---

c. *The Reasonable Care Defense*

Unlike Rule 10b-5, Section 12(a)(2) does not require the plaintiff to prove that the defendant acted with scienter. Section 12(a)(2) does, however, allow the defendant to avoid liability by establishing a reasonable care defense, namely, that "he did not know, and in the exercise of reasonable care could not have known," about the materially misleading misstatement or omission.

How does Section 12(a)(2)'s reasonable care defense compare with Section 11's due diligence defenses? Courts struggle with this issue. See, e.g., *In re Software Toolworks, Inc. Sec. Litig.*, 50 F.3d 615, 621 (9th Cir. 1994) (describing them as "similar, if not identical"). Consider *Sanders v. John Nuveen & Co.*, 619 F.2d 1222 (7th Cir. 1980), a Section 12(a)(2) action against the exclusive underwriter of an exempt offering of unsecured promissory notes as to which the issuer (WH) had defaulted. The default had been the result of a fraud perpetrated by WH and its accountants over a ten year period. The underwriter "was not aware of the fraud and held 'the mistaken but honest belief that financial statements (of WH) prepared by certified public accountants correctly represented the condition of' WH." Id. at 1224 (quoting *Sanders v. John Nuveen & Co.*, 524 F.2d 1064, 1066 (7th Cir. 1975)). The court concluded that the underwriter had not established its reasonable care defense:

> It is not at all clear that Congress intended to impose a higher standard of care under § 11 than under § 12(2). The difference in language appeared in the House bill and was retained in the Act as agreed to by the Joint Conference Committee and as passed by both Houses. The Conference Committee report, in its discussion of the standard of liability imposed for a misleading registration statement, describes the standard adopted not as one of "reasonable investigation," but one of "reasonable care." More specifically, Congress does not appear to have intended that a different standard apply to underwriters. Thus, the House Report draws no distinction between an underwriter's burden in the case of misleading statements in a prospectus, for which it can be liable only under § 12(2), and its § 11 duty to conduct a "reasonable investigation." The difference in language can be explained not as an attempt to impose different duties of care under §§ 11 and 12, but by the fact that § 12(2) imposes the duty on all sellers of securities, while § 11 imposes liability only on specified groups of persons having such a close relationship with the registration statement that the 1933 Act, before it was amended the following year, treated them as fiduciaries. See Securities Act, § 11(c); Securities Exchange Act § 206(c). Thus the general duty of reasonable care, the specific requirements of which are determined by the circumstances of the case, was to be applied in § 11 only to persons who had a stronger connection with a registration statement than a seller necessarily has to a prospectus, so a more stringent articulation of the standard was appropriate.

> In the circumstances of this case, the reasonable care standard required [a] reasonable investigation *** . Since what constitutes reasonable care under § 12(2) depends upon the circumstances, we, of course, do not intimate that the duty of a seller under § 12(2) is always the same as that of an underwriter in a registration offering under § 11.

Id. at 1228.

The Supreme Court denied certiorari in *Sanders*, but Justice Powell wrote a dissenting opinion (in which Justice Rehnquist joined). In that opinion, Justice Powell maintained that the Seventh Circuit had been wrong about the reasonable care defense:

> The Court of Appeals' opinion may be read as holding that petitioner's duty of "reasonable care" under § 12(2) required it independently to *investigate* the accuracy and completeness of the certified financial statements. It was customary, however — and in my view entirely reasonable — for petitioner to rely on these statements as accurately reflecting W&H's financial condition. Even under § 11 of the Act, an underwriter is explicitly absolved of the duty to investigate with respect to "any part of the registration statement purporting to be made on the authority of an expert" such as a certified accountant if "he had no reasonable ground to believe and did not believe" that the information therein was misleading. § 11(b)(3)(C) of the Act; see § 11(a)(4). This provision is in the Act because, almost by definition, it *is* reasonable to rely on financial statements certified by public accountants. Yet, in this case, the Court of Appeals nevertheless seems to have imposed the higher duty prescribed by § 11 to investigate, but denied petitioner the right to rely on "the authority of an expert" that also is provided by § 11. ***
>
> *** Dealers may believe that they must undertake extensive independent financial investigations rather than rely on the accuracy of the certified financial statements. If this is so, the efficiency of the short- term financial markets will be impaired. I would grant certiorari.

450 U.S. 1005, 1009-11 (1981). Cf. *Associated Randall Bank v. Griffin, Kubik, Stephens & Thompson, Inc.*, 3 F.3d 208, 213 (7th Cir. 1993) (noting that no court has "pursued the implication of [the Seventh Circuit in] *Sanders*, that broker-dealers must investigate the securities they sell").

The SEC set forth its position on the relationship between the reasonable care and due diligence defenses in its release adopting the 2005 reforms:

> We believe *** that the standard of care under Section 12(a)(2) is less demanding than that prescribed by Section 11, or, put another way, that Section 11 requires a more diligent investigation than Section 12(a)(2). Moreover, we believe that any practices or factors that would be considered favorably under Section 11, including pursuant to Rule 176, also would be considered as favorably under the reasonable care standard of Section 12(a)(2).

SEC, Securities Offering Reform, Release 33-8591, 70 Fed. Reg. 44722, 44770 (Aug.3, 2005). The SEC had taken essentially the same position in its amicus brief filed in *Sanders* in the Seventh Circuit. See *John Nuveen & Co. v. Sanders*, 450 U.S. 1005, 1009 (1981) (Powell, J., dissenting from the denial of certiorari) (quoting the SEC's Seventh Circuit brief).

NOTES AND QUESTIONS

1. **Competing Views.** Which position do you find more persuasive – the Seventh Circuit's or Justice Powell's? If Congress intended to equate the due diligence and reasonable care defenses, why didn't it use the same language in each? What is the legal status of the SEC's position as expressed in its 2005 release? Is the SEC's endorsement of Rule 176 for Section 12(a)(2) purposes likely to prove useful?

2. ***A Facts and Circumstances Approach?*** Consider the views of Professor Maynard on the *Sanders* decision in particular and the reasonable care defense in general:

> *Sanders* suggests that the reasonable care standard of section 12(2) should be interpreted flexibly and that the nature of the defendant is a crucial factor in defining the relevant standard. Moreover, *Sanders* suggests that the exercise of reasonable care may, but does not automatically, require the defendant-seller to conduct an investigation to establish her exercise of reasonable care. Again, the nature of the defendant-seller is a critical factor in determining whether there is an affirmative obligation to make a reasonable investigation to establish the section 12(2) reasonable care defense. Finally, *Sanders* indicates that, where an investigation is required to show the defendant's exercise of reasonable care, the scope of any required investigation will be defined in substantial part by the nature of the defendant-seller and her involvement in, and relationship to, the plaintiff's purchase of the securities at issue. ***
>
> Since section 12(2) essentially embodies a negligence standard, the exercise of reasonable care will presumably be defined by the facts and circumstances of each case.

Therese H. Maynard, The Affirmative Defense of Reasonable Care Under Section 12(2) of the Securities Act of 1933, 69 Notre Dame L. Rev. 57, 94-95 (1993). Do you agree with her interpretation of *Sanders*? Does she suggest a workable approach to the reasonable care defense?

3. ***Possible Irrationality.*** Notice that an issuer that has made a registered offering has a reasonable care defense under Section 12(a)(2) but is strictly liable under Section 11. Professor Horwich regards this discrepancy as "difficult, if not impossible to rationalize." Alan Horwich, Section 11 of the Securities Act: The Cornerstone Needs Some Tuckpointing, 58 Bus. Law. 1, 23 (2002). Do you agree?

PROBLEM 3-5

"Dare to be Great" (DTBG) was a fraudulent pyramid scheme that attracted investors by holding meetings that were exciting and emotional. At these meetings, fraudulent written materials were also distributed. Interests in DTBG constituted securities under the federal securities laws. The offering was not registered with the SEC. Nor did it fit any exemption from registration.

From February through July of 2010, Ace Loan Company provided secured loans to people who wanted to purchase interests in DTBG. After Ace had made some of these loans, DTBG contacted an Ace employee (Joe) about future loan business. Joe attended several DTBG meetings, at which he supplied those in attendance with Ace loan applications. He also gave a speech at each of these meetings about obtaining financing through Ace. In these speeches, he represented that DTBG was a terrific investment.

In July 2010, Joe's supervisor (Drew) became aware of Joe's activities involving DTBG. Drew quickly realized that DTBG was a sham. He thereupon ordered Joe to stop engaging in such activities immediately.

DTBG declared bankruptcy in November 2010. Shortly thereafter, Fred, who purchased an interest in DTBG based on a loan from Ace obtained through Joe, brought a Section 12(a)(2) action against Joe. Is Joe an appropriate defendant? Assuming that he is, can he establish his reasonable care defense?

Cf. *Davis v. Avco Fin. Serv., Inc.*, 739 F.2d 1057 (6th Cir. 1984).

d. Damages and Negative Causation

Damages under Section 12(a)(2) are rescissory in nature, regardless of whether the plaintiff has sold the securities in question. Thus, if the plaintiff has not sold the securities, he is entitled to "the consideration paid for such security with interest thereon, less the amount of any income received." If the plaintiff has sold the securities, he has the right to rescissory damages — "a return of the consideration paid, reduced by the amount realized when he sold the security and any 'income received' on the security." *Randall v. Loftsgaarden*, 478 U.S. 647, 655-56 (1986). See also id. at 667 (holding that recovery under Section 12(a)(2), as well as under Rule 10b-5, need not be offset by tax benefits received).

A defendant in a Section 12(a)(2) action can reduce — or even eliminate entirely — the amount of money that the plaintiff would otherwise recover. Authorization comes from Section 12(b):

> [I]f the person who offered or sold such security proves that any portion or all of the amount recoverable under subsection (a)(2) represents other than the depreciation in value of the subject security resulting from such part of the prospectus or oral communication, with respect to which the liability of that person is asserted, not being true or omitting to state a material fact required to be stated therein or necessary to make the statement not misleading, then such portion or amount, as the case may be, shall not be recoverable.

The "negative causation" defense – enacted in 1995 as part of the PSLRA – is analogous to Section 11's negative causation defense and thus *Akerman v. Oryx Communications, Inc.*, 810 F.2d 336 (2d Cir. 1987), which you read in connection with Section 11, is relevant to Section 12(a)(2) as well. By enacting Section 12(b), Congress confirmed that a Section 12(a)(2) plaintiff has no obligation to prove causation.

NOTES AND QUESTIONS

1. Obligatory Resale. Once a plaintiff discovers the material misstatement or omission at issue, is she obliged to sell her securities in order to mitigate damages under Section 12(a)(2)? See 9 Louis Loss & Joel Seligman, Securities Regulation 4195 (3d ed. rev. 2004) (raising the question).

2. Delaying Tactics. As mentioned, the Supreme Court has held that recovery under Section 12(a)(2) need not be offset by the amount of a tax benefit already received. *Randall v. Loftsgaarden*, 478 U.S. 647, 667 (1987). But suppose that a plaintiff intentionally delays filing his Section 12(a)(2) action in order to realize a tax benefit not yet received from the securities in question. Would the court be entitled to take this delay into account for the purpose of calculating the amount of his recovery? What other risks are incurred by a plaintiff who pursues such a strategy?

3. ***Making Comparisons.*** How does the measure of calculating damages under Section 12(a)(2) compare with that of Section 11? With that of Rule 10b-5?

PROBLEM 3-6

a. On the recommendation of her broker, Thalia purchased 1000 shares of Dog.com that were sold at $5 per share in a firm commitment initial public offering (IPO) in which the broker's firm acted as underwriter. The broker did not tell Thalia that analysts at the broker's firm had been giving Dog.com a "buy" recommendation under heavy pressure from the underwriting side of the firm. He told Thalia that he himself thought the stock was a "great buy," but he made no other material misrepresentations to her about Dog.com. There were also no material misrepresentations in the prospectus. Two months later, Dog.com stock had become worthless. Can Thalia sue her broker and his firm under Section 12(a)(2)?

b. Assume instead that Thalia bought the Dog.com stock on the secondary market in large part relying upon oral statements made on the television show Wall Street Beat by a renowned Internet stock analyst, James Botchit. Botchit does not work for the firm that sold Thalia her stock; instead, he works for another broker-dealer that also participated in the underwriting. Can Thalia sue Botchit and his firm under Section 12(a)(2)?

3. Additional Shared Features of Sections 11 and 12(a)(2)

Sections 11 and 12(a)(2) have the following features in common: (i) a materiality requirement; (ii) an applicable provision for the liability of controlling persons; (iv) a discovery stay provision; (iv) pleading standards; (v) a statute of limitations; and (vi) concurrent state and federal jurisdiction. We will briefly consider each of these.

a. Materiality

To be actionable under Sections 11 and 12(a)(2), the misstatement or omission at issue must be material in nature. As is true under Rule 10b-5, the basic definition of materiality comes from *TSC Indus., Inc. v. Northway, Inc.*, 426 U.S. 438 (1976): "a substantial likelihood that a reasonable shareholder would consider [the information] *** important" or "a substantial likelihood that the disclosure of the omitted fact would have been viewed by the reasonable investor as having significantly altered the 'total mix' of information made available." Id. at 449. See, e.g., *Litwin v. Blackstone Group, LP*, 634 F.3d 706, 716-17 (2d Cir. 2011) (applying *Northway* standard to Sections 11 and 12(a)(2)).

The Supreme Court recently reaffirmed the *Northway* standard in the Rule 10b-5 context in *Matrixx Initiatives, Inc. v. Siracusano*, 131 S.Ct. 1309

(2011). Emphasizing the context-specific nature of the materiality inquiry, the Court refused to allow the materiality of an issuer's statements about drug side effects to turn on whether those side effects met the threshold of "statistical significance." See generally supra Chapter 2.B (discussing the materiality requirement under Rule 10b-5). In addition, the bespeaks caution doctrine (Chapter 2.B.3.b supra) and the puffery doctrine (see Note 2 on page 63) are typically available under Sections 11 and 12(a)(2) in circumstances in which they would also be available under Rule 10b-5.

Sections 11 and 12(a)(2) also share a statutory safe harbor for forward-looking statements that is set forth in Section 27A of the Securities Act. This safe harbor closely resembles its Exchange Act counterpart — Section 21E — which you examined with reference to Rule 10b-5 in Chapter 2.B.3.c. As is with Section 21E, Section 27A applies only when the issuer is subject to the reporting requirements of the Exchange Act. See Section 27A(a)(1). See also Chapter 1.A.2.c (discussing Exchange Act reporting requirements). Likewise as with Section 21E, Section 27A does not apply to IPOs and to certain other transactions. See Section 27A(b).

b. Controlling Person Liability

Persons who control those who violate Sections 11 and 12(a)(2) are liable under Section 15 of the Securities Act, which reads as follows:

> Every person who, by or through stock ownership, agency, or otherwise, or who, pursuant to or in connection with an agreement or understanding with one or more other persons by or through stock ownership, agency, or otherwise, controls any person liable under Sections 11 or 12, shall also be liable jointly and severally with and to the same extent as such controlled person to any person to whom such controlled person is liable, unless the controlling person had no knowledge of or reasonable ground to believe in the existence of the facts by reason of which the liability of the controlled person is alleged to exist.

You have previously examined Section 15's Exchange Act counterpart — Section 20(a) — in connection with Rule 10b-5. See Chapter 2.H.3.

Enacted more than half a century ago, Section 15 appears well designed to deal with a set of twenty-first century scenarios involving offerings of mortgage-backed and other asset-backed securities (ABS). In these scenarios, the issuers are separately incorporated special purpose entities set up by investment banks or other financial institutions that act not only as underwriters but also as control persons. Frequently the same financial institution controlled a separate entity that had acquired the underlying assets of the ABS in the first place from a loan originator or other intermediary. Cf. *In re Charles Schwab Corp. Sec. Litig.*, 257 F.R.D. 534, 550 (N.D. Cal. 2009) (denying motion to dismiss claim that, in the words of the complaint, the "'parent company of the Charles Schwab financial services complex,' the 'parent company of [the asset management company] and the principal underwriter and distributor for [the] shares,' the entity that 'over[saw] the asset management and administration of the [fund],' and the registrant and issuer of the shares, were each in a position to exercise actual power and control over the contents of the registration statements and reports at issue").

c. Discovery Stay

Section 11 and Section 12(a)(2) claims are subject to Section 27(b) of the Securities Act. Section 27(b) empowers a court to stay discovery in all private actions under the Securities Act during the pendency of a motion to dismiss. You previously encountered Section 27(b)'s Exchange Act counterpart — Exchange Act Section 21D(b)(3)(B) — in connection with Rule 10b-5. See supra Chapter 2.D.2.

d. Pleading Standards

Sections 11 and 12(a)(2) are also identically situated with respect to applicable pleading standards. These standards include Fed. R. Civ. P. 8, which governs all civil complaints filed in federal court and provides that plaintiffs need plead only "a short and plain statement of the claim showing that [they are] entitled to relief."

Sections 11 and 12(a)(2) are not, however, subject to the heightened pleading requirements enacted as part of the PSLRA. Indeed, the PSLRA added the heightened pleading requirements to the Exchange Act (see Exchange Act Section 21D(b)) but not to the Securities Act. Therefore the conclusion seems unavoidable that the heightened pleading requirements — applicable to private claims under Rule 10b-5 — do not apply to claims under Sections 11 and 12(a)(2). See Sale, supra, 76 Wash. U. L. Q. at 586-93 (showing that this result follows from the PSLRA as well as from the nature of the Securities Act itself).

But do claims under Sections 11and 12(a)(2) nonetheless need to satisfy Fed. R. Civ. P. 9(b), which requires particularity in the pleading of fraud or mistake? The circuits are divided on this question, with most "hold[ing] that Rule 9(b) applies when the misrepresentation justifying relief under the Securities Act is also alleged to support a claim for fraud under the Exchange Act and Rule 10b-5." *Wagner v. First Horizon Pharm. Corp.*, 464 F.3d 1273, 1277 (11th Cir. 2006) (collecting cases). Under these circumstances, the Securities Act claims are said to "sound in fraud." *Rombach v. Chang*, 355 F.3d 164 (2d Cir. 2004). But cf. Hillary A. Sale, Heightened Pleading and Discovery Stays: An Analysis of the Effect of the PSLRA's Internal-Information Standard on '33 and '34 Act Claims, 76 Wash.U.L.Q. 537, 584-86 (1998) (discussing the inapplicability of Rule 9(b) to Sections 11 and 12(a)(2) actions).

There remains the question of how to treat Securities Act claims that the pleadings make clear are negligence-based. The few decisions to address this question have held that Rule 9(b) does not apply under these circumstances. See, e.g., *In re Suprema Specialties, Inc. Sec. Litig.*, 438 F.3d 256, 272-73 (3d Cir. 2006); *In re Refco, Inc. Sec. Litig.*, 503 F. Supp. 2d 611, 633 (S.D.N.Y. 2007) (finding *Suprema* to be persuasive). See Marc I. Steinberg & Brent A. Kirby, The Assault on Section 11 of the Securities Act: A Study in Judicial Activism, 63 Rutgers L. Rev. 1, 38-42 (2010).

e. Statute of Limitations

The statute of limitations for both Sections 11 and 12(a)(2) is set forth in Section 13 of the Securities Act:

> No action shall be maintained to enforce any liability created under Section 11 or Section 12(a)(2) unless brought within one year after the discovery of the

> untrue statement or the omission, or after such discovery should have been made by the exercise of reasonable diligence ***. In no event shall any such action be brought to enforce a liability created under Section 11 *** more than three years after the security was bona fide offered to the public, or under Section 12(a)(2) more than three years after the sale.

But with the enactment of the Sarbanes-Oxley Act of 2002 (SOX), an important question arises. Recall from our discussion of Rule 10b-5's limitations period (in Chapter 2.I) that SOX replaced the period's one year/three year structure with a two year/five year structure. See Section 804 of the SOX, enacted as 28 U.S.C. § 1658(b), set out on page 249. Notice that the latter provision does not refer to Rule 10b-5 (or to Section 10(b)) as such. Rather, the reference is to private securities law "claim[s] of fraud, deceit, manipulation, or contrivance." Is it possible that this language embraces some or all claims under Sections 11 or 12(a)(2)? As a general matter, courts have rejected this argument. See *In re Alstom SA Sec. Litig.*, 406 F. Supp. 2d 402, 413 & n.5 (S.D.N.Y. 2005) (collecting cases). The rationale offered for the rejection is that the SOX provision encompasses only those claims requiring proof of scienter, whereas Sections 11 and 12(a)(2) do not require such proof. See id.

But that rationale raises yet another question: whether the SOX provision applies to those Section 11 and Section 12(a)(2) claims that "sound in fraud" (and are subject to Rule 9(b)). Consider the following justification for why the answer is no:

> To rule otherwise would give rise to an anomaly. It would place the determination of the relevant statute of limitations in plaintiffs' hands and identify its source with the pleadings in the Complaint. In essence, plaintiffs in actions under the securities laws, as their own convenience suited, would be able to prescribe what statute of limitations would apply to their claims by how skillfully they draft the complaint, effectively contracting or expanding the limitations period for claims brought under Sections 11 and 12(a)(2) on the basis of their artful pleading of fraud, even though they would not be put to the test of proving fraud to make out a case under those statutes. Exacting reasonable disclosure of the particulars of time, place and manner constituting an averment of fraud that does not actually have to be proved should not warrant a substantial extension of the otherwise applicable statute of limitations.
>
> The Court is mindful of the difficulties inherent in this case, and grants that the application of the longer limitations period of Section 804 to claims averring fraud, even when proof of such conduct is not required for liability to attach under the legal claims asserted, may be a reasonably arguable proposition. On balance, the Court finds the arguments against the application of the longer limitations period are the more compelling. *** It was the Second Circuit that applied the pleading standards of Rule 9(b) to such claims. If the principles underlying the *Rombach* decision mandate the application of the Section 804 period of limitations to claims under Sections 11 and 12(a)(2) that sound in fraud, it should be left to the Circuit Court to so rule. This Court declines to enlarge Section 804's reach in this respect.

Alstom, 406 F. Supp. 2d at 418. But see *Amorosa v. Ernst & Young, LLP*, 682 F. Supp. 2d 351, 369 (S.D.N.Y. 2010) (observing that Section 1568(b) applies to Section 11 claims sounding in fraud). Do you agree?

f. Concurrent State and Federal Jurisdiction

Section 11 and 12(a)(2) claims may be brought in state or federal court in accordance with Section 22(a) of the Securities Act. If, however, the complaint is a class action and alleges a material misstatement or omission in connection with the sale of a "nationally traded security" (encompassing those listed on the New York Stock Exchange, the American Stock Exchange, or the NASDAQ), it may be filed in federal court only. See Section 16 of the Securities Act.

In contrast to the Securities Act, the Exchange Act has always provided for exclusive federal jurisdiction. Why does the Exchange Act embrace exclusive federal jurisdiction, in contrast to not only the Securities Act but also to all the other federal securities statutes? See Margaret V. Sachs, Exclusive Federal Jurisdiction for Implied Rule 10b-5 Actions: The Emperor Has No Clothes, 49 Ohio St. L.J. 559, 580-81 (1988) (linking the Exchange Act's exclusive federal jurisdiction with the onerousness of that Act's express private actions).

B. SECTION 17(a): FRAUD IN THE OFFER OR SALE OF SECURITIES

Section 17(a) prohibits fraud in the offer or sale of securities. We begin with a general consideration of Section 17(a), which is frequently invoked by both the SEC and the DOJ. We then consider the (non)existence of an implied private action under the Section.

1. In General

Section 17(a) of the Securities Act provides as follows:

> It shall be unlawful for any person in the offer or sale of any securities by ... the use of any means or instruments of transportation or communication in interstate commerce or by the use of the mails, directly or indirectly —
>
> (1) to employ any device, scheme, or artifice to defraud, or
>
> (2) to obtain money or property by means of any untrue statement of a material fact or any omission to state a material fact necessary in order to make the statements made, in the light of the circumstances under which they were made, not misleading, or
>
> (3) to engage in any transaction, practice, or course of business which operates or would operate as a fraud or deceit upon the purchaser.

The similarity between Section 17(a) and Rule 10b-5 is no accident. When drafting Rule 10b-5 in 1942, the SEC used Section 17(a) as a model.

In the decision that follows, the Supreme Court addressed whether Section 17(a) requires proof of scienter.

AARON v. SEC
446 U.S. 680 (1980)

JUSTICE POTTER STEWART:

*** We granted certiorari to resolve the conflict in the federal courts as to whether the Commission is required to establish scienter — an intent on the part of the defendant to deceive, manipulate, or defraud [5] — as an element of a Commission enforcement action to enjoin violations of § 17(a), § 10(b), and Rule 10b-5. ***

[*The Court held that the SEC must prove scienter under Rule 10b-5*].

*** The language of Section 17(a) strongly suggests that Congress contemplated a scienter requirement under § 17(a)(1), but not under § 17(a)(2) or § 17(a)(3). The language of § 17(a)(1), which makes it unlawful "to employ any device, scheme, or artifice to defraud," plainly evinces an intent on the part of Congress to proscribe only knowing or intentional misconduct. Even if it be assumed that the term "defraud" is ambiguous, given its varied meanings at law and in equity, the terms "device," "scheme," and "artifice" all connote knowing or intentional practices.[13] Indeed, the term "device," which also appears in § 10(b), figured prominently in the Court's conclusion in *Hochfelder* that the plain meaning of Section 10(b) embraces a scienter requirement.

By contrast, the language of § 17(a)(2), which prohibits any person from obtaining money or property "by means of any untrue statement of a material fact or any omission to state a material fact," is devoid of any suggestion whatsoever of a scienter requirement. As a well-known commentator has noted, "[t]here is nothing on the face of Clause (2) itself which smacks of *scienter* or intent to defraud." 3 L. Loss, Securities Regulation 1442 (2d ed. 1961). In fact, this Court in *Hochfelder* pointed out that the similar language of Rule 10b-5(b) "could be read as proscribing ... any type of material misstatement or omission ... that has the effect of defrauding investors, whether the wrongdoing was intentional or not." 425 U.S., at 212.

Finally, the language of § 17(a)(3), under which it is unlawful for any person "to engage in any transaction, practice, or course of business which *operates* or *would operate* as a fraud or deceit," (emphasis added) quite plainly focuses upon the *effect* of particular conduct on members of the investing public, rather than upon the culpability of the person responsible. This reading follows directly from *Capital Gains*, which attributed to a similarly worded provision in § 206(2) of the Investment Advisers Act of 1940 a meaning that does not require a "showing [of] deliberate dishonesty as a condition precedent to protecting investors." 375 U.S., at 200.

It is our view, in sum, that the language of § 17(a) requires scienter under § 17(a)(1), but not under § 17(a)(2) or § 17(a)(3). Although the parties

---

5. The term "scienter" is used throughout this opinion, as it was in *Ernst & Ernst v. Hochfelder*, 425 U.S. 185, 194, n. 12 (1976), to refer to "a mental state embracing intent to deceive, manipulate, or defraud." We have no occasion here to address the question, reserved in *Hochfelder*, ibid., whether, under some circumstances, scienter may also include reckless behavior.

13. Webster's International Dictionary (2d ed. 1934) defines (1) "device" as "[t]hat which is devised, or formed by design; a contrivance; an invention; project; scheme; often, a scheme to deceive; a stratagem; an artifice," (2) "scheme" as "[a] plan or program of something to be done; an enterprise; a project; as, a business scheme[, or] [a] crafty, unethical project," and (3) "artifice" as a "[c]rafty device; trickery; also, an artful stratagem or trick; artfulness; ingeniousness."

have urged the Court to adopt a uniform culpability requirement for the three subparagraphs of § 17(a), the language of the section is simply not amenable to such an interpretation. *** Indeed, since Congress drafted § 17(a) in such a manner as to compel the conclusion that scienter is required under one subparagraph but not under the other two, it would take a very clear expression in the legislative history of congressional intent to the contrary to justify the conclusion that the statute does not mean what it so plainly seems to say. ***

NOTES AND QUESTIONS

*1. **The Scienter Question.*** The Court held that the Commission must prove scienter when proceeding under Section 10(b) of the Exchange Act and Rule 10b-5, but not under Sections 17(a)(2) and (3) of the Securities Act. Yet the latter provisions are almost identical to Rule 10b-5 (and, along with Section 17(a)(1), served as the model for drafting Rule 10b-5). How can virtually identical language give rise to such a sharp difference with respect to the scienter requirement?

*2. **Broad Scope.*** Section 17(a) is not limited to initial offerings of securities, despite the fact that such offerings are the principal focus of the Securities Act. As the Supreme Court explained in *United States v. Naftalin*, 441 U.S. 768 (1979):

> Although it is true that the 1933 Act was primarily concerned with the regulation of new offerings, *** the antifraud prohibition of § 17(a) was meant as a major departure from that limitation. Unlike much of the rest of the act, it was intended to cover any fraudulent scheme in an offer or sale of securities, whether in the course of an initial distribution or in the course of ordinary market trading. This is made abundantly clear both by the statutory language, which makes no distinctions between the two kinds of transactions, and by the Senate Report ***. Respondent is undoubtedly correct that the two Acts prohibit some of the same conduct. But "[t]he fact that there may well be some overlap is neither unusual nor unfortunate." *SEC v. National Securities, Inc.*, 393 U.S., at 468.

Id. at 777-78 (applying Section 17(a) to a customer who defrauded his broker through a short-selling scheme).

*3. **Powerful Weapon for the Government.*** Section 17(a) provides the SEC with a powerful litigation weapon. Not only can liability be imposed on someone who was merely careless (under Sections 17(a)(2) and (a)(3)), whether in the context of an initial offering or in secondary market trading. In addition, the material misstatement or omission need not appear in (or be linked to) an official document such as a registration statement or prospectus. Thus, it makes sense for the SEC, whenever it can, to allege violations of Section 17(a) together with violations of Rule 10b-5.

The DOJ likewise makes use of Section 17(a)'s broad scope in bringing criminal securities actions. But unlike the SEC, the DOJ cannot sidestep proof of scienter when proceeding under Section 17(a). The reason lies with Section 24 of the Securities Act, which conditions criminal liability for all Securities Act violations on proof that the defendant acted "willfully." See generally infra

Chapter 11.A.1.

2. *The (Non)Existence of An Implied Private Action*

Section 17(a) says nothing about a private action. The Supreme Court has reserved the question of whether to recognize a private action by implication. See *Herman & MacLean v. Huddleston,* 459 U.S. 375, 378 n. 2 (1983); *Int'l Bhd. of Teamsters v. Daniel,* 439 U.S. 551, 557 n. 9 (1979). The consensus among the lower federal courts, however, is that Section 17(a) should be available to the government only. Consider the following decision.

MALDONADO v. DOMINGUEZ

137 F.3d 1 (1st Cir. 1998)

JUAN R. TORRUELLA, CHIEF JUDGE:

Plaintiffs invested in and became directors of a corporation called the Puerto Rico International Bank ("PRIBANK"), which was designed to create huge profits for its investor-directors by leveraging its collateral with low interest loans in order to purchase higher interest mortgage obligations. When PRIBANK failed, the plaintiffs brought this suit, claiming that the investment bankers marketing the PRIBANK stock defrauded them by failing to mention the possibility that PRIBANK's securities would be "called" in the event of an interest rate adjustment. The investors filed this suit under sections 12(2) and 17(a) of the Securities Act of 1933, as well as section 10(b) of the Securities Act of 1934, and Rule 10(b)(5) ***. The district court dismissed all of these claims on a motion to dismiss. We affirm. ***

Section 17(a) of the 1933 Act

*** Courts and law enforcement agencies have the authority to enforce section 17(a) of the 1933 Act via injunction and criminal prosecution. However, for years circuit courts have struggled with the question of whether an implied private right of action to enforce section 17(a) also exists. The Supreme Court has never answered the question. ***

This issue has caused confusion because, while neither the language nor the history of section 17(a) clearly indicates a congressional intent to create a private right of action, see *Newcome v. Esrey*, 862 F.2d 1099, 1103-07 (4th Cir.1988), section 10(b) of the 1934 Act — with substantially similar language — has always been interpreted to provide for a private right of action. See *Herman & MacLean v. Huddleston*, 459 U.S. 375, 385-87 (1983) (expressly interpreting section 10(b)'s private right of action as consistent with securities laws' "broad remedial purposes"). While some courts did not find the requisite congressional intent to infer a private right of action from section 17(a), see *Touche Ross & Co. v. Redington*, 442 U.S. 560, 574-76 (1979) (legislative intent is the primary factor to consider when addressing whether a private right of action exists), other circuits found no meaningful distinction between section 17(a) and section 10(b). Compare *Daniel v. Teamsters*, 561 F.2d 1223, 1244-46 (7th Cir.1977) (holding that a private right of action exists), and *SEC v. Texas Gulf Sulphur Co.*, 401 F.2d 833, 867 (2d Cir.1968) (Friendly, J., concurring) (same), with *Landry v. All American Assur. Co.*, 688 F.2d 381, 384-91 (5th Cir.1982) (holding that no private right of action exists), and *Stephenson v. Calpine Conifers II, Ltd.*, 652 F.2d 808, 815 (9th Cir.1981) (same).

However, in *Aaron v. SEC*, 446 U.S. 680, 695-97 (1980), the Supreme Court held that, unlike section 10(b) of the Exchange Act, section 17(a) of the Securities Act does not require proof of scienter. Thus, while the implied cause of action under 10(b) would expose only the deceitful to private causes of action, an implied cause of action under 17(a) would impose such liability on merely negligent wrongdoers. Furthermore, the Court had ruled four years earlier that a judicially created cause of action, such as the one implied under section 10(b), could not be extended to actions premised on negligent wrongdoing. See *Ernst & Ernst v. Hochfelder*, 425 U.S. 185, 210 (1976).

Aaron and *Ernst* highlighted for courts a significant distinction between implying private causes of action under the two sections. While the 10(b) implied cause of action has continued to enjoy unanimous recognition and the imprimatur of a unanimous Supreme Court in *Huddleston*, the 17(a) cause of action has been held up to renewed scrutiny. In recent years, every circuit to have addressed the issue has refused to recognize a private right of action under section 17(a), including four circuits which originally had held otherwise. We now come to the same conclusion.

In determining whether an implied private right of action exists in a statute, we look to congressional intent, see *Touche Ross*, 442 U.S. at 574-76, keeping in mind that there is a strong presumption against such inferences. In this case, we do not find sufficient evidence of congressional intent to overcome the presumption. As the district court observed, Congress *explicitly* provided for private causes of action in sections 11 and 12 of the 1933 Act. While the fact that other provisions of a complex statutory scheme create express remedies does not in itself prove that Congress did not imply a private remedy in another section, see *Cannon v. University of Chicago*, 441 U.S. 677, 690 n. 13 (1979), where the explicit remedies in the same statute address much of the same conduct and benefit the same parties as a potential implied private cause of action, the circumstances militate against that inference. Furthermore, the legislative history of section 17(a) does not, on the whole, favor an implied private right of action. See *Newcome*, 862 F.2d at 1103-07 (conducting an in-depth examination of the legislative history of this provision). Therefore, the district court did not err in dismissing the plaintiffs' claim under section 17(a) of the 1933 Act. ***

NOTES AND QUESTIONS

*1. **Result-Oriented Reasoning?*** The Court asserts that *Hochfelder* held that "a judicially created cause of action, such as the one implied under section 10(b), could not be extended to actions premised on negligent wrongdoing." Is this an accurate characterization of *Hochfelder*?

Does the court refuse to recognize an implied private action under Section 17(a) based on *Aaron's* rejection of a scienter requirement for some Section 17(a) actions and *Hochfelder*'s imposition of a scienter requirement for the implied private action under Rule 10b-5? Do these two issues — the existence of an implied private action and the existence of a scienter requirement — have anything to do with each other? Is this decision an example of result-oriented reasoning?

2. The Impact of **Gustafson.** Recall that prior to the Supreme Court's *Gustafson* decision, Section 12(a)(2) was widely considered applicable to private offerings as well as to secondary trading. Thus, most of the decisions cited by *Maldonado* were issued at a time when Sections 12(a)(2) and 17(a) encompassed many of the same types of transactions, thereby making recognition of an implied action under Section 17(a) arguably unnecessary. After *Gustafson*, however, this argument loses much of its force, a fact not acknowledged (or perhaps not even recognized) by *Maldonado*.

Is it likely that Congress would have left purchasers in private offerings and secondary markets without a private action for material misstatements and omissions under the Securities Act? If *Gustafson* was rightly decided, does it follow that the courts are now wrong in refusing to recognize a private action under Section 17(a)? Alternatively, should courts recognize an implied private action under Section 17(a) in order to right the wrong of *Gustafson* (assuming that the decision constitutes a wrong)? Or should the task of restoring a private action under the Securities Act for private offering and secondary market purchasers be left to Congress? Is a private action needed, given the availability of the implied private action under Rule 10b-5? In considering this question, recall from Chapter 2 the many obstacles that a Rule 10b-5 plaintiff must face.

3. An Imperfect Consensus. Section 17(a) private actions may not be altogether off the checkerboard, however. According to a relatively recent district court decision, such actions are still viable in the Sixth Circuit. See *AFA Private Equity Fund 1 v. Miresco Inv. Servs.*, 2005 WL 2417116 (E.D. Mich. 2005) (relying on *Craighead v. E.F. Hutton & Co.*, 899 F.2d 485 (6th Cir. 1990), to deny the defendant's summary judgment motion on the plaintiff's Section 17(a) claim). Cf. *Trustcash Holdings, Inc. v. Moss,* 668 F. Supp. 2d 650, 655 (D.N.J. 2009) (rejecting implied action under Section 17(a) for non-purchaser of securities and noting "the almost universal trend" to this effect). On the other hand, pleading a Section 17(a) claim in a circuit that has unambiguously declared such a claim to be a dead letter can be costly. See *Crookham v. Crookham,* 914 F.2d 1027 (8th Cir. 1990) (affirming district court's imposition of $10,000 sanction on lawyers who filed Section 17(a) claim in the Eighth Circuit).

Chapter 4

PROXY FRAUD—SECTION 14(a) OF THE EXCHANGE ACT AND RULE 14a-9

Shareholders in public corporations typically vote by proxy when electing directors or approving mergers or other corporate transactions. Section 14(a) and Rule 14a-9 help to protect the integrity of shareholder decision-making on these matters.

Consider first Section 14(a), which gives the SEC a broad mandate to adopt rules bearing on the solicitation of proxies:

> It shall be unlawful for any person, by the use of the mails or by any means or instrumentality of interstate commerce or of any facility of a national securities exchange or otherwise, in contravention of such rules and regulations as the Commission may prescribe as necessary or appropriate in the public interest or for the protection of investors, to solicit or to permit the use of his name to solicit any proxy or consent or authorization in respect of any security (other than an exempted security) registered pursuant to section 12 of this title.

SEC rules adopted pursuant to this mandate require (among other things) that shareholders receive, in conjunction with a proxy solicitation, a "proxy statement" disclosing specified information about the matter as to which their votes are sought. SEC rules also allow shareholders who satisfy explicit criteria to submit proposals for inclusion in management's proxy statement. See generally Jill E. Fisch, From Legitimacy to Logic: Reconstructing Proxy Regulation, 46 Vand. L. Rev. 1129 (1993). On the other hand, it is state law that determines the matters on which shareholders are entitled to vote and the percentage of shares necessary to approve each of those matters.

Among the rules adopted by the SEC under Section 14(a) is Rule 14a-9, subsection (a) of which prohibits material omissions or misrepresentations in proxy solicitations:

> No solicitation subject to this regulation shall be made by means of any proxy statement, form of proxy, notice of meeting or other communication, written or oral, containing any statement which, at the time and in the light of the circumstances under which it is made, is false or misleading with respect to any material fact, or which omits to state any material fact necessary in order to make the statements therein not false or misleading or necessary to correct any statement in any earlier communication with respect to the solicitation of a proxy for the same meeting or subject matter which has become false or misleading.

While nothing in the Rule (or Section 14(a)) authorizes private enforcement, the Supreme Court has held that a private action under the Rule exists by implication. *J. I. Case Co. v. Borak*, 377 U.S. 426 (1964).

As is no doubt becoming obvious, Rule 14a-9 resembles Rule 10b-5 in several critical respects. Like Rule 10b-5, Rule 14a-9 bars material omissions and misrepresentations and has given rise to a judicially created private action. Moreover, like Rule 10b-5, Rule 14a-9 can be enforced not only in private actions (of the individual, class, or derivative, variety) but also in SEC and criminal actions. Finally, like Rule 10b-5, Rule 14a-9 has been construed primarily by the courts rather than by the Commission.

Yet Rule 14a-9 and Rule 10b-5 likewise have several very important differences. First, Rule 10b-5 applies regardless of the size of the corporation that has issued the securities, whereas Rule 14a-9 applies only to Section 12 companies, defined on page 7). Second, Rule 10b-5 applies when investors buy or sell securities, whereas Rule 14a-9 applies when their proxies are solicited, regardless of whether they (or others) are engaged in securities trading at the time. A third difference between Rules 10b-5 and 14a-9 involves the frequency with which each is utilized by the SEC and the DOJ. While SEC and DOJ actions are relatively commonplace under Rule 10b-5, they are quite rare under Rule 14a-9. Hence, to a far greater degree than with Rule 10b-5, the enforcement of Rule 14a-9 falls to investors.

The evolution of Rule 14a-9 has been enormously affected by that of Rule 10b-5 (and to some extent vice versa). Thus, judicial hostility to private Rule 10b-5 actions appears to have aggravated judicial hostility to private Rule 14a-9 actions. See, e.g, *Virginia Bankshares, Inc. v Sandberg,* 501 U.S. 1083, 1105 (1991) (evaluating the threat of vexatious Rule 14a-9 litigation by analogizing to the threat of such litigation under Rule 10b-5).

Moreover, the Private Securities Litigation Reform Act (PSLRA), aimed primarily at Rule 10b-5, has enveloped Rule 14a-9 as well. Rule 14a-9 class actions must comply with requirements for class actions established by the PSLRA (which you will encounter in Chapter 6). Other PSLRA provisions applicable to private Rule 14a-9 actions include the safe harbor for forward-looking statements (Section 21E); the loss causation requirement (Section 21D(b)(4)); stiffened requirements for pleading material omissions and misstatements (Section 21D(b)(1)); the automatic stay of discovery during the pendency of motions to dismiss for failure to satisfy the pleading requirements (Section 21D(b)(3)(A)); and proportionate liability (Section 21D(f)). The circuits currently are divided over the applicability to Rule 14a-9 of the provision on pleading state of mind (Section 21D(b)(2)). That division is considered later in this Chapter .

This Chapter examines the elements of Rule 14a-9 with emphasis on the implied private action. We begin with judicial recognition of the implied private action (Section A) and then address the requirements of materiality (Section B), state of mind (Section C), and causation (Section D). Later chapters draw upon these elements in connection with class actions (Chapter 6); SEC enforcement (Chapter 9); and criminal enforcement (Chapter 11).

As you consider Section 14(a) and Rule 14a-9, think about the following questions. Should courts draw sharper distinctions between Rule 14a-9 and Rule 10b-5 than they do at present? To what extent is judicial interpretation of Rule 14a-9 affected by fear of the possible impact on Rule 10b-5, even if that fear is not stated explicitly? When interpreting Rule 14a-9, what weight (if any) should be given to the fact that investors are the Rule's principal enforcers? What accounts for the seeming lack of interest in Rule 14a-9 on the part of the SEC and the Department of Justice (DOJ)?

A. JUDICIAL RECOGNITION OF THE IMPLIED PRIVATE ACTION

In the landmark decision that follows, the Supreme Court recognized an implied private action for violations of Rule 14a-9.

J. I. CASE COMPANY v. BORAK

377 U.S. 426 (1964)

JUSTICE THOMAS C. CLARK:

This is a civil action brought by respondent, a stockholder of petitioner J. I. Case Company, charging deprivation of the pre-emptive rights of respondent and other shareholders by reason of a merger between Case and the American Tractor Corporation. It is alleged that the merger was effected through the circulation of a false and misleading proxy statement by those proposing the merger. The complaint was in two counts, the first based on diversity and claiming a breach of the directors' fiduciary duty to the stockholders. The second count alleged a violation of §14(a) of the Securities Exchange Act of 1934 with reference to the proxy solicitation material. The trial court held that as to this count it had no power to redress the alleged violations of the Act but was limited solely to the granting of declaratory relief thereon under § 27 of the Act.[2] The court held Wis. Stat. 1961, § 180.405(4), which requires posting security for expenses in derivative actions, applicable to both counts, except that portion of Count 2 requesting declaratory relief. It ordered the respondent to furnish a bond in the amount of $75,000 thereunder and, upon his failure to do so, dismissed the complaint, save that part of Count 2 seeking a declaratory judgment. On interlocutory appeal the Court of Appeals reversed on both counts, holding that the District Court had the power to grant remedial relief and that the Wisconsin statute was not applicable. *** We consider only the question of whether § 27 of the Act authorizes a federal cause of action for rescission or damages to a corporate stockholder with respect to a consummated merger which was authorized pursuant to the use of a proxy statement alleged to contain false and misleading statements violative of § 14(a) of the Act. ***

---

2. Section 27 of the Act provides in part:

The district courts of the United States, the Supreme Court of the District of Columbia, and the United States courts of any territory or other place subject to the jurisdiction of the United States shall have exclusive jurisdiction of violations of this title or the rules and regulations thereunder, and of all suits in equity and actions at law brought to enforce any liability or duty created by this title or the rules and regulations thereunder. Any criminal proceeding may be brought in the district wherein any act or transaction constituting the violation occurred. Any suit or action to enforce any liability or duty created by this title or rules and regulations thereunder, or to enjoin any violation of such title or rules and regulations, may be brought in any such district or in the district wherein the defendant is found or is an inhabitant or transacts business, and process in such cases may be served in any other district of which the defendant is an inhabitant or wherever the defendant may be found.

I.

Respondent, the owner of 2000 shares of common stock of Case acquired prior to the merger, brought this suit based on diversity jurisdiction seeking to enjoin a proposed merger between Case and the American Tractor Corporation (ATC). *** The injunction was denied and the merger was thereafter consummated. *** The claims pertinent to the asserted violation of the Securities Exchange Act were predicated on diversity jurisdiction as well as on § 27 of the Act. They alleged: that petitioners, or their predecessors, solicited or permitted their names to be used in the solicitation of proxies of Case stockholders for use at a special stockholders' meeting at which the proposed merger with ATC was to be voted upon; that the proxy solicitation material so circulated was false and misleading in violation of § 14(a) of the Act and Rule 14a-9 *** ; that the merger was approved at the meeting by a small margin of votes and was thereafter consummated; that the merger would not have been approved but for the false and misleading statements in the proxy solicitation material; and that Case stockholders were damaged thereby. The respondent sought judgment holding the merger void and damages for himself and all other stockholders similarly situated, as well as such further relief "as equity shall require." ***

II.

It appears clear that private parties have a right under § 27 to bring suit for violation of § 14(a) of the Act. Indeed, this section specifically grants the appropriate District Courts jurisdiction over "all suits in equity and actions at law brought to enforce any liability or duty created" under the Act. The petitioners make no concessions, however, emphasizing that Congress made no specific reference to a private right of action in § 14(a); that, in any event, the right would not extend to derivative suits and should be limited to prospective relief only. In addition, some of the petitioners argue that the merger can be dissolved only if it was fraudulent or non-beneficial, issues upon which the proxy material would not bear. But the causal relationship of the proxy material and the merger are questions of fact to be resolved at trial, not here. We therefore do not discuss this point further.

III.

While the respondent contends that his Count 2 claim is not a derivative one, we need not embrace that view, for we believe that a right of action exists as to both derivative and direct causes.

right of action applies to both direct and derivative claims

The purpose of § 14(a) is to prevent management or others from obtaining authorization for corporate action by means of deceptive or inadequate disclosure in proxy solicitation. The section stemmed from the congressional belief that "[f]air corporate suffrage is an important right that should attach to every equity security bought on a public exchange." H.R.Rep. No. 1383, 73d Cong., 2d Sess., 13. It was intended to "control the conditions under which proxies may be solicited with a view to preventing the recurrence of abuses which ... [had] frustrated the free exercise of the voting rights of stockholders." Id., at 14. "Too often proxies are solicited without explanation to the stockholder of the real nature of the questions for which authority to cast his vote is sought." S. Rep. No.792, 73d Cong., 2d Sess., 12. These broad remedial purposes are evidenced in the language of the section which makes it "unlawful for any person

... to solicit or to permit the use of his name to solicit any proxy or consent or authorization in respect of any security ... registered on any national securities exchange in contravention of such rules and regulations as the Commission may prescribe as necessary or appropriate in the public interest *or for the protection of investors*." (Italics supplied.) While this language makes no specific reference to a private right of action, among its chief purposes is "the protection of investors," which certainly implies the availability of judicial relief where necessary to achieve that result.

The injury which a stockholder suffers from corporate action pursuant to a deceptive proxy solicitation ordinarily flows from the damage done the corporation, rather than from the damage inflicted directly upon the stockholder. The damage suffered results not from the deceit practiced on him alone but rather from the deceit practiced on the stockholders as a group. To hold that derivative actions are not within the sweep of the section would therefore be tantamount to a denial of private relief. Private enforcement of the proxy rules provides a necessary supplement to Commission action. As in anti-trust treble damage litigation, the possibility of civil damages or injunctive relief serves as a most effective weapon in the enforcement of the proxy requirements. The Commission advises that it examines over 2,000 proxy statements annually and each of them must necessarily be expedited. Time does not permit an independent examination of the facts set out in the proxy material and this results in the Commission's acceptance of the representations contained therein at their face value, unless contrary to other material on file with it. Indeed, on the allegations of respondent's complaint, the proxy material failed to disclose alleged unlawful market manipulation of the stock of ATC, and this unlawful manipulation would not have been apparent to the Commission until after the merger.

We, therefore, believe that under the circumstances here it is the duty of the courts to be alert to provide such remedies as are necessary to make effective the congressional purpose. As was said in *Sola Electric Co. v. Jefferson Electric Co.*, 317 U.S. 173, 176 (1942):

> When a federal statute condemns an act as unlawful, the extent and nature of the legal consequences of the condemnation, though left by the statute to judicial determination, are nevertheless federal questions, the answers to which are to be derived from the statute and the federal policy which it has adopted.

It is for the federal courts "to adjust their remedies so as to grant the necessary relief" where federally secured rights are invaded. "And it is also well settled that where legal rights have been invaded, and a federal statute provides for a general right to sue for such invasion, federal courts may use any available remedy to make good the wrong done." *Bell v. Hood*, 327 U.S. 678, 684 (1946). Section 27 grants the District Courts jurisdiction "of all suits in equity and actions at law brought to enforce any liability or duty created by this title...." In passing on almost identical language found in the Securities Act of 1933, the Court found the words entirely sufficient to fashion a remedy to rescind a fraudulent sale, secure restitution and even to enforce the right to restitution against a third party holding assets of the vendor. *Deckert v. Independence Shares Corp.*, 311 U.S. 282 (1940). This significant language was used:

> The power *to enforce* implies the power to make effective the right of recovery afforded by the Act. And the power to make the right of recovery effective implies the power to utilize any of the procedures or actions normally available to the litigant according to the exigencies of the particular case. At 288 of 311 U.S.

Nor do we find merit in the contention that such remedies are limited to prospective relief. This was the position taken in *Dann v. Studebaker-Packard Corp.*, 6 Cir., 288 F.2d 201, where it was held that the "preponderance of questions of state law which would have to be interpreted and applied in order to grant the relief sought ... is so great that the federal question involved ... is really negligible in comparison." At 214. But we believe that the overriding federal law applicable here would, where the facts required, control the appropriateness of redress despite the provisions of state corporation law, for it "is not uncommon for federal courts to fashion federal law where federal rights are concerned." *Textile Workers Union of America v. Lincoln Mills*, 353 U.S. 448, 457 (1957). In addition, the fact that questions of state law must be decided does not change the character of the right; it remains federal. As Chief Justice Marshall said in *Osborn v. Bank of United States*, 9 Wheat. 738 (1824):

> If this were sufficient to withdraw a case from the jurisdiction of the federal Courts, almost every case, although involving the construction of a law, would be withdrawn.... At 819-820 of 9 Wheat.

Moreover, if federal jurisdiction were limited to the granting of declaratory relief, victims of deceptive proxy statements would be obliged to go into state courts for remedial relief. And if the law of the State happened to attach no responsibility to the use of misleading proxy statements, the whole purpose of the section might be frustrated. Furthermore, the hurdles that the victim might face (such as separate suits *** , security for expenses statutes, bringing in all parties necessary for complete relief, etc.) might well prove insuperable to effective relief.

IV.

Our finding that federal courts have the power to grant all necessary remedial relief is not to be construed as any indication of what we believe to be the necessary and appropriate relief in this case. We are concerned here only with a determination that federal jurisdiction for this purpose does exist. Whatever remedy is necessary must await the trial on the merits. ***

NOTES AND QUESTIONS

1. ***The Advantages of Federal Court.*** Why did Borak prefer to litigate his claims in federal court rather than in state court?

2. ***"[B]oth Derivative and Direct."*** The Court observed that "[t]he injury which a stockholder suffers from corporate action pursuant to a deceptive proxy solicitation ordinarily flows from the damage done the corporation, rather than from the damages inflicted directly upon the stockholder." Why then did the Court hold that Borak's claim was "both derivative and direct" rather than simply derivative? In what sense was his claim direct?

3. ***Derivative Claims and the Demand Requirement.*** A Rule 14a-9 plaintiff who sues on a derivative basis must make a demand on the board of directors in accordance with the law of the state of incorporation or, alternatively, show that demand would be futile (provided that a futility exception exists under state law). See, e.g., *Shaev v. Saper*, 320 F.3d 373, 377-78 (3d Cir. 2003); *Resnik v. Boskin*, 2011 WL 689617 at * 8 (D.N.J. 2011); *In re Bank of Am. Corp. Sec., Deriv. & ERISA Litig.*, 757 F. Supp. 2d 260, 331 (S.D.N.Y. 2010); *In re CNET Networks, Inc., S'holder Deriv. Litig.*, 483 F. Supp. 2d 947 (N.D. Cal. 2007).

At least one federal district court has held the demand requirement inapplicable to Rule 14a-9 on the ground that the board does not employ "business judgment" in deciding what to include in the proxy statement. See *Vides v. Amelio*, 265 F. Supp. 2d 273, 275-76 (S.D.N.Y. 2003). Other such courts have expressly rejected this perspective, however. See *Bader v. Blankfein*, 2008 WL 5274442 at *5-6 (E.D.N.Y. 2008) (collecting cases), aff'd on other grds, 356 F. App'x 471 (2d Cir. 2009).

4. The Range of Potential Defendants. Notice that Borak sued defendants who, in the words of Section 14(a), had either "solicited or permitted their names to be used in the solicitation of proxies." This statutory language encompasses not only corporate insiders but also outsiders identified by name in the solicitation process. Compare *City P'ship Co. v. Lehman Bros., Inc.*, 344 F. Supp. 2d 1241, 1246 (D. Colo. 2004) (allowing Rule 14a-9 claim against "an investment banking firm issuing a fairness opinion that it knows will be used for proxy solicitation and relied on by voting constituents"); with *New Jersey v. Sprint Corp.*, 314 F. Supp. 2d 1119, 1149 (D. Kan. 2004) (disallowing Rule 14a-9 claim against accounting firm that had made no representations in proxy statement). Does a private action under Rule 10b-5 reach a similar range of defendants?

5. Rationalizing the Implied Private Action. The Court offered two grounds for its recognition of an implied private action under Rule 14a-9: (i) Section 27 of the Exchange Act and (ii) the view that a private action "would provide a necessary supplement to Commission action." Years later, when faced with the question of whether to recognize an implied private action under Section 17(a) of the Exchange Act, the Court revisited both of these grounds and disavowed them:

> Section 27 grants jurisdiction to the federal courts and provides for venue and service of process. It creates no cause of action of its own force and effect; it imposes no liabilities. The source of plaintiffs' rights must be found, if at all, in the substantive provisions of the 1934 Act which they seek to enforce, not in the jurisdiction provision. The Court in *Borak* found a private cause of action implicit in Section 14(a). We do not now question the actual holding of that case, but we decline to read the opinion so broadly that virtually every provision of the securities Acts gives rise to an implied private cause of action.
>
> The invocation of the "remedial purposes" of the 1934 Act is similarly unavailing. Only last Term, we emphasized that generalized references to the "remedial purposes" of the 1934 Act will not justify reading a provision "more broadly than its language and the statutory scheme reasonably permit." *SEC v. Sloan,* 436 U.S. 103, 116 (1978). Certainly the mere fact that § 17(a) was designed to provide protection for brokers' customers does not require the implication of a private damages action in their behalf. To the extent our analysis in today's decision differs from that of the Court in *Borak*, it suffices to

> say that in a series of cases since *Borak* we have adhered to a stricter standard for the implication of private causes of action, and we follow that stricter standard today. The ultimate question is one of congressional intent, not one of whether this Court thinks that it can improve upon the statutory scheme that Congress enacted into law.

Touche Ross & Co. v. Redington, 442 U.S. 560, 577-78 (1979). See *Stoneridge Inv. Partners, LLC v. Scientific Atlanta., Inc.*, 552 U.S. 148, 164 (2008) (characterizing as "settled" the centrality of congressional intent to the question of whether to recognize an implied private action). Is this sensible? If Congress intends a private action, why would it fail to create one explicitly?

6. The Future of the Rule 14a-9 Private Action. As the preceding note shows, the Supreme Court has undercut the two grounds set forth in *Borak* for recognizing an implied private action under Rule 14a-9. Does it follow that the Court will eventually disavow the Rule 14a-9 implied private action itself? See generally C. Steven Bradford, The Possible Future of Private Rights of Action for Proxy Fraud: The Parallel Between *Borak* and *Wilko*, 70 Neb. L. Rev. 306 (1991) (answering this question in the affirmative). As you read the Supreme Court (and other) decisions that follow, ask yourself whether there is any indication that the action is at risk.

B. THE MATERIALITY REQUIREMENT

The Supreme Court addressed the definition of materiality under Rule 14a-9 in *TSC Indus., Inc. v. Northway, Inc.*, 426 U.S. 438 (1976):

> In formulating a standard of materiality under Rule 14a-9, we are guided, of course, by *** the Rule's broad remedial purpose. That purpose is not merely to ensure by judicial means that the transaction, when judged by its real terms, is fair and otherwise adequate, but to ensure disclosures by corporate management in order to enable the shareholders to make an informed choice. *** And particularly in view of the prophylactic purpose of the Rule and the fact that the content of the proxy statement is within management's control, it is appropriate that these doubts be resolved in favor of those the statute is designed to protect.
>
> We are aware, however, that the disclosure policy embodied in the proxy regulations is not without limit. Some information is of such dubious significance that insistence on its disclosure may accomplish more harm than good. The potential liability for a Rule 14a-9 violation can be great indeed, and if the standard of materiality is unnecessarily low, not only may the corporation and its management be subjected to liability for insignificant omissions or misstatements, but also management's fear of exposing itself to substantial liability may cause it simply to bury the shareholders in an avalanche of trivial information—a result that is hardly conducive to informed decisionmaking. ***
>
> The general standard of materiality that we think best comports with the policies of Rule 14a-9 is as follows: An omitted fact is material if there is a substantial likelihood that a reasonable shareholder would consider it important in deciding how to vote. *** It does not require proof of a substantial likelihood that disclosure of the omitted fact would have caused the reasonable investor to change his vote. What the standard does contemplate is a showing of a substantial likelihood that, under all the circumstances, the omitted fact would have assumed actual significance in the deliberations of the reasonable investor as having significantly altered the "total mix" of information available. ***

Id. at 448-49. See *Seinfeld v. Gray*, 404 F.3d 645, 650-51 (2d Cir. 2005) (applying *Northway* and finding the alleged misrepresentation immaterial based on language located elsewhere in the proxy statement). The *Northway* definition of materiality is apt to sound familiar to you, since it was adopted for Rule 10b-5 purposes in *Basic Inc. v. Levinson,* 485 U.S. 224 (1988). See also *Matrixx Initiatives, Inc. v. Siracusano*, 131 S.Ct. 1309, 1318 (2011) (reaffirming the applicability of the *Northway/Basic* standard to Rule 10b-5). See generally supra Chapter 2.B.2.

The materiality definition under Rules 14a-9 and 10b-5 may not be altogether co-extensive in application, however. Recall that when a Rule 10b-5 action involves securities traded in an efficient market, the "total mix" of information encompasses information known to the market, even if not known to the shareholder bringing the action. See supra Chapter 2.B.1. Contrast *United Paperworkers Int'l Union v. Int'l Paper Co.*, 985 F.2d 1190 (2d Cir. 1993), a Rule 14a-9 action involving management's response to a shareholder proposal that urged adoption of certain environmental policies. At issue was whether, in assessing the materiality of the alleged omissions and misrepresentations, the "total mix" of information should include news reports as well as the company's 10-K report filed with the SEC. The Second Circuit held that the "total mix" did not reach that far:

> Corporate documents that have not been distributed to the shareholders entitled to vote on the proposal should rarely be considered part of the total mix of information reasonably available to those shareholders.
>
> *** [W]hen the subject of a proxy solicitation has been widely reported in readily available media, shareholders may be deemed to have constructive notice of the facts reported, and the court may take this into consideration in determining whether representations in or omissions from the proxy statement are materially misleading. However, the mere presence in the media of sporadic news reports does not give shareholders sufficient notice that proxy solicitation statements sent directly to them by the company may be misleading, and such reports should not be considered to be part of the total mix of information that would clarify or place in proper context the company's representations in its proxy materials.
>
> In the present case, the district court properly rejected Paper Co.'s contention that public press reports and its 10-K Report should be viewed as part of the total mix of information reasonably available to shareholders. Though the Company argued that news articles should be considered, the articles were few in number, narrow in focus, and remote in time. ***
>
> Nor was the Company's 10-K Report part of the reasonably available mix. That report was filed with the SEC, not distributed to shareholders. Nothing in any of the documents sent to shareholders highlighted the 10-K Report. ***

Id. at 1199.

NOTES AND QUESTIONS

*1. **Different Causes of Action, Different "Total Mixes."*** Rule 14a-9 and Rule 10b-5 encompass different types of shareholder decisions – voting decisions in the former versus trading decisions in the latter. Does this distinction help explain why the scope of the "total mix" tends to be narrower under Rule 14a-9 than under Rule 10b-5? Cf. *In re Keyspan Corp. Sec. Litig.*, 383 F. Supp. 2d 358, 374 n.6 (E.D.N.Y. 2003) (observing that "the universe of information a shareholder would consider when voting in a proxy contest concerning a specific issue is smaller than, or at least different from, the corresponding universe an investor would consider when deciding whether to purchase or a retain a publicly traded stock in the first instance").

*2. **Our Post-Internet World.*** Notice that the *United Paperworkers* decision was issued in 1993, prior to "the explosion in Internet availability and use generally, and the institution of mandatory filing on EDGAR in particular." *In re Keyspan Corp. Sec. Litig.*, 383 F. Supp. 2d 358, 374 n.6 (E.D.N.Y. 2003). Should twenty-first century courts adjudicating Rule 14a-9 routinely treat SEC filings as part of the "total mix"? Cf. *Charming Shoppes, Inc. v. Crescendo Partners II, L.P.*, 557 F. Supp. 2d 621, 628-29 (E.D. Pa. 2008) (implicitly answering this question in the affirmative).

What types of information remain not readily accessible to shareholders (and thereby presumably outside the Rule 14a-9 "total mix")? Cf. *Koppel v. 4987 Corp.*, 167 F.3d 125, 132 (2d Cir. 1999) (finding that the "total mix" did not include a document that the proxy solicitation indicated was available in a specified New York City office partly because of "[t]he difficulty of obtaining the *** [document] — particularly for those *** who do not live in New York City").

*3. **Puffery Revisited.*** Recall the puffery doctrine that you encountered in connection with materiality under Rule 10b-5. See Note 2 on page 63. Is that doctrine applicable to Rule 14a-9?

C. THE STATE OF MIND REQUIREMENT

The Supreme Court has twice reserved the question of whether Rule 14a-9 requires proof of scienter. See *Virginia Bankshares v. Sandberg*, 501 U.S. 1083,1090 n.5 (1991); *TSC Indus., Inc. v. Northway, Inc.*, 426 U.S. 438, 444 n. 7 (1976). In general, lower courts have found negligence to be sufficient. See, e.g., *California Public Employees' Ret. Sys. v. Chubb Corp.*, 394 F.3d 126, 143-44 (3d Cir. 2004); *In re Bank of Am. Sec., Deriv. & ERISA Litig.*, 757 F. Supp. 2d 260, 321 (S.D.N.Y. 2010). *In re J.P. Morgan Chase Sec. Litig.*, 363 F. Supp. 2d 595, 636 (S.D.N.Y. 2005).

The following analysis by Judge Friendly of the Second Circuit has been influential in the development of this consensus:

> Although the language of Rule 14a-9(a) closely parallels that of Rule 10b-5, and neither says in so many words that scienter should be a requirement, one of the primary reasons that this court has held that this is required in a private action under Rule 10b-5 is a concern that without some such requirement the Rule might be invalid as exceeding the Commission's authority under section 10(b) to regulate "manipulation or deceptive devices." In contrast, the scope of the rulemaking authority granted under section 14(a) is broad, extending to all

> proxy regulation "necessary or appropriate in the public interest or for the protection of investors" and not limited by any words connoting fraud or deception. This language suggests that rather than emphasizing the prohibition of fraudulent conduct on the part of insiders to a securities transaction, as we think section 10(b) does, in section 14(a) Congress was somewhat more concerned with protection of the outsider whose proxy is being solicited. *** We note also that while an open-ended reading of Rule 10b-5 would render the express civil liability provisions of the securities acts largely superfluous, *** a reading of Rule 14a-9 as imposing liability without scienter in a case like the present is completely compatible with the statutory scheme.[18]
>
> Although this does not mean that scienter should never be required in an action under Rule 14a-9, a number of considerations persuade us that it would be inappropriate to require plaintiffs to prove it in the context of this case. First, many 10b-5 cases relate to statements issued by corporations, without legal obligation to do so, as a result of what the SEC has properly called "a commendable and growing recognition on the part of industry and the investment community of the importance of informing security holders and the public generally with respect to important business and financial developments." Securities Act Release No. 3844 (Oct. 8, 1957). Imposition of too liberal a standard with respect to culpability would deter this, particularly in light of the almost unlimited liability that may result. Such considerations do not apply to a proxy statement required by the Proxy Rules, especially to one, like that in the present case, which serves many of the same functions as a registration statement. Rather, a broad standard of culpability here will serve to reinforce the high duty of care owed by a controlling corporation to minority shareholders in the preparation of a proxy statement seeking their acquiescence in this sort of transaction, a consideration which is particularly relevant since liability in this case is limited to the stockholders whose proxies were solicited. While "privity" is not required for most actions under the securities laws, its existence may bear heavily on the appropriate standard of culpability.
>
> Furthermore, the common law itself finds negligence sufficient for tort liability where a person supplies false information to another with the intent to influence a transaction in which he has a pecuniary interest. This is particularly so when the transaction redounded directly to the benefit of the defendant, in which case the common law would provide the remedies of rescission and restitution without proof of scienter. It is unlikely that section 14(a) and Rule 14a-9 contemplated less.

Gerstle v. Gamble-Skogmo, Inc., 478 F.2d 1281, 1299-1300 (2d Cir. 1973). See *Wilson v. Great Am. Indus., Inc.*, 855 F.2d 987, 995 (2d Cir. 1988); *Brown v. Brewer*, 2010 WL 2472182 at *24 (C.D. Cal. 2010); *Bond Opportunity Fund v.*

---

18. It has been argued that imposing liability for negligent misrepresentations or omissions under Rule 14a-9 would be inconsistent with the congressional intent in enacting section 18 of the 1934 Act, which expressly creates liability in a private civil action for making materially false or misleading statements in any document filed with the Commission but provides that no liability shall be imposed if the defendant "acted in good faith and had no knowledge that such statement was false and misleading." But section 18 applies broadly to any document filed with the Commission, whereas section 14 was specifically directed at proxy regulation. Moreover, most of the documents within the scope of section 18 are not distributed to stockholders for the purpose of inducing action; we see nothing anomalous about applying a different standard of culpability in actions concerning misrepresentations in proxy statements which are so distributed than in those involving reports which were merely filed with the Commission. ***

Unilab Corp., 2003 WL 21058251 at *4 (S.D.N.Y. 2003) (citing *Gerstle* and collecting cases), aff'd, 87 Fed. App'x 772 (2d Cir. 2004).

NOTES AND QUESTIONS

1. Pleading Negligence. As part of the PSRLA, Congress enacted a uniform standard for pleading state of mind in connection with claims brought by private plaintiffs seeking money damages:

> **Section 21D(b)(2)** – In any private action arising under [the Exchange Act] in which the plaintiff may recover money damages only on proof that the defendant acted with a particular state of mind, the complaint shall, with respect to each act or omission alleged to violate [the Exchange Act], state with particularity facts giving rise to a strong inference that the defendant acted with the required state of mind.

You encountered this provision previously in connection with Rule 10b-5. See Chapter 2.D.2.

Does this provision likewise govern the pleading of negligence under Rule 14a-9? The courts are divided. Compare *Beck v. Dobrowski*, 559 F.3d 680, 682 (7th Cir. 2009) (holding provision inapposite because "negligence is not a state of mind") with *Little Gem Life Sciences, LLC v. Orphan Medical, Inc.*, 537 F.3d 913, 917 (8th Cir. 2008) (holding provision applicable because negligence is a state of mind).

Recall from your study of Section 21D(b)(2) in the Rule 10b-5 context the Supreme Court's decision in *Tellabs, Inc. v. Makor Issues & Rights, Ltd.*, 551 U.S. 308 (2007). If Section 21D(b)(2) applies to negligence-based claims under Rule 14a-9, does the *Tellabs* interpretation of the provision apply as well?

2. The Sufficiency of Non-Negligent Conduct. Did the *Gerstle* decision establish negligence as the rock-bottom minimum for Rule 14a-9 liability? See *Beck v. Dobrowski*, 559 F.3d 680, 682 (7th Cir. 2009) (suggesting that less than negligence would be acceptable). Cf. *Ash v. LFE Corp.*, 525 F.2d 215, 220 (3d Cir. 1975) (declining to require proof of negligence when the plaintiff sought equitable relief and noting that "[w]hatever may be the rule with respect to scienter when other remedies such as damages or rescission of a sale are sought, we have no hesitancy in recognizing that for prospective relief looking to the protection of the franchise, the test for the purposes of Rule 14a-9 is the objective sufficiency of the disclosure").

3. The Inescapableness of Scienter. As noted at the beginning of this Section, the Supreme Court reserved the question of whether Rule 14a-9 requires scienter in *Virginia Bankshares v. Sandberg*, 501 U.S. 1083,1090 n.5 (1991). See also *TSC Indus., Inc. v. Northway, Inc.*, 426 U.S. 438, 444 n.7 (1976). Yet the following passage from *Virginia Bankshares* initially prompted some courts and commentators to infer that scienter might nonetheless sometimes have a role:

> *** We consider first the actionability *per se* of statements of reasons, opinions, or belief. Because such a statement by definition purports to express what is consciously on the speaker's mind, we interpret the jury verdict as finding that the directors' statements of belief and opinion were made with knowledge that the directors did not hold the beliefs or opinions expressed, and we confirm our

> discussion to statements so made.[5] That such statements may be materially significant raises no serious question. ***
>
> *** Provable facts either furnish good reasons to make a conclusory commercial judgment, or they count against it, and expressions of such judgments can be uttered with knowledge of truth or falsity just like more definite statements, and defended or attacked through the orthodox evidentiary process that either substantiates their underlying justifications or tends to disprove their existence. ***
>
> *** Under § 14(a), then, a plaintiff is permitted to prove a specific statement of reason knowingly false or misleadingly incomplete, even when stated in conclusory terms. ***

Id. at 1090, 1093-94. See, e.g., *In re Reliance Sec. Litig.*, 135 F. Supp.2d 480, 515 (D.Del. 2001) (concluding that after *Virginia Bankshares*, liability for a misleading opinion requires that the defendants act "recklessly or intentionally"); Marc I. Steinberg & William A. Reece, The Supreme Court, Implied Rights of Action, and Proxy Regulation, 54 Ohio St. L. J. 67, 92-93 (1993) (concluding from *Virginia Bankshares* that "the culpability level [under Rule 14a-9] may no longer be simple negligence, at least in certain instances").

These initial inferences failed to snowball, however. One significant reason was that the imposition of a scienter requirement would have likely lengthened the limitations period. To understand why this is so, some brief background is in order.

Perhaps not surprisingly, the Exchange Act as originally enacted contained no explicit limitations period for implied private actions. The Supreme Court initially filled the gap for implied actions under Rule 10b-5 with a one year/three year structure: "one year after the discovery of the facts constituting the violation and within three years after the violation." *Lampf, Pleva, Lipkind, Prupis & Petigrow v. Gilbertson*, 501 U.S. 350, 364 (1991). Lower courts applied this structure to implied actions under Rule 14a-9 as well. See, e.g., *Westinghouse Elec. Corp. by Levit v. Franklin*, 993 F.2d 349, 353 (3d Cir. 1993).

Then, in 2002, as part of the Sarbanes-Oxley Act, Congress established a two year/five year structure for "a claim of fraud, deceit, manipulation, or contrivance" under the Exchange Act (as well as under other federal securities statutes). See 18 U.S.C. § 1658(b), set forth supra page 249.

Does Section 1658(b)'s two year/five year structure apply to Rule 14a-9? Lower courts to date have given a negative answer based on Section 1658(b)'s fraud-deceit-manipulation-contrivance language. Reasoning that this language embraces only those actions that require scienter, the courts insist that the limitations period for Rule 14a-9 continues to be the one year/three year structure upheld in *Lampf*, supra. See, e.g., *In re Exxon Mobil Corp. Sec. Litig.*, 500 F.3d 189, 202 (3d Cir. 2002); *Lane v. Page*, 649 F. Supp. 2d 1256, 1298 (D.N.M. 2009), *In re Maxim Integrated Prods., Inc., Deriv. Litig.*, 574 F. Supp.

---

5. In *TSC Industries, Inc. v. Northway, Inc.*, 426 U.S. 438, 444 n. 7 (1976), we reserved the question whether scienter was necessary for liability generally under § 14(a). We reserve it still.

2d 1046, 1072 (N.D. Cal. 2008).

But dispensing with Section 1658(b) altogether in the Rule 14a-9 context may not be so easy. What if the Rule 14a-9 claim "sounds in fraud"? What if it involves a forward-looking statement? Cf. Exchange Act Section 21E. What if the defendant is an outside accountant? See *Adams v. Standard Knitting Mills, Inc.*, 623 F.2d 422, 428 (6th Cir. 1980) (adopting scienter requirement for such a lawsuit). But see *Herskowitz v. Nutri/System, Inc.*, 857 F.2d 179, 190 (3d Cir. 1988) (rejecting scienter requirement in action against investment banker).

4. Individual vs. Corporate Liability. In *SEC v. Bank of Am. Corp*, 653 F. Supp. 2d 507 (S.D.N.Y. 2009), the court considered whether to approve a proposed consent judgment resolving the SEC's claim that Bank of America (Bank) had misled its shareholders about executive bonuses to be paid in the aftermath of Bank's acquisition of Merrill Lynch. Disapproving that judgment, the court observed:

> [T]he Consent Judgment would effectively close the case without the S.E.C. adequately accounting for why, in contravention of its own policy *** it did not pursue charges against either Bank management or the lawyers who allegedly were responsible for the false and misleading proxy statements. The S.E.C. says this is because charges against individuals for making false proxy statements require, at a minimum, proof that they participated in the making of the false statements knowing the statements were false or recklessly disregarding the high probability the statements were false. ***

Id. at 510-11. Do you agree with the SEC's assessment of the requisite state of mind for individuals charged with violations of Rule 14a-9? After many months of pre-trial discovery, the court ultimately approved a second proposed consent judgment that included, among other things, Bank's payment of a $150 million civil penalty (up from the less "meaningful" figure of $33 million under the terms of the first proposed consent judgment). The court determined "only that the S.E.C.'s conclusion that the Bank and its officers acted negligently, rather than intentionally, in causing the nondisclosures . . . is a reasonable conclusion, supported by substantial evidence, that a reasonable regulator could draw." *SEC v. Bank of Am. Corp*, 2010 WL 624581 at *3 (S.D.N.Y. 2010). If the SEC can charge a corporation with violating Rule 14a-9 based on its merely negligent conduct, does it make sense to apply a scienter standard to the individuals responsible for the false and misleading statements?

SEC says negligence / for corps, scienter for individuals

D. CAUSATION

A private action under Rule 14a-9 brings into play both transaction causation and loss causation. These two forms of causation are addressed in the subsections that follow.

1. Transaction Causation

In a private action under Rule 14a-9, what relationship (if any) must the plaintiff establish between the proxy statement and the merger (or other transaction)? The Supreme Court addressed this question in *Mills v. Electric Auto-Lite Co.*, 396 U.S. 375 (1970) and also in *Virginia Bankshares, Inc. v. Sandberg*, 501 U.S. 1083 (1991). *Mills* laid down the basic parameters of Rule

14a-9 causation analysis. *Virginia Bankshares* addressed causation in the situation where management controls enough shares to obtain approval of the transaction, thereby rendering the votes of the public shareholders unnecessary.

a. The Basic Parameters

The Supreme Court decision that follows is significant not only for its analysis of causation under Rule 14a-9 but also for its analysis of the scope of relief available in private actions under the Rule.

MILLS v. ELECTRIC AUTO-LITE COMPANY

396 U.S. 375 (1970)

JUSTICE JOHN M. HARLAN:

This case requires us to consider a basic aspect of the implied private right of action for violation of § 14(a) of the Securities Exchange Act of 1934, recognized by this Court in *J. I. Case Co. v. Borak*, 377 U.S. 426 (1964). As in *Borak* the asserted wrong is that a corporate merger was accomplished through the use of a proxy statement that was materially false or misleading. The question with which we deal is what causal relationship must be shown between such a statement and the merger to establish a cause of action based on the violation of the Act.

I

Petitioners were shareholders of the Electric Auto-Lite Company until 1963, when it was merged into Mergenthaler Linotype Company. They brought suit on the day before the shareholders' meeting at which the vote was to take place on the merger against Auto-Lite, Mergenthaler, and a third company, American Manufacturing Company, Inc. The complaint sought an injunction against the voting by Auto-Lite's management of all proxies obtained by means of an allegedly misleading proxy solicitation; however, it did not seek a temporary restraining order, and the voting went ahead as scheduled the following day. Several months later petitioners filed an amended complaint, seeking to have the merger set aside and to obtain such other relief as might be proper.

In Count II of the amended complaint, which is the only count before us, petitioners predicated jurisdiction on § 27 of the 1934 Act. They alleged that the proxy statement sent out by the Auto-Lite management to solicit shareholders' votes in favor of the merger was misleading, in violation of § 14(a) of the Act and SEC Rule 14a-9 thereunder. Petitioners recited that before the merger Mergenthaler owned over 50% of the outstanding shares of Auto-Lite common stock, and had been in control of Auto-Lite for two years. American Manufacturing in turn owned about one-third of the outstanding shares of Mergenthaler, and for two years had been in voting control of Mergenthaler and, through it, of Auto-Lite. Petitioners charged that in light of these circumstances the proxy statement was misleading in that it told Auto-Lite shareholders that their board of directors recommended approval of the merger without also informing them that all 11 of Auto-Lite's directors were nominees of Mergenthaler and were under the "control and domination of Mergenthaler." Petitioners asserted the right to complain of this alleged violation both derivatively on behalf of Auto-Lite and as representatives of the class of all its minority shareholders.

On petitioners' motion for summary judgment with respect to Count II, the District Court *** ruled as a matter of law that the claimed defect in the proxy statement was, in light of the circumstances in which the statement was made, a material omission. The District Court concluded, from its reading of the *Borak* opinion, that it had to hold a hearing on the issue whether there was "a causal connection between the finding that there has been a violation of the disclosure requirements of § 14(a) and the alleged injury to the plaintiffs" before it could consider what remedies would be appropriate.

After holding such a hearing, the court found that under the terms of the merger agreement, an affirmative vote of two-thirds of the Auto-Lite shares was required for approval of the merger, and that the respondent companies owned and controlled about 54% of the outstanding shares. Therefore, to obtain authorization of the merger, respondents had to secure the approval of a substantial number of the minority shareholders. At the stockholders' meeting, approximately 950,000 shares, out of 1,160,000 shares outstanding, were voted in favor of the merger. This included 317,000 votes obtained by proxy from the minority shareholders, votes that were "necessary and indispensable to the approval of the merger." The District Court concluded that a causal relationship had thus been shown, and it granted an interlocutory judgment in favor of petitioners on the issue of liability, referring the case to a master for consideration of appropriate relief.

The District Court made the certification required by 28 U.S.C. § 1292(b), and respondents took an interlocutory appeal to the Court of Appeals for the Seventh Circuit. That court affirmed the District Court's conclusion that the proxy statement was materially deficient, but reversed on the question of causation. The court acknowledged that, if an injunction had been sought a sufficient time before the stockholders' meeting, "corrective measures would have been appropriate." However, since this suit was brought too late for preventive action, the courts had to determine "whether the misleading statement and omission caused the submission of sufficient proxies," as a prerequisite to a determination of liability under the Act. If the respondents could show, "by a preponderance of probabilities, that the merger would have received a sufficient vote even if the proxy statement had not been misleading in the respect found," petitioners would be entitled to no relief of any kind.

The Court of Appeals acknowledged that this test corresponds to the common-law fraud test of whether the injured party relied on the misrepresentation. However, rightly concluding that "[r]eliance by thousands of individuals, as here, can scarcely be inquired into," the court ruled that the issue was to be determined by proof of the fairness of the terms of the merger. If respondents could show that the merger had merit and was fair to the minority shareholders, the trial court would be justified in concluding that a sufficient number of shareholders would have approved the merger had there been no deficiency in the proxy statement. In that case respondents would be entitled to a judgment in their favor. ***

II

As we stressed in *Borak*, § 14(a) stemmed from a congressional belief that "[f]air corporate suffrage is an important right that should attach to every equity security bought on a public exchange." H.R.Rep.No.1383, 73d Cong., 2d Sess., 13. The provision was intended to promote "the free exercise of the voting rights of stockholders" by ensuring that proxies would be solicited with "explanation to the stockholder of the real nature of the questions for which authority to cast his vote is sought." Id. at 14; S.Rep.No.792, 73d Cong., 2d Sess., 12; see 377 U.S., at 431. The decision below, by permitting all liability to be foreclosed on the basis of a finding that the merger was fair, would allow the stockholders to be by-passed, at least where the only legal challenge to the merger is a suit for retrospective relief after the meeting has been held. A judicial appraisal of the merger's merits could be substituted for the actual and informed vote of the stockholders.

The result would be to insulate from private redress an entire category of proxy violations — those relating to matters other than the terms of the merger. Even outrageous misrepresentations in a proxy solicitation, if they did not relate to the terms of the transaction, would give rise to no cause of action under § 14(a). Particularly if carried over to enforcement actions by the Securities and Exchange Commission itself, such a result would subvert the congressional purpose of ensuring full and fair disclosure to shareholders.

Further, recognition of the fairness of the merger as a complete defense would confront small shareholders with an additional obstacle to making a successful challenge to a proposal recommended through a defective proxy statement. The risk that they would be unable to rebut the corporation's evidence of the fairness of the proposal, and thus to establish their cause of action, would be bound to discourage such shareholders from the private enforcement of the proxy rules that "provides a necessary supplement to Commission action." *J. I. Case Co. v. Borak*, 377 U.S., at 432.[5]

Such a frustration of the congressional policy is not required by anything in the wording of the statute or in our opinion in the *Borak* case. Section 14(a) declares it "unlawful" to solicit proxies in contravention of Commission rules, and SEC Rule 14a-9 prohibits solicitations "containing any statement which ... is false or misleading with respect to any material fact, or which omits to state any material fact necessary in order to make the statements therein not false or

---

5. The Court of Appeals' ruling that "causation" may be negated by proof of the fairness of the merger also rests on a dubious behavioral assumption. There is no justification for presuming that the shareholders of every corporation are willing to accept any and every fair merger offer put before them; yet such a presumption is implicit in the opinion of the Court of Appeals. That court gave no indication of what evidence petitioners might adduce, once respondents had established that the merger proposal was equitable, in order to show that the shareholders would nevertheless have rejected it if the solicitation had not been misleading. Proof of actual reliance by thousands of individuals would, as the court acknowledged, not be feasible, see R. Jennings & H. Marsh, Securities Regulation, Cases and Materials 1001 (2d ed. 1968); and reliance on the *nondisclosure* of a fact is a particularly difficult matter to define or prove, see 3 L. Loss, Securities Regulation 1766 (2d ed. 1961). In practice, therefore, the objective fairness of the proposal would seemingly be determinative of liability. But, in view of the many other factors that might lead shareholders to prefer their current position to that of owners of a larger, combined enterprise, it is pure conjecture to assume that the fairness of the proposal will always be determinative of their vote.

misleading..." Use of a solicitation that is materially misleading is itself a violation of law, as the Court of Appeals recognized in stating that injunctive relief would be available to remedy such a defect if sought prior to the stockholders' meeting. *** In the present case there has been a hearing specifically directed to the causation problem. The question before the Court is whether the facts found on the basis of that hearing are sufficient in law to establish petitioners' cause of action, and we conclude that they are.

Where the misstatement or omission in a proxy statement has been shown to be "material," as it was found to be here, that determination itself indubitably embodies a conclusion that the defect was of such a character that it might have been considered important by a reasonable shareholder who was in the process of deciding how to vote.[6] This requirement that the defect have a significant *propensity* to affect the voting process is found in the express terms of Rule 14a-9, and it adequately serves the purpose of ensuring that a cause of action cannot be established by proof of a defect so trivial, or so unrelated to the transaction for which approval is sought, that correction of the defect or imposition of liability would not further the interests protected by § 14(a).

There is no need to supplement this requirement, as did the Court of Appeals, with a requirement of proof of whether the defect actually had a decisive effect on the voting. Where there has been a finding of materiality, a shareholder has made a sufficient showing of causal relationship between the violation and the injury for which he seeks redress if, as here, he proves that the proxy solicitation itself, rather than the particular defect in the solicitation materials, was an essential link in the accomplishment of the transaction. This objective test will avoid the impracticalities of determining how many votes were affected, and, by resolving doubts in favor of those the statute is designed to protect, will effectuate the congressional policy of ensuring that the shareholders are able to make an informed choice when they are consulted on corporate transactions.[7]

---

6. In this case, where the misleading aspect of the solicitation involved failure to reveal a serious conflict of interest on the part of the directors, the Court of Appeals concluded that the crucial question in determining materiality was "whether the minority shareholders were sufficiently alerted to the board's relationship to their adversary to be on their guard." An adequate disclosure of this relationship would have warned the stockholders to give more careful scrutiny to the terms of the merger than they might to one recommended by an entirely distinterested board. Thus, the failure to make such a disclosure was found to be a material defect "as a matter of law," thwarting the informed decision at which the statute aims, regardless of whether the terms of the merger were such that a reasonable stockholder would have approved the transaction after more careful analysis.

7. We need not decide in this case whether causation could be shown where the management controls a sufficient number of shares to approve the transaction without any votes from the minority. Even in that situation, if the management finds it necessary for legal or practical reasons to solicit proxies from minority shareholders, at least one court has held that the proxy solicitation might be sufficiently related to the merger to satisfy the causation requirement, see *Laurenzano v. Einbender*, 264 F. Supp. 356 (E.D.N.Y.1966). But see *Hoover v. Allen*, 241 F. Supp. 213, 231-232 (S.D.N.Y.1965).

III

Our conclusion that petitioners have established their case by showing that proxies necessary to approval of the merger were obtained by means of a materially misleading solicitation implies nothing about the form of relief to which they may be entitled. We held in *Borak* that upon finding a violation the courts were "to be alert to provide such remedies as are necessary to make effective the congressional purpose," noting specifically that such remedies are not to be limited to prospective relief. In devising retrospective relief for violation of the proxy rules, the federal courts should consider the same factors that would govern the relief granted for any similar illegality or fraud. One important factor may be the fairness of the terms of the merger. Possible forms of relief will include setting aside the merger or granting other equitable relief, but, as the Court of Appeals below noted, nothing in the statutory policy "requires the court to unscramble a corporate transaction merely because a violation occurred." In selecting a remedy the lower courts should exercise "'the sound discretion which guides the determinations of courts of equity'," keeping in mind the role of equity as "the instrument for nice adjustment and reconciliation between the public interest and private needs as well as between competing private claims." *Hecht Co. v. Bowles*, 321 U.S. 321, 329-330 (1944), quoting from *Meredith v. Winter Haven*, 320 U.S. 228, 235 (1943). ***

Monetary relief will, of course, also be a possibility. Where the defect in the proxy solicitation relates to the specific terms of the merger, the district court might appropriately order an accounting to ensure that the shareholders receive the value that was represented as coming to them. On the other hand, where, as here, the misleading aspect of the solicitation did not relate to terms of the merger, monetary relief might be afforded to the shareholders only if the merger resulted in a reduction of the earnings or earnings potential of their holdings. In short, damages should be recoverable only to the extent that they can be shown. If commingling of the assets and operations of the merged companies makes it impossible to establish direct injury from the merger, relief might be predicated on a determination of the fairness of the terms of the merger at the time it was approved. These questions, of course, are for decision in the first instance by the District Court on remand, and our singling out of some of the possibilities is not intended to exclude others.

IV

*** The absence of express statutory authorization for an award of attorneys' fees in a suit under § 14(a) does not preclude such an award in cases of this type. In a suit by stockholders to recover short-swing profits for their corporation under § 16(b) of the 1934 Act, the Court of Appeals for the Second Circuit has awarded attorneys' fees despite the lack of any provision for them in § 16(b), "on the theory that the corporation which has received the benefit of the attorney's services should pay the reasonable value thereof." *Smolowe v. Delendo Corp.*, 136 F.2d 231, 241 (2d Cir. 1943). The court held that Congress' inclusion in §§ 9(e) and 18(a) of the Act of express provisions for recovery of attorneys' fees in certain other types of suits "does not impinge [upon] the result we reach in the absence of statute, for those sections merely enforce an additional penalty against the wrongdoer." ***

While the general American rule is that attorneys' fees are not ordinarily recoverable as costs, both the courts and Congress have developed exceptions to this rule for situations in which overriding considerations indicate the need for such a recovery. A primary judge-created exception has been to award expenses where a plaintiff has successfully maintained a suit, usually on behalf of a class, that benefits a group of others in the same manner as himself. To allow the others to obtain full benefit from the plaintiff's efforts without contributing equally to the litigation expenses would be to enrich the others unjustly at the plaintiff's expense. This suit presents such a situation. The dissemination of misleading proxy solicitations was a "deceit practiced on the stockholders as a group," *J. I. Case Co. v. Borak*, 377 U.S., at 432, and the expenses of petitioners' lawsuit have been incurred for the benefit of the corporation and the other shareholders.

The fact that this suit has not yet produced, and may never produce, a monetary recovery from which the fees could be paid does not preclude an award based on this rationale. ***

*** [I]n shareholders' derivative actions, where the courts increasingly have recognized that the expenses incurred by one shareholder in the vindication of a corporate right of action can be spread among all shareholders through an award against the corporation, regardless of whether an actual money recovery has been obtained in the corporation's favor. For example, awards have been sustained in suits by stockholders complaining that shares of their corporation had been issued wrongfully for an inadequate consideration. A successful suit of this type, resulting in cancellation of the shares, does not bring a fund into court or add to the assets of the corporation, but it does benefit the holders of the remaining shares by enhancing their value. ***

*** [A]n increasing number of lower courts have acknowledged that a corporation may receive a "substantial benefit" from a derivative suit, justifying an award of counsel fees, regardless of whether the benefit is pecuniary in nature. A leading case is *Bosch v. Meeker Cooperative Light & Power Assn.*, 257 Minn. 362 (1960), in which a stockholder was reimbursed for his expenses in obtaining a judicial declaration that the election of certain of the corporation's directors was invalid.***

In many suits under § 14(a), particularly where the violation does not relate to the terms of the transaction for which proxies are solicited, it may be impossible to assign monetary value to the benefit. Nevertheless, the stress placed by Congress on the importance of fair and informed corporate suffrage leads to the conclusion that, in vindicating the statutory policy, petitioners have rendered a substantial service to the corporation and its shareholders. Whether petitioners are successful in showing a need for significant relief may be a factor in determining whether a further award should later be made. But regardless of the relief granted, private stockholders' actions of this sort "involve corporate therapeutics," and furnish a benefit to all shareholders by providing an important means of enforcement of the proxy statute. To award attorneys' fees in such a suit to a plaintiff who has succeeded in establishing a cause of action is not to saddle the unsuccessful party with the expenses but to impose them on the class that has benefitted from them and that would have had to pay them had it brought the suit. ***

NOTES AND QUESTIONS

*1. **The Presumption of Transaction Causation.*** What is the Court's rationale for presuming causation once the plaintiff establishes the materiality of the omission or misrepresentation? Are defendants entitled to rebut this presumption? If so, how can they do so?

*2. **Transaction Causation in the Backdating Context.*** A number of recent Rule 14a-9 cases have involved the backdating of stock options. See, e.g., *Edward J. Goodman Life Income Trust v. Jabil Circuit, Inc.*, 594 F.3d 783 (11th Cir. 2010); *Police & Ret. Sys. of the City of Detroit v. SafeNet, Inc.*, 645 F. Supp. 2d 210 (S.D.N.Y. 2009); *Hulliung v. Bolen*, 548 F. Supp. 2d 336 (N.D. Tex. 2008). Consider the following description of how transaction causation plays out in this context:

> Transactional causation for stock option grant manipulation customarily involves a three-step-process. First, there is a stock option grant manipulation that pre-dates a proxy statement. Then, there is a false or misleading proxy statement that leads to approval of the recommended action, generally the reelection of directors or the amendment of the Company's stock option plan. Finally, these directors grant additional manipulated stock options. ***

In re IBasis, Inc. Deriv. Litig., 532 F. Supp. 2d 214, 223 (D. Mass. 2007).

*3. **The Necessity of Individual Reliance.*** Suppose a shareholder who was not misled by a fraudulent proxy statement thereafter voted against the merger or other transaction. Is she entitled to challenge the proxy statement pursuant to which the merger (or other transaction) received the requisite shareholder approval? The D.C. Circuit has given an affirmative answer:

DC circ said SH who voted no w/ fraud proxy that went through is entitled to challenge

> The injury Cowin alleges was not caused by his individual reliance on deceptive proxy solicitations. Rather, his claim is that other shareholders elected appellees as directors because they were misled by the proxy materials. The installation of appellees as directors and their subsequent actions has injured appellant. This injury is totally divorced from any reliance, or lack of reliance, on Cowin's part and falls precisely into the scope of injury Congress sought to protect. Requiring reliance in these circumstances would serve no legitimate policy and we decline to do so.

Cowin v. Bresler, 741 F.2d 410, 427 (D.C. Cir. 1984) ; *Kaplan v. First Hartford Corp.*, 447 F. Supp. 2d 3, 9 (D. Mass. 2006); *Tracinda Corp. v. DaimlerChrysler AG*, 364 F. Supp. 2d 362, 414 n. 24 (D. Del. 2005). See also *Stahl v. Gibraltar Fin. Corp.*, 967 F.2d 335 (9th Cir.1992) Do you agree? Must she nonetheless allege the reliance of the other shareholders? See *Bender v. Jordan*, 439 F. Supp. 2d 139, 164 (D.D.C. 2006).

*4. **The Relevance of Fairness.*** While rejecting the fairness of the merger terms as a stand-in for transaction causation, the *Mills* Court nonetheless made the fairness of those terms an "important factor" in fashioning relief. Seizing upon this statement on remand, the Seventh Circuit held "that the terms of the merger were fair and that the plaintiffs should recover no damages." *Mills v. Electric Auto-Lite Co.*, 552 F.2d 1239, 1249 (7th Cir. 1977). Does it follow that the *Mills* litigation was not worthwhile?

b. When Management Controls Sufficient Shares to Approve the Transaction; Lost State Remedies

In footnote 7 of *Mills*, the Supreme Court left open the appropriateness of presuming causation in those situations where management controls enough shares to obtain approval of the transaction without the votes of the public shareholders. The Court divided 5-4 on this question in the decision that follows.

VIRGINIA BANKSHARES v. SANDBERG

501 U.S. 1083 (1991)

JUSTICE DAVID H. SOUTER:

*** In December 1986, First American Bankshares, Inc. (FABI), a bank holding company, began a "freeze-out" merger, in which the First American Bank of Virginia (Bank) eventually merged into Virginia Bankshares, Inc. (VBI), a wholly owned subsidiary of FABI. VBI owned 85% of the Bank's shares, the remaining 15% being in the hands of some 2,000 minority shareholders. FABI hired the investment banking firm of Keefe, Bruyette & Woods (KBW) to give an opinion on the appropriate price for shares of the minority holders, who would lose their interests in the Bank as a result of the merger. Based on market quotations and unverified information from FABI, KBW gave the Bank's executive committee an opinion that $42 a share would be a fair price for the minority stock. The executive committee approved the merger proposal at that price, and the full board followed suit.

Although Virginia law required only that such a merger proposal be submitted to a vote at a shareholders' meeting, and that the meeting be preceded by circulation of a statement of information to the shareholders, the directors nevertheless solicited proxies for voting on the proposal at the annual meeting set for April 21, 1987.[3] In their solicitation, the directors urged the proposal's adoption and stated they had approved the plan because of its opportunity for the minority shareholders to achieve a "high" value, which they elsewhere described as a "fair" price, for their stock.

Although most minority shareholders gave the proxies requested, respondent Sandberg did not, and after approval of the merger she sought damages in the United States District Court for the Eastern District of Virginia from VBI, FABI, and the directors of the Bank. She pleaded two counts, one for soliciting proxies in violation of § 14(a) and Rule 14a-9, and the other for breaching fiduciary duties owed to the minority shareholders under state law. Under the first count, Sandberg alleged, among other things, that the directors had not believed that the price offered was high or that the terms of the merger were fair, but had recommended the merger only because they believed they had no alternative if they wished to remain on the board. At trial, Sandberg invoked language from this Court's opinion in *Mills v. Electric Auto-Lite Co.*, 396 U.S. 375, 385 (1970), to obtain an instruction that the jury could find for her without

3. Had the directors chosen to issue a statement instead of a proxy solicitation, they would have been subject to an SEC antifraud provision analogous to Rule 14a-9. See 17 CFR § 240.14c-6 (1990). See also 15 U.S.C. § 78n(c).

a showing of her own reliance on the alleged misstatements, so long as they were material and the proxy solicitation was an "essential link" in the merger process.

jury found for P / 4th circ affirmed

The jury's verdicts were for Sandberg on both counts, after finding violations of Rule 14a-9 by all defendants and a breach of fiduciary duties by the Bank's directors. The jury awarded Sandberg $18 a share, having found that she would have received $60 if her stock had been valued adequately. ***

On appeal, the United States Court of Appeals for the Fourth Circuit affirmed the judgments, holding that certain statements in the proxy solicitation were materially misleading for purposes of the Rule, and that respondents could maintain their action even though their votes had not been needed to effectuate the merger. 891 F.2d 1112 (1989).[4] ***

III

The second issue before us, left open in *Mills v. Electric Auto-Lite Co.*, 396 U.S., at 385, n. 7, is whether causation of damages compensable through the implied private right of action under § 14(a) can be demonstrated by a member of a class of minority shareholders whose votes are not required by law or corporate bylaw to authorize the transaction giving rise to the claim. *J.I. Case Co. v. Borak,* 377 U.S. 426 (1964), did not itself address the requisites of causation, as such, or define the class of plaintiffs eligible to sue under § 14(a). But its general holding, that a private cause of action was available to some shareholder class, acquired greater clarity with a more definite concept of causation in *Mills,* where we addressed the sufficiency of proof that misstatements in a proxy solicitation were responsible for damages claimed from the merger subject to complaint.

Although a majority stockholder in *Mills* controlled just over half the corporation's shares, a two-thirds vote was needed to approve the merger proposal. After proxies had been obtained, and the merger had carried, minority shareholders brought a *Borak* action. *Mills,* 396 U.S., at 379. The question arose whether the plaintiffs' burden to demonstrate causation of their damages traceable to the § 14(a) violation required proof that the defect in the proxy solicitation had had "a decisive effect on the voting." Id., at 385. The *Mills* Court avoided the evidentiary morass that would have followed from requiring individualized proof that enough minority shareholders had relied upon the misstatements to swing the vote. Instead, it held that causation of damages by a material proxy misstatement could be established by showing that minority proxies necessary and sufficient to authorize the corporate acts had been given in accordance with the tenor of the solicitation, and the Court described such a causal relationship by calling the proxy solicitation an "essential link in the accomplishment of the transaction." Ibid. In the case before it, the Court found the solicitation essential, as contrasted with one addressed to a class of minority shareholders without votes required by law or bylaw to authorize the action

4. The Court of Appeals reversed the District Court, however, on its refusal to certify a class of all minority shareholders in Sandberg's action. Consequently, it ruled that petitioners were liable to all of the Bank's former minority shareholders for $18 per share. 891 F.2d, at 1119.

proposed, and left it for another day to decide whether such a minority shareholder could demonstrate causation. Id., 396 U.S., at 385, n. 7.

In this case, respondents address *Mills'* open question by proffering two theories that the proxy solicitation addressed to them was an "essential link" under the *Mills* causation test. They argue, first, that a link existed and was essential simply because VBI and FABI would have been unwilling to proceed with the merger without the approval manifested by the minority shareholders' proxies, which would not have been obtained without the solicitation's express misstatements and misleading omissions. On this reasoning, the causal connection would depend on a desire to avoid bad shareholder or public relations, and the essential character of the causal link would stem not from the enforceable terms of the parties' corporate relationship, but from one party's apprehension of the ill will of the other.

In the alternative, respondents argue that the proxy statement was an essential link between the directors' proposal and the merger because it was the means to satisfy a state statutory requirement of minority shareholder approval, as a condition for saving the merger from voidability resulting from a conflict of interest on the part of one of the Bank's directors, Jack Beddow, who voted in favor of the merger while also serving as a director of FABI. Under the terms of Va.Code Ann. § 13.1-691(A) (1989), minority approval after disclosure of the material facts about the transaction and the director's interest was one of three avenues to insulate the merger from later attack for conflict, the two others being ratification by the Bank's directors after like disclosure and proof that the merger was fair to the corporation. On this theory, causation would depend on the use of the proxy statement for the purpose of obtaining votes sufficient to bar a minority shareholder from commencing proceedings to declare the merger void.

Although respondents have proffered each of these theories as establishing a chain of causal connection in which the proxy statement is claimed to have been an "essential link," neither theory presents the proxy solicitation as essential in the sense of *Mills'* causal sequence, in which the solicitation links a directors' proposal with the votes legally required to authorize the action proposed. As a consequence, each theory would, if adopted, extend the scope of *Borak* actions beyond the ambit of *Mills* and expand the class of plaintiffs entitled to bring *Borak* actions to include shareholders whose initial authorization of the transaction prompting the proxy solicitation is unnecessary.

Assessing the legitimacy of any such extension or expansion calls for the application of some fundamental principles governing recognition of a right of action implied by a federal statute, the first of which was not, in fact, the considered focus of the *Borak* opinion. The rule that has emerged in the years since *Borak* and *Mills* came down is that recognition of any private right of action for violating a federal statute must ultimately rest on congressional intent to provide a private remedy, *Touche Ross & Co. v. Redington,* 442 U.S. 560, 575 (1979). From this the corollary follows that the breadth of the right once recognized should not, as a general matter, grow beyond the scope congressionally intended.

This rule and corollary present respondents with a serious obstacle, for we can find no manifestation of intent to recognize a cause of action (or class of plaintiffs) as broad as respondents' theory of causation would entail. At first blush, it might seem otherwise, for the *Borak* Court certainly did not ignore the matter of intent. Its opinion adverted to the statutory object of "protection of investors" as animating Congress' intent to provide judicial relief where "necessary," 377 U.S., at 432, and it quoted evidence for that intent from House and Senate Committee Reports, id., at 431-432. *Borak's* probe of the congressional mind, however, never focused squarely on private rights of action, as distinct from the substantive objects of the legislation, and one Member of the *Borak* Court later characterized the "implication" of the private right of action as resting modestly on the Act's "'exclusively procedural provision' affording access to a federal forum." *Bivens v. Six Unknown Fed. Narcotics Agents,* 403 U.S. 388, 403, n. 4 (1971) (Harlan, J., concurring in judgment). In fact, the importance of enquiring specifically into intent to authorize a private cause of action became clear only later, see *Cort v. Ash,* 422 U.S., at 78,, and only later still, in *Touche Ross,* was this intent accorded primacy among the considerations that might be thought to bear on any decision to recognize a private remedy. There, in dealing with a claimed private right under § 17(a) of the Act, we explained that the "central inquiry remains whether Congress intended to create, either expressly or by implication, a private cause of action." 442 U.S., at 575-576.

Looking to the Act's text and legislative history mindful of this heightened concern reveals little that would help toward understanding the intended scope of any private right. According to the House Report, Congress meant to promote the "free exercise" of stockholders' voting rights, H.R.Rep. No. 1383, 73d Cong., 2d Sess., 14 (1934), and protect "[f]air corporate suffrage," id., at 13, from abuses exemplified by proxy solicitations that concealed what the Senate Report called the "real nature" of the issues to be settled by the subsequent votes, S.Rep. No. 792, 73d Cong., 2d Sess., 12 (1934). While it is true that these Reports, like the language of the Act itself, carry the clear message that Congress meant to protect investors from misinformation that rendered them unwitting agents of self-inflicted damage, it is just as true that Congress was reticent with indications of how far this protection might depend on self-help by private action. The response to this reticence may be, of course, to claim that § 14(a) cannot be enforced effectively for the sake of its intended beneficiaries without their participation as private litigants. *Borak,* supra, 377 U.S., at 432. But the force of this argument for inferred congressional intent depends on the degree of need perceived by Congress, and we would have trouble inferring any congressional urgency to depend on implied private actions to deter violations of § 14(a), when Congress expressly provided private rights of action in §§ 9(e), 16(b), and 18(a) of the same Act.[11]

---

11. The object of our enquiry does not extend further to question the holding of either *J. I. Case Co. v. Borak,* 377 U.S. 426 (1964), or *Mills v. Electric Auto-Lite Co.,* 396 U.S. 375 (1970), at this date, any more than we have done so in the past, see *Touche Ross & Co. v. Redington,* 442 U.S. 560, 577 (1979). Our point is simply to recognize the hurdle facing any litigant who urges us to enlarge the scope of the action beyond the point reached in *Mills.*

The congressional silence that is thus a serious obstacle to the expansion of cognizable *Borak* causation is not, however, a necessarily insurmountable barrier. This is not the first effort in recent years to expand the scope of an action originally inferred from the Act without "conclusive guidance" from Congress, see *Blue Chip Stamps v. Manor Drug Stores,* 421 U.S., at 737, and we may look to that earlier case for the proper response to such a plea for expansion. There, we accepted the proposition that where a legal structure of private statutory rights has developed without clear indications of congressional intent, the contours of that structure need not be frozen absolutely when the result would be demonstrably inequitable to a class of would-be plaintiffs with claims comparable to those previously recognized. Faced in that case with such a claim for equality in rounding out the scope of an implied private statutory right of action, we looked to policy reasons for deciding where the outer limits of the right should lie. We may do no less here, in the face of respondents' pleas for a private remedy to place them on the same footing as shareholders with votes necessary for initial corporate action.

A

Blue Chip Stamps set an example worth recalling as a preface to specific policy analysis of the consequences of recognizing respondents' first theory, that a desire to avoid minority shareholders' ill will should suffice to justify recognizing the requisite causality of a proxy statement needed to garner that minority support. It will be recalled that in *Blue Chip Stamps* we raised concerns about the practical consequences of allowing recovery, under § 10(b) of the Act and Rule 10b-5, on evidence of what a merely hypothetical buyer or seller might have done on a set of facts that never occurred, and foresaw that any such expanded liability would turn on "hazy" issues inviting self-serving testimony, strike suits, and protracted discovery, with little chance of reasonable resolution by pretrial process. Id., at 742-743. These were good reasons to deny recognition to such claims in the absence of any apparent contrary congressional intent.

The same threats of speculative claims and procedural intractability are inherent in respondents' theory of causation linked through the directors' desire for a cosmetic vote. Causation would turn on inferences about what the corporate directors would have thought and done without the minority shareholder approval unneeded to authorize action. A subsequently dissatisfied minority shareholder would have virtual license to allege that managerial timidity would have doomed corporate action but for the ostensible approval induced by a misleading statement, and opposing claims of hypothetical diffidence and hypothetical boldness on the part of directors would probably provide enough depositions in the usual case to preclude any judicial resolution short of the credibility judgments that can only come after trial. Reliable evidence would seldom exist. Directors would understand the prudence of making a few statements about plans to proceed even without minority endorsement, and discovery would be a quest for recollections of oral conversations at odds with the official pronouncements, in hopes of finding support for *ex post facto* guesses about how much heat the directors would have stood in the absence of minority approval. The issues would be hazy, their litigation

P's first theory would invite hypothetical P's strike suits and little resolution from pre-trial process protracted, and their resolution unreliable. Given a choice, we would reject any theory of causation that raised such prospects, and we reject this one.[12]

B

The theory of causal necessity derived from the requirements of Virginia law dealing with postmerger ratification seeks to identify the essential character of the proxy solicitation from its function in obtaining the minority approval that would preclude a minority suit attacking the merger. Since the link is said to be a step in the process of barring a class of shareholders from resort to a state remedy otherwise available, this theory of causation rests upon the proposition of policy that § 14(a) should provide a federal remedy whenever a false or misleading proxy statement results in the loss under state law of a shareholder plaintiff's state remedy for the enforcement of a state right. Respondents agree with the suggestions of counsel for the SEC and FDIC that causation be recognized, for example, when a minority shareholder has been induced by a misleading proxy statement to forfeit a state-law right to an appraisal remedy by voting to approve a transaction, cf. *Swanson v. American Consumers Industries, Inc.,* 475 F.2d 516, 520-521 (CA7 1973), or when such a shareholder has been deterred from obtaining an order enjoining a damaging transaction by a proxy solicitation that misrepresents the facts on which an injunction could properly have been issued. Cf. *Healey v. Catalyst Recovery of Pennsylvania, Inc.,* 616 F.2d 641, 647-648 (CA3 1980); *Alabama Farm Bureau Mutual Casualty Co. v. American Fidelity Life Ins. Co.,* 606 F.2d 602, 614 (CA5 1979). Respondents claim that in this case a predicate for recognizing just such a causal link exists in Va. Code Ann. § 13.1-691(A)(2) (1989), which sets the conditions under which the merger may be insulated from suit by a minority shareholder seeking to void it on account of Beddow's conflict.

This case does not, however, require us to decide whether § 14(a) provides a cause of action for lost state remedies, since there is no indication in the law or facts before us that the proxy solicitation resulted in any such loss. The contrary appears to be the case. Assuming the soundness of respondents' characterization of the proxy statement as materially misleading, the very terms of the Virginia statute indicate that a favorable minority vote induced by the solicitation would not suffice to render the merger invulnerable to later attack on the ground of the conflict. The statute bars a shareholder from seeking to avoid a transaction tainted by a director's conflict if, *inter alia,* the minority shareholders ratified the transaction following disclosure of the material facts

12. In parting company from us on this point, Justice Kennedy emphasizes that respondents in this particular case substantiated a plausible claim that petitioners would not have proceeded without minority approval. FABI's attempted freeze-out merger of a Maryland subsidiary had failed a year before the events in question when the subsidiary's directors rejected the proposal because of inadequate share price, and there was evidence of FABI's desire to avoid any renewal of adverse comment. The issue before us, however, is whether to recognize a theory of causation generally, and our decision against doing so rests on our apprehension that the ensuing litigation would be exemplified by cases far less tractable than this. Respondents' burden to justify recognition of causation beyond the scope of *Mills* must be addressed not by emphasizing the instant case but by confronting the risk inherent in the cases that could be expected to be characteristic if the causal theory were adopted.

of the transaction and the conflict. Va. Code Ann. § 13.1-691(A)(2) (1989). Assuming that the material facts about the merger and Beddow's interests were not accurately disclosed, the minority votes were inadequate to ratify the merger under state law, and there was no loss of state remedy to connect the proxy solicitation with harm to minority shareholders irredressable under state law.[13] Nor is there a claim here that the statement misled respondents into entertaining a false belief that they had no chance to upset the merger, until the time for bringing suit had run out.[14]

JUSTICE ANTHONY M. KENNEDY, WITH WHOM JUSTICE MARSHALL, JUSTICE BLACKMUN, AND JUSTICE STEVENS JOIN, CONCURRING IN PART AND DISSENTING IN PART:

A

*** The severe limits the Court places upon possible proof of nonvoting causation in a § 14(a) private action are justified neither by our precedents nor by any case in the courts of appeals. These limits are said to flow from a shift in our approach to implied causes of action that has occurred since we recognized the § 14(a) implied private action in *J.I. Case Co. v. Borak,* 377 U.S. 426 (1964).

I acknowledge that we should exercise caution in creating implied private rights of action and that we must respect the primacy of congressional intent in that inquiry. Where an implied cause of action is well accepted by our own cases and has become an established part of the securities laws, however, we should enforce it as a meaningful remedy unless we are to eliminate it altogether. As the Court phrases it, we must consider the causation question in light of the underlying "policy reasons for deciding where the outer limits of the right should lie."

According to the Court, acceptance of non-voting causation theories would "extend the scope of *Borak* actions beyond the ambit of *Mills.*" But *Mills v. Electric Auto-Lite Co.,* 396 U.S. 375 (1970), did not purport to limit the scope of *Borak* actions, and as footnote 7 of *Mills* indicates, some courts have applied nonvoting causation theories to *Borak* actions for at least the past 25 years.

To the extent the Court's analysis considers the purposes underlying § 14(a), it does so with the avowed aim to limit the cause of action and with undue emphasis upon fears of "speculative claims and procedural intractability." The result is a sort of guerrilla warfare to restrict a well-established implied

13. In his opinion dissenting on this point, Justice Kennedy suggests that materiality under Virginia law might be defined differently from the materiality standard of our own cases, resulting in a denial of state remedy even when a solicitation was materially misleading under federal law. Respondents, however, present nothing to suggest that this might be so.

14. Respondents do not claim that any other application of a theory of lost state remedies would avail them here. It is clear, for example, that no state appraisal remedy was lost through a § 14(a) violation in this case. *** "Va. Code § 6.1-43 specifically excludes bank mergers from application of § 13.1-730 [the Virginia appraisal statute]." ***

right of action. If the analysis adopted by the Court today is any guide, Congress and those charged with enforcement of the securities laws stand forewarned that unresolved questions concerning the scope of those causes of action are likely to be answered by the Court in favor of defendants.

B

The Court seems to assume, based upon the footnote in *Mills* reserving the question, that Sandberg bears a special burden to demonstrate causation because the public shareholders held only 15 percent of the stock of First American Bank of Virginia (Bank). Justice Stevens is right to reject this theory. Here, First American Bankshares, Inc. (FABI), and Virginia Bankshares, Inc. (VBI), retained the option to back out of the transaction if dissatisfied with the reaction of the minority shareholders, or if concerned that the merger would result in liability for violation of duties to the minority shareholders. The merger agreement was conditioned upon approval by two-thirds of the shareholders, and VBI could have voted its shares against the merger if it so decided. To this extent, the Court's distinction between cases where the "minority" shareholders could have voted down the transaction and those where causation must be proved by nonvoting theories is suspect. Minority shareholders are identified only by a *post hoc* inquiry. The real question ought to be whether an injury was shown by the effect the nondisclosure had on the entire merger process, including the period before votes are cast.

The Court's distinction presumes that a majority shareholder will vote in favor of management's proposal even if proxy disclosure suggests that the transaction is unfair to minority shareholders or that the board of directors or majority shareholder is in breach of fiduciary duties to the minority. If the majority shareholder votes against the transaction in order to comply with its state-law duties, or out of fear of liability, or upon concluding that the transaction will injure the reputation of the business, this ought not to be characterized as nonvoting causation. Of course, when the majority shareholder dominates the voting process, as was the case here, it may prefer to avoid the embarrassment of voting against its own proposal and so may cancel the meeting of shareholders at which the vote was to have been taken. For practical purposes, the result is the same: Because of full disclosure the transaction does not go forward and the resulting injury to minority shareholders is avoided. The Court's distinction between voting and nonvoting causation does not create clear legal categories.

III

Our decision in *Mills v. Electric Auto-Lite Co.*, supra, at 385, rested upon the impracticality of attempting to determine the extent of reliance by thousands of shareholders on alleged misrepresentations or omissions. A misstatement or an omission in a proxy statement does not violate § 14(a) unless "there is a substantial likelihood that a reasonable shareholder would consider it important in deciding how to vote." *TSC Industries, Inc. v. Northway, Inc.*, 426 U.S. 438, 449 (1976). If minority shareholders hold sufficient votes to defeat a management proposal and if the misstatement or omission is likely to be considered important in deciding how to vote, then there exists a likely causal link between the proxy violation and the enactment of the proposal; and one can justify recovery by minority shareholders for damages resulting from enactment of management's proposal.

If, for sake of argument, we accept a distinction between voting and nonvoting causation, we must determine whether the *Mills* essential link theory applies where a majority shareholder holds sufficient votes to force adoption of a proposal. The merit of the essential link formulation is that it rests upon the likelihood of causation and eliminates the difficulty of proof. Even where a minority lacks votes to defeat a proposal, both these factors weigh in favor of finding causation so long as the solicitation of proxies is an essential link in the transaction.

A

The Court argues that a nonvoting causation theory would "turn on 'hazy' issues inviting self-serving testimony, strike suits, and protracted discovery, with little chance of reasonable resolution by pretrial process." The Court's description does not fit this case and is not a sound objection in any event. Any causation inquiry under § 14(a) requires a court to consider a hypothetical universe in which adequate disclosure is made. Indeed, the analysis is inevitable in almost any suit when we are invited to compare what was with what ought to have been. The causation inquiry is not intractable. On balance, I am convinced that the likelihood that causation exists supports elimination of any requirement that the plaintiff prove the material misstatement or omission caused the transaction to go forward when it otherwise would have been halted or voted down. This is the usual rule under *Mills,* and the difficulties of proving or disproving causation are, if anything, greater where the minority lacks sufficient votes to defeat the proposal. A presumption will assist courts in managing a circumstance in which direct proof is rendered difficult. See *Basic Inc. v. Levinson,* 485 U.S. 224, 245 (1988) (discussing presumptions in securities law).

B

There is no authority whatsoever for limiting § 14(a) to protecting those minority shareholders whose numerical strength could permit them to vote down a proposal. One of § 14(a)'s "chief purposes is 'the protection of investors.'" *J. I. Case Co. v. Borak,* 377 U.S., at 432. Those who lack the strength to vote down a proposal have all the more need of disclosure. The voting process involves not only casting ballots but also the formulation and withdrawal of proposals, the minority's right to block a vote through court action or the threat of adverse consequences, or the negotiation of an increase in price. The proxy rules support this deliberative process. These practicalities can result in causation sufficient to support recovery.

The facts in the case before us prove this point. ***

The theory that FABI would not have pursued the transaction if full disclosure had been provided and the shareholders had realized the inadequacy of the price is supported not only by the trial testimony but also by notes of the meeting of the Bank's board, which approved the merger. The inquiry into causation can proceed not by "opposing claims of hypothetical diffidence and hypothetical boldness," but through an examination of evidence of the same type the Court finds acceptable in its determination that directors' statements of reasons can lead to liability. Discussion at the board meeting focused upon matters such as "how to keep PR afloat" and "how to prevent adverse reac[tion]/perception," demonstrating the directors' concern that an unpopular merger proposal could injure the Bank.

Only a year or so before the Virginia merger, FABI had failed in an almost identical transaction, an attempt to freeze out the minority shareholders of its Maryland subsidiary. FABI retained Keefe, Bruyette & Woods (KBW) for that transaction as well, and KBW had given an opinion that FABI's price was fair. The subsidiary's board of directors then retained its own adviser and concluded that the price offered by FABI was inadequate. The Maryland transaction failed when the directors of the Maryland bank refused to proceed; and this was despite the minority's inability to outvote FABI if it had pressed on with the deal.

In the Virginia transaction, FABI again decided to retain KBW. Beddow, who sat on the boards of both FABI and the Bank, discouraged the Bank from hiring its own financial adviser, out of fear that the Maryland experience would be repeated if the Bank received independent advice. Directors of the Bank testified they would not have voted to approve the transaction if the price had been demonstrated unfair to the minority. Further, approval by the Bank's board of directors was facilitated by FABI's representation that the transaction also would be approved by the minority shareholders. ***

I conclude that causation is more than plausible; it is likely, even where the public shareholders cannot vote down management's proposal. Causation is established where the proxy statement is an essential link in completing the transaction, even if the minority lacks sufficient votes to defeat a proposal of management.

IV

The majority avoids the question whether a plaintiff may prove causation by demonstrating that the misrepresentation or omission deprived her of a state-law remedy. I do not think the question difficult, as the whole point of federal proxy rules is to support state-law principles of corporate governance. Nor do I think that the Court can avoid this issue if it orders judgment for petitioners. The majority asserts that respondents show no loss of a state-law remedy, because if "the material facts about the merger and Beddow's interests were not accurately disclosed, the minority votes were inadequate to ratify the merger under state law." This theory requires us to conclude that the Virginia statute governing director conflicts of interest, Va. Code Ann. § 13.1-691(A)(2) (1989), incorporates the same definition of materiality as the federal proxy rules. I find no support for that proposition. If the definitions are not the same, then Sandberg may have lost her state-law remedy. For all we know, disclosure to the minority shareholders that the price is $42 per share may satisfy Virginia's requirement. If that is the case, then approval by the minority without full disclosure may have deprived Sandberg of the ability to void the merger.

In all events, the theory that the merger would have been voidable absent minority shareholder approval is far more speculative than the theory that FABI and the Bank would have called off the transaction. Even so, this possibility would support a remand, as the lower courts have yet to consider the question. We are not well positioned as an institution to provide a definitive resolution to state-law questions of this kind. Here again, the difficulty of knowing what would have happened in the hypothetical universe of full disclosure suggests that we should "resolv[e] doubts in favor of those the statute is designed to protect" in order to "effectuate the congressional policy of ensuring that the shareholders are able to make an informed choice when they are consulted on corporate transactions." *Mills,* 396 U.S., at 385. ***

NOTES AND QUESTIONS

1. ***The Corollary.*** *Virginia Bankshares* announced a "corollary" to its rule that a court should recognize an implied private action only when Congress intended the action to exist: an implied private action "should not, as a general matter, grow beyond the scope Congress intended." How important was the corollary to the *Virginia Bankshares* decision? What is the likely impact of the corollary on judicial interpretation of Rule 14a-9? Cf. *Stoneridge Inv. Partners, LLC v. Scientific Atlanta, Inc.,* 552 U.S. 148, 165 (2008) (invoking the *Virginia Bankshares* corollary to restrict the implied action under Rule 10b-5).

2. ***Vexatious Litigation Threat?*** The Court suggested that Rule 14a-9 presents a threat of vexatious litigation essentially comparable to that of Rule 10b-5. Do you agree?

3. ***Solicitations to Foster Shareholder Relations.*** The plaintiff claimed that management had solicited proxies in order to foster shareholder relations, but the Court rejected this argument as too speculative. Is it any more speculative than the reasoning that led to the presumption of causation in *Mills*?

4. ***Lost State Remedies.*** Are causation arguments based on lost state remedies viable in the wake of *Virginia Bankshares*? If so, must the plaintiff show that she would have prevailed on her state law remedy? Or would it be sufficient for her to show that she had a prima facie case for the remedy? Must she show that she would have pursued the state law remedy if the proxy statement had not been misleading?

5. ***Varieties of State Law.*** State laws can vary considerably with respect to the remedies provided to shareholders in any given situation. Thus, assume two corporations (X and Y) incorporated in different states, each of which issued a proxy statement to its shareholders containing a comparable material misrepresentation. The shareholders of X Corporation might be able to claim loss of a state remedy (and hence entitlement to sue under Rule 14a-9), whereas the shareholders of Y Corporation might not have had a state remedy to lose (and hence lack entitlement to sue under Rule 14a-9). Does this state of affairs conflict with the last paragraph of Part III of *Borak*? From the standpoint of policy, should the vagaries of state law determine whether Rule 14a-9 is available?

6. ***How Bright a Line?*** Can a plaintiff distinguish *Virginia Bankshares* (and thereby avail himself of the *Mills* presumption) by proving that at least some of the shares under management's "control" would have been voted

against the merger if the proxy statement had not been misleading? One district court has given a negative answer:

> *Virginia Bankshares* *** apparently establishes a bright line rule that courts should not look behind an affirmative shareholder vote where a majority of the shareholders indicate in the proxy statement *** their intent to cast an affirmative vote in the face of speculative claims that, absent some statement in the proxy materials, a controlling shareholder would have voted differently.

In re Reliance Sec. Litig., 135 F. Supp. 2d 480, 517 (D. Del. 2001). Do you agree?

***7. A Wider Role for* Virginia Bankshares?** The Second Circuit relied upon *Virginia Bankshares* to dismiss a Rule 14a-9 action brought by shareholders whose votes were necessary to the approval of a merger:

> We may assume that the omitted information would have been important to a reasonable shareholder in determining how to vote on the proposed merger with Astoria and thus meets the standard definition of materiality. See *TSC Indus., Inc. v. Northway, Inc.*, 426 U.S. 438, 449 (1976). However, in the proxy context this definition of materiality assumes that the omitted information would have influenced a reasonable shareholder against the proposed transaction for which proxies were sought. Here, the omitted information would not have made a reasonable shareholder any less likely to favor the objected to transaction, and such an omission, material or not, could not have caused the injury for which damages are sought.
>
> In *Virginia Bankshares, Inc. v. Sandberg,* 501 U.S. 1083 (1991), the Supreme Court held that a materially misleading proxy solicitation was not actionable where the controlling shareholder had enough votes to approve the objected-to transaction without seeking proxies. See id. at 1099-1108. The rationale of that holding applies equally to cases where the omissions would have caused a reasonable shareholder to favor rather than disfavor the transaction. In *Virginia Bankshares,* the omissions were not actionable because the disputed transaction would have occurred even if the proxy statement had been complete and accurate. See id. at 1107-08. That is also the case here. Had a reasonable Greater New York shareholder been fully informed, that shareholder would not have been any less likely to vote for the Astoria merger knowing of the cataloged information than being ignorant of it.

Minzer v. Keegan, 218 F.3d 144, 149-50 (2d Cir. 2000). See *Bond Opportunity Fund v. Unilab Corp.*, 2003 WL 21058251 at *9 (S.D.N.Y. 2003) (following *Minzer*), aff'd, 87 Fed. App'x 772 (2d Cir. 2004). Could the *Minzer* court have reached the same result without invoking *Virginia Bankshares*?

PROBLEM 4-1

Whiz, Inc. is a manufacturer of surgical supplies, including a device (the "direx") used in the performance of abortions. Whiz's stock is listed on the New York Stock Exchange. Management does not control a majority of the shares.

Eliza, a Whiz shareholder, submitted a shareholder proposal recommending to the board that it halt manufacture of the direx. The proxy statement containing Eliza's proposal included an argument from management urging shareholders to vote against her proposal. Management's argument was that the direx was not used exclusively in connection with abortions. Rather, management maintained, the direx had multiple surgical uses outside the abortion context. This argument had no basis in fact.

The shareholders defeated Eliza's proposal. Eliza then filed a Rule 14a-9 action that challenged management's statement regarding the direx. She asked the court to declare void the shareholder vote on her proposal and to order the company to resubmit her proposal to the shareholders at the next annual meeting.

Whiz responded with a motion to dismiss Eliza's action for failure to state a claim. According to Whiz, the board would have been entitled to disregard Eliza's proposal even if a majority of the shareholders had voted for it. Thus, Whiz argued, the proxy solicitation was not "an essential link in the accomplishment of [a corporate] action," as the Supreme Court requires.

Should the court grant Whiz's motion?

In the decision that follows, the court confronted an argument mentioned but not addressed in *Virginia Bankshares* — that the shareholders would have pursued their appraisal rights if the proxy statement had not been misleading.

WILSON v. GREAT AMERICAN INDUSTRIES, INC.

979 F.2d 924 (2d Cir. 1992)

RICHARD J. CARDAMONE, CIRCUIT JUDGE:

Defendants appeal and plaintiffs cross appeal from two decisions and orders of the United States District Court *** that awarded damages to plaintiffs because of misrepresentations contained in a joint proxy/prospectus issued in connection with a merger of defendant Chenango Industries, Incorporated (Chenango) into defendant Great American Industries, Incorporated (Great American). Defendants assert that the intervening Supreme Court decision in *Virginia Bankshares, Inc. v. Sandberg,* 501 U.S. 1083, (1991), compels dismissal of plaintiffs' causes of action on the grounds that as minority shareholders, without power to influence the proposed merger, they suffered no compensable damages under § 14(a) of the Security Exchange Act, notwithstanding that their votes were solicited by proxies containing material misrepresentations. Defendants and plaintiffs also claim the district court incorrectly calculated damages. ***

*** The thrust of plaintiffs' complaint is that the material misstatements induced them to exchange their shares of Chenango common stock for new preferred stock in Great American. Defendants at the time of the merger owned 73 percent of Chenango's stock, well over the two thirds necessary under New York law to approve a corporate merger. New York law only required that defendants hold a shareholders' meeting prior to which Chenango was required to give each shareholder notice of the meeting accompanied by a "copy of the plan of merger." N.Y.Bus.Corp. Law § 903(a)(1) (McKinney 1986). Because Chenango stock was registered under § 12(g) of the Act, defendants were also required to provide shareholders with an "Information Statement" pursuant to § 14(c) of the Act. Nonetheless, defendants mailed out joint proxy and registration statements seeking Chenango minority shareholders' approval of the merger.

The misrepresentations or omissions contained in the proxy created an unfair exchange ratio, plaintiffs assert, by overvaluing Great American's stock and undervaluing Cherango's stock. ***

I.

A. *Intervening Supreme Court Decision*

The Supreme Court in *Virginia Bankshares* did not hold that minority shareholders whose votes number too few to affect the outcome of a shareholder vote may *never* recover damages under § 14(a) or that *no* implied private cause of action for such shareholders is provided under that section of the Act. And, it expressly declined to decide whether § 14(a) provides an implied federal remedy for minority shareholders deprived of certain state remedies as a result of deceptive proxy solicitations. 501 U.S. at [1108] & n. 14. To the extent that this Circuit recognizes such a remedy, defendants incorrectly contend therefore that *Virginia Bankshares* precludes plaintiffs from seeking such relief. ***

B. *Plaintiff's Theories of Recovery*

*** Plaintiffs set forth two theories of causation to support their claims. They assert first that an implied action under any of the four securities law provisions pleaded should be recognized because 85 percent of the voting shares, or 12 percent of the minority shareholders in addition to the controlling majority shareholders, had to approve the merger in order for the exchange of stock to take place without tax consequences. Although an opinion letter stated the merger might have tax-free consequences for the majority shareholders if 85 percent of the shareholders approved it, such an approval level was not a requirement of the merger. If it was not an express condition of the merger, the higher rate of dissenting voters could only prevent the merger were it to influence the controlling majority. Such a speculative and hypothetical causal connection would make liability "turn on 'hazy' issues [and invite] self-serving testimony, strike suits, and protracted discovery, with little chance of reasoned resolution by pretrial process." *Virginia Bankshares,* 501 U.S. at 1105 (rejecting causal theory promised on majority's desire for "cosmetic" vote and avoidance of minority shareholders' ill-will). Thus, we reject this theory of causation.

Plaintiffs' second theory of causation — one with more merit and upon which § 14(a) causes of action have been sustained in the past — is that their deceptively procured vote in favor of the merger deprived them of their state appraisal rights under N.Y. Bus. Corp. Law §§ 623(a), (b); § 910(a)(1). We and other courts have recognized that plaintiffs might prevail on such a § 14(a) theory. See *Cole v. Schenley Indus., Inc.*, 563 F.2d 35, 39-40 (2d Cir.1977) (on a motion to dismiss complaint, implied right recognized when insignificant minority shareholders had state law alternatives to accepting merger); *Schlick v. Penn-Dixie Cement Corp.*, 507 F.2d 374, 381-84 (2d Cir.1974) (though insignificant minority shareholders had no appraisal rights under state law, deprivation of measures other than casting proxies may support implied right to recovery under § 14(a)).

As noted, *Virginia Bankshares* left open the possibility that § 14(a) might include this type of implied right to recover and did not address whether the causal relationship between a deceptive proxy and lost state remedies was sufficient to support a federal remedy. Defendants, having failed to contest causation prior to the present appeal, should hardly be allowed to argue the point now, especially when to permit such puts them in a better position than if they had made this objection earlier and lost.

We continue to believe that a minority shareholder, who has lost his right to a state appraisal because of a materially deceptive proxy, may make "a sufficient showing of causal relationship between the violation and the injury for which he seeks redress." *Mills,* 396 U.S. at 385. The transaction effected by a proxy involves not only the merger of the corporate entities, and the attendant exchange of stock, but also the forfeiture of shareholders' appraisal rights. The injury sustained by a minority shareholder powerless to affect the outcome of the merger vote is not the merger but the loss of his appraisal right. The deceptive proxy plainly constitutes an "essential link" in accomplishing the forfeiture of this state right.

That the causal nexus between the merger and the proxy is absent when the minority stockholder's vote cannot affect the merger decision does not necessarily mean a causal link between the proxy and some other injury may not exist. We recognize that loss causation or economic harm to plaintiffs must be shown, as well as proof that the misrepresentations induced plaintiffs to engage in the subject transaction, that is, transaction causation. Here loss causation may be established when a proxy statement prompts a shareholder to accept an unfair exchange ratio for his shares rather than recoup a greater value through a state appraisal. And transaction causation may be shown when a proxy statement, because of material misrepresentations, causes a shareholder to forfeit his appraisal rights by voting in favor of the proposed corporate merger. See *Schlick,* 507 F.2d at 380; Note, Causation and Liability in Private Actions for Proxy Violations, 80 Yale L.J. 107, 123-27 (1970).

Even though the proxy was not legally required in this case, when defendants choose to issue a proxy plaintiffs have a right to a truthful one. With the Securities Exchange Act of 1934, Congress sought to promote fair corporate suffrage with respect to "'every equity security'" by requiring an "'explanation to the stockholder of the real nature of the questions for which authority to cast his vote is sought.'" *Mills,* 396 U.S. at 381 (quoting H.R. Rep. No. 1383, 73d Cong., 2d Sess. 13-14 (1934)); see also *J.I. Case Co. v. Borak,* 377 U.S. 426, 431-32 (1964). Congress' interest in the protection of investors and the "'free exercise of [their] voting rights,'" *Borak,* 377 U.S. at 431 (quoting H.R. Rep. No. 1383, 73d Cong., 2d Sess. 14 (1934)), should not vary in degree according to the ability of the shareholder to affect the merger, if the vote nevertheless may result in a different sort of injury which full disclosure might have avoided.

The statute does not suggest that the prohibition of material misrepresentation in a proxy extends only to necessary proxies that are mailed to shareholders the solicitation of whose votes may affect the outcome of the proposed corporate action. That a controlling group of shareholders may accomplish any corporate change they want does not insulate them from liability for injury occasioned when they commit the sort of fraud that § 14(a) seeks to prevent. See *Swanson v. American Consumer Indus., Inc.,* 415 F.2d 1326, 1331-32 (7th Cir.1969). To decline to extend the protection of § 14(a) to plaintiffs, we think, might sanction overreaching by controlling shareholders when the minority shareholders most need § 14(a)'s protection. See *Schlick,* 507 F.2d at 383. At the same time, allowing the action does not pose a threat of "speculative claims and procedural intractability," *Virginia Bankshares,* 501 U.S. at 1105, because the forfeiture of state appraisal rights is a question separate from the effectuation of the merger and does not require courts to guess how or whether the majority shareholders would have proceeded in the face of minority dissent.

Although a finding of materiality in a proxy solicitation may satisfy the elements of loss and transaction causation for forfeited state appraisal rights, plaintiffs must also prove that they in fact lost state appraisal rights. See *Virginia Bankshares,* at [1108] & n. 14. *** Accordingly, we must remand this matter for the limited purpose of determining whether the proxy solicitation actually resulted in the loss of any remedies available to plaintiffs under New York law. ***

II

Given the possibility that on remand defendants may again have liability imposed against them under § 14(a), we think it prudent to reach those aspects of the appeal and cross-appeal that challenge the trial court's calculation of damages. ***

The benefit of the bargain rule set forth in *Janigan v. Taylor,* 344 F.2d 781 (1st Cir. 1965), is the appropriate measure of damages in this matter. *Janigan* held a shareholder induced by fraud into selling his shares for less than fair consideration may recover future accretions in value of the stock, even if those damages are not foreseeable. Id. at 786-87. This rule applies to mergers involving fraudulent proxies as well as to face-to-face transactions under § 10(b). See *Osofsky v. Zipf,* 645 F.2d 107, 114 (2d Cir.1981). The goal of preventing the speculative fraud resulting when damages are awarded only for the difference in the values of the exchanged stocks, see id. (citing Restatement (Second) of Torts § 549(2), cmts. g, i (1977)), applies with as much force when appraisal rights are fraudulently forfeited as it does when a merger is fraudulently effected.

But to place plaintiffs in substantially the same position they would have occupied absent the fraud, they should be entitled to the profits attributable to the extra stock they would have received had the proxy provided a fair exchange ratio. Although the fraud may not be the proximate cause of the merger, it did cause the forfeiture of appraisal rights, which in turn prevented plaintiffs from realizing a fair exchange ratio. Thus the injury caused by the fraud cannot be measured by the shares that were exchanged, rather by the value of the additional shares that should have been exchanged but because of the fraud were not. The benefit of the bargain rule in the context of lost state appraisal rights would apply only to the stock never received, and not to the shares actually received. ***

NOTES AND QUESTIONS

1. ***Speculativeness Again.*** As a general matter, shareholders pursue appraisal rights relatively rarely because to do so is expensive and time-consuming and may result in their receipt of a per share price that is less than

that offered in the merger. See generally Robert B. Thompson, Exit, Liquidity, and Majority Rule: Appraisal's Role in Corporate Law, 84 Geo. L. J. 1 (1995). Does allowing shareholders to recover for lost appraisal rights entail a level of speculativeness that is unacceptable in light of *Virginia Bankshares*?

*2. **The Benefit of the Bargain.*** Should the *Wilson* court have limited the plaintiffs' recovery to the amount likely to have been forthcoming from the appraisal action that they did not pursue?

PROBLEM 4-2

Quincy Corporation issued a proxy statement that urged its shareholders to approve a merger with Dunster Corporation. The proxy statement included a forward-looking statement containing a material misrepresentation. Approval of the merger was a given, since management controlled eighty percent of the shares.

Jillian, one of the public shareholders, voted against the merger but did not perfect her appraisal rights. After the merger was consummated, she brought a Rule 14a-9 action that challenged the forward-looking statement. She claimed that had the proxy statement not been misleading, she would have perfected her appraisal rights and initiated an appraisal proceeding.

Quincy Corporation moved to dismiss Jillian's action. It contended that Jillian's causation argument is supported neither by *Virginia Bankshares* nor *Wilson* and therefore should be rejected.

Should the court grant the motion? Are there additional facts that would be useful to know in answering this question?

Cf. *Howing Co. v. Nationwide Corp.*, 972 F.2d 700 (6th Cir. 1992).

2. Loss Causation

Pursuant to the PSLRA, loss causation has become a requirement that all Exchange Act plaintiffs have to prove:

> In any private action arising under this title, the plaintiff shall have the burden of proving that the act or omission of the defendant alleged to violate this title caused the loss for which the plaintiff seeks to recover damages.

Exchange Act § 21D(b)(4). According to the Supreme Court, this language requires that loss causation be alleged as well. See *Dura Pharm., Inc. v. Broudo*, 544 U.S. 336, 346 (2005) (interpreting loss causation in the Rule 10b-5 context).

The difficulties involved in pleading loss causation under Rule 14a-9 parallel those arising under Rule 10b-5. See, e.g., *Amorosa v. Ernst & Young, LLP,* 682 F. Supp. 2d 351, 364 (S.D.N.Y. 2010) (failure to claim that a disclosure to which the market reacted corrected the alleged falsehoods in the proxy statement); *Edward J. Goodman Life Income Trust v. Jabil Circuit, Inc.*, 595 F. Supp. 2d 1253, 1279 (M.D. Fla. 2009) (failure to link proxy statement to the decline in share price), aff'd on other grds, 594 F.3d 783 (5th Cir. 2010).

PROBLEM 4-3

Preston, Inc., is a Section 12 company. Last year its annual proxy statement inflated the credentials of management's slate of candidates for the board of directors, none of whom had previously served on the board . There was no alternative slate of candidates. Preston utilizes plurality voting .

Once on the board, the directors voted in favor of two transactions which proved to be financial disasters for Preston. Neither transaction required shareholder approval.

Preston shareholders Carlie and Erik have sued under Rule 14a-9. They allege that if the proxy statement had accurately described the respective backgrounds of the director candidates, those candidates would not have been elected to the board and thus would not have cast votes in favor of the two disastrous transactions. Carlie and Erik seek to recover on behalf of the company the losses that those transactions precipitated.

Will Carlie and Erik be able to plead and prove loss causation? Why or why not?

Chapter 5

TENDER OFFER FRAUD — SECTION 14(e) OF THE EXCHANGE ACT

Section 14(e) of the Exchange Act prohibits fraud in connection with tender offers. An important weapon in contests for corporate control, Section 14(e) did not appear in the Exchange Act as originally enacted. It was added in 1968, along with a number of other provisions on tender offer regulation. The 1968 amendments, encompassing Section 14(e) together with Sections 13(d), 13(e), 14(d), and 14(f), are known collectively as the Williams Act.

We begin our study of Section 14(e) with an overview of tender offers and the Williams Act (Section A). We then turn to litigation under Section 14(e) and contrast it with litigation under other fraud provisions of the federal securities laws, especially Section 10(b) and Rule 10b-5 (Section B). The Chapter concludes with a brief discussion of the critical role of state law in tender offer litigation (Section C).

A. AN OVERVIEW OF TENDER OFFERS AND THE WILLIAMS ACT

The material that follows is intended to provide a context for our discussion of Section 14(e). Some students may have encountered this material previously in courses in corporations or mergers and acquisitions, whereas others will find it altogether new.

1. Tender Offers in General

A tender offer enables a company (the "bidder") to acquire control of another company (the "target"). In a tender offer, the bidder offers to purchase all or some of the target's shares directly from the target's shareholders, typically at a premium over the market price. The bidder and the target are usually different companies, although occasionally a company makes a tender offer for its own shares in a transaction known as a "self tender offer."

Like a proxy contest, a tender offer provides a means of accomplishing an acquisition that is opposed by the target's management. An acquisition supported by the target's management is usually achieved through a "friendly" merger rather than a friendly tender offer. A "friendly" tender offer is by no means unknown, however.

When the bidder's goal is to control the target, a tender offer is often preferable to a proxy contest. Indeed, the winner in a proxy contest obtains seats on the board, whereas a successful bidder in a tender offer owns the shares and hence is guaranteed the control that such ownership provides. But a tender offer has the disadvantage of being expensive, both because the bidder has to buy the shares and also because the target's management can commence litigation against the bidder or implement defensive tactics designed to frustrate the offer.

Prior to the enactment of the Williams Act, tender offers were only minimally regulated by the federal securities laws (or by state law). To be sure, the registration and civil liability provisions of the Securities Act came into play in "exchange" offers — tender offers in which shareholders are asked to exchange their shares for securities rather than for cash. But these provisions do not apply when, as is common, cash is the sole consideration. And while it is true that fraud in connection with the bidder's purchase of the tendered shares is prohibited by Section 10(b) of the Exchange Act and Rule 10b-5, those provisions do nothing for the defrauded non-tendering shareholder.

The relative absence of federal regulation of tender offers contrasted sharply with the comprehensive federal regulation of proxy contests provided by Section 14(a) of the Exchange Act and SEC rules promulgated thereunder. Thus, by using a tender offer, hostile acquirers could avoid the mandatory disclosure and procedural regulations to which they would have been subject if they had instead conducted a proxy contest.

Without laws mandating disclosure, bidders often provided little information regarding such matters as their background and their plans for the target. Accordingly, shareholders were forced to decide whether to tender with little knowledge of the relevant facts. Congress recognized their plight when discussing the need for federal tender offer regulation in 1967:

> [A shareholder] has many alternatives. He can tender all of his shares immediately and hope they are all purchased. However, if the offer is for less than all the outstanding shares, perhaps only a part of them will be taken. In these instances, he will remain a shareholder in the company, under a new management which he has helped to install without knowing whether it will be good or bad for the company.
>
> The shareholder, as another alternative, may wait to see if a better offer develops, but if he tenders late, he runs the risk that none of his shares will be taken. He may also sell his shares in the market or hold them and hope for the best. Without knowledge of who the bidder is and what he plans to do, the shareholder cannot reach an informed decision.

S. Rep. No. 90-550 at 2 (1967).

Moreover, prior to the enactment of the Williams Act, a lack of information was not the sole difficulty besetting shareholders faced with a tender offer. Common practices included giving shareholders only a short time to decide whether to tender, prohibiting withdrawals of tendered shares, giving some shareholders a better price than others, and offering to buy less than 100% of the shares (a "partial tender offer") while purchasing shares on a "first come, first served" basis. Partial tender offers coupled with "first come, first served" purchases caused Congress particular concern because bidders frequently used two-tiered transactions — first, a partial tender offer at an inadequate amount of cash per share, typically for a percentage of shares sufficient to give the bidder control, followed shortly thereafter by a second transaction squeezing out the remaining shareholders on even less desirable terms (e.g., junk bonds rather than cash). Confronting the decision whether to tender in the first tier, shareholders found themselves in a situation analogous to the prisoner's dilemma commonly used in game theory. Indeed, because the price paid in the first tier surpassed the price paid in the second tier, they were often coerced into tendering quickly, even though all shareholders would have been better off if none of them tendered.

Of course, even with disclosure, the decision whether to tender is frequently not an easy one to make. Consider a partial tender offer by a bidder with a good track record who has no present plans to acquire the remaining shares. A shareholder might plausibly refuse to tender in order to reap the benefits of a company controlled by responsible management. But she cannot be certain that the bidder will receive enough shares in the tender offer to achieve control in the first place.

2. The Williams Act

Prompted by an upsurge in tender offers in the 1960s, Congress enacted the Williams Act in 1968. That Act amended the Exchange Act to require disclosure and impose various other substantive and procedural protections on behalf of shareholders faced with the decision whether to tender their shares.

While providing shareholders with these protections, Congress sought to avoid playing favorites in the contest for control. In the words of the Supreme Court:

> The purpose of the Williams Act is to insure that public shareholders who are confronted by a cash tender offer for their stock will not be required to respond without adequate information regarding the qualifications and intentions of the offering party. By requiring disclosure of information to the target corporation as well as the Securities and Exchange Commission, Congress intended to do no more than give incumbent management an opportunity to express and explain its position. The Congress expressly disclaimed an intention to provide a weapon for management to discourage takeover bids or prevent large accumulations of stock which would create the potential for such attempts. Indeed, the Act's draftsmen commented upon the "extreme care" which was taken "to avoid tipping the balance of regulation either in favor of management or in favor of the person making the takeover bid." S. Rep. No. 550, 90th Cong., 1st Sess., 3 (1967); H.R. Rep. No. 1711, 90th Cong., 2d Sess., 4 (1968).

Rondeau v. Mosinee Paper Corp., 422 U.S. 49, 58-59 (1975).

The Williams Act does not regulate the defensive tactics employed by the target's management. Such tactics are instead governed by the law of the target's state of incorporation (see Section C infra).

The Williams Act is embodied in Sections 13(d), 13(e), 14(d), 14(e), and 14(f) of the Exchange Act. Some of these Sections apply to acquisitions accomplished by any means, whereas others apply to tender offers only. Thus, after examining the various Sections and the manner of their enforcement, we will take a look at how "tender offer" is defined.

a. Section 13(d)

Section 13(d) provides the marketplace with an early indication that control of a company may be "in play." The Section applies to any acquirer (whether by tender offer or otherwise) of more than 5% of the shares of a class of equity security of a Section 12 company. (For a discussion of Section 12 companies, see page 7). Such an acquirer must, within 10 days of making the acquisition, or, as amended by the Section 929R of the Dodd-Frank Act, "within such shorter time as the Commission may establish by rule," provide the SEC with a report (the Schedule 13D) that discloses his identity, background, source of financing, and any plans to make a later tender offer for the target. (The same Dodd-Frank Section eliminated from Section 13(d) the acquirer's obligation to provide the Schedule 13D to the issuer and any exchanges on which the security trades).

The filing of a Schedule 13D has a several-fold impact. First, such a filing is likely to trigger an immediate sharp increase in the target's share price, particularly if it discloses that a tender offer is in the offing. Thus, if a tender offer does occur, the offering price is apt to be higher than it would have been in the absence of the Schedule 13D. Hence Schedule 13D makes tender offers more expensive for bidders and arguably for this reason may deter some tender offers altogether. Moreover, by mandating disclosure of future plans to launch a tender offer, Schedule 13D gives the target's management the opportunity to undertake defensive measures.

The question of how the SEC should exercise its new authority to contract the 10 day window has generated considerable debate. That window has long afforded hostile acquirers the opportunity to significantly increase their holdings under the radar. Thus, Wachtel Lipton Rosen and Katz (WLRK), a prominent law firm that represents takeover targets and whose partner, Martin Lipton, created the poison pill takeover defense several decades ago, has urged the SEC to shrink the window to one day. See WLRK Petition, available at www.sec.gov/rules/petitions/2011/petn4-624.pdf On the other hand, Professor Jonathan Macey has argued against such a change: "Since the target company's stock price jumps significantly when these public filings are made, this rule change *** would make activist investments prohibitively expensive by increasing the price that these investors would have to pay for all shares acquired just one day after the 5% threshold is passed." Jonathan Macey, Uncle Sam and the Hostile Takeover, Wall St. J., March 21, 2011, at A17.

The Dodd-Frank Act gives the SEC new authority over Section 13(d)'s reporting requirement in another respect as well – namely, in connection with its applicability to security-based swap agreements: contracts in which the parties agree to exchange payments that turn on the price of a referenced security. Thus, Section 766 of the Dodd-Frank Act creates a new Section 13(o), which lets the SEC determine by rule that a person acquires a beneficial ownership of the security underlying a swap if it decides that "the purchase or sale of such swap, or class of swap, provides incidents of ownership comparable to ownership of the underlying security." To provide clarity while it considers how to proceed, the SEC has adopted a rule retaining the beneficial ownership reporting requirements as they existed prior to Dodd-Frank's enactment. See Beneficial Ownership Reporting Requirements and Security-Based Swaps, Release No. 34-64628 (June 14, 2011). Such a rule was deemed necessary in order to foreclose the argument that Section 13(o), which became effective after July 16, 2011, repealed the status quo. Among the proposals that the SEC is widely understood to be contemplating are those made in the petition by WLRK.

b. Section 14(d)

Unlike Section 13(d), Section 14(d) applies to tender offers specifically. Regulation under Section 14(d) takes several forms.

Under Section 14(d)(1), anyone who makes a tender offer for more than 5% of a class of equity security of a Section 12 company must file a Schedule TO with the SEC. Schedule TO requires disclosure of many items called for by Schedule 13D, along with the terms of the offer and the bidder's financial statements if "material" to the offer. Rules 14d-4 and 14d-6 govern the disclosures that must be made to the target's shareholders about the tender offer.

Under Section 14(d)(4), anyone (including the target) who makes a solicitation or recommendation to the target's shareholders concerning a tender offer must file a Schedule 14D-9 with the SEC. Schedule 14D-9 mandates many of the same disclosures called for by Schedule TO. In addition, it requires the target to indicate whether it is negotiating with another bidder (a "white knight").

Other subsections of Section 14(d) are designed to reduce shareholder coercion. Thus, the bidder must accept the tendered shares on a pro rata rather than a first-come-first-served basis (Section 14(d)(6) and Rule 14d-8); the shareholders may withdraw their tendered shares during the period that the tender offer remains open (Section 14(d)(5) and Rule 14d-7); and all tendering shareholders must be paid the same price (Section 14(d)(7) and Rule 14d-10). Shareholder coercion is also reduced by Rule 14e-1. That Rule, promulgated under Section 14(e), requires that the offer remain open for twenty business days. We return to Rule 14e-1 later in this Chapter when we discuss the SEC's rule-making authority under Section 14(e).

c. Section 14(f)

Section 14(f) applies to acquisitions governed by both Sections 13(d) and 14(d). Section 14(f) requires disclosure of arrangements involving a change in the membership of a majority of the target's board of directors that occurs other than by a vote of the shareholders. The disclosure must be made to the SEC as well as to the shareholders denied their franchise not less than 10 days before the new directors assume office.

d. Section 13(e)

Sections 13(d) and 14(d) are each inapplicable when a company purchases its own stock. Such purchases fall instead under Section 13(e), which prohibits a Section 12 company from "purchas[ing] any equity security issued by it" if doing so would violate rules adopted by the SEC. Thus, Section 13(e) and the rules adopted pursuant to it regulate issuer "buy-backs," so-called "going private transactions" (often structured as leveraged buyouts (LBOs)), and issuer self-tender offers.

e. Section 14(e)

Section 14(e) prohibits fraud in connection with any tender offer. In 1970, Congress added a final sentence to the Section that gives the SEC rulemaking authority. Section 14(e) is the exclusive focus of the next section of this Chapter.

In contrast to Sections 13(d), 13(e), and 14(d), Section 14(e) applies to all tender offers regardless of whether the target of the acquisition is a Section 12 company. Moreover, in contrast to Sections 13(d) and 14(d), Section 14(e) applies regardless of whether the offer is for more than 5% of the shares.

f. Enforcement

Enforcement of the Williams Act can take several forms. The SEC enforces the Williams Act by means of administrative and judicial actions. See, e.g., *SEC v. First City Fin. Corp.,* 890 F.2d 1215 (D.C. Cir. 1989) (affirming injunctive and disgorgement orders for violations of Section 13(d) in connection with attempted hostile takeover of Ashland Oil Co.), set forth in Chapter 9.C.1. There is also the possibility (albeit remote) of a criminal prosecution by the Department of Justice (DOJ).

The Williams Act says nothing, however, about private enforcement. While courts have recognized implied private actions, their willingness to do so is in general greater when the relief sought is an injunction rather than damages. See, e.g., *Hallwood Realty Partners, LP v. Gotham Partners, LP,* 286 F.3d 613, 620-21 & n.9 (2d Cir. 2002) (rejecting issuer's right to sue for damages under Section 14(e) but acknowledging its right to sue for injunction under that Section); *Bender v. Jordan,* 439 F. Supp. 2d 139, 159-161 (D.D.C. 2006) (rejecting shareholders' right to sue for damages under Section 13(d) but upholding their right to sue for injunction under that Section); *Drobbin v. Nicolet Instrument Corp.,* 631 F. Supp. 860, 908-914 (S.D.N.Y. 1986) (assuming that shareholders have right to sue for injunction under Section 14(f)). In the next section of this Chapter, we will give close attention to the implied private action under Section 14(e).

3. The Definition of a Tender Offer

As noted, some Williams Act provisions apply to tender offers specifically. Questions sometimes arise concerning the application of these provisions to transactions which, while admittedly not conventional tender offers, nonetheless arguably call for the sort of regulation that the Williams Act provides. These questions cannot be answered by reference to a statutory definition of "tender offer" because the Williams Act does not provide one. Instead, the Act delegates the definition question to the courts, which in turn have generated two principal approaches.

One approach, known as the *Wellman v. Dickinson* eight-factor approach, determines the existence of a tender offer by reference to the following:

> (1) active and widespread solicitation of public shareholders for the shares of an issuer;
>
> (2) solicitation made for a substantial percentage of the issuer's stock;
>
> (3) offer to purchase made at a premium over the prevailing market price;
>
> (4) terms of the offer are firm rather than negotiable;

> (5) offer contingent on the tender of a fixed number of shares, often subject to a fixed maximum number to be purchased;
>
> (6) offer open only for a limited period of time;
>
> (7) offeree subjected to pressure to sell his stock;
>
> (8) public announcements of a purchasing program concerning the target company precede or accompany rapid accumulation of a large amount of target company's securities.

See *Wellman v. Dickinson,* 475 F. Supp. 783, 823-25 (S.D.N.Y. 1979) (applying the factors to solicitations made privately to institutions and to individuals), aff'd on other grounds, 682 F.2d 355 (2d Cir. 1982). See *SEC v. Carter Hawley Hale Stores*, 760 F.2d 945 (9th Cir. 1985) (applying the factors to a target's purchases of its own stock on the open market in response to a hostile tender offer); *Brown v. Kinross Gold, USA*, 378 F. Supp. 2d 1280, 1285-86 (D. Nev. 2005) (applying the factors to bidder's transaction occurring prior to public tender offer). All of the *Wellman* factors do not have to be present in order to conclude that a tender offer has occurred. See *Wellman,* supra, 475 F. Supp. at 824 ("depending upon the circumstances ***, one or more of the [factors] may be more compelling and determinative than the others"); *Brown,* supra, 378 F. Supp. 2d at 1285 ("Not all factors need to be present to find a tender offer").

The other approach to the definition of a tender offer, set forth in *Hanson Trust PLC v. SMC Corp.*, 774 F.2d 47 (2d Cir. 1985), looks to whether the offerees require Williams Act protection:

> [T]he question of whether a solicitation constitutes a "tender offer" *** turns on whether, viewing the transaction in the light of the totality of the circumstances, there appears to be a likelihood that unless the pre-acquisition filing structures of that statutes are followed there will be a substantial risk that solicitees will lack information needed to make a carefully considered appraisal of the principal put before them.

Id. at 57 (applying this approach to five privately negotiated purchases and one open market purchase). See *E.ON, AG v. Acciona*, SA, 468 F. Supp. 2d 559, 581 (S.D.N.Y. 2007) (applying *Hanson* approach).

NOTES AND QUESTIONS

*1. **Enforcing the Williams Act.*** What accounts for the complete absence of express private actions in the Williams Act? Did Congress drop the ball? Did it assume that courts would recognize implied private actions under some (or all) of the Act's provisions? Or did it intend to leave enforcement of the Williams Act to the SEC (and to the DOJ)?

*2. **Victims of Noncompliance.*** Consider Sections 13(d), 13(e), 14(d), and 14(f). Who is harmed, potentially, when the requisite disclosures are not made? Who is harmed the most? Whose interests did Congress most seek to protect? Other than an implied private action, what litigation vehicles are available to private plaintiffs who wish to challenge the failure to make the disclosures called for by the Williams Act?

*3. **The Breadth of Section 14(e).*** Recall that Section 14(e) applies to a tender offer regardless of whether the target is a Section 12 company and regardless of whether the bidder seeks more than 5% of the target's shares. The

Section's broad reach may have been an instance of congressional foresight. Consider "mini-tender offers" — tender offers that seek to sidestep the strictures of Section 14(d) by seeking less than 5% of the shares of the target (which in addition is frequently not a Section 12 company). Some bidders offer a below-market price in mini-tender offers and thereby take advantage of uninformed shareholders who assume that a tender offer always involves a premium. See generally Commission Guidance on Mini-Tender Offers and Limited Partnership Tender Offers, Exch. Act Rel. No. 43069, 72 SEC Docket 2245 (July 24, 2000). The SEC has brought and settled a number of Section 14(e) actions against such bidders. See, e.g., SEC v. Gaines, Litig. Rel. No. 18535, 81 SEC Docket 3430 (Jan. 9, 2004); SEC v. Leach, Litig. Rel. No. 18077, 79 SEC Docket 3053 (April 9, 2003). Is it sensible for the SEC to use Section 14(e) in the mini-tender offer context? Or should these investors be expected to protect themselves by ascertaining the market price of their stock before deciding to tender? See generally Miriam R. Albert, Because We Said So: The SEC's Overreaching Efforts to Regulate Mini-Tender Offers, 45 Ariz. L. Rev. 897 (2003).

B. LITIGATION UNDER SECTION 14(e)

Section 14(e) comes into play in the vast majority of contested tender offers. It reads as follows:

> It shall be unlawful for any person to make any untrue statement of a material fact or omit to state any material fact necessary in order to make the statements made, in the light of the circumstances under which they are made, not misleading, or to engage in any fraudulent, deceptive, or manipulative acts or practices, in connection with any tender offer or request or invitation for tenders, or any solicitation of security holders in opposition to or in favor of any such offer, request, or invitation. The Commission shall, for the purposes of this subsection, by rules and regulations define, and prescribe means reasonably designed to prevent, such acts and practices as are fraudulent, deceptive, or manipulative.

Compare Section 14(e) with the Exchange Act's general antifraud provisions (Section 10(b) and Rule 10b-5) and its proxy antifraud provisions (Section 14(a) and Rule 14a-9). Compare Section 14(e) also with the Securities Act's general antifraud provision (Section 17(a)). What are the similarities and differences?

Why does Section 14(e) say nothing about the use of interstate commerce, in contrast to Sections 10(b), 14(a), and 17(a)? Does this omission carry significance?

In turning to litigation under Section 14(e), we leave aside such litigation insofar as it involves insider trading. We take up that subject in Chapter 7.C.

Section 14(e) has much in common with Section 10(b) and Rule 10b-5. To begin with, both bar misstatements and omissions, apply regardless of the size of the company issuing the securities, and are enforceable in an implied private action (as well as in actions by the SEC and the DOJ). Moreover, private actions under Section 14(e), like those under Rule 10b-5, must satisfy various Exchange Act provisions that were enacted in 1995 as part of the PSLRA. These provisions require the plaintiff to establish loss causation when seeking damages (Section 21D(b)(4)), create a scheme of proportionate liability (Section 21D(f)), and stiffen pleading requirements (Section 21D(b)). In addition, Section 14(e) class actions must satisfy PSLRA class action provisions that you will encounter in Chapter 6.

Yet as we shall see, Section 14(e) and Rule 10b-5 part company in various respects as well. One example involves the safe harbor for forward-looking statements set forth in Section 21E of the Exchange Act. That safe harbor plays an important role in private litigation under Rule 10b-5 (see generally Chapter 2.B.3.c), but it specifically does not apply to litigation involving tender offers (see Section 21E(b)(2)(c)). Another difference involves the form that enforcement is likely to take. While the SEC and the DOJ bring Rule 10b-5 actions relatively frequently, they bring actions under Section 14(e) relatively infrequently (at least where insider trading is not at issue). Thus, much more than is the case with Rule 10b-5, Section 14(e) is enforced by investors. In this respect at least, Section 14(e) resembles Section 14(a) and Rule 14a-9. See generally Chapter 4.

Our examination of litigation under Section 14(e) is divided into three parts. They are (1) the necessity of proving misrepresentation or nondisclosure; (2) standing to sue; and (3) (further) comparisons between Section 14(e) and Rule 10b-5.

As you consider Section 14(e), think about the following questions. Should courts analogize Section 14(e) as much (or more) to Rule 14a-9 as to Rule 10b-5? Is judicial interpretation of Section 14(e) compromised by fear of the possible impact on Rule 10b-5, even if that fear is not expressly stated? When interpreting Section 14(e), what significance should be attached to the fact that it is a statute and not a rule? To the fact that it is enforced mainly in private actions? What accounts for the seeming lack of interest in tender offer fraud on the part of the SEC and the DOJ (at least when insider trading is not at issue)? Do the pleading requirements imposed by the PSLRA create any special difficulties in the context of tender offers?

1. The Necessity of Misrepresentation or Nondisclosure

In the following decision, the Supreme Court addressed whether Section 14(e) requires proof of a misrepresentation or nondisclosure. The Court had previously resolved this issue for purposes of Rule 10b-5 in *Santa Fe Indus., Inc. v. Green*, 430 U.S. 462 (1977), set forth supra in Chapter 2.A.1.a. Notice how the Court used the *Santa Fe* precedent in particular and the Rule 10b-5 analogy in general.

SCHREIBER v. BURLINGTON NORTHERN, INC.

472 U.S. 1 (1985)

CHIEF JUSTICE WARREN E. BURGER:

We granted certiorari to resolve a conflict in the Circuits over whether misrepresentation or nondisclosure is a necessary element of a violation of § 14(e) of the Securities Exchange Act of 1934.

I

On December 21, 1982, Burlington Northern, Inc., made a hostile tender offer for El Paso Gas Co. Through a wholly owned subsidiary, Burlington proposed to purchase 25.1 million El Paso shares at $24 per share. Burlington reserved the right to terminate the offer if any of several specified events occurred. El Paso management initially opposed the takeover, but its shareholders responded favorably, fully subscribing the offer by the December 30, 1982, deadline.

Burlington did not accept those tendered shares; instead, after negotiations with El Paso management, Burlington announced on January 10, 1983, the terms of a new and friendly takeover agreement. Pursuant to the new agreement, Burlington undertook, inter alia, to (1) rescind the December tender offer, (2) purchase 4,166,667 shares from El Paso at $24 per share, (3) substitute a new tender offer for only 21 million shares at $24 per share, (4) provide procedural protections against a squeeze-out merger[1] of the remaining El Paso shareholders, and (5) recognize "golden parachute"[2] contracts between El Paso and four of its senior officers. By February 8, more than 40 million shares were tendered in response to Burlington's January offer, and the takeover was completed.

The rescission of the first tender offer caused a diminished payment to those shareholders who had tendered during the first offer. The January offer was greatly oversubscribed and consequently those shareholders who retendered were subject to substantial proration. Petitioner Barbara Schreiber filed suit on

---

1. A "squeeze-out" merger occurs when Corporation A, which holds a controlling interest in Corporation B, uses its control to merge B into itself or into a wholly owned subsidiary. The minority shareholders in Corporation B are, in effect, forced to sell their stock. The procedural protection provided in the agreement between El Paso and Burlington required the approval of non-Burlington members of El Paso's board of directors before a squeeze-out merger could proceed. Burlington eventually purchased all the remaining shares of El Paso for $12 cash and one-quarter share of Burlington preferred stock per share. The parties dispute whether this consideration was equal to that paid to those tendering during the January tender offer.

2. Petitioner alleged in her complaint that respondent Burlington failed to disclose that four officers of El Paso had entered into "golden parachute" agreements with El Paso for "extended employment benefits in the event El Paso should be taken over, which benefits would give them millions of dollars of extra compensation." The term "golden parachute" refers generally to agreements between a corporation and its top officers which guarantee those officers continued employment, payment of a lump sum, or other benefits in the event of a change of corporate ownership. As described in the Schedule 14D-9 filed by El Paso with the Securities and Exchange Commission on January 12, 1983, El Paso entered into "employment agreements" with two of its officers for a period of not less than five years, and with two other officers for a period of three years. The Schedule 14D-9 also disclosed that El Paso's Deferred Compensation Plan had been amended "to provide that for the purposes of such Plan a participant shall be deemed to have retired at the instance of the Company if his duties as a director, officer or employee of the Company have been diminished or curtailed by the Company in any material respect."

behalf of herself and similarly situated shareholders, alleging that Burlington, El Paso, and members of El Paso's board of directors violated § 14(e)'s prohibition of "fraudulent, deceptive, or manipulative acts or practices ... in connection with any tender offer." She claimed that Burlington's withdrawal of the December tender offer coupled with the substitution of the January tender offer was a "manipulative" distortion of the market for El Paso stock. Schreiber also alleged that Burlington violated § 14(e) by failing in the January offer to disclose the "golden parachutes" offered to four of El Paso's managers. She claims that this January nondisclosure was a deceptive act forbidden by § 14(e).

The District Court dismissed the suit for failure to state a claim. The District Court reasoned that the alleged manipulation did not involve a misrepresentation, and so did not violate § 14(e). The District Court relied on the fact that in cases involving alleged violations of § 10(b) of the Securities Exchange Act, this Court has required misrepresentation for there to be a "manipulative" violation of the section.

The Court of Appeals for the Third Circuit affirmed. The Court of Appeals held that the acts alleged did not violate the Williams Act, because "§ 14(e) was not intended to create a federal cause of action for all harms suffered because of the proffering or the withdrawal of tender offers." The Court of Appeals reasoned that § 14(e) was "enacted principally as a disclosure statute, designed to insure that fully-informed investors could intelligently decide how to respond to a tender offer." It concluded that the "arguable breach of contract" alleged by petitioner was not a "manipulative act" under § 14(e).

We granted certiorari to resolve the conflict.[3] We affirm.

II

A

We are asked in this case to interpret § 14(e) of the Securities Exchange Act. The starting point is the language of the statute. ***

Petitioner relies on a construction of the phrase, "fraudulent, deceptive, or manipulative acts or practices." Petitioner reads the phrase "fraudulent, deceptive, or manipulative acts or practices" to include acts which, although fully disclosed, "artificially" affect the price of the takeover target's stock. Petitioner's interpretation relies on the belief that § 14(e) is directed at purposes broader than providing full and true information to investors.

Petitioner's reading of the term "manipulative" conflicts with the normal meaning of the term. We have held in the context of an alleged violation of § 10(b) of the Securities Exchange Act:

---

3. The Court of Appeals for the Sixth Circuit has held that manipulation does not always require an element of misrepresentation or nondisclosure. *Mobil Corp. v. Marathon Oil Co.*, 669 F.2d 366 (1981). The Courts of Appeals for the Second and Eighth Circuits have applied an analysis consistent with the one we apply today. *Feldbaum v. Avon Products, Inc.*, 741 F.2d 234 (C.A.8 1984); *Buffalo Forge Co. v. Ogden Corp.*, 717 F.2d 757 (C.A.2 1983).

> Use of the word "manipulative" is especially significant. It is and was virtually a term of art when used in connection with the securities markets. It connotes intentional or willful conduct *designed to deceive or defraud* investors by controlling or artificially affecting the price of securities. *Ernst & Ernst* v. *Hochfelder*, 425 U.S. 185, 199 (1976) (emphasis added).

Other cases interpreting the term reflect its use as a general term comprising a range of misleading practices:

> The term refers generally to practices, such as wash sales, matched orders, or rigged prices, that are intended to mislead investors by artificially affecting market activity.... Section 10(b)'s general prohibition of practices deemed by the SEC to be "manipulative" — in this technical sense of artificially affecting market activity in order to mislead investors — is fully consistent with the fundamental purpose of the 1934 Act "'to substitute a philosophy of full disclosure for the philosophy of *caveat emptor*....'" ... Indeed, nondisclosure is usually essential to the success of a manipulative scheme.... No doubt Congress meant to prohibit the full range of ingenious devices that might be used to manipulate securities prices. But we do not think it would have chosen this 'term of art' if it had meant to bring within the scope of § 10(b) instances of corporate mismanagement such as this, in which the essence of the complaint is that shareholders were treated unfairly by a fiduciary. *Santa Fe Industries, Inc.* v. *Green*, 430 U.S. 462, 476-477 (1977).

The meaning the Court has given the term "manipulative" is consistent with the use of the term at common law,[4] and with its traditional dictionary definition.[5]

She argues, however, that the term "manipulative" takes on a meaning in § 14(e) that is different from the meaning it has in § 10(b). Petitioner claims that the use of the disjunctive "or" in § 14(e) implies that acts need not be deceptive or fraudulent to be manipulative. But Congress used the phrase "manipulative or deceptive" in § 10(b) as well, and we have interpreted "manipulative" in that context to require misrepresentation.[6] Moreover, it is a "'familiar principle of statutory construction that words grouped in a list should be given related meaning.'" *Securities Industry Assn. v. Board of Governors, FRS*, 468 U.S. 207, 218 (1984). All three species of misconduct, *i. e.*, "fraudulent, deceptive, or manipulative," listed by Congress are directed at failures to disclose. The use of the term "manipulative" provides emphasis and guidance

---

4. For example, the seminal English case of *Scott v. Brown, Doering, McNab & Co.*, [1892] 2 Q.B. 724 (C.A.), which broke new ground in recognizing that manipulation could occur without the dissemination of false statements, nonetheless placed emphasis on the presence of deception. As Lord Lopes stated in that case, "I can see no substantial distinction between false rumours and false and fictitious acts." Id., at 730. See also *United States v. Brown*, 5 F. Supp. 81, 85 (S.D.N.Y. 1933) ("[E]ven a speculator is entitled not to have any present fact involving the subject matter of his speculative purchase or the price thereof misrepresented by word or act").

5. See Webster's Third New International Dictionary 1376 (1971) (Manipulation is "management with use of unfair, scheming, or underhanded methods").

6. *Santa Fe Industries, Inc. v. Green*, 430 U.S. 462, 476-477, 97 (1977); *Piper v. Chris-Craft Industries, Inc.*, 430 U.S. 1, 43 (1977); *Ernst & Ernst v. Hochfelder*, 425 U.S. 185, 199 (1976).

to those who must determine which types of acts are reached by the statute; it does not suggest a deviation from the section's facial and primary concern with disclosure or congressional concern with disclosure which is the core of the Act.

B

Our conclusion that "manipulative" acts under § 14(e) require misrepresentation or nondisclosure is buttressed by the purpose and legislative history of the provision. Section 14(e) was originally added to the Securities Exchange Act as part of the Williams Act. "The purpose of the Williams Act is to insure that public shareholders who are confronted by a cash tender offer for their stock will not be required to respond without adequate information." *Rondeau v. Mosinee Paper Corp.*, 422 U.S. 49, 58 (1975).

It is clear that Congress relied primarily on disclosure to implement the purpose of the Williams Act. Senator Williams, the bill's Senate sponsor, stated in the debate:

> Today, the public shareholder in deciding whether to accept or reject a tender offer possesses limited information. No matter what he does, he acts without adequate knowledge to enable him to decide rationally what is the best course of action. This is precisely the dilemma which our securities laws are designed to prevent. 113 Cong. Rec. 24664 (1967).

The expressed legislative intent was to preserve a neutral setting in which the contenders could fully present their arguments.[8] The Senate sponsor went on to say:

> We have taken extreme care to avoid tipping the scales either in favor of management or in favor of the person making the takeover bids. S. 510 is designed solely to require full and fair disclosure for the benefit of investors. The bill will at the same time provide the offeror and management equal opportunity to present their case. Ibid.

To implement this objective, the Williams Act added §§ 13(d), 13(e), 14(d), 14(e), and 14(f) to the Securities Exchange Act. Some relate to disclosure; §§ 13(d), 14(d), and 14(f) all add specific registration and disclosure provisions. Others — §§ 13(e) and 14(d) — require or prohibit certain acts so that investors will possess additional time within which to take advantage of the disclosed information.

Section 14(e) adds a "broad antifraud prohibition," *Piper v. Chris-Craft Industries, Inc.*, 430 U.S. 1, 24 (1977), modeled on the antifraud provisions of

---

8. The process through which Congress developed the Williams Act also suggests a calculated reliance on disclosure, rather than court-imposed principles of "fairness" or "artificiality," as the preferred method of market regulation. For example, *** [Section 13(e)] which imposes specific disclosure duties on corporations purchasing stock and grants broad regulatory power to the Securities and Exchange Commission to regulate such repurchases. Congress stopped short, however, of imposing specific substantive requirements forbidding corporations to trade in their own stock for the purpose of maintaining its price. The specific regulatory scheme set forth in § 13(e) would be unnecessary if Congress at the same time had endowed the term "manipulative" in § 14(e) with broad substantive significance.

§ 10(b) of the Act and Rule 10b-5.[10] It supplements the more precise disclosure provisions found elsewhere in the Williams Act, while requiring disclosure more explicitly addressed to the tender offer context than that required by § 10(b).

While legislative history specifically concerning § 14(e) is sparse, the House and Senate Reports discuss the role of § 14(e). Describing § 14(e) as regulating "fraudulent transactions," and stating the thrust of the section:

> This provision would affirm the fact that persons engaged in making or opposing tender offers or otherwise seeking to influence the decision of investors or the outcome of the tender offer are under an obligation to make *full disclosure* of material information to those with whom they deal." H. R. Rep. No. 1711, 90th Cong., 2d Sess., 11 (1968) (emphasis added); S. Rep. No. 550, 90th Cong., 1st Sess., 11 (1967) (emphasis added).

Nowhere in the legislative history is there the slightest suggestion that § 14(e) serves any purpose other than disclosure, or that the term "manipulative" should be read as an invitation to the courts to oversee the substantive fairness of tender offers; the quality of any offer is a matter for the marketplace.

To adopt the reading of the term "manipulative" urged by petitioner would not only be unwarranted in light of the legislative purpose but would be at odds with it. Inviting judges to read the term "manipulative" with their own sense of what constitutes "unfair" or "artificial" conduct would inject uncertainty into the tender offer process. An essential piece of information — whether the court would deem the fully disclosed actions of one side or the other to be "manipulative" — would not be available until after the tender offer had closed. This uncertainty would directly contradict the expressed congressional desire to give investors full information.

Congress' consistent emphasis on disclosure persuades us that it intended takeover contests to be addressed to shareholders. In pursuit of this goal, Congress, consistent with the core mechanism of the Securities Exchange Act, created sweeping disclosure requirements and narrow substantive safeguards. The same Congress that placed such emphasis on shareholder choice would not at the same time have required judges to oversee tender offers for substantive fairness. It is even less likely that a Congress implementing that intention would express it only through the use of a single word placed in the middle of a provision otherwise devoted to disclosure.

C

We hold that the term "manipulative" as used in § 14(e) requires misrepresentation or nondisclosure. It connotes "conduct designed to deceive or defraud investors by controlling or artificially affecting the price of securities."

---

10. *** Because of the textual similarities, it is often assumed that § 14(e) was modeled on § 10(b) and Rule 10b-5. See, e.g., *Panter v. Marshall Field & Co.*, 646 F.2d 271, 283 (7th Cir. 1981). For the purpose of interpreting the term "manipulative," the most significant changes from the language of § 10(b) were the addition of the term "fraudulent," and the reference to "acts" rather than "devices." Neither change bears in any obvious way on the meaning to be given to "manipulative."

Similar terminology is also found in § 15(c) of the Securities Exchange Act [and] § 17(a) of the Securities Act of 1933 ***.

Ernst & Ernst v. *Hochfelder*, 425 U.S., at 199. Without misrepresentation or nondisclosure, § 14(e) has not been violated.

Applying that definition to this case, we hold that the actions of respondents were not manipulative. The amended complaint fails to allege that the cancellation of the first tender offer was accompanied by any misrepresentation, nondisclosure, or deception. The District Court correctly found: "All activity of the defendants that could have conceivably affected the price of El Paso shares was done openly."

Petitioner also alleges that El Paso management and Burlington entered into certain undisclosed and deceptive agreements during the making of the second tender offer. The substance of the allegations is that, in return for certain undisclosed benefits, El Paso managers agreed to support the second tender offer. But both courts noted that petitioner's complaint seeks only redress for injuries related to the cancellation of the first tender offer. Since the deceptive and misleading acts alleged by petitioner all occurred with reference to the making of the second tender offer — when the injuries suffered by petitioner had already been sustained — these acts bear no possible causal relationship to petitioner's alleged injuries. The Court of Appeals dealt correctly with this claim.

III

The judgment of the Court of Appeals is affirmed.

NOTES AND QUESTIONS

1. Section 14(e)'s Two Prongs. Notice that Section 14(e) has two prongs. The first prong prohibits making a material misstatement or omission in connection with a tender offer. The second prong — separated from the first prong by an "or" — prohibits "engag[ing] in any fraudulent, deceptive, or manipulative acts or practices." Does the Court acknowledge the existence of these two prongs? If not, why not? What do you suppose prompted Congress to draft the statute in this fashion?

2. "Fraudulent, Deceptive, or Manipulative." The Court suggested that the terms "fraudulent," "manipulative," and "deceptive" were duplicative. Why would Congress have intended duplication? But if Congress didn't intend duplication, why did it use all three terms? Might the term "fraudulent" have been intended to embrace the concept of constructive fraud, which would prohibit at least some acts of corporate mismanagement?

Why didn't Burlington's withdrawal of the December tender offer, coupled with substitution of the January tender offer at a lower price, not amount to a "manipulative" distortion of the market, as plaintiff alleged? Why did it not amount to deception, as the plaintiff also alleged?

3. The* Santa Fe *Precedent. Did the Supreme Court's *Santa Fe* decision render the result in *Schreiber* inevitable? Why or why not? To what extent do *Santa Fe* and *Schreiber* involve similar reasoning? To what extent is their reasoning different?

4. The Road Not Taken. The lower court in *Schreiber* had likewise upheld the necessity of proving a misrepresentation or nondisclosure, but primarily for reasons of policy rather than statutory language. Consider its analysis:

> Absent a requirement of deception, the Williams Act would mandate that the federal courts supervise the substantive fairness of practically all tender offers. Mindful of the Supreme Court's instruction in *Santa Fe* that we should be reluctant to federalize state corporate law, we decline to adopt *Mobil's* expansive view of § 14(e) and hold that deception is an essential element of a manipulative act.

Schreiber v. Burlington Northern, Inc., 731 F.2d 163, 166 (3d Cir. 1984). Is it likely that the Supreme Court was also averse to federalizing state corporate law? If so, why did the Court not make its aversion explicit?

5. The Nondisclosure Allegation. Notice the plaintiff's allegation that Burlington had failed to disclose the "golden parachute" agreements. Why did this allegation fail to state a claim under Section 14(e)?

6. Analogizing to Rule 10b-5. To what extent does *Schreiber* direct lower courts to analogize to Rule 10b-5 when interpreting Section 14(e)?

7. False Tender Offers. Suppose Burlington had made the December tender offer without intending to consummate it but simply for the purpose of extracting the "golden parachute" agreements that accompanied the January tender offer. Would such conduct have constituted a violation of Section 14(e) as construed by *Schreiber*? Cf. *Wharf (Holdings) Ltd. v. United Int'l Holdings, Inc.,* 532 U.S. 588 (2001) (holding that a secret intention not to honor an option to buy stock satisfies the deception element of Section 10(b) and Rule 10b-5). In 1999, the SEC adopted Rule 14e-8, which reads as follows:

> It is a fraudulent, deceptive or manipulative act or practice within the meaning of section 14(e) of the Act for any person to publicly announce that the person (or a party on whose behalf the person is acting) plans to make a tender offer that has not yet been commenced, if the person:
>
> > (a) Is making the announcement of a potential tender offer without the intention to commence the offer within a reasonable time and complete the offer;
> >
> > (b) Intends, directly or indirectly, for the announcement to manipulate the market price of the stock of the bidder or subject company; or
> >
> > (c) Does not have the reasonable belief that the person will have the means to purchase securities to complete the offer.

What types of evidence would assist the SEC or private plaintiffs in pleading and proving a violation of Rule 14e-8? Is there phraseology in the Rule that can be described as "slippery" and the likely "locus of future litigation"? See *Hartmarx Corp. v. Abboud,* 326 F.3d 862, 868 (7th Cir. 2003).

8. Two-Track Litigation Framework. In the wake of *Schreiber,* claims involving breach of fiduciary duty in a tender offer must be filed in state court. Section 14(e) claims must be filed in federal court, however, since Section 27 of the Exchange Act calls for exclusive federal jurisdiction. Who benefits from this two-track litigation framework? Does it promote judicial economy?

PROBLEM 5-1

WRG is an advertising firm established in 1997. The majority of the shares belonged to the WRG directors until 2005, when the company made a public offering. The directors netted $5 million in that offering.

In the years following, WRG was highly profitable. Its common stock traded at $30-35 a share, but fell to about $5 a share in a depressed market.

It was at the time of the depressed market that the directors decided to take the company private by making a tender offer for the publicly owned shares. Given the depressed market, the directors were able to offer a much lower price than would have been possible under other circumstances. The offering price was $3 cash plus an $8 note.

Glenn, a WRG shareholder, filed an action under Section 14(e) to enjoin the tender offer. He claimed that the offer to buy back the publicly held shares at a price much lower than that paid by the public shareholders violated Section 14(e). He also challenged the failure of the offering documents to state the price at which the WRG directors bought the shares prior to the IPO.

Defendants made a motion to dismiss for failure to state a claim under Section 14(e). Should the court grant the motion?

Cf. *Kaufmann v. Lawrence*, 386 F. Supp. 12 (S.D.N.Y. 1974).

2. Standing to Sue

In the decision that follows, the Supreme Court addressed whether to grant a bidder standing to sue for damages. In so doing, it shed light on the general question of standing to sue under Section 14(e).

PIPER v. CHRIS-CRAFT INDUSTRIES, INC.

430 U.S. 1 (1977)

CHIEF JUSTICE WARREN E. BURGER:

[*Chris Craft and Bangor Punta battled for control of Piper, and Bangor Punta prevailed. Chris Craft sued Bangor Punta and Piper for damages under Section 14(e). Chris Craft claimed that they had made fraudulent representations which had undermined its efforts to gain control of Piper.*]

*** [W]e must consider whether § 14(e), which is entirely silent as to private remedies, permits this Court to read into the statute a damages remedy for unsuccessful tender offerors. To resolve that question we turn to the legislative history to discern the congressional purpose underlying the specific statutory prohibition in § 14(e). Once we identify the legislative purpose, we must then determine whether the creation by judicial interpretation of the implied cause of action asserted by Chris-Craft is necessary to effectuate Congress' goals. ***

The legislative history *** shows that Congress was intent upon regulating takeover bidders, theretofore operating covertly, in order to protect the shareholders of target companies. ***

Congress was indeed committed to a policy of neutrality in contests for control, but its policy of evenhandedness does not go either to the purpose of the legislation or to whether a private cause of action is implicit in the statute. Neutrality is, rather, but one characteristic of legislation directed toward a different purpose — the protection of investors. ***

*** In *Borak*, the Court emphasized that § 14(a), the proxy provision, was adopted expressly for "the protection of investors," the very class of persons there seeking relief. The Court found no difficulty in identifying the legislative objective and concluding that remedies should be available if necessary "to make effective the congressional purpose." *Borak* did not involve, and the statements in the legislative history relied upon by Chris-Craft do not implicate, the interests of parties such as offeror-bidders who are outside the scope of the concerns articulated in the evolution of this legislation.[22] ***

The legislative history *** shows that the sole purpose of the Williams Act was the protection of investors who are confronted with a tender offer. *** We find no hint in the legislative history *** that Congress contemplated a private cause of action for damages by one of several contending offerors against a successful bidder or by a losing contender against the target corporation.

*** It is clear *** that Chris-Craft has not asserted standing under § 14(e) as a Piper shareholder. The reason is not hard to divine. As a tender offeror actively engaged in competing for Piper stock, Chris-Craft was not in the posture of a target shareholder confronted with the decision of whether to tender or retain its stock. Consequently, Chris-Craft could scarcely have alleged a need for the disclosures mandated by the Williams Act. In short, the fact that Chris-Craft necessarily acquired Piper stock as a means of taking over Piper adds nothing to its § 14(e) standing arguments. ***

Chris-Craft argues, however, that Congress intended standing under § 14(e) to encompass tender offerors since the statute, unlike §10(b), does not contain the limiting language, "in connection with the purchase or sale" of securities. Instead, in § 14(e), Congress broadly proscribed fraudulent activities "in connection with any tender offer ... or any solicitation ... in opposition to or in favor of any such offer...."

The omission of the purchaser-seller requirement does not mean, however, that Chris-Craft has standing to sue for damages under § 14(e) in its capacity as a takeover bidder. It may well be that Congress desired to protect, among others, shareholder-offerees who decided not to tender their stock due to fraudulent misrepresentations by persons opposed to a takeover attempt. See generally 1 A. Bromberg, Securities Law: Fraud § 6.3 (1021), p. 122.17 (1969). See also Senate Report 2; House Report 3. These shareholders, who might not

---

22. In this connection, Chris-Craft emphasizes Congress' intent to treat tender offers in the same way as proxy solicitations, since both are devices for seeking corporate control. This argument, however, does not support the proposition that Chris-Craft should have a cause of action for damages, since this Court had not then held, nor has it since, that defeated insurgents in a proxy fight, suing in a capacity other than that of a shareholder, have a cause of action for damages. There is no occasion to resolve that question in this case.

enjoy the protection of § 10(b) under *Blue Chip Stamps v. Manor Drugs Stores*, 421 U.S. 723 (1975), could perhaps state a claim under § 14(e), even though they did not tender their securities.[25] But increased protection, if any, conferred upon the class of shareholder-offerees by the elimination of the purchaser-seller restriction can scarcely be interpreted as giving protection to the entirely separate and unrelated class of persons whose conduct the statute is designed to regulate.

*** As a disclosure mechanism aimed especially at protecting shareholders of target corporations, the Williams Act cannot consistently be interpreted as conferring a monetary remedy upon regulated parties, particularly where the award would not redound to the direct benefit of the protected class. Although it is correct to say that the $36 million damages award indirectly benefits those Piper shareholders who became Chris-Craft shareholders when they accepted Chris-Craft's exchange offer, it is equally true that the damages award injures those Piper shareholders who exchanged their shares for Bangor Punta's stock and who, as Bangor Punta shareholders, would necessarily bear a large part of the burden of any judgment against Bangor Punta. The class sought to be protected by the Williams Act are the shareholders of the *target* corporation; hence it can hardly be said that their interests as a class are served by a judgment in favor of Chris-Craft and against Bangor Punta. Moreover, the damages are awarded to the very party whose activities Congress intended to curb; Chris-Craft did not sue in the capacity of an injured Piper shareholder, but as a defeated tender offeror.

Nor can we agree that an ever-present threat of damages against a successful contestant in a battle for control will provide significant additional protection for shareholders in general. The deterrent value, if any, of such awards can never be ascertained with precision. More likely, however, is the prospect that shareholders may be prejudiced because some tender offers may never be made if there is a possibility of massive damages claims for what courts subsequently hold to be an actionable violation of § 14(e).[26] Even a contestant who "wins the battle" for control may well wind up exposed to a costly "war" in a later and successful defense of its victory. Or at worst on Chris-Craft's damages theory the victorious tender offeror or the target corporation might be subject to a large substantive judgment, plus high costs of litigation. ***

*** [A]warding damages to parties other than the protected class of shareholders has only a remote, if any, bearing upon implementing the congressional policy of protecting shareholders who must decide whether to

---

25. These cases, of course, do not present that issue, and we express no view on it.

26. *** The legal uncertainties that inevitably pervade this area of the law call into question whether "deterrence" of § 14(e) violations is a meaningful goal, except possibly with respect to the most flagrant sort of violations which no reasonable person could consider lawful. Such cases of flagrant misconduct, however, are not apt to occur with frequency, and to the extent that the violations are obvious and serious, injunctive relief at an earlier stage of the contest is apt to be the most efficacious form of remedy.

tender or retain their stock.[28] Indeed, as we suggested earlier, a damages award of this nature may well be inconsistent with the interests of many members of the protected class and of only indirect value to shareholders who accepted the exchange offer of the defeated takeover contestant.

We therefore conclude that Chris-Craft, as a defeated tender offeror, has no implied cause of action for damages under § 14(e). ***

NOTES AND QUESTIONS

1. ***The Bidder and Standing to Sue.*** While holding that a bidder lacks standing to sue for damages under Section 14(e), the Court did not resolve whether a bidder has standing to sue for an injunction. What (if anything) did it imply about this matter? Subsequent to *Piper*, various lower courts have upheld a bidder's standing to sue for an injunction. One such court has synthesized the reasons for so doing as follows:

> Three tenets are relied on *** in reaching the conclusion that tender offerors have standing to seek injunctive relief under the Williams Act. First, in corporate control contests, injunctive relief at an early stage is "apt to be the most efficacious form of remedy." *Chris-Craft*, 430 U.S. at 40 n. 26. Second, tender offerors are more likely to be in a position to discover violations of the Act than other shareholders. Finally, if the plaintiffs' allegations are proven, the target company's shareholders benefit when the requested relief is granted.

Torchmark Corp. v. Bixby, 708 F. Supp. 1070, 1079 (W.D. Mo. 1988). See *E.ON, AG v. Acciona, SA*, 468 F. Supp. 2d 537, 550 (S.D.N.Y. 2006) (following *Bixby*). Is this reasoning sound? Is it consistent with *Piper?* Is it sensible to disallow standing in a damages action but to allow standing in an injunctive action?

2. ***The Target and Standing to Sue.*** In the wake of *Piper*, a number of courts have upheld a target's standing to sue for injunctive relief under Section 14(e) (typically for corrected disclosures). See, e.g., *Polaroid Corp. v. Disney*, 862 F.2d 987, 1003 (3d Cir. 1988) (collecting cases). One court explained its reasons for so doing as follows:

> In most cases, shareholders simply cannot protect their own interests; they lack the resources to confirm the accuracy of information in a Schedule 13D of 14D-1. The SEC simply cannot police every tender offer or major acquisition subject to the Williams Act. The issuer is frequently in the best position to seek corrective disclosures within a time frame that will optimize the benefit to shareholders of such disclosures. See *GAF Corp. v. Milstein*, 453 F.2d 709, 721 (2d Cir.1971). We conclude that it is necessary to grant this private right of action to issuers in order for the Williams Act to be effective.

Florida Commercial Banks v. Culverhouse, 772 F.2d 1513, 1519 (11th Cir. 1985). Is this reasoning sound? Is it consistent with *Piper?* Would *Piper* allow a court to grant a target standing to sue for damages?

---

28. Our holding is a limited one. Whether shareholder-offerees, the class protected by § 14(e), have an implied cause of action under § 14(e) is not before us, and we intimate no view on the matter. Nor is the target corporation's standing to sue in issue in this case. We hold only that a tender offeror, suing in its capacity as a takeover bidder, does not have standing to sue for damages under § 14(e). ***

*3. **The Target's Shareholders and Standing to Sue.*** What does *Piper* suggest about whether to grant the target's shareholders standing to sue? Does *Schreiber* shed light on this question? What is the value of Section 14(e) to a tendering shareholder, given the availability of Rule 10b-5?

PROBLEM 5-2

Apex, Inc., owned 7% of the stock of Lincoln, Inc. Apex initiated a tender offer for Lincoln, making various misrepresentations in connection with that offer. Shortly thereafter, Apex withdrew the tender offer. In fact, Apex never intended to make the tender offer for Lincoln. Its reason for initiating the offer was to enable it to sell its Lincoln shares at artificially inflated prices on the open market.

April is a Lincoln shareholder who refrained from selling her shares on the open market in anticipation of tendering her shares. Does she have standing to sue Apex for damages under Section 14(e)?

---

3. (Further) Comparisons Between Section 14(e) and Rule 10b-5

Thus far in our consideration of Section 14(e), we have made a number of comparisons with Section 10(b) and Rule 10b-5. We pursue additional such comparisons in connection with the following decision.

WARDROP v. AMWAY ASIA PACIFIC LTD.

2001 WL 274067 (S.D.N.Y. 2001), aff'd, 26 F. App'x 89 (2d Cir. 2002)

DENNY CHIN, DISTRICT JUDGE:

This proposed class action arises from a tender offer for stock of defendant Amway Asia Pacific, Ltd. ("AAP") at $18 per share. The tender offer was announced on November 15, 1999, the same day that an agreement between China and the United States permitting China to join the World Trade Organization (the "WTO") was announced. The news of the WTO agreement caused the market value of companies with business related to China to increase. Plaintiffs brought this action, before the tender offer period expired, alleging that $18 per share was not a fair price and that defendants engaged in fraud by not considering the impact of the WTO agreement on the value of AAP's stock. Defendants move to dismiss the amended complaint for failure to state a claim pursuant to Fed. R. Civ. P. 12 (b)(6) and failure to comply with Fed. R. Civ. P. 9(b).

The motion is granted, for the federal securities laws require not that a tender offer price be substantively fair, but only that full and accurate disclosure be made. Here, plaintiffs do not allege that defendants withheld any material information, nor do plaintiffs contend that defendants acted on the basis of any inside information. Rather, the factors that purportedly affected the value of the stock — the WTO agreement and China's impending entry into the WTO — were announced to the public. Moreover, plaintiffs brought suit before their time to tender expired. In other words, plaintiffs knew that the stock was purportedly underpriced before the time to tender their shares had expired, and thus they could have rejected the offer and chosen not to sell their shares. The amended complaint is dismissed for failure to state a claim upon which relief may be granted.

BACKGROUND

A. *Facts*

The facts alleged in the amended complaint are assumed to be true for the purposes of this motion and are as follows:

1. *The Parties*

Plaintiffs are former shareholders of AAP stock who sold their shares in connection with the tender offer. Plaintiffs sue individually and as proposed class representatives on behalf of all persons, excluding defendants, who held shares of AAP common stock on November 18, 1999, and sold their shares as a result of the tender offer.

Defendants include the "Principal Shareholders" of AAP, directors and officers of AAP, members of a special committee appointed by the AAP board of directors to consider the fairness of the tender offer price, and Goldman, Sachs & Co. ("Goldman, Sachs"), which was retained to render an opinion as to the fairness of the tender offer price.

AAP, a Bermuda company, is the exclusive distributor in the Asian Pacific region for Amway Corporation ("Amway"), a manufacturer and retailer of home and personal care products.

2. *The Tender Offer*

In 1998, the Principal Shareholders began discussions about taking AAP private. In October 1999, AAP's board formed a special committee to evaluate and negotiate any such proposal. On November 15, 1999, AAP and the Principal Shareholders announced that the Principal Shareholders intended to commence a cash tender offer to purchase, for $18 per share, the 15% of AAP stock that they did not own. Pursuant to the Offer to Purchase, which was issued on November 18th, shareholders had the opportunity to tender their shares or revoke a decision to tender their shares for one month, until the tender offer period expired on December 17, 1999. The Offer to Purchase represented that the special committee and disinterested directors had determined that the offer was fair. As stated in the Offer to Purchase, under Bermuda law shareholders who questioned the fairness of the tender offer price could apply to the Bermuda court for a court appraisal of the fair market value of the shares.

3. *The WTO Agreement*

After 13 years of discussions, China and the United States reached an agreement permitting China to join the WTO. The agreement and the $18 per share tender offer were both announced on November 15, 1999. As a result of the WTO announcement, companies with business related to China increased in value.

B. *Procedural History*

Plaintiffs commenced this action by filing a complaint on December 16, 1999 alleging that defendants committed securities fraud pursuant to § 14(e) of the Securities Exchange Act of 1934 (the "Exchange Act"). On June 26, 2000, plaintiffs filed an amended complaint, adding claims for violations of § 10(b) of the Exchange Act, Rule 10b-5, and § 20(a) of the Exchange Act, against the individual defendants. Plaintiffs also added a claim based on Bermuda common law against the Principal Shareholders. Plaintiffs allege that defendants knew that the market would react strongly to the news about the WTO and that defendants sought to announce the $18 tender offer price before the WTO news was made public. Plaintiffs further allege that defendants committed securities fraud by failing to consider the anticipated impact of China's entry into the WTO in determining a fair tender offer price, and by failing to recalculate a fair price after the WTO agreement was reached. Plaintiffs seek rescission, damages, and costs.

This motion followed.

DISCUSSION

A. *Applicable Law*

1. *Motions to Dismiss*

When reviewing a motion to dismiss, a court must accept as true the facts presented in the complaint and must view the pleadings in the light most favorable to, and draw reasonable inferences in favor of, the non-moving party. A court shall dismiss a complaint only when "it appears beyond doubt that the plaintiff can prove no set of facts in support of his claim which would entitle him to relief." *Conley v. Gibson,* 355 U.S. 41, 45-56 (1957). The issue "is not whether a plaintiff will ultimately prevail but whether the claimant is entitled to offer evidence to support its claims." *Village Pond, Inc. v. Darien,* 56 F.3d 375, 378 (2d Cir. 1995). In considering a motion to dismiss, a court may consider only the allegations of the pleadings and documents that are integrated in the pleading by reference.

2. *Securities Laws*

Plaintiffs sue under §§ 10(b), 14(e), and 20(a) of the Exchange Act and Rule 10b-5 and Bermuda common law.

To state a cause of action under § 10(b) and Rule 10b-5, plaintiffs must allege: (1) in connection with a purchase or sale of securities; (2) each defendant, acting with scienter; (3) made a material false representation, or omitted to disclose material information, or engaged in a scheme to defraud; (4) to each plaintiff's detrimental reliance. *Ganino v. Citizens Utils. Co.*, 228 F.3d 154, 161 (2d Cir. 2000). Section 14(e) is modeled after § 10(b) and applies specifically to tender offers. *Schreiber v. Burlington N., Inc.*, 472 U.S. 1, 10 (1985). Accordingly, as with a claim under § 10(b), to properly plead a violation of § 14(e), plaintiffs must assert that they relied upon defendants' alleged misrepresentation and that this reliance caused them injury. *Lewis v. McGraw*, 619 F.2d 192, 194-95 (2d Cir. 1980).

Section 20(a) of the Exchange Act provides that "every person who ... controls any person liable [for violation of §§ 10(b), 14(e) or Rule 10b-5] ... shall also be liable jointly and severally with and to the same extent as such controlled person." To withstand a motion to dismiss a § 20(a) claim, plaintiffs must allege: (1) an underlying primary violation by the controlled person; (2) control over the controlled person; and (3) particularized facts as to the controlling person's culpable participation in the fraud perpetrated by the controlled person. *Securities and Exchange Comm'n v. First Jersey Secs., Inc.*, 101 F.3d 1450, 1472 (2d Cir. 1996). Plaintiffs' allegation of a § 20(a) violation will not survive a motion to dismiss unless plaintiffs properly allege an underlying primary violation. ***

B. *Application*

Defendants move to dismiss, inter alia, on the following grounds: plaintiffs' allegations do not fall within the scope of the federal securities laws; plaintiffs fail to allege a prima facie claim of a federal securities fraud violation; and the Court should not exercise supplemental jurisdiction over plaintiffs' Bermuda law claim.

1. *Scope of §§ 10(b) and 14(e)*

Defendants argue that plaintiffs' claims do not fall within the scope of the federal securities laws relied on in this case. I agree.

Plaintiffs allege that defendants violated §§ 10(b) and 14(e) because they failed to factor into the tender offer price the impact of the anticipated outcome of the negotiations regarding China's entry into the WTO. According to plaintiffs, it was apparent that if China were to join the WTO, the value of AAP stock would increase, and that had defendants considered the possibility that an agreement would soon be reached, a fair tender offer price would have exceeded $18 per share. Plaintiffs further allege that presenting $18 per share as a fair offer was materially false and misleading. Plaintiffs also assert that defendants violated the federal securities laws by failing to reconsider the fairness of the tender offer price during the three days between the announcement of China's inclusion in the WTO and the date that the Offer to Purchase went into effect.

These claims, however, fall outside the ambit of §§ 10(b) and 14(e). The fundamental purpose of the Exchange Act is to ensure full disclosure so that investors may make intelligent and informed decisions. *Santa Fe Indus., Inc. v. Green*, 430 U.S. 462, 477-78 (1977) (in § 10(b) case, describing the Exchange Act as "implementing a philosophy of full disclosure"); see also *Schreiber*, 472 U.S. at 5 (stating the same regarding § 14(e)). The scope of § 10(b) does not include instances of corporate mismanagement. *Santa Fe*, 430 U.S. at 477. The Supreme Court, in examining the scope of § 14(e), observed that "nowhere in the legislative history is there the slightest suggestion that § 14(e) serves any purpose other than disclosure ... or that the ... [provision] should be read as an invitation to the courts to oversee the substantive fairness of tender offers; the quality of any offer is a matter for the marketplace." *Schreiber*, 472 U.S. at 11-12. This Court has held that an "allegation that defendants falsely characterized the tender offer price as fair and failed to disclose that it was unfair does not state a claim under § 14(e)." *In re Phlcorp Secs. Tender Offer Litig.*, 700 F. Supp. 1265, 1269 (S.D.N.Y. 1988).

Plaintiffs' claims that defendants failed to factor the WTO negotiations and agreement into the determination of the tender offer price are not allegations of nondisclosure. Even assuming that the defendants did anticipate that the WTO news would increase the value of AAP shares, but did not reveal this information, plaintiffs have not stated a claim of fraud because the news of the WTO agreement was publicly available. As the Supreme Court has held, a private cause of action under the antifraud provisions of the Exchange Act may be brought only where it is necessary to ensure the fulfillment of Congress's intent to implement full disclosure. *Santa Fe*, 430 U.S. at 477-78. Here, where the information that defendants allegedly failed to disclose was publicly disseminated, investors did not need to rely on disclosure statutes to ensure that they were fully informed.

While plaintiffs' allegations arguably may constitute claims of negligence or breach of fiduciary duty, they do not fall within the purview of the federal securities laws relied on in this case. See *Santa Fe*, 430 U.S. at 479-80 ("There may well be a need for uniform federal fiduciary standards to govern mergers ... but those standards should not be supplied by judicial extension of § 10(b) and Rule 10b-5 to cover the corporate universe."); *Chiarella v. United States*, 445 U.S. 222, 232 (1980) ("not every instance of financial unfairness constitutes fraudulent activity under § 10(b)").

For the reasons stated above, plaintiffs' §§ 10(b) and 14(e) and Rule 10b-5 claims are dismissed.

2. *Requisite Elements of §§ 10(b) and 14(e) Claims*

Plaintiffs' allegations of federal securities fraud are also dismissed for failure to sufficiently plead the requisite elements.

To properly plead a cause of action pursuant to §§ 10(b) and 14(e), plaintiffs must allege detrimental reliance on defendants' alleged misrepresentation. See *Lewis*, 619 F.2d at 194-95. Here, even assuming defendants knowingly and falsely represented that $18 per share was a fair price by omitting information about the impending entry of China into the WTO, plaintiffs could not have reasonably relied to their detriment on that misrepresentation. First, the announcement of the WTO agreement was made the same day the tender offer was announced. Hence, the allegedly withheld information was publicly available in any event. Second, plaintiffs could have chosen not to sell their shares. They had until December 17, 1999 to tender their shares or to withdraw any shares that had been tendered. Plaintiffs' attorneys executed the original complaint on December 15th and filed it on December 16th. Accordingly, plaintiffs were aware of the alleged fraud before the tender offer period expired. Indeed, plaintiffs filed the complaint asserting these allegations when they still had a choice: they could have chosen not to tender their shares. Moreover, in those instances where they had already tendered, they still could have revoked their decision to tender.

Plaintiffs argue that reliance is not a necessary element of their claims or alternatively that reliance is presumed. The cases cited by plaintiffs, however, are distinguishable. For example, plaintiffs cite to *Lewis*, 619 F.2d 192, for the proposition that reliance should be presumed. In *Lewis*, however, the Second Circuit held that reliance may be presumed in situations in which "reliance is possible, and even likely, but is unduly burdensome to prove." *Lewis*, 619 F.2d at 195. The Second Circuit further held that "we presume reliance only where it is logical to do so.... Where no reliance was possible under any imaginable set of facts, such a presumption would be illogical in the extreme." Id. Here, plaintiffs could not have relied on the alleged false and misleading representation because the information was publicly available and plaintiffs filed the complaint before the tender offer period expired. Similarly, plaintiffs also cite to *Herbst v. International Tel. & Tel. Corp.*, 495 F.2d 1308 (2d Cir. 1974), and *Affiliated Ute Citizens v. United States*, 406 U.S. 128, 153-54 (1972). Those cases are also distinguishable. The issue in *Herbst* was whether proof of reliance by each class member is necessary for recovery of a securities fraud class action. That, however, is not the issue here. The issue in the instant case is whether plaintiffs alleged reliance sufficient for a well-pleaded securities fraud case, not whether class action is appropriate. The Supreme Court's ruling in *Affiliated Ute*, is also not relevant because *Affiliated Ute* involved a situation where some of the plaintiffs could have relied (and, in fact, likely did rely) on the defendants' misrepresentation. In the instant case, however, none of the plaintiffs could have relied on the alleged misrepresentation. Accordingly, plaintiffs' claims pursuant to §§ 10(b) and 14(e) and Rule 10b-5 are also dismissed for failing to sufficiently allege reliance.

3. *Section 20(a)*

Because plaintiffs do not allege a viable federal securities claim under §§ 10(b) or 14(e) or the corresponding rules, plaintiffs' § 20(a) claim is also dismissed. See *First Jersey Secs.*, 101 F.3d at 1472.

4. *Bermuda Common Law*

Plaintiffs assert a claim of oppression of minority shareholders under Bermuda common law against the Principal Shareholders. In light of the dismissal of plaintiffs' federal causes of action, I decline to exercise supplemental jurisdiction over plaintiffs' Bermuda law claim. With no federal claims and no allegation of diversity jurisdiction, plaintiffs' Bermuda law claim is dismissed without prejudice for lack of subject matter jurisdiction. ***

NOTES AND QUESTIONS

1. Inside Information? According to the court, the plaintiffs did not claim that the defendants "acted on the basis of any inside information." Do you agree?

2. The Materiality Requirement. Courts employ the same definition of materiality under Section 14(e) that they employ under Rule 14a-9 and Rule 10b-5: "An omitted [or misrepresented] fact is material if there is a "substantial likelihood that a reasonable shareholder would consider it important" or if there is a substantial likelihood that *** the omitted [or misrepresented] fact would have *** significantly altered the 'total mix' of information made available." *TSC Indus., Inc. v. Northway, Inc.*, 426 U.S. 438, 448-49 (1976) (decision under Rule 14a-9). See *Nobles v. First Carolina Commc'ns, Inc,* 929 F.2d 141, 145 (4th Cir. 1991) (applying *Northway to* Section 14(e)); *In re N.Y. Comty. Bancorp, Inc. Sec. Litig.*, 448 F. Supp. 2d 466, 478 (E.D.N.Y. 2006) (equating the materiality standards under § 14(e), Rule 14a-9, and Rule 10b-5). See also *Basic Inc. v.*

Levinson, 485 U.S. 224 (1988) (adopting *Northway* standard for Rule 10b-5 purposes); *Matrixx Initiatives, Inc. v. Siracusano,* 131 S.Ct. 1309 (2011) (reaffirming *Northway* standard for Rule 10b-5 purposes).

In an apparent reference to the materiality requirement, *Wardrop* concluded that "plaintiffs have not stated a claim of fraud because the news of the WTO agreement was publicly available." Is the court suggesting that the information was already part of the "total mix" of information available to shareholders deciding whether to tender? Or is it suggesting instead that by virtue of being publicly available, the information would already have been impounded in the market price? Possibly both? Is the court's failure to clarify this point simply accidental?

3. ***Forward-Looking Statements.*** As noted at the beginning of this Chapter, the Exchange Act's safe harbor for forward-looking statements explicitly excludes tender offers. See Exchange Act Section 21E(b)(2)(c). What is the rationale for this exclusion? The SEC has the authority to expand the safe harbor and override this (or any) statutory exclusion from it. See Exchange Act Section 21E(b). Should it override the exclusion for tender offers?

Recall the bespeaks caution doctrine, another shield for defendants charged with making fraudulent forward-looking statements. See generally Chapter 2.B.3.b (discussing the bespeaks caution doctrine in the context of Rule 10b-5). Does that doctrine offer sufficient protection for defendants who are charged with making fraudulent forward-looking statements in the tender offer context?

4. ***The Scienter Requirement.*** According to Professors Loss and Seligman, the relevance of scienter to Section 14(e) turns on which portion of the Section is at issue:

> Section 14(e), though not quite as broad as Rule 14a-9, is similar to § 17(a) of the 1933 Act; and, unlike Rule 10b-5, is a statute — not a rule. Therefore the Supreme Court's construction of § 17(a) [in *Aaron v. SEC,* 446 U.S.680 (1980)] should govern so as to conclude that scienter (whatever its meaning) is required by the "fraudulent" and "deceptive" clause of § 14(e), which more or less tracks § 17(a)(1) of the 1933 Act and § 10(b) of the 1934 Act, but not by the untrue statement clause, which *precisely* tracks § 17(a)(2).

5 Louis Loss & Joel Seligman, Securities Regulation 165 (4th ed. 2010). Does their analysis clash with that of *Schreiber* and/or *Waldrop*? Should the definition of scienter under Section 14(e) be the same as it is under Rule 10b-5? See *In re Digital Island Sec. Litig.*, 357 F.3d 322, 328 (3d Cir. 2004) (answering affirmatively); *Rubke v. Capital Bancorp Ltd.*, 460 F. Supp. 2d 1124, 1150 (N.D. Cal. 2006) (same), aff'd on other grounds, 551 F.3d 1156 (9th Cir. 2009).

5. ***The Reliance Requirement.*** In its affirmance in *Wardrop,* the Second Circuit stated as follows: "The district court did not err in dismissing the complaint on the ground, inter alia, that it failed adequately to plead the reliance element of plaintiffs' claims or to present any logical basis on which reliance could be proven or presumed." 89 F. App'x 89, 90. Do you agree?

To support its view as to the impossibility of reliance in *Wardop*, the district court cited *Lewis v. McGraw*, 619 F.2d 192, 194-95 (2d Cir. 1980), where reliance had been literally impossible because the tender offer had been withdrawn. Was reliance in *Wardrop* literally impossible?

Assume that the named plaintiffs in *Wardrop* did not rely on the fraud. Is it arguable that they were nonetheless injured by the decisions of less knowledgeable shareholders who did rely? Cf. *Kahn v. Lynden, Inc.*, 705 F. Supp. 1458, 1463-64 (W.D. Wash. 1989) (noting that "[w]hile the plaintiffs themselves had adequate information, their cause of action [under Section 14(e)] is based on the allegation that the other public shareholders did not and that the defendants' fraud consequently caused the majority to tender and assured the success of the tender offer, forcing the plaintiffs to sell [in a subsequent squeeze-out merger] and resulting in their injury").

Should there be a reliance requirement under Section 14(e) in the first place? The answer may depend on whether to analogize to Rule 10b-5 or to Rule 14a-9. Recall that in contrast to Rule 10b-5, Rule 14a-9 does not have a reliance requirement. See generally Chapter 4.D.1. The status of the reliance requirement under Section 14(e) appears to be an open question in the courts. Compare *Melnyk v. Consonus, Inc.*, 2005 WL 2263950 at *6 n.2 (D. Utah 2005) (collecting cases requiring reliance under § 14(e)) with *Rubke v. Capitol Bancorp Ltd.*, 460 F. Supp. 2d 1124, 1131 (N.D. Cal. 2006) (noting that the Ninth Circuit seems not to require reliance under § 14(e)), aff'd on other grounds, 551 F.3d 1156 (9th Cir. 2009)..

6. Presuming Reliance. In *Wardrop*, both the Second Circuit and the district court indicate a general willingness to presume reliance under Section 14(e). Under what circumstances would a presumption be appropriate? What about a presumption when the allegation involves the omission of material information, as there is under Rule 10b-5? See *Affiliated Ute v. United States*, 406 U.S. 128 (1972) ? See generally Chapter 2.F.1.a. Cf. *In re Piedmont Office Trust, Inc., Sec. Litig.*, 264 F.R.D. 693, 701 (N.D. Ga. 2010) (applying *Affiliated Ute* presumption to Section 14(e) claim). What about a presumption based on fraud-on-the-market, as there is under Rule 10b-5? See *Basic Inc. v. Levinson*, 485 U.S. 224 (1988). See generally Chapter 2.F.1.b. The latter presumption assumes the existence of an efficient market. See generally id. In the context of a tender offer, is the market efficient? More efficient than usual? Less so, or only efficient regarding some types of information?

7. Reasonable Reliance. *Wardrop* also suggests that the plaintiff's reliance must be "reasonable." Why should there be a reasonable reliance requirement under Section 14(e)? Is the requirement based on an analogy to Rule 10b-5 (where it is sometimes called the justifiable reliance requirement)? See generally Chapter 2.F.1.d. In the Rule 10b-5 context, reasonable reliance issues arise primarily in the context of face-to-face transactions. See generally id. Is it sensible to import such a requirement into the tender offer context?

8. Loss Causation. Pursuant to the PSLRA, loss causation has become a requirement that all Exchange Act plaintiffs have to prove:

> In any private action arising under this title, the plaintiff shall have the burden of proving that the act or omission of the defendant alleged to violate this title caused the loss for which the plaintiff seeks to recover damages.

Exchange Act Section 21D(b)(4). According to the Supreme Court, this language requires that loss causation be alleged as well. *Dura Pharm., Inc. v. Broudo*, 544

U.S. 336, 346 (2005). Suppose the defendants obtained control of the company by means of a fraudulent tender offer and then used that control to loot the company. Can the shareholders use Section 14(e) to recover for the looting? See *Gorman v. Coogan*, 2004 WL 60271 (D. Me. 2004).

9. Damages. Section 14(e) says nothing about the measure of damages in a private action. This silence is not surprising, given that the private action is implied. Courts typically require a Section 14(e) plaintiff to establish specific damages that flowed from the defendant's violation. The burden of so doing can be daunting. One court put it this way: "While Congress has determined that accurate disclosure is important to shareholders, it would often be impossible for shareholders to prove that on the facts of their particular tender offer accurate disclosure would have affected their decision making in a particular way with concomitant quantifiable monetary loss." *Polaroid Corp. v. Disney*, 862 F.2d 987, 1006-07 (3d Cir. 1988) (directing the lower court to order a preliminary injunction on behalf of the target, partly because of the difficulty in establishing damages). Moreover, when it comes to damages sought by shareholders, a court may take into account whether the price they received for their shares was fair: "While the issue of fairness is relevant to the issue of damages, it does not necessarily defeat a plaintiff's claim of injury." *Plaine v. McCabe,* 797 F.2d 713, 721 (9th Cir. 1986). See also *Horowitz v. Pownall,* 582 F. Supp. 665, 668 (D. Md. 1984) (nontendering shareholders must show damages resulting from retention of their shares).

10. The Relevance of Policy Debates. Debates swirl over whether shareholders benefit from the regulation of tender offers. See, e.g., John Armour & Daivd A. Skeel, Jr., Who Writes the Rules for Hostile Takeovers and Why?-- The Peculiar Divergence of U.S. and U.K. Takeover Regulation, 95 Geo. L. J. 1727 (2007); Lucian A. Bebchuk & Allen Ferrell, A New Approach to Tender Offer Law and Regulatory Competition, 87 Va. L. Rev. 111 (2001); Sharon Hannes, The Market for Tender Offer Defenses, 101 Nw. U. L. Rev. 125 (2007); Gregg A. Jarrell & Michael Bradley, The Economic Effects of Federal and State Regulations of Cash Tender Offers, 23 J. L. & Econ. 371 (1980); Jonathan R. Macey, Displacing Delaware: Can the Feds do a Better Job than the States in Regulating Takeovers?, 57 Bus. Law. 1025 (2002); Roberta Romano, A Guide to Takeovers: Theory, Evidence and Regulation, 9 Yale J. on Reg. 119 (1992). Because this is not a casebook on mergers and acquisitions, we do not systematically address these economic and policy issues. But a lawyer who is familiar with these issues can enhance a litigation team in a tender offer case. Indeed, policy reasons for and against regulatory intervention can be used to strengthen legal arguments, particularly with respect to damages or injunctive remedies once a violation is found to have occurred.

PROBLEM 5-3

Red, Inc., made a partial tender offer for the shares of Blue, Inc. Shares had to be delivered by midnight on December 10, 2002 in order to be in the proration pool. On December 11, Red issued a press release stating that the pool consisted of 50 million Blue shares.

Zoe, a Blue shareholder, relied on the size of the pool as stated in the press release to calculate the number of shares that would be returned to her.

Knowing that the market price for the unpurchased and returned shares would be substantially lower than the price being paid under the tender offer, she attempted to reduce her losses by engaging in various hedging transactions involving the shares to be returned, including selling calls and/or buying puts as well as option transactions and short sales.

The actual size of the proration pool turned out to be 70 million shares. Thus, on January 15, 2003, more shares were returned unpurchased to Zoe and other Blue shareholders than could have been expected based on the press release.

On February 1, 2003, Zoe sued Red under Section 14(e). She claimed that the press release misrepresented the size of the proration pool and that by relying on that misrepresentation, she incurred losses in connection with her hedging transactions and thus with the disposition of her unpurchased shares.

Red responded with a motion to dismiss. It argues that because there is no claim that its statements affected a decision whether to tender or to withdraw tendered shares, Section 14(e) does not apply. Should Red's motion be granted?

Cf. *Pryor v. United States Steel Corp.*, 591 F. Supp. 942 (S.D.N.Y. 1984).

PROBLEM 5-4

Catherine filed a damages action under Section 14(e) 18 months after discovering the facts concerning the fraud described in Problem 5-3, supra. Is her claim barred on statute of limitations grounds?

4. The SEC's Rulemaking Authority

Recall the final sentence of Section 14(e): "The Commission shall, for the purposes of this subsection, by rules and regulations define, and prescribe means reasonably designed to prevent, such acts and practices as are fraudulent, deceptive, or manipulative." Thus, the SEC's rulemaking authority has two aspects — definition and prevention.

The above-quoted sentence constitutes a departure from Section 10(b), which allows the SEC merely to prohibit "manipulative or deceptive device[s] or contrivance[s]." The sentence instead parallels Exchange Act Section 15(c)(2)(D), which focuses on broker-dealers in the over the counter market. Under Section 15(c)(2)(D), the SEC is authorized to "define, and prescribe means reasonably designed to prevent, such [broker-dealer] practices as are fraudulent, deceptive, and manipulative." See *United States v. O'Hagan*, 521 U.S. 642, 672 n.16 (1997) (identifying examples of SEC rulemaking under Section 15(c)(2)(D) that "reach beyond common law fraud").

The Supreme Court considered the SEC's rulemaking authority under Section 14(e) in *United States v. O'Hagan*, supra. At issue in *O'Hagan* was the validity of Rule 14e-3(a), which prohibits insider trading in connection with a tender offer. The Court upheld the Rule as an appropriate exercise of the SEC's power to prevent fraud. The Court was thus able to avoid addressing the government's argument that the SEC's authority to define fraud under Section 14(e) was broader than its authority to define fraud under Section 10(b). (The *O'Hagan* decision receives extensive attention in Chapter 7 on insider trading.)

The SEC's rulemaking authority is an important issue under Section 14(e) outside the insider trading context. Recall that earlier in this Chapter we mentioned Rule 14e-1, adopted by the SEC pursuant to its authority under Section 14(e). Rule 14e-1 requires a bidder to keep the tender offer open for at least twenty business days, presumably to give shareholders sufficient time to ponder the disclosures that are required to be made under Section 14(d). It would seem, however, to be a stretch to say that a tender offer that is held open for 10 days — or 19 days — is a fraudulent, deceptive, or manipulative tender offer. If Rule 14e-1 is a valid exercise of the SEC's rulemaking authority under Section 14(e), it must be as a prophylactic measure to prevent fraud, not as a prohibition of fraud itself. See generally *Polaroid Corp. v. Disney*, 862 F.2d 987 (3d Cir. 1988) (considering SEC's authority to adopt Rule 14d-10, which requires that all shareholders in a tender offer receive the same price for their shares). Why do you suppose that the SEC adopted the twenty day rule under Section 14(e) rather than under Section 14(d)?

C. THE CRITICAL ROLE OF STATE LAW IN TENDER OFFER LITIGATION

In most hostile tender offers, litigation between the target and the bidder can generally be expected. In many instances, target shareholders may also become parties to the lawsuit, with shareholders who wish to accept the bidder's offer aligning with the bidder, and other shareholders sometimes aligning with the target's management.

Litigation over the offer is in many cases simultaneously conducted in federal court (under the Williams Act) and in state court (under state law governing the fiduciary duties of the target's management in responding to the tender offer). In situations where the bidder does not have standing to sue the target, a target shareholder often sues the target management, sometimes with the bidder's encouragement.

Directors of target corporations routinely respond to hostile tender offers with a wide variety of measures designed to thwart the bidder's plan to take control of the company. These defensive measures, often described in artful words and phrases, include seeking a friendly acquirer (a "white knight"); granting preferential options on stock or assets to white knights or persons other than the hostile bidder ("lock-up options"); selling the corporation's most valuable assets ("sale of crown jewels"); implementing rights plans that entitle existing shareholders to large amounts of stock, debt securities, or cash if a hostile bidder gains control ("poison pills"); launching a bid for the bidder itself (the "Pac Man Defense"); paying off the hostile bidder in return for it agreeing to go away ("green mail"); and contractually binding the target corporation tomake large severance payments to incumbent managers in the event of a change of control ("golden parachutes").

Because of the *Schreiber* decision, state law continues to govern these defensive tactics. The law that applies is that of the state of incorporation (typically Delaware, which is the traditional favorite of large corporations), and the forum for litigating these defensive tactics is almost always state court (again typically Delaware), in contrast to the federal court forum that is used for Section 14(e) litigation.

When the bidder and/or target shareholders challenge the validity of these defensive measures, courts in Delaware as well as other states apply a "modified business judgment rule" that requires the target's directors to show that after a "good faith and reasonable investigation," they saw a danger to corporate policy and effectiveness. See *Cheff v. Mathes,* 199 A.2d 548 (Del. 1964). The business judgment rule applied in the tender offer context thus is different from the business judgment rule applied to most other decisions by corporate directors. Courts recognize that hostile tender offers present target directors with an inherent conflict of interest (their jobs are probably on the line) and have accordingly modified the traditional business judgment rule to reflect this reality. Although Delaware courts justify the enhanced scrutiny of defensive tactics as a means to protect target company shareholders, many decisions defer to those tactics and thereby protect incumbent management. Unlike federal courts addressing claims under the Williams Act, which is supposedly neutral between the bidder and target company management, state courts hearing fiduciary duty claims can and do take sides.

Delaware courts generally apply a two part test to determine whether a target's defensive tactics survive review under this modified business judgment rule. Both parts of the test were set out in *Unocal Corp. v. Mesa Petroleum Co.*, 493 A.2d 946, 955 (Del. 1985), where the court looked to (i) whether directors had reasonable grounds for perceiving a threat to the corporation from the takeover bid, and (ii) whether the defensive measures used were "reasonable in relation to the threat posed." Thus, an injunction against a target's defensive measures may be warranted where a bidder's hostile offer does not appear to threaten the corporation, its shareholders, or non-shareholder constituencies (e.g., the offer is all cash, substantially above market price and for 100% of the target company's stock, and the bidder does not plan to radically restructure the company). A court might also enjoin a defensive measure that is very costly to the corporation or its shareholders (e.g., a lock-up option or sale of crown jewels at an unreasonably low price), particularly if the threat that existed was not very great. Even in these situations, however, courts accord substantial deference to the judgment of target company directors. Indeed, most decisions under *Unocal* have permitted defensive measures to remain in place. See, e.g., *Moran v. Household Int'l, Inc.*, 500 A.2d 1346 (Del. 1985) (upholding a "flip over" poison pill providing that if an acquirer sought to merge the corporation into itself after a hostile tender offer, the remaining shareholders would be entitled to buy $200 worth of the acquirer's stock for $100).

Yet when a corporation is faced with multiple bidders, Delaware courts impose additional restrictions on directors' conduct. Under *Revlon v. MacAndrews & Forbes Holdings, Inc.*, 506 A.2d 173 (Del. 1985), once the board concludes that a sale of the company is inevitable, or the board takes steps to put the corporation up for sale (such as structuring a leveraged buyout, a sale of substantially all the corporation's assets, or a merger with a white knight), the role of the board changes substantially. At that point, a corporation is in the "*Revlon* mode," and the directors must obtain the highest price for the shareholders. Defensive measures that were permissible when the company was in the *Unocal* mode may now be a breach of directors' fiduciary duty, and directors have less discretion to take into consideration interests of non-shareholder stakeholders (e.g., employees or customers).

Delaware courts are therefore faced with the challenge of distinguishing between transactions that put a company into the *Revlon* mode from transactions that do not. Compare *Paramount Commc'ns v. QVC Network, Inc.*, 637 A.2d 34 (Del. 1994) with *Paramount Commc'ns v. Time, Inc.*, 571 A.2d 1140 (Del. 1989). Generally, a transaction that contemplates a change in control of the target company triggers *Revlon* duties, whereas a transaction that involves no change of control does not. Directors who seek to sell a control block of the target's stock to a single person or corporation (as in *QVC*) thus have an obligation to sell to the highest bidder, whereas directors who sell less than a control block, transfer a control block to a white knight's dispersed public shareholders, or cause the target company to incur massive debt to buy the stock of another corporation (as in *Time*) retain the far greater discretion allowed under a *Unocal* analysis.[a]

Delaware courts continue to uphold poison pills that can be shown to be reasonably related to the interests of shareholders, while subjecting poison pills to greater scrutiny in other circumstances. Compare *Yucaipa American Alliance Fund II, L.P. v. Riggio,* 1 A.3d 310 (Del. Ch. 2010) (upholding poison pill implemented by the directors of Barnes & Noble even though its founder and chairman controlled about 30% of the company's stock, because the company had proven that its pill was a good faith, reasonable response to a hostile bidder's threat to the company and its shareholders), aff'd mem., 15 A.3d 218 (Del Supr. Ct. 2011) with *eBay Domestic Holdings, Inc. v. Newmark,* 16 A.3d 1 (Del. Ch. 2010) (rescinding a poison pill implemented by the directors of Craigslist on the ground that it was intended to punish eBay, the holder of approximately 28% of Craigslist's outstanding stock, rather than to protect Craigslist or its shareholders from economic harm).

How do the goals sought by the Delaware legislature and courts compare with those sought by Congress in the Williams Act? Is the resultant regime for the regulation of tender offers an intelligible one? Are lawyers the primary beneficiaries? For illustrative recent commentary, see Stephen M. Bainbridge, *Unocal* at 20: Director Primacy in Corporate Takeovers, 31 Del. J. Corp. L. 769 (2006); Richard E. Kihlstrom & Michael L. Wachter, Corporate Policy and the Coherence of Delaware Takeover Law, U. Pa. L. Rev. 523 (2003); Symposium on Takeover Bids in the Boardroom: 25 Years Later, 60 Bus. Law. 1369 (2005).

Another set of concerns involves the constitutionality of state anti-takeover statutes – specifically, whether they survive scrutiny under the Constitutions's dormant commerce clause and avoid preemption under the Williams Act. These concerns emerged in the 1980s when several states enacted

---

a. This modified business judgment rule of Delaware and other American jurisdictions stands in sharp contrast to the regulatory regime under the London City Code and other European jurisdictions which prohibit target company directors from deploying defensive measures without prior authorization obtained from target company shareholders after commencement of the tender offer (the "strict neutrality rule"). See Christian Kirchner & Richard W. Painter, A European Modified Business Judgment Rule for Takeover Law, 2 Eur. Bus. Org. L. Rev. 353 (2000) (comparing this strict neutrality rule with the American modified business judgment rule and proposing that continental Europe consider adopting a variation of the latter).

anti-takeover laws at the behest of labor unions and corporate managers who joined political forces to persuade state legislatures to oppose hostile bids. See *Edgar v MITE*, 457 U.S. 624 (1982) (reviewing an Illinois anti-takeover statute that required approval by the Illinois Secretary of State of any takeover of a corporation, regardless of where incorporated, if 10% or more of its stock was owned by persons located in Illinois, and holding that the Illinois statute imposed burdens on interstate commerce that were excessive in light of the local interests the statute purported to further)

More recently, academics have focused attention on the constitutionality of Delaware's takeover statute, Section 203 of the D.G.C.L. That provision bars a publicly-held Delaware corporation for three years from combining with any entity that owns more than 15% of its stock unless that entity owns at least 85% of its stock or receives approval (i) from the corporation's board of directors prior to the entity's acquiring more than 15% of the corporation's stock, or (ii) from a subsequent board plus approval from two-thirds of the corporation's stockholders. Important empirical research has examined whether Section 203 gives bidders a meaningful opportunity for success. See Guhan Subramanian, et al., Is Delaware's Antitakeover Statute Unconstitutional? Evidence from 1988–2008, 65 Bus. Law. 685 (2010). Professor Subramanian and his co-authors studied a sample of "hostile" or "unsolicited" tender offers for Delaware target companies from January 1, 1988, to December 31, 2008 and found that hostile bidders had a sufficiently low chance of success such that the constitutionality of Section 203 is "up for grabs." Id. at 688. Other commentators dispute this finding. See A. Gilchrist Sparks and Helen Bowers, After Twenty-Two Years, Section 203 of the Delaware General Corporation Law Continues to Give Hostile Bidders a Meaningful Opportunity for Success, 65 Bus. Law. 761 (2010).

Chapter 6

CLASS ACTIONS

Class actions are a prominent feature of American law. The Supreme Court has described their function thus:

> The class-action device was designed as "an exception to the usual rule that litigation is conducted by and on behalf of the individual named parties only." *Califano v. Yamasaki*, 442 U.S. 682, 700-701 (1979). Class relief is "peculiarly appropriate" when the "issues involved are common to the class as a whole" and when they "turn on questions of law applicable in the same manner to each member of the class." Id., at 701. For in such cases, "the class-action device saves the resources of both the courts and the parties by permitting an issue potentially affecting every [class member] to be litigated in an economical fashion under Rule 23." Ibid.

General Tel. Co. of the Southwest v. Falcon, 457 U.S. 147, 155 (1982).

For federal securities law in particular, class actions loom large. The major form of private action, they account for the vast majority of this casebook's principal cases filed by a non-government plaintiff. See, e.g., *Janus Capital Group, Inc. v. First Derivative Traders,* 131 S.Ct. 2296 (2011); *Tellabs, Inc. v. Makor Issues & Rights, Ltd.*, 551 U.S. 308 (2007); *Dura Pharm., Inc. v. Broudo*, 544 U.S. 336 (2005); *Central Bank of Denver, N.A. v. First Interstate Bank of Denver, N.A.*, 511 U.S. 164 (1994); *Virginia Bankshares, Inc. v. Sandberg*, 501 U.S. 1083 (1991); *Basic, Inc. v. Levinson*, 485 U.S. 224 (1988); *Schreiber v. Burlington Northern, Inc.*, 472 U.S. 1 (1985); *Blue Chip Stamps v. Manor Drug Stores*, 421 U.S. 723 (1975). The remaining principal non-government cases include derivative actions — actions filed by shareholders on the corporation's behalf. See, e.g., *J.I. Case Co. v. Borak,* 377 U.S. 426 (1964) (derivative as well as class action). They also include a few actions brought solely on behalf of a single individual or a small group. See, e.g., *Gustafson v. Alloyd Co.*, 513 U.S. 561 (1995).

Certain recent developments involving securities class actions have attracted considerable attention. First, there is the matter of unprecedented settlement size, with all of the top ten settlements approved since 2000 surpassing one billion: Enron Corp. ($7.24 billion); WorldCom, Inc. ($6.16 billion); Cendant Corp. ($3.56 billion); Tyco International, Ltd. ($3.20 billion); AOL Time Warner, Inc. ($2.65 billion); Nortel Networks I ($1.14 billion); Royal Ahold, NV ($1.10 billion); Nortel Networks II ($1.07 billion); McKesson HBOC, Inc. ($1.04 billion); American International Group ($1.01 billion). See Jordan Milev, et al., NERA Econ. Consulting, Trends 2010 Year-End Update: Securities Class Action Filings Accelerate in Second Half of 2010; Median Settlement Value at an All-Time High 21 (2011).

Second, for the first time, some individual defendants have had to fund the settlements from their own pockets. See, e.g., Lucian Bebchuk, Op-Ed, What's $13 Million Among Friends?, N.Y. Times, Jan. 17, 2005 at A17 (noting that "ten former directors of Enron have agreed to pay $13 million from their own pockets to settle a class actions suit stemming from Enron's collapse"). Finally, the number of federal securities class actions filed in 2010 exceeded the number for 2009 and was basically in line with the average post-PSLRA yearly tally. See Milev, NERA Economic Consulting, Trends 2010 Year-end Update, supra, at 2.

Securities class actions are steeped in controversy, the numerous recent corporate scandals notwithstanding. These actions are charged with failing in their mission to compensate because investors typically receive only a fraction of their losses. See Barbara Black, Eliminating Securities Fraud Class Actions Under the Radar, 2009 Colum. Bus. L. Rev. 807, 811-14 (examining this argument). These actions are likewise said to fail at deterrence because individual wrongdoers, shielded by insurance, almost never have to contribute funds of their own. See id. (critiquing this argument). The claim is also often made that securities class actions are inherently circular, since a subset of the shareholders recover money at the expense of the shareholders as a whole. See generally Jill E. Fisch, Confronting the Circularity Problem in Private Securities Litigation, 2009 Wis. L. Rev. 333.

Federal securities class actions are subject to two types of restrictions: (i) those relevant to all private securities actions and (ii) those applicable to class actions only. The first type has been addressed in previous Chapters. It includes restrictions that are largely judicial creations (e.g., Rule 10b-5's purchaser/seller requirement and Rule 14a-9's causation requirement). It also includes restrictions spawned by the Private Securities Litigation Reform Act (PSLRA), such as the safe harbor for forward looking statements, the loss causation requirement, the heightened pleading requirements, the discovery stay upon the filing of a motion to dismiss, and the mandatory penalties for violating Rule 11 of the Federal Rules of Civil Procedure.

This Chapter focuses on the second type of restriction – those applicable to class actions only. Some restrictions of this type apply to all class actions filed in federal court, irrespective of the subject matter. Others originate in the PSLRA or in the Securities Litigation Uniform Standards Act of 1998 (SLUSA) and target securities class actions specifically.

The fact that there are restrictions aimed squarely at securities class actions attests to the quantum of hostility that such actions provoke. But this hostility is, at least to a limited degree, tempered by ambivalence. Thus, the PSLRA and the SLUSA notwithstanding, Congress has declined to do what would bring most federal securities class actions to a grinding halt – enact a statute that overturns the Supreme Court's decision in *Basic, Inc.* v. *Levinson*, 485 U.S. 224 (1988). In *Basic*, the Court authorized a presumption of reliance which, when applicable, eliminates the need for separate inquiries into each plaintiff's reliance. By allowing common reliance issues to predominate over individual ones, the presumption makes many class actions possible.

This Chapter is divided into six Sections. It begins with the appointment of the lead plaintiff and the lead counsel (Section A) and then turns to the certification of the class (Section B), settlement (Section C), the preemption of state law class actions (Section D), and the interplay between securities class actions and shareholder derivative litigation (Section E). It concludes with the current debate over whether, and to what extent, securities class actions successfully compensate and deter (Section F).

A. SELECTION OF THE LEAD PLAINTIFF AND THE LEAD COUNSEL

Probably the most innovative development to emerge from the PSLRA is the court-appointed "lead plaintiff." See generally Elliott J. Weiss & John S. Beckerman, Let the Money Do the Monitoring: How Institutional Investors Can Reduce Agnecy Costs in Securities Class Actions, 104 Yale L.J. 2054 (1995) (proposing the concept of the "lead plaintiff"). As the name suggests, the lead plaintiff assumes a leadership role in the litigation. The PSLRA's legislative history suggests that the ideal lead plaintiff is an institution. See *Ravens v. Iftikar*, 174 F.R.D. 651, 661 (N.D. Cal. 1997) (collecting comments in the legislative history to this effect). The text of the PSLRA itself, however, leaves this preference unstated.

When the PLSRA was first enacted, institutional lead plaintiffs were relatively few and far between. Stephen J. Choi, et al., Do Institutions Matter? The Impact of the Lead Plaintiff Provision of the Private Securities Litigation Reform Act, 83 Wash. U. L. Q. 869, 877 (2005). In 2010, in contrast, institutions accounted for in excess of sixty-seven percent of the lead plaintiff total. See Ellen M. Ryan & Laura E. Simmons, Cornerstone Research, Securities Class Action Settlements: 2010 Review and Analysis 8 (2011). Participation rates vary, however, by institutional type: public pension funds serve as lead plaintiffs relatively often, whereas mutual funds, banks, and insurance companies almost never do. See Stephen J. Choi & Robert B. Thompson, Securities Litigation and Its Lawyers: Changes During the First Decade After the PLSRA, 106 Colum. L. Rev. 1489, 1504 (2006). As you read this Chapter, think about why so many institutions stay on the sidelines.

Whether institutional lead plaintiffs actually make a difference remains unclear. On the one hand, they are associated with larger recoveries. Id. at 1505. On the other hand, that association may simply reflect the cases in which they choose to participate. Id. at 1506. See also James D. Cox and Randall S. Thomas, Does the Plaintiff Matter? An Empirical Analysis of Lead Plaintiffs in Securities Class Actions, 106 Colum. L. Rev. 1587 (2006).

Prior to the PSLRA, securities class action litigation was typically directed by the lawyer whose client managed to be the first to file the class action complaint. To wrest control from that lawyer, the PSLRA establishes the following:

The Notice Requirement. Under the PSLRA, the first filer must notify the other members of the purported class that the action is pending and that they each have the right to seek appointment as the lead plaintiff:

> Not later than 20 days after the date on which the complaint is filed, the plaintiff or plaintiffs shall cause to be published, in a widely circulated

> national business-oriented publication or wire service, a notice advising members of the purported plaintiff class –
>
> (I) of the pendency of the action, the claims asserted therein, and the purported class period; and
>
> (II) that, not later than 60 days after the date on which the notice is published, any member of the purported class may move the court to serve as lead plaintiff of the purported class.

Securities Act § 27(a)(3)(A); Exchange Act § 21D(a)(3)(A). See *Waldman v. Wachovia Corp.*, 2009 WL 2950362 at *1 (S.D.N.Y. 2009) (noting the necessity of republication "where the amended complaint substantially alters the claims or class members") (collecting cases). The goal is to reach the most plausible lead plaintiff candidates, not necessarily every class member as such. See *Greebel v. FTP Software, Inc.*, 939 F. Supp. 57, 63 (D. Mass. 1996).

The Presumption in Favor of the Investor With the Largest Financial Interest. Under the PLRSA, the lead plaintiff candidate with the largest financial interest in the relief sought receives a presumption as follows:

> (I) In general
>
> *** [T]he court shall adopt a presumption that the most adequate plaintiff *** is the person or group of persons that –
>
> (aa) has either filed the complaint or made a motion in response to a notice under subparagraph (A)(i);
>
> (bb) in the determination of the court, has the largest financial interest in the relief sought by the class; and
>
> (cc) otherwise satisfies the requirements of Rule 23 of the Federal Rules of Civil Procedure.
>
> (II) Rebuttal evidence
>
> The presumption *** may be rebutted only upon proof by a member of the purported plaintiff class that the presumptively most adequate plaintiff –
>
> (aa) will not fairly and adequately protect the interests of the class; or
>
> (bb) is subject to unique defenses that render such plaintiff incapable of adequately representing the class.

Securities Act § 27(a)(3)(B)(iii); Exchange Act § 21D(a)(3)(B)(iii).

Notice that the presumption brings into play two requirements from Rule 23 of the Federal Rules of Civil Procedure – the typicality and adequacy. Typicality focuses on whether the movant with the largest financial interest "has claims or defenses *** [that] are typical of the claims and defenses of the class." Rule 23(a)(3). Adequacy focuses on whether she "will fairly and adequately protect the interests of the class." Rule 23(a)(4). The court must decide whether she "has made a prima facie showing of typicality and adequacy" before the presumption even attaches. Then, if she receives the presumption, other members of the class can endeavor to rebut it by disproving her typicality or adequacy (or both). See *In re Cendant Corp. Litig.*, 264 F.3d 201, 263-68 (3d Cir. 2001). These inquiries into typicality and adequacy tend to be less exhaustive than those made at the certification stage. See, e.g., *In re eSpeed Inc. Sec. Litig.*, 232 F.R.D. 95, 102 (S.D.N.Y. 2005).

Availability of Discovery. The above presumption anticipates a competition among lead plaintiff candidates. Accordingly, discovery "relating to whether a member or members of the purported plaintiff class is the most adequate plaintiff " is available to the plaintiff who "demonstrates a reasonable basis for a finding that the presumptively most adequate plaintiff is incapable of adequately representing the class." Securities Act § 27(a)(3)(B)(iv); Exchange Act § 21D(a)(3)(B)(iv).

Restriction on Professional Plaintiffs. The PSLRA restricts the participation of "professional plaintiffs" – those who frequently file lawsuits against the numerous companies in which they own shares. The restriction is prompted by concern that professional plaintiffs will function merely as lawyers' pawns. But the participation of such plaintiffs is not barred outright:

> Except as the court may otherwise permit, consistent with the purposes of this section, a person may be a lead plaintiff, or an officer, director, or fiduciary of a lead plaintiff, in no more than 5 securities class actions brought as plaintiff class actions pursuant to the Federal Rules of Civil Procedure during any 3-year period.

Securities Act § 27(a)(3)(B)(vi); Exchange Act § 21D(a)(3)(B)(vi). Why is there no outright bar? The probable reason is that a bar would lead to the frequent disqualification of institutions, Congress's preferred lead plaintiffs. Cf. *In re Vicuron Pharm., Inc. Sec. Litig.*, 225 F.R.D. 508, 511-12 (E.D. Pa. 2004) (appointing an institution as the lead plaintiff despite its having served in this capacity more than five times in three years).

Selection of the Lead Counsel. Prior to the PSLRA, the named plaintiffs in securities class actions were often chosen by the lawyers. See *Gluck v. CellStar Corp.*, 976 F. Supp. 542, 549 (N.D. Tex. 1997). To turn this around and allow the plaintiffs to do the choosing, the PSRLA provides:

> The most adequate plaintiff shall, subject to the approval of the court, select and retain counsel to represent the class.

Securities Act § 27(a)(3)(B)(v); Exchange Act § 21D(a)(3)(B)(v). See *Cohen v. U.S. Dist. Ct. for N. Dist. of Cal.*, 586 F.3d 703 (9th Cir. 2009) (granting writ of mandamus when a federal district court itself selected the lead counsel).

IRON WORKERS LOCAL NO. 25 PENSION FUND v. CREDIT-BASED ASSET SERVICING & SECURITIZATION, LLC

616 F. Supp. 2d 461 (S.D.N.Y. 2009)

JED S. RAKOFF, DISTRICT JUDGE:

By motions filed earlier this year, the two respective plaintiffs in these consolidated class actions each sought to be appointed "lead plaintiff," a position that carries with it enhanced responsibility for the conduct of the litigation and-dare one mention it-increased legal fees for the law firm representing whichever plaintiff is chosen to lead. The choice presented a classic dilemma, in the sense of a choice between two less-than-perfect plaintiffs. Still, a choice had to be made if the case were to proceed, and so on April 23, 2009, the Court issued a "bottom-line" Order granting the motion of the Public Employees'

Retirement System of Mississippi ("MissPERS") to be lead plaintiff, appointing one of MissPERS' counsel, Bernstein Litowitz Berger & Grossmann LLP ("Bernstein Litowitz"), as lead counsel, and denying the motion of Iron Workers Local No. 25 Pension Fund ("Iron Workers Fund") to be lead plaintiff. This Opinion states the reasons for those rulings.

Each of the plaintiffs sought to represent a putative class of investors who purchased from defendant Merrill Lynch & Co., Inc. and/or its affiliates "certificates" backed by pools of subprime mortgages and the like. The central thrust of the complaints was that defendants failed to disclose the extent of the underlying risk. The complaints sufficiently overlapped that the Court ordered them consolidated (two other actions have been similarly consolidated since), and both plaintiffs sought to be appointed lead plaintiff in the consolidated action pursuant to the relevant provisions of the Private Securities Litigation and Reform Act of 1995 ("PSLRA").[1]

After receiving written submissions, the Court held an evidentiary hearing on April 1, 2009, at which the Court was made aware of problematic relationships between plaintiffs and their counsel (discussed below) that arguably affected the pending motions. The Court therefore invited, and received, further briefing before issuing its "bottom-line" ruling on April 23, 2009.

It is axiomatic, and the parties here do not dispute, that the lead plaintiff provisions of the PSLRA were intended to curtail the vice of "lawyer-driven" litigation, *i.e.,* lawsuits that, because of the huge potential fees available in contingent securities fraud class actions, were initiated and controlled by the lawyers and appeared to be litigated more for their benefit than for the benefit of the shareholders they ostensibly represented. See, e.g., *In re Doral Fin. Corp. Sec. Litig.,* 414 F.Supp.2d 398, 401 (S.D.N.Y.2006) ("[the PSLRA] was enacted to address perceived abuses in securities fraud class actions created by lawyer-driven litigation"); *In re Pfizer Inc. Sec. Litig.,* 233 F.R.D. 334, 337 (S.D.N.Y.2005) ("One of the principal legislative purposes of the PSLRA was to prevent lawyer-driven litigation."). To help combat this problem, the lead plaintiff provisions of the PSLRA required that a court "appoint as lead plaintiff the member or members of the purported plaintiff class that the court determines to be most capable of adequately representing the interests of class members." 15 U.S.C. § 77z-1(a)(3)(B)(i). Further, the provisions created a "rebuttable presumption" that the "most adequate" plaintiff is, *inter alia,* the person or group of persons that "has the largest financial interest in the relief sought by the class." 15 U.S.C. § 77z-1(a)(3)(B)(iii)(I)(bb). "The theory of these provisions was that if an investor with a large financial stake in the litigation was made lead plaintiff, such a plaintiff-frequently a large institution or otherwise sophisticated investor-would be motivated to act like a 'real' client, carefully choosing counsel and monitoring counsel's performance to make sure that adequate representation was delivered at a reasonable price." *In re*

---

1. 15 U.S.C. § 77z-1 is the part of the PSLRA applicable to cases, like this, brought under the Securities Act of 1933. Parallel provisions of the PSLRA applicable to cases brought under the Securities Exchange Act of 1934 are found at 15 U.S.C. § 78u-(4).

Razorfish, Inc. Sec. Litig., 143 F.Supp.2d 304, 307 (S.D.N.Y.2001) (citing Elliott J. Weiss & John S. Beckerman, Let the Money Do the Monitoring: How Institutional Investors Can Reduce Agency Costs in Securities Class Actions, 104 Yale L.J. 2053, 2089 (1995)).

Accordingly, each of the plaintiffs, in their initial papers on these motions, focused much of their attention on demonstrating that they had a substantial financial interest. MissPERS, in particular, emphasized that it had purchased 177,500 of the underlying certificates, compared with the Iron Workers Funds' 100,000. But the Iron Workers Fund argued that it alone held an interest in one of the classes of certificates at issue here, and that MissPERS could therefore "not fairly and adequately protect the interests of the class." 15 U.S.C. § 77z-1(a)(3)(B)(iii)(II)(bb).

At the evidentiary hearing, however, the Court was made aware of an arrangement between the Iron Workers Fund and its counsel, Coughlin Stoia Geller Rudman & Robbins LLP ("Coughlin Stoia"), that cast in doubt the adequacy of the Fund to serve as lead plaintiff in any event. Specifically, the evidence showed the Fund had entered into a contractual arrangement with Coughlin Stoia whereby, in return for Coughlin Stoia's providing free "monitoring" of the Funds' investments, the Fund agreed that, if Coughlin Stoia recommended bringing a securities class action and the Fund approved doing so, Coughlin Stoia would be retained, on a contingent fee basis, to represent the Fund. As Dennis Kramer, the Fund's administrator, testified:

> Q. [by the Court] ... what you've chosen to enter into, as I understand it, is a contract where the monitoring counsel will also be the counsel who represents you if a lawsuit is brought, is that right?
>
> A. [by Mr. Kramer] Yes, that's true.
>
> Q. And the only way they get paid is if they bring such a lawsuit and recover, is that right?
>
> A. Correct.

Transcript, April 1, 2009 ("Tr.") at 8.

Going far beyond any traditional contingency arrangement of which the Court is aware, this practice, on its face, creates a clear incentive for Coughlin Stoia to discover "fraud" in the investments it monitors and to recommend to the Fund's non-lawyer administrator (and, through him, to the trustees) that the Fund, at no cost to itself, bring a class action lawsuit. In other words, the practice fosters the very tendencies toward lawyer-driver litigation that the PSLRA was designed to curtail.

At the evidentiary hearing, the Court also questioned whether the seeming conflict of interest inherent in this arrangement violated ethical prohibitions. See, e.g., ABA Code of Professional Responsibility, Disciplinary Rule 5-101 ("[a] lawyer shall not accept or continue employment if the exercise of professional judgment on behalf of the client will be or reasonably may be affected by the lawyer's own financial, business, property, or personal interests...."). At the time, Coughlin Stoia's chief response was a variation on everybody-does-it: "this portfolio monitoring is not something that's unique to our firm." Tr. at 11. There was also a suggestion that free monitoring was of special benefit in this time of economic hardship-in apparent disregard of the ever-applicable adage that there is no such thing as a free lunch.

Subsequently, however, Coughlin Stoia identified two reported cases in which district courts had appeared untroubled by this kind of arrangement, see *In re Am. Italian Pasta Co. Sec. Litig.*, 2007 WL 927745 (W.D.Mo.2007) ("the Court is not surprised Lead Plaintiff has arranged for a law firm to keep it apprised of events (including lawsuits) that might be of interest"); *Plumbers & Pipefitters Local 572 Pension Fund v. Cisco Sys.*, 2004 WL 5326262 (C.D.Cal.2004) ("Nothing about these [monitoring agreements] renders Carpenters inadequate as a class representative."). Additionally, Coughlin Stoia submitted a sworn declaration from a well-known expert on legal ethics, Prof. Geoffrey C. Hazard, Jr. of the Hastings College of the Law, University of California, who, while noting the Court's "legitimate concern" with the apparent conflict of interest, concluded that "in my opinion, there is no *improper* conflict of interest." Declaration of Geoffrey C. Hazard, Jr. dated April 8, 2009 ("Hazard Decl.") (emphasis added). Prof. Hazard reached this conclusion "based on discussion of the issue with experienced lawyers on both sides," that convinced him that "a plaintiff's lawyer, in a securities case that is worth bringing on a contingent basis, has every incentive to proceed only if the claim is reasonably viable on the basis of informed professional judgment," and that, while "[t]here are plaintiff cases brought on the basis of contingent fees that should not have been brought [,m]y impression is that the lawyers in such cases are inexperienced or unrealistic, and that they do not long remain in contingent fee practice," "Accordingly, on the question of the viability of the claim, the interests of an experienced plaintiff's counsel in contingent fee cases, not only in securities litigation but generally, are aligned with the claimant."

Although the Court has the very greatest respect for Prof. Hazard, it must be noted that these are quite sweeping conclusions to be reached on the basis of little more than "discussions" with unnamed "experienced lawyers." One might have supposed that defendants in securities class actions, facing potentially huge damages, might be prepared to pay substantial sums to settle even those actions where the chances of plaintiffs' ultimately prevailing were remote and that this might give plaintiffs' lawyers a motive to bring even dubious actions if a compliant plaintiff could be found. Professor Hazard, indeed, acknowledges that "[m]any observers have had similar suppositions," but opines, in somewhat conclusory fashion, that they are "not accurate."

This Court need not resolve this debate in the abstract, for if Prof. Hazard were correct, Congress would never have enacted the PSLRA in the first place, because it would have agreed with Prof. Hazard that experienced securities class action lawyers would almost never be motivated to bring abusive lawsuits, let alone to convince their clients to come along (cost-free) for the ride. But, as noted, it was Congress' conclusion that abusive lawyer-driven litigation existed in this context that gave rise to the PSLRA. Indeed, Congress even included in the PSLRA, under the title "Sanctions for abusive litigation," a requirement that a court at the end of any such action make specific findings of whether litigation abuse had been present at any stage and, if so, impose mandatory sanctions. 15 U.S.C. 77z-1(c). Congress, then, has rejected Prof. Hazard's primary suppositions, and this Court must be guided accordingly.

Prof. Hazard goes on, however, to assert that, in any event, "[i]n the field of contemporary securities claims and litigation, most of the clients are sophisticated and have access to sophisticated advisers, financial and legal, in determining whether to bring suit." But, even if true elsewhere, this is not true in the case of the Iron Workers Fund. The Court, from its own observation of the testimony and demeanor of the Fund's administrator, readily perceived that he was not particularly sophisticated in evaluating securities class actions and, indeed, had only a rough idea of what this lawsuit was all about. But who were the "sophisticated advisers, financial and legal" who would advise him and the Fund "in determining whether to bring suit"? – why, the very lawyers who would be bringing the suit, Coughlin Stoia. Accordingly, the Court need not determine whether there here exists a conflict of interest that violates ethical rules. What is crystal clear to the Court is that the Iron Workers Fund is in no position to adequately monitor the conduct of this complex litigation when it has not even taken the necessary steps to assure itself that the advice it is getting from its monitors is disinterested, let alone take the necessary steps to find out much about the lawsuit it is being asked to oversee.

This is not to say that the alternative lead plaintiff, MissPERS, is without blemish. It too employs plaintiffs' firms to "monitor" its investments free of charge, although there are a number of important differences that serve to mitigate, though not entirely eliminate, the dangers outlined above. First, MissPERS relies on something like twelve different firms to monitor its investments, and no such firm is guaranteed that it will be selected to bring the potential lawsuit it identifies in the course of its monitoring. On the contrary, MissPERS "play[s] off one against the other," both in terms of determining whether a given lawsuit should be brought and in determining the fee arrangement. Second, the ultimate evaluation of the monitoring firms' recommendations, and the oversight of such litigation as is then brought, is entrusted to a group of lawyers in the Attorney General's Office of the State of Mississippi, who bring their own expertise to bear. Here, Special Assistant Attorney General George W. Neville, the MissPERS client representative responsible for this case, who testified at the evidentiary hearing, plainly had a sophisticated knowledge of such matters. Third, as it happens, the basis for this particular litigation was brought to MissPERS' attention, not by any of its monitoring firms, but by another Mississippi law firm, Pond Gadow & Tyler, P.A. ("Pond Gadow"), which will *not* be serving as lead counsel in this case (though it will be involved). All these circumstances render it much more likely that MissPERS can adequately oversee this litigation than could the Iron Workers Fund.

The Fund, however, argues that, precisely because MissPERS is involved in fifteen securities fraud actions under Mr. Neville's supervision, MissPERS is a "professional plaintiff" of the kind that the PSLRA disfavors. Specifically, the relevant provision of the PSLRA provides that "[e]xcept as the court may otherwise permit, consistent with the purposes of this section, a person may be a lead plaintiff ... in no more than 5 securities class actions brought as plaintiff class actions pursuant to the Federal Rules of Civil Procedure during any 3-year period." 15 U.S.C. § 77z-1(3)(B)(vi). Even in the abstract, however, it would seem that this provision might apply with less force when the plaintiff is a state agency-after all, a state regularly brings suit in hundreds of cases-and, as already noted, in this case, where the alternative lead plaintiff, the Iron Workers Fund, seems to have little real expertise in handling such cases, the accumulated experience of MissPERS in pursuing multiple securities fraud actions seems a benefit more than a detriment. Moreover, as many courts have noted, the provision of the PSLRA restricting the use of professional plaintiffs was largely directed at private individuals, and courts have routinely waived the restriction in the case of qualified institutional investors.[2] See, e.g., *Kuriakose v. Fed. Home Loan Mortgage Co.*, 2008 WL 4974839, at *8 (S.D.N.Y. Nov. 24, 2008); *In re Fannie Mae Sec. Litig.*, 355 F.Supp.2d 261, 264 (D.D.C.2005); *In re Vicuron Pharms., Inc. Sec. Litig.*, 225 F.R.D. 508, 512 (E.D.Pa.2004).

As for the objection, noted previously, that MissPERS did not own an interest in one of the class of certificates at issues in this consolidated litigation, the record presently before the Court does not suggest that this matters, for the central allegations here are the same for all classes of certificates. Nevertheless, the Court holds open the possibility that additional lead plaintiffs (such as from the other two cases more recently consolidated into this action) may have to be added if subsequent circumstances warrant.

Finally, there is the question of which law firm(s) should represent MissPERS as lead plaintiff. MissPERS recommends the two firms that have represented it thus far: Bernstein Litowitz and Pond Gadow. But, concededly, only the former is experienced in securities class actions, and the Court sees no need for two firms to represent the lead plaintiff. Hence, the Court appoints Bernstein Litowitz as the sole lead lawyer.[3]

For the foregoing reasons, the Court hereby reaffirms its Order of April 23, 2009 appointing MissPERS as lead plaintiff and Bernstein Litowitz as lead counsel.

NOTES AND QUESTIONS

1. ***Portfolio Monitoring.*** Portfolio monitoring is a reasonably new practice with which courts selecting lead plaintiffs have only begun to grapple.

---

2. See H.R. Conf. Rep. No. 104-369 at *35, reprinted in 1995 U.S.C.C.A.N. 730, 734 ("Institutional investors seeking to serve as lead plaintiff may need to exceed this limitation and do not represent the type of professional plaintiff this legislation seeks to restrict. As a result, the Conference Committee grants courts discretion to avoid the unintended consequences of disqualifying institutional investors from serving more than five times in three years. The Conference Committee does not intend for this provision to operate at cross purposes with the 'most adequate plaintiff' provision.").

3. The Court is not unaware of disturbing allegations that state entities not unlike MissPERS, and law firms not unlike Bernstein Litowitz, have engaged in "pay-for-play" arrangements, by which such an entity will not even consider hiring such a law firm unless the law firm has contributed to the campaign fund of the relevant state elected official, such as the attorney general. *See, e.g.,* John C. Coffee, Jr., *'Pay-to-Play' Reform: What, How, and Why?,* New York Law Journal, May 21, 2009, p. 5. But no such allegations are presently before the Court in this case.

Cf. *In re Gen'l Elec. Sec. Litig.*, 2009 WL 2259502 at *6 (S.D.N.Y. 2009) (observing that "whether monitoring by law firms truly presents a conflict of interest is an open question"). Might certain institutional investors have a particular need for portfolio monitoring assistance? See John C. Coffee, Jr., "Pay to Play" Reform: What, How and Why, N.Y.L.J. at 5 (May 21, 2009) (observing that thinly-staffed pension funds often fail to file claims after the settlement of class actions that cover them). As Professor Coffee sees it, instead of inherently closing or corrupting a market, portfolio monitoring may actually enhance competition. Accordingly, his principal concern would "be whether the law firm can 'capture' the client in this fashion, and he points out that "this is less a conflict of interest problem than an issue of 'adequacy' under Rule 23(a) of the Federal Rules of Civil Procedure." Id. He concludes that:

> Ultimately, the dividing line here probably should be between institutional investors that have an active in-house counsel and those that do not. In the latter case, the law firm effectively controls the client, and thus the problems that the PSLRA sought to end with its lead plaintiff reform resurface again. But when there is a competent house counsel who makes the litigation decisions, the provision of monitoring services should not be viewed as questionable or disqualifying.

Id. Are Professor Coffee's views in cinque with those of Judge Rakoff?

2. Pay to Play. Judge Rakoff noted that there had been no allegations of pay to play in *Iron Workers*. Concerning the appropriate judicial response to "pay to play," the Third Circuit has had this to say:

> [W]e observe that actual *proof* of pay-to-play would constitute strong (and, quite probably, dispositive) evidence that the presumption had been rebutted. A movant that was willing to base its choice of class counsel on political contributions instead of professional considerations would, it seems to us, have quite clearly demonstrated that it would "not fairly and adequately protect the interests of the class."

In re Cendant Corp Litig., 264 F.3d 201, 269 (3d Cir. 2001). What would constitute proof of "pay to play"? How readily can the other lead plaintiff candidates obtain such proof?

For a discussion of what the SEC could do to combat "pay to play," see John C. Coffee, Jr., The Attorney as Gatekeeper: An Agenda for the SEC, 103 Colum. L. Rev. 1293, 1315 n.61 (2003). But cf. David H. Webber, Is "Pay to Play" Driving Public Pension Fund Activism in Securities Class Actions? An Empirical Study, 90 B. U. L. Rev. 2031 (2010) (calling into question the significance of the "pay to play" dynamic).

3. Then There Were None. Suppose that Iron Workers had been the only lead plaintiff candidate. Would Judge Rakoff have been entitled to lower the bar in order to allow the lawsuit to go forward? See generally *In re Cavanaugh*, 306 F.3d 726, 731 n.7 (9th Cir. 2002) (noting that such discretion might exist but not resolving whether it does).

4. Determining Who Has the Greatest Financial Interest. Judge Rakoff appeared to have relatively little trouble determining whose financial interest was greater. This determination is typically made by applying the four factors articulated in *Lax v. First Merchants Acceptance Corp.*, 1997 WL 461036

(N.D. Ill. 1997). These factors – known as the *Lax* factors – consist of the following:

> (1) the number of shares purchased; (2) the number of net shares purchased; (3) the total net funds expended by the plaintiffs during the class period; and (4) the approximate losses suffered by the plaintiffs.

Id. at *5. See, e.g., *Janbay v. Canadian Solar, Inc.*, 272 F.R.D. 112, 118 (S.D.N.Y. 2010). The fourth factor is widely understood to be the most important, but divisions abound about how to measure it. See, e.g., *Foley v. Transocean, Ltd.*, 272 F.R.D. 126, 129-30 & n.7 (S.D.N.Y. 2011) (noting divisions regarding whether to use LIFO or FIFO as well as whether to borrow the 90 day look-back rule mandated by the PLRSA for use in calculating damages). While Judge Rakoff did not cite the *Lax* factors, to what extent (if at all) did he seem to be drawing upon them?

Consider this description of the difficulties that can arise when applying the *Lax* factors:

> [S]ome applicants will not have made all their purchases of the issuer's securities during the purported class period or will not have held all securities they purchased until the period's end. Some will have held securities at the time the class period began and then sold some or all of them during the class period at allegedly inflated prices (arguably realizing some benefit from the alleged fraud). Others will have made all of their securities purchases during the class period but sold some of those securities before that period's end. Some may have done both. Moreover, two common occurrences can make the computation of applicants' losses even more complex. First, a major portion of an applicant's losses (at least arguably) may be due to adverse business developments, not the alleged fraud. Second, corrective disclosures often enter the market piecemeal, rather than all at once, and one or more applicants may have purchased or sold securities after the first partial corrective disclosure, but before the last.

Elliott J. Weiss, The Lead Plaintiff Provisions of the PLSRA After a Decade, or "Look What's Happened to My Baby," 61 Vand. L. Rev. 543, 568-69 (2008).

Should Congress have anticipated these uncertainties? If it had, could it have generated a superior solution?

Instead of favoring the lead plaintiff candidate with the greatest financial interest, would it be better to favor the candidate with the greatest financial sophistication? Why or why not?

5. Groups as Lead Plaintiffs. The PSRLA presumes in favor of the lead plaintiff candidate that meets the specified criteria, regardless of whether that candidate is a "person or group of persons." Courts have divided over the interpretation of the phrase "group of persons." Some insist that a group can serve as lead plaintiff only if its members had a pre-existing relationship. *Ruland v. InfoSonics Corp.*, 2006 WL 3746716 at *4 (S.D. Cal. 2006) (maintaining that the "[a]ppointment of lead counsel should not depend on which law firm can accumulate the most class action members"). The majority of courts permit service by a group without such a relationship so long as its members offer evidence that they can "function cohesively and *** effectively manage the litigation apart from their lawyers." *Varghese v. China Shenghuo Pharm. Holdings, Inc.*, 589 F. Supp. 2d 388, 392 (S.D.N.Y. 2008).

According to Professor Burch, courts should stop prioritizing cohesion and pre-existing relationships because, according to the social science literature, these characteristics jeopardize high-quality decision-making. Elizabeth Chamblee Burch, Optimal Lead Plaintiffs, 64 Vand. L. Rev. 1109 (2011). Instead, she argues, courts should seek groups that reflect the range of perspectives that comprise the class. Id. What do you think?

6. Co-Lead Plaintiffs. Judge Rakoff acknowledged the "possibility" that he would need to appoint additional lead plaintiffs "if subsequent circumstances warrant." Courts have offered the following justifications for appointing co-lead plaintiffs – because the novel substantive questions at issue would benefit from a range of perspectives, see *Pirelli Armstrong Tire Corp. Retiree Medical Benefits Trust v. Labranche & Co.*, 229 F.R.D. 395, 420 (S.D.N.Y. 2004); because it would permit "diverse representation, including *** a state pension fund, significant individual investors, and a large institutional investor," *In re Oxford Health Plans, Inc. Sec. Litig.*,182 F.R.D. 42, 49 (S.D.N.Y.1998); because distinguishing between two (or more) lead plaintiff candidates is difficult, if not impossible, see *Gluck v. CellStar Corp.*, 976 F. Supp. 542, 549-50 (N.D. Tex. 1997). Which (if any) of these justifications do you find persuasive?

On the other hand, the Ninth Circuit has, albeit in dictum, suggested that appointing co-lead plaintiffs conflicts with the statutory language: "While the PSLRA allows a group to serve as lead plaintiff, it also consistently refers to the lead plaintiff and most adequate plaintiff in the singular, suggesting that the district court should appoint only one lead plaintiff, whether an individual or a group." *Cohen v. U.S. Dist. Ct. for N. Dist. of Cal.*, 586 F.3d 703, 711 n.4 (9th Cir. 2009). Do you agree?

Contrast co-lead plaintiffs with a lead plaintiff consisting of a group of unrelated members. Is there a difference that should make a difference?

7. Selecting the Lead Counsel. Most courts regard the most adequate plaintiff as entitled to receive the lead counsel of her choice, unless that choice is so outrageous that making it demonstrates inadequacy to serve as the lead plaintiff in the first place. See, e.g., *In re Cavanaugh*, 306 F.3d 726, 732-33 (9th Cir. 2002). See also *Cohen v. U.S. Dist. Ct. for the N. Dist. of Cal.*, 586 F.2d 703 (9th Cir. 2009) (mandamusing the federal district court that had chosen the lead counsel itself). But cf. *In re Copper Mountain Sec. Litig.*, 305 F. Supp. 2d 1124, 1128 (N.D. Cal. 2004) (lambasting interpretations of the lead counsel provisions that "straightjacket" courts and prevent them from doing what is best for investors).

Would it be outrageous to choose a law firm which, ten years earlier, had received an order from the SEC to cease and desist from securities law violations? Cf. *In re Leapfrog Enters., Inc. ,Sec. Litig.*, 2005 WL 3801587 (N.D. Cal. 2005) (approving such a law firm and distinguishing its situation from one in which the wrongdoing consisted of a felony fraud conviction). See generally Lisa L. Casey, Reforming Securities Class Actions from the Bench: Judging Fiduciaries and Fiduciary Judging, 2003 B.Y.U. L. Rev. 1239.

8. Unhappily Ever After. Suppose that after being appointed, the lead plaintiff decides that the lead counsel is performing his duties unsatisfactorily and asks the court to name a replacement. Should the court accept the lead plaintiff's assessment at face value? If not, how should the court proceed? Cf. Panel Discussion, The Private Securities Law Reform Act: Is It Working?, 71 Fordham L. Rev. 2363, 2384 (2003) (questions raised by Professor Jill E. Fisch). Does the court have an ongoing responsibility to monitor the conduct of the lead counsel? See generally Theresa A. Gabaldon, Milberg Weiss: Of Studied Indifference and Dying of Shame, 2 J. Bus. & Tech. L. 207 (2007).

9. Opting Out. A significant number of institutions have been opting out of federal actions in order to bring individual actions in state court under state law, most of which settle on more lucrative terms. Among the reasons that those opting out fare better is that they sidestep the application of the PSLRA. See John C. Coffee, Jr., Accountability and Competition in Securities Class Actions: Why "Exit" Works Better than "Voice," 30 Cardozo L. Rev. 407, 429-33 (2008) (discussing why those opting out "do better").

What are the consequences of the opt-out phenomenon? Consider the following view:

> [T]he securities class action could become the vehicle of last resort for only those smaller claimants who cannot economically afford to opt out. Below some minimum level of damages, it becomes uneconomic for a class member to opt out because its losses are too small to justify individual litigation. ***
>
> The larger question will be the impact of opt-outs on defendants. Will they insist on settling the class action for a lower amount per claimant because they expect to pay more to opt-outs? Although defendants will certainly wish to reduce the class settlement, class counsel know that any reduction in the per-claimant recovery will likely further motivate those class members at the margin to opt out. Thus, class counsel have increased reason to resist a weak settlement. Still, if the per-claimant recovery does fall as the result of increased opting out, then the gain to opt-outs can be said to come at the expense of the smaller class members, thereby complicating the issue of whether public policy should seek to encourage opting out.

John C. Coffee, Jr., Litigation Governance: Taking Accountability Seriously, 110 Colum. L. Rev. 288, 314 (2010).

PROBLEM 6-1

Fast-Track, Inc. is a computer company with shares traded on the New York Stock Exchange. In a Rule 10b-5 action against Fast-Track premised on the fraud-on-the market doctrine, candidates A, B, and C vy for appointment as the lead plaintiff. The three have equivalent financial losses as measured by the *Lax* factors.

a. Evaluate the likelihood of success of the following argument by Candidate A: that the question of who has the largest financial interest should be answered by reference to who lost the highest percentage of her wealth through trades of Fast-Track shares during the class period.

b. Assume that the court rejected the argument made in part (a). In support of their motions for appointment, Candidates A, B, and C filed memoranda that, taken together, reveal that:

(i) Candidate A sold her Fast-Track shares based on her own independent research into the computer industry. That research showed that the market price was inaccurate and would soon fall;

(ii) Candidate B sold his shares in a private negotiation at the same time that the other investors sold theirs on the open market;

(iii) Candidate C sold half his Fast-Track shares and retained the other half.

Who should become the lead plaintiff?

B. CERTIFICATION OF THE CLASS

To proceed as a class action, the court must certify the class in accordance with Rule 23 of the Federal Rules of Civil Procedure. No doubt you studied Rule 23 in your Civil Procedure course. You may recall that the Rule applies to all class actions, regardless of subject matter. Here we examine the pivotal role played by the Rule in securities class actions in particular.

The court's decision on certification carries enormous significance for all concerned. If certification is denied, most (and possibly all) members of the might-have-been class will lose the opportunity to recover because they lack the resources to sue individually. On the other hand, a grant of certification "may so increase the defendant's potential damages liability and litigation costs that he may find it economically prudent to settle and to abandon a meritorious defense." *Coopers & Lybrand v. Livesay*, 437 U.S. 463, 478 (1978).

The plaintiff's certification motion often precedes her motion for the appointment of the lead plaintiff and the lead counsel. See, e.g., *Desai v. Deutche Bank Secs., Ltd.*, 573 F.3d 931, 935-36 (9th Cir. 2009); *Teamster Local 445 Freight Div. Pension Fund v. Bombardier, Inc.*, 546 F.3d 196, 198 (2d Cir. 2008). Occasionally, however, these matters are resolved simultaneously. See, e.g., *In re Turkcell Iletisim Hizmetler, A.S. Sec. Litig.*, 209 F.R.D. 353 (S.D.N.Y. 2002).

In order for the court to grant certification, the plaintiff must satisfy Rule 23(a) as well as one of the three subsections of Rule 23(b), typically Rule 23(b)(3). Rule 23(a) imposes four requirements:

(1) *Numerosity*. The class is so numerous that joinder of all members is impracticable.

(2) *Commonality*. There are questions of law or fact common to the class.

(3) *Typicality*. The claims or defenses of the representative parties are typical of the claims or defenses of the class.

(4) *Adequacy*. The representative parties will fairly and adequately protect the interests of the class.

Rule 23(a). These four requirements often overlap:

> The commonality and typicality requirements of Rule 23(a) tend to merge. Both serve as guideposts for determining whether under the particular circumstances maintenance of a class action is economical and whether the named plaintiff's claim and the class claims are so interrelated that the interests of the class

> members will be fairly and adequately protected in their absence. Those requirements therefore also tend to merge with the adequacy-of-representation requirement, although the latter requirement also raises concerns about the competency of class counsel and conflicts of interest.

Wal-Mart Stores, Inc. v. Dukes, 131 S.Ct. 2541, 2551 n.5 (2011) (quoting *General Tel. Co. of the Southwest v. Falcon,* 457 U.S.147, 157 n.13 (1982)).

Rule 23(b)(3) sets forth the following two additional requirements:

(1) *Predominance.* The questions of law or fact common to the members of the class predominate over any questions affecting only individual members, and

(2) *Superiority.* A class action is superior to other available methods for the fair and efficient adjudication of the controversy. The matters pertinent to the findings include:

> (A) the interest of members of the class in individually controlling the prosecution or defense of separate actions;
>
> (B) the extent and nature of any litigation concerning the controversy already commenced by or against members of the class;
>
> (C) the desirability or undesirability of concentrating the litigation of the claims in the particular forum;
>
> (D) the difficulties likely to be encountered in the management of a class action.

Rule 23(b)(3).

The certification inquiry does not purport to address the substantive strength of the plaintiff's claim(s). The certification inquiry sometimes reaches the merits, however, to the extent that becomes necessary to determine the plaintiff's compliance with one (or more) of the certification requirements. See *Wal-Mart Stores, Inc. v. Dukes,* 131 S.Ct. 2541, 2551-52 (2011).

The following decision addresses the relationship between certification and the merits in the context of the following question: should certification of a Rule 10b-5 action for fraud-on-the-market be conditioned on proof of "loss causation"?

ERICA P. JOHN FUND, INC. v. HALLIBURTON CO..

131 S.Ct. 2179 (2011)

CHIEF JUSTICE JOHN G. ROBERTS, JR.:

To prevail on the merits in a private securities fraud action, investors must demonstrate that the defendant's deceptive conduct caused their claimed economic loss. This requirement is commonly referred to as "loss causation." The question presented in this case is whether securities fraud plaintiffs must also prove loss causation in order to obtain class certification. We hold that they need not.

I

Petitioner Erica P. John Fund, Inc. (EPJ Fund), is the lead plaintiff in a putative securities fraud class action filed against Halliburton Co. and one of its executives (collectively Halliburton). The suit was brought on behalf of all investors who purchased Halliburton common stock between June 3, 1999, and December 7, 2001.

EPJ Fund alleges that Halliburton made various misrepresentations designed to inflate its stock price, in violation of § 10(b) of the Securities Exchange Act of 1934 and Securities and Exchange Commission Rule 10b–5.. The complaint asserts that Halliburton deliberately made false statements about (1) the scope of its potential liability in asbestos litigation, (2) its expected revenue from certain construction contracts, and (3) the benefits of its merger with another company. EPJ Fund contends that Halliburton later made a number of corrective disclosures that caused its stock price to drop and, consequently, investors to lose money.

After defeating a motion to dismiss, EPJ Fund sought to have its proposed class certified pursuant to Federal Rule of Civil Procedure 23. The parties agreed, and the District Court held, that EPJ Fund satisfied the general requirements for class actions set out in Rule 23(a): The class was sufficiently numerous, there were common questions of law or fact, the claims of the representative parties were typical, and the representative parties would fairly and adequately protect the interests of the class.

The District Court also found that the action could proceed as a class action under Rule 23(b)(3), but for one problem: Circuit precedent required securities fraud plaintiffs to prove "loss causation" in order to obtain class certification. Id.,at 4a, and n. 2 (citing *Oscar Private Equity Invs. v. Allegiance Telecom, Inc.,* 487 F.3d 261, 269 (C.A.5 2007)). As the District Court explained, loss causation is the "'causal connection between the material misrepresentation and the [economic] loss' " suffered by investors (quoting *Dura Pharmaceuticals, Inc. v. Broudo,* 544 U.S. 336, 342 (2005)). After reviewing the alleged misrepresentations and corrective disclosures, the District Court concluded that it could not certify the class in this case because EPJ Fund had "failed to establish loss causation with respect to any" of its claims. The court made clear, however, that absent "this stringent loss causation requirement," it would have granted the Fund's certification request.

The Court of Appeals affirmed the denial of class certification. It confirmed that, "[i]n order to obtain class certification on its claims, [EPJ Fund] was required to prove loss causation, i.e., that the corrected truth of the former falsehoods actually caused the stock price to fall and resulted in the losses." Like the District Court, the Court of Appeals concluded that EPJ Fund had failed to meet the "requirements for proving loss causation at the class certification stage."

We granted the Fund's petition for certiorari to resolve a conflict among the Circuits as to whether securities fraud plaintiffs must prove loss causation in order to obtain class certification. Compare 597 F.3d, at 334 (case below), with *In re Salomon Analyst Metromedia Litigation,* 544 F.3d 474, 483 (2nd Cir. 2008) (not requiring investors to prove loss causation at class certification stage); *Schleicher v. Wendt,* 618 F.3d 679, 687 (7th Cir. 2010) (same); *In re DVI, Inc. Securities Litigation,* 639 F.3d 623, 636 – 637 (3rd Cir. 2011) (same; decided after certiorari was granted).

II

EPJ Fund contends that the Court of Appeals erred by requiring proof of loss causation for class certification. We agree.

A

As noted, the sole dispute here is whether EPJ Fund satisfied the prerequisites of Rule 23(b)(3). In order to certify a class under that Rule, a court must find "that the questions of law or fact common to class members predominate over any questions affecting only individual members, and that a class action is superior to other available methods for fairly and efficiently adjudicating the controversy." Fed. Rule Civ. Proc. 23(b)(3). Considering whether "questions of law or fact common to class members predominate" begins, of course, with the elements of the underlying cause of action. The elements of a private securities fraud claim based on violations of § 10(b) and Rule 10b–5 are: " '(1) a material misrepresentation or omission by the defendant; (2) scienter; (3) a connection between the misrepresentation or omission and the purchase or sale of a security; (4) reliance upon the misrepresentation or omission; (5) economic loss; and (6) loss causation.' " *Matrixx Initiatives, Inc. v. Siracusano,* 131 S.Ct. 1309, 1317 (2011) (quoting *Stoneridge Investment Partners, LLC v. Scientific–Atlanta, Inc.,* 552 U.S. 148, 157 (2008)).

Whether common questions of law or fact predominate in a securities fraud action often turns on the element of reliance. The courts below determined that EPJ Fund had to prove the separate element of loss causation in order to establish that reliance was capable of resolution on a common, classwide basis.

"Reliance by the plaintiff upon the defendant's deceptive acts is an essential element of the § 10(b) private cause of action." *Stoneridge*, supra, at 159. This is because proof of reliance ensures that there is a proper "connection between a defendant's misrepresentation and a plaintiff's injury." *Basic, Inc. v. Levinson*, 485 U.S. 224, 243 (1988). The traditional (and most direct) way a plaintiff can demonstrate reliance is by showing that he was aware of a company's statement and engaged in a relevant transaction — e.g., purchasing common stock — based on that specific misrepresentation. In that situation, the plaintiff plainly would have relied on the company's deceptive conduct. A plaintiff unaware of the relevant statement, on the other hand, could not establish reliance on that basis.

We recognized in *Basic*, however, that limiting proof of reliance in such a way "would place an unnecessarily unrealistic evidentiary burden on the Rule 10b–5 plaintiff who has traded on an impersonal market." Id., at 245. We also observed that "[r]equiring proof of individualized reliance from each member of the proposed plaintiff class effectively would" prevent such plaintiffs "from proceeding with a class action, since individual issues" would "overwhelm[ ] the common ones." Id., at 242.

The Court in *Basic* sought to alleviate those related concerns by permitting plaintiffs to invoke a rebuttable presumption of reliance based on what is known as the "fraud-on-the-market" theory. According to that theory, "the market price of shares traded on well-developed markets reflects all publicly available information, and, hence, any material misrepresentations." Id., at 246. Because the market "transmits information to the investor in the processed form of a market price," we can assume, the Court explained, that an investor relies on public misstatements whenever he "buys or sells stock at the price set by the market." Id., at 244, 247; see also *Stoneridge*, supra, at 159. *Dura Pharmaceuticals,* 544 U.S., at 341–342. The Court also made clear that the presumption was just that, and could be rebutted by appropriate evidence. See *Basic,* supra, at 248.

B

It is undisputed that securities fraud plaintiffs must prove certain things in order to invoke *Basic*'s rebuttable presumption of reliance. It is common ground, for example, that plaintiffs must demonstrate that the alleged misrepresentations were publicly known (else how would the market take them into account?), that the stock traded in an efficient market, and that the relevant transaction took place "between the time the misrepresentations were made and the time the truth was revealed." *Basic,* 485 U.S., at 248, n. 27; id., at 241–247; see also *Stoneridge*, supra, at 159.

According to the Court of Appeals, EPJ Fund also had to establish loss causation at the certification stage to "trigger the fraud-on-the-market presumption." 597 F.3d, at 335. The court determined that, in order to invoke a rebuttable presumption of reliance, EPJ Fund needed to prove that the decline in Halliburton's stock was "because of the correction to a prior misleading statement" and "that the subsequent loss could not otherwise be explained by some additional factors revealed then to the market." Id., at 336. This is the loss causation requirement as we have described it. See *Dura Pharmaceuticals, supra,* at 342; see also 15 U.S.C. § 78u–4(b)(4).

The Court of Appeals' requirement is not justified by *Basic* or its logic. To begin, we have never before mentioned loss causation as a precondition for invoking *Basic* 's rebuttable presumption of reliance. The term "loss causation" does not even appear in our *Basic* opinion. And for good reason: Loss causation addresses a matter different from whether an investor relied on a misrepresentation, presumptively or otherwise, when buying or selling a stock.

We have referred to the element of reliance in a private Rule 10b–5 action as "transaction causation," not loss causation. *Dura Pharmaceuticals,* supra, at 341–342 (citing *Basic,* supra, at 248–249). Consistent with that description, when considering whether a plaintiff has relied on a misrepresentation, we have typically focused on facts surrounding the investor's decision to engage in the transaction. See *Dura Pharmaceuticals,* supra, at 342. Under *Basic*'s fraud-on-the-market doctrine, an investor presumptively relies on a defendant's misrepresentation if that "information is reflected in [the] market price" of the stock at the time of the relevant transaction. See *Basic,* 485 U.S., at 247.

Loss causation, by contrast, requires a plaintiff to show that a misrepresentation that affected the integrity of the market price *also* caused a subsequent economic loss. As we made clear in *Dura Pharmaceuticals,* the fact that a stock's "price on the date of purchase was inflated because of [a] misrepresentation" does not necessarily mean that the misstatement is the cause of a later decline in value. 544 U.S., at 342. We observed that the drop could instead be the result of other intervening causes, such as "changed economic circumstances, changed investor expectations, new industry-specific or firm-specific facts, conditions, or other events." Id., at 342–343. If one of those factors were responsible for the loss or part of it, a plaintiff would not be able to prove loss causation to that extent. This is true even if the investor purchased the stock at a distorted price, and thereby presumptively relied on the misrepresentation reflected in that price.

According to the Court of Appeals, however, an inability to prove loss causation would prevent a plaintiff from invoking the rebuttable presumption of reliance. Such a rule contravenes *Basic*'s fundamental premise — that an investor presumptively relies on a misrepresentation so long as it was reflected in the market price at the time of his transaction. The fact that a subsequent loss may have been caused by factors other than the revelation of a misrepresentation has nothing to do with whether an investor relied on the misrepresentation in the first place, either directly or presumptively through the fraud-on-the-market theory. Loss causation has no logical connection to the facts necessary to establish the efficient market predicate to the fraud-on-the-market theory.

The Court of Appeals erred by requiring EPJ Fund to show loss causation as a condition of obtaining class certification.

C

Halliburton concedes that securities fraud plaintiffs should not be required to prove loss causation in order to invoke *Basic* 's presumption of reliance or otherwise achieve class certification. Halliburton nonetheless defends the judgment below on the ground that the Court of Appeals did not actually require plaintiffs to prove loss causation" as we have used that term. According to Halliburton, "loss causation was merely "shorthand" for a different analysis. The lower court's actual inquiry, Halliburton insists, was whether EPJ Fund had demonstrated "price impact" — that is, whether the alleged misrepresentations affected the market price in the first place. See Tr. of Oral Arg. 27 (stating that the Court of Appeals' "test is simply price impact" and that EPJ Fund's "only burden under the Fifth Circuit case law was to show price impact").[4]

"Price impact" simply refers to the effect of a misrepresentation on a stock price. Halliburton's theory is that if a misrepresentation does not affect market price, an investor cannot be said to have relied on the misrepresentation

4. Halliburton further concedes that, even if its conception of what the Court of Appeals meant by "loss causation" is correct, the Court of Appeals erred by placing the initial burden on EPJ Fund. See Tr. of Oral Arg. 29 ("We agree ... that the Fifth Circuit put the initial burden of production on the plaintiff, and that's contrary to *Basic* "). According to Halliburton, a plaintiff must prove price impact only after *Basic* 's presumption has been successfully rebutted by the defendant. We express no views on the merits of such a framework.

merely because he purchased stock at that price. If the price is unaffected by the fraud, the price does not reflect the fraud.

We do not accept Halliburton's wishful interpretation of the Court of Appeals' opinion. As we have explained, loss causation is a familiar and distinct concept in securities law; it is not price impact. While the opinion below may include some language consistent with a "price impact" approach, we simply cannot ignore the Court of Appeals' repeated and explicit references to "loss causation," see [597 F.3d], at 334 (three times), 334 n. 2, 335, 335 n. 10 (twice), 335 n. 11, 336, 336 n. 19, 336 n. 20, 337, 338, 341 (twice), 341 n. 46, 342 n. 47, 343, 344 (three times).

Whatever Halliburton thinks the Court of Appeals meant to say, what it said was loss causation: "[EPJ Fund] was required to prove loss causation, *i.e.*, that the corrected truth of the former falsehoods actually caused the stock price to fall and resulted in the losses." 597 F.3d, at 334; see id., at 335 ("we require plaintiffs to establish loss causation in order to trigger the fraud-on-the-market presumption" (internal quotation marks omitted)). We take the Court of Appeals at its word. Based on those words, the decision below cannot stand. ***

Because we conclude the Court of Appeals erred by requiring EPJ Fund to prove loss causation at the certification stage, we need not, and do not, address any other question about *Basic,* its presumption, or how and when it may be rebutted. To the extent Halliburton has preserved any further arguments against class certification, they may be addressed in the first instance by the Court of Appeals on remand. The judgment of the Court of Appeals is vacated, and the case is remanded for further proceedings consistent with this opinion. ***

NOTES AND QUESTIONS

1. ***The Non-Connection Between Loss Causation and Market Efficiency.*** According to the Court, loss causation bears "no logical connection" to fraud on the market's efficient market prerequisite. The Court thereby rejected the following attempt by the Fifth Circuit to establish such a connection:

> First, it might be that even though the market for the defendant's shares has been demonstrated efficient by the usual indicia, the market is actually inefficient with respect to the particular type of information conveyed by the material misrepresentation, *i.e,.* analysts and market makers do poorly at digesting line-count information. Thus our approach gives effect to information-type inefficiencies, recognizing that "the market price of a security will not be uniformly efficient as to all types of information." A second possible explanation for a misrepresentation's failure to move the market is that the market was strong-form efficient with respect to that type of information ***. Both explanations resist application of the semi-strong efficient-market hypothesis, the theory on which the presumption of classwide reliance depends. ***

Oscar Private Equity Inv. v. Allegiance Telecom, Inc., 487 F.3d 261, 269 (5th Cir. 2007), abrogated by *Erica P. John Fund, Inc. v. Halliburton, Inc.*, 131 S.Ct. 2179 (2011). Is the Fifth Circuit's analysis wide off the mark? Why or why not?

2. Practicalities. If the Court had conditioned certification on proof of loss causation, what would have been the likely practical impact? Prior to *Halliburton*, Judge Easterbrook offered this assessment:

> It would make certification impossible in many securities suits, because when true and false statements are made together it is often impossible to disentangle the effects with any confidence. The court suggested (perhaps required) that this be done by showing what happened when the truth was announced. Yet truth can come out, and affect the market price, in advance of a formal announcement. ***
>
> *** After a class has been certified, and other elements of the claim have been established, the court will need to pin down when the stock's price was affected by any fraud. That decision, like the other issues, can be made on a class-wide basis, because it affects investors in common. It gets the cart before the horse to insist that it be made before any class can be certified.***

Schleicher v. Wendt, 618 F.3d 679, 686-87 (7th Cir. 2010). Why do you suppose that such considerations went unmentioned by the *Halliburton* Court?

3. Rebuttal and Certification. The *Halliburton* Court affirmatively steered clear of addressing whether a defendant can rebut the presumption of reliance at the certification stage or whether he must wait until trial (or summary judgment). The circuits currently divide on this question. Compare *In re Salomon Analyst Metromedia Litig.*, 544 F.3d 474, 485 (2d Cir. 2008) (rebuttal permissible at certification) with *In re Polymedica Corp. Sec. Litig.*, 432 F.3d 1, 17,19 (1st Cir. 2005) (rebuttal not permissible at certification).

In *Basic*, the Court suggested that rebuttal could not occur at certification:

> We note there may be a certain incongruity between the assumption that Basic shares are traded on a well-developed, efficient, and information-hungry market, and the allegation that such a market could remain misinformed, and its valuation of Basic shares depressed, for 14 months, on the basis of three public statements. Proof of that sort is a matter for trial, throughout which the District Court retains the authority to amend the certification order as may be appropriate. Thus, we see no need to engage in the kind of factual analysis the dissent suggests that manifests the "oddities" of applying a rebuttable presumption of reliance in this case.

Basic, Inc. v. Levinson, 485 U.S. 224, 249 n.29 (1988). But cf. *In re DVI, Inc. Sec. Litig,*, 639 F.3d 623, 637 n.20 (3d Cir. 2011) (dismissing significance of *Basic*'s footnote 29 on the ground that it was not critical to the holding, directed at the dissent, and would, if "[t]aken literally, *** may even appear to preclude a court from evaluating evidence presented by a defendant at class certification to demonstrate the market is inefficient").

Viewed through the prism of Rule 23 and *Halliburton*, should rebuttal be fair game at certification? To what extent (if at all) does the answer turn on the form of rebuttal undertaken – for example, a rebuttal to overcome a prerequisite versus one to show that the market was not fooled? To what extent does it matter whether the focus is typicality or adequacy on the one hand or predominance on the other hand?

4. The Relevance of Wal-Mart *– Part I.* Only weeks after issuing its decision in *Halliburton*, the Supreme Court addressed certification again in

Wal-Mart Stores, Inc. v. Dukes, 131 S.Ct. 2541 (2011). In that case, female Wal-Mart employees charged that the company's grant of discretion to local managers fueled gender discrimination and was tantamount to a discrimination policy. The Court split 5-4 on whether the plaintiff's commonality showing sufficed. The majority found that it did not:

> In this case, proof of commonality necessarily overlaps with respondents' merits contention that Wal–Mart engages in a *pattern or practice* of discrimination. That is so because, in resolving an individual's Title VII claim, the crux of the inquiry is "the reason for a particular employment decision," *Cooper v. Federal Reserve Bank of Richmond*, 467 U.S. 867, 876 (1984). Here respondents wish to sue about literally millions of employment decisions at once. Without some glue holding the alleged reasons for all those decisions together, it will be impossible to say that examination of all the class members' claims for relief will produce a common answer to the crucial question *why was I disfavored.*

131 S.Ct. at 2552. According to the dissent, the majority had impermissibly transformed the inquiry into the existence of common questions into an inquiry into the existence of "common answer[s]." In so doing, the dissent maintained, the majority had, under cover of commonality, examined the requirements of predominance and superiority that are supposed to come into play only in connection with Rule 23(b)(3).

What (if anything) does *Wal-Mart* imply for securities class actions? Perhaps little or nothing, since securities class actions rarely founder on the shoals of commonality. But the opposite view is also worth considering: *Wal-Mart* may demonstrate the Court's adoption of a demanding approach to certification in general (rather than only to commonality in particular). Relatedly, the decision may evidence an enhanced willingness to rationalize excursions into merits territory, regardless of the subsection of Rule 23 at issue, the specific result in *Halliburton* notwithstanding.

What do you think? In assessing the impact of *Wal-Mart*, consider also the Note immediately following.

*5. **The Relevance of** Wal-Mart – **Part II.*** Prior to *Wal-Mart*, the Supreme Court had said virtually nothing about what constitutes "proof" at the certification stage. Is it a merely a preliminary showing, or the essential equivalent of that which would be required at trial, or something in between? Cf. *In re Hydrogen Peroxide Antitrust Litig.*, 552 F.3d 305, 315-16 (3d Cir. 2008) (noting the paucity of Supreme Court guidance on the question). Against this backdrop of uncertainty came *Wal-Mart*, which, drawing on the fraud-on-the-market presumption , made the following observation: "[T]he plaintiffs *** must prove that their shares were traded on an efficient market, an issue they will surely have to prove *again* at trial in order to make out their case on the merits." *Wal-Mart*, supra, 131 S.Ct. at 2552 n.6. Does the reference to "prove" (at certification) and then to "prove *again*" (at trial) suggest that the proof required at the two stages is virtually identical?

6. Appellate Review of Certification Orders. Certification orders are not appealable as of right. In *Halliburton*, the Fifth Circuit granted leave to appeal the certification order pursuant to F.R.Civ. P. 23(f). Adopted in 1998, Rule 23(f) reads in pertinent part as follows:

> A court of appeals may in its discretion permit an appeal from an order of a district court granting or denying class action certification under this rule if application is made to it within ten days after entry of the order.

Notice that this Rule effectively gives the appellate courts complete control of their certification docket (but for the 10 day window). Patterns and practices under Rule 23(f) vary widely among the circuits. See generally Barry Sullivan & Amy Kobelski Trueblood, Rule 23(f): A Note on Law and Discretion in the Courts of Appeals, 246 F.R.D. 277 (2008).

PROBLEM 6-2

Dorcas has filed a fraud-on- the-market action under Rule 10b-5. The defendant is a securities analyst, who allegedly defrauded the market by publishing fraudulent reports. In the jurisdiction where Dorcas has filed, there is as yet no precedent regarding whether securities analysts can be sued on a fraud-on-the-market theory. Dorcas has filed a motion for certification.

A) Must Dorcas establish the falsity of the analysts' reports as a prerequisite to receiving the presumption of reliance?

B) Must Dorcas establish that a fraud on the market cause of action exists against securities analysts as a prerequisite to receiving the presumption of reliance?

C) Assume that unlike the plaintiffs in *Basic, Inc. v. Levinson*, or most other fraud on-the-market plaintiffs, Dorcas did not plead in the alternative a traditional Rule 10b-5 claim of direct reliance on the fraud. What is the impact (if any) on her certification motion?

C. SETTLEMENT

Because most securities class actions are settled rather than tried, the settlement stage is highly significant. Settlements can be as mammoth as the litigation that precedes them. Thus, for example, one recently approved settlement – for $586 million, with approximately $170 million in attorneys' fees – following eight years of litigation that entailed the following:

> Over one thousand initial complaints were filed. The actions were filed against fifty-five securities underwriters, over three hundred issuers, and one thousand officers and directors of the issuers. Defendants were represented by over 110 law firms, not including the law firms that represented insurance companies with an interest in the litigation.
>
> Plaintiffs' counsel submitted more than three hundred amended pleadings in the actions, successfully defended against and opposed numerous motions to dismiss, and briefed and argued three hotly contested class certification motions. In addition, counsel engaged in extensive discovery efforts, including the serving of over six hundred third-party subpoenas and the retention of twelve experts.

In re Initial Public Offering Sec. Litig., 671 F. Supp. 2d 467, 508 (S.D.N.Y. 2009).

Studies have indicated a positive link between settlement amounts and the underlying merits. See Stephen J. Choi, The Evidence on Securities Class Actions, 57 Vand. L. Rev. 1465, 1522-23 (2004). This link has been enhanced by the PSLRA. See id.

The parameters of settlement are set by Rule 23(e) of the Federal Rules of Civil Procedure as well as by certain PSLRA provisions.

Rule 23(e) establishes requirements for the settlement of all class actions filed in federal court. These requirements include the following:

> (1)(A) The court must approve any settlement ***.
>
> (B) The court must direct notice in a reasonable manner *** to all class members who would be bound by a proposed settlement ***.
>
> (C) The court may approve a settlement *** that would bind class members only after a hearing and on finding that the settlement *** is fair, reasonable, and adequate. ***
>
> (3) In an action previously certified as a class action under Rule 23(b)(3), the court may refuse to approve a settlement unless it affords a new opportunity to request exclusion to individual class members who had an earlier opportunity to request exclusion but did not do so.

Rule 23(e). The court is also entitled to award "reasonable attorneys' fees." Rule 23(h).

For class actions brought under the federal securities laws, the following additional PSLRA requirements come into play: (i) the need to include specified information in the notice to class members, see Securities Act § 27(a)(7), Exchange Act § 21D(a)(7); (ii) a prohibition against awarding class representatives more than other class members, see Securities Act § 27(a)(4); Exchange Act § 21D(a)(4); and (iii) a prohibition against awarding attorneys' fees that "exceed a reasonable percentage of the amount of any damages and prejudgment interest actually paid to the class," Securities Act § 27(a)(6), Exchange Act § 21D(a)(6).

The PSLRA is silent, however, concerning the role to be played by the lead plaintiff in the settlement process. Consider the following decision.

IN RE BANKAMERICA CORP. SEC. LITIG.

350 F.3d 747 (8th Cir. 2003)

MICHAEL J. MELLOY, CIRCUIT JUDGE:

In this class action under the Private Securities Litigation Reform Act of 1995 (the "Act"), the district court determined that it possessed the authority to approve a global settlement involving all plaintiff classes notwithstanding the fact that some members of a lead plaintiff group for one of four certified plaintiff classes objected to the settlement. We affirm.

I. Background

The plaintiffs in this class action alleged losses caused by misrepresentations and omissions surrounding the 1998 merger of NationsBank and BankAmerica to form Bank of America. After consolidating numerous state and federal actions from multiple jurisdictions, the district court certified four plaintiff classes: the NationsBank and BankAmerica, Holder and Purchaser classes. Membership in the classes depended on whether plaintiffs held or purchased NationsBank or BankAmerica shares during designated periods of time. As required under the Act, the district court appointed lead plaintiffs or lead plaintiff groups who in turn selected class counsel. The district court also designated some of these lead plaintiffs as class representatives under Fed.R.Civ.P. 23.

The district court appointed a seven-member lead plaintiff group to represent the NationsBank classes. Members of this group included Earl J. Gates, Robert Hepworth, Pamela Wootton, Appellees Joseph Hempen and Kevin Kloster, and Appellants John M. Koehler and David P. Oetting. The district court appointed a six-member lead plaintiff group to represent the BankAmerica classes. Members of this group included David Fike, Elizabeth Menkes, Patricia A. Thomas, and Appellees Selma Kaiser, Brian Markee, and Walter E. Ryan, Jr. No members of the lead plaintiff groups were large institutional investors nor did they have relationships with one another prior to this litigation. The lead plaintiffs for the NationsBank classes owned, collectively, less than one tenth of one percent of the outstanding shares in NationsBank. Institutional investors owned more than forty percent of NationsBank, but no institutional investor came forward to serve as a lead plaintiff.

Shortly before trial, class counsel, defendants, and some members of the lead plaintiff groups participated in a mediation that led to the signing of a memorandum of understanding with the defendants regarding a $490 million global settlement of all claims. Under the global settlement, Bank of America was to pay the NationsBank classes approximately $333 million and the BankAmerica classes approximately $157 million. While many of the circumstances and statements surrounding the mediation are disputed, it is undisputed that class counsel signed the memorandum of understanding with the defendants after members of the lead plaintiff group for the NationsBank class left the mediation.

In response to a motion for the district court's approval of the global settlement, three members of the NationsBank lead plaintiff group, Appellants Oetting and Koehler and Appellee Kloster, filed objections. They alleged that class counsel instructed them to leave the mediation because it was futile, but that class counsel remained and reached the proposed global settlement for an amount far below that which they had authorized. Based on these allegations, they argued that the district court should not approve the global settlement because: class counsel negotiated the settlement without their approval as lead plaintiffs; the settlement provided inadequate compensation to the NationsBank classes; and the settlement improperly structured compensation to be paid in cash rather than stock thus resulting in adverse tax consequences and a depletion of the cash reserves of the new, merged bank (in which most plaintiffs owned shares).

After sending notice to, and soliciting objections from, the hundreds of thousands of eligible class members, the district court received a total of ten objections. No institutional investors objected. The joint objection from Appellants Oetting and Koehler and Appellee Kloster was the only objection filed by any members of the NationsBank lead plaintiff group. Regarding the other NationsBank lead plaintiffs, Appellee Hepworth supported the global settlement; Gates died prior to the mediation; Hempen was not available for comment; and Wootton stated that she would defer to the decision of the group.

Faced with the fractured positions of the NationsBank lead plaintiff group, the lack of a singular voice to advocate a position for the group, and the lack of clear guidance in the Act regarding the power of a fraction of one lead plaintiff group to disapprove settlement, the district court looked to cases under Fed.R.Civ.P. 23 to determine the proper weight to place on the objections from Oetting, Koehler, and Kloster. The district court held a fairness hearing and issued an order in which it determined, inter alia, that it had the authority to approve the settlement even over the objections raised by the three members of the NationsBank lead plaintiff group.

In determining that it had the authority to conduct a fairness/adequacy review and approve the settlement over Appellants' objections, the district court emphasized its duty to act in the best interest of class members. It noted that Appellants' estimations of the settlement value of the case were so high as to be "bordering on fantasy." It expressed concern that, because the global settlement amount far exceeded what had been previously offered to the separate classes, the Appellants potentially were jeopardizing a favorable settlement. The district court was intimately familiar with the case, having spent over three years with the case prior to ruling on the settlement. In light of this familiarity, the district court clearly expressed its opinion that, based on working with the attorneys in the case, this was not the kind of lawyer-driven, lawyer-initiated lawsuit that fails to protect class interest and that Congress targeted with the Act.

Ultimately, the district court approved the settlement as fair and adequate by applying those factors we have listed as relevant in the context of Rule 23 fairness determinations. See *Van Horn v. Trickey*, 840 F.2d 604, 607 (8th Cir.1988). In particular, the district court noted the adequacy of the settlement in light of the apparent merits of the plaintiffs' cases and in light of the risks and the high level of uncertainty that the litigation would entail if allowed to proceed to trial. The district court further noted the absence of objections from institutional investors and the relatively slight number of shares owned by the objecting lead plaintiffs.

On appeal, Appellants Koehler and Oetting argue that we should reverse the district court's decision and hold that the district court erred as a matter of law in approving the global settlement over their objections. They interpret the Act as prohibiting the district court from approving a settlement unless the district court either receives approval from the lead plaintiff, or lead plaintiff group, or disqualifies the lead plaintiff for acting in a manner inimical to class interests. All parties concede that the Act does not expressly provide for such a requirement, and Appellees argue that we should not read such a requirement into the Act.

Alternatively, Appellees argue that we are not required to address the broader issue of how much power the Act grants to lead plaintiff groups to control and settle litigation. Appellees characterize the narrow issue presented for review as relating only to whether the district court abused its discretion when it acted to approve a settlement over objections from some members of a fractured lead plaintiff group that failed to speak with one voice. In other words, Appellees argue that this case does not concern the relative roles that class counsel, lead plaintiffs and the supervising district court should play under the

Act, but rather, is simply a case about how a district court is to deal with a fractured lead plaintiff group.

We note that NationsBank lead plaintiff group member Kloster changed his position after the district court proceedings and now appears before us as an appellee to argue in support of the global settlement. Further, as expressly conceded by Appellants during oral argument, the district court's findings of fairness and adequacy are not contested on appeal. Therefore, the only issue on appeal is whether the district court properly determined that it had the authority, over the objections of Koehler and Oetting, to review and approve the settlement.

II.

Congress enacted the Private Litigation Securities Reform Act of 1995 to address problems related to class action securities litigation. In particular, Congress sought to create mechanisms to ensure the protection of class members' interests in securities litigation that was widely perceived as being lawyer- instituted and lawyer-driven. See *In re Cendant Corp. Litig.*, 264 F.3d 201, 254-68 (3rd Cir.2001). One way in which the Act provides this protection is by requiring the district courts to appoint a lead plaintiff or lead plaintiff group to represent aggrieved shareholders and requiring these lead plaintiffs to select counsel. See 15 U.S.C. § 78u-4(a)(3)(B)(i); 15 U.S.C. § 78u-4(a)(3)(B)(v). To further ensure that class members' interests and not the interests of class counsel drive the litigation, the Act contains a rebuttable presumption that the most adequate plaintiff is the "person or group of persons that ... has the largest financial interest in the relief sought by the class." 15 U.S.C. § 78u-4(a)(3)(B)(iii)(I)(bb).[2]

While the Act is explicit on the lead plaintiff's authority to select and retain counsel, it is silent on the other responsibilities and rights that lead plaintiffs have to control, direct, and manage class action securities litigation. In particular, the Act says nothing about whether the lead plaintiff must either approve a settlement or be replaced for actions inimical to class interests before a district court may review and approve a proposed settlement. In addition, it says nothing regarding how a district court should deal with a fractured lead plaintiff group that advocates inconsistent positions.

We agree with Appellees that the present case does not squarely present the broad question of whether the Act grants a lead plaintiff or lead plaintiff group sufficient control over litigation to block a district court's approval of a proposed settlement. Looking at the narrow issue that is presented, namely, what weight a district court must give to objections from a fraction of a fractured lead plaintiff group, we find no guidance in the Act and find that the district court properly relied on decisions under Rule 23 when it determined that it possessed the necessary authority to approve the settlement.

2. Although we noted that the lead plaintiffs in this case are not institutional investors and do not have the largest financial interest in the relief sought by the classes, the district court's selection of lead plaintiffs is not the subject of this appeal .

"Under Rule 23(e) the district court acts as a fiduciary who must serve as guardian of the rights of absent class members." *Grunin v. Int'l House of Pancakes*,752 513 F.2d 114, 123 (8th Cir.1975). It is appropriate for the district court to serve this role as guardian for absent class members because the district court is heavily involved in the management of class actions and, therefore, "'is exposed to the litigants, and the strategies, positions and proofs.'" Id. (quoting *Ace Heating & Plumbing Co. v. Crane Co.*, 453 F.2d 30, 34 (3d Cir.1971)). In light of this exposure to the litigants and litigation, we defer to district courts' approvals of settlement agreements in class actions under an abuse of discretion standard ***.

We believe this abuse of discretion standard is also appropriate for our review of the district court's decision to approve the global settlement over the objection of Appellants Koehler and Oetting. The Act does not expressly divest the district court of its Rule 23(e) authority or discretion by explicitly granting a veto power to lead plaintiffs. Further, it seems clear that the Act was intended to supplement rather than replace Rule 23. This strongly suggests that Congress did not intend to remove discretion from the district courts or usurp the district courts' traditional responsibility to guard the interests of absent class members.

Reviewing the district court's decision only for abuse of discretion, then, we find that the district court, which was intimately familiar with this lengthy and complex matter, did not abuse its discretion in overruling the objections of a fraction of the NationsBank lead plaintiff group. The district court properly determined that it bore a responsibility to safeguard the interests of class members, expressly noted that this case was not lawyer-driven, understood the risks attendant to trial and the strengths and weaknesses of the plaintiffs' cases, and emphatically noted what it viewed as the unrealistic expectations of the objecting lead plaintiffs. In light of these determinations and the absence of guidance in the Act, it was not an abuse of discretion for the district court to proceed under Rule 23 and approve the settlement over Appellants' objections. We leave for another day a determination of how much control over litigation the Act confers on a singular lead plaintiff or unified lead plaintiff group.

Accordingly, the judgment of the district court is affirmed.

NOTES AND QUESTIONS

1. ***Why Bother.*** If the objectors in *Bankamerica* regarded the settlement as fair, why did they appeal the trial court's decision? At least one of the objectors continued to fight by suing the attorneys for the class for conspiracy, breach of fiduciary duty, and violation of the PSLRA. See *Koehler v. Brody*, 483 F.3d 590 (8th Cir. 2007) (rejecting collateral attack on settlement).

2. ***The Complexities of Institutional Behavior.*** Would the court have given the objectors greater deference if they had been institutions and/or had owned more shares? The institutional investors remained aloof – neither objecting to the settlement nor volunteering to serve as lead plaintiffs in the first place. Institutional investors also often fail to file settlement claims for the money to which they are entitled. See James D. Cox & Randall S. Thomas, Letting Billions Slip Through Your Fingers: Empirical Evidence and Legal Implications of the Failure of Financial Institutions to Participate in Securities

Class Action Settlements, 58 Stan. L. Rev. 411, 454 (2005). What might account for such passivity?

On the other hand, institutional lead plaintiffs are associated with the biggest settlement amounts. See James D. Cox, There Are Plaintiffs And . . . There are Plaintiffs: An Empirical Analysis of Securities Class Action Settlements, 61 Vand. L. Rev. 355, 370 (2008). One possible contributing factor is that such lead plaintiffs "cherry pick" the cases in which they compete to serve. See id. at 372.

3. Groups Revisited. Does the *Bankamerica* decision affect your view of whether it is advisable to appoint lead plaintiff groups? Should the trial court insist that a lead plaintiff candidate consisting of a group provide a plan for managing dissent within its ranks? Cf. Elizabeth Chamblee Burch, Optimal Lead Plaintiffs, 64 Vand. L. Rev. 1109, 1180 (2011) (mentioning alternatives including supermajority voting and voting weighted in terms of amount of loss).

4. Controlling Attorneys' Fees. The problem of excessive attorneys' fees was supposed largely to disappear under the watchful eyes of the lead plaintiff, backstopped by the statutory cap on those fees of a "reasonable percentage" of the settlement. See Securities Act § 27(a)(6); Exchange Act § 21D(a)(6). But problems persist:

> [T]he PSLRA has not eliminated all difficulties with establishing fair and reasonable attorneys' fees in class action suits. As objectors note, the adversarial process is often "diluted" or entirely "suspended" during fee proceedings, and fee requests often go unchallenged. Lead plaintiffs, having previously negotiated a fee arrangement with lead counsel, will rarely oppose a fee request. Class members may have little incentive to oppose a fee request, since any reduction will only result in a minor increase in their share of the settlement. And defendants have little incentive to oppose a fee request, since usually they are not impacted by the way in which the settlement fund is distributed.

In re AT & T Corp. Sec. Litig., 455 F.3d 160, 168 (3d Cir. 2006).

5. Professional Objectors. Some investors make a habit of objecting to settlements. See, e.g., *In re Initial Public Offering Sec. Litig.*, 671 F. Supp. 2d 496, 497 n. 219 (S.D.N.Y. 2009). The motive can be to extract money to step aside from the class counsel or the parties so that the settlement process can go forward smoothly. How should the trial judge respond to this phenomenon? See generally Bruce D. Greenberg, Keeping the Flies Out of the Ointment: Restricting Objectors to Class Action Settlements, 84 St. John's L. Rev. 949 (2010).

PROBLEM 6-3

In August 2010, a Rule 10b-5 action was filed against Hall Corp. (which is traded on the New York Stock Exchange) and some of its officers and directors on behalf of a purported class of investors who bought Hall stock on the open market at allegedly inflated prices. In December 2010, the court appointed four lead plaintiffs – Gabriel, Paul, the Private Asset Management Group (PAM), and the Archdiocese of Milwaukee Priests' Pension Fund (AMPPF). It also named the law firm of Barrow & Smith as the lead counsel.

Two months later, in February 2011, Peter Barrow, of Barrow & Smith, initiated settlement negotiations with lawyers for the defendants. These negotiations continued through March and led to an agreement in principle in April. Barrow did not obtain the permission of AMPPF to begin the negotiations. Nor did he inform AMPPF that an agreement in principle had been reached. AMPPF learned about the agreement in principle by happenstance after the fact.

On behalf of Gabriel, Paul, and PAM, Barrow has sought judicial approval of the settlement, which provides approximately $3 million for the 800,000 class members. In addition, the settlement encompasses derivative claims that were not as yet alleged. The notices to the class members have generated six objections (none from institutions).

None of the pro-settlement plaintiffs appeared at the hearing to explain why they supported the settlement. Nor did they submit affidavits. The AMPPF, however, did send a representative.

At the hearing, Barrow made only conclusory allegations as to why the settlement was fair, just, and reasonable. The lawyer for the AMPPF was likewise conclusory in arguing the opposite.

Is the court likely to approve the settlement? Why or why not?

Cf. *Moore v. Halliburton Co.*, 2004 WL 2092019 (N.D. Tex. 2004).

D. THE SECURITIES LITIGATION UNIFORM STANDARDS ACT OF 1998

Following enactment of the PSLRA, some plaintiffs sought to avoid the PSLRA's restrictions by filing securities class actions in state court under state law. See generally Richard W. Painter, Responding to A False Alarm: Federal Preemption of State Securities Fraud Causes of Action, 84 Cornell L. Rev. 1 (1998); Michael A. Perino, Fraud and Federalism: Preempting Private State Securities Fraud Causes of Action, 50 Stan. L. Rev. 273 (1998). To eliminate this tactic, Congress enacted the SLUSA. In brief, the SLUSA preempts most class actions filed under state common law and state securities statutes.

To understand the SLUSA, it is necessary to begin with a brief look at the Securities Act and the Exchange Act as originally enacted. Both statutes contained broad anti-preemption provisions, ensuring that the newly enacted causes of action under federal law would supplement — rather than supplant — existing remedies under the common law and blue sky laws of the states. See Section 16(a) of the Securities Act ("the rights and remedies provided by this title shall be in addition to any and all other rights and remedies that may exist at law or in equity"); and Section 28(a) of the Exchange Act ("the rights and remedies provided by this title shall be in addition to any and all other rights and remedies that may exist at law or in equity"). And courts that subsequently interpreted federal securities remedies routinely emphasized the availability of alternative state remedies. See, e.g., *Marine Bank v. Weaver*, 455 U.S. 551, 556 (1982) (noting that "we are satisfied that Congress, in enacting the securities laws, did not intend to provide a broad federal remedy for all fraud."); *Blue Chip Stamps v. Manor Drug Stores*, 421 U.S. 723, 738 n. 9 (1975) (observing that the disadvantages of requiring the plaintiff to be a purchaser or seller of securities in order to have standing under Rule 10b-5 are "attenuated to the extent that remedies are available to nonpurchasers and nonsellers under state law").

As amended by the SLUSA, Section 16 of the Securities Act provides as follows:

> (b) Class Action Limitations. – No covered class action based upon the statutory or common law of any State or subdivision thereof may be maintained in any State or Federal court by any private party alleging –
>
> > (1) an untrue statement or omission of a material fact in connection with the purchase or sale of a covered security; or
> >
> > (2) that the defendant used or employed any manipulative or deceptive device or contrivance in connection with the purchase or sale of a covered security.
>
> (c) Removal of covered class actions. – Any covered class action brought in any State court involving a covered security, as set forth in paragraph (b), shall be removable to the Federal district court for the district in which the action is pending, and shall be subject to paragraph (b).

Virtually identical language appears in the Exchange Act. See Sections 28(f)(1) and 28(f)(2).

As is apparent, these provisions turn on the meaning of the terms "covered security" and "covered class action." The term "*covered security*" encompasses those listed on the New York Stock Exchange, the National Market System of the NASDAQ Stock Market, or other comparable national securities exchange. See Securities Act Section 18(b); Exchange Act Section 28(f)(5)(E). The term "*covered class action*" includes three types of class actions:

> (1) a lawsuit in which "damages are sought on behalf of more than 50 persons or prospective class members, and questions of law or fact common to those persons or members of the prospective class, without reference to issues of individualized reliance on an alleged misstatement or omission, predominate over any questions affecting only individual persons or members;" or
>
> (2) a lawsuit in which "one or more named parties seek to recover damages on a representative basis on behalf of themselves and other unnamed parties similarly situated, and questions of law or fact common to those persons or members of the prospective class predominate over any questions affecting only individual persons or members;" or
>
> (3) a group of lawsuits "filed in or pending in the same court and involving common questions of law or fact, in which "damages are sought on behalf of more than 50 persons" and "the lawsuits are joined, consolidated, or otherwise proceed as a single action for any purpose."

Securities Act Section 16(f)(2). See also Exchange Act Section 28(f)(5)(B). Note that all three types of class actions involve requests for *damages*. See *Feitelberg v. Merrill Lynch & Co.*, 234 F. Supp. 2d 1043, 1047-49 (N.D. Cal. 2002) (holding that "damages" encompasses restitution and disgorgement), aff'd mem., 353 F.3d 765 (9th Cir. 2003). Thus, a class action seeking solely an injunction is generally outside SLUSA's scope. See *Wald v. C.M. Life Ins. Co.*, 2001 WL 256179 at *6 (N.D. Tex. 2001) (granting remand motion because complaint requests injunction only and "there is simply no indication that Plaintiff is attempting to manipulate the system").

The SLUSA contains certain significant explicit exclusions. Among them are class actions grounded on the law of the issuer's state of incorporation that involve either (1) purchases or sales of securities exclusively between the issuer (or an affiliate) and the issuer's current equity security holders; and (2) communications to the issuer's current equity security holders by the issuer (or an affiliate) that pertain to "decisions of those equity holders with respect to voting their securities, acting in response to a tender or exchange offer, or exercising dissenters' or appraisal rights." See, e.g., *Madden v. Cowen & Co.*, 576 F.3d 957 (9th Cir. 2009) (remanding the case to determine the applicability of the Delaware carve-out). These exclusions are frequently referred to as "the Delaware carve-out." Likewise beyond the SLUSA's reach are actions exclusively derivative in nature as well as those brought by states (including their subdivisions and pension plans). See Securities Act Section 16(d)(2) and Exchange Act Section 28(f)(3)(B).

One other aspect of the SLUSA merits attention – its attempt to prevent federal securities plaintiffs from utilizing state court litigation *not* precluded by the SLUSA as a means of circumventing the discovery stay provision of the PSLRA. Thus, the SLUSA provides that "[u]pon a proper showing, a [federal] court may stay discovery proceedings in a State court as necessary in aid of its jurisdiction, or to protect or effectuate its judgments, in an action subject to a stay of discovery" entered pursuant to the PSLRA. Securities Act Section 27(b)(4); Exchange Act Section 21(D)(b)(3)(D). See, e.g., *In re Cardinal Health, Inc., Sec. Litig.*, 365 F. Supp. 2d 866 (S.D. Ohio 2005) (staying discovery in state court derivative action to safeguard integrity of PSLRA's discovery stay provision which was not then in play because motion to dismiss the federal securities action had yet to be filed).

The Supreme Court made two forays into SLUSA territory in 2006: the decision set out below as well as *Kircher v. Putnam Funds Trust*, 547 U.S. 633 (2006), discussed at Note 5 in the Notes and Questions that follow.

MERRILL LYNCH, PIERCE, FENNER & SMITH INC. v. DABIT

547 U.S. 71 (2006)

JUSTICE JOHN PAUL STEVENS:

Title I of the Securities Litigation Uniform Standards Act of 1998 (SLUSA) provides that "[n]o covered class action" based on state law and alleging "a misrepresentation or omission of a material fact in connection with the purchase or sale of a covered security" "may be maintained in any State or Federal court by any private party." § 101(b), 112 Stat. 3227 (codified at 15 U.S.C. § 78bb(f)(1)(A)). In this case the Second Circuit held that SLUSA only pre-empts state-law class-action claims brought by plaintiffs who have a private remedy under federal law. A few months later, the Seventh Circuit ruled to the contrary, holding that the statute also pre-empts state-law class action claims for which federal law provides no private remedy. *Kircher v. Putnam Funds Trust*, 403 F.3d 478 (C.A.7 2005). The background, the text, and the purpose of SLUSA's pre-emption provision all support the broader interpretation adopted by the Seventh Circuit.

I

Petitioner Merrill Lynch, Pierce, Fenner & Smith, Inc. (Merrill Lynch), is an investment banking firm that offers research and brokerage services to investors. Suspicious that the firm's loyalties to its investment banking clients had produced biased investment advice, the New York attorney general in 2002 instituted a formal investigation into Merrill Lynch's practices. The investigation sparked a number of private securities fraud actions, this one among them.

Respondent, Shadi Dabit, is a former Merrill Lynch broker. He filed this class action in the United States District Court for the Western District of Oklahoma on behalf of himself and all other former or current brokers who, while employed by Merrill Lynch, purchased (for themselves and for their clients) certain stocks between December 1,1999, and December 31, 2000. Rather than rely on the federal securities laws, Dabit invoked the District Court's diversity jurisdiction and advanced his claims under Oklahoma state law.

The gist of Dabit's complaint was that Merrill Lynch breached the fiduciary duty and covenant of good faith and fair dealing it owed its brokers by disseminating misleading research and thereby manipulating stock prices.[2] Dabit's theory was that Merrill Lynch used its misinformed brokers to enhance the prices of its investment banking clients' stocks: The research analysts, under management's direction, allegedly issued overly optimistic appraisals of the stocks' value; the brokers allegedly relied on the analysts' reports in advising their investor clients and in deciding whether or not to sell their own holdings; and the clients and brokers both continued to hold their stocks long beyond the point when, had the truth been known, they would have sold. The complaint further alleged that when the truth was actually revealed (around the time the New York attorney general instituted his investigation), the stocks' prices plummeted.

Dabit asserted that Merrill Lynch's actions damaged the class members in two ways: The misrepresentations and manipulative tactics caused them to hold onto overvalued securities, and the brokers lost commission fees when their clients, now aware that they had made poor investments, took their business elsewhere.

In July 2002, Merrill Lynch moved to dismiss Dabit's complaint. It argued, first, that SLUSA pre-empted the action and, second, that the claims alleged were not cognizable under Oklahoma law. The District Court indicated that it was "not impressed by" the state-law argument, but agreed that the federal statute pre-empted at least some of Dabit's claims. The court noted that the complaint alleged both "claims and damages based on wrongfully-induced

---

2. The complaint alleged, for example, that the prices of the subject stocks were "artificially inflated as a result of the manipulative efforts" of Merrill Lynch, and that Merrill Lynch, "acting as a central nerve center in the manipulation of various stocks..., perpetrated this stock manipulation through a variety of deceptive devices, artifices, and tactics that are the hallmarks of stock manipulation."

purchases" and "claims and damages based on wrongfully-induced holding." While the "holding" claims, the court suggested, might not be pre-empted, the "purchasing" claims certainly were. The court dismissed the complaint with leave to amend to give Dabit the opportunity to untangle his "hopeless melange of purchase-related and holding-related assertions."

Dabit promptly filed an amended complaint that omitted all direct references to purchases. What began as a class of brokers who "purchased" the subject securities during the class period became a class of brokers who "owned and continued to own" those securities.

Meanwhile, dozens of other suits, based on allegations similar to Dabit's, had been filed against Merrill Lynch around the country on both federal- and state-law theories of liability. The Judicial Panel on Multidistrict Litigation transferred all of those cases, along with this one, to the United States District Court for the Southern District of New York for consolidated pretrial proceedings. Merrill Lynch then filed its second motion to dismiss Dabit's complaint. Senior Judge Milton Pollack granted the motion on the ground that the claims alleged fell "squarely within SLUSA's ambit."

The Court of Appeals for the Second Circuit, however, vacated the judgment and remanded for further proceedings. It concluded that the claims asserted by holders did not allege fraud "in connection with the purchase or sale" of securities under SLUSA. Although the court agreed with Merrill Lynch that that phrase, as used in other federal securities laws, has been defined broadly by this Court, it held that Congress nonetheless intended a narrower meaning here-one that incorporates the "standing" limitation on private federal securities actions adopted in *Blue Chip Stamps v. Manor Drug Stores,* 421 U.S. 723 (1975). Under the Second Circuit's analysis, fraud is only "in connection with the purchase or sale" of securities, as used in SLUSA, if it is alleged by a purchaser or seller of securities. Thus, to the extent that the complaint in this action alleged that brokers were fraudulently induced, not to sell or purchase, but to retain or delay selling their securities, it fell outside SLUSA's pre-emptive scope.[3]

After determining that the class defined in Dabit's amended complaint did not necessarily exclude purchasers, the panel remanded with instructions that the pleading be dismissed without prejudice. The court's order would permit Dabit to file another amended complaint that defines the class to exclude "claimants who purchased in connection with the fraud and who therefore could meet the standing requirement" for a federal damages action, and to include only those "who came to hold [a Merrill Lynch] stock before any relevant misrepresentation." Under the Second Circuit's analysis, a class action so limited could be sustained under state law. For the reasons that follow, we disagree.

---

3. The Court of Appeals also concluded that Dabit's lost commission claims escaped pre-emption under SLUSA because they did not "allege fraud that 'coincide[s]' with the sale or purchase of a security." 395 F.3d, at 47 (quoting *SEC v. Zandford,* 535 U.S. 813, 82 (2002)). That determination is not before this Court for review.

II

The magnitude of the federal interest in protecting the integrity and efficient operation of the market for nationally traded securities cannot be overstated. In response to the sudden and disastrous collapse in prices of listed stocks in 1929, and the Great Depression that followed, Congress enacted the Securities Act of 1933 (1933 Act), and the Securities Exchange Act of 1934 (1934 Act). Since their enactment, these two statutes have anchored federal regulation of vital elements of our economy.

*** Rule 10b-5, promulgated in 1942 pursuant to § 10(b) of the 1934 Act, is an important part of that regulatory scheme. The Rule, like § 10(b) itself, broadly prohibits deception, misrepresentation, and fraud "in connection with the purchase or sale of any security." The SEC has express statutory authority to enforce the Rule. Although no such authority is expressly granted to private individuals injured by securities fraud, in 1946 Judge Kirkpatrick of the United States District Court for the Eastern District of Pennsylvania, relying on "the general purpose" of the Rule, recognized an implied right of action thereunder. *Kardon v. National Gypsum Co.,* 69 F.Supp. 512, 514. His holding was adopted by an "overwhelming consensus of the District Courts and Courts of Appeals," *Blue Chip Stamps,* 421 U.S., at 730, and endorsed by this Court in *Superintendent of Ins. of N.Y. v. Bankers Life & Casualty Co.,* 404 U.S. 6 (1971).

A few years after *Kardon* was decided, the Court of Appeals for the Second Circuit limited the reach of the private right of action under Rule 10b-5. In *Birnbaum v. Newport Steel Corp.,* 193 F.2d 461 (C.A.2 1952), a panel composed of Chief Judge Swan and Judges Augustus and Learned Hand upheld the dismissal of a suit brought on behalf of a corporation and a class of its stockholders alleging that fraud "in connection with" a director's sale of his controlling block of stock to third parties violated Rule 10b-5. The court held that the Rule could only be invoked by a purchaser or seller of securities to remedy fraud associated with his or her own sale or purchase of securities, and did not protect those who neither purchased nor sold the securities in question but were instead injured by corporate insiders' sales to third parties. While the *Birnbaum* court did not question the plaintiffs' "standing" to enforce Rule 10b-5, later cases treated its holding as a standing requirement. See *Eason v. General Motors Acceptance Corp.,* 490 F.2d 654, 657 (C.A.7 1973).

By the time this Court first confronted the question, literally hundreds of lower court decisions had accepted "*Birnbaum's* conclusion that the plaintiff class for purposes of § 10(b) and Rule 10b-5 private damages actions is limited to purchasers and sellers." *Blue Chip Stamps,* 421 U.S., at 731-732. Meanwhile, however, cases like *Bankers Life & Casualty Co.* had interpreted the coverage of the Rule more broadly to prohibit, for example, "deceptive practices *touching* [a victim's] sale of securities as an investor." 404 U.S., at 12-13 (emphasis added). The "judicial oak which ha[d] grown from little more than a legislative acorn," as then-Justice Rehnquist described the rules governing private Rule 10b-5 actions, *Blue Chip Stamps,* 421 U.S., had thus developed differently from the law defining what constituted a substantive violation of Rule 10b-5. Ultimately, the Court had to decide whether to permit private parties to sue for any violation of Rule 10b-5 that caused them harm, or instead to limit the private remedy to plaintiffs who were themselves purchasers or sellers.

Relying principally on "policy considerations" which the Court viewed as appropriate in explicating a judicially crafted remedy, and following judicial precedent rather than "the many commentators" who had criticized the *Birnbaum* rule as "an arbitrary restriction which unreasonably prevents some deserving plaintiffs from recovering damages," the Court in *Blue Chip Stamps* chose to limit the private remedy. The main policy consideration tipping the scales in favor of precedent was the widespread recognition that "litigation under Rule 10b-5 presents a danger of vexatiousness different in degree and in kind from that which accompanies litigation in general." Even weak cases brought under the Rule may have substantial settlement value, the Court explained, because "[t]he very pendency of the lawsuit may frustrate or delay normal business activity." Cabining the private cause of action by means of the purchaser-seller limitation would, in the Court's view, minimize these ill effects. The limitation of course had no application in Government enforcement actions brought pursuant to Rule 10b-5. See id., at 751, n. 14.

III

Policy considerations similar to those that supported the Court's decision in *Blue Chip Stamps* prompted Congress, in 1995, to adopt legislation targeted at perceived abuses of the class-action vehicle in litigation involving nationally traded securities. While acknowledging that private securities litigation was "an indispensable tool with which defrauded investors can recover their losses," the House Conference Report accompanying what would later be enacted as the Private Securities Litigation Reform Act of 1995 (Reform Act), identified ways in which the class action device was being used to injure "the entire U.S. economy." H.R.Rep. No. 104-369, p. 31 (1995). According to the Report, nuisance filings, targeting of deep-pocket defendants, vexatious discovery requests, and "manipulation by class action lawyers of the clients whom they purportedly represent" had become rampant in recent years. Proponents of the Reform Act argued that these abuses resulted in extortionate settlements, chilled any discussion of issuers' future prospects, and deterred qualified individuals from serving on boards of directors. Id., at 31-32.

Title I of the Reform Act, captioned "Reduction of Abusive Litigation," represents Congress' effort to curb these perceived abuses. Its provisions limit recoverable damages and attorney's fees, provide a "safe harbor" for forward-looking statements, impose new restrictions on the selection of (and compensation awarded to) lead plaintiffs, mandate imposition of sanctions for frivolous litigation, and authorize a stay of discovery pending resolution of any motion to dismiss. See 15 U.S.C. § 78u-4. Title I also imposes heightened pleading requirements in actions brought pursuant to § 10(b) and Rule 10b-5; it "insists that securities fraud complaints 'specify' each misleading statement; that they set forth the facts 'on which [a] belief' that a statement is misleading was 'formed'; and that they 'state with particularity facts giving rise to a strong inference that the defendant acted with the required state of mind.' " *Dura Pharmaceuticals, Inc. v. Broudo,* 544 U.S. 336, 345 (quoting15 U.S.C. §§ 78u-4(b)(1), (2)).

The effort to deter or at least quickly dispose of those suits whose nuisance value outweighs their merits placed special burdens on plaintiffs seeking to bring federal securities fraud class actions. But the effort also had an unintended consequence: It prompted at least some members of the plaintiffs' bar to avoid the federal forum altogether. Rather than face the obstacles set in their path by the Reform Act, plaintiffs and their representatives began bringing class actions under state law, often in state court. The evidence presented to Congress during a 1997 hearing to evaluate the effects of the Reform Act suggested that this phenomenon was a novel one; state-court litigation of class actions involving nationally traded securities had previously been rare. See H.R.Rep. No. 105-640, p. 10 (1998); S.Rep. No. 105-182, pp. 3-4 (1998). To stem this "shif[t] from Federal to State courts" and "prevent certain State private securities class action lawsuits alleging fraud from being used to frustrate the objectives of" the Reform Act, SLUSA §§ 2(2),(5), Congress enacted SLUSA.

IV

The core provision of SLUSA reads as follows:[6]

> ***No covered class action based upon the statutory or common law of any State or subdivision thereof may be maintained in any State or Federal court by any private party alleging-
>
> (A) a misrepresentation or omission of a material fact in connection with the purchase or sale of a covered security; or
>
> (B) that the defendant used or employed any manipulative or deceptive device or contrivance in connection with the purchase or sale of a covered security.

Id., at 3230 (codified as amended at 15 U.S.C. § 78bb(f)(1)).[7]

***Respondent does not dispute that both the class and the securities at issue in this case are "covered" within the meaning of the statute, or that the complaint alleges misrepresentations and omissions of material facts. The only disputed issue is whether the alleged wrongdoing was "in connection with the purchase or sale" of securities.

Respondent urges that the operative language must be read narrowly to encompass (and therefore pre-empt) only those actions in which the purchaser-seller requirement of *Blue Chip Stamps* is met. Such, too, was the Second Circuit's view. But insofar as the argument assumes that the rule adopted in *Blue Chip Stamps* stems from the text of Rule 10b-5-specifically, the "in connection with" language, it must be rejected. Unlike the *Birnbaum* court, which relied on Rule 10b-5's text in crafting its purchaser-seller limitation, this Court in *Blue Chip Stamps* relied chiefly, and candidly, on "policy considerations" in adopting that limitation. 421 U.S., at 737. The *Blue Chip Stamps* Court purported to define the scope of a private right of action under Rule 10b-5-not to define the words "in connection with the purchase or sale." Id., at 749 ("No language in either [§ 10(b) or Rule 10b-5] speaks at all to the

6. SLUSA amends the 1933 Act and the 1934 Act in substantially identical ways. For convenience and because they are more pertinent here, we quote the amendments to the 1934 Act.

7. Another key provision of the statute makes all "covered class actions" filed in state court removable to federal court. 112 Stat. 3230 (codified at 15 U.S.C. § 78bb(f)(2)).

contours of a private cause of action for their violation"). Any ambiguity on that score had long been resolved by the time Congress enacted SLUSA. See *United States v. O'Hagan,* 521 U.S. 642, 656, 664 (1997); *United States v. Naftalin,* 441 U.S. 768, 774, n. 6 (1979); see also 395 F.3d, at 39 (acknowledging that "[t]he limitation on standing to bring [a] private suit for damages for fraud in connection with the purchase or sale of securities is unquestionably a distinct concept from the general statutory and regulatory prohibition on fraud in connection with the purchase or sale of securities").

Moreover, when this Court *has* sought to give meaning to the phrase in the context of § 10(b) and Rule 10b-5, it has espoused a broad interpretation. A narrow construction would not, as a matter of first impression, have been unreasonable; one might have concluded that an alleged fraud is "in connection with" a purchase or sale of securities only when the plaintiff himself was defrauded into purchasing or selling particular securities. After all, that was the interpretation adopted by the panel in the *Birnbaum* case. But this Court, in early cases like *Superintendent of Ins. of N.Y. v. Bankers Life & Casualty Co.,* 404 U.S. 6 (1971), and most recently in *SEC v. Zandford,* 535 U.S. 813, 820, 822 (2002), has rejected that view. Under our precedents, it is enough that the fraud alleged "coincide" with a securities transaction-whether by the plaintiff or by someone else. See *O'Hagan,* 521 U.S., at 651. The requisite showing, in other words, is "deception 'in connection with the purchase or sale of any security,' not deception of an identifiable purchaser or seller." Id., at 658. Notably, this broader interpretation of the statutory language comports with the longstanding views of the SEC. See *Zandford,* 535 U.S., at 819-820.[10]

Congress can hardly have been unaware of the broad construction adopted by both this Court and the SEC when it imported the key phrase-"in connection with the purchase or sale"- into SLUSA's core provision. And when "judicial interpretations have settled the meaning of an existing statutory provision, repetition of the same language in a new statute indicates, as a general matter, the intent to incorporate its ... judicial interpretations as well." *Bragdon v. Abbott,* 524 U.S. 624, 645 (1998). Application of that presumption is particularly apt here; not only did Congress use the same words as are used in § 10(b) and Rule 10b-5, but it used them in a provision that appears in the same statute as § 10(b). Generally, "identical words used in different parts of the same statute are ... presumed to have the same meaning." *IBP, Inc. v. Alvarez,* 546 U.S. 1144 (2005).

The presumption that Congress envisioned a broad construction follows not only from ordinary principles of statutory construction but also from the particular concerns that culminated in SLUSA's enactment. A narrow reading of the statute would undercut the effectiveness of the 1995 Reform Act and thus run contrary to SLUSA's stated purpose, viz., "to prevent certain State private securities class action lawsuits alleging fraud from being used to frustrate the objectives" of the 1995 Act. SLUSA § 2(5), 112 Stat. 3227. As the *Blue Chip Stamps* Court observed, class actions brought by holders pose a special risk of vexatious litigation. 421 U.S., at 739. It would be odd, to say the least, if

10. *** Here, too, the SEC supports a broad reading of the "in connection with" language.

SLUSA exempted that particularly troublesome subset of class actions from its pre-emptive sweep.

Respondent's preferred construction also would give rise to wasteful, duplicative litigation. Facts supporting an action by purchasers under Rule 10b-5 (which must proceed in federal court if at all) typically support an action by holders as well, at least in those States that recognize holder claims. The prospect is raised, then, of parallel class actions proceeding in state and federal court, with different standards governing claims asserted on identical facts. That prospect, which exists to some extent in this very case,[11] squarely conflicts with the congressional preference for "national standards for securities class action lawsuits involving nationally traded securities." SLUSA § 2(5).[12]

In concluding that SLUSA pre-empts state-law holder class-action claims of the kind alleged in Dabit's complaint, we do not lose sight of the general "presum[ption] that Congress does not cavalierly pre-empt state-law causes of action." *Medtronic, Inc. v. Lohr,* 518 U.S. 470, 485 (1996). But that presumption carries less force here than in other contexts because SLUSA does not actually pre-empt any state cause of action. It simply denies plaintiffs the right to use the class action device to vindicate certain claims. The Act does not deny any individual plaintiff, or indeed any group of fewer than 50 plaintiffs, the right to enforce any state-law cause of action that may exist.

Moreover, the tailored exceptions to SLUSA's pre-emptive command demonstrate that Congress did not by any means act "cavalierly" here. The statute carefully exempts from its operation certain class actions based on the law of the State in which the issuer of the covered security is incorporated, actions brought by a state agency or state pension plan, actions under contracts between issuers and indenture trustees, and derivative actions brought by shareholders on behalf of a corporation. 15 U.S.C. §§ 78bb(f)(3)(A)-(C), (f)(5)(C). The statute also expressly preserves state jurisdiction over state agency enforcement proceedings. § 78bb(f)(4). The existence of these carve-outs both evinces congressional sensitivity to state prerogatives in this field and makes it inappropriate for courts to create additional, implied exceptions.

Finally, federal law, not state law, has long been the principal vehicle for asserting class-action securities fraud claims. See, *e.g.,* H.R. Conf. Rep. No. 105-803, p. 14 (1998) ("Prior to the passage of the Reform Act, there was essentially no significant securities class action litigation brought in State court"). More importantly, while state-law holder claims were theoretically available both before and after the decision in *Blue Chip Stamps,* the actual assertion of such claims by way of class action was virtually unheard of before SLUSA was

---

11. See 2003 WL 1872820, *1 (S.D.N.Y., Apr.10, 2003) (observing that Dabit's holder claims rested "on the very same alleged series of transactions and occurrences asserted in the federal securities actions" filed against Merrill Lynch).

12. See H.R.Rep. No. 105-640, p. 10 (1998) (the "solution" to circumvention of the Reform Act "is to make Federal court the exclusive venue for securities fraud class action litigation"); S.Rep. No. 105-182, p. 3 (1998) (identifying "the danger of maintaining differing federal and state standards of liability for nationally-traded securities").

enacted; respondent and his *amici* have identified only *one* pre-SLUSA case involving a state-law class action asserting holder claims.[13] This is hardly a situation, then, in which a federal statute has eliminated a historically entrenched state-law remedy.

V

The holder class action that respondent tried to plead, and that the Second Circuit envisioned, is distinguishable from a typical Rule 10b-5 class action in only one respect: It is brought by holders instead of purchasers or sellers. For purposes of SLUSA pre-emption, that distinction is irrelevant; the identity of the plaintiffs does not determine whether the complaint alleges fraud "in connection with the purchase or sale" of securities. The misconduct of which respondent complains here-fraudulent manipulation of stock prices-unquestionably qualifies as fraud "in connection with the purchase or sale" of securities as the phrase is defined in *Zandford,* 535 U.S., at 820, 822 and *O'Hagan,* 521 U.S., at 651.

The judgment of the Court of Appeals for the Second Circuit is vacated, and the case is remanded for further proceedings consistent with this opinion.***

NOTES AND QUESTIONS

1. ***Claims vs. Actions.*** Assume that a complaint contains both a class action claim and a shareholder derivative claim. If the court dismisses the class action claim on the ground that it is precluded by the SLUSA, must it dismiss the shareholder derivative claim as well? Compare *Proctor v. Vishnay Intertech., Inc.*, 584 F.3d 1208 , 1226 (9th Cir. 2009) (giving negative answer) and *In re Lord Abbett Mut. Funds Fee Litig.*, 553 F.3d 248, 255-56 (3d Cir. 2009) (same) with *Superior Partners v. Chang*, 471 F. Supp. 2d 750 (S.D. Tex. 2007) (giving positive answer) and *Greaves v. McAuley*, 264 F. Supp. 2d 1078, 1085 (N.D. Ga. 2003) (same).

2. ***Big Investors vs. Small.*** Is the impact of *Dabit* essentially the same for all investors, big and small alike?

3. ***Escape Hatch?*** The SLUSA seeks to prevent plaintiffs from circumventing the PSLRA by filing *state law* class actions. But what about plaintiffs who attempt such circumvention by filing in a state court class action premised on Section 11 or Section 12(a)(2) of the Securities Act of 1933 (both of which provisions are addressed in Chapter 3)? In thinking about this question, bear in mind that the Securities Act Section 22(a) specifically prohibits removal of Securities Act actions filed in state court: "No case arising under the Securities Act and brought in any state court of competent jurisdiction shall be removed to any of the courts of the United States."

Courts and commentators are deeply divided. Some courts say that the SLUSA's language flatly precludes such removal. See, e.g., *In re Tyco Internat'l,*

---

13. See Brief for Respondent 5 (citing *Weinberger v. Kendrick,* 698 F.2d 61, 78 (C.A.2 1982) (approving a settlement that included holder claims brought pursuant to New York law).

Ltd. Multidist. Litig,, 322 F. Supp. 2d 116, 120 (D.N.H. 2004). Others disagree, reasoning that "[a]fter SLUSA, state courts were no longer 'courts of competent jurisdiction' to hear covered class actions raising 1933 Act claims." *Knox v. Agria Group*, 613 F. Supp. 2d 419, 425 (S.D.N. Y. 2009). Still others allow removal so as to prevent SLUSA from becoming "meaningless." *Brody v. Homestore, Inc.*, 240 F. Supp. 2d 1122, 1124 (C.D. Cal. 2003). Compare Jordan A. Costa, Note, Removal of Securities Act of 1933 Claims After SLUSA: What Congress Changed, and What It Left Alone, 78 St. John's L. Rev. 1193 (2004) (arguing that the Democratically-controlled Congress that enacted the SLUSA would have balked at a provision explicitly authorizing removal of all Securities Act class actions) with William B. Snyder, Jr., Comment, The Securities Act of 1933 After SLUSA: Federal Class Actions Belong in Federal Court, 85 N.C.L. Rev. 669 (2007). What do you think?

4. ***The Plight of Defrauded Securities Holders.*** With *Dabit*, those defrauded into holding their shares lost the possibility of bringing state law-based class actions. Previously foreclosed to such holders was the right to sue under Rule 10b-5 (whether on behalf of a class or individually). See *Blue Chip Stamps v. Manor Drug Stores*, 421U.S. 723 (1975).

The vulnerability of defrauded securities holders was highlighted by the wave of corporate scandals at companies such as Enron and Worldcom. Those employees claimed to have been duped into retaining company stock in which their pension plans were invested. See generally Susan J. Stabile, I Believed My Employer and Didn't Sell My Company Stock: Is There an ERISA (or '34 Act) Remedy for Me?, 36 Conn. L. Rev. 385 (2004). Prompted at least in part by this history, the California Supreme Court has held that California law protects defrauded security holders. See *Small v. Fritz Cos.*, 65 P.3d 1255, 1264 (Cal. 2003) (noting that in the wake of the scandals, "[e]liminating barriers that deny redress to actual victims of fraud now assumes an importance equal to that of deterring nonmeritorious suits").

Why do you suppose that the scandals had no discernible impact on the *Dabit* Court? What accounts for the Court's description of holders' claims as "especially vexatious"? Did the claims of the *Dabit* plaintiffs involve unsympathetic facts? If so, how much did that matter to the ultimate result?

Should Congress or the Supreme Court intervene on behalf of defrauded securities holders? If so, what should they do? See generally Robert W. Taylor, Note, Re-Evaluating Holder Actions: Giving Defrauded Securities Holders a Fighting Chance, 86 Notre Dame L. Rev. 413 (2011).

5. ***Holder Lawsuits – The Supreme Court Round Two.*** In general, defendants cannot appeal orders remanding cases that they previously removed to federal court. See 28 U.S.C. § 1447(d). The Supreme Court's decision in *Kircher v. Putnam Funds Trust*, 547 U.S. 633 (2006), addressed whether this holds true for removals based on the SLUSA. Answering affirmatively, the Court held that SLUSA did not change the basic rules regarding remands and appealability: "there is no indication whatsoever in the [SLUSA] that, apart from its purpose to preclude certain vexing state-law class actions, Congress intended to add other state-law cases to the federal dockets." Id. at 644. Accordingly, the Court overturned the Seventh Circuit's reversal of the federal district court's remand order and returned the case to the Seventh Circuit with instructions that it dismiss the appeal for lack of jurisdiction. The Seventh Circuit ordered a remand to the state court. *In the Matter of Mutual Fund Market Timing Litig.*, 468 F.3d 439 (7th Cir. 2006). Back in state court, the plaintiffs amended their complaint and removed the action once again to the federal district court. See *Spurgeon v. Pacific Life Ins. Co.*, 2006 WL 3841811 (S.D. Ill. 2006) (ordering a status conference).

The federal district court had issued its original remand order prior to the Supreme Court's *Dabit* decision. That order had reasoned that the SLUSA did not come into play because the plaintiffs were "holders" of securities rather than purchasers or sellers. See *Kircher*, supra, 547 U.S. at 638. More specifically, the *Kircher* plaintiffs were holders of shares in mutual funds which they alleged were devalued due to "market timing" activity by arbitrageurs. The defendants were the mutual funds and the investment advisers for the funds who allegedly permitted such market timing in violation of their fiduciary duties to the plaintiffs. Suppose that upon returning to state court, the plaintiffs had not amended the complaint and re-removed. Under those circumstances, what should the state court have done? What litigation alternatives remain for injured holders in mutual funds?

6. Preclusion vs. Federalism. Did Congress make the correct decision in enacting the SLUSA? How would you assess the benefits and costs of the uniformity that comes as the result of the SLUSA?

7. Beyond the SLUSA. The *Dabit* Court declared that "[t]he magnitude of the federal interest in protecting the integrity and efficient operation of the market for nationally traded securities cannot be overstated." Does this statement have implications that extend beyond the SLUSA?

PROBLEM 6-4

Joe has filed a class action in state court under state law, in which he alleges a misrepresentation in connection with the purchase of securities. Decide whether the SLUSA would preclude the action under each of the following circumstances:

a. The defendant allegedly acted negligently, but not recklessly.

b. The defendant's role in the transaction is alleged to have been solely that of aidor and abettor.

c. Joe brought the action on behalf of 48 people. Several days earlier, he filed another virtually identical action on behalf of 45 other people in another trial court of the same state.

d. Joe is the county sheriff and sued on behalf of the state pension plan.

e. Joe filed the action not under the law of a state of the United States, but rather under the law of Switzerland.

E. THE INTERPLAY BETWEEN SECURITIES FRAUD CLASS ACTIONS AND SHAREHOLDER DERIVATIVE LITIGATION

The material misstatements and omissions that typically fuel securities class action litigation often spawn shareholder derivative litigation as well.

Investors typically initiate class action litigation against issuers and others who allegedly defrauded them in connection with their securities transactions, whereas one or more shareholders initiate derivative litigation on behalf of the corporation against those who allegedly injured the corporation, often through the breach of a fiduciary duty. Accordingly, harm to the corporation – not harm to investors – is the subject of the derivative lawsuit, with the corporation ordinarily receiving any recovery that is obtained.

Under the "internal affairs doctrine," the law of the state of incorporation governs the substantive allegations in a derivative complaint, even if that complaint is filed in the court of a different state or in a federal court. Scholars have given the lion's share of attention to derivative lawsuits against the officers and directors of Delaware corporations, but broader inquiries hold much value because, as at least one recent study has shown, "most shareholder derivative suits are filed in federal court and nearly half are filed on behalf of companies incorporated outside of Delaware." Jessica Erickson, Corporate Governance in the Courtroom: An Empirical Analysis, 51 Wm. & Mary L. Rev. 1749, 1754 (2010). Indeed, according to Professor Erickson, "[s]hareholders actually file more shareholder derivative suits than securities class actions." Id.

Although shareholders file a derivative lawsuit on behalf of the corporation, the reality is a bit more complex. The corporation can act only through its officers and directors – and those are often the very same people who, according to the shareholders, committed the breach of fiduciary duty on which their lawsuit is based. Thus, as Judge Ralph Winter has explained:

> The derivative action is the common law's inventive solution to the problem of actions to protect shareholder interests. In its classic form, a derivative suit involves two actions brought by an individual shareholder: (i) an action against the corporation for failing to bring a specified suit and (ii) an action on behalf of the corporation for harm to it identical to the one which the corporation failed to bring. The technical structure of the derivative suit is thus quite unusual.

Joy v. North, 692 F.2d 880, 887 (2d Cir. 1982).

Because directors, rather than shareholders, ordinarily make the corporation's litigation decisions, the law of the state of incorporation generally requires the complaining shareholders to justify the maintenance of the derivative lawsuit in the absence of the directors' approval. Some states – so-called universal demand jurisdictions – require the shareholders to make a demand upon the board to file the lawsuit against the alleged wrongdoers. If, as virtually always happens, the board rejects the demand, the shareholders may proceed with the derivative lawsuit provided they can establish that the demand was wrongly rejected, say, because the directors had a conflict of interest or failed to act with a proper business purpose or on an informed basis. Other jurisdictions – so-called demand excused jurisdictions (with Delaware as the most prominent example) – allow shareholders to forego the formality of the demand if they can show, on the basis of the allegations in the derivative complaint, that demand would be futile. See *Aronson v. Lewis*, 473 A.2d 805, 814 (Del. 1984) (stating that "in determining demand futility, the Court of Chancery in the proper exercise of its discretion must decide whether, under the particularized facts alleged, a reasonable doubt is created that: (1) the directors are disinterested and independent, [or] the challenged transaction was otherwise the product of a valid exercise of business judgment"). See also David Skeel, The Accidental Elegance of *Aronson v. Lewis*, in The Iconic Cases in Corporate Law (Macey, J., ed., 2008) (discussing *Aronson*'s framework and comparing it to the framework for direct lawsuits by shareholders under state corporate law or in securities fraud class actions).

Although the requirements for derivative litigation may differ depending on the substantive law of the state of incorporation as well as on the applicable procedural rules (whether in a federal or state court), the threshold inquiry is largely the same: should the directors or the shareholders decide whether the lawsuit should proceed? Only if this threshold issue is resolved in a manner that allows the lawsuit to go forward will the underlying substantive allegations of the lawsuit be reached and decided.

Professor Erickson's research illuminates the intriguing phenomenon that shareholders who file parallel derivative and class action litigation often make use of overlapping allegations. She observes that:

> Derivative plaintiffs typically use two approaches to turn federal securities claims into the basis of a derivative claim. First, *** many plaintiffs allege *** that the corporation was injured by an officer or director's false or misleading statements. Second, many plaintiffs use so-called *Caremark* or other good faith claims to turn federal securities claims into state fiduciary duty claims. In a *Caremark* claim, the shareholder typically alleges that the board breached its fiduciary duty by failing to exercise proper oversight over the plaintiff corporation. For example, the plaintiff in a securities class action may allege that the corporation and its officers and directors violated the federal securities laws by lying to the market. The plaintiff in a parallel derivative suit can then take this same allegation and assert that the officers and directors breached their fiduciary duty to the corporation by causing the corporation to make false statements or by causing the underlying financial problems resulting from the misstatements.

Erickson, supra, at 1777.

To be sure, successful derivative lawsuits (through adjudication or settlement) may culminate in the payment of money damages resulting from the defendants' alleged breaches of fiduciary duty. Most often, however, the principal recovery entails prospective reforms in corporate governance, with relatively few derivative suits actually resulting in "the corporation receiving a meaningful financial benefit." Erickson, supra, at 1754. The *Caremark* case referenced in the excerpt above provides a notable example, see *In re Caremark Int'l Inc. Deriv. Litig.*, 698 A.2d 959 (Del. Ch. 1996) (approving as "fair and reasonable" proposed settlement whereby corporation agreed to establish a compliance and ethics committee composed of four directors and to reform business practices relating to dealings with health care providers). Attorney fees for the successful shareholder in a derivative lawsuit are either awarded as part of a judgment or are agreed upon as part of the settlement and then approved by the court.

The practice of filing so-called tagalong derivative lawsuits appears to be on the rise. As Professor Erickson explains:

> Following the enactment of the PSLRA, shareholders tried to get around the Act by filing state law securities class actions. Congress quickly determined that these state suits were "frustrat[ing] the objectives of the [PSLRA]" and enacted the Securities Litigation Uniform Standards Act of 1998, or SLUSA. SLUSA preempts a significant number of securities class actions filed under state law, preventing shareholders from using these claims as a backdoor around the PSLRA. Congress, however, did not use its preemption power to bar derivative suits, even though these suits also often mirror the allegations in a securities class action. The end result of these statutory enactments is that Congress has drastically limited the ability of shareholders to file securities class actions—whether under federal or state law—but left intact their ability to file derivative suits. It is therefore not surprising that many shareholders are filing derivative suits that look quite similar to federal securities class actions.

Erickson, supra, at 1778-79. Specifically, the SLUSA added a new Section 28(f)(5)(c) to the Exchange Act which makes clear that "[t]he term 'covered class action' does not include the exclusively derivative action brought by one or more shareholders on behalf of a corporation."

What are some of the issues that arise when shareholders file parallel securities fraud class actions and derivative lawsuits premised on the same general allegations of corporate wrongdoing? Should most stock-drop actions under Rule 10b-5 be re-characterized as derivative rather than direct claims? See Richard A. Booth, Direct and Derivative Claims in Securities Fraud Litigation, 4 Va. L. & Bus. Rev. 277, 283 (2010) (contending that "federal law (mistakenly) [relies] on class actions rather than derivative actions to deal with securities fraud claims" and that "courts have the power and the duty to clean up the mess"). You should reconsider both of these questions after you have read the materials in the final section below.

F. THE DEBATE ABOUT SECURITIES CLASS ACTIONS

Securities class actions have long been the subject of vociferous debate, with particular controversy surrounding the question of whether corporations should be held liable for damages in "open market" frauds. The following excerpts offer differing views on the benefits and costs of "entity liability."

MAKING SECURITIES FRAUD CLASS ACTIONS VIRTUOUS

by James D. Cox

39 Ariz. L. Rev. 497 (1997)

Few things are as American as the class action. Housed in this single procedural device is the mechanism that accords equal footing to the common man in his dispute with the large corporation. Where the single claimant could not proceed individually because her expenses would dwarf the expected recovery, the class action can be brought on behalf of all who are similarly situated. And the sheer size of the aggregated claim attracts not only the entrepreneurial instincts of the class lawyer but also commands the full attention of the defendant. The class action thereby has an important deterrent feature which gives it a quasi-public character; it can thus be seen as an extension of the state's enforcement arm and an expression of society's will.***

A reason that the securities class action poorly serves both a compensatory and a deterrent objective is the circuity problem that arises when the source of a settlement is the corporation that commits the misrepresentation.

Though the inanimate character of the business entity assures that misrepresentations can physically be committed only by its personnel, it is the entity, and not its actors, that provides the settlement funds. For a variety of reasons, its responsible officers and directors only rarely contribute to the recovery. The corporation's payment for the sins committed by its personnel is, transparently, a payment made proportionately by all its owners. Hence, a circularity problem arises for settlements of securities class actions involving securities class actions arising from the misleading reports of corporate defendants. If plaintiffs recover a settlement of $10 million from Alpha Inc. for misrepresentations in its annual report that induced the plaintiffs to purchase their Alpha shares, and assuming no insurance, the plaintiffs necessarily provide, albeit indirectly, some portion of their own settlement recovery. The degree of circularity involved by such a settlement depends primarily on what portion of the company is owned by the members of the class action, a consideration that likely is dependent on the length over which the fraud was committed, the relative turnover of the company's shares, and the number of class members who pursued a buy-and-hold-strategy versus an in-and-out-strategy. If we assume that the class represents 5% of Alpha's shares when the settlement occurs, then effectively 5% of the settlement was paid by members of the class. And, if the corporation bears the full economic weight of the settlement, though it was its personnel who committed the offense, then 95% of the settlement's effects are borne by Alpha's non-class member shareholders.

Though the rejoinder to the concern for circularity is that most of the class's recovery does not come from the class members themselves, so that circularity occurs only at the margins, we may still question why we should continue a system of liability whose impact falls on parties as innocent as the class members – the Alpha stockholders who were not members of the class. This innocent set of stockholders can easily be seen as also victims; their managers betrayed their owners' trust by committing the securities violation. On this point, consider the findings of one study of securities class actions that most such cases arise from managers purposely either concealing the financial problems of the firm, or otherwise projecting a false appearance of financial stability, as part of their desperate attempt to "turn things around." This is the so-called last period agency problem where the managers commit frauds that can be seen as both furthering their own interests of avoiding their incurring the repercussions of the reporting firm's poor performance as well as the managers striving to further the firm's interest by attempting to overcome the causes for its present financial distress.*** Because the managers' interest so clearly dominates their reasons for committing the violation, questions abound why the fault should not, as it is in the instance of insider trading, be solely that of the managers. That is, the class action's critics question why should any portion of the loss fall on the innocent owners of the employing company?

That managers may act to serve their interest at their owner's expense is neither unexpected nor isolated to securities violations. Too frequently managers engage in antisocial behavior – concealing the defects of the company's products, conspiring to fix prices or flaunting environmental standards – for reasons that are consistent with advancing their careers, preserving perquisites, or avoiding dismissal. All such conduct has given rise to class action recoveries against the corporate employer with consequential effects on the firm's passive, and innocent, stockholders. The question of entity liability is not, therefore, limited to securities law violations and there seems little reason to so isolate the debate of the propriety of entity liability to securities violations. Managerial misbehavior, after all, is a portion of the risk that accompanies ownership. It is a risk internalized through the concept of entity liability.

The financial burdens of a securities fraud settlement borne by the innocent stockholders of the corporate violator is indistinguishable from the burden borne by the shareholders of the corporation that produces a defective product or violates the environmental laws. Being a burden of ownership, it is inherent in the feature of enterprise liability that the enterprise internalize the costs of its activities. Though the last period agency problem appears to be advancing the personal rather than the corporation's interest, this clearly is too narrow a view of the managers' motivation. Managers who defraud securities markets as part of their attempt to rescue the firm from financial failure cannot be seen as acting solely without a consciousness of the corporation's interests. Even the increasingly prevalent instances in which managers proffer unreasonably optimistic financial forecasts, the managers' act with their corporation's interest at heart. Professor Langevoort observes that the corporate culture seems to breed the type of optimism that invites class action suits for misleading financial forecasts.[49] To the extent this is the case, it would seem to argue for owner responsibility since it was their enterprise that gave rise to the culture calling for such optimism; and since ambiguity will most certainly exist with respect to whether the manager was acting at least in part to serve her employer's interest, the case for entity responsibility becomes even stronger. Though the burden of the innocent Alpha stockholders is as unexpected, and certainly unwanted, as knowledge that the company's management has knowingly infringed on a competitor's product, it nevertheless is a risk and cost properly shared proportionately among its owners.

There is a rich body of literature on the appropriateness of entity liability, as opposed to liability only for the managers who committed the violation. Entity liability provides incentives for owners to employ efficient strategies to reduce costly violations of the law. One such strategy is the use of outside directors and another is according a strong oversight role to the audit committee with respect to the company's financial reporting. For example, whatever may be the personal incentive of the full-time officers to misrepresent the company's financial position and performance, their ability to coerce the firm's outside accountants into acceding to management's disclosure choices is greatly reduced by the presence of a truly independent audit committee when one of the functions of the committee is to mediate disagreements between management and the auditors. The audit committee members' independence and judgment in such matters is formed not solely because they have professional lives outside the organization, but because their responsibility is to oversee management's stewardship of the firm. The presence of entity liability, therefore, not only underscores the importance of the outside directors' task, but also gives content to the discharge of that task. ***

---

49. See Langevoort, [Capping Damages for Open Market Securities Fraud, 38 Ariz. L. Rev.639], 656 (1996).

REFORMING THE SECURITIES CLASS ACTION: AN ESSAY ON DETERRENCE AND ITS IMPLEMENTATION

By John C. Coffee, Jr.

106 Colum. L. Rev. 1534 (2006)

*** The essential circularity of the securities class action in the secondary market context has not escaped the attention of legal academics. But their responses have diverged radically. One school – best typified by Professor James Cox – argues that holding the nontrading corporation liable for secondary market purchases is justifiable because it is consistent with the standard rule of enterprise liability that prevails across tort law generally.[97] ***

***Those who point to tort law's general preference for enterprise liability as a justification for the status quo miss what is most distinctive about the securities class action. When a corporation is fined or incurs liability in a class action because of a defective product or environmental pollution, society is imposing a cost on the corporation (and indirectly its shareholders) to induce it to monitor the behavior of its managers more diligently. Shareholders are not themselves the primary victims of the offense. Instead, a negative externality is being internalized (at least partially) by shifting costs from the victims of the tort to the corporation and its shareholders. But in the case of at least the "secondary market" securities class action, the victims and the shareholders are largely the same (at least if we assume the shareholders to be diversified). Thus, enterprise liability in this context is a strategy akin to punishing the victims of burglary for their failure to take greater precautions. Although this strategy might produce some enhanced monitoring, it offends social norms, including the public's basic sense of fairness, to punish the victim for conduct that it did not cause. Thus, the more this strategy becomes transparent, the more it will predictably encounter both political and judicial resistance. Nor is punishing the victim terribly effective, as victims are generally not the best-suited persons to detect and prevent the offense (which is ultimately why they became victims).

Defenders of the current system of enterprise liability tend to assume that the corporation's agents and employees are engaging in legal violations to maximize profits for the corporation. But again securities litigation is distinctive. Although this assumption is generally valid when the corporation sells a defective product or pollutes the environment, the corporate manager usually has more self-interested reasons for inflating the firm's earnings. Except in the case where the corporation is itself issuing shares, securities fraud appears to be primarily motivated by the manager's own personal interests. Typically, managers hide bad news because they fear loss of their jobs (either from a dismissal or a hostile takeover), and they overstate favorable developments or inflate earnings in order to maximize the value of their stock options and other equity compensation. After analyzing a large sample of class actions, Professors Arlen and Carney report that managerial self-interest seems to be the dominant motivation underlying securities fraud, with managers frequently engaging in behavior that closely resembles insider trading. If so,

97. See James D. Cox, Making Securities Class Actions Virtuous, 39 Ariz. L. Rev. 497, 509-12 (1997). ***

enterprise liability may work less well than a strategy that focuses directly on the managers themselves. ***

A deeper question also lurks here that this Essay will not attempt to resolve: How much deterrence is needed? *** [S]ome economists argue that to truly deter, the expected penalty should equal the expected social harm. Yet, this in turn raises even more perplexing questions: What is the overall social harm in securities fraud? How should it be measured?

Here, one school of thought tends to view the harm as simply the loss to the victimized investors, whose loss is more or less counterbalanced by the gains received by the usually equally innocent investors on the other side of these transactions. But this is overly narrow and myopic accounting. The deeper problem in securities fraud is the impact of fraud on investor confidence and thus the cost of equity capital. Here, it is impossible to quantify the impact of any individual scandal, but clearly the cumulative impact of Enron, WorldCom, and a host of other scandals in the 2000 to 2002 era made stockholders wary, chilled the initial public offering market, and caused investors to demand a higher return based on the perceived higher risks – in short, the cost of capital rose. When the cost of capital rises, the economy as a whole suffers, as Gross National Product declines or stagnates, and unemployment may increase. As a result, not only investors, but also citizens throughout society experience a loss. In addition, fundamental misallocations of resources may result because of what might best be termed a "contagion effect." That is, companies in the same industry may feel compelled to copy the accounting tricks of an industry leader, lest their stock price fall far behind and they become a takeover target. Other firms may simply abandon a market or industry in the belief that they cannot effectively compete with the seemingly dominant competitor (who is in fact using crooked accounting). Considerable evidence suggests that Enron and WorldCom had this impact on other firms within their respective industries. ***

> *[Professor Coffee goes on to offer a number of proposals that would shift the incidence of damage awards in securities class actions to agents/mangers of the corporation rather than the corporation itself.]*

All the prior proposals in this section pale in comparison to this final recommendation: The SEC can and should exempt the non-trading corporate issuer from private liability for monetary damages under Rule 10b-5. Effectively, this would require plaintiffs' attorneys to sue the corporate insiders and the corporation's gatekeepers (e.g., its investment bankers, auditors, and attorneys), not the issuer, in order to obtain their recovery. At a stroke, this would eliminate entity insurance (because the corporation now could not be sued), and it would compel the insider defendants to apply to the corporation for indemnification when they settled (thereby activating the board's role in monitoring indemnification requests). Today, the board seldom has to face the issue of indemnification because the corporation contributes the entire settlement and then turns to its insurer for repayment.

But does the SEC have the authority to "disimply" Rule 10b-5 – that is, to deny a private cause of action under it? This issue has been elaborately debated in the past. But whether these earlier advocates were right or wrong is no longer the issue. Following an earlier debate over the Commission's authority, Congress in 1996 added section 36 ("General Exemptive Authority") to the Securities Exchange Act of 1934, which authorizes the SEC to "conditionally or unconditionally exempt any person, security, or transaction, or any class or classes of persons, securities, or transactions, from any provision or provisions of this chapter or of any rule or regulation thereunder, to the extent that such exemption is necessary or appropriate in the public interest, and is consistent with the protection of investors."

Because Rule 10b-5 is a rule under the Exchange Act, the Commission's authority to grant an exemption from it seems clear on the face of the statute, so long as the Commission can plausibly make the requisite findings. If this Essay's analysis is correct, Rule 10b-5 litigation in the secondary market "stock drop" context essentially produces pocket-shifting wealth transfers that injure shareholders and do not protect the public interest. Predictably, some will respond that exempting the corporation will create a haven for fraud. But this is a shallow response. Because no exemption would be given to those officers, employees, or agents who act on the corporation's behalf or who control it, the real impact of such an exemption would not be to end Rule 10b-5 litigation, but to focus it on the culpable. Exempting the non-trading corporation from Rule 10b-5 litigation effectively moves us at least a significant distance from a system of enterprise liability toward a system of managerial liability.

Of course, such a change would also alter the market for D&O insurance. Now threatened, executives would demand more insurance and would reexamine the corporation's bylaws to make certain they were guaranteed broad indemnification rights. Such insurance would fund sufficiently large recoveries to continue to motivate plaintiffs' attorneys to bring suit (even if the overall scale of the recoveries might decline). Because of the SEC's ban on indemnification of securities law liabilities (when they result in judgments), executives would remain under strong pressure to settle and to seek indemnification. Outside directors would thus be required to consider carefully and dispassionately whether these defendants acted "in good faith" and in a manner "reasonably believed to be in or not opposed to the best interests of the corporation."[183] Alternatively, insider defendants might forego indemnification and simply rely on their insurance policies, but now they would face a heightened danger that the insurer would seek to cancel the policy for fraud in the application. Although plaintiffs' attorneys will predictably collude with defendants to resist any attempt to terminate the insurance policy, these disputes are still likely to be settled on a basis that places some liability on the individual defendant. Minimum deductibles on D&O insurance policies might also come into greater use. At this point, real deterrence would begin to emerge.

Finally, the limited exemption from Rule 10b-5 here contemplated would not apply when the corporation sold its shares during the class period. In such cases, the corporation is benefiting from the fraud and should sensibly be made a cost bearer. This position is consistent with the SEC's own position on financial penalties.

---

183. This is the language of Del. Code Ann. tit. § 145(a) (2001).

Some will respond that executives will not bear greater risk without demanding higher compensation. But the contemporary evidence is that executives already receive high rents in the form of executive compensation, and the danger that individuals would be deterred from becoming chief executive seems laughably remote.

The key idea is that by removing the corporate defendant from most Rule 10b-5 cases, we reduce the extent to which it serves as the residual cost bearer and thereby passes the costs of the litigation onto the shareholders.

To the extent that contemporary securities litigation imposes its costs almost exclusively on the corporation and its insurers, this system benefits three sets of actors – corporate insiders, plaintiffs' attorneys, and insurance companies – but not shareholders. Viewed in this way, the plaintiff's attorney is less a champion of shareholders and more a participant in a process by which the parties shift liabilities created by corporate managers onto shareholders through the medium of costly insurance paid for by shareholders. Because the repeat players – managers, attorneys, and insurers – all benefit from this system, it remains stable, and the outcome is usually the same: settlement.***

Of course, this would increase the risk that plaintiffs' attorneys assumed in such litigation, and it might scale down the recoveries. Precisely for this reason, attorneys' fees should be higher with regard to that percentage of the settlement that comes from officers and third parties in order to incentivize the plaintiffs' bar to pursue personal liability against such persons. Once securities litigation becomes more adversarial than it is today, the next step would be for the SEC to recognize that the settlement of a securities class action represents an acute conflict of interest, one requiring independent directors to review it as carefully as they would a management buy out proposal.

For the SEC to take such action and curtail private Rule 10b-5 litigation, it must first acknowledge an inescapable fact: The securities class action is unlikely to afford significant compensation to shareholders. That realization should lead not to the abolition of the class action (as some critics have proposed), but to its reconfiguration into a mechanism for deterrence. Deterrence through private enforcement is possible, but punishing the victim is both unnecessary and unjust. ***

The debate about securities class actions continues to be volatile and full of surprises. As reported on the front page of the Wall Street Journal, the SEC was "exploring a new policy that could permit companies to resolve complaints by aggrieved shareholders through arbitration, limiting shareholders' ability to sue in court." Kara Scannell, SEC Explores A Wider Role for Arbitration – Agency May Consider Letting Firms Head Off Lawsuits by Investors, Wall St. J. at A1 (April 16, 2007). The SEC's Chairman, however, later clarified in congressional testimony that no such policy was pending before the Commission. Is mandatory arbitration of securities class actions an idea worth pursuing? See generally Barbara Black, Eliminating Securities Fraud Class Actions Under the Radar, 2009 Colum. Bus. L. Rev. 802.

Chapter 7

INSIDER TRADING

> "This is not securities litigation. This is cops and robbers. The issue is, 'Did you get the information and did you trade on it.'"
>
> Former U.S. Attorney for the S.D.N.Y. Otto G. Obermaier, quoted in Stephen Labaton and David Leonhardt, Whispers Inside, Thunder Outside: A New Hunt is on for Insider Trading, N.Y. Times at C1, 14, June 30, 2002

> "Unfortunately from what I can see,*** illegal insider trading is rampant and may even be on the rise. And the people who are cheating the system include bad actors not only at Wall Street firms, but also at Main Street companies."
>
> U.S. Attorney for the S.D.N.Y. Preet Bharara before the New York City Bar Association, October 20, 2010 (prepared remarks)

The media tends to follow closely allegations of insider trading because the public enjoys the drama generated by the government's investigations and prosecutions. Much attention, for example, was directed at the home designer-entrepreneur Martha Stewart, and the former CEO of ImClone Systems, Dr. Samuel Waksal, whose stock trades or attempted trades were the subject of high-profile investigations and prosecutions by the SEC and the Department of Justice (DOJ). More recently, the spotlight has focused on hedge funds and their possible use of material nonpublic information received in the form of tips from Wall Street employees and "expert network" consultants with routine access to confidential information. For weeks and months on end, newspaper headlines were fixated on the prosecution – and ultimate conviction – of billionaire hedge fund manager Raj Rajaratnam, the co-founder of the Galleon Group. The media was likewise abuzz over his intricate web of tippers and traders, more than two dozen of whom ultimately were convicted of or pled guilty to securities fraud.

Although it is impossible to deny the "cops and robbers" aspect of investigations and prosecutions for insider trading, it also is important to recognize that insider trading raises complex questions under the federal securities laws. This Chapter highlights such complexities by tracing the development of the law of insider trading, and by posing questions and problems that require application of doctrine to specific facts. Section A discusses early attempts by state courts, Congress, and lower federal courts to deal with the problem of insider trading under the common law and the federal securities laws. Section B then turns to the Supreme Court decisions establishing or endorsing the classical and misappropriation theories of insider trading liability under Rule 10b-5 and examines lower court decisions and SEC rulemaking that build on those decisions. Section C focuses on Rule 14e-3's prohibition of insider trading in connection with tender offers and explores whether the rule constitutes a valid exercise of SEC authority. The Insider Trading Sanctions Act of 1984 (ITSA) and the Insider Trading and Securities Fraud Enforcement Act of 1988 (ITSFEA) are discussed in Section D. Section E highlights the difficulties often faced in cases where proof of insider trading must be established by circumstantial evidence. And Section F examines Regulation FD, an SEC initiative designed to prevent the practice of trading securities based on selectively disclosed information.

As you read and analyze the material in these first six sections, keep in mind the following questions: What, if anything, is wrong with insider trading? Who is harmed by the practice? Does insider trading produce any benefits (other than, of course, the profits to the traders)? Does the offense merit severe sanction? Prison sentences? These fundamental policy issues will be revisited in Section G at the conclusion of the Chapter.

A. INITIAL EFFORTS TO COMBAT AND CURTAIL INSIDER TRADING

1. Insider Trading Under the Common Law

The earliest litigation in the United States over insider trading took the form of lawsuits filed in state court by shareholders against corporate officers and directors under a theory of fraudulent nondisclosure. Although an affirmative misstatement is generally required for a plaintiff to plead and prove common law fraud, courts have long recognized a number of circumstances under which a defendant's "pure silence" about material facts in a business transaction may constitute fraudulent or deceptive conduct. One such circumstance involves transactions in which the parties stand in a fiduciary relationship.

Common law courts, however, varied widely on the question of whether shareholders stood in a fiduciary relationship with corporate insiders. Under the so-called "majority rule," a traditional insider of a corporation (such as an officer or director) was said to owe fiduciary duties to the corporation itself but not to individual shareholders of the corporation. Thus, in most jurisdictions, corporate insiders were free to remain silent about material facts in transactions with shareholders, and could freely exploit whatever informational advantage they were fortunate enough to possess. See, e.g., *Bawden v. Taylor*, 98 N.E. 941, 942 (Ill. 1912); *Barth v. Fid. & Columbia Trust Co.*, 224 S.W. 351, 356 (Ky. 1920). See also Fletcher Cyc. Corp § 1168.10 (Perm. Ed) (citing cases and concluding that "[t]he 'majority rule' is that directors do not occupy a trust relation with shareholders with respect to their shares because dealing in the corporation's stock is not a corporate function").

The common law "minority rule," in contrast, viewed officers and directors as fiduciaries not only to the corporation but also to its shareholders. Thus, as a fiduciary, a traditional insider was obligated to share with an ignorant shareholder all material facts in his possession prior to consummating a transaction. See, e.g., *Dawson v. Nat'l Life Ins. Co.*, 157 N.W. 929, 938 (Iowa 1916) (recognizing cause of action for fraud in securities trading when corporate officer fails to make "full disclosure of all facts bearing thereon known to such officer and unknown to the shareholder"); *Stewart v. Harris*, 77 P. 277, 281 (Kan. 1904) (holding that "before any director or managing officer *** can rightfully purchase the stock of one not actively engaged in the management of its affairs, such director or managing officer must inform such stockholder of the true condition of the affairs of the corporation").

Other jurisdictions purposefully sidestepped the fiduciary duty issue, and scrutinized acts of insider trading under the so-called "special facts" doctrine, which imposed disclosure duties when one party to a transaction had access to highly significant facts that were unknown to the other party. See, e.g., *Strong v. Repide*, 213 U.S. 419 (1908). However, because it was often a traditional insider's status that provided him with access to "special facts," legal analysis under the minority rule and special facts doctrine often tended to blend together. In *Strong v. Repide*, for example, the Supreme Court granted recission in a case where the plaintiff-shareholder had sold her stock to an agent of the defendant-insider. The company soon after concluded negotiations to sell valuable real estate to the Philippine government, thereby substantially increasing the worth of the company's shares. The Court had no trouble finding that "the negotiations and their probable result were a most material fact affecting the value of the shares of stock of the company." Id. at 432. The Court also found that the plaintiff's agent "would not have sold them at the price he did had he known the actual state of the negotiations as to the lands and that it was the defendant who was seeking to purchase the stock." Id. The Court stated further:

> That the defendant was a director of the corporation is but one of the facts upon which the liability is asserted, the existence of all the others in addition making such a combination as rendered it the plain duty of the defendant to speak. He was not only a director, but he owned three-fourths of the shares of its stock, and was, at the time of the purchase of the stock, administrator general of the company, with large powers, and engaged in the negotiations which finally led to the sale of the company's lands (together with all the other friar lands) to the Government at a price which very greatly enhanced the value of the stock. He was the chief negotiator for the sale of all the lands, and was acting substantially as the agent of the shareholders of his company by reason of his ownership of the shares of stock in the corporation and by the acquiescence of all the other shareholders, and the negotiations were for the sale of the whole of the property of the company. By reason of such ownership and agency, and his participation as such owner and agent in the negotiations then going on, no one knew as well as he the exact condition of such negotiations. No one knew as well as he the probability of the sale of the lands to the Government. No one knew as well as he the probable price that might be obtained on such sale. The lands were the only valuable asset owned by the company. *** Concealing his identity when procuring the purchase of the stock, by his agent, was in itself strong evidence of fraud on the part of the defendant. *** If, under all these facts, he purchased the stock from the plaintiff, the law would indeed be impotent if the sale could not be set aside or the defendant cast in damages for his fraud. ***

Id. at 431-33.

Plaintiffs alleging insider trading under the common law of fraud and deceit had other hurdles to scale, even in those jurisdictions that generally adhered to the minority rule or special facts doctrine. Two principles, in particular, limited a court's ability to impose liability for an insider's fraudulent nondisclosure. First, officers and directors were said to owe shareholders a disclosure duty only in face-to-face securities transactions. The minority rule and the special facts doctrine thus left insider trading in impersonal markets unfettered. See *Goodwin v. Agassiz*, 186 N.E. 659, 660 (Mass. 1933) (refusing to recognize the breach of a disclosure duty when the traditional insider's securities transactions were carried out over the Boston Stock Exchange). The court in *Goodwin* noted that:

> The identity of the buyers and seller of the stock in question in fact was not known to the parties and perhaps could not readily have been ascertained. The defendants caused the shares to be bought through brokers on the stock exchange. They said nothing to anybody as to the reasons actuating them. The plaintiff was no novice. He was a member of the Boston stock exchange and had kept record of sales of [the company] stock. *** He made no inquiries of the defendants or of other officers of the company. The result is that the plaintiff cannot prevail.

Id. at 661-62. The other limiting principle was that traditional insiders were regarded as fiduciaries only with respect to those investors with pre-existing relationships with the corporation. Thus, even in minority rule jurisdictions, there was nothing to prevent corporate insiders from selling their stock to investors who did not already own shares in the corporation. See A.C. Pritchard, *United States v. O'Hagan*: Agency Law and Justice Powell's Legacy for the Law of Insider Trading, 78 B.U. L. Rev. 13, 26 (1998) (noting that "the fiduciary obligation of corporate officers and directors *** does not extend to prospective shareholders who may purchase their shares for the first time when an insider sells").

Mitigating the harshness of these common law limitations on recovery for fraud and deceit, a number of jurisdictions—notably Delaware, see *Brophy v. Cities Service Co.*, 70 A.2d 5, 8 (Del. Ch. 1949) and New York, see *Diamond v. Oreamuno*, 248 N.E.2d 910, 912 (N.Y. 1969)—permitted shareholders to institute derivative actions against officers and directors who had used the corporation's confidential information to reap "secret profits" in securities transactions. The Court in *Diamond* explained its decision in the following manner:

> It is well established, as a general proposition, that a person who acquires special knowledge or information by virtue of a confidential or fiduciary relationship with another is not free to exploit that knowledge or information for his own personal benefit but must account to his principal for any profits derived therefrom. This, in turn, is merely a corollary of the broader principle, inherent in the nature of the fiduciary relationship, that prohibits a trustee or agent from extracting secret profits from his position of trust.
>
> ***[T]he defendants take the position that, although it is admittedly wrong for an officer or director to use his position to obtain trading profits for himself in the stock of his corporation, the action ascribed to them did not injure or damage [the corporation] in any way. Accordingly, the defendants continue, the corporation should not be permitted to recover the proceeds. They acknowledge that, by virtue of the exclusive access which officers and directors

> have to inside information, they possess an unfair advantage over other shareholders and, particularly, the persons who had purchased the stock from them but, they contend, the corporation itself was unaffected and, for that reason, a derivative action is an inappropriate remedy.
>
> It is true that the complaint before us does not contain any allegation of damages to the corporation but this has never been considered to be an essential requirement for a cause of action founded on a breach of fiduciary duty. This is because the function of such an action, unlike an ordinary tort or contract case, is not merely to compensate the plaintiff for wrongs committed by the defendant but, as this court declared many years ago "to *prevent* them, by removing from agents and trustees all inducement to attempt dealing for their own benefit in matters which they have undertaken for others, or to which their agency or trust relates."
>
> Just as a trustee has no right to retain for himself the profits yielded by property placed in his possession but must account to his beneficiaries, a corporate fiduciary, who is entrusted with potentially valuable information, may not appropriate that asset for his own use even though, in so doing, he causes no injury to the corporation. The primary concern, in a case such as this, is not to determine whether the corporation has been damaged but to decide, as between the corporation and the defendants, who has a higher claim to the proceeds derived from the exploitation of the information. In our opinion, there can be no justification for permitting officers and directors, such as the defendants, to retain for themselves profits which, it is alleged, they derived solely from exploiting information gained by virtue of their inside position as corporate officials.
>
> In addition, it is pertinent to observe that, despite the lack of any specific allegation of damage, it may well be inferred that the defendants' actions might have caused some harm to the enterprise. Although the corporation may have little concern with the day-to-day transactions in its shares, it has a great interest in maintaining a reputation of integrity, an image of probity, for its management and in insuring the continued public acceptance and marketability of its stock. When officers and directors abuse their position in order to gain personal profits, the effect may be to cast a cloud on the corporation's name, injure stockholder relations and undermine public regard for the corporation's securities. ***

Id. at 912. As you read the *O'Hagan* decision set out in Section B.3 of this Chapter, consider the extent to which the intellectual underpinnings of what is today known as the "misappropriation theory" of insider trading liability can be traced to "secret profits" cases like *Diamond* and *Brophy*. Why might shareholders prefer to file derivative actions in state court rather than federal actions against officers and directors under Rule 10b-5? For a recent decision reaffirming *Brophy* and holding that derivative plaintiffs may assert insider trading claims without pleading harm to the corporation, see *Kahn v. Kolberg Kravis Roberts & Co., L.P.*, 23 A.3d. 831, 840 (Del. 2011) ("Delaware law dictates that the scope of recovery for a breach of the duty of loyalty is not to be determined narrowly, [and] we find no reasonable public policy ground to restrict the scope of disgorgement remedy in *Brophy* cases—irrespective of arguably parallel remedies grounded in federal securities law") (internal quotes omitted).

2. *A Brief Look at Section 16(b)*

The legislative history of the Exchange Act reveals that the problem of insider trading was very much on the minds of its congressional drafters. Yet, rather than defining the offense of insider trading and prohibiting it outright, Congress chose only to regulate certain trading practices of officers, directors, and shareholders beneficially owning more than 10 percent of issuers with a security registered pursuant to Section 12 of the Exchange Act. The congressional concern with these key "insiders" is reflected in the following passage from the 1934 Report of the Senate Banking and Currency Committee:

> Among the most vicious practices unearthed at the hearings before the subcommittee was the flagrant betrayal of their fiduciary duties by directors and officers of corporations who used their positions of trust and the confidential information which came to them in such positions, to aid them in their market activities. Closely allied to this type of abuse was the unscrupulous employment of inside information by large stockholders who, while not directors and officers, exercised sufficient control over the destinies of their companies to enable them to acquire and profit by information not available to others.

S. Rep. No. 73-1455 at 55 (1934). Section 16 of the Exchange Act constitutes Congress's initial solution to the problem of insider trading.

Section 16(a) imposes a reporting obligation upon every officer or director of a company with an equity security registered under Section 12 of the Exchange Act, as well as every person "who is directly or indirectly the beneficial owner of more than 10 percent of any class of any equity security" so registered. Pursuant to this obligation, such high level insiders must file with the SEC an initial report on Form 3 within ten days of becoming an officer, director, or 10 percent beneficial shareholder of the corporation. When such persons change their beneficial ownership (either through purchases or sales of the company's equity securities), they must file supplementary reports on a Form 4 within two business days. This two business day requirement was a statutory change brought about by the Sarbanes-Oxley Act of 2002. Prior to that legislation, Form 4 reports were required to be filed within ten days of the close of each calendar month in which any additional purchases or sales of the corporation's equity securities had been made. What factors may have prompted Congress to substantially shorten the filing deadline?

To be sure, the mere obligation to report all purchases and sales in a corporation's equity securities is bound to deter some insiders from trading on the basis of confidential corporate information. But Congress intended the principal deterrent for insider trading to stem from Section 16(b), which makes officers, directors, and 10 percent shareholders liable to the corporation, or to shareholders suing on its behalf, for any profits they obtain from "short swing" trading of the corporation's stock. Specifically, Section 16(b) provides that:

> For the purpose of preventing the unfair use of information which may have been obtained by such beneficial owner, director, or officer by reason of his relationship to the issuer, any profit realized by him from any purchase and sale, or any sale and purchase, of any equity security of such issuer (other than an exempted security) *** within any period of less than six months, unless such security *** was acquired in good faith in connection with a debt previously contracted, shall inure to and be recoverable by the issuer, irrespective of any intention on the part of such beneficial owner, director, or

> officer in entering into such transaction of holding the security *** purchased or of not repurchasing the security *** sold for a period exceeding six months.

The reporting obligation imposed on insiders by Section 16(a) substantially assists the corporation and its shareholders with enforcing the disgorgement provision in Section 16(b).

Obviously, as it relates to insider trading, Section 16(b)'s disgorgement net is both too wide and too narrow: it catches legitimate trades by corporate insiders who lack any knowledge of material nonpublic information, and it allows to slip through those trades that *are* based on inside information when the insider has sold stock that was held for at least six months, or when the insider is patient enough to wait for six months to reap the profit off a new purchase. Indeed, as the Second Circuit recently emphasized, Section 16(b) "operates mechanically, and makes no moral distinctions, penalizing technical violators of pure heart, and bypassing corrupt insiders who skirt the letter of the prohibition." *Magma Power Co. v. Dow Chem. Co.*, 136 F.3d 316, 320-21 (2d Cir. 1998). For the view that Congress had additional objectives in enacting Section 16, see Steve Thel, The Genius of Section 16: Regulating the Management of Publicly Held Companies, 42 Hastings L. J. 391, 399, 414-15 (1991) (contending that "[t]hose who secured the enactment of Section 16 *** were probably more concerned with reforming the way public corporations conduct their business than with the interests of securities traders. *** Section 16 works to focus the attention of corporate managers on corporate business. Automatic forfeiture of short-swing profits eliminates the incentive to speculate for the short swing, and thus helps to keep corporate managers from being distracted from the business of running publicly held companies"). See also Karl S. Okamoto, Rereading Section 16(b) of the Securities Exchange Act, 27 Ga. L. Rev. 183, 205 (1992) (stating that "[s]ince the market will view [an insider's] trading as a signal of information, the insider can manipulate stock prices simply by trading. *** [The six-month limit] serves as the basis for a presumption as to the motivation of the insider trader. If an insider reverses her position within six months, it is more likely that her initial trading was itself a false signal").

Because of its unduly wide and narrow net, Section 16(b) was only somewhat successful in preventing officers and directors from trading corporate stock on the basis of material nonpublic information. But after the SEC promulgated Rule 10b-5 in 1942, another—and very wide—federal regulatory avenue opened. The text of Rule 10b-5 is set out on page 23 in Chapter 2.

3. *Insider Trading as a Violation of Rule 10b-5*

Like common law fraud and deceit actions brought by shareholders against traditional insiders, the first Rule 10b-5 cases that permitted shareholders to sue a traditional insider for insider trading involved face-to-face securities transactions. In *Kardon v. Nat'l Gympsum Co.*, 73 F. Supp. 798 (E.D. Penn. 1947), the first decision to recognize a private right of action under Section 10(b) and Rule 10b-5, the court expressly held that "these provisions apply to directors and officers who, in purchasing the stock of the corporation from others, fail to disclose a fact coming to their knowledge by reason of their position, which would materially affect the judgment of the other party to the transaction." Id. at 800. The two plaintiffs in *Kardon* had sold their stock directly to the defendant-insiders who had been in possession of material, nonpublic information.

The scope of Rule 10b-5 expanded quite extraordinarily in 1961 when the Commission decided *In re Cady, Roberts & Co.*, 40 SEC 907 (1961). The Enforcement Division of the SEC brought this landmark case as an administrative broker-dealer disciplinary proceeding against a brokerage firm and a securities broker employed by that firm. The Enforcement Division alleged that the broker had engaged in fraud by selling on the NYSE a company's securities (held in personal and client accounts) on the basis of confidential bad news about a reduction in dividends that had been tipped to the broker by a director of the company. After an administrative hearing, the Commission held that Rule 10b-5 prohibited the tippee-broker's stock sales because "insiders must disclose material facts which are known to them by virtue of their position but which are not known to persons with whom they deal." Id. at 911. The Commission opined that:

> Analytically, the obligation [to disclose or abstain] rests on two principal elements; first, the existence of a relationship giving access, directly or indirectly, to information intended to be available only for a corporate purpose and not for the personal benefit of anyone, and second, the inherent unfairness involved where a party takes advantage of such information knowing it is unavailable to those with whom he is dealing.

Id. at 912. Thus, in *Cady, Roberts*, the Commission construed the term "insider" quite broadly to include those persons, such as the tippee-broker before it, who were in positions of access to confidential corporate information. The Commission also construed Rule 10b-5 to support a broad definition of fraud that was not limited by the common law distinction between face-to-face transactions and stock market trading. Even today, commentators continue to be struck by the Commission's groundbreaking decision to bring an administrative enforcement action against the tippee-broker and by the "new corporation law" that was announced in its decision. See Donald C. Langevoort, Rereading *Cady, Roberts*: The Ideology and Practice of Insider Trading Regulation, 99 Colum. L. Rev. 1319, 1320 (1999) (quoting *Cady, Roberts*, 40 SEC at 910).

In the years following *Cady, Roberts*, the Commission continued to expand the scope of the duty to disclose or abstain from securities trading while in possession of material nonpublic information. See, e.g., *In re Investors Mgmt. Co.*, 44 SEC 633 (1971), where the Commission imposed Rule 10b-5 liability against non-insider securities professionals who knew or had reason to know that the information they possessed was confidential.

The view that insider trading over anonymous securities markets constitutes a violation of Rule 10b-5 also won acceptance from the federal courts, particularly in the Second Circuit.

SEC v. TEXAS GULF SULPHUR CO.

401 F.2d 833 (2d Cir. 1968, en banc)

STERRY R. WATERMAN, CIRCUIT JUDGE:

This action was commenced in the United States District Court for the Southern District of New York by the Securities and Exchange Commission (the SEC) pursuant to Sec. 21(e) of the Securities Exchange Act of 1934 (the Act) against Texas Gulf Sulphur Company (TGS) and several of its officers, directors and employees, to enjoin certain conduct *** said to violate Section 10(b) of the Act and Rule 10b-5 (the Rule), promulgated thereunder ***. The complaint alleged (1) that defendants Fogarty, Mollison, Darke, Murray, Huntington, O'Neill, Clayton, Crawford, and Coates had either personally or through agents purchased TGS stock or calls thereon from November 12, 1963 through April 16, 1964 on the basis of material inside information concerning the results of TGS drilling in Timmins, Ontario, while such information remained undisclosed to the investing public generally or to the particular sellers; [and] (2) that defendants Darke and Coates had divulged such information to others for use in purchasing TGS stock or calls[3] or recommended its purchase while the information was undisclosed to the public or to the sellers; ***

THE FACTUAL SETTING

This action derives from the exploratory activities of TGS begun in 1957 on the Canadian Shield in eastern Canada. In March of 1959, aerial geophysical surveys were conducted over more than 15,000 square miles of this area by a group led by defendant Mollision, a mining engineer and a Vice President of TGS. The group included defendant Holyk, TGS's chief geologist, defendant Clayton, an electrical engineer and geophysicist, and defendant Darke, a geologist. These operations resulted in the detection of numerous anomalies, i.e., extraordinary variations in the conductivity of rocks, one of which was on the Kidd 55 segment of land located near Timmins, Ontario.

On October 29 and 30, 1963, Clayton conducted a ground geophysical survey on the northeast portion of the Kidd 55 segment which confirmed the presence of an anomaly and indicated the necessity of diamond core drilling for further evaluation. Drilling of the initial hole, K-55-1, at the strongest part of the anomaly was commenced on November 8 and terminated on November 12 at a depth of 655 feet. Visual estimates by Holyk of the core of K-55-1 indicated an average copper content of 1.15% and an average zinc content of 8.64% over a length of 599 feet. This visual estimate convinced TGS that it was desirable to acquire the remainder of the Kidd 55 segment, and in order to facilitate this acquisition TGS President Stephens instructed the exploration group to keep the results of K-55-1 confidential and undisclosed even as to other officers, directors, and employees of TGS. The hole was concealed and a barren core was intentionally drilled off the anomaly. Meanwhile, the core of K-55-1 had been shipped to Utah for chemical assay which, when received in early December, revealed an average mineral content of 1.18% copper, 8.26% zinc, and 3.94% ounces of silver per ton over a length of 602 feet. These results were so remarkable that neither Clayton, an experienced geophysicist, nor four other TGS expert witnesses, had ever seen or heard of a comparable initial exploratory drill hole in a base metal deposit. *** By March 27, 1964, TGS decided that the land acquisition program had advanced to such a point that the company might well resume drilling, and drilling was resumed on March 31.

---

3. A "call" is a negotiable option contract by which the bearer has the right to buy from the writer of the contract a certain number of shares of a particular stock at a fixed price on or before a certain agreed-upon date.

During this period, from November 12, 1963 when K-55-1 was completed, to March 31, 1964 when drilling was resumed, certain of the individual defendants *** and persons *** said to have received "tips" from them, purchased TGS stock or calls thereon. Prior to these transactions these persons had owned 1135 shares of TGS stock and possessed no calls; thereafter they owned a total of 8235 shares and possessed 12,300 calls.***

When drilling was resumed on March 31, hole K-55-3 was commenced***. Daily progress reports of the drilling of this hole K-55-3 and of all subsequently drilled holes were sent to defendants Stephens and Fogarty (President and Executive Vice President of TGS) by Holyk and Mollison. Visual estimates of K-55-3 revealed an average mineral content of 1.12% copper and 7.93% zinc over 641 of the hole's 876-foot length. On April 7, drilling of a third hole, K-55-4, *** was commenced and mineralization was encountered over 366 of its 579-foot length. Visual estimates indicated an average content of 1.14% copper and 8.24% zinc. Like K-55-1, both K-55-3 and K-55-4 established substantial copper mineralization on the eastern edge of the anomaly. On the basis of these findings relative to the foregoing drilling results, the trial court concluded *** that "There was real evidence that a body of commercially mineable ore might exist." Id. at 281- 82.

On April 8 TGS began with a second drill rig to drill another hole, K-55-6, 300 feet easterly of K-55-1.*** While no visual estimates of its core were immediately available, it was readily apparent by the evening of April 10 that substantial copper mineralization had been encountered over the last 127 feet of the hole's 569-foot length. On April 10, a third drill rig commenced drilling yet another hole, K-55-5 ***. By the evening of April 10 in this hole, too, substantial copper mineralization had been encountered over the last 42 feet of its 97-foot length.

Meanwhile, rumors that a major ore strike was in the making had been circulating throughout Canada. On the morning of Saturday, April 11, Stephens at his home in Greenwich, Conn. read in the New York Herald Tribune and in the New York Times unauthorized reports of the TGS drilling which seemed to infer a rich strike from the fact that the drill cores had been flown to the United States for chemical assay. Stephens immediately contacted Fogarty at his home in Rye, N.Y., who in turn telephoned and later that day visited Mollison at Mollison's home in Greenwich to obtain a current report and evaluation of the drilling progress. The following morning, Sunday, Fogarty again telephoned Mollison, inquiring whether Mollison had any further information and told him to return to Timmins with Holyk, the TGS Chief Geologist, as soon as possible "to move things along." With the aid of one Carroll, a public relations consultant, Fogarty drafted a press release designed to quell the rumors, which release, after having been channeled through Stephens and Huntington, a TGS attorney, was issued at 3:00 P.M. on Sunday, April 12, and which appeared in the morning newspapers of general circulation on Monday, April 13.

*[The press release was rather gloomy and downplayed the significance to the company of the exploratory activities. Later in the opinion, in a section omitted here but discussed in Chapter 2.C supra, the court held that the company had violated Rule 10b-5 through the issuance of this materially misleading press release.]****

Meanwhile, drilling operations continued. By morning of April 13, in K-55-5, the fifth drill hole, substantial copper mineralization had been encountered *** [and] [v]isual estimates revealed an average content of 0.82% copper and 4.2% zinc over a 525-foot section. Also by 7:00 A.M. on April 13, K-55-6 had found mineralization to the 946-foot mark. On April 12 a fourth drill rig began to drill K-55-7 ***

While drilling activity ensued to completion, TGC officials were taking steps toward ultimate disclosure of the discovery. On April 13, a previously-invited reporter for The Northern Miner, a Canadian mining industry journal, visited the drillsite, interviewed Mollison, Holyk and Darke, and prepared an article which confirmed a 10 million ton ore strike. This report, after having been submitted to Mollison and returned to the reporter unamended on April 15, was published in the April 16 issue. A statement relative to the extent of the discovery, in substantial part drafted by Mollison, was given to the Ontario Minister of Mines for release to the Canadian media. Mollison and Holyk expected it to be released over the airways at 11 P.M. on April 15th, but, for undisclosed reasons, it was not released until 9:40 A.M. on the 16th. An official detailed statement, announcing a strike of at least 25 million tons of ore, based on the drilling data set forth above, was read to representatives of American financial media from 10:00 A.M. to 10:10 or 10:15 A.M. on April 16, and appeared over Merrill Lynch's private wire at 10:29 A.M. and, somewhat later than expected, over the Dow Jones ticker tape at 10:54 A.M.

Between the time the first press release was issued on April 12 and the dissemination of the TGS official announcement on the morning of April 16, the only defendants before us on appeal who engaged in market activity were Clayton and Crawford and TGS director Coates. Clayton ordered 200 shares of TGS stock through his Canadian broker on April 15 and the order was executed that day over the Midwest Stock Exchange. Crawford ordered 300 shares at midnight on the 15th and another 300 shares at 8:30 A.M. the next day, and these orders were executed over the Midwest Exchange in Chicago at its opening on April 16. Coates left the TGS press conference and called his broker son-in-law Haemisegger shortly before 10:20 A.M. on the 16th and ordered 2,000 shares of TGS for family trust accounts of which Coates was a trustee but not a beneficiary; Haemisegger executed this order over the New York and Midwest Exchanges, and he and his customers purchased 1500 additional shares.

During the period of drilling in Timmins, the market price of TGS stock fluctuated but steadily gained overall. On Friday, November 8, when the drilling began, the stock closed at 17 3/8 ; on Friday, November 15, after K- 55-1 had been completed, it closed at 18. After a slight decline to 16 3/8 by Friday, November 22, the price rose to 20 7/8 by December 13, when the chemical assay results of K-55-1 were received, and closed at a high of 24 1/8 on February 21 ***. It had reached a price of 26 by March 31, after the land acquisition program had been completed and drilling had been resumed, and continued to ascend to 30 1/8 by the close of trading on April 10, at which time the drilling progress up to then was evaluated for the April 12th press release. On April 13, the day on which the April 12 release was disseminated, TGS opened at 30 1/8, rose immediately to a high of 32 and gradually tapered off to close at 30 7/8. It closed at 30 1/4 the next day, and at 29 3/8 on April 15. On April 16, the day of the official announcement of the Timmins discovery, the price climbed to a high of 37 and closed at 36 3/8. By May 15, TGS stock was selling at 58 1/4.

I. THE INDIVIDUAL DEFENDANTS

A. Introductory

Rule 10b-5 on which this action is predicated *** was promulgated pursuant to the grant of authority given the SEC by Congress in Section 10(b) of the Securities Exchange Act of 1934. By that Act Congress purposed to prevent inequitable and unfair practices and to insure fairness in securities transactions generally, whether conducted face-to-face, over the counter, or on exchanges. The Act and the Rule apply to the transactions here, all of which were consummated on exchanges. Whether predicated on traditional fiduciary concepts, see, e.g., *Hotchkiss v. Fisher*, 136 Kan. 530, 16 P.2d 531 (Kan.1932), or on the "special facts" doctrine, see, e.g., *Strong v. Repide*, 213 U.S. 419 (1909), the Rule is based in policy on the justifiable expectation of the securities marketplace that all investors trading on impersonal exchanges have relatively equal access to material information. The essence of the Rule is that anyone who, trading for his own account in the securities of a corporation has "access, directly or indirectly, to information intended to be available only for a corporate purpose and not for the personal benefit of anyone" may not take "advantage of such information knowing it is unavailable to those with whom he is dealing," i.e., the investing public. *Matter of Cady, Roberts & Co.*, 40 SEC 907, 912 (1961). Insiders, as directors or management officers are, of course, by this Rule, precluded from so unfairly dealing, but the Rule is also applicable to one possessing the information who may not be strictly termed an "insider" within the meaning of Sec. 16(b) of the Act. *Cady, Roberts*, supra. Thus, anyone in possession of material inside information must either disclose it to the investing public, or, if he is disabled from disclosing it in order to protect a corporate confidence, or he chooses not to do so, must abstain from trading in or recommending the securities concerned while such inside information remains undisclosed. So, it is here no justification for insider activity that disclosure was forbidden by the legitimate corporate objective of acquiring options to purchase the land surrounding the exploration site; if the information was, as the SEC contends, material, its possessors should have kept out of the market until disclosure was accomplished. *Cady, Roberts*, supra at 911.

B. Material Inside Information

An insider is not, of course, always foreclosed from investing in his own company merely because he may be more familiar with company operations than are outside investors. An insider's duty to disclose information or his duty to abstain from dealing in his company's securities arises only in "those situations which are essentially extraordinary in nature and which are reasonably certain to have a substantial effect on the market price of the security if (the extraordinary situation is) disclosed." Fleischer, Securities Trading and Corporate Information Practices: The Implications of the Texas Gulf Sulphur Proceeding, 51 Va.L.Rev. 1271, 1289 [1965].

Nor is an insider obligated to confer upon outside investors the benefit of his superior financial or other expert analysis by disclosing his educated guesses or predictions. The only regulatory objective is that access to material information be enjoyed equally, but this objective requires nothing more than the disclosure of basic facts so that outsiders may draw upon their own evaluative expertise in reaching their own investment decisions with knowledge equal to that of the insiders.

This is not to suggest *** that the materiality of facts is to be assessed solely by measuring the effect the knowledge of the facts would have upon prudent or conservative investors. *** The speculators and chartists of Wall and Bay Streets are also "reasonable" investors entitled to the same legal protection afforded conservative traders. Thus, material facts include not only information disclosing the earnings and distributions of a company but also those facts which affect the probable future of the company and those which may affect the desire of investors to buy, sell, or hold the company's securities.

In each case, then, whether facts are material within Rule 10b-5 when the facts relate to a particular event and are undisclosed by those persons who are knowledgeable thereof will depend at any given time upon a balancing of both the indicated probability that the event will occur and the anticipated magnitude of the event in light of the totality of the company activity. Here, notwithstanding the trial court's conclusion that the results of the first drill core, K-55-1, were "too 'remote' *** to have had any significant impact on the market, i.e., to be deemed material," 258 F.Supp. at 283, knowledge of the possibility, which surely was more than marginal, of the existence of a mine of the vast magnitude indicated by the remarkably rich drill core located rather close to the surface (suggesting mineability by the less expensive openpit method) within the confines of a large anomaly (suggesting an extensive region of mineralization) might well have affected the price of TGS stock and would certainly have been an important fact to a reasonable, if speculative, investor in deciding whether he should buy, sell, or hold. After all, this first drill core was "unusually good and ... excited the interest and speculation of those who knew about it." 258 F. Supp. at 282.

Our disagreement with the district judge on the issue does not, then, go to his findings of basic fact, as to which the "clearly erroneous" rule would apply, but to his understanding of the legal standard applicable to them. Our survey of the facts found below conclusively establishes that knowledge of the results of the discovery hole, K-55-1, would have been important to a reasonable investor and might have affected the price of the stock.[12] On April 16, The Northern Miner, a trade publication in wide circulation among mining stock specialists, called K- 55-1, the discovery hole, "one of the most impressive drill

---

12. We do not suggest that material facts must be disclosed immediately; the timing of disclosure is a matter for the business judgment of the corporate officers entrusted with the management of the corporation within the affirmative disclosure requirements promulgated by the exchanges and by the SEC. Here, a valuable corporate purpose was served by delaying the publication of the K-55-1 discovery. We do intend to convey, however, that where a corporate purpose is thus served by withholding the news of a material fact, those persons who are thus quite properly true to their corporate trust must not during the period of non-disclosure deal personally in the corporation's securities or give to outsiders confidential information not generally available to all the corporations' stockholders and to the public at large.

holes completed in modern times." Roche, a Canadian broker whose firm specialized in mining securities, characterized the importance to investors of the results of K-55-1. He stated that the completion of "the first drill hole" with "a 600 foot drill core is very very significant *** anything over 200 feet is considered very significant and 600 feet is just beyond your wildest imagination." He added, however, that it "is a natural thing to buy more stock once they give you the first drill hole." Additional testimony revealed that the prices of stocks of other companies, albeit less diversified, smaller firms, had increased substantially solely on the basis of the discovery of good anomalies or even because of the proximity of their lands to the situs of a potentially major strike. ***

Finally, a major factor in determining whether the K-55-1 discovery was a material fact is the importance attached to the drilling results by those who knew about it. In view of other unrelated recent developments favorably affecting TGS, participation by an informed person in a regular stock-purchase program, or even sporadic trading by an informed person, might lend only nominal support to the inference of the materiality of the K-55-1 discovery; nevertheless, the timing by those who knew of it of their stock purchases and their purchases of *short-term* calls—purchases in some cases by individuals who had never before purchased calls or even TGS stock—virtually compels the inference that the insiders were influenced by the drilling results. This insider trading activity, which surely constitutes highly pertinent evidence and the only truly objective evidence of the materiality of the K-55-1 discovery, was apparently disregarded by the court below in favor of the testimony of defendants' expert witnesses, all of whom "agreed that one drill core does not establish an ore body, much less a mine," 258 F.Supp. at 282- 283. Significantly, however, the court below, while relying upon what these defense experts said the defendant insiders *ought* to have thought about the worth to TGS of the K-55-1 discovery, and finding that from November 12, 1963 to April 6, 1964 Fogarty, Murray, Holyk and Darke spent more than $100,000 in purchasing TGS stock and calls on that stock, made no finding that the insiders were motivated by any factor other than the extraordinary K-55-1 discovery when they bought their stock and their calls. No reason appears why outside investors, perhaps better acquainted with speculative modes of investment and with, in many cases, perhaps more capital at their disposal for intelligent speculation, would have been less influenced, and would not have been similarly motivated to invest if they had known what the insider investors knew about the K-55-1 discovery.

Our decision to expand the limited protection afforded outside investors by the trial court's narrow definition of materiality is not at all shaken by fears that the elimination of insider trading benefits will deplete the ranks of capable corporate managers by taking away an incentive to accept such employment. Such benefits, in essence, are forms of secret corporate compensation, see Cary, Corporate Standards and Legal Rules, 50 Calif. L. Rev. 408, 409-10 (1962), derived at the expense of the uninformed investing public and not at the expense of the corporation which receives the sole benefit from insider incentives. Moreover, adequate incentives for corporate officers may be provided by properly administered stock options and employee purchase plans of which there are many in existence. In any event, the normal motivation induced by stock ownership, i.e., the identification of an individual with corporate progress, is ill-promoted by condoning the sort of speculative insider activity which occurred here; for example, some of the corporation's stock was sold at market in order to purchase short-term calls upon that stock, calls which would never be exercised to increase a stockholder equity in TGS unless the market price of that stock rose sharply.

The core of Rule 10b-5 is the implementation of the Congressional purpose that all investors should have equal access to the rewards of participation in securities transactions. It was the intent of Congress that all members of the investing public should be subject to identical market risks,—which market risks include, of course the risk that one's evaluative capacity or one's capital available to put at risk may exceed another's capacity or capital. The insiders here were not trading on an equal footing with the outside investors. They alone were in a position to evaluate the probability and magnitude of what seemed from the outset to be a major ore strike; they alone could invest safely, secure in the expectation that the price of TGS stock would rise substantially in the event such a major strike should materialize, but would decline little, if at all, in the event of failure, for the public, ignorant at the outset of the favorable probabilities would likewise be unaware of the unproductive exploration, and the additional exploration costs would not significantly affect TGS market prices. Such inequities based upon unequal access to knowledge should not be shrugged off as inevitable in our way of life, or, in view of the congressional concern in the area, remain uncorrected.

We hold, therefore, that all transactions in TGS stock or calls by individuals apprised of the drilling results of K-55-1 were made in violation of Rule 10b-5. Inasmuch as the visual evaluation of that drill core (a generally reliable estimate though less accurate than a chemical assay) constituted material information, those advised of the results of the visual evaluation as well as those informed of the chemical assay traded in violation of law. The geologist Darke possessed undisclosed material information and traded in TGS securities. Therefore we reverse the dismissal of the action as to him and his personal transactions. The trial court also found that Darke, after the drilling of K-55-1 had been completed and with detailed knowledge of the results thereof, told certain outside individuals that TGS "was a good buy." These individuals thereafter acquired TGS stock and calls. *** [W]e *** hold that Darke violated Rule 10b-5(3) and Section 10(b) by "tipping" and we remand, pursuant to the agreement of the parties, for a determination of the appropriate remedy. As Darke's "tippees" are not defendants in this action, we need not decide whether, if they acted with actual or constructive knowledge that the material information was undisclosed, their conduct is as equally violative of the Rule as the conduct of their insider source, though we note that it certainly could be equally reprehensible.

With reference to Huntington, the trial court found that he "had no detailed knowledge as to the work" on the Kidd-55 segment. Nevertheless, the evidence shows that he knew about and participated in TGS's land acquisition program which followed the receipt of the K-55-1 drilling results, and that on February 26, 1964 he purchased 50 shares of TGS stock. Later, on March 16, he helped prepare a letter for Dr. Holyk's signature in which TGS made a substantial offer for lands near K-55-1, and on the same day he, who had never before purchased calls on any stock, purchased a call on 100 shares of TGS stock. We are satisfied that these purchases in February and March, coupled with his readily inferable and probably reliable, understanding of the highly favorable nature of preliminary operations on the Kidd segment, demonstrate that Huntington possessed material inside information such as to make his purchase violative of the Rule and the Act.

C. When May Insiders Act?

Appellant Crawford, who ordered the purchase of TGS stock shortly before the TGS April 16 official announcement, and defendant Coates, who placed orders with and communicated the news to his broker immediately after the official announcement was read at the TGS-called press conference, concede that they were in possession of material information. They contend, however, that their purchases were not proscribed purchases for the news had already been effectively disclosed. We disagree.

Crawford telephoned his orders to his Chicago broker about midnight on April 15 and again at 8:30 in the morning of the 16th, with instructions to buy at the opening of the Midwest Stock Exchange that morning. The trial court's finding that "he sought to, and did, 'beat the news,'" 258 F. Supp. at 287, is well documented by the record. The rumors of a major ore strike which had been circulated in Canada and, to a lesser extent, in New York, had been disclaimed by the TGS press release of April 12, which significantly promised the public an official detailed announcement when possibilities had ripened into actualities. The abbreviated announcement to the Canadian press at 9:40 A.M. on the 16th by the Ontario Minister of Mines and the report carried by The Northern Miner, parts of which had sporadically reached New York on the morning of the 16th through reports from Canadian affiliates to a few New York investment firms, are assuredly not the equivalent of the official 10-15 minute announcement which was not released to the American financial press until after 10:00 A.M. Crawford's orders had been placed before that. Before insiders may act upon material information, such information must have been effectively disclosed in a manner sufficient to insure its availibility to the investing public. Particularly here, where a formal announcement to the entire financial news media had been promised in a prior official release known to the media, all insider activity must await dissemination of the promised official announcement.

Coates was absolved by the court below because his telephone order was placed shortly before 10:20 A.M. on April 16, which was after the announcement had been made even though the news could not be considered already a matter of public information. 258 F.Supp. at 288. This result seems to have been predicated upon a misinterpretation of dicta in *Cady, Roberts*, where the SEC instructed insiders to "keep out of the market until the established procedures for public release of the information are *carried out* instead of hastening to execute transactions in advance of, and in frustration of, the objectives of the release," 40 SEC at 915. The reading of a news release, which prompted Coates into action, is merely the first step in the process of dissemination required for compliance with the regulatory objective of providing all investors with an equal opportunity to make informed investment judgments. Assuming that the contents of the official release could instantaneously be acted upon, at the minimum Coates should have waited until the news could reasonably have been expected to appear over the media of widest circulation, the Dow Jones broad tape, rather than hastening to insure an advantage to himself and his broker son-in-law. ***

CONCLUSION

In summary, therefore, we affirm the finding of the court below that appellants Richard H. Clayton and David M. Crawford have violated [Section 10(b)] and Rule 10b-5; we reverse the judgment order entered below dismissing the complaint against appellees Charles F. Fogarty, Richard H. Clayton, Richard D. Mollison, Walter Holyk, Kenneth H. Darke, Earl L. Huntington, and Francis G. Coates, as we find that they have violated [Section 10b-5] and Rule 10b-5. As to these eight individuals we remand so that in accordance with the agreement between the parties the Commission may notice a hearing before the court below to determine the remedies to be applied against them. ***

NOTES AND QUESTIONS

1. Silence in Securities Trading vs. Silence in Real Estate Transactions. The Second Circuit made quite clear in *Texas Gulf Sulphur* that Rule 10b-5 imposed on TGS's insiders a duty to disclose the confidential information about the ore strike or to abstain from trading in the company's shares. The choice to remain silent, then, was clearly an unacceptable alternative when corporate shares were the object of an insider's purchase. But TGS insiders also remained silent about the ore strike when they sought to acquire for the company additional land in close proximity to the original strikes. Was this fair to the potential sellers of the land? Was such silence fraudulent under the common law?

Consider a person's liability for nondisclosure under Section 551 of the Restatement (Second) of Torts (1976), which is set out at page 59 in Chapter 2. What additional information would be relevant in assessing whether the landowners could state a claim for fraud against TGS?

In 1969, when the Ontario High Court of Justice considered claims brought by landowners who had sold property to TGS, the Court had this to say about the company's tactics:

> [O]bviously Texas Gulf could not push the negotiations too hard without causing the prospective vendors to suspect that a discovery had been made, in which event either purchases would have become impossible or prices grossly inflated. Under the circumstances, I believe Texas Gulf did what any prudent mining company would have done to acquire property in which it knew a very promising anomaly lay.

Leitch GoldMines, Ltd. v. Texas Gulf Sulphur Co., 3 D.L.R. 3(d) 161, 184-85 (1969). Rather than chastise the company for its silence, the Court expressed a grudging admiration.

How can potential land sellers protect themselves from disparities of information in transactions with potential buyers? Might such disparities counsel adherence to a rule of caveat emptor in real estate transactions? Do national securities markets lend themselves to a caveat emptor approach? What other factors might justify treating securities transactions differently from real estate or other commercial transactions?

*2. **Federal Regulation of Insider Trading Through Rule 10b-5.*** As we saw in Chapter 2, the SEC promulgated Rule 10b-5 in 1942 based on its rulemaking powers under Section 10(b) of the Exchange Act. And since then, the contours of the Rule 10b-5 cause of action have been shaped almost entirely by the SEC and the federal judiciary. Moreover, in the context of the regulation of insider trading, the SEC and the courts had to employ particularly creative reasoning because the template for common law fraud did not fit well over insider trading. Was this activism on the part of the SEC and the courts justified? Should Congress have acted to prohibit insider trading outright, rather than acquiesce in its regulation by the SEC and courts under Rule 10b-5? What problems would Congress have encountered in drafting such a prohibition? We will revisit this question in the last subsection of this Chapter.

*3. **The Remedy for Insider Trading.*** Notice that the Second Circuit found only that the corporate insiders had violated Rule 10b-5 by purchasing stock in TGS (or tipping others) while in possession of material nonpublic information. The court then remanded the case to the district court for imposition of a remedy. On remand, the district judge ordered Holyk, Huntington, Clayton, and Darke to pay to TGS the difference between the average price of TGS stock on April 17, 1964, when news of the ore strike was known to the investing public, and the purchase price of the shares. (Darke also had to pay to TGS the profits that his tippees had derived from sale of TGS stock.) *SEC v. Texas Gulf Sulphur Co.*, 312 F. Supp. 77, 96-97 (S.D.N.Y. 1970). TGS, however, was obliged to hold the money in escrow for five years, subject to disposition in any manner that the court should direct on its own motion, or by application from the SEC or any other interested person. The district court also enjoined defendants Clayton and Crawford from future violations of Rule 10b-5. The Second Circuit later affirmed the district court's order in its entirety. See 446 F.2d 1301 (2d Cir. 1971).

In its affirmance, the Second Circuit rejected the defendants' claims that Section 21(e) of the Exchange Act provided only for injunctive relief and that the required restitution constituted a penalty that could be imposed only in a criminal action brought pursuant to Section 32(a):

> [W]e do not read § 21(e) as restricting the remedies which the SEC can pursue to injunctive relief. *** [I]n other contexts the Supreme Court has upheld the power of the Government without specific statutory authority to seek restitution, and has upheld the lower courts in granting restitution, as an ancillary remedy in the exercise of the courts' general equity powers to afford complete relief. *** Restitution of the profits on these transactions merely deprives the appellants of the gains of their wrongful conduct. Nor does restitution impose a hardship in this case.*** The court's order requires only restitution of the profits made by the violators prior to general knowledge of the ore strike on April 17, 1964, and, in effect, leaves the appellants all the profits accrued after that date. It would severely defeat the purposes of the Act if a violator of Rule 10b-5 were allowed to retain the profits from his violation. ***
>
> As to the requirement that Darke make restitution for the profits derived by his tippees, admittedly more of a hardship is imposed. However, without such a remedy, insiders could easily evade their duty to refrain from

> trading on the basis of inside information. Either the transactions so traded could be concluded by a relative or an acquaintance of the insider, or implied understandings could arise under which reciprocal tips between insiders in different corporations could be given.

Id. at 1307-08.

Today, courts routinely impose injunctions and orders of disgorgement in insider trading cases in which the SEC has established federal securities law violations, although the funds disgorged typically are paid to the SEC, rather than to the company whose stock was traded. See Rory C. Flynn, SEC Distribution Plans in Insider Trading Cases, 48 Bus. Law. 107 (1992). Moreover, since 1984, the SEC has had the authority to seek a monetary penalty in insider trading cases up to three times the profit gained or loss avoided by the defendant. And, as we will see in the *Chiarella* decision that follows, the government may choose to prosecute an insider trading case criminally and seek the imposition of a prison sentence. Section D of this Chapter explores these remedial issues more fully.

4. Implied Private Rights of Action for Insider Trading. Could private plaintiffs have asserted an implied right of action under Rule 10b-5 against the TGS insiders who purchased company stock while in possession of the confidential information about the ore strike? Who would have standing to sue? What would have been the plaintiffs' damages? In view of the fact that the TGS insiders purchased their TGS stock over exchanges, could plaintiffs make the requisite showing of causation? That is, wouldn't those shareholders who sold their TGS stock in early April 1964 have done so even if the TGS insiders had abstained from trading?

Federal courts confronted questions like these shortly after *Texas Gulf Sulphur* and began to develop law, particularly in the Second Circuit, that recognized a private right of action for insider trading, at least in circumstances where the defendants were corporate insiders. See, e.g., *Shapiro v. Merrill Lynch, Pierce, Fenner & Smith, Inc.*, 495 F.2d 228, 241 (2d Cir. 1974) (recognizing standing for all persons purchasing shares in company stock from the date of the insiders' sales until disclosure was made by the company); *Wilson v. Comtech Telecomm. Corp.*, 648 F.2d 88, 93 (2d Cir. 1981) (limiting *Shapiro* and restricting the plaintiff class to those investors who traded contemporaneously with the defendants); *Moss v. Morgan Stanley, Inc.*, 719 F.2d 515 (2d Cir. 1983) (denying standing of plaintiffs who sold stock contemporaneously with defendants who had purchased company stock based on information that was stolen from the corporation, because defendants were not fiduciaries of the plaintiffs, and therefore did not owe a duty of disclosure). The Sixth Circuit, however, adopted a harder line on the complicated issues of standing, causation, and damages. See *Fridrich v. Bradford*, 542 F.2d 307, 318 (6th Cir. 1976) (holding that in the absence of proof of a direct causal relationship, shareholders who sold stock over an exchange could not recover from directors who purchased stock based on inside knowledge).

As we will see in Section D, Congress resolved this controversy in 1988 when it added a new Section 20A to the Exchange Act, granting "contemporaneous traders" an express right of action against persons who have violated the federal securities laws through illegal insider trading or tipping.

Under Section 20A, those shareholders who sold TGS stock "contemporaneously" with the insiders' purchases would have been entitled to recover damages in the amount of the insiders' illegal profits, offset by any amount paid in disgorgement to the SEC. Why did Congress choose to limit plaintiff's recovery to the amount of defendant's illegal profits?

5. "Material Nonpublic Information." An insider's obligation under Rule 10b-5 to "disclose or abstain" attaches only when the information can be said to be both "material" and "nonpublic." On what reasoning did the *Texas Gulf Sulphur* court base its decision that the information about the ore findings was material? How does the court's analysis compare to the tests for materiality that were explored in Chapter 2.B—namely the "total mix" formulation from *TSC Indus., Inc. v. Northway,* 426 U.S. 438 (1976) and, for so-called contingent information, the probably/magnitude measure from *Basic Inc. v. Levinson*, 485 U.S. 224 (1988)?

The *Texas Gulf Sulphur* court also concluded that the information used by the insiders in their securities transactions was nonpublic. According to the court, when can information be said to be "public?" The *Texas Gulf Sulphur* standard for determining whether information is public was echoed in *In re Faberge*, 45 SEC 249, 256 (1973) (indicating that information must be disclosed "in a manner calculated to reach the securities market place in general through recognized channels of distribution, and public investors must be afforded a reasonable waiting period to react to the information"). Pursuant to the decisions in *Texas Gulf Sulphur* and *Faberge,* what steps would have to be taken before a company's previously confidential information could be regarded as in the public realm?

There is an alternative theory for determining whether information is public, predicated on the efficient capital markets hypothesis (discussed in Chapter 1.G). The theory postulates that information is "public" when it is known by a sufficient number of securities analysts or other professionals in the financial community. The Second Circuit adopted this theory in *United States v. Libera*, 989 F.2d 596 (2d Cir. 1993), where it maintained that:

> information may be considered public for Section 10(b) purposes even though there has been no public announcement and only a small number of people know of it. The issue is not the number of people who possess it but whether their trading has caused the information to be fully impounded into the price of the particular stock. Once the information is fully impounded in price, such information can no longer be misused by trading because no further profit can be made.

Id. at 601. Why, even today, might the SEC favor the *Texas Gulf Sulphur* approach? Which approach would you favor?

6. Parity of Information vs. Parity of Access to Information. The Second Circuit's approach in *Texas Gulf Sulphur* has often been characterized as "the parity of information" theory of insider trading liability. This characterization, however, is somewhat of a misnomer because the court postulates only an equality *of access* to information, not complete equality of information. The difference is important because, under the equal access approach, those investors who lawfully search out information are clearly entitled to the benefits of their research. See Victor Brudney, Insiders,

Outsiders, and Informational Advantages Under the Federal Securities Laws, 93 Harv. L. Rev. 322, 339-41 (1979) (questioning whether an "egalitarian utopia" could even be achieved, and highlighting the values gained by encouraging lawful exploration for relevant corporate and economic information). See also *Chiarella v. United States*, 445 U.S. 222, 252 n. 2 (1980) (Blackmun, J., dissenting) (noting that "there is a significant conceptual distinction between parity of information and parity of *access* to material information" and emphasizing that the "latter gives free rein to certain kinds of informational advantages that the former might foreclose, such as those that result from differences in diligence or acumen").

Do you agree with the Second Circuit's premise in *Texas Gulf Sulphur* that there is a "justifiable expectation of the securities marketplace that all investors trading on impersonal exchanges have relatively equal access to material information?" It is with this premise that the Supreme Court takes issue in the decision that immediately follows.

B. THE SUPREME COURT SPEAKS ON INSIDER TRADING AND RULE 10b-5

1. The Classical Theory of Insider Trading

CHIARELLA v. UNITED STATES

445 U.S. 222 (1980)

JUSTICE LOUIS F. POWELL:

The question in this case is whether a person who learns from the confidential documents of one corporation that it is planning an attempt to secure control of a second corporation violates § 10(b) of the Securities Exchange Act of 1934 if he fails to disclose the impending takeover before trading in the target company's securities.

I

Petitioner is a printer by trade. In 1975 and 1976, he worked as a "markup man" in the New York composing room of Pandick Press, a financial printer. Among documents that petitioner handled were five announcements of corporate takeover bids. When these documents were delivered to the printer, the identities of the acquiring and target corporations were concealed by blank spaces or false names. The true names were sent to the printer on the night of the final printing.

The petitioner, however, was able to deduce the names of the target companies before the final printing from other information contained in the documents. Without disclosing his knowledge, petitioner purchased stock in the target companies and sold the shares immediately after the takeover attempts were made public. By this method, petitioner realized a gain of slightly more than $30,000 in the course of 14 months. Subsequently, the Securities and Exchange Commission (Commission or SEC) began an investigation of his trading activities. In May 1977, petitioner entered into a consent decree with the Commission in which he agreed to return his profits to the sellers of the shares. On the same day, he was discharged by Pandick Press.

In January 1978, petitioner was indicted on 17 counts of violating

§ 10(b) of the Securities Exchange Act of 1934 (1934 Act) and SEC Rule 10b-5. After petitioner unsuccessfully moved to dismiss the indictment, he was brought to trial and convicted on all counts.

The Court of Appeals for the Second Circuit affirmed petitioner's conviction. We granted certiorari and we now reverse.

II

***This case concerns the legal effect of the petitioner's silence. The District Court's charge permitted the jury to convict the petitioner if it found that he willfully failed to inform sellers of target company securities that he knew of a forthcoming takeover bid that would make their shares more valuable. In order to decide whether silence in such circumstances violates § 10(b), it is necessary to review the language and legislative history of that statute as well as its interpretation by the Commission and the federal courts.

Although the starting point of our inquiry is the language of the statute, *Ernst & Ernst v. Hochfelder*, 425 U.S. 185, 197 (1976), § 10(b) does not state whether silence may constitute a manipulative or deceptive device. Section 10(b) was designed as a catch-all clause to prevent fraudulent practices. *[Hochfelder]*, 425 U.S., at 202, 206. But neither the legislative history nor the statute itself affords specific guidance for the resolution of this case. When Rule 10b-5 was promulgated in 1942, the SEC did not discuss the possibility that failure to provide information might run afoul of § 10(b).

The SEC took an important step in the development of §10(b) when it held that a broker-dealer and his firm violated that section by selling securities on the basis of undisclosed information obtained from a director of the issuer corporation who was also a registered representative of the brokerage firm. In *Cady, Roberts & Co.*, 40 SEC 907 (1961), the Commission decided that a corporate insider must abstain from trading in the shares of his corporation unless he has first disclosed all material inside information known to him. The obligation to disclose or abstain derives from

> "[a]n affirmative duty to disclose material information[, which] has been traditionally imposed on corporate 'insiders,' particular officers, directors, or controlling stockholders. We, and the courts have consistently held that insiders must disclose material facts which are known to them by virtue of their position but which are not known to persons with whom they deal and which, if known, would affect their investment judgment."

Id., at 911. The Commission emphasized that the duty arose from (i) the existence of a relationship affording access to inside information intended to be available only for a corporate purpose, and (ii) the unfairness of allowing a corporate insider to take advantage of that information by trading without disclosure. Id., at 912, and n. 15.[8]

---

8. In *Cady, Roberts*, the broker-dealer was liable under § 10(b) because it received nonpublic information from a corporate insider of the issuer. Since the insider could not use the information, neither could the partners in the brokerage firm with which he was associated. The transaction in *Cady, Roberts* involved sale of stock to persons who previously may not have been shareholders in the corporation. 40 SEC, at 913, and n. 21. The Commission embraced the reasoning of Judge Learned Hand that

That the relationship between a corporate insider and the stockholders of his corporation gives rise to a disclosure obligation is not a novel twist of the law. At common law, misrepresentation made for the purpose of inducing reliance upon the false statement is fraudulent. But one who fails to disclose material information prior to the consummation of a transaction commits fraud only when he is under a duty to do so. And the duty to disclose arises when one party has information "that the other [party] is entitled to know because of a fiduciary or other similar relation of trust and confidence between them." [Restatement (Second) of Torts § 551(2)(a) (1976)]. In its *Cady, Roberts* decision, the Commission recognized a relationship of trust and confidence between the shareholders of a corporation and those insiders who have obtained confidential information by reason of their position with that corporation. This relationship gives rise to a duty to disclose because of the "necessity of preventing a corporate insider from ... tak[ing] unfair advantage of the uninformed minority stockholders." *Speed v. Transamerica Corp.*, 99 F.Supp. 808, 829 (D.Del.1951).

The federal courts have found violations of § 10(b) where corporate insiders used undisclosed information for their own benefit. E. g., *SEC v. Texas Gulf Sulphur Co.*, 401 F.2d 833 (CA2 1968). The cases also have emphasized, in accordance with the common-law rule, that "[t]he party charged with failing to disclose market information must be under a duty to disclose it." *Frigitemp Corp. v. Financial Dynamics Fund, Inc.*, 524 F.2d 275, 282 (CA2 1975). Accordingly, a purchaser of stock who has no duty to a prospective seller because he is neither an insider nor a fiduciary has been held to have no obligation to reveal material facts. See *General Time Corp. v. Talley Industries, Inc.*, 403 F.2d 159, 164 (CA2 1968).

This Court followed the same approach in *Affiliated Ute Citizens v. United States*, 406 U.S. 128 (1972). ***

Thus, administrative and judicial interpretations have established that silence in connection with the purchase or sale of securities may operate as a fraud actionable under §10(b) despite the absence of statutory language or legislative history specifically addressing the legality of nondisclosure. But such liability is premised upon a duty to disclose arising from a relationship of trust and confidence between parties to a transaction. Application of a duty to disclose prior to trading guarantees that corporate insiders, who have an obligation to place the shareholder's welfare before their own, will not benefit personally through fraudulent use of material, nonpublic information.[12]

"the director or officer assumed a fiduciary relation to the buyer by the very sale; for it would be a sorry distinction to allow him to use the advantage of his position to induce the buyer into the position of a beneficiary although he was forbidden to do so once the buyer had become one." Id., at 914, n. 23, quoting *Gratz v. Claughton*, 187 F.2d 46, 49 (CA2 1951).

12. "Tippees" of corporate insiders have been held liable under § 10(b) because they have a duty not to profit from the use of inside information that they know is confidential and know or should know came from a corporate insider, *Shapiro v. Merrill Lynch, Pierce, Fenner & Smith, Inc.*, 495 F.2d 228, 237-238 (CA2 1974). The tippee's obligation has been viewed as arising from his role as a participant after the fact in the insider's breach of a fiduciary duty.

III

In this case, the petitioner was convicted of violating § 10(b) although he was not a corporate insider and he received no confidential information from the target company. Moreover, the "market information" upon which he relied did not concern the earning power or operations of the target company, but only the plans of the acquiring company. Petitioner's use of that information was not a fraud under § 10(b) unless he was subject to an affirmative duty to disclose it before trading. In this case, the jury instructions failed to specify any such duty. In effect, the trial court instructed the jury that petitioner owed a duty to everyone; to all sellers, indeed, to the market as a whole. The jury simply was told to decide whether petitioner used material, nonpublic information at a time when "he knew other people trading in the securities market did not have access to the same information."

The Court of Appeals affirmed the conviction by holding that "*[a]nyone*—corporate insider or not—who regularly receives material nonpublic information may not use that information to trade in securities without incurring an affirmative duty to disclose." Although the court said that its test would include only persons who regularly receive material, nonpublic information, its rationale for that limitation is unrelated to the existence of a duty to disclose.

The Court of Appeals, like the trial court, failed to identify a relationship between petitioner and the sellers that could give rise to a duty. Its decision thus rested solely upon its belief that the federal securities laws have "created a system providing equal access to information necessary for reasoned and intelligent investment decisions." The use by anyone of material information not generally available is fraudulent, this theory suggests, because such information gives certain buyers or sellers an unfair advantage over less informed buyers and sellers.

This reasoning suffers from two defects. First not every instance of financial unfairness constitutes fraudulent activity under § 10(b). See *Santa Fe Industries, Inc. v. Green*, 430 U.S. 462, 474-477 (1977). Second, the element required to make silence fraudulent—a duty to disclose—is absent in this case. No duty could arise from petitioner's relationship with the sellers of the target company's securities, for petitioner had no prior dealings with them. He was not their agent, he was not a fiduciary, he was not a person in whom the sellers had placed their trust and confidence. He was, in fact, a complete stranger who dealt with the sellers only through impersonal market transactions.

We cannot affirm petitioner's conviction without recognizing a general duty between all participants in market transactions to forgo actions based on material, nonpublic information. Formulation of such a broad duty, which departs radically from the established doctrine that duty arises from a specific relationship between two parties, should not be undertaken absent some explicit evidence of congressional intent.

As we have seen, no such evidence emerges from the language or legislative history of § 10(b). Moreover, neither the Congress nor the Commission ever has adopted a parity-of-information rule. Instead the problems caused by misuse of market information have been addressed by detailed and sophisticated regulation that recognizes when use of market information may not harm operation of the securities markets. For example, the Williams Act limits but does not completely prohibit a tender offeror's purchases of target corporation stock before public announcement of the offer. Congress' careful action in this and other areas contrasts, and is in some tension, with the broad rule of liability we are asked to adopt in this case.

Indeed, the theory upon which the petitioner was convicted is at odds with the Commission's view of § 10(b) as applied to activity that has the same effect on sellers as the petitioner's purchases. "Warehousing" takes place when a corporation gives advance notice of its intention to launch a tender offer to institutional investors who then are able to purchase stock in the target company before the tender offer is made public and the price of shares rises. In this case, as in warehousing, a buyer of securities purchases stock in a target corporation on the basis of market information which is unknown to the seller. In both of these situations, the seller's behavior presumably would be altered if he had the nonpublic information. Significantly, however, the Commission has acted to bar warehousing under its authority to regulate tender offers after recognizing that action under §10(b) would rest on a "somewhat different theory" than that previously used to regulate insider trading as fraudulent activity.

We see no basis for applying such a new and different theory of liability in this case. As we have emphasized before, the 1934 Act cannot be read "'more broadly than its language and the statutory scheme reasonably permit.'" *Touche Ross & Co. v. Redington*, 442 U.S. 560, 578, (1979). Section 10(b) is aptly described as a catchall provision, but what it catches must be fraud. When an allegation of fraud is based upon nondisclosure, there can be no fraud absent a duty to speak. We hold that a duty to disclose under § 10(b) does not arise from the mere possession of nonpublic market information. The contrary result is without support in the legislative history of § 10(b) and would be inconsistent with the careful plan that Congress has enacted for regulation of the securities markets. *** The judgment of the Court of Appeals is reversed.

[The concurring opinions of Justices Stevens and Brennan, and the dissenting opinion of Chief Justice Burger, raise the issue of an alternative "misappropriation theory" of insider trading liability, and are discussed infra at Section B.3]

JUSTICE HAROLD A. BLACKMUN, WITH WHOM JUSTICE MARSHALL JOINS, DISSENTING:

***The Court continues to pursue a course, charted in certain recent decisions, designed to transform § 10(b) from an intentionally elastic "catchall" provision to one that catches relatively little of the misbehavior that all too often makes investment in securities a needlessly risky business for the uninitiated investor. See, e.g., *Ernst & Ernst v. Hochfelder*, 425 U.S. 185, (1976); *Blue Chip Stamps v. Manor Drug Stores*, 421 U.S. 723 (1975). Such confinement in this case is now achieved by imposition of a requirement of a "special relationship" akin to fiduciary duty before the statute gives rise to a duty to disclose or to abstain from trading upon material, nonpublic information. The Court admits that this conclusion finds no mandate in the language of the statute or its legislative history. Yet the Court fails even to attempt a justification of its ruling in terms of the purposes of the securities laws, or to square that ruling with the long-standing but now much abused principle that the federal securities laws are to be construed flexibly rather than with narrow technicality. See *Affiliated Ute Citizens v. United States*, 406 U.S. 128, 151 (1972); *Superintendent of Insurance v. Bankers Life & Casualty Co.*, 404 U.S. 6, 12 (1971); *SEC v. Capital Gains Research Bureau*, 375 U.S. 180, 186 (1963).

I, of course, agree with the Court that a relationship of trust can establish a duty to disclose under § 10(b) and Rule 10b-5. But I do not agree that a failure to disclose violates the Rule only when the responsibilities of a relationship of that kind have been breached. As applied to this case, the Court's approach unduly minimizes the importance of petitioner's access to confidential information that the honest investor no matter how diligently he tried, could not legally obtain. In doing so, it further advances an interpretation of §10(b) and Rule 10b-5 that stops short of their full implications. Although the Court draws support for its position from certain precedent, I find its decision neither fully consistent with developments in the common law of fraud, nor fully in step with administrative and judicial application of Rule 10b-5 to "insider" trading.

The common law of actionable misrepresentation long has treated the possession of "special facts" as a key ingredient in the duty to disclose. See *Strong v. Repide*, 213 U.S. 419, 431-433 (1909); 1 F. Harper & F. James, Law of Torts § 7.14 (1956). Traditionally, this factor has been prominent in cases involving confidential or fiduciary relations, where one party's inferiority of knowledge and dependence upon fair treatment is a matter of legal definition, as well as in cases where one party is on notice that the other is "acting under a mistaken belief with respect to a material fact." *Frigitemp Corp. v. Financial Dynamics Fund, Inc.*, 524 F.2d 275, 283 (CA2 1975); see also Restatement of Torts § 551 (1938). Even at common law, however, there has been a trend away from strict adherence to the harsh maxim *caveat emptor* and toward a more flexible, less formalistic understanding of the duty to disclose. See, e. g., Keeton Fraud—Concealment and Non-Disclosure, 15 Texas L.Rev. 1, 31 (1936). Steps have been taken toward application of the "special facts" doctrine in a broader array of contexts where one party's superior knowledge of essential facts renders a transaction without disclosure inherently unfair. See James & Gray, Misrepresentation—Part II, 37 Md.L.Rev. 488, 526-527 (1978); 3 Restatement (Second) of Torts § 551(e), Comment *l* (1977).

By its narrow construction of § 10(b) and Rule 10b-5, the Court places the federal securities laws in the rearguard of this movement, a position opposite to the expectations of Congress at the time the securities laws were enacted. I cannot agree that the statute and Rule are so limited. The Court has observed that the securities laws were not intended to replicate the law of fiduciary relations. *Santa Fe Industries, Inc. v. Green*, 430 U.S. 462, 474-476 (1977). Rather, their purpose is to ensure the fair and honest functioning of impersonal national securities markets where common-law protections have proved inadequate. Cf. *United States v. Naftalin*, 441 U.S. 768, 775 (1979). As Congress itself has recognized, it is integral to this purpose "to assure that dealing in securities is fair and without undue preferences or advantages among investors."

Indeed, the importance of access to "special facts" has been a recurrent theme in administrative and judicial application of Rule 10b-5 to insider trading. Both the SEC and the courts have stressed the insider's misuse of secret knowledge as the gravamen of illegal conduct. The Court, I think, unduly minimizes this aspect of prior decisions.

Cady, Roberts & Co., 40 SEC 907 (1961), which the Court discusses at some length, provides an illustration. In that case, the Commission *** regarded the insider "relationship" primarily in terms of *access* to nonpublic information, and not merely in terms of the presence of a common-law fiduciary duty or the like. This approach was deemed to be in keeping with the principle that "the broad language of the anti-fraud provisions" should not be "circumscribed by fine distinctions and rigid classifications," such as those that prevailed under the common law. Ibid. The duty to abstain or disclose arose, not merely as an incident of fiduciary responsibility, but as a result of the "inherent unfairness" of turning secret information to account for personal profit. This understanding of Rule 10b-5 was reinforced when *Investors Management Co.*, 44 SEC 633, 643 (1971), specifically rejected the contention that a "special relationship" between the alleged violator and an "insider" source was a necessary requirement for liability.

A similar approach has been followed by the courts. In *SEC v. Texas Gulf Sulphur Co.*, 401 F.2d 833, 848 (CA2 1968) (en banc), the court specifically mentioned the common-law "special facts" doctrine as one source for Rule 10b-5, and it reasoned that the Rule is "based in policy on the justifiable expectation of the securities marketplace that all investors trading on impersonal exchanges have relatively equal access to material information." See also *Lewelling v. First California Co.*, 564 F.2d 1277, 1280 (CA9 1977); *Speed v. Transamerica Corp.*, 99 F.Supp. 808, 829 (D.Del.1951). ***

I believe, and surely thought, that this broad understanding of the duty to disclose under Rule 10b-5 was recognized and approved in *Affiliated Ute Citizens v. United States*, 406 U.S. 128 (1972). That case held that bank agents dealing in the stock of a Ute Indian development corporation had a duty to reveal to mixed-blood Indian customers that their shares could bring a higher price on a non-Indian market of which the sellers were unaware. The Court recognized that "by repeated use of the word 'any,'" the statute and Rule "are obviously meant to be inclusive." Although it found a relationship of trust between the agents and the Indian sellers, the Court also clearly established that the bank and its agents were subject to the strictures of Rule 10b-5 because of their strategic position in the marketplace. The Indian sellers had no knowledge of the non-Indian market. The bank agents, in contrast, had intimate familiarity with the non-Indian market, which they had promoted actively, and from which they and their bank both profited. In these circumstances, the Court held that the bank and its agents "possessed the affirmative duty under the Rule" to disclose market information to the Indian sellers, and that the latter "had the right to know" that their shares would sell for a higher price in another market.

It seems to me that the Court gives *Affiliated Ute Citizens* an unduly narrow interpretation. As I now read my opinion there for the Court, it lends strong support to the principle that a structural disparity in access to material information is a critical factor under Rule 10b-5 in establishing a duty either to disclose the information or to abstain from trading. Given the factual posture of the case, it was unnecessary to resolve the question whether such a structural disparity could sustain a duty to disclose even absent "a relationship of trust and confidence between parties to a transaction." Nevertheless, I think the rationale of *Affiliated Ute Citizens* definitely points toward an affirmative answer to that question. Although I am not sure I fully accept the "market insider" category created by the Court of Appeals, I would hold that persons having access to confidential material information that is not legally available to others generally are prohibited by Rule 10b-5 from engaging in schemes to exploit their structural informational advantage through trading in affected securities. To hold otherwise, it seems to me, is to tolerate a wide range of manipulative and deceitful behavior. [S]ee generally Brudney, Insiders, Outsiders, and Informational Advantages under the Federal Securities Laws, 93 Harv.L.Rev. 322 (1979).

Whatever the outer limits of the Rule, petitioner Chiarella's case fits neatly near the center of its analytical framework. He occupied a relationship to the takeover companies giving him intimate access to concededly material information that was sedulously guarded from public access. The information, in the words of *Cady, Roberts & Co.* was "intended to be available only for a corporate purpose and not for the personal benefit of anyone." Petitioner, moreover, knew that the information was unavailable to those with whom he dealt. And he took full, virtually riskless advantage of this artificial information gap by selling the stocks shortly after each takeover bid was announced. By any reasonable definition, his trading was "inherent[ly] unfai[r]." This misuse of confidential information was clearly placed before the jury. Petitioner's conviction, therefore, should be upheld, and I dissent from the Court's upsetting that conviction.

NOTES AND QUESTIONS

1. ***Disclosure Duties at Common Law.*** Does the *Chiarella* Court suggest that disclosure duties under Rule 10b-5 arise only out of pre-existing fiduciary relationships? Is such a suggestion consistent with Section 551(2) of the Restatement of Torts (Second), set out on page 59 of Chapter 2? What may have prompted the Court to focus on the existence of a fiduciary relationship between the parties to a securities transaction?

2. **Chiarella*'s Departures From the Common Law.*** *Chiarella*'s classical theory was clearly an effort by the Court to curtail the SEC's and the Second Circuit's more expansive approach to insider trading; but it is also important to recognize that *Chiarella* itself construed Rule 10b-5 in a manner that departed from at least two common law limitations on recovery for a fiduciary's silence. What justified those departures?

3. ***Identifying Insiders.*** By the very terms of the majority opinion, *Chiarella*'s classical theory of insider trading liability applies to officers, directors, and controlling shareholders of the corporation who trade in the company's stock. Are other employees of the corporation included in this circle? For example, can an attendant in a company's mailroom be viewed as a corporate fiduciary owing disclosure duties to shareholders? Courts have indeed been willing to do so. (Recall the geologists held liable for insider trading in *Texas Gulf Sulphur.*) Is the circle wide enough to include the issuer itself? Again the answer appears to be yes. See, e.g., *Shaw v. Digital Equip. Corp.*, 82 F.3d 1194, 1203 (1st Cir. 1996) (observing that numerous courts "have treated a corporation trading in its own securities as an 'insider' for purposes of the 'disclose or abstain' rule"); *McCormick v. Fund Am. Cos.*, 26 F.3d 869, 876 (9th Cir. 1994) (emphasizing that "the corporate issuer in possession of material nonpublic information, must, like other insiders in the same situation, disclose that information to its shareholders or refrain from trading with them"). For a more nuanced analysis, see Mark J. Loewenstein & William K.S. Wang, The Corporation as Insider Trader, 30 Del J. Corp. L. 45 (2005).

4. The "Possession vs. Use" Debate. Under the classical theory of insider trading liability, is a traditional insider required to abstain from trading securities while that insider is "in possession of" material nonpublic information, or is the insider required to abstain only from trading securities "on the basis of" material nonpublic information? This question is often phrased in terms of whether liability for insider trading under Rule 10b-5 should be determined pursuant to a "knowing possession" test or a "use" test.

For many years, the controversy over the proper test to apply in Rule 10b-5 cases persisted without direct judicial attention, primarily because persons facing substantial monetary penalties and possible prison sentences for alleged insider trading offenses seldom defended themselves by maintaining that although they possessed material nonpublic information, they did not trade securities on the basis of such information. But in *SEC v. Adler,* 137 F.3d 1325 (11th Cir. 1998), and *United States v. Smith*, 155 F.3d 1051 (9th Cir. 1998), two federal courts of appeals squarely confronted this question in the context of insider trading claims against a corporate director (in *Adler*) and a corporate officer (in *Smith*). Both circuits rejected the Commission's "knowing possession" position, holding that Rule 10b-5's disclose or abstain obligation prohibits securities trading only *on the basis of* material nonpublic information. The Second Circuit reached precisely the opposite conclusion in *United States v. Teicher*, 987 F.2d 112 (2d Cir. 1993), but the court's views on the issue of "possession vs. use" constituted dictum rather than a holding. For extensive analysis of these decisions, see Donna M. Nagy, The "Possession vs. Use" Debate in the Context of Securities Trading by Traditional Insiders: Why Silence Can Never Be Golden, 67 U. Cin. L. Rev. 1129 (1999).

Rather than reconciling the circuits' conflicting positions through case-by-case adjudication, the Commission, in August 2000, opted to use its authority under Section 10(b) to promulgate a rule intended to resolve the debate once and for all. The result—Rule 10b5-1—comes close to endorsing a "knowing possession" standard because it focuses liability on whether a person traded securities while "aware" of material nonpublic information.

5. Rule 10b5-1 and its Affirmative Defenses. Rule 10b5-1 stands as the SEC's first rule designed to regulate insider trading outside the specific context of tender offers. It begins with a "preliminary note" stating that:

> This provision defines when a purchase or sale constitutes trading "on the basis of" material nonpublic information in insider trading cases brought under Section 10(b) of the Act and Rule 10b-5 thereunder. The law of insider trading

> is otherwise defined by judicial opinions construing Rule 10b-5, and Rule 10b5-1 does not modify the scope of insider trading law in any other respect.

Rule 10b5-1(a) then sets out a general rule providing that:

> The "manipulative and deceptive devices" prohibited by Section 10(b) of the Act and Rule 10b-5 thereunder include, among other things, the purchase or sale of a security of any issuer, *on the basis of* material nonpublic information about that security or issuer, in breach of a duty of trust or confidence that is owed directly, indirectly, or derivatively, to the issuer of that security or the shareholders of that issuer, or to any person who is the source of the material non-public information.

Id. (emphasis added). Subject to several narrowly drawn affirmative defenses, trading "on the basis of" is defined in Rule 10b5-1(b) as trading by someone who "was aware of the material, nonpublic information." Does it make sense to define "on the basis of" in terms of a person's awareness of information? The *Adler* and *Smith* courts used the phrase "on the basis of" in a manner that made it interchangeable with the "use" test referred to in the preceding Note. Do the affirmative defenses in Rule 10b5-1(c) shed light on the SEC's choice of the "on the basis of" syntax?

According to the SEC's Adopting Release, Rule 10b5-1(c)'s affirmative defenses are designed to provide "appropriate flexibility to persons who wish to structure securities trading plans and strategies when they are not aware of material nonpublic information, and do not exercise any influence over the transaction once they do become aware of such information." Selective Disclosure and Insider Trading, Exchange Act Release No. 43154 (Aug. 23, 2000). To that end, Rule 10b5-1(c)(1)(i) provides that:

> a person's purchase or sale is not "on the basis of" material nonpublic information if the person making the purchase or sale demonstrates that:

A. Before becoming aware of the information, the person had:

1. Entered into a binding contract to purchase or sell the security,

2. Instructed another person to purchase or sell the security for the instructing person's account, or

3. Adopted a written plan for trading securities;

B. The contract, instruction, or plan described in paragraph (c)(1)(i)(A) of this Section:

1. Specified the amount of securities to be purchased or sold and the price at which and the date on which the securities were to be purchased or sold;

2. Included a written formula or algorithm, or computer program, for determining the amount of securities to be purchased or sold and the price at which and the date on which the securities were to be purchased or sold; or

3. Did not permit the person to exercise any subsequent influence over how, when, or whether to effect purchases or sales; provided, in

addition, that any other person who, pursuant to the contract, instruction, or plan, did exercise such influence must not have been aware of the material nonpublic information when doing so; and

C. The purchase or sale that occurred was pursuant to the contract, instruction, or plan.

Rule 10b5-1(c)(1)(ii) makes clear that the availability of these affirmative defenses is strictly limited to circumstances in which the contract, plan or instruction to trade is "entered into in good faith, and not as part of a plan or scheme to evade the prohibitions of the rule."

What are the principal benefits of Rule 10b5-1? Are there costs or disadvantages? Should the Commission have included affirmative defenses for pre-existing trading plans? Can such defenses be reconciled with *Chiarella*'s "disclose or abstain" rule? With the common law of fraud and deceit?

6. Financial Institutions and Chinese Walls. Financial institutions such as Goldman Sachs and Morgan Stanley are generally organized into many separate departments, some of which routinely come into contact with material nonpublic information about securities issuers. To prevent confidential information in one sector of the firm (such as an investment banking department) from being imputed to persons working in another sector (such as a trading department), firms typically erect so-called "Chinese Walls." And for decades, the SEC has assured firms that their properly walled-off departments could continue to trade securities for client and proprietary accounts without incurring liability for insider trading. See Ralph C. Ferrara, Donna M. Nagy, and Herbert C. Thomas, Ferrara on Insider Trading and the Wall (2d ed. 2001).

Rule 10b5-1(c)(2) now codifies the practice of creating Chinese Walls as a separate affirmative defense available to "non-natural" persons. To invoke the affirmative defense, a firm must demonstrates that:

> 1. The individual making the investment decision on behalf of the [firm] to purchase or sell the securities was not aware of the information; and
>
> 2. The [firm] had implemented reasonable policies and procedures, taking into consideration the nature of the [firm's] business, to ensure that individuals making investment decisions would not violate the laws prohibiting trading on the basis of material nonpublic information. These policies and procedures may include those that restrict any purchase, sale, and causing any purchase or sale of any security as to which the [firm] has material nonpublic information, or those that prevent such individuals from becoming aware of such information.

PROBLEM 7-1

Jonathan Bryant is a Senior Vice President for Chrontonic, Inc., which provides contract manufacturing services to original equipment manufacturers in the electronics industry. He also sits on the company's Board of Directors. For several years, Bryant has received a sizable amount of Chrontonic shares as part of his year-end compensation bonus. In January 2010, his broker and financial adviser recommended that he diversify his stock portfolio by periodically selling some shares in Chrontonic and investing the proceeds in companies outside the electronics industry. Believing this diversification strategy to be a good one, Bryant developed a written plan whereby his broker would sell 1000 shares of Chrontonic stock at the market price on January 15, 2010 and the first day of every quarter thereafter. At the time, Bryant was not aware of any material nonpublic information concerning Chrontonic. And in accordance with this plan, sales were made for Bryant's account on January 15, April 15, July 15, and October 15 for the years 2010 and 2011.

During November and December of 2011, Chrontonic began receiving decreased orders from one of its largest customers, Jonners Peripherals ("Jonners"). On January 5, 2012, Chrontonic's CEO informed its Board of Directors that the company was expecting a complete termination in the orders from Jonners due to that company's decision to move much of its manufacturing off-shore. The CEO expressed the view that when this information was disseminated to the public, Chrontonic's stock price was likely to drop substantially. After the Board meeting, Bryant did nothing to alter his broker's standing instructions, and on January 15, 2012, 1000 shares of Chrontonic shares were sold for Bryant's account. A number of other officers and directors of Chrontonic had adhered to similar written trading plans, and shares for their account were also sold pursuant to those plans on January 15, 2012.

On January 17, 2012, Chrontonic issued a press release announcing its cessation of business with Jonners. In response to the press release, the price of Chrontonic stock dropped from $30.50 to $18.25 over the next two trading days. Shareholders of Chrontonic maintain that by selling 1,000 shares of Chrontonic stock before the January 17 press release, Bryant avoided $12,250 in losses. In addition, other officers and directors avoided similar losses, to a combined total of more than $400,000.

Has Bryant violated Rule 10b-5? What if another director had sold Chrontonic stock on January 15, but decided only that morning to trade? Would he have violated Rule 10b-5? What if a third director had been planning to sell a portion of her Chrontonic stock on January 10—the due date for her daughter's college tuition for the second semester? Does the CEO's January 5 announcement to the Board preclude her from selling?

Suppose that, instead of the confidential bad news announced at the board meeting on January 5, the CEO had announced confidential good news that the company would be receiving double its expected orders from Jonners. If Bryant had then called his broker to cancel the sales to occur on January 15, would this have been a violation of Rule 10b-5?

If you were a corporation's general counsel, what advise would you give its officers and directors who wish to set up trading plans like the one developed by Bryant?

PROBLEM 7-2

In January 2010, Brentwood Management LLP ("Brentwood") issued ten-year bonds to finance its acquisition of a shopping center in a downtown area of the city that urban planners had hoped to revitalize. Over the next two years, largely due to effective marketing on the part of Brentwood, many retail stores signed long-term leasing agreements with the company. The shopping center proved to be a very profitable venture for Brentwood in that its goal of maximum occupancy was reached. Indeed, Brentwood even has a "wait list" for any tenant vacancies that might come available. The bonds now trade in a small over-the-counter market.

In January 2012, an employee in Brentwood's marketing department learned from a current tenant confidential information relating to plans by a competing company to construct a mega-mall to be located in the near suburbs. The competing company has yet to publicly announce this project because it has not yet finalized its negotiations with the owners of the land on which the mall will be built. Fearing that the construction of the mall will spell doom for the shopping center (and therefore Brentwood), the employee sold his bonds in the market. Under the classical theory of insider trading, has the employee committed a violation of Rule 10b-5?

2. *Tippees and Temporary Insiders*

A footnote in *Chiarella*'s majority opinion expressed the view that "tippees" of corporate insiders may incur liability under Rule 10b-5 "because they have a duty not to profit from the use of inside information that they know is confidential and know or should know came from a corporate insider," and that "[t]he tippee's obligation has been viewed as arising from his role as a participant after the fact in the insider's breach of a fiduciary duty." See *Chiarella v. United States*, 445 U.S. 222, 231 n.12 (1980). The Supreme Court elaborated on the scope of tippee liability in the following decision.

DIRKS v. SEC

463 U.S. 646 (1983)

JUSTICE LOUIS F. POWELL:

Petitioner Raymond Dirks received material nonpublic information from "insiders" of a corporation with which he had no connection. He disclosed this information to investors who relied on it in trading in the shares of the corporation. The question is whether Dirks violated the antifraud provisions of the federal securities laws by this disclosure.

I

In 1973, Dirks was an officer of a New York broker-dealer firm who specialized in providing investment analysis of insurance company securities to institutional investors. On March 6, Dirks received information from Ronald Secrist, a former officer of Equity Funding of America. Secrist alleged that the assets of Equity Funding, a diversified corporation primarily engaged in selling life insurance and mutual funds, were vastly overstated as the result of fraudulent corporate practices. Secrist also stated that various regulatory agencies had failed to act on similar charges made by Equity Funding employees. He urged Dirks to verify the fraud and disclose it publicly.

Dirks decided to investigate the allegations. He visited Equity Funding's headquarters in Los Angeles and interviewed several officers and employees of the corporation. The senior management denied any wrongdoing, but certain corporation employees corroborated the charges of fraud. Neither Dirks nor his firm owned or traded any Equity Funding stock, but throughout his investigation he openly discussed the information he had obtained with a number of clients and investors. Some of these persons sold their holdings of

Equity Funding securities, including five investment advisers who liquidated holdings of more than $16 million.

While Dirks was in Los Angeles, he was in touch regularly with William Blundell, the Wall Street Journal's Los Angeles bureau chief. Dirks urged Blundell to write a story on the fraud allegations. Blundell did not believe, however, that such a massive fraud could go undetected and declined to write the story. He feared that publishing such damaging hearsay might be libelous.

During the 2-week period in which Dirks pursued his investigation and spread word of Secrist's charges, the price of Equity Funding stock fell from $26 per share to less than $15 per share. This led the New York Stock Exchange to halt trading on March 27. Shortly thereafter California insurance authorities impounded Equity Funding's records and uncovered evidence of the fraud. Only then did the Securities and Exchange Commission (SEC) file a complaint against Equity Funding and only then, on April 2, did the Wall Street Journal publish a front-page story based largely on information assembled by Dirks. Equity Funding immediately went into receivership.

The SEC began an investigation into Dirks' role in the exposure of the fraud. After a hearing by an Administrative Law Judge, the SEC found that Dirks had aided and abetted violations of § 17(a) of the Securities Act of 1933, § 10(b) of the Securities Exchange Act of 1934, and SEC Rule 10b-5 by repeating the allegations of fraud to members of the investment community who later sold their Equity Funding stock. The SEC concluded: "Where 'tippees'—regardless of their motivation or occupation—come into possession of material 'corporate information that they know is confidential and know or should know came from a corporate insider,' they must either publicly disclose that information or refrain from trading." Recognizing, however, that Dirks "played an important role in bringing [Equity Funding's] massive fraud to light," the SEC only censured him.

Dirks sought review in the Court of Appeals for the District of Columbia Circuit. The court entered judgment against Dirks "for the reasons stated by the Commission in its opinion." ***

In view of the importance to the SEC and to the securities industry of the question presented by this case, we granted a writ of certiorari. We now reverse.

II

In the seminal case of *In re Cady, Roberts & Co.,* 40 SEC 907 (1961), the SEC recognized that the common law in some jurisdictions imposes on "corporate 'insiders,' particularly officers, directors, or controlling stockholders" an "affirmative duty of disclosure ... when dealing in securities." Id., at 911, and n. 13. The SEC found that not only did breach of this common-law duty also establish the elements of a Rule 10b-5 violation, but that individuals other than corporate insiders could be obligated either to disclose material nonpublic information before trading or to abstain from trading altogether. In *Chiarella,* we accepted the two elements set out in *Cady Roberts* for establishing a Rule 10b-5 violation: "(i) the existence of a relationship affording access to inside information intended to be available only for a corporate purpose, and (ii) the unfairness of allowing a corporate insider to take advantage of that information by trading without disclosure." 445 U.S., at 227. In examining whether *Chiarella* had an obligation to disclose or abstain, the Court found that there is no general duty to disclose before trading on material nonpublic information, and held that "a duty to disclose under § 10(b) does not arise from the mere possession of nonpublic market information." Id., at 235. Such a duty arises rather from the existence of a fiduciary relationship. See id., at 227-235.

Not "all breaches of fiduciary duty in connection with a securities transaction," however, come within the ambit of Rule 10b-5. *Santa Fe Industries, Inc. v. Green*, 430 U.S. 462, 472 (1977). There must also be "manipulation or deception." Id., at 473. In an inside-trading case this fraud derives from the "inherent unfairness involved where one takes advantage" of "information intended to be available only for a corporate purpose and not for the personal benefit of anyone." *In re Merrill Lynch, Pierce, Fenner & Smith, Inc.*, 43 SEC 933, 936 (1968). Thus, an insider will be liable under Rule 10b-5 for inside trading only where he fails to disclose material nonpublic information before trading on it and thus makes "secret profits." *Cady, Roberts,* [40 SEC], at 916, n. 31.

III

We were explicit in *Chiarella* in saying that there can be no duty to disclose where the person who has traded on inside information "was not [the corporation's] agent, ... was not a fiduciary, [or] was not a person in whom the sellers [of the securities] had placed their trust and confidence." 445 U.S., at 232. Not to require such a fiduciary relationship, we recognized, would "depar[t] radically from the established doctrine that duty arises from a specific relationship between two parties" and would amount to "recognizing a general duty between all participants in market transactions to forgo actions based on material, nonpublic information." Id., at 232, 233. This requirement of a specific relationship between the shareholders and the individual trading on inside information has created analytical difficulties for the SEC and courts in policing tippees who trade on inside information. Unlike insiders who have independent fiduciary duties to both the corporation and its shareholders, the typical tippee has no such relationships.[14] In view of this absence, it has been unclear how a

---

14. Under certain circumstances, such as where corporate information is revealed legitimately to an underwriter, accountant, lawyer, or consultant working for the corporation, these outsiders may become fiduciaries of the shareholders. The basis for recognizing this fiduciary duty is not simply that such persons acquired nonpublic corporate information, but rather that they have entered into a special confidential relationship in the conduct of the business of the enterprise and are given access to information solely for corporate purposes. See *SEC v. Monarch Fund*, 608 F.2d 938, 942 (CA2 1979); *In re Investors Management Co.*, 44 SEC 633, 645 (1971); *In re Van Alystne, Noel & Co.*, 43 SEC 1080, 1084-1085 (1969); *In re Merrill Lynch, Pierce, Fenner & Smith, Inc.*, 43 SEC 933, 937 (1968); *Cady, Roberts,* 40 SEC, at 912. When such a person breaches his fiduciary relationship, he may be treated more properly as a tipper than a tippee. See *Shapiro v. Merrill Lynch, Pierce, Fenner & Smith, Inc.*, 495 F.2d 228, 237 (CA2 1974) (investment banker had access to material information when working on a proposed public offering for the corporation). For such a duty to be imposed, however, the corporation must expect the outsider to keep the disclosed nonpublic information

tippee acquires the *Cady, Roberts* duty to refrain from trading on inside information.

A

The SEC's position, as stated in its opinion in this case, is that a tippee "inherits" the *Cady, Roberts* obligation to shareholders whenever he receives inside information from an insider:

> "In tipping potential traders, Dirks breached a duty which he had assumed as a result of knowingly receiving confidential information from [Equity Funding] insiders. Tippees such as Dirks who receive non-public, material information from insiders become 'subject to the same duty as [the] insiders.' *Shapiro v.*

Merrill Lynch, Pierce, Fenner & Smith, Inc. 495 F.2d 228, 237 (CA2 1974). *** 21 SEC Docket, at 1410, n. 42.

This view differs little from the view that we rejected as inconsistent with congressional intent in *Chiarella.*[15] ***

In effect, the SEC's theory of tippee liability in both cases appears rooted in the idea that the antifraud provisions require equal information among all traders. This conflicts with the principle set forth in *Chiarella* that only some persons, under some circumstances, will be barred from trading while in possession of material nonpublic information. *** We reaffirm today that "[a] duty [to disclose] arises from the relationship between parties ... and not merely from one's ability to acquire information because of his position in the market." [445 U.S.] at 232-233, n. 14.

Imposing a duty to disclose or abstain solely because a person knowingly receives material nonpublic information from an insider and trades on it could have an inhibiting influence on the role of market analysts, which the SEC itself recognizes is necessary to the preservation of a healthy market. It is commonplace for analysts to "ferret out and analyze information," 21 SEC, at 1406, and this often is done by meeting with and questioning corporate officers and others who are insiders. And information that the analysts obtain normally may be the basis for judgments as to the market worth of a corporation's securities. The analyst's judgment in this respect is made available in market letters or otherwise to clients of the firm. It is the nature of this type of information, and indeed of the markets themselves, that such information

---

confidential, and the relationship at least must imply such a duty.

15. Apparently, the SEC believes this case differs from *Chiarella* in that Dirks' receipt of inside information from Secrist, an insider, carried Secrist's duties with it, while Chiarella received the information without the direct involvement of an insider and thus inherited no duty to disclose or abstain. The SEC fails to explain, however, why the receipt of nonpublic information from an insider automatically carries with it the fiduciary duty of the insider. As we emphasized in *Chiarella,* mere possession of nonpublic information does not give rise to a duty to disclose or abstain; only a specific relationship does that. And we do not believe that the mere receipt of information from an insider creates such a special relationship between the tippee and the corporation's shareholders. ***

cannot be made simultaneously available to all of the corporation's stockholders or the public generally.

B

The conclusion that recipients of inside information do not invariably acquire a duty to disclose or abstain does not mean that such tippees always are free to trade on the information. The need for a ban on some tippee trading is clear. Not only are insiders forbidden by their fiduciary relationship from personally using undisclosed corporate information to their advantage, but they also may not give such information to an outsider for the same improper purpose of exploiting the information for their personal gain. Similarly, the transactions of those who knowingly participate with the fiduciary in such a breach are "as forbidden" as transactions "on behalf of the trustee himself." *Mosser v. Darrow*, 341 U.S. 267, 272 (1951). As the Court explained in *Mosser,* a contrary rule "would open up opportunities for devious dealings in the name of the others that the trustee could not conduct in his own." 341 U.S., at 271. Thus, the tippee's duty to disclose or abstain is derivative from that of the insider's duty. As we noted in *Chiarella,* "[t]he tippee's obligation has been viewed as arising from his role as a participant after the fact in the insider's breach of a fiduciary duty." [445 U.S.] at 230, n. 12.

Thus, some tippees must assume an insider's duty to the shareholders not because they receive inside information, but rather because it has been made available to them *improperly*. And for Rule 10b-5 purposes, the insider's disclosure is improper only where it would violate his *Cady, Roberts* duty. Thus, a tippee assumes a fiduciary duty to the shareholders of a corporation not to trade on material nonpublic information only when the insider has breached his fiduciary duty to the shareholders by disclosing the information to the tippee and the tippee knows or should know that there has been a breach. As Commissioner Smith perceptively observed in *In re Investors Mgmt. Co.:* "[T]ippee responsibility must be related back to insider responsibility by a necessary finding that the tippee knew the information was given to him in breach of a duty by a person having a special relationship to the issuer not to disclose the information...." [44 SEC] at 651 (concurring in the result). Tipping thus properly is viewed only as a means of indirectly violating the *Cady, Roberts* disclose-or-abstain rule.

C

In determining whether a tippee is under an obligation to disclose or abstain, it thus is necessary to determine whether the insider's "tip" constituted a breach of the insider's fiduciary duty. All disclosures of confidential corporate information are not inconsistent with the duty insiders owe to shareholders. In contrast to the extraordinary facts of this case, the more typical situation in which there will be a question whether disclosure violates the insider's *Cady, Roberts* duty is when insiders disclose information to analysts. In some situations, the insider will act consistently with his fiduciary duty to shareholders, and yet release of the information may affect the market. For example, it may not be clear—either to the corporate insider or to the recipient analyst—whether the information will be viewed as material nonpublic information. Corporate officials may mistakenly think the information already has been disclosed or that it is not material enough to affect the market. Whether disclosure is a breach of duty therefore depends in large part on the purpose of the disclosure. This standard was identified by the SEC itself in *Cady, Roberts:* a purpose of the securities laws was to eliminate "use of inside information for personal advantage." 40 SEC, at 912, n. 15. Thus, the test is whether the insider personally will benefit, directly or indirectly, from his disclosure. Absent some personal gain, there has been no breach of duty to stockholders. And absent a breach by the insider, there is no derivative breach. As Commissioner Smith stated in *Investors Management Co.:* "It is important in this type of case to focus on policing insiders and what they do ... rather than on policing information *per se* and its possession...." 44 SEC, at 648 (concurring in the result).

The SEC argues that, if inside-trading liability does not exist when the information is transmitted for a proper purpose but is used for trading, it would be a rare situation when the parties could not fabricate some ostensibly legitimate business justification for transmitting the information. We think the SEC is unduly concerned. In determining whether the insider's purpose in making a particular disclosure is fraudulent, the SEC and the courts are not required to read the parties' minds. Scienter in some cases is relevant in determining whether the tipper has violated his *Cady, Roberts* duty. But to determine whether the disclosure itself "deceive[s], manipulate[s], or defraud[s]" shareholders, *Aaron v. SEC*, 446 U.S. 680, 686 (1980), the initial inquiry is whether there has been a breach of duty by the insider. This requires courts to focus on objective criteria, *i.e.*, whether the insider receives a direct or indirect personal benefit from the disclosure, such as a pecuniary gain or a reputational benefit that will translate into future earnings. Cf. Brudney, Insiders, Outsiders, and Informational Advantages Under the Federal Securities Laws, 93 Harv. L. Rev. 324, 348 (1979) ("The theory ... is that the insider, by giving the information out selectively, is in effect selling the information to its recipient for cash, reciprocal information, or other things of value for himself...."). There are objective facts and circumstances that often justify such an inference. For example, there may be a relationship between the insider and the recipient that suggests a *quid pro quo* from the latter, or an intention to benefit the particular recipient. The elements of fiduciary duty and exploitation of nonpublic information also exist when an insider makes a gift of confidential information to a trading relative or friend. The tip and trade resemble trading by the insider himself followed by a gift of the profits to the recipient.

Determining whether an insider personally benefits from a particular disclosure, a question of fact, will not always be easy for courts. But it is essential, we think, to have a guiding principle for those whose daily activities must be limited and instructed by the SEC's inside-trading rules, and we believe that there must be a breach of the insider's fiduciary duty before the tippee inherits the duty to disclose or abstain. In contrast, the rule adopted by the SEC in this case would have no limiting principle.

IV

Under the inside-trading and tipping rules set forth above, we find that there was no actionable violation by Dirks. It is undisputed that Dirks himself was a stranger to Equity Funding, with no pre-existing fiduciary duty to its shareholders. He took no action, directly or indirectly, that induced the shareholders or officers of Equity Funding to repose trust or confidence in him. There was no expectation by Dirks' sources that he would keep their information in confidence. Nor did Dirks misappropriate or illegally obtain the information about Equity Funding. Unless the insiders breached their *Cady, Roberts* duty to shareholders in disclosing the nonpublic information to Dirks, he breached no duty when he passed it on to investors as well as to the Wall Street Journal.

It is clear that neither Secrist nor the other Equity Funding employees violated their *Cady, Roberts* duty to the corporation's shareholders by providing information to Dirks. The tippers received no monetary or personal benefit for revealing Equity Funding's secrets, nor was their purpose to make a gift of valuable information to Dirks. As the facts of this case clearly indicate, the tippers were motivated by a desire to expose the fraud. In the absence of a breach of duty to shareholders by the insiders, there was no derivative breach by Dirks. Dirks therefore could not have been "a participant after the fact in [an] insider's breach of a fiduciary duty." *Chiarella*, 445 U.S., at 230, n. 12.

V

We conclude that Dirks, in the circumstances of this case, had no duty to abstain from use of the inside information that he obtained. The judgment of the Court of Appeals therefore is reversed.

JUSTICE HAROLD A. BLACKMUN, WITH WHOM JUSTICES BRENNAN AND MARSHALL JOIN, DISSENTING:

The Court today takes still another step to limit the protections provided investors by § 10(b) of the Securities Exchange Act of 1934. See *Chiarella v. United States*, 445 U.S. 222, 246 (1980) (dissenting opinion). The device employed in this case engrafts a special motivational requirement on the fiduciary duty doctrine. This innovation excuses a knowing and intentional violation of an insider's duty to shareholders if the insider does not act from a motive of personal gain. Even on the extraordinary facts of this case, such an innovation is not justified. ***

No one questions that Secrist himself could not trade on his inside information to the disadvantage of uninformed shareholders and purchasers of Equity Funding securities. Unlike the printer in *Chiarella,* Secrist stood in a fiduciary relationship with these shareholders. As the Court states, corporate insiders have an affirmative duty of disclosure when trading with shareholders of the corporation. See *Chiarella*, 445 U.S. at 227. This duty extends as well to purchasers of the corporation's securities. Id., at 227, n. 8.

The Court also acknowledges that Secrist could not do by proxy what he was prohibited from doing personally. *Mosser v. Darrow*, 341 U.S. 267, 272 (1951). But this is precisely what Secrist did. Secrist used Dirks to disseminate information to Dirks' clients, who in turn dumped stock on unknowing purchasers. Secrist thus intended Dirks to injure the purchasers of Equity Funding securities to whom Secrist had a duty to disclose. ***

The Court holds, however, that Dirks is not liable because Secrist did not violate his duty; according to the Court, this is so because Secrist did not have the improper purpose of personal gain. In so doing, the Court imposes a new, subjective limitation on the scope of the duty owed by insiders to shareholders. The novelty of this limitation is reflected in the Court's lack of support for it.

The insider's duty is owed directly to the corporation's shareholders. See Langevoort, Insider Trading and the Fiduciary Principle: A Post-*Chiarella* Restatement, 70 Calif. L. Rev. 1, 5 (1982). As *Chiarella* recognized, it is based on the relationship of trust and confidence between the insider and the shareholder. That relationship assures the shareholder that the insider may not take actions that will harm him unfairly. The affirmative duty of disclosure protects against this injury. ***

The fact that the insider himself does not benefit from the breach does not eradicate the shareholder's injury. Cf. Restatement (Second) of Trusts § 205, Comments c and d (1959) (trustee liable for acts causing diminution of value of trust); 3 A. Scott, Law of Trusts § 205, p. 1665 (1967) (trustee liable for any losses to trust caused by his breach). It makes no difference to the shareholder whether the corporate insider gained or intended to gain personally from the transaction; the shareholder still has lost because of the insider's misuse of nonpublic information. The duty is addressed not to the insider's motives, but to his actions and their consequences on the shareholder. Personal gain is not an element of the breach of this duty.

This conclusion is borne out by the Court's decision in *Mosser v. Darrow*, 341 U.S. 267 (1951). There, the Court faced an analogous situation: a reorganization trustee engaged two employee-promoters of subsidiaries of the companies being reorganized to provide services that the trustee considered to be essential to the successful operation of the trust. In order to secure their services, the trustee expressly agreed with the employees that they could continue to trade in the securities of the subsidiaries. The employees then turned their inside position into substantial profits at the expense both of the trust and of other holders of the companies' securities.

The Court acknowledged that the trustee neither intended to nor did in actual fact benefit from this arrangement; his motives were completely selfless and devoted to the companies. [341 U.S.], at 275. The Court, nevertheless, found the trustee liable to the estate for the activities of the employees he authorized. The Court described the trustee's defalcation as "a willful and deliberate setting up of an interest in employees adverse to that of the trust." Id., at 272. The breach did not depend on the trustee's personal gain, and his motives in violating his duty were irrelevant; like Secrist, the trustee intended that others would abuse the inside information for their personal gain.

As *Mosser* demonstrates, the breach consists in taking action disadvantageous to the person to whom one owes a duty. In this case, Secrist owed a duty to purchasers of Equity Funding shares. The Court's addition of the bad-purpose element to a breach of fiduciary duty claim is flatly inconsistent with the principle of *Mosser*. I do not join this limitation of the scope of an insider's fiduciary duty to shareholders. ***

The improper-purpose requirement not only has no basis in law, but it rests implicitly on a policy that I cannot accept. The Court justifies Secrist's and Dirks' action because the general benefit derived from the violation of Secrist's duty to shareholders outweighed the harm caused to those shareholders—in other words, because the end justified the means. Under this view, the benefit conferred on society by Secrist's and Dirks' activities may be paid for with the losses caused to shareholders trading with Dirks' clients.

Although Secrist's general motive to expose the Equity Funding fraud was laudable, the means he chose were not. Moreover, even assuming that Dirks played a substantial role in exposing the fraud, he and his clients should not profit from the information they obtained from Secrist. *** As a citizen, Dirks had at least an ethical obligation to report the information to the proper authorities. The Court's holding is deficient in policy terms not because it fails to create a legal norm out of that ethical norm, but because it actually rewards Dirks for his aiding and abetting.

Dirks and Secrist were under a duty to disclose the information or to refrain from trading on it. I agree that disclosure in this case would have been difficult. I also recognize that the SEC seemingly has been less than helpful in its view of the nature of disclosure necessary to satisfy the disclose-or-refrain duty. The Commission tells persons with inside information that they cannot trade on that information unless they disclose; it refuses, however, to tell them how to disclose. See *In re Faberge, Inc.,* 45 SEC 249, 256 (1973) (disclosure requires public release through public media designed to reach investing public generally). This seems to be a less than sensible policy, which it is incumbent on the Commission to correct. The Court, however, has no authority to remedy the problem by opening a hole in the congressionally mandated prohibition on insider trading, thus rewarding such trading.

In my view, Secrist violated his duty to Equity Funding shareholders by transmitting material nonpublic information to Dirks with the intention that Dirks would cause his clients to trade on that information. Dirks, therefore, was under a duty to make the information publicly available or to refrain from actions that he knew would lead to trading. Because Dirks caused his clients to trade, he violated § 10(b) and Rule 10b-5. Any other result is a disservice to this country's attempt to provide fair and efficient capital markets. I dissent.

NOTES AND QUESTIONS

1. ***The "Personal Benefit" Test.*** If a corporate officer breaches her company's well-delineated policy of confidentiality by sharing confidential information with a friend, and if her friend is aware of that breach, should it matter for purposes of Rule 10b-5 liability whether the insider personally benefitted from the breach of this duty?

2. ***Tippees and Fiduciary Duties.*** As the *Dirks* Court recognized, the typical tippee stands as a complete stranger to the shareholders of the corporations whose securities are being purchased on the basis of material nonpublic information. Yet the Court extends the classical theory of insider trading to cover these clear outsiders. What policy reasons does the Court provide to justify this departure from the common law?

3. ***Identifying Temporary or Constructive Insiders.*** In footnote 14, the *Dirks* Court points out that the "disclose or abstain" rule applies as well to temporary insiders of a corporation, such as attorneys, accountants, and investment bankers, who are provided with confidential corporate information.

In the Court's view, these "outsiders may become fiduciaries of the shareholders." Yet other than noting that "the relationship itself must at least imply such a duty [to keep the disclosed information confidential]," *Dirks* does little to shed light on how else one attains this "special status." Lower courts must therefore articulate their own standards. See, e.g., *SEC v. Ingram*, 694 F. Supp. 1437 (C.D. Cal. 1988) (temporary insider status accorded to stockbroker who had assisted the company with finding a merger partner, and who had been invited to attended pre-merger negotiations where there was an absolute expectation of confidentiality); *SEC v. Mayhew*, 916 F. Supp. 123, 129 (D. Conn. 1995) (concluding that SEC had failed to establish that a business consultant was the "functional equivalent of a fiduciary") aff'd without discussion of this issue, 121 F.3d 44 (2d Cir. 1997). *Mayhew* involved a luncheon conversation in which a company executive revealed to a human resources consultant that his company was discussing merger possibilities. The court noted that "there was never any formal agreement" between the consultant's firm and the takeover target, and emphasized that "the fact that [the company executive] expected [the consultant] to keep the substance of the lunch conversation confidential did not, in itself, give rise to a fiduciary duty." Id. at 129-30. Weighing the testimony of both the consultant and the company executive, the court concluded that the consultant's "ambiguous and ambivalent role at the time [of the] lunch when he obtained the insider information was much more akin to the proverbial 'old boys networking' *** lacking indicia of de facto control and dominance resulting from the confidence imposed." Id. at 130. Do you agree? For arguments favoring a broader construction of the temporary insider category, see Robert A. Prentice, Permanently Reviving the Temporary Insider, 36 J. Corp. L. 343, 388 (2011) (arguing that persons "who voluntarily receive confidential corporate information for a business purpose should be deemed to owe a quasi-fiduciary duty to the source of that information when they know or should know that the source reasonably expects them to keep the information confidential").

4. Securities Analysts and the Problem of Selective Disclosure. Issuers and their corporate officials regularly interact with securities analysts, often providing them with publicly available information through telephone conversations, letters, in-person meetings, and other types of communications. In addition, to maintain an active level of interest in their company's securities, corporate officials are often tempted to share with analysts certain information that has yet to be released to the public. This practice of "selective disclosure" may create potential insider trading problems for securities issuers, their officials, and the analysts who cover the company. That is, such selective disclosure raises questions as to whether the issuer and its officials can be characterized as "tippers," and whether the analysts can be characterized as "tippees," engaged in acts and practices prohibited by Rule 10b-5. Such questions, though, are complicated by *Dirks*'s requirement that for tippee liability to be present, the tipper must have acted for a personal benefit.

If a company's CEO informs an analyst of lower than expected quarterly returns, and if that CEO shares this information "to protect and enhance his reputation," does the CEO act with the requisite motivation to trigger tipper liability under *Dirks*? See *SEC v. Stevens*, 48 SEC Docket 739 (Mar. 19, 1991) (consent order sanctioning CEO of Ultrasystems Corporation). Assuming that a "reputational benefit" constitutes sufficient motivation, how likely is that the

SEC could demonstrate at trial that this was, in fact, a CEO's motivation? What if a CEO acted solely to bolster favorable publicity about his company? Could an analyst share the negative earnings with his clients and advise them to sell off their shares in the company? Could an analyst sell short the company's stock?

The SEC has taken the position that the practice of selective disclosure "leads to a loss of investor confidence in the integrity of our capital markets." See Selective Disclosure and Insider Trading, Exchange Act Release No. 43154, 2000 WL 1201556 at *2 (Aug. 15, 2000). Do you agree?

5. Regulation FD. Regulation FD (which took effect in October 2000) is predicated on the belief that all investors should have access to an issuer's material disclosures at the same time. Regulation FD does not characterize the practice of selective disclosure as a fraudulent act or device under Exchange Act Section 10(b) and Rule 10b-5. Rather, Regulation FD was promulgated pursuant to Exchange Act Section 13(a), which empowers the SEC to regulate the disclosure practices of reporting companies. Although Regulation FD's provisions are somewhat lengthy, it sets forth a basic rule that requires that whenever:

> (1) an issuer, or person acting on its behalf,
>
> (2) discloses material nonpublic information,
>
> (3) to certain enumerated persons (in general, securities market professionals or holders of the issuer's securities who may well trade on the basis of the information) unless they agree to keep that information confidential,
>
> (4) the issuer must make public disclosure of that same information: (a) simultaneously (for intentional disclosures), or (b) "promptly" (for non-intentional disclosures).

Id. at *6-7 (summarizing Rule 100 of Regulation FD). Accordingly, while Regulation FD does not automatically require covered issuers to promptly disclose all material events as they occur, it does in fact require that when an issuer chooses to disclose material nonpublic information to a person covered by the regulation, "it must do so in a manner that provides general public disclosure, rather than through selective disclosure" to a favored few. Selective Disclosure Release, supra, 2000 WL 1201556 at *7.

If you were a member of the Commission, would you have voted to adopt Regulation FD? Why or why not? Regulation FD is examined more extensively in Section F of this Chapter.

PROBLEM 7-3

Dylan is an outside attorney with a law firm retained by Merff, Inc., one of the nation's largest biotechnology companies. In counseling Merff in connection with certain patent applications, Dylan learned that Merff will soon announce to the public its development of a new drug for the treatment of Alzheimer's disease. While continuing to advise Merff in connection with its patent applications, Dylan secretly purchased 1000 shares of stock in Merff, expecting to make a huge profit when the news of the drug is announced.

Shortly after his purchase of the stock in Merff, Dylan began to experience nightmares, which kept him wide awake for several nights in a row. Exhausted and a bit remorseful, he confided in a psychiatrist who had counseled him a few years earlier in the wake of his divorce. In the course of his therapy session, Dylan told the psychiatrist the entire story behind his purchases of stock in Merff, including the information about the soon to be released drug. The psychiatrist listened intently, prescribed sleeping pills for Dylan, and scheduled another session to meet with him in two weeks. As soon as Dylan left his office, the psychiatrist phoned his broker and placed an order for the purchase of 2000 shares of stock in Merff.

Once the development of its Alzheimer's drug was announced, the market price of Merff rose substantially and Dylan and the psychiatrist made a substantial profit from selling their shares. Has Dylan violated Rule 10b-5? Has the psychiatrist violated Rule 10b-5?

3. The Misappropriation Theory

The government raised the misappropriation theory in its brief to the Supreme Court in *Chiarella*, where it argued that Chiarella had "committed fraud against both the acquiring corporations whose information he converted and the investors who sold him securities in ignorance of forthcoming market events of critical importance." Brief for the Petitioner at 24, *Chiarella v. United States*, 445 U.S. 222 (1980) (No. 78-1202). That is, the government contended that Chiarella's "secret conversion of confidential information operated as a fraud on the corporation that entrusted him with that information" and also that his "purchase of securities based on material non-public information obtained by misappropriation constituted fraud on the sellers of those securities." Id. at 28, 38-39. Yet the *Chiarella* majority ruled on the validity of neither version of the misappropriation theory because, in its view, neither had been presented to the jury. Misappropriation theories were, however, discussed at length by a total of five Justices in separate concurring or dissenting opinions.

Chief Justice Burger and Justices Brennan, Blackmun, and Marshall all agreed that Rule 10b-5 liability would be triggered by any person who purchased or sold securities on the basis of material nonpublic information that was improperly obtained or converted for a personal benefit. Thus, four Justices in *Chiarella* endorsed a broad version of the misappropriation theory that recognized a general disclosure obligation owed to any investors with whom a misappropriator trades: "a person who has misappropriated nonpublic information has an absolute duty to disclose that information or to refrain from trading." *Chiarella v. United States*, 445 U.S. 222, 240 (1980) (Burger, J. dissenting). A fifth member of the Court, Justice Stevens, indicated that while he did not accept the existence of a general duty owed to all securities investors on the other side of Chiarella's transactions, "[r]espectable arguments could be made" that Chiarella's actions had defrauded the acquiring companies that had entrusted his employer with confidential tender offer information, and that this fraud occurred " 'in connection with the purchase or sale of any security.' " Justice Stevens's concurring opinion therefore raised the possibility of a narrower version of the misappropriation theory premised on a "fraud on the source" of the misappropriated information. Id. at 238 (Stevens, J., concurring). Yet he thought the Court wise for "leav[ing] the resolution of this issue for another day." Id.

Encouraged by its positive reception from the concurring and dissenting Justices in *Chiarella*, the SEC and the DOJ advanced the misappropriation theory of insider trading liability in instances where the government wished to pursue Section 10(b) and Rule 10b-5 actions against individuals who did not owe fiduciary duties to the shareholders of the companies in which securities transactions had been made. Specifically, the government began to emphasize the argument set forth by Justice Stevens in *Chiarella*, that trading securities based on nonpublic information obtained in breach of a pre-existing duty of confidentiality defrauded the source of the information in connection with the purchase or sale of securities. And the Second Circuit was quick to give this theory a warm embrace. See, e.g., *United States v. Newman*, 664 F.2d 12 (2d Cir. 1981) (affirming criminal conviction in misappropriation case against investment bank employees); *SEC v. Materia*, 745 F.2d 197, 202 (2d Cir. 1984) (affirming injunction and disgorgement in a case against a financial printer involving facts almost identical to those of *Chiarella*); *SEC v. Musella*, 578 F. Supp. 425, 439 (S.D.N.Y. 1984) (enjoining tippees of an administrative staff employee of a law firm who purchased shares of a companies targeted for takeover by the law firm's clients); and *United States v. Carpenter*, 791 F.2d 1024 (2d Cir. 1986), aff'd by an equally divided Court, 484 U.S. 19 (1987) (affirming conviction of Wall Street Journal reporter who had traded on the basis of information in a soon to be released column). Other circuits soon followed. See, e.g., *Rothberg v. Rosenbloom*, 771 F.2d 818 (3d Cir. 1985) (tippee who traded on the basis of confidential merger information obtained from corporate official), rev'd on other grounds after remand, 808 F.2d 252 (3d Cir. 1986); *SEC v. Cherif*, 933 F.2d 403, 410 (7th Cir. 1991) (individual who broke into his former place of employment to steal nonpublic information about his former employer's clients and then used that information to trade securities); *SEC v. Clark*, 915 F.2d 439 (9th Cir. 1990) (employee who tipped and traded in the securities of a company he knew to be a takeover target of his employer).

The unanimity among the federal circuits dissipated in 1995 when the Fourth Circuit decided *United States v. Bryan*, 58 F.3d 933 (4th Cir. 1995) (overturning conviction of state lottery official who had purchased the stock of companies that were slated to receive contracts from the Virginia Lottery Commission). The Eighth Circuit also rejected the misappropriation theory the following year in *United States v. O'Hagan*, 92 F.3d 612, 620 (8th Cir. 1996). The Supreme Court granted certiorari to resolve the split in the federal circuits.

UNITED STATES v. O'HAGAN

521 U.S. 642 (1997)

JUSTICE RUTH BADER GINSBURG:

I

Respondent James Herman O'Hagan was a partner in the law firm of Dorsey & Whitney in Minneapolis, Minnesota. In July 1988, Grand Metropolitan PLC (Grand Met), a company based in London, England, retained Dorsey & Whitney as local counsel to represent Grand Met regarding a potential tender offer for the common stock of the Pillsbury Company, headquartered in Minneapolis. Both Grand Met and Dorsey & Whitney took precautions to protect the confidentiality of Grand Met's tender offer plans. O'Hagan did no work on the Grand Met representation. Dorsey & Whitney withdrew from representing Grand Met on September 9, 1988. Less than a month later, on October 4, 1988, Grand Met publicly announced its tender offer for Pillsbury stock.

On August 18, 1988, while Dorsey & Whitney was still representing Grand Met, O'Hagan began purchasing call options for Pillsbury stock. Each option gave him the right to purchase 100 shares of Pillsbury stock by a specified date in September 1988. Later in August and in September, O'Hagan made additional purchases of Pillsbury call options. By the end of September, he owned 2,500 unexpired Pillsbury options, apparently more than any other individual investor. O'Hagan also purchased, in September 1988, some 5,000 shares of Pillsbury common stock, at a price just under $39 per share. When Grand Met announced its tender offer in October, the price of Pillsbury stock rose to nearly $60 per share. O'Hagan then sold his Pillsbury call options and common stock, making a profit of more than $4.3 million.

The Securities and Exchange Commission initiated an investigation into O'Hagan's transactions, culminating in a 57-count indictment. The indictment alleged that O'Hagan defrauded his law firm and its client, Grand Met, by using for his own trading purposes material, nonpublic information regarding Grand Met's planned tender offer. According to the indictment, O'Hagan used the profits he gained through this trading to conceal his previous embezzlement and conversion of unrelated client trust funds. O'Hagan was charged with 20 counts of mail fraud, in violation of 18 U.S.C. § 1341; 17 counts of securities fraud, in violation of § 10(b) of the Securities Exchange Act of 1934 and SEC Rule 10b-5; 17 counts of fraudulent trading in connection with a tender offer, in violation of § 14(e) of the Exchange Act and SEC Rule 14e-3(a); and 3 counts of violating federal money laundering statutes. A jury convicted O'Hagan on all 57 counts, and he was sentenced to a 41-month term of imprisonment.

A divided panel of the Court of Appeals for the Eighth Circuit reversed all of O'Hagan's convictions. 92 F.3d 612 (1996). ***

II

We address first the Court of Appeals' reversal of O'Hagan's convictions under § 10(b) and Rule 10b-5. Following the Fourth Circuit's lead, see *United States v. Bryan*, 58 F.3d 933, 943-959 (1995), the Eighth Circuit rejected the misappropriation theory as a basis for § 10(b) liability. We hold, in accord with several other Courts of Appeals, that criminal liability under § 10(b) may be predicated on the misappropriation theory.[4]

4. Twice before we have been presented with the question whether criminal liability for violation of § 10(b) may be based on a misappropriation theory. In *Chiarella v. United States*, 445 U.S. 222, 235-237 (1980), the jury had received no misappropriation theory instructions, so we declined to address the question. In *Carpenter v. United States*, 484 U.S. 19, 24 (1987), the Court divided evenly on whether, under the circumstances of that case, convictions resting on the misappropriation theory should be affirmed.

A

***Liability under Rule 10b-5, our precedent indicates, does not extend beyond conduct encompassed by § 10(b)'s prohibition. See *Ernst & Ernst v. Hochfelder*, 425 U.S. 185, 214 (1976) (scope of Rule 10b-5 cannot exceed power Congress granted Commission under § 10(b)); see also *Central Bank of Denver, N.A. v. First Interstate Bank of Denver, N. A.*, 511 U.S. 164, 173 (1994) ("We have refused to allow [private] 10b-5 challenges to conduct not prohibited by the text of the statute.").

Under the "traditional" or "classical theory" of insider trading liability, § 10(b) and Rule 10b-5 are violated when a corporate insider trades in the securities of his corporation on the basis of material, nonpublic information. Trading on such information qualifies as a "deceptive device" under § 10(b), we have affirmed, because "a relationship of trust and confidence [exists] between the shareholders of a corporation and those insiders who have obtained confidential information by reason of their position with that corporation." *Chiarella v. United States*, 445 U.S. 222, 228 (1980). That relationship, we recognized, "gives rise to a duty to disclose [or to abstain from trading] because of the 'necessity of preventing a corporate insider from ... tak[ing] unfair advantage of ... uninformed ... stockholders.'" Id., at 228-229. The classical theory applies not only to officers, directors, and other permanent insiders of a corporation, but also to attorneys, accountants, consultants, and others who temporarily become fiduciaries of a corporation. See *Dirks v. SEC*, 463 U.S. 646, 655, n. 14 (1983).

The "misappropriation theory" holds that a person commits fraud "in connection with" a securities transaction, and thereby violates § 10(b) and Rule 10b-5, when he misappropriates confidential information for securities trading purposes, in breach of a duty owed to the source of the information. Under this theory, a fiduciary's undisclosed, self-serving use of a principal's information to purchase or sell securities, in breach of a duty of loyalty and confidentiality, defrauds the principal of the exclusive use of that information. In lieu of premising liability on a fiduciary relationship between company insider and purchaser or seller of the company's stock, the misappropriation theory premises liability on a fiduciary-turned-trader's deception of those who entrusted him with access to confidential information.

The two theories are complementary, each addressing efforts to capitalize on nonpublic information through the purchase or sale of securities. The classical theory targets a corporate insider's breach of duty to shareholders with whom the insider transacts; the misappropriation theory outlaws trading on the basis of nonpublic information by a corporate "outsider" in breach of a duty owed not to a trading party, but to the source of the information. The misappropriation theory is thus designed to "protec[t] the integrity of the securities markets against abuses by 'outsiders' to a corporation who have access to confidential information that will affect th[e] corporation's security price when revealed, but who owe no fiduciary or other duty to that corporation's shareholders." [Brief for the United States at 14].

In this case, the indictment alleged that O'Hagan, in breach of a duty of trust and confidence he owed to his law firm, Dorsey & Whitney, and to its client, Grand Met, traded on the basis of nonpublic information regarding Grand Met's planned tender offer for Pillsbury common stock. This conduct, the Government charged, constituted a fraudulent device in connection with the purchase and sale of securities.

B

We agree with the Government that misappropriation, as just defined, satisfies § 10(b)'s requirement that chargeable conduct involve a "deceptive device or contrivance" used "in connection with" the purchase or sale of securities. We observe, first, that misappropriators, as the Government describes them, deal in deception. A fiduciary who "[pretends] loyalty to the principal while secretly converting the principal's information for personal gain," Brief for United States 17, "dupes" or defrauds the principal. See Aldave, Misappropriation: A General Theory of Liability for Trading on Nonpublic Information, 13 Hofstra L. Rev. 101, 119 (1984).

We addressed fraud of the same species in *Carpenter v. United States*, 484 U.S. 19 (1987), which involved the mail fraud statute's proscription of "any scheme or artifice to defraud." Affirming convictions under that statute, we said in *Carpenter* that an employee's undertaking not to reveal his employer's confidential information "became a sham" when the employee provided the information to his co-conspirators in a scheme to obtain trading profits. A company's confidential information, we recognized in *Carpenter*, qualifies as property to which the company has a right of exclusive use. The undisclosed misappropriation of such information, in violation of a fiduciary duty, the Court said in *Carpenter*, constitutes fraud akin to embezzlement—"'the fraudulent appropriation to one's own use of the money or goods entrusted to one's care by another.'" Id., at 27. *Carpenter's* discussion of the fraudulent misuse of confidential information, the Government notes, "is a particularly apt source of guidance here, because [the mail fraud statute] (like Section 10(b)) has long been held to require deception, not merely the breach of a fiduciary duty." Brief for United States 18, n. 9.

Deception through nondisclosure is central to the theory of liability for which the Government seeks recognition. As counsel for the Government stated in explanation of the theory at oral argument: "To satisfy the common law rule that a trustee may not use the property that [has] been entrusted [to] him, there would have to be consent. To satisfy the requirement of the Securities Act that there be no deception, there would only have to be disclosure." Tr. of Oral Arg. 12; see generally Restatement (Second) of Agency §§ 390, 395 (1958) (agent's disclosure obligation regarding use of confidential information).[6]

---

6. Under the misappropriation theory urged in this case, the disclosure obligation runs to the source of the information, here, Dorsey & Whitney and Grand Met. Chief Justice Burger, dissenting in *Chiarella*, advanced a broader reading of § 10(b) and Rule 10b-5; the disclosure obligation, as he envisioned it, ran to those with whom the misappropriator trades. 445 U.S., at 240 ("a person who has misappropriated nonpublic information has an absolute duty to disclose that information or to refrain from trading"); see also id., at 243, n. 4. The Government does not propose that we adopt a misappropriation theory of that breadth.

The misappropriation theory advanced by the Government is consistent with *Santa Fe Industries, Inc. v. Green*, 430 U.S. 462 (1977), a decision underscoring that § 10(b) is not an all-purpose breach of fiduciary duty ban; rather, it trains on conduct involving manipulation or deception. See id., at 473-476. In contrast to the Government's allegations in this case, in *Santa Fe Industries*, all pertinent facts were disclosed by the persons charged with violating § 10(b) and Rule 10b-5; therefore, there was no deception through nondisclosure to which liability under those provisions could attach. Similarly, full disclosure forecloses liability under the misappropriation theory: Because the deception essential to the misappropriation theory involves feigning fidelity to the source of information, if the fiduciary discloses to the source that he plans to trade on the nonpublic information, there is no "deceptive device" and thus no § 10(b) violation—although the fiduciary-turned-trader may remain liable under state law for breach of a duty of loyalty.

We turn next to the § 10(b) requirement that the misappropriator's deceptive use of information be "in connection with the purchase or sale of [a] security." This element is satisfied because the fiduciary's fraud is consummated, not when the fiduciary gains the confidential information, but when, without disclosure to his principal, he uses the information to purchase or sell securities. The securities transaction and the breach of duty thus coincide. This is so even though the person or entity defrauded is not the other party to the trade, but is, instead, the source of the nonpublic information. See Aldave, 13 Hofstra L.Rev., at 120 ("a fraud or deceit can be practiced on one person, with resultant harm to another person or group of persons"). A misappropriator who trades on the basis of material, nonpublic information, in short, gains his advantageous market position through deception; he deceives the source of the information and simultaneously harms members of the investing public.

The misappropriation theory targets information of a sort that misappropriators ordinarily capitalize upon to gain no-risk profits through the purchase or sale of securities. Should a misappropriator put such information to other use, the statute's prohibition would not be implicated. The theory does not catch all conceivable forms of fraud involving confidential information; rather, it catches fraudulent means of capitalizing on such information through securities transactions.

The Government notes another limitation on the forms of fraud § 10(b) reaches: "The misappropriation theory would not ... apply to a case in which a person defrauded a bank into giving him a loan or embezzled cash from another, and then used the proceeds of the misdeed to purchase securities." Brief for United States 24, n. 13. In such a case, the Government states, "the proceeds would have value to the malefactor apart from their use in a securities transaction, and the fraud would be complete as soon as the money was obtained." In other words, money can buy, if not anything, then at least many things; its misappropriation may thus be viewed as sufficiently detached from a subsequent securities transaction that § 10(b)'s "in connection with" requirement would not be met.

Justice Thomas' charge that the misappropriation theory is incoherent because information, like funds, can be put to multiple uses misses the point.

The Exchange Act was enacted in part "to insure the maintenance of fair and honest markets," and there is no question that fraudulent uses of confidential information fall within § 10(b)'s prohibition if the fraud is "in connection with" a securities transaction. It is hardly remarkable that a rule suitably applied to the fraudulent uses of certain kinds of information would be stretched beyond reason were it applied to the fraudulent use of money.

Justice Thomas does catch the Government in overstatement. Observing that money can be used for all manner of purposes and purchases, the Government urges that confidential information of the kind at issue derives its value *only* from its utility in securities trading. See Brief for United States 10, 21. Substitute "ordinarily" for "only," and the Government is on the mark. ***

The misappropriation theory comports with § 10(b)'s language, which requires deception "in connection with the purchase or sale of any security," not deception of an identifiable purchaser or seller. The theory is also well tuned to an animating purpose of the Exchange Act: to insure honest securities markets and thereby promote investor confidence. See 45 Fed. Reg. 60412 (1980) (trading on misappropriated information "undermines the integrity of, and investor confidence in, the securities markets"). Although informational disparity is inevitable in the securities markets, investors likely would hesitate to venture their capital in a market where trading based on misappropriated nonpublic information is unchecked by law. An investor's informational disadvantage vis-a-vis a misappropriator with material, nonpublic information stems from contrivance, not luck; it is a disadvantage that cannot be overcome with research or skill. See Brudney, Insiders, Outsiders, and Informational Advantages Under the Federal Securities Laws, 93 Harv. L. Rev. 322, 356 (1979) ("If the market is thought to be systematically populated with ... transactors [trading on the basis of misappropriated information] some investors will refrain from dealing altogether, and others will incur costs to avoid dealing with such transactors or corruptly to overcome their unerodable informational advantages.")

In sum, considering the inhibiting impact on market participation of trading on misappropriated information, and the congressional purposes underlying § 10(b), it makes scant sense to hold a lawyer like O'Hagan a § 10(b) violator if he works for a law firm representing the target of a tender offer, but not if he works for a law firm representing the bidder. The text of the statute requires no such result. The misappropriation at issue here was properly made the subject of a § 10(b) charge because it meets the statutory requirement that there be "deceptive" conduct "in connection with" securities transactions. ***

Vital to our decision that criminal liability may be sustained under the misappropriation theory, we emphasize, are two sturdy safeguards Congress has provided regarding scienter. To establish a criminal violation of Rule 10b-5, the Government must prove that a person "willfully" violated the provision. [See Section 32(a) of the Exchange Act.] Furthermore, a defendant may not be imprisoned for violating Rule 10b-5 if he proves that he had no knowledge of the Rule. See ibid. O'Hagan's charge that the misappropriation theory is too indefinite to permit the imposition of criminal liability thus fails not only because the theory is limited to those who breach a recognized duty. In addition, the statute's "requirement of the presence of culpable intent as a necessary element of the offense does much to destroy any force in the argument that application of the [statute]" in circumstances such as O'Hagan's is unjust. *Boyce Motor Lines, Inc. v. United States*, 342 U.S. 337, 342 (1952). ***

III

[The Court's discussion regarding the validity of Rule 14e-3(a) appears in Section C of this Chapter]

IV

Based on its dispositions of the securities fraud convictions, the Court of Appeals also reversed O'Hagan's convictions for mail fraud. Reversal of the securities convictions, the Court of Appeals recognized, "d[id] not as a matter of law require that the mail fraud convictions likewise be reversed." Id., at 627 (citing *Carpenter*, 484 U.S., at 24, in which this Court unanimously affirmed mail and wire fraud convictions based on the same conduct that evenly divided the Court on the defendants' securities fraud convictions). But in this case, the Court of Appeals said, the indictment was so structured that the mail fraud charges could not be disassociated from the securities fraud charges, and absent any securities fraud, "there was no fraud upon which to base the mail fraud charges."

The United States urges that the Court of Appeals' position is irreconcilable with *Carpenter*: Just as in *Carpenter*, so here, the "mail fraud charges are independent of [the] securities fraud charges, even [though] both rest on the same set of facts." Brief for United States 46-47. We need not linger over this matter, for our rulings on the securities fraud issues require that we reverse the Court of Appeals judgment on the mail fraud counts as well. ***

The judgment of the Court of Appeals for the Eighth Circuit is reversed, and the case is remanded for further proceedings consistent with this opinion.

JUSTICE ANTONIN SCALIA, CONCURRING IN PART AND DISSENTING IN PART:

I join Parts I, III, and IV of the Court's opinion. I do not agree, however, with Part II of the Court's opinion, containing its analysis of respondent's convictions under § 10(b) and Rule 10b-5. ***

While the Court's explanation of the scope of § 10(b) and Rule 10b-5 would be entirely reasonable in some other context, it does not seem to accord with the principle of lenity we apply to criminal statutes (which cannot be mitigated here by the Rule, which is no less ambiguous than the statute). See *Reno v. Koray*, 515 U.S. 50, 64-65 (1995) (explaining circumstances in which rule of lenity applies); *United States v. Bass*, 404 U.S. 336, 347-348 (1971) (discussing policies underlying rule of lenity). In light of that principle, it seems to me that the unelaborated statutory language: "[t]o use or employ, in connection with the purchase or sale of any security ... any manipulative or deceptive device or contrivance," § 10(b), must be construed to require the manipulation or deception of a party to a securities transaction.

JUSTICE CLARENCE THOMAS, WITH WHOM CHIEF JUSTICE REHNQUIST JOINS, CONCURRING IN THE JUDGMENT IN PART AND DISSENTING IN PART:

Today the majority upholds respondent's convictions for violating § 10(b) of the Securities Exchange Act of 1934, and Rule 10b-5 promulgated thereunder, based upon the Securities and Exchange Commission's "misappropriation theory." Central to the majority's holding is the need to interpret § 10(b)'s requirement that a deceptive device be "use[d] or employ[ed], in connection with the purchase or sale of any security." Because the Commission's misappropriation theory fails to provide a coherent and consistent interpretation of this essential requirement for liability under § 10(b), I dissent. ***

I do not take issue with the majority's determination that the undisclosed misappropriation of confidential information by a fiduciary can constitute a "deceptive device" within the meaning of § 10(b). Nondisclosure where there is a pre-existing duty to disclose satisfies our definitions of fraud and deceit for purposes of the securities laws. See *Chiarella v. United States*, 445 U.S. 222, 230 (1980).

Unlike the majority, however, I cannot accept the Commission's interpretation of when a deceptive device is "use[d] ... in connection with" a securities transaction. ***

The Commission's construction of the relevant language in § 10(b), and the incoherence of that construction, become evident as the majority attempts to describe why the fraudulent theft of information falls under the Commission's misappropriation theory, but the fraudulent theft of money does not. The majority correctly notes that confidential information "qualifies as property to which the company has a right of exclusive use." It then observes that the "undisclosed misappropriation of such information, in violation of a fiduciary duty, ... constitutes fraud akin to embezzlement—the fraudulent appropriation to one's own use of the money or goods entrusted to one's care by another." So far the majority's analogy to embezzlement is well taken, and adequately demonstrates that undisclosed misappropriation can be a fraud on the source of the information.

What the embezzlement analogy does not do, however, is explain how the relevant fraud is "use[d] or employ[ed], in connection with" a securities transaction. And when the majority seeks to distinguish the embezzlement of funds from the embezzlement of information, it becomes clear that neither the Commission nor the majority has a coherent theory regarding § 10(b)'s "in connection with" requirement.

***The touchstone required for an embezzlement to be "use[d] or employ[ed], in connection with" a securities transaction is not merely that it "coincide" with, or be consummated by, the transaction, but that it is *necessarily* and *only* consummated by the transaction. Where the property being embezzled has value "apart from [its] use in a securities transaction"—even though it is in fact being used in a securities transaction—the Government contends that there is no violation under the misappropriation theory.

My understanding of the Government's proffered theory of liability, and its construction of the "in connection with" requirement, is confirmed by the Government's explanation during oral argument:

> "[Court]: What if I appropriate some of my client's money in order to buy stock?.....
>
> "[Court]: Have I violated the securities laws?
>
> "[Counsel]: I do not think that you have.
>
> "[Court]: Why not? Isn't that in connection with the purchase of securit[ies] just as much as this one is?
>
> "[Counsel]: It's not just as much as this one is, because in this case it is the use of the information that enables the profits, pure and simple. There would be no opportunity to engage in profit—
>
> "[Court]: Same here. I didn't have the money. The only way I could buy this stock was to get the money. ...
>
> "[Counsel]: The difference ... is that once you have the money you can do anything you want with it. In a sense, the fraud is complete at that point, and then you go on and you can use the money to finance any number of other activities, but *the connection is far less close than in this case, where the only value of this information for personal profit for respondent was to take it and profit in the securities markets by trading on it. . . .*
>
> "[Court]: So what you're saying is, is in this case the misappropriation can only be of relevance, or is of substantial relevance, is with reference to the purchase of securities.
>
> "[Counsel]: Exactly.
>
> "[Court]: When you take the money out of the accounts you can go to the racetrack, or whatever.
>
> "[Counsel]: That's exactly right, and because of that difference, [there] can be no doubt that this kind of misappropriation of property is in connection with the purchase or sale of securities.
>
> "Other kinds of misappropriation of property may or may not, but this is a unique form of fraud, unique to the securities markets, in fact, because *the only way in which respondent could have profited through this information is by either trading on it or by tipping somebody else to enable their trades.*" Tr. of Oral Arg. 16-19 (emphases added).

As the above exchange demonstrates, the relevant distinction is not that the misappropriated information *was* used for a securities transaction (the money example met that test), but rather that it could *only* be used for such a transaction. ***

The Government's construction of the "in connection with" requirement—and its claim that such requirement precludes coverage of financial embezzlement—also demonstrates how the majority's described distinction of financial embezzlement is incomplete. Although the majority claims that the fraud in a financial embezzlement case is complete as soon as the money is obtained, and before the securities transaction is consummated, that is not uniformly true, and thus cannot be the Government's basis for claiming that such embezzlement does not violate the securities laws. It is not difficult to imagine an embezzlement of money that takes place via the mechanism of a securities transaction—for example where a broker is directed to purchase stock for a client and instead purchases such stock—using client funds—for his own account. The unauthorized (and presumably undisclosed) transaction is the very act that constitutes the embezzlement and the "securities transaction and the breach of duty thus coincide." What presumably distinguishes monetary embezzlement for the Government is thus that it is not *necessarily* coincident with a securities transaction, not that it *never* lacks such a "connection."

Once the Government's construction of the misappropriation theory is accurately described and accepted—along with its implied construction of § 10(b)'s "in connection with" language—that theory should no longer cover cases, such as this one, involving fraud on the source of information where the source has no connection with the other participant in a securities transaction. It seems obvious that the undisclosed misappropriation of confidential information is not necessarily consummated by a securities transaction. In this case, for example, upon learning of Grand Met's confidential takeover plans, O'Hagan could have done any number of things with the information: He could have sold it to a newspaper for publication; he could have given or sold the information to Pillsbury itself; or he could even have kept the information and used it solely for his personal amusement, perhaps in a fantasy stock trading game.

Any of these activities would have deprived Grand Met of its right to "exclusive use," of the information and, if undisclosed, would constitute "embezzlement" of Grand Met's informational property. Under *any* theory of liability, however, these activities would not violate § 10(b) and, according to the Commission's monetary embezzlement analogy, these possibilities are sufficient to preclude a violation under the misappropriation theory even where the informational property *was* used for securities trading. That O'Hagan actually did use the information to purchase securities is thus no more significant here than it is in the case of embezzling money used to purchase securities. In both cases the embezzler *could have* done something else with the property, and hence the Commission's necessary "connection" under the securities laws would not be met.[2] If the relevant test under the "in connection with" language is whether the fraudulent act is *necessarily* tied to a securities transaction, then the misappropriation of confidential information used to trade no more violates § 10(b) than does the misappropriation of funds used to trade. As the Commission concedes that the latter is not covered under its theory, I am at a loss to see how the same theory can coherently be applied to the former. ***

[T]he majority also points to various policy considerations underlying the securities laws, such as maintaining fair and honest markets, promoting investor confidence, and protecting the integrity of the securities markets. But

---

2. Indeed, even if O'Hagan or someone else thereafter used the information to trade, the misappropriation would have been complete before the trade and there should be no § 10(b) liability. The most obvious real-world example of this scenario would be if O'Hagan had simply tipped someone else to the information. The mere act of passing the information along would have violated O'Hagan's fiduciary duty and, if undisclosed, would be an "embezzlement" of the confidential information, regardless of whether the tippee later traded on the information.

the repeated reliance on such broad-sweeping legislative purposes reaches too far and is misleading in the context of the misappropriation theory. It reaches too far in that, regardless of the overarching purpose of the securities laws, it is not illegal to run afoul of the "purpose" of a statute, only its letter. The majority's approach is misleading in this case because it glosses over the fact that the supposed threat to fair and honest markets, investor confidence, and market integrity comes not from the supposed fraud in this case, but from the mere fact that the information used by O'Hagan was nonpublic. ***

The majority's statement that a "misappropriator who trades on the basis of material, nonpublic information, in short, *gains his advantageous market position through deception; he deceives the source of the information and simultaneously harms members of the investing public,*" ante (emphasis added), thus focuses on the wrong point. Even if it is true that trading on nonpublic information hurts the public, it is true whether or not there is any deception of the source of the information. Moreover, as we have repeatedly held, use of nonpublic information to trade is not itself a violation of § 10(b). E.g., *Chiarella*, 445 U.S., at 232-233. Rather, it is the use of fraud "in connection with" a securities transaction that is forbidden. Where the relevant element of fraud has no impact on the integrity of the subsequent transactions as distinct from the nonfraudulent element of using nonpublic information, one can reasonably question whether the fraud was used in connection with a securities transaction. And one can likewise question whether removing that aspect of fraud, though perhaps laudable, has anything to do with the confidence or integrity of the market.

The absence of a coherent and consistent misappropriation theory and, by necessary implication, a coherent and consistent application of the statutory "use or employ, in connection with" language, is particularly problematic in the context of this case. The Government claims a remarkable breadth to the delegation of authority in § 10(b), arguing that "the very aim of this section was to pick up unforeseen, cunning, deceptive devices that people might cleverly use in the securities markets." Tr. of Oral Arg. 7. As the Court aptly queried, "[t]hat's rather unusual, for a criminal statute to be that open-ended, isn't it?" Unusual indeed. Putting aside the dubious validity of an open-ended delegation to an independent agency to go forth and create regulations criminalizing "fraud," in this case we do not even have a formal regulation embodying the agency's misappropriation theory. Certainly Rule 10b-5 cannot be said to embody the theory—although it deviates from the statutory language by the addition of the words "any person," it merely repeats, unchanged, § 10(b)'s "in connection with" language. Given that the validity of the misappropriation theory turns on the construction of that language in § 10(b), the regulatory language is singularly uninformative. ***

[The dissenters' discussion regarding the invalidity of Rule 14e-3(a)

appears in Section C of this Chapter; the discussion concurring with the majority's judgment to sustain the mail fraud conviction is omitted.]

NOTES AND QUESTIONS

1. ***"Fraud on the Source" vs. "Fraud on Investors."*** As discussed in the material preceding the *O'Hagan* decision, after *Chiarella*, the SEC and the DOJ gravitated toward Justice Stevens's "fraud on the source" misappropriation theory. What explains that preference? Was a broader misappropriation theory possible in light of the holdings in *Chiarella* and *Dirks*? In other words, could an argument be made that while traders do not owe a general duty to investors in the marketplace to disclose all material nonpublic information or to refrain from trading, traders nonetheless owe all investors a duty of disclosure when they obtained that information through misappropriation or other illegal means? See Donna M. Nagy, Reframing the Misappropriation Theory of Insider Trading Liability: A Post-*O'Hagan* Suggestion, 59 Ohio St. L.J. 1223 (1998) (arguing that the common law of fraud and deceit, the text of Section 10(b), and prior court precedents can all be read to support this broader version of a misappropriation theory).

2. ***Rule of Lenity.*** Justice Scalia referenced the principle of lenity that is applicable to criminal statutes. What is this principle? In light of the fact that the remedies for Rule 10b-5 violations are both criminal and civil, would it be possible for the misappropriation theory to apply to civil violations but not to criminal violations? What types of problems would this create? These matters will be examined in more detail in Chapter 11.A.2 infra.

3. ***Tippee Trading.*** The defendant-attorney in *O'Hagan* had misappropriated confidential client information to personally profit from his own securities trading. Accordingly, the Court had no occasion to address directly the application of the misappropriation theory to cases involving tippee trading. Prior to *O'Hagan*, tippees who traded on the basis of misappropriated information were viewed as co-participants in the misappropriator's breach of fiduciary duty. Thus, tippees incurred Rule 10b-5 liability for their own trading when they knew or should have known that their tippers had breached a fiduciary duty owed to the initial source of the information.

Will the SEC encounter problems in cases where the securities are traded by a misappropriator's tippee? In particular, consider whether a tippee's trading would satisfy Section 10(b)'s "in connection with" requirement, as that requirement was explained by the Court in *O'Hagan*. Does the tipper-misappropriator's breach of duty to the source of the information "coincide" with the tippee's securities transaction?

Focusing on this question in *United States v. Falcone*, 257 F.3d 226, 233 (2d Cir. 2001), the Second Circuit acknowledged that "the coincidence of a securities transaction and breach of duty" was not present where a tipper conveyed confidential information to a third party but did not himself trade." The court, however, maintained that "*O'Hagan* did not purport to set forth the sole combination of factors necessary to establish the requisite connection in all contexts." In the court's view, "*O'Hagan*'s requirement that the misappropriated information 'ordinarily' be valuable due to 'its utility in securities trading' appears to be a more generally applicable factor in determining whether section

10(b)'s 'in connection with' requirement is satisfied." Id. at 234. Do you agree with this conclusion?

*4. **Identifying Fiduciary-Like Relationships.*** Does *O'Hagan* offer insight into the type of relationships that would trigger a duty owed to the source of the information to disclose an intent to trade? What problems are lower courts likely to encounter in defining the scope of this duty? For a decision upholding the misappropriation theory against a psychiatrist who traded stock on the basis of material nonpublic information told to him by a patient, see *United States v. Willis*, 778 F. Supp. 205, 209 (S.D.N.Y. 1991) (emphasizing that "[a] treating psychiatrist's relationship to his patient is a traditional inherently fiduciary relationship"). For a decision upholding the misappropriation theory against a contractor handling the electrical work for a corporation, see *SEC v. Falbo*, 14 F. Supp.2d 508, 523 (S.D.N.Y. 1998) (stating that while not a traditional fiduciary, contractor was nonetheless placed "in a position of trust and confidence" which he violated when he "used for personal benefit information obtained during the course of his association"). Cases on this issue are often difficult to reconcile. Compare *United States v. Kim*, 184 F. Supp.2d 1006 (N.D. Cal. 2002) (member of the "Young Presidents Association," a national organization of company presidents under the age of 50, did not owe a duty of trust and confidence to fellow club member, despite the club's written requirement that all members must comply with a "confidentiality commitment") with *SEC v. Kirch*, 263 F. Supp.2d 1144,1147 (N.D. Ill. 2003) (member of a business roundtable owed a "duty of loyalty and confidentiality" to a fellow member where there was an "express policy and understanding that such [nonpublic business] matters were indeed to be kept confidential").

Not surprisingly, particularly thorny issues have arisen in the context of misappropriations by family members. See, e.g., *United States v. Reed*, 601 F. Supp. 685 (S.D.N.Y. 1985) (applying misappropriation theory against son who traded on the basis of nonpublic information obtained from father, a corporate director), rev'd in part on other grounds, 773 F.2d 477 (2d Cir. 1985); *United States v. Chestman*, 947 F.2d 551, 568 (2d Cir. 1991) (en banc) (reversing conviction of securities broker on the ground that his alleged tipper did not owe a duty of trust and confidence to his wife who had shared with him confidential information about an upcoming transaction involving the sale of her family's company); *SEC v. Yun*, 327 F.3d 1263, 1272 (11th Cir. 2003) (disagreeing with *Chestman* and reasoning that a court's insistence "on either an express agreement of confidentiality or a strictly defined fiduciary relationship" would ignore "the many instances in which a spouse has a reasonable expectation of confidentiality").

*5. **Rule 10b5-2.*** Recognizing the uncertainty surrounding whether a particular relationship qualifies as "fiduciary-like," the SEC in 2000 promulgated Rule 10b5-2, subsection (b) of which provides that a person trading or tipping on the basis of material nonpublic information breaches a duty of "trust or confidence" in any one of three circumstances:

> (1) when the person receiving the information has agreed to maintain that information in confidence;

(2) when the persons involved in the communication "have a history, pattern, or practice of sharing confidences" that results in a reasonable expectation of confidentiality; and

(3) when the person receives such information from a spouse, parent, child or sibling, unless the person can show affirmatively, based on the particular facts and circumstances of that family relationship, that "he or she neither knew nor reasonably should have known that the person who was the source of the information expected that the person would keep the information confidential ***"

What legal issues are likely to be raised by the rule?

Thus far, challenges to Rule 10b5-2's validity have met with mixed success. Compare *United States v. Corbin*, 729 F. Supp.2d 607, 616 (S.D.N.Y. 2010) (holding that Rule 10b5-2(b)(3)'s rebuttable presumption of a fiduciary-like relationship between spouses is a reasonable exercise of the SEC's rulemaking authority under Section 10(b) and does not violate defendant's constitutional right to due process) with *SEC v. Cuban*, 634 F. Supp.2d 713, 730-31 (N.D. Tex. 2009) (dismissing complaint and holding that Rule 10b5-2(b)(1) is invalid and unenforceable insofar as it predicates liability on a defendant's mere agreement to maintain information in confidence), vacated and remanded, 620 F.3d 551 (5th Cir. 2010). Yet the lower court in *Cuban* also held that a fiduciary-like relationship between a defendant and the source of the information was not essential to liability under the misappropriation theory because the necessary element of deception could be established by a breach of a promise "not to trade on or otherwise use the information for personal benefit." Id. at 730. Is this ruling consistent with *O'Hagan*'s reasoning? On appeal, the Fifth Circuit vacated the judgment of dismissal and remanded the case for discovery because, in its view, there was "more than a plausible basis to find that the understanding between the [defendant and the source] was that he was not to trade, that it was more than a simple confidentiality agreement." *Cuban*, 620 F.3d at 557. But, at least at this juncture, the Fifth Circuit did nothing to disturb the district court's holdings with respect to Rule 10b5-2(b)(1)'s validity.

PROBLEM 7-4

Which of the following scenarios would constitute a violation of Rule 10b-5 under the misappropriation theory endorsed by the *O'Hagan* Court? Which scenarios lie beyond *O'Hagan*'s reach? Do the "not-reached" scenarios demonstrate a significant weakness in the Court's theory?

1. A computer hacker manages to gain access to the internal e-mail system of the nation's largest biotechnology company. After several days of reading not very interesting confidential e-mails between corporate executives, she stumbles upon a message revealing that company engineers have developed a new wonder drug for treating diabetes. The computer hacker purchases 200 call options on the company, and reaps a tremendous profit when she exercises those options after the drug breakthrough is announced.

2. You are an outside attorney for the nation's largest biotechnology company. You often take work home with you, and on one of those

occasions, you inadvertently leave in your living room the notes you took at a recent meeting with your clients. The notes make clear that the company will soon announce the development of a new wonder drug for treating diabetes. Your unemployed younger brother, who has been staying for the last two weeks as a guest in your home, finds your notes as he is channel surfing through the soap-operas the following day. A bit resentful of your many successes, your brother decides to take for himself a piece of the action, and asks his girlfriend to lend him the money so that he can purchase 500 shares of stock in the company. He tells her he has found a sure way to double that money in less than a week and purchases shares in the company.

3. A taxi driver overhears a conversation between two passengers who appear to be engineers for a large biotechnology company. The passengers discuss the new wonder drug for treating diabetes and their company's anticipated public announcement of this breakthrough later in the week. The taxi driver notices on the briefcase of one of the passengers a well known corporate logo. He later opens an investment account with Ameritrade and purchases 1000 shares of that company, whose stock price doubles two days later after the news about the drug is announced to the public.

4. The biotechnology company's assistant director of public relations helps to plan the announcement of the newly developed diabetes drug. The day before the announcement, she resigns her position, and leaves the country for the Caymen Islands. Her resignation letter expresses her unhappiness with the company, and informs her supervisors that she has given her broker instructions to purchase 1000 shares of the company at the opening of the NYSE the next morning. She is confident that the company will do nothing to detract attention from its impending announcement.

5. Instead of resigning and purchasing the stock for herself, the assistant director of public relations for the biotech company secretly sells the information about the newly developed drug to a third party for $100. Two days later, the third party purchases 500 call options on the company. The assistant director continues to perform all other aspects of her job responsibilities quite satisfactorily.

6. The U.S. Commissioner of the Federal Food and Drug Administration informs the U.S. House Subcommittee on Health that the FDA will soon approve a new wonder drug for treating diabetes. The FDA Commissioner also reveals the name of the pharmaceutical company that will manufacture the drug and makes clear to the subcommittee members that no public announcement has yet been made. A congressman on the committee and a legislative aide each purchases 1000 shares of the company at the opening of the NYSE the following morning.

PROBLEM 7-5

Nathan Nottingham was pursuing his MBA degree as an evening student at a prestigious New York business school. He was also a part-time word processor assigned by the temporary agency for which he worked to two Wall Street investment banking firms. As a "temp" for these firms, Nottingham was able to gain access to material nonpublic information regarding numerous merger and acquisition transactions. As is the customary practice on Wall Street, each firm had Nottingham sign a confidentiality agreement which contained an explicit warning that material nonpublic information learned in the course of employment must not be shared with anyone outside the firm and may under no circumstances be used for purposes of personal profit.

In May 2010, Nottingham "met" Adam Appelson, an insurance agent, in an Internet chat room devoted to the performance of a stock in which both had invested and lost money. In the course of their on-line communications, Nottingham mentioned to Appelson the names of his temporary Wall Street employers. The two then agreed upon a plan to profit from any inside information Nottingham could learn about merger and acquisition transactions being planned by the firm's clients. Specifically, Appelson agreed to give Nottingham one quarter of any profits made by him through the use of the confidential information.

Over the course of the next year, Nottingham and Appelson each had purchased stock in more than 20 companies based on information garnered by Nottingham as a temporary employee. Appelson also shared his profits with Nottingham in accordance with the original agreement.

Nottingham and Appelson were also very generous in providing the confidential merger and acquisition information to their friends and relatives, often sending them e-mails containing "hot stock tips." On April 1, 2011, Appelson sent an e-mail to his brother-in-law Timothy Tyler, who has also an insurance agent, urging him to purchase stock in ABC Corp. because it was a "sure thing." The e-mail did not disclose any additional information, but Tyler was well aware of his brother-in-law's increasingly lavish lifestyle. Tyler then purchased 1000 shares of ABC Corp. for his own account. He also passed this tip on to two of his neighbors, who each bought 1000 shares in the company. When the neighbors asked about the source of the tip, Tyler responded, "you don't want to know." One of these neighbors shared the tip with his dentist, and the dentist purchased 500 shares in ABC.

On April 5, 2011, ABC Corp. announced publicly that it was being acquired by XYZ Corp., a client of one of the Wall Street firms that had employed Nottingham. ABC stock, which was trading at $28 dollars a share prior to the announcement, had skyrocketed to $42 a share by the end of the trading day. On five other occasions during the summer of 2011, Appelson sent an e-mail to his brother-in-law suggesting a "sure thing" stock, and the brother-in-law, his two neighbors, and the neighbors' dentist each purchased a sizable amount of shares in the recommended company. The pattern ceased only when Nottingham was arrested by federal marshals working with the Securities and Commodities Fraud Task Force in the Office of the United States Attorney for the Southern District of New York.

After *O'Hagan*, there is little doubt that Nottingham has engaged in multiple violations of Rule 10b-5 when he purchased for his own account stock in the targets of his employer's client. But is he liable for Appelson's purchases? The brother-in-law's? The neighbors'? The dentist's? When, if ever, is the tipper-tippee relationship too remote to impose liability? What about individual liability on the part of these tippees? Has each of these traders violated Rule 10b-5?

The case on which this problem was loosely based resulted in civil charges against 19 defendants, most of whom chose to settle with the SEC. See SEC v. Freeman, Litigation Release No. 16469 (March 14, 2000). For an older case discussing and deciding liability for remote tippees, see *SEC v. Musella*, 678 F. Supp. 1060 (S.D.N.Y. 1988).

4. Deceptive Acquisition – A Third Basis for Insider Trading Liability?

Reconsider Problem 7-4(1) involving the computer hacker. The Second Circuit confronted a strikingly similar scenario in the following case.

SEC v. DOROZHKO
547 F.3d 42 (2d Cir. 2009)

JOSE A. CABRANES, CIRCUIT JUDGE:

We are asked to consider whether, in a civil enforcement lawsuit brought by the United States Securities and Exchange Commission ("SEC") under Section 10(b) of the Securities Exchange Act of 1934 ("Section 10(b)"), computer hacking may be "deceptive" where the hacker did not breach a fiduciary duty in fraudulently obtaining material, nonpublic information used in connection with the purchase or sale of securities. For the reasons stated herein, we answer the question in the affirmative. ***

On January 8, 2008, in a thoughtful and careful opinion, the District Court denied the SEC's request for a preliminary injunction because the SEC had not shown a likelihood of success. Specifically, the District Court ruled that computer hacking was not "deceptive" within the meaning of Section 10(b) as defined by the Supreme Court. According to the District Court, "a breach of a fiduciary duty of disclosure is a required element of any 'deceptive' device under § 10b." *Dorozhko*, 606 F.Supp.2d at 330. The District Court reasoned that since defendant was a corporate outsider with no special relationship to IMS or Thomson [the sources of the material, nonpublic information], he owed no fiduciary duty to either. Although computer hacking might be fraudulent and might violate a number of federal and state criminal statutes, the District Court concluded that this behavior did not violate Section 10(b) without an accompanying breach of a fiduciary duty. ***This appeal followed. ***

The District Court concluded that in *Chiarella*, *O'Hagan*, and *Zandford*, the Supreme Court developed a requirement that any "deceptive device" requires a breach of a fiduciary duty. In applying that interpretation to the instant case, the District Court ruled that "[a]lthough [defendant] may have broken the law, he is not liable in a civil action under § 10(b) because he owed no fiduciary or similar duty either to the source of his information or to those he transacted with in the market." *Dorozhko*, 606 F.Supp.2d at 324. ***

In our view, none of the Supreme Court opinions relied upon by the District Court – much less the sum of all three opinions – establishes a fiduciary duty requirement as an element of every violation of Section 10(b). In *Chiarella*, *O'Hagan*, and *Zandford*, the theory of fraud was silence or nondisclosure, not an affirmative misrepresentation. The Supreme Court held that remaining silent was actionable only where there was a duty to speak, arising from a fiduciary relationship.

*** While *Chiarella*, *O'Hagan*, and *Zandford* all dealt with fraud *qua* silence, an affirmative misrepresentation is a distinct species of fraud. Even if a person does not have a fiduciary duty to "disclose or abstain from trading," there is nonetheless an affirmative obligation in commercial dealings not to mislead. *See, e.g., Basic Inc. v. Levinson*, 485 U.S. 224, 240 n. 18 (1988) (distinguishing "situations where insiders have traded in abrogation of their duty to disclose or abstain," from "affirmative misrepresentations by those under no duty to disclose (but under the ever-present duty not to mislead)"). ***

[T]he SEC has not alleged that defendant fraudulently remained silent in the face of a "duty to disclose or abstain" from trading. Rather, the SEC argues that defendant affirmatively misrepresented himself in order to gain access to material, nonpublic information, which he then used to trade. We are aware of no precedent of the Supreme Court or our Court that forecloses or prohibits the SEC's straightforward theory of fraud. Absent a controlling precedent that "deceptive" has a more limited meaning than its ordinary meaning, we see no reason to complicate the enforcement of Section 10(b) by divining new requirements. *** Accordingly, we adopt the SEC's proposed interpretation of *Chiarella* and its progeny: "misrepresentations are fraudulent, but ... silence is fraudulent only if there is a duty to disclose." Appellant's Br. 44. ***

In its ordinary meaning, "deceptive" covers a wide spectrum of conduct involving cheating or trading in falsehoods. See WEBSTER'S INTERNATIONAL DICTIONARY 679 (2d ed.1934) (defining "deceptive" as "tending to deceive," and defining "deceive" as "[t]o cause to believe the false, or to disbelieve the true" or "[t]o impose upon; to deal treacherously with; cheat"). In light of this ordinary meaning, it is not at all surprising that Rule 10b-5 equates "deceit" with "fraud." See 17 C.F.R. § 240.10b-5 (prohibiting "any untrue statement of a material fact ... or ... any act, practice, or course of business which operates or would operate as a *fraud* or *deceit* upon any person, in connection with the purchase or sale of any security" (emphases added)). Indeed, we have previously observed that the conduct prohibited by Section 10(b) and Rule 10b-5 "irreducibly entails some act that gives the victim a false impression." *United States v. Finnerty*, 533 F.3d 143, 148 (2d Cir.2008).

The District Court - summarizing the SEC's allegations - described the computer hacking in this case as "employ[ing] electronic means to trick, circumvent, or bypass computer security in order to gain unauthorized access to computer systems, networks, and information ... and to steal such data." *Dorozhko*, 606 F.Supp.2d at 329. On appeal, the SEC adds a further gloss, arguing that, in general, "[computer h]ackers either (1) 'engage in false identification and masquerade as another user['] ... or (2) 'exploit a weakness in [an electronic] code within a program to cause the program to malfunction in a way that grants the user greater privileges.'" Appellant's Br. 22-23. In our view, misrepresenting one's identity in order to gain access to information that is otherwise off limits, and then stealing that information is plainly "deceptive" within the ordinary meaning of the word. It is unclear, however, that exploiting a weakness in an electronic code to gain unauthorized access is "deceptive," rather than being mere theft. Accordingly, depending on how the hacker gained access, it seems to us entirely possible that computer hacking could be, by definition, a "deceptive device or contrivance" that is prohibited by Section 10(b) and Rule 10b-5.

However, we are hesitant to move from this general principle to a particular application without the benefit of the District Court's views as to whether the computer hacking in this case - as opposed to computer hacking in general - was "deceptive." ***Having established that the SEC need not demonstrate a breach of fiduciary duty, we now remand to the District Court to consider, in the first instance, whether the computer hacking in this case involved a fraudulent misrepresentation that was "deceptive" within the ordinary meaning of Section 10(b). The District Court may, in its informed discretion, enter a new order on the basis of the existing record or reopen the preliminary injunction hearing to consider such additional testimony regarding the nature of the hacking in this particular case as it deems appropriate in the circumstances.***

For the foregoing reasons, the District Court's January 8, 2008 order denying the SEC's motion for a preliminary injunction is Vacated. The cause is remanded for further proceedings consistent with this opinion.

NOTES AND QUESTIONS

1. Insider Trading Based on Deceptively Acquired Information. After *Dorozhko*, is it now correct to say that there are three theories for establishing Rule 10b-5 liability for insider trading: a classical theory, a misappropriation theory, and a "deception acquisition" theory? Would the Supreme Court be likely to endorse this alternative theory?

2. The Final Chapter. On remand from the Second Circuit, the district court granted the SEC's unopposed motion for summary judgment. The district court directed Dorozhko to disgorge illegal gains of $286,456 and to pay a penalty in an equal amount. The court also entered an order enjoining him from future violations of federal securities laws. SEC v. Dorozhko, Litigation Release No. 21465 (Mar. 29, 2010). What if, instead, Dorozhko had responded to the SEC's motion with compelling evidence that he accomplished the hacking by exploiting a weakness in the electronic code? Could the SEC have argued that even this type of conduct is deceptive within the ordinary meaning of Section 10(b)? Can a person "deceive" a computer system or computer network?

3. Insider Trading Liability for Wrongful Use of Information. The proposed – but never enacted – "Insider Trading Proscriptions Act of 1987" would have amended the Exchange Act to prohibit the use of material nonpublic information to purchase or sell any security if a "person knows (or recklessly disregards) that such information has been obtained wrongfully, or if the purchase or sale would constitute a wrongful use of such information." See S. 1380, 100th Cong, 1st Sess. (1987). The proposed legislation further provided that:

> For the purposes of this subsection, such trading while in possession of material, nonpublic information is wrongful only if such information has been obtained by, or its use would constitute, directly or indirectly, (A) theft, bribery, misrepresentation, espionage (through electronic or other means) or (B) conversion, misappropriation, or a breach of any fiduciary duty, any personal or other relationship of trust and confidence, or any contractual or employment relationship.

Are there insider trading scenarios currently outside the reach of Rule 10b-5 that this proposed legislation would prohibit? Should Congress once again consider a statutory definition/prohibition of insider trading? Is dusting off the proposed 1987 legislation a good place to start? See generally Donna M. Nagy, Insider Trading and the Gradual Demise of Fiduciary Principles, 94 Iowa L. Rev. 1315 (2009).

PROBLEM 7-6

Reconsider the taxi driver hypothetical in Problem 7-4(3). Assume that the passenger's briefcases did not bear the biotechnology company's well-known corporate logo. Rather, the taxi driver learned the identity of the company which was soon to announce the diabetes wonder drug breakthrough by listening intently to his passengers' conversation in the backseat. Would the following additional facts change your analysis?

The taxi driver picked up the two passengers at LaGuardia Airport in Queens, NY and drove them to midtown Manhattan. The most direct route for this trip involves passage through the Queens-Midtown Tunnel (the "Midtown Tunnel") under the East River. It was late in the evening, and the trip at that time typically takes 25 minutes and the fare is usually $40.

To the driver's dismay, as he approached the expressway exit for the Midtown tunnel, his passengers had not yet identified the name of the biotechnology company. Hopeful that with some additional time in the taxi they would do so, the driver intentionally passed the exit for the Midtown tunnel and continued on the expressway. "Hey," yelled one of the passengers. "Why aren't we going through the Midtown tunnel?" The driver thought quickly and stated falsely that: "The Midtown tunnel is backed-up with traffic from a car accident; so I'll take you over the Williamsburg Bridge. That's the quickest way for us to avoid the traffic delay."

The passengers resumed their conversation about the impending announcement, and moments before they arrived at their midtown Manhattan destination, one of passengers let it slip that the company was "TYE Pharmaceutical." The taxi trip from the airport took 45 minutes, and the fare on the meter was $65.

The driver went home that evening and verified on the Internet that TYE Pharmaceutical had yet to make a public announcement about a new wonder drug for treating diabetes. He then opened an investment account with Ameritrade and depleted all of his savings ($10,000) to purchase 1000 shares of TYE Pharmaceutical stock. Two days later, after the public announcement of the drug breakthrough, he sold those shares, reaping a tremendous profit.

Did the taxi driver violate Rule 10b-5 when he purchased stock in TYE Pharmaceutical?

C. RULE 14e-3—INSIDER TRADING IN THE CONTEXT OF TENDER OFFERS

As we saw from the *O'Hagan* decision in Section B.3, corporate transactions involving tender offers frequently present particularly tempting opportunities to profit unlawfully from the use of material nonpublic information. Although "tender offer" is not defined in Section 14(e) of the Exchange Act or in Rule 14e-3, the phrase typically refers to a publicized offer, sometimes by a hostile bidder, to buy shares of a publicly owned company at an advertised price within a confined time period. Recall that the material nonpublic information to which attorney James O'Hagan had access involved the confidential plans of Grand Metropolitan to launch a tender offer for shares in Pillsbury. Thus, in addition to violations of Section 10(b) and Rule 10b-5, the government charged him with, and the jury convicted him for, illegal trading under Section 14(e) and Rule 14e-3(a). The Supreme Court's analysis of this aspect of the case is set forth below.

UNITED STATES v. O'HAGAN

521 U.S. 642 (1997)

JUSTICE RUTH BADER GINSBURG:

***A sole question is before us as to [O'Hagan's convictions for fraudulent trading in connection with a tender offer, in violation of § 14(e) of the Exchange Act and SEC Rule 14e-3(a)]: Did the Commission, as the Court of Appeals held, exceed its rulemaking authority under § 14(e) when it adopted Rule 14e-3(a) without requiring a showing that the trading at issue entailed a breach of fiduciary duty? We hold that the Commission, in this regard and to the extent relevant to this case, did not exceed its authority.

The governing statutory provision, § 14(e) of the Exchange Act, reads in relevant part:

> "It shall be unlawful for any person ... to engage in any fraudulent, deceptive, or manipulative acts or practices, in connection with any tender offer.... The [SEC] shall, for the purposes of this subsection, by rules and regulations define, and prescribe means reasonably designed to prevent, such acts and practices as are fraudulent, deceptive, or manipulative."

Section 14(e)'s first sentence prohibits fraudulent acts in connection with a tender offer. This self-operating proscription was one of several provisions added to the Exchange Act in 1968 by the Williams Act. The section's second sentence delegates definitional and prophylactic rulemaking authority to the Commission. Congress added this rulemaking delegation to § 14(e) in 1970 amendments to the Williams Act.

Through § 14(e) and other provisions on disclosure in the Williams Act,[14] Congress sought to ensure that shareholders "confronted by a cash tender offer for their stock [would] not be required to respond without adequate information." *Rondeau v. Mosinee Paper Corp.*, 422 U.S. 49, 58 (1975); see *Lewis v. McGraw*, 619 F.2d 192, 195 (C.A.2 1980) ("very purpose" of Williams Act was "informed decisionmaking by shareholders"). As we recognized in *Schreiber v. Burlington Northern, Inc.*, 472 U.S. 1 (1985), Congress designed the Williams Act to make "disclosure, rather than court imposed principles of 'fairness' or 'artificiality,' ... the preferred method of market regulation." Id., at 9, n. 8. Section 14(e), we explained, "supplements the more precise disclosure provisions found elsewhere in the Williams Act, while requiring disclosure more explicitly addressed to the tender offer context than that required by § 10(b)." Id., at 10-11.

Relying on § 14(e)'s rulemaking authorization, the Commission, in 1980, promulgated Rule 14e-3(a). That measure provides:

> (a) If any person has taken a substantial step or steps to commence, or has commenced, a tender offer (the 'offering person'), it shall constitute a fraudulent, deceptive or manipulative act or practice within the meaning of section 14(e) of the [Exchange] Act for any other person who is in possession of material information relating to such tender offer which information he knows or has reason to know is nonpublic and which he knows or has reason to know has been acquired directly or indirectly from:
>
> > (1) The offering person,
> >
> > (2) The issuer of the securities sought or to be sought by such tender offer, or
> >
> > (3) Any officer, director, partner or employee or any other person acting on behalf of the offering person or such issuer,
>
> to purchase or sell or cause to be purchased or sold any of such securities or any securities convertible into or exchangeable for any such securities or any option or right to obtain or to dispose of any of the foregoing securities, unless within a reasonable time prior to any purchase or sale such information and its source are publicly disclosed by press release or otherwise.

As characterized by the Commission, Rule 14e-3(a) is a "disclose or abstain from trading" requirement. 45 Fed.Reg. 60410 (1980). The Second Circuit concisely described the Rule's thrust:

> "One violates Rule 14e-3(a) if he trades on the basis of material nonpublic information concerning a pending tender offer that he knows or has reason to know has been acquired 'directly or indirectly' from an insider of the offeror or issuer, or someone working on their behalf. Rule 14e-3(a) is a disclosure provision. It creates a duty in those traders who fall within its ambit to abstain

---

14. In addition to § 14(e), the Williams Act and the 1970 amendments added to the Exchange Act the following provisions concerning disclosure: § 13(d) (disclosure requirements for persons acquiring more than five percent of certain classes of securities); § 13(e) (authorizing Commission to adopt disclosure requirements for certain repurchases of securities by issuer); § 14(d) (disclosure requirements when tender offer results in offeror owning more than five percent of a class of securities); § 14(f) (disclosure requirements when tender offer results in new corporate directors constituting a majority).

> or disclose, *without regard to whether the trader owes a pre-existing fiduciary duty* to respect the confidentiality of the information."

United States v. Chestman, 947 F.2d 551, 557 (1991) (en banc) (emphasis added)(1992). See also *SEC v. Maio*, 51 F.3d 623, 635 (C.A.7 1995) ("Rule 14e-3 creates a duty to disclose material non-public information, or abstain from trading in stocks implicated by an impending tender offer, *regardless of whether such information was obtained through a breach of fiduciary duty*." (emphasis added)); *SEC v. Peters*, 978 F.2d 1162, 1165 (C.A.10 1992) (as written, Rule 14e-3(a) has no fiduciary duty requirement).

In the Eighth Circuit's view, because Rule 14e-3(a) applies whether or not the trading in question breaches a fiduciary duty, the regulation exceeds the SEC's § 14(e) rulemaking authority. Contra, *Maio*, 51 F.3d, at 634-635(CA7); *Peters*, 978 F.2d, at 1165-1167 (C.A.10); *Chestman*, 947 F.2d, at 556-563(CA2) (all holding Rule 14e-3(a) a proper exercise of SEC's statutory authority). In support of its holding, the Eighth Circuit relied on the text of § 14(e) and our decisions in *Schreiber* and *Chiarella*.

The Eighth Circuit homed in on the essence of § 14(e)'s rulemaking authorization: "[T]he statute empowers the SEC to 'define' and 'prescribe means reasonably designed to prevent' 'acts and practices' which are 'fraudulent.' " Id., at 624. All that means, the Eighth Circuit found plain, is that the SEC may "identify and regulate," in the tender offer context, "acts and practices" the law already defines as "fraudulent"; but, the Eighth Circuit maintained, the SEC may not "create its own definition of fraud." Ibid.

This Court, the Eighth Circuit pointed out, held in *Schreiber* that the word "manipulative" in the § 14(e) phrase "fraudulent, deceptive, or manipulative acts or practices" means just what the word means in § 10(b): Absent misrepresentation or nondisclosure, an act cannot be indicted as manipulative. See 92 F.3d, at 625 (citing *Schreiber*, 472 U.S., at 7-8, and n. 6). Section 10(b) interpretations guide construction of § 14(e), the Eighth Circuit added, see 92 F.3d, at 625, citing this Court's acknowledgment in *Schreiber* that § 14(e)'s "'broad antifraud prohibition' ... [is] modeled on the antifraud provisions of § 10(b) ... and Rule 10b-5," 472 U.S., at 10; see id., at 10-11, n. 10.

For the meaning of "fraudulent" under § 10(b), the Eighth Circuit looked to *Chiarella*. In that case, the Eighth Circuit recounted, this Court held that a failure to disclose information could be "fraudulent" under § 10(b) only when there was a duty to speak arising out of " 'a fiduciary or other similar relation of trust and confidence.' " *Chiarella*, 445 U.S., at 228 (quoting Restatement (Second) of Torts § 551(2)(a) (1976)). Just as § 10(b) demands a showing of a breach of fiduciary duty, so such a breach is necessary to make out a § 14(e) violation, the Eighth Circuit concluded.

As to the Commission's § 14(e) authority to "prescribe means reasonably designed to prevent" fraudulent acts, the Eighth Circuit stated: "Properly read, this provision means simply that the SEC has broad regulatory powers in the field of tender offers, but the statutory terms have a fixed meaning which the SEC cannot alter by way of an administrative rule." 92 F.3d, at 627.

The United States urges that the Eighth Circuit's reading of § 14(e) misapprehends both the Commission's authority to define fraudulent acts and the Commission's power to prevent them. "The 'defining' power," the United States submits, "would be a virtual nullity were the SEC not permitted to go beyond common law fraud (which is separately prohibited in the first [self-operative] sentence of Section 14(e))." Brief for United States 11; see id., at 37.

In maintaining that the Commission's power to define fraudulent acts under § 14(e) is broader than its rulemaking power under § 10(b), the United States questions the Court of Appeals' reading of *Schreiber*. See Brief for United States at 38-40. Parenthetically, the United States notes that the word before the Schreiber Court was "manipulative"; unlike "fraudulent," the United States observes, " 'manipulative' ... is 'virtually a term of art when used in connection with the securities markets.' " Brief for United States at 38, n. 20 (quoting *Schreiber*, 472 U.S., at 6). Most tellingly, the United States submits, *Schreiber* involved acts alleged to violate the self-operative provision in § 14(e)'s first sentence, a sentence containing language similar to § 10(b). But § 14(e)'s second sentence, containing the rulemaking authorization, the United States points out, does not track § 10(b), which simply authorizes the SEC to proscribe "manipulative or deceptive device[s] or contrivance[s]." Brief for United States 38. Instead, § 14(e)'s rulemaking prescription tracks § 15(c)(2)(D) of the Exchange Act, which concerns the conduct of broker-dealers in over-the-counter markets. See Brief for United States 38-39. Since 1938, § 15(c)(2) has given the Commission authority to "define, and prescribe means reasonably designed to prevent, such [broker-dealer] acts and practices as are fraudulent, deceptive, or manipulative." When Congress added this same rulemaking language to § 14(e) in 1970, the Government states, the Commission had already used its § 15(c)(2) authority to reach beyond common-law fraud. See Brief for United States 39, n. 22.

We need not resolve in this case whether the Commission's authority under § 14(e) to "define ... such acts and practices as are fraudulent" is broader than the Commission's fraud-defining authority under § 10(b), for we agree with the United States that Rule 14e-3(a), as applied to cases of this genre, qualifies under § 14(e) as a "means reasonably designed to prevent" fraudulent trading on material, nonpublic information in the tender offer context.[17] A prophylactic measure, because its mission is to prevent, typically encompasses more than the core activity prohibited. As we noted in *Schreiber*, § 14(e)'s rulemaking authorization gives the Commission "latitude," even in the context of a term of art like "manipulative," "to regulate nondeceptive activities as a 'reasonably designed' means of preventing manipulative acts, without suggesting any

17. We leave for another day, when the issue requires decision, the legitimacy of Rule 14e-3(a) as applied to "warehousing," which the Government describes as "the practice by which bidders leak advance information of a tender offer to allies and encourage them to purchase the target company's stock before the bid is announced." Reply Brief 17. As we observed in *Chiarella*, one of the Commission's purposes in proposing Rule 14e-3(a) was "to bar warehousing under its authority to regulate tender offers." 445 U.S., at 234. The Government acknowledges that trading authorized by a principal breaches no fiduciary duty. See Reply Brief 17. The instant case, however, does not involve trading authorized by a principal; therefore, we need not here decide whether the Commission's proscription of warehousing falls within its § 14(e) authority to define or prevent fraud.

change in the meaning of the term 'manipulative' itself." 472 U.S., at 11, n. 11. We hold, accordingly, that under § 14(e), the Commission may prohibit acts not themselves fraudulent under the common law or § 10(b), if the prohibition is "reasonably designed to prevent ... acts and practices [that] are fraudulent."

Because Congress has authorized the Commission, in § 14(e), to prescribe legislative rules, we owe the Commission's judgment "more than mere deference or weight." *Batterton v. Francis*, 432 U.S. 416, 424-426 (1977). Therefore, in determining whether Rule 14e-3(a)'s "disclose or abstain from trading" requirement is reasonably designed to prevent fraudulent acts, we must accord the Commission's assessment "controlling weight unless [it is] arbitrary, capricious, or manifestly contrary to the statute." *Chevron U.S.A. Inc. v. Natural Resources Defense Council, Inc.*, 467 U.S. 837, 844 (1984). In this case, we conclude, the Commission's assessment is none of these.

In adopting the "disclose or abstain" rule, the SEC explained:

> The Commission has previously expressed and continues to have serious concerns about trading by persons in possession of material, nonpublic information relating to a tender offer. This practice results in unfair disparities in market information and market disruption. Security holders who purchase from or sell to such persons are effectively denied the benefits of disclosure and the substantive protections of the Williams Act. If furnished with the information, these security holders would be able to make an informed investment decision, which could involve deferring the purchase or sale of the securities until the material information had been disseminated or until the tender offer had been commenced or terminated.

45 Fed. Reg. 60412 (1980).

The Commission thus justified Rule 14e-3(a) as a means necessary and proper to assure the efficacy of Williams Act protections.

The United States emphasizes that Rule 14e-3(a) reaches trading in which "a breach of duty is likely but difficult to prove." Reply Brief 16. "Particularly in the context of a tender offer," as the Tenth Circuit recognized, "there is a fairly wide circle of people with confidential information," *Peters*, 978 F.2d, at 1167, notably, the attorneys, investment bankers, and accountants involved in structuring the transaction. The availability of that information may lead to abuse, for "even a hint of an upcoming tender offer may send the price of the target company's stock soaring." *SEC v. Materia*, 745 F.2d 197, 199 (C.A.2 1984). Individuals entrusted with nonpublic information, particularly if they have no long-term loyalty to the issuer, may find the temptation to trade on that information hard to resist in view of "the very large short-term profits potentially available [to them]." *Peters*, 978 F.2d, at 1167.

"[I]t may be possible to prove circumstantially that a person [traded on the basis of material, nonpublic information], but almost impossible to prove that the trader obtained such information in breach of a fiduciary duty owed either by the trader or by the ultimate insider source of the information." Ibid. The example of a "tippee" who trades on information received from an insider illustrates the problem. Under Rule 10b-5, "a tippee assumes a fiduciary duty to the shareholders of a corporation not to trade on material nonpublic information only when the insider has breached his fiduciary duty to the shareholders by disclosing the information to the tippee and the tippee knows or should know that there has been a breach." *Dirks*, 463 U.S., at 660. To show that a tippee who traded on nonpublic information about a tender offer had breached a fiduciary duty would require proof not only that the insider source breached a fiduciary duty, but that the tippee knew or should have known of that breach. "Yet, in most cases, the only parties to the [information transfer] will be the insider and the alleged tippee." *Peters*, 978 F.2d, at 1167.

In sum, it is a fair assumption that trading on the basis of material, nonpublic information will often involve a breach of a duty of confidentiality to the bidder or target company or their representatives. The SEC, cognizant of the proof problem that could enable sophisticated traders to escape responsibility, placed in Rule 14e-3(a) a "disclose or abstain from trading" command that does not require specific proof of a breach of fiduciary duty. That prescription, we are satisfied, applied to this case, is a "means reasonably designed to prevent" fraudulent trading on material, nonpublic information in the tender offer context. See *Chestman*, 947 F.2d, at 560 ("While dispensing with the subtle problems of proof associated with demonstrating fiduciary breach in the problematic area of tender offer insider trading, [Rule 14e-3(a)] retains a close nexus between the prohibited conduct and the statutory aims."); accord, *Maio*, 51 F.3d, at 635, and n. 14; *Peters*, 978 F.2d, at 1167. Therefore, insofar as it serves to prevent the type of misappropriation charged against O'Hagan, Rule 14e-3(a) is a proper exercise of the Commission's prophylactic power under § 14(e).

As an alternate ground for affirming the Eighth Circuit's judgment, O'Hagan urges that Rule 14e-3(a) is invalid because it prohibits trading in advance of a tender offer—when "a substantial step ... to commence" such an offer has been taken—while § 14(e) prohibits fraudulent acts "in connection with any tender offer." See Brief for Respondent 41-42. O'Hagan further contends that, by covering pre-offer conduct, Rule 14e-3(a) "fails to comport with due process on two levels": The Rule does not "give fair notice as to when, in advance of a tender offer, a violation of § 14(e) occurs," id., at 42; and it "disposes of any scienter requirement," id., at 43. The Court of Appeals did not address these arguments, and O'Hagan did not raise the due process points in his briefs before that court. We decline to consider these contentions in the first instance. The Court of Appeals may address on remand any arguments O'Hagan has preserved. ***

JUSTICE CLARENCE THOMAS, WITH WHOM CHIEF JUSTICE REHNQUIST JOINS, CONCURRING IN THE JUDGMENT IN PART AND DISSENTING IN PART:

***I find neither of the Commission's justifications for Rule 14e-3(a) acceptable in misappropriation cases. With regard to the Commission's claim of authority to redefine the concept of fraud, I agree with the Eighth Circuit that the Commission misreads the relevant provision of § 14(e).

> "Simply put, the enabling provision of § 14(e) permits the SEC to identify and regulate those 'acts and practices' which fall within the § 14(e) legal definition of 'fraudulent,' but it does not grant the SEC a license to redefine the term." 92 F.3d 612 at 624 (1996).

This conclusion follows easily from our similar statement in *Schreiber v. Burlington Northern, Inc.*, 472 U.S. 1, 11, n. 11 (1985), that § 14(e) gives the "Commission latitude to regulate nondeceptive activities as a 'reasonably designed' means of preventing manipulative acts, without suggesting any change in the meaning of the term 'manipulative' itself."

Insofar as the Rule 14e-3(a) purports to "define" acts and practices that "are fraudulent," it must be measured against our precedents interpreting the scope of fraud. The majority concedes, however, that Rule 14e-3(a) does not prohibit merely trading in connection with fraudulent nondisclosure, but rather it prohibits trading in connection with *any* nondisclosure, regardless of the presence of a pre-existing duty to disclose. The Rule thus exceeds the scope of the Commission's authority to define such acts and practices as "are fraudulent."

Turning to the Commission's second justification for Rule 14e-3(a), although I can agree with the majority that § 14(e) authorizes the Commission to prohibit nonfraudulent acts as a means reasonably designed to prevent fraudulent ones, I cannot agree that Rule 14e-3(a) satisfies this standard.***

In order to be a valid prophylactic regulation, Rule 14e-3(a) must be reasonably designed not merely to prevent *any* fraud, but to prevent persons from engaging in "fraudulent, deceptive, or manipulative acts or practices, *in connection with* any tender offer." Insofar as Rule 14e-3(a) is designed to prevent the type of misappropriation at issue in this case, such acts are not legitimate objects of prevention because the Commission's misappropriation theory does not represent a coherent interpretation of the statutory "in connection with" requirement ***. Even assuming that a person misappropriating information from the bidder commits fraud on the bidder, the Commission has provided no coherent or consistent explanation as to why such fraud is "in connection with" a tender offer, and thus the Commission may not seek to prevent indirectly conduct which it could not, under its current theory, prohibit directly.

Finally, even further assuming that the Commission's misappropriation theory is a valid basis for direct liability, I fail to see how Rule 14e-3(a)'s elimination of the requirement of a breach of fiduciary duty is "reasonably designed" to prevent the underlying "fraudulent" acts. The majority's primary argument on this score is that in many cases "'a breach of duty is likely but difficult to prove.'" Although the majority's hypothetical difficulties involved in a tipper-tippee situation might have some merit in the context of "classical" insider trading, there is no reason to suspect similar difficulties in "misappropriation" cases. In such cases, Rule 14e-3(a) requires the Commission to prove that the defendant "knows or has reason to know" that the nonpublic information upon which trading occurred came from the bidder or an agent of the bidder. Once the source of the information has been identified, it should be a simple task to obtain proof of any breach of duty. After all, it is the bidder itself that was defrauded in misappropriation cases, and there is no reason to suspect that the victim of the fraud would be reluctant to provide evidence against the perpetrator of the fraud. There being no particular difficulties in proving a breach of duty in such circumstances, a rule removing the requirement of such a breach cannot be said to be "reasonably designed" to prevent underlying violations of the misappropriation theory. ***

While enhancing the overall efficacy of the Williams Act may be a reasonable goal, it is not one that may be pursued through § 14(e), which limits its grant of rulemaking authority to the prevention of fraud, deceit, and manipulation. As we have held in the context of § 10(b), "not every instance of financial unfairness constitutes fraudulent activity." *Chiarella*, supra, at 232. Because, in the context of misappropriation cases, Rule 14e-3(a) is not a means "reasonably designed" to prevent persons from engaging in fraud "in connection with" a tender offer, it exceeds the Commission's authority under § 14(e), and respondent's conviction for violation of that Rule cannot be sustained.

NOTES AND QUESTIONS

1. ***Rule 14e-3 and Parity Of Access to Information.*** The SEC promulgated Rule 14e-3 in 1980, a few months after the government's defeat in *Chiarella*. Did the SEC use its rulemaking powers under Section 14(e) to enact the "equal access to information" approach that the Court had rejected in the context of Rule 10b-5 liability? Does Section 14(e) give the SEC the power to (re)define fraud in the context of tender offers?

2. ***"As Applied to Cases of this Genre."*** The *O'Hagan* Court endorsed the validity of Rule 14e-3(a), but only "insofar as it serve[d] to prevent the type of misappropriation charged against O'Hagan." What is meant by this qualification? Does it mean that Rule 14e-3(a)'s validity has been established only in misappropriation cases?

3. ***The Practice of Warehousing.*** The *O'Hagan* Court stated explicitly that the legality of warehousing was an issue left for resolution another day. How does the Court define the practice of warehousing? Why doesn't warehousing constitute fraudulent conduct under Rule 10b-5?

SEC studies done in the 1970s indicated not only that warehousing tactics were often used, but also that such conduct was widespread across many different tender offers with different bidders. The SEC repeatedly pointed to these findings in order to justify its promulgation of Rule 14e-3. See SEC Release No. 33-6022, 44 Fed. Reg. 9956, 9957 (Feb. 15, 1979) ("[T]he Commission is proposing a rule which is designed to curb a serious abuse in tender offer practice by certain persons trading in [target] securities prior to the bidder's announcement of an intention to make a tender offer."). See also id. at 9976-77 ("In some instances, the leaking of the intention to make a tender offer may be deliberate. The [Institutional Investor Study Report] found that bidders frequently gave institutions advance notice in either general or specific terms of proposed tender offers. Whether deliberate or not, the leaking of the bidder's intention to make a tender offer when coupled with trading on such non-public market information is a matter of serious concern to the Commission").

Why would a warehouser tip someone to buy target shares in advance of the public announcement of its tender offer? Since such action may increase the demand for target shares, how would the warehouser benefit from action leading to an upward pressure on the target share price? Who is disadvantaged? Do you think the Supreme Court would be likely to endorse the validity of Rule 14e-3(a) in a case in which the facts directly involved warehousing? See T. Andrew Eckstein. "The Prohibition of Warehousing Under Rule 14e-3," 30 Sec. Reg. L.J. 401 (2002).

*4. **The Substantial Step Requirement.*** Rule 14e-3(a)'s prohibitions apply only when "the offering person" has "taken a substantial step or steps to commence, or has commenced a tender offer." For examples of what constitutes a substantial step, see *SEC v. Ginsburg,* 362 F.3d 1292, 1304 (11th Cir. 2004) (requirement was met where "there was a meeting between executives, which was followed by due diligence procedures, a confidentiality agreement, and by a meeting between" the defendant and an executive of the target); *SEC v. Mayhew*, 121 F.3d 44, 53 (2d Cir. 1997) (noting that retaining a consulting firm, signing a confidentiality agreement, and holding meetings between company officials constitute "substantial steps"); *SEC v. Maoi,* 51 F.3d 623, 636 (7th Cir. 1995) (officials in a meeting "much more serious than any previous discussion between the parties" satisfies substantial step requirement); *SEC v. Musella,* 578 F. Supp. 425, 443-444 (S.D.N.Y. 1984) (retaining a law firm constitutes a "substantial step"). These cases comport with the SEC definition of "substantial steps" that was set out in the adopting release. See Tender Offers, Exchange Act Release No. 17120, 20 SEC Docket 1241, 1248 n. 23 (Sept. 4, 1980) ("activities which substantially facilitate the offer" engaged in after "the formulation of a plan or proposal to make a tender offer by the offeror or person(s) acting on behalf of the offeror").

*5. **Knowledge on the Part of the Defendant.*** For liability to attach under Rule 14e-3(a), must the defendant actually know that substantial steps to commence a tender offer have been taken? On remand from the Supreme Court, the Eighth Circuit Court of Appeals addressed this question in response to a challenge by O'Hagan to the following jury instruction:

> With respect to [the Rule 14e-3(a) counts], you must find that Grand Met had taken one or more substantial steps to commence its tender offer for Pillsbury stock at the time that O'Hagan had purchased the relevant Pillsbury securities. It is not necessary for a bidder to make a tender offer for you to find that substantial steps toward such an offer have been taken or made. *Nor is it necessary that you find that the defendant knew that the substantial steps had been taken.* It is enough that you find one or more substantial steps were in fact taken.

United States v. O'Hagan, 139 F.3d 641, 650 (8th Cir. 1998) (quoting Trial Tr. Vol. XII at 39) (emphasis by 8th Circuit). The Eighth Circuit had no trouble with the instruction, maintaining that Rule 14e-3(a) "does not require the defendant to have knowledge of [the substantial steps]. Instead, the defendant need only 'know[ ] or have reason to know' that the material information is 'nonpublic and has been acquired directly or indirectly from' the tender offeror in some way." Id.

Moreover, for liability to attach under Rule 14e-3 (a), must the defendant even know that the information in his possession pertains to a tender offer? See *SEC v. Sargent*, 229 F.3d 68, 78 (1st Cir. 2000) (holding that "there is simply no language in the Rule indicating that a defendant must know that the nonpublic information in his possession relates to a tender offer"); *SEC v. Ginsburg*, 362 F.3d 1292, 1304 (11th Cir. 2004) (holding that "Rule 14e-3, by its terms, does not require that the offender know or have reason to know that the information relates to a tender offer, so long as the information in fact does relate to a tender offer and the offender knows or has reason to know the information is nonpublic and was acquired by a person with the required status"). Can a person know or have reason to know that information came from a "tender offeror," if that person is not aware that the information pertained to a tender offer? Might the issue be resolved differently in the context of a criminal proceeding? See *United States v. Cassese*, 290 F. Supp.2d 443 (S.D.N.Y. 2003) (emphasizing the requirement of willfulness in Exchange Act Section 32(a), and concluding that "since there is 'no general duty to refrain from trading on material nonpublic information,' the defendant must have believed that the information related to, or most likely related to, a tender offer in order to impose criminal liability"), aff'd on other grounds, 428 F.3d 92 (2d Cir. 2005).

PROBLEM 7-7

Reconsider each of the factual scenarios in Problems 7-4 with the following modification: instead of the impending announcement of a new wonder drug for diabetes, assume that the material nonpublic information at issue concerns a tender offer launched by the biotech company. Assume further that all traders had purchased shares of stock in the target. Which scenarios would result in liability under Rule 14e-3? Note how your answers would change once again if the takeover were accomplished through a friendly merger or proxy solicitation rather than through a tender offer.

PROBLEM 7-8

Your spouse received a phone call last night from your next door neighbor asking for a favor. The neighbor was sick in bed with the flu, and she asked your spouse to drive her children to school in the morning. The neighbor hated to put your spouse to that trouble, and told your spouse that her husband was not able to drive to the school himself because his company was being sold and he has been working around the clock throughout the last five days. Your spouse quickly agreed to act as chauffeur and wished your neighbor a speedy recovery. Your spouse then relayed the entire conversation to you.

Because you have lived next door to this couple for the last five years, you are well aware that the "around-the-clock" working husband is a Senior Vice President of Digamax, a medium size company that manufactures compact discs. At this point, your curiosity is peaked, and you surf the Internet to see whether the news about Digamax is public. What you find are several recent references to Digamax in a trade publication indicating that the company is considered by many to be ripe for a takeover.

If you purchase Digamax stock while in possession of the information learned from your neighbor, would you be liable under Rule 14e-3(a)?

D. CONGRESS SPEAKS ON INSIDER TRADING—ITSA, ITSFEA, AND SUBSEQUENT LEGISLATION

In enforcing the federal prohibition against insider trading prior to 1984, the SEC had a relatively limited arsenal of enforcement weapons on which to draw, none of which were tailored to insider trading specifically. Thus, enforcement actions brought against persons for insider trading—whether litigated or settled—typically resulted in an injunction against future violations and an order that the defendant disgorge the ill-gotten profit gained or loss avoided from the illegal transactions. (Recall that this was the remedy upheld by the Second Circuit in *Texas Gulf Sulphur*.) Alternatively, if the case involved insider trading by a securities professional—such as a broker-dealer or investment adviser—the SEC could pursue an administrative action, and impose sanctions including censure (as it did in the *Cady, Roberts* and *Dirks* cases), temporary suspension, or a permanent bar from the industry. A final possible enforcement avenue took the case down the path of the criminal law where, as in *Chiarella*, the DOJ could prosecute the defendant in federal court and typically seek a prison sentence. The SEC, however, could only refer matters to the DOJ for criminal prosecutions; as you will be reminded again in Chapters 9 and 11, the SEC does not itself have the power to seek criminal sanctions against violators of the federal securities laws.

Recognizing that these remedies resulted in an unacceptably low level of deterrence, Congress sought to expand the arsenal of remedies available in insider trading cases, first in 1984 with the enactment of the Insider Trading Sanctions Act (ITSA), and then in 1988 when it enacted the Insider Trading and Securities Fraud Enforcement Act (ITSFEA).

ITSA's most important provision accorded the SEC—for the first time ever—the authority to seek in federal district court a civil penalty of up to three times the profit gained or loss avoided through a defendant's illegal insider trading. This penalty, which can be imposed for illegal tipping as well as trading, is clearly in addition to any disgorgement or criminal fine that may also be ordered. ITSA's civil penalty provision is now set out in Section 21A of the Exchange Act:

> **Section 21A—Civil penalties for insider trading**
>
> (a) Authority to impose civil penalties
>
> (1) Judicial actions by Commission authorized. Whenever it shall appear to the Commission that any person has violated any provision of this chapter or the rules or regulations thereunder by purchasing or selling a security *** while in possession of material, nonpublic information in, or has violated any such provision by communicating such information in connection with, a transaction on or through the facilities of a national securities exchange or from or through a broker or dealer, *** the Commission–
>
> > (A) may bring an action in a United States district court to seek, and the court shall have jurisdiction to impose, a civil penalty to be paid by the person who committed such violation; ***
>
> (2) Amount of penalty for person who committed violation. The amount of the penalty which may be imposed on the person who committed such violation shall be determined by the court in light of the facts and circumstances, but shall not exceed three times the profit gained or loss avoided as a result of such unlawful purchase, sale, or communication.

Notice the artful wording that enabled Congress to provide substantial penalties for insider trading without having to define precisely the conduct that is subject to sanction.

ITSA also clarified the law of insider trading as it pertains to options by adding a new Section 20(d) to the Exchange Act. This provision specifies that where trading or tipping on an issuer's securities would violate the Exchange Act, so too would a trade or tip that resulted in the purchase or sale of an option or similar right with respect to that security. Thus, option traders were put on equal footing with shareholders, in terms of their ability to be protected from those with access to material, nonpublic information. Prior to the enactment of Section 20(d), what hurdles may have prevented the government or private plaintiffs from suing those who purchased options on the basis of material, nonpublic information? See *Laventhall v. Gen. Dynamics Corp.*, 704 F.2d 407 (8th Cir, 1983); *O'Connor & Assocs. v. Dean Witter Reynolds, Inc.*, 600 F. Supp. 702 (S.D.N.Y. 1985).

With ITSA in place, the SEC quickly escalated its enforcement efforts with respect to insider trading. Yet a number of high-profile scandals in the mid-1980s primed Congress for action on the SEC's claim that further measures of deterrence and enforcement were needed. The scandals involved the types of facts that eventually found their way into Hollywood movies: extremely wealthy entrepreneurs being led out of their Wall Street offices in handcuffs. But for a while, the scandals themselves were what the public closely watched, and Ivan Boesky, Michael Milkin, Dennis Levine and others soon became well-known villains. Concerned that the scandals represented "far more than the transgressions of a few individuals," Congress set out to send a clear message that "insider trading will not be tolerated in our markets." H.R. Rep. No. 100-910 at 14 (1988).

The legislative response took the form of ITSFEA – the Insider Trading and Securities Fraud Enforcement Act of 1988. One of ITSFEA's most important provisions extended the treble penalty provision in what is now Section 21A to those persons or entities who "control" a person found liable for illegal trading or tipping. Pursuant to Section 21A(a)(1)(B), the SEC may seek a penalty in federal district court against such controlling persons provided it satisfies the following provision:

> **Section 21A(b)(1)—Liability of controlling persons**
>
> No controlling person shall be subject to a penalty *** unless the Commission establishes that:
>
> (A) such controlling person knew or recklessly disregarded the fact that such controlled person was likely to engage in the act or acts constituting the violation and failed to take appropriate steps to prevent such act or acts before they occurred; or
>
> (B) such controlling person knowingly or recklessly failed to establish, maintain, or enforce any policy or procedure required under [Section 15(f) of the Exchange Act or Section 204A of the Investment Advisers Act] and such failure substantially contributed to or permitted the occurrence of the act or acts constituting the violation.

Section 21A(3) provides that a court shall determine the penalty imposed on a controlling person "in light of the facts and circumstances," but that it "shall not exceed the greater of $1,000,000 [now 1.2 million (adjusted for inflation)], or three times the amount of the profit gained or loss avoided as a result of such controlled person's violation." Moreover, in cases where the controlled person's violation involved tipping, the profit gained or loss avoided by the controlled person is to be calculated based on the transactions of the person or persons who directly received the tip from the controlled person. In other words, profits made or losses avoided by so-called remote tippees are disregarded when calculating the maximum penalty for a person found to have controlled a person liable for tipping.

Important questions prompted by this provision include who qualifies as a "control person" and what does it mean to "recklessly" disregard someone's likelihood of engaging in illegal tipping or trading. The legislative history relevant to both questions shows that Congress intended to put economic pressure on employers—particularly, but not exclusively, those on Wall Street—to better supervise those persons who have regular access to material, nonpublic information. But the House Committee Report also makes clear that the case law interpreting that term in Section 20(a) of the Act (see supra Chapter 2.H.3) applies here, such that "control" broadly includes any person "with the power to influence or control the direction of management, policies or activities of another person." H.R. Rep. No. 100-910 at 17 (1988). That said, Congress was not looking to impose a scheme of strict liability for employers in connection with their employees' bad acts, and explicitly provided in Section 21A(b)(2) that no person shall be subject to a penalty "solely by reason of employing another person who is subject to a penalty under such subsection." The House Report further stated that, for a penalty to be imposed, "the Commission must establish that a controlling person objectively disregarded a risk that a controlled person was engaged in violations of the insider trading laws," and that the risk involved "must be such that to disregard it would constitute a gross deviation from the standard of care that a reasonable person would exercise in such a situation." House Report at 18. Notice however, that Section 20(a) provides controlling persons with a "good faith" defense to liability whereas no such defense is provided for controlling persons under Section 21A. Does the recklessness standard in Section 21A(b)(1)(A) effectively ensure that no one acting in good faith could be subject to a penalty under that provision?

Another important provision of ITSFEA added Section 20A to the Exchange Act, a provision that establishes an express private right of action for violations of the federal securities laws involving illegal insider trading or tipping. Note once again how Congress managed to establish a remedy for insider trading without specifically defining the insider trading offense.

> **Section 20A—Liability to contemporaneous traders for insider trading**
>
> (a) Private rights of action based on contemporaneous trading. Any person who violates any provision of this chapter or the rules or regulations thereunder by purchasing or selling a security while in possession of material, nonpublic information shall be liable in an action in any court of competent jurisdiction to any person who, contemporaneously with the purchase or sale of securities that is the subject of such violation, has purchased (where such violation is based on a sale of securities) or sold (where such violation is based on a purchase of securities) securities of the same class. ***
>
> (c) Joint and several liability for communicating. Any person who violates any provision of this chapter or the rules or regulations thereunder by communicating material, nonpublic information shall be jointly and severally liable under subsection (a) of this section with, and to the same extent as, any person or persons liable under subsection (a) of this section to whom the communication was directed.

Note also that Section 20A eliminates the need for private plaintiffs to show that the insider trader owed them a disclosure duty. Instead, plaintiffs have to establish merely the existence of a predicate violation—typically, that the defendant violated Rule 10b-5 by trading while in possession of material, nonpublic information. Recall the facts of *United States v. O'Hagan*. Under Section 20A, Pillsbury shareholders and option traders who sold contemporaneously with James O'Hagan's purchases could have sued O'Hagan for damages even though, under the Court's misappropriation theory, it was Grand Metropolitan and the law firm of Dorsey & Whitney who were the actual victims of O'Hagan's fraud. Why should contemporaneous traders who were not defrauded nonetheless be entitled to an insider trader's profits? Do Dorsey & Whitney and Grand Metropolitan have a stronger normative claim for O'Hagan's profits? Would either have had a legal claim against O'Hagan under Section 20A? Could either have sued O'Hagan under the implied right of action under Rule 10b-5?

What does it mean to say that a plaintiff purchased a security contemporaneously with a defendant's sale? Congress chose not to define the term "contemporaneously," preferring instead to rely on the definition that had developed through the case law. Today, most courts agree that a plaintiff trades "contemporaneously" by trading on the same day or no more than a few days after an illegal trade. Just how many days after is an issue of some dispute. Compare *In re Oxford Heath Plans, Inc. Sec. Litig.*, 187 F.R.D. 133, 144 (S.D.N.Y. 1999) (concluding that "[f]ive trading days is a reasonable period between the insider's sales and the plaintiff's purchase to be considered contemporaneous") with *Backman v. Polaroid Corp.*, 540 F. Supp. 667, 671 (D. Mass. 1982) (concluding that purchases two business days after defendant's sales were not contemporaneous) and *Copland v. Grumet*, 88 F. Supp. 2d 326, 338 (D.N.J. 1999) (requiring the plaintiff to have bought the stock "on the same dates on which the defendant's sales took place").

In addition to restricting the right of recovery to persons who trade contemporaneously with (and opposite) the unlawful trade, Congress took other steps to see that the amount of liability to private plaintiffs would not be draconian. First, Section 20A(b)(1) caps the total amount of available damages to "the profit gained or loss avoided in the transaction or transactions that are the subject of the violation." Second, Section 20A(b)(2) provides that any funds that were paid to the SEC as disgorgement may be offset by the "total amount of damages imposed against any person" for the same transaction or transactions. Finally, Section 20A(b)(3) clarifies that "[n]o person shall be liable under this section solely by reason of employing another person who is liable under this section, but the liability of a controlling person under this section shall be subject to [Section 20(a)]." In view of these limitations on liability, is Section 20A a particularly effective deterrent against insider trading? In what types of fact patterns would you most expect to see Section 20A claims asserted?

ITSFEA amended the Exchange Act in other significant ways. It increased the individual criminal fine available under Section 32(a) to a maximum of $1,000,000 and raised the maximum available prison term from 5 to 10 years. For non-natural persons, it increased the maximum criminal fine to 2.5 million. (As you will see when you study criminal enforcement in Chapter 11, the Sarbanes-Oxley Act subsequently amended Section 32(a) to increase the maximum prison sentence to 20 years, and to increase the maximum fine to $5,000,000 for individuals and $25,000,000 for non-natural persons). ITSFEA also added a "bounty program" to Section 21A(e) of the Exchange Act. This provision authorized the SEC or the Attorney General to pay informants a sum, not to exceed ten percent of the penalty recovered, where an informant's information leads to the imposition of a penalty for illegal trading or tipping. (But as you will see when you study SEC enforcement in Chapter 9, the Dodd-Frank Act repealed Section 21A(e) when it amended the Exchange Act to include a new Section 21F that *mandates* the payment of bounties to informants whenever "original information" leads to the successful prosecution of *any* violation of the federal securities laws resulting in monetary sanctions exceeding a million dollars).

With the enactment of ITSA and ITSFEA, did Congress achieve its stated objectives? This question, of course, can be answered on a number of levels. To be sure, one measure of success might be the legislation's effect on the types of securities professionals that prompted Congress's intervention in the first place. And, for at least some period of time, there was good reason for congressional satisfaction. Indeed, toward the end of the 1990s, the SEC's Enforcement Director shared his observation that "we have not seen arbitragers and investment banking professionals end up in the caption *** of complaints or charged in criminal cases. *** This is a group of people that understands seeing their name on the front page of the New York Times and the possibility of going to jail." See Micro Cap Fraud, Staffing Issues Top Enforcement Agenda, 29 Sec. Reg. & L. Rep. 1769, 1772 (BNA) (Dec. 19, 1997) (quoting statements by former SEC Enforcement Director William McLucas). Attorneys, legal assistants, and other law firm personnel also appeared to have heeded the warnings. See, e.g., Crime: Former NY Prosecutor Admits to Insider Trading, Bribery Scheme, 33 Sec. Reg. & L. Rep. 215 (BNA) (February 12, 2001) (reporting guilty plea in criminal case where defendant offered $50,000 to a paralegal at the law firm of Skadden Arps in return for confidential information regarding deals that the law firm was handling; the paralegal refused and reported the offer to Skadden Arps's management, who in turn notified federal authorities). There were, of course notable exceptions. See id. (incredibly, the defendant who pled guilty was formerly a prosecutor for the state of New York). See also *United States v. O'Hagan*, 521 U.S. 642 (1997), supra, Section B.3.

Yet, as the second introductory quote to this chapter reflects, the SEC and the DOJ are once again mounting an aggressive campaign against insider trading by Wall Street professionals and others with routine access to material nonpublic information. Assuming that insider trading on Wall Street is once again on the rise, what factors might explain this development?

Since the enactment of ITSA and ITSFEA, Congress has expanded substantially the SEC's arsenal of remedies in enforcement actions for violations of the federal securities laws. In the Securities Enforcement Remedies and Penny Stock Reform Act of 1990 (discussed in Chapter 9.C.1, infra), Congress added new provisions to the Securities Act and Exchange Act which authorized federal courts to impose orders barring individuals from future service as an officer or director of a publicly traded company, upon the SEC's showing that the person committed fraud in violation of Section 10(b) of the Exchange Act or SEC rules thereunder or Section 17(a)(1) of the Securities Act and that the person was "substantially unfit" to serve. Federal courts often imposed this remedy in insider trading cases, although SEC officials contended that the statutory language of "substantial unfitness" courts interpreted in an overly restrictive manner. See Stephen M. Cutler, SEC Director, Division of Enforcement, Remarks at the Glasser LegalWorks 20th Annual Federal Securities Institute (Feb. 15, 2002) (discussing insider trading cases in which federal courts imposed liability for violating Rule 10b-5 but refused to bar defendants from future corporate service).

In the wake of the scandals at Enron and WorldCom, Congress acceded to the SEC's requests to modify this bar order remedy. Under Section 20(e) of the Securities Act and Section 21(d)(2) of the Exchange Act, federal courts may now impose a bar order upon the SEC's showing of an individual's mere "unfitness" to serve. The Act also amended Section 8A of the Securities Act and Section 21C of the Exchange Act to authorize the SEC to impose such bar orders in administrative proceedings. Although only time will tell the extent to which the SEC actually utilizes these additional enforcement weapons, one can certainly expect that insider trading cases will present fact patterns that lead the SEC to seek to impose a greater number of officer and director bars.

The Dodd-Frank Act also added several new enforcement-related provisions to the Exchange Act, including an amendment to Sections 21B, which now authorizes the SEC to impose a civil monetary penalty against *any* person in *any* cease-and-desist proceeding upon the establishment of a violation of the Exchange Act, provided that such a penalty is in the public interest. Prior to this change, only regulated persons such as broker-dealers and their associated persons could be subject to civil penalties in administrative proceedings. Might this new penalty authority prompt the SEC to change its prior practice of filing almost all insider trading cases in federal court? Why or why not?

Although Congress has yet to enact a broad statutory ban on insider trading, the Enron and WorldCom scandals did inspire the very first express prohibition, albeit in a very narrow context. And once again, as with Section 16(b)'s disgorgement provision for short-swing profits (see Section A.2, supra), Congress did so without any regard to whether the trading insiders possess any material nonpublic information. Section 306 of the Sarbanes-Oxley Act, entitled "Insider Trades During Pension Fund Blackout Periods," provides that:

> it shall be unlawful for any director or executive officer of an issuer of any equity security (other than an exempted security), directly or indirectly, to purchase, sell, or otherwise acquire any equity security *** during any blackout period with respect to such equity security if such director or officer acquires such equity security in connection with his or her service or employment as a director or executive officer.

A "blackout period" is defined, subject to certain exceptions, as "any period of more than 3 consecutive business days during which the ability of not fewer than 50 percent of the participants" in an individual account plan (as defined in ERISA) maintained by the issuer, to make trades in the issuer's equity securities "is temporarily suspended by the issuer or by a fiduciary of the plan." See id. at Section 306(a)(4). As a remedy for breaches of its trading prohibition, Section 306(a)(2) provides that an action to recover the profits of the director or executive officer may be instituted at law or in equity in any court of competent jurisdiction by the issuer or on behalf of the issuer if the issuer fails to bring such a suit within 60 days.

Should Congress have used the occasion of the Sarbanes-Oxley Act to legislatively overhaul the regulation of insider trading rather than merely tinker around its peripheral edges? Should Congress have done so in connection with the Dodd-Frank Act? The final section of this Chapter explores the pros and cons of a statutory definition.

PROBLEM 7-9

Ben Brittle, a registered representative with the national brokerage firm of Ferris Morton, had been generating tremendous profits, both for his own accounts and for the proprietary accounts that he manages for Ferris Morton. His immediate supervisors had suspected for some time that he is up to no good, but they had no specific evidence of illegal activity. The supervisors shared their suspicions with the Senior Vice President in Charge of Compliance (the "Compliance Director"), who formulated an enhanced supervisory plan pursuant to which any of the broker's transactions above $5,000 would require pre-approval by the branch manager or assistant manager. When informed of this new procedure, Brittle complained to the Executive Vice President in Charge of Sales, who then pressured the Compliance Director into rescinding the special supervisory measures.

As it turned out, Brittle was one of several people who had been receiving information directly from an analyst who worked at Connelly, Inc., a venture capital firm that recently made a number of highly lucrative acquisitions. One of Connelly's recent deals involved the takeover of Harris Industries. When Connelly first became interested in Harris, its stock had been trading steadily for more than a year in or around $16 a share. Throughout the weeks of negotiations and due diligence, Harris's stock price crept up gradually to $19 a share. Connelly negotiated a friendly deal with management at $21 a share for the 1 million shares outstanding, though it was convinced that the deal could have been consummated at a lower price had Harris continued to trade at the $16 level. The SEC also focused attention on the stock price spike in the days prior to the merger announcement and quickly identified the employee-analyst who was the source of the tips. This employee is cooperating with the SEC and the U.S. Attorney in return for a penalty that will not involve jail time.

The SEC identified Brittle as a tippee who purchased stock in Harris on the basis of the misappropriated information. Brittle agreed to settle the action with the SEC, and consented to a permanent bar from association with a broker-dealer, disgorgement in the sum of $120,000 (representing the profit from the Harris transaction as well as several other ones), and a penalty of $240,000.

Can the SEC bring an action against Ferris Morton, Brittle's broker-dealer employer? Against officials at Ferris Morton? On what theory? What remedies can it seek?

Can Connolly seek damages under Rule 10b-5 to recoup some of the money it spent in acquiring Harris at the $21 price? Whom can it sue? How would damages be calculated?

What about those who sold stock in Harris on the day that Brittle made his purchases? Do they have an incentive to sue?

E. LITIGATING INSIDER TRADING CASES—THE PROBLEM OF CIRCUMSTANTIAL EVIDENCE

An overwhelming percentage of enforcement actions brought by the SEC are settled rather than litigated, and insider trading cases present no exception to this pattern. But what about the infrequent case that is tried? How does the SEC prove all of the elements necessary to establish a violation of Rule 10b-5 (or Rule 14e-3)?

Insider trading cases often raise particularly difficult questions of proof because the evidence that one was aware of material nonpublic information at the time of a transaction is often in the sole control of the individual trader or her tipper. If the trader denies such awareness (as is typical in cases brought to trial), and if the suspected tipper denies that information was imparted (or if the suspected tipper cannot be identified), the SEC has no choice but to make its case circumstantially. Although the SEC may work with criminal prosecutors to seek court-orders for wiretaps based on probable cause (as it did in connection with the investigation and prosecution of hedge fund trader Raj Rajaratnam and a host of defendants in related actions), wiretap evidence of illegal tipping and trading activity is likely to remain the exception rather than the rule.

SEC officials readily acknowledge that "virtually all insider trading cases hinge on circumstantial evidence" because it "is rare to find a 'smoking gun.'" United States Senate Committee on the Judiciary Hearings on Illegal Insider Trading , 109 Cong. 143, Sept. 26, 2006 (written testimony of Linda Thomsen, Director, SEC Division of Enforcement). But SEC officials also emphasize that when suspicious trading is detected, the staff of the Enforcement Division reviews all relevant trading reports, bank statements, and brokerage records, and "has become particularly adept at sifting through all available forms of evidence, including phone records, emails, instant messages, and the electronic footprints of internet protocol data." Id.

The SEC's challenge in civil litigation is to prove unlawful trading or tipping by a preponderance of evidence. One illustrative case is *SEC v. Geon Indus., Inc.*, 531 F.2d 39 (2d Cir. 1976), in which Geon's CEO was alleged to have tipped a stockbroker about the company's upcoming merger. Although there was no direct evidence of the tip, the court held that the circumstantial evidence of their telephone conversations followed by substantial stock purchases by the stockbroker supported the trial court's inference that material nonpublic information had passed between them. In so concluding, the court emphasized that the broker had asserted a privilege against self-incrimination and that the CEO had claimed "inability to recall the subject-matter of most of their numerous talks." Id. at 46.

Circumstantial evidence is also used routinely in a criminal insider trading trial, where the DOJ must establish the defendant's guilt beyond a reasonable doubt. One well-publicized recent example is *U.S. v. McDermott*, 245 F. 3d 133 (2d Cir. 2001), in which the court reviewed a jury's finding that James McDermott, CEO and Chairman of an investment bank, had tipped his "adult film" star girlfriend, Kathryn Gannon, as to to confidential merger information. The court held that "although the government was unable to produce direct evidence" of the tips, "rational minds could have inferred such a conclusion" from the following evidence:

> (1) that McDermott and Gannon were having an affair involving incessant telephone conversations; (2) that Gannon, who was up until this point an amateur trader, opened a trading account funded by monies given to her by McDermott; (3) that during the alleged conspiracy period, Gannon traded twenty-one times in twelve different stocks based upon McDermott's recommendations; (4) that Gannon traded in non-blue chip stocks, many of which were banks subject to non-public negotiations with [McDermott's investment bank]; (5) that Gannon was quite successful in her trading and in the timing of her trades; (6) that telephone conversations between Gannon and McDermott coincided with Gannon's trading activity; and (7) that Gannon shared her recommendations with [a third party who acted on those recommendations].

Id. at 138. The court noted specifically that "[c]ircumstantial evidence is a legitimate form of evidence in this Circuit, and in fact-intensive cases such as this, requiring careful examination of trading records and a myriad of public information, the jury is the appropriate body to determine a defendant's guilt or innocence." Id. at 139. Although the court found that the evidence was sufficient to convict McDermott on the insider trading charges, it nonetheless ordered a new trial due to prejudicial errors committed with respect to joining certain conspiracy charges. See id. at 139-40. McDermott subsequently pled guilty to the insider trading charges rather than be retried. See Crime: Former Wall Street Exec. Pleads Guilty to Insider Charges in Lieu of Second Trial, 33 Sec. Reg. & L. Rep. 1003 (BNA) (July 9, 2001). How would you have weighed the circumstantial evidence in the following case?

SEC v. MORAN

922 F. Supp. 867 (S.D.N.Y. 1996)

BERNARD NEWMAN, SENIOR JUDGE:*

The United States Securities and Exchange Commission, brings this civil securities fraud enforcement action against Frederick Augustus Moran ("Moran Sr."), Frederick Winston Moran ("Moran Jr."), Moran Asset Management Inc. ("Moran Asset"), and Moran & Associates, Inc., Securities Brokerage ("Moran Brokerage"). Specifically, the SEC alleges that Moran Sr., Moran Jr., Moran Asset, and Moran Brokerage engaged in insider trading thereby violating Section 10(b) of the Securities Exchange Act of 1934 ["the Exchange Act"] ***The SEC seeks judgment permanently enjoining each of the defendants from violating the pertinent provisions of the Exchange Act *** disgorgement of all illegal profits, prejudgment interest arising from the alleged insider trading, [and a] payment of three time civil penalties based on the insider trading ***. The defendants deny each of the allegations lodged against them and seek dismissal of the complaint.

***[T]he only issues presented to the court at this juncture are the liability of the defendants for the charges in the complaint. The case was tried to the court in a twelve day bench trial. In conformity with F.R.C.P.Rule 52(a), the following constitutes the court's findings of fact and conclusions of law.

---

*. Senior Judge of the United States Court of International Trade, sitting as United States District Judge by designation.

THE RECORD

In its direct case, the SEC presented eight witnesses: John Reddan, executive vice-president and security analyst for Moran & Associates Securities Brokerage from May 1985 until October 31, 1995; defendant Frederick Winston Moran, a vice-president at Salomon Brothers; defendant Frederick Augustus Moran, president of Moran Asset Management and Moran & Associates Brokerage;[2] Richard Scribner, chief compliance officer for Salomon Brothers, Inc.; Edward Meyercord, vice-president in investment banking for Salomon Brothers; Frank Poli, an attorney, who in 1993 was the head trader for Moran Asset Management; Peter D. Crawford, executive director of investor relations and share owner relations for Bell Atlantic Corporation; and Kevin Tarrant, manager of investor relations for Bell Atlantic Corporation. Defendants did not present any witnesses. On rebuttal plaintiff called Raymond Liguori, who was employed as the telecommunication analyst for Salomon Brothers in October 1993. Pursuant to agreement by counsel and F.R.C.P. Rule 32(a)(3)(E), the depositions of Susan Putnam, vice-president of Moran Asset and Moran Brokerage, Katherine Dietze Courage, a director at Salomon Brothers, Richard Holbein, the president of Pension Asset Consulting Associates Inc., and Jennifer Netterville, the investment officer of Louisiana Teacher's Retirement Fund, were admitted into evidence. The parties moved 213 exhibits into evidence.

CONTENTIONS OF THE PARTIES

The SEC alleges that Moran Sr. and his companies acted upon inside information about two cable companies provided by Moran Jr., his son. According to the SEC, Moran Jr. "tipped" Moran Sr. with respect to a merger between Bell Atlantic and Telecommunications Incorporated ("TCI"). This circumstantial case revolves around the fact that Moran Jr., as an employee of Salomon Brothers, was in possession of material, non-public information with respect to the Bell Atlantic-TCI merger. Moran Sr. who had previously been reticent to trade cable stocks, after a series of phone conversations with Moran Jr., made [a] large purchase of Liberty, TCI and other cable company stocks on October 11, 1993, two days before the October 13, 1993 official announcement of the merger. The SEC argues that because Moran Sr. and his companies had lost substantial money and clients as the result of a very unsuccessful prior investment in Chamber Development stock, Moran Sr. needed a "sure winner." Moreover, plaintiff contends that Moran Jr. had a history of violating Salomon Brothers' policies regarding confidential information in order to benefit Moran Sr.'s firms, thereby demonstrating an intent on the part of Moran Jr. to provide his father with confidential information. Finally, plaintiff alleges that because Moran Sr. had previously been bearish on cable, these October 11th stock purchases constituted an aberrant trading pattern for Moran Sr., there were several phone calls between Moran Sr. and Jr., including one for over forty minutes the week before Moran Sr. made the stock purchases, and Moran Sr. faxed to Moran Jr. the Moran "morning meeting notes" specifying the switch in cable policy on the morning of the stock purchases indicates that the defendants traded the cable securities as a result of material, non-public information in violation of the Exchange Act and Rules thereunder. ***

2. Moran Sr. and Moran Jr. were called as hostile witnesses by the SEC.

Defendants deny each of the charges. Specifically, Moran Sr. and Moran Jr. respond that Moran Jr. in no way "tipped" any material non-public information with respect to the Bell Atlantic-TCI merger. Defendants maintain that Moran Sr.'s change of heart regarding the cable stocks came about as a result of the actions of Dr. John Malone, a "giant" in the cable industry. Moran Sr. claims that his return to purchasing cable stocks resulted from following Malone's lead. Indeed, defendants additionally point out that news of the impending merger was made public through newspaper articles in the New York Times and the Wall Street Journal. Moran Sr. argues that it was during the weekend of October 9-10, after reading a Wall Street Journal article about a merger between TCI and Liberty, that he made his final decision to begin investment in cable stocks.***

FINDINGS OF FACT

Frederick Augustus Moran ("Moran Sr.") is the president and principal portfolio manager of Moran Asset Management Inc., as well as the president and director of research of Moran & Associates, Inc. Securities Brokerage. Frederick Winston Moran Jr. ("Moran Jr.") is Moran Sr.'s eldest son and has been employed since March 1993 by Salomon Brothers Inc. as an analyst specializing in the cellular telephone and wireless communications industries. In July 1993, while working for Salomon Brothers, Moran Jr. expanded his focus to the cable television industry for Salomon Brothers. Moran Asset Management, Inc. ("Moran Asset") since 1986 has been a registered investment adviser. Moran & Associates, Inc. Securities Brokerage ("Moran Brokerage") since 1987 has been a registered broker-dealer. Moran Sr. and his wife Joan, during the periods in question each owned 50% of the stock of Moran Asset and Moran Brokerage.

The Insider Trading Claim

Overview of Events

On October 3, 1993, Moran Jr. was "brought over the wall" at Salomon Brothers with regard to a proposed merger between Telecommunication Incorporated ("TCI") and Bell Atlantic. Moran Jr. was told that the official announcement of the merger would come "within a week to two weeks" (R. 437). On Wednesday, October 6, Moran Jr. was briefed on the details of the proposed Bell Atlantic/TCI merger and told by Edward Meyercord that the announcement was expected to take place early the following week. Moran Jr.'s understanding was that the announcement date "would probably be the 13th, or certainly the 12th, 13th, or 14th" (R. 437). On Thursday, October 7, the Wall Street Journal published an article entitled "TCI Reported In Talks To Buy Liberty Media" (Exhibit 11).

Moran Jr. attended a meeting at Bell Atlantic headquarters in Philadelphia on October 9, 1993. The purpose of the meeting was twofold. First, there were discussions about how to best market the Bell Atlantic/TCI merger. Second, the speech that the president of Bell Atlantic would deliver when the deal was announced was drafted. At this meeting Salomon Brothers representatives, including Moran Jr., learned for the first time that the definitive date of the announcement regarding the merger was October 13. According to Meyercord, "there was a very detailed media plan that was put together and ... there was to be a public announcement in New York City in the morning in which the analyst community would be present" (R. 894). This media plan also set forth October 13 as the date of the public announcement (Exh. 1).

On October 11, 1993 Moran Sr. bought approximately 340,000 and 203,000 shares of TCI and Liberty stock respectively. During the evening of October 12, Moran Jr. told employees of Moran Asset and John Reddan about the merger. The proposed merger of Bell Atlantic and TCI was publicly announced by a press release issued at approximately 7:00 a.m. on October 13.

Moran Sr.'s Trading Practice

From 1987 through 1991 Moran Sr. invested at least 35% and as much as 45% of his clients' managed funds in cable television stocks. In 1991, Dr. John Malone, the President and Chief Executive Officer of TCI, the largest cable company in the world, began moving his personal wealth out of TCI, a cable television operator company, and into Liberty, a programing company. Moran Sr. testified that at the time of Malone's transaction, the move did not seem significant "because [Moran Asset's] impression was that [Malone] had exercised only half of his rights and [Moran Sr.] thought that was therefore a case of saying to the world I am not abandoning Liberty and it was something he did with that in mind and he had not exercised all of his rights" (R. 1406-07; 1411 Moran Sr. Exh. CX). At that juncture, Moran Sr. believed that Malone was actually increasing his backing of TCI and therefore Moran Sr. increased his purchases of TCI stocks. In fact, however, Dr. Malone was tendering all of his TCI shares in exchange for increased stocks in Liberty (R. 773, 1413; Moran Sr. Exhs. CW, CQ). From October 25, 1991, when Dr. Malone publicly disclosed his venture into Liberty, and until Liberty recombined with TCI, Liberty's stock price had increased by 3000 percent. During this time Moran Sr. was still a proponent of cable stocks.

Beginning in 1992 Moran Sr.'s view of the cable industry began to change. In addition, Moran Sr. learned on January 7, 1992 that Malone had actually liquidated his TCI holdings to pay for his investment in Liberty. Moran Sr. was further aware that Malone was an outspoken critic of government regulation of the cable industry and predicted a negative impact would result. In response to the problems he believed would result from increased regulation of the cable industry, as well as the discovery that Malone had in fact been divesting himself from TCI holdings, Moran Sr. began selling cable stocks in Moran Asset's client accounts beginning in 1992 (R. 780-82; Exhs. 39-40). On January 8, 1992 Moran Sr. began selling TCI and Comcast stock and within several weeks Moran Asset sold out all its cable stock positions almost completely. According to Moran Sr., the decision to sell was made by him without first consulting Moran Jr. or John Reddan.

In addition to selling TCI stock, Moran Sr. decided to cover the short position he had in Liberty stock. According to Reddan, the short position was closed at a substantial loss. With respect to Moran Sr.'s reaction after these transactions, Reddan testified that "[Moran Sr.] said we've got to learn our lesson here. Malone has a tremendous following. [Moran Sr.] never wanted to go against him again. And it was more—our feeling that Malone's following was more powerful than we had estimated" (R. 775).[8] During 1993, Malone appeared to be moving further into programming and away from cable television. This move was well documented in Moran Brokerage Morning Meeting Notes. Specifically, the notes stated:

> There is a rumor that TCI will purchase Liberty Media's cable properties. This would mean 1) John Malone would be reducing further his cable interests and moving further into programming inhibits the cable companies ability to pass on programming price increases.

(Morning Meeting Note May 27, 1993, Moran Sr. Exh. K).

> NYT article:—Cable television John Malone is moving further into programming in response to regulatory and technological changes.

(Morning Meeting Note, June 1, 1993, Moran Sr. Exh. L).

> Fortune article: John Malone calls President Clinton a bold face liar. Two possible reasons for this unguarded behavior are: 1) he is so frustrated with what Congress has done to the cable industry, or 2) won't be around to bear the consequences. Recently he has begun to say it is too much trouble for him to be Chairman of both Liberty Media and Telecommunications.

(Morning Meeting Note, June 14, 1993, Moran Sr. Exh, M).

> [Liberty Media is] rumored to be planning to swap its interests in cable system for TCI's interest in programming assets—especially Turner Broadcasting and Discovery Channel. Malone is moving away from cable systems and toward programming.

(Morning Meeting Note, September 20, 1993, Moran Sr. Exh. N).

It is undisputed that from 1992 and into August 1993 Moran Sr. was "bearish" on cable stocks. Indeed, published materials from Moran Brokerage clearly demonstrate Moran Sr.'s unfavorable view of cable stock. In Moran Asset's morning meeting notes from March, April, and June 1993, Moran Sr. predicted that "cable TV stocks, as a group, offer modest upside potential and substantial downside risk," that regulation "was more severe than our forecasted worst case scenario," and that "the focus on technology in cable is causing investors to overlook a serious negative—reregulation" (Exhs. 38 and 45). Included in Moran Sr.'s negative view of the cable television industry was TCI. Aside from completely liquidating all of the Moran Asset's holdings in TCI in 1992, Moran Asset's good relationship with TCI came to an end because according to Reddan, "we had become negative on the cable industry" (R. 61). In the Moran Morning Meeting notes of July 20, 1993, Moran Brokerage concluded that:

> [TCI] Conference call regarding effects of reregulation: effect is somewhat less than expected. Annual revenue is reduced roughly 3% to 4% compared to a 6% to 8% expected.... Even with relatively mild effects, six of TCI's credit agreements will go into technical default. Continue to recommend strength as growth will be very tough over next year.

---

8. Following Malone with respect to the cable industry is a well recognized practice on Wall Street. Malone had been characterized as "the cable industries most brilliant and creative player," a "multimedia god," and that investing along side Malone "has proved to be profitable," "has continuing merit."

(Exh. 107). Even as late as September 24, 1993 Moran's morning meeting note stated that "Sumner Redstone's antitrust lawsuit against TCI, Liberty Media and QVC has very serious long term negative implications for those companies. It is likely to ... increase regulatory scrutiny or pressure on those companies" (Exh. 38 at 55; R. 1172-73).

Moran Sr.'s position on cable stocks becomes an issue of dispute between the parties starting in September 1993. The last recommendation to sell cable stocks appeared in Moran Brokerage's morning meeting note for August 26, 1993 (Moran Sr. Exh. BF). While future morning meeting notes, up until the time in question did not include a recommendation to buy cable stocks, the recommendation was the more neutral "hold." According to Reddan, Moran Sr. "began to soften his views in September of 1993, and in October of 1993 he changed his views" (R. 782).

In support of his claim that he was changing his view of cable stocks, Moran Sr. points to the fact that he, along with Susan Putnam, attended a Donaldson Lufkin & Jenrette media conference relating in part to the cable industry from September 20 to September 22, 1993. While there, Moran Sr. learned both that the industry was developing the technology to compete with local telephone companies for long distance access charges by enabling cable companies to carry long distance service over coaxial telephone lines and that Bell Atlantic was permitting cable companies to access its research related to video service over the "twisted pair" copper wires which carry telephone service (R. 1464-1468; Moran Sr. Exh. O). Moran Sr. also learned of technological advances being made by cable companies with respect to their potential long distance capabilities on September 23, 1993 at a Scientific Atlanta meeting. Believing that this innovation could produce an "enormous revenue stream" for cable companies, Moran Sr.'s notes made at the conference read: "Conclusions—sell [local exchange carriers] ... buy cable" (R. 1468-1471; Moran Sr. Exh. P). In fact, Moran Sr. set forth in the Moran Brokerage Morning Meeting Notes of September 24, 1993 that:

> Bottom Line: Of all these competitors, the telcos are in poorest position to compete in video services. Cable companies will enter the long distance telephone business. Cable companies in nine months will attach unit to outside of the home that will reverse amplifiers on existing coax reverse line, will carry the telephone signal. Long distance calls will be offered. AT & T wants the cable companies there to reduce the access charges. Cable companies will be looking at an enormous revenue stream

Moran Sr. Exh. S. Thus, Moran Sr. asserts, the evidence demonstrates that he was now "primed to get back into cable." See Frederick A. Moran's Post Trial Brief, p. 19.

The SEC, on the other hand, argues that the Moran Sr.'s claim that he was turning bullish on cable stocks beginning in August 1993 is contradicted "not only by the morning meeting notes, but also by the testimony of Susan Putnam." See Plaintiff's Proposed Finding of Fact and Conclusions of Law, p. 35. In support of this claim, the SEC points to the morning meeting note of September 24, 1993 addressing the Redstone anti-trust lawsuit against TCI (Exh. 55). In addition, Putnam stated that after seeing a presentation with respect to the Jones Intercable on September 23, 1993, she suggested to Moran Sr. that it might be an "interesting" investment idea (Putnam Deposition, p. 88).

Putnam recalled Moran Sr. telling her that "he felt regulation was still a major problem." (Id.). The SEC maintains that this evidence demonstrates that Moran Sr. was not interested in investing in cable. With respect to the other proof relied upon by Moran Sr., the SEC suggests that the very technology Moran Sr. claims he was impressed with, was actually nothing more than innovations which Reddan had been expecting "for some time during the year 1993" (R. 822). Coupled with the fact that Moran did not buy any cable stock after attending the conferences and assigned Scientific Atlanta to Susan Putnam for further study, the SEC concludes that Moran Sr. was still "bearish" on cable.

In resolving this dispute of fact, the court finds that while there is no suggestion that Moran Sr. turned "bullish" on cable stocks in September 1993, there is ample credible evidence that Moran Sr. had begun to soften his view on the cable industry. Indeed, the SEC admits that Moran Sr.'s "firm decided to do more research on the cable phone." SEC Proposed Findings of Fact and Conclusions of Law, p. 36. Additionally, while the conversation with Putnam indicates Moran Sr. was still concerned with regulation of the cable industry, the court will not ignore the documentary evidence with respect to telecommunications, which Moran Sr. would reasonably consider in deciding upon a position to take about cable stocks. Moreover, contrary to Moran Asset's practice since 1992, after August 26, 1993, Moran Morning Meeting Notes no longer included a "sell" recommendation with respect to cable stocks. Significantly, on August 24, 1993, Bell Atlantic won a lawsuit challenging the 1984 Cable Act, which prohibited telephone companies and their affiliates from providing video programming to subscribers in their own telephone service area. While this decision paved the way for competition in the cable television industry, Moran Sr. viewed the "competition as an alternative to regulation" (R. 1459). Knowing that its monopoly status was behind the regulation of the cable industry, Moran Sr. reasoned that "if you had competition in place instead of regulation, you wouldn't need regulation" (R. 1459). Finally, Moran Sr. did not fear the idea of competition in the cable industry because he "had clearly determined the cable companies would be overwhelming winners" (R. 1459). Referring to a report Moran Sr. had previously published he stated, "[a]s far back as 1988 we made that decision" (R. 1459; Moran Sr. Exh. A).

While the SEC argues that "one would most reasonably expect that if the Moran firms were again to take a long position in cable stocks, they would do so either (a) in an orderly fashion; (b) on the basis of careful, detailed and documented research into the fundamentals of cable companies; and/or (c) over an extended period of time," (SEC Proposed Finding of Facts and Conclusions of Law, p. 36), the evidence in this case amply demonstrates that was not the way Moran Sr. typically operated. Reddan testified that "Fred's style is to jump in with both feet. Over the course of our ten-year relationship, we've had many of these disagreements primarily because of a difference in approach. I'm more cautious; Fred is more—acts more decisively" (R. 139). Accordingly, the court finds that the evidence supports defendants' contention that Moran Sr. was softening his view on the cable industry.

The Alleged Motive and Intent of Moran Jr. to Give and Moran Sr. to Trade Using Material Non-Public Information

The SEC alleges that because of a very negative experience with Chamber's Development stock, Moran Sr. had a motive to want a "sure thing." In addition, the SEC further claims that Moran Jr.'s conduct[9] demonstrates that he had the intent to provide his father with inside information. Moran Sr. responds that the losses sustained by his venture into Chambers stock were over with, that his company was doing well, and that even if his company were to fold, he could have comfortably retired. Moran Jr. maintains that none of the actions raised by the SEC constitute any breach of securities law or in any way indicates he would act inappropriately to benefit his father's firm.

It is undisputed that the decision by Moran Sr. to invest in Chambers Development Company resulted in significant financial losses for Moran Sr.'s clients as well as his personal account. Shortly after an announcement in March 1992 that Chambers' net income was far less than had been previously reported, Moran Sr. began aggressively purchasing Chambers stock for his clients. By the end of 1992, Moran Sr., Moran Asset, and Moran Brokerage had become the largest or second largest outside shareholder of Chambers. While Moran Asset continued to purchase Chambers stock during 1992, the price of the stock steadily declined. At one point the price of Chamber stock fell approximately 60 percent. Because of the losses being sustained by Moran Sr.'s clients, Reddan testified that beginning in 1992, business began to fall off. Specifically he stated:

> [w]e no longer were beating the market, we were lagging the market and that was beginning to catch up. I think about it, 1990 we had a bad year because several factors, the credit crunch and this was the first wave of cable regulation. '91 we did fairly well, but in '92 we began to lag the market and cumulatively the business wasn't going that well.

(R. 109). In fact, Moran Sr. characterized Chambers as the worst investment experience of his entire business career and in terms of dollars, Chambers represented the largest loss that Moran Sr. had ever suffered on a single stock. Moran Sr. also conceded that one of the reasons that Moran Asset decreased its long position in Turner Broadcasting in 1993, was "because clients were leaving us" (R. 1299).

There is no question that Moran Jr. was aware of the problems the Chambers stock investment was causing for his father. Moran Jr. specifically testified that he had knowledge of his father's big investment in Chambers stock, and that Moran Sr. was suffering losses. Moran Jr. "knew that ... two things

---

9. The court permitted the SEC to introduce evidence that Moran Jr. provided his father with confidential information from Salomon Brothers in violation of Salomon Brothers' regulation and other information which his father was not entitled to receive. See, Order dated October 30, 1995. The sole purpose that the court allowed this evidence was to the extent that it purported to show Moran Jr.'s state of mind and intent to communicate the material non-public information at issue in this case. See, *United States v. Zackson*, 6 F.3d 911, 921 (2d Cir.1993); Federal R. Evid. 404(b). The introduction of the evidence was not permitted for the purpose of demonstrating that Moran Jr. had a propensity to violate securities law, nor did the court make any such inference when it received this evidence.

were occurring; one, that Chambers was not quite performing up to expectations, and I knew that, given several years of less-than-superior performance, [Moran Sr.] was losing clients" (R. 281). By the beginning of October 1993, Moran Jr. was cognizant of the losses Moran Sr. was sustaining owing to the Chambers stock investment.

Moran Sr. responds that while it is true that the Chambers stock was a bad investment, the bulk of the paper losses in Chambers occurred a full year before the Bell Atlantic merger. While in October 1993 the stock was not doing particularly well, the drop in price of Chambers had reached a plateau. In addition, the firms' financial condition in October 1993 was much better than a year earlier. The firms had no debt, and profits for the quarter ending September 1993 were up more than 60% from a year earlier. Finally, Moran Sr. testified that if he were to retire in October 1993 he could have lived at the same comfort level for the rest of his life. In short, Moran Sr. argues that it would be "ridiculous" to conclude that the losses sustained in Chambers stock had anything to do with his decision to reinvest in cable stocks.

After hearing all of the evidence and examining the documentary exhibits, the court concludes that the losses in Chambers did not put Moran Sr. in any dire position by October 1993. Undoubtedly Chambers was a bad investment causing Moran Sr.'s clients to suffer large monetary losses as the price of the stock plummeted. Certainly because of the losses that were incurred Moran Sr.'s business was negatively affected. However, the evidence is compelling that by October 1993, Moran Sr. had already experienced the worst of the Chambers fallout. While Moran Sr., like any other investor, would desire to pick a winner in the market, there was no special urgency created by the Chambers stock fallout for Moran Sr. to produce a successful stock pick. The court finds that Moran Sr. was in no worse position than any other analyst who seeks to recommend a stock that would significantly increase in value.

The SEC also maintains that Moran Jr. engaged in a pattern of deceptive conduct that indicates he would favor his father's firm even if it meant disclosing confidential material. In support of this assertion, the SEC claims that Moran Jr. was not forthright with Salomon Brothers regarding his directorships and outside business interests, that Moran Jr. through subterfuge allowed Moran Asset to listen in to the TCI conference call, and that Moran Jr. was reprimanded because he improperly sent his research publications to Moran Asset. The SEC asserts that this conduct demonstrates a manifest intent by Moran Jr. to provide special assistance to his father's firms. Moran Jr. counters that the incidents pointed to by the SEC do not even demonstrate wrongdoing on his part, and certainly do not establish an intent to violate the law in order to benefit his father. The court shall address each allegation in turn.

With respect to his position as a director and his trust accounts,[10] the court finds that Moran Jr. did not initially know that he was placed on the board of directors but upon learning of his position, did inform Salomon Brothers about the directorships. Moran Sr. testified that he did not disclose to either of his sons that he had appointed them to the director positions. The fact that Moran Jr. did not participate in running these companies supports the court's conclusion that he had no knowledge of his position. It is not likely that there would have been a need to forge Moran Jr.'s signature on resolutions, if he had been aware that he was on the board of directors. At trial, it was quite clear that the signatures on all the Directors' resolutions that purported to be of Moran Jr. were not genuine. The SEC did not dispute that the resolutions lacked Moran Jr.'s genuine signature and that they were signed without his permission or authority. Moreover, when Moran Jr. learned of his positions, he informed Salomon Brothers and subsequently resigned the positions.

Similarly, with respect to the trust accounts, Moran Sr. specifically confirmed that he did not disclose their existence to Moran Jr. or his other children who were also beneficiaries. Considering this testimony, the Court finds that Moran Jr. was not aware of these trust accounts and consequently, could not disclose his interest to Salomon Brothers. When the existence of these accounts was discovered, Salomon was notified by Moran Jr. and "Salomon Brothers approved [Moran Jr.] being a beneficiary of these trusts and just requested that confirmation statements be sent to Salomon Brothers" (R. 646). Therefore, with respect to the trust accounts and his position as a director, the court finds that the only reason Moran Jr. failed to disclose this information to Salomon Brothers was that he was unaware of his position and status. Hence, the court finds that these holdings do not demonstrate any intent on the part of Moran Jr. to benefit his father or father's firms.

Moran Jr. admits that while using Salomon's office telephone system, he allowed John Reddan to listen to analyst conference calls conducted by TCI after TCI had specifically excluded Reddan and Moran Asset from these calls. Reddan concurred that at his request Moran Jr. gave him access to the conference calls. Moreover, by his own testimony, Moran Jr. concedes that he made no attempt to inform TCI that he was engaging in this practice. In response, Moran Jr. maintains that there was no requirement that TCI be informed as to who was listening in on the calls. More, Moran Jr. attempts to support his conclusion that his actions do not constitute any wrongdoing by pointing out that he did not in any way attempt to conceal from Salomon Brothers that he was allowing Reddan to listen in on these conference calls.

While the court is of the view that Moran Jr.'s actions did not constitute either a violation of law or even Salomon Brothers' policy, Moran Jr.'s actions do demonstrate an intent to help his father's companies beyond any effort he would

---

10. The court finds no impropriety with respect to Moran Jr.'s interest in International Tel-Cel. The court credits Moran Jr.'s explanation that he "didn't realize the necessity of disclosing it, as [he] had no involvement in it other than ownership interest" allocated to him by Moran Sr. (R. 351). Significantly, when Salomon Brothers was informed of Moran Jr.'s interest, the compliance department allowed Moran Jr. to maintain his interest in the company (R. 355; 648).

make for any other firm. While Moran Jr. may not have concealed his actions to Salomon Brothers, the fact that he would allow a member of his father's firms access to a conference call that his father's firm was specifically banned, clearly demonstrates an intent on the part of Moran Jr. to assist his father's firm where he could, even under questionable circumstances. The court finds that Moran Jr. concealed his actions from TCI and that there was no evidence that Moran Jr. ever gave such assistance to any other entity.

The SEC also claims that Moran Jr. was officially reprimanded by Salomon Brothers because he mailed copies of his research publications marked "Internal Use Only" to Moran Asset. Moran Jr. responds that the information contained in the memorandum was not confidential and that he was not reprimanded. As far as Moran Jr. understood, the meeting with the Salomon compliance department was "to advise him of certain aspects of his conduct that the firm—wished to bring to his attention" (R. 873).

The parties agree that on Wednesday October 11 [sic –13], 1993, at approximately 6:30 a.m., Moran Jr. faxed to Moran Asset a summary he prepared which contained his insights as to the proposed Bell Atlantic/TCI transaction (Exh. 5). The document was marked in several areas "For Internal Use Only." Moran Jr. never sought or received approval from anyone at Salomon Brothers to send the document to Moran Asset. Sometime after Moran Jr. used the document to make a presentation at Salomon's morning meeting, the compliance department told Moran Jr. not to put the document on the First Call system, which would have distributed the document to the investment community, because the Salomon involvement in the merger was on an advisory basis. Despite being aware of the decision not to use the First Call system, Moran Jr. did not tell anyone at Salomon Brothers that he had already faxed the document to Moran Asset. When Salomon eventually learned of the fax, Moran Jr. had a meeting with Scribner, the Chief Compliance Officer for Salomon Brothers. At that meeting Moran Jr. was told that "it was contrary to Firm policy for him to have sent "internal use only" material to persons outside of the Firm, and that he must not do it again" (Exh. 6). The SEC characterizes the meeting as a reprimand while Moran Jr. states that he "doesn't know if it qualifies as a reprimand or not" (R. 594). Moreover, Moran Jr. believed that the Internal Use Only designation was "a technical compliance procedure that was used very loosely in this business." See Moran Jr. Post-Trial Brief at 22.

After evaluating all of the evidence, including the testimony of Scribner, the court finds that Moran Jr. was given a "reprimand." Scribner testified that the meeting and subsequent memo was "to advise him of certain aspects of his conduct that the firm wished to—bring to his attention" (R. 873). Scribner explained that the designation of "Internal Use Only" "is that the document on which the—on which that legend appears is not to be distributed outside the firm itself, that is to say, the document, not necessarily—not the information that the document contains" (R. 873). Indeed, other Salomon employees such as Meyercord and Dietze-Courage understood that such a designation meant that the document was not to be distributed to clients or anyone outside the firm (R. 900; Dietze-Courage Deposition, at 59). It is clear that from the tone of the memo regarding Scribner's conversation with Moran Jr. that Salomon Brothers was not pleased that Moran Jr. sent the memo to his father. All of this evidence, coupled with the fact that Scribner warned Moran Jr. not to release such documents again, lead to the unmistakable conclusion that Moran Jr. engaged in a practice that violated Salomon policies in order to benefit his father. Further, there was no evidence that Moran Jr. faxed this document to any other outside parties, other than Moran Asset.

The court notes that the information contained in that memorandum was not confidential. Scribner agreed that there was "absolutely no prohibition for the sales force to discuss the contents of that document with the institutional clients of Salomon Brothers" and that "the prohibition as it stands is merely for the fact of faxing out the document itself rather than the information it contains" (R. 879). Accordingly, after reviewing each of the SEC's allegations regarding Moran Jr.'s conduct, the court finds that the evidence in this case, while not showing an intent on the part of Moran Jr. to violate the law in order to assist his father, nonetheless illustrates Moran Jr.'s willingness to provide information to his father, even if doing so is contrary to the established policies of Salomon Brothers or the wishes of his firm's clients.

Events From October 3, 1993 to October 11, 1993

On October 3, 1993, Moran Jr. was officially brought "over the wall" by Salomon Brothers, meaning that he was made aware of the proposed merger between Bell Atlantic and TCI. According to Meyercord, the purpose of involving Moran Jr. was to have him "meet with the company and to discuss how to tell the [merger] story ... to the investment community ... so that he could provide his insight and information on how to tell the story and best position the story to the market place" (R. 893). At that time Moran Jr. was told that "the announcement would come within a week to two weeks" (R. 437).

After being informed about the details of the proposed merger, Moran Jr. left on a previously scheduled business trip to San Francisco. On the night of Monday October 4, Moran Jr. placed two telephone calls from his hotel to the residence of Moran Sr. Upon his return from San Francisco, Moran Jr. reviewed materials relating to the Bell Atlantic/TCI merger plan which he had received in San Francisco. Included in these materials were the details of the merger and an indication that its public announcement would be made in October 1993.

On the morning of October 6, 1993, Moran Jr. attended a meeting at Salomon where he received a full briefing regarding the transaction. During this meeting where Moran Jr. learned the details of the merger, a firm date for the merger's public announcement had not been set. Nonetheless, Moran Jr. was told by Meyercord that the announcement "was going to occur either at the end of the week or in the middle of the following week, and more likely the middle of the following week" (R. 671). Moran Jr. understood that the announcement date "would probably be the 13th, or certainly the 12th, 13th, or 14th" (R. 437). Moran Jr. also received a draft of the press release for the Bell Atlantic/TCI merger which indicated an unspecified announcement day of October 1993. In a telephone conversation that same day, Moran Jr. spoke to either his father or an employee of Moran Asset. Also on October 6, 1993, Furman Selz, a broker dealer issued a report which opined that TCI might reacquire Liberty. Specifically it stated: "To date investing alongside Malone has proved to be profitable. We suspect Liberty might be bought back by TCI. This would make TCI more attractive to a regional Bell investor." In fact, Bell Atlantic sought to acquire Liberty as well as TCI and as a result, TCI and Liberty entered into merger negotiations.

On October 7, the Wall Street Journal published an article entitled "TCI Reported in Talks to Buy Liberty Media" (Exh. 11). In that Wall Street Journal article a Furman Selz analyst speculated that such a merger might "attract a huge investment from a regional Bell phone company." In addition to several brief phone calls between Moran Jr.'s office and Moran Asset as well as Moran Sr.'s home, there was one call where Moran Jr. spoke to Moran Sr. for approximately 43 minutes (R. 720; Exh. 7). Although Moran Jr. remembered that he spoke with Moran Jr. during that period of time, he said "I can't recall the exact specifics, but I believe [Moran Sr.] mentioned something to the effect of Infinity Broadcasting and/or Westwood One during that phone conversation and we talked about that, but I can't remember the specifics of that conversation very well." (R. 427). Moran Jr. further testified that he did not believe there was any discussion of the rumor regarding the rumored TCI/Liberty merger, or the Wall Street Journal article.

Moran Sr. agreed that he had in fact spoken to Moran Jr. during the 43 minute phone conversation. Relative to that conversation, Moran Sr. stated: "To the best of my recollection, my recollection having been helped by two factors, I now believe that I spoke to him about Infinity Broadcasting, and I believe I spoke to him about a party that we were going to have for family and friends at our house sometime in the near future" (R. 1198). Moran Sr. identified the "two factors" stating:

> Well, I studied our buy and sell orders because of this case, and I noticed that we started buying Infinity for the first time I believe it was on October 5th, and I knew Fred followed Infinity, or followed it, and so I believe and I kind of now do recall it, that I talked to him about Infinity, what I thought about it, asked him what he thought about it and so on. The other situation was that, having studied the telephone records and spoken to my wife, I believe—and think it's—let me see—yes, which has to do with my home, perhaps both of those calls were calls to her, or from her—let me see, Frederick A.—yes, that's my wife calling Fred at his office because I had told her to because we were—he wanted her to talk to him about this party that we were going to have, and it had to do with his then fiancee, Michelle, singing at the party and Fred and Michelle coming to the party.

(R. 1198-1199). Moran Sr. also remembered that he did not discuss the rumors regarding the TCI/Liberty merger or the Wall Street Journal Article. October 7, represented the last documented phone conversations between Moran Sr. and Moran Jr. until Monday October 11.

On Friday, October 8, TCI and Liberty announced that they had agreed in principle to a combination of the two companies. An effect of the combination is that John Malone whose holdings in Liberty Stock were valued in excess of $600 million, while his holdings in TCI were $15 million, was diluting his percentage of holdings invested in programming stocks by allocating that wealth to a cable operator. It is undisputed that Moran Sr. did not purchase any TCI or Liberty stock on October 8. In a morning meeting note authored by Reddan, Moran Brokerage reported that "we believe Liberty's real motive is to use TCI's balance sheet to acquire Paramount" (Moran Sr. Exh. AC). This represented the speculation on Wall Street with regard the reasoning behind the merger. Moran

Sr. testified that on October 8, he "had no opinion because I really hadn't focused on it" (R. 1482). There was no documented contact between Fred Sr. and Fred Jr. on October 8, 1993.

On Saturday, October 9, 1993, Moran Jr. attended a meeting at Bell Atlantic's headquarters in Philadelphia with co-workers from Salomon Brothers and personnel from Bell Atlantic's Investor Relations Department. Moran Jr.'s purpose in attending the meeting was to discuss the "spin" that would be put on the merger, so as to create the most favorable reaction to the merger from the investment community (R. 912-13). As part of this plan, Bell Atlantic arranged to give advance notice to important members of the investment community "providing notification of a special Bell Atlantic meeting at 8:00 a.m. the following day" through a "blast fax" (Exh. 1). Additionally, it was decided that the Bell's investor relations staff would make phone calls to individual analysts in order to demonstrate the significance of the announcement.

During the weekend of October 9-10, Moran Sr. claims that he began to focus "on what was happening with TCI and Liberty" (R. 1485). After speaking with his wife on October 9th about the possibility of investing in cable stocks, on Sunday October 10th, Moran Sr. telephoned Reddan. Moran Sr. stated that he did not agree with Reddan's view that TCI was acquiring Liberty to help Liberty in its effort to back an acquisition of Paramount. Stating that "my concept was that there were many easier ways to accomplish that [backing of the Paramount acquisition] without having John Malone move all of his wealth from cable—from programming to cable, and I recited the various ways to John [Reddan] that could have been done," Moran Sr. gave his assessment to Reddan (R. 1487). Reddan testified that "at the outset of the conversation I did not agree with him. By the end of the conversation I came around to agree that it represented an endorsement of Telecommunications, Inc. by John Malone and that I thought we should recommend only Telecommunications, Inc. and Liberty Media and we should not recommend other cable television operator stocks or invest in them" (R. 132-33).

Moran Sr. explained to Reddan that beyond Liberty and TCI, the action "was an endorsement of John Malone of the cable TV business and therefore all of the stocks" (R. 1488). Accordingly, Moran Sr. told Reddan that he "wanted to buy all the cable companies and that we were not going to sit by while Malone moved into cable and miss what was happening in the area that had built our reputation and was our forte" (R. 1489). It was the belief of Moran Sr., this was action constituted the appropriate response to Malone's apparent course of conduct. Moran Sr. further explained that "it was a case of following the substance of what John Malone was doing and not limiting [Moran Asset] to the limitation [Malone] had placed on himself of investing only in TCI and Liberty, just like we didn't buy Liberty when he moved into Liberty" (R. 1489). As a result of his analysis, Moran Sr. detailed to Reddan his strategy for buying cable stocks. He testified that "the strategy was to buy almost all the cable TV companies and to move quickly before the rest of Wall Street caught on to what we were doing, because you must understand that everybody was following John Malone, and the logic of my scenario was plain and clear in my opinion, and everybody would end up doing what we were doing, so we wanted to move quickly" (R. 1489). Reddan, while agreeing that there was a basis to buy into TCI and Liberty, urged more caution.

On Monday October 11, 1995 Moran Sr. prepared a written plan to purchase stock in Liberty, TCI and other cable companies for client accounts so that each client would have 25% of its portfolio invested in cable stock (Moran Sr. Exh. W). Prior to the opening of the market, Moran Sr. directed his traders to purchase, through Moran Asset and Moran Brokerage, stock in TCI, Liberty, as well as other cable companies. According to Reddan, Moran Sr. announced to the staff that he had changed his position on cable television operator stocks, and summarized his reasons for doing so. Although Moran Sr. was adamant about his position, Reddan testified that, "there was a general feeling that we should go—everybody was urging caution, and I think that was the feeling of the people in the meeting" (R. 135). In fact, the item in the morning meeting note relating to cable was specifically caption "Fred Moran's Cable TV Industry Comments" because Reddan, who usually co-authored the morning meeting notes, did not agree in total with Moran Sr.'s view. With respect to the Cable TV industry the morning meeting note stated:

> Through the merger of TCI and Liberty Media, John Malone has signaled his plans to transfer the vast majority of his personal wealth, estimated a $700 million, from a company that is roughly half cable TV and half programming, to a company that is very predominantly cable.... Despite the negative of poor government and poor customer relations, the economics of this business are so powerful that they will overshadow the regulatory negative.

(Exh. 41). The morning meeting note was distributed to all of Moran Brokerage's institutional clients. At the opening of the market, Fred Sr. began aggressively purchasing cable stocks, including Liberty and TCI. These stocks were bought for both Moran Sr.'s client accounts and Moran Sr.'s personal and family accounts. His traders were told to be active buyers but don't "chase" stocks which would push the prices higher.

Later on October 11, Moran Asset's Investment Policy Committee ("IPC") held a meeting so that views could be exchanged with respect to the change in strategy. According to Reddan, the purpose "was to talk about the decision to re-recommend the cable television stocks and to invest in those stocks" (R. 143). At the meeting, the general recommendations to Moran Sr. were to adopt a go slow approach and several people wished to engage in more research. The conclusion of the IPC meeting was that "[w]e were going to investigate further change in the cable television industry. We were going to talk to other companies in the cable industry and other investors in cable television" (R. 146). There was no change, however, in the way the stocks were being purchased.[11]

At approximately 3:17 p.m. on October 11, Moran Sr. faxed to Moran Jr. that day's Moran Brokerage Morning Meeting note. Moreover, during the afternoon, Moran Sr. and Moran Jr. spoke via telephone with respect to Moran Sr.'s analysis of cable stocks. Moran Jr.'s recollection of the conversation was that he "was the listener in that conversation. That day [Moran Sr.] called me

---

11. Although Reddan advocated the "go slow approach," he was not surprised that it was not heeded by Moran Sr. of whom he stated "Fred has a mentality to jump in with both feet and act decisively" (R. 802). Indeed, Reddan testified that he had observed [Moran Sr.] act this way "half a dozen or a dozen times over the course of my ten years" (R. 803).

or I called him and he told me about his change of position on the cable stocks, and basically all I said was your points are well presented or something to that effect" (R. 725). Moran Jr. claimed that he never mentioned Bell Atlantic at any time during the conversation and that the reason he did not respond to Moran Sr.'s inquiry with a "no comment" was because that "could be a signal to [Moran Sr.] that I was working on something, and I purposely avoided signaling anything to him in any way" (R. 725-26). Similarly, Moran Sr. recalled that the conversation regarding the morning meeting note was brief and that Moran Jr. "just said he thought it was well done and that the institutions who [Moran Sr.] sent it to should think well of it, or something to that effect" (R. 1347). While Moran Jr. did not have specific knowledge that Moran Sr.'s new strategy included buying TCI, he testified that "my assumption was that he was probably buying TCI" (R. 459).

On the evening of Tuesday, October 12, Moran Jr. concedes that he spoke to an employee of Moran Asset with respect to the Bell Atlantic proposed merger. Moran Jr. testified that he could not remember if he spoke to Kevin Martin or Brian Kelly, and stated:

> What happened is these two gentlemen answered the telephone when I was trying to reach my father and one of them asked me, you know, is something going on, and I said to one of them, I don't remember which one specifically, but I said to them there is, you know, a big deal that's going to be announced tomorrow at the merger of Bell Atlantic and TCI.

(R. 499-500). At the time he disseminated this information, Moran Jr. opined that there was no need to caution either Martin or Kelly because he felt that the information was no longer confidential. Moran Jr. explained that:

> The stock market had already closed, the Wall Street Journal and New York Times were being apprised of the transaction as were the rating agencies, and the announcement would come before the opening of trading the next day, so there would be no way of acting on the information anyway. Plus, they would understand that as professionals in the industry.

(R. 502).

Having failed to reach his father, sometime between 6:30 and 7:00 p.m., Moran Jr. placed a telephone call to Reddan. According to Reddan, the substance of the conversation was that Moran Jr. "told [Reddan] that Bell—there was going to be an announcement in the morning that Bell Atlantic was going to take over Telecommunications, Inc. He asked me if I had heard" (R. 146-47). While Reddan had received a fax from Bell Atlantic which told of an upcoming announcement the next morning, the fax did not include any details such as what the announcement was going to pertain to or if any other parties were involved. Reddan continued, stating that he and Moran Jr. talked a little bit about that, and then Moran Jr. asked me if I knew where his father was" (R. 147). Moran Jr. recalled that he briefed Reddan "on some of the details of the merger at that time" (R. 518). In addition, Moran Jr. left a message on Moran Sr.'s answering machine stating that "there will be a big announcement tomorrow morning essentially creating a merger between Bell Atlantic and TCI" (R. 517).

The reason Moran Jr. believed that the information he disclosed in the evening of October 12 was public was based on his assertion that at the October

9 meeting it was discussed that top investors and the newspapers were to be advised of the transaction prior to the official announcement. When asked who said that the merger was going to be revealed before the public announcement, Moran Jr. stated:

> It was discussed that in general notifying the general public the night of Tuesday, October 12, 1993, that was discussed between Peter Crawford, Kevin Tarrant, Wendy Dietze, Ed Meyercord, Ray Ligouri and myself at the October 12—at the October 9th, 1993 meeting at Bell Atlantic headquarters. Whether they specifically said individual X will notify the Wall Street Journal, I don't remember us discussing that, but they said we will be apprising the investment community in general, which includes the two biggest newspapers.

(R. 506-07). To contradict this assertion by Moran Jr., the SEC called to the stand four of the five individuals Moran Jr. named and offered the deposition of the fifth, and each contradicted Moran Jr.'s recollection.

Specifically, Crawford of Bell Atlantic testified that "there was absolutely no discussion about preannouncing this transaction to any newspapers" (R. 1045). In fact, Crawford continued that Bell Atlantic was "very concerned that there would be no leakage, whether to the investment community or to the newspapers or any other community, for that matter, of the terms and conditions or the announcement itself prior to 7:30 in the morning on the 13th" (R. 1046). After a stipulation that Tarrant would testify on direct to the same facts as Crawford, on redirect Tarrant stated that the policy with respect to media inquiries made on October 12, "would be neither confirm nor deny rumors or choose to comment on that" (R. 1120, 1128). Tarrant stated that the policy was the same until the public announcement on October 13. Katherine Dietze-Courage of Salomon Brothers testified that she did not learn of any Salomon Brothers employees who had disseminated information regarding the merger or disclosed the identities of the companies (Deposition of Katherine Dietze-Courage, at 63). Meyercord and Ligouri of Salomon Brothers each told the court that their understanding of the policies concerning disclosure of the merger details was that public dissemination would take place in the morning on October 13 and that neither of them contacted the newspapers with this information, nor knew of anyone who did so. Further undermining the claim that the information was public in the evening of October 12 is documentary evidence that contradicts Moran Jr.'s recollection. In the story published by the Wall Street Journal on October 13, it was reported that TCI and Bell Atlantic officials would not comment on the rumored merger (Moran Sr. Exh. AL). Moreover, Moran Jr.'s own exhibit, a chronology of events prepared by Bell Atlantic states:

> Calls start coming in to media relations and other Bell Atlantic employees from the New York Times and the Wall Street Journal news reporters indicating that they have some information about the deal and asking for more. Bell Atlantic neither confirms nor denies per routine corporate policy.

(Moran Jr. Exh. AS). Even Reddan, who had already received the blast fax; testified before the court that he did not know the identities of all the parties and the details until he was told by Moran Jr. Thus, the issue of whether the information Moran Jr. passed to Reddan and Moran Asset was still confidential is vehemently contested.

In resolving this factual dispute, the court has examined all of the relevant testimony and documentary evidence. The court finds that the merger details relayed by Moran Jr. on the evening of October 12 were still confidential non- public information. Whether Moran Jr. merely misunderstood the timing of disclosure or intentionally neglected to follow the guidelines, the evidence is overwhelming that the policy was not to disclose the details of the merger to the public as a whole, including the newspapers, until October 13. Every person named by Moran Jr. contradicted his account of the meeting and Moran Jr. was never able to tell the court who specifically authorized disclosure to the public at large on October 12. Therefore, the court is constrained to find that by engaging in these conversations, Moran Jr. disclosed confidential, non-public information.

At 6:36 a.m. on October 13, Moran Jr. sent by fax to Moran Asset a summary of the proposed Bell Atlantic/TCI transaction that he had helped to prepare[13] (R. 153, 464; Exh. 5). This was the same summary Moran Jr. used at Salomon's morning meeting on October 13, to make a presentation. Reddan found this document helpful in interpreting the Bell Atlantic/TCI deal because "it was Fred's [Moran Jr.] analysis of the transaction, and ... took that as a starting point to do our own analysis" (R. 155). Later that morning, but before the market opened, Bell Atlantic, TCI and Liberty announced their agreement in principle to merge. On that day, TCI Class A stock closed up $3.00 per share and Liberty Class A stock rose $2.625 per share (Exh. 24).***

CONCLUSIONS OF LAW

***The SEC alleges that Moran Jr. disclosed material non-public confidential information to Moran Sr., who then purchased stock as a result of that information. There are several possible scenarios proposed by the SEC that it claims constitutes insider trading. Initially, the SEC argues that sometime during the October 7, 1993 forty minute phone call between Moran Jr. and Sr., Moran Jr. disclosed to Moran Sr. material non-public information regarding the merger. The SEC further maintains that the evidence supports its theory that Moran Jr. "tipped" Moran Sr. or relayed additional material non-public information from a public phone during the weekend October 9-10. More, the SEC contends that Moran Jr.'s statements to Moran Sr. during their October 11 telephone conversation constituted a tip of material, non-public information, in that Moran Jr. signaled Moran Sr. that it was advantageous for him to continue to purchase cable stocks. Finally, although not clearly set forth, the SEC implies that Moran Jr.'s disclosure to Reddan and other employees of Moran Asset during the evening of October 12, constituted a violation of Section 10(b) of the Exchange Act and Rule 10b-5 thereunder. For the following reasons, the court finds that the SEC has not proved its claims by a preponderance of the evidence.

To establish that the defendants violated Section 10(b) of the Exchange Act and Rule 10b-5 thereunder, the SEC must show by a preponderance of the

---

13. The summary was marked "For Internal Use Only" and when Salomon learned that Moran Jr. had faxed the document to Moran Asset, Moran Jr. was told that "it was contrary to Firm policy for him to have sent "internal use only" material to persons outside the firm, he must not do so again," and his father's firm should not receive any better treatment than any other firm would ordinarily receive (Exh. 6).

evidence that the defendants made improper use of confidential material information in connection with the purchase or sale of securities and that the defendants acted with scienter. *Dirks v. SEC,* 463 U.S. 646, 659-660 (1983); *Aaron v. SEC,* 446 U.S. 680, 695 (1980); *United States v. Carpenter*, 791 F.2d 1024, 1033-34 (2d Cir.1986), aff'd by an evenly divided court, *Carpenter v. United States,* 484 U.S. 19 (1987). A person makes improper use of confidential information when that person obtains material, non-public information intended to be used for a proper purpose and uses it in a breach of a fiduciary duty owed to his employer. *Dirks*, 463 U.S. at 663-64; *United States v. Newman*, 664 F.2d 12, 16-19 (2d Cir.1981).

On October 3, 1993, Moran Jr. was "brought over the wall" with regard to the Bell Atlantic/TCI proposed merger. It is beyond dispute that the information he obtained was confidential and non-public. Indeed, Moran Jr., himself, demonstrated that he knew he was in possession of non-public confidential information, specifically testifying that he had admonished two of his research assistants, who had mistakenly seen related information in Moran Jr.'s office, that they had a duty to maintain as strictly confidential the information they had seen. Consequently, as an "insider" Moran Jr. had the requisite fiduciary duty requiring non-disclosure of this material. *SEC v. Texas Gulf Sulphur*, 401 F.2d 833 (2d Cir.1968); *SEC v. Musella*, 748 F.Supp. 1028 (S.D.N.Y.1989), aff'd, 898 F.2d 138 (2d Cir.1990) ("*Musella II*").

A "tippee" inherits the tipper's duty if the tipper disclosed the nonpublic information and the tippee knows or should know of the tipper's breach of duty. *SEC v. Carpenter*, 791 F.2d at 1024; *SEC v. Musella*, 578 F.Supp. 425, 438-39 (S.D.N.Y.1984) ("*Musella I*"). Accordingly, "a tippee who knows or is reckless in not knowing that he was trading on misappropriated non-public information violates Rule 10b-5." *Musella II*, 748 F.Supp. at 1038; see also *Dirks v. SEC*, 463 U.S. at 660; *SEC v. Vaskevitch*, 657 F.Supp. 312, 314 (S.D.N.Y.1987). If Moran Jr. did tip Moran Sr., it would be unfathomable that Moran Sr. would not know or be expected to know that such information was misappropriated by Moran Jr. from his position at Salomon Brothers. Therefore, any resulting stock trades made by Moran Sr. and his companies would subject him to liability as a tippee. Because both Moran Sr. and Jr. would have known that details regarding the merger were confidential misappropriated information, any trading based on a tip would have been made with the requisite scienter necessary to violate federal insider trading statutes. Scienter is established if it is shown that the defendants acted with a "mental state embracing intent to deceive, manipulate, or defraud." *Ernst & Ernst v. Hochfelder*, 425 U.S. 185, 193 (1976); *SEC v. Drexel Burham Lambert*, 837 F.Supp. 587, 608 (S.D.N.Y.1993), aff'd, *SEC v. Posner*, 16 F.3d 520 (2d Cir.1994).

The record further indicates that the information was material. Moran Jr. allegedly informed his father that Liberty and TCI were about to merge, as well as when the announcement was going to take place. The Supreme Court has stated that for actions arising under Federal securities laws, a fact is material "if there is a substantial likelihood that a reasonable [investor] will consider it important in deciding how to [invest]." *Basic Inc. v. Levinson*, 485 U.S. 224, 231 (1988); *TSC Indus., Inc. v. Northway, Inc.*, 426 U.S. 438, 449 (1976); *Azrielli v. Cohen Law Offices*, 21 F.3d 512, 518 (2d Cir.1994); *Sable v. Southmark/Envicon Capital Corp.*, 819 F.Supp. 324, 334 (S.D.N.Y.1993). Here, information of this magnitude was certain to have an effect on cable stocks. Both Moran Jr. and Sr. were specifically knowledgeable about the cable industry. Accordingly, it is beyond peradventure that each defendant would realize the significance of the information regarding the proposed merger and the likely effect that cable stocks would increase in value. Information regarding an impending transaction that is expected to increase the value of a security is certainly of the type that would be considered by a reasonable investor important with respect to deciding how to invest. *SEC v. Shapiro*, 494 F.2d 1301, 1305 (2d Cir.1974); *Musella II*, 748 F.Supp. at 1040.

Hence, the only issue left for the court to resolve with respect to this allegation is whether the SEC has proved by a preponderance of the evidence that Moran Jr. did, in fact, disclose information about the proposed merger to Moran Sr. before such information was public. As previously stated, if Moran Jr. tipped Moran Sr. as to the proposed merger, they would each be liable for securities violations. The court, however, finds that the evidence does not so prove. With the exception of the claims regarding Moran Jr.'s comments to Moran Sr. about his morning meeting notes and the call to Reddan the evening before the announcement was made, the SEC presented no direct evidence of a tip by Moran Jr. to Moran Sr. The court is mindful that "proof of insider trading can well be made through an inference from circumstantial evidence and not solely upon direct testimonial confession." *SEC v. Singer*, 786 F.Supp. 1158, 1164 (S.D.N.Y.1992). Notwithstanding such recognition, however, if the totality of the evidence suggests an equally or more compelling inference than the SEC's allegation, the plaintiff will not have met its burden of proving its case by preponderance of the evidence. The court finds that the SEC has not established its case.

Surely one possible inference that can reasonably be drawn from the evidence presented in this case is that Moran Sr. purchased cable security stocks based on material non-public information provided to him by Moran Jr. This inference, however, is not the most likely scenario suggested by the proof. The court finds that the testimony and documentary exhibits suggest that Moran Sr. made his stock purchases on October 11, 1993 as a result of following John Malone, the announcement of the TCI/Liberty merger on October 8, and Moran Sr.'s softening position on cable stocks. Moreover, the court also finds that the amount of purchases were not aberrational to Moran Sr.'s style of investing in securities. Further, upon closely examining the SEC assertions, the court declines to accept their proposed inferences regarding the alleged telephone tip, and finds the SEC's argument to be inconsistent. Lastly, the court finds that the statements Moran Jr. made to Moran Sr. with respect to the morning meeting notes on October 11, 1993 do not constitute a tip and that while Moran Jr. may have disclosed non-public information during the evening October 12, 1993, there were no trades made by Moran Sr. as a result of such disclosure. In making this determination, the court relies not only on the testimony of Moran Sr. and Jr., but also that of Reddan, who the court finds completely credible, other workers for Moran Sr., and the voluminous documentary evidence, much of which dates well before October 3, 1993, when Moran Jr. was brought "over the wall."

Contrary to the claims of the SEC, the evidence is overwhelming that Moran Sr. followed Malone. In fact, the record is uncontroverted that the one time Moran Sr. did not react to Malone, he vowed never to be on the wrong side of Malone again. Moran Sr. testified at length as to the power that Malone has over the cable industry. The court credits Moran Sr.'s testimony that he believed Malone to be [the] leader in the cable industry. As previously discussed, there is ample outside evidence such as other broker publications and media articles that lend support to Moran Sr.'s view of Malone. While the SEC is correct that one reason for Moran Sr.'s bearish view on cable was increased government regulation of the industry, another significant reason was that Moran Sr. learned that Malone had liquidated his position in TCI. Reddan testified that concern about regulation and following Malone was virtually "flip sides of the same coin" (R. 781-82). Additionally, Reddan confirmed that Moran Sr. did follow Malone and advised his clients to do the same.

In making its argument that Moran Sr. did not follow Malone, the SEC apparently assumes that "following" Malone is the same as "copying" Malone's investments. Moran Sr. explained, "we don't follow John Malone literally, we follow the substance of what he is doing and then apply it to what makes the most sense given the areas of—the alternative selections that we can make, which are not the same as his because he is limited. As I said before, he chooses to be limited" (R. 1148-49). Moreover, during the period of January 8, 1992 to October 11, 1993, Moran Sr. maintained his holdings in programming, increased his clients' weighting in programming stocks, and purchased most if not all of the Liberty/TCI publicly owned programmers, and followed Malone into the United Kingdom cable television companies (R. 779-781, 1438-39, 1446-51; Exh. 40). The short of the matter is that while Moran Sr. did not simply duplicate investments made by Malone, the evidence before the court nonetheless illustrates a demonstrative pattern of moves made by Moran Sr. that identify his reliance on Malone. Thus, the court finds that Moran Sr. did follow Malone and as discussed at length in the factual section of this opinion, the court finds that by October 1993, Moran Sr. was softening his view on the cable television industry.

The court is therefore presented with circumstantial evidence that indicates Moran Sr. made his investments on October 11, not because of inside information, but rather because he became aware of Malone's actions which indicated that cable stocks would become lucrative. Aside from the testimony of Moran Sr.[20] there is ample evidence which supports Moran Sr.'s innocent explanation of his purchases. The Liberty/TCI merger took place on October 8, 1993. Over the weekend, Reddan testified that Moran Sr. told him about his game plan to invest in cable stocks. Contrary to the SEC argument, Reddan did not disagree with Moran Sr.'s analysis, but urged a "go slow" approach. The court finds no significance that Moran Sr. did not heed Reddan's or his analysts' warnings to go slow, since Moran Sr. typically disregarded such analysis. Additionally, Moran Sr. has a demonstrated history for buying stocks in large quantities. Indeed, his holdings of cable stocks prior to 1992 and investment in Chambers demonstrates that large percentage acquisitions were common place

20. The SEC reasonably argues that Moran Sr. is now manufacturing a "cover story" to hide the fact that his real reason for investing was inside information. The court certainly takes this possibility into account and accordingly looks to evidence beyond that of Moran Sr.'s testimony.

for Moran Sr. By virtue of the evidence as to how Moran Sr. typically engaged in stock purchases, the court finds that the fact that he bought large amounts of cable stocks for himself and clients is not aberrational.

Merely because the defendants present a reasonable inference from the circumstances which suggests no illegality, does not mean that the plaintiff has failed to fulfill its burden. However, the court finds several troubling aspects to the SEC's theory of liability. Initially, the SEC argues an inconsistent position. On the one hand, the SEC argues that Moran Jr. and Sr. should be considered "a sophisticated tipper and tippee," and that would explain why there was no documented contact between October 9 and October 11. See, Plaintiff's Proposed Finding of Fact and Conclusions of Law, p. 21. Since the defendants presumably understood that the SEC's attention would have been drawn by contact during that period, the SEC argues that Moran Sr. and Jr. distanced themselves from each other. On its own this is not an unreasonable proposition, however, under the same theory, the SEC also wants the court to accept that Moran Jr. and Sr. would be foolish enough to give and receive a tip during a 40 minute phone conversation from Moran Jr.'s office to Moran Sr.'s office. A conversation which could be and was documented. Not only that, the SEC asks the court to find that during the time that Moran Sr. was actually engaged in the alleged illegal trade, he would fax his morning meeting notes to Moran Jr., the very morning meeting notes that included the recommendation to buy cable stocks. The court is puzzled as to why Moran Sr. would send these notes to Moran Jr., if as the SEC claims, Moran Sr. was already tipped as to the proposed merger.

Lastly, the SEC asks this court to accept that Moran Jr., "the sophisticated tipper," who had already given the information regarding the merger to his father, would then call his father's firm on the evening before the official announcement and disclose the details of the same merger to at least one employee of Moran Asset and later to Reddan. Considering that Moran Sr. had already made the trades in issue, there is no reason for Moran Jr. to call his father with this information. If he had already tipped his father earlier, as claimed by the SEC, it would have been utterly nonsensical for Moran Jr. to place this call.

The court also has difficulty with the SEC's claim that the fact that there was no documented contact between Moran Sr. and Jr. from October 8 until October 11, is somehow indicative of guilt because it shows that they were attempting to distance themselves from one another or that it was then that the actual tip took place. While this argument is a possible theory, there are other equally possible theories that do not suggest any wrongdoing. One such theory is that the lack of documented contact between Moran Sr. and Jr. was because they truly did not have any contact with each other during that time period. Indeed, the SEC's allegation regarding theoretical secret phone calls from public telephones is nothing more than conjecture which cannot be substituted for evidence. Indeed, even if the court were to assume that there was a tip during that time period or that the defendants were merely attempting to distance themselves, the court is at a loss to explain Moran Sr.'s subsequent fax to Moran Jr. on October 11 and Moran Jr.'s disclosure of the information during the evening of October 12. Certainly, the exchange of this information would be the opposite of distancing. The more logical inference is that there was no tip from Moran Jr. to Moran Sr. in this aspect.

The next claim asserted by the SEC is that Moran Jr.'s statements to Moran Sr. during their October 11 telephone conversation constituted a tip of material, nonpublic information, because it signaled Moran Sr. that it was advantageous to continue purchasing cable stocks. Encouragement to continue to purchase a stock, even if the specific advantageous information is not included in the conversation, and a resulting purchase of the security can be a violation of the prohibition against insider trading. See, *SEC v. Drexel Burnham Lambert, Inc.*, 837 F.Supp. 587, 597-98 (S.D.N.Y.1993), aff'd, *SEC v. Posner*, 16 F.3d 520 (2d Cir.1994); *SEC v. First City Financial Corp.*, 688 F.Supp. 705, 712-13 (D.D.C.1988), aff'd, 890 F.2d 1215 (D.C. Cir.1989). But in this case, the court finds that Moran Jr.'s statements that the morning meeting notes were "well presented" do not constitute a tip for the purposes of the securities law. Moran Jr. testified that he used that response rather than just say no comment because he believed that if he refused to provide an answer, Moran Jr.'s silence would have communicated to his father that there was something imminently about to happen in the cable industry. Specifically Moran Jr. stated, "if I told him no comment that could be a signal to him that I was working on something, and I purposely avoided signaling anything to him in any way" (R. 725-6). Considering that the morning meeting notes did not address any possibility of a merger, it was entirely proper for Moran Jr. to answer the way he did. If he had refused comment, Moran Sr. might then have realized that there was some other aspect to consider. Moreover, considering the conversation took place in the late afternoon after most of the trading was already completed, the conversation between Moran Sr. and Jr., does not appear to be a tip. Additionally, there is no proof that Moran Sr. ever had any hesitancy regarding his purchase of cable stocks. Actually, the evidence demonstrates just the opposite, despite the fact that Moran Sr.'s employees wanted him to slow down, he ignored their requests. Therefore, it is not likely that Moran Sr. was worried about seeking any confirmation from Moran Jr. as to whether the stock purchase was still a good idea. Thus, the court finds that the conversation on October 11, 1993 between Moran Sr. and Jr. does not constitute a violation of the Exchange Act.

The last theory, apparently advanced by the SEC, suggests that Moran Jr.'s October 12th disclosures of the merger details, somehow constituted insider trading. The court rejects this theory. The evidence, in part, leaves no question that the details disclosed by Moran Jr. were material, non-public, and confidential information. The mere disclosure of the information, however, is not sufficient to establish a violation of the Exchange Act. In order to violate § 10(b) of the Exchange Act, the fraud must be "in connection with the purchase or sale of any security registered on a national security exchange or any security not so registered." In this case, the purchases of the securities at issue had previously occurred on October 11. Since it is undisputed that there were no security purchases of cable stock after Moran Jr. disclosed the merger information and prior to the public announcement of the merger, there can be no liability for insider trading. Consequently, since the SEC has not demonstrated by a preponderance of the credible evidence that Moran Sr.'s stock purchases were made as a result of material non-public information disclosed by Moran Jr., the court finds for the defendants with respect to that charge.***

CONCLUSION

The court finds that:

Frederick W. Moran, Frederick A. Moran, Moran Asset Management, and Moran & Associates Securities Brokerage did not violate Section 10(b) of the Exchange Act and Rule 10b-5 thereunder and therefore the court dismisses that claim with prejudice; ***

NOTES AND QUESTIONS

1. ***Bench Trial vs. Jury Trial.*** Because the SEC was seeking the imposition of a civil monetary penalty against each of the Morans, the Morans could have asserted a Seventh Amendment right to a trial by jury. Why might the Morans have preferred a bench trial? Did the bench trial offer the SEC any advantages? We will explore more fully the issue of a constitutional right to a jury trial in civil prosecutions by the SEC in Chapter 9.

2. ***SEC and SRO Surveillance.*** The SEC began an investigation of the proposed Bell Atlantic-TCI merger almost immediately following the deal's public announcement. What may have alerted the SEC to the possibility of insider trading? How do you suppose the SEC identified Moran Sr. as a possible insider trader? In addition to Bell Atlantic, TCI, Liberty, and Salomon Brothers, what other entities would most likely have been asked to supply the SEC with information?

Note that the case involving the Morans was one of three SEC enforcement actions brought against persons for insider trading in connection with the Bell Atlantic-TCI merger. In the second case, a member of the board of directors of Liberty was alleged to have told his wife of the proposed merger, who then purchased TCI stock for her own account and advised her son to do the same. After a district judge upheld the validity of the SEC's misappropriation theory as a matter of law, see *SEC v. Lenfest*, 949 F. Supp. 341, (E.D. Pa. 1996), the case was tried to a jury, but the judge issued a directed verdict against the SEC. See *SEC v. Lenfest*, Civil Action No. 95-7597 (E.D. Pa. 1998). The third case was brought against the son of a TCI employee in Denver, who was alleged to have misappropriated information on the proposed deal from his father, avoiding $22,781 in losses on call contracts and making a $14,000 profit. The son settled with the SEC in December 1994, agreeing to pay a civil penalty of $36,781 and to disgorge the sum of $40,113 ($22,781 for losses avoided, $14,000 for gains that would have been realized, and $3,332.72 in prejudgement interest). *SEC v. William K. Fisher*, Litigation Release No. 14362, 58 SEC Docket 1309 (Dec. 20, 1994).

3. ***Constructing the Circumstantial Case.*** Do you agree with the trial judge that the 40 minute phone call on Thursday, October 7 was done too openly and conspicuously to support the inference that an illegal tip was communicated between Moran Jr. and Moran Sr.? Speculate as to what types of facts may have provided stronger support for this inference. What if the SEC had been able to introduce evidence of a call from a pay phone to the Moran Sr. residence on Sunday, October 10, the evening prior to Moran Sr.'s stock purchases?

Consider the SEC's evidence regarding Moran Sr.'s prior investments and trading practices. What types of documents would the SEC have been likely to seek from Moran Sr.? How did the SEC attempt to establish that Moran Sr. had been reticent about cable stocks prior to his purchases in TCI and Liberty? Did the SEC's contention that Moran Sr. needed a "sure thing" to recover from his substantial losses in Chamber Development strengthen or detract from its case?

Consider also the SEC's contention that Moran Jr. had violated Salomon Brothers' procedures on a number of occasions. From where did the SEC likely get evidence to support this contention? For what purpose was this evidence admitted at trial?

*4. **Violations of the Advisers Act and the Exchange Act.*** Although the trial judge dismissed the SEC's Rule 10b-5 allegations against both of the Morans, the trial judge held Moran Sr. and Moran Asset liable for violating Sections 204, 206(2), and 207 of the Investment Advisers Act of 1940 and Rule 204-1(b)(1) thereunder. The trial judge also imposed liability for Moran Sr.'s and Moran Brokerage's violation of Section 15(b) of the Exchange Act and Rule 15b3-1 thereunder. *SEC v. Moran*, 922 F. Supp 867, 902 (S.D.N.Y. 1996) (*Moran I*). The Section 206(2) of the Advisers Act violations were based on Moran Sr.'s breach of fiduciary duty through a negligent decision to allocate purchases of Liberty stock to his personal and family trading accounts rather than to the accounts of his client. *Moran I*, 922 F. Supp. at 897-98. For these violations, the court ordered disgorgement in the amount of $9,551, a permanent injunction against both Moran Sr. and Moran Asset, and a civil penalty of $5,000 and 25,000, respectively. See *SEC v. Moran*, 944 F. Supp. 286, 295-96 (S.D.N.Y. 1996) (*Moran II*). With respect to the other violations of the Advisers Act, and the violations of the Exchange Act, the court found that Moran Asset had willfully failed to amend its Forms ADV, and Moran Brokerage had willfully failed to amend its Form BD, to reflect the fact that Moran's Sr.'s wife and two sons held directorships. *Moran I*, 922 F. Supp. at 900-01. For these violations, the court ordered permanent injunctions against Moran Sr., Moran Asset, and Moran Brokerage, and imposed a civil penalty of $20,000, $25,000, and $25,000 respectively. *Moran II*, 944 F. Supp. at 298.

*5. **Collateral Consequences.*** After the trial judge announced his initial decision in the case brought against both of the Morans, Moran Sr. shared these sentiments with reporters: "I feel beaten up, bloodied, worn-out. All I want to do at this point is go in a corner and hide for fear that [the SEC] will come back and beat me up some more." He is also reported to have said that the Advisers Act and Exchange Act violations found by the judge were "administrative nonsense." See Frances A. McMorris, Moran and Son are Cleared in Insider Case, Wall St. J. at B2 (Apr. 3, 1996). Moran Sr. commented that "[T]he hurt will never go away. [The SEC] knew from the beginning they had no evidence against us.... They didn't care. They proceeded to destroy my business and my son's career. It cost us over $1 million in legal fees." Sharon Walsh, Securities Analyst, Father Cleared of Insider Trading, Both Men Critical of SEC's High-Profile Case, Wash. Post at G3 (April 3, 1996). Press reports note that Moran Sr.'s firm managed $540 million in assets when the SEC began its investigations, but had only $4 million under management when the judge's decision was announced. Id. Reports further state that Moran Sr.'s profit figures alleged by the SEC were based on " 'paper' estimates of how much the stock position gained in value on the day the takeover bid was announced." See

Jeffrey Taylor & Amy J. Schatz, SEC Accuses Moran and His Son of Insider Trading, Wall St. J. at B8 (June 16, 1995). Most of the TCI and Liberty stock was not "sold for several months and eventually resulted in a substantial loss after the takeover deal later collapsed." Id. With respect to Moran Jr., it was reported that Salomon Brothers suspended him from dealing with clients when the SEC filed its complaint, and that while the firm kept him on the payroll and paid for much of his legal fees, "the firm has been essentially pushing him out." John M. Higgins, Judge Clears Morans on Insider Trading, Multichannel News (April 1996), 1996 WL 13824595. See also Walsh, supra, Wash. Post. at G3. In view of all this, did the government extract a significant penalty from both of the Morans notwithstanding the judge's findings and official sanctions? Based on your review of the circumstantial evidence, would you have taken this case to trial?

*6. **Suspicious Trading as Proof of Possession.*** What if SEC officials are convinced that a person traded securities based on material nonpublic information but have no evidence to establish that the defendant had access to that information at the time of the trades? It is well established that suspicious trading activity (in terms of timing and/or amount) can provide circumstantial evidence of possession. But can it ever, by itself, support such an inference? At least one court has concluded that the answer is no. See *SEC v. Truong*, 98 F. Supp. 2d 1086, 1097 (N.D. Cal. 2000) ("[a]llowing the SEC to tell a jury that 'because the [defendant's] trading was suspicious, the [defendant] must have possessed some material nonpublic information,' would relieve the SEC of its burden to identify the information, prove its materiality, and prove possession and use by the [defendant]"). Would facts showing mere access to material nonpublic information, when coupled with evidence of suspicious trading, support such an inference? Was this basically the SEC's argument in *Moran*?

*7. **Using Circumstantial Evidence to Establish Scienter.*** Even in cases in which it is easy to establish that the defendant was aware of material, nonpublic information at the time of his trade, liability under Rule 10b-5 will attach only if it can also be shown that the defendant acted with "scienter," a "mental state embracing intent to deceive, manipulate, or defraud." *Ernst & Ernst v. Hochfelder*, 425 U.S. 185, 193-94 n. 12 (1976). As we have seen, this showing is generally made in insider trading cases through proof that the defendant knew, or was reckless in not knowing, that the information in his possession was both material and nonpublic. And in cases in which a tip has been given, the defendant-tippee must also have known or should have known that the tipped information stemmed from a breach of duty on the part of the tipper. Not surprisingly, the government often uses evidence of uncharacteristically large, speculative, or otherwise suspicious trading in proving the defendant's scienter. See, e.g., *SEC v. Warde*, 151 F.3d 42, 48 (2d Cir. 1998) (noting that co-defendants tipper and tippee "engaged in uncharacteristic, substantial and exceedingly risky investments in [ ] warrants shortly after speaking with one another, suggesting that they discussed not only the inside information, but also the best way to profit from it"); *SEC v. Willis*, 777 F. Supp. 1165, 1173 are (S.D.N.Y. 1991) (stating that scienter was plead sufficiently with allegation in complaint concerning "the volume and timing of the trading"); *SEC v. Musella*, 748 F. Supp. 1028, 1039 (S.D.N.Y. 1989) (inferring scienter in part from "the amounts involved and the financing of the trades"). From what other types of facts can a defendant's scienter be inferred?

F. REGULATION FD

Regulation FD is summarized in Note 5 on page 509. Failure to comply with it subjects reporting companies to a host of sanctions, including cease-and-desist orders, civil injunctions, and monetary penalties. The SEC may also initiate enforcement actions against the company officials responsible for causing (or aiding and abetting) the violation.

Former SEC Chairman Arthur Levitt recounts the following policy rationale:

> Reg FD would require companies to release important information to all investors at the same time, and not just to a favored few. Such "selective disclosure" had gotten out of hand in the 1990s, and put small investors at a disadvantage to the analysts, brokers, and institutional investors who were routinely getting advance information on corporate earnings ahead of the rest of the market. That was wrong, plan and simple.

Arthur Levitt, Take on the Street 87 (2002). If trading on advance information is "wrong, plan and simple," why isn't such trading illegal, plain and simple? The answer, of course, lies with the so-called "personal benefit" requirement for tipper-tippee liability under Rule 10b-5 (see *Dirks v. SEC* and Note 4, Section B.2 supra).

As you read the decision below, consider whether the benefits sought by the SEC in promulgating Reg FD outweigh its costs. Would the public have been better served by a re-thinking of *Dirks*'s requirement of a personal benefit? Why or why not?

SEC v. SIEBEL SYSTEMS, INC.

384 F. Supp. 2d 694 (S.D.N.Y. 2005)

GEORGE B. DANIELS, DISTRICT JUDGE:

Plaintiff, the Securities and Exchange Commission ("SEC"), commenced this action, against Siebel Systems, Inc. ("Siebel Systems"), Siebel Systems's Chief Financial Officer, Kenneth Goldman, and one of Siebel Systems's Senior Vice Presidents, Mark Hanson. The SEC charges the defendants with, *inter alia,* violations of, or aiding and abetting in the violation of, Regulation FD ("Fair Disclosure"), 17 C.F.R. § 243.100. In general terms, Regulation FD prohibits a company and its senior officials from privately disclosing any material nonpublic information regarding the company or its securities to certain persons such as analysts and institutional investors.

Defendants moved, pursuant to Fed.R.Civ.P. 12(b)(6), to dismiss the complaint for failure to state a claim upon which relief may be granted on the grounds that the statements disclosed were neither material nor nonpublic. Defendants' motion is granted. The nature and content of the statements that the SEC alleges violate Regulation FD do not support the Commission's claim that Siebel Systems or its senior officials privately disclosed material nonpublic information.

Regulation FD requires an issuer, to make public material information disclosed to security market professionals or holders of the issuer's securities who are reasonably likely to trade on the basis of that information. 17 C.F.R §§ 243.100; 242.101(c), (f). Where the issuer's selective disclosure of material nonpublic information is intentional, the issuer is to simultaneously make public disclosure. 17 C.F.R. § 243.100(a)(1). In the case of non-intentional disclosure, public disclosure must be promptly made. 17 C.F.R. § 243(a)(2). "'Promptly' means as soon as reasonably practicable (but in no event after the later of 24 hours or the commencement of the next day's trading on the New York Stock Exchange) after a senior official of the issuer, ... learns that there has been a non-intentional disclosure by the issuer or person acting on behalf of the issuer of information that the senior official knows, or is reckless in not knowing, is both material and nonpublic." 17 C.F.R. § 243.101(d).

The gravamen of the complaint is that defendant Goldman made positive comments about the company's business activity levels and sales transaction pipeline at two private events on April 30th, 2003, attended by institutional investors and by defendant Hanson. The SEC alleges that, at these two events, Mr. Goldman privately disclosed material nonpublic information by stating that Siebel Systems's activity levels were "good" or "better," that new deals were coming back into the pipeline, that the pipeline was "building" and "growing," and that "there were some $5 million deals in Siebel's pipeline." The complaint alleges that immediately following the disclosure of this information or soon thereafter, certain attendants of the meetings and their associates made substantial purchases of shares of Siebel Systems's stock. The SEC alleges "by disclosing that Siebel's business activity levels were 'good' and 'better,' and that its sales transaction pipeline was 'growing' and 'building,' Goldman communicated to his private audiences that Siebel's business was improving as the result of new business, and that the increase in the Company's guidance for the second quarter was not simply because deals that had slipped from the first quarter were closing."

The SEC claims that these statements materially contrasted with public statements made by Thomas Siebel during conference calls on April 4th and 23rd, and at an April 28th conference. In the complaint, the SEC sets forth, in great detail, the contents of Mr. Siebel's public statements of April 4th, April 23rd, and April 28th. Those statements provided information about the company's "performance in the first quarter of 2003 and its expected performance in the second quarter of 2003." The SEC alleges that in these statements it was reported that: (1) Siebel Systems's first quarter results were poor because the economy was poor and because some deals that were expected to close in the previous quarter did not, *i.e.,* deals had "slipped" into the second quarter; (2) Siebel Systems's software license revenues were expected to be higher in the second quarter than in the first quarter, but the company conditioned its estimate on the performance of the overall economy; and (3) there were no indications that the existing poor economic conditions were approving. "In each statement, the Company [allegedly] characterized the economy negatively (as not improved or not improving)." The complaint further states that, with regard to the guidance for the second quarter of fiscal year 2003, "[t]he Company conditioned its estimate on the performance of the overall economy. It said that if the economy improved, Siebel's business would improve, and that, conversely, if the economy did not improve, then Siebel's business would not improve." The SEC alleges that the public statements "linked the Company's prospective performance to the economy's performance--that is, if the economy improved, Siebel's business would improve."

The SEC contends that "[b]ased on these disclosures, the total mix of information available to investors was that Siebel's business had performed poorly in the first quarter and would improve in the second quarter only if the economy improved." Allegedly, Mr. Goldman's "statements materially contrasted with the public statements that Thomas Siebel made during the April 4 and 23 conference calls and at the ... conference on April 28. For example, in contrast to the apocalyptic economic environment that Thomas Siebel described at the [April 28th] conference, Goldman's disclosure at the April 30 [events] were significantly more positive and upbeat. Unlike the Company's prior public disclosure about its prospective performance in the second quarter, Goldman's statements about the Company's business were not linked to or conditioned upon the performance of the economy."

The complaint further alleges that analysts, who were participating in the April 23rd conference call and the April 28th conference, "wanted to know how much of the projected increase in software license revenues in the second quarter compared to the first quarter revenues was attributable to the deals that slipped from the first quarter as opposed to the Company's expectation that it would generate new business in the second quarter." The SEC alleges that when the analysts repeatedly inquired about the impact of the slipped deals on Siebel Systems's second quarter guidance, Mr. Siebel "avoided," "evaded," and "directly declined to answer the question." The SEC maintains that, publicly, "the total mix of information available to investors did not include information that would enable either analysts or investors to determine whether the increased guidance for the second quarter represented an improvement over the first quarter."

The complaint further alleges that Siebel Systems failed to file the requisite Form 8-K disclosing the material nonpublic information that Mr. Goldman had disclosed at the private meetings within the time frame specified by the SEC's rules, nor did it "disseminate that information through another method of disclosure reasonably designed to provide broad, non-exclusionary distribution of the information to the public."

***

VIOLATION OF REGULATION FD

The complaint alleges four nonpublic material disclosures made by Mr. Goldman which are the basis for the SEC's claims for violations of Regulation FD: (1) that there were some *five million dollar deals* in the company's pipeline for the second quarter of 2003; (2) that *new deals* were coming into the sales pipeline; (3) that the company's sales pipeline was "*growing* " or "*building;* " and (4) that the company's sales or business activity levels were "*good* " or "*better*." The complaint relies on no statements regarding specific earnings or sales figures. Defendants argue that dismissal of the complaint is warranted because the four statements at issue cannot support a conclusory allegation that these statements were either material or nonpublic.

Regulation FD does not contain definitions for the terms "material" or "nonpublic." In the SEC's release discussing the proposed adoption of the regulation ("Proposing Release"), the SEC "recognize[d] that materiality judgments can be difficult." *Proposed Rule: Selective Disclosure and Insider Trading,* 64 Fed.Reg. 72590, 72594 (Dec. 28, 1999). The SEC observed that the proposed regulation could have a "chilling effect" in that "[c]orporate officials [might] become more cautious in communicating with analysts or selected investors," especially since such communications may take the form of "unrehearsed question-and-answer sessions, and responses to unsolicited inquiries." Id. Thus, the SEC noted it was "mindful of the potential burdens of requiring instant materiality judgments to be made by those put in the position of responding immediately to questions." Id. Despite the SEC's concession that materiality determinations are difficult, the SEC nevertheless suggested that in most cases, the question of whether information was material will be reasonably clear. The SEC explained,

> Although materiality issues do not lend themselves to a bright-line test, we believe that the majority of cases are reasonably clear. At one end of the spectrum, we believe issuers should avoid giving guidance or express warnings to analysts or selected investors about important upcoming earnings or sales figures; such earnings or sales figures will frequently have a significant impact on the issuer's stock price. On the other end of the spectrum, more generalized background information is less likely to be material. Id. at 72595.

In the SEC's Adopting Release, the SEC again noted the frequently expressed concern that the regulation would not lead to broader dissemination of information, but would instead have a "chilling effect" on disclosure of information by the issuer. 65 Fed.Reg. 51716, 51718. The potential chilling effect could conceivably result in the issuers "speak[ing] less often out of fear of liability based on a post hoc assessment that disclosed information was material," and "such a chilling effect result[ing] from Regulation FD [ ] would be a cost to the overall market efficiency and capital formation." Id. at 51733.

In response to this concern and in recognizing that the market is best served by more, rather than less, disclosure of information by issuers, the SEC modified the proposed Regulation FD to include certain safeguards to narrow the applicability of Regulation FD so as not to diminish the flow of information.[7] Despite its previous acknowledgment, in the Proposing Release, that materiality judgments can be difficult, the SEC did not find that the "appropriate answer to this difficulty is to set forth a bright-line test, or an exclusive list of material items for purpose of Regulation FD." *Id.* at 51721.

---

7. "In response to the comments [the SEC] received on the proposal, [the SEC has] made several modifications ... in the final rules." *Id.* at 51716. "These modifications include narrowing the scope of the regulation so that it does not apply to all communications with persons outside the issuer, narrowing the types of issuer personnel covered by the regulation to senior officials and those who would normally be expected to communicate with securities market professionals or security holders, and clarifying that where the regulation requires 'knowing or reckless' conduct, liability will attach only when the issuer's personnel know or are reckless in not knowing that the information selectively disclosed is both material and nonpublic. Additionally, ... [the SEC] added an express provision in the regulation's text designed to remove any doubt that private liability will not result from a Regulation FD violation." Id. at 51733, see also, Id. at 51719.

Although the SEC declined to set forth an all-inclusive list of what matters are to be deemed material, it did provide seven categories of information or events that have a higher probability of being considered material. The seven enumerated categories are:

> (1) Earnings information; (2) mergers, acquisitions, tender offers, joint ventures, or changes in assets; (3) new products or discoveries, or developments regarding customers or supplies (e.g., the acquisition or loss of a contract); (4) changes in control or in management; (5) change in auditors or auditor notification that the issuer may no longer rely on an auditor's audit report; (6) events regarding the issuer's securities-- e.g., defaults on strict securities, calls of securities for redemption, repurchase plans, stock splits or changes in dividends, changes to rights of security holders, public or private sales of additional securities; and (7) bankruptcies and receiverships. Id.

The specific matters included in the list, however, are not *per se* material.[8]

Although Regulation FD does not contain definitions for the terms "material" or "nonpublic," the Adopting Release advises that those terms are to be defined as they have been in previous case law. With regard to the "nonpublic" element, the Adopting Release relied on the finding in *SEC v. Texas Sulphur Co.*, 401 F.2d 833, 854 (2d Cir.1968), that information is nonpublic if it has not been disseminated in a manner sufficient to ensure its availability to the investing public. Id. As the Second Circuit Court of Appeals explained, in *SEC v. Mayhew*, 121 F.3d 44 (2d Cir.1997):

> Information becomes public when disclosed to achieve a broad dissemination to the investing public generally and without favoring any special person or group, or when, although known only by a few persons, their trading on it has caused the information to be fully impounded into the price of the particular stock.

Mayhew, 121 F.3d at 50.

---

8. On November 1, 2000, approximately a week after Regulation FD became effective, then-Director of the SEC Division of Enforcement, Richard H. Walker, gave a speech before the Compliance and Legal Division of the Securities Industry Association regarding the enforcement perspective of Regulation FD. Former-Director Walker indicated that in enforcing Regulation FD, the SEC was "not going to second-guess close calls regarding the materiality of a potential disclosure" noting that "[a]n issuer's incorrect determination that information is not material must represent an extreme departure from standards of reasonable care in order for [the SEC] to allege a violation of FD." He further stated, "Regulation FD's adopting release ... spells out seven items that should be reviewed carefully to determine whether they are material ... This list puts the world on notice that an intentional or reckless selective disclosure of information falling into one of these categories is likely to draw the attention of the Enforcement Division. The views expressed in Mr. Walker's speech were his own and did not necessarily reflect the views of the SEC or its staff. However, in [a submission to Congress in] May of 2001, the SEC quoted and summarized portions of Mr. Walker's speech, wherein he indicated "that Regulation FD was not designed as a 'trap for the unwary' and that enforcement cases will not be based on second-guessing reasonable judgments made in good faith by issuers, including judgments about materiality. The SEC noted that "[t]hese remarks ... have indicated that Commission enforcement of the regulation will be focused on clear violations." *Id.*

With regard to the definition of "materiality," the Adopting Release embraced the definition set forth in *TSC Indus., Inc. v. Northway, Inc.,* 426 U.S. 438 (1976), concluding that "[i]nformation is material if 'there is a substantial likelihood that a reasonable shareholder would consider it important' in making an investment decision." Fed.Reg. 51716, 51721 (quoting *TSC Indus., Inc.,* 426 U.S. at 449 (1976)). To satisfy the materiality element, there must be a substantial likelihood that a reasonable investor would have considered the information as having significantly altered the 'total mix' of information made available. *Id.* (quoting *TSC Indus., Inc.,* 426 U.S. at 449); *see also Basic Inc. v. Levinson,* 485 U.S. 224, 231-32 (1988). The "total mix" of information includes all information that is reasonably available to the public. *Starr v. Georgeson Shareholder, Inc.,* 412 F.3d 103, 110 (2d Cir.2005). It is not a prerequisite to a finding of materiality that had a reasonable investor been privy to the information, the investor would necessarily have changed his or her investment decision as a result of that information. *TSC Indus., Inc.,* 426 U.S. at 449; *see also, Folger Adam Co. v. PMI Indus., Inc.,* 938 F.2d 1529, 1533 (2d Cir.1991) ("material fact need not be outcome-determinative," but rather it is sufficient that the information would assume actual significance to a reasonable investor). Information that would affect the probable future of the company and which may affect an investor's desire to buy, sell, or hold the company's securities is material. *Texas Gulf Sulphur Co.,* 401 F.2d at 849. "Some information is of such dubious significance that insistence on its disclosure may accomplish more harm than good. * * * [I]f the standard of materiality is unnecessary low, not only may the company and its management be subjected to liability for insignificant [nonpublic selective disclosure], but also management's fear of exposing itself to substantial liability may cause it simply to bury the shareholders in an avalanche of trivial information, a result that is hardly conducive to informed decisionmaking." *TSC Indus., Inc.,* 426 U.S. at 448-49.

The question of materiality generally presents a mixed question of law and fact, as it involves the application of a legal standard to a particular set of facts. *TSC Indus., Inc.,* 426 U.S. at 450. The question of materiality is, however, an objective one, involving the significance of the information to a reasonable investor. *TSC Indus., Inc.,* 426 U.S. at 445. "[S]ince the importance of a particular piece of information depends on the context in which it is given, materiality has become one of the most unpredictable and elusive concepts of the federal securities laws." *SEC v. Bausch & Lomb Inc.,* 565 F.2d 8, 10 (2d Cir.1977). A determination with regard to materiality is a fact-specific inquiry to be determined on a case-by-case basis. *Basic,* 485 U.S. at 240, 250. A complaint may only be dismissed on the grounds that the alleged private disclosure of information was immaterial if the subject information is "so obviously unimportant to a reasonable investor that reasonable minds could not differ on the question of [its] importance." *Goldman v. Belden,* 754 F.2d 1059, 1067 (2d Cir.1985). Hence, where the subject statements are so blatantly unimportant, it is appropriate for the Court to rule, as a matter of law, that the statements do not meet the materiality threshold, and to dismiss the complaint. *See, Schoenhaut v. Am. Sensors, Inc.,* 986 F.Supp. 785, 790-91 (S.D.N.Y.1997) (quoting *In re Burlington Coat Factory Securities Litig.,* 114 F.3d at 1429).

In applying the aforementioned principles to the case at bar, the allegations in the complaint fail to demonstrate that Regulation FD was violated. Regulation FD was never intended to be utilized in the manner attempted by the SEC under these circumstances. The statements relied upon in the complaint cannot support a conclusion that material information privately provided by Mr. Goldman was unavailable to the public. Specifically, Mr. Goldman's private statement regarding the existence of five million dollar deals in the company's pipeline for the second quarter was equivalent in substance to the information previously disclosed by Mr. Siebel. With regard to the guidance for the second quarter, Mr. Siebel stated at the April 23rd conference call:

> Our guidance and license revenue for the quarter is 120 to 140 million range. I think that we'll see lots of small deals. We'll see some medium deals. We'll see a number of deals over a million dollars. And I suspect we'll see some *greater than five*. And now that's what the mix will look like.

The SEC argues that Mr. Goldman's statement, in contrast, was in the *present* tense, and hence constitutes a factually different material statement than that made by Mr. Siebel. The SEC contends that unlike Mr. Goldman's statement, Mr. Siebel's statement was in the *future* tense, and Mr. Siebel's use of the word "suspect" indicates his statement was not a present fact, but rather was forward looking.

It would appear that in examining publicly and privately disclosed information, the SEC has scrutinized, at an extremely heightened level, every particular word used in the statement, including the tense of verbs and the general syntax of each sentence. No support for such an approach can be found in Regulation FD itself, or in the Proposing and Adopting Releases. Such an approach places an unreasonable burden on a company's management and spokespersons to become linguistic experts, or otherwise live in fear of violating Regulation FD should the words they use later be interpreted by the SEC as connoting even the slightest variance from the company's public statements.

Regulation FD does not require that corporate officials only utter verbatim statements that were previously publicly made. In *Kennecott Copper Corp. v. Curtiss-Wright Corp.*, 584 F.2d 1195, 1200 (2d Cir.1978), which concerned the adequacy of a proxy disclosure, the Second Circuit advised that, in analyzing the disclosure of material statements, "nit-picking should not become the name of the game. * * * There is no requirement that a material fact be expressed in certain words or in a certain form of language. Fair accuracy, not perfection, is the appropriate standard." To require a more demanding standard, in the context of Regulation FD, could compel companies to discontinue any spontaneous communications so that the content of any intended communication may be examined by a lexicologist to ensure that the proposed statement discloses the exact information in the same form as was publicly disclosed. If Regulation FD is applied in such a manner, the very purpose of the regulation, *i.e.*, to provide the public with a broad flow of relevant investment information, would be thwarted.

Mr. Goldman's private statement regarding the existence of five million dollars deals in the company's pipeline for the second quarter was equivalent in substance to the information publicly disclosed by the company in that it conveyed the same material information. As long as the private statement conveys the same material information that the public statement publicly conveyed, Regulation FD is not implicated, and hence no greater form of disclosure, pursuant to the regulation, is required. Although Mr. Goldman's statement was not literally a word for word recitation of Mr. Siebel's disclosure, both provided the same information, and Mr. Goldman's statement did not add, contradict, or significantly alter the material information available to the general public. It therefore cannot constitute a sufficient factual basis on which to allege a nonpublic disclosure of material information in violation of Regulation FD.

Similarly unavailing are the SEC's claims that Mr. Goldman's private statements regarding new business in the pipeline and that the pipeline was "growing" or "building" was information which was not previously disclosed to the public. The SEC argues that Mr. Siebel "did not describe the status of the Company's pipeline." However, at the April 23rd conference call, a question was posed regarding the makeup of the pipeline with respect to "new versus exist[ing] customers." The verbatim transcript on which the SEC relies indicates that in response thereto, Mr. Siebel publicly stated, "every quarter will be some place between 45 and 55 percent of our business with new customers." Such a statement clearly indicated that the second quarter pipeline would include new deals.

Mr. Goldman's private description of the pipeline as "growing" or "building" provides no additional material information that was not previously publicly disclosed by the company. The complaint acknowledges Siebel Systems's April 23rd and 28th public statements that "the Company projected that its software license revenues would be in the range of $120 to $140 million, which was more than the Company's reported revenues for the first quarter." Moreover, the company publicly disclosed that the projected total revenues for the second quarter appeared to be in the 340 to 360 million dollar range, which was greater than the reported total revenues for the first quarter. Additionally, at the April 23rd conference call, Mr. Siebel explained that the anticipated increase in the license revenues was based on an analysis of the pipeline. At the April 28th conference, Mr. Siebel again explained that the projected increase was Siebel Systems's "best professional judgment based upon the pipeline with the deals that we saw ..." Siebel Systems's public statements clearly disclosed that it was projecting an increase in revenues in the second quarter, and that this expectation was based, in part, upon an analysis of the pipeline. Based on this information, a reasonable investor would be aware that the sales pipeline was "growing" and "building." Hence Mr. Goldman's private wording, to that effect, added nothing to the total mix of information publicly available.

The SEC further alleges that Regulation FD was violated as a result of Mr. Goldman's private statements that Siebel Systems's sales or business activity levels were "good" or "better." Mr. Goldman's private statement that the activity levels were "good" or "better" was based on information available to the public since Siebel Systems publicly reported that it anticipated a future increase in the company's performance. The terms "better" and "good" are merely generalized descriptive labels based on the underlying quantitative information provided publicly by Siebel Systems. Given the detailed and specific information revealed in the company's public disclosures, Mr. Goldman's description of the company's performance and activity level as being "good" and "better" imparted no greater information to his private audiences than Siebel Systems had already disclosed to the public at large. Hence, the statements regarding the company's performance or activity levels being "good" or "better" did not alter the total mix of information already available to the reasonable investor.

The SEC maintains that Mr. Goldman's statements constituted nonpublic material information because his statements forecasted overall positive growth for the company, whereas the company's public statements avoided making such a positive affirmation. Although the SEC is not disputing that the public information was that the second quarter guidance was higher than the first quarter's actual results, the SEC asserts that this is not dispositive of whether business was improving. However, the information available to the public provides a sufficient factual basis for a reasonable investor to conclude that business was improving.

The SEC places great emphasis on the alleged actions taken by certain individuals who were in attendance at Mr. Goldman's private speaking engagements. The complaint alleges that certain attendees, and other individuals with whom they communicated, purchased Siebel Systems stock almost immediately after Mr. Goldman's private statements or soon thereafter, causing the market for Siebel Systems stock to significantly rise and for trading to surge. The SEC argues that taking these allegations as true, and drawing all reasonable inferences in its favor, leads to the conclusion that Mr. Goldman disclosed information that was both new and material.

A major factor in determining whether information is material is the importance attached to it by those who were exposed to the information as may be expressed by their reaction to the information. *Mayhew,* 121 F.3d at 52 (citing *Texas Gulf Sulphur Co.,* 401 F.2d at 851); *Elkind v. Liggett & Myers, Inc.,* 635 F.2d 156, 166-67 (2d Cir.1980). Although stock movement is a relevant factor to be considered in making the determination as to materiality, it is not, however, a sufficient factor alone to establish materiality. *United States v. Bilzerian,* 926 F.2d 1285, 1298 (2d Cir.1991).

An examination of the public and private statements do not support a conclusory allegation that Mr. Goldman's statements were the disclosure of nonpublic material information. The actions taken by those in attendance at Mr. Goldman's speaking engagements, although a relevant consideration, do not change the nature or content of Mr. Goldman's statements. Regulation FD deals exclusively with the disclosure of material information. The regulation does not prohibit persons speaking on behalf of an issuer, from providing mere positive or negative characterizations, or their optimistic or pessimistic subjective general impressions, based upon or drawn from the material information available to the public. The mere fact that analysts might have considered Mr. Goldman's private statements significant is not, standing alone, a basis to infer that Regulation FD was violated. *See,* 65 Fed.Reg. 51716, 51722 ("Regulation FD will not be implicated where an issuer discloses immaterial information whose significance is discerned by the analyst. * * * The focus of Regulation FD is on whether the issuer discloses material nonpublic information, not on whether an analyst, through some combination of persistence, knowledge, and insight, regards as material information whose significance is not apparent to the reasonable investor.").

The SEC further argues that Mr. Goldman's statements "constituted new information" because they were not "conditioned upon nor qualified by the performance of the economy," and therefore they "contrasted with the Company's prior statements and altered the total mix of information available to investors," which included, "that Siebel's business had performed poorly in the first quarter and would improve in the second quarter only if the economy improved.

It would be an unusual rule, indeed, to require that forecasts must repeatedly be accompanied by a warning that company performance might be affected by an improving or worsening economy. However, even if the potential effects of the economy constituted material information, Siebel Systems had publicly disclosed that the performance of the company was linked to the performance of the economy. What Regulation FD does not require is that an individual, speaking privately on behalf of an issuer, repeat material information which has already been previously publicly proclaimed. *See, Spielman v. Gen. Host Corp.,* 402 F.Supp. 190, 195 (S.D.N.Y.1975), *aff'd,* 538 F.2d 39 (2d Cir.1976). Mr. Goldman's alleged failure to qualify his private statement about the company's performance, by linking it to, or conditioning it upon, the performance of the economy, cannot be alleged as a private disclosure of nonpublic information. Regulation FD only pertains to the required public disclosure of information, not the failure to repeat a particular public statement in private.[14]

Significantly, none of the statements challenged by the SEC falls squarely within the seven enumerated categories listed by the SEC, in the Adopting Release, as being more likely to be considered material. Applying Regulation FD in an overly aggressive manner cannot effectively encourage full and complete public disclosure of facts reasonably deemed relevant to investment decisionmaking. It provides no clear guidance for companies to conform their conduct in compliance with Regulation FD. Instead, the enforcement of Regulation FD by excessively scrutinizing vague general comments has a potential chilling effect which can discourage, rather than, encourage public disclosure of material information.

In accepting the factual allegations in the complaint as true and drawing all reasonable inferences in the SEC's favor, the statements relied upon in the complaint fail to support its conclusory allegation that material information disclosed by Mr. Goldman in private, had not already been publicly disclosed by Siebel Systems. Accordingly, the complaint fails to sufficiently allege that Regulation FD was violated.[15] * * *

---

14. Although Regulation FD pertains solely to disclosure of information, the challenged communication need not be an expressed verbal or written statement. Tacit communications, such as a wink, nod, or a thumbs up or down gesture, may give rise to a Regulation FD violation.

15. Defendants additionally raise the following constitutional challenges to Regulation FD: (1) the SEC lacked the statutory authority to promulgate the regulation; (2) the regulation abridges the freedom of speech protected by the First Amendment; (3) the regulation is void for vagueness in violation of the Due Process Clause of the Fifth Amendment; and (4) the regulation is unconstitutional as applied. The issues regarding

The defendants' motion to dismiss the complaint, pursuant to Fed.R.Civ.P. 12(b)(6), is granted. The case is dismissed in its entirety.

NOTES AND QUESTIONS

1. ***Parity of Access Revisited?*** In their briefs to the district court in *Siebel*, the defendants and the U.S. Chamber of Commerce as *amicus curiae* argued that Regulation FD was a repudiation of the Supreme Court's decisions in *Chiarella* and *Dirks* and an effort to resurrect the "parity of access" rule that the Court rejected in those decisions. Is that a fair claim? Why or why not?

2. ***Stock Price Movements.*** If the court was correct in concluding that the CEO's private statements did not constitute material nonpublic information, what explains the substantial purchases of Siebel System's stock by the recipients of that information and by individuals with whom they communicated "almost immediately after Mr. Goldman's private statements or soon thereafter"? In determining whether selectively disclosed information is both material and nonpublic, how much evidentiary weight should be given to the movement of the company's stock?

3. ***Changed Times, Changed Norms?*** Regulation FD provides that an issuer may satisfy the requirements for a "public disclosure" by filing a Form 8-K with the SEC or by disseminating "the information through another method (or combination of methods) of disclosure that is reasonably designed to provide broad, non-exclusionary distribution of the information to the public." Rule 101(e). Would a posting on a company's website constitute a "broad, non-exclusionary distribution"? When the SEC proposed Regulation FD in December 1999, it took the position that such a website posting would "not by itself be considered a sufficient method of public disclosure." Has the ubiquity of the Internet rendered this position outdated? If posting on a corporate website is now sufficient to satisfy the SEC's requirement of a broad non-exclusionary distribution, what about a posting on a corporate blog? What if the blog were linked to the corporation's home page? See Peter Lattman, Should the SEC Let Sun's CEO Break News on His Blog? Wall Street Journal Law Blog, October 5, 2006.

4. ***Reg FD and the First Amendment.*** Footnote 15 of the *Siebel* decision notes that the U.S. Chamber of Commerce and a group of law professors filed *amicus curiae* briefs offering opposing views as to whether Regulation FD violates the First Amendment. See also Antony Page & Katy Yang, Controlling Corporate Speech: Is Regulation Fair Disclosure Unconstitutional?, 39 U.C. Davis L. Rev. 1 (2005). How does Regulation FD compare with other securities law provisions that regulate corporate speech?

---

the SEC's authority to adopt Regulation FD and whether the regulation violates the First Amendment's right to free speech were raised in an *amicus curiaei* brief, submitted by the Chambers of Commerce of the United States in support of the defendants' motion to dismiss, and addressed in an *amicus curiae* brief, submitted by a group of law professors in opposition to the motion. Since the complaint itself fails to allege a cognizable cause of action for violation of Regulation FD, this Court declines to opine on the constitutional challenges raised.

*5. **Reg FD and Rule 10b-5.*** Rule 102 of Regulation FD states specifically that: "No failure to make a public disclosure required solely by Rule 100 shall be deemed to be a violation of Rule 10b-5 under the Securities Exchange Act." What purposes does this provision serve?

*6. **Enhanced Confidence vs. Reduced Efficiency.*** From the time Regulation FD was first proposed in December 1999, the possibility that it might chill corporate disclosures was considered its principal cost. Although empirical studies offer an array of conclusions, the initial (and highly publicized) fears on Wall Street – that Regulation FD would substantially reduce information flow and increase price volatility– do not seem to have materialized. For a discussion of the empirical research, see Page & Yang, supra, 39 U.C. Davis L. Rev. at 26-33; Jill E. Fisch & Hillary A. Sale, The Securities Analyst as Agent: Rethinking the Regulation of Analysts, 88 Iowa L. Rev. 1035, 1065-68 (2003).

PROBLEM 7-10

Digatech, Inc.'s common stock trades on the New York Stock Exchange. On January 12, 2011 the company held a live webcast analyst conference call, during which Digatech officials discussed the company's fourth quarter 2006 results and estimated first quarter 2011 sales at $9.8 billion and earnings at 13 cents per share.

On February 22, 2011 the company issued a press release stating that "as a result of significant weakness in first-quarter order input across its business segments, the company does not expect to achieve the first-quarter 2007 sales guidance of $9.8 billion or the earnings guidance of 13 cents per share given on Jan. 12, 2011." Later that day, during a live webcast analyst conference call, Digatech's CEO explained that the company was "experiencing significant weakness in orders and sales versus our expectations at the beginning of the quarter." He also stated that Digatech was "experiencing lower sales and significantly lower orders. All markets are down compared with the same period last year."

a. On February 28, Digatech's CEO contacted by phone ten sell-side analysts who cover the company. In the course of these private phone calls, Digatech's CEO stated that when Digatech "uses the terms 'significant' or 'significantly' it intends a rate of change of 25% or more." Did Digatech violate Regulation FD? See Report of Investigation Pursuant to Section 21(a) of the Exchange Act, Motorola, Inc., Release No. 34-46898 (Nov. 25, 2002).

b. Instead of making the calls described above, Digatech's CEO had private meetings with the portfolio managers of four institutional investors, three of which were Digatech's largest shareholders. At each of these meetings, which occurred on March 1 and 2 over lunch or dinner, the CEO stated in a very somber tone that Digatech was going to take a "very hard hit to earnings" and that "the street" had not sufficiently lowered earnings estimates for the first quarter of 2011. Did Digatech violate Regulation FD? See In the Matter of Schering-Plough Corp., Exchange Act Release No. 34-48461 (Sept. 9, 2003).

c. At one of the above referenced meetings, when Digatech's CEO was asked how things looked for the remainder of 2011, he shook his head from side to side, and made a nose-dive gesture with his right arm. Did Digatech violate Regulation FD?

d. From March 1 - March 3, Digatech's stock price fell by more than 17 percent, from $21.32 to 17.64 per share, with volume each day averaging more than four times the stock's typical daily volume. Digatech's officials knew of this volume increase and price decline, and knew that the institutional investors that had met with the CEO each sold more than 7 million shares during that three day period, accounting for more than 30% of the overall volume. How do these facts affect your answers to b and c above?

e. Could the SEC bring an enforcement action against Digatech's CEO and/or the institutional investors for insider trading? What if at the outset of each meeting, the CEO had sought and received a promise of confidentiality from the portfolio managers?

G. POLICY RATIONALES FOR FEDERAL REGULATION OF INSIDER TRADING AND THE SEARCH FOR A DEFINITION

All of the preceding material in this Chapter relates to the question of *how* the federal securities laws operate to prevent, detect, and remedy offenses involving insider trading. What follows are various arguments as to *why* insider trading should—or should not—be subject to federal prohibition and why the offense of insider trading should—or should not—be specifically defined. While the chosen excerpts shed much light on the most important policy concerns, they intended to provide only a flavor of what is out there in a very rich universe of insider trading literature.

1. The Policy Debate Over the Harms and Benefits of Insider Trading

a. Insider Trading and its Effects on Corporate Management

IN DEFENSE OF INSIDER TRADING

by Henry G. Manne

Harv. Bus. Rev. 113-19 (Nov.- Dec. 1966)

In April 1965, when the Securities and Exchange Commission announced its action against executives of the Texas Gulf Sulphur Company for alleged violations of rules against insider trading, there was an outcry of public indignation against the defendants. It was as though men who were highly respected members of the community had suddenly been found out in heinous crime.

But this is only one more manifestation of a long and persistent trend. The main push came with the Pecora hearings in Congress in 1933-1934, where the activities of prominent executives who conceded playing some part in insider trading were characterized as "immoral," "unscrupulous," "unfair," a "betrayal of fiduciary duties," and a "vicious practice." Since that time, leading academic figures, lawyers, businessmen, and spokesmen for the SEC with almost boring uniformity, have castigated insider trading as being costly to shareholders and giving unfair and undeserved gains to insiders. The tone of most discussions on this subject suggests that there is no doubt whatever: insider trading is a sin, and the war against it is a holy one.

But, as in most holy wars, self-righteousness and hypocrisy may be the true order of the day. In the entire literature on insider trading there does not exist one careful analysis of the subject. Lawyers have been having a field day arguing about the meaning of words or the reach of the last case or any of a thousand technical and legal issues. Unfortunately, however, most lawyers do not have the skills to develop a careful economic analysis of the subject, and economists have offered no assistance. The tone of debate has remained essentially moralistic and question-begging. Logic has been totally lost to emotion.

It is very likely, however, that unless businessmen, commentators, and the courts wake up, far more than logic will be lost. For the current attack on insider trading may prove to be a fundamental attack on free capital markets and entrepreneurial capitalism. It would be a shame to lose the battle by default. ***

This article constitutes at least a starting point for logical analysis of the subject. In particular, I shall argue that insider trading is the best, if not the only, method of adequately compensating corporate innovators ***

Stimulus to Innovation

***I should begin this discussion with some explanation of what is meant by the "entrepreneurial function." The term is used here in a technical, economic sense, and the function differs in critical respects from that performed by managers:

Entrepreneur—An Innovator. Fundamentally the entrepreneur is a man who finds a new product or a new way to make or sell an old one. He may reorganize corporate administration, or he may be responsible for the merger of two companies. He may be a corporate promoter, or he may perform the job of selecting and guiding the managers. In short, he is the individual responsible for having or taking a new idea and causing it to be put into effect. A critical part of this definition is the "new idea," but there is no payoff unless the idea is put into effect successfully.

Since the value of an entrepreneur's contribution cannot be known until it has been made, there is rarely any way of appraising his services in advance. This is undoubtedly why early economists, including Adam Smith, did not see the entrepreneurial function as being distinct from the capitalist's function, for in the eighteenth century one was generally required to risk his own money to prove the value of his innovation. The return for successful innovation looks, superficially at least, like the return to the owner of capital.

Today, however, a sizable portion of economic literature, introduced principally by the late Joseph A. Schumpeter of Harvard University, has been built on the distinction between the entrepreneur and the capitalist, though it has not yet had a great impact on popular thinking.

Manager—A Technician. The management function is, in the pure sense, simply to administer a business along lines already determined. Though it may be extraordinarily complex and highly paid, the manager's job is basically that of a technician. As soon as he begins to reorganize the existing arrangement, then and only then is the executive performing an innovational or entrepreneurial activity, rather than a management function. Again the distinction between functions remains even though the same individual performs both. As Schumpeter commented, it is "just as rare for anyone always to remain an entrepreneur through the decades of his active life as it is for a businessman never to have a moment in which he is an entrepreneur, to however modest a degree."[2]

Reward for Performance

In return for performing its function, management receives its compensation, generally termed by economists the "wage." This wage is simply the market price for managerial skills. No one knowingly pays more or takes less. Similarly, the capitalist receives "interest," which, whatever the legal form might be called, is the economic return to him. It may be relatively certain, as in the case of bonds, or it may be very indefinite, as with speculative securities; but its economic nature remains the same. Although the degrees of risk may vary greatly, interest is the price that has to be paid for the use of money over time.

But in the sense that wages and interest are the market return for capital and management, there is no such thing as a market price for entrepreneurial skills. In fact, almost by definition, it is impossible to value entrepreneurial activities *before they have paid off in some other form.* Economic theorists do, however, have a word for the entrepreneurial return; it is termed "profit," although that particular usage of the word has not received popular acceptance. But, aside from having a word for it, we have little knowledge about the particular form that this "profit" may take, or even whether it can redound to the benefit of entrepreneurs in large corporations. ***

Compensation Not Enough

To provide an effective incentive, entrepreneurial compensation has to be available when the benefits are realized by the corporation, and it must vary with the value of the contribution. Since neither of these eventualities can ordinarily be predicted in advance, most existing compensation plans are inadequate for the task. Obviously, salary is inappropriate. The amount of salary has to be decided on in advance, it does not allow for distinguishing the manager who only manages from one who also innovates, and it is not flexible enough to reward particular contributions.

At first glance the bonus does seem to answer most of these objections. However, most bonuses today are formulated in advance and depend on total profits rather than individual contributions. Bonus plans are incentive devices, but they probably tend to generate managerial improvements, such as small cost-cutting, rather than radical innovations. The bonus plan, as opposed to the special bonus, will not serve the entrepreneur's purpose.

The special bonus can, of course, be used to reward great innovations, though there are legal restrictions if authorization is not established in advance. But the main drawback is that the true value of a particular contribution, in the form of higher profits, may not be known for many years. So there frequently

2. Joseph Alois Schumpeter, The Theory of Economic Development, translated by Redvers Opie (Cambridge, Harvard University Press, 1934), p.78.

are gross disparities in judgment between the bonus committee and the executive as to the latter's true worth. This misjudgment may become even more serious if the innovation has caused the price of the stock to rise but has not yet affected profits, though the stock price rise is precisely what the entrepreneur should be rewarded for.

In addition, the entrepreneurial type who is motivated by the possibility of "getting rich quick" probably does not like the idea of negotiating his reward after his contribution has been made. This distinction is like that between a patent system and a system of bonuses or government awards for inventions. Few will be found to argue that the latter system encourages as much invention as the former.

Stock options also add some incentive to efficiency for managers, but it is doubtful that they can serve the needs of the entrepreneur for massive reward for great innovations. The difficulty should be obvious. The number of shares to be optioned to various executives normally has to be determined in advance of any entrepreneurial innovation. If the options are granted after the innovation, they are the same as the special bonus, except that payment is made in the form of a free call on corporate stock rather than in the form of cash. Stock options undoubtedly add greatly to incentive, but they may still promise too little to entrepreneurial types with ambition, enthusiasm, and a large measure of self-confidence.

Incentives from Trading

On the other hand, free trading by insiders in a company's securities meets the objections mentioned for other compensation schemes and has special advantages of its own. Perhaps this can best be seen by comparing systems of compensation for patentable and nonpatentable innovations.

Basically the patent system is designed to allow inventors to receive an appropriate reward for successful innovations by preventing others from copying and participating in profits which we might say were not earned by them. The granting of a temporary monopoly to the patentee assures two goals: (1) it excludes the would-be interloper; (2) it provides the patentee with a substantial reward for his idea, although that reward will vary with the economic importance of the invention.

The patent system seems to work reasonably well, but only for patentable ideas. How can we guarantee a similar reward to inventors of non-patentable ideas? In this area our legal system has been rather weak and ineffective; it has developed few really successful techniques for the protection of such ideas. Most businessmen recognize that secrecy and speed of marketing are the two principal devices for realizing substantial profits for their companies from nonpatentable innovations—secrecy to keep competitors away and speed because they cannot be kept away for long. But nothing in this scheme provides any protection or reward for the individual who has an important, nonpatentable idea which he personally is in no position to exploit.

For the man who has not founded his own business to exploit his idea—historically the traditional course for an entrepreneur—trading in the stock market on inside information provides a reward system, and is the only effective device available for the entrepreneur who is employed by a large corporation.

Insider trading allows any individual who works for a publicly traded corporation to play the entrepreneurial role, a very important advantage. Individuals can, in effect, sell their own ideas without the necessity of having large amounts of capital available. The increase in stock price, though not perfect, will provide as accurate a gauge of the value of the innovation as can be found, and it will leave little room for argument about an individual's worth.

Large corporations will be able to compete more effectively for entrepreneurial talent with closely owned companies, since they can now hold out the promise of very great rewards for the successful innovator. The image of corporate executives as gray bureaucrats can and should be erased. Large corporations can furnish as much romance, excitement, and opportunity for rapid economic and social advancement as any other avenues pursued today. But if corporations get hung up on foolish moralizing, such as characterizes most discussions of insider trading, they cannot hope to compete successfully or to survive the subtle attacks of government agencies.

If there really is an economic service or function that can be termed entrepreneurship, then we must have some way of compensating it. The cases are legion of new corporate managers bringing in fresh, imaginative, but often untested ideas. If these individuals were to be limited to the same compensation as their dull unimaginative, and overly conservative predecessors, what incentive would they have to innovate? Their salaries, bonuses, and pensions are usually secure, and few large companies face imminent bankruptcy. Their stock options and bonus plans will give some motivation to improve things, but not to take very great personal risks. For the true entrepreneur, the possibility of great riches will elicit more risk-taking activities and enterprise than will the possibility of smaller though more certain gain.

It might also be added that this promise attracts a different type of personality as well, one with which successful American businessmen have traditionally been proud to identify—the self-made, rags-to-riches, "Horatio Alger" hero. There is still room for such characters in the large modern corporation.***

Critics of Professor Manne's "entrepreneur compensation" argument—and through the years there have been many—respond chiefly that insider trading is a particularly poor method of compensating corporate executives because:

- it tempts officials to engage in overly risky projects because greater trading profits can be extracted in companies with more volatile stock prices. See Frank Easterbrook, Insider Trading, Secret Agents, Evidentiary Privileges, and the Production of Information, 1981 Sup. Ct. Rev. 309, 323;
- it allows corporate executives to profit from bad news and negative corporate developments as well as the good (thus creating perverse incentives on the part of management). See

Richard A. Posner and Kenneth E. Scott, Economics of Corporation Law and Securities Regulation 154 (1980).

- it encourages corporate executives and employees to keep secrets from each other thereby decreasing the firm's internal operational efficiency. See Robert J. Haft, The Effect of Insider Trading Rules on the Internal Efficiency of the Large Corporation, 80 Mich. L. Rev. 1051 (1982);
- it allows for rewards to all officials—even those who shirk responsibilities and are largely unproductive. See Iman Anabtawi, Note, Toward a Definition of Insider Trading, 41 Stan. L. Rev. 377, 392-93 (1989); and
- it hides from corporate shareholders the total benefits that are being received by management. See Robert C. Clark, Agency Costs Versus Fiduciary Duties 55, in Principals and Agents: The Structure of Business (John W. Pratt & Richard J. Zeckhauser eds., 1985).

b. The Effects of Insider Trading on Stock Market Price Efficiency

In addition to its value as potential compensation for corporate executives, the practice of insider trading has also been defended on the theory that it contributes to efficiency in stock market pricing. Professors Dennis Carlton and Daniel Fischel, two of the most prominent proponents of this "stock market efficiency" theory, advance the following argument:

> Since the firm's shareholders value the ability to control information that flows to the stock market, they may also value insider trading because it gives the firm an additional method of communicating and controlling information. If insiders trade, the share price will move closer to what it would have been had the information been disclosed. How close will depend on the amount of "noise" surrounding the trade. The greater the ability of market participants to identify insider trading, the more information such trading will convey. At the extreme, trading by insiders is as fully revealing as complete disclosure. But since insiders will limit the size of their positions because of risk aversion and will camouflage their trading to some degree, they convey less information by trading than that conveyed by (credible) full disclosure.
>
> Several reasons explain why communicating information through insider trading may be of value to the firm. Through insider trading, a firm can convey information it could not feasibly announce publicly because an announcement would destroy the value of the information, would be too expensive, not believable, or-owing to the uncertainty of the information-would subject the firm to massive damage liability if it turned out ex post to be incorrect. Conversely, firms also could use insider trading to limit the amount of information to be reflected in price. Controlling the number of traders who have access to information may be easier than controlling how much information gets announced over time. In other words, announcement of information need not be continuous, while trading on inside information can be. Thus, insider trading gives firms a tool either to increase or to decrease the amount of information that is contained in share prices.

Dennis W. Carlton and Daniel R. Fischel, The Regulation of Insider Trading, 35 Stan. L. Rev. 857, 868 (1983).

Critics of the "stock market efficiency" defense point out that insider trading is a highly inefficient way to impound information into a company's stock price. As Professor James Cox has argued:

> [c]ertainly price changes will occur more quickly and efficiently through disclosure of the material nonpublic information than through the manager's use of personal resources and time to trade in his firm's stock. The insider's trading simply has too much "noise" associated with it to be an efficient substitute for a clarion corporate announcement.

James D. Cox, Insider Trading and Contracting: A Critical Response to the "Chicago School." 1986 Duke L.J. 628, 646. Moreover, although widespread trading among insiders and their tippees would be more likely to produce a signaling effect than, as noted above, would individual and isolated trading, such widespread trading would expose the company to substantial risks in its internal operations.

Arguments about stock price efficiency have also been launched from the other direction. For example, Professor Schotland and others have argued that a ban on insider trading promotes efficiency by eliminating the personal profit incentive that otherwise would come from delaying disclosure of corporate events:

> Allowing any trading on undisclosed material information makes improper delay of disclosure more likely. We must not forget that if disclosure is improperly delayed, we cannot find out until all or at least some of the harm is done, and often we will not find out at all. To ensure timely disclosure—an end to which the SEC and the self-regulatory bodies are equally dedicated—it is obvious that we must avoid encouraging motivations for improper delay, however subconscious they may be. If we abandon restraints on insider trading, we tempt insiders to delay disclosure so that they can buy more shares or arrange financing for more buying; we also invite the timing of disclosure to get maximum market response. *** It is difficult enough to time disclosure properly for corporate reasons, without adding an extraneous, easily avoidable conflict of interest.

Roy Schotland, Unsafe at Any Price: A Reply to Manne, Insider Trading and the Stock Market, 53 Va. L. Rev. 1425, 1448-49 (1967).

Moreover, some argue that insider trading contributes to inefficient stock prices because it forces specialists and market makers to protect themselves by widening the spreads between their bid and ask prices. This argument was summarized succinctly by amici urging the Supreme Court's endorsement of the misappropriation theory:

> Trading in organized securities markets is usually effected through specialized intermediaries (e.g., market makers in dealer markets or specialists on the exchanges), who determine a bid-ask spread at which they trade with public customers. The width of the spread between the prices at which intermediaries will buy or sell (the bid-ask spread) is essentially a measure of the efficiency of the market for a security. While dealers and specialists are the initial victims of those who trade on misappropriated material nonpublic information, they pass this injury along to public customers through a widened bid-ask spread. To the extent it is foreseeable that people will trade with misappropriated material nonpublic information, intermediaries must protect themselves in advance by widening the bid-ask spread. Thus trading by those who misappropriate

> material nonpublic information for personal profit necessarily injures all public customers by decreasing the price at which they can sell to intermediaries (the bid) and increasing the price at which they can buy from intermediaries (the ask). Indeed, customers trading other securities will also be injured, because dealers cannot anticipate which securities will be traded by those in possession of material nonpublic information and will consequently widen the bid-ask spread for all securities that may be the subject of such information.

Amicus Curiae Brief of North Amer. Sec. Administrators Ass'n., Inc. and Law Professors in Support of Petitioner, at 8, *United States v. O'Hagan*, 521 U.S. 642 (1997) (No. 96-842).

The debate over stock market efficiency has taken yet another turn with several scholars advancing the view that insider trading serves as a useful signaling device that alerts capital markets to fraud and other corporate wrongdoings. See Jonathan R. Macey, Getting the Word Out About Fraud: A Theoretical Analysis of Whistleblowing and Insider Trading, 105 Mich. L. Rev. 1899, 1903 (2007) (contending that a "limited and tightly regulated ability to 'sell short' can credibly signal to the market that the trader has negative information about a company"); Bruce H. Kobayashi & Larry E. Ribstein, Outsider Trading as an Incentive Device, 40 U.C. Davis L. Rev. 21, 67-69 (2006) (contending that low-level employees and former employees would have greater incentives to report corporate wrongdoing if they could reap trading profits by selling or shorting the issuer's securities prior to blowing the whistle). For a critique of these arguments, see Robert A. Prentice & Dain C. Donelson, Insider Trading as a Signaling Device, 47 Am. Bus. L. J. 1, 59 (2010) (emphasizing that "[r]ewards or bounties carry several advantages over insider trading as incentive devices to encourage whistleblowing").

c. *Identifying the "Victims" of Insider Trading*

Clearly, one of the most contentious issues in the policy debate over insider trading involves the identification of actual victims. To be sure, the persons on the other side of an insider's transactions would not have traded at that same time and price had they known of the material nonpublic information in the insider's possession. But can these persons properly be thought of as "victims" of the insider trader? If such an insider had obeyed the law and simply abstained from trading, these contemporaneous traders would still have traded in ignorance, and still would have suffered financial damage when the company revealed the material nonpublic information. Thus, in this sense, it is difficult to regard those who traded with the insider as the victims of his unlawful act.

The above excerpt from the *O'Hagan* brief argues that everyone is in one sense a victim of insider trading to the extent that we all must trade in less efficient securities markets. Professor William Wang's "law of conservation of securities" provides an even more precise identification of the victims of insider trading.

STOCK MARKET INSIDER TRADING: VICTIMS, VIOLATORS AND REMEDIES—INCLUDING AN ANALOGY TO FRAUD IN THE SALE OF A USED CAR WITH A GENERIC DEFECT

by William K.S. Wang

45 Vill. L. Rev. 27, 28-38 (2000)

*** The presence of victims is important to the [insider trading] debate. Analogous to this issue is the controversy about regulating pornography. Some argue that pornography is a victimless crime. Others contend that pornography increases sex crimes or undermines respect for women. Whether pornography has victims does not resolve the question of how to regulate it. Nevertheless, society is more likely to regulate pornography strictly if it has victims. Similarly, whether insider trading is a victimless crime does not resolve the question of how to regulate it. Nevertheless, society is more likely to regulate insider trading strictly if it has victims.

In fact, each *act* of stock market insider trading has *specific* victims. This part of the Article will discuss the victims of the *act* of insider trading. These victims are those who would be better off, but for the *act* of insider trading. This part of the Article will not focus on the victims of the *nondisclosure* accompanying a stock market insider trade.

Assume that the outstanding number of shares of a company remains constant between the time of the insider trade and public disclosure. Let us focus on the shares outstanding at the time of public disclosure.

With an insider *purchase* of stock, the insider has more of that issue at public disclosure. Someone else must have less. That someone is worse off because of the insider trade.

With an insider *sale* of shares, the insider has less of that issue at public disclosure. Someone else must have more. That someone is worse off because of the insider trade.

Paraphrasing "the law of conservation of mass-energy," I call this phenomenon "the law of conservation of securities." I label as "trade victims" those harmed by the phenomenon of the "law of conservation of securities."

Who are those harmed by the phenomenon of the "law of conservation of securities"? The victims are those whose transactions were either preempted or induced by the insider trade. To paraphrase Milton Friedman, there is no such thing as a free insider trade.

To explain preempted and induced traders, I shall use an analogy to used cars. The used automobile market is roughly comparable to the securities market. Over the counter dealers, stock exchange specialists and large block positioning firms often trade stock for their own account with the public. All these market-makers are somewhat like used car dealers.

Many commentators assume that stock exchange transactions are anonymous. This is an oversimplification, at least with large block trades between an institutional investor and a block positioner. In fact, if Prudential Life Insurance Company wants to sell a large block of IBM stock, Prudential may sell to Goldman Sachs, a block positioner. Prudential and Goldman Sachs know each other's identity before, during and after the trade.

They could even ask each other questions before the transaction. At least conceivably, Goldman Sachs could ask Prudential: "Do you have any material, nonpublic information about IBM?" At least conceivably, Prudential might lie in response. In other words, much trading in New York Stock Exchange listed shares has aspects of face-to-face dealing. This strengthens the analogy between stock market and used car transactions.

To illustrate how induced and preempted stock traders are harmed by insider trading under the law of conservation of securities, I shall use two analogies to used car trading:

(1) the *solitary* defect hypothetical, and

(2) the *generic* defect hypothetical.

In the solitary defect hypothetical, only one automobile is a lemon. In contrast, in the generic defect situation, many individuals are buying and selling cars, *all* the same year model and *all* with the same defect. Even a slight change in price may dissuade or induce trading. Stock market insider trading resembles the *generic* defect used car hypothetical.

The *generic* defect used car analogy will demonstrate two points: First, each act of stock market insider trading has one or more particular victims. Second, these victims are anonymous. They exist, but, practically, cannot be identified.

I shall start with the *solitary* defect used car hypothetical. Suppose Mr. Greedie owns a 1998 Cadillac. He discovers that his particular automobile has a major defect. He goes to a car dealer and sells the car for the going price, $25,000.

Assume in the alternative that:

(1) the dealer does not ask Greedie about any defect, or

(2) the dealer asks Greedie about defects, and Greedie *lies*.

The dealer discovers the defect and is stuck with a lemon. The victim of Greedie's sale is clearly the dealer.

Suppose the dealer does not discover the defect and resells the car to Mr. Public Buyer. This resale is illustrated in Figure 1 below:

FIGURE 1:

SOLITARY DEFECT HYPOTHETICAL

(ONLY GREEDIE'S 1998 CADILLAC HAS DEFECT)

GREEDIE ————>	DEALER ————>	MR. PUBLIC BUYER,
SELLS LEMON TO	SELLS SAME LEMON TO	THE VICTIM

Assume that Mr. Public Buyer is now stuck with a lemon. Who is the victim of Greedie's sale? Only *one* 1998 Cadillac is a lemon. If Greedie had not sold his lemon to the dealer, the dealer would not have been able to resell the lemon to Mr. Public Buyer. The victim of Greedie's sale is Mr. Public Buyer.

Now, I shall turn to the generic defect example. (This hypothetical is analogous to stock market insider trading.)

Suppose Mr. Greedie is an employee of General Motors. Through his job at GM, Greedie receives material, nonpublic information that *all* 1998 Cadillacs have a major defect. By coincidence, Greedie personally owns a 1998 Cadillac. He immediately sells his Cadillac to a car dealer for the going price, $25,000.

Again, assume in the alternative that:
(1) the dealer does not ask Greedie about any defect, or
(2) the dealer asks Greedie about defects, and Greedie *lies*.

When GM announces the news of the defect to the public, the price of the 1998 Cadillac falls by $10,000. Greedie is clearly better off.

Who is the victim of Greedie's sale? Who in the universe would be better off had Greedie not sold? Is it the car dealer who bought the Cadillac? The answer is not necessarily.

Suppose, *without changing its prices*, the dealer resold Greedie's Cadillac to Mr. Public Buyer before announcement of the defect. Mr. Public Buyer is stuck with the lemon after the announcement.

Nevertheless, Mr. Public Buyer is also not necessarily the victim of Greedie's sale. *All* 1998 Cadillacs are lemons, although only Greedie knows this. Had Mr. Public Buyer not bought Greedie's car, he might have purchased *another* 1998 Cadillac.

These transactions are illustrated in Figure 2 below:

FIGURE 2:

GENERIC DEFECT HYPOTHETICAL

(ALL 1998 CADILLACS HAVE THE SAME DEFECT)

GREEDIE ————>	DEALER ————>	MR. PUBLIC BUYER,
SELLS LEMON TO	WITH *NO CHANGE IN PRICE*, DEALER SELLS SAME LEMON TO	NOT NECESSARILY THE VICTIM

What is the difference between this *generic* defect hypothetical and the *solitary* defect hypothetical? In the *solitary* defect hypothetical, Greedie's car was the only one with the defect. In the *solitary* defect hypothetical, had Greedie not sold his Cadillac, and had Mr. Public Buyer bought another 1998 Cadillac, Mr. Public Buyer would have been *better off*.

In the *generic* defect hypothetical, *all* 1998 Cadillacs have the same defect. Innocent individuals without Greedie's information compete with Greedie to sell 1998 Cadillacs with the same defect. Had Greedie *not* sold his Cadillac, and had Mr. Public Buyer bought another 1998 Cadillac instead of Greedie's, Mr. Public Buyer would have been *equally worse off*.

This phenomenon has prompted some commentators to conclude that each act of insider trading has *no* specific victims. This conclusion is wrong.

In the *generic defect* example, the insider trade has a specific victim. Identifying this victim is easier if we assume that the dealer does not sell Greedie's automobile to Mr. Public Buyer and still owns Greedie's car at the time of public disclosure (as illustrated in Figure 3 below).

FIGURE 3:

THE VICTIM IN THE GENERIC DEFECT HYPOTHETICAL (ASSUME THAT DEALER STILL OWNS GREEDIE'S CAR AT TIME OF PUBLIC DISCLOSURE)

GREEDIE ———>	DEALER,
SELLS LEMON TO	MAY OR MAY NOT BE VICTIM DEPENDING ON SIZE OF INVENTORY AT DISCLOSURE
DEALER MAY *LOWER PRICES*, AND	*MAY* INDUCE MR. POTENTIAL TO BUY ANOTHER 1998 CADILLAC (INDUCED BUYER);
OR	*MAY* DISSUADE MS. MARGINAL FROM SELLING (PREEMPTED SELLER)

Even if the dealer still owns Greedie's car at the time of the public announcement of the defect, the dealer is not necessarily the victim of Greedie's sale. Prior to public disclosure, the dealer *may* have passed the harm to someone else.

The dealer desires a certain inventory level. Because of Greedie's sale, the dealer's inventory of 1998 Cadillacs increased. The dealer sets a price at which it will purchase a car *from* the public. The dealer sets a *higher* price at which it will sell *to* the public. In an attempt to reduce inventory, the dealer may have slightly reduced both its buying and selling prices for 1998 Cadillacs.

Assume that Mr. Potential was interested in purchasing a 1998 Cadillac. The lower price *may* have induced him to buy *another* 1998 Cadillac (other than Greedie's) from the dealer. All 1998 Cadillacs have the same defect. As an induced purchaser, Mr. Potential may be the victim of Greedie's sale.

Alternatively, assume that Ms. Marginal owned a 1998 Cadillac and was thinking about selling her automobile. The lower price *may* have dissuaded her from selling the car to the dealer. She may still hold the car at the time of the public announcement of the defect. As a *preempted* seller, Ms. Marginal may be the victim of Greedie's sale.

What is the difference between this generic defect hypothetical and the solitary defect hypothetical? In the *solitary* defect situation, Greedie's automobile was the only one with the defect. In the *solitary* defect hypothetical, if the dealer owned Greedie's particular car at discovery of the defect, the dealer was worse off. *The size of the dealer's total inventory of 1998 Cadillacs at discovery of the solitary defect was not relevant.*

In the *generic* defect hypothetical, *all* 1998 Cadillacs have the defect.

The size of the dealer's inventory of 1998 Cadillacs at public disclosure is crucial. The size of the inventory determines the dealer's damage.

The dealer is only worse off as a result of Greedie's sale if his sale causes the dealer's inventory at disclosure to be higher than it otherwise would have been. Initially, Greedie's sale increased the dealer's inventory. Nevertheless, the dealer may have *decreased* its inventory by lowering prices. The dealer *may* have shifted the harm to a preempted seller or induced buyer.

In practice, identifying the preempted seller or induced buyer is impossible. In order to identify the victim, one must determine the prices the dealer would have charged absent Greedie's sale. Then, one must ascertain how the public would have reacted to these prices. This information is unknowable. Nevertheless, the victim still exists.

At the time of the defect's announcement, there are a fixed number of 1998 Cadillacs. If Greedie has one less Cadillac at the time of the announcement, someone else must have one more. That someone is the victim of Greedie's sale. I call this "the law of conservation of used automobiles."

If the sale of one car on inside information to the car dealer causes even a slight lowering of the dealer's prices for 1998 Cadillacs, that decline may dissuade or induce a transaction. If the dealer's prices do not change (or if the price declines fail to dissuade or induce a trade), the loss falls on the automobile dealer (an induced buyer). Under the "law of conservation of used automobiles," Greedie's sale *must* induce a purchase or preempt a sale.

Only one victim exists: either a preempted seller, like Ms. Marginal, or an induced buyer, like Mr. Potential or the dealer. The loss is not spread among a large number of victims. The price decline after disclosure falls on this *one* victim; that loss corresponds to Greedie's gain.

The law of conservation of used automobiles is similar to the law of conservation of *securities*. Each stock market insider trade has one or more specific victims, either induced and/or preempted traders.

One may make the following objection. Suppose an innocent individual fortuitously sells *stock* in advance of an announcement of adverse, material information. Under the law of conservation of securities, does not this innocent sale also cause harm? Does not this innocent sale either preempt a sale or induce a purchase? The answer is yes.

Clearly, society will not impose liability on traders who *unknowingly*, fortuitously make advantageous trades prior to public disclosure. Therefore, causing harm under the law of conservation of securities is not *sufficient* in itself to impose liability.

Unlike innocent traders, however, stock market insider traders *knowingly* profit by taking advantage of others. This difference alone may or may not be sufficient to impose liability. (Suppose an analyst discovers material nonpublic information about a corporation through diligent outside research with no contact with company employees. If the analyst's firm traded on this information, the transaction would harm preempted or induced traders. Nevertheless, the analyst and the firm might not be liable.)

One analogy is to but-for causation and proximate causation. The law of conservation of securities demonstrates that the insider trade is a *but-for* cause of injury to specific victims. Whether the insider trade is a *proximate* cause of harm is a separate issue. Nevertheless, if the insider trade is not even a but-for cause of injury, liability is much less likely. As mentioned earlier, as with pornography, whether insider trading has victims, affects, but does not resolve the question of how strictly to regulate it.

The analysis above deals with the specific ex post victims of a stock market insider trade. What are *some* of the broader possible adverse effects of insider trading?

If the public becomes aware of insider trading, the prices of stocks generally may decline (although estimating the risk may be difficult). If the employees of a *particular* corporation acquire a reputation for trading on nonpublic information, that specific company's stock may decline in price. *Such declines would increase the cost of capital of particular companies or of publicly traded corporations generally.*

Ex ante, these price decreases might partially compensate new buyers for the risk of being victims of stock market insider trading (although, as mentioned earlier, estimating the risk would be difficult). Nevertheless, ex post the harm of insider trading would not be spread equally. An insider trade has arbitrary, but specific victims. These victims are *disproportionately* harmed by the trade. (Some victims, preempted buyers, may never own stock in the issuer.)

Even ex ante, a decline in the price of all publicly traded stocks (or of a particular stock) would not adequately compensate all investors for the risk of being victims of a stock market insider trade. This risk of harm is associated with the act of trading (or of *almost* trading, in the case of a preempted trader). Consequently, the risk varies with the frequency of one's trades (or "near trades").

Even if the return on all publicly traded stocks (or of a particular stock) were slightly higher because of the risk of harm from insider trading, the higher return would not adequately compensate *frequent* traders for incurring that risk. Nor would risk-averse investors who trade *often* be able to diversify away the risk of becoming a victim.

In short, ex post, victims of a stock market insider trade are *disproportionately* injured even if they originally purchased their stock at a price that accurately reflected the possibility of insider trading. Even ex ante, frequent traders definitely suffer harm from insider trading.

To analogize, suppose apartment rents in one neighborhood are slightly lower because a small percentage of arbitrarily chosen residents will be mugged and/or assaulted. Ex post, the unfortunate victims suffer disproportionately and are only minimally compensated by the lower rents. Ex ante, residents who take walks often are not adequately compensated because they take more risk than others. ***

d. Investor Confidence in Securities Markets

As we saw in Section C of this Chapter, the policy argument that has seemed to carry the day with at least a majority of the Supreme Court is that insider trading "'undermines the integrity of, and investor confidence in, the securities markets.'" See *O'Hagan* at 658 (quoting the Government's brief). See also id. at 653 ("the misappropriation theory is ... designed to protec[t] the integrity of the securities markets against abuses by 'outsiders' to a corporation who have access to confidential information that will affect th[e] corporation's security price when revealed"); id. at 658 (observing that "investors likely would hesitate to venture their capital in a market where trading based on misappropriated nonpublic information is unchecked by law").

Congress also invoked investor confidence and market integrity arguments as the principal justification for enhancing the sanctions available to the government in insider trading cases. See H. Rep. No. 98-355, ITSA, at 2 (noting that "[c]apital formation and our nation's economic growth and stability depend on investor confidence in the fairness and integrity of our capital markets" and that "[i]nsider trading threatens these markets by undermining the public's expectations of honest and fair securities markets where all participants play by the same rules"). These congressional sentiments were echoed four years later with the enactment of ITSFEA:

> [T]he far greater number of commentators support efforts to curb insider trading, viewing such efforts as crucial to the capital formation process that depends on investor confidence in the fairness and integrity of our securities markets. Insider trading damages the legitimacy of the capital market and diminishes the public's faith. The investing public has a legitimate expectation that the prices of actively traded securities reflect publicly available information about the issuer of such securities. *** [T]he small investor will be—and has been—reluctant to invest in the market if he feels it is rigged against him.

H. Rep. No. 100-910 at 8.

Critics of the "investor confidence/market integrity" rationale have a variety of counter arguments. Some highlight its lack of empirical support. See, e.g., Dennis S. Karjala, Statutory Regulation of Insider Trading in Impersonal Markets, 1982 Duke L.J. 627, 629 (noting that a formula to measure loss of investor confidence does not exist). Others argue that if insider trading were legal, investors could easily protect themselves by discounting the price they are willing to pay for shares in companies that allow insider trading. In other words, "if the existence of insider trading is known, *** outsiders will not be disadvantaged because the price they pay will reflect the risk of insider trading." Carlton & Fischel, supra, 35 Stan. L. Rev. at 881. Still others say that the investor confidence rationale is undercut by the experiences of other countries such as Japan, India, and Hong Kong, all of which have very active stock markets but insider trading prohibitions and enforcement provisions that are quite lax. See, e.g., Jonathan R. Macey, Insider Trading: Economics, Politics, and Policy 44 (1991). There is, however, recent empirical evidence demonstrating that countries with more prohibitive insider trading laws generally have more dispersed equity ownership, more informative stock prices, and more liquid stock markets. See Laura N. Beny, Insider Trading Laws and Stock Markets Around the World: An Empirical Contribution to the Theoretical Law and Economics Debate, 32 J. Corp. L. 237, 240 (2007) (reporting results using financial, legal and institutional data from a cross-section of thirty-three countries).

e. *Fairness and Morality*

Of course, there are those who urge the regulation of insider trading principally as a matter of fairness and morality. Indeed, as a former Chairman of the SEC once remarked: "[t]he American people see it, bluntly, as a form of cheating." Arthur Levitt, A Question of Integrity: Promoting Investor Confidence By Fighting Insider Trading, Vital Speeches of the Day, Vol. LXIV, 354, 355 (April 1, 1998). See also Robert C. Clark, Corporate Law 271 (1986) (bemoaning that "many people, including judges and legislators, feel no need to say anything [other than] *** it is simply *** unfair for some investors (insiders and their tip[p]ees) to have preferential access to information").

But there have also been very thoughtful arguments against insider trading advanced from perspectives of fairness and morality. Professor Kim Lane Scheppele, for example, uses "contractarian ethics" to support her "equality of access" approach to the regulation of insider trading, an approach similar to the one advanced by Justice Blackmun in his dissent in *Chiarella*. Professor Scheppele explains that:

> Equal access to information is the moral concept on which a prohibition on insider trading would be grounded. When one person has special knowledge and nonetheless trades with those who do not, the offense is not just that a secret is kept. The offense lies in the fact that the secret is withheld under conditions in which those with whom the secret-keeper trades cannot discover the information as easily (or, *** as legally) as those who have the secret information. The target of the secret and the secret-keeper do not have *equal access* to information, and that is the problem.
>
> Consider the following hypothetical. If an insider were to trade with another insider, few would have moral qualms about the transaction. Under those circumstances, the two parties to the deal would be on equal footing; such equality of access to information underwrites the moral argument about secret-keeping. But the contractarian argument reveals what is wrong when insiders trade with those who do not have *access* to knowledge equal to theirs (not equal knowledge), particularly where the insiders trade using deep secrets. People would not agree to be part of a system where their disadvantage in access to knowledge could be turned into disadvantages in the distribution of other resources. They might be willing to take their chances on a system that required them to work as hard as anyone else at acquiring this knowledge, but they would not be willing to enter into transactions with people who are clearly advantaged relative to them at the starting point. When insiders trade with people who are in no position, or a distinctly disadvantageous position, to acquire the information that the insiders now want to use, the insiders should have an obligation to disclose the information or refrain from trading with these unequal trading partners.
>
> This obligation should extend not just to those unproblematically thought to be insiders, like officers and directors employed by a particular firm, but also to anyone whose position gives them special *access* to knowledge that others cannot acquire. In the complicated world of corporate transactions, an insider should be considered to be any person whose position allows access to information unavailable to those with whom the insider is interacting. This does not mean that all traders must have equal information; rather, all traders should face *roughly equal search costs* in locating relevant information. Without

> such a level playing field at the start, it is unlikely that rational consenters would agree to such rules in advance. After all, why should one sign onto a system in which one may be permanently disadvantaged? It is the *structural* imbalance in access to information, as Justice Blackmun started to argue in *Chiarella*, that gives rise to the duty to disclose. This argument is grounded not only in existing equitable rules about fair dealing that courts have long invoked in determining fraud, but also in contractarian ethics.

Kim Lane Scheppele, "It's Just Not Right:" The Ethics of Insider Trading, 56 Law & Contemp. Probs. 123, 162-63 (Summer 1993).

Reasoned moral arguments against the practice of insider trading can also be found in Alan Strudler and Eric W. Orts, Moral Principle in the Law of Insider Trading, 78 Tex. L. Rev. 375, 383 (1999) (maintaining that the "hard problems in insider trading law are paradigmatically moral, such as whether nondisclosure of material nonpublic information deprives a participant in a public securities market of the ability to make an autonomous choice, or whether an inside securities trader uses information that is stolen, converted to an improper use, or otherwise morally tainted").

f. Protecting Private Property

One additional policy justification for the regulation of insider trading merits our close attention. It involves the very valuable role that information plays in our society and the harms that would flow from a legal system's failure to protect a corporation's right to the information it produces.

INSIDER TRADING REGULATION: THE PATH DEPENDENT CHOICE BETWEEN PROPERTY RIGHTS AND SECURITIES FRAUD

by Stephen M. Bainbridge

52 S.M.U. L. Rev. 1589, 1606-08 (1999)

*** There is a growing consensus that the federal insider trading prohibition is more easily justified as a means of protecting property rights in information than as a way of protecting investors. As I have elsewhere defended in some detail, a property rights-based approach to insider trading regulation, a brief recapitulation will suffice here. Consider the prototypical insider trading transaction, in which an insider trades in her employer's stock on the basis of information learned solely because of her position with the firm. The property right must be assigned to either the corporation or the inside trader. A rule allowing insider trading assigns the property right to the insider, while a rule prohibiting insider trading assigns it to the corporation.

The rationale for assigning the property right to the firm is precisely the same as the rationale for prohibiting patent infringement or theft of trade secrets: protecting the economic incentive to produce socially valuable information. As the theory goes, the readily appropriable nature of information makes it difficult for the developer of a new idea to recoup the sunk costs incurred in developing it. For example, if an inventor develops a better mousetrap, he cannot profit on that invention without selling mousetraps and thereby making the new design available to potential competitors. Assuming both the inventor and his competitors incur roughly equivalent marginal costs to produce and market the trap, the competitors will be able to set a market price at which the inventor will likely be unable to earn a return on his sunk costs. *Ex post*, the rational inventor should ignore his sunk costs and go on producing the improved mousetrap. *Ex ante*, however, the inventor will anticipate that he will be unable to generate positive returns on his up-front costs, and therefore will be deterred from developing socially valuable information. As Judge Ralph Winter explained in his separate opinion in *United States v. Chestman*:

> Information is ... expensive to produce, and, because it involves facts and ideas that can be easily photocopied or carried in one's head, there is a ubiquitous risk that those who pay to produce information will see others reap the profit from it. Where the profit from an activity is likely to be diverted, investment in that activity will decline. If the law fails to protect property rights in commercial information, therefore, less will be invested in generating such information. [947 F.2d 551, 576-77 (2d Cir. 1991) (Winter, J., concurring in part and dissenting in part)]

Accordingly, society provides incentives for inventive activity by using the patent system to give inventors a property right in new ideas. By preventing competitors from appropriating the idea, the patent allows the inventor to charge monopolistic prices for the improved mousetrap, thereby recouping his sunk costs. Trademark, copyright, and trade secret law are all justified on similar grounds.

Granted, this argument may not provide quite as compelling a justification for the insider trading prohibition as it does for the patent system. Legalizing insider trading would likely have a much smaller impact on the corporation's incentive to develop new information than would, say, legalizing patent infringement. It seems plausible, however, that insider trading will have at least some impact on the incentive to produce new information. Again, Judge Winter explains:

> [I]nsider trading creates a risk that information will be prematurely disclosed by such trading, and the corporation will lose part or all of its property in that information. Although trades by an insider may rarely affect market price, others who know of the insider's trading may notice that a trader is unusually successful, or simply perceive unusual activity in a stock and guess the information and/or make piggyback trades. A broker who executes a trade for [an insider] may well draw relevant conclusions. Or, as in the instant matter, the trader . . . may tell his or her broker about the inside information, who may then trade on his or her account, on clients' accounts, or may tell friends and relatives. One inside trader has publicly attributed his exposure in part to the fact that the bank through which he made trades piggybacked on the trades, as did the broker who made the trades for the bank. Once activity in a stock reaches an unusual stage, others may guess the reason for the trading—the corporate secret. Insider trading thus increases the risk that confidential information acquired at a cost may be disclosed. If so, the owner of the information may lose its investment. [*U.S. v. Libera*, 947 F. 2d 551, 577-78 (2d Cir. 1991) (Winter, J., concurring in part and dissenting in part)].

Even if one is skeptical that insider trading poses the sort of threats Winter identifies, the affirmative case for assigning the property right to the corporation is demonstrably stronger than the one for assigning it to the insider, as I have explained elsewhere. The law, therefore, should assume (although the assumption may sometimes be wrong) that assigning the property right to the firm maximizes the social incentives for the production of valuable new information.

There are essentially two ways of assigning a property right to information: (1) allowing the owner to enter into transactions without disclosing the information; or (2) prohibiting others from using the information. In effect, the federal insider trading prohibition vests a property right of the latter type in the owner of nonpublic information. To be sure, enforcement of the insider trading prohibition differs rather dramatically from enforcement of, say, trespassing laws. In context, however, the prohibition's enforcement mechanisms are not inconsistent with a property rights analysis. Where public policy argues for giving someone a property right, but the costs of enforcing such a right would be excessive, the state often uses its regulatory powers as a substitute for granting a property right. Insider trading poses such a situation. Private enforcement of the insider trading laws is rare and usually parasitic on public enforcement proceedings. Indeed, *** the very nature of insider trading makes public regulation essential precisely because private enforcement is almost impossible. The insider trading prohibition's regulatory nature thus need not preclude a property rights-based analysis. ***

In addition to Professor Bainbridge, other notable law and economics scholars, including Judge Frank Easterbrook and Professor Jonathan Macey, have endorsed the private property rationale for regulating insider trading. But the rationale has also been criticized:

> The property rights theory appeals to those who believe that securities regulation should be predicated on principles of economics, rather than on principles of fairness. However, the federal securities laws were based on the principle that when an issuer goes public, investors are entitled to information about its business and affairs. The easiest criticism of the property rights theory is that when Congress passed and subsequently amended the Exchange Act, it was concerned about fairness and the protection of investors, not the protection of property rights in information held by issuers and traders. Protecting the source of confidential information is illogical when the parties injured by traders possessing informational advantages are those who purchase or sell securities without access to the material information. Further, the property rights theory seems to be concerned with interests in information that are generally protected by state law. The federal securities laws impose disclosure duties on issuers, bidders, and other market participants and the insider trading laws should be viewed as a means to enforce the investing public's right to this information.

Roberta S. Karmel, Outsider Trading on Confidential Information—A Breach in Search of a Duty, 20 Cardozo L. Rev. 83, 112-13 (1998). More specifically, Professor Karmel proposes that:

> the ban on insider trading be related to the disclosure obligations of issuers, bidders, and other market participants under the federal securities laws, as a means to enforce those obligations and accelerate the release of material information. Although the ban is regulatory, its necessity arises from gaps in the disclosure system administered by the SEC, gaps that can only be filled by the disclose or abstain doctrine.

Id. at 113. Professor Karmel contends that this link between the insider trading prohibition and the mandatory disclosure provision in the federal securities laws "seems self-evident." Yet, in her view, "the SEC, the courts, and the commentators seem to have become so bogged down in the details of the misappropriation theory, as well as other theories, that they have overlooked [this] basic rationale ***." Id. at 133. For additional critique of the property rights rationale, see Kimberly D. Krawiec, Fairness, Efficiency, and Insider Trading: Deconstructing the Coin of the Realm in the Information Age, 95 Nw. U.L. Rev. 443 (2001) (situating insider trading regulation within the larger body of intellectual property law).

2. The Debate Over a Statutory Definition of Insider Trading

Despite numerous calls to do so, Congress has not provided a statutory definition of insider trading. Some of its reasons for failing to act are set forth in the material that follows.

U.S. HOUSE REPORT, ENERGY AND COMMERCE COMMITTEE, INSIDER TRADING SANCTIONS ACT OF 1984

No. 98-355 at 13-14

September 15, 1983

Because insider trading is pursued under the broad anti-fraud provisions of the federal securities laws, some witnesses suggested that the Committee should add to the legislation specific language defining the scope of the violation for purposes of the triple penalty provided by the legislation. They suggested that judicial interpretations have not provided clear boundaries of acceptable conduct and that the case-by-case approach, while appropriate for a remedial sanction such as an injunction, would not be appropriate for the civil penalty provided under the legislation.

Others testified that a definition of insider trading would not be desirable. For example, Arnold S. Jacobs testified that hundreds of cases clarify the insider trading prohibition of Rule 10b-5. He noted that: "As with any broad anti-fraud remedy, the fringes of what constitutes the prohibited act are occasionally fuzzy. This, however, does not justify placing a definition in the bill; unscrupulous traders would skirt around any definition constructed." He warned: "Even if H.R. 559 were redrafted to include a caveat that any definition of insider trading contained in H.R. 559 is not to be applied to private rights of action or actions by the SEC for injunctions, it is highly probable that any definition in H.R. 559 (although limited by its terms to the triple-profit sanctions) would become the definition for all purposes of the federal securities laws...."

The Committee believes that the law with respect to insider trading is sufficiently well-developed at this time to provide adequate guidance. Further, the Committee believes that the Commission has used its broad rulemaking authority to respond to marketplace developments; that the adoption of a statutory definition could reduce flexibility; and that any new definition which might be adopted would be likely to create new ambiguities, thereby increasing rather than limiting uncertainty.

The deliberations of the American Law Institute and the American Bar Association Securities Law Committee in drafting the Proposed Federal

Securities Code are also instructive on this point. Those deliberations were publicly and democratically conducted over a period of 12 years under conditions where every segment of the securities bar was thoroughly involved. The result was sections 1602(a)(1) and 1603 of the Code as supplemented by definitional and remedial provisions. The conclusion was that hard-core insider trading could be vaguely defined in section 1603 but that all other types of questionable conduct involving illicit misappropriation of market and insider information must be left to the courts which must determine whether the particular conduct amounts to a "fraudulent act" or a "misrepresentation" under Section 1602(a)(1). Comment 3(d) to section 1603 states, after full analysis, "this area must be left to further judicial development."

Hence, evidence seems to show that any effort to define insider trading would result in, at best, a slightly less generalized rule than 10b-5 and, at worst, a rule that leaves gaping holes, previously referred to in hearings on the Code as "large enough to drive a truck through."

Further, the clarification made to the scope of the persons liable for the penalty answers the definitional concerns of some commentators. Finally, the Committee believes that the adoption of a definition (which would inevitably affect to some degree the substantive law) is not necessary to achieve the basic purpose of the bill: to increase the sanctions available under the law as it now exists and as it continues to evolve.

Since the seminal cases of *In re Cady, Roberts & Co.*, and *SEC v. Texas Gulf Sulphur Co.*, it has been clear that trading by corporate officials and employees on information gained in their employment violates fiduciary duties and violates the federal securities laws. These cases and their progeny do not, however, proscribe legitimate business communications. The Committee does not intend that the legislation reach legitimate business transactions.

U.S. HOUSE REPORT, ENERGY AND COMMERCE COMMITTEE, INSIDER TRADING AND SECURITIES FRAUD ENFORCEMENT ACT

No. 100-910 at 10-11

September 9, 1988

The Committee clearly has recognized the continuing concern over a definition of insider trading. The securities bar and the Congress have debated this issue for a number of years, including during consideration of the adoption of the Insider Trading Sanctions Act of 1984. During this Congress, such definitional questions have been the focus of much attention in Senate inquiries on this subject.

While cognizant of the importance of providing clear guidelines for behavior which may be subject to stiff criminal and civil penalties, the Committee nevertheless declined to include a statutory definition in this bill for several reasons. First, the Committee believed that the court-drawn parameters of insider trading have established clear guidelines for the vast majority of traditional insider trading cases, and that a statutory definition could potentially be narrowing, and in an unintended manner facilitate schemes to evade the law. Second, the Committee did not believe that the lack of consensus over the proper delineation of an insider trading definition should impede progress on the needed enforcement reforms encompassed within this legislation. Accordingly, the Committee does not intend to alter the substantive law with respect to insider trading with this legislation. The legal principles governing insider trading cases are well- established and widely-known.

Consider this call by one of your casebook authors for a congressional definition of insider trading.

DON'T ASK, JUST TELL: INSIDER TRADING AFTER *UNITED STATES V. O'HAGAN*

by Richard W. Painter, Kimberly D. Krawiec, and Cynthia A. Williams

84 Va. L. Rev. 153, 211-12, 219-228 (1998)

Virtually every other country that has joined the United States in prohibiting trading on the basis of material, nonpublic information has done so through statutes that define with specificity such terms as "insider" and "inside information" as well as the circumstances in which trading is prohibited. The United Kingdom, for example, enacted a specific prohibition in 1980, Italy did so in 1991, and Germany followed in 1994. The United States stands alone in allowing judges to develop a common law prohibition against insider trading, and now against trading on the basis of misappropriated information, from a general antifraud statute that does not even mention insiders, inside information, insider trading, or misappropriation. The Supreme Court's analysis, or perhaps lack of analysis, of Section 10(b) in *Chiarella*, *Dirks*, and now *O'Hagan*, makes a compelling case that the United States should abandon its common law approach to trading on material, nonpublic information and follow Europe***

[A]s the Commission has begun more vigorously to enforce insider trading prohibitions over the last fifteen years, and as the penalties for such trading have been enhanced, the ABA's Task Force on the Regulation of Insider Trading and others have called on Congress to specify when trading on material, nonpublic information is illegal, so far without success.

In spite of its reluctance to act, Congress may be the best institution to make these determinations. Trading on inside and misappropriated information is a complex area of law that has engendered an outpouring of scholarship and disagreement. Much of the disagreement arises from a lack of consensus among scholars, regulators, and judges about the purpose to be served by regulation. The numerous possible purposes include protection of investors, prevention of unfair information asymmetries in trading transactions, promotion of confidence in the market, promotion of disclosure, prevention of fraud, protection of proprietary information, enforcement of fiduciary duties, or some combination of the foregoing purposes. As Professor Louis Loss and Dean Joel Seligman have emphasized, a legislative determination "could address a fundamental question that the Supreme Court believed that it could not: whether a legislative approach ought to be limited to a fraud rubric?"[264] A legislative determination, like a formal SEC rulemaking procedure, also offers the advantage of public participation to develop a consensus on the purposes of the regulation.

Moreover, Congress can define prohibited trading on material, nonpublic information in a systematic way, in the context of the federal securities laws as a whole, so the development of the law will not depend on the serendipity of what cases happen to arise after *O'Hagan*. To be sure, Congress's failure to define insider trading in 1988, even after the SEC finally endorsed a proposed definition, does not bode well for congressional action now, notwithstanding *O'Hagan*. And yet there are any number of approaches Congress could take that would have the benefits of logical consistency and clarity not now found in this area of law.

For instance, Congress could establish a pre-*United States v. Chiarella* equality of access approach, even for outsiders, and then carve out exceptions, if necessary, for securities analysts and perhaps others who are perceived to benefit securities markets through their use of nonpublic information. This is the approach Joel Seligman advocated after *Dirks v. Securities and Exchange Commission* and *Chiarella*.[269] His proposal suggested a general prohibition on trading while in possession of material, nonpublic information modeled on the *Securities and Exchange Commission v. Texas Gulf Sulphur Co.* approach, with certain provisions to "harmonize the new standard with other parts of the securities law." [Id. at 1138]. Those provisions included 1) an exception for potential acquirers prior to their acquisition of five percent of the target, necessary to parallel the Williams Act; 2) a legitimization of the "Chinese wall" defense for securities firms, whereby traders can continue to buy and sell the securities of issuers that have provided their underwriting departments with material, nonpublic information, so long as firm procedures are adequate to prevent information from leaking from the underwriters to the traders; 3) recognition that securities analysts could continue to search out immaterial, nonpublic information and make recommendations on the basis of that information; and 4) permission for "stock or options exchange specialists, market-makers or floor traders to trade while in possession of material nonpublic information about trading activity on the floor of an exchange to the extent . . . permitted by section 11 of the Securities Exchange Act or Stock Exchange rules." [Id.]

A somewhat narrower approach was suggested by Professor Victor Brudney: a ban on trading based on "unerodable informational advantages."[276] Professor Brudney recognized that allocative efficiency goals are furthered by

---

264. Louis Loss & Joel Seligman, 8 Securities Regulation 3763 (3d ed. 1991). The "alternative approach would involve simply prohibiting certain undesirable practices the same way that wash sales and certain short sales are prohibited." Id.

269. Joel Seligman, "The Reformulation of Federal Securities Law Concerning Nonpublic Information," 73 Geo. L.J. 1083 (1985).

276. Victor Brudney, "Insiders, Outsiders, and Informational Advantages Under the Federal Securities Laws," 93 Harv. L. Rev. 322, 326-39 (1979).

providing incentives for outsiders to search for relevant corporate and economic information; thus people ought to be able to benefit from the informational advantages that their searches provide by freely trading on such advantages. Professor Brudney's suggestion therefore does not follow a pure equality of access approach. Yet he argued that the law should "deny an informational advantage to those who seek to use otherwise nonpublic information which they are precluded by legal restrictions from disclosing to public investors" or which the public cannot lawfully acquire, notwithstanding diligent effort. [Id. at 355-56].

Professor Jill Fisch has suggested a still narrower approach, one that focuses on the duties of insiders to the market, particularly disclosure duties.[280] Her proposal concentrates on defining the insider class, since the harm to be prevented by insider trading regulation is "not only superior access to information but also the opportunity [by insiders] to manipulate the timing and quality of [market] disclosure" to capitalize on informational advantages. [Id. at 239-40] Professor Fisch's insiders would include "primary insiders" such as officers, directors, and ten percent stockholders, and "secondary insiders" such as lower-level employees and outsiders such as lawyers and investment bankers who have irregular access to material, nonpublic information. Both categories would be prohibited from trading or tipping while in possession of material, nonpublic information obtained by virtue of their status as an insider.

In addition, Congress could look either to the detailed codes adopted in Great Britain and Germany or to the insider trading provisions of the Federal Securities Code, developed over ten years by the ALI under the guidance of Louis Loss, but never enacted into law.[285] Professor Loss's Code set out a specific provision prohibiting insider trading, while recognizing that Section 10(b)'s broad antifraud analogue stood available as a backstop in the event a particular egregious case did not fall within the parameters of the insider trading section. Section 1603 of the Securities Code endorsed an abstain or disclose rule for insiders who know "fact[s] of special significance" concerning the issuer or the security, while defining insiders broadly, to include any "person who, by virtue of his relationship or former relationship to the issuer, knows a fact of special significance about the issuer or the security in question that is not generally available." This formulation does not ground liability by reference to a fiduciary relationship or a relationship of trust and confidence with the issuer. Rather, any passage of material, inside information, coupled with any relationship with the issuer, suffices as a basis to impose a duty to abstain from trading. This provision thus avoids the complexities inherent in importing a separate body of law—that of fiduciary duty—into the insider trading prohibition. Moreover, this formulation more directly addresses concerns of inappropriate information asymmetries among investors than does the misappropriation theory. The latter does not reach outsiders' trading on inside information in the absence of a fiduciary relationship, nor under *O'Hagan,* does it reach outsiders who disclose

---

280. Jill E. Fisch, "Start Making Sense: An Analysis and Proposal for Insider Trading Regulation," 26 Ga. L. Rev. 179, 238-39 (1991).

285. Fed. Sec. Code §§ 1602, 1603 (1978).

to the principal their intention to trade. Although Section 1603 is animated by policy concerns closer to the equality of access theory, by imposing disclosure duties only on insiders, even as broadly defined, Section 1603 specifically disclaims complete equality of access among investors.

Congress may conclude, however, that Section 1603 is only a starting place. As Professor Loss recognized, a category of outsiders remains, who are not reached by Section 1603's definition. Congress may determine that:

> It would be convenient to have a new category of 'quasi-insider' that would cover people like (i) judges' clerks who trade on information in unpublished opinions, (ii) Federal Reserve Bank employees who trade with knowledge of an imminent change in the margin rate, [and] (iii) printers of tender offer literature who buy the target company's stock . . . [Id. §1603 cmt. d.]

Professor Loss was concerned that this quasi-insider category would be difficult to define. Perhaps, though, with Section 1603 as a starting point, and given the existence of Rule 14e-3 in the tender offer context, Congress could work to define the quasi-insider category with substantially more precision than the courts have used in defining the misappropriation theory. Indeed, the fact that this quasi-insider category is difficult to define with precision is a strong argument for Congress to undertake the task rather than leave it to the courts.

One aspect of the ALI approach, which was echoed in 1985 by the ABA Task Force on Regulation of Insider Trading, is avoiding reliance on the law of fraud altogether, and instead simply prohibiting specific types of conduct.[294] This approach recognizes that the misuse of informational advantages is an analytically different problem than fraud, and that regulating the former through an approach designed for the latter is problematic:

> Because section 10(b) of the 1934 Act is an antifraud rather than an unfair-trading provision, any rulemaking initiative based on section 10(b), whether an expansion of present rule 10b-5 or a new rule aimed specifically at abuse of informational advantages like rule 14e-3, may be subject to some of the same problems that have accompanied development of the case law under rule 10b-5.
>
> ... If, as the task force believes, more specific guidance is required as to what conduct is forbidden, then a legislative definition based on legislative policy determinations is highly desirable, if not essential....
>
> ... Both proposals [set out by the Task Force] depart from the fraud-based framework of section 10(b) and the *Chiarella* and *Dirks* decisions, and instead directly regulate trading and tipping regardless of whether such conduct may be characterized as "fraud." [Id. at 253]

The Task Force suggested two alternative statutes, one very specific and comprehensive, the other much simpler. Yet under both approaches the prohibited conduct was directly defined and regulated, rather than relying upon the analytic construct of fraud. Similarly, in response to those legislative proposals by the Task Force (introduced in the Senate in 1987), the SEC ultimately, if reluctantly, supported a statutory definition that departed from

---

294. See Committee on Federal Regulation of Securities, American Bar Association, Report of the Task Force on Regulation of Insider Trading: Part I: Regulation Under the Antifraud Provisions of the Securities Exchange Act of 1934, 41 Bus. Law. 223, 253 (1985).

the fraud construct towards direct regulation of certain prohibited conduct.

Finally, Congress could develop a statutory definition of the proscribed conduct based on a theory of property rights in information, and clearly define the relationship between the property rights in information and the trading transaction necessary to give rise to liability. Jonathan Macey has advocated this approach, defining the primary concern of prohibitions on trading on material, nonpublic information as the misuse of corporate property (information).[300] Given this view of the harm to be prevented, Macey has argued that companies should be permitted to allow insiders to trade on proprietary company information.

Regardless of which proposal Congress adopts, it might consider bifurcating criminal liability from civil liability and SEC enforcement actions, in order to allow broader liability in the civil context while setting clear, very specific standards for the imposition of criminal sanctions. For example, Congress could empower the Commission to designate which categories of professionals and other fiduciaries could be held criminally liable for trading on misappropriated information and which categories would be subject only to civil liability to contemporaneous traders under Section 20A.

The above ideas are not meant to be exhaustive. Indeed, some commentators have suggested that insider trading should be legalized entirely. It may even be the case that as securities trading becomes more sophisticated, global, and instantaneous, any regulatory regime aimed at illegal informational advantages will become increasingly difficult to enforce in all but the most egregious cases. When an American can buy call options in Switzerland on securities traded in Japan, it may not be possible to detect unusual trading patterns that suggest illegal trading on material, nonpublic information. Perhaps in light of these realities, the expanded, real-time disclosure of corporate information that Professor Langevoort has suggested may be the most effective means to achieve the regulatory goals of investor protection and fundamental fairness.[304] The point of this wide-ranging enumeration of possible legislative approaches is not to advocate any one idea. Rather, the point is to suggest that the proper institution to consider these and other suggestions and to make the necessary policy choices is Congress. Absent congressional action, the definition of illegal trading on proscribed informational advantages will remain incomplete, unsystematic, and analytically unsatisfying, particularly after *O'Hagan*.

The preceding arguments for a congressional definition of insider trading were made prior to the SEC's adoption of Rule 10b5-1 and Rule 10b5-2. Do these

---

300. Jonathan R. Macey, Insider Trading: Economics, Politics, and Policy, 67 (1991).

304. Donald C. Langevoort, Toward More Effective Risk Disclosure for Technology-Enhanced Investing, 75 Wash. U. L.Q. 753 (1997) (analyzing the problems of risk disclosure in public disclosure documents, and suggesting that, in an electronic disclosure environment, annual and quarterly filings should be replaced with a company file that is required to be relatively accurate and up-to-date on a real-time basis).

new rules lessen the need for a congressional definition? Or have they only compounded the problem? How difficult would it be to draft a statutory prohibition of insider trading? Consider once again the proposed "Insider Trading Proscriptions Act of 1987" set out in Note 3 on page 529 of this chapter. Would prohibiting the "wrongful use" of material nonpublic information add greater clarity to insider trading law or would it merely replace the uncertainties surrounding a fraud-based rubric with an equally malleable new offense?

When faced with the task of drafting a statutory prohibition of insider trading, the European Community first issued to its Member States a directive aimed at coordinating regulations. See Council Directive 89/592/EEC of 13 November 1989, Coordinating Regulations of Insider Dealing, OJ 1989 L334/30. In January 2003, the European Union adopted a common set of rules, as set forth in the following pages. Should Congress enact a version of this Directive? What if the Directive's prohibitions against insider trading were only a floor upon which the SEC could build through its rulemaking powers?

DIRECTIVE 2003/6/EC OF THE EUROPEAN PARLIAMENT AND OF THE COUNCIL OF THE EUROPEAN UNION

of 28 January 2003

On Inside Dealing and Market Manipulation (Market Abuse)

***

Article 1

For the purposes of this Directive:

1. 'Inside information' shall mean information of a precise nature which has not been made public, relating, directly or indirectly, to one or more issuers of financial instruments or to one or more financial instruments and which, if it were made public, would be likely to have a significant effect on the prices of those financial instruments or on the price of related derivative financial instruments.***

For persons charged with the execution of orders concerning financial instruments, 'inside information' shall also mean information conveyed by a client and related to the client's pending orders, which is of a precise nature, which relates

directly or indirectly to one or more issuers of financial instruments or to one or more financial instruments, and which, if it were made public, would be likely to have a significant effect on the prices of those financial instruments or on the price of related derivative financial instruments.

***

Article 2

1. Member States shall prohibit any person referred to in the second subparagraph who possesses inside information from using that information by acquiring or disposing of, or by trying to acquire or dispose of, for his own account or for the account of a third party, either directly or indirectly, financial instruments to which that information relates.

The first subparagraph shall apply to any person who possesses that information:

(a) by virtue of his membership of the administrative, management or supervisory bodies of the issuer; or

(b) by virtue of his holding in the capital of the issuer; or

(c) by virtue of his having access to the information through the exercise of his employment, profession or duties; or

(d) by virtue of his criminal activities.

2. Where the person referred to in paragraph 1 is a legal person, the prohibition laid down in that paragraph shall also apply to the natural persons who take part in the decision to carry out the transaction for the account of the legal person concerned.

3. This Article shall not apply to transactions conducted in the discharge of an obligation that has become due to acquire or dispose of financial instruments where that obligation results from an agreement concluded before the person concerned possessed inside information.

Article 3

Member States shall prohibit any person subject to the prohibition laid down in Article 2 from:

(a) disclosing inside information to any other person unless such disclosure is made in the normal course of the exercise of his employment, profession or duties;

(b) recommending or inducing another person, on the basis of inside information, to acquire or dispose of financial instruments to which that information relates.

Article 4

Member States shall ensure that Articles 2 and 3 also apply to any person, other than the persons referred to in those Articles, who possesses inside information while that person knows, or ought to have known, that it is inside information.

***

Article 8

The prohibitions provided for in this Directive shall not apply to trading in own shares in 'buy-back' programmes or to the stabilisation of a financial instrument provided such trading is carried out in accordance with implementing measures adopted in accordance with the procedure laid down in Article 17(2).

***

Article 13

The obligation of professional secrecy shall apply to all persons who work or who have worked for the competent authority or for any authority or market undertaking to whom the competent authority has delegated its powers, including auditors and experts instructed by the competent authority. Information covered by professional secrecy may not be disclosed to any other person or authority except by virtue of provisions laid down by law.

***

Chapter 8

MARKET MANIPULATION

The term "market manipulation," according to the Supreme Court, "connotes intentional or willful conduct designed to deceive or defraud investors by controlling or artificially affecting the price of securities." *Ernst & Ernst v. Hochfelder*, 425 U.S. 185, 199 (1976). That definition, however, raises many more questions than it settles. For example, what, precisely, does it mean to "control" the price of a security? And how is it possible to ascertain whether a security is trading at an "artificial" price? Even more basically, what is the difference between an artificially and a non-artificially priced security?

Courts must necessarily struggle with these questions because the terms "manipulation" and "manipulative" appear in, but are not defined by, the federal securities laws. As we have seen in previous chapters, Section 10(b) of the Exchange Act accords the SEC broad authority to proscribe the use of "any manipulative or deceptive device or contrivance" in connection with the purchase or sale of securities, and Section 14(e) of the Exchange Act specifically prohibits "fraudulent, deceptive, or manipulative acts or practices" in connection with tender offers. The terms are also set out in the titles of Section 9 ("Manipulation of Security Prices") and Section 10 ("Regulation of the Use of Manipulative and Deceptive Devices") of the Exchange Act. As we shall see in this Chapter, Section 9 proscribes a number of particular practices designed to create the appearance of active securities trading (e.g., washed sales and matched orders). A catchall provision in Section 9(a)(2) makes it unlawful for any person to effect a transaction that creates actual or apparent active securities trading "for the purpose of inducing the purchase or sale of such security by others." Section 10(a) authorizes the SEC to regulate short sales and stop-loss orders. A final important provision is Section 15(c) of the Exchange Act, prohibiting "manipulative, deceptive or other fraudulent" conduct by broker-dealers. Taken together, these statutory sections evidence a strong congressional concern that the federal securities markets be free of conduct that interferes with the "natural" forces of supply and demand.

The types of manipulative conduct and schemes that have captured the attention of securities regulators have varied markedly over time. When the federal securities laws were first enacted in 1933 and 1934, Congress's desire to eradicate manipulative activity from the securities markets was propelled, in large part, by testimony and reports of stock pools and other conspiratorial trading schemes thought to have contributed to the stock market crash a few years earlier. Typically, the pools operated to effectuate a series of transactions in a particular security that created the illusion of rapidly rising prices, and the operators would then systematically unload the security to the unsuspecting public before the price dropped and their scam was exposed. Boiler room operations became the concern in the 1950s, and securities regulators sought to slow down, or put out of business altogether, those unscrupulous broker-dealers who used high pressure (and generally misleading) sales tactics over the telephone to generate market activity in stocks of fledgling companies. In the 1980s, with the scandals that made Michael Milken, Ivan Boesky, and Dennis Levine virtually household names, attention was focused on Wall Street and the staggering profits that could be generated in the securities markets through manipulative activity. In contrast to these high-flying defendants, many of today's market manipulation cases involve far more ordinary types of characters—auto mechanics, tree trimmers, and even law school students—who have managed to use the Internet to perpetrate wide-spread schemes at a speed and in a manner that would have been unimaginable only a decade ago.

Practices on Wall Street also continue to occupy the enforcement agenda of the SEC and the Department of Justice (DOJ) as well as the Financial Industry Regulatory Authority (FINRA) (formed in 2007 when the NASD consolidated with the enforcement, member regulatory, and arbitration divisions of the NYSE). In 2003, these federal regulators, together with the Attorneys General from all fifty states, entered into a historic "global settlement" with twelve of the nation's largest investment banks, resolving charges that the firms engaged in fraud and market manipulation through questionable IPO allocation practices and conflicts of interest affecting securities analysts' research reports. In the aftermath of the 2008 financial crisis, the SEC and other securities regulators turned their attention toward allegations that massive short selling was largely responsible for the sharp declines in the stock prices of the nation's largest financial firms. Some commentators even went so far as to blame manipulative short sellers for the ultimate demise of Bear Stearns (subsequently acquired by J.P. Morgan Chase) and Lehman Brothers (which, prior to its bankruptcy in 2008, was the fourth largest investment bank in the U.S).

Reflecting the various types of market manipulation cases that the SEC pursues through the initiation of enforcement actions and, though less frequently, through criminal referrals to the DOJ, this Chapter is organized into three sections: Section A, which focuses on manipulation in the context of so-called "fictitious" securities transactions; Section B, which centers on actual trading activity that is alleged to have been motivated by a manipulative purpose; and Section C, which focuses on misleading recommendations and material misstatements about particular securities—conduct that forms the basis of schemes known as "pump and dumps" and "distort and short." Section C also discusses conflicts of interest on Wall Street. Issues relating to private actions for market manipulation are discussed in notes following the primary material.

A. PRACTICES THAT CREATE THE APPEARANCE OF ACTIVE TRADING

On three separate occasions, the Supreme Court has emphasized that manipulation is "virtually a term of art when used in connection with securities markets." See *Ernst & Ernst v. Hochfelder*, 425 U.S. 185, 199 (1976), *Sante Fe Indus., Inc. v. Green*, 430 U.S. 462, 476 (1977), and *Schreiber v. Burlington Northern, Inc.*, 472 U.S. 1, 6 (1985). It has also stated that the "term refers generally to practices, such as wash sales, matched orders, or rigged prices, that are intended to mislead investors by artificially affecting market activity." *Schreiber*, 472 U.S. at 6 (quoting *Sante Fe*, 430 U.S. at 476).

As you read the following SEC enforcement action alleging market manipulation in violation of Section 10(b) and Rule 10b-5, consider the ways in which the defendants' actions could be said to have intentionally misled investors.

SEC v. U.S. ENVIRONMENTAL, INC.

155 F.3d 107 (2d Cir. 1998)

JOHN M. WALKER, JR., CIRCUIT JUDGE:

Plaintiff-appellant Securities and Exchange Commission ("SEC") appeals from the [district court order] dismissing, pursuant to Fed.R.Civ.P. 12(b)(6), the SEC's claim that defendant-appellee John Romano engaged in market manipulation in violation of Section 10(b) of the Securities Exchange Act of 1934 and Rule 10b-5 thereunder.

We hold that Romano can be primarily liable under § 10(b) for following a stock promoter's directions to execute stock trades that Romano knew, or was reckless in not knowing, were manipulative, even if Romano did not share the promoter's specific overall purpose to manipulate the market for that stock. We therefore vacate the order of the district court and remand for further proceedings.

Background

The following facts are taken exclusively from the SEC's amended complaint, which on a motion to dismiss at the pleading stage must be read in the light most favorable to the SEC.

Romano was employed as a trader and registered representative of defendant Castle Securities Corporation ("Castle"), a securities broker-dealer. Castle agreed to participate in a scheme whereby it and other defendants, including Romano, would manipulate upward the price of the stock of U.S. Environmental, Inc. ("USE"). At the direction of stock promoter Mark D'Onofrio ("D'Onofrio"), certain of the defendants or their nominees traded USE shares among themselves "for the purpose of creating the appearance of an actual market for trading USE shares" and thus raising USE's stock price.

The complaint alleges that

> Romano knowingly or recklessly participated in and furthered a market manipulation by:
>
> (a) effecting offers, purchases, and sales of USE securities in return for promises of risk-free profit for engaging in such trades;
>
> (b) effecting directed and controlled trades of USE securities;
>
> (c) effecting "wash sales" and "matched orders"; and
>
> (d) effecting trades involving undisclosed nominees.

Wash sales are "transactions involving no change in beneficial ownership" and matched orders are "orders for the purchase [or] sale of a security that are entered with the knowledge that orders of substantially the same size, at substantially the same time and price, have been or will be entered by the same or different persons for the sale/purchase of such security." *Ernst & Ernst v. Hochfelder,* 425 U.S. 185, 205 n.25 (1976). The complaint states further that

> Romano agreed to advise D'Onofrio continuously as Castle received buy and sell orders for USE shares during each trading day. Romano agreed to execute trades as directed by D'Onofrio, and Romano also agreed to move, or adjust, the price Castle quoted for USE shares at D'Onofrio's direction. In return, D'Onofrio assured Romano that Castle would receive a profit on the transactions D'Onofrio directed.

In a typical manipulative transaction,

> (a) D'Onofrio would direct a buy order from one of the ... brokerage accounts controlled by the D'Onofrio group [consisting of stock promoters Ramon N. D'Onofrio, Richard Kirschbaum, and D'Onofrio] to a market maker other than Castle;
>
> (b) D'Onofrio would arrange in advance that the other market maker would contact Romano at Castle to buy the same number of shares;
>
> (c) D'Onofrio would alert Romano that the other market maker would be calling Romano for stock;
>
> (d) D'Onofrio, specifying number of shares and price, would instruct Romano to sell shares of USE to the other market maker; and
>
> (e) D'Onofrio would supply Castle with the specified number of shares at a discount, enabling Romano to complete the transaction at a price at which both Castle and the other market maker received a risk-free profit on the transaction, as had been prearranged with Castle ... and Romano.

Romano, Castle, and the D'Onofrio group "intentionally engaged" in such "manipulative conduct ... between September 1989 and December 1989." As a result of these manipulative trades, the price of USE stock rose from $.05 to approximately $5.00 per share in this period. In June or early July 1990, Castle sold approximately 15,000 shares of USE stock to retail customers at $6.00 per share. Between September 1989 and August 1990, Castle made a profit of approximately $175,000 as a result of its market-making activity for USE.

The SEC then commenced the instant action, alleging that defendants violated various provisions of the securities laws in connection with their manipulation of USE stock and other aspects of an illegal scheme involving USE. Romano moved, pursuant to Fed R. Civ. P. 12(b)(6), to dismiss the SEC's manipulation claim under Section 10(b) of the Securities Exchange Act of 1934 and Rule 10b-5 thereunder. The district court granted the motion on the sole ground that the SEC had failed to allege that Romano was a "primary violator[ ]," as required by the Supreme Court in *Central Bank of Denver, N.A. v. First Interstate Bank of Denver, N.A.,* 511 U.S. 164, 191 (1994). Rather, the district court held that Romano was alleged only to be an aider/abettor of securities violations, because Romano "follow[ed] directions from D'Onofrio in carrying out buy or sell orders" and "did not himself make wash sales, match orders, or use undisclosed nominees to artificially affect the price of securities."[a] ***

Discussion

In reviewing the district court's dismissal of the SEC's claim pursuant to Fed.R.Civ.P. 12(b)(6), we are "required to accept the material facts alleged in the complaint as true" and will vacate the dismissal "unless it appears beyond doubt that the plaintiff can prove no set of facts in support of [its] claim which would entitle [it] to relief." Our review is *de novo.*

Romano's principal contention on appeal, with which the district court agreed, is that he cannot be primarily liable under § 10(b) for following a stock promoter's directions to execute trades that Romano knew, or was reckless in not knowing, were manipulative, where Romano did not share the promoter's ultimate "manipulative ... purpose" to raise the stock price. We disagree.

*** In *Central Bank,* the Supreme Court held that private civil liability under § 10(b) applies only to those who "engage in the manipulative or deceptive practice," but not to those "who aid and abet the violation." 511 U.S. at 167. The Court observed that "[a]iding and abetting is a method by which courts create secondary liability in persons *other than* the violator [or violators] of the statute." Id. at 184. We have noted further that a primary violator is one who "participated in the fraudulent scheme" or other activity proscribed by the securities laws. *SEC v. First Jersey Secs., Inc.,* 101 F.3d 1450, 1471 (2d Cir.1996).

Under the foregoing standards, we believe that, as alleged in the complaint, Romano falls well within the boundaries of primary liability. *** We [therefore] disagree with the district court's view that "[e]ven if Romano knew that [the buyers and sellers] were D'Onofrio and undisclosed nominees of D'Onofrio, and hence knew that D'Onofrio was manipulating USE stock, [Romano] did not himself manipulate USE stock because he did not himself have a manipulative purpose." ***

A. Scienter

Of course, to establish Romano's liability under § 10(b), the complaint must as a threshold matter allege that Romano acted with sufficient scienter. The complaint's allegation that Romano "knowingly or recklessly participated in and furthered a market manipulation by ... effecting 'wash sales' and 'matched orders'" and that he "intentionally engaged" in "manipulative conduct" is plainly sufficient to satisfy that requirement. It is well-settled that knowledge of the proscribed activity is sufficient scienter under § 10(b). See *Ernst & Ernst,* 425 U.S. at 197 ("[t]he words 'manipulative or deceptive' ... strongly suggest that

---

a. Ed. Note—At the conclusion of its opinion, the court observed that although Section 20(e) of the Exchange Act, enacted after the Supreme Court's decision in *Central Bank,* now provides the SEC with the authority to assert aiding and abetting claims under Section 10(b), there was some question as to whether the SEC could bring aiding and abetting claims based on conduct occurring before Section 20(e) was on the books. The court did not address this alternative ground for vacating the district court's dismissal order because the SEC did not make this argument before the district court or on appeal.

§ 10(b) was intended to proscribe knowing or intentional misconduct"); *SEC v. Lorin,* 76 F.3d 458, 460 (2d Cir.1996) (per curiam) (affirming liability against defendant who "knew of the manipulation agreement and knowingly participated in carrying it out"); cf. Restatement (Second) of Torts, § 8A (1965) ("If the actor knows that the consequences are certain, or substantially certain, to result from his act, and still goes ahead, he is treated by the law as if he had in fact desired to produce the result."). Therefore, the allegation that Romano executed trades that he knew were for a manipulative purpose sufficiently alleged scienter in a manner supporting § 10(b) liability.

Although we need not rely on this point, we also note that the complaint's claim that Romano recklessly participated in the manipulation also alleges sufficient scienter. See *San Leandro Emergency Med. Group Profit Sharing Plan v. Philip Morris Cos.,* 75 F.3d 801, 813 (2d Cir.1996) ("In order to establish scienter ..., [it is sufficient that] the plaintiffs ... identify circumstances indicating conscious or reckless behavior by the defendants"); see also Louis Loss & Joel Seligman, Securities Regulation, Vol. VIII, ch.9, § B(6), at 3665-67 n. 521 (3d ed.1991) (noting holdings of eleven circuits that recklessness can constitute sufficient scienter); cf. *Ernst & Ernst,* 425 U.S. at 193 n. 12 (leaving open question whether "reckless behavior" is sufficient to establish § 10(b) liability).

Moreover, as long as Romano, with scienter, effected the manipulative buy and sell orders, Romano's personal motivation for manipulating the market is irrelevant in determining whether he violated § 10(b). Even if Romano were motivated by a desire to obtain compensation rather than by a desire to change USE's market price, as D'Onofrio was, Romano is liable under § 10(b) if, with scienter, he effected the manipulative trades.

B. *Primary Violator or Aider and Abettor*

It is plain to us that the complaint alleged Romano to be a primary violator. Romano "participated in the fraudulent scheme," *First Jersey Secs.,* 101 F.3d at 1471, i.e., the manipulation of USE's stock, by effecting the very buy and sell orders that artificially manipulated USE's stock price upward. Indeed, if the trader who executes manipulative buy and sell orders is not a primary violator, it is difficult to imagine who would remain liable after *Central Bank.*

*** [I]t is of no relevance that D'Onofrio, not Romano, masterminded the USE stock manipulation and that D'Onofrio's group "directed" Romano to effect the illegal trades. *** The Supreme Court in *Central Bank* never intended to restrict § 10(b) liability to supervisors or directors of securities fraud schemes while excluding from liability subordinates who also violated the securities laws. In sum, the complaint alleges that Romano is primarily liable under § 10(b) and Rule 10b-5 for the manipulation of USE stock. ***

NOTES AND QUESTIONS

1. Manipulation as a Sub-Category of Fraud and Deception. When a defendant's conduct involves securities trading that is designed to create the impression that multiple buyers and sellers are actively engaging in securities transactions, is the separate concept of market manipulation even necessary to state a claim under Section 10(b) and Rule 10b-5? See Daniel R. Fischel and David J. Ross, Should the Law Prohibit "Manipulation" in Financial Markets?,

105 Harv. L. Rev. 503, 510-11 (1991) (contending that fictitious transactions—such as wash sales and matched orders—are "a form of fraud by conduct" and that "the concept of manipulation for this category of cases is superfluous"). Can fictitious trades be analogized to material misrepresentations or omissions prohibited under the explicit text of Rule 10b-5(b)? What assumptions underlie this analogy? Decide whether you agree with the following statement:

> When an outsider, a member of the public, reads the price quotations of a stock listed on an exchange, he is justified in supposing that the quoted price is an appraisal of the value of that stock due to a series of actual sales between various persons dealing at arm's length in a free and open market on the exchange, and so represents a true chancering of the market value of that stock thereon under the process of attrition due to supply operating against demand.

United States v. Brown, 5 F. Supp. 81, 85 (S.D.N.Y. 1933), aff'd on other grounds, 79 F.2d 321 (2d Cir. 1935). Consider the text of Rule 10b-5(a) (unlawful "to employ any device, scheme, or artifice to defraud") and Rule 10b-5(c) (unlawful "to engage in any act, practice, or course of business which operates *** as a fraud or deceit upon any person"). In light of that explicit text, is a Rule 10b-2(b) analogy for fictitious trades even necessary? See *Stoneridge Inv. Partners, LLC v. Scientific-Atlanta, Inc.*, 552 U.S. 148, 158 (2008). ("Conduct itself can be deceptive;" there need not be "a specific oral or written statement before there could be liability under § 10(b) or Rule 10b–5").

2. Section 9(a) of the Exchange Act. Although it is Section 9(a)(1) of the Exchange Act that expressly prohibits wash sales and matched orders, most market manipulation cases involving these so-called fictitious trading practices are brought by the SEC under the more generally worded provisions in Section 10(b) and Rule 10b-5. A principal historical reason was that Section 9(a)'s prohibitions initially extended only to practices involving securities listed on national securities exchanges. In the Dodd-Frank Act of 2010, however, Congress extended Section 9's reach to all securities except government securities. Had this statutory change been in force at the time of the manipulative activity at issue in *US Environmental*, would the SEC have been able to satisfy the other elements necessary to state a claim against Romano under Section 9(a)(1)? What about under the catch-all provisions in Section 9(a)(2)? These sections now read as follows:

> **Section 9(a).** It shall be unlawful for any person, directly or indirectly, by the use of the mails or any means or instrumentality of interstate commerce, or of any facility of any national securities exchange, or for any member of a national securities exchange—***
>
> (1) For the purpose of creating a false or misleading appearance of active trading in any security other than a government security, or a false or misleading appearance with respect to the market for any such security,(A) to effect any transaction in such security which involves no change in the beneficial ownership thereof, or (B) to enter an order or orders for the purchase of such security with the knowledge that an order or orders of substantially the same size, at substantially the same time, and at substantially the same price, for the sale of any such security, has been or will be entered by or for the same or different parties, or (C) to enter any order or orders for the sale of any such security with the knowledge that an order or orders of substantially the same size, at substantially the same time, and at substantially the same price, for the

purchase of such security, has been or will be entered by or for the same or different parties.

(2) To effect, alone or with one or more other persons, a series of transactions in any security other than a government security or in connection with any security-based swap agreement *** with respect to such security creating actual or apparent active trading in such security, or raising or depressing the price of such security, for the purpose of inducing the purchase or sale of such security by others.

3. Section 9(e)'s Express Private Right of Action. Under Section 9(e) of the Exchange Act, any person who "willfully participates in any act or transaction" in violation of Section 9 shall be liable "to any person who shall purchase or sell any security at a price which was affected by such act or transaction" for "the damages sustained as a result of any such act or transaction." The provision also authorizes courts, in their discretion, "to assess reasonable costs, including reasonable attorneys' fees, against either party litigant." Although Section 9(e) constitutes one of only a few express private remedies in the Exchange Act, at least prior to the Dodd-Frank Act, it was generally viewed as "a dead letter so far as producing recoveries is concerned." 9 Louis Loss & Joel Seligman, Securities Regulation 4279 (3d ed. 2004). Is it likely that Section 9(e) will be utilized more frequently now that Dodd-Frank has removed the "listed on a national securities exchange" limitation from Section 9? What other factors might account for the dearth of Section 9(e) cases?

4. Implied Right of Action Under Rule 10b-5 for Market Manipulation. Rule 10b-5 is typically the weapon of choice for private plaintiffs seeking damages against alleged market manipulators. Such plaintiffs must allege that "(1) they were injured; (2) in connection with the purchase or sale of securities; (3) by relying on a market for securities; (4) controlled or artificially affected by defendant's deceptive or manipulative conduct; and (5) the defendants engaged in the manipulative conduct with scienter." *In re Blech Sec. Litig.*, 961 F. Supp. 569, 582 (S.D.N.Y. 1997) (citing *Ernst & Ernst v. Hochfelder*, 425 U.S. 185, 199 (1976)). As the Second Circuit recently summarized:

> Because a claim for market manipulation is a claim for fraud, it must be pled with particularity under [Fed. R. Civ. Pro.] Rule 9(b). A claim of manipulation, however, can involve facts solely within the defendant's knowledge; therefore, at the early stages of litigation, the plaintiff need not plead manipulation to the same degree of specificity as a plain misrepresentation claim.
>
> Accordingly, a manipulation complaint must plead with particularity the nature, purpose, and effect of the fraudulent conduct and the roles of the defendants. General allegations not tied to the defendants or resting upon speculation are insufficient. This test will be satisfied if the complaint sets forth, to the extent possible, "what manipulative acts were performed, which defendants performed them, when the manipulative acts were performed, and what effect the scheme had on the market for the securities at issue." *Baxter v. A.R. Baron & Co.*, No. 94 Civ. 3913, 1995 WL 600720 at *6. This standard meets the goals of Rule 9(b) while also considering which specific facts a plaintiff alleging manipulation can realistically plead at this stage of the litigation.
>
> Because a claim for market manipulation requires a showing of scienter, the PSLRA's heightened standards for pleading scienter also apply.

> Therefore, the complaint must plead with particularly facts giving rise to a strong inference that the defendant intended to deceive investors by artificially affecting the market price of securities. See 15 U.S.C. § 78u-4(b)(2). This pleading requirement is particularly important in manipulation claims because in some cases scienter is the only factor that distinguishes legitimate trading from improper manipulation.

ATSI Commc'ns, Inc. v. Shaar Fund, Ltd., 493 F.3d 87, 101-02 (2d Cir. 2007).

How do the elements for market manipulation compare with claims for alleged material misrepresentations or omissions? Consider, in particular, the element of reliance. As we saw in Chapter 2.F.1, Rule 10b-5 plaintiffs frequently establish reliance through the use of either the *Affiliated Ute* presumption or the fraud-on-the-market presumption. Are either of these presumptions available to plaintiffs alleging market manipulation? With respect to the *Affiliated Ute* presumption, most courts have answered no. See *Desai v. Deutsche Bank Sec., Ltd.*, 573 F.3d 931, 941 (9th Cir. 2009) ("'Any fraudulent scheme requires some degree of concealment, both of the truth and of the scheme itself. We cannot allow the mere fact of this concealment to transform the alleged malfeasance into an omission rather than an affirmative act. To do otherwise would permit the *Affiliated Ute* presumption to swallow the reliance requirement almost completely,'" quoting *Joseph v. Wiles*, 223 F.3d 1155, 1163 (10th Cir.2000)). But see *In re Sterling Foster & Co., Inc., Sec. Litig.*, 222 F.Supp.2d 216, 275 (E.D.N.Y.2002) (finding that the *Affiliated Ute* presumption applied because "the majority of the complaint focuses on the defendants' failure to disclose" defendant's manipulative scheme). Likewise, the fraud-on-the market presumption of reliance has not brought plaintiffs in manipulation cases much success. Although courts generally agree that the presumption is theoretically available, manipulative schemes are most often perpetrated on *in*efficient markets involving thinly-traded over-the-counter stocks. For an article questioning the wisdom of requiring plaintiffs to establish an efficient market in order to gain the benefit of the fraud-on-the-market presumption in market manipulation cases, see Charles R. Korsmo, Mismatch: The Misuse of Market Efficiency in Market Manipulation Class Actions, 52 Wm. & Mary L. Rev 1111 (2011).

Should private plaintiffs alleging market manipulation receive a presumption that they relied on "the integrity of the market" in making their trades? In other words, should they be presumed to have traded under a (mistaken) belief that the market for the security was free of manipulation? When the plaintiffs in *Desai*, supra, urged the Ninth Circuit to accept this theory, they were rebuffed and the district court's order denying class certification was affirmed. Id. at 573 F.3d at 942 ("We are chary. *** 'Though it remains the law, the § 10(b) private right should not be extended beyond its present boundaries,'" quoting *Stoneridge Inv. Partners, LLC v. Scientific-Atlanta, Inc.*, 552 U.S. 148, 165 (2008)). If a court were to presume a plaintiff's reliance on the integrity of the market, how else could a court ensure that the alleged manipulations actually affected prices to the plaintiff's detriment? See Korsmo, supra, at 1174-79 (proposing that class action plaintiffs in market manipulation cases should be presumed to have relied on the integrity of the market, but should be required to demonstrate loss causation at the class certification stage).

Consider again the express private right of action available to investors under Exchange Act Section 9(e). To alleviate the reliance requirement essential to private claims under Rule 10b-5, might an investor in a thinly-traded over-the-counter security be more likely after Dodd-Frank to allege market manipulation under Section 9(e)?

PROBLEM 8-1

Smith & Jones, one of the nation's largest investment banks, served as managing underwriter for more than 30 initial public offerings (IPOs) between 1998-2000. Private plaintiffs and the SEC have alleged that, as a routine course of conduct in many of these offerings, Smith & Jones brokers conditioned allocations of shares at the offering price on agreements to purchase shares in the aftermarket (so-called "Tie-in Agreements"). For example, in an IPO in which the offering price was $75 per share, a favored client would be allocated 1000 shares provided she agreed to purchase 2000 additional shares in the aftermarket at successively higher prices.

During this time period, more than fifty investment banks may have utilized such tie-in agreements, thereby engaging in a practice which came to be known as "IPO laddering." As the Wall Street Journal reported when the scandal unfolded,

> Steering hot IPOs to big investors who signaled plans to buy additional shares * * * could have stimulated additional demand for technology stocks during the stock-market bubble, contributing to the huge first-day price gains that eventually worsened losses suffered by individual investors who – lacking access to the actual IPOs – bought on the open market after trading began.

Randall Smith, IPO "Laddering" Case Expands, Wall Street Journal at C1 (Feb. 26, 2003).

Assume that the SEC and private plaintiffs have garnered evidence supporting the claim that laddering occurred in connection with specific IPOs. Under which provisions of the federal securities laws might the investment banks be liable? What arguments would you anticipate that the banks would make by way of defense?

SEC settlements resolving charges of illegal IPO allocation practices include: SEC v. Morgan Stanley & Co., Litigation Release No. 19050 (Jan. 25, 2005) ($40 million penalty); SEC v. Goldman Sachs & Co., Litigation Release No. 19051 (Jan. 25, 2005) ($40 million penalty); SEC v. J.P. Morgan Secs., Inc., Litigation Release No. 18385 (Oct. 1, 2003) ($25 million penalty). Without admitting or denying liability, these firms agreed to settle charges that they had violated Rule 101 of Regulation M, promulgated under Section 10(b) of the Exchange Act. Rule 101 states:

> *Unlawful Activity.* In connection with a distribution of securities, it shall be unlawful for a distribution participant or an affiliated purchaser of such person, directly or indirectly, to bid for, purchase, or attempt to induce any person to bid for or purchase, a covered security during the applicable restricted period.

17 C.F.R. § 242.101. Years before these settlements, the SEC's Division of Market Regulation had issued Staff Legal Bulletin No. 10, which made clear that Regulation M prohibits solicitations and "tie-in" agreements:

> Tie-in agreements are a particularly egregious form of solicited transactions prohibited by Regulation M. *** [T]ie-in agreements for aftermarket purchases are manipulative because they undermine the integrity of the market as an independent pricing mechanism for the offered security. Solicitations for aftermarket purchases give purchasers in the offering the impression that there is a scarcity of the offered securities. This can stimulate demand and support the pricing of the offering. Moreover, traders in the aftermarket will not know that the aftermarket demand, which may appear to validate the offering price, has been stimulated by the distribution participants. Underwriters have an incentive to artificially influence aftermarket activity because they have underwritten the risk of the offering, and a poor aftermarket performance could result in reputational and subsequent financial loss.

http://www.sec.gov/interps/legal/slbmr10.htm In addition to (or instead of) Rule 101 of Regulation M, could the SEC have charged these investments banks with violating Rule 10b-5? If so, why were there no Rule 10b-5 violations alleged in the complaints?

Illegal IPO allocation practices were also alleged in more than 1,000 private lawsuits, with alleged damages totaling more than $55 billion. These suits were later consolidated into a single proceeding in the Southern District of New York, see *In re IPO Sec. Litig.*, 241 F. Supp. 2d 281 (S.D.N.Y. 2003) (denying motions to dismiss), and class actions were certified in six "focus" cases, *In re IPO Sec. Litig.*, 227 F.R.D. 65 (S.D.N.Y. 2004), but the Second Circuit subsequently vacated the class certifications after concluding that the plaintiffs had failed to establish the predominance of common questions over the individual questions. See *In re IPO Sec. Litig.*, 471 F.3d 24 (2d Cir. 2006).

Note also that investment banks were not the only defendants pursued in private litigation: hundreds of securities issuers were also named as defendants in the consolidated proceeding. After the district court rejected in large part their motion to dismiss, see *IPO Sec. Litig.*, 241 F. Supp. 2d at 297-98, the issuers agreed to settle with the plaintiffs, guaranteeing a payment of at least $1 billion. But this agreed-upon settlement was subject to court approval and the settlement was subsequently nullified in light of the Second Circuit's ruling on the question of class certification.

The consolidated class action then continued, albeit with a more modest class definition reflecting, among other things, the exclusion of institutional investors. And eventually, after almost ten years of litigation involving at least 55 investment banks, 300 issuers, 1000 individual defendants associated with these issuers, and more than seven million potential class members, the action then settled with the payment of $586 million. See *In re IPO Sec. Litig*, 671 F.Supp.2d 467 (S.D.N.Y. 2009). In a lengthy opinion discussing its overall conclusion that the settlement was "fair, reasonable and adequate" in accordance with Fed. R. Civ. Pro. 23(e), the court observed that:

> Plaintiffs concede that "establishing liability is, at best, uncertain." They contend that defendants have denied any wrongdoing in the case, arguing that the tie-in agreements were really "underwriters gauging 'indications of interest' as part of the IPO price discovery process." Plaintiffs admit that it is

> possible that a jury might find defendants' version of events to be more compelling, reducing their recovery to nothing. Plaintiffs also acknowledge that if history is any indication, their chances of success at trial is-at best-fifty percent.

Id. at 482 (quoting Plaintiff's Memorandum of Law in Support of Motion for Final Approval of Settlement, Plan of Distribution, and Class Certification). How would you have assessed the plaintiffs chances at trial?

B. ACTUAL TRADING CONDUCTED FOR A MANIPULATIVE PURPOSE

Recall that in *US Environmental*, the Second Circuit held that a broker's personal motivation for executing sell and buy orders was irrelevant because the trades themselves were manipulative acts proscribed by Section 10(b) and Rule 10b-5. The following decision demonstrates the very important role that motive plays in a market manipulation case in which the defendant has engaged in bona fide, arms-length, securities transactions.

UNITED STATES v. MULHEREN

938 F.2d 364 (2d Cir. 1991)

JOSEPH M. MCLAUGHLIN, CIRCUIT JUDGE:

In the late 1980's a wide prosecutorial net was cast upon Wall Street. Along with the usual flotsam and jetsam, the government's catch included some of Wall Street's biggest, brightest, and now infamous—Ivan Boesky, Dennis Levine, Michael Milken, Robert Freeman, Martin Siegel, Boyd L. Jeffries, and Paul A. Bilzerian—each of whom either pleaded guilty to or was convicted of crimes involving illicit trading scandals. Also caught in the government's net was defendant-appellant John A. Mulheren, Jr., the chief trader at and general partner of Jamie Securities Co. ("Jamie"), a registered broker-dealer.

Mulheren was charged in a 42-count indictment handed-up on June 13, 1989. The indictment alleged that he conspired to and did manipulate the price on the New York Stock Exchange (the "NYSE") of the common stock of Gulf & Western Industries, Inc. ("G & W" or the "company") in violation of [Section 10(b) of the Exchange Act and Rule 10b-5] *** by purchasing 75,000 shares of G & W common stock on October 17, 1985 for the purpose of raising the price thereof to $45 per share (Counts One through Four) ***.

***[A jury found Mulheren guilty and he] was sentenced to concurrent terms of one year and one day imprisonment, a $1,681,700 fine and a $200 special assessment.

This appeal thus focuses solely on the convictions concerning Mulheren's alleged manipulation of G & W common stock. The government sought to prove that on October 17, 1985, Mulheren purchased 75,000 shares of G & W common stock with the purpose and intent of driving the price of that stock to $45 per share. This, the government claimed, was a favor to Boesky, who wanted to sell his enormous block of G & W common stock back to the company at that price. Mulheren assails the convictions on several grounds.

First, Mulheren claims that the government failed to prove beyond a reasonable doubt that when he purchased the 75,000 shares of G & W common stock on October 17, 1985, he did it for the sole purpose of raising the price at which it traded on the NYSE, rather than for his own investment purposes. Second, Mulheren argues that even if his sole intent had been to raise the price of G & W stock, that would not have been a crime because, he claims, (1) he neither misrepresented any fact nor failed to disclose any fact that he was under a duty to disclose concerning his G & W purchases; (2) his subjective intent in purchasing G & W stock is not "material"; and (3) he did not act for the purpose of deceiving others. ***

Although we harbor doubt about the government's theory of prosecution, we reverse on Mulheren's first stated ground because we are convinced that no rational trier of fact could have found the elements of the crimes charged here beyond a reasonable doubt.

BACKGROUND

Reviewing the evidence "in the light most favorable to the government, and construing all permissible inferences in its favor," the following facts were established at trial.

In 1985, at the suggestion of his long-time friend, Carl Icahn, a prominent arbitrageur and corporate raider, Ivan Boesky directed his companies to buy G & W stock, a security that both Icahn and Boesky believed to be "significantly undervalued." Between April and October 1985, Boesky's companies accumulated 3.4 million shares representing approximately 4.9 percent of the outstanding G & W shares. According to Boesky, Icahn also had a "position of magnitude."

On September 5, 1985, Boesky and Icahn met with Martin Davis, the chairman of G & W. At the meeting, Boesky expressed his interest in taking control of G & W through a leveraged buyout or, failing that, by increasing his position in G & W stock and securing seats on the G & W board of directors. Boesky told Davis that he held 4.9 percent of G & W's outstanding shares. Davis said he was not interested in Boesky's proposal, and he remained adamant in subsequent telephone calls and at a later meeting on October 1, 1985.

At the October 1, 1985 meeting, which Icahn also attended, Boesky added a new string to his bow: if Davis continued to reject Boesky's attempts at control, then G & W should buy-out his position at $45 per share. At that time, G & W was, indeed, reducing the number of its outstanding shares through a repurchase program, but, the stock was trading below $45 per share. Davis stated that, although he would consider buying Boesky's shares, he could not immediately agree to a price. Icahn, for his part, indicated that he was not yet sure whether he would sell his G & W stock.

During—and for sometime before—these negotiations, Mulheren and Boesky also maintained a relationship of confidence and trust. The two had often shared market information and given each other trading tips. At some point during the April-October period when Boesky was acquiring G & W stock, Mulheren asked Boesky what he thought of G & W and whether Icahn held a position in the stock. Boesky responded that he "thought well" of G & W stock and that he thought Icahn did indeed own G & W stock. Although Boesky told Mulheren that G & W stock was "a good purchase and worth owning," Boesky never told Mulheren about his meetings or telephone conversations with Davis because he considered the matter "very confidential." Speculation in the press, however, was abound. Reports in the August 19, 1985 issue of *Business Week* and the September 27, 1985 issue of the *Wall Street Journal* indicated that Boesky and Icahn each owned close to five percent of G & W and discussed the likelihood of a take-over of the company. Mulheren, however, testifying in his own behalf, denied reading these reports and denied knowing whether Boesky and Icahn held positions in G & W.

On October 3, 1985, two days after his meeting with Boesky and Icahn, Davis met with Mulheren. Mulheren stated that he had a group of investors interested in knowing whether G & W would join them in acquiring CBS. According to Davis, Mulheren also volunteered that he could be "very helpful in monitoring the activities of Ivan Boesky [in G & W stock;] [Mulheren] knew that [Davis] considered Mr. Boesky adversarial;" and Mulheren agreed with Davis' unflattering assessment of Boesky. In a telephone conversation sometime between this October 3 meeting and a subsequent meeting between the two on October 9, 1985, Mulheren told Davis that he believed that Boesky did not own any G & W securities. Mulheren also said that he did not own any G & W stock either. When Davis and Mulheren met again on October 9, they spoke only about Mulheren's CBS proposal.

In the meantime, Boesky continued to press Davis to accept his proposals to secure control of G & W. When Boesky called Davis after their October 1, 1985 meeting, Davis "told [Boesky] as clearly as [he] could again that [G & W] had no interest whatsoever in doing anything with [Boesky]." Boesky then decided to contact his representative at Goldman, Sachs & Co. to arrange the sale of his massive block of stock to G & W. Boesky advised Goldman, Sachs that G & W common stock was not trading at $45 per share at the time, "but that should it become 45," he wanted to sell. A Goldman, Sachs representative met with Davis shortly thereafter regarding the company's repurchase of Boesky's G & W shares.

Sometime after the close of the market on October 16, 1985, Boesky called Davis, offering to sell his block of shares back to G & W at $45 per share. NYSE trading had closed that day at $44 3/4 per share, although at one point during that day it had reached $45. Davis told Boesky that the company would buy his shares back, but only at the "last sale"—the price at which the stock traded on the NYSE at the time of the sale—and that Boesky should have his Goldman, Sachs representative contact Kidder Peabody & Co. to arrange the transaction.

After this conversation with Davis, but before 11:00 a.m. on October 17, 1985, Boesky called Mulheren. According to Boesky's testimony, the following, critical exchange took place:

> Boesky: Mr. Mulheren asked me if I liked the stock on that particular day, and I said yes, I still liked it. At the time it was trading at 44 3/4 . I said I liked it; however, I would not pay more than 45 for it and it would be great if it traded at 45. The design for the comment—
>
> DEFENSE COUNSEL MR. PUCCIO: Objection to the "design of the comment." I would ask [ ] only for the conversation.

A.U.S.A. GILBERT: What if anything did he say to you?

BOESKY: I understand.

Shortly after 11:00 a.m. on October 17, 1985, Jamie (Mulheren's company) placed an order with Oliver Ihasz, a floor broker, to purchase 50,000 shares of G & W at the market price. Trading in G & W had been sluggish that morning (only 32,200 shares had traded between 9:30 a.m. and 11:03 a.m.), and the market price was holding steady at $44 3/4, the price at which it had closed the day before. At 11:04 a.m., Ihasz purchased 16,100 shares at $44 3/4 per share. Unable to fill the entire 50,000 share order at $44 3/4, Ihasz purchased the remaining 33,900 shares between 11:05 a.m. and 11:08 a.m. at $44 7/8 per share.

At 11:09 a.m., Ihasz received another order from Jamie; this time, to purchase 25,000 shares of G & W for no more than $45 per share. After attempting to execute the trade at $44 7/8, Ihasz executed the additional 25,000 share purchase at $45 per share at 11:10 a.m. In sum, between 11:04 a.m. and 11:10 a.m., Jamie purchased a total of 75,000 shares of G & W common stock, causing the price at which it traded per share to rise from $44 3/4 to $45. At 11:17 a.m., Boesky and Icahn sold their G & W stock—6,715,700 shares between them—back to the company at $45 per share. Trading in G & W closed on the NYSE on October 17, 1985 at $43 5/8 per share. At the end of the day, Jamie's trading in G & W common stock at Mulheren's direction had caused it to lose $64,406.

DISCUSSION

A convicted defendant, of course, bears "a very heavy burden" to demonstrate that the evidence at trial was insufficient to prove his guilt beyond a reasonable doubt. "A jury's verdict will be sustained if there is *substantial evidence,* taking the view most favorable to the government, to support it." Where "'*any* rational trier of fact could have found the essential elements of the crime,' the conviction must stand."

On this appeal, however, we are reminded that "in America we still respect the dignity of the individual, and [a defendant] ... is not to be imprisoned except on definite proof of a specific crime." To that end, it is "imperative that we not rend the fabric of evidence and examine each shred in isolation; rather, the reviewing court 'must use its experience with people and events in weighing the chances that the evidence correctly points to guilt against the possibility of innocent or ambiguous inference.'"

The government's theory of prosecution in this case is straightforward. In its view, when an investor, who is neither a fiduciary nor an insider, engages in securities transactions in the open market with the sole intent to affect the price of the security, the transaction is manipulative and violates Rule 10b-5.[2]

---

2. The government also appears to argue in the alternative that the violation occurs not by simply engaging in a securities transaction with the intent to affect the price of a security, but rather by failing to disclose that subjective intent to the market. The government contends that all investors are under a "general duty" not to manipulate; thus, absent disclosure of an intent to manipulate, Rule 10b-5 is violated.

Unlawful manipulation occurs, the argument goes, even though the investor has not acted for the "purpose of inducing the purchase or sale of such security by others," an element the government would have had to prove had it chosen to proceed under the manipulation statute, § 9(a)(2). Mulheren was not charged with violating § 9(a)(2). When the transaction is effected for an investment purpose, the theory continues, there is no manipulation, even if an increase or diminution in price was a foreseeable consequence of the investment.

Although we have misgivings about the government's view of the law, we will assume, without deciding on this appeal, that an investor may lawfully be convicted under Rule 10b-5 where the purpose of his transaction is solely to affect the price of a security. The issue then becomes one of Mulheren's subjective intent. The government was obligated to prove beyond a reasonable doubt that when Mulheren purchased 75,000 shares of G & W common stock on October 17, 1985, he did it with the intent to raise its price, rather than with the intent to invest. We conclude that the government failed to carry this burden.

In order to convict, the government had to demonstrate, in the first place, that Mulheren was aware that Boesky had a stake in G & W. In proof of knowledge, the government makes three arguments.

First, the government suggests that Boesky himself told Mulheren of his G & W positions. Boesky, however, never so testified; and the greatest puzzle in this record is why that critical question was never directly put to Boesky.

Second, the government relies on the speculation reported in the media, specifically the *Wall Street Journal* and *Business Week,* and the rumors floating on Wall Street that Boesky and Icahn owned substantial positions in G & W. There was no evidence, however, that Mulheren read these articles or heard these rumors. On the contrary, Mulheren flatly denied knowing of their existence. Moreover, knowledge of a rumor, particularly one on Wall Street, can hardly substitute for knowledge of a fact.

Third, the government contends that Mulheren's knowledge of Boesky's position is evident in the October 3, 1985 meeting between Davis and Mulheren. In that meeting, Mulheren told Davis that he knew that Davis and Boesky had an "adversarial" relationship and Mulheren "understood" Davis' "position" and offered to help Davis "in any way he could" to "monitor" Boesky's G & W transactions. While this evidence, taken in isolation, might create an inference that Mulheren knew of Boesky's G & W holdings (as the source of the Boesky-Davis adversarial relationship), the rest of Davis' testimony casts a considerable shadow on the inference. Davis went on to testify that in a telephone conversation sometime between their October 3 and October 9 meetings Mulheren stated that he did not believe Boesky owned any G & W stock at all. By this time, of course, Boesky had already told Davis (at their September 5 meeting) that he owned 4.9 percent of G & W's outstanding shares. Given that Mulheren was at the time attempting to curry favor from Davis in connection with Mulheren's CBS proposal, it was hardly in Mulheren's best interest to lie to Davis by telling him that Boesky owned *no* shares, if in fact Mulheren knew

---

We express no view on this theory.

that Boesky owned 3.4 million shares. In sum, the evidence of Mulheren's knowledge that Boesky had an interest in G & W rests on a very slender reed.

Even were we to conclude otherwise, however, the convictions still could not be sustained. Assuming that Mulheren knew that Boesky held a substantial position in G & W stock, the government nevertheless failed to prove that Mulheren agreed to and then purchased the 75,000 shares for the sole purpose of raising the price at which G & W common stock traded.

The strongest evidence supporting an inference that Mulheren harbored a manipulative intent, is the telephone conversation between Boesky and Mulheren that occurred either late in the day on October 16 or before 11:00 a.m. on October 17, 1985. In discussing the virtues of G & W stock, Boesky told Mulheren that he "would not pay more than 45 for it and it would be great if it traded at 45." To this Mulheren replied "I understand." The meaning of this cryptic conversation is, at best, ambiguous, and we reject the government's contention that this conversation "*clearly* conveyed Boesky's request that the price of the stock be pushed up to $45 ... [and Mulheren's] agreement to help." Boesky never testified (again, he was not asked) what he meant by his words.[4]

We acknowledge that, construed as an innocent tip—*i.e.* G & W would be a "great" buy at a price of $45 or below—the conversation appears contradictory. It seems inconsistent for Boesky to advise, on one hand, that he would not pay more than $45, yet on the other to exclaim that it would be a bargain ("great") at $45. The conversation does not make any more sense, however, if construed as a request for illicit manipulation. That Boesky put a limit on the price he would pay for the stock ("I would not pay more than 45 for it") seems inconsistent with a request to drive up the price of the stock. If a conspiracy to manipulate for his own selfish benefit had been Boesky's intent, and if Davis were poised to repurchase the shares at the "last sale," Boesky would obviously have preferred to see Mulheren drive the trading in G & W stock to a price above $45. In this regard, it is noteworthy that there was *no* evidence whatever that Mulheren knew of Boesky's demand to get $45 per share from G & W. Moreover, during the four to six weeks preceding this conversation, Mulheren repeatedly asked Boesky what he thought of G & W—evincing Mulheren's predisposition (and Boesky's knowledge thereof) to invest in the company. In fact, Mulheren took a position in G & W when he shorted a broker 25,000 shares of G & W after the market closed on October 16.

Clearly, this case would be much less troubling had Boesky said "I want you to bring it up to 45" or, perhaps, even, "I'd like to see it trading at 45." But to hang a conviction on the threadbare phrase "it would be great if it traded at 45," particularly when the government does not suggest that the words were some sort of sinister code, defies reason and a sense of fair play. Any doubt about this is dispelled by the remaining evidence at trial.

First, and perhaps most telling, is that Jamie *lost* over $64,000 on Mulheren's October 17th transactions. This is hardly the result a market

---

4. Defense counsel objected after Boesky testified "[t]he design of the comment...." No ruling was made on the objection and the government—for reasons known only to itself—abandoned further inquiry into Boesky's state of mind.

manipulator seeks to achieve. One of the hallmarks of manipulation is some profit or personal gain inuring to the alleged manipulator. See, e.g., *Baum v. Phillips, Appel & Walden, Inc.*, 648 F. Supp. 1518, 1531 (S.D.N.Y. 1986), aff'd per curiam, 867 F.2d 776 (2d Cir. 1989); *Walck v. American Stock Exchange, Inc.*, 565 F. Supp. 1051, 1065-66 (E.D. Pa. 1981), aff'd, 687 F.2d 778 (3rd Cir. 1982); *SEC v. Commonwealth Chemical Securities, Inc.*, 410 F. Supp. 1002, 1013 (S.D.N.Y.1976), aff'd in part, modified on other grounds, 574 F.2d 90 (2d Cir. 1978).

Second, the unrebutted trial testimony of the G & W specialist demonstrated that if raising the price of G & W to $45 per share was Mulheren's sole intent, Mulheren purchased significantly more shares (and put Jamie in a position of greater risk) than necessary to achieve the result. The G & W specialist testified that at the time Jamie placed its second order, 5,000 shares would "definitely" have raised the trading price from $44 7/8 to $45 per share. Yet, Jamie bought 25,000 shares.

Although there was no evidence that Mulheren received a *quid pro quo* from Boesky for buying G & W stock, the government, nevertheless, claims that Mulheren had a "strong pecuniary interest" in accommodating Boesky in order to maintain the close and mutually profitable relationship they enjoyed. With this argument the government is hoist with its own petard. Precisely because of this past profitable relationship, the more reasonable conclusion is that Mulheren understood Boesky's comment as another tip—this time to buy G & W stock. Indeed, there was no evidence that Boesky had ever asked Mulheren to rig the price of a stock in the past.

None of the traditional badges of manipulation are present in this case. Mulheren conspicuously purchased the shares for Jamie's account in the open market. Compare *United States v. Scop*, 846 F.2d 135, 137 (matched orders through fictitious nominees) (2d Cir.1988); *United States v. Gilbert*, 668 F.2d 94, 95 (2d Cir. 1981) (matched orders and wash sales); *United States v. Minuse*, 114 F.2d 36, 38 (2d Cir. 1940) (fictitious accounts, matched orders, wash sales, dissemination of false literature). The government argues that Mulheren's deceptive intent can be inferred from the fact that (1) he purchased the G & W shares through Ihasz, a floor broker whom the government claims was used only infrequently by Jamie; and (2) Ihasz never informed anyone that the purchases were made for Jamie. These arguments are factually flawed.

There was no evidence that there was anything unusual about Ihasz's execution of the trades. Oliver Ihasz testified that Jamie was a customer of his company. There was no testimony that his company was used infrequently, or that Mulheren's request was in any way out of the ordinary. Nor is there anything peculiar about the fact that Ihasz disclosed only the name of the clearing broker and not Jamie, as the purchaser, when he executed the trade. As Ihasz testified, in an open market transaction, the only information the floor broker provides to the seller is the name of the clearing broker, not the ultimate buyer. Jamie was conspicuously identified as the ultimate buyer of the G & W securities on Ihasz's order tickets, where it is supposed to appear.

The government also argues that manipulative intent can be inferred from the fact that Mulheren's purchase on October 17, 1985 comprised 70 percent of the trading in G & W common stock during the period between the opening of the market and 11:10 a.m. Such market domination, the government contends, is indicative of manipulation. While we agree, as a general proposition, that market domination is a factor that supports a manipulation charge, the extent to which an investor controls or dominates the market at any given period of time cannot be viewed in a vacuum. For example, if only ten shares of a stock are bought or sold in a given hour and only by one investor, that investor has created 100 percent of the activity in that stock in that hour. This alone, however, does not make the investor a manipulator. The percent of domination must be viewed in light of the time period involved and other indicia of manipulation. Taken in this context, the cases upon which the government relies, *United States v. Gilbert*, 668 F.2d 94 (2d Cir. 1981); *United States v. Stein*, 456 F.2d 844 (2d Cir. 1972); *In re Delafield & Delafield,* [1967- 69 Transfer Binder] Fed. Sec. L. Rep. (CCH) § 77, 648 (SEC 1969), are readily distinguishable.

Gilbert, for example, involved the manipulation of the shares of Conrac Corporation where, over a *one-year period,* the defendant's trading constituted more than 50 percent of the overall trading. See *United States v. Gilbert*, [1981-82 Transfer Binder] Fed. Sec. L. Rep. (CCH) § 98, 244, at 91,602, 91,605, 1981 WL 1662 (S.D.N.Y.1981), aff'd, 668 F.2d at 95. In *Stein*, the manipulator's transactions accounted for 28.8 percent of the daily exchange volume of transactions in Buckeye Corporation stock over a *four month period.* When domination is sustained over such an extended period of time, evidence of manipulation is strong. But, if the percentage of control be measured in terms of minutes or hours, anyone could find himself labeled as a manipulator.

In re Delafield & Delafield is the only case that gives us pause. There, the respondents entered into a consent decree with the Securities and Exchange Commission concerning allegations that they had manipulated the Class A common stock of the Mary Carter Paint Company by selling 17,600 shares of the stock between 2:00 p.m. and the close of the market on January 9, 1968. Respondents' transactions represented 83 percent of the transactions in the stock during that period. Significantly, however, the sales "were effected in the name of two foreign banks to conceal the identity" of the true seller. No such chicanery exists here. Thus, in the absence of other indicia of manipulation—and there are none—the fact that Mulheren dominated the market between 9:30 a.m. and 11:10 a.m. on October 17, 1985 (noting that Mulheren's purchases represented a small fraction of the total October 17th activity in G & W stock) carries little weight.

The government also urges that Mulheren's manipulative intent—as opposed to investment intent—can be inferred from certain of Mulheren's actions after his purchase of the G & W shares. For example, Mulheren sold G & W call options in the afternoon of October 17, 1985 that were designed to create a hedge in the event of a drop in the price of stock. Had Mulheren known, however, that Boesky and Icahn were going to unload 6.7 million shares of G & W stock—which had the inevitable effect of driving the price down—surely Mulheren would have had the foresight to write the options *before* Boesky and Icahn had a chance to sell. That Mulheren wrote the options in the afternoon suggests only that he was attempting to mitigate his losses.

Finally, the government contends that the fact that Mulheren continued to do favors for Boesky after G & W repurchased Boesky and Icahn's shares is inconsistent with his claim that he was "duped" by Boesky into purchasing the 75,000 G & W shares. We disagree. First, the evidence of "favors" rests largely on the unproven "stock parking" charges. Second, Mulheren's conduct after his G & W purchases is equally consistent with that of a sophisticated businessman who turns the other cheek after being slapped by the hand that usually feeds him.

We acknowledge that this case treads dangerously close to the line between legitimate inference and impermissible speculation. We are persuaded, however, that to come to the conclusion it did, "the jury must have engaged in false surmise and rank speculation." At best, Mulheren's convictions are based on evidence that is "at least as consistent with innocence as with guilt," and "on inferences no more valid than others equally supported by reason and experience." Accordingly, the judgments of conviction are reversed and Counts One through Four of the indictment are dismissed.

NOTES AND QUESTIONS

*1. **The Government's Legal Theories.*** The *Mulheren* court expressed "misgivings" about the government's argument that a person violates Rule 10b-5 by trading securities in the open market with the sole purpose of affecting the price of a security. The court also noted, but "expressed no view" on, the government's alternative theory that Rule 10b-5 is violated by the failure to disclose the subjective "manipulative" intent behind one's trading decisions.

The government's latter argument found acceptance with another Second Circuit panel in *United States v. Regan*, 937 F.2d 823 (2d Cir. 1991), a case decided less than two weeks before *Mulheren*. At trial, the government alleged, and ultimately convinced a jury, that Lee Newberg, a bond trader at Drexel, Burnham, Lambert (Drexel) had sought to depress the price of C.O.M.B. common stock by arranging with Charles Zarzecki, a trader at the arbitrage firm of Princeton/Newport (PN), to sell short a substantial amount of C.O.M.B. stock. Drexel had agreed to underwrite a $25 million dollar offering of convertible bonds for C.O.M.B., and a lower C.O.M.B. stock price would have enabled Drexel to command a higher interest rate for the convertible bonds and therefore make the issue more easy to sell. In effecting the short sales, Zarzecki did not disclose that PN was the short seller or that "Drexel was the moving party behind the entire deal." Id. at 829.

The bond traders argued on appeal that because they did not stand in a fiduciary relationship with the parties on the other side of their short sales, they were free to remain silent about their motivations for trading, even if they did engage in short sales with the hope of affecting the market price of C.O.M.B. stock. The court rejected this argument, and affirmed the jury's finding that Section 10(b) and Rule 10b-5 had been violated. The following constitutes the court's analysis on this issue:

> In enacting section 10(b), "Congress meant to prohibit the full range of ingenious devices that might be used to manipulate securities prices." *Santa Fe Indus. v. Green*, 430 U.S. 462, 477 (1977). *** The plan conceived by Newberg and Zarzecki fits comfortably within this "full range" of wrongful acts. "Failure to disclose that market prices are being artificially depressed operates as a

> deceit on the market place and is an omission of a material fact." *United States v. Charnay*, 537 F.2d 341, 351 (9th Cir. 1976). Appellants' argument that a fiduciary relationship must exist before liability can be found is without merit. The case of *Chiarella v. United States*, 445 U.S. 222 (1980), upon which appellants rely involved trading on the basis of nonpublic information; here, appellants are charged with market manipulation.

Regan, 937 F.2d at 829.

Did the *Regan* court come to terms with the defendants' argument? To be sure, *Chiarella* was an insider trading case, but the Supreme Court's holding that silence may operate as a fraud under Rule 10b-5 only if there is a duty to speak has never been limited to that narrow context. See, e.g., *Basic Inc. v. Levinson*, 485 U.S. 224, 239 n. 17 (1988) (stating that "[s]ilence, absent a duty to disclose, is not misleading under Rule 10b-5"). (See also Chapter 2.A.2 supra.) What, if anything, is special about manipulative conduct that imposes a duty to disclose "subjective motivations?"

Does the government stand on firmer footing when it asks courts to view manipulation not as a disclosure violation but as a form of active conduct that serves to deceive investors? In its brief to the Supreme Court opposing Zarzecki's petition for certiorari, the DOJ argued that the traders "engaged in affirmative conduct designed to deceive investors by creating an artificial market price for C.O.M.B. stock." Brief for the U.S. in Opposition at 10-11, *Zarzecki v. U.S.*, 504 U.S. 940 (1992) (No. 91-1233). Leaving aside the uncertainty surrounding the meaning of "artificial," is this argument otherwise consistent with the Supreme Court's view that manipulative acts require either misrepresentation or nondisclosure? See *Schreiber*, supra, 472 U.S. at 8 ("[a]ll three species of misconduct, i.e., 'fraudulent, deceptive, or manipulative,' listed by Congress are directed at failures to disclose"); *Santa Fe*, 430 U.S. at 477 ("nondisclosure is generally essential to the success of a manipulative scheme"). How do the Court's statements in *Stoneridge* factor into this mix? See *Stoneridge Inv. Partners, LLC v. Scientific–Atlanta, Inc.*, 552 U.S. 148, 158 (2008) ("Conduct itself can be deceptive;" there need not be "a specific oral or written statement before there could be liability under § 10(b) or Rule 10b–5").

2. Artificial v. Non-Artificial Prices. Professors Fischel and Ross have recognized that the task of defining the difference between artificial and non-artificial securities prices is an exceedingly difficult one. Consider their analysis:

> One possible definition is that any price change that results from trading designed to produce such a price change is an artificial price. This definition is unsatisfactory because trading with the purpose of producing a price change is not necessarily harmful. Consider *** the example of an issuer that purchases its own shares to signal investors that the shares are undervalued. In this example, the trading moves prices in the correct direction and thus the resulting price change should not be labeled "artificial."
>
> An alternate approach is to focus on whether the trading moves prices closer to or away from their correct level. But what is the "correct level"? One possibility is the price that reflects long-run conditions of supply and demand. Manipulation could then be defined as trades that "do not move price more quickly in the direction that reflects long-run conditions of supply and demand." *** But this definition is also unsatisfactory. What if the trades do not move

prices at all or move prices in the direction that reflects short-run conditions of supply and demand? Most importantly, what happens if the trades move prices in one direction because the trader genuinely believes that prices will move in this direction, but the trader turns out to be wrong and prices ultimately move in the opposite direction? Trading based on a genuine belief that prices will ultimately move in the direction of the trades is the essence of nonmanipulative trading.

To avoid the need to distinguish between short-run and long-run conditions of supply and demand, the correct level of prices could be defined as the level prices would be if all relevant information were publicly disclosed. But this definition is also unhelpful. "All relevant information" includes not only the information possessed by the trader, but also the trades themselves. If prices move in response to trades, the price cannot be said to be "artificial" unless the trades are defined as illegitimate in some way. Once again we are faced with the problem of circularity—improper trades are trades that produce an artificial price and artificial price is defined as a price produced by improper trades.

Defining manipulation by reference to whether the trades move prices closer to their correct level has another flaw: it jeopardizes property rights in information. Absent a fiduciary relationship or other special circumstance, traders do not have a duty to disclose the information they possess that motivates their trades. Disclosure would cause the information to lose its value and thus eliminate the incentive to acquire the information in the first place. Without such an incentive, no one would search for information and securities markets—which depend on new information to cause price changes—would be destroyed. But trades, as well as disclosures, can reveal information. The more information the trade reveals, the closer the trade comes to a direct disclosure, which decreases the trader's ability to capture the value of the private information in his possession. For markets to exist, therefore, trades cannot be fully revealing. Traders must be allowed to disguise their trades to avoid disclosing the information they possess to other traders. Accordingly, manipulation cannot be defined as trading that does not move prices closer to their "correct" level. Such a definition would deny traders the ability to disguise their trades to capture the value of the information they possess.

Thus, there is no objective definition of manipulation. The only definition that makes any sense is subjective—it focuses entirely on the intent of the trader. Manipulative trades could be defined as profitable trades made with "bad" intent—in other words, trades that meet the following conditions: (1) the trading is intended to move prices in a certain direction; (2) the trader has no belief that the prices would move in this direction but for the trade; and (3) the resulting profit comes solely from the trader's ability to move prices and not from his possession of valuable information. Traders who trade with "good" intent—for the purpose of moving prices in the direction they believe prices will move—are not engaged in manipulation. Similarly, traders with private information who disguise their trades with the effect that prices do not move in the correct direction, or even move in the wrong direction, also trade with "good" intent and thus are not engaged in manipulation because their ultimate profit is attributable to the private information they possess.

Daniel R. Fischel and David J. Ross, Should the Law Prohibit "Manipulation" in Financial Markets?, 105 Harv. L. Rev. 503, 508-10 (1991).

3. Proving "Bad Intent" With Circumstantial Evidence. *Mulheren* reveals some of the problems that the government (or a private plaintiff) will typically encounter when it seeks to prove that actual stock trades were made with "bad intent." Indeed, because "it is impossible to probe into the depths of a man's mind, it is necessary in the usual case (that is, absent an admission) that the finding of manipulative purpose be based on inferences drawn from circumstantial evidence." In re Federal Corp., Exchange Act Release No. 3909, 25 SEC 227, 230 (Jan. 29, 1947).

In *Regan*, the government prosecutors were fortunate to have a recording of the conversation between the Drexel and PN bond traders, wherein Newberg told Zarzecki about the upcoming Drexel underwriting of C.O.M.B.'s convertible bonds and said:

> The stock is sixteen bid, up from fifteen and three eighths.
>
> I don't want this thing to be sixteen bid.
>
> I want, y-y- you know, to get rid of it, y—, ah, you know. I want, I want it down to at least fifteen and three quarters and hopefully lower. Umm ..., I wouldn't mind you selling a little bit first. And um ..., you're indemnified, uh, you know, my—, it's, y—, you know what I'm saying.

Information, *United States v. Drexel Burnham Lambert, Inc.* (S.D.N.Y. Mar. 29, 1989) (89 Cr. 41) at 22-23 (quoted in Lewis D. Lowenfels & Alan R. Bromberg, Securities Market Manipulations: An Examination and Analysis of Domination and Control, Frontrunning, and Parking, 55 Alb. L. Rev. 293, 352 (1991)). While hardly an unequivocal "smoking gun," the recorded conversation certainly did much to bolster the government's case that the bond traders' sole intent in shorting the C.O.M.B stock was to depress the price for Drexel's benefit in the upcoming bond offering.

Can you identify other areas of law—apart from federal securities law—where the legality of a person's conduct turns exclusively on a person's subjective motivations? In such cases, what types of facts would support a claim that the law was violated?

4. Manipulative Activity Designed to Restore Value. What if a person sincerely believes that others in the market are acting to artificially affect the price of a security and therefore trades with the ultimate goal of *restoring* the stock's price to its "true" value? For example, there was evidence in *Regan* that Drexel believed that C.O.M.B. was itself manipulating—"levitat[ing]," to use the court's term—the price of its common stock into a higher range. *Regan,* 937 F.2d at 829. If Drexel acted with the purpose of counteracting C.O.M.B's activity, is it fair to say that the bond traders acted with the requisite "bad intent?" The court in *United States v. Hall,* 48 F. Supp.2d 386, 387 (S.D.N.Y. 1999) had this to say about "correcting" the market:

> A fraudulent scheme to manipulate is unlawful, even if the defendant is trying in his mind to correct the market. Even assuming Hall was genuinely trying to bring the price of HealthTech stock up to where he believed it should be, the ends do not justify the means and he could not seek to do so through unlawful means.

Assuming that the defendant's trades did not involve wash sales, matched orders, or other such fictitious trading practices, does *Hall* reach a sound conclusion?

*5. **The Costs and Benefits of Market Manipulation.*** In *Mulheren*, among other evidence, the Second Circuit found "most telling" that Mulheren's firm lost over $64,000 on the G & W stock purchases and concluded that "this is hardly the result a market manipulator seeks to achieve." Given the government's contention that Mulheren's trading was motivated by a desire to assist Boesky, shouldn't the economic inquiry have been on the profit made by Boesky? Professor Steve Thel points out that the 1/4 point rise in the price of G & W due to Mulheren's trading resulted in Boesky receiving about $850,000 more for his 3.4 million shares than he would have received had Mulheren not effected the trades. And if the overall benefit of the alleged manipulation scheme is measured to include the increase in value for Carl Icahn's shares, the profit earned through the Mulheren trades becomes $1,678,925. See Steve Thel, $850,000 in Six Minutes—The Mechanics of Securities Manipulation, 79 Cornell L. Rev. 219, 255 (1994).

*6. **"Real" Trades Revisited.*** In *Markowski v. SEC*, 274 F.3d 525 (D.C. Cir. 2001), the court affirmed an SEC order sustaining a disciplinary action taken by the NASD against Michael Markowski, the Chairman, CEO, and majority shareholder of Global America, Inc (then an NASD member firm that specialized in emerging growth companies), and Joseph Riccio, Global's trader. The order imposed liability under Rule 10b-5 for manipulating the stock market. Specifically, in connection with an initial public offering of Mountaintop Corporation underwritten by Global, Markowski and Riccio were found to have artificially supported the price of Mountaintop securities by "(1) maintain[ing] high bid prices for Mountaintop securities, and (2) absorb[ing] all unwanted securities into inventory, thereby preventing sales from depressing market prices." Id. at 527. The D.C. Circuit had this to say about the defendants' argument that "because Global's bids and trades in this case were 'real'—they involved real customers, real transactions, and real money—the trades cannot be classified as an unlawful manipulation":

> Liability for manipulation wholly independent of fictitious transactions in fact raises interesting questions. Without such transactions, the core of the offense can be obscure. It may be hard to separate a "manipulative" investor from one who is simply over-enthusiastic, a true believer in the object of investment. Both may amass huge inventories and place high bids, even though there are scant objective data supporting the implicit estimate of the stock's value. Legality would thus depend entirely on whether the investor's intent was "an investment purpose" or "solely to affect the price of [the] security." *United States v. Mulheren*, 938 F.2d 364, 368 (2d Cir.1991). Given the typical ambiguity of intent, commentators have suggested that imposing liability may chill investors from transactions that actually contribute to the efficiency of securities markets. Daniel R. Fischel & David J. Ross, "Should the Law Prohibit 'Manipulation' in Financial Markets?," 105 Harv. L. Rev. 503, 523 (1991) (expressing concerns about the manipulation doctrine's over-deterrence effects); see also *Mulheren*, 938 F.2d at 368 (expressing misgivings about basing 10b-5 violations purely on whether or not a "transaction is effected for an investment purpose").
>
> Commentators have also suggested that where manipulative behavior is solely defined in terms of the actor's purpose, it may well be self-deterring as

a general matter, so that any need for an external sanction is slight. Purely "trade-based" manipulation schemes, in which the manipulator simply buys a security in order to induce higher prices and then sells to take advantage of the price change, are likely to fail. First, it is difficult unilaterally to cause price to rise. Second, it is even more difficult to sell subsequently at a price high enough to cover both purchase costs *and* transaction costs. For one thing, if the actor's purchases are such as to give the market a material upward thrust, his later sales may equivalently drive it down. See Fischel & Ross, supra, at 512-19. But see Steve Thel, "$850,000 in Six Minutes—The Mechanics of Securities Manipulation," 79 Cornell L. Rev. 219 (1994) (suggesting that manipulators may profit from very small, short-lived price changes).

These arguments, however, are of little use to Markowski and Riccio. Whatever the practical concerns, we cannot find the Commission's interpretation to be unreasonable in light of what appears to be Congress's determination that "manipulation" can be illegal solely because of the actor's purpose. See *Chevron U.S.A., Inc. v. Natural Resources Defense Council, Inc.*, 467 U.S. 837, 843-44(1984). Section 9(a)(2) of the Securities Exchange Act manifests this idea by declaring it unlawful

> [t]o effect ... a series of transactions in any security registered on a national securities exchange creating actual or apparent active trading in such security or raising or depressing the price of such security, for the purpose of inducing the purchase or sale of such security by others.

Id. This provision is quite separate from the subsections of § 9 prohibiting manipulation through fraudulent devices such as wash sales, [Exchange Act Section 9(a)(1)(A)], matched sales, id. at [Section 9(a)(1)(B)-(C)], and false statements, id. at [Section 9(a)(4)]. Given Congress's clear endorsement for sanctions against this sort of manipulation, the Commission's inclusion of it within the phrase "manipulative ... device" in § 10(b) cannot have been unreasonable.

The Commission's interpretation is also consistent with its rules governing an issuer's purchases of its own securities. See Securities Exchange Act of 1934, Rule 10b-18. Issuer repurchases are perfectly real transactions. But the Commission has created a safe harbor measured in terms of timing, volume, and price; purchases outside the safe harbor are subject to possible enforcement action as manipulations. See Purchases of Certain Equity Securities by the Issuer and Others; Adoption of Safe Harbor, 47 Fed. Reg. 53,333 (1982).

Further, to the extent that the case against liability for "trade-based" manipulation depends on its inherently self-deterring character, petitioners' situation may be distinguishable. The activity in Mountaintop furthered an external purpose. At least in the short term, Global supported Mountaintop's price not to profit from later sales of Mountaintop, but to maintain customer interest in Global generally and to sustain confidence in its other securities. As James Shanley, Global's chief operating officer, testified, petitioner Riccio explained his refusal to lower his bid price: "If we do that on one stock, they [presumably, holders of Global's stocks] will hit us on all the stocks." Thus, the prospects of losing some money on Mountaintop in the short run would not deter Global from manipulating—if that cost was worth the benefit of keeping its customers and preserving confidence in its other stocks.

Id. at 528-29. Was *Markowski's* reasoning sound?

PROBLEM 8-2

Frank Franklin is a very sophisticated investor who has recently reduced his work schedule as an architect so that he can spend more time at home researching companies and "day-trading" his stock portfolio through his on-line investment account. On many mornings throughout the last several months, Frank has bought substantial amounts of low priced stocks in companies that he believes the market is overlooking and, therefore, undervaluing. Frank has noticed that his early morning trading often seems to spark others' interest in his selected stock, such that he can make a reasonable profit by selling off his holdings at the close of the business day.

Are there any aspects of Frank's day-trading strategy that could be considered manipulative? Could the government prove that his actions were in violation of the federal securities laws? Should it try?

Would your answer change if, after he purchased his chosen stocks, Frank routinely sent postings to on-line bulletin boards stating that "now is the time to buy X stock" or "I strongly recommend X stock"?

What if, instead, Frank's preferred trading strategy involves short selling? Assume that he frequently targets particular companies for massive amounts of short selling, even though Frank does not believe that the company's stock is overpriced. Instead, he seeks to profit from the effects of his own trading activity: in a series of separate transactions, he sells short substantial blocks of a company's shares, with the knowledge that his sales will push down the company's stock price and thereby trigger stop-loss orders placed by investors and institutions with long positions. Frank recognizes, of course, that he must repurchase the same number of shares at a later time in order to cover the stock that he borrowed to effectuate the short. But he is confident that he'll be able to purchase that stock at a price that is substantially lower than the price at which he sold. Is Frank engaging in illegal market manipulation? Who, possibly, is harmed by this activity? Is Frank likely to be successful over time?

Would your answer change if, after he shorted his chosen stocks, Frank sent postings to on-line bulletin boards spreading negative and false rumors about the respective companies?

Short selling involves the execution of a sell order placed by a person who does not actually own the security that is being sold. Instead, the order is filled with borrowed stock, and the short seller expects that he will be able to cover what is essentially an IOU held by his broker through the purchase of stock at a later time for a lower price. The short seller is therefore hoping to sell high and buy low, in contrast to the more conventional strategic hope of buying low and selling high. Short sellers perform an important market role by increasing liquidity, promoting efficient price discovery, and facilitating hedging and other risk management activities. However, as the SEC has observed:

> Although short selling serves useful market purposes, it also may be used *** to illegally manipulate stock prices. One example is the "bear raid" where an equity security is sold short in an effort to drive down the price of the security by creating an imbalance of sell-side interest. This unrestricted short selling could exacerbate a declining market in a security by increasing pressure from

> the sell-side, eliminating bids, and causing a further reduction in the price of a security by creating an appearance that the security's price is falling for fundamental reasons, when the decline, or the speed of the decline, is being driven by other factors.

SEC Final Rule — Amendments to Regulation SHO, Exchange Act Release No. 61595, Feb. 26, 2010. In the problem above, is Frank's massive short selling essentially a bear raid? Note here the Second Circuit's caution in *ATSI Commc'ns, Inc. v. Shaar Fund, Ltd.*, 493 F.3d 87, 101 (2d Cir. 2007) that "short selling – even in high volumes – is not, by itself, manipulative. *** To be actionable as a manipulative act, short selling must be willfully combined with something more to create a false impression of how market participants value a security." What is the "more" that occurs in a bear raid?

To counteract the destabilizing effects of manipulative short selling, the SEC used its authority under Section 10(a) of the Exchange Act to adopt former Rule 10a-1, which for more than 60 years, applied an "uptick" test on short sales. This uptick test effectively prohibited short sales in a declining market by allowing only short sale transactions at a price equal to or above the price of the last reported sale. The SEC abolished Rule 10a-1 in July 2007 in response to decades of claims from economists that the uptick test was undermining market efficiency.

One year later, as financial markets were imploding, debates about short selling took center stage, with some observers going so far as to blame manipulative short sellers for the collapses of Bear Stearns and Lehman Brothers. Although the SEC emphasized that "we are not aware of specific empirical evidence that the elimination of short sale price tests has contributed to the increased volatility in U.S. markets," SEC officials were concerned nonetheless that short selling in the securities of a wide range of financial institutions "may be causing sudden and excessive fluctuations of the prices of such securities in such a manner so as to threaten fair and orderly markets." Emergency Order Taking Temporary Action to Respond to Market Developments, Exchange Act Release No. 58592, 73 Fed. Reg. 55,169 (Sept. 18, 2008). To "prevent short selling from being used to drive down the share prices of issuers even where there is no fundamental basis for a price decline other than general market conditions," the SEC instituted a temporary ban on the short selling of securities in almost 800 financial companies. The unprecedented ban was lifted a month later after the federal government rescued the financial industry with an unprecedented bailout package.

After the dust settled, the SEC adopted a number of new measures to more effectively regulate short selling activity. These rulemaking initiatives amended Regulation SHO, which the SEC had enacted in 2004 as an initial attempt to modernize its short selling rules. One set of initiatives was directed at the practice of "naked-short selling," *i.e.,* selling shares short without first having borrowed them. Although Reg SHO still does not explicitly prohibit "naked shorts," the SEC has placed increasingly stringent requirements on the market professionals who facilitate short sale transactions. For example, Rule 204, first adopted on a temporary basis and then made permanent in summer 2009, requires broker-dealers promptly to purchase or borrow securities to deliver on a short sale (or to have reasonable grounds to believe that the short seller has made appropriate arrangements for borrowing) and promptly to close out positions where there have been repeated failures to deliver. The SEC also adopted an antifraud rule, Rule 10b-21, aimed at short sellers who deceive broker-dealers or other specified persons about their intention or ability to deliver securities in time for settlement. Given that deceptive short selling already constituted a violation of Section 10(b) and Rule 10b-5 (and/or Section 17(a)(1) of the Securities Act, see *United States v. Naftalin*, 441 U.S. 768 (1979)), why nonetheless might the SEC have chosen to adopt the explicit prohibitions in Rule 10b-21?

Further amendments to Reg SHO became effective in spring 2010, with an alternative uptick rule (Rule 201) that imposes restrictions on short selling when a stock has triggered a "circuit breaker" by experiencing a price decline of ten percent or more in one day. At that point, short selling would be permitted during that day and the one following only if the transaction price is above the current national best bid. Will this modified uptick rule successfully thwart short selling schemes along the lines of the one set out in Problem 8-2 above?

For additional background and analysis, see Merritt B. Fox et al., Short Selling and the News: A Preliminary Report on an Empirical Study, 54 N.Y.L.S. Rev. 645 (2010); Douglas M. Branson, Nibbling at the Edges – Regulation of Short Selling: Policing Fails to Deliver and Restoration of an Uptick Rule, 65 Bus. Law. 67 (2009).

C. MISLEADING RECOMMENDATIONS AND MATERIAL MISSTATEMENTS DESIGNED TO AFFECT MARKET PRICES

1. Scalping and "Pump and Dumps"

The SEC's complaint that follows this prefatory material charges a Georgetown law student with Rule 10b-5 violations in connection with a stock scalping scheme that was conducted over the Internet with the assistance of three other law students. Although sometimes viewed and prosecuted as a type of insider trading (see discussion of *Carpenter v. United States* in Chapter 7), scalping can be more generally described as the practice of recommending the purchase of a security to a group of investors while one is selling, or intending to sell, that security at the same time. To be sure, the scalper is purchasing securities on the basis of the nonpublic information that he is about to publicize a positive recommendation about a security. But unlike the typical insider trading case, the scalper controls—indeed creates—the very information that, when released, is bound to affect the security's market price. Accordingly, when recommendations are made for the avowed purpose of profiting from their effect, the practice of scalping can be viewed as a type of market manipulation. Once again, then, the role of motive is key.

The Supreme Court first considered the legality of scalping in *SEC v. Capital Gains Research Bureau, Inc.*, 375 U.S. 180 (1963), a case which involved recommendations issued by the publishers of a monthly investment report who were registered investment advisers. The SEC argued, and the Court agreed, that the advisers had committed acts which "operat[ed] as a fraud or deceit" in violation of Section 206 of the Investment Advisers Act of 1940. Id. at 181. The Court focused specifically on the advisers' failure to disclose to their clients their "practice of purchasing shares of a security for [their] own account shortly before recommending that security for long-term investment and then immediately selling the shares at a profit upon the rise in the market price following the recommendation." Id. at 181. In the Court's view, it did not matter whether the advisers' "advice was 'honest' in the sense that they believed it was sound and did not offer it for the purpose of furthering personal pecuniary objectives." Id. at 200. Rather, the Court found in the legislative history an intent "to eliminate, *or at least to expose*, all conflicts of interest which might incline an investment adviser—consciously or unconsciously—to render advice which was not disinterested." Id. at 191-192 (emphasis added). Absent from the case was any suggestion that the investment advisers had sought to intentionally manipulate the market.

An inquiry into the unlawfulness of scalping becomes a bit more complex when we depart from the context of recommendations by investment advisers or broker-dealers who clearly owe fiduciary duties of disclosure to their clients. Yet in *Zweig v. Hearst Corp.*, 594 F.2d 1261 (9th Cir.1979), the court had little trouble concluding that a newspaper columnist had violated Rule 10b-5 when he touted a stock in his column without disclosing that he had recently purchased 5,000 shares of that stock from the issuer at a discounted price and intended to sell the stock after the column's publication. (The plaintiff's case was no doubt strengthened when he was able to show that the columnist had written similar columns about 21 other securities which he had purchased shortly before and had sold shortly after each column was published.) In finding an omission of a material fact in violation of Rule 10b-5, the court concluded that "[c]olumnists *** ordinarily have no duty to disclose facts about their personal financial affairs ***" but that here "the defendant assumed those duties when, with knowledge of the stock's market and an intent to gain personally, he encouraged purchases of the securities in the market." Id. at 1268. Although the facts of the case may well have supported it, the court in *Zweig* did not consider the theory that the newspaper columnist had violated Rule 10b-5 by engaging in acts that were intended to have a manipulative effect on the market.

The *Zweig* court's conclusion that the failure to disclose an intention to scalp violates Rule 10b-5 was reached prior to the Supreme Court's holding in *Chiarella* that silence, absent a duty to disclose, is not actionable as fraud under Rule 10b-5. Is *Zweig's* conclusion still valid? At least one court has answered affirmatively, at least in the context where, like a newspaper columnist, the defendant was found to have stood in a relationship of trust and confidence with the recipients of his stock recommendations. See *SEC v. Park (a.k.a."Tokyo Joe")*, 99 F. Supp.2d 889 (N.D. Ill. 2000) (refusing to dismiss Rule 10b-5 scalping allegations against defendant, a former burrito vendor and present-day "internet guru," who operated a stock-pick and investment advice website for fee-paying subscribers).

Consider the allegations in the following complaint:

SEC v. DOUGLAS W. COLT

COMPLAINT

CV-1:00CV00423 (D.C.D.C) (EGS)

March 2, 2000

Plaintiff Securities and Exchange Commission ("the Commission") alleges:

NATURE OF THE ACTION

1. During February and March 1999, defendant Douglas Colt, a student at a Washington, D.C. area law school, carried out an illegal scheme to manipulate the price of four stocks using a free subscription internet website called "Fast-Trades.com."

2. Through his scheme centered on recommending stocks, Colt drove up the short-term price for each stock by as much as 700%. By trading in advance of the stock recommendations, Colt generated more than $345,000 in total profits for himself, four individuals who assisted him in the scheme, and two of Colt's friends. At times, some of them garnered profits exceeding 500% within one hour. Within a few hours after the recommendations were disseminated to subscribers, the price of each of the four stocks decreased significantly from its intraday high.

3. Colt targeted low priced, thinly traded stocks knowing that his trades and trades by subscribers would artificially increase the price of the stocks selected. For each of the four manipulated stocks, Colt and the other participants collectively purchased a significant volume of the selected stock -in three cases more than 150% of the total average daily volume [the average number of shares bought and sold each day for approximately 200 business days immediately preceding the selection of the stock by the Fast-Trades.com website]. For all four stock selections, Fast-Trades purchases were made shortly before the website disseminated the recommendations to its subscribers.

4. After making these purchases and before the recommendations to purchase the stock were e-mailed to subscribers, Colt and the other participants entered sell limit orders or had orders entered on their behalf. Colt expected that unwitting subscribers would buy the recommended stock. Colt further expected that the purchases would drive the price higher still, triggering the sell limit orders. This is precisely what happened.

5. Subscriber purchases were essential to the scheme. Thus, Colt constantly needed to maintain and expand Fast-Trades subscriber rolls. To attract new subscribers, Colt recruited and trained his roommates, Kenneth Terrell and Jason Wyckoff, along with Adam Altman—all law school classmates—to help him promote the site by posting false and misleading messages on hundreds of publicly accessible internet message boards. These messages disguised the authors' connection with the site and misrepresented the investment success they achieved from following Fast-Trades' recommendations. Partly through these postings, the subscriber base grew to more than 9,000 people over a two month period.

6. Colt also included a false "track record" on the Fast-Trades.com website, where he touted the performance of several stocks that he claimed were past Fast-Trades selections. In fact, several of these stocks had not been selected by Fast-Trades.

7. The Fast-Trades.com website also contained a misleading disclaimer crafted by Colt, Terrell, Wyckoff and Altman that misrepresented their trading intentions to their subscribers. The disclaimer stated that Fast-Trades representatives "may" trade Fast-Trades selections "at any time." In fact, for each of the four stocks, Colt had already purchased the selected stock *and* entered sell limit orders before Fast-Trades even distributed the selection to its subscribers.

8. By engaging in the transactions, acts, practices and courses of business alleged herein, defendant Colt violated the antifraud provisions of the federal securities laws.

JURISDICTION

9. The Commission brings this action pursuant to Section 21(d)(1) of the Securities Exchange Act of 1934 ("Exchange Act").

10. This Court has jurisdiction of this action pursuant to Section 27 of the Exchange Act.

11. The defendant, directly or indirectly, has engaged in, and unless restrained and enjoined by this Court will continue to engage in, transactions, acts, practices, and courses of business that violate Section 10(b) of the Exchange Act and Rule 10b-5 promulgated thereunder.

12. In connection with the transactions, acts, practices, and courses of business described in this Complaint, the defendant, directly or indirectly, has made use of the means and instrumentalities of interstate commerce, of the mails, and/or of the facilities of national securities exchanges.

THE DEFENDANT

13. Defendant Douglas Colt, age 24, is a permanent resident of Colorado Springs, Colorado, and a third-year law student at a Washington, D.C. area law school. During the time of the violations alleged herein, Colt resided in Arlington, Virginia, in an apartment he shared with two law school classmates, Kenneth Terrell and Jason Wyckoff.

CLAIM FOR RELIEF

Violations of Section 10(b) of the Exchange Act
and Rule 10b-5 Promulgated Thereunder

COLT LAYS THE GROUNDWORK FOR THE FAST-TRADES.COM SCHEME

14. Douglas Colt began trading stocks in the summer of 1998, when he opened a margin account at Charles Schwab & Co. Through 1998 and early 1999, he predominantly traded technology and penny stocks, holding most positions for only a few days or weeks. In total, he bought and sold approximately thirteen positions before he began making recommendations on the Fast-Trades website.

Colt's trading in these thirteen stocks yielded a total net profit of approximately $24.

15. In late January 1999, Colt created Fast-Trades.com, an internet stock selection subscription website. Fast-Trades offered a free "six month trial period," which the website represented was a "limited time" offer, and no subscriber ever paid a fee. Subscribers received the stock selections from Fast-Trades in one of two ways: either through a password protected area of the Fast-Trades website that allowed subscribers to learn the selection twenty-four hours before it was available to the public; or by having the selection e-mailed to them at the same time it became available to subscribers on the website.

16. The website consisted of an introduction page describing the site, a page that allowed visitors to the site to register as subscribers, and a page listing the current stock selection and providing information about the company selected, and displaying a disclaimer. The introduction page also included a "track record" that listed alleged previous stock picks, the highest price the stock reached after that pick, and a "stable high" price purportedly showing a price at which the stock settled after Fast-Trades selected it.

17. The "track record" of alleged previous stock picks that Colt included on the Fast-Trades website was materially false and misleading. In his posted track record, Colt included the names and short term performance of some stocks that had never been selected by Fast-Trades. He did this in order to artificially enhance Fast-Trades stock-picking credibility with potential subscribers. In fact, in an April 27, 1999 online message board posting, Colt revealed his understanding of this part of the scheme when he accused a competing stock picking website of doing the same thing. Using an alias, Colt attacked the other website's track record, calling it an "extremely fraudulent practice." Colt noted that on the first day the competing site appeared, "they somehow had a `track record' of about five picks." The posting continued: "Hmmm ... think they just made those up so that investors would be fooled into thinking [the unrelated stock picking website] actually knew something about picking stocks? You bet."

18. Colt created the website and selected all of Fast-Trades' recommendations, purportedly after researching various companies. Colt's "research," however was illusory. In an April 29, 1999 online message board posting criticizing an unrelated stock picking website, and again using an alias, Colt set forth an eleven-point blueprint for a price manipulation scheme. Colt's blueprint posting stated: screen for thinly traded stocks in the $1 to $2 range; get rid of all the oil and gas stocks because "they're not trendy"; modify the screen to find companies that have shown revenue increases in the last quarter, "so you can justify this gem to the world"; of the remaining stocks, look for one with very low average volume and low float; pull together information from optimistic company press releases; "throw in some bull*** about the company being an internet wonder"; "buy a bunch of this garbage stock"; "tell your idiot subscribers about how great the stock is, and, like sheep, they will run out and buy it"; "dump the shares you bought a few hours ago to all of these suckers"; "watch the stock steadily tank for the next month"; and "laugh all the way to the bank."

19. Before investing, Colt conducted a test to determine what impact dissemination of his stock recommendation would have on the market. On February 1, 1999, Colt recommended the test selection, Electrosource, Inc.

(ticker: ELSI). Colt observed ELSI's price increase by thirty-five percent after the selection was announced.

COLT ENLISTS HIS ROOMMATES TO JOIN FAST-TRADES

20. During the 1998-99 academic year, Colt shared an apartment with two other law students, Kenneth Terrell and Jason Wyckoff. Shortly after Colt started the Fast-Trades website in late January, Colt offered his roommates the opportunity to participate in Fast-Trades. Colt told them he had posted a selection on the website and monitored the market to see how his selection affected the stock. If they agreed to help, Colt would allow them to trade on Fast-Trades selections through his account.

21. Terrell and Wyckoff agreed to participate with Colt, and during February and March 1999, the two spent numerous hours posting materially false and misleading messages on several hundred different Yahoo! internet message boards promoting the site to potential subscribers. Colt's roommates each gave Colt money to purchase shares on their behalf in Colt's brokerage account. Neither Terrell nor Wyckoff had any prior experience investing in stocks.

THE FAST-TRADES.COM SCHEME

22. After observing the upward price movement stemming from his recommendation of Electrosource, Colt began purchasing stock in advance of Fast-Trades selections. From February 16 through March 10, Colt, one or more Fast-Trades participants, and as many as two friends purchased shares in the next four Fast-Trades selections before they were provided to subscribers. As the chart below illustrates, participants in the Fast-Trades scheme and their two friends collectively purchased an increasing number of shares with each selection.

Security	Fast-Trades Related Purchases	Avg. Daily Volume	% of Avg. Daily Volume
Apache Medical	5,000	11,694	43%
Option Care	24,000	13,823	174%
American Education	36,283	3,454	1050%
Artecon	51,512	33,341	154%

23. For all four stock selections, Fast-Trades purchases drove up the price and volume of the stock selected even before the selection was sent out to subscribers. Non-subscribing investors who observed the increase in price and volume of the selected stock and purchased shares—both before and after the release of the stock pick—also helped create a price increase. The rising price usually triggered the sell limit orders that Colt and the other Fast-Trades participants who traded had previously entered. Colt, his mother Joanne Colt (who was a participant in the Fast-Trades scheme), Terrell and Wyckoff monitored the run up by watching real time market quotes.

COLT, TERRELL AND WYCKOFF PURCHASE AMSI ON FEBRUARY 16

24. Apache Medical Systems, Inc. (ticker: AMSI) was the first Fast-Trades selection in which Fast-Trades participants traded. The AMSI selection was sent out to subscribers at approximately 2:45 p.m. on February 16, 1999.

25. Less than an hour before sending out the selection, Colt purchased 5,000 shares at $1.0625 per share in his account: 4,000 for himself and 500 each for his two roommates. Colt then entered a sell limit order of $4.00 per share just before the message recommending the stock was sent to subscribers. Colt set the sell limit order based on his observing the extent of the price movement on ELSI.

26. Colt's purchase of 5,000 shares spurred an increase in the price and volume of AMSI stock. Colt's purchase represented more than 40% of the 11,700 share total average daily volume of AMSI. In addition, between 2:25 p.m., the time that Colt's purchase was reported, and 2:45 p.m., when the Fast-Trades selection was sent out, an additional 44,600 shares of AMSI were traded, and the price rose to $1.50, a 41% increase over a twenty minute period.

27. After the Fast-Trades selection was sent to subscribers, the trading volume and price of AMSI increased significantly. The stock had a reported one day trading volume of 1,085,600 shares and reached an intraday high of $7.9375 per share—a price movement of $6.875, more than 600% higher than the price of Colt's first purchase. As the price of AMSI rose far above Colt's $4.00 sell limit price, Colt, watching the real-time price movement on a computer, chased the market, raising his sell price twice in a matter of minutes just after the selection went out to subscribers. Colt finally set his sell limit price at $6.00 per share, and his order was filled in 1000 share lots at prices ranging from $6.00 up to $7.75 per share. In the end, Colt, Terrell and Wyckoff reaped a collective profit of $27,937.50 on their AMSItrading in just thirty minutes. Within just a few hours after the recommendation was distributed to subscribers, the price of AMSI collapsed. Within a few days, AMSI was back to trading within pennies of its price at the time the recommendation was disseminated.

COLT, TERRELL, WYCKOFF AND JOANNE COLT PURCHASE OPTN ON FEBRUARY 24

28. Fast-Trades' next selection was Option Care, Inc. (ticker: OPTN). The OPTN selection went out to subscribers shortly after 11:00 a.m. on February 24, 1999. Through his account, Colt purchased twice as many shares—10,000—of OPTN as he had of AMSI. Colt purchased these shares at a price of $1.625: 8000 for himself and 1,000 for each of his two roommates, just minutes before he sent out the selection to subscribers. Colt then entered a sell limit order of $5.00 for the shares—more than 200% above his purchase price. Colt believed that there was a "strong possibility" that OPTN would increase in price after the selection was announced.

29. Before Colt's 10,000 share purchase around 11:00 a.m., there were no trades in OPTN on February 24. The 10,000 share purchase represented approximately 70% of the roughly 14,000 share total average daily volume of OPTN.

30. After the Fast-Trades selection went out to subscribers, the price and volume of OPTN climbed rapidly. On February 24, OPTN had a reported one day trading volume of 1,290,100 shares and reached an intraday high of $5.875—a

price movement of $4.25, more than 250% higher than the price of Colt's first purchase. Colt's sell limit order was filled at $5.375 shortly after the Fast-Trades announcement. Colt, Terrell and Wyckoff reaped a collective profit of $37,500. Within just a few hours after the recommendation was distributed to subscribers, the price of OPTN collapsed. Within a few days, OPTN was back to trading within pennies of its price at the time the recommendation was disseminated.

31. Joanne Colt, the defendant's mother, purchased 14,000 shares of OPTN in the same manner as other subscribers: she waited until she received the Fast-Trades e-mail, then placed her purchase orders. Joanne Colt lost more than $24,000 in approximately twenty-five minutes trading on the recommendation from the Fast-Trades website. After losing more than $24,000 in one day trading in OPTN, Joanne Colt withdrew $15,000 from her individual retirement account at a penalty and borrowed $11,000 from her life insurance policy to replace her losses and accumulate funds in her brokerage account to use to buy the next Fast-Trades selection.

COLT, THE PARTICIPANTS, AND
FRIENDS PURCHASE AEDU ON MARCH 5

32. The next Fast-Trades selection was American Education Corporation (ticker: AEDU), which Fast-Trades sent to subscribers at approximately 2:45 p.m. on March 5. The total average daily volume for AEDU as of that date was approximately 3,500 shares. Starting around four hours before the selection was sent out, Colt purchased a total of 19,000 AEDU shares in his account: 10,000 for himself, 4,000 each for his two roommates, and 1,000 for Adam Altman, another law school classmate who had agreed to become a participant in Fast-Trades. The shares were purchased in six separate market orders at ascending prices: the first 1,000 shares were purchased at $1.25, while the last 3,000 shares were purchased at $1.62. Colt then entered a sell limit order at $6.50 per share.

33. At Colt's direction, one of his friends, another fellow law student, purchased an additional 2,000 shares. Colt then instructed this friend to enter a sell limit order at $5.00 per share. Both Colt's and his friend's sell orders were entered before the message recommending AEDU was sent to subscribers.

34. Shortly before sending out the AEDU selection, Colt told Joanne Colt that AEDU would be the March 5 selection. Joanne Colt then called her friend. Joanne Colt then purchased 10,750 shares of AEDU and quickly placed sell limit orders staggered between $4.50 and $7.00 per share. Joanne Colt's friend—who had not purchased a stock on the open market in approximately eight years—purchased 4,533 shares, and quickly entered sell limit orders ranging from $4.00 to $5.00 per share.

35. These purchases spurred a dramatic increase in the price and volume of AEDU stock. The 36,283 shares bought by Fast-Trades participants and their friends represented over 1000% of the 3,500 share total average daily volume of AEDU. On March 5 there was only one trade reported for 1,000 shares at $1.25 per share before Colt and the others began buying. From 10:47 a.m., Douglas Colt's first trade, through the 2:45 p.m. dissemination of the Fast-Trades

recommendation, over 100,000 shares of AEDU changed hands, and the price of AEDU rose to $1.625, a 30% increase in three and a half hours of trading.

36. Moreover, Colt knew that his purchases, along with those of the other Fast-Trades participants and friends, were impacting the price of AEDU, because as his multiple purchase orders were filled over the course of the day, he paid progressively higher prices for the stock. Colt paid $1.25 for his first 1,000 shares at around 10:45 a.m., and paid incrementally higher prices until his last purchase of 3,000 shares at 2:19 p.m. at $1.625 per share.

37. After Fast-Trades recommended AEDU to subscribers, the price and volume of the stock rose dramatically. On March 5, AEDU had a reported one day trading volume of 842,600 shares and reached an intraday high of $10.00—a price movement of $8.75, 700% higher than the price at Colt's first purchase. Colt's account reaped a profit of $41,093.75, and Colt's friend made a profit of $3,500. Joanne Colt made $59,984.37, and her friend made $15,899. Within just a few hours, the price of AEDU collapsed, plummeting several dollars. Within a few days, AEDU was back to trading within pennies of its price at the time the recommendation was disseminated.

COLT, THE PARTICIPANTS, AND
FRIENDS ALL PURCHASE ARTE ON MARCH 10

38. The fourth and final Fast-Trades selection purchased by Colt and the other participants was Artecon, Inc. (ticker: ARTE). The ARTE selection went out to subscribers at approximately 11:30 a.m. on March 10. Starting an hour and twenty minutes before the selection was sent out, Colt used six separate orders to purchase a total of 18,282 ARTE shares in his account: 9,282 for himself, 4,000 each for his two roommates, and 1,000 for the other law student. Colt's friend also purchased 4,000 shares at Colt's direction.

39. Colt also telephoned Joanne Colt and told her about ARTE, and Joanne Colt immediately called her friend. Joanne Colt purchased 17,500 shares and her friend purchased 11,730 shares, increasing the total number of shares purchased by the group to 51,512. All entered sell limit orders before the recommendation went out to subscribers.

40. These purchases of ARTE spurred an increase in the price and volume of ARTE stock. The purchases of 51,512 shares by Fast-Trades participants and their friends represented over 150% of the 33,000 share total average daily volume of ARTE. On March 10, before Colt began buying ARTE, only 800 shares changed hands and the price remained steady at $1.125 per share. From 10:11 a.m., when Colt's first trade was reported, until 11:30 when the recommendation went out, total trading volume of ARTE increased to 164,500 shares and the price rose to $1.375, a 22% increase in two hours.

41. As with his AEDU trading, Colt could see the effect of his purchases on the market because over the course of his purchases he paid progressively more for ARTE shares. Colt's first purchase of ARTE was at $1.125, but over the next eighty minutes Colt made ARTE purchases at $1.1875 and then $1.25 a share, and by the time of his last purchase before the selection was announced he paid $1.375 per share.

42. After the Fast-Trades recommendation went out to subscribers, the price and volume of ARTE went higher still. On March 10, ARTE had a reported one day trading volume of 4,581,000 shares and reached an intraday high of $6.00—a price movement of $4.875, more than 400% higher than the price of Colt's first purchase. The orders by Fast-Trades participants and their two friends were filled shortly after the recommendation went out. Douglas Colt's account reaped a profit of $66,516.36, Colt's friend made $15,474.37, Joanne Colt made $47,081.25, and her friend made $34,937. Within just a few hours after the recommendation, the price of ARTE collapsed, plummeting several dollars. Within a few days, ARTE was back to trading within pennies of its price at the time the recommendation was disseminated.

COLT AND OTHER PARTICIPANTS
POST MESSAGES ON THE INTERNET

43. As part of the Fast-Trades scheme, Colt, Terrell, Wyckoff and Altman posted hundreds of false or misleading messages on internet message boards. The vast majority of these messages were advertisements used to promote the Fast-Trades website to attract new subscribers. The purpose of these messages was to build the subscriber base by inducing readers of the message boards to visit the website, to review its recommendations and to become subscribers, so that they would in turn purchase Fast-Trades selected stocks and help drive up the price of the selection. Colt, Terrell, Wyckoff and later, Altman, all made such postings. Colt taught each of them how to create on-line "identities," and how to post messages to internet message boards at financial websites such as Yahoo.com and RagingBull.com.

44. Colt instructed them not to disclose their affiliation with Fast-Trades and to use multiple identities in order to enhance the credibility of their messages. Colt also instructed them to misrepresent substantive information, such as their investment successes from following Fast-Trades recommendations, to draw readers of the message boards to the Fast-Trades site.

45. For example, a February 9, 1999, posting by Colt to the Electrosource message bulletin board contains false information regarding his age and geographic location, conveys that he was not a participant in Fast-Trades when in fact he was, and misrepresents that Colt had made profits from Fast-Trades' recommendation of Electrosource, when in fact he had not traded in the stock.

46. Through these and hundreds of other postings containing false or misleading information, Colt expected to induce individuals to visit the Fast-Trades website and become subscribers so that they would then purchase Fast-Trades selections and drive up the price of the selected stocks. At Colt's direction, Wyckoff, Terrell and Altman all made numerous false or misleading postings similar to Colt's that failed to disclose their identities or their ties to Fast-Trades, and misrepresented their trading activity or success in trading Fast-Trades selections.

47. In addition to these "advertising" postings, Colt also posted messages on the internet defending Fast-Trades against investors who accused the site of price manipulation. In those messages, Colt misrepresented his identity and geographic location, and argued that Fast-Trades' activities were lawful. Indeed, Colt tried to discourage individuals from informing the SEC about the Fast-

Trades scheme, at times taunting those who posted internet messages stating that they were going to contact the SEC about the website.

THE DISCLAIMER ON THE FAST-TRADES.COM WEBSITE

48. From the first time Fast-Trades published a recommendation, it included a disclaimer on the webpage that purported to describe the trading intentions of Fast-Trades representatives. This disclaimer was revised after the AMSI selection. With the first selection the participants traded in, Apache Medical Systems on February 16, the disclaimer stated: "We may buy or sell our picks at any time." After that selection, Colt, Terrell, and Wyckoff, along with the new participant Altman, revised various aspects of the disclaimer, including the portion addressing their trading in Fast-Trades selections. From that point on, through the remaining three selections they traded in, the disclaimer read, in relevant part: "FastTrades representatives may, and in many cases do, invest or hold positions in the companies that FastTrades recommends; FastTrades representatives reserve the right to buy or sell securities recommended by FastTrades at any time."

49. Both versions were materially misleading as to the real trading intent or trading activities of the participants. By the time the subscribers received the Fast-Trades recommendation, the Fast-Trades participants already had purchased shares in the recommended stock, and already had placed orders to sell the stock, which they expected to be filled by the increase in price and volume caused by the purchases of their own subscribers. If Fast-Trades had accurately disclosed their trading intentions, subscribers would have been able to deduce that the only reason Colt offered his "free" service was so he could further influence the market price movement initiated by his purchase of the recommended stock just before the announcement. In this way, Colt could condition the market and then profit at the expense of his subscribers by executing pre-set sales of the recommended stock at inflated prices to a market which was likely to include subscribers.

50. By reason of the foregoing, Douglas Colt violated Section 10(b) of the Exchange Act and Rule 10b-5 thereunder.

PRAYER FOR RELIEF

WHEREFORE, the Commission respectfully requests that this Court:

I.

Issue a Final Judgment of Permanent Injunction permanently restraining and enjoining Douglas Colt from violating Section 10(b) of the Exchange Act and Rule 10b-5 thereunder.

II.

Issue a Final Judgment requiring Colt to disgorge all illicit profits from the manipulative scheme alleged herein, with prejudgment interest.

III.

Issue a Final Judgment requiring Colt to pay appropriate civil penalties pursuant to Section 21(d)(3)(A) of the Exchange Act.

IV.

Grant such other relief as this Court may deem just and appropriate.

Dated: March 2, 2000

Respectfully submitted.

____

Attorneys for Plaintiff
SECURITIES AND EXCHANGE COMMISSION

NOTES AND QUESTIONS

*1. **Settlement with the SEC.*** Simultaneously with the filing of the Complaint set out above, Douglas Colt, "without admitting or denying the allegations," consented to the entry of a final judgment permanently enjoining him from committing or causing any violation or future violation of Section 10(b) and Rule 10b-5. Pursuant to this settlement, the SEC waived payment of disgorgement and prejudgment interest based on Colt's "demonstrated financial inability to pay" and did not seek the imposition of a civil monetary penalty. *Douglas M. Colt*, Litigation Release No. 16461 (Mar. 2, 2000).

At the same time it settled its case against Douglas Colt, the SEC also entered an administrative order and "without admitting or denying the Commission's findings," Kenneth Terrell, Jason Wyckoff, Adam Altman and Joanne Colt consented to an Order directing them to cease and desist from committing or causing any violation and any future violation of Section 10(b) of the Exchange Act and Rule 10b-5, and ordering Terrell, Wyckoff and Joanne Colt to pay disgorgement of all illicit profits with prejudgment interest. See *In re Kenneth Terrell, Jason Wyckoff, Adam Altman and Joanne Colt*, Exchange Act Release No. 42483, 2000 WL 248549 (Mar. 2, 2000). As in its settlement with Douglas Colt, based on Terrell's, Wyckoff's and Joanne Colt's "demonstrat[ed] financial inability to pay," the Commission waived payment of disgorgement and prejudgment interest.

A number of commentators expressed surprise at the SEC's willingness to resolve these actions without at least insisting on the recovery of the "ill-gotten gains." Some have even questioned whether it reflected the SEC's doubts of the merits of its case. See Ellen Rosen, SEC May Lack Basis to Bar Stock Touting, Nat'l L. J. at A1 (March 20, 2000) (quoting Professor John Coffee's statements that "[t]he facts justify the fraud prosecution, but the settlement is so weak [that it appears to express] the SEC's own doubts of the merits" and that it is "rare to quantify ill-gotten gains with no attempt to get restitution"). Is it likely that the SEC's enforcement action could have been resolved at the summary judgment stage? Based on the allegations in the complaint, what difficulties would you expect the SEC to have faced at trial? Consider the legal discussion from the SEC's administrative order:

> Colt effected a series of transactions and through the Fast-Trades.com website disseminated stock recommendations without completely and accurately describing those transactions in the website's disclaimer. Those transactions created actual trading activity causing the price of the selected stocks to

> increase. Colt's purpose was to induce the purchase of the Fast-Trades.com stock recommendation by both subscribers and non-subscribers. Colt's purchases, recommendations and misleading statements and omissions about his trading in the recommended stocks were material to reasonable investors deciding whether to purchase the securities recommended by the Fast-Trades.com website. As a result of his conduct, Colt violated Section 10(b) of the Exchange Act and Rule 10b-5, thereunder, and Terrell, Wyckoff, Altman and Joanne Colt knew or should have known that their acts or omissions to act would contribute to such violations.

In re Kenneth Terrell, supra, 2000 WL 248549 at *9. Can you identify both the stronger and the weaker aspects of the SEC's legal theories? Might *Stoneridge*'s brief reminder that "[c]onduct itself can be deceptive" bolster aspects of the SEC's argument above? See *Stoneridge Inv. Partners, LLC v. Scientific-Atlanta, Inc.*, 552 U.S. 148, 158 (2008).

*2. **The SEC's Cyberforce***. There is little doubt that the SEC regarded the *Colt* case as an old wine in a new bottle. In announcing the settlement, Richard H. Walker, Director of the SEC's Division of Enforcement, emphasized that "[t]he Internet has replaced the boiler room as the stock manipulator's tool of choice" and that "[i]ts low cost and ease of use has attracted a new breed of persons seeking to profit at the expense of innocent investors." See SEC News Digest 2000-40 (March 2, 2000). Reflecting a similar theme, the SEC's administrative order cautioned that the "type of activity involved in [the Colt] case *** was a variation of a "pump and dump" scheme," and maintained that the only novelty was in "the way that internet technology was used to promote the stocks and deceive investors." The publicity surrounding the *Colt* case was clearly used by the SEC to send the message that "[a]ttempts to deceive investors or disrupt the securities markets, whether such schemes are perpetrated on the internet or by more traditional means, will not be tolerated." *In re Kenneth Terrell,* supra, 2000 WL 248549 at *10.

The *Colt* case constitutes only one of several hundred Internet-related enforcement actions initiated by the SEC over the decade spanning from 1995-2005. The agency began its surveillance of the Internet in 1995 with a very small task force. In 1998, the SEC had in place an "Office of Internet Enforcement" (OIE), which coordinated the activities of its"CyberForce"—a group of over 250 SEC attorneys, investigators, and accountants who were charged with responsibility for Internet surveillance. Specifically, the OIE:

- identified areas of surveillance;
- formulated investigative procedures;
- provided strategic and legal guidance to Enforcement staff nationwide;
- conducted Internet investigations and prosecutions (a task it shared with the entire Enforcement staff);
- performed training for Commission staff and outside agencies and;
- served as a resource on Internet matters for the entire Commission.

John Reed Stark, EnforceNet Redux: A Retrospective of the SEC's Internet Program Four Years After Its Genesis, 57 Bus. Law. 105, 112-13 (2001). In addition to surveillance efforts by the SEC, the OIE also worked to coordinate Internet-related efforts with various U.S. Attorneys, the FBI and the self-regulatory organizations that form the Intermarket Surveillance Group.

The OIE also conducted a number of "Internet sweeps"—described in a speech by SEC Commissioner Laura Unger as "a relatively new enforcement technique involving the simultaneous investigation of numerous individuals, broker-dealers or issuers, with multiple actions being announced on the same day for maximum deterrent effect." See Speech by SEC Commissioner Laura S. Unger, Empowering Investors in an Electronic Age, IOSCO Annual Conference, May 17, 2000. These Internet sweeps generated extensive media coverage, and highlighted to the investing public what might seem to be the rather obvious risks of acting on investment advice from strangers over the Internet.

To be sure, market manipulation has not been the only type of fraudulent activity swept up by the SEC's recent attention to the Internet. But the SEC maintains that of the many types of fraud, "market manipulations are by far the most prevalent on the Internet." Unger Speech, supra. In addition to the classic "pump and dump" scheme alleged to have been perpetrated by the law students, can you identify other types of manipulative conduct that is facilitated by widespread usage of the Internet?

As we shall see in Chapter 9, the SEC's Division of Enforcement reorganized in 2010, with numerous changes including the creation of five new speciality units: Asset Management, Market Abuse, Structured and New Products, Foreign Corrupt Practices, and Municipal Securities and Public Pensions. These new units were designed to increase the SEC's effectiveness in focusing in on particular markets and practices and in identifying patterns of wrongdoing. However, one former SEC Commissioner has claimed that "insufficient attention is being paid to 'boots-on-the-ground' investigative resources to combat the pernicious frauds that prey on individual investors." Statement of Paul S. Atkins, Senate Banking, Housing and Urban Affairs Committee Hearing on Enhanced Investor Protection After the Financial Crisis, July 12, 2011, at 15. With limited funding, the SEC enforcement staff cannot possibly be everywhere. Is a robust Internet enforcement program perhaps less essential today than a decade ago?

3. Not a Minor Problem. The following quotations, from an adoring father and a frustrated SEC Enforcement Director, represent what are no doubt polar opinions as to the legality—and indeed morality—of Jonathan Lebed's stock trading practices:

> "I'm more proud of him now than ever. He's a smart boy and he's done a good job.... He earned it. He did a lot of work. He didn't sit behind a garage smoking pot or stealing wheels off a car."
>
> *Greg Lebed (60 Minutes, CBS television broadcast, Oct. 22, 2000).*
>
> "I wonder how many investors who've lost money as a result of Jonathan's manipulations would agree with this sentiment. A hubcap is worth about $20. Smoking pot—as harmful and foolish as it may be—does not injure innocent bystanders. Securities manipulation, by contrast, deprives people of hard-earned dollars needed for retirement, education and the like. So Mr. Lebed is

right in saying his son's conduct is different from smoking pot or stealing hubcaps. It's worse."

> *Richard Walker, Director, SEC Division of Enforcement, "Regulation vs. Enforcement in an On-Line World," Speech Delivered to the Bond Market Association, October 25, 2000.*

Jonathan Lebed undoubtedly stands as one of the country's most famous stock traders, having been the subject of a featured story in the New York Times Magazine (see Michael Lewis, Jonathan Lebed's Extracurricular Activities, Feb. 25, 2001 at 26) in addition to the segment on 60 Minutes noted above.

The SEC charged Lebed with numerous violations of Rule 10b-5. The case was settled (without admission or denial of liability) rather than litigated, with the SEC issuing an Order requiring Lebed to cease and desist from further violations and to pay $272,826, an amount said to constitute the ill-gotten gains from his Internet schemes. See *In re Jonathan G. Lebed*, Exchange Act Release No. 43307, 2000 WL 1353040 (Sept. 20, 2000).

According to the SEC, on eleven separate occasions between August 1999 and February 2000, Lebed had

> purchased large blocks of thinly traded microcap stocks and, within hours of making such purchases, sent numerous false and/or misleading messages, or "spam," over the Internet touting the stocks he had just purchased. Lebed then sold all of these shares, usually within 24 hours, profiting from the increased price his messages had caused.

Id. at *1. The SEC's Order sets out the following as a "representative transaction":

> On January 5, 2000, Lebed purchased 18,000 shares of [Man Sang Holdings, Inc. (ticker symbol "MSHI")] at prices ranging from $1.375 to $2.00 per share. The trading volume on December 30, 1999 was 100 shares with a closing price of $1.125 per share. On January 5, 2000, the volume was 60,700 shares at a closing price of $1.8125. At 11:46 p.m. on January 5, 2000, Lebed posted messages on Yahoo!Finance message boards claiming that MSHI was "the most undervalued stock in history" and would be trading at more than $20 per share "very soon." On January 6, 2000, in response to the messages posted by Lebed, the volume of trading skyrocketed to 1,074,900 shares at a high of $4.6875 per share. On that date, Lebed sold all 18,000 shares of MSHI at prices ranging from $3.8125 to $4.00 per share. His net profit was $34,959. MSHI issued no press releases and there was no news in the marketplace during this time period to account for the rise in price and volume.
>
> Three weeks later, Lebed again manipulated the price of MSHI stock. From January 27, 2000, the date he purchased MSHI and posted his spams touting the stock (again predicting a price of $20 "very soon"), until the following day, January 28, 2000, the date he liquidated his entire position, the volume of the stock increased from 71,500 to 1,879,000 shares, and the price jumped from $2.25 to a high of $5.125. Both the price and volume were 52-week highs. Lebed realized a net profit of $37,901.

Id. at *2.

With respect to the MSHI transactions set out above, what legal arguments might have been made in Lebed's defense against Rule 10b-5 liability? In this regard, consider the so-called puffery exception to the element of materiality discussed on page 63. Consider also the Supreme Court's conclusion in *Virginia Bankshares* as to when statements of opinion may be found to be materially misleading. See page 44. In his Internet postings, did Lebed have a duty to disclose his substantial holdings in the recommended stocks? Why or why not?

For contrasting views on difficult doctrinal questions, compare Richard H. Walker & David M. Levine, "You've Got Jail:" Current Trends in Civil and Criminal Enforcement of Internet Securities Fraud, 38 Am. Crim. L. Rev. 405 (2001) and Judith R. Starr & David Herman, The Same Old Wine in a Brand New Bottle: Applying Traditional Market Manipulation Principles to Internet Stock Scams, 29 Sec. Reg. L.J. 236 (2001) with Donald C. Langevoort, Taming the Animal Spirits of the Stock Markets: A Behavioral Approach to Securities Regulation, 97 Nw. U. L. Rev. 135,156-63 (2002).

4. Dial M for Manipulation. The SEC and the DOJ have prosecuted a bevy of cases involving phony fax scams and phony voice message scams. In the prototypical case, the defendant is alleged to have purposely dialed wrong numbers, providing recipients of the fax or the answering machine message with a phony stock tip designed to drive up the price of the touted security. Automated calling technology allows for thousands of such "wrong number" calls to be placed in a very short period of time. In one instance, where defendants were charged with sending collectively more than one million faxes, recipients of the phony stock tips included the SEC's San Francisco Regional office and the office of the U.S. Attorney for the S.D.N.Y. (clearly wrong, wrong numbers!) See Richard Hill, Indictment Charges Promoters With Using Fake Faxes to Dupe Recipients, 37 Sec. Reg. L. Rep. 1252 (BNA) (July 25, 2005). In another, three defendants allegedly conspired to leave on thousands of answering machines messages such as the following:

> Hey Tracy, it's Debbie! I couldn't find your old number and Tammy said this was your new one — I hope it's the right one. Anyway, remember Evan, that hot stock exchange guy I'm dating? He gave my dad that stock tip on [stock symbol] and it went from under a buck to like three bucks in two weeks and you were mad I didn't call you? Well I'm calling you now. This new company is supposed to be like the next Tommy Bahama and they're making some big news announcement this week. The stock symbol is [stock symbol]. He said it's cheap now, like $0.50. Sorry I'm eating but I'm starving. Its $.50 now and its going up to, like, 5 or 6 bucks this week, so get as much as you can. Call me on my cell - I'm still in Orlando. Its [phone number]. Dad and I are buying a bunch tomorrow and I already called Kelly and Ron, too. Anyway, I miss you. Give me a call. Bye.

SEC v. Boling, Litigation Release No. 20192 (July 11, 2007) (announcing guilty pleas in criminal securities fraud case and hyperlinking transcript of message).

What hurdles might the government face in litigating such phony fax/voice message scams under Rule 10b-5? Is there anything that may render the purchasers of securities based on such phony stock tips less sympathetic than other investors duped by pump and dump schemes?

5. Distort and Short Schemes. As discussed in Section A of this Chapter, in the midst of the 2007-08 financial crisis, age-old concerns reemerged about market manipulation through dissemination of false rumors. As then-SEC Chairman Christopher Cox explained:

> When an irrational panic is fueled by false rumors that investors believe must be acted on immediately — lest everyone else get out first — market integrity is threatened. In such circumstances, it is the job of market cops to provide a measure of confidence that information about public companies is accurate — and when it is not, to punish those responsible.
>
> Who profits from intentionally false information in the marketplace? Those who are in on the scam and positioned to benefit from the predictable response of people who believe the fraudulent information to be true.
>
> The classic "pump and dump" scheme, in which a stock is inflated through false information and then dumped on unsuspecting investors when the perpetrators flee, is one example of how this works. "Distort and short" is the same thing in reverse.

SEC Chairman Christopher Cox, What the SEC Really Did on Short Selling, Wall St. J., July 24, 2008, at A15 (Op-ed). As part of its investigation into the possibility of widespread rumor mongering during the financial crisis, the SEC joined forces with FINRA and the NYSE to inspect and examine the supervisory and compliance controls put in place by broker-dealers and investment advisers over their employees, and to assess whether those controls were reasonably designed to prevent this and other types of manipulative conduct. For a settled enforcement action against a Wall Street trader, see SEC v. Berliner, Litigation Release No. 20537 (Apr. 24, 2008) (settling securities fraud charges that defendant had unlawfully profited by short selling ADS stock and covering those sales as his false rumors caused the price of ADS stock to fall).

---

2. *Conflicts of Interest on Wall Street*

Do securities analysts engage in fraud or market manipulation when they publish "buy" recommendations in research reports to brokerage firm customers while simultaneously holding the view that those recommended stocks are "dogs," "crap," or "junk?" What if it could be shown that these analysts intentionally misled investors about the quality of the stocks in order to win lucrative investment banking business for their firms?

These questions and many related ones were at one time at the top of the enforcement agendas for the SEC, DOJ, State Attorneys General, and the NYSE and NASD. Indeed, throughout the 2002-03 time period, newspapers were filled with weekly, and often daily, accounts of the various investigations into securities analysts' conflicts of interest, culminating in a historic "global settlement" that required the nation's twelve largest investments banks to pay a combined total of more than $1.4 billion in fines, disgorgement, and funding for independent research and investor education. See Federal Court Approves Global Research Analyst Settlement, Litigation Release No. 18438 (Oct. 31, 2003). Two individual analysts were identified and included in the settlement: Jack Grubman, an analyst once at Salomon Smith Barney, who agreed to a lifetime bar from the securities industry and the payment of $15 million in fines, and Henry Blodget, an analyst once at Merrill Lynch, who agreed to a lifetime bar from the securities industry and the payment of $4 million in fines. The global settlement further required the firms to adopt substantial structural changes to ensure that analysts' stock recommendations would not be tainted by efforts to secure investment banking-related bonuses.

The topic of conflicts of interest on Wall Street also received much attention from Congress in the months preceding the Sarbanes-Oxley Act of 2002. As noted in the Senate Report:

> The Committee [on Banking, Housing, and Urban Affairs] heard persuasive testimony that a serious problem exists regarding conflicts of interest between Wall Street stock analysts and their employing brokerage firms, on the one hand, and the public companies that the stock analysts cover on the other hand. Growing knowledge of these conflicts is harming the integrity and credibility to the public of stock analyst recommendations. ***
>
> The Committee feels that it is critical to restore investor confidence in this area. The bill is intended to prevent certain pressures on analysts which could compromise their objectivity and to provide disclosure to investors of certain conflicts of interest that can also influence the objectivity of the analyst in preparing a research report.

Senate Report 107-205, 107th Cong. 2d Session, Committee on Banking, Housing, and Urban Affairs, July 3, 2002 at 32-33.

Responding to these concerns, Section 501 of the Sarbanes-Oxley Act added a new Section 15D to the Exchange Act:

Section 15D—Securities Analysts And Research Reports

(a) Analyst protections—The Commission, or upon the authorization and direction of the Commission, a registered securities association or national securities exchange, shall have adopted, not later than 1 year after the date of enactment of this section [enacted July 30, 2002], rules reasonably designed to address conflicts of interest that can arise when securities analysts recommend equity securities in research reports and public appearances, in order to improve the objectivity of research and provide investors with more useful and reliable information, including rules designed—

> (1) to foster greater public confidence in securities research, and to protect the objectivity and independence of securities analysts, by—
>
> > (A) restricting the prepublication clearance or approval of research reports by persons employed by the broker or dealer who are engaged in investment banking activities, or persons not directly responsible for investment research, other than legal or compliance staff;
> >
> > (B) limiting the supervision and compensatory evaluation of securities analysts to officials employed by the broker or dealer who are not engaged in investment banking activities; and
> >
> > (C) requiring that a broker or dealer and persons employed by a broker or dealer who are involved with investment banking activities may not, directly or indirectly, retaliate against or threaten to retaliate against any securities analyst employed by that broker or dealer or its affiliates as a result of an adverse, negative, or otherwise unfavorable research report that may adversely affect the present or prospective investment banking relationship of the broker or dealer with the issuer that is the subject of the research report, except that such rules may not limit the authority of a broker or dealer to discipline a securities analyst for causes other than such research report in accordance with the policies and procedures of the firm;

(2) to define periods during which brokers or dealers who have participated, or are to participate, in a public offering of securities as underwriters or dealers should not publish or otherwise distribute research reports relating to such securities or to the issuer of such securities;

(3) to establish structural and institutional safeguards within registered brokers or dealers to assure that securities analysts are separated by appropriate informational partitions within the firm from the review, pressure, or oversight of those whose involvement in investment banking activities might potentially bias their judgment or supervision; and

(4) to address such other issues as the Commission, or such association or exchange, determines appropriate.

(b) Disclosure—The Commission, or upon the authorization and direction of the Commission, a registered securities association or national securities exchange, shall have adopted, not later than 1 year after the date of enactment of this section [enacted July 30, 2002], rules reasonably designed to require each securities analyst to disclose in public appearances, and each registered broker or dealer to disclose in each research report, as applicable, conflicts of interest that are known or should have been known by the securities analyst or the broker or dealer, to exist at the time of the appearance or the date of distribution of the report, including—

(1) the extent to which the securities analyst has debt or equity investments in the issuer that is the subject of the appearance or research report;

(2) whether any compensation has been received by the registered broker or dealer, or any affiliate thereof, including the securities analyst, from the issuer that is the subject of the appearance or research report, subject to such exemptions as the Commission may determine appropriate and necessary to prevent disclosure by virtue of this paragraph of material non-public information regarding specific potential future investment banking transactions of such issuer, as is appropriate in the public interest and consistent with the protection of investors;

(3) whether an issuer, the securities of which are recommended in the appearance or research report, currently is, or during the 1-year period preceding the date of the appearance or date of distribution of the report has been, a client of the registered broker or dealer, and if so, stating the types of services provided to the issuer;

(4) whether the securities analyst received compensation with respect to a research report, based upon (among any other factors) the investment banking revenues (either generally or specifically earned from the issuer being analyzed) of the registered broker or dealer; and

(5) such other disclosures of conflicts of interest that are material to investors, research analysts, or the broker or dealer as the Commission, or such association or exchange, determines appropriate.

Many of the rules required under new Section 15D of the Exchange Act had been proposed by the NASD and NYSE and approved by the SEC in May 2002, more than two months before the enactment of the Sarbanes-Oxley Act. See Commission Approves Rules to Address Analyst Conflicts, SEC Press Release 2002-63, May 8, 2002. The following year the NASD and NYSE proposed additional rules which the SEC approved. See SEC Announces Approval of SRO Rules Addressing Research Analyst Conflicts of Interest, Press Release 2003-89 (July 29, 2003). Note also that in February 2003, the SEC adopted Regulation

Analyst Certification (Regulation AC), 17 C.F.R. §§242.500-242.505, which requires "research analysts to certify the truthfulness of the views they express in research reports and public appearances, and to disclose whether they have received any compensation related to the specific recommendations or views expressed in those reports and appearances." SEC Press Release 2003-21, Feb. 6, 2003.

Do you think the enactment of Section 15D reflects a congressional judgment that manipulative activity was pervasive in the stock market? Assuming that conflicts of interest were pervasive, does that necessarily mean that the practices were manipulative?

Professor Jill Fisch has questioned whether regulators should "attempt to protect investors from bad decisions that may be the result of irrational behavior." See Jill E. Fisch, Regulatory Responses to Investor Irrationality: The Case of the Research Analyst, 10 Lewis & Clark L. Rev. 57 (2006). Should they?

PROBLEM 8-3

Susan Shore is a securities analyst with Shaker Hanley, a Wall Street investment bank/brokerage firm with an international reputation. A few years ago, Susan's firm acquired a stake in a start-up business, Betatech, by obtaining shares in exchange for financial services. Betatech later made the decision to go public and, not surprisingly, Shaker Hanley acted as the lead underwriter in the IPO. The firm's shares in Betatech were subject to a 180 day lock-up period which was to expire on July 23, 2001.

On July 20, 2001, Susan issued a favorable research report on Betatech and rated the stock a "strong buy." The report was contained in Shaker's monthly newsletter to clients, the back page of which contained disclaimers reading: "The firm and/or affiliates and employees have or may have a long or short position or holding in the securities, options on securities, or other related investments of issuers mentioned herein" and "The firm may have, within the last three years, served as manager or co-manager of a public offering of or makes markets in the securities of any or all of the companies mentioned." The following day, Susan appeared on WallStreet Beat, a cable TV show, where she repeated her favorable view of Betatech and her "strong buy" recommendation.

Betatech's shares steadily rose in value on July 20, 21st, and 22nd, and Shaker Hanley reaped a substantial profit when it sold its shares on July 23rd. Has Susan, Betatech, or Shaker Hanley violated the federal securities laws? On what theory?

Note that such "booster shots" are now prohibited under FINRA Rule 2711(f)(4), which provides that:

> No member that has acted as a manager or co-manager of a securities offering may publish or otherwise distribute a research report or make a public appearance concerning a subject company 15 days prior to and after the expiration, waiver or termination of a lock-up agreement or any other agreement that the member has entered into with a subject company or its shareholders that restricts or prohibits the sale of securities held by the subject company or its shareholders after the completion of a securities offering.

The NASD promulgated this rule in response to the congressional mandate in Section 15D(a)(2) of the Exchange Act, set out above.

What lessons can be drawn from the conflict of interest scandal and its aftermath?

Chapter 9

SEC ENFORCEMENT OF THE FEDERAL SECURITIES LAWS

Although in any given year the sheer volume of enforcement proceedings initiated by the SEC pales in comparison to the volume of private securities litigation, familiarity with the SEC's enforcement process is essential to representing corporate clients. One reason is that, regardless of whether enforcement action is actually initiated, SEC investigations have a tremendous impact on the persons or companies involved. Indeed, as we have seen from our previous study of insider trading and market manipulation, investigations by the SEC are often long and detailed, typically demanding significant amounts of time and attention on the part of numerous people. And Congress has given the SEC broad powers to investigate whether the federal securities laws have been, are being, or are likely to be violated. A second reason is that once securities law violations have been established, the SEC has at its disposal a wide arsenal of enforcement remedies, most of which are not available in private litigation. These remedies run the gamut from an order by the Commission to "cease and desist," to the imposition of substantial monetary penalties by a federal district court judge, to a broker-dealer disciplinary proceeding that results in a permanent suspension. SEC officials also have the power to refer securities law violations to the Department of Justice (DOJ) for criminal prosecution. One cannot represent a corporate client effectively without being well versed in the possible enforcement stakes—including the sanctions that may be imposed by courts or directly by the SEC and the collateral consequences that may flow from them.

This Chapter is divided into six sections. Section A provides a brief introduction to the SEC's Division of Enforcement, the division that is generally responsible for investigating and prosecuting suspected violations of the federal securities laws. Section B then explores the investigatory process in more detail and highlights some procedural issues that often arise in the course of investigations. It also examines the process by which an investigation may result in a consensual settlement with the SEC. Section C turns to the important topic of remedies and looks at how, and in what fora, such remedies may be employed, and Section D focuses on litigation with the SEC. Section E shifts attention to the enforcement powers of the self-regulatory organizations (SROs) in the securities industry, with particular emphasis on the New York Stock Exchange, Inc. (NYSE) and the National Association of Securities Dealers, Inc. (NASD), which in 2007 consolidated with the enforcement, member regulatory, and arbitration divisions of the NYSE to form the Financial Industry Regulatory Authority (FINRA). The Chapter concludes with Section F, which examines the law governing so-called parallel proceedings—concurrent or subsequent investigations and litigation that may be conducted by the SEC, federal criminal prosecutors, the SROs, and/or state officials.

Securities enforcement issues are also subject to extensive examination in Chapter 10 (focusing on the new enforcement regimes for attorneys and accountants created by the Sarbanes-Oxley Act of 2002 (SOX)) and Chapter 11 (focusing on criminal enforcement). In addition, international securities enforcement is discussed in Chapter 12 (focusing on international securities fraud).

A. THE SEC's DIVISION OF ENFORCEMENT

First organized in 1972 as a separate Division of the SEC, the Division of Enforcement investigates possible violations of the federal securities laws, recommends action to the Commission when appropriate, negotiates settlements on behalf of the Commission, and litigates in federal court or in administrative proceedings before the agency. The Division also refers cases to the DOJ, and the various U.S. Attorney's offices throughout the country, when criminal prosecution for securities law violations appears to be warranted. Of all the SEC's Divisions, it is the Enforcement Division that is the most visible to the public, in large part due to the publicity that typically surrounds its investigations and prosecutions.

The Division is composed of more than 1250 attorneys, accountants, and other professionals ("the staff"), most of whom are based at the SEC's headquarters in Washington, D.C. Staff members in the SEC's 11 regional offices also pursue enforcement matters within their respective jurisdictions. The Division is headed by a Director who is appointed by the SEC's Chairperson. There are also at least two Associate Directors of Enforcement, each of whom are typically supported by a number of Assistant Directors. The Division also has its own Chief Counsel. Although this traditional structure remains intact, in 2010 the Enforcement Division adopted a host of new policies and structural initiatives. The changes were prompted by a number of factors and events, not least of which was the public outcry over the multi-billion dollar Ponzi scheme perpetrated by Bernard Madoff and the stinging criticism directed at SEC enforcement officials from sources that included the SEC Office of Inspector General.

As part of its 2010 enforcement overhaul, the Division created five nationwide specialized units, each headed by its own unit chief, to concentrate on high-priority areas of enforcement: Asset Management (hedge funds and investment advisers), Market Abuse (high-volume and computer-driven trading strategies, large-scale insider trading, and market manipulation schemes), Structured and New Products (particularly derivative products), Foreign Corrupt Practices Act, and Municipal Securities and Public Pensions. The Division also created a new Office of Market Intelligence to handle tips, complaints, and referrals, and to house the Whistleblower Office mandated by the Dodd-Frank Act of 2010. According to SEC Director of Enforcement Robert Khuzami, these structural changes bolster the Division's ability to meet the "[t]wo great challenges fac[ing] every enforcement authority policing our securities markets — the complexity and high-velocity pace of innovation in financial products, transactions, and markets, and the willingness of violators to use every trick to cover their tracks." SEC Press Release 2010-5 (Jan. 13, 2010). For insightful commentary, see Jayne M. Barnard, Evolutionary Enforcement at the Securities and Exchange Commission, 71 Pitt. L. Rev. 403 (2010); Douglas M. Branson, Trekking Toward Uber Regulation: Prospects for Meaningful Change at SEC Enforcement?, 71 Pitt. L. Rev. 545 (2010).

Along with capturing the lion's share of public attention, the Enforcement Division also receives far more funding than any other division of the SEC. For fiscal year 2002, the SEC received $439 million in funding, approximately a third of which was allocated to the Division of Enforcement. The following year, in the wake of the scandals at Enron and WorldCom, Congress nearly doubled the SEC's appropriations, authorizing $776 million in the SOX, with most of the increase directed toward the enhancement of the SEC's investigative and enforcement efforts. Then, in response to the financial crisis occurring at the decade's end, the Dodd-Frank Act pre-authorized a series of increases in SEC funding over the next five years from $1.3 billion in 2011 to $2.25 billion in 2016. However, shifting priorities on Capitol Hill (toward deficit reduction and away from spending) prompted Congress to retreat from this plan. Although SEC Chairman Mary Schapiro frequently has emphasized that enhanced funding is essential to the agency's implementation and execution of its added responsibilities under the Act,, the House Appropriations Committee released an appropriations bill in June 2011 that funded the SEC at $1.2 billion for fiscal year 2012 (an amount equal to the agency's FY 2011 funding level). More than a third of that funding will be allocated to the Division of Enforcement.

Not surprisingly, the SEC has been quick to point out that all monies received by the Division of Enforcement are in fact very well spent. In FY 2010, for example, the SEC reported that "while numbers do not tell the whole story," the Enforcement Division obtained at least $2.8 billion in penalties and disgorgement, and returned more than $2.2 billion of that to harmed investors. 2010 Annual Report at 11-12. In addition, in FY 2010, the Division:

- sought orders barring 71 defendants and respondents from serving as officers or directors of public companies;
- sought emergency relief from federal courts in the form of temporary restraining orders (TROs) to halt ongoing fraudulent conduct in 37 actions and sought asset freezes in 57 actions; and
- halted trading in securities of 254 issuers about which there was inadequate public disclosure.

Moreover, in SEC-related criminal cases in FY 2010, prosecutors filed indictments, informations, or contempts in 139 cases. See Enforcement Milestones, 2010 SEC Select and Market Data, at Table 1.

Select SEC and Market Data from 2006-10 (available on the SEC's website) set forth the total number of SEC enforcement actions initiated over this five year period:

Enforcement Actions Initiated

	FY06	FY07	FY08	FY09	FY10
Civil Injunctive Actions	218	262	285	312	252
Administrative Proceedings	356	393	386	352	429
Total	574	655	671	664	681

The following chart provides a FY 2006-2010 snapshot of the Enforcement Division's distribution of cases across core enforcement areas:

Year-by-Year SEC Enforcement Statistics

Enforcement Actions by Fiscal Year	**2006**	**2007**	**2008**	**2009**	**2010**
Financial Disclosure / Reporting	138	219	154	143	126
Broker-Dealer	75	89	67	109	70
Investment Adviser/Investment Co.	87	79	87	76	113
Securities Offering	61	68	115	141	144
Delinquent Filings	91	52	113	92	106
Insider Trading	46	47	61	37	53
Market Manipulation	27	36	53	39	34
Other	49	65	21	27	35
Total Enforcement Actions	**574**	**655**	**671**	**664**	**681**

www.sec.gov/news/newsroom/images/enfstats.pdf

The SEC describes the Enforcement Division's key FY 2010 cases and going-forward priorities as follows:

> **Financial Crisis**. In the aftermath of the financial crisis, the SEC filed many cases involving mortgage-related securities and mortgage-related products linked to the crisis.
>
> **Pay-to-Play.** Another enforcement focus was on "pay-to-play" arrangements, in which lucrative financial management deals are struck between municipalities and firms who reward the well-connected individuals who arrange those deals with cash, campaign contributions or other favors. Contracts based on connections - rather than competence - potentially harm both taxpayers and the beneficiaries of these funds, through higher fees and lower performance.
>
> **Auditors.** Investors rely on accurate financial information to make critical financial decisions. By focusing on the auditors who sign off on companies'

reporting, the SEC helps deter Enron-type accounting fraud that might cost investors billions.

Insider Trading. The SEC continues to focus on insider trading - both by individuals and by large-scale institutional traders - through its new Market Abuse Unit.

Offering Frauds/Ponzi Schemes. The SEC's efforts to hold accountable perpetrators of offering frauds and Ponzi schemes - aided by the adoption of significant post-Madoff reforms and the establishment of the Asset Management Unit - continue to uncover numerous large-scale frauds.

Foreign Corrupt Practices Act. The SEC continues to prosecute companies that make illegal payments to win business overseas. A renewed focus on these practices in recent years, coupled with the efforts of the FCPA Unit, continues to yield significant settlements.

Financial Fraud. Financial fraud can cost investors billions in lost equity. Both companies and corporate officers are accountable to shareholders for timely and, especially, honest reporting.

Municipal Securities and Public Pensions. As the financial health of municipalities and its effect on the securities they issue become a matter of greater concern, the SEC has focused on ensuring that investors are aware of factors which could affect the ability of municipalities to meet their financial obligations.

SEC FY 2010 Performance and Accountability Report at 11-14.

Professors James Cox and Randall Thomas have raised an interesting threshold question concerning the very existence of the SEC's authority to enforce the federal securities laws: "Why did Congress not instead empower the SEC with only rulemaking authority and the general authority to review disclosures, leaving private parties to pursue violations of the agency's directives?" They posit answers on multiple fronts:

> One answer to why the SEC has enforcement authority is that of path dependency. When Congress enacted the securities laws, class action procedures were not as developed as they are today. The harm of financial frauds leading up to the market collapse of the Great Depression was seen by the New Deal Congress through its political lens as most significantly impacting the small investor. There did not then exist the experience, as there is today, with class action procedures, not to mention a well-funded private plaintiffs' bar, to empower the small investor with the means not only to recoup her losses, but also protect herself against any ongoing violations. *** Hence, within the legal landscape that existed in 1933 and 1934, Congress chose a fork in the road that included both private and public enforcement. It granted the agency the authority to proceed administratively and judicially to address violations committed, as well as those about to be committed, while providing private suits in selective areas.
>
> More significantly, numerous regulatory provisions of the securities laws create problems that prevent the meaningful pursuit of violations by private plaintiffs. In many cases, the loss suffered by the plaintiff or even a group of plaintiffs may not rise to a sufficient level to attract the interest of the entrepreneurial plaintiffs' attorney. And, the expected gains of the suit may be heavily discounted by both the plaintiff and his attorney, due to problematic elements such as establishing or even pleading key elements of the case. *** It can also be the case that the violation is simply of the type for which no private

> action exists. The net capital requirements of brokers, the requirement of reliable internal controls and records, and compliance with the independence requirements of auditors and audit committee members are examples of such provisions. The absence of a private action may well be because the nature of the regulation is one that focuses not on investor protection as such, but rather on achieving desired efficiency or general confidence in the market. Violation of such a broadly based social objective is a poor candidate to isolate particular investor harm and, therefore, to equip the investor with a private enforcement remedy, let alone to exclude the SEC from enforcement. If the SEC then is to have an enforcement mission, why not allow its actions to cover those violations where there may also be private harms that arise from the violation. A related factor is the a priori concern that private actions may well be fortuitous, but that SEC actions may be more deliberate in their focus. ***

James D. Cox & Randall S. Thomas, SEC Enforcement Heuristics: An Empirical Inquiry, 53 Duke L. J. 737, 743-44 (2003).

B. SEC INVESTIGATIONS

Investigations by the SEC staff are often described as "the heart of the securities enforcement practice." The following analysis by experienced defense counsel offers several reasons why.

SEC INVESTIGATIONS: THE HEART OF SEC ENFORCEMENT PRACTICE

by Richard M. Phillips, Glenn R. Reichardt, Michael J. Missal, and Robyn J. Lipton *in* The Securities Enforcement Manual: Tactics and Strategies (1997)

***First, the staff typically conducts a comprehensive investigation before recommending enforcement action by the Commission. The investigation often involves extensive document production and the testimony of numerous witnesses. By the time the staff recommends an enforcement action, it usually has amassed a great deal of evidence and has developed a detailed theory of the alleged liability of the targets of the staff's investigation. At the conclusion of its investigation, the staff will normally invite a potential target of its enforcement recommendation to file a Wells Submission, in which counsel can argue why the Commission ought not institute a public enforcement proceeding. The ability to prepare a persuasive Wells Submission will depend on the factual record developed during the staff's investigation. Accordingly, the best opportunity to influence the outcome of an SEC investigation occurs **during** the staff's investigation, rather than **after** its completion.

Second, for most persons who are confronted by an SEC enforcement action, the staff's investigation will represent their only "day in court" because the vast majority of cases brought by the Commission are settled at the time or shortly after they are instituted. SEC investigations generally are confidential, whereas formal enforcement proceedings are matters of public record. The publicity associated with the institution of a public enforcement proceeding can cause more reputational and business damage than the formal sanctions that may ultimately be imposed as a result of the proceeding. Thus, a primary focus of defense counsel during an SEC investigation is to persuade the Commission not to initiate a public enforcement proceeding, to reduce the gravity of the charges made in an enforcement proceeding, or to lay the foundation for a satisfactory settlement in which the client accepts certain findings and sanctions without admitting or denying any wrongdoing.

Third, the witnesses called to testify or produce documents in SEC investigations greatly exceed in number the defendants named in enforcement actions that result from those investigations. Thus, the number of firms and individuals requiring representation will be greatest at the investigatory stage. The investigatory stage is also a time when many issues will arise regarding joint representation, e.g., whether one law firm can represent both a securities firm and its individual officers or employees. Often, to avoid potential conflicts of interest, firms and individuals will retain separate counsel during the investigatory stage.

Finally, SEC enforcement actions are expensive and difficult to defend successfully. More often than not, the SEC prevails in litigated enforcement actions, not only in administrative proceedings before the SEC's own administrate law judges, but also in court. Accordingly, in most cases the subjects of an SEC investigation and their counsel devote their efforts toward developing a favorable record during the staff's investigation; they do not delay their defense in the hope or expectation of a successful result in a formal enforcement proceeding.

The SEC's Rules of Practice applicable to investigations do not explicitly provide for an active role for counsel representing the subjects of an investigation. Nevertheless, experienced counsel typically have ample opportunity to influence an investigation's outcome. Through a proactive approach with the staff, counsel can often allay the staff's concerns and otherwise help to shape the staff's investigative conclusions. Moreover, through negotiating reasonable accommodations and developing a professionally credible relationship with the staff, counsel can influence the scope and time frame for the production of documents as well as the number of witnesses and the nature and location of their testimony.

To have the maximum impact, counsel must be closely involved in an investigation from its outset. An investigation generally should not be treated like discovery in a civil case, in which the presumed strategy often is "the less said, the better." Instead, in many cases the most effective strategy is to present the client's defense at every stage of the investigation. Such an approach requires a thorough evaluation of the client's case at an early stage. This evaluation will help determine whether to: (a) present the client's defenses to the staff in an aggressive fashion by freely furnishing information even beyond that requested, or (b) take a more defensive "sit back and wait" approach, furnishing to the staff only the minimum information necessary to comply with the staff's subpoenas.

If the first strategy is chosen, the potential target will want to present its affirmative defenses to the staff's factual allegations and legal theories through discussions with the staff, document production, testimony and, if necessary, through Wells Submissions and post-Submission discussions with the staff. If, on the other hand, a "sit back and wait" strategy is appropriate, the potential target of the investigation may provide only the minimum information required and may rely heavily on privileges, such as the attorney-client privilege and the privilege against self-incrimination, to limit the evidence that might be used against the potential target in subsequent proceedings.

While the nature of each client's defense will depend upon the particular circumstances of each investigation, anyone with potential exposure should approach an SEC investigation with the same careful attention and preparation that he or she would devote to the defense of civil litigation. Otherwise counsel will not be in a position to counteract and dispel the staff's prosecutorial suspicions—suspicions that may be assisted by the often misguided inclination of other potential targets to deflect the staff's attention from themselves by pointing fingers at others.

Of course, each investigation varies in scope and tone, depending upon the severity of the potential violations being investigated, the reputation of the parties under investigation, the interest of the press or the Congress in the subject matter of the investigation, the culture and priorities of the particular SEC office (i.e., headquarters or a regional office) in which the investigation originates, and the personalities of the individual staff members actually conducting the investigation. Nevertheless, there are certain characteristics that are common to many staff investigations.***

---

1. The Investigatory Process

The above excerpt emphasizes the enormous sweep of the SEC's investigatory powers. The source of these broad powers can be found in each of the five securities acts administered and enforced by the SEC, all of which authorize the Commission to investigate past, ongoing, or prospective violations of the federal securities laws, the SEC rules or regulations promulgated thereunder, and the rules and regulations of the various SROs. See Sections 20(a) and 8(e) of the Securities Act; Sections 21(a)(1) and (2) of the Exchange Act; Section 209(a) of the Advisers Act; Section 42(a) of the Investment Company Act; and Section 321(a) of the Trust Indenture Act. Section 21(a)(1) of the Exchange Act provides an example:

> The Commission may, in its discretion, make such investigations as it deems necessary to determine whether any person has violated, is violating, or is about to violate any provision of this title, the rules or regulations thereunder, the rules of a national securities exchange or registered securities association of which such person is a member or a person associated with a member, [and] *** is authorized in its discretion, to publish information concerning any such violations, and to investigate any facts, conditions, practices, or matters which it may deem necessary or proper to aid in the enforcement of such provisions, in the prescribing of rules and regulations under this title, or in securing information to serve as a basis for recommending further legislation concerning the matters to which this title relates.

The conduct of these investigations is governed by the SEC's Rules of Informal and Other Procedures, 17 C.F.R. §§ 202.1 et seq. (particularly § 202.5(a)-(f), which governs enforcement activities) and the SEC's Rules Relating to Investigations, 17 C.F.R. §§ 203.1-203.8. The SEC's Rules of Practice, 17 C.F.R. § 201.100 et seq., also have some relevance in the investigatory phase. Moreover, in response to a 2007 Senate report recommending that the SEC standardize its investigative procedures, the SEC made its Enforcement Manual available on its website. See **http://www.sec.gov/divisions/**enforce/ enforcementmanual.pdf Although the Manual states clearly at the outset that it is intended to provide guidance only to the staff of the Enforcement Division and "does not, and may not be relied upon to create any rights, substantive or procedural, enforceable at law by any party in any matter civil or criminal," securities law practitioners nonetheless heralded this development as a means to bring added "'transparency to the process—it enables defense counsel to know the expectations of the SEC's enforcement staff and to respond appropriately.' " Yin Wilczek, SEC's Enforcement Division Publishes Enforcement Manual; Lawyers Welcome Move, SEC's Enforcement Division Publishes, 40 Sec. Reg. & L. Rep. 1635 (BNA) (Oct. 13, 2008) (quoting Stephen J. Crimmins, a partner at Mayer, Brown in Washington, D.C., and a former SEC deputy chief litigation counsel).

Courts have routinely emphasized Congress's intent to grant federal agencies broad discretion in the conduct of their investigations and have generally refused to interfere in judgments by SEC officials that investigations are warranted. A decision often cited is *United States v. Morton Salt Co.*, 338 U.S. 632 (1950), where the Supreme Court stated that:

> Even if one were to regard the request for information in this case as caused by nothing more than official curiosity, nevertheless, law-enforcing agencies have a legitimate right to satisfy themselves that corporate behavior is consistent with the law and the public interest *** [I]t is sufficient if the inquiry is within the authority of the agency, the demand is not too indefinite and the information sought is reasonably relevant.

Id. at 652. See *SEC v. Brigadoon Scotch Distributing* Co., 480 F.2d 1047, 1052-53 (2d Cir. 1973) (emphasizing that "[t]he Commission must be free without undue interference or delay to conduct an investigation which will adequately develop a factual basis for a determination as to whether particular activities come within the Commission's regulatory authority"); *Treats Int'l Enter., Inc. v. SEC*, 828 F. Supp. 16, 19 (S.D.N.Y. 1993) (refusing to enjoin SEC investigation where the agency had shown "some good faith basis for investigating"). For an exceptional decision in which a court displayed a willingness to second-guess SEC officials, see *SEC v. Wheeling-Pittsburgh Steel Corp.*, 648 F. 2d 118 (3d Cir. 1981). In this very famous case, Wheeling-Pittsburgh put forth compelling evidence that SEC subpoenas of company officials resulted from pressure by Senator Lowell Weicker who was in turn acting under pressure from Wheeling-Pittsburgh's leading competitor. The mere fact that the SEC was investigating Wheeling-Pittsburgh could have been very damaging to the company, because Senator Weicker had introduced a bill in Congress that would have barred any corporation that was under investigation by the SEC from receiving federal loan guarantees. It appeared that both the Senator and the competitor knew that Wheeling-Pittsburgh was seeking a loan guarantee from the Department of Commerce.

Section 202.5(a) of the SEC's Informal and Other Procedures suggests some of the far more typical sources of SEC investigations, noting specifically that "complaints received from members of the public, communications from Federal or State agencies, examination of filings made with the Commission, or otherwise" may trigger an inquiry by the staff. Other likely sources of SEC investigations include:

- market surveillance and internet surveillance units in the Division of Enforcement;
- referrals from other offices and divisions within the SEC (such as Corporation Finance and Market Regulation);
- periodic inspections of broker-dealers, investment advisers, and investment companies by the SEC or SROs;
- press accounts of troubled companies and other news stories;
- complaints from disgruntled customers and whistleblowing employees;
- referrals from foreign governments;
- referrals from the SROs; and
- informants (including those seeking bounties pursuant to the SEC's new whistleblower program discussed infra at subsection B.2).

As history reflects, even the smallest of leads can trigger a major investigation. For example, officials from the Fort Worth District office of the SEC have credited a Wall Street Journal article on Enron's financial woes as the initial source of its investigation into Enron's alleged violations of the federal securities laws. See Brenda S. Jeffreys, Extra Funds, Political Pressure Help Once-Strapped Office Rise to Enforcement Challenge, Tex. Law. at 1 (Sept. 16, 2002).

As with Enron, SEC investigations most often begin with a preliminary inquiry, which may be conducted by the staff without any need to obtain formal approval. On other occasions, however, the staff may launch an investigation with a "formal order of investigation" that carries with it the authority to subpoena documents and testimony. Both types of investigations are nonpublic, except in the very rare instances where the Commission authorizes otherwise. Although for decades, formal orders of investigation could not be issued in the absence of approval by the Commission, as part of the recent efforts to reinvigorate SEC enforcement, the Commissioners have delegated their approval authority to the Director of Enforcement who, in turn, has sub-delegated his authority to senior officials throughout the Division. See Enforcement Manual at § 2.3.3. In highly practical terms, this change "means that if defense counsel resist the voluntary production of documents or witnesses, or fail to be complete and timely in responses or engage in dilatory tactics, there will very likely to be a subpoena on [their] desk the next morning." Robert Khuzamii, Remarks Before the New York City Bar: My First 100 Days as Director of Enforcement, August 5, 2009.

Additional insight into the SEC's investigatory process can be drawn from the following article by two leading defense attorneys. The first co-author once served as the SEC's General Counsel; the second served as Senior Counsel in the Enforcement Division.

SEC ENFORCEMENT PROCEEDINGS: STRATEGIC CONSIDERATIONS FOR WHEN THE AGENCY COMES CALLING

by Ralph C. Ferrara and Philip S. Khinda

51 Admin. L. Rev. 1143, 1148-1165 (1999)

****The Informal Inquiry*

When the SEC learns of possible violations of the federal securities laws, it generally conducts a preliminary investigation. The enforcement staff will usually refer to such a preliminary matter as an informal inquiry or, less frequently, as an "MUI," an abbreviation for "matter under inquiry."

The enforcement staff uses the informal inquiry to conduct a preliminary review of certain facts and circumstances that it believes may involve violative conduct. The staff will generally review documents and other information in order to determine whether further investigation is warranted. At a minimum, the staff will need to obtain background information regarding the subject matter and activities that prompted its inquiry. In a preliminary investigation, "no process is issued or testimony compelled." [17 C.F.R. § 202.5(a)] The success of a preliminary investigation depends almost entirely on the voluntary cooperation of the individuals or entities approached by the SEC staff.

In an initial meeting or telephone call, the SEC staff may identify certain corporate personnel or officers with whom they wish to speak, either through an in-person or telephone interview or under oath. The enforcement staff's policy regarding requests for information from corporate personnel is to direct its inquiries to the corporate general counsel's office, or to outside counsel if the staff has been so notified.

The staff may ask that the company voluntarily produce or supply particular information from corporate records, such as schedules, indexes, or chronologies. The staff may also present counsel with a request list seeking documents relevant to particular subjects. To the extent that the recipient of such a request intends to supply any information to the staff, counsel should review all of the same considerations it would in producing information pursuant to a subpoena, particularly with respect to confidentiality.

In evaluating these considerations, counsel should bear in mind that a refusal to provide such information, or an extended delay in doing so, may serve as the basis for the enforcement staff's seeking to obtain a formal order of investigation (and, in turn, subpoena power) *** to further its fact-finding efforts.

If the SEC staff seeks to examine a witness during the course of an informal inquiry, counsel should request that it be done via an interview rather than through testimony, i.e., not under oath and without the use of a court reporter. Interviews are generally preferable whenever parallel proceedings or litigation exists or is likely, as such discussions with the staff will not generate witness transcripts (as would be the case with formal testimony) that may be discoverable and later used to challenge the witness or otherwise impair the witness's or the company's defense in other actions.

During preliminary inquiries and formal investigations, the staff occasionally may wish or agree to interview a witness "informally"—that is, not in the presence of a court reporter or stenographer. If the staff does so, it will usually begin the session with a number of notices and warnings that should be considered carefully. The witness should be told (1) that the conversation is voluntary; (2) whether or not a formal order has been granted ***; (3) that he or she has the right to have counsel present during the interview; (4) that the staff will be taking notes during the interview that will be subject to the SEC's routine uses for such information; and (5) that, although the witness is not under oath, he or she should understand that knowingly and willfully providing false information to the staff in connection with such an inquiry is a crime.

Whether a witness provides testimony voluntarily or agrees to be interviewed by the staff, here as in a formal proceeding, the staff will provide the witness and/or counsel with a standard form setting forth several important notices, warnings, and routine uses applicable to any information provided to the staff. Any information given to the SEC may be forwarded to a number of government and regulatory entities, among others.

While noting that compliance with its requests is voluntary at this point, the SEC staff may nevertheless insist that the witness appear to testify. A voluntary appearance before the staff should be treated in the same manner as one required by subpoena in a formal investigation, discussed below. Procedurally, the testimony will differ from its formal counterpart only in that a notary public (the court reporter or stenographer), rather than a member of the enforcement staff, will administer the oath and the witness will be informed that he or she may decline to answer any question. It is important to bear in mind that a witness's refusal to answer questions may serve as the basis for a staff recommendation seeking a formal order of investigation.

****The Formal Investigation*

If the enforcement staff's concerns are not resolved through the informal inquiry, it may request that the Commission [ed. note – now, a senior supervisory official] authorize a formal investigation. The regulations suggest, but do not require, that a formal investigation occur after the completion of a preliminary investigation. [See 17 C.F.R.§ 202.5]

***It is important to bear in mind that the commencement of an SEC investigation initiates only a fact-finding proceeding and not an adjudication. The Supreme Court has held that an SEC investigation is "an administrative investigation [which] adjudicates no legal rights." [*SEC v. O'Brien, Inc.*, 467 U.S. 735, 742 (1984)]. It is also important to note that, unlike criminal investigations, SEC investigations do not have formal targets or subjects. Rather, the enforcement staff will assert that it has made no final judgments regarding the potential liability of any individual or entity involved in an investigation, although its actions may suggest otherwise.

The SEC initiates a formal investigation with the entry of an "Order Directing Private Investigation and Designating Officers to Take Testimony," generally referred to as a formal order. *** [As part of its request for a formal order], the enforcement staff will generally describe the facts and circumstances that have raised concerns, the potential securities law violations, and its need for subpoena power to further its investigative efforts. *** [I]t is often sufficient to claim that [violations] may have occurred, may be occurring, or may be about to occur. Indeed, in certain types of inquiries, the issuance of a formal order seems to be a routine matter.

Although the graduation of an informal SEC inquiry to a formal investigation may be of little legal consequence, it represents a significant milestone in the agency's enforcement process. Specifically, a formal investigation represents a certain degree of entrenchment on the part of the enforcement staff with respect to the matter, both with regard to its resolve in exploring further and as a matter of internal administrative practice. A formal investigation has a sense of importance and perhaps an impetus, as compared with an informal inquiry, that will be harder to stop.

Moreover, even when a formal investigation that will not yield an enforcement action has wound down, it often develops an inertia that is difficult to overcome. Administrative practices within the SEC may add to this apparent sense of permanence. The closure of a formal investigation requires the staff to prepare a memorandum that accounts for all of the actions it took in exploring the issues that raised concern and explains why further investigation is unwarranted. This closing memorandum must then be reviewed and approved by one or more senior members of the Division of Enforcement staff, usually an Assistant Director, among others.***

The formal order of investigation is itself an important document that should be reviewed carefully by counsel. Drafted by the Division of Enforcement, the order generally outlines the scope of the investigation that the Commission has authorized. The order also delegates to members of the enforcement staff designated as officers of the SEC the power to issue subpoenas *ad testificandum* and *duces tecum* and to administer oaths. A formal order is generally a blend of general boilerplate recitations and specific language dealing with the conduct and concerns that prompted the inquiry.

Structurally, the formal order of investigation usually consists of six sections: the caption, a recitation of information from the SEC's "public files," a staff report, a statement of purpose and order, a designation of officers, and authentications. Two of these sections are of special importance. The first two paragraphs of the "purpose and order" section should contain a list of the specific statutory provisions that are given as grounds for ordering the commencement of a formal investigative proceeding. In addition, the "staff report" section of the formal order summarizes facts relating to each potential statutory violation. Although these descriptions are usually general, they may be helpful in determining the enforcement staff's factual awareness and areas of interest.

Copies of the formal order are furnished to parties upon request only with the approval of the appropriate staff member, generally the Assistant Director overseeing the matter, who find such production to be consistent with both the protection of privacy of the persons involved in the investigation, and the unimpeded conduct of the investigation. The release of a copy of the formal order is usually limited to individuals and entities contacted by the staff and/or their respective counsel.

1. SEC Subpoenas

The subpoena power *** provides the Division of Enforcement with its most important tool in conducting formal investigations. Under the Commission's revised Rules of Practice, the general service provisions of Rule 150 apply to the issuance of subpoenas for the purposes of an investigation. [See 17 C.F.R. §§ 201.150, 201.232(c), 203.8] Such service may be made in person, through the United States mail, via courier or express delivery, or by facsimile. The reach of an SEC subpoena is nationwide.*** In practice, however, the staff is free to, and often does, negotiate the location of witness testimony before and after a subpoena is issued based on the particular circumstances of the witness and the case. When not taking place at its Washington, D.C. headquarters, SEC testimony generally is taken at one of the Commission's regional or district offices or in an available federal office building.***

2. Producing Documents in Response to an SEC Subpoena

If a corporation determines that it will comply with a subpoena for documents, it will benefit from a number of preliminary considerations. Practical considerations for the production of documents in response to an SEC subpoena are, in most respects, the same as those for production in response to a grand jury or judicially-issued subpoena. A discussion or meeting with the SEC staff—like one with opposing counsel or a meeting with a criminal prosecutor—provides an opportunity to propose a procedure for making documents available to the staff and potentially to limit the scope of its requests.

A threshold question for counsel is whether the staff should be invited to examine original documents or, alternatively, whether copies of requested materials should be reproduced and delivered to the staff. The staff will generally accept copies in lieu of original records with the understanding that the originals will be preserved and that the reproduction costs will be borne by the recipient of the subpoena.

***Ordinarily, off-site review of documents by the SEC staff is highly preferable for the recipient of a subpoena. The delivery of relevant documents to the SEC (or to outside counsel's office) eliminates the disruption and possible inadvertent contacts of an on-site visit. In addition, off-site review of photocopies provides a superior procedure for organizing documents, identifying the documents produced, withholding documents on grounds of privilege, and preventing inadvertent loss or misplacement of original documents. The location and arrangement of original documents can be accurately described when groups of documents are correctly marked and their sources identified.

Before any records are made available to the SEC staff, they should be reviewed carefully to determine whether any applicable legal privilege, such as the attorney-client privilege or work product doctrine, might shield them from production. In addition, any production of documents to the SEC should be made in compliance with its various rules regarding confidentiality [to third parties].

3. Witness Examinations

Formal investigations invariably involve the taking of testimony by the members of the staff of the Commission's Division of Enforcement who have been designated as officers of the Commission for the purposes of the investigation in question. Such testimony may be required by a subpoena *ad testificandum* (requiring only that the witness appear) or a subpoena *duces tecum* (requiring that the witness appear in connection with the production of certain documents).

Pursuant to Rule 7(b) of the SEC's Rules Relating to Investigations [17 C.F.R. §203.7(b)], witnesses are entitled to be "accompanied, represented, and advised" by counsel of their choice in connection with any formal investigative proceedings at which the witness personally appears. The right to counsel affords the witness the right to consult his or her attorney before, during, and after the examination. During the examination, the attorney may also question the witness briefly to clarify his or her answers, and the attorney may take summary notes during the examination for the witness's subsequent use.

Following an opening statement by the staff, counsel should use an invitation to make an opening statement to place any relevant assertion or request to the staff on the record. Some practitioners use this opportunity to assert a statement of the witness's rights. Others reserve making such assertions until they are given an opportunity to clarify the record, generally towards the close of the proceeding.

If multiple witnesses are called to appear, corporate counsel should consider certain preliminary issues. The backdrop for these considerations is the SEC's sequestration rule, which provides that witnesses and their counsel be sequestered at the discretion of any of the enforcement staff members designated as officers of the Commission. In other words, a witness's testimony is generally closed to other witnesses and counsel.

Outside counsel may not represent both the corporation and its officers if differing or divergent interests are present. Similarly, counsel cannot represent multiple witnesses if such conflicting interests appear. Counsel bears the responsibility of determining at the outset of the engagement whether a possible conflict exists.***

Counsel for the corporation may request the SEC staff's permission to attend the examination of a company officer, director, or employee not represented by corporate counsel, but no right to do so has been recognized by the courts. Counsel for the corporation is most likely to be permitted to appear as co-counsel on behalf of the witness in the witness's capacity as a corporate employee, officer, and/or director in addition to the witness's personal counsel.

Witnesses should be prepared for testimony before the SEC in accordance with counsel's usual witness preparation practice, with certain considerations given added emphasis. The customary instructions should underscore the witness's obligation to testify truthfully, and review features typical of SEC examinations. Questioning in the course of an investigation may be primarily in the format of cross-examination and may focus the witness's attention largely upon documents. Witnesses should be given the practical advice that their demeanor and attitude—whether captured in a transcribed record or not—may influence the recommendations of the staff with respect to further enforcement inquiries or actions.

Similarly, any statement made in the presence of the staff may be used for any purpose it chooses. Even if a statement is made after a staff member advises that communications are "off the record" and is not recorded by the court reporter, the statement may be used for the same purposes as statements made on the record. In short, statements made in the presence of the staff are never "off the record." Such communications, even if not transcribed, may influence the recommendation of the staff with respect to an enforcement action. They may also implicate the United States Code provision that provides criminal penalties for knowingly and willfully providing false information to a government agent. [18 U.S.C. § 1001]

A witness's speculation and surmise are especially dangerous as other witnesses, whose testimony and identity will not be known, may be called to testify on the same matters. Further, counsel for the witness will not have had the opportunity to cross-examine these other witnesses. Although this right is available in court and in administrative proceedings, it is not generally available during investigations.

Irrespective of the issues being pursued, the SEC staff will routinely ask the witness a series of personal questions regarding, among other things, biographical and educational background; employment history; personal securities brokerage accounts and trading activity; corporate offices held; the location of bank accounts and loans; residence(s); telephone number(s); telephone calling card and credit card numbers; and prior testimony in securities-related and fraud-related proceedings. Counsel may be successful in limiting some of these lines of questioning insofar as the witness's personal conduct or contacts are not at issue. ***

[4.] Confidentiality Considerations

Anyone who supplies information to the SEC (whether in the form of documents or testimony) should carefully comply with its rules regarding confidentiality. These rules provide a procedure for requesting that information not be released in response to a request under the Freedom of Information Act (FOIA), the statute that provides for public access to documents held by the federal government. [5 U.S.C. § 552; 17 C.F.R. § 200.83]. Confidentiality may be requested for documentary or oral information (to the extent that oral information is memorialized in writing) submitted to the SEC, and applies to information produced pursuant to subpoena as well as information produced voluntarily. The two general grounds for a request are personal privacy and business confidentiality, although other reasons are permitted by law.

NOTES AND QUESTIONS

1. ***Cooperating with the SEC.*** Because SEC staff members conducting an informal investigation lack the power to subpoena documents or testimony, a client's initial inclination may well be to refuse to voluntarily produce any requested material. Yet experienced defense counsel often advise that cooperation with the SEC staff generally constitutes a superior strategy.

What, precisely, is meant by the term "cooperation?" Does it involve more than producing voluntarily what the staff could otherwise obtain only through its subpoena power? What benefits are to be gained from cooperation? What are some drawbacks? Are there particular types of cases where the cooperation strategy would seem clearly preferable? Are there particular types of cases where that strategy may be counter-productive? The materials in Subsection 3 infra include an SEC Report and Release discussing the types of "credit" that the SEC may give for a company's or individual's cooperation.

Consider also the excerpt by Phillips et al., supra, which expresses the view that an SEC investigation "should not be treated like discovery in a civil case, in which the presumed strategy is 'the less said the better.'" Upon what are these differences based? Acting on this view, what advice might you give in preparing your client (or clients) for interviews or testimony with the SEC staff? Are there particular types of cases where "the less said" strategy may well be the superior one?

2. Multiple Representations. Assume you represent a corporation that has received an SEC subpoena for documents with an accompanying letter indicating that the staff intends to subpoena testimony from a number of the corporation's top officials in the upcoming months. What are some of the factors you should consider in determining whether your ethical responsibilities permit you to engage in multiple representations?

State professional responsibility rules, often drawn from the ABA's Model Rules of Professional Conduct, will play a key role in your analysis. In this regard, consider ABA Model Rule 1.13, captioned the "organization as client." Rule 1.13(a) states unequivocally that a " lawyer employed or retained by an organization represents the organization acting through its duly authorized constituents" and Rule 1.13(f) makes clear that "in dealing with an organization's directors, officers, employees, members, shareholders or other constituents, a lawyer shall explain the identity of the client when the lawyer knows or reasonably should know that the organization's interests are adverse to those of the constituents with whom the lawyer is dealing." Rule 1.13(g) then goes on to state that a:

> lawyer representing an organization may also represent any of its directors, officers, employees, members, shareholders or other constituents, subject to the provisions of Rule 1.7. If the organization's consent to the dual representation is required by Rule 1.7, the consent shall be given by an appropriate official of the organization other than the individual who is to be represented, or by the shareholders.

ABA Model Rule 1.13(g).

ABA Model Rule 1.7 concerns conflicts of interest involving current clients. Rule 1.7(a) states the general rule, subject to an exception in paragraph b, that a "lawyer shall not represent a client if the representation involves a concurrent conflict of interest." It then explains that a concurrent conflict of interest exists if "the representation of one client will be directly adverse to another client" or if "there is a significant risk that the representation of one or more clients will be materially limited by the lawyer's responsibilities to another client, a former client or a third person or by a personal interest of the lawyer."

The exception in Rule 1.7(b) provides that, notwithstanding the existence of a concurrent conflict of interest, a lawyer may represent a client if:

> (1) the lawyer reasonably believes that the lawyer will be able to provide competent and diligent representation to each affected client;
>
> (2) the representation is not prohibited by law;
>
> (3) the representation does not involve the assertion of a claim by one client against another client represented by the lawyer in the same litigation or other proceeding before a tribunal; and
>
> (4) each affected client gives informed consent, confirmed in writing.

ABA Model Rule 1.7(b).

For a decision concluding that a single law firm could continue its simultaneous representation of a brokerage firm and 47 registered representatives under investigation by the SEC for securities fraud, see *In the Matter of Merrill Lynch, Pierce, Fenner & Smith, Inc.*, [1973-74 Transfer Binder] Fed. Sec. L. Rep. ¶ 79,608, 83,630 at 83,633 (Ullman, ALJ) (Dec. 6, 1973) (maintaining that "where it is not clear that a conflict of interests will occur between two or more clients of an attorney, the informed consent of the client or clients whose interests more likely would suffer in the event a conflict should develop can provide justification for the continuation of multiple representations"). From the clients' perspective, what are some of the advantages and disadvantages of engaging in a multiple representation on such a large scale? For additional discussion of this issue, see John F.X. Peloso & Ben A. Indek, Ethical Minefield: Multiple Representation in Government Probes, N. Y. L. J. at 3 (Oct. 19, 2005); Richard W. Painter, Advance Waiver of Conflicts, 13 Geo. J. Legal Ethics 289 (2000); Marc I. Steinberg & Timothy U. Sharpe, Attorney Conflicts of Interest: The Need for a Coherent Framework, 66 Notre Dame L. Rev. 1 (1990). See also Karl A. Groskaufmanis, Ethics for Securities Lawyers, 111 PLI/NY 219 (Nov. 2001).

*3. **Tell the Truth.*** It should go without saying that counsel representing clients under investigation by the SEC should do everything in their power to encourage their clients to tell the truth to SEC officials under all sets of circumstances, no matter how formal or seemingly informal the interview or testimony. Among other reasons, counsel can emphasize that: (a) it is the morally right thing to do; (b) the truth typically comes out eventually; (c) making knowingly false statements to a federal official is a crime in and of itself under 18 U.S.C. § 1001; and (d) lying to the SEC is one of the surest ways of turning even the most routine civil securities infraction into a criminal case. For elaboration on the latter point, see Phyllis Diamond, SEC Official Outlines Factors Triggering Criminal Referrals, 28 Sec. Reg. & L. Rep. 970 (BNA) (Aug.9, 1996) (discussing statement by SEC Southeast Regional Director that "while there is no 'checklist' of factors that will turn a civil investigation into a criminal action, failing to be truthful to the Securities and Exchange Commission staff during a civil investigation is increasingly likely to trigger a Justice Department referral"). For a high profile criminal prosecution involving false statements to government officials investigating possible insider trading, see *United States v. Stewart*, 433 F.3d 273 (2d Cir. 2006) (affirming conviction of home designer/

entrepreneur Martha Stewart and her stockbroker, Peter Bacanovic, for making false statements and obstructing an agency proceeding).

*4. **Obstruction of Justice.*** Whereas concerns about truth telling are typically directed to witnesses and potential targets in SEC investigations, it is critical that all of the potential participants in an SEC investigation—including witnesses, targets and their agents (particularly attorneys and accountants)—be aware of the broad sweep of the federal laws against the obstruction of justice. One example of the enormous liability risk for obstructing justice is the verdict issued against the now defunct accounting firm of Arthur Andersen, LLP, for alleged document destruction and other actions taken in connection with the SEC's investigation into the collapse of Enron, a long-time audit client of the firm. Although that conviction was later reversed by a unanimous Supreme Court, see *Arthur Andersen LLP v. United States*, 544 U.S. 696 (2005) (holding that the jury was improperly instructed), the case continues to serve as an important reminder of the ancillary issues that may develop in the course of government investigations for possible violations of the federal securities laws. Indeed, Arthur Andersen was prosecuted in part for the conduct of one of its attorneys, who was alleged to have instructed others at the firm to shred Enron-related documents. See Symposium Transcript, Twenty Years of Legal Ethics: Past, Present and Future, 20 Geo. J. of Legal Ethics 321, 329 (2006).

"Obstruction of justice" is a broad phrase that may extend to "any attempt to impede the due administration of justice." *United States v. Cihak*, 137 F.3d 252, 262 (5th Cir. 1998). As such, it encompasses conduct involving document destruction as well as witness or evidence tampering. The crime of obstruction of justice may be prosecuted under an array of federal statutes, including 18 U.S.C. § 1519, which was enacted by Congress as part of SOX.

> **18 U.S.C. § 1519 Destruction, Alteration, or Falsification of Records in Federal Investigations and Bankruptcy**
>
> Whoever knowingly alters, destroys, mutilates, conceals, covers up, falsifies, or makes a false entry in any record, document, or tangible object with the intent to impede, obstruct, or influence the investigation or proper administration of any matter within the jurisdiction of any department or agency of the United States or any case filed under title 11, or in relation to or contemplation of any such matter or case, shall be fined under this title, imprisoned not more than 20 years, or both.

In view of 18 U.S.C. § 1519's obvious breadth, what specific advice would you give to clients at the outset of an investigation by the SEC? What suggestions would you give an attorney who is advising a client under investigation?

*5. **SEC Investigations and the Duty to Disclose.*** When a company learns that it is under investigation by the SEC, must it disclose this information to its shareholders? Does it matter whether the investigation takes the form of a preliminary inquiry or a formal investigation authorized by the Commission? Even absent a legal duty, should it disclose the investigation? Consider the important judgments—both legal and business—that must be made by the issuer. What role should an attorney play in assisting a corporate client with this decision?

*6. **Applicable Privileges.*** As in depositions or document discovery conducted under the Federal Rules of Civil Procedure, persons subject to an SEC subpoena or an SEC request for testimony or documents possess constitutional and other legal rights to withhold such testimony or materials. What types of privileges might you expect to see asserted in the course of an SEC investigation? What are some of the consequences that flow from a client's decision to assert an applicable privilege?

*7. **The Power to Subpoena Documents and Testimony.*** SEC subpoenas are not self-enforcing. This means that if a subpoena recipient fails to produce documents or fails to attend scheduled testimony, the SEC must take the subsequent step of applying for a judicial order to enforce the subpoena. The SEC may bring this action by filing a motion and an "order to show cause" in the federal district court where the investigation is being conducted or in any jurisdiction where the subpoenaed party resides. See, e.g., Exchange Act Section 21(c). Such actions are conducted as "summary proceedings" under Rule 81(a)(3) of the Federal Rules of Civil Procedure (i.e., there is no complaint and no discovery), and the burden of proof is on the opposing party to demonstrate why the judge should not enforce the SEC subpoena. As we saw earlier, courts are typically reluctant to second guess the SEC's broad investigatory power, and only in the most extraordinary cases will they refuse to use their judicial power to enforce an agency subpoena of non-privileged materials.

In cases involving valid claims of privilege, persons or companies under investigation by the SEC may also file objections to an SEC motion seeking judicial enforcement of a subpoena to a third party. However, because SEC investigations are generally confidential, the investigation's target may not even be aware that the agency has called for documents or testimony. This situation is illustrated in the following case.

SEC v. JERRY T. O'BRIEN, INC.

467 U.S. 735 (1984)

JUSTICE THURGOOD MARSHALL:

The Securities and Exchange Commission (SEC or Commission) has statutory authority to conduct nonpublic investigations into possible violations of the securities laws and, in the course thereof, to issue subpoenas to obtain relevant information. The question before us is whether the Commission must notify the "target" of such an investigation when it issues a subpoena to a third party.

I

This case represents one shard of a prolonged investigation by the SEC into the affairs of respondent Harry F. Magnuson and persons and firms with whom he has dealt. The investigation began in 1980, when the Commission's staff reported to the Commission that information in their possession tended to show that Magnuson and others had been trading in the stock of specified mining companies in a manner violative of the registration, reporting, and antifraud provisions of the Securities Act of 1933 and the Securities Exchange Act of 1934. In response, the Commission issued a Formal Order of Investigation authorizing employees of its Seattle Regional Office to initiate a "private investigation" into the transactions in question and, if necessary, to subpoena testimony and documents "deemed relevant or material to the inquiry."

Acting on that authority, members of the Commission staff subpoenaed financial records in the possession of respondent Jerry T. O'Brien, Inc. (O'Brien), a broker-dealer firm, and respondent Pennaluna & Co. (Pennaluna). O'Brien voluntarily complied, but Pennaluna refused to disgorge the requested materials. Soon thereafter, in response to several inquiries by O'Brien's counsel, a member of the SEC staff informed O'Brien that it was a "subject" of the investigation.

O'Brien, Pennaluna, and their respective owners promptly filed a suit in the District Court for the Eastern District of Washington, seeking to enjoin the Commission's investigation and to prevent Magnuson from complying with subpoenas that had been issued to him.[3] Magnuson filed a cross-claim, also seeking to block portions of the investigation. O'Brien then filed motions seeking authority to depose the Commission's officers and to conduct expedited discovery into the Commission's files.

The District Court denied respondents' discovery motions and soon thereafter dismissed their claims for injunctive relief. The principal ground for the court's decision was that respondents would have a full opportunity to assert their objections to the basis and scope of the SEC's investigation if and when the Commission instituted a subpoena enforcement action. The court did, however, rule that the Commission's outstanding subpoenas met the requirements outlined in *United States v. Powell*, 379 U.S. 48 (1964), for determining whether an administrative summons is judicially enforceable. Specifically, the District Court held that the Commission had a legitimate purpose in issuing the subpoenas, that the requested information was relevant and was not already in the Commission's possession, and that the issuance of the subpoenas comported with pertinent procedural requirements.

Following the District Court's decision, the SEC issued several subpoenas to third parties. In response, Magnuson and O'Brien renewed their request to the District Court for injunctive relief, accompanying the request with a motion, pursuant to Rule 62(c) of the Federal Rules of Civil Procedure, for a stay pending appeal. For the first time, respondents expressly sought notice of the subpoenas issued by the Commission to third parties. Reasoning that respondents lacked standing to challenge voluntary compliance with subpoenas by third parties, and that, in any subsequent proceeding brought by the SEC, respondents could move to suppress evidence the Commission had obtained from third parties through abusive subpoenas, the District Court denied the requested relief.

A panel of the Court of Appeals for the Ninth Circuit affirmed the District Court's denial of injunctive relief with regard to the subpoenas directed

---

3. The principal bases of O'Brien's suit were that the SEC's Formal Order of Investigation was defective, that the investigation did not have a valid purpose, that the Commission should have afforded the subjects of the investigation a chance to comment upon it, and that the issues around which the case revolved had been litigated and settled in another proceeding. Complaint 9-15.

at respondents themselves, agreeing with the lower court that respondents had an adequate remedy at law for challenging those subpoenas. However, the Court of Appeals reversed the District Court's denial of respondents' request for notice of subpoenas issued to third parties. In the Court of Appeals' view, "targets" of SEC investigations "have a right to be investigated consistently with the *Powell* standards." To enable targets to enforce this right, the court held that they must be notified of subpoenas issued to others.

The Court of Appeals denied the Commission's request for rehearing and rejected its suggestion for rehearing en banc. ***

We granted certiorari because of the importance of the issue presented. We now reverse.

II

***No provision in the complex of statutes governing the SEC's investigative power expressly obliges the Commission to notify the "target" of an investigation when it issues a subpoena to a third party. If such an obligation is to be imposed on the Commission, therefore, it must be derived from one of three sources: a constitutional provision; an understanding on the part of Congress, inferable from the structure of the securities laws, regarding how the SEC should conduct its inquiries; or the general standards governing judicial enforcement of administrative subpoenas enunciated in *United States v. Powell*, 379 U.S. 48 (1964), and its progeny. Examination of these three potential bases for the Court of Appeals' ruling leaves us unpersuaded that the notice requirement fashioned by that court is warranted.

A

Our prior cases foreclose any constitutional argument respondents might make in defense of the judgment below. The opinion of the Court in *Hannah v. Larche*, 363 U.S. 420 (1960), leaves no doubt that neither the Due Process Clause of the Fifth Amendment nor the Confrontation Clause of the Sixth Amendment is offended when a federal administrative agency, without notifying a person under investigation, uses its subpoena power to gather evidence adverse to him. The Due Process Clause is not implicated under such circumstances because an administrative investigation adjudicates no legal rights, id., at 440-443, and the Confrontation Clause does not come into play until the initiation of criminal proceedings, id., at 440, n. 16. These principles plainly cover an inquiry by the SEC into possible violations of the securities laws.

It is also settled that a person inculpated by materials sought by a subpoena issued to a third party cannot seek shelter in the Self-Incrimination Clause of the Fifth Amendment. The rationale of this doctrine is that the Constitution proscribes only *compelled* self-incrimination, and, whatever may be the pressures exerted upon the person to whom a subpoena is directed, the subpoena surely does not "compel" anyone else to be a witness against himself. *Fisher v. United States*, 425 U.S. 391, 397 (1976); *Couch v. United States*, 409 U.S. 322, 328-329 (1973). If the "target" of an investigation by the SEC has no Fifth Amendment right to challenge enforcement of a subpoena directed at a third party, he clearly can assert no derivative right to notice when the

Commission issues such a subpoena.

Finally, respondents cannot invoke the Fourth Amendment in support of the Court of Appeals' decision. It is established that, when a person communicates information to a third party even on the understanding that the communication is confidential, he cannot object if the third party conveys that information or records thereof to law enforcement authorities. *United States v. Miller*, 425 U.S. 435, 443 (1976). Relying on that principle, the Court has held that a customer of a bank cannot challenge on Fourth Amendment grounds the admission into evidence in a criminal prosecution of financial records obtained by the Government from his bank pursuant to allegedly defective subpoenas, despite the fact that he was given no notice of the subpoenas. Id., at 443, and n. 5. See also *Donaldson v. United States*, 400 U.S. 517, 522 (1971) (Internal Revenue summons directed to third party does not trench upon any interests protected by the Fourth Amendment). These rulings disable respondents from arguing that notice of subpoenas issued to third parties is necessary to allow a target to prevent an unconstitutional search or seizure of his papers.

B

The language and structure of the statutes administered by the Commission afford respondents no greater aid. The provisions vesting the SEC with the power to issue and seek enforcement of subpoenas are expansive. ***

More generally, [these] statutes vest the SEC with "power to make such rules and regulations as may be necessary or appropriate to implement [their] provisions...." 15 U.S.C. §§ 77s(a), 78w(a)(1). Relying on this authority, the SEC has promulgated a variety of rules governing its investigations, one of which provides that, "[u]nless otherwise ordered by the Commission, all formal investigative proceedings shall be non-public." 17 CFR § 203.5 (1983). In other words, the Commission has formally adopted the policy of not routinely informing anyone, including targets, of the existence and progress of its investigations. To our knowledge, Congress has never questioned this exercise by the Commission of its statutory power. And, in another context, we have held that rulemaking authority comparable to that enjoyed by the SEC is broad enough to empower an agency to "establish standards for determining whether to conduct an investigation publicly or in private." *FCC v. Schreiber*, 381 U.S. 279, 292 (1965).

It appears, in short, that Congress intended to vest the SEC with considerable discretion in determining when and how to investigate possible violations of the statutes administered by the Commission. We discern no evidence that Congress wished or expected that the Commission would adopt any particular procedures for notifying "targets" of investigations when it sought information from third parties.

The inference that the relief sought by respondents is not necessary to give effect to congressional intent is reinforced by the fact that, in one special context, Congress has imposed on the Commission an obligation to notify persons directly affected by its subpoenas. In 1978, in response to this Court's decision in *United States v. Miller*, supra, Congress enacted the Right to Financial Privacy Act, 92 Stat. 3697, 12 U.S.C. § 3401 et seq. That statute accords customers of banks and similar financial institutions certain rights to be notified of and to challenge in court administrative subpoenas of financial records in the possession of the banks. The most salient feature of the Act is the narrow scope of the entitlements it creates. Thus, it carefully limits the kinds of customers to whom it applies, §§ 3401(4), (5), and the types of records they may seek to protect, § 3401(2). A customer's ability to challenge a subpoena is cabined by strict procedural requirements. For example, he must assert his claim within a short period of time, § 3410(a), and cannot appeal an adverse determination until the Government has completed its investigation, § 3410(d). Perhaps most importantly, the statute is drafted in a fashion that minimizes the risk that customers' objections to subpoenas will delay or frustrate agency investigations. Thus, a court presented with such a challenge is required to rule upon it within seven days of the Government's response, § 3410(b), and the pertinent statutes of limitations are tolled while the claim is pending, § 3419. Since 1980, the SEC has been subject to the constraints of the Right to Financial Privacy Act. When it made the statute applicable to the SEC, however, Congress empowered the Commission in prescribed circumstances to seek *ex parte* orders authorizing it to delay notifying bank customers when it subpoenas information about them, thereby further curtailing the ability of persons under investigation to impede the agency's inquiries.

Considerable insight into the legislators' conception of the scope of the SEC's investigatory power can be gleaned from the foregoing developments. We know that Congress recently had occasion to consider the authority of the SEC and other agencies to issue and enforce administrative subpoenas without notifying the persons whose affairs may be exposed thereby. In response, Congress enacted a set of carefully tailored limitations on the agencies' power, designed "to strike a balance between customers' right of privacy and the need of law enforcement agencies to obtain financial records pursuant to legitimate investigations." H.R. Rep. No. 95-1383, p. 33 (1978). The manner in which Congress dealt with this problem teaches us two things. First, it seems apparent that Congress assumed that the SEC was not and would not be subject to a general obligation to notify "targets" of its investigations whenever it issued administrative subpoenas. Second, the complexity and subtlety of the procedures embodied in the Right to Financial Privacy Act suggest that Congress would find troubling the crude and unqualified notification requirement ordered by the Court of Appeals.

C

The last of the three potential footings for the remedy sought by respondents is some other entitlement that would be effectuated thereby. Respondents seek to derive such an entitlement from a combination of our prior decisions. Distilled, their argument is as follows: A subpoena issued by the SEC must comport with the standards set forth in our decision in *United States v. Powell*, 379 U.S., at 57-58.[18] Not only the recipient of an SEC subpoena, but also

18. The holding of *Powell* was that the Commissioner of Internal Revenue need not demonstrate probable cause in order to secure judicial enforcement of a summons issued pursuant to § 7602 of the Internal Revenue Code. The Court then went on to sketch the requirements that the Commissioner would be obliged to satisfy:

"He must show that the investigation will be conducted pursuant to a legitimate any person who would be affected by compliance therewith, has a substantive right, under *Powell*, to insist that those standards are met. A target of an SEC investigation may assert the foregoing right in two ways. First, relying on *Reisman v. Caplin*, 375 U.S. 440, 445 (1964), and *Donaldson v. United States*, 400 U.S., at 529, the target may seek permissive intervention in an enforcement action brought by the Commission against the subpoena recipient. Second, if the recipient of the subpoena threatens voluntarily to turn over the requested information, the target "might restrain compliance" by the recipient, thereby forcing the Commission to institute an enforcement suit. See *Reisman v. Caplin*, supra, 375 U.S., at 450. A target can avail himself of these options only if he is aware of the existence of subpoenas directed at others. To ensure that ignorance does not prevent a target from asserting his rights, respondents conclude, the Commission must notify him when it issues a subpoena to a third party.

There are several tenuous links in respondents' argument. Especially debatable are the proposition that a target has a substantive right to be investigated in a manner consistent with the *Powell* standards and the assertion that a target may obtain a restraining order preventing voluntary compliance by a third party with an administrative subpoena. Certainly we have never before expressly so held. For the present, however, we may assume, *arguendo*, that a target enjoys each of the substantive and procedural rights identified by respondents. Nevertheless, we conclude that it would be inappropriate to elaborate upon those entitlements by mandating notification of targets whenever the Commission issues subpoenas.

Two considerations underlie our decision on this issue. First, administration of the notice requirement advocated by respondents would be highly burdensome for both the Commission and the courts. The most obvious difficulty would involve identification of the persons and organizations that should be considered "targets" of investigations. The SEC often undertakes investigations into suspicious securities transactions without any knowledge of which of the parties involved may have violated the law. To notify all potential wrongdoers in such a situation of the issuance of each subpoena would be virtually impossible. The Commission would thus be obliged to determine the point at which enough evidence had been assembled to focus suspicion on a manageable subset of the participants in the transaction, thereby lending them the status of "targets" and entitling them to notice of the outstanding subpoenas directed at others. The complexity of that task is apparent. Even in cases in which the Commission could identify with reasonable ease the principal targets of its inquiry, another problem would arise. In such circumstances, a person not

---

> purpose, that the inquiry may be relevant to that purpose, that the information sought is not already within the Commissioner's possession, and that the administrative steps required by the Code have been followed.... [A] court may not permit its process to be abused. Such an abuse would take place if the summons had been issued for an improper purpose, such as to harass the taxpayer or to put pressure on him to settle a collateral dispute, or for any other purpose reflecting on the good faith of the particular investigation."

379 U.S., at 57-58. *** Because of the manner in which we dispose of this case, we have no occasion to pass upon respondents' characterization or application of our decision in *Powell*.

considered a target by the Commission could contend that he deserved that status and therefore should be given notice of subpoenas issued to others. To assess a claim of this sort, a district court would be obliged to conduct some kind of hearing to determine the scope and thrust of the ongoing investigation. Implementation of this new remedy would drain the resources of the judiciary as well as the Commission.

Second, the imposition of a notice requirement on the SEC would substantially increase the ability of persons who have something to hide to impede legitimate investigations by the Commission. A target given notice of every subpoena issued to third parties would be able to discourage the recipients from complying, and then further delay disclosure of damaging information by seeking intervention in all enforcement actions brought by the Commission. More seriously, the understanding of the progress of an SEC inquiry that would flow from knowledge of which persons had received subpoenas would enable an unscrupulous target to destroy or alter documents, intimidate witnesses, or transfer securities or funds so that they could not be reached by the Government. Especially in the context of securities regulation, where speed in locating and halting violations of the law is so important, we would be loathe to place such potent weapons in the hands of persons with a desire to keep the Commission at bay.

We acknowledge that our ruling may have the effect in practice of preventing some persons under investigation by the SEC from asserting objections to subpoenas issued by the Commission to third parties for improper reasons. However, to accept respondents' proposal "would unwarrantedly cast doubt upon and stultify the [Commission's] every investigatory move," *Donaldson v. United States*, 400 U.S., at 531. Particularly in view of Congress' manifest disinclination to require the Commission to notify targets whenever it seeks information from others, we refuse so to curb the Commission's exercise of its statutory power.

III

Nothing in this opinion should be construed to imply that it would be improper for the SEC to inform a target that it has issued a subpoena to someone else. But, for the reasons indicated above, we decline to curtail the Commission's discretion to determine when such notice would be appropriate and when it would not. Accordingly, the judgment of the Court of Appeals is reversed, and the case is remanded for further proceedings consistent with this opinion.

NOTES AND QUESTIONS

1. ***Balancing Burdens.*** Do you agree with the Court that requiring notice to the target of a third party subpoena would impose an undue administrative burden on the SEC? Did the Court give adequate consideration to the legitimate concerns of persons who become subject to SEC investigations? What potentially negative consequences to the target could be avoided were the SEC required to provide such notice? Is there anything unique about the securities industry that, from the target's perspective, makes "secret investigations" by the SEC particularly harmful? See Therese Maynard, *SEC v. Jerry T. O'Brien, Inc.:* Has the Supreme Court Overruled *United States v.*

Powell?, 18 Loy. L.A. L. Rev. 643, 645-46 (1985). Has the SEC's recent experience with Enron and its auditor Arthur Andersen bolstered the case for investigative secrecy?

*2. **Lessons to Draw.*** Does the Court's decision in *O'Brien* impact the advice that you would give clients who wish to retain agents, such as accountants or consultants, to provide assistance with matters where confidentiality is key? Assuming that an engagement letter will be executed, what specific provisions can be included to ensure that your client is not surprised by an agent's release of its information to a government agency such as the SEC?

---

2. *Whistleblowers: Monetary Incentives and Protections Against Retaliation*

Identified by many securities law practitioners as a clear "game-changer" with respect to SEC enforcement, Section 922 of the Dodd-Frank Act established a new program aimed at encouraging corporate employees (and others) to "blow the whistle" on suspected securities law violations. As we saw in Chapter 7.D's discussion of the Insider Trading and Securities Fraud Enforcement Act of 1988 (ITSFEA), the SEC for decades has had the discretionary authority to award so-called bounties in successful insider trading prosecutions. But in Dodd-Frank, Congress repealed that ITSFEA provision and placed in its stead a new Section 21F of the Exchange Act, which is broadly directed toward the reporting of *all* types of possible securities law violations. Specifically, if a qualifying whistleblower provides the SEC with "original information" about a possible securities law violation that leads to a successful SEC enforcement action resulting in civil monetary sanctions of more than $1 million (including fines and disgorgement), Section 21F *requires* the SEC to pay that whistleblower an award (i.e.,a bounty) worth between 10% to 30% of the sanctions collected. The SEC must also pay such awards in certain instances in which a whistleblower's information leads to enforcement action by the DOJ, another federal agency, an SRO, or a state attorney general. Significantly, if a whistleblower is dissatisfied with the SEC's determination regarding an award, Section 21F(f) grants a right to appeal "to the appropriate court of appeals of the United States not more than 30 days after the determination is issued by the Commission." Like many other provisions in Dodd-Frank, Section 21F sets out a general framework that requires the SEC to flush out the all-important details through rulemaking.

Less than a year after the enactment of Dodd-Frank, a divided Commission (3-2) announced the final rules for this new whistleblower program. See Final Rule: Implementation of the Whistleblower Provisions of Section 21F of the Securities Exchange Act of 1934, Exchange Act Release No. 64545 (May 25, 2011), codified at 17 C.F.R. Parts 240.21F *et seq.* The most controversial aspect of this rulemaking concerned whether to require whistleblowers to report suspected violations first to their employer (through the company's internal compliance system) before reporting that information to the SEC. To be sure, the final rules include provisions aimed at encouraging the utilization of a company's internal compliance and reporting system (for example, by considering internal reporting as a positive factor with the potential to increase the percentage to be awarded and by allowing persons who report internally to collect a whistleblowing payment if the company subsequently reports the information to the SEC). But the final rules clearly permit whistleblowers to report violations directly to the SEC instead of first utilizing the employer's internal compliance channels. What specific concerns was the SEC attempting to balance by encouraging – but not requiring – internal reporting as a pre-condition to Section 21F awards? In your opinion, did the SEC strike the appropriate balance with these final rules? Not surprisingly, this was the principal question that divided the five SEC Commissioners.

Prior to the adoption of the final rules, there was also a controversy concerning the categories of persons who should be ineligible for Section 21F awards. The possibility of payments to attorneys for whistleblowing raised issues that were particularly thorny. As we shall see in Chapter 10.B.4, SEC Rule 21F-4(b)(4) now specifies that attorneys (and others) who are privy to client confidences, or otherwise become aware of privileged information, may not receive whistleblower awards unless state professional responsibility rules or SEC rules permit attorney disclosure of the reported information. Does this provision properly balance the need to protect the lawyer-client relationship with the need to root out securities law violations? Other categories of ineligible whistleblowers include an entity's compliance and internal audit officials as well as outside auditors who already have reporting responsibilities pursuant to Section 10A of the Exchange Act. See generally Rule 21F-8 (specifying categories of ineligible persons).

Another question that was raised in the rulemaking concerned direct communications between SEC officials (many of whom are attorneys) and corporate agents or employees. Indeed, most states have in place professional responsibility rules similar to ABA Model Rule 4.2, which provides that unless authorized by law, an attorney is prohibited from communicating with a person represented by counsel in a matter without first obtaining consent from that person's counsel. Rule 4.2 has been construed to prohibit contacts with directors and some employees of a corporation without the prior consent of corporate counsel. However, SEC Rule 21F-17(b) now specifies that SEC staff may communicate directly with a "director, officer, member, agent, or employee of an entity that has counsel ***regarding [that person's report of a] possible securities law violation without seeking the consent of the entity's counsel." Does SEC Rule 21F-17(b) provide the authorization "by law" that is contemplated under ABA Model Rule 4.2? The SEC has answered yes and argues that protection of the anonymity of the whistleblower precludes seeking consent from corporate counsel. Might state bar officials argue otherwise?

Section 922 of the Dodd-Frank Act also enhanced the whistleblower protections that were first enacted as part of the SOX. That is, in the wake of the scandals at Enron and WorldCom, Congress created a private civil action for employees of publicly traded companies who believe that they have suffered retaliation for providing information to any federal agency or Congress about suspected fraud. See 18 U.S.C. § 1514A. The SOX in addition created a new crime for "Retaliation Against Informants":

> Whoever knowingly, with the intent to retaliate, takes any action harmful to any person, including interference with the lawful employment or livelihood of any person, for providing to a law enforcement officer any truthful information relating to the commission or possible commission of any Federal offense, shall be fined under this title or imprisoned not more than 10 years, or both.

18 U.S.C. § 1513(e).

Following the 2008 financial crisis, however, Congress determined that potential whistleblowers needed even greater statutory protections against the possibility of retaliation. To that end, Dodd-Frank amended the private right of action in 18 U.S.C. § 1514A to extend the statute of limitations, to prohibit the enforcement of pre-dispute arbitration clauses or pre-dispute waivers of retaliation rights and remedies, and to clarify that § 1514A applies to employees of subsidiaries of publicly-traded companies "whose financial information is included in the consolidated financial statements of [a publicly] traded company." Section 1057 of the Dodd-Frank Act in addition created a new private right of action for employees in the financial services industry who suffer retaliation for disclosing suspected misconduct relating to the offering or provision of a consumer financial product or service.

How do the whistleblower anti-retaliation provisions in SOX and Dodd-Frank affect the advice that you would give a corporate client whom the SEC is investigating?

3. Concluding an SEC Investigation

The staff of the Enforcement Division cannot by itself initiate enforcement actions against persons or companies who may have violated the federal securities laws. Rather, if the staff believes that enforcement action is warranted, a recommendation to that effect must be made to the Commission. This recommendation typically includes the staff's analysis of the facts and the law, and their views with respect to appropriate sanctions. Even in instances where a person or company is willing to settle and consent to a sanction that is also acceptable to the SEC staff, such a settlement can be accepted only by the Commission.

Important aspects of the process by which the Commission considers staff recommendations are described in the following excerpt. At the time of its publication, the article's first co-author was the Director of the SEC's Enforcement Division.

A PRACTITIONER'S GUIDE TO THE SEC'S INVESTIGATIVE AND ENFORCEMENT PROCESS

by William R. McLucas, J. Lynn Taylor, and Susan A. Mathews[a]

70 Temple L. Rev. 53, 111-116 (1997)

*** *A. Staff Recommendation*

---

a. The Securities and Exchange Commission, as a matter of policy, disclaims responsibility for any private publication by any of its employees. The views expressed herein are those of the authors and do not necessarily reflect the views of the Commission or its staff. See 17 C.F.R. § 200.735-4(e).

At the conclusion of an investigation, the staff may determine to take no action or to recommend that the Commission bring enforcement proceedings. The staff is not required to inform a witness or an individual or entity whose activities were under scrutiny if the investigation is terminated without action. The staff may, in its discretion, use a "closing letter" to advise a witness that its investigation has been terminated.

Historically, the staff issued these letters only when counsel made a request for such a communique. Recognizing that the uncertainty of the status of an investigation may have adverse consequences for individuals and businesses, the staff changed its practice. Currently, the staff notifies individuals and entities whose activities were under scrutiny of the termination of an investigation. If an investigation is terminated without the staff recommending or the Commission authorizing an action, the staff will notify those persons and entities: (1) named in the formal order of investigation or (2) provided with a Wells submission notification. Other persons or entities involved in the investigation, such as those subpoenaed or whose activities were under scrutiny, also may request such notification. Notification of the termination of an investigation is not an exoneration or an indication that no enforcement action ultimately may result from the staff's investigation. Rather, such notification simply means that the staff has completed its investigation and is not, as of the date of the letter, recommending enforcement action to the Commission.

If the staff determines that remedial action is necessary as a result of its investigation, it will make a recommendation to the Commission that identifies the proposed defendants or respondents, states the evidentiary and legal bases supporting the claimed violations, and sets forth a proposed remedy and the rationale therefor. The staff, at the time that it makes its recommendation, will forward to the Commission any Wells Submissions received from proposed defendants.

B. Wells Submissions ***

In Securities Act Release 5310, the Commission discussed its discretionary practice "of permitting persons involved in an investigation to present a statement to [the Commission] setting forth their interests and position." [Sec. Act Release No. 5310 (Sept. 27, 1972)]. In order to advise the public of its practice, the Wells Committee procedure was set forth in the Commission's regulations relating to Informal and Other Procedures. [17 C.F.R.§ 202.5(c).]

In Release 5310, the Commission indicated that interested persons may find it useful to discuss the matter under investigation with the staff. To that end, the Commission stated that the staff, in its discretion, may advise prospective defendants of the general nature of the investigation and violations contemplated by the staff and permit the proposed defendant to submit a response to the allegations within a time frame determined by the staff. The Commission viewed the submissions from the proposed defendants to be of the greatest benefit when addressing questions of policy or law. The Commission indicated that it did not view a discussion of factual disagreements between the staff and proposed defendants as particularly useful. Notwithstanding the language of the Release, many Wells Submissions do address factual issues, evidentiary matters, and the inference and/or weight to be given the evidence, and they often highlight factual disagreements with the staff's position. Generally, unless circumstances otherwise warrant, the staff will describe in its Wells notice the proposed enforcement recommendation, and provide a summary of the evidence and legal theories on which the staff relies.

The Wells Submission practice has not created, nor has the Commission employed, any formal, pre-proceeding notification or solicitation procedure. Release 5310 was not intended to, and did not, confer any rights upon the subjects of Commission investigations. While there is no requirement that the Commission provide a Wells notice to persons or entities which may be the subject of an enforcement recommendation by the staff, and although no due process rights attach to this practice, the staff generally provides the opportunity for such a submission as an investigation nears completion. The Commission, however, does not provide such an opportunity when there are concerns about dissipation of assets, destruction of documents, or any other situations which may require the Commission to act quickly to protect the public interest.

***Strategic Considerations in Making Wells Submissions

A substantial number of proposed respondents and defendants do make Wells Submissions. The submissions are evaluated carefully, not only by the Commissioners and by the enforcement staff, but also by other offices and divisions within the Commission which may have an interest in the matters involved in the case. While statistics are not maintained on the number of successful submissions, the Commission staff often has modified its recommendations, or dropped individuals altogether, after evaluating a submission. The Commission has done likewise in considering whether to authorize an enforcement action. The following points regarding Wells Submissions bear noting:

(a) A submission may highlight factual and legal deficiencies in a proposed enforcement action.

(b) The Division of Enforcement takes the position that a submission may be utilized subsequently as an admission or for impeachment purposes.

(c) Submissions may be particularly helpful in analyzing the role of "peripheral" defendants or persons charged with "aiding and abetting" violations.

(d) Novel, unique, or unusual policy issues may be highlighted, especially the nature of relief sought and the statutory provisions alleged to have been violated.

(e) A concise submission is likely to be more effective than a lengthy discourse. Currently, Commission policy is that Wells Submissions should be limited to no more than 40 pages.

(f) The Commission's current policy is that a videotaped statement by counsel of no more than twelve minutes may be submitted in lieu of a written Wells Submission. A transcript of the videotaped statement also should be submitted.

(g) A submission must be timely. In general, a one-month period for the submission of Wells statements is permitted, although the time frame may vary somewhat depending upon the complexity of a case. Extensions of time are granted in certain circumstances, but should not be counted upon as they are not granted as a matter of course. ***

In general, after the completion of an enforcement proceeding, Wells Submissions may become available under the FOIA [Freedom of Information Act] unless

i) Disclosure would "constitute an unwarranted invasion of personal privacy" [or] "disclose the identity of a confidential source"; [5 U.S.C. § 552(b)(7)(C), (D)]

(ii) It is likely that additional proceedings may be brought, even if a particular enforcement action has been concluded;

(iii) Disclosure would deprive a person of a fair trial or impartial adjudication in proceedings other than the Commission's action; [5 U.S.C. § 552(b)(7)(B)] or

(iv) Disclosure would disclose Commission investigative techniques or procedures; [5 U.S.C. § 552(b)(7)(E)]

Notwithstanding the above, it is important to note that § 552 of the Administrative Procedures Act contemplates disclosure of "any reasonably segregable portion of a record" and thus, disclosure of nonexempt portions of a Wells Submission may be appropriate. Further, considerations of personal privacy do not apply to Wells Submissions made solely on behalf of a corporate entity. ***

NOTES AND QUESTIONS

*1. **The Costs and Benefits of Drafting a Wells Submission.*** The above excerpt highlights some strategic considerations in deciding whether to prepare a Wells submission on a client's behalf. Can you identify some of the other potential advantages and disadvantages of preparing a Wells submission? Are there particular types of cases where a Wells submission on behalf of a client may be particularly harmful? Particularly useful? For additional guidance, see Kenneth B. Winer & Samuel J. Winer, Effective Representation in the SEC Wells Process, 34 Rev. Sec. & Comm. Reg. 59 (2001).

*2. **Commission Adoption of Staff Recommendations.*** SEC staff members work long and hard in gathering the facts, analyzing the law, and preparing the memorandum that is eventually presented to the Commission along with a recommendation that enforcement action be instituted against the subject of a pending investigation. Could it therefore be argued that the Commission has an inherent bias that favors its staff in reviewing Wells Submissions and deciding whether to institute enforcement action? Should the Commissioners view the facts and the law presented by the enforcement staff at the prosecutorial stage any differently from how they view those facts and law when sitting in an adjudicative capacity? For an insightful essay focusing on the

Commission's role as prosecutor, see Roberta S. Karmel, Creating Law at the Securities and Exchange Commission: The Lawyer as Prosecutor, 61 Law & Contemp. Probs. 33 (1998). Note in particular former Commissioner Karmel's observation that "[i]t is psychologically and politically difficult to decline to institute a case involving bad facts or to accept a questionable settlement." Id. at 41.

3. A Congressionally-Dictated Time Clock. In an effort to accelerate the pace of SEC enforcement, the Dodd-Frank Act added a new Section 4E to the Exchange Act. Subject to exceptions for certain complex actions, Section 4E(a) specifies that, not later than 180 days after the SEC staff provides a written Wells notification to any person, it must either file an action against that person or provide notice to the Director of the Division of Enforcement of its intent not to file an action. The same complex action exception and 180 day deadline applies to SEC reports setting out findings and requests for corrective action in connection with compliance inspections and examinations. The determination that an investigation or examination is "complex" must be made by a senior SEC official, who may authorize a 180 day extension after notifying the SEC Chairman. Any additional 180 day extensions require approval by the Commission. Although a speedier SEC enforcement process is generally thought to benefit both persons under investigation and the public at large, do the deadlines and procedures in Section 4E raise any concerns? How might these new deadlines affect counsel advising persons under investigation?

What factors are likely to be considered by the Commission in determining whether to initiate enforcement action against entities and individuals? The following Report, issued by the Commission pursuant to its authority under Section 21(a) of the Exchange Act, provides important insights with respect to crediting entities for cooperation. Immediately following that Report is an SEC Release setting forth a framework for evaluating cooperation by individuals.

REPORT OF INVESTIGATION PURSUANT TO SECTION 21(a) OF THE SECURITIES EXCHANGE ACT OF 1934 AND COMMISSION STATEMENT ON THE RELATIONSHIP OF COOPERATION TO AGENCY ENFORCEMENT DECISIONS

Exchange Act Release No. 44969 (Oct. 23, 2001)

Today, we commence and settle a cease-and-desist proceeding against Gisela de Leon-Meredith, former controller of a publicly traded company's subsidiary. [Exchange Act Release No. 44970 (October 23, 2001)] Our order finds that Meredith caused the parent company's books and records to be inaccurate and its periodic reports misstated, and then covered up those facts. We are not taking action against the parent company, given the nature of the conduct and the company's responses. Within a week of learning about the apparent misconduct, the company's internal auditors had conducted a preliminary review and had advised company management who, in turn, advised the Board's audit committee, that Meredith had caused the company's books and records to be inaccurate and its financial reports to be misstated. The full Board was advised and authorized the company to hire an outside law firm to conduct a thorough inquiry. Four days later, Meredith was dismissed, as were two other employees who, in the company's view, had inadequately supervised Meredith; a day later, the company disclosed publicly and to us that its financial statements would be restated. The price of the company's shares did not decline after the announcement or after the restatement was published. The company pledged and gave complete cooperation to our staff. It provided the staff with all information relevant to the underlying violations. Among other things, the company produced the details of its internal investigation, including notes and transcripts of interviews of Meredith and others; and it did not invoke the attorney-client privilege, work product protection or other privileges or protections with respect to any facts uncovered in the investigation

The company also strengthened its financial reporting processes to address Meredith's conduct—developing a detailed closing process for the subsidiary's accounting personnel, consolidating subsidiary accounting functions under a parent company CPA, hiring three new CPAs for the accounting department responsible for preparing the subsidiary's financial statements, redesigning the subsidiary's minimum annual audit requirements, and requiring the parent company's controller to interview and approve all senior accounting personnel in its subsidiaries' reporting processes.

Our willingness to credit such behavior in deciding whether and how to take enforcement action benefits investors as well as our enforcement program. When businesses seek out, self-report and rectify illegal conduct, and otherwise cooperate with Commission staff, large expenditures of government and shareholder resources can be avoided and investors can benefit more promptly. In setting forth the criteria listed below, we think a few caveats are in order:

First, the paramount issue in every enforcement judgment is, and must be, what best protects investors. There is no single, or constant, answer to that question. Self-policing, self-reporting, remediation and cooperation with law enforcement authorities, among other things, are unquestionably important in promoting investors' best interests. But, so too are vigorous enforcement and the imposition of appropriate sanctions where the law has been violated. Indeed, there may be circumstances where conduct is so egregious, and harm so great, that no amount of cooperation or other mitigating conduct can justify a decision not to bring any enforcement action at all. In the end, no set of criteria can, or should, be strictly applied in every situation to which they may be applicable.

Second, we are not adopting any rule or making any commitment or promise about any specific case; nor are we in any way limiting our broad discretion to evaluate every case individually, on its own particular facts and circumstances. Conversely, we are not conferring any "rights" on any person or entity. We seek only to convey an understanding of the factors that may influence our decisions.

Third, we do not limit ourselves to the criteria we discuss below. By definition, enforcement judgments are just that—judgments. Our failure to mention a specific criterion in one context does not preclude us from relying on that criterion in another. Further, the fact that a company has satisfied all the criteria we list below will not foreclose us from bringing enforcement proceedings that we believe are necessary or appropriate, for the benefit of investors.

In brief form, we set forth below some of the criteria we will consider in determining whether, and how much, to credit self-policing, self-reporting, remediation and cooperation—from the extraordinary step of taking no enforcement action to bringing reduced charges, seeking lighter sanctions, or including mitigating language in documents we use to announce and resolve enforcement actions.

1. What is the nature of the misconduct involved? Did it result from inadvertence, honest mistake, simple negligence, reckless or deliberate indifference to indicia of wrongful conduct, willful misconduct or unadorned venality? Were the company's auditors misled?

2. How did the misconduct arise? Is it the result of pressure placed on employees to achieve specific results, or a tone of lawlessness set by those in control of the company? What compliance procedures were in place to prevent the misconduct now uncovered? Why did those procedures fail to stop or inhibit the wrongful conduct?

3. Where in the organization did the misconduct occur? How high up in the chain of command was knowledge of, or participation in, the misconduct? Did senior personnel participate in, or turn a blind eye toward, obvious indicia of misconduct? How systemic was the behavior? Is it symptomatic of the way the entity does business, or was it isolated?

4. How long did the misconduct last? Was it a one-quarter, or one-time, event, or did it last several years? In the case of a publicly traded company, did the misconduct occur before the company went public? Did it facilitate the company's ability to go public?

5. How much harm has the misconduct inflicted upon investors and other corporate constituencies? Did the share price of the company's stock drop significantly upon its discovery and disclosure?

6. How was the misconduct detected and who uncovered it?

7. How long after discovery of the misconduct did it take to implement an effective response?

8. What steps did the company take upon learning of the misconduct? Did the company immediately stop the misconduct? Are persons responsible for any misconduct still with the company? If so, are they still in the same positions? Did the company promptly, completely and effectively disclose the existence of the misconduct to the public, to regulators and to self-regulators? Did the company cooperate completely with appropriate regulatory and law enforcement bodies? Did the company identify what additional related misconduct is likely to have occurred? Did the company take steps to identify the extent of damage to investors and other corporate constituencies? Did the company appropriately recompense those adversely affected by the conduct?

9. What processes did the company follow to resolve many of these issues and ferret out necessary information? Were the Audit Committee and the Board of Directors fully informed? If so, when?

10. Did the company commit to learn the truth, fully and expeditiously? Did it do a thorough review of the nature, extent, origins and consequences of the conduct and related behavior? Did management, the Board or committees consisting solely of outside directors oversee the review? Did company employees or outside persons perform the review? If outside persons, had they done other work for the company? Where the review was conducted by outside counsel, had management previously engaged such counsel? Were scope limitations placed on the review? If so, what were they?

11. Did the company promptly make available to our staff the results of its review and provide sufficient documentation reflecting its response to the situation? Did the company identify possible violative conduct and evidence with sufficient precision to facilitate prompt enforcement actions against those who violated the law? Did the company produce a thorough and probing written report detailing the findings of its review? Did the company voluntarily disclose information our staff did not directly request and otherwise might not have uncovered? Did the company ask its employees to cooperate with our staff and make all reasonable efforts to secure such cooperation?

12. What assurances are there that the conduct is unlikely to recur? Did the company adopt and ensure enforcement of new and more effective internal controls and procedures designed to prevent a recurrence of the misconduct? Did the company provide our staff with sufficient information for it to evaluate the company's measures to correct the situation and ensure that the conduct does not recur?

13. Is the company the same company in which the misconduct occurred, or has it changed through a merger or bankruptcy reorganization?

We hope that this Report of Investigation and Commission Statement will further encourage self-policing efforts and will promote more self-reporting, remediation and cooperation with the Commission staff. We welcome the constructive input of all interested persons. We urge those who have contributions to make to direct them to our Division of Enforcement. The public can be confident that all such communications will be fairly evaluated not only by our staff, but also by us. We continue to reassess our enforcement approaches with the aim of maximizing the benefits of our program to investors and the marketplace.

POLICY STATEMENT OF THE SECURITIES AND EXCHANGE COMMISSION CONCERNING COOPERATION BY INDIVIDUALS IN ITS INVESTIGATIONS AND RELATED ENFORCEMENT ACTIONS

Exchange Act Release No. 61340 (Jan. 13, 2010), 17 CFR Part 202

Cooperation by individuals and entities in the Commission's investigations and related enforcement actions can contribute significantly to the success of the agency's mission. Cooperation can enhance the Commission's ability to detect violations of the federal securities laws, increase the effectiveness and efficiency of the Commission's investigations, and provide important evidence for the Commission's enforcement actions. There is a wide spectrum of tools available to the Commission and its staff for facilitating and rewarding cooperation by individuals, ranging from taking no enforcement action to pursuing reduced charges and sanctions in connection with enforcement actions. As with any cooperation program, there exists some tension between the objectives of holding individuals fully accountable for their misconduct and providing incentives for individuals to cooperate with law enforcement authorities. This policy statement sets forth the analytical framework employed by the Commission and its staff for resolving this tension in a manner that ensures that potential cooperation arrangements maximize the Commission's law enforcement interests. Although the evaluation of cooperation requires a case-by-case analysis of the specific circumstances presented, as described in greater detail below, the Commission's general approach is to determine whether, how much, and in what manner to credit cooperation by individuals by evaluating four considerations: the assistance provided by the cooperating individual in the Commission's investigation or related enforcement actions ("Investigation"); the importance of the underlying matter in which the individual cooperated; the societal interest in ensuring that the cooperating individual is held accountable for his or her misconduct; and the appropriateness of cooperation credit based upon the profile of the cooperating individual. In the end, the goal of the Commission's analysis is to protect the investing public by determining whether the public interest in facilitating and rewarding an individual's cooperation in order to advance the Commission's law enforcement interests justifies the credit awarded to the individual for his or her cooperation.

(a) Assistance provided by the individual. The Commission assesses the assistance provided by the cooperating individual in the Investigation by considering, among other things:

(1) The value of the individual's cooperation to the Investigation including, but not limited to:

(i) Whether the individual's cooperation resulted in substantial assistance to the Investigation;

(ii) The timeliness of the individual's cooperation, including whether the individual was first to report the misconduct to the Commission or to offer his or her cooperation in the Investigation, and whether the cooperation was provided before he or she had any knowledge of a pending investigation or related action;

(iii) Whether the Investigation was initiated based on information or other cooperation provided by the individual;

(iv) The quality of cooperation provided by the individual, including whether the cooperation was truthful, complete, and reliable; and

(v) The time and resources conserved as a result of the individual's cooperation in the Investigation.

(2) The nature of the individual's cooperation in the Investigation including, but not limited to:

(i) Whether the individual's cooperation was voluntary or required by the terms of an agreement with another law enforcement or regulatory organization;

(ii) The types of assistance the individual provided to the Commission;

(iii) Whether the individual provided non-privileged information, which information was not requested by the staff or otherwise might not have been discovered;

(iv) Whether the individual encouraged or authorized others to assist the staff who might not have otherwise participated in the Investigation; and

(v) Any unique circumstances in which the individual provided the cooperation.

(b) Importance of the underlying matter. The Commission assesses the importance of the Investigation in which the individual cooperated by considering, among other things:

(1) The character of the Investigation including, but not limited to:

(i) Whether the subject matter of the Investigation is a Commission priority;

(ii) The type of securities violations;

(iii) The age and duration of the misconduct;

(iv) The number of violations; and

(v) The isolated or repetitive nature of the violations.

(2) The dangers to investors or others presented by the underlying violations involved in the Investigation including, but not limited to:

(i) The amount of harm or potential harm caused by the underlying violations;

(ii) The type of harm resulting from or threatened by the underlying violations; and

(iii) The number of individuals or entities harmed.[1]

(c) Interest in holding the individual accountable. The Commission assesses the societal interest in holding the cooperating individual fully accountable for his or her misconduct by considering, among other things:

(1) The severity of the individual's misconduct assessed by the nature of the violations and in the context of the individual's knowledge, education, training, experience, and position of responsibility at the time the violations occurred;

(2) The culpability of the individual, including, but not limited to, whether the individual acted with scienter, both generally and in relation to others who participated in the misconduct;

(3) The degree to which the individual tolerated illegal activity including,

1. Cooperation in Investigations that involve priority matters or serious, ongoing, or widespread violations will be viewed most favorably.

but not limited to, whether he or she took steps to prevent the violations from occurring or continuing, such as notifying the Commission or other appropriate law enforcement agency of the misconduct or, in the case of a violation involving a business organization, by notifying members of management not involved in the misconduct, the board of directors or the equivalent body not involved in the misconduct, or the auditors of such business organization of the misconduct;

(4) The efforts undertaken by the individual to remediate the harm caused by the violations including, but not limited to, whether he or she paid or agreed to pay disgorgement to injured investors and other victims or assisted these victims and the authorities in the recovery of the fruits and instrumentalities of the violations; and

(5) The sanctions imposed on the individual by other federal or state authorities and industry organizations for the violations involved in the Investigation.

(d) Profile of the individual. The Commission assesses whether, how much, and in what manner it is in the public interest to award credit for cooperation, in part, based upon the cooperating individual's personal and professional profile by considering, among other things:

(1) The individual's history of lawfulness, including complying with securities laws or regulations;

(2) The degree to which the individual has demonstrated an acceptance of responsibility for his or her past misconduct; and

(3) The degree to which the individual will have an opportunity to commit future violations of the federal securities laws in light of his or her occupation -- including, but not limited to, whether he or she serves as: a licensed individual, such as an attorney or accountant; an associated person of a regulated entity, such as a broker or dealer; a fiduciary for other individuals or entities regarding financial matters; an officer or director of public companies; or a member of senior management -- together with any existing or proposed safeguards based upon the individual's particular circumstances.

Note to § 202.12. Before the Commission evaluates an individual's cooperation, it analyzes the unique facts and circumstances of the case. The above principles are not listed in order of importance nor are they intended to be all-inclusive or to require a specific determination in any particular case. Furthermore, depending upon the facts and circumstances of each case, some of the principles may not be applicable or may deserve greater weight than others. Finally, neither this statement, nor the principles set forth herein creates or recognizes any legally enforceable rights for any person.

NOTES AND QUESTIONS

1. A Typical Case? Note the quick and decisive actions taken by officials at Seaboard Corporation, the publicly traded company that was the subject of the SEC's Section 21(a) report. All within a two week period, Seaboard officials conducted an internal inquiry which confirmed the subsidiary's inaccurate financial statements; terminated the subsidiary's former controller and two of her supervisors; and notified the public and the SEC that the company would be restating its financial statements. The report also reveals that Seaboard's stock price was unaffected by the restatement of its financial statements and that the company had taken steps to strengthen its financial reporting processes. In view of these facts, can Seaboard's "enforcement story" be considered a typical one? In particular, how likely is it that the discovery and revelation of material errors in an issuer's financial statements will have no impact on that issuer's stock price? Is this a report about a company's cooperation or merely an instance where enforcement action against the parent company would serve no identifiable public good?

*2. **Waiver of Privilege.*** In footnote 3 of its Seaboard Report, the Commission stated that "[i]n some cases, the desire to provide information to the Commission staff may cause companies to consider choosing not to assert the attorney-client privilege, the work product protection and other privileges, protections and exemptions with respect to the Commission." Recognizing that these privileges, protections and exemptions "serve important social interests," the Commission stated that it "does not view a company's waiver of a privilege as an end in itself, but only as a means (where necessary) to provide relevant and sometimes critical information to the Commission staff." What limitations, if any, should be placed on the SEC's ability to factor privilege waivers into its enforcement decisions? For contrasting views, compare Rachel McTague, Thomsen Describes Privilege Waiver Policy at SEC, Says Staff "Judicious" in Requests, 39 Sec. Reg. L. Rep. 793 (BNA) (May 21, 2007) with BNA editorial staff, ABA Asks SEC to Revise Policy on Waiver of Lawyer/Client Privilege, 39 Sec. Reg. L. Rep. 284 (BNA) (Feb. 26, 2007). See also William R. McLucas et al., The Decline of the Attorney-Client Privilege in the Corporate Setting, 96 J. Crim. L. & Criminology 621 (2006).

What risks are associated with a client's decision to waive vis-a-vis the SEC otherwise applicable privileges such as attorney-client or work product protections? In particular, can a client waive a privilege in an SEC investigation or proceeding and then reassert that privilege in litigation brought by third parties? There is a split of authority on this issue of "selective" or "limited" waiver. Compare *Westinghouse Elec. Corp. v. Republic of the Philippines*, 951 F.2d 1414 (3d Cir. 1991) (waiver to SEC in the course of investigation waives privilege to all third parties) and *In re Subpoena Duces Tecum,* 738 F.2d 1367 (D.C. Cir. 1984) (same) with *Diversified Indus., Inc. v. Meredith*, 572 F.2d 596 (8th Cir. 1977) (holding that a corporation participating in the SEC's voluntary disclosure program retains a privilege as to all third party litigants, and noting that "[t]o hold otherwise may have the effect of thwarting the developing procedure of corporations to employ independent outside counsel to investigate and advise them in order to protect stockholders, potential stockholders and customers"). Consider also the decision in *In re Steinhardt Partners*, 9 F.3d 230 (2d Cir. 1993). There the court ruled that voluntary disclosure of work product to the SEC waived the privilege for all parties but left open the possibility that limited waiver may be appropriate where the SEC has explicitly agreed with the disclosing party to maintain the confidentiality of the disclosed materials. Id. at 236. Are the policy reasons behind the doctrine of selective disclosure compelling ones? As a matter of course, should the SEC enter into confidentiality agreements to encourage voluntary disclosure? What concerns are raised by the SEC's willingness to enter into these agreements?

3. Section 21(a) Reports. Section 21(a) authorizes the SEC "to publish information" concerning its investigations of possible violations of the federal securities laws. The Commission tends to use its authority under this provision to articulate novel legal theories or standards of conduct. By including its views in a report, rather than in an SEC order resolving an enforcement action, the Commission is able to draw public attention without placing the agency in the uncomfortable position of applying its views retroactively to justify the imposition of a sanction. The vehicle of a Section 21(a) report also eliminates the need to hold a hearing to establish the violation and forecloses any judicial review of the theories and standards articulated in the report.

On several occasions, the SEC has issued reports of investigations that address the roles and responsibilities of boards of directors in ensuring their company's compliance with the federal securities laws. See Report of Investigation Pursuant to Section 21(a) of the Securities Exchange Act of 1934 Concerning the Conduct of Certain Former Officers and Directors of W.R. Grace & Co., Exchange Act Release No. 39157 (Sept. 30, 1997); Report of Investigation in the Matter of the Cooper Companies, Inc. as it Relates to the Conduct of Cooper's Board of Directors, Exchange Act Release No. 35082, 58 SEC Docket 591 (Dec. 12, 1994); Report of Investigation In the Matter of Stirling Homex Corporation Relating to Activities of the Board of Directors of Stirling Homex Corporation, Exchange Act Release No. 11516, 7 SEC Docket 298 (July 2, 1975); Report of Investigation In the Matter of Nat'l Tel. Co., Relating to Activities of the Outside Directors of Nat'l Tel. Co., Exchange Act Release 14380, 13 SEC Docket 1393 (Jan. 16, 1978). In each of these reports, the SEC subjected the board to substantial criticism for their lax procedures and inadequate diligence in overseeing management. Assuming that the subjects of the report could have prevented or at least cut short the period of management's misconduct, why might the SEC have nonetheless been reluctant to officially sanction those directors?

As we will see in Section C of this Chapter, in 1990 Congress gave the SEC broad authority to issue "cease and desist" orders, a vehicle that allows the SEC to settle with the party under investigation and thereby publicize its views concerning conduct that may not warrant the imposition of a federal court-ordered injunction. Does the ready availability of this congressionally authorized sanction raise an issue as to the SEC's continued use of Section 21(a) reports?

4. Cooperation Tools. In January 2010, the SEC announced that it was making available to its Enforcement Division a number of "cooperation tools" that the Justice Department has traditionally used in its criminal investigations and prosecutions. These new tools, which are described more fully in the Enforcement Manual at § 6.2, include:

> Cooperation Agreements — Formal written agreements in which the Enforcement Division agrees to recommend to the Commission that a cooperator receive credit for cooperating in investigations or related enforcement actions if the cooperator provides substantial assistance such as full and truthful information and testimony.
>
> Deferred Prosecution Agreements — Formal written agreements in which the Commission agrees to forego an enforcement action against a cooperator if the

individual or company agrees, among other things, to cooperate fully and truthfully and to comply with express prohibitions and undertakings during a period of deferred prosecution.

Non-prosecution Agreements — Formal written agreements, entered into under limited and appropriate circumstances, in which the Commission agrees not to pursue an enforcement action against a cooperator if the individual or company agrees, among other things, to cooperate fully and truthfully and comply with express undertakings.

SEC Press Release 2010-6, SEC Announces Initiative to Encourage Individuals and Companies to Cooperate and Assist in Investigations, Jan. 13, 2010. What changes might you expect to see if the SEC adopts a highly "prosecutorial" approach to the enforcement of the federal securities laws?

*5. **Creating Law Through the Initiation of Enforcement Actions.*** The SEC has many vehicles available for creating rules and standards that become a part of the federal securities laws. One vehicle—and undoubtedly the most obvious one—is to promulgate rules and regulations under either specific or general rulemaking authorization from Congress. For example, the Commission has issued a number of rules that establish criteria for so-called limited offerings and private offerings under the Securities Act. See, e.g., Regulation D, Rules 504, 505, 506.

The SEC may also create new law through litigated proceedings, either directly through adjudicating administrative proceedings or indirectly through initiating civil enforcement actions in federal district court. In *SEC v. Chenery Corp.*, 332 U.S. 194 (1947), the Supreme Court recognized that announcing new regulatory interpretations in the course of a litigated proceeding would necessarily have a retroactive effect on respondents. But the court made clear that "the choice made between proceeding by general rule or by individual, ad hoc litigation is one that lies primarily in the informed discretion of the administrative agency." Id. at 203. What are some of the advantages and disadvantages of creating law through the SEC enforcement process? Can you identify contexts in which the SEC seems drawn to this litigation approach? Can you identify other contexts where the SEC initially created law through litigation but later clarified the law through explicit rulemaking? For elaboration of some of the advantages of "ad hoc litigation," see William R. McLucas et al., Common Sense, Flexibility, and Enforcement of the Federal Securities Laws, 51 Bus. Law. 1221, 1222-23 (1996) (emphasizing that "the SEC has tried to adopt a reasoned, common sense application of the basic requirements of the federal securities laws to new market conditions as they have evolved over the years"). For in-depth analysis of some disadvantages, see Roberta S. Karmel, Regulation by Prosecution: The Securities and Exchange Commission vs. Corporate America 96 (1982) (strongly disfavoring prosecutorial strategies for developing law, in part because "[o]ther regulated persons who will become subject to that regulatory policy do not have the opportunity to object or to comment upon the new interpretation or rule, as they would have in a rulemaking proceeding").

---

4. Consent Decrees and Settlements with the SEC

The vast majority of SEC enforcement actions are resolved through a consensual settlement (often termed a "consent decree") between the party charged with securities law violations and the SEC, though the timing of the settlement may vary. Invariably, the party's "Offer of Settlement" as well as the resulting Order will make clear that the party has consented to the imposed sanction "without either admitting or denying the allegations in the Commission's complaint" (in actions pursued in district court) or "without either admitting or denying the Commission's findings of fact and conclusions of law" (in actions pursued administratively). As we shall see in subsequent sections of this Chapter, many variables determine whether the SEC brings and settles an enforcement action in federal district court or as an administrative proceeding, including the types of remedies available in each of those fora. We shall also see that SEC settlements are often the highly preferred avenue for parties charged with securities law violations because litigating with the SEC and losing may collaterally estop a defendant from re-litigating facts and issues in related actions filed by private plaintiffs.

In many cases, even before the Commission has authorized enforcement action, the staff of the Enforcement Division negotiates with defense counsel the tentative terms of an SEC settlement and presents its recommendation for enforcement to the Commission together with the party's offer of settlement as a "package" for approval and authorization. If the Commission agrees to act on the staff's recommendation, the Commission issues a release that announces to the public the enforcement action and its resolution. The discussions that lead to this type of early settlement are generally initiated by defense counsel.

A significant and increasing number of settlements occur after the Commission has authorized an enforcement action but before it files a complaint in court or commences an administrative proceeding. A smaller, but still sizable, number of settlements occur after the staff files its complaint in federal district court or issues an order instituting administrative proceedings. As one might expect, only a few cases are settled on the courthouse steps.

What benefits might flow from deciding to negotiate an offer of settlement with the SEC staff before the Commission has authorized enforcement action? What are some drawbacks? Note that even in cases where an early settlement is pursued, counsel should still consider preparing a Wells Submission. A well-drafted Wells Submission—setting out both the facts and the law from the client's perspective—will often be a useful starting point in discussions with the staff. Then, once an agreement in principle is reached with the staff, the offer of settlement, the Wells Submission (or a modified version), and the staff's recommendation memorandum can be presented to the Commission simultaneously.

The following excerpt sheds significant light on a rather basic question: why are most SEC enforcement actions settled and not litigated? The Task Force was chaired by Harvey L. Pitt almost a decade before he became SEC Chairperson.

REPORT OF THE TASK FORCE ON SEC SETTLEMENTS PREPARED BY THE SUBCOMMITTEE ON CIVIL LITIGATION AND SEC ENFORCEMENT MATTERS OF THE FEDERAL REGULATION OF SECURITIES COMMITTEE OF THE ABA'S SECTION ON BUSINESS LAW

47 Bus. Law. 1083, 1092-1094 (1992)

*** Although settlement of pending claims is a common method of resolving disputes between private parties as well as between private parties and the government, such as the SEC, the two processes differ in a number of significant respects. In a wholly private settlement, the plaintiff generally is motivated by a desire to maximize its own individual position vis-a-vis the defendant. Any effect upon non-parties is, at best, a tangential concern. In the case of a "public" plaintiff, however, and certainly in the case of the SEC, the agency's position reflects a strong public interest dimension. Unlike private litigants, the agency is motivated by an inherent desire to affect the rights and interests of the public and of particular parties and/or interest groups who are not directly involved in the proceeding to be settled.

As a result, the respondent and the SEC generally approach a settlement with differing, although not necessarily opposing, objectives. The respondent will seek a minimal sanction pursuant to the statutory provision which suggests the lowest degree of culpability. The respondent also will seek the elimination of any inflammatory language from the release issued by the Commission upon settlement of the enforcement proceeding (the "Settlement Release" or "Release"). The Commission, on the other hand, may feel compelled to impose a harsh sanction and, moreover, to "send a message" to industry participants through a strongly worded Release which applies the relevant law to as broad a range of conduct as possible.

Both the Commission and the respondent possess considerable incentive to reach a settlement rather than become embroiled in lengthy litigation. The caseload of the SEC is enormous, and its resources are limited. Nevertheless, it is clear that the Commission will litigate the cases it deems necessary to vindicate important principles. In order to utilize its Staff efficiently, the SEC must choose with particularity those matters it will pursue, and which matters it will litigate. Thus, if the Commission chooses to take action against a company or an individual, the odds are high that the SEC views its position as strong. Litigation risks the certainty of a result (since the SEC could and does lose) while occupying the time of personnel who otherwise could be conducting other investigations. To litigate all of these cases would burden the Commission tremendously. ***

As great an incentive as the Commission has to avoid the demands of full-blown judicial litigation, the incentive of respondents to do the same is, perhaps, even greater. For the private party, litigation is extremely expensive. It creates a drain on both financial and human resources. These tangible costs of litigation, and the related, intangible costs (including the harm to the individual's and/or company's reputation with customers and others in the business environment, the ability to obtain employment or to recruit new employees and the uncertainty resulting from prolonged litigation), provide a powerful incentive to settle a pending charge.

In addition to these relatively direct costs of litigation, other, less obvious, costs exist for the respondent. Personal costs, including harm from adverse publicity resulting from having been accused of wrongdoing, should not be overlooked. In addition, regardless of the final disposition of the matter, many respondents still must coexist with the Commission. Thus, the company or individual accused of a violation may be reluctant to earn a reputation for being uncooperative by resisting, even when it does not believe it is in the wrong. Finally, although the collateral consequences of settling an action with the SEC can be significant, a negative outcome in litigation will likely open up the Commission's findings to discovery in private litigation and may even eliminate the respondent's right to deny the relevant conduct in such proceedings.

With both sides hoping for settlement, the process by which settlements are finalized becomes particularly sensitive. The divergence in the parties' marginal propensity towards settlement creates uneven bargaining power, with the Commission holding the upper hand. Short of an unacceptable sanction or inflammatory language, many respondents will consent to the violation(s) the Commission wants to allege, including an expansive enunciation of the applicable legal principles, in return for a few cosmetic changes in the settlement documents.

For these reasons, with the likelihood that the settlement documents and the SEC's public release describing the settlement will be viewed as precedent in subsequent SEC cases, and particularly with the advent of increased actions and higher consequences resulting from the Remedies Act, the language of settlement documents and the procedures in the settlement process become increasingly significant. ***

NOTES AND QUESTIONS

*1. **Neither Admitting nor Denying Liability.*** The SEC's willingness to allow parties to settle without either "admitting or denying" the allegations in the complaint or administrative order clearly promotes settlements. This terminology, however, imposes significant restraints on the settling parties long into the future. Indeed, SEC rules provide "that in any civil lawsuit brought by it or in any administrative proceeding of an accusatory nature pending before it, it is important to avoid creating, or permitting to be created, an impression that a decree is being entered or a sanction imposed, when the conduct alleged did not, in fact, occur." 17 C.F.R. § 202.5(e). Thus, the SEC has announced a "policy not to permit a defendant or respondent to consent to a judgment or order that imposes a sanction while denying the allegations in the complaint or order for proceedings." Id. And enforcement staff officials have stated their view that a settling party's subsequent public denial of such allegations constitutes an abrogation of the express terms of settlement, such that the SEC "will not hesitate to seek to vacate a settled proceeding if the terms of the settlement are breached by the defendant or counsel." See William R. McLucas & John Polise, A Critical Examination of the SEC's Enforcement Process, InSights at 3 (Jan. 1994). In light of the foregoing, what advice would you give to a client about how to respond to an inquiry from the press about his or her SEC settlement?

*2. **The Settlement Documents.*** Settlements of SEC enforcement actions are matters of public record, and the actual settlement documents are relatively easy to obtain: most complaints filed in federal district court are posted on the SEC's web site, and SEC orders in administrative proceedings can be accessed through the web site as well as through databases on Westlaw and Lexis. Although the specific terms of the settlement generally protect the settling party from third party claims of collateral estoppel (see Section D.2.c infra), private litigants, business competitors, and members of the media can all be expected to take particular interest in such documents. In anticipation of this heavy public scrutiny, defense counsel typically reviews draft settlement documents with painstaking care and often negotiates about the precise wording with the SEC staff. Can you identify other important points or issues involving the settlement documents that defense counsel might wish to negotiate?

*3. **Undertakings.*** As we have seen, a party's settlement with the SEC may include one or more "undertakings," which are prospective, and typically remedial, acts and measures not specifically authorized by statutory provisions. (Section C of this Chapter provides extensive detail of the SEC's statutory remedies.) Both defense counsel and the SEC staff have been very creative in crafting such undertakings, which over the years have included the retention of independent consultants or committees to conduct reviews of the party's operations, the adoption of internal training programs for company personnel, and the appointment of new officers and directors or the removal of existing ones. See Cristie L. Ford, Toward a New Model for Securities Law Enforcement, 57 Admin. L. Rev. 757, 797-805 (2005); ABA Committee on Federal Regulation of Securities, Report of the Task Force on SEC Settlements, 47 Bus. Law. 1083, 1128-30 (1992). The ABA Task Force specifically endorsed this vehicle for "creative relief" in SEC settlements, emphasizing that it "can offer both the Commission and the defendant the opportunity to tailor a settlement to the unique needs of the case at hand." Id. at 1127. Does this settlement practice raise concerns? What are the consequences if a settling party fails to adequately fulfill an undertaking to which he agrees?

*4. **It Ain't Over 'Til it's Over.*** As the excerpt from the Task Force Report on SEC Settlements makes clear, a powerful incentive for settling rather than litigating an enforcement action with the SEC is the desire for closure by the subject of an investigation. In light of the following provision from Rule 202.5(f) of the Commission's "Informal and Other Procedures," what advice regarding "closure" would you provide to your client before he or she makes a decision to settle an enforcement action with the SEC?

> It is the policy of the Commission [that the disposition of any investigation, civil lawsuit, or administrative proceeding] may not, expressly or impliedly, extend to any criminal charges that have been, or may be, brought against any such person or any recommendation with respect thereto. Accordingly, any person involved in an enforcement matter before the Commission who consents, or agrees to consent, to any judgment or order does so solely for the purpose of resolving the claims against him in that investigative, civil, or administrative matter and not for the purpose of resolving any criminal charges that have been, or might be, brought against him. This policy reflects the fact that neither the Commission nor its staff has the authority or responsibility for instituting, conducting, settling, or otherwise disposing of criminal proceedings. That authority and responsibility are vested in the Attorney General and representatives of the Department of Justice.

How would the SEC's enforcement program be affected if, after the settlement and public announcement of an SEC action, the DOJ initiated criminal investigations or proceedings routinely? Periodically? Seldomly? Note also that in addition to subsequent criminal proceedings, parties that settle with the SEC must also consider their status vis-a-vis the self-regulatory organizations such as the NYSE or the NASD as well as with state securities regulators and state bar or other professional organizations.

Assume that a client will consent to a settlement with the SEC only if it is part of a "global settlement" resolving all potential federal and state actions for the same underlying conduct. Is such a settlement possible? What would be some of the risks in pursuing this strategy?

5. The Role of Federal District Judges. If a settlement between the SEC and an individual or entity involves relief that must emanate from a court, such as an injunction, that settlement has to receive court approval. Although the vast majority of proposed settlements are approved without fanfare, federal district court judges have, on occasion, withheld approval, effectively forcing the SEC and the defendant back to the negotiation table. See, e.g., *SEC v. Bank of Am. Corp*, 2010 WL 624581 (S.D.N.Y. 2010) (ultimately approving a second proposed settlement which included, among other things, an injunction and a $150 million civil penalty (up from the less "meaningful" figure of $33 million under the terms of the first proposed settlement) (discussed supra in Chapter 4.C–Proxy Fraud). See also Edward Wyatt, Judge Accepts Citigroup's Settlement With SEC, N. Y. Times, September 25, 2010 at B2 (observing that the court approval process took several months and required multiple hearings which ultimately culminated in a final judgment ordering, among other things, an injunction and the payment of a $75 million penalty). High profile enforcement actions such as these have prompted some to criticize courts for overstepping their bounds. See Jonathan J. Lerner & Robert A. Fumerton, Federal Courts as Public Watchdogs: Have Judges Exceeded Their Authority By Refusing to Approve Government Settlements With Financial Institutions?, 42 Sec. Reg. & L. Rep. 2126 (BNA) (Nov. 8, 2010). Others would like to see even more extensive judicial scrutiny of SEC settlements. What is your view on this issue?

6. Creating New Law Through Settled Proceedings. Concerns about the SEC's "regulation by prosecution" have already been discussed in this Chapter. Does the creation of new law through *settled* proceedings raise additional issues? Note that the ABA Task Force on SEC Settlements emphasized the likelihood that settlement documents and SEC releases will be viewed as "precedent" in subsequent cases. The Report further pointed out that SEC administrative orders in settled cases actually take the form of opinions by the Commission and contain lengthy findings of fact and conclusions of law. As such, they are particularly susceptible to being quoted in subsequent orders and judicial opinions as statements of "the law." See Task Force Report, supra, 47 Bus. Law. at 1148-49. Consider this view of one commentator, who was also a member of the Task Force:

> If a respondent elects not to settle, the SEC initiates an action almost immediately and seeks penalties even greater than those offered in the settlement. As a practical matter, respondents confront a Hobbesian choice: to accept whatever severe penalties are being imposed to conclude the matter or

> to face the uncertainty and expense that will result from a decision to resist. Consequently, the SEC has tremendous leverage in fashioning the final outcome of the case. Interested persons such as industry representatives play no role in shaping the content of an individual settled order even though that order establishes how the SEC expects persons similarly situated to the respondents to conduct themselves in the future.

Anne C. Flannery, Time for Change: A Re-Examination of the Settlement Policies of the Securities and Exchange Commission, 51 Wash. & Lee L. Rev. 1015, 1018 (1994). Should settled cases be viewed as precedent stating the law? Even if one is troubled by this practice, is there a feasible way to avoid it?

The SEC's use of settlements to create new law has also drawn sharp criticism from former SEC Commissioner Roberta Karmel. During her tenure, Commissioner Karmel objected particularly to the SEC's practice of issuing Section 21(a) reports that contain a subject's admission of misconduct as well as his agreement to specific undertakings:

> In my view, publication by the Commission under Section 21(a) of a negotiated statement by a person under investigation setting forth admissions and undertakings constitutes, in effect, a sanction. Moreover, the publication would not necessarily announce a Commission determination as to whether or not the facts set forth in the submitted statements constitute a violation of the securities laws. I do not believe the imposition of a sanction is proper unless the Commission makes such a determination and then announces it. It is wrong for a government prosecutor to impose sanctions based on factual admissions, as contrasted to violations of law. If the Commission is unwilling to authorize administrative or injunctive proceedings based on the facts uncovered in an enforcement investigation, it should exercise its prosecutorial discretion by simple terminating the investigation.
>
> I appreciate *** the need for administrative flexibility and the public policy favoring the settlement of cases. Nevertheless, I believe that flexibility can only go so far as a statute reasonably permits and that extra caution with respect to those limitations must be taken when the prosecutorial function is involved. The appropriate channel for enhancement of the Commission's law enforcement capability is a request to Congress for additional administrative jurisdiction, rather than the formulation of a new administrative remedy.

The Commission's Practice Relating to Reports of Investigations and Statements Submitted to the Commission Pursuant to Section 21(a) of the Securities Exchange Act of 1934, Exchange Act Release No. 15664, 17 SEC Docket 18, 20 (Mar. 21, 1979). As you read the following materials, consider whether Congress may have answered this objection when it enacted the Securities Enforcement Remedies and Penny Stock Reform Act of 1990.

C. CIVIL REMEDIES FOR VIOLATIONS OF THE SECURITIES LAWS

"What can the SEC do to me?" "How much money will I have to pay?" "Will an action be filed in federal court?" "Can my case be resolved administratively?" "What collateral consequences result from a finding that I violated the securities laws?" "What effects can SEC sanctions have in private litigation?"

The above questions, and questions like them, have been posed to counsel by concerned clients since the SEC's creation in 1934. Yet, while the questions may not have changed, their answers certainly have, as Congress has added more and more to the SEC's arsenal of enforcement remedies.

As originally contemplated, violations of the federal securities laws were to be remedied principally through the filing of civil injunctive actions in federal district court. To this end, each of the six federal securities statutes authorized the SEC to seek injunctive relief. Any additional relief sought in court by the SEC came not from provisions in the federal securities laws but from the exercise of the considerable equitable powers possessed by federal district judges. Congress had also authorized the SEC to pursue relief administratively, but only against specific categories of regulated persons, such as broker-dealers, investment advisers, and reporting companies. Regulated persons could be subject to an array of sanctions ranging from censure, to temporary suspensions, to permanent bars from the industry (in the case of securities professionals), and orders to comply (in the case of publicly traded companies).

The modern landscape is quite different. We have already seen that 1984 was an important year, since it was then that Congress for the first time authorized the SEC to seek civil monetary penalties in insider trading cases. But an even more drastic sea change occurred six years later, when Congress passed and the President signed the "Securities Enforcement Remedies and Penny Stock Reform Act of 1990" (the "Remedies Act"). This legislation significantly enhanced the remedies previously available by authorizing the SEC to seek civil monetary penalties in federal district courts for virtually any violation of the federal securities laws and, in cases involving securities fraud, judicial orders barring individuals from service as corporate officers and directors upon a showing of "substantial unfitness" to serve. The Remedies Act also broadened considerably the SEC's administrative remedies, providing for the imposition of cease-and-desist orders against anyone found to have violated—or to have caused someone else to violate—the federal securities laws. It also allowed the SEC to impose civil monetary penalties in administrative proceedings brought against certain securities professionals, including broker-dealers, investment advisers, and their associated personnel.

Congress further expanded the SEC's enforcement arsenal in SOX. First, the Act facilitated the SEC's ability to obtain officer and director bar orders in federal court by changing the former "substantial unfitness" standard to one of mere "unfitness." Congress also acceded to the SEC's request for new authority to impose bar orders in administrative proceedings without any judicial involvement. Second, in an effort to provide an even more solid foundation for remedies that had been traditionally viewed as part of a federal court's equitable authority, the Act authorized the SEC to seek and federal courts to impose "any equitable relief that may be appropriate or necessary for the benefit of investors." Third, the Act authorized court-ordered temporary asset freezes to prevent publicly traded companies under investigation by the SEC from making "extraordinary payments" to any of its directors, officers, agents, or employees. The Act also authorized courts, in an SEC injunctive action, to bar persons from participating in penny stock offerings if their alleged misconduct related to an offering of penny stock. In addition, the Act contained two significant expansions of SEC enforcement power that will be dealt with extensively in Chapter 10: authority for the SEC to censure, suspend, or deny any person the privilege of appearing or practicing before the Commission; and the establishment of a new independent regulatory body, the "Public Company Accounting Oversight Board," over which the SEC has significant control.

In the wake of the financial crisis of 2008, Congress once again expanded the enforcement remedies available to the SEC. Most notably, the Dodd-Frank Act authorized the SEC to impose civil monetary penalties in cease-and-desist proceedings brought against *any* person or entity. As noted above, prior to this change, only regulated persons and entities were subject to civil monetary sanctions in administrative proceedings. The Dodd-Frank Act also authorized the SEC to impose so-called collateral bar orders preventing securities law violators from associating with *any* regulated entity (e.g., in a broker-dealer disciplinary action under Exchange Act 15(b)(6)(A), the respondent's sanction can now prohibit future association with investment advisers and municipal securities dealers, in addition to broker-dealers). In addition, the Act clarifies that the SEC may bring enforcement action against and seek applicable remedies in cases in which persons served in a regulated capacity at the time of the alleged violations (e.g., *former* broker-dealers, investment advisers, officer and directors of SROs).

The chart on the next several pages sketches out this modern landscape and highlights the most important types of judicial and administrative relief available to the SEC. The cases and materials that follow provide a closer inspection of the statutory framework and demonstrate some of the complex determinations that must be made by courts and the SEC in fashioning appropriate remedies. The significant collateral consequences of SEC sanctions are explored at the end of this section.

Judicial Relief Available	***Statutory Authority***	***Brief Overview***
Preliminary Injunctions & Temp. Restraining Orders	Exchange Act § 21(d) Securities Act § 20(d) Advisers Act § 209(d) Inv. Company Act § 42(d)	SEC may seek a preliminary injunction or TRO against "any person" who may be violating or about to violate any provision of the federal securities laws
Temporary Asset Freezes	Exchange Act § 21C(c)	SEC may request court to temporarily freeze assets to prevent a publicly traded company from making "extraordinary payments" to corporate officials
Permanent Injunctions	Exchange Act § 21(d) Securities Act § 20(d) Advisers Act § 209(d) Inv. Company Act § 42(d)	SEC must establish a securities law violation and demonstrate a reasonable likelihood that the defendant will engage in future violations
Equitable Relief—Including Disgorgement	Exchange Act § 21(d)(5)	In any action instituted by the SEC under the federal securities laws, the SEC may seek and any federal court may grant "any equitable relief that may be appropriate or necessary for the benefit of investors"
Civil Monetary Penalties	Exchange Act § 21(d)(3) Securities Act § 20(d) Advisers Act § 209(e) Inv. Company Act § 42(e)	SEC may seek monetary penalties against "any" person for "any" violation of the securities laws or the violation of a cease and desist order issued by the SEC; penalty, in accordance with a three-tiered structure, must be "in the public interest"
Civil Monetary Penalties in Insider Trading Cases	Exchange Act § 21A(a)	SEC may seek penalty of up to three times the profit gained or loss avoided by any person who has engaged in illegal insider trading or tipping
CEO and CFO Bonus and Trading Profit Clawback	15 U.S.C. § 7243(a)	SEC may seek disgorgement if issuer is required to restate financial statements because of error due to misconduct

Judicial Relief Available	***Statutory Authority***	***Brief Overview***
Bar Orders Against Future Service as an Officer or Director of a Publicly Traded Company	Exchange Act § 21(d)(2) Securities Act § 20(e)	Court may bar defendant from future corporate service where SEC establishes a violation of Exchange Act § 10(b) or any rule thereunder, or Securities Act § 17(a)(1), where the SEC has demonstrated "unfitness to serve"
Bar Orders Against Future Participation in Penny Stock Offerings	Exchange Act § 21(d)(6)	In an injunctive proceeding initiated by the SEC, court may bar defendant in penny stock offering if defendant's misconduct involved an offering of penny stock

Admin. Relief Available	***Statutory Authority***	***Brief Overview***
Permanent Cease-and-Desist Orders	Exchange Act § 21C(a) Securities Act § 8A(a) Advisers Act § 203(k)(1) Inv. Company Act § 9(f)(1)	SEC, after notice and opportunity for a hearing, may publish findings and issue order against "any person" found to have violated "any provision" of the federal securities laws or to have caused any such violation. The SEC may also order the respondent to "comply" with the relevant provision and/or to take steps to ensure future compliance
Accounting & Disgorgement	Exchange Act § 21B(e) Securities Act § 8A(e) Advisers Act § 203(k)(5) Inv. Company Act § 9(e)	Where a violation has been shown in any permanent cease-and-desist proceeding, or in any action in which the SEC may impose a monetary penalty, the SEC may order the retention of an accountant to calculate the profit from the unlawful activity, and may order the payment of that profit

Admin. Relief Available	***Statutory Authority***	***Brief Overview***
Disciplinary proceedings against broker-dealers and their associated persons	Exchange Act § 15(b)(4) and § 15(b)(6)	Instituted for violations of the securities laws, or a person's "failure to reasonably supervise" another person who has violated the securities laws. Possible sanctions, after notice and the opportunity for a hearing, include censures, temporary suspensions, or permanent bars (including collateral bars)
Disciplinary proceedings against investment advisers and their associated persons	Advisers Act §§ 203(e) & 203(f)	Same as above
Disciplinary proceedings against persons associated with investment companies	Inv. Company Act § 9(b)	Instituted for "willful" violations of the securities laws. After notice and opportunity for a hearing, sanctions may include baring person from future employment or service with a registered investment company
Civil Monetary Penalties in Administrative Proceedings	Exchange Act § 21B Securities Act § 8A(g) Advisers Act § 203(i) Inv. Company Act § 9(d)	SEC, after notice and hearing, may impose monetary penalties according to a three-tiered structure for violating, or causing a violation, of the securities laws. Penalties may also be imposed against broker-dealers, investment advisers, and their associated persons for "failure to reasonably supervise"
Temporary Cease-and-Desist Orders	Exchange Act § 21C(c) Securities Act § 8A(c) Advisers Act § 203(k)(3) Inv. Company Act § 9(f)(3)	In extraordinary cases, SEC may issue orders ex parte against the regulated persons specified in the statutes

Admin. Relief Available	***Statutory Authority***	***Brief Overview***
Orders to comply with filing and other reporting obligations imposed by Sections 12, 13, 14, or 15(d) of the Ex-change Act	Exchange Act § 15(c)(4)	After notice and opportunity for a hearing, and a finding that one has failed to comply or caused another person's failure to comply with the relevant statutory provision, an order may be issued requiring respondent to "comply, or take steps to effect compliance with [the relevant] provision *** upon such terms and conditions and within such time as the Commission may specify"
Summary Suspensions of Exchange Trading or OTC Trading	Exchange Act §§ 12(k) & 15(c)(5)	Extraordinary remedy to be used for periods of limited duration
Stop Orders to Suspend Effectiveness of Registration Statement	Securities Act § 8(d)	SEC may issue a stop order if it finds, after notice and opportunity for a hearing, that a registration statement is false or misleading
Bar Orders Against Future Service as an Officer or Director of a Public Company	Exchange Act § 21C(f) Securities Act § 8A(f)	SEC, after notice and a hearing, may bar respondent from future corporate service if SEC finds a violation of Exchange Act § 10(b) or any rule thereunder, or Securities Act § 17(a)(1), and finds an "unfitness to serve"
Proceedings Against Professionals Who Practice Before the Commission	Exchange Act § 4C 17 C.F.R. § 201.102(e)	The SEC may suspend or bar a person from future practice, if, after notice and opportunity for a hearing, it is established that the person violated the federal securities laws or that the person "engaged in unethical or improper professional conduct"

1. *Judicial Remedies*

a. *Injunctions, Disgorgement, and Officers & Director Bar Orders*

SEC v. FIRST CITY FINANCIAL CORP.

890 F.2d 1215 (D.C. Cir. 1989)

LAURENCE H. SILBERMAN, CIRCUIT JUDGE:

Section 13(d) of the Securities Exchange Act of 1934 requires any person who has directly or indirectly obtained the beneficial ownership of more than 5 percent of any registered equity security to disclose within 10 days certain information to the issuer, the exchanges on which the security trades, and to the Securities and Exchange Commission ("SEC").[1] The SEC charged appellants, First City Financial Corporation, Ltd. ("First City") and Marc Belzberg, with deliberately evading section 13(d) and its accompanying regulations in their attempted hostile takeover of Ashland Oil Company ("Ashland") by filing the required disclosure statement after the 10 day period. The district court concluded that appellants had violated the statute; it then enjoined them from further violations of section 13(d) and ordered them to disgorge all profits derived from the violation. We think that the district court's findings were not clearly erroneous and that the injunction and disgorgement orders were lawful and appropriate remedies for appellants' violations. We therefore affirm.

I.

The SEC's case is based on its contention that on March 4, 1986 Marc Belzberg, a vice-president of First City, telephoned Alan ("Ace") Greenberg, the Chief Executive Officer of Bear Stearns, a large Wall Street brokerage firm, and asked Greenberg to buy substantial shares of Ashland for First City's account. Appellants claim that Greenberg "misunderstood" Belzberg: the latter intended only to recommend that Bear Stearns buy Ashland for its own account.

First City is a diversified Canadian corporation founded and controlled by the Belzberg family and engaged in, among other things, investing in the publicly-traded securities of United States corporations. Samuel Belzberg, Marc's father, is the Chairman and Chief Executive Officer of the company. Samuel Belzberg and his two brothers own at least 70 percent of the stock of First City. Marc Belzberg managed the company's fifteen-person New York City subsidiary. The New York office apparently evaluated potential investments for the parent First City.

On February 3, 1986, a New York stockbroker, Alan D. Alan, wrote a

---

1. Section 13(d) of the Act provides in pertinent part:

> Any person who, after acquiring directly or indirectly the beneficial ownership of any equity security ... is directly or indirectly the beneficial owner of more than 5 per centum of such class shall, within ten days after such acquisition, send to the issuer of the security at its principal executive office, ... to each exchange where the security is traded, and file with the Commission, a statement containing ... the following information, and such additional information, as the Commission may prescribe ... as necessary or appropriate in the public interest or for the protection of investors.

letter to Samuel Belzberg describing Ashland as a "sensational business opportunity" and stating that "the circumstances and timing could hardly be better for the '*Sam Belzberg Effect.*' " (emphasis in original). In a second letter sent several days later, Alan presented Samuel Belzberg with additional financial information on Ashland, including its break-up valuation. After Marc Belzberg received copies of this information, he instructed two financial analysts in the New York office to begin to study Ashland and its component divisions. Armed with their favorable preliminary analysis, on February 11 Marc and Samuel Belzberg purchased 61,000 shares of Ashland stock for First City using Goldman Sachs, another large Wall Street investment banking house. Throughout the month, First City also steadily acquired large blocks of Ashland stock through Katz-Goldring, Alan's smaller brokerage firm. By February 26, First City had accumulated more than 1.3 million shares, approximately 4.8 percent of Ashland's total outstanding stock. Around the same time, Marc Belzberg discontinued purchasing Ashland stock through Katz-Goldring and began acquiring shares through Greenberg at Bear Stearns. Greenberg had enjoyed a longstanding business relationship with First City and Samuel Belzberg. Additional purchases of approximately 53,000 shares of Ashland stock through Greenberg between February 26 and 28 pushed First City's holdings to 1.4 million shares, or just over 4.9 percent of all Ashland stock.

During this period, First City employed several commonly accepted measures to maintain the secrecy of its purchases, since public knowledge that First City was acquiring a large stake in Ashland would likely drive up the price of the stock. For instance, First City bought the Ashland stock through nominee accounts established at Katz-Goldring specifically for the Ashland purchases. Confirmations of the stock purchases were mailed under the nominee name to the home of Robi Blumenstein, an officer in First City's New York subsidiary.

On Friday, February 28, First City received a favorable report from Pace Consultants, a Texas consulting firm hired to assess Ashland's petroleum-related businesses. Pace valued these segments of Ashland at $726 million. The following Monday, on March 3, Pace revised its estimate upward to $844 million. The next day, on March 4, Marc Belzberg telephoned Greenberg and engaged him in a short conversation that would be the centerpiece of this litigation. At his deposition Greenberg described the conversation in the following manner:

> [Marc Belzberg] called me and said something to the effect that—something like, "It wouldn't be a bad idea if you bought Ashland Oil here," or something like that. And I took that to mean that we were going to do another put and call arrangement that we had done in the past.... I was absolutely under the impression I was buying at their risk and I was going to do a put and call.

While Greenberg interpreted Marc Belzberg's call as an order to purchase Ashland stock on behalf of First City, Marc Belzberg later claimed that he intended only to recommend that Greenberg buy stock for himself, that is, for Bear Stearns, and that Greenberg apparently misunderstood Belzberg. Immediately after the phone call, Greenberg purchased 20,500 Ashland shares. If purchased for First City, those shares would have pushed First City's Ashland holdings above 5 percent and triggered the beginning of the 10 day filing period of section 13(d). In that event, First City would have been obliged to file a Schedule 13D disclosure statement on March 14 with the SEC.

Between March 4 and 14, Greenberg purchased an additional 330,700 shares of Ashland stock for First City costing more than $14 million. Greenberg called Marc Belzberg periodically during those ten days to discuss various securities, including Ashland. In these conversations, Greenberg reported to Marc Belzberg the increasing number of Ashland shares Greenberg had accumulated. According to Greenberg, Belzberg replied to these reports by saying, "'Fine, keep going,' or something to that effect." Greenberg also characterized Belzberg's response as "grunt[ing]" approvingly. Belzberg did not squarely deny that testimony; he testified that he, Belzberg, said "uh-huh, I think it's cheap." Over the March 15-16 weekend, Marc Belzberg met with his father and uncles in Los Angeles to discuss Ashland. On Sunday, March 16, Samuel Belzberg decided that First City should continue to buy Ashland stock. Marc Belzberg then advised his father that Greenberg had accumulated a block of Ashland shares that "First City could acquire quickly." Samuel Belzberg later testified that he had no prior knowledge of the Greenberg purchases.

Returning to New York the next morning, March 17, Marc Belzberg called Greenberg and arranged a written put and call agreement for the 330,700 shares Bear Stearns had accumulated. During that conversation, Marc Belzberg did not mention a price to Greenberg. Several days later, Marc Belzberg received the written agreement with a "strike price," or the price Bear Stearns was charging First City, of $43.96 per share. This price was well below the then market price of $45.37; thus, the total March 17 put and call price was almost $500,000 below market. Marc Belzberg apparently expressed no surprise that Bear Stearns was charging almost half a million dollars less than market value. He later testified that he believed that Bear Stearns was acting as a "Santa Claus" and that Greenberg was giving him "a bit of a break" to gain more business from First City in the future.

When Blumenstein, the officer responsible for ensuring First City's compliance with the federal securities laws, noticed the strike price, he immediately met with Marc Belzberg. Blumenstein recognized that the computation of the price reflected only the cost to Bear Stearns of acquiring the stock over the two week period before the written agreement (plus interest and commission), thus creating an inference that First City was the beneficial owner of the securities before March 17. After Blumenstein outlined the problem to Belzberg, the two men called Greenberg on a speakerphone. Belzberg later testified, "I informed Mr. Greenberg [during that conversation] that the letter [the written agreement] was incorrect, that I didn't care what the price of the stock was that he bought for himself, I didn't care what day he made the trades for himself, that I was buying stock from him as of today." Belzberg then testified that Greenberg said, "[Y]ou're right, the letter's wrong, I didn't read it before it went out, throw it out and I will send you a corrected copy." Greenberg, however, testified that Belzberg referred only to an error in the calculation of interest and not to the date on which First City acquired the stock. At the end of the conversation, Belzberg suggested he pay $44.00 per share, 4 cents per share higher than the original strike price but still $1.36, or a total of nearly $450,000, below the market price. At trial, Belzberg admitted to picking the $44 figure "out of the air" and that he "did not want the price [he] was paying to relate to [Greenberg's] cost." Between March 17 and 25, on Marc Belzberg's instructions, Greenberg bought another 890,100 Ashland shares on behalf of First City using several put and call agreements.

After these purchases, Samuel Belzberg sent a letter to Ashland's management, informing them of First City's holdings in their stock and proposing a friendly takeover of the company. Ashland rejected the offer, and on the morning of March 25 the company issued a press release disclosing that First City held between 8 and 9 percent of Ashland's stock. Almost immediately, the price of Ashland stock rose 10 percent to $52.25. The next day, on March 26, First City filed the Schedule 13D disclosure statement required by section 13(d). The statement indicated that First City had accumulated 9 percent of Ashland stock and intended to launch a tender offer for the remaining shares at $60 per share. The market price of Ashland stock then rose to $55, peaking at $55.75 per share the next day.

At Ashland's urging, the Kentucky legislature passed legislation hampering First City's ability to obtain financing for the tender offer. Soon thereafter, First City abandoned the attempted tender offer. On March 31, Ashland agreed to buy back First City's shares for $51 per share, or $134.1 million, resulting in a $15.4 million profit for First City. In return, First City agreed not to purchase any Ashland shares for the next 10 years.

Around the time of the buy-back agreement, the SEC began an informal inquiry into the timeliness of First City's Schedule 13D filing and requested that both First City and Bear Stearns provide a detailed chronology of events describing their contacts with each other relating to the Ashland purchases. After deposing Greenberg and Marc Belzberg, the SEC filed a civil complaint against Marc Belzberg and First City, alleging that they crossed the 5 percent threshold on March 4 but filed the required disclosure statement on March 26, twelve days past the section 13(d) deadline.

The district court found that Marc Belzberg and First City entered into an informal put and call agreement on March 4 and then deliberately violated the 10 day filing requirement of section 13(d). The district court, in an extensive opinion, relied primarily on First City's acknowledged ultimate purpose to take over Ashland, Greenberg's understanding of his March 4 telephone conversation with Marc Belzberg, the subsequent conversations between Belzberg and Greenberg, and the suspicious price of the March 17 written agreement. The court discounted Marc Belzberg's "misunderstanding" explanation as "self-serving, inconsistent with his later actions and [not] squar[ing] with the objective evidence." Belzberg, to put it bluntly, was not credited. The court also refused to consider Greenberg's later testimony that there might have been an "honest misunderstanding" since Greenberg reached that conclusion based only on Belzberg's suggestions and statements.

The district court permanently enjoined appellants from future violations of section 13(d) because they violated the statute deliberately, showed no "remorse," and were engaged in a business which presented opportunities to violate the statute in the future. The court also ordered appellants to disgorge approximately $2.7 million, representing their profits on the 890,000 shares of Ashland stock acquired between March 14 and 25. The court reasoned that appellants were able to purchase these shares at an artificially low price due to their failure to make the section 13(d) disclosure on March 14. Appellants *** contend that the district court abused its discretion in ordering the injunction and disgorgement remedies. ***

Appellants challenge the injunction the district court granted as unwarranted on the facts of this case. Since a district judge has wide latitude in fashioning a remedy, we will not disturb the trial court's remedial choice unless there is no reasonable basis for the decision. See *United States v. W.T. Grant Co.*, 345 U.S. 629, 634 (1953); *SEC v. Bausch & Lomb, Inc.*, 565 F.2d 8, 18 (2d Cir.1977). Appellants claim such an abuse of discretion here because the SEC did not show "that there [was] a *reasonable likelihood* of further violation[s] in the future." *SEC v. Savoy Indus.*, 587 F.2d 1149, 1168 (D.C. Cir.1978) (emphasis in original); see also *SEC v. Bausch & Lomb, Inc.*, 565 F.2d at 18.

Under our *Savoy Industries* test, the district judge should consider whether a defendant's violation was isolated or part of a pattern, whether the violation was flagrant and deliberate or merely technical in nature, and whether the defendant's business will present opportunities to violate the law in the future. See *Savoy Indus.*, 587 F.2d at 1168; *Commonwealth Chem.*, 574 F.2d at 100; *SEC v. National Student Mktg.*, 457 F.Supp. 682, 715-16 (D.D.C. 1978). No single factor is determinative; instead, the district court should determine the propensity for future violations based on the totality of circumstances. See *SEC v. Youmans,* 729 F.2d 413, 415 (6th Cir. 1984); *SEC v. Bausch & Lomb, Inc.,* 565 F.2d at 18.

Appellants raise two troubling points about the injunction order. First, in explaining the injunction the district court said, "[T]here is also a public perception that defendants have been recent and active participants in heated takeover battles and unfriendly mergers." Justifying an injunction, even in part, in terms of propitiating public sentiment, is objectionable as a matter of law. Second, the district court misconstrued our precedents in suggesting that another basis for justifying the injunction was appellants' "lack of remorse." See *SEC v. Savoy Indus.*, 587 F.2d 1149, 1168 (D.C. Cir. 1978). The district court compared Belzberg's "unrepentant demeanor" with defendants in other cases who "express[ ] immediate and vociferous remorse for [their] errors." The government's appellate brief compounds this mistake by urging us to consider, as further evidence of lack of remorse, appellants' *counsel's* arguments and appellants' willingness to pursue this case on appeal. The securities laws do not require defendants to behave like Uriah Heep in order to avoid injunctions. They are not to be punished because they vigorously contest the government's accusations. We think "lack of remorse" is relevant only where defendants have previously violated court orders, see *SEC v. Koenig,* 469 F.2d 198, 202 (2d Cir. 1972), or otherwise indicate that they did not feel bound by the law, see *Savoy Indus.,* 587 F.2d at 1168. As such, it is really only another indication as to whether it is "reasonably likely" that future violations will occur in the absence of an injunction.

The district court, then, appeared to rely in part on two inappropriate factors to support the injunction. Typically we would remand to the district court under these circumstances for reconsideration of the injunction. We do not do so here, however, because we have made an independent determination that the injunction is appropriate, i.e. a reasonable likelihood of future violations exist. Appellants do not even deny that their business will offer many opportunities in the future to violate the securities laws. Instead, appellants quarrel primarily with the district court's determination that Belzberg *deliberately* violated section 13(d). As our prior discussion—particularly our appraisal of Belzberg's testimony—should make clear, we think the district court's determination as to Belzberg's state of mind is not subject to serious challenge. That this is First City's first section 13(d) violation is no bar to the issuance of an injunction. See *SEC v. National Student Mktg. Corp.*, 360 F.Supp. 284, 299 (D.D.C. 1973) (stating that a single violation may justify an injunction if committed willfully and knowingly); see also *SEC v. Bausch & Lomb, Inc.,* 565 F.2d 8, 18 (2d Cir. 1977) (approving injunctions for single acts in some circumstances). ***

The district court directed disgorgement of profits, and appellants' challenge to this aspect of the order presents an issue of first impression—whether federal courts have the authority to employ that remedy with respect to section 13(d) violations and whether it is appropriate in this sort of case. Appellants also claim that the amount ordered disgorged is excessive. We reject both arguments and affirm the district court's order on these issues as well.

Appellants, by claiming that Congress did not explicitly authorize a monetary remedy for section 13(d) violations, misapprehend the source of the court's authority. Disgorgement is an equitable remedy designed to deprive a wrongdoer of his unjust enrichment and to deter others from violating the securities laws. See *SEC v. Tome,* 833 F.2d 1086, 1096 (2d Cir. 1987); *SEC v. Blavin,* 760 F.2d 706, 713 (6th Cir. 1985); *SEC v. Texas Gulf Sulphur Co.,* 446 F.2d 1301, 1307 (2d Cir. 1971). "Unless otherwise provided by statute, all the inherent equitable powers of the District Court are available for the proper and complete exercise of that jurisdiction." *Porter v. Warner Holding Co.,* 328 U.S. 395, 398 (1946); see also *Mitchell v. Robert DeMario Jewelry, Inc.,* 361 U.S. 288, 291-92 (1960). We see no indication in the language or the legislative history of the 1934 Act that even implies a restriction on the equitable remedies of the district courts. See *Mills v. Electric Auto-Lite Co.,* 396 U.S. 375, 391 (1970). Disgorgement, then, is available simply because the relevant provisions of the Securities Exchange Act of 1934, sections 21(d) and (e), vest jurisdiction in the federal courts.

Indeed, appellants concede that disgorgement is rather routinely ordered for insider trading violations despite a similar lack of specific authorizations for that remedy under the securities law. But they seek to distinguish section 13(d) violations as a "technical" transgression of reporting rules that really do not cause injury. In contrast, they argue, insider trading under modern theory is tantamount to theft; an actual injury is inflicted on the individual or institution entitled to confidentiality. Section 13(d), however, is the pivot of the entire Williams Act regulation of tender offers. To be sure, some may doubt the usefulness of that statute generally or the section 13(d) requirement specifically, but it is hardly up to the judiciary to second-guess the wisdom of Congress' approach to regulating takeovers. Suffice it for us to note that section 13(d) is a crucial requirement in the congressional scheme, and a violator, it is legislatively assumed, improperly benefits by purchasing stocks at an artificially low price because of a breach of the duty Congress imposed to disclose his investment position. The disclosure of that position—a holding in excess of 5 percent of another company's stock—suggests to the rest of the market a likely takeover and therefore may increase the price of the stock. Appellants circumvented that scheme, and the theory of the statute, by which we are bound, is that the circumventions caused injury to other market participants who sold stock without knowledge of First City's holdings. We therefore see no relevant distinction between disgorgement of inside trading profits and disgorgement of post-section 13(d) violation profits.

There remains, of course, the question of how the court measures those illegal profits. Appellants vigorously dispute the $2.7 million figure that the district court arrived at by simply calculating all of the profits First City realized (in its eventual sale back to Ashland) on the 890,000 shares First City purchased between March 14 and 25. The SEC's claim to disgorgement, which the district court accepted, is predicated on the assumption that had First City made its section 13(d) disclosure on March 14, at the end of the statutory 10 day period, the stock it purchased during the March 14-25 period would have been purchased in a quite different and presumably more expensive market. That hypothetical market would have been affected by the disclosure that the Belzbergs had taken a greater than 5 percent stake in Ashland and would soon propose a tender offer.

Since disgorgement primarily serves to prevent unjust enrichment, the court may exercise its equitable power only over property causally related to the wrongdoing. The remedy may well be a key to the SEC's efforts to deter others from violating the securities laws, but disgorgement may not be used punitively. See *SEC v. Blatt,* 583 F.2d 1325, 1335 (5th Cir. 1978); *SEC v. Manor Nursing Centers, Inc.,* 458 F.2d 1082, 1104 (2d Cir. 1972). Therefore, the SEC generally must distinguish between legally and illegally obtained profits. Appellants assert that the hypothetical market between March 14-25 that the SEC urged and the district court accepted was simplistic, quite unrealistic, and so *de facto* punitive. It did not take into account other variables—besides the section 13(d) disclosure—which caused the post-March 25 price of the stock to rise above that which prevailed during the March 14-25 period. At trial appellants' expert witness testified that four independent factors combined to increase the stock price to the level it reached on March 25 and that these factors were not present on March 14, when the defendants should have disclosed. He identified these factors as: (1) the Belzbergs by the 25th held between 8 and 9 percent of Ashland, (2) the Belzbergs had prior to the 25th communicated to Ashland the size of their holdings, (3) Ashland publicly disclosed the Belzbergs' position on the 25th before the 13(d) disclosure, and (4) by the 25th, rumors swirled of an imminent takeover bid at $55 per share. In an attempt to hypothesize how the Belzbergs would have acted—had they disclosed on March 14—and how the market would have responded to those actions, the witness presented three alternative scenarios that in his view more accurately measured the impact of the nondisclosure and which yielded disgorgement figures of zero, $496,050, and $864,588. Perhaps not surprisingly, appellants' witness testified that the most realistic scenario required no disgorgement at all.[23]

---

23. The expert witness concluded that disgorgement was unnecessary because if First City had disclosed on March 14, as the SEC claims it should have, we should assume that the 890,000 shares actually bought in the March 17-25 period (the 10-day

If exact information were obtainable at negligible cost, we would not hesitate to impose upon the government a strict burden to produce that data to measure the precise amount of the ill-gotten gains. Unfortunately, we encounter imprecision and imperfect information. Despite sophisticated econometric modelling, predicting stock market responses to alternative variables is, as the district court found, at best speculative. Rules for calculating disgorgement must recognize that separating legal from illegal profits exactly may at times be a near-impossible task. See, e.g., *Elkind v. Liggett & Myers, Inc.,* 635 F.2d 156, 171 (2d Cir.1980).

Accordingly, disgorgement need only be a reasonable approximation of profits causally connected to the violation. ***

Although the SEC bears the ultimate burden of persuasion that its disgorgement figure reasonably approximates the amount of unjust enrichment, we believe the government's showing of appellants' actual profits on the tainted transactions at least presumptively satisfied that burden. Appellants, to whom the burden of going forward shifted, were then obliged clearly to demonstrate that the disgorgement figure was not a reasonable approximation. Defendants in such cases may make such a showing, for instance, by pointing to intervening events from the time of the violation. In *SEC v. MacDonald,* 699 F.2d 47 (1st Cir.1983) (en banc), the First Circuit reversed a district court order requiring the defendant to disgorge all profits from an illegal insider trade when the defendant had held on to the stock for more than a year. The court restricted the amount to a figure based on the price of the stock "a reasonable time after public dissemination of the inside information." Id. at 55. Similarly, the Second Circuit in *SEC v. Manor Nursing Centers, Inc.,* 458 F.2d 1082 (2d Cir.1972), refused to extend the disgorgement remedy to income subsequently earned on the initial illegal profits. In those cases, the defendant demonstrated a clear break in or considerable attenuation of the causal connection between the illegality and the ultimate profits.

Here, appellants took a different approach using a sophisticated expert witness. As we noted, they maintained that the post-March 25 price was influenced by four other independent factors besides the belated section 13(d) disclosure, so even if First City had disclosed on March 14, the price would not have run up then to the extent it did after March 25. The difficulty we see with appellants' argument is that none of the four factors are independent of the section 13(d) disclosure determination. Thus, although by March 25 First City had accumulated 8-9 percent of Ashland, whereas on March 14 it had slightly over 5 percent (and although the market might react more strongly to the higher figure), we do not see why we should not assume that First City would have acquired 8-9 percent before March 14—if they knew they had to disclose on the earlier date. Second, it seems likely that First City would have notified Ashland's management on March 13 if they had planned to disclose on the next

---

window in Belzberg's view) would have been purchased in the lawful March 4-14 10-day window. Since Ashland prices were lower in the March 4-14 period than during March 17-25, the witness believed that no disgorgement was appropriate. This analysis, however, does not consider the impact of buying these 890,000 shares within this 10-day period—in addition to the 330,000 shares the Belzbergs actually purchased then—which presumably would have itself pushed up the price.

day, just as they did on March 25. Third, Ashland's premature disclosure of First City's holdings (prior to the section 13(d) notice) would likely have also occurred. And finally, the March 25 market takeover rumors were probably associated with all of the above activity, which is inextricably linked with the impending section 13(d) notice. We therefore agree with the district court that appellants' efforts to hypothesize both the takeover efforts of a First City that complied with section 13(d) and the market reaction to that are impossibly speculative.

Placing the burden on the defendants of rebutting the SEC's showing of actual profits, we recognize, may result, as it has in the insider trader context, in actual profits becoming the typical disgorgement measure. But the line between restitution and penalty is unfortunately blurred, and the risk of uncertainty should fall on the wrongdoer whose illegal conduct created that uncertainty. See *SEC v. MacDonald,* 699 F.2d 47, 55 (1st Cir. 1983) (en banc); *Elkind v. Liggett & Myers, Inc.,* 635 F.2d 156, 171 (2d Cir. 1980).

***We [therefore] uphold the permanent injunction and disgorgement orders. Accordingly, the judgment of the district court is affirmed.

SEC v. PATEL

61 F.3d 137 (2d Cir. 1995)

ROGER J. MINER, CIRCUIT JUDGE:

Defendant-appellant Ratilal K. Patel appeals from a judgment entered in the United States District Court for the Southern District of New York (Patterson, J.) in an action brought against him by plaintiff-appellee Securities and Exchange Commission ("SEC") for violations of federal securities laws. The judgment permanently enjoins Patel from future violations, orders him to disgorge $453,203 in illegal profits plus prejudgment interest and bars him from serving as an officer or director of any publicly traded company. On appeal, Patel contends *** that the district court considered improper factors in barring him permanently from serving as an officer or director of any publicly traded company.

BACKGROUND

The parties have no dispute regarding the factual background of this case. Patel was a founder, director and senior vice president for research and development of Par Pharmaceutical, Inc. ("Par"), a manufacturer of generic drugs. In November of 1987, Par submitted to the Food and Drug Administration ("FDA") an Abbreviated New Drug Application ("the Application") for a generic version of the drug known as Maxzide, which is used for the treatment of hypertension. The Application falsely represented that Par's generic Maxzide, of which sodium bicarbonate was an ingredient, had been tested in bioequivalency studies required by the FDA. This misrepresentation came in the form of a certificate of analysis for sodium bicarbonate. The certificate was backdated to conceal the fact that the bioequivalency studies were performed with a formulation of Maxzide that did not contain the sodium bicarbonate. Patel knew that the Application was false and, in February and March of 1988, sold 75,000 shares of common stock in Par. The average sale price was approximately $21.00 per share, and Patel realized a total of $1,576,358. It was not until July 24, 1989 that Par publicly disclosed that it was recalling its Maxzide tablets.

Par had experienced a number of adverse events before it revealed its problems with Maxzide. In July of 1988, a congressional subcommittee (the Dingell Subcommittee), which had begun an investigation into the generic pharmaceutical industry, focused on Par. A subcommittee subpoena for Par records was served on July 5, 1988, and the press later reported that Par was involved in the Dingell Subcommittee's inquiry into allegations of bribes and payoffs to FDA officials. It seems certain that this information had a negative impact on the price of Par's stock. Another, more serious, decline in the price of the stock occurred in October of 1988, following Par's announcement that it was a target of a grand jury investigation into various improprieties, including bribery, in the generic drug industry.

In April of 1989, the press reported that Ashok Patel, another Senior Vice President of Par, had resigned his position with Par and had agreed to plead guilty to unspecified charges. Later that month, the press reported the indictment of two FDA officials on bribery charges, in an article that referred to Par, Ashok Patel and Dilip Shah. Shah later resigned from the Board of Directors of a Par subsidiary known as Quad Pharmaceuticals, Inc. In May of 1989, the Dingell Subcommittee held public hearings in connection with its investigation into the generic drug approval process. The following month, there were negative press reports on the relationship between FDA officials and Ashok Patel and Dilip Shah. Thereafter, on July 11, it was reported that a third FDA employee had been criminally charged and, on July 17, it was reported that Par had agreed to plead guilty to a charge of providing an unlawful gratuity to an FDA employee. As was to be expected, all the negative news resulted in depressions in the price of Par stock.

When Par announced on July 24, 1989 that it was recalling its Maxzide product and suspending all shipments of the drug, it also announced that it had intentionally furnished a false report to the FDA during a recent inspection; that Ratilal Patel was taking a leave of absence from the company; that its vice president for regulatory affairs and its executive vice-president were taking leaves of absence from the Board of Directors; and that the company was postponing its annual shareholders' meeting in light of the ongoing investigation. Following that announcement, the price of Par stock closed on July 24 at $8.375 per share, down $1.625 from the $10 closing price on Friday, July 21, the previous trading day. On July 25, the next trading day, the stock closed at $7.125 per share. The total decline from the July 21 closing price was $2.875 or 28.75%. On July 26, 1989, the third day after the disclosure, Par stock rallied from $7.125 to close at $7.625.

On September 8, 1989, Patel resigned as a director and senior vice president of Par and as a director of its subsidiary, Quad Pharmaceuticals, Inc. In March of 1992, he settled a securities fraud class action claim with the payment of 500,000 shares of Par stock valued at approximately $3,000,000. In January of 1993, Patel pled guilty to conspiracy to defraud the FDA in connection with the generic Maxzide Application and thereafter was sentenced to a 27-month term of imprisonment, two years of supervised release and a $25,000 fine.

The enforcement action giving rise to this appeal was commenced by the filing of a complaint by the SEC on July 7, 1993. In the complaint, the SEC alleged violations by Patel of various antifraud provisions of the federal securities laws: Section 17(a) of the Securities Act of 1933, Section 10(b) of the Securities Exchange Act of 1934, and Rule 10b-5 promulgated thereunder. Injunctive relief was sought, along with disgorgement of "avoided losses" plus prejudgment interest, assessment of civil penalties under the provisions of the Insider Trading Sanctions Act of 1984, [Exchange Act Section 21A], and an order barring Patel from ever serving as an officer or director of a publicly traded company. Following a motion for summary judgment by the SEC, Patel conceded that he had violated the antifraud provisions and agreed that a permanent injunction against future violations would be appropriate. The district court denied the relief sought under the Insider Trading Sanctions Act but ordered the disgorgement of Patel's avoided losses plus interest in accordance with the computation suggested by the SEC. The district court also imposed a lifetime bar against Patel's service as an officer or director of any publicly traded company. As he did in the district court, Patel here challenges *** the permanent employment ban imposed upon him.

DISCUSSION

****Injunction Against Service as Officer and Director*

For violations of the antifraud provisions of the securities laws,

> the court may prohibit, conditionally or unconditionally, and permanently or for such period of time as it shall determine, any person who violated [the applicable provisions] from acting as an officer or director [of a publicly traded company] if the person's conduct demonstrates substantial unfitness to serve as an officer or director....

[Securities Act Section 20(e); Exchange Act Section 21(d)(2)].

In permanently enjoining Patel from serving as an officer or director of any publicly traded company at the behest of the SEC, the district court necessarily determined that Patel was substantially unfit to hold such positions. The court identified six factors that it considered in resolving the issue of substantial unfitness: "(1) the 'egregiousness' of the underlying securities law violation; (2) the defendant's 'repeat offender' status; (3) the defendant's 'role' or position when he engaged in the fraud; (4) the defendant's degree of scienter; (5) the defendant's economic stake in the violation; and (6) the likelihood that misconduct will recur." These factors were suggested in a law review article by Jayne W. Barnard entitled When is a Corporate Executive "Substantially Unfit to Serve"?, 70 N.C.L.Rev. 1489, 1492-93 (1992).

Applying the factors suggested by Professor Barnard, the district court found: that Patel's violations were not egregious in comparison with those of others and in view of the size of the loss avoided; that Patel was a first-time offender; that in his position as officer and director of Par, Patel allowed the false Application to be submitted and obstructed the FDA investigation of the Application by providing a "switched sample" of Maxzide to an FDA inspector; that Patel "showed some scienter in his actions, although he did not engage in clandestine trading"; that he was the sole economic beneficiary of his insider trading; and that, because he was a founder of Par and abused his position as officer and director, "the likelihood of future misconduct is sufficient to warrant the imposition of the injunctive relief requested."

Patel contends that the district court improperly applied the factors it considered "by 'mixing' Patel's 'insider trading' with Par's submission of the false [application] to the FDA." He further contends that, although his "conduct in the Maxzide affair gave rise to his 'insider' knowledge, it was not part of any 'scheme' to commit the securities law violation[s], and is not relevant to an analysis of his conduct" in respect of the violations. Patel claims that the district court's application of the six-factor test results in an almost even "split" between those factors that cut in his favor and those factors that cut against him. Moreover, Patel thinks that the district court should have taken into account the fact that criminal sanctions were imposed upon him and that he voluntarily settled the class action suit brought against him.

The district court properly considered Patel's involvement in the "Maxzide affair" as part and parcel of his conduct in the securities law violations. His deception of the FDA, although perhaps not originally designed to obtain profits or avoid losses in the sale of his stock, set in motion the scheme that culminated in his breach of fiduciary duties and in the resultant detriment to investors. Also, the district court properly took into account the six factors that it identified in evaluating substantial unfitness. These factors are useful in making the unfitness assessment, although we do not mean to say that they are the only factors that may be taken into account or even that it is necessary to apply all these factors in every case. A district court should be afforded substantial discretion in deciding whether to impose a bar to employment in a publicly traded company.

We do find a problem in this case, however, with the district court's finding regarding the likelihood of future misconduct, which is always an important element in deciding whether the substantial unfitness found justifies the imposition of a lifetime ban. The only findings that the district court made in this regard were that "Patel was a founder of Par and used his position as an officer and director to engage in misconduct." This is merely a general statement of events and can in no way justify the prediction that future misconduct will occur.

Moreover, we think that it was error for the district court to say that the likelihood of future misconduct based on the foregoing statement "is sufficient to warrant the imposition of the injunctive relief requested." The loss of livelihood and the stigma attached to permanent exclusion from the corporate suite certainly requires more. In a case in which we approved lifetime banishment as a common law remedy, we noted that the defendants "had committed securities law violations with a 'high degree of scienter' and that their past securities law violations and lack of assurances against future violations demonstrated that such violations were likely to continue." [*SEC v.*] *Posner*, 16 F.3d [520, 521-22 (2d Cir. 1994)]. Although it is not essential for a lifetime ban that there be past violations, we think that it is essential, in the absence of such violations, that a district court articulate the factual basis for a finding of the likelihood of recurrence.

Finally, we take note of the fact that the governing statute provides that a bar on service as an officer or director that is based on substantial unfitness may be imposed "conditionally or unconditionally" and "permanently or for such period of time as [the court] shall determine." We take these provisions to suggest that, before imposing a permanent bar, the court should consider whether a conditional bar (e.g., a bar limited to a particular industry) and/or a bar limited in time (e.g., a bar of five years) might be sufficient, especially where there is no prior history of unfitness. In this connection, we do not think that it would be improper for the district court to take into account any prior punishment that may have been imposed in a criminal proceeding. If the district court decides that a conditional ban or a ban limited in time is not warranted, it should give reasons why a lifetime injunction is imposed.

CONCLUSION

We affirm the judgment to the extent that it enjoins future securities law violations and orders the disgorgement of avoided losses. We reverse so much of the judgment as imposes a lifetime injunction on Patel's service as an officer or director of any publicly traded company, and we remand for further consideration of the issue in accordance with the foregoing.

NOTES AND QUESTIONS

1. Injunctions—"Mild Prophylactic" or "Drastic Remedy?" Although viewed at one time as a "mild prophylactic," *SEC v. Capital Gains Research Bureau, Inc.*, 375 U.S. 180, 193 (1963), a court-ordered injunction against future securities law violations is today widely recognized to be a rather "drastic remedy." *Aaron v. SEC*, 446 U.S. 680, 703 (1980) (Burger, C.J., concurring). What is it about an injunction that makes it more than a mere slap on the wrist? Aren't defendants obliged to obey the law in the future even in the absence of a court-ordered injunction?

2. Injunctions—The Operative Standard. Because the federal securities laws provide the SEC with a statutory basis for obtaining permanent injunctive relief, see, e.g., Exchange Act Section 21(d), the SEC does not have to satisfy the traditional test for equitable relief, which generally requires the plaintiff to plead and prove irreparable injury and inadequacy of remedies at law. Instead, courts may grant "permanent or temporary injunction[s] or restraining order[s]" upon "a proper showing." According to *First Financial,* what evidence must the SEC put forth to make this "proper showing?" In cases where the SEC establishes an underlying violation of the securities laws, how likely is it that courts will refuse to enjoin a defendant from future violations? For examples of such instances, see *SEC v. Sargent,* 329 F.3d 34, 39 (1st Cir. 2003) (emphasizing that tippee's violation was a first-time offense, was not egregious (in that he neither traded himself nor profited from the tip), and that his current employment did not facilitate his coming into contact with material nonpublic information); *SEC v. Pros Int'l, Inc.*, 994 F.2d 767 (10th Cir. 1993) (holding that the lower court did not abuse its discretion in denying motion for injunction, since there was no showing that the defendant-accountant intended to defraud investors, accountant did not profit from transaction, and it was unlikely that future violations of securities laws would occur). See also Daniel J. Morrissey, SEC Injunctions, 68 Tenn. L. Rev. 427, 467-470 (2001); Daniel F.

Levy, The Impact of the Remedies Act on the SEC's Ability to Obtain Injunctive Relief, 44 Am. U. L. Rev. 645, 656-69 (1994).

Are there limits to the enforceability of "obey-the-law" type injunctions that simply mirror the language of the allegedly violated statute or SEC rule? In elaborate dicta, the Eleventh Circuit has pointed to the Federal Rules of Civil Procedure:

> This Circuit has held repeatedly that "obey the law" injunctions are unenforceable. The specificity requirement of Rule 65(d) is no mere technicality; "[the] command of specificity is a reflection of the seriousness of the consequences which may flow from a violation of an injunctive order." An injunction must be framed so that those enjoined know exactly what conduct the court has prohibited and what steps they must take to conform their conduct to the law.

SEC v. Smyth, 420 F.3d 1225, 1233 n. 14 (11th Cir. 2005). How would the SEC's enforcement program be affected if other circuits were to adopt the position set out in *Smyth*? See David M. Weiss, Reexamining the SEC's Use of Obey-the-Law Injunctions, 7 U.C. Davis Bus. L. J. 6 (2006).

3. Preliminary Injunctions, Temporary Restraining Orders, and Temporary Asset Freezes. In addition to permanent relief, Section 21(d) of the Exchange Act authorizes the SEC to seek both preliminary injunctions and temporary restraining orders. In what types of cases would the SEC be likely to seek these remedies? What standards should govern their issuance?

In *SEC v. Unifund SAL*, 910 F.2d 1028 (2d Cir. 1990), the Second Circuit held that the SEC's requests for preliminary or temporary relief must be judged against a "likelihood of success" standard. However, pointing to the "very serious consequences" that may flow from such relief, the court emphasized that district judges, exercising their equitable discretion, should "bear in mind the nature of the preliminary relief the Commission is seeking, and should require a more substantial showing of likelihood of success, both as to violation and risk of recurrence, whenever the relief sought is more than preservation of the status quo." Id. at 1039. In applying this standard to the relief ordered by the lower court in a case involving allegations of insider trading, the Second Circuit affirmed (with modifications) a temporary asset freeze, which was imposed to preserve the SEC's "opportunity to collect funds that may be yet ordered disgorged." Id. at 1041. But the Second Circuit reversed the lower court's order of a preliminary injunction, finding that the SEC had not produced sufficient evidence to warrant a remedy that "accomplishes significantly more than preserving the status quo." Id. at 1040. Among other deficiencies, the court noted that the SEC had yet to establish the identity of the tipper, and had yet to demonstrate that the defendants had breached a fiduciary duty in trading on the material nonpublic information. Id.

New authority for temporary asset freezes was among the remedies made available to the SEC in SOX. Specifically, the Act added Section 21C(c)(3)(A)(i) to the Exchange Act:

> Whenever, during the course of a lawful investigation involving possible violations of the Federal securities laws by an issuer of publicly traded securities or any of its directors, officers, partners, controlling persons, agents, or employees, it shall appear to the Commission that it is likely that the issuer

> will make extraordinary payments (whether compensation or otherwise) to any of the foregoing persons, the Commission may petition a Federal district court for a temporary order requiring the issuer to escrow, subject to court supervision, those payments in an interest-bearing account for 45 days.

Without the SEC's initiation of an enforcement proceeding charging a violation of the federal securities laws, the order may be extended only up to an additional 45 days, provided the SEC establishes "good cause." Exchange Act Section 21C(c)(3)(A)(iv). The order, however, may continue subject to court approval if a violation of the federal securities laws is charged, though an issuer or other affected person has the right to petition the court for review. See Exchange Act Section 21C(c)(3)(B)(i).

Consider the ways in which this new provision authorizing temporary asset freezes is actually more limiting than the provision for temporary restraining orders in Section 21(d). What constraints, if any, does this new authority place on the general equitable powers of federal courts (particularly as now bolstered by new Section 21(d)(5), which authorizes federal courts to grant "any equitable relief that may be appropriate or necessary for the benefit of investors")? Would you expect to see the SEC make significant use of its specific authority to seek temporary asset freezes in instances where it appears likely that an issuer may make extraordinary payments to corporate officials?

4. The Permanence of Permanent Injunctions. Unless specifically limited in duration (a relatively rare occurrence), court-ordered injunctions against future violations of the federal securities laws are permanent. That said, SEC injunctions may be modified or even dissolved by a subsequent court on a defendant's petition, though the granting of such relief is also a rare occurrence. Indeed, both the SEC and courts routinely point to *United States v. Swift & Co.*, 286 U.S. 106, 119 (1932), which held that the appropriate standard for vacating an injunction is "[n]othing less than a clear showing of grievous wrong evoked by new and unforeseen conditions." See, e.g., *SEC v. Blinder, Robinson & Co.*, 855 F.2d 677, 680 (10th Cir. 1988) (confirming that *Swift* articulates the applicable standard and emphasizing the necessity of clear proof of "unforeseen conditions" flowing from the injunction). Yet there have been occasions when a court's power "to do equity" resulted in modification or dissolution. See, e.g., *SEC v. Warren*, 583 F.2d 115, 121-22 (3d Cir. 1978) (dissolving injunction imposed five years earlier pursuant to a consent decree, finding that the defendant's unlawful conduct was "a single isolated offense in an esoteric area of the law *** and never again renewed," and which caused him "personal humiliation and business embarrassment"). As a matter of policy, would you favor a change in the law to provide for automatic dissolution of SEC injunctions after a certain number of years? After five years? Ten years? Twenty? For additional discussion and suggested standards, see Marc I. Steinberg, SEC and Other Permanent Injunctions—Standards for Their Imposition, Modification, and Dissolution, 66 Cornell L. Rev. 27 (1980).

5. Officer and Director Bars. Section 20(e) of the Securities Act and Section 21(d)(2) of the Exchange Act specifically identify the statutory provisions that, if violated, may be remedied through a court order barring a person from future service as an officer or director of a publicly traded company. What are these provisions and why did Congress impose this limitation? As we saw in *Patel*, Congress originally conditioned the availability of this remedy on the

SEC's showing of "a substantial unfitness to serve." Did the factors enumerated by the *Patel* court (prompted by Professor Barnard's law review article) provide sufficient standards? How would you have decided Patel's appeal based on these (or other) factors?

Note the SOX amendments to Securities Act Section 20(e) and Exchange Act Section 21(d)(2), which authorize federal courts to issue officer and director bar orders upon the lesser showing of a person's "unfitness" to serve. The legislative history of SOX reflects congressional agreement with the SEC's argument that "the 'substantial unfitness' standard for imposing bars [was] inordinately high, causing courts to refrain from imposing bars even in cases of egregious misconduct." Sen. Rep. 107-205, at 27 (July 3, 2002). Do these amendments entail a congressional judgment that *Patel* was wrongly decided? Was Congress's decision to do away with the "substantial unfitness" standard a wise one? Should Professor Barnard's six-factor test continue to play a role in a judge's analysis of whether to order a bar under the new standard of "unfitness?" See generally, Jayne W. Barnard, SEC Disbarment of Officers and Directors After Sarbanes-Oxley, 59 Bus. Law. 391 (2004).

Note also that prior to the passage of the Remedies Act, courts on a number of occasions had issued consent decrees enjoining defendants from future corporate service. Such equitable relief was also ordered in litigated proceedings, though less frequently. See, e.g., *SEC v. Posner*, 16 F.3d 520 (2d Cir. 1994) (holding that order enjoining officers from acting as officers or directors of any publicly traded company was within the district court's well-established equitable power). Do Section 20(e) of the Securities Act and Section 21(d)(2) of the Exchange Act merely provide statutory authorization for a remedy that could otherwise be ordered through the exercise of a federal court's equitable powers?

The officer and director bar remedy was in fact one of the more controversial aspects of the Remedies Act, in part because it called into question the interplay between the federal securities laws and state corporate law. Consider, for example, how this remedy impacts the corporate shareholder franchise and who, in fact, should determine the minimum qualifications for director and officer service. On this point, in his testimony before Congress, then-SEC Chairperson Richard Breeden stated the following:

> The Commission recognizes that corporate governance issues are generally regulated by state law. The purpose of the corporate bar provisions is not to establish federal standards governing the qualifications of corporate officers or directors. Rather, the purpose of this provision is to protect public investors from persons who have already demonstrated a propensity to abuse a position of corporate trust. Where a person's conduct is such that the disclosure provisions of the federal securities laws, even when supplemented by the coercive power of a federal court injunction, are insufficient to protect investors from further loss, the availability of such a provision is necessary. ***

Written Testimony of Chairperson Richard C. Breeden, Securities and Exchange Commission, Before the Subcomm. on Securities of the Comm. on Banking, Housing and Urban Affairs Concerning S. 647, The "Securities Law Enforcement Remedies Act of 1989," at 63 (Feb. 1, 1990). Do you agree? Have the massive financial frauds by publicly traded companies such as Enron and WorldCom created a need for even greater use of the bar order remedy? Congress apparently thought so, since it granted the SEC the new authority to issue such bar orders in administrative proceedings. See SOX, Section 1105 (adding a new Section 8A(f) to the Securities Act and a new Section 21C(f) to the Exchange Act). Was this a wise decision?

*6. **Disgorgement and Other Equitable Relief.*** As is reflected in both *First Financial* and *Patel*, the equitable remedy of disgorgement is likely to be sought and ordered in almost any case in which the SEC is able to prove that a defendant has wrongfully profited from a violation of the securities laws. Both cases also reflect the SEC's routine decision to seek, and the federal courts' routine decisions to order, the defendant to pay "pre-judgment interest" on the amount subject to disgorgement. Can the ordering of pre-judgment interest be described as remedial?

As we have seen from the material on SEC settlements, a number of courts have also used their equitable power to approve consent decrees that impose "creative relief" such as additional reporting requirements, the prohibition of exercising voting control, the appointment of additional independent directors on a corporate board, and the appointment of "corporate overseers" to ensure compliance with federal securities laws. See Section B.4 supra. Yet the argument was often made that Congress's enactment of specific statutory remedies in the Remedies Act should restrict a court's ability to fashion additional equitable remedies and that it was particularly inappropriate for courts to order "creative relief" in the absence of the defendant's express agreement. See ABA Committee on Federal Regulation of Securities, Report of the Task Force on SEC Settlements, 47 Bus. Law. 1083, 1127 (1992) (stating that "there should be no question that these unauthorized remedies are appropriate solely in the context of settled enforcement matters"). How does Section 21(d)(5) of the Exchange Act factor into this debate?

*7. **Clawbacks and Accounting Restatements.*** Section 304(a) of the SOX provides:

> a) *Additional Compensation Prior to Noncompliance With Commission Financial Reporting Requirements.* If an issuer is required to prepare an accounting restatement due to the material noncompliance of the issuer, as a result of misconduct, with any financial reporting requirement under the securities laws, the chief executive officer and chief financial officer of the issuer shall reimburse the issuer for-
>
> (1) any bonus or other incentive-based or equity-based compensation received by that person from the issuer during the 12-month period following the first public issuance or filing with the Commission (whichever first occurs) of the financial document embodying such financial reporting requirement; and
>
> (2) any profits realized from the sale of securities of the issuer during that 12-month period.

15 U.S.C. § 7243(a). Notice that the provision is written to be self-executing. In the wake of an accounting restatement, is it likely that CEOs and CFOs will voluntarily reimburse the issuer for the value of their bonuses or trading profits? What if a CEO or CFO does not voluntarily reimburse the issuer? Although the text is silent as to whether Section 304 may be enforced in a private action brought on behalf of the securities issuer, courts have been consistent in viewing this provision as enforceable only by the SEC. See, e.g., *Cohen v. Viray*, 622 F.3d

188 (2d Cir. 2010); *In re Digimarc Corp. Deriv. Litig.*, 549 F.3d 1223 (9th Cir. 2008). Likewise, while the text references "misconduct," the text is silent as to whether that "misconduct" must be by the officer who is the subject of the action. The only federal court directly to address this issue held that Section 304's text and legislative history does not require misconduct on the part of the CEO or CFO, and ruled that the SEC may proceed with a clawback action "even if the CEO was unaware of the misconduct leading to misstated financials." *SEC v. Jenkins*, 718 F. Supp. 2d 1070, 1075 (D. Ariz. 2010). What policy arguments support SEC clawback actions even in "no-fault" situations? What are the arguments against? For SEC settlements in the two other clawback actions where the CEO was not charged with any wrongdoing, see SEC v. McCarthy, Litigation Release No. 21873 (Mar. 4, 2011); SEC v. Diebold, Inc., Litigation Release No. 21543 (June 2, 2010).

In Section 954 of the Dodd-Frank Act, Congress added a new Section 10D to the Exchange Act, which requires the SEC to develop rules directing national securities exchanges to prohibit the listing of any issuer's security unless the issuer develops and implements a clawback policy adhering to certain requirements. The SEC's rules (which are expected to be proposed in fall 2011) will substantially expand the SOX Section 304 landscape because a listed company's clawback policy: (1) must apply to any current or former "executive officer;" (2) would be triggered by any accountant restatement due to material non-compliance, regardless of whether there is "misconduct;" and (3) must provide a look-back period of not less than three years. Presumably, as a written corporate policy, clawback obligations will be enforced by the listed company (and likely by shareholders in derivative litigation), and failures to develop and implement a clawback policy could also subject the listed company to an enforcement action by the stock exchange. Congress could have imposed the new clawback requirements on public companies directly. What might explain why it chose instead to direct the SEC to order the stock exchanges to impose those requirements on listed companies?

b. Civil Monetary Penalties

In 1990, Congress gave the SEC the power to seek civil monetary penalties in virtually any federal court case involving virtually any violation of the federal securities laws. The power to seek such sanctions was perhaps the most controversial aspect of the Securities Enforcement Remedies and Penny Stock Reform Act. The breadth of these penalty provisions is exemplified by Section 21(d)(3) of the Exchange Act, which provides:

> **Section 21(d)(3). Money penalties in civil actions.**
>
> A. Authority of Commission. Whenever it shall appear to the Commission that any person has violated any provision of this title, the rules or regulations thereunder, or a cease- and-desist order entered by the Commission pursuant to section 21C, other than by committing a violation subject to a penalty pursuant to section 21A, the Commission may bring an action in a United States district court to seek, and the court shall have jurisdiction to impose, upon a proper showing, a civil penalty to be paid by the person who committed such violation.
>
> B. Amount of penalty.
>
> i. First tier. The amount of the penalty shall be determined by the court in light

of the facts and circumstances. For each violation, the amount of the penalty shall not exceed the greater of (I) $5,000 for a natural person or $50,000 for any other person, or (II) the gross amount of pecuniary gain to such defendant as a result of the violation.

ii. Second tier. Notwithstanding clause (i), the amount of penalty for each such violation shall not exceed the greater of (I) $50,000 for a natural person or $250,000 for any other person, or (II) the gross amount of pecuniary gain to such defendant as a result of the violation, if the violation described in subparagraph (A) involved fraud, deceit, manipulation, or deliberate or reckless disregard of a regulatory requirement.

iii. Third tier. Notwithstanding clauses (i) and (ii), the amount of penalty for each such violation shall not exceed the greater of (I) $100,000 for a natural person or $500,000 for any other person, or (II) the gross amount of pecuniary gain to such defendant as a result of the violation, if--

(aa) the violation described in subparagraph (A) involved fraud, deceit, manipulation, or deliberate or reckless disregard of a regulatory requirement; and

(bb) such violation directly or indirectly resulted in substantial losses or created a significant risk of substantial losses to other persons.

The SEC's power to seek civil monetary penalties raises general questions about the purposes and effects of this sanction: Is punishment a proper goal of civil enforcement? Are civil penalties necessary for effective deterrence of securities law violations? Is it possible to distinguish between these two goals? See Mary M. Cheh, Constitutional Limits on Using Civil Remedies to Achieve Criminal Law Objectives: Understanding and Transcending the Criminal-Civil Law Distinction, 42 Hastings L.J. 1325, 1355 (1991); Kenneth Mann, Punitive Civil Sanctions: The Middleground Between Criminal and Civil Law, 101 Yale L.J. 1795, 1803-10 (1992).

Civil monetary penalties also raise a specific question when the defendant in an SEC enforcement proceeding is a public corporation: Is the imposition of a monetary penalty fair to the shareholders of that corporation? In the wake of the scandals at Enron and WorldCom, the penalties obtained by the SEC increased substantially, both in size and frequency, with some corporate penalties exceeding $100 million. Do penalties of this magnitude unjustifiably hurt the corporation's shareholders who have already been hurt by a drop in stock price resulting from the corporation's damaged reputation? What are the arguments in favor of seeking substantial corporate penalties? Consider these questions in light of the following statement, issued by a unanimous Commission, setting forth objective standards for imposing monetary penalties on corporations.

STATEMENT OF THE SECURITIES AND EXCHANGE COMMISSION CONCERNING FINANCIAL PENALTIES

SEC Release No. 2006-4 (January 4, 2006)

***The question of whether, and if so to what extent, to impose civil penalties against a corporation raises significant questions for our mission of investor protection. The authority to impose such penalties is relatively recent in the Commission's history, and the use of very large corporate penalties is more recent still. Recent cases have not produced a clear public view of when and how the Commission will use corporate penalties, and within the

Commission itself a variety of views have heretofore been expressed, but not reconciled.

The Commission believes it important to provide the maximum possible degree of clarity, consistency, and predictability in explaining the way that its corporate penalty authority will be exercised. To this end, we are issuing this statement describing with particularity the framework for our penalty determinations ***

In 1990, Congress passed the Securities Enforcement Remedies and Penny Stock Reform Act (the "Remedies Act"), which gave the Commission authority generally to seek civil money penalties in enforcement cases. The penalty provisions added by the Remedies Act expressly authorize the Commission to obtain money penalties from entities, including corporate issuers. These provisions also enhanced the Commission's authority to fine individuals. Today, we limit our discussion to penalties against corporations, although we view penalties against individual offenders as a critical component in punishing and deterring violative conduct.

The Remedies Act legislative history contains express references to penalty assessments against corporate issuers of securities. In its Report on the legislation, the Senate Committee on Banking, Housing, and Urban Affairs expressly noted both that the civil money penalty provisions would be applicable to corporate issuers, and that shareholders ultimately may bear the cost of penalties imposed on corporate issuers. According to the Report, such penalties should be assessed when the securities law violation that is the basis of the penalty has resulted in an improper benefit to the shareholders. It also cautioned that the Commission and courts should, in considering corporate issuer penalties, take into account whether the penalty would be paid by shareholders who had been the principal victims of the violation:

> The Committee believes that the civil money penalty provisions should be applicable to corporate issuers, and the legislation permits penalties against issuers. However, because the costs of such penalties may be passed on to shareholders, the Committee intends that a penalty be sought when the violation results in an improper benefit to shareholders. In cases in which shareholders are the principal victims of the violations, the Committee expects that the SEC, when appropriate, will seek penalties from the individual offenders acting for a corporate issuer. Moreover, in deciding whether and to what extent to assess a penalty against the issuer, the court may properly take into account whether civil penalties assessed against corporate issuers will ultimately be paid by shareholders who were themselves victimized by the violations. The court also may consider the extent to which the passage of time has resulted in shareholder turnover. [S. Rep. No. 337, 101st Cong., 2d Sess. at 17 (1990)].

As this discussion indicates, a key question for the Commission is whether the issuer's violation has provided an improper benefit to the shareholders, or conversely whether the violation has resulted in harm to the shareholders. Where shareholders have been victimized by the violative conduct, or by the resulting negative effect on the entity following its discovery, the Commission is expected to seek penalties from culpable individual offenders acting for a corporation. This same point was made in the SEC's memorandum in support of the Remedies Act, which the then Chairman of the SEC, David

Ruder, transmitted to the Senate in a January 18, 1989 letter.

In addition to the benefit or harm to shareholders, the statute and its legislative history suggest several other factors that may be pertinent to the analysis of corporate issuer penalties. For example, the need for effective deterrence is discussed throughout the legislative history of the Remedies Act. The Senate Report also notes the importance of good compliance programs and observes that the availability of penalties may encourage development of such programs. The Senate Report also observes that penalties may serve to decrease the temptation to violate the law in areas where the perceived risk of detection of wrongdoing is small. Other factors discussed in the legislative history include whether there was fraudulent intent, harm to innocent third parties, and the possibility of unjust enrichment to the wrongdoer.

The Sarbanes-Oxley Act of 2002 changed the ultimate disposition of penalties. Section 308 of Sarbanes-Oxley (the Fair Funds provision) allows the Commission to take penalties paid by individuals and entities in enforcement actions and add them to disgorgement funds for the benefit of victims. Penalty moneys no longer always go to the Treasury. Under Fair Funds, penalty moneys instead can be used to compensate the victims for the losses they experienced from the wrongdoing. If the victims are shareholders of the corporation being penalized, they will still bear the cost of issuer penalty payments (which is the case with any penalty against a corporate entity). When penalty moneys are ultimately returned to all or some of the investors who were victims of the violation, the amounts returned are less the administrative costs of the distribution. While the legislative history of the Fair Funds provision is scant, there are two general points that can be discerned. First, the purpose of the provision is to provide an additional source of compensation to victims of securities law violations. Second, the provision applies to all penalties and makes no distinction between penalties against individuals or entities.

We have considered the legislative histories of both the Remedies Act and the Fair Funds provisions of the Sarbanes-Oxley Act in reaching the decisions we announce today.

We proceed from the fundamental principle that corporate penalties are an essential part of an aggressive and comprehensive program to enforce the federal securities laws, and that the availability of a corporate penalty, as one of a range of remedies, contributes to the Commission's ability to achieve an appropriate level of deterrence through its decision in a particular case.

With this principle in mind, our view of the appropriateness of a penalty on the corporation in a particular case, as distinct from the individuals who commit a securities law violation, turns principally on two considerations:

The presence or absence of a direct benefit to the corporation as a result of the violation. The fact that a corporation itself has received a direct and material benefit from the offense, for example through reduced expenses or increased revenues, weighs in support of the imposition of a corporate penalty. If the corporation is in any other way unjustly enriched, this similarly weighs in support of the imposition of a corporate penalty. Within this parameter, the strongest case for the imposition of a corporate penalty is one in which the shareholders of the corporation have received an improper benefit as a result of the violation; the weakest case is one in which the current shareholders of the corporation are the principal victims of the securities law violation.

The degree to which the penalty will recompense or further harm the injured shareholders. Because the protection of innocent investors is a principal objective of the securities laws, the imposition of a penalty on the corporation itself carries with it the risk that shareholders who are innocent of the violation will nonetheless bear the burden of the penalty. In some cases, however, the penalty itself may be used as a source of funds to recompense the injury suffered by victims of the securities law violations. The presence of an opportunity to use the penalty as a meaningful source of compensation to injured shareholders is a factor in support of its imposition. The likelihood a corporate penalty will unfairly injure investors, the corporation, or third parties weighs against its use as a sanction.

In addition to these two principal considerations, there are several additional factors that are properly considered in determining whether to impose a penalty on the corporation. These are:

The need to deter the particular type of offense. The likelihood that a corporate penalty will serve as a strong deterrent to others similarly situated weighs in favor of the imposition of a corporate penalty. Conversely, the prevalence of unique circumstances that render the particular offense unlikely to be repeated in other contexts is a factor weighing against the need for a penalty on the corporation rather than on the responsible individuals.

The extent of the injury to innocent parties. The egregiousness of the harm done, the number of investors injured, and the extent of societal harm if the corporation's infliction of such injury on innocent parties goes unpunished, are significant determinants of the propriety of a corporate penalty.

Whether complicity in the violation is widespread throughout the corporation. The more pervasive the participation in the offense by responsible persons within the corporation, the more appropriate is the use of a corporate penalty. Conversely, within this parameter, isolated conduct by only a few individuals would tend not to support the imposition of a corporate penalty. Whether the corporation has replaced those persons responsible for the violation will also be considered in weighing this factor.

The level of intent on the part of the perpetrators. Within this parameter, the imposition of a corporate penalty is most appropriate in egregious circumstances, where the culpability and fraudulent intent of the perpetrators are manifest. A corporate penalty is less likely to be imposed if the violation is not the result of deliberate, intentionally fraudulent conduct.

The degree of difficulty in detecting the particular type of offense. Because offenses that are particularly difficult to detect call for an especially high level of deterrence, this factor weighs in support of the imposition of a corporate penalty.

Presence or lack of remedial steps by the corporation. Because the aim of the securities laws is to protect investors, the prevention of future harm, as well as the punishment of past offenses, is a high priority. The Commission's decisions in particular cases are intended to encourage the management of corporations accused of securities law violations to do everything within their power to take remedial steps, from the first moment that the violation is brought to their attention. Exemplary conduct by management in this respect weighs against the use of a corporate penalty; failure of management to take remedial steps is a factor supporting the imposition of a corporate penalty.

Extent of cooperation with Commission and other law enforcement. Effective compliance with the securities laws depends upon vigilant supervision, monitoring, and reporting of violations. When securities law violations are discovered, it is incumbent upon management to report them to the Commission and to other appropriate law enforcement authorities. The degree to which a corporation has self reported an offense, or otherwise cooperated with the investigation and remediation of the offense, is a factor that the Commission will consider in determining the propriety of a corporate penalty.

This framework for the consideration of the propriety of corporate penalties is grounded in the Commission's statutory authority and supported by the legislative history underlying that authority. It is the Commission's intent that the elucidation of these principles will provide a high degree of transparency to our decisions in these and future cases, and will be of assistance to the Commission's professional staff, to corporate issuers and their counsel, and to the public.

NOTES AND QUESTIONS

1. ***Monetary Penalties in* First Financial?** Reconsider the *First Financial* case set out in the previous sub-section. Had the defendants in that case been "eligible" for a civil monetary penalty, would you expect the SEC to have sought and a court to have imposed such penalties? Note that the Remedies Act civil penalty provisions require a "proper showing" for the ordering of a penalty. Would the SEC's evidence support such a showing? From your review of the three tiers in Exchange Act Section 21(d)(3)(B), what would you estimate to be the maximum amount of a possible penalty against the *First Financial* defendants?

2. ***"Show Me the Money."*** Prior to the enactment of SOX, the SEC typically distributed disgorgement monies obtained through enforcement action to investors injured by a defendant's wrongful conduct, provided that such persons could be identified. Civil monetary penalties, on the other hand, were directed to the U.S. Treasury. In a provision of the Act entitled "Fair Funds for Investors," Congress altered this scheme by specifying that in any judicial or administrative action brought by the SEC under the federal securities laws, any amounts disgorged and any civil penalties imposed "shall, on the motion or at the direction of the Commission, be added to and become part of the disgorgement fund for the benefit of the victims of such violation." 15 U.S.C. § 7246(a). The Act further authorized the SEC to add to this fund any "gifts, bequests and devises of property, both real and personal." Id. at § 7246(b). In the Dodd-Frank Act, Congress amended this Fair Fund provision to allow the SEC to add civil monetary sanctions imposed in enforcement actions to a "distribution fund" for the victims of the violation regardless of whether the SEC obtains disgorgement as part of that action.

How might the Commission's authority to distribute funds to injured investors affect its deliberations on corporate penalties? What logistical problems do you foresee with the SEC's ability to carry out Congress's rather clear intention that victims of securities fraud be made as whole as possible? Is the Fair Funds provision fair to the creditors of a bankrupt corporation? See *SEC v. WorldCom Inc.*, 273 F.Supp.2d 431, 435 (S.D.N.Y. 2003) (approving settlement imposing a $750 million penalty that would be distributed to WorldCom shareholders pursuant to the Fair Funds provision, but acknowledging that any SEC penalty "premised primarily" on compensating defrauded shareholders "might arguably run afoul of the provisions of the [Bankruptcy] Code that subordinate shareholder claims below all others"); Marvin E. Sprouse III, A Collision of Fairness: Sarbanes-Oxley and §510(B) of the Bankruptcy Code, 24 Am. Bankr. Inst. J. 8 (2005). For additional background and analysis regarding Fair Fund distribution, see Barbara Black, Should the SEC Be a Collection Agency for Defrauded Investors?, 63 Bus. Law. 317 (2008).

PROBLEM 9-1

Shortly after its announcement of the framework for the imposition of corporate penalties, the SEC sought substantial penalties in several enforcement actions, including the following: SEC v. American Int'l Group, Inc., Litigation Release No. 19560 (Feb. 9, 2006) ($700 million disgorgement, $100 million penalty in accounting fraud case); In the Matter of Prudential Equity Group LLC, Exchange Act Release No. 54371 (Aug. 28, 2006) ($270 million penalty in mutual funds market timing case). The SEC also sought substantial corporate penalties in several enforcement actions relating to the financial crisis, including: SEC v. Goldman, Sachs & Co., Litigation Release No. 21592 (July 15, 2010) ($550 million penalty for misleading investors with respect to collateralized debt obligations); In the Matter of State St. Bank and Trust Co., Securities Act Release No. 9107 (Feb. 4, 2010) ($300 million penalty for misleading investors about their exposure to subprime investments while selectively disclosing more complete information to specific investors). All of these cases were settled rather than litigated, with the corporation neither admitting nor denying liability.

After accessing the litigation release or administrative proceedings section of the SEC's web site (www.sec.gov), review a release announcing one or more of these settlements, or a releases from another case that you may be familiar with from the news. To what extent does the imposed penalty reflect the considerations set out in the SEC's Statement Concerning Financial Penalties?

2. Administrative Remedies

RIZEK v. SEC

215 F.3d 157 (1st Cir. 2000)

SANDRA L. LYNCH, CIRCUIT JUDGE:

Al Rizek was a vice president of PaineWebber Incorporated of Puerto Rico. Over a ten-month period in 1993 he churned the accounts of five customers, causing losses of approximately $195,000 on accounts with average balances that totaled about $700,000. This violated Section 10(b) of the

Securities Exchange Act of 1934 and Rule 10b-5. Although his customers indicated that they had conservative investment objectives, Rizek pursued the extremely risky strategy of trading U.S. Treasury bonds in an attempt to take advantage of short-term fluctuations in the market. He magnified the risk by trading the accounts on margin.

In 1999, the Securities and Exchange Commission ordered that Rizek be permanently barred from the securities industry, cease and desist from violations, pay a civil penalty of $100,000, and disgorge over $120,000. In doing so, the SEC departed from the recommendations of its own Administrative Law Judge, who would have imposed a disgorgement of over $275,000, but only a two-year suspension. See generally *In re Al Rizek,* Exchange Act Release No. 41,725 (Aug. 11, 1999), available in 1999 WL 600427.

Rizek, by petition for review of the SEC order, challenges the permanent bar order and the civil penalty; he does not challenge the findings that he excessively traded the accounts. The essence of his argument is that the SEC was wrong in finding he had the degree of scienter required for such a sanction: while his investment strategy may have been wrong, he had a good faith belief in it, he meant no harm, and he is remorseful. From this he argues that a permanent bar from the industry where he has supported himself and his family for fifteen years is arbitrary and capricious, and so should be reversed. He also urges that this court adopt a rule that when the Commission imposes a permanent bar, the most drastic sanction available, it must show that a less drastic remedy would not suffice to protect the public.

We decline that invitation and affirm the Commission order.

I.

There is very little dispute about the underlying facts, which we take from the record before the Commission. The parties disagree, however, as to the conclusions that may be drawn from those facts.

The five customers in question—Eddie Figueroa, Jorge Donato, Jose Acevedo, Hector Torres Nadal, and Herminio R. Cintron—opened their accounts with Rizek in 1990 and 1991. Only Donato and Cintron had some prior experience investing in securities. Acevedo and Torres had purchased CDs or similar investment products, while Figueroa had previously kept his money in a savings account.

Four of the customers' new account forms listed "speculation" last among possible investment objectives, while Rizek's record of Torres's account does not mention speculation at all. Donato told Rizek that he was primarily interested in long-term bonds and the "safety of [his] investment." Acevedo testified that he was looking for a long-term investment; he was not willing to speculate or risk any of his principal. Cintron was planning for his retirement and his children's education; he testified that he was looking for "something that was safe"; Torres was also saving for retirement and described himself as "very cautious" and interested in "something that was protected and secure." Figueroa testified that he was willing to take "any type of risk," but that Rizek had counseled him that "given the small amount of money that [he] had, the most convenient thing was to put most of the savings into some safe investments and devote a small amount to moderate type of risk." ***

In early 1993, Rizek recommended a strategy of short-term trading of zero-coupon bonds to certain of his customers, including the five whose accounts are at issue here. Zero-coupon bonds are U.S. government instruments that accumulate interest until maturity, rather than paying interest periodically. The value of a zero-coupon bond is very sensitive to changes in interest rates. Rizek recommended that his customers purchase the bonds on margin, which significantly increased the face value amounts of the trades, thus magnifying the potential gains and losses. Purchasing on margin meant that the customers had to make monthly margin interest payments to PaineWebber; it also placed them at risk of being forced to sell at a loss to meet a margin call.

The SEC Division of Enforcement's expert witness testified that there was no economic logic to Rizek's trading strategy of swapping zero-coupon bonds, because bond prices move in parallel with each other. The expert stated that only a "very sophisticated, experienced investor" could have understood Rizek's strategy and its risks. On the other hand, Rizek's expert witness testified that trading zero-coupon bonds was an "accepted trading strategy," but conceded that Rizek's customers would have had to be able to tolerate "aggressive risk" for the strategy to have been appropriate for them.

Figueroa, Torres, and Cintron testified that they always followed Rizek's investment recommendations, while Donato said that he followed them "ninety-nine percent" of the time. Acevedo testified that he could not remember refusing any of Rizek's recommendations during the relevant period.

During the fifteen-month period from January 1993 to March 1994, the five accounts had average monthly balances of approximately $50,000; $85,000; $86,000; $165,000; and $312,000. During this time, Rizek carried out approximately $24 million in transactions on the accounts, generating tens of thousands of dollars in commissions and margin interest fees. For example, Rizek effected $1.6 million in transactions on the account with the $50,000 average balance, incurring average annual commissions of about $16,000 and interest fees of over $5,000. On the largest account, Rizek carried out $9.3 million in transactions, which generated average annual commissions of more than $82,000 and interest fees of over $30,000. All told, Rizek's strategy led to losses of approximately $195,000 on the five accounts, which had average monthly balances totaling about $700,000.

II.

A sanctions order of the Commission must be upheld unless the order is a "gross abuse of discretion." *A.J. White & Co. v. SEC*, 556 F.2d 619, 624 (1st Cir. 1977).

Congress has charged the Commission with protecting the investing public. See *Pierce v. SEC*, 239 F.2d 160, 163 (9th Cir. 1956) ("The Commission is given the duty to protect the public. What will protect the public must involve, of necessity, an exercise of discretionary determination."). And so the question of the appropriate remedy is "peculiarly a matter for administrative competence." *American Power & Light Co. v. SEC*, 329 U.S. 90 (1946). As a result, the Commission's sanctions must be affirmed unless "unwarranted in law or ... without justification in fact." *American Power & Light,* 329 U.S. at 112-13.

Rizek contends that his conduct was at most negligent and naive. He says that the violations involved only five of his 400 customers; that his strategy relied on predictions from Paine Webber's chief economist; and that he stopped investing in zero-coupon bonds when his customers began to lose money. He also points to the fact that he has given assurances against future violations. Rizek claims that the bar is improperly punitive in nature and not meant to protect the investing public.

Rizek argues that this court should follow *Steadman v. SEC,* 603 F.2d 1126 (5th Cir. 1979), aff'd on other grounds, 450 U.S. 91 (1981). Rizek claims *Steadman* held that a court should not affirm a permanent bar, the most drastic sanction available, unless the SEC has shown that no lesser remedy will suffice to protect the public interest.

We think Rizek's argument confuses two concepts. We understand *Steadman* to articulate no more than the well-established rule that agencies must sufficiently articulate the grounds of their decisions so that appellate courts are able to perform their function of judicial review meaningfully. The Supreme Court made this point about the need for adequate SEC findings in *SEC v. Chenery Corp.,* 318 U.S. 80, 94 (1943) ("[T]he orderly functioning of the process of review requires that the grounds upon which the administrative agency acted be clearly disclosed and adequately sustained."). This court has made the point in various contexts involving judicial review of administrative actions, and at times has remanded to the agency when it has not provided such an explanation.

To say that the Commission must adequately set forth its grounds is far different from saying that the agency's discretion as to remedy is curtailed by judge-made rules, such as a rule that a permanent bar may be imposed only if the agency has explained to the satisfaction of a court why no lesser remedy will do. *** Section 15(b)(6)(A) of the Securities Exchange Act authorizes the Commission to issue a permanent bar if it finds that such a bar "is in the public interest." Considerable deference should be given the Commission's ultimate judgment about what will best protect the public.

We also note that the term "permanent bar" is more than a bit of a misnomer. It does not literally mean that the sanctioned person may never reenter the securities industry. In fact, there are two routes back in. First, Rizek may later apply to the SEC for consent to associate with an entity that is not a member of a self-regulatory organization such as the National Association of Securities Dealers (NASD). See SEC Rule of Practice 193, 17 C.F.R. § 201.193(a). Second, Rizek may find a NASD member firm willing to employ him, and that firm may apply to NASD to have Rizek become associated with it. See By-Laws of The National Association of Securities Dealers, Inc., art. III, § 3(d). NASD's approval of any such application is subject to whatever further action the Commission may take. See id., art. III, § 3(f). This is a remarkably porous definition of a permanent bar.

The Commission said it was imposing a permanent bar on Rizek because of the egregiousness of his violation; because there was little basis to credit his claim of remorse (he was remorseful about the losses, but not about using the strategy which caused the losses); and because Rizek, who was at the time president of his own investment company, posed a substantial threat to public investors.

The activity was egregious. These five clients were unsophisticated in the world of investing and trusted Rizek to handle their savings conservatively. In some instances these were their life savings, their funds for retirement, or their funds for educating their children. On average balances in the five accounts totaling $700,000, Rizek engaged in over $24 million in transactions over a ten month period. The transaction costs equaled roughly 40% of the account balances; one customer lost about 50% of his account. While his customers lost $195,000, Rizek received about $125,000 in commissions.

There is no doubt that Rizek churned the accounts. Churning is commonly said to have three elements: (1) control of the customer's account by the broker, either explicit or de facto; (2) excessive trading in light of the customer's investment objectives; and (3) scienter—the required state of mind for liability under Section 10(b) and Rule 10b-5. See *Tiernan v. Blyth, Eastman, Dillon & Co.,* 719 F.2d 1, 2 (1st Cir. 1983). Rizek focuses on the third element. ***

Rizek argues that while the Commission may have been entitled to find that he had the degree of scienter needed to establish a churning violation, a greater degree of scienter is needed to justify the sanctions imposed. There is no statutory basis to distinguish between the scienter needed to establish a violation for which a sanction may be imposed administratively and the scienter needed to warrant a particular penalty. At most, Rizek's argument goes to the Commission's exercise of its discretion. And the Commission found that even if Rizek had a good faith belief in the efficacy of his strategy, "he had no justification for recommending it to unsophisticated customers who were incapable of making an independent judgment, when he knew that the extremely high risk was directly contrary to the customers' conservative investment objectives." That finding is adequate support for the remedy.

In any event, this case involves churning plus. The Commission also found that "Rizek was well aware that he had acted improperly in recommending his strategy, and tried to conceal his conduct from his firm." Id. Rizek both misled his firm's management and attempted to mislead the Commission. Paine Webber management had become concerned about Rizek's trading strategy and questioned him about it at four meetings. Rizek responded by giving the firm a list of clients whose strategies, he said, had changed so that "speculation" was now a high ranking objective. In addition, at the hearings before the ALJ, Rizek testified that he had called all of the customers in November 1993 and all of them agreed to the reordering of their investment objectives. But the facts were to the contrary: none of the customers testified that Rizek had sought or received their permission to change their investment objectives. There was ample evidence to support the Commission's conclusion that Rizek acted willfully and recklessly.

Under these circumstances, there is simply no viable argument that the permanent bar was an abuse of discretion, or that it was punitive and not meant to protect the investing public.

III.

Rizek also challenges the imposition of a $100,000 civil penalty. Under Section 21B(b) of the Act, there is a three-tiered system for assessing civil penalties, ranging from a first tier penalty of $5,000 to a third tier penalty of $100,000. See [Exchange Act Section 21B(b)]. The requirements for imposition of the third tier penalty are set forth at [Exchange Act Section 21B(b)(3)]:

> (3) Third tier
>
> Notwithstanding paragraphs (1) and (2), the maximum amount of penalty for each such act or omission shall be $100,000 for a natural person or $500,000 for any other person if—
>
> > (A) the act or omission described in subsection (a) of this section involved fraud, deceit, manipulation, or deliberate or reckless disregard of a regulatory requirement; and
> >
> > (B) such act or omission directly or indirectly resulted in substantial losses or created a significant risk of substantial losses to other persons or resulted in substantial pecuniary gain to the person who committed the act or omission.

In turn, the statute sets forth six factors which the Commission may consider in assessing monetary penalties:

> (1) whether the act or omission for which such penalty is assessed involved fraud, deceit, manipulation, or deliberate or reckless disregard of a regulatory requirement;
>
> (2) the harm to other persons resulting either directly or indirectly from such act or omission;
>
> (3) the extent to which any person was unjustly enriched, taking into account any restitution made to persons injured by such behavior;
>
> (4) whether such person previously has been found by the Commission, another appropriate regulatory agency, or a self-regulatory organization to have violated the Federal securities laws, State securities laws, or the rules of a self-regulatory organization, has been enjoined by a court of competent jurisdiction from violations of such laws or rules, or has been convicted by a court of competent jurisdiction of violations of such laws or of any felony or misdemeanor described in [Exchange Act Section 15(b)(4)(b)];
>
> (5) the need to deter such person and other persons from committing such acts or omissions; and
>
> (6) such other matters as justice may require.

[Exchange Act Section 21B(c)] To the extent Rizek argues he is unable to pay the penalty, we note that he did not raise the argument before the Commission, and so it is waived. See [Exchange Act Section 25(c)(1)]. For the same reasons there was no abuse of discretion in the permanent bar order, there was no abuse of discretion in the imposition of the civil penalty.

We affirm the Commission's order.

IN THE MATTER OF JEFFRY L. FELDMAN
Administrative Proceeding File No. 3-8063
Securities Act Release No. 7014 / September 20, 1993

FINDINGS AND CEASE AND DESIST ORDER PURSUANT TO SECTION 8A OF THE SECURITIES ACT OF 1933

I.

By Order dated May 27, 1993, the Commission instituted administrative proceedings pursuant to Section 8A of the Securities Act of 1933 ("Securities Act") against Jeffry Feldman ("Feldman") to determine whether Feldman caused violations of Sections 5(a) and 5(c) of the Securities Act. Feldman has submitted an Offer of Settlement which the Commission has determined to accept. Solely for the purpose of these proceedings and any other proceeding brought by or on behalf of the Commission or to which the Commission is a party, Feldman consents to the issuance of these Findings and Cease and Desist Order Pursuant to Section 8A of the Securities Act of 1933 ("Order"), without admitting or denying the matters set forth herein.

II.

FACTS

Based on the foregoing, the Commission finds the following:

A. Respondent

Feldman, age 46, is admitted to practice law in the State of New York. Feldman is a partner with the New York law firm of Dunn & Zuckerman. Feldman's practice consists of commercial law, bankruptcy, commercial litigation and banking law.

B. The Pakistani Banks Proposed to Offer and Sell Foreign Exchange Bearer Certificates

In 1985, the Islamic Republic of Pakistan ("Pakistan") formulated a plan to offer rupee denominated foreign exchange bearer certificates ("FEBC"), issued and guaranteed by Pakistan, in foreign countries, including the United States. The offer and sale of FEBCs was administered by the State Bank of Pakistan, Pakistan's central bank, and carried out in the United States through the United States branches of nationalized Pakistani commercial banks.

In June 1985, the Karachi headquarters offices of three Pakistani commercial banks, National Bank of Pakistan, Habib Bank, Ltd., and United Bank, Ltd., informed their New York offices about the proposal to offer and sell FEBCs in the United States. The Karachi offices requested that the New York offices determine what legal or regulatory restrictions applied to the sale and purchase of the FEBCs, including restrictions imposed by "exchange or securities authorities," and make arrangements to comply with any applicable regulations.

C. Feldman Was Asked to Determine the Applicability of the Federal Securities Laws to the FEBCs

Officials of the New York offices of the Pakistani banks sought to fulfill the directives of their Karachi offices by seeking the advice of counsel and through independent inquiries to state and federal regulatory agencies. In June or July of 1985, officials of each of the New York offices of the Pakistani banks began to communicate with Feldman, whose law firm had a long-established relationship with the Pakistani banks.

The New York offices of the Pakistani banks requested that Feldman identify all regulatory barriers to the offer and sale of the FEBCs in New York and take the steps necessary to comply with regulatory requirements. To assist Feldman in evaluating the regulatory obstacles, the Pakistani banks provided Feldman with numerous documents describing the characteristics of the FEBC program.

Feldman understood that the Pakistani banks wanted him to determine the applicability of the federal securities laws to the offer and sale of the FEBCs. Neither Feldman nor any other member of Dunn & Zuckerman had any background in the practice of law relating to the offer and sale of securities.

In addition to engaging the services of Feldman, in July 1985, an officer of the National Bank of Pakistan (the "Bank Officer") independently contacted the Commission both by telephone and by letter concerning the proposed program. In a letter dated July 8, 1985, the Bank Officer described the FEBC program and asked the Commission to confirm that it would have "no objection to the proposed sale of the Bonds."

On July 19, 1985, a staff member of the Division of Corporation Finance responded orally to that inquiry. The staff member informed the Bank Officer that registration on Schedule B was required. On July 23, 1985, Feldman received a handwritten note from the Bank Officer informing him about the staff member's conclusion regarding registration on Schedule B and stating that "[w]e have to know precisely which forms need to be filed with the SEC." Despite these circumstances, Feldman took no steps to effect registration of the FEBCs with the Commission.

D. Feldman Told the Pakistani Banks That the Offer and Sale of the FEBCs Did Not Need to Be Registered

The only measure taken by Feldman on behalf of the Pakistani banks to comply with regulatory requirements was submitting applications to the New York Superintendent of Banks seeking permission for the New York branches to exercise fiduciary powers to sell and encash the FEBCs. These applications were submitted for each of the three banks between September 3, 1985, and January 21, 1986.

National Bank of Pakistan's application to the New York Superintendent of Banks was approved in November 1985, Habib Bank's in January 1986, and United Bank's in February 1986. Once the first application for the exercise of fiduciary powers was approved by the New York Superintendent of Banks, Feldman began telling the Pakistani banks that they had no obligation to take the additional step of registering the offer of the FEBCs with the Commission. In December 1985, Feldman wrote to the legal department of Habib Bank in

Karachi stating that the activities of selling and purchasing FEBCs "do not involve what can be considered securities" and recommending that "no further action be taken with those agencies [SEC and New York State securities authorities] for the time being." In January 1986, Feldman again told the Karachi office that the offer and sale of the FEBCs did not require Commission "authorization." Feldman made identical statements to the other two Pakistani banks. Feldman had no basis for his statement that the FEBCs were not securities and thus exempt from the registration requirements of Section 5.

E. Feldman Took No Notice of Further Indications That The Offer and Sale of the FEBCs Must Be Registered

In March 1986, after the New York offices of the Pakistani commercial banks had begun selling the FEBCs, the Washington, D.C. branch of the National Bank of Pakistan submitted an application to the Office of the Comptroller of the Currency ("OCC") to obtain permission to sell the FEBCs in Washington, D.C. The OCC responded with a letter warning that "[t]he Certificates may be securities subject to registration under the securities laws" and that "[i]f the Certificates are securities, the branch may be subject to registration with the Securities and Exchange Commission as a broker-dealer." The OCC sent a copy of this letter to the New York Superintendent of Banks.

In a letter to Feldman dated June 26, 1986, the Bank Officer enclosed a copy of the OCC letter and requested that Feldman draft responses both to the OCC and the New York Superintendent of Banks. As requested, Feldman wrote to the New York State Superintendent of Banks, in a letter dated July 1, 1986, arguing that the bearer certificates were analogous to certificates of deposit that were not required to be registered under the federal securities laws. Feldman's letter also stated that "the National Bank of Pakistan did, in fact, request the Securities & Exchange Commission to comment upon the prospective activities of the Bank in connection with the sale/encashment of Foreign Exchange Bearer Certificates" and that "[t]o date, no written response has been received from the Securities & Exchange Commission." Feldman did not inform the Superintendent of Banks that, as he knew, the National Bank of Pakistan had received an oral response in July 1985 in which Commission staff stated that registration on Schedule B was required.

Feldman did not respond to the OCC. Instead, on August 12, 1986, Feldman wrote another officer of the New York office of the National Bank of Pakistan, warning that registration of the FEBCs with the Commission would be "cumbersome, time consuming and expensive," and recommending that the National Bank of Pakistan "make no further attempt to obtain authorization to transact the sale of Foreign Exchange Bearer Certificates by the Washington, D.C. Branch." Feldman warned that, in light of the OCC letter, which indicated that the offering of FEBCs may need to be registered with the Commission, pursuing the application would only "open a 'can of worms' which may adversely affect the ongoing activities of the State Bank of Pakistan in continuing sale of Foreign Exchange Bearer Certificates [in New York] pursuant to State Banking Law authorization."

As a consequence of Feldman's actions, more than $8 million of FEBCs were offered and sold in the United States without registration from 1986 through March 1992. Sales of the FEBCs were halted in April 1992.

III.

OPINION

Feldman aided and abetted the Pakistani banks' violations of Section 5 of the Securities Act. See, e.g., *Metge v. Baehler*, 762 F.2d 621, 624 (8th Cir.1985); *Woodward v. Metro Bank of Dallas*, 522 F.2d 84, 94-95 (5th Cir.1975) (discussing standards for aiding and abetting liability). The first element of aiding and abetting liability—a primary violation of Section 5—is clearly established. The FEBCs were securities the offer and sale of which was required to be registered with the Commission. Section 5(a) of the Securities Act prohibits any person, directly or indirectly, from selling a security in interstate commerce unless a registration statement is in effect as to such security. Section 5(c) of the Securities Act prohibits the offer or sales of a security unless a registration statement has been filed as to the security. A security is defined to include a "note" or "evidence of indebtedness" or "bond." [Securities Act Section 2(1)]. On their face, the FEBCs come within the definition of a security. Each FEBC represented a promise by the issuing entity, Pakistan, to repay the principal amount, plus accrued interest at a specified rate, within a specified time period or on demand.

The offer and sale of FEBCs did not fall within any exemption from the registration requirements of Section 5. For example, the FEBCs were not exempt as government-issued securities. Section 3(a)(2) of the Securities Act exempts from registration only securities issued or guaranteed by the United States government or by state or local governments. Nor were the FEBCs exempt pursuant to Sections 3(a)(2) or 3(a)(5) of the Securities Act as securities or certificates of deposit issued or guaranteed by a financial institution because the FEBCs were issued by the government of Pakistan and not by a financial institution. Furthermore, the FEBCs were not certificates of deposit because the purchase of a FEBC did not create a deposit in the Pakistani commercial banks on behalf of the purchaser. Rather, the Pakistani commercial banks were to remit the proceeds to the government of Pakistan and receive a one percent sales commission from the State Bank of Pakistan for FEBCs sold at each U.S. branch.

Feldman substantially assisted the Pakistani banks' violations of Section 5 of the Securities Act. The Pakistani banks relied on Feldman to inform them of what obligations, if any, they had under the federal securities laws with respect to their offer and sale of FEBCs. Feldman substantially contributed to the Pakistani banks' violations of Section 5 because the banks did not register the FEBC offering after Feldman told them repeatedly that they did not have to do so. Feldman persisted in his erroneous position even though he had been put on notice by the Commission staff of the need for registration. Feldman knew when he told the Pakistani banks that the offering and sale of FEBCs did not need to be registered that the Commission staff had expressed a contrary view to the Bank Officer. Feldman did not do anything to resolve this discrepancy.

Soon after the sales of FEBCs commenced, Feldman was confronted with additional indications that his conclusion was wrong when the OCC informed one of the Pakistani banks that the FEBCs may be securities subject to registration with the Commission. Instead of addressing the OCC's concerns,

Feldman told the Pakistani bank simply to abandon its plans to sell the FEBCs at the Washington, D.C. branch, since any further contact with the OCC could "open a 'can of worms' that could "adversely affect" the banks' ongoing unregistered sales of FEBCs. Although he knew that the Bank Officer had spoken with a member of the Commission staff, who had indicated that registration was required on Schedule B in connection with the offering, he informed the New York banking authorities who learned of the OCC's concerns only that "to date, no written response" had been received from the Commission concerning the need to register the offering of FEBCs.

IV.

FINDINGS

Based on the above, the Commission finds that Feldman aided and abetted and caused violations of Sections 5(a) and 5(c) of the Securities Act.

V.

ORDER

Accordingly, it is hereby ordered, pursuant to Section 8A of the Securities Act, that Feldman permanently cease and desist from committing or causing any violation of, and committing or causing any future violation of, Section 5 of the Securities Act.

NOTES AND QUESTIONS

*1. **Permanent Cease-and-Desist Orders.*** Consider how the addition of administrative cease-and-desist authority has affected the SEC's enforcement program. Prior to 1990, when the Commission believed that enforcement action was warranted against a non-regulated person or entity, what remedies were available? What policy goals were served by including cease-and-desist authority in the Remedies Act? Note that the Remedies Act also empowers the Commission to seek an accounting and disgorgement in any permanent cease-and-desist proceeding. See, e.g., Exchange Act Section 21C(e).

Note the text of Exchange Act Section 21C(a), which sets out the Commission's authority for issuing cease-and-desist orders in connection with violations of the Exchange Act or rules and regulations thereunder. The authority that this Section gives the Commission is wide-ranging:

> In addition to ordering a person to cease and desist from committing or causing violations or future violations, the Commission is also authorized to order a person to comply with a provision or to take steps to effect compliance. The Commission may also prescribe specific terms and conditions that a person must observe in order to effect compliance and may specify the time frame within which compliance must be effected. Thus, the Commission is authorized to require a person to take action to correct an existing condition resulting from a violation and to specify the steps to be taken. Most importantly, the Commission may issue orders requiring a person to comply in the future with, or requiring the person to take steps to effect future compliance with, a provision, rule or regulation with respect to any security, any issuer or any other person. The Commission may order such relief permanently, or for such period as it determines appropriate. For example, the Commission may direct a corporate respondent to add directors and to form specific committees to monitor certain corporate activities, or to resolicit proxies obtained by deficient

> proxy materials. Similarly, the Commission could order a brokerage firm to retain counsel to conduct a review of the firm's compliance with applicable provisions.

Ralph C. Ferrara et al., Hardball! The SEC's New Arsenal of Enforcement Weapons, 47 Bus. Law. 33, 58-59 (1991). Is the statutory text of Section 21C(a) broad enough to enable the SEC and the courts to circumvent the statutory requirements of other administrative or judicial remedies? Ferrara points out, for example, that if the Commission were to use its authority to direct a respondent corporation to terminate an officer in order to effect compliance with an Exchange Act reporting provision, "the Commission would undermine the Congressional determination to vest in the district courts the power to enter orders suspending or barring persons from serving as an officer or director based only upon a violation of the antifraud provisions or proof of *** unfitness." See id. at 59. What checks operate on the SEC's ability to use its cease and desist authority in this way?

2. Permanent Cease-and-Desist Orders—The Operative Standard. Must the Commission find a likelihood of future violations in order to impose a permanent cease-and-desist order? In order words, should a cease-and-desist order be analogized to a court-ordered injunction, in that both remedies are forward-looking?

In an enforcement action against the accounting firm of KPMG, the Commission decided that, although there must be "some" risk of future violations, the amount of risk "need not be very great," since "[a]bsent evidence to the contrary, a finding of violation raises a sufficient risk of future violation." *In the Matter of KPMG Peat Marwick LLP,* Exchange Act Release No. 43862, 2001 WL 47245 at *24 (Jan. 19, 2001).

The Commission then went on to hold that it would consider a laundry list of "traditional factors" in deciding whether a cease-and-desist order is an appropriate sanction:

> Along with the risk of future violations, we will continue to consider our traditional factors in determining whether a cease-and-desist order is an appropriate sanction based on the entire record. Many of these factors are akin to those used by courts in determining whether injunctions are appropriate, including the seriousness of the violation, the isolated or recurrent nature of the violation, the respondent's state of mind, the sincerity of the respondent's assurances against future violations, the respondent's recognition of the wrongful nature of his or her conduct, and the respondent's opportunity to commit future violations. In addition, we consider whether the violation is recent, the degree of harm to investors or the marketplace resulting from the violation, and the remedial function to be served by the cease-and-desist order in the context of any other sanctions being sought in the same proceedings. This inquiry is a flexible one and no one factor is dispositive. This inquiry is undertaken not to determine whether there is a "reasonable likelihood"of future violations but to guide our discretion.

Id. at * 26. Moreover, in a footnote, the Commission observed:

> "In some instances, we may also consider the function that a cease-and-desist order serves in alerting the public that a respondent has violated the securities laws."

Id. at n.148.

On review, the D.C. Circuit questioned whether "a single violation" would suffice to show that there was "some" risk of a future violation, but the court ultimately concluded that a remand was unnecessary because the Commission's findings of fact had included multiple violations. *KPMG, LLP v. SEC*, 289 F.3d 109 (D.C. Cir. 2002). For a decision vacating a cease-and-desist order on the grounds that the Commission failed to adhere to its own standards, see *WHX Corp. v. SEC*, 362 F.3d 854, 861 (D.C. Cir. 2004) (finding that defendant WHX "committed (at most) a single, isolated violation" of a tender offer rule, and that the Commission "has offered no reason to doubt WHX's assurances that it will not violate the rule in the future").

3. Causing vs. Aiding and Abetting Liability. Contrast Securities Act Section 8A's provision (or Exchange Act Section 21C(a)'s provision) for cease-and-desist orders against persons who "cause" another person's securities law violation with the SEC's statutory authority to pursue "aiders and abetters" in federal district court. What if Feldman had "recklessly" rendered substantial assistance to the Pakistani banks in their violation of the Securities Act's registration provisions? Could the SEC have sought judicial relief for "aiding and abetting?" Prior to the Dodd-Frank Act, the SEC's authority to pursue aiders and abetters who acted "recklessly" (as opposed to "knowingly") was unclear and, in any event, only the Exchange Act contained an explicit provision authorizing the SEC to pursue federal court actions for aiding and abetting another person's securities law violation. But in Dodd-Frank, Congress amended Section 20(e) of the Exchange Act to impose aiding and abetting liability on persons who "knowingly or recklessly" provide substantial assistance to those who violate the Exchange Act. Congress also added new, similarly worded aiding and abetting provisions to Section 15(b) of the Securities Act, Section 48(b) of the Investment Company Act, and Section 209(f) of the Investment Advisers Act.

What is the mental state necessary to trigger liability under Exchange Act Section 21C(a) and Securities Act Section 8A for "causing" another person's securities law violation? In the *KPMG* order discussed above, the Commission made a number of factual findings, including that KPMG's lack of independence as an outside auditor had caused its client to violate Section 13(a) of the Exchange Act and Rule 13a-1 thereunder, which require every issuer with securities registered pursuant to Section 12 to include financial statements certified by independent auditors in their annual reports. The Commission further found that KPMG had acted negligently in determining that it was independent from its client and, among other sanctions, it issued a cease-and-desist order in connection with KPMG's having "caused" its client's primary violations. See *In the Matter of KPMG Peat Marwick LLP,* supra.

In its petition for review to the D.C. Circuit, KPMG challenged, among numerous other issues, the propriety of a negligence standard under Section 21C, particularly for accountants who are also subject to professional discipline under SEC Rule 102(e). In denying this petition, the D.C. Circuit emphasized that "the Commission was virtually compelled by Congress' choice of language in enacting Section 21C to interpret the phrase 'an act or omission the person *knew or should have known* would contribute to such violation' as setting a negligence standard." *KPMG, LLP v. SEC*, 289 F.3d 109, 120 (D.C. Cir. 2002) (emphasis in original).

As a matter of policy, should the Commission make a practice of initiating cease-and-desist proceedings against attorneys and accountants for conduct that may constitute a single act of negligence? What would be some of the costs and benefits of such a practice? Note that we will revisit this issue in our discussion of Rule 102(e) in Chapter 10.

*4. **Ex Parte Orders.*** The Remedies Act also empowers the SEC to issue temporary cease-and-desist orders against certain regulated entities and associated persons, and such orders may be issued ex parte if the Commission "determines that notice and hearing prior to entry would be impractical or contrary to the public interest." Exchange Act Section 21C(c)(1); Securities Act Section 8A(c)(1). What types of facts would justify the imposition of such temporary relief? As originally proposed to Congress by the Commission, the SEC's authority to issue temporary cease-and-desist orders would have extended to any person. Was Congress's decision to limit this authority to regulated entities and persons a wise one? Note that in SOX, Congress amended Section 21C(c)(2) to include a "registered public accounting firm" among the entities which may be subject to ex parte orders.

*5. **Civil Monetary Penalties in Administrative Proceedings.*** The *Rizek* court considered the SEC's authority under Exchange Act Section 21B to assess a monetary penalty in a broker-dealer proceeding brought pursuant to Exchange Act Sections 15(b)(4) and (6). Can you identify some of the differences between the administrative remedy in Section 21B and the judicial remedy in Section 21(d)(3)?

In the wake of Enron, WorldCom, and other massive financial frauds in 2001-02, the SEC had asked Congress for the power to impose civil penalties on publicly traded companies and their officers and directors in administrative proceedings. See Chairperson Harvey Pitt, Written Testimony Concerning Accounting and Investor Protection Issues Raised by Enron and Other Public Companies, Before the Sen. Comm. on Banking, Housing and Urban Affairs, March 21, 2002. Although Congress declined to authorize this additional administrative enforcement remedy in the SOX, it eventually expanded the SEC's authority even further in the Dodd-Frank Act, when it amended Exchange Act Section 21B (and the other securities statutes) to provide for civil monetary penalties against any person for any violation of the federal securities laws (or for causing such a violation). Why might Congress have withheld this authority for such a long period? What may account for the change? Consider the SEC enforcement action statistics for 2006-10 which are set out at the beginning of this Chapter. In upcoming years, would you expect the relative breakdown between judicial actions and administrative proceedings to remain the same? Why or why not?

*6. **Collateral Bar Orders.*** The *Rizek* court also reviewed the SEC's decision to permanently bar Rizek from "association with any broker, dealer, member of a national securities exchange, or member of a registered securities association." In re Al Rizek, Exchange Act Release No. 41725 (Aug. 11, 1999). Note how the D.C. Circuit inaccurately characterized this sanction as a permanent bar "from the securities industry." This overly broad characterization has significance because, until relatively recently, the SEC's ability to impose so-called "collateral bars" (or industry-wide bars) was a hotly contested issue. See *Teicher v. SEC*, 177 F.3d 1016, 1020 (D.C. Cir. 1999) (finding that the respondent's bar from the securities industry had exceeded the SEC's authority under Section 15(b)(6) of the Exchange Act because Congress's "repeated use of a nexus requirement focus[ing] on a single branch of the industry *** underscore[s] a congressional determination to create separate sets of sanctions, each triggered by an individual's satisfying the industry-specific nexus"). In the Dodd-Frank Act, however, Congress amended the federal securities laws to provide that the SEC may collaterally bar persons "from being associated with a broker, dealer, investment adviser, municipal securities dealer, municipal advisor, transfer agent, or nationally recognized statistical rating organization."

7. ***Administrative Proceedings Under Exchange Act Section 15(c)(4).*** Section 15(c)(4) of the Exchange Act provides an administrative remedy where the Commission finds a failure to comply with Sections 12, 13, 14, or 15(d) of the Exchange Act or any rule or regulation thereunder. A remedy is also available against any person "who was a cause of the failure [of another person] to comply due to an act or omission the person knew or should have known would contribute to the failure to comply." Specifically, after notice and an opportunity for a hearing, the Commission may issue an order requiring the respondent "to comply, or to take steps to effect compliance with [the relevant] provision *** upon such terms and conditions and within such time as the Commission may specify."

In *In re George C. Kern, Jr.*, Exchange Act Release No. 29356, 49 SEC Docket 422 (June 21, 1991), the Commission upheld an administrative law judge's finding that George Kern, a highly respected securities lawyer and partner at the New York firm of Sullivan & Cromwell, had caused his corporate client's violation of Exchange Act Section 14(d)(4) and Rule 14d-9(b), which require the target of a tender offer to promptly disclose to the SEC any material changes in the information provided in the target's initial SEC filing. Yet the Commission refused to issue the relief requested by the Enforcement Division, which was an order that would require Kern to comply, and to take steps to see that his future clients comply, with Section 14(d). The staff's suggested order was phrased broadly in terms of future compliance because Kern's client in the tender offer dispute was no longer in business. In rejecting the Division's recommendation, the Commission held that it lacked the power under Section 15(c)(4) to issue such an order of "general compliance." Instead, it pointed to legislative history indicating that the provision was to be used "primarily as a means of compelling issuers to correct false or inaccurate periodic reports."

The tender offer events underlying the violations by Kern's corporate client occurred in 1986. Had these violations occurred a decade later, what enforcement remedies wold have been available to the SEC? Would it surprise you to learn that the SEC now invokes Section 15(c)(4) only on rare occasions?

---

3. *Collateral Consequences of SEC Sanctions*

SEC sanctions must be evaluated with reference to their possible collateral consequences. The following excerpt draws a useful comparison between court-ordered injunctions and administrative cease-and-desist orders.

SEC CEASE-AND-DESIST ORDERS

by Andrew M. Smith

51 Admin. L. Rev. 1197, 1217-1225 (1999)

******Direct Effects: Enforcement of Order if Violated*

The direct effect of an injunction is that it compels the person charged by it to obey the law, or be found in contempt of the court issuing the injunction. Being found in contempt of court might carry with it fines, imprisonment, or other civil and criminal penalties.

A cease-and-desist order is a command from the SEC to refrain from violating the securities laws. If violated, the SEC can seek an injunction requiring compliance with the order. In addition, the SEC can bring an action in a federal court for a civil money penalty.

In the injunctive proceeding, the SEC would be required to show the violation of its order and a reasonable likelihood that its order will be violated in the future. The SEC would not be required to prove the violation that was the subject of the underlying cease-and-desist order. Contempt proceedings could be initiated if this subsequent injunction were violated. ***

Because a violation of an injunction subjects one immediately to contempt proceedings, the direct consequences of an injunction generally are more serious than those of a cease-and-desist order. However, the SEC's option to seek money penalties for violations of cease-and-desist orders, might work to make such violations more serious under certain circumstances.

******Additional SEC Disciplinary Action*

Another collateral effect of an injunction is that it might subject one to further SEC disciplinary action, including a bar from the securities industry or from practicing before the SEC. Exchange Act sections 15(b)(4)(C) and 15(b)(6)(A) authorize the SEC to censure, suspend, or bar broker-dealers and associated persons who have been enjoined from committing securities violations. Investment Advisers Act sections 203(e) and 203(f) authorize the SEC to censure, suspend, or bar investment advisers and associated persons who have been enjoined from committing securities violations. While there is no analogous provision authorizing the SEC to place limitations on persons who have been sanctioned administratively, these laws do allow the SEC to censure, suspend, or bar broker-dealers, investment advisers, and associated persons who have "willfully violated" the securities laws or who have "willfully aided, abetted, counseled, commanded, induced, or procured" such a violation. There is no authority on whether these provisions would allow the SEC to bootstrap a suspension, censure, or bar from a cease-and-desist order imposed in an administrative hearing. Presumably, however, if the public interest warranted, the SEC could find a "willful" violation and censure, suspend, or bar a person under Exchange Act section 15(b) or Investment Advisers Act section 203 in the initial proceeding, in addition to imposing upon him a cease-and-desist order.

i. Disciplinary Action Against Professionals

Commission Rule of Practice 102(e) provides that attorneys, accountants, engineers, and other professionals who are "found by the [SEC] ... to have engaged in unethical or improper professional conduct; or [t]o have willfully violated, or willfully aided and abetted" securities violations may be suspended or barred by the SEC from appearing or practicing before it. The SEC also may temporarily suspend any person permanently enjoined from committing securities violations or found by the SEC in an administrative proceeding to have violated the securities law or to have aided and abetted violations of the securities laws. In other words, for the purposes of Rule 102(e), cease-and-desist orders and injunctions appear to be equally serious.

ii. Investment Company Act Restrictions

A person who is enjoined from violating the securities laws automatically becomes ineligible to serve as an employee, officer, director, investment adviser, or depositor of an investment company or as an underwriter of an open- end investment company, unit investment trust, or face-amount certificate company. [See Investment Company Act Section 9(a)] While there is no analogous provision making ineligible persons who have been sanctioned administratively, this law allows the SEC to prohibit persons who have "willfully violated" the securities laws or who have "willfully aided, abetted, counseled, commanded, induced, or procured" such a violation from serving as an employee, officer, director, investment adviser, underwriter, or depositor of an investment company. [Investment Company Act Section 9(b)]

iii. Statutory Disqualification

A person enjoined from securities violations also becomes subject to a "statutory disqualification." [Exchange Act Section 3(a)(39)(F)] Self-regulatory organizations, i.e., the NASD [now FINRA], securities exchanges, and clearing agencies, may deny membership to any person subject to a statutory disqualification. Moreover, they *shall* deny such membership when ordered to do so by the SEC. Persons subject to SEC cease-and-desist orders are not subject automatically to a statutory disqualification, although, like Exchange Act section 15(b)(4) and Investment Company Act section 9(b), persons who have "willfully violated" the securities laws or who have "willfully aided, abetted, counseled, commanded, induced, or procured" such a violation are subject to a statutory disqualification.

****Other Sanctions*

i. Unavailability of Registration Exemptions

An injunction also disqualifies an issuer of securities from taking advantage of certain exemptions from the securities registration process. For instance, Regulation A provides that its exemption shall be denied to any issuer that has been enjoined from engaging in a practice involving the making of a false filing with the SEC, and to any issuer with a director, officer, general partner, promoter, or ten percent shareholder who has been enjoined from committing certain securities violations. Regulation A does not include restrictions on issuers that are subject to SEC cease-and-desist orders or on issuers with a director, officer, general partner, promoter, or ten percent shareholder who is subject to an SEC cease-and-desist order.

ii. Disclosure of Violation

An injunction must be disclosed in many instances, with concomitant damage to one's reputation. For instance, disclosure is required if one has been enjoined from violating the securities laws within the last five years and (1) one is a director or officer of a publicly traded company, or is nominated to become a director or officer of a publicly traded company; (2) one is bidding to acquire a publicly traded company; (3) one becomes a five-percent shareholder of a publicly traded company; or (4) one engages in a going-private transaction. Each of these disclosures also must be made, however, when a person is subject to a cease-and-desist order issued by the SEC. For instance, Regulation S-K requires disclosure whenever a person has been found by the SEC to have violated a federal or state securities or commodities law, and the judgment has not been reversed, suspended, or vacated.

Both an injunction and a cease-and-desist order also must be disclosed on a Form U-4, the form filed by broker-dealers with the National Association of Securities Dealers (NASD) [now FINRA] to register associated persons. Form ADV, for registration with the SEC as an investment adviser, also requires disclosures of both injunctions and cease-and-desist orders.

iii. Nasdaq Delisting

The NASD has broad discretion to delist from Nasdaq the securities of an issuer, where the NASD "deems it necessary to prevent fraudulent and manipulative acts and practices, to promote just and equitable principles of trade, or to protect investors and the public interest." [NASD Sec. Dealers Man. (CCH) Rule 4330(a)(3)] Presumably, the NASD could use this authority to delist or refuse to list the securities of an issuer who has associated with it a person who has been enjoined from violating the securities laws, and, by the same token, an issuer who has associated with it a person who is subject to an SEC cease-and-desist order.

iv. State Disciplinary Action

The laws of many, if not all, states, allow the securities administrator of the state to suspend or revoke the broker, dealer, or investment adviser registration of any person who has been enjoined by a "court of competent jurisdiction" from "engaging in ... any aspect of the securities business." While these same laws also provide that a state securities administrator may suspend or revoke the broker, dealer, or investment adviser registration of any person who 'is the subject of an order entered by [the SEC] denying or revoking' such registration, they generally do not specifically address cease-and-desist orders entered by the SEC. However, there are several notable exceptions to this general rule—at least 17 state codes provide that the state securities administrator may suspend or revoke the registration of a person who is the subject of an SEC cease-and-desist order.

Many state laws also provide that licensing authorities may deny, suspend, or revoke non-securities professional licenses where the licensee has been enjoined from committing securities violations or is subject to an SEC cease-and-desist order. For instance, Arizona law provides that the state real estate commissioner may deny, suspend, or revoke the real estate license of any person who has "violated any federal or state law, regulation or rule that relates to real estate or securities or that involves forgery, theft, extortion, fraud, substantial misrepresentation, [or] dishonest dealings." Under this law, the effect of a securities violation, whether sanctioned by an injunction or by a cease-and-desist order, would be the same. It appears, however, that the effect on a non-securities license of any civil violation of the securities laws would be limited, given that states tend to deny, suspend, or revoke licenses on the basis of factors relevant to the licensee's character and fitness to practice that particular profession. ***

NOTES AND QUESTIONS

1. ***The Power of the Press.*** Although the regulatory consequences of SEC sanctions may often be grave, consider also the impact of an SEC release reporting a settlement or announcing a judicial or administrative decision. In assessing the consequences of SEC settlements, the ABA Task Force specifically noted that:

> Although publicity is not necessarily a legal consequence collateral to the settlement, in many circumstances, publicity can be the most devastating of all collateral consequences and should not be overlooked or treated as insignificant by the Commission or practitioners. Often, information about the settling party that has never before been released becomes public, such as an officer or director's involvement with other United States or foreign entities, his or her personal financial condition, or business or personal relationships. Persons and entities previously eager to do business with the settling party may refuse to do so upon hearing of the settlement or may, while continuing to do business, cause the working relationship to be affected. Lenders may consider the settlement a negative factor in determining whether to provide financing. Even personal relationships may become strained because, although the settling party would not have admitted wrongdoing when entering the settlement, the party would have rejected the opportunity to be pronounced innocent by a factfinder. These significant consequences should not be ignored when examining the legal consequences that also may result from settlement with the Commission.

ABA Committee on Federal Regulation of Securities, Report of the Task Force on SEC Settlements, 47 Bus. Law. 1083, 1149-50 (1992). What constraints do SEC rules impose on a settling party's ability to respond to media inquiries about the reasons for settlement?

2. ***Litigation and Evidentiary Consequences.*** As we shall see in Section D.2.c of this Chapter, the Supreme Court's decision in *Parklane Hosiery Co. v. Shore*, 439 U.S. 322 (1979), imposes significant collateral consequences on those who litigate with the SEC and lose. Indeed, after *Parklane*, such defendants face the risk that principles of collateral estoppel will be invoked in subsequent private litigation to prevent them from re-litigating those issues of fact and law that were necessarily determined in the prior proceeding with the SEC. And even when collateral estoppel is inapplicable, such as where the defendant has settled and has "neither admitted nor denied liability," sanctions imposed by a court or the SEC, as well as any findings relating thereto, may be admissible as evidence in subsequent litigation. For what purposes may a court admit such evidence? What arguments can a defendant make to exclude such evidence?

3. Neither Admitting nor Denying Liability Revisited. Recall from Section B.4 of this Chapter that almost all settlements with the SEC include a provision making clear that the party consents to the settlement without either "admitting or denying" the allegations in the complaint or administrative order. Consider how this practice comports with Exchange Act or Advisers Act "disciplinary" provisions, which permit the SEC to suspend or bar from association with a broker-dealer or investment adviser any person who has been enjoined from committing securities violations. May a person who consents to an injunction deny the facts alleged in the injunctive complaint in a subsequent proceeding to suspend or bar that person from the industry? In 2003, the SEC clarified its view that the answer is no:

> [T]he Advisers Act and Exchange Act draw no distinction between injunctions entered after litigation or by consent. We do not believe that the statutes require the Enforcement Division to prove the allegations of an injunctive complaint in a follow-on administrative proceeding before any disciplinary action can be taken. If the contrary were true, then in the many cases involving willful misconduct, a disciplinary action under [Exchange Act] Section 15(b)(4)(C) based on an injunction would become indistinguishable from one under Section 15(b)(4)(D) based on a willful violation. The injunction would make no difference and have no force in the disciplinary proceeding. We do not believe that Congress, having made an injunction a ground for commencing the proceeding, intended for the parties to conduct the proceeding as if the injunction had never been entered, disregarding the allegations underlying the injunction. ***
>
> For purposes of consent injunctions that are agreed to and entered by a court after issuance of this opinion, we will construe the "neither admit nor deny" language as precluding a person who has consented to an injunction in a Commission enforcement action from denying the factual allegations of the injunctive complaint in a follow-on proceeding before this agency. *** Moreover, those allegations potentially can be dispositive of what remedial action is appropriate in the public interest. ***

The Commission further emphasized that the collateral consequences of an injunction for fraud will be particularly severe:

> The fact that a person has been "permanently or temporarily enjoined by order, judgment, or decree of any court of competent jurisdiction" from violating the antifraud provisions has especially serious implications for the public interest. Based on our experience enforcing the federal securities laws, we believe that ordinarily, and in the absence of evidence to the contrary, it will be in the public interest to revoke the registration of, or suspend or bar from participation in the securities industry, or prohibit from participation in an offering of penny stock, a respondent who is enjoined from violating the antifraud provisions.

In the Matter of Marshall E. Melton, Inv. Adv. Act Release No. 2151 (July 25, 2003).

PROBLEM 9-2

Microchip, Inc. launched an initial public offering (IPO) in March 2010 at the price of $10 per share. Microchip's registration statement, in its "use of proceeds" section, stated that all of the offering proceeds would be used for research on new technologies for the production of computer microchips. The national accounting firm of Reilly & Whitman audited the financial statements that were included in the registration statement. The lead underwriter was Wilson, Hartley, & Co. The IPO netted $10 million exclusive of costs.

Hooker & Faye had been a member of the syndicate in the Microchip IPO. In the months following the public offering, office managers at Hooker & Faye encouraged their brokers to recommend to clients the purchase of Microchip stock in the aftermarket. Hooker & Faye also featured Microchip as the "stock of the month" in its April 2010 investment newsletter. Steve Swanson and Emma Emerald were among the Hooker & Faye brokers that participated in the hyping of Microchip. Both brokers were particularly aggressive in soliciting their clients to buy Microchip, which was trading in the aftermarket at $12 per share. However, neither broker—nor any other broker at Hooker—revealed to those clients that in March 2010, a small group of favored clients had been allotted shares from the Microchip IPO on the condition that they purchase additional Microchip stock in the aftermarket at prices higher than the offering price of $10. The brokers also did not reveal to their present clients that as a result of this "laddering" activity with the favored clients, the current market price of Microchip stock was probably inflated.

Microchip's three most senior officials were Jerry Johnson, Peter Passet, and Carol Clarkson who were Chief Executive Officer, President, and Chief Operating Officer respectively. At the time of the IPO, these three officers, all also directors of Microchip, expected that at least 60% of the offering proceeds would be used to satisfy a multi-million dollar past-due account owed to its principal supplier. According to a report from Microchip's Chief Financial Officer, Wilma Wilkins, dated January 2010, the offering proceeds represented the only way to meet this obligation. Ms. Wilkins's report, however, was shown only to Johnson, Passet, and Clarkson, and they did not share it with Microchip's four other directors, all of whom were independent directors not employed by the company.

In April 2010, Microchip paid its supplier $6 million from the IPO proceeds. The other $4 million from the IPO was spent on research on new technologies for the production of computer microchips as described in the use of proceeds section of the prospectus.

After the IPO, Microchip filed periodic forms 10-K and 10-Q as required by the Exchange Act. Between March 2010 and March 2012, none of these reports disclosed that its supplier had received any of the proceeds from the IPO. The financial statements included in these periodic reports, like the financial statements included in the earlier registration statement, were audited by Reilly & Whitman. Microchip's stock declined slowly during 2010 and 2011 from its post-IPO aftermarket price of $12 to a price of $7 per share at the beginning of March, 2012.

On March 10, 2012, Microchip finally disclosed that the company had used 60% of the IPO proceeds to satisfy an obligation owed its supplier. Microchip's stock quickly dropped from a trading price of $7 per share to $2 per share on the same day. The price thereafter tumbled to $1 per share after Suzy Squeal, a former internal auditor for Microchip, announced at a press conference her belief that Johnson, Passet, and Clarkson had intentionally obscured from shareholders and the investing public the payment to the supplier and the consequent diversion of funds from research. She also voiced a suspicion that the funds had been unavailable to pay the supplier in March 2010 because all three officers and directors had been embezzling from the company for years.

Assume that all of the above facts and suspicions have been confirmed by SEC staff members in the course of an informal investigation. What enforcement alternatives are available to the SEC? Against whom can enforcement actions be instituted? What remedies would the SEC be most likely to seek?

D. LITIGATING WITH THE SEC

Although the overwhelming majority of enforcement actions initiated by the SEC are settled, an increasing number of them are litigated, either in an administrative proceeding or in federal court. Often, a case that the staff would have been willing to settle administratively with, for example, the issuance of a cease-and-desist order, may be litigated as an injunctive action in federal district court with the SEC also seeking the imposition of a monetary penalty. (Under these circumstances, the added threat of a federal court action coupled with a possible injunction and monetary fine constitute additional costs to the party in refusing to settle.) Other types of litigated actions—particularly those against regulated entities such as broker-dealers, investment advisers, and investment companies—are almost always brought administratively, in part because of the wide array of sanctions that Congress has empowered the Commission to impose. The choice of whether to pursue an administrative action or a judicial action is one that generally rests entirely with the Commission. But see *Gupta v. SEC*, __F.Supp.2d ___ 2011 WL 2674840 (S.D.N.Y 2011) (refusing to grant SEC's motion for dismissal because complaint pled facts sufficient to state a claim that the SEC's decision to treat plaintiff, a respondent in an administrative proceeding, differently from 28 other defendants in related insider trading federal court cases was irrational, arbitrary, and discriminatory).

This section first describes the process of litigation with the SEC—in both administrative proceedings and in federal court. It then examines three issues common to both types of enforcement proceedings: burdens of proof, statutes of limitations, and collateral estoppel.

1. *The Litigation Process*

a. *SEC Administrative Proceedings*

Although administrative proceedings vary widely depending on the particular type that is instituted by the SEC—for example, stop order proceedings against publicly traded companies are very different from disciplinary proceedings brought against broker-dealers—there are certain shared characteristics. First, administrative proceedings are governed by the Commission's Rules of Practice. See 17 C.F.R. § 201.100 et seq. Second, they typically are initiated with the Commission's issuance of an "Order of Proceedings" that specifies the charges against the "respondent" and there is typically a 20 day period for the respondent to file an answer. See § 201.220(b). Third, administrative proceedings that require evidentiary hearings are generally conducted by administrative law judges (ALJs), who are employees of the Commission. ALJs address pre-hearing motions, see § 201.221(c)(5), supervise the limited process of discovery, see § 201.230, evaluate the testimony and cross-examinations of the witnesses presented by the enforcement staff and the respondent, see § 201.326, and render a written decision, see § 201.360, often after the receipt of post-hearing briefs submitted by both the respondent and the staff, see § 201.340(c). In an evidentiary hearing conducted by an ALJ, neither the Federal Rules of Civil Procedure nor the Federal Rules of Evidence apply. Such a hearing is thus very different from a hearing in federal district court.

The initial decision issued by the ALJ generally includes findings of fact and conclusions of law (supported by reasons for those findings and conclusions) and a recommended sanction. This initial decision is final unless either party files a petition for review with the Commission within the time limit specified by the ALJ, generally not to exceed 21 days from the date of decision. See 17 C.F.R. §§ 201.360(b), 201.410. The Commission may also order review on its own initiative. See § 201.411(c). On review, the Commission may affirm, reverse, modify, or set aside the ALJ's initial decision, or may remand the case to the ALJ for further proceedings, and may make "any findings or conclusions that in its judgment are proper and on the basis of the record." § 201.411(a). In other words, the Commission's authority on review is *de novo*. If no review is sought, or if the Commission declines review where it has discretion to do so, see § 201.411(b), the Commission issues a final order which sets the date on which the sanction recommended by the ALJ, if any, takes effect. See § 201.360(e).

Some have argued that conflict inheres in the Commission's quasi-judicial function of adjudicating administrative proceedings that it itself has authorized. Even in the Commission's very early years, it was thought that "there is something abhorrent in the idea that any single group may make laws, may act as a public prosecutor in enforcing those laws, and may then determine the guilt or innocence of the person it has accused." Roland L. Redmond, The Securities Exchange Act of 1934: An Experiment in Administrative Law, 47 Yale L.J. 622, 636-37 (1938). Do you agree? Is the conflict, if any, ameliorated by the availability of judicial review?

In this regard, consider that each of the federal securities laws provides for judicial review of a final order by the Commission in the United States Court of Appeals for the circuit in which the respondent resides or has his principal place of business or in the District of Columbia Circuit. See, e.g., Section 25(a)(1) of the Exchange Act. The statutes specify that an appeal must be commenced within sixty days after the entry of the Commission's final order, see, e.g., id., and that the SEC's factual findings, if supported by substantial evidence, are conclusive. See, e.g., Section 25(a)(4) of the Exchange Act. A respondent may seek circuit court review of an administrative proceeding only if she has already pursued and exhausted all administrative remedies available.

b. Federal Court Proceedings

At first blush it may seem, from a private litigant's perspective, that litigating in federal court is a superior alternative to the administrative process because the fact finder—whether judge or jury—is very much independent of the SEC. But consider whether this independence comes with a level of formality that is often avoided in an administrative hearing. What are the consequences when the SEC (literally) makes a federal case out of a suspected securities law violation? In this regard, consider even seemingly simple things, such as the fact that, in federal court, the SEC files a "complaint" against a "defendant" in an action captioned "SEC v. *defendant*." How does this differ from the administrative nomenclature? Consider also the fact that the Federal Rules of Civil Procedure and the Federal Rules of Evidence now apply. In what ways would this benefit a defendant? Are there ways in which this constitutes a tactical disadvantage?

As we have seen from the preceding Section of this Chapter, enforcement actions initiated by the SEC in federal court are typically filed as injunctive actions pursuant to provisions in one or more of the federal securities laws. See, e.g., Section 21(d)(1) of the Exchange Act. The action commences with the filing of the SEC's complaint, which in cases alleging fraud, must meet the particularity requirements of Rule 9(b) of the Federal Rules of Civil Procedure. In most cases, this is hardly a hurdle because the SEC typically files complaints of considerable length and detail, often described by defense counsel as "speaking complaints."

Although both pre-trial and trial practice with the SEC follows a similar course with the same rules as private litigation, it would be extremely unwise to regard the SEC as an ordinary litigant. Consider this view from the defense counsel's perspective:

> First, the Commission, as a law enforcement agency, enters many courts on an important public mission and with an aura of credibility, advantages not often held by private plaintiffs. Second, its investigative powers give the Commission substantial advantages when seeking a TRO or preliminary injunction. The Commission usually goes to court with the benefit of many months and sometimes several years of "discovery" through the investigative process. Even the best funded and best prepared of defendants often can assemble only a few pieces of the mosaic that the staff has had months or years to complete. The Commission also enjoys immunity from certain legal defenses and tactics that may be available in private actions. Finally, the Commission now holds a wide array of flexible "remedies" to rectify and punish violations of the law.

Jeffrey B. Maletta, Litigating SEC Injunctive Actions: The SEC's Traditional Enforcement Mechanism, in the Securities Enforcement Manual: Tactics and Strategies 204 (Richard M. Philips, ed., 1997).

As with private litigation, the defendant in an SEC injunctive action may file any number of pre-trial motions, including motions to dismiss under Fed. R. Civ. P. 12(b)(6) and motions for summary judgment under Rule 56. The SEC also frequently submits motions for summary judgment, or partial summary judgment, in cases where it is the law rather than the facts that are in dispute. Unresolved issues of material fact must proceed to trial.

Because SEC injunctive actions are "equitable" in nature, they are typically tried before a judge. However, in cases where the SEC is seeking the imposition of a civil monetary penalty, a defendant may invoke a Seventh Amendment right to a trial by jury. As the Supreme Court made clear in *Tull v. United States*, 481 U.S. 412 (1987), this right applies only to the determination of the defendant's liability; the determination of the penalty amount occurs in a subsequent phase conducted by a judge. What tactical considerations may influence a defendant's choice between a bench trial or a jury trial? In penalty cases where the defendant chooses not to assert the jury right, can this right be asserted by the SEC?

2. *Legal Issues in SEC Litigation*

a. Burden of Proof

As this next decision and the notes that follow make clear, controversy has surrounded the issue of the SEC's burden of proof at trial and in administrative hearings. Although at one time it appeared that a higher standard should govern in at least some actions brought by the Commission, today there is little doubt that "preponderance of the evidence" is the standard that the SEC must meet in virtually all of its civil litigation.

STEADMAN v. SEC

450 U.S. 91 (1981)

JUSTICE WILLIAM J. BRENNAN, JR.:

In administrative proceedings, the Securities and Exchange Commission applies a preponderance-of-the-evidence standard of proof in determining whether the antifraud provisions of the federal securities laws have been violated. The question presented is whether such violations must be proved by clear and convincing evidence rather than by a preponderance of the evidence.

I

In June 1971, the Commission initiated a disciplinary proceeding against petitioner and certain of his wholly owned companies. The proceeding against petitioner was brought pursuant to § 9(b) of the Investment Company Act of 1940 and § 203(f) of the Investment Advisers Act of 1940. The Commission alleged that petitioner had violated numerous provisions of the federal securities laws in his management of several mutual funds registered under the Investment Company Act.

After a lengthy evidentiary hearing before an Administrative Law Judge and review by the Commission in which the preponderance-of-the-evidence standard was employed, the Commission held that between December 1965 and June 1972, petitioner had violated antifraud, reporting, conflict of interest, and proxy provisions of the federal securities laws. Accordingly, it entered an order permanently barring petitioner from associating with any investment adviser or affiliating with any registered investment company, and suspending him for one year from associating with any broker or dealer in securities.

Petitioner sought review of the Commission's order in the United States Court of Appeals for the Fifth Circuit on a number of grounds, only one of which is relevant for our purposes. Petitioner challenged the Commission's use of the preponderance-of-the-evidence standard of proof in determining whether he had violated antifraud provisions of the securities laws. He contended that, because of the potentially severe sanctions that the Commission was empowered to impose and because of the circumstantial and inferential nature of the evidence that might be used to prove intent to defraud, the Commission was required to weigh the evidence against a clear-and-convincing standard of proof. The Court of Appeals rejected petitioner's argument, holding that in a disciplinary proceeding before the Commission violations of the antifraud provisions of the securities laws may be established by a preponderance of the evidence. Because this was contrary to the position taken by the United States Court of Appeals for the District of Columbia Circuit, see *Whitney v. SEC*, 604 F.2d 676 (1979);

Collins Securities Corp. v. SEC, 562 F.2d 820 (1977), we granted certiorari to resolve the conflict. We affirm.

II

Where Congress has not prescribed the degree of proof which must be adduced by the proponent of a rule or order to carry its burden of persuasion in an administrative proceeding, this Court has felt at liberty to prescribe the standard, for "[i]t is the kind of question which has traditionally been left to the judiciary to resolve." *Woodby v. INS*, 385 U.S. 276, 284 (1966). However, where Congress has spoken, we have deferred to "the traditional powers of Congress to prescribe rules of evidence and standards of proof in the federal courts" absent countervailing constitutional constraints. *Vance v. Terrazas*, 444 U.S. 252, 265 (1980). For Commission disciplinary proceedings initiated pursuant to [Section 9(b) of the Investment Company Act and Section 203(f) of the Investment Advisers Act] we conclude that Congress has spoken, and has said that the preponderance-of-the-evidence standard should be applied.

The securities laws provide for judicial review of Commission disciplinary proceedings in the federal courts of appeals and specify the scope of such review. Because they do not indicate which standard of proof governs Commission adjudications, however, we turn to § 5 of the Administrative Procedure Act (APA), 5 U.S.C. § 554, which "applies ... in every case of adjudication required by statute to be determined on the record after opportunity for an agency hearing," except in instances not relevant here. Section 5(b) makes the provisions of § 7, 5 U.S.C. § 556, applicable to adjudicatory proceedings. The answer to the question presented in this case turns therefore on the proper construction of § 7.

The search for congressional intent begins with the language of the statute. Section 7(c) states in pertinent part:

> Except as otherwise provided by statute, the proponent of a rule or order has the burden of proof. Any oral or documentary evidence may be received, but the agency as a matter of policy shall provide for the exclusion of irrelevant, immaterial, or unduly repetitious evidence. A sanction may not be imposed or rule or order issued except on consideration of the whole record or those parts thereof cited by a party and supported by and *in accordance with* the reliable, probative, and *substantial evidence*. (Emphasis added.)

The language of the statute itself implies the enactment of a standard of proof. By allowing sanctions to be imposed only when they are "in accordance with ... *substantial* evidence," Congress implied that a sanction must rest on a *minimum quantity* of evidence. The word "substantial" denotes quantity. The phrase "in accordance with ... substantial evidence" thus requires that a decision be based on a certain quantity of evidence. Petitioner's contention that the phrase "reliable, probative, and substantial evidence" sets merely a standard of *quality* of evidence is, therefore, unpersuasive.

The phrase "in accordance with" lends further support to a construction of § 7(c) as establishing a standard of proof. *** [This section] provides that an agency may issue an order only if that order is "supported by and *in accordance with* ... substantial evidence" (emphasis added). The additional words "in accordance with" suggest that the adjudicating agency must weigh the evidence and decide, based on the weight of the evidence, whether a disciplinary order should be issued. The language of § 7(c), therefore, requires that the agency decision must be "in accordance with" the weight of the evidence, not simply supported by enough evidence " 'to justify, if the trial were to a jury, a refusal to direct a verdict when the conclusion sought to be drawn from it is one of fact for the jury.' " *Consolo v. FMC*, 383 U.S. 607, 620 (1966), quoting *NLRB v. Columbian Enameling & Stamping Co.*, 306 U.S. 292, 300 (1939). Obviously, weighing evidence has relevance only if the evidence on each side is to be measured against a standard of proof which allocates the risk of error. See *Addington v. Texas*, 441 U.S. 418, 423 (1979). *** Thus, petitioner's argument that § 7(c) merely establishes the scope of judicial review of agency orders is unavailing.

While the language of § 7(c) suggests, therefore, that Congress intended the statute to establish a standard of proof, the language of the statute is somewhat opaque concerning the precise standard of proof to be used. The legislative history, however, clearly reveals the Congress' intent. The original Senate version of § 7(c) provided that "no sanction shall be imposed ... except as supported by relevant, reliable, and probative evidence." S. 7, 79th Cong., 1st Sess. (1945). After the Senate passed this version, the House passed the language of the statute as it reads today, and the Senate accepted the amendment. Any doubt as to the intent of Congress is removed by the House Report, which expressly adopted a preponderance-of-the-evidence standard:

> [W]here a party having the burden of proceeding has come forward with a prima facie and substantial case, he will prevail unless his evidence is discredited or rebutted. In any case the agency must decide 'in accordance with the evidence.' Where there is evidence pro and con, the agency must weigh it and decide *in accordance with the preponderance.* In short, these provisions require a conscientious and rational judgment on the whole record in accordance with the proofs adduced." H.R. Rep. No. 1980, 79th Cong., 2d Sess., 37 (1946) (emphasis added)

Nor is there any suggestion in the legislative history that a standard of proof higher than a preponderance of the evidence was ever contemplated, much less intended. Congress was primarily concerned with the elimination of agency decisionmaking premised on evidence which was of poor quality—irrelevant, immaterial, unreliable, and nonprobative—and of insufficient quantity—less than a preponderance. See id., at 36-37 and 45; S. Doc. No. 248, 79th Cong., 2d Sess., 320-322 and 376-378 (1946); n. 21, supra.

The language and legislative history of § 7(c) lead us to conclude, therefore, that § 7(c) was intended to establish a standard of proof and that the standard adopted is the traditional preponderance-of-the-evidence standard.

III

Our view of congressional intent is buttressed by the Commission's longstanding practice of imposing sanctions according to the preponderance of the evidence. As early as 1938, the Commission rejected the argument that in a proceeding to determine whether to suspend, expel, or otherwise sanction a brokerage firm and its principals for, *inter alia*, manipulation of security prices in violation of § 9 of the Securities Exchange Act of 1934 a standard of proof greater than the preponderance-of-the-evidence standard was required. *In re*

White, 3 S.E.C. 466, 539-540 (1938). Use of the preponderance standard continued after passage of the APA, and persists today. E.g., *In re Cea*, 44 S.E.C. 8, 25 (1969); *In re Pollisky*, 43 S.E.C. 458, 459-460 (1967). The Commission's consistent practice, which is in harmony with § 7(c) and its legislative history, is persuasive authority that Congress intended that Commission disciplinary proceedings, subject to § 7 of the APA, be governed by a preponderance-of-the- evidence standard. See *Andrus v. Sierra Club*, 442 U.S. 347, 358 (1979); *United States v. National Association of Securities Dealers, Inc.*, 422 U.S. 694, 719 (1975); *Skidmore v. Swift & Co.*, 323 U.S. 134, 140 (1944).

In *Vermont Yankee Nuclear Power Corp. v. Natural Resources Defense Council, Inc.*, 435 U.S. 519, 524 (1978), we stated that § 4 of the APA established the "maximum procedural requirements which Congress was willing to have the courts impose upon agencies in conducting rulemaking procedures." In § 7(c), Congress has similarly expressed its intent that adjudicatory proceedings subject to the APA satisfy the statute where determinations are made according to the preponderance of the evidence. Congress was free to make that choice, *Vance v. Terrazas*, 444 U.S., at 265-266, and, in the absence of countervailing constitutional considerations, the courts are not free to disturb it.

JUSTICE LOUIS F. POWELL, JR., WITH WHOM JUSTICE STEWART JOINS, DISSENTING:

The Securities and Exchange Commission (SEC), acting under the antifraud provisions of the Investment Company Act of 1940 and the Investment Advisers Act of 1940, has imposed severe sanctions on petitioner. He has been barred permanently from practicing his profession and also forced to divest himself of an investment at a substantial loss. In making its findings of fraud and imposing these penalties, the SEC applied the "preponderance of the evidence" standard of proof. ***

The SEC acted in this case under § 9(b) of the Investment Company Act of 1940 and § 203(f) of the Investment Advisers Act of 1940. Sanctions imposed under these sections are the functional equivalent of penalties for fraud. At common law, it was plain that allegations of fraud had to be proved by clear and convincing evidence. E.g., *Addington v. Texas*, 441 U.S. 418, 424 (1979); *Woodby v. INS*, 385 U.S. 276, 285, n. 18 (1966); *Weininger v. Metropolitan Fire Insurance Co.*, 359 Ill. 584, 598 (1935); *Bank of Pocahontas v. Ferimer*, 161 Va. 37, 40-41 (1933); *Bowe v. Gage*, 127 Wis. 245, 251 (1906). Congress enacted the Investment Company and Investment Advisers Acts against this common-law background. There is no evidence that Congress, when it adopted these Acts, intended to authorize the SEC to abandon the then-applicable standard of proof in fraud adjudications. See *Whitney v. SEC*, 604 F.2d 676 (1979); *Collins Securities Corp. v. SEC*, 562 F.2d 820 (1977).

The APA, upon which the Court relies, did not become law for some seven years after the enactment of the two statutes under which the SEC imposed these penalties. Again, the Court points to no specific evidence that Congress intended the APA to supplant the burden-of-proof rule generally applicable when the securities laws were enacted. Thus, the APA—the *general* statute applicable only where a *specific* statute is not—should have no bearing on the proof burden in this case.

I imply no opinion on the question whether the evidence supports the SEC's allegations against petitioner. It is clear, however, that the SEC's finding of fraud and its imposition of harsh penalties have resulted in serious stigma and deprivation. Cf. *Addington v. Texas,* supra.[1] In the absence of any specific demonstration of Congress' purpose, we should not assume that Congress intended the SEC to apply a lower standard of proof than the prevailing common-law standard for similar allegations. With all respect, it seems to me that the Court's decision today lacks the sensitivity that traditionally has marked our review of the Government's imposition upon citizens of severe penalties and permanent stigma.

NOTES AND QUESTIONS

1. ***Civil Proceedings vs. Criminal Proceedings.*** Consider Justice Powell's reference in the footnote of his dissenting opinion to the "beyond a reasonable doubt" standard of the criminal law. Given some of the severe sanctions that Congress has authorized the SEC to seek against securities law violators, does it make sense to distinguish a person's rights based on whether enforcement is civil or criminal? In addition to the higher burden of proof, what additional protections—constitutional or otherwise—attach only to criminal proceedings? As a matter of policy, should any of these be extended to defendants/respondents in litigation with the SEC? How much should turn on whether a sanction is deemed to be "remedial" or "punitive"? How much should turn on the technical description of a sanction as criminal or civil? In this regard, consider the Supreme Court's decision in *Hudson v. United States* discussed in Section F.3 infra. Consider also the material in Section D.2.b infra dealing with whether statutes of limitations are applicable to enforcement actions brought by the Commission.

2. ***Burden of Proof in SEC Injunctive Actions.*** *Steadman* established preponderance of the evidence as the standard of proof in administrative proceedings brought by the Commission. Does this standard apply as well in enforcement actions brought by the Commission in federal court?

Although there have been a few twists in the road in the past, today one can expect that in seeking injunctive relief in federal court, the SEC will be held to a preponderance of the evidence standard. That there was ever any controversy is somewhat surprising in light of the Supreme Court's clear statement in *SEC v. C.M. Joiner Leasing Corp.*, 320 U.S. 344, 355 (1943), that "[w]here *** proof is offered in a civil action *** a preponderance of the evidence will establish the case." *Joiner* was an injunctive action brought by the SEC for violations of Section 17(a) of the Securities Act. The issue arose again in *Herman & MacLean v. Huddleston*, 459 U.S. 375 (1983), which involved a private action for damages under Rule 10b-5. Because the latter action involved allegations of fraud, the Fifth Circuit maintained that clear and convincing

---

1. Petitioner has practiced the profession of investment adviser for many years. He has been forever barred from resuming that profession. Many penalties imposed under our criminal laws—such as monetary fines and probation—are far less severe, and yet these can be imposed only under the "beyond a reasonable doubt" standard of the criminal law.

evidence was the appropriate standard of proof. The Supreme Court disagreed, noting that "[a] preponderance-of-the-evidence standard allows both parties to 'share the risk of error in roughly equal fashion,' " id. at 390, and that the plaintiffs should recover if "they prove that it is more likely than not that they were defrauded." Id. Courts routinely cite *Herman & MacLean* in the context of Section 10(b) injunctive actions brought by the Commission. See, e.g., *SEC v. Lorin*, 877 F. Supp. 192, 195 (S.D.N.Y. 1995), aff'd in part, vacated in part on other grounds, 76 F.3d 458 (2d Cir. 1996); *SEC v. Musella*, 678 F. Supp. 1060, 1063 (S.D.N.Y. 1988).

*3. **Loss of Livelihood.*** In *SEC v. Moran*, 922 F. Supp. 867, 887-88 (S.D.N.Y. 1996), an insider trading case that we studied in Chapter 7, the court considered the defendants' claim that because "they [were] subjected to money damages, an injunction, and loss of livelihood in [a] wholly circumstantial case, the higher standard proof, clear and convincing evidence, is necessitated." In so doing, the court noted that:

> Historically, there are relatively few areas of the law which impose upon the plaintiff the burden of proving its case by clear and convincing evidence. Those examples are limited to cases in which the defendant faces a judgement which could potentially impose penalties such as loss of liberty, deportation, termination of parental rights, or deprivation of ability to engage in ones livelihood. See e.g., *Santosky v. Kramer*, 455 U.S. 745 (1982) (proceeding to terminate parental rights); *Addington v. Texas*, [441 U.S. 418, 427 (1979)] (due process requires that in a commitment proceeding the state must "justify confinement by proof more substantial than a mere preponderance of the evidence"); *Woodby v. INS*, [385 U.S. 276, 285-86 (1966)] (deportation proceedings governed by clear and convincing standard); *In re Ryder*, 263 F.Supp. 360, 361 (E.D.Va.), aff'd, 381 F.2d 713 (4th Cir.1967) (disbarment proceeding governed by clear and convincing standard).

Moran, 922 F. Supp. at 889. The court further cited to *Collins Sec. Corp. v. SEC*, 562 F.2d 820, 825-26 (D.C. Cir. 1977) where the D.C. Circuit had stated that the clear and convincing standard would govern an action brought by the SEC seeking revocation of a defendant's broker and dealer registration, expulsion from membership in NASD, and barring association with any other broker or dealer. See *Moran*, 922 F. Supp. at 889.

The *Moran* court ultimately rejected the defendants' request for a higher proof burden, distinguishing the injunctive relief sought against the insider trading defendants from the relief of a permanent bar sought against the securities broker in *Collins*. See id. at 889 (stating that "there is significant difference between a defendant who will in fact be deprived of his livelihood and one who will 'effectively' be deprived"). But in so doing, the *Moran* court seemed to assume that *Collins*' "loss of livelihood" rationale for a clear and convincing standard survives the Supreme Court's decision in *Steadman*. Does it?

b. Statutes of Limitations

With the single exception of the five year period specified in Section 21A(d)(5) for civil monetary penalties in insider trading cases, the federal securities laws do not specify any statutes of limitations for enforcement actions brought by the SEC. And the SEC's unequivocal and long-standing position had been that no such statute of limitations should be implied. The SEC's position met with complete success the few times it was litigated, until 1995, when the

D.C. Circuit decided *Johnson v. SEC*, the principal case that follows.

Prior to *Johnson*, the most important case to consider this statute of limitations issue was *SEC v. Rind*, 991 F.2d 1486 (1993). The underlying conduct at issue involved the well-publicized collapse of ZZZZ Best Company ("Z Best"). In August 1990, more than three years after Z Best's declaration of bankruptcy, the SEC filed a civil injunction action against Rind and thirteen other defendants. Because twelve of these defendants had consented to judgments against them and another one defaulted, Rind was the only defendant left in the case.

The SEC's complaint alleged that Rind had concocted a fraudulent transaction (from which he gained at least $700,000 in profits) which allowed Z Best to overstate its assets vastly, thereby enabling the company to raise millions of dollars in capital. The SEC sought a permanent injunction prohibiting Rind from violating Securities Act Section 17(a), Exchange Act Section 10(b), and Rule 10b-5 in the future and requiring disgorgement of his unlawful gains. Rind sought dismissal on the ground that the SEC must adhere to the same one year/ three year limitations rule applicable to private plaintiffs by the Supreme Court's decision in *Lampf, Pleva, Lipkind, Prupis & Petigrow v. Gilbertson*, 501 U.S. 350 (1991). The district court had granted the SEC's motion to strike that defense but certified the question for interlocutory appeal.

In rejecting Rind's arguments, the Ninth Circuit drew a stark contrast between private actions for securities fraud and enforcement actions brought by the SEC, emphasizing that:

> [T]he Commission sues as part of its statutory mandate to enforce the federal securities laws. As such, civil enforcement actions promote economic and social policies independent of the claims of individual investors. The fact that disgorgement involves money does not change the nature of the remedy. The Commission seeks disgorgement in order to deprive the wrongdoer of his or her unlawful profits and thereby eliminate the incentive for violating the securities laws. The theory behind the remedy is deterrence and not compensation. Indeed, a district court may grant the Commission's request for disgorgement even where no injured investors can be identified. In light of the important public function served by Commission enforcement activity, we therefore cannot conclude, as did the Court in *Lampf*, that the express time limits for private claims "accommodate a balance of interests very similar to that at stake here."

Rind, 991 F.2d at 1490.

Having determined that the Supreme Court's decision in *Lampf* did not establish a statute of limitations for SEC enforcement actions, the Ninth Circuit next considered whether such a limitations period should nonetheless be implied. Although the court observed that Congress's silence regarding a statute of limitations often has been interpreted to require "borrowing" from analogous state statutes, the court pointed to the exception that:

> [s]tate limitations periods do not bind the United States when it sues to vindicate a public right or interest, absent a clear showing of congressional intent to the contrary. This doctrine, which has its origins in the ancient principle that time does not run against the king, finds its modern justification in the policy that public rights, revenues, and property should not be forfeited due to the negligence of public officials. See *Guaranty Trust Co. v. United States,* 304 U.S. 126, 132 (1938).

Rind, 991 F.2d at 1491. The court then stated that:

> When the Commission sues to enforce the securities laws, it vindicates public rights and furthers the public interest. The public character of Commission action is reflected in the introduction to the 1934 Act: "[T]ransactions in securities ... are affected with a national public interest which makes it necessary to provide for regulation and control of such transactions." Congress entrusted the Commission with the vital mission of ensuring the honesty and fairness of the capital markets. "The entire purpose and thrust of a [Commission] enforcement action is to expeditiously safeguard the public interest by enjoining securities violations. The claims asserted in such an action stem from, and are colored by, the intense public interest in [Commission] enforcement of these laws." *SEC v. Asset Management Corp.*, 456 F. Supp. 998, 1000 (S.D. Ind. 1978). ***

Rind, 991 F.2d at 1491.

The court further emphasized the central role that disgorgement plays in the enforcement of the securities laws and the complexity of many of the securities fraud cases pursued by the Commission. It noted specifically that "[b]y deterring violations of the securities laws, disgorgement actions further the Commission's public policy mission of protecting investors and safeguarding the integrity of the markets." Id. at 1491. It also observed that "the Commission must expend considerable time and energy investigating alleged violations of the securities laws" and that "securities fraud may involve multiple parties and transactions of mind-boggling complexity." Id. at 1492. Quoting the Supreme Court's decision in *Occidental Life Ins. Co. v. EEOC*, 432 U.S. 355, 367 (1977), it therefore concluded that "[p]lacing strict time limits on Commission enforcement actions *** would quite plainly 'frustrate or interfere with the implementation of national policies.'" *Rind*, 991 F.2d at 1492.

As you read the following decision, consider whether it signals a potential turning of the tide.

JOHNSON v. SEC

87 F.3d 484 (D.C. Cir. 1996)

PATRICIA M. WALD, CIRCUIT JUDGE:

*** In this case, we decide that a Securities and Exchange Commission ("SEC") proceeding resulting in a censure and a six-month disciplinary suspension of a securities industry supervisor was a proceeding "for the enforcement of any civil fine, penalty, or forfeiture, pecuniary or otherwise," within the meaning of [the five-year statute of limitations in 28 U.S.C.] § 2462. Accordingly we grant petitioner Patricia A. Johnson's petition for review and vacate the SEC's order imposing sanctions on her.

I. BACKGROUND

Patricia A. Johnson was the branch manager of PaineWebber, Inc.'s Beverly Hills, California office from November 1984 to April 1991. Among the employees she supervised was David Zetterstrom, an account representative who allegedly stole more than $114,000 from his customers between 1987 and 1988 by writing unauthorized checks against their accounts. Though Johnson was unaware of these thefts, she had received other complaints about Zetterstrom's handling of customer accounts which eventually led her to place him on probation, and then fire him, on June 10, 1988. Three days after he was fired, Zetterstrom committed suicide.

After terminating Zetterstrom's employment, Johnson further investigated his activities and learned for the first time that he had stolen clients' funds. PaineWebber began an internal audit, and notified the SEC, which began its own investigation in June 1988. More than five years later, on October 26, 1993, the SEC brought formal charges against Johnson, alleging that she had "failed reasonably to supervise [Zetterstrom] ... within the meaning of Section 15(b)(4)(E) of the Exchange Act." Order Instituting Public Administrative Proceedings. The SEC alleged that Johnson had allowed Zetterstrom to issue checks drawn from his customers' accounts without first obtaining from them the required letters of authorization, and that Johnson—even after preliminary evidence of Zetterstrom's wrongdoing had come to light—had allowed him continued access to customers' funds, thereby facilitating his thievery.

In the administrative proceedings, Johnson conceded that Zetterstrom had stolen money from his customers, but disputed the SEC's allegation that her supervision of him was unreasonable. In addition, Johnson claimed that the SEC's action was barred by the general five-year statute of limitations of 28 U.S.C. § 2462:

> Except as otherwise provided by Act of Congress, an action, suit or proceeding for the enforcement of any civil fine, penalty, or forfeiture, pecuniary or otherwise, shall not be entertained unless commenced within five years from the date when the claim first accrued....

The SEC denied Johnson's motion to dismiss under § 2462, holding in February 1994 that "[s]ection 2462 does not apply to Commission administrative proceedings." The SEC's position, however, was severely undercut less than two weeks later when this court decided [*3M Co. v. Browner*, 17 F.3d 1453 (D.C.Cir.1994)] rejecting the view that § 2462 applies only to *judicial* proceedings and holding that § 2462 applies to administrative proceedings as well. 17 F.3d at 1457.

Notwithstanding the *3M* decision, an SEC Administrative Law Judge ("ALJ") held hearings and issued a decision in Johnson's case, finding that she had failed reasonably to supervise Zetterstrom, and imposing a six-month "supervisory suspension" on her. Johnson petitioned the SEC for review of the ALJ's decision, again seeking dismissal based on the statute of limitations.

Evaluating Johnson's second petition in light of *3M*, the SEC articulated another theory for rejecting her claim, holding this time that § 2462 should not apply because the "proceeding before us does not seek to impose a *civil penalty,* but rather to determine the appropriate *remedial action.* The intent of Johnson's suspension is to protect the public from future harm at her hands." Opinion of the Commission at 11. Finally, the SEC affirmed the ALJ's finding that Johnson had failed reasonably to supervise Zetterstrom, and issued an order saying:

> On the basis of the Commission's opinion issued this day, it is ordered that Patricia A. Johnson be, and hereby is, censured and suspended from acting in a supervisory capacity with any broker or dealer for six months. ***

II. DISCUSSION

The sole question in this case is whether the SEC proceeding which resulted in the sanctions imposed on Johnson was "an action, suit, or proceeding for the enforcement of any civil fine, penalty, or forfeiture, pecuniary or otherwise" within the meaning of 28 U.S.C. § 2462. Because § 2462 is a statute of general applicability rather than one whose primary administration has been delegated to the SEC, we interpret it *de novo*.

A. *The Meaning of "Penalty" Under* § 2462

The term "penalty" is nowhere defined in § 2462, so we must be guided here by the Supreme Court's common-sense rule that "[c]ourts properly assume, absent sufficient indication to the contrary, that Congress intends the words in its enactments to carry 'their ordinary, contemporary, common meaning.' " *Pioneer Inv. Servs. Co. v. Brunswick Assoc. Ltd. Partnership*, 507 U.S. 380, 388 (1993).

In common usage, a penalty is "the suffering in person, rights or property which is annexed by law or judicial decision to the commission of a crime or public offense." Webster's Third New International Dictionary 1668 (1976). For at least a century, legal dictionaries have similarly defined penalty. See Black's Law Dictionary 1020 (5th ed.1979) ("A punishment imposed by statute as a consequence of the commission of an offense."); Ballentine's Law Dictionary 948 (1930) ("An exaction in the nature of a punishment for the nonperformance of an act, or for the performance of an unlawful act, and involving the idea of punishment, whether enforced by a civil or criminal action or proceeding."); 2 Burrill's Law Dictionary (1871) ("A punishment; a punishment imposed by statute as a consequence of the commission of a certain act."); 2 Bouvier's Law Dictionary 323 (1866) ("By penalty is understood, also, the punishment inflicted by law for its violation....").

In *Huntington v. Attrill*, 146 U.S. 657 (1892), the Supreme Court addressed the question of whether a judgment in a state court was "penal," and thus could not be enforced in another state under the Constitution's Full Faith and Credit Clause. The Court explained that "[p]enal laws, strictly and properly, are those imposing punishment for an offense committed against the state.... The test whether a law is penal, in the strict and primary sense, is whether the wrong sought to be redressed is a wrong to the public, or a wrong to the individual...." 146 U.S. at 667-68. Put another way, the question of whether a law is penal depends on whether its purpose "is to punish an offense against the public justice of the State, or to afford a private remedy to a person injured by the wrong." Id. at 673-74.

Thus where a legal action is essentially private in nature, seeking only compensation for the damages suffered, it is not an action for a penalty. ***

In many other situations the courts have reaffirmed that a sanction which only remedies the damage caused by the defendant does not trigger the protections of § 2462. ***

In sum, we conclude that a "penalty," as the term is used in § 2462, is a form of punishment imposed by the government for unlawful or proscribed conduct, which goes beyond remedying the damage caused to the harmed parties by the defendant's action.

B. *The Sanctions Here*

We turn next to the specific sanctions imposed here, asking whether the suspension of a supervisor or broker fits within this definition of penalty.

At the outset, we agree with the SEC that the test for whether a sanction is sufficiently punitive to constitute a "penalty" within the meaning of § 2462 is an objective one, not measured from the subjective perspective of the accused (which would render virtually every sanction a penalty). It is obviously not enough that the person subjected to a sanction feels pain or finds the sanction disagreeable; as the Supreme Court has pointed out, "even remedial sanctions carry the sting of punishment." *United States v. Halper*, 490 U.S. 435, 447 n. 7 (1989).***

Here, the sanctions imposed by the SEC—censure and a six-month suspension—clearly resemble punishment in the ordinary sense of the word. The SEC not only restricted Johnson's ability to earn a living as a supervisor during her six-month suspension, but the suspension was also likely to have longer-lasting repercussions on her ability to pursue her vocation. Suspended brokers must forever after disclose the sanction, and it becomes part of their permanent public file. See Form ADV, 17 C.F.R. § 279.1, Part I, Item 11(C)(4) (must disclose whether SEC has "entered an order denying, suspending, or revoking the applicant's ... registration"). Congress has also required securities associations such as the National Association of Securities Dealers to set up a toll-free number for investors and other members of the public to check whether brokers or other brokerage employees have been subject to disciplinary actions. See 15 U.S.C. § 78o-3(i). These collateral consequences of the censure and suspension, while not the central determinant in whether a sanction reaches penalty status, do suggest its punishment-like qualities.

This sanction would less resemble punishment if the SEC had focused on Johnson's current competence or the degree of risk she posed to the public. Despite the SEC's claims to the contrary, however, it is evident that the sanctions here were not based on any general finding of Johnson's unfitness as a supervisor, nor any showing of the risk she posed to the public, but rather were based on Johnson's alleged failure reasonably to supervise Zetterstrom, as required by section 15(b) of the Securities Exchange Act of 1934 ("Exchange Act"). The SEC initiated these proceedings with an indictment-like document entitled "Order Instituting Public Administrative Proceedings Pursuant to Sections 15(b) and 19(h) of the Securities Exchange Act of 1934," which alleged, *inter alia,* that:

> C. From approximately August 1987 through June 1988, a registered representative in PaineWebber's Beverly Hills branch office willfully violated Section 17(a) of the Securities Act of 1933 ..., Section 10(b) of the Securities Exchange Act of 1934 ... and Rule 10b-5 thereunder in that he misappropriated funds from the accounts of customers without their knowledge or consent.
>
> D. During the period from approximately August 1987 through June 1988, Johnson failed reasonably to supervise the registered representative described in paragraph C above with a view to preventing his violations of Section 17(a) of the Securities Act, Section 10(b) of the Exchange Act and Rule 10b-5 thereunder.

Consistent with this charge, the SEC inquiry appears to have focused almost exclusively on Johnson's failure reasonably to supervise, not her current competence or risk to the public.

Although the ALJ held two days of hearings, with three witnesses and 22 exhibits, the SEC cites not a single piece of evidence in the record explicitly supporting its finding that suspension of Johnson was necessary due to Johnson's current unfitness to be a supervisor. In its final order of more than 11 single-spaced pages, the SEC included only one conclusory paragraph concerning the sanction:

> We believe the sanctions of censure and six months suspension from acting in a supervisory capacity with any broker or dealer imposed by the law judge to be warranted. Johnson displayed a lack of hands-on involvement with her staff and a lack of responsiveness to serious violations by a registered representative under her supervision. Her deficiencies permitted further violations to occur. Accordingly, we affirm the law judge's sanctions against Johnson.

This statement, which justifies the sanction solely in view of Johnson's past misconduct, belies the SEC's assertion in this litigation that the sanctions were imposed not as punishment for past dereliction, but primarily because of Johnson's present danger to the public.[9] To the contrary, we conclude that any inquiry into Johnson's current competence or the danger she posed to the public (and the SEC cites to no such inquiry) was at most *pro forma*. In substance, this proceeding was directed toward one thing only—determining whether Johnson had failed reasonably to supervise Zetterstrom within the meaning of the Exchange Act—and the resultant sanction was inflicted on Johnson for that failure.

C. *Exception for Statutes Protecting the Public?*

The SEC argues nonetheless that a license suspension should not constitute punishment or a penalty where the government's purpose is to protect the public. See, e.g., *Hawker v. New York*, 170 U.S. 189, 200 (1898) (law barring convicted felons from practicing medicine did not violate *ex post facto* clause); *Ex parte Wall*, 107 U.S. 265, 287 (1883) (disbarment of attorney could proceed without grand jury indictment or jury trial); *United States v. Stoller*, [78 F.3d 724 (1st Cir. 1996)] (debarment of individual from banking industry did not violate double jeopardy clause); *DiCola v. FDA*, 77 F.3d 504, 507 (D.C.Cir.1996) (exclusion of an individual from further activities in the pharmaceutical industry was "solely remedial" and thus did not constitute punishment for double jeopardy or *ex post facto* purposes).

While these cases do hold that a license suspension—if motivated by a *bona fide* goal of protecting the public—may not be punishment in various *constitutional* contexts, they do not control the question of whether license

9. If the SEC really viewed Johnson as a clear and present danger to the public, it is inexplicable why it waited *more than five years* to begin the proceedings to suspend her.

suspension is a *penalty for purposes of § 2462.*[10] In the constitutional cases cited by the SEC, the chief concern has been whether a putatively civil or regulatory sanction is in actuality a back-door form of punishment, such that certain constitutional protections should be triggered. Accordingly, the main focus of these cases has been on whether the law imposing the sanctions has an overall remedial *purpose* of protecting the public (with the sanctions being the reasonable means of achieving that purpose). In interpreting § 2462, however, the court's concern is not whether Congress legislated the sanction as part of a regulatory scheme to protect the public, but rather whether the sanction is itself a form of punishment of the individual for unlawful or proscribed conduct, going beyond compensation of the wronged party.

Thus in *Meeker* [*v. Lehigh Valley R.R.*I, 236 U.S. 412, 423 (1915)], the sanction was "strictly remedial" because it only required the defendant to return overcharges to the plaintiff, and did not impose any punishment. Similarly, where the effect of the SEC's action is to restore the *status quo ante,* such as through a proceeding for restitution or disgorgement of ill-gotten profits, § 2462 will not apply. See, e.g., *SEC v. Lorin*, 869 F. Supp. 1117, 1122-23 (S.D.N.Y. 1994) (reading *Meeker* to support proposition that disgorgement is not a "fine, penalty, or forfeiture" within the meaning of § 2462 since such sanction is "strictly remedial").

The sanctions imposed here, however, are certainly not "remedial" in the sense that term is used in *Meeker* and its progeny, for they are not directed toward correcting or undoing the effects of Johnson's allegedly faulty supervision. Unlike restitution or disgorgement, the sanctions here do not attempt to restore the stolen funds to their rightful owner. To the contrary, the sanctions in this case impose a punishment for Johnson's violation of a standard laid down in the Exchange Act, and qualify therefore as a "penalty" within the meaning of § 2462.

D. *Public Policy Exception?*

Finally, the SEC suggests that we should narrowly construe "penalty" in this case, in light of the fact that its proceedings "serve[ ] public policy by preserving public rights, revenues and interests," SEC Brief at 33. While we do not doubt the public importance of SEC proceedings, the Supreme Court has admonished us that:

> Whatever prejudice there may have been in ancient times against statutes of limitations, it is a cardinal principle of modern law and of this court, that they are to be treated as statutes of repose, and are not to be construed so as to defeat their obvious intent to secure the prompt enforcement of claims during

---

10. The SEC's own position on what constitutes a penalty appears to vary with the context. In *SEC v. Telsey*, 144 B.R. 563 (Bankr.S.D.Fla.1992), the court agreed with the SEC that disgorgement orders are not dischargeable in bankruptcy because they have a deterrent purpose and thus *are* a "fine, penalty, or forfeiture." The SEC never explains why the position it took in *that* case should not apply here as well.

> the lives of the witnesses, and when their recollection may be presumed to be still unimpaired.[14]

Campbell v. City of Haverhill, 155 U.S. 610, 617 (1895). The SEC also directs us toward cases which serve up maxims about the need for strict construction of statutes of limitation, *see* SEC Brief at 32. But as we pointed out in *3M*, 17 F.3d at 1457, such cases—including their maxims—are unpersuasive, as they run counter to the Supreme Court's basic position on the subject, first stated by Chief Justice Marshall:

> In a country where not even treason can be prosecuted, after a lapse of three years, it would scarcely be supposed, that an individual would remain for ever liable to a pecuniary forfeiture.

Adams v. Woods, 6 U.S. (2 Cranch) 336, 341 (1805).

Finally, any public policy concerns in this case are greatly attenuated because § 2462 applies "[e]xcept as otherwise provided by Act of Congress," and thus Congress, should it believe a five-year statute of limitations is too burdensome in any particular situation, can simply put in a longer limitations period. We therefore find no reason based on public policy or general concerns about statutes of limitation to depart from the "ordinary, contemporary, common meaning" of the word "penalty," as a sanction imposed by the government for unlawful or proscribed conduct which goes beyond remedying the damage caused to the harmed party.

III. CONCLUSION

We find that the five-year statute of limitations set forth in § 2462 does apply to SEC proceedings under section 15(b) of the Securities and Exchange Act of 1934 which seek to censure and suspend a securities supervisor. Accordingly, we grant Johnson's petition for review, and vacate the SEC's order imposing sanctions on her.

NOTES AND QUESTIONS

1. ***Distinctions and Differences.*** Can the D.C. Circuit's decision in *Johnson* be reconciled with the Ninth Circuit's decision in *Rind?* Are there circumstances under which an SEC action for injunctive relief could be considered an action for a penalty? Note the *Johnson* court's footnote highlighting the SEC's characterization of disgorgement as a "penalty" for purposes of the "no discharge" provisions in the bankruptcy code. Are there other circumstances under which disgorgement may be viewed as a penalty? In this regard, note that the *Johnson* court cited with approval the district court's holding in *SEC v. Lorin* that § 2462 does not apply to SEC actions for disgorgement.

2. ***Balancing the Public Interest.*** The *Rind* court emphasized that its refusal to impose a "borrowed" statute of limitations on the SEC accorded with the common law doctrine *nullum tempus occurrit regi* (time does not run

---

14. In addition, the SEC argues that enforcing § 2462 would "hobble efforts to prevent future harm to the public." SEC Brief at 33. It is equally likely, however, that once the SEC has delayed more than five years in proceeding against a broker it considers a grave threat to the public, the bulk of the harm has already been done.

against the king). As a matter of policy, should there be an outside time limit in which the SEC must act to use its enforcement powers under the federal securities laws? Would such a limit jeopardize the SEC's ability to protect the public? What would be an appropriate limit? Five years? Less? More?

*3. **Starting the Clock.*** Section 2462 does not define the phrase "first accrued." How should that phrase be interpreted? Compare *SEC v. Scrushy*, 2005 WL 3279894 (N.D. Ala. 2005) ("the appropriate start of the statute of limitations [for § 2462] is the date of the violations for which the civil penalties are sought, not the discovery of such violations") with *SEC v. Buntrock*, 2004 WL 1179423 (N.D.Ill. 2004) ("the date of accrual of the five-year statute of limitations of 28 U.S.C. § 2462 for securities fraud cases is governed by the 'discovery of violation' rule"). In *3M Co. v. Browner,* 17 F.3d 1453, 1462-63 (D.C. Cir. 1994), the EPA advanced the "discovery rule" and the court specifically rejected it as "unworkable; outside the language of the statute; inconsistent with judicial interpretations of §2462; unsupported by the discovery of injury rule adopted in non-enforcement, remedial cases; and incompatible with the functions served by a statute of limitations in penalty cases." In determining when the clock should start for purposes of an SEC enforcement action for monetary penalties, how much weight should be accorded to the *3M Co.* decision? The underlying allegations in *3M Co.* did not involve a claim of fraud. Does that fact affect your answer?

c. Collateral Estoppel

As we noted previously, one explanation for the overwhelming number of enforcement actions resolved through consensual settlement is the potential collateral estoppel ramifications of litigating with the SEC and losing. The following case vividly illustrates why collateral estoppel constitutes such a serious collateral consequence.

PARKLANE HOSIERY CO. v. SHORE
439 U.S. 322 (1979)

JUSTICE POTTER STEWART:

This case presents the question whether a party who has had issues of fact adjudicated adversely to it in an equitable action may be collaterally estopped from relitigating the same issues before a jury in a subsequent legal action brought against it by a new party.

The respondent brought this stockholder's class action against the petitioners in a Federal District Court. The complaint alleged that the petitioners, Parklane Hosiery Co., Inc. (Parklane), and 13 of its officers, directors, and stockholders, had issued a materially false and misleading proxy statement in connection with a merger. The proxy statement, according to the complaint, had violated §§ 14(a), 10(b), and 20(a) of the Securities Exchange Act of 1934, as well as various rules and regulations promulgated by the Securities and Exchange Commission (SEC). The complaint sought damages, rescission of the merger, and recovery of costs.

Before this action came to trial, the SEC filed suit against the same defendants in the Federal District Court, alleging that the proxy statement that had been issued by Parklane was materially false and misleading in essentially the same respects as those that had been alleged in the respondent's complaint. Injunctive relief was requested. After a 4-day trial, the District Court found that the proxy statement was materially false and misleading in the respects alleged, and entered a declaratory judgment to that effect. The Court of Appeals for the Second Circuit affirmed this judgment.

The respondent in the present case then moved for partial summary judgment against the petitioners, asserting that the petitioners were collaterally estopped from relitigating the issues that had been resolved against them in the action brought by the SEC. The District Court denied the motion on the ground that such an application of collateral estoppel would deny the petitioners their Seventh Amendment right to a jury trial. The Court of Appeals for the Second Circuit reversed, holding that a party who has had issues of fact determined against him after a full and fair opportunity to litigate in a nonjury trial is collaterally estopped from obtaining a subsequent jury trial of these same issues of fact. The appellate court concluded that "the Seventh Amendment preserves the right to jury trial only with respect to issues of fact, [and] once those issues have been fully and fairly adjudicated in a prior proceeding, nothing remains for trial, either with or without a jury." [*Shore v. Parklane Hosiery Co.*, 565 F.2d 815, 819 (2d Cir. 1977)], at 819. Because of an inter-circuit conflict, we granted certiorari.

I

The threshold question to be considered is whether, quite apart from the right to a jury trial under the Seventh Amendment, the petitioners can be precluded from relitigating facts resolved adversely to them in a prior equitable proceeding with another party under the general law of collateral estoppel. Specifically, we must determine whether a litigant who was not a party to a prior judgment may nevertheless use that judgment "offensively" to prevent a defendant from relitigating issues resolved in the earlier proceeding.[4]

A

Collateral estoppel, like the related doctrine of res judicata,[5] has the dual purpose of protecting litigants from the burden of relitigating an identical issue with the same party or his privy and of promoting judicial economy by preventing needless litigation. *Blonder-Tongue Laboratories, Inc. v. University of Illinois Foundation,* 402 U.S. 313, 328-329. Until relatively recently, however, the scope of collateral estoppel was limited by the doctrine of mutuality of

---

4. In this context, offensive use of collateral estoppel occurs when the plaintiff seeks to foreclose the defendant from litigating an issue the defendant has previously litigated unsuccessfully in an action with another party. Defensive use occurs when a defendant seeks to prevent a plaintiff from asserting a claim the plaintiff has previously litigated and lost against another defendant.

5. Under the doctrine of res judicata, a judgment on the merits in a prior suit bars a second suit involving the same parties or their privies based on the same cause of action. Under the doctrine of collateral estoppel, on the other hand, the second action is upon a different cause of action and the judgment in the prior suit precludes relitigation of issues actually litigated and necessary to the outcome of the first action. 1B J. Moore, Federal Practice ¶ 0.405[1], pp. 622-624 (2d ed. 1974).

parties. Under this mutuality doctrine, neither party could use a prior judgment as an estoppel against the other unless both parties were bound by the judgment. Based on the premise that it is somehow unfair to allow a party to use a prior judgment when he himself would not be so bound, the mutuality requirement provided a party who had litigated and lost in a previous action an opportunity to relitigate identical issues with new parties.

By failing to recognize the obvious difference in position between a party who has never litigated an issue and one who has fully litigated and lost, the mutuality requirement was criticized almost from its inception. Recognizing the validity of this criticism, the Court in *Blonder-Tongue Laboratories, Inc. v. University of Illinois Foundation, supra*, abandoned the mutuality requirement, at least in cases where a patentee seeks to relitigate the validity of a patent after a federal court in a previous lawsuit has already declared it invalid. The "broader question" before the Court, however, was "whether it is any longer tenable to afford a litigant more than one full and fair opportunity for judicial resolution of the same issue." 402 U.S., at 328. The Court strongly suggested a negative answer to that question. ***

B

The *Blonder-Tongue* case involved defensive use of collateral estoppel—a plaintiff was estopped from asserting a claim that the plaintiff had previously litigated and lost against another defendant. The present case, by contrast, involves offensive use of collateral estoppel—a plaintiff is seeking to estop a defendant from relitigating the issues which the defendant previously litigated and lost against another plaintiff. In both the offensive and defensive use situations, the party against whom estoppel is asserted has litigated and lost in an earlier action. Nevertheless, several reasons have been advanced why the two situations should be treated differently.

First, offensive use of collateral estoppel does not promote judicial economy in the same manner as defensive use does. Defensive use of collateral estoppel precludes a plaintiff from relitigating identical issues by merely "switching adversaries." Thus defensive collateral estoppel gives a plaintiff a strong incentive to join all potential defendants in the first action if possible. Offensive use of collateral estoppel, on the other hand, creates precisely the opposite incentive. Since a plaintiff will be able to rely on a previous judgment against a defendant but will not be bound by that judgment if the defendant wins, the plaintiff has every incentive to adopt a "wait and see" attitude, in the hope that the first action by another plaintiff will result in a favorable judgment. Thus offensive use of collateral estoppel will likely increase rather than decrease the total amount of litigation, since potential plaintiffs will have everything to gain and nothing to lose by not intervening in the first action.

A second argument against offensive use of collateral estoppel is that it may be unfair to a defendant. If a defendant in the first action is sued for small or nominal damages, he may have little incentive to defend vigorously, particularly if future suits are not foreseeable. Allowing offensive collateral estoppel may also be unfair to a defendant if the judgment relied upon as a basis for the estoppel is itself inconsistent with one or more previous judgments in favor of the defendant Still another situation where it might be unfair to apply offensive estoppel is where the second action affords the defendant procedural opportunities unavailable in the first action that could readily cause a different result.[15]

C

We have concluded that the preferable approach for dealing with these problems in the federal courts is not to preclude the use of offensive collateral estoppel, but to grant trial courts broad discretion to determine when it should be applied. The general rule should be that in cases where a plaintiff could easily have joined in the earlier action or where, either for the reasons discussed above or for other reasons, the application of offensive estoppel would be unfair to a defendant, a trial judge should not allow the use of offensive collateral estoppel.

In the present case, however, none of the circumstances that might justify reluctance to allow the offensive use of collateral estoppel is present. The application of offensive collateral estoppel will not here reward a private plaintiff who could have joined in the previous action, since the respondent probably could not have joined in the injunctive action brought by the SEC even had he so desired. Similarly, there is no unfairness to the petitioners in applying offensive collateral estoppel in this case. First, in light of the serious allegations made in the SEC's complaint against the petitioners, as well as the foreseeability of subsequent private suits that typically follow a successful Government judgment, the petitioners had every incentive to litigate the SEC lawsuit fully and vigorously. Second, the judgment in the SEC action was not inconsistent with any previous decision. Finally, there will in the respondent's action be no procedural opportunities available to the petitioners that were unavailable in the first action of a kind that might be likely to cause a different result.[19]

We conclude, therefore, that none of the considerations that would justify a refusal to allow the use of offensive collateral estoppel is present in this case. Since the petitioners received a "full and fair" opportunity to litigate their claims in the SEC action, the contemporary law of collateral estoppel leads inescapably to the conclusion that the petitioners are collaterally estopped from

15. If, for example, the defendant in the first action was forced to defend in an inconvenient forum and therefore was unable to engage in full scale discovery or call witnesses, application of offensive collateral estoppel may be unwarranted. Indeed, differences in available procedures may sometimes justify not allowing a prior judgment to have estoppel effect in a subsequent action even between the same parties, or where defensive estoppel is asserted against a plaintiff who has litigated and lost. The problem of unfairness is particularly acute in cases of offensive estoppel, however, because the defendant against whom estoppel is asserted typically will not have chosen the forum in the first action. See [Restatement (Second) of Judgments] § 88(2) and Comment *d.*

19. It is true, of course, that the petitioners in the present action would be entitled to a jury trial of the issues bearing on whether the proxy statement was materially false and misleading had the SEC action never been brought—a matter to be discussed in Part II of this opinion. But the presence or absence of a jury as factfinder is basically neutral, quite unlike, for example, the necessity of defending the first lawsuit in an inconvenient forum.

relitigating the question of whether the proxy statement was materially false and misleading.

II

The question that remains is whether, notwithstanding the law of collateral estoppel, the use of offensive collateral estoppel in this case would violate the petitioners' Seventh Amendment right to a jury trial.***[20]

"[T]he thrust of the [Seventh] Amendment was to preserve the right to jury trial as it existed in 1791." *Curtis v. Loether*, 415 U.S. 189, 193. At common law, a litigant was not entitled to have a jury determine issues that had been previously adjudicated by a chancellor in equity.

***The petitioners contend that since the scope of the Amendment must be determined by reference to the common law as it existed in 1791, and since the common law permitted collateral estoppel only where there was mutuality of parties, collateral estoppel cannot constitutionally be applied when such mutuality is absent.

The petitioners have advanced no persuasive reason, however, why the meaning of the Seventh Amendment should depend on whether or not mutuality of parties is present. A litigant who has lost because of adverse factual findings in an equity action is equally deprived of a jury trial whether he is estopped from relitigating the factual issues against the same party or a new party. In either case, the party against whom estoppel is asserted has litigated questions of fact, and has had the facts determined against him in an earlier proceeding. In either case there is no further factfinding function for the jury to perform, since the common factual issues have been resolved in the previous action. Cf. *Ex parte Peterson*, 253 U.S. 300, 310 ("No one is entitled in a civil case to trial by jury, unless and except so far as there are issues of fact to be determined").

The Seventh Amendment has never been interpreted in the rigid manner advocated by the petitioners. On the contrary, many procedural devices developed since 1791 that have diminished the civil jury's historic domain have been found not to be inconsistent with the Seventh Amendment. See *Galloway v. United States*, 319 U.S. 372, 388-393 (directed verdict does not violate the Seventh Amendment); *Gasoline Products Co. v. Champlin Refining Co.*, 283 U.S. 494, 497-498 (retrial limited to question of damages does not violate the Seventh Amendment even though there was no practice at common law for setting aside a verdict in part); *Fidelity & Deposit Co. v. United States*, 187 U.S. 315, 319-321 (summary judgment does not violate the Seventh Amendment). ***

The law of collateral estoppel, like the law in other procedural areas defining the scope of the jury's function, has evolved since 1791. Under the rationale of the *Galloway* case, these developments are not repugnant to the Seventh Amendment simply for the reason that they did not exist in 1791. Thus if, as we have held, the law of collateral estoppel forecloses the petitioners from relitigating the factual issues determined against them in the SEC action,

---

20. The Seventh Amendment provides: "In Suits at common law, where the value in controversy shall exceed twenty dollars, the right to jury trial shall be preserved...."

nothing in the Seventh Amendment dictates a different result, even though because of lack of mutuality there would have been no collateral estoppel in 1791. ***

NOTES AND QUESTIONS

*1. **Stacking the Decks for Settlement?*** Key to the Supreme Court's decision in *Parklane Hosiery* was that the issues to be precluded from the private litigation had already been "fully and fairly" adjudicated in the defendant's prior proceeding with the SEC. What if the Parklane defendants had entered into a settlement with the SEC and agreed to be bound by a consent decree ordering an injunction and disgorgement? Could principles of collateral estoppel preclude such defendants from relitigating liability in a subsequent action brought by private plaintiffs? At least in the typical case where a settlement with the SEC has been entered into "for purposes of this proceeding only" and "without admitting or denying" the SEC's allegations, the answer is almost assuredly no. See, e.g., *In re Cenco Inc. Sec. Litig.*, 529 F. Supp. 411, 413-15 (N.D. Ill. 1982). See also ABA Committee on Federal Regulation of Securities, Report of the Task Force on SEC Settlements, 47 Bus. Law. 1083, 1155 (1992) (emphasizing that "SEC settlement documents should have no collateral estoppel effect").

The conclusion that settlements with the SEC lack collateral estoppel effect also captured the attention of Justice Rehnquist, who wrote the sole dissent in *Parklane Hosiery.* Justice Rehnquist chastised the majority for ruling in a way that could "coerc[e] defendants to agree to consent orders or settlements in agency enforcement actions in order to preserve their right to jury trial in the private actions." 439 U.S. at 355-56 (Rehnquist, J., dissenting). Thus, in his view, "for no compelling reason," the majority had "simply added a powerful club to the administrative agencies' arsenals that even Congress was unwilling to provide them." Id. at 356. How would the *Parklane* majority likely respond?

*2. **Collateral Estoppel Ramifications of SEC Administrative Proceedings.*** Although the defendants in *Parklane* were estopped from relitigating the factual and legal issues that had been necessarily determined in a prior injunctive action brought by the SEC in federal district court, the doctrine of collateral estoppel is also potentially applicable to adverse findings made in the course of an SEC administrative proceeding. Support for this conclusion dates back more than 35 years, to the Supreme Court's statement in *United States v. Utah Constr. & Mining Co.*, 384 U.S. 394, 422 (1966), that "[w]hen an administrative agency is acting in a judicial capacity and resolves disputed issues of fact properly before it which the parties have had an adequate opportunity to litigate, the courts have not hesitated to apply *res judicata* to enforce repose." See also *Univ. of Tenn. v. Elliott*, 478 U.S. 788, 797 (1986) (endorsing the practice of applying "principles of issue preclusion to the fact-finding of administrative bodies acting in a judicial capacity"). Although there has yet to be a litigated case directly on point, commentators generally advise respondents in SEC proceedings to weigh heavily this possibility in calculating the consequences of litigation. See, e.g., Andrew M. Smith, SEC Cease-and-Desist Orders, 51 Admin. L. Rev. 1197, 1219-20 (1999) (stating that "an SEC cease-and-desist order might easily be given nonmutual offensive preclusive effect"). See also Edmund H. Kerr & Robert J. Stillman, Collateral Estoppel Implications of SEC Adjudications, 42 Bus. Law. 441 (1987).

3. Collateral Estoppel in SEC Litigation. The SEC often invokes the doctrine of collateral estoppel to prevent a defendant in a civil case from relitigating issues that were "fully and fairly" decided in a criminal trial. See, e.g., *SEC v. Grossman*, 887 F. Supp. 649 (S.D.N.Y. 1995), aff'd, 101 F.3d 109 (2d Cir. 1996). The SEC has also successfully argued for collateral estoppel in cases in which the defendant has resolved the prior criminal action through a guilty plea. See *Palmisano* (set out in Section F.3 of this Chapter). See also *SEC v. McCaskey*, 2001 WL 1029053 (S.D.N.Y. 2001). Should the SEC be able to use collateral estoppel to preclude a defendant in a subsequent civil action from relitigating issues resolved in a prior sentencing proceeding? See *SEC v. Monarch Funding Corp.*, 192 F.3d 295 (2d Cir. 1999) (rejecting the use of collateral estoppel but declining to adopt a bright-line rule).

4. The Importance of Jury Trials. As noted above, Justice Rehnquist was the sole dissenter from the Court's opinion in *Parklane*, arguing strongly that the defendant's Seventh Amendment right to a jury trial would be violated by the application of collateral estoppel. In his view, "developments in the judge-made doctrine of collateral estoppel, however salutary, cannot, consistent with the Seventh Amendment, contract in any material fashion the right to a jury trial that a defendant would have enjoyed in 1791." 439 U.S. at 347 (Rehnquist, J., dissenting).

Justice Rehnquist also maintained that notwithstanding the Seventh Amendment, it was highly "unfair" to apply estoppel in this case because the company never had the opportunity to have the facts determined by a jury. Thus, based on the majority's own standards for the use of non-mutual offensive collateral estoppel, Justice Rehnquist would not have applied the doctrine to estop the company from relitigating in front of a jury the issues determined in the SEC's injunctive action.

Justice Rehnquist reasoned that "the use of offensive collateral estoppel in this case runs counter to the strong federal policy favoring jury trials." Id. at 351. He also argued that "the opportunity for a jury trial in the second action could easily lead to a different result from that obtained in the first action before the court," id. at 353, and took particular issue with the majority's footnote 19:

> [T]hose who drafted the Declaration of Independence and debated so passionately the proposed Constitution during the ratification period, would indeed be astounded to learn that the presence or absence of a jury is merely "neutral," whereas the availability of discovery, a device unmentioned in the Constitution, may be controlling. It is precisely because the Framers believed that they might receive a different result at the hands of a jury of their peers than at the mercy of the sovereign's judges, that the Seventh Amendment was adopted. And I suspect that anyone who litigates cases before juries in the 1970's would be equally amazed to hear of the supposed lack of distinction between trial by court and trial by jury. ***
>
> Contrary to the majority's supposition, juries can make a difference, and our cases have, before today at least, recognized this obvious fact. Thus, in *Colgrove v. Battin*, [413 U.S. 149, 157 (1973),] we stated that "the purpose of the jury trial in ... civil cases [is] to assure a fair and equitable resolution of factual issues." And in *Byrd v. Blue Ridge Rural Electrical Cooperative*, [356 U.S. 525,

> 537 (1958),] the Court conceded that "the nature of the tribunal which tries issues may be important in the enforcement of the parcel of rights making up a cause of action or defense . . . . It may well be that in the instant personal-injury case the outcome would be substantially affected by whether the issue of immunity is decided by a judge or a jury." Jurors bring to a case their common sense and community values; their "very inexperience is an asset because it secures a fresh perception of each trial, avoiding the stereotypes said to infect the judicial eye." H. Kalven & H. Zeisel, The American Jury 8 (1966).

Parklane Hosiery, 439 U.S. at 354-55 (Rehnquist, J., dissenting). Are you persuaded that the use of collateral estoppel against Parklane would have been unfair?

E. SROs AS ENFORCERS OF THE FEDERAL SECURITIES LAWS

Although Congress established the SEC as the principal enforcer of its newly created federal securities laws, even in 1934, Congress clearly envisioned that the stock exchanges—particularly the New York Stock Exchange (NYSE)—would continue to play a major role in regulating the conduct of exchange members and their associated persons. Four years later, the National Association of Securities Dealers (NASD) was added to this scheme of self-regulation, when Congress enacted the Maloney Act of 1938, which extended federal regulation to the non-exchange, or over-the-counter (OTC), market.

1. Self-Regulation and SEC Oversight

The legislative history that immediately follows reflects a decision by Congress in 1975 to change significantly many of the aspects of self-regulation that had existed in the decades prior. As you read the Senate Report, consider the role that Congress expected the SROs to play in the enforcement of the federal securities laws.

P.L. 94-29, SECURITIES ACTS AMENDMENTS OF 1975 SENATE REPORT (BANKING, HOUSING AND URBAN AFFAIRS COMMITTEE)

No. 94-75, Apr. 14, 1975 (To accompany S. 249)

The Committee on Banking, Housing and Urban Affairs *** reports favorably upon S. 249 as amended and recommends without objection that the bill do pass.***

A. NATIONAL MARKET SYSTEM AND SELF-REGULATORY ORGANIZATIONS ***

Because of the unique system of self-regulation in the securities industry, the principal markets for securities, i.e., the exchanges, are also the principal regulators of the activities of broker-dealers using those markets. Meaningful reform of this country's securities trading mechanisms will, therefore, be impossible unless there is also a reform of the method and manner by which the self-regulatory organizations operate and in the way that the SEC oversees the performance of their regulatory responsibilities.

Accordingly, S. 249 would significantly amend the provisions of the Exchange Act dealing with the powers of the self-regulatory organizations and the oversight authority of the SEC with respect to these organizations. The Committee believes that self-regulation should be preserved in the securities industry, but it also believes that the self-regulatory organizations must display a greater responsiveness to their statutory obligations and to the need to coordinate their functions and activities. In the new regulatory environment created by this bill, self-regulation would be continued, but the SEC would be expected to play a much larger role than it has in the past to ensure that there is no gap between self-regulatory performance and regulatory need and, when appropriate, to provide leadership for the development of a more coherent and rational regulatory structure to correspond to and to police effectively the new national market system. ***

II. SELF-REGULATION AND SEC OVERSIGHT***

S. 249 contains a number of provisions which would clarify the scope of the self-regulatory responsibilities of national securities exchanges and registered securities associations (which are defined in section 3(a)(26) as "self-regulatory organizations") and the manner in which they are to exercise those responsibilities. The bill would also clarify and strengthen the Commission's oversight role with respect to the self-regulatory organizations.

The Committee has found a common and serious misunderstanding of the nature and limits of the concept of self-regulation. All too frequently, the view is expressed that self-regulation is an arrangement whereby the exchanges and the NASD, rather than the federal government, police the conduct and strengthen the professional standards of securities firms. In other words, self-regulation is thought to mean that the securities industry regulates itself and therefore is not regulated by the government. Such a conception of self-regulation is seriously misleading in that it fails to recognize the essential and continuing role of the federal government. Industry regulation and government regulation are not alternatives, but complementary components of the self-regulatory process.

In enacting the Exchange Act, the Congress balanced the limitation and dangers of permitting the securities industry to regulate itself against "the sheer ineffectiveness of attempting to assure [regulation] directly through the government on a wide scale." The result was a unique pattern of regulation combining both industry and government responsibility. The fundamental pattern established in 1934 has not been essentially changed since then:

> The SEC has the authority and responsibility to assure compliance by all broker-dealers with the legal requirements of the Exchange Act and of the rules which the SEC is authorized to promulgate under the Exchange Act.
>
> Industry organizations, i.e., the exchanges and the NASD, are delegated governmental power in order to enforce, at their own initiative, compliance by members of the industry with both the legal requirements laid down in the Exchange Act and ethical standards going beyond those requirements.
>
> The SEC is charged with supervising the exercise of this self-regulatory power in order to assure that it is used effectively to fulfill the responsibilities assigned to the self-regulatory agencies, and that it is not used in a manner inimical to the public interest or unfair to private interests.

In an effort to emphasize the fact that both the industry and the government have regulatory responsibilities under the Exchange Act, it has become commonplace to refer to the "partnership" between the self-regulatory organizations and the SEC, or to the "cooperative" character of the regulatory system. The Committee concurs in the need to emphasize the mutual regulatory responsibilities of the industry and the SEC. However, it believes care should be exercised, lest the use of phrases such as "partnership" and "cooperative regulation" lead to the impression that the industry and the government fulfill the same function in the regulatory framework or that they enjoy the same order of authority or deserve the same degree of deference, whether by firms, courts or the Congress. The self-regulatory organizations exercise authority subject to SEC oversight. They have no authority to regulate independently of the SEC's control.

The self-regulatory roles of the exchanges and the NASD have been major elements of the regulatory scheme of the Exchange Act since 1934 and 1938, respectively. Although self-regulation has not always performed up to expectations, on the whole it has worked well, and the Committee believes it should be preserved and strengthened. S. 249 is designed to accomplish this, not only by clarifying regulatory responsibilities at all levels but also by assuring that the self-regulatory organizations follow effective and fair procedures, that their activities are not anticompetitive and that the Commission's oversight powers are ample and its responsibility to correct self-regulatory lapses is unmistakable. The intent of the bill is not to diminish the role of self-regulation but to strengthen the total regulatory fabric.

A. THE CONCEPT OF MEMBERSHIP

The concept of "membership"—i.e., voluntary association with an industry organization—is fundamental to the self-regulatory system established by the Exchange Act. However, because of certain changes in the operation of the markets a change in the definition of "member" appears desirable.***

Section 3(a)(3) as amended by the bill would redefine "member" to mean any natural person permitted to effect transactions without the services of a broker and any registered broker or dealer with which such a natural person is associated, any registered broker or dealer permitted to designate as a representative such a natural person and any registered broker or dealer which agrees to be regulated by such exchange and with respect to which the exchange undertakes to enforce compliance with its rules and the Exchange Act. An exchange's or association's undertaking to regulate a broker or dealer would not be discretionary with respect to persons qualified for membership. In other words, if a person meets the requirements for membership he must be admitted. (Sections 6(b)(2) and 15A(b)(3)). And with respect to a person admitted, i.e., a member, an exchange or association must enforce compliance with its rules, the Exchange Act, and the rules and regulations thereunder. (Section 19(g)). ***

B. PROCEDURAL STANDARDS FOR SELF-REGULATORY ACTION

The self-regulatory organizations exercise government power, and they do so in basically three ways which may adversely affect the interests of particular persons: (1) by imposing a disciplinary sanction, broadly defined, on a member or person affiliated with a member, (2) by denying membership to an applicant, and (3) by requiring members to cease doing business entirely or in specified ways with a particular non-member or with respect to a particular security.

The self-regulatory organizations must exercise governmental-type powers if they are to carry out their responsibilities under the Exchange Act. When a member violates the Act or a self-regulatory organization's rules, the organization must be in a position to impose appropriate penalties or to revoke relevant privileges. Similarly, a self-regulatory organization must be able to prevent an unqualified person from obtaining access to facilities and business opportunities by denying membership. And members' transactions and relationships with non-members must be regulated, as the Supreme Court pointed out in the *Silver* case, in order that "... contact with an unreliable non-member [does not] injure the member or the member's customer on whose behalf the contract is made and [thus] ultimately imperil the future status of the [self-regulatory organization] by sapping public confidence." [*Silver v. New York Stock Exch.*, 373 U.S. 341, 356 (1963)].

Recognizing that the self-regulatory organizations utilize governmental-type powers in carrying out their responsibilities under the Exchange Act highlights the fact that these organizations must be required to conform their activities to fundamental standards of due process.

The Exchange Act presently requires that the NASD's disciplinary actions be conducted in accordance with rules which provide "a fair and orderly procedure," including the obligation that the self-regulatory organization bring "specific charges," give notice, provide an opportunity for hearing, and identify in any adverse determination the act or practice which constitutes the violation of a "specific rule or rules." [Section 19(d)(1)]. The Exchange Act also provides for Commission review of NASD disciplinary actions both on the Commission's own motion and by petition of an aggrieved person. [Section 19(d)(2)]. In contrast to the provisions under which the NASD must operate, the Exchange Act contains no requirements as to an exchange's disciplinary procedures and no provision for Commission review of an exchange's enforcement actions. Sections 6(b)(7), 15A(b)(8), 19(d) and 19(e) would eliminate these statutory anomalies and establish uniform standards to which both exchange and NASD rules would be required to conform and in accordance with which SEC review would be available.

The Exchange Act presently requires that in a proceeding to determine whether an applicant is to be denied membership, the NASD must notify the applicant of "the specific grounds for denial ... which are under consideration;" give him an opportunity to be heard on those grounds; keep a record; and set forth in the determination "the specific grounds upon which the denial ... is based." [Section 15(h)(2)]. The Exchange Act also provides for Commission review of the NASD's denial of a membership application on its own motion and by petition of an aggrieved person. [Section 19(d)(2)]. There are no comparable provisions with respect to an exchange's procedure for denial of a membership application or Commission review thereof.

The Committee is well aware of the historical differences between "membership" in an exchange and in the NASD. The limited number of "seats" on an exchange, as contrasted with the availability of NASD membership to all qualified brokers and dealers, is only the most obvious of these differences. However, the Committee does not believe that the substantive differences in the two concepts of membership justify any less attention to procedural fairness in the case of the exchanges than in that of the NASD. Sections 6(b)(7), 15A(b)(8),

19(d) and 19(f) would establish the same procedural requirements and review rights for exchange and NASD actions concerning membership applications.

With respect to non-members, the Committee believes the Exchange Act should be amended to require all self-regulatory agencies to adopt procedures which will afford constitutionally adequate due process to non-members directly affected by self-regulatory action. The bill would accomplish this in Sections 6(b)(7) and 15A(b)(8) by establishing a formal procedure that must be followed before a self-regulatory organization could take any action directly affecting a non-member. Sections 19(e) and 19(f) would establish a right to obtain review of such an action by the appropriate regulatory agency as defined in Section 3(a)(34).

With respect to all three types of quasi-adjudicatory self-regulatory proceedings—the disciplining of a member, the denial of membership, and the limitation or prohibition of a person's access to requested services—the Committee believes that final action should be open to public scrutiny. ***Accordingly, Section 19(d) would require the self- regulatory organizations to file with the appropriate regulatory agency for the self-regulatory organization, and with the appropriate regulatory agency for the member, participant, applicant or other person affected (if other than the appropriate regulatory agency for the self-regulatory organization), notice of all final quasi-adjudicatory actions affecting members and nonmembers. That agency would have the power to prescribe the information to be included in the notices, and it would be required to make all notices available for public inspection. [Section 19(d)(1)].

C. SCOPE OF SELF-REGULATORY AUTHORITY

***Under the bill the scope of the rule-making authority and responsibility of all self-regulatory organizations would be defined in terms of purposes and standards rather than subject matters. The purposes to be served by self- regulatory rules would be expressed affirmatively and negatively (what the rules must be, and what they may not be, designed to accomplish). New Sections 6(b)(5) and 15A(b)(6) would require the rules of any self-regulatory organization to be designed to prevent fraudulent and manipulative acts and practices, to promote just and equitable principles of trades, to foster cooperation and coordination with persons engaged in regulating, clearing, settling, processing information with respect to, and facilitating transactions in securities, to remove impediments to and perfect the mechanism of a national market system, and, in general, to protect investors and the public interest. Similarly, by reason of the same sections, a self-regulatory organization's rules must not be designed to permit unfair discrimination between customers, issuers, brokers, or dealers or to regulate, by virtue of any authority conferred by the Exchange Act, matters not related to the purposes of the Exchange Act or the administration of such self-regulatory organization.

Under procedures established by the bill whereby self-regulatory rule changes would have to be justified to and reviewed by the Commission after opportunity for public comment, the Commission's action in approving any such change would constitute a determination by the Commission that the rule was within the permitted purposes, and in conformity with the specified standards, of the Exchange Act. [Section 19(b)]. ***

D. SELF-REGULATORY RULE-MAKING

The Exchange Act says very little about the internal decision-making processes of the self-regulatory organizations. These bodies do not act just like Government agencies, whose procedures and functions are derived from, and often prescribed by, statutes rather than from the decisions of those who choose to become members, and the Committee believes the distinction is essential to the concept of self-regulation. This does not mean that the decision-making processes of the self-regulatory bodies cannot be improved. Quite to the contrary, but in the Committee's view it would be self-defeating to saddle the self-regulatory organizations with the wholly panoply of Governmental administrative procedure.

One of the advantages of self-regulation is the flexibility and informality of its decision-making procedures. Further, self-regulatory organizations differ as to their membership, regulatory responsibilities, and economic power. It would be difficult to prescribe a single "proper" decision-making procedure appropriate to the circumstances of every self-regulatory organization, and it is doubtful that any such formal procedure would better serve the goal of effective securities regulation than the present practice of encouraging each organization to develop procedures which best serve its needs and those of public investors.

The increased use of public governors, providing an opportunity for public comment on proposed rule changes, and the delegation of increased authority to professional staffs are only some of the positive steps that are being taken by the self-regulatory organizations in the area of policy formation. The Committee encourages the self-regulatory organization to continue their healthy experimentation and innovation with regard to decision-making processes, keeping in mind at all times that they were quasi-public organizations, not private clubs, and that one of their principal goals is the prevention of inequitable and unfair practices and the advancement of the public interest.

Without qualifying its general support for preserving flexibility in self-regulatory decision-making, the Committee believes there are several respects in which the rule-making processes of the self-regulatory organizations should be improved by legislation.

First, although all self-regulatory organizations are required to file proposed rule changes with the SEC, there is no requirement that they file an explanation or justification for their proposals. In order to facilitate expeditious Commission review and evaluation of such proposals and to assure informed public comment on them, Section 19(b)(1) would require all self-regulatory organizations to file with the SEC in connection with any proposed rule change a "concise general statement of the basis and purpose" of the proposed rule change. It is the Committee's intention in adopting this standard to hold the self-regulatory organizations to the same standards of policy justification that the Administrative Procedure Act imposes on the SEC.

Second, the Committee believes interested persons should have a meaningful opportunity to obtain accurate information about proposed changes in self-regulatory rules and to comment on the need or justification for these changes. Section 19(b)(1) would require the SEC to give notice and provide an opportunity for interested persons to participate in the process of reviewing a proposed change in a self-regulatory organization's rules. In addition, this section would require that all comments and all correspondence between the SEC and the self-regulatory agency concerning the proposal be available for public inspection. Section 19(b)(2) would give the SEC sufficient flexibility to fashion a proceeding appropriate to the particular self-regulatory proposal being considered. In many, perhaps most, situations, notice and an opportunity for written comment would be sufficient and there would undoubtedly be few, if any, comments. In cases in which fundamental policy issues are involved, however, oral hearings or publicly announced conferences might be most appropriate.

Third, the Exchange Act at present creates the anomalous situation whereby an exchange, which may not lawfully do business until its rules have undergone official scrutiny in relation to statutory standards, is free to change those rules at any time thereafter without similar advance scrutiny or approval. Section 19(b)(2) would fill this regulatory gap by providing that, subject to certain exceptions specified in Section 19(b)(3), no change in the rules of any self-regulatory organization may become effective until the SEC finds it to be consistent with the registration requirements for the organization and the purposes of the Exchange Act. The Committee believes the Commission has a responsibility to see that self-regulatory rules are fully responsive to regulatory needs. By explicitly providing that the Commission's oversight authority encompasses major self-regulatory policies, the bill would make this responsibility clear and substantially decrease the possibility of slippage between regulatory need and self-regulatory performance.***

E. SEC TO CHANGE SELF-REGULATORY RULES

*** Under the bill, the SEC would have uniform authority to "abrogate, add to, or delete from" any self-regulatory organization's rules. (Section 19(c)). Moreover, where the Commission has exercised its rulemaking authority under Section 19(c) of the Exchange Act to abrogate, add to, or delete from the rules of any self-regulatory organization, any rule of a self-regulatory organization inconsistent with such Commission rule adopted pursuant to Section 19(c) shall be null and void.

***[T]here has been a continuing controversy as to the precise scope of the SEC's power to amend the rules of a self-regulatory organization. The bill would give the SEC clear authority to amend any self-regulatory organization's rules in any respect consistent with the objectives of the Exchange Act (Section 19(c)).

***[T]here is also a controversy over the procedures that the SEC must follow in order to force a change in the rules of a self-regulatory organization. In recognition of the quasi-legislative, policy-making nature of an SEC determination to require such a change, Section 19(c) would provide that the Commission's action shall be by "rule". Accordingly, the basic procedures the Commission would be required to follow are specified in the Administrative Procedure Act (5 U.S.C. § 553) for rulemaking not on the record. The bill would, however, also require the Commission to (1) provide all interested persons an opportunity to present their views in person as well as in writing; (2) keep a transcript of all oral presentations; and (3) publish a statement of its reasons for taking the action it did, including an identification of the facts, if any, it has relied upon in reaching its conclusion. (Section 19(c)). ***

F. COORDINATION OF SELF-REGULATORY RESPONSIBILITIES

***[T]he Committee believes the SEC can do a great deal more than it has in the past to foster the development of a more rational self-regulatory framework. The Committee agrees with the recommendation of the Commission's Advisory Committee on Enforcement Policies and Practices that "the Commission should play an affirmative role in allocating inspection and enforcement responsibilities among the self-regulatory organizations...." Further, as the Advisory Committee on Broker-Dealer Reports and Registration Requirements recommends: "... for reporting purposes each broker-dealer [should] be assigned to a designated principal self-regulator or government regulator who will be responsible for determining the broker-dealer's operating and financial status." Section 17(d) would provide the SEC with unquestioned authority to accomplish these objectives. It is the Committee's hope that the SEC would use this authority to lay the foundation for a restructured self-regulatory system appropriate to the national market system.

***Section 19(g) would obligate a self-regulatory organization "absent any reasonable justification or excuse" to enforce compliance by its members or participants with applicable provisions of the Exchange Act and its own rules. In Section 19(h)(1), the SEC or other appropriate regulatory agency would be authorized to sanction any self-regulatory organization which fails to enforce compliance by its members "without reasonable justification or excuse." The Committee believes the standard in these Sections appropriately defines the responsibility of the self-regulatory organizations. Such organizations should never be placed in the position of being insurers of their members' compliance. They do, however, have an obligation to enforce applicable provisions of the Exchange Act and their own rules which they should not be permitted to avoid except for good cause.

G. SEC ENFORCEMENT POWERS

***The SEC's "reserved control" over the self-regulatory organizations is of several sorts ranging from the draconian remedy of suspending or withdrawing registration to highly flexible rulemaking authority. Although it has become commonplace to refer to the SEC's oversight authority as a "big stick" or a "shotgun behind the door," the Committee found the SEC also has available certain, albeit limited, powers to act in specific ways to correct identified instances of inappropriate self-regulatory activity.

The Commission's oversight responsibility with respect to the self-regulatory agencies is to insure that they exercise their delegated governmental power effectively to meet regulatory needs in the public interest and that they do not exercise that delegated power in a manner inimical to the public interest or unfair to private interests. To the degree that there may have been undue deference to the self-regulatory organizations because of the cumbersomeness of the oversight mechanisms or the unavailability of appropriately focused remedies, the Committee believes the Exchange Act should be amended to correct the problem. However, the Committee also believes that the successful performance of the Commission's oversight task necessarily involves the willingness to take steps to assure that the self-regulatory agencies comply with and advance the policies of the Exchange Act. This willingness to act can be encouraged by legislation but it cannot be compelled.

In order to enhance the oversight powers of the Commission and the other appropriate regulatory agencies, as defined in Section 3(a)(34), and to provide them with greater regulatory flexibility, the bill would significantly increase the regulatory options available to them to deal with perceived self-regulatory shortcomings.

First, Section 19(h)(1) would authorize them, by order and upon appropriate findings, to censure and place restrictions on the activities, functions, and operations of a self-regulatory agency. These powers are in addition to suspension and deregistration and are intended to provide more usable sanctions than the SEC's traditional "big stick."

Second, Section 19(h)(1) would also expand and make uniform the grounds on which the Commission may sanction a self-regulatory organization. The appropriate regulatory agency would be able to take appropriate action directly against any self-regulatory organization upon a finding that it had failed to enforce its own rules or failed to enforce the Exchange Act or the rules thereunder.

Third, Section 19(h)(4) would authorize the appropriate regulatory agency to censure or remove from office any officer or director of a self-regulatory organization who had willfully failed to enforce compliance with the Exchange Act, the rules thereunder, or the organization's own rules.

Fourth, Sections 21(e) and 21(f) would empower the SEC to apply to a federal court for an order to (1) enjoin the violation of the rules of a self-regulatory organization, (2) command a member of a self-regulatory organization to comply with the rules of such organization, or (3) command a self-regulatory organization to enforce compliance by its members with the Exchange Act, the rules thereunder, and the organization's own rules. Before exercising a power described in (1) or (2), it must appear to the commission (1) that the self-regulatory organization was unable or unwilling to take appropriate action or (2) that such action is otherwise necessary in the public interest or for the protection of investors.

The Committee expects the additional enforcement powers provided by the bill to lead to an increased willingness on the part of the Commission to take formal action where needed to assure adequate self-regulatory performance. Although the Congress cannot mandate such a willingness, the Committee has no reason to believe that the Commission and the other agencies granted regulatory authority under S. 249 would not be responsive to such an explicit expression of congressional intent. It is important, however, for the Congress to monitor the performance of the Commission and the other regulatory agencies with oversight responsibilities with respect to self-regulatory organizations. Section 23(b) would require the Commission and the other regulatory agencies in their annual report to the Congress to describe fully their activities with respect to the self-regulatory organizations. The SEC would be required to include in its annual reports information as to (1) its program for inspecting the self-regulatory organizations; (2) the expenses and operations of each self-regulatory organization in connection with performance of its responsibilities under the Exchange Act; (3) the development of a national market system and a national system for clearance and settlement; (4) steps the Commission has taken toward the discontinuance of the physical movement of securities certificates in connection with the settlement of securities transactions and any recommendations for legislation to eliminate the use of securities certificates; (5) the number of exemptions requested from provisions of the Exchange Act, the number granted, and the basis for exemptions granted; (6) the Commission's regulatory activities with respect to municipal securities dealers and brokers for which it is not the appropriate regulatory agency; *** and (8) the time elapsed between the Commission's receipt and its publication of reports filed pursuant to Section 13(f) of the Exchange Act.

H. JUDICIAL REVIEW

The bill would substantially revise Section 25 of the Exchange Act concerning judicial review of SEC action. ***

The Exchange Act now establishes a procedure for review of SEC "orders" in the Court of Appeals. *** The bill would (1) simplify and clarify the provisions relating to the review of Commission orders and (2) establish a statutory review procedure for certain SEC rules, including those approving and disapproving self-regulatory actions.

The changes with respect to review of SEC orders are included in Section 25(a). These changes are intended to codify existing law and would not alter in any fundamental respect the availability of court review of orders or the manner in which such review is exercised. ***[They are also] designed to create a more logical and realistic review procedure without impairing the due process protections presently afforded parties to administration adjudications before the SEC.

The bill's major innovation in the area of judicial review relates to SEC rule-making. *** Section 25(b), as amended by the bill, would give to any person adversely affected a right to preenforcement review in the Court of Appeals of any rule promulgated under Sections 6, [19(h)(2)], 11, 11A, 15(c)(5)- (6), 15A, 17, 17A or 19 of the Exchange Act—i.e., any provision directly relating to the operation or regulation of the national market system, a national clearing system, or the SEC's oversight of the self-regulatory organizations.

By establishing a scheme for the preenforcement review of rules, the Committee believes the bill would expedite final resolution of the major policy determinations the Commission will be called upon to make with respect to the national market system and the rationalization of the self-regulatory system. The changes, however, are not intended to change the existing law with respect to finality or standing in connection with pre-enforcement review of agency rule-making. The Court of Appeals appears to provide the most appropriate forum for this review in light of the fact that the District Court's fact finding function is rarely necessary and the questions subject to review are likely to end up in the higher court anyway. ***

In 2007, the securities industry's self-regulatory landscape changed dramatically when the SEC formally approved the consolidation of the NASD and the enforcement, member regulatory, and arbitration divisions of the NYSE into a single self-regulatory organization to be known as the Financial Industry Regulatory Authority (FINRA). According to the SEC,

> The consolidation is intended to help streamline the broker-dealer regulatory system, combine technologies, and permit the establishment of a single set of rules governing membership matters, with the aim of enhancing oversight of U.S. securities firms and assuring investor protection.
>
> FINRA will operate under SEC oversight. It will be responsible for regulating all securities firms that do business with the public, including with respect to professional training, testing and licensing of registered persons, arbitration and mediation. FINRA also will be responsible, by contract, for regulating The Nasdaq Stock Market, Inc., the American Stock Exchange LLC, and the International Securities Exchange, LLC. Finally, FINRA will be responsible for operating industry utilities, such as trade reporting facilities and other over-the-counter operations.***

SEC Press Release 2007-151, SEC Gives Regulatory Approval for NASD and NYSE Consolidation (July 26, 2007).

Subsequent years have resulted in further consolidation. Indeed, in 2011, FINRA reported that, in addition to its regulatory authority over member firms and their associated persons, it was responsible for "surveillance, investigation, and enforcement of more than 80 percent of U.S. equity trading." See FINRA 2010 Year in Review and Annual Financial Report at 3. FINRA's sweeping authority over multiple markets stems from regulatory service agreements entered into with NYSE Euronext and most of the regional exchanges. Thus, as explained on its website:

> The Financial Industry Regulatory Authority (FINRA) is the largest independent regulator for all securities firms doing business in the United States. FINRA's mission is to protect America's investors by making sure the securities industry operates fairly and honestly. All told, FINRA oversees nearly 4,525 brokerage firms, about 163,530 branch offices and approximately 631,085 registered securities representatives.
>
> FINRA touches virtually every aspect of the securities business—from registering and educating industry participants to examining securities firms; writing rules; enforcing those rules and the federal securities laws; informing and educating the investing public; providing trade reporting and other industry utilities; and administering the largest dispute resolution forum for investors and registered firms. We also perform market regulation under contract for the major U.S. stock markets, including the New York Stock Exchange, NYSE Arca, NYSE Amex, The NASDAQ Stock Market and the International Securities Exchange.
>
> FINRA has approximately 3,000 employees and operates from Washington, DC, and New York, NY, with 20 regional offices around the country.

http://www.finra.org/AboutFINRA/

Consider how this new unitary framework compares with the multiple SRO system that had been in place for decades. Do the benefits brought about by consolidation outweigh the disadvantages?

NOTES AND QUESTIONS

1. The Benefits and Costs of Self-Regulation. What factors help to explain why self-regulation in the securities industry is a workable alternative to regulation by the government? Should there be serious concerns about the proverbial "fox guarding the chicken coop?" To what extent has consolidation mitigated such concerns? For recent analysis of the benefits and costs of self-regulation in the securities industry, see Roberta S. Karmel, Should Securities Industry Self-Regulatory Organizations Be Considered Government Agencies?, 14 Stan. J.L. Bus. & Fin. 151, 197 (2008); Onnig H. Dombalagian, Self and Self-Regulation: Solving the SRO Identity Crisis, 1 Brook. J. of Corp., Fin. & Com. L. 317 (2007); Jonathan R. Macey & Maureen O'Hara, From Markets to Venues: Securities Regulation in an Evolving World, 58 Stan. L. Rev. 563 (2005). For analysis considering the possibility of new SROs in related industries, see Saule T. Omarova, Wall Street as a Community of Fate: Toward Financial Industry Self-Regulation, 159 U. Pa. L. Rev. 411 (2011); Donna M. Nagy, Regulating the Mutual Fund Industry, 1 Brook. J. of Corp., Fin. & Com. L. 11 (2006).

In the Dodd-Frank Act, Congress ordered four separate studies involving the merits of creating new SROs: a General Accountability Office (GAO) study on a possible SRO for hedge funds and other private funds; a GAO study of an independent professional analyst organization for credit rating analysts; an SEC study on a possible SRO for investment advisers (or the possible extension of FINRA's mandate to include investment advisor oversight); and an SEC study of the feasibility of establishing an SRO to pair credit rating agencies with the issuers of structured finance products. What factors might explain this congressional fascination with self-regulation?

2. SEC Involvement in Self-Regulation. How would you characterize the SEC's relationship to FINRA? How did Congress characterize the SEC's relationship to national securities exchanges and national securities associations when it enacted the 1975 amendments to the Exchange Act? How does the SEC's involvement in self-regulation relate to the question of whether SROs are private actors or state actors? Note that this question will be revisited in the materials that follow.

3. Voluntary Association? As we shall see, courts that refuse to recognize SRO action as state action often emphasize that SROs are private organizations in which membership is voluntary. Is this a fair characterization? In this regard, consider Exchange Act Section 15(d)(8), which states that "[i]t shall be unlawful for any [SEC] registered broker-dealer to effect any transaction in *** any security (other than commercial paper, bankers' acceptances or commercial bills), unless such broker or dealer is a member of a securities association registered pursuant to Section 15A of this title or effects transactions solely on a national securities exchange of which it is a member."

4. Demutualization and Shareholder-Owned SROs. In an extensive on-line gallery, the SEC Historical Society has recounted many of the radical changes that have occurred in securities industry self-regulation over the last two decades. As the framework essay for the gallery observes:

> Membership organizations once seemed well suited to operating exchanges, a fact confirmed when the 1934 Exchange Act enveloped them within a newly-constructed scheme of federal securities regulation. This was a practical

> decision, but the framers of the 1934 Act had reasons beyond expediency. They believed that member organizations were potentially better able to discipline market participants for unethical as well as illegal conduct.
>
> But member organizations also moved slowly and could not mobilize the capital necessary to make big acquisitions or investments. There was an alternative: turn the member organization into a shareholder-owned entity. The "demutualization" of member-owned exchanges was soon well under way.

SEC Historical Society, The Institution of Experience: Self-Regulatory Organizations in the Securities Industry, 1792-2010, at http://www.sechistorical.org/museum/galleries/sro/sro06b. See generally Roberta S. Karmel, Turning Seats into Shares: Causes and Implications of Demutualization of Stock and Futures Exchanges, 53 Hastings L.J. 367 (2002).

Today, NYSE-Euronext and NASDAQ, like many of the smaller national securities exchanges, are publicly-owned corporations. Does demutualization raise the concern that the profit motive of a shareholder-owned SRO could detract from rigorous and effective self-regulation? Does this concern shed any light on the consolidation of regulatory authority through regulatory service agreements between most of the national securities exchanges and FINRA?

FINRA, in contrast, is a nonprofit membership corporation. It is governed by a board composed of a majority of independent directors (i.e., persons who have no material business relationships with its broker-dealer members or the securities exchanges which it regulates). See FINRA By-Laws, § 4(a). In 2011, the Board of Governors consists of 11 seats held by Public Governors, 10 seats held by Industry Governors, and one seat held by FINRA's CEO. The presence of a non-industry majority on the Board and key committees of FINRA has prompted some to contend that there is little "self" left in securities industry self-regulation. Others, however, disagree and emphasize that member firms and associated persons are actively engaged in all aspects of FINRA's work.

---

2. *SROs and the State Action Debate*

As the following decision makes clear, major consequences turn on whether SROs are characterized as private—rather than state—actors.

UNITED STATES v. SOLOMON

509 F.2d 863 (2d Cir. 1975)

HENRY J. FRIENDLY, CIRCUIT JUDGE:

In mid-April 1973 Arthur Levine and Sol Leit, the chairman and president of Weis Securities, Inc. (Weis), a brokerage and investment banking firm which was a member of the New York Stock Exchange (NYSE), notified the Exchange that the firm was in financial difficulty and that there might have been certain "bookkeeping inadequacies" which had resulted in an understatement by as much as $2.5 million of its reported operating losses over the prior several months. Despite the officers' urging that NYSE refrain, at least temporarily, from sending in examiners, NYSE commenced a full investigation on the following day. During the next two weeks, a number of financial irregularities were discovered in Weis' accounts, including an understatement of losses and bank loans. In accordance with its statutory duty, NYSE advised the Securities and Exchange Commission (SEC) of the probable violations of its rules and regulations and began transmitting, on an almost daily basis, reports containing the results of its investigatory activities and contemplated actions.

On May 17, Alan C. Solomon, who as a Weis officer and director was an allied member of NYSE, was summoned to appear before the Department of Member Firms and testify. Article XIV of NYSE's Constitution provided:

> Whenever it is adjudged in a proceeding under this Article that a member, allied member or approved person has been required by the Board or any committee, officer or employee of the Exchange authorized thereby ... to furnish information to or to appear and testify before or to cause any such employee to appear and testify before the Board or any such committee, officer, or employee and has refused or failed to comply with such requirement, such member or allied member may be suspended or expelled and such approved person may have his approval withdrawn.

Accompanied by his then counsel, Solomon appeared and was questioned at some length, first off the record and then on the record. The chief interrogator was Dennis Pape, special counsel to NYSE. According to an affidavit by Solomon, he "was aware of the provisions of Article XIV of the New York Stock Exchange Constitution which empowered the Exchange to suspend me if I refused to cooperate and answer all the questions put to me during the May 17th interrogation." He averred also that "Mr. Pape and his cohorts in the off-the-record discussions which preceded their formal interrogation, also reminded me of the sanction of suspension which would be imposed if I did not testify." Under questioning Solomon admitted that he had originated the idea of seeking to create an appearance of a better financial situation for Weis by "taking a position in Pan American convertible bonds 4 1/2's 1986, which were selling at around 52, and misvaluating them as Pan Am's 4 1/2's 1984, which were selling around 80."

Two days prior to Solomon's testimony before the Department of Member Firms, the SEC entered an order of investigation and on May 16 served a subpoena requiring NYSE to turn over all material developed in its investigation. NYSE immediately submitted depositions already taken; considering the subpoena to be a continuing one, it later furnished Solomon's. On a complaint by the SEC alleging that Weis did not have sufficient capital under the Securities Exchange Act and the implementing rules of the Commission and NYSE and had been filing false financial reports with both bodies in an effort to conceal this, Weis was placed in receivership at the end of May by the District Court for the Southern District of New York. That action was followed in July by an eighteen count indictment, in the same court, of five of Weis' officers and directors, including Solomon.

The indictment charged in part a conspiracy to violate and a number of substantive violations of the recordkeeping and reporting regulations promulgated by the SEC under § 17(a) of the Securities Exchange Act. Each of the other defendants pleaded guilty to at least one substantive count and three to the conspiracy count as well. After a bench trial on stipulated facts which included a transcript of his deposition before the Department of Member Firms, Solomon was found guilty on one substantive count of creating and maintaining false books and records. With the Government's agreement the other counts were dismissed with prejudice. The judge placed him on a supervised probation program for a year and imposed a $5,000 fine.

The sole point on appeal is the use, both before the grand jury and at trial, of Solomon's self-incriminating testimony to the Department of Member Firms, allegedly in violation of *Garrity v. New Jersey*, 385 U.S. 493 (1967). The complete deposition containing his admissions had been presented to the grand jury and constituted an important basis for the indictment. Solomon's present counsel moved to dismiss the indictment and to suppress use of the testimony or any of its fruits at trial. The judge denied the motion both before and again after an evidentiary hearing. ***[On appeal] Solomon again claims that the indictment should have been dismissed since the allegedly tainted testimony is claimed to have been the only evidence before the grand jury on the count on which he was convicted; alternatively he seeks a reversal and remand for a hearing to determine whether the Government possesses sufficient evidence not derived directly or derivatively through investigation from the deposition testimony to justify a retrial. We do not reach the question of remedy since we find no taint.

I.

The United States suggests, in an elaborate footnote to its brief, that we could affirm without reaching the question whether interrogation by NYSE is to be deemed governmental action. The most appealing basis asserted is the lack of any evidence that Solomon claimed his privilege against self-incrimination. Even when the inquiry is by a body having power to compel testimony, the rule is "that when an *ordinary witness* is on the stand and an incriminating fact, relevant to the issue, is desired to be proved through him, the question may be asked, and it is for him then to say, in terms which the court may reasonably be expected to understand to be a claim of privilege, that he will exercise the option given him by the law," 8 Wigmore, Evidence § 2268 at 402 (McNaughton rev. 1961) (emphasis in original); per contra with respect to the accused in a criminal case, id. at 406. The former principle, which governs a witness before a grand jury, or a Congressional investigating committee, would seem clearly applicable here. When Solomon appeared before the Department of Member Firms he was a subject of investigation for possible future NYSE disciplinary proceedings, not a person accused of crime.

The first problem with taking this smooth road to affirmance is that except for a possible ground of distinction noted below the same reasoning would have led to a result in *Garrity* opposite to that reached by the Supreme Court. There the New Jersey Deputy Attorney General had advised the defendants, who at the time were still only unindicted witnesses, of the privilege, but had added that this was "limited to the extent that you as a police officer once sworn and asked questions pertaining to your office and your conduct therein, if you refuse to answer, you may then be subject to a proceeding to have you removed from the department." *State v. Naglee*, 44 N.J. 209, 212 (1965); the officers then proceeded to answer without protest. Although the State's brief before the Supreme Court did not argue the point that appellants had not claimed their privilege, the Court was surely aware of the usual necessity for this in the case of an ordinary witness. Insofar as the decision rested on a violation of the privilege, the Court evidently considered an exception to that principle to be required when invocation of the privilege was clogged by *certain* forfeiture of office and pension rights and permanent disability from future state employment. *** We thus prefer to place decision on the basic ground that interrogation by the New York Stock Exchange in carrying out its own legitimate investigatory purposes does not trigger the privilege against self-incrimination or, at least under the circumstances here, render Solomon's statement involuntary.

II.

Most of the provisions of the Fifth Amendment, in which the self-incrimination clause is embedded, are incapable of violation by anyone except government in the narrowest sense. No private body, however close its affiliations with the government, can hold a person "to answer for a capital or otherwise infamous crime" without an indictment, or subject a person "for the same offense to be twice put in jeopardy of life or limb." No one can take property for public use except the government or a person on whom the government has expressly bestowed that power. Solomon argues, however, that the remaining provision of the Fifth Amendment, the due process clause, has been extended in some instances to action by private persons having certain types of connection with the government, see, e.g., *Burton v. Wilmington Parking Authority*, 365 U.S. 715 (1961); that NYSE has close connections with the government; and that the self-incrimination clause as explicated in *Garrity* should therefore apply.

There is no need for us to add to the extensive discussion of the history of the privilege against self-incrimination in 8 Wigmore, Evidence § 2250, and Professor Leonard W. Levy's The Origins of the Fifth Amendment (1968). Whatever differences in the precise details of its origin and historic scope may exist among scholars, there can be no doubt that the privilege was in large part developed to protect the individual in what was thought to be an unequal contest with the state. The Supreme Court has frequently referred to Wigmore's statement, 8 Evidence § 2251 at 317:

> The privilege contributes toward a fair state-individual balance by requiring the government to leave the individual alone until good cause is shown for disturbing him and by requiring the government in its contest with the individual to shoulder the entire load.

Murphy v. Waterfront Commission, 378 U.S. 52, 55 (1968); *Tehan v. United States ex rel. Shott*, 382 U.S. 406, 415 (1966). The Court has also said that the origin and history of the Fourth Amendment "clearly show that it was intended as a restraint upon the activities of sovereign authority, and was not intended to be a limitation upon other than governmental agencies ...", *Burdeau v. McDowell*, 256 U.S. 465, 475 (1921). Relying in part on that statement and the fact that *Burdeau* itself dismissed a self-incrimination claim, we have held the same to be true of the self-incrimination clause of the Fifth, in the context, quite pertinent here, of the application of *Miranda v. Arizona*, 384 U.S. 436 (1966), to interrogation by private security guards at a pier. *United States v. Antonelli*, 434 F.2d 335 (2 Cir. 1970). Accord *United States v. Birnstihl*, 441 F.2d 368 (9 Cir. 1971) (per curiam) (store security officer); *United States v. Casteel*, 476 F.2d 152 (10 Cir. 1973) (employees of private security firm).

Solomon argues that despite all this, interrogation by NYSE must be deemed the equivalent of interrogation by the United States because the Exchange has become in effect the arm of the Government in administering portions of the Securities Exchange Act. He relies on various provisions of the Act, such as the reporting requirements of § 17(a) and the regulations thereunder and the many other powers over exchanges and their members conferred on the SEC by § 19(a), (b), see *Gordon v. New York Stock Exchange, Inc.*, 498 F.2d 1303, 1306-1307 (2 Cir. 1974). Particular emphasis is placed on *Silver v. New York Stock Exchange*, 373 U.S. 341, 350-353 (1963), where, after discussing the proved inadequacies of "ungoverned self-regulation" by the exchanges and the consequent need for government supervision, the Court said:

> The pattern of governmental entry, however, was by no means one of total displacement of the exchanges' traditional process of self-regulation. The intention was rather, as Mr. Justice Douglas said, while Chairman of the SEC, one of "letting the exchanges take the leadership with Government playing a residual role. Government would keep the shotgun, so to speak, behind the door, loaded, well oiled, cleaned, ready for use but with the hope it would never have to be used." Douglas, Democracy and Finance (Allen ed. 1940), 82. ***

Thus arose the federally mandated duty of self-policing by exchanges.

Solomon misconceives the thrust of the Act and the Court's discussion of it. The exchanges' "traditional process of self-regulation" was not displaced. See H.R.Rep. No. 1383, 73d Cong., 2d Sess. 15 (1934); S.Rep. No. 792, 73d Cong., 2d Sess. 13 (1934) (stressing the broad responsibility left with the exchanges to administer their own affairs). Rather the SEC was given the power and the duty to make sure that the responsibility was diligently and effectively used. See *Gordon v. New York Stock Exchange*, supra, 498 F.2d at 1306-1307, and sources cited therein. NYSE's inquiry into Weis was in pursuance of its own interests and obligations, not as an agent of the SEC. It is not enough to create an agency relationship that Solomon's conduct violated both a rule of NYSE, thereby subjecting him to disciplinary action by that body, and federal law, with consequent liability to civil and criminal enforcement proceedings by the Government.

***[W]e see no principled basis whereby acceptance of Solomon's argument could be confined to interrogation by stock exchanges; this is but one of many instances where government relies on self-policing by private organizations to effectuate the purposes underlying federal regulating statutes. Under the Commodity Exchange Act, § 5, 7 U.S.C.§ 7, boards of trade have self-policing functions quite similar to those of stock exchanges under the Securities Exchange Act. Airline and steamship conferences have elaborate enforcement machinery to bring to light the charging of less than prescribed rates, the payment of more than agreed commissions to travel and freight agents, or violations of any of the many other regulations concerning the conduct of their members. Whether or not the agreements provide explicitly for suspension or expulsion for refusal to furnish needed records or testimony, a member is aware that any such refusal will likely involve this or some other heavy penalty and will have methods of making this known to refractory employees. One purpose of the provision of the Elkins Act, 32 Stat. 847 (1903), as amended, 49 U.S.C. § 41(2), imposing criminal liability on shippers and carriers for railroad rebates resulting from "the act, omission, or failure of any officer, agent, or other person acting for or employed by any common carrier, or shipper, acting within the scope of his employment" was surely to enlist the aid of the carriers and shippers in policing their employees; clearly a refusal to answer an employer's questions about a rebate on the ground of self-incrimination would lead to discharge, and an employee discharged on that account would be unlikely to gain employment elsewhere in the industry at least for some time. We cite these only as examples that come readily to mind; there would be a complete breakdown in the regulation of many areas of business if employers did not carry most of the load of keeping their employees in line and have the sanction of discharge for refusal to answer what is essential to that end. ***

We find no basis for a different conclusion in the many "state action" cases in wholly different contexts cited by Solomon's counsel. Analysis of the particular constitutional provision at issue must be among the first, if not the very first, step in the process of "sifting facts and weighing circumstances" needed to attribute "true significance" to "the nonobvious involvement of the State in private conduct" dictated by *Burton v. Wilmington Parking Authority*, supra, 365 U.S. at 722. It is one thing to say that the exclusion of blacks is no more permissible for a restaurant which is a lessee of a state parking authority than it would be for the authority itself; it would be altogether different to say that a lease of state property carries the privilege against self-incrimination on its back. Nothing in *Burton* remotely suggests that if the proprietor of the Eagle Coffee Shoppe had interrogated a waiter suspected of snatching a patron's purse, under the same kind of threat that refusal to answer would lead to discharge and a report to a restaurant trade association as would be made by other employers, the answer could not be used in evidence at a criminal trial. We need not here decide whether stock exchanges may be subject to some due process requirements for certain types of action as stated in dictum in *Intercontinental Industries, Inc. v. American Stock Exchange*, 452 F.2d 935, 941 (5 Cir. 1971) (delisting of corporation's stock), *Crimmins v. American Stock Exchange, Inc.*, 346 F.Supp. 1256, 1259 (S.D.N.Y. 1972) (disciplinary hearing), and *Villani v. New York Stock Exchange*, 348 F.Supp. 1185, 1188 n.1 (S.D.N.Y. 1972), aff'd sub nom. *Sloan v. New York Stock Exchange*, 489 F.2d 1 (2 Cir. 1973) (same), although the recent decision in *Jackson v. Metropolitan Edison Co.*, 419 U.S. 345 (1974), would suggest the need for some caution on this score. We deal here with special factors concerning the privilege against self-incrimination and, although we do not think this decisive, even with that only in a preliminary investigation rather than a formal disciplinary proceeding.

III.

There remains for consideration the ground of involuntariness on which *Garrity* may have been rested. This interpretation of *Garrity* seems to have been accepted in *United States ex rel. Sanney v. Montanye*, [500 F.2d 411 (2d Cir. 1974)], although the majority there held that the economic threat to Sanney—discharge from a job as driver's assistant which he had held for one or two days—was not sufficiently serious to bring the case within the *Garrity* doctrine. Both *Garrity* and *Sanney* are distinguishable from this case. In

Garrity there was clearly government action. Similarly, the *Sanney* court found that the private employer was "admittedly acting as an agent for the police". While it therefore could perceive no consequence from the fact that the coercive threat was conveyed in that manner "rather than through a person on the public payroll", it repeatedly stressed that government action was involved, 500 F.2d at 415. Here, as we have concluded above, it was not.

It is settled law that the common law rule excluding confessions induced by a threat is limited to inducement by "a person in authority"; what is generally required is "a legal interest in the prosecution" and "not the mere existence of actual control or influence growing out of the social or commercial relations of the persons." 3 Wigmore, Evidence, § 829 at 443 (Chadbourn rev. 1970). There is more debate about what "a legal interest in the prosecution" means. Under the leading English case a master or mistress is deemed "a person in authority" for purposes of the rule excluding involuntary confessions when and only when the offense concerns him or her. *R. v. Moore*, 2 Den.C.C. 522 (1852). *** Most American courts have opted for a "middle way" in which "[t]he injured person, or the master of a servant, is not regarded as necessarily having a control sufficient to vitiate confessions made by his inducement ..." and "[e]ach case is decided upon its own circumstances, and the actual state of the relation between him [the master] and the confessor is inquired into with reference to the probable strength of the inducement", 3 Wigmore, supra § 830 at 446-47 and cases cited in n.5.

Whatever may be the ultimate solution of the question how far coercion by non-governmental sources can ever demand exclusion as distinguished from consideration by the fact-finder, in the instant case, on this issue of involuntariness in fact we find the distinction [from] *Garrity* *** to be important. There the penalty for a claim of a right to remain silent was mandatory dismissal from office, loss of accrued pension benefits and permanent disability from state or municipal employment. Here there was no certainty what penalty NYSE would prescribe if Solomon refused to speak. It seems plain to us that Solomon, who had conferred with counsel and had his lawyer present during the off-the-record and the later on-the-record interrogation, decided it would be to his advantage to make a clean breast of falsifications that were bound to be discovered, or, indeed, very likely had been, rather than add another item to the case against him. To be sure, Solomon's position was not a particularly pleasant one. But the rule excluding involuntary confessions does not protect against hard choices when a person's serious misconduct has placed him in a position where these are inevitable. Of course, if there were any question whether Solomon was responsible for the false entries in Weis' books, he would have been entitled to have a trier of the facts consider whether the circumstances under which he admitted having conceived the plan affected the reliability of his statement. But there was none. It would be a wholly unwarranted extension of the principle with respect to involuntary confessions to include Solomon's statement to the Exchange.

NOTES AND QUESTIONS

1. The Relevance of the 1975 Exchange Act Amendments. Note that the *Solomon* decision preceded the 1975 amendments to the Exchange Act set out in the previous subsection of this Chapter. Had this legislation been in place at the time, would it likely have changed Judge Friendly's analysis in any significant respect?

*2. **Refusals to Testify and Failures to Cooperate.*** To what extent did Judge Friendly base his determination as to the voluntariness of Solomon's confession on the ground that there was "no certainty" about the consequences of failing to testify in an NYSE investigation? Today, there is little doubt that a person's refusal to testify or cooperate in an SRO investigation typically results in a permanent suspension from association with a member organization. See, e.g., *In the Matter of the Application of Warren E. Turk*, Exchange Act Release No. 55942 (June 22, 2007), set out immediately following these Notes and Questions. See also John Falvey & Stephanie Gibson, The NASD's Invitation to Testify: An Offer You Can't Refuse, 16 No. 6 White-Collar Crime Rep. 1 (June 2002) (maintaining that a client's "refusal to testify will likely mean expulsion"). Yet, as reflected in the *Turk* opinion, courts and the SEC routinely cite *Solomon* when declining to recognize a Fifth Amendment privilege in an SRO proceeding.

*3. **Immunity for SRO Officials.*** A number of courts have recognized that SROs perform a quasi-governmental role in enforcing the federal securities laws and have held SRO officials—or the SRO itself—subject to absolute immunity for damages in private actions. See, e.g., *D'Alessio v. NYSE,* 258 F.3d 93, 105 (2d Cir. 2001) (stating that "[t]he NYSE, as a SRO, stands in the shoes of the SEC in interpreting the securities laws for its members and in monitoring compliance with those laws. It follows that the NYSE should be entitled to the same immunity enjoyed by the SEC when it is performing functions delegated to it under the SEC's broad oversight authority"); *Barbara v. NYSE,* 99 F.3d 49, 59 (2d Cir. 1996) (holding that "absolute immunity is particularly appropriate in the unique context of the self-regulation of the national securities exchanges," where the NYSE "performs a variety of regulatory functions that would, in other circumstances, be performed by [the SEC]"); *Austin Mun. Sec., Inc. v. Nat'l Ass'n of Sec. Dealers, Inc.*, 757 F.2d 676, 690-91 (5th Cir. 1985) (stating that the "NASD disciplinary officers serve as surrogates for the SEC, and should receive the same immunity their principles [sic] possess"). See also *D'Alessio*, supra, 258 F.3d at 105 (quoting lower court's statement that "according the NYSE absolute immunity when it performs regulatory functions that would otherwise be performed by the SEC 'is a matter not simply of logic but of intense practicality, since, in the absence of such immunity, the [NYSE's] exercise of its quasi-governmental functions would be unduly hampered by disruptive and recriminatory lawsuits' "). Are these cases reconcilable with *Solomon* and its progeny?

*4. **The Supreme Court and Controversies Over State Action.*** In *Brentwood Academy v. Tenn. Secondary School Athletic Ass'n*, 531 U.S. 288, 291 (2001), a closely divided Supreme Court found that a nominally private statewide association that regulated interscholastic athletic competition engaged in state action when it enforced a rule against a member school, in light of the "pervasive entwinement of state school officials in the structure of the association." Other decisions have held that a challenged activity may be state action when it results from the government's exercise of "coercive power," ***Blum** v. Yaretsky*, 457 U.S. 991, 1004 (1982), when the government provides "significant encouragement, either overt or covert," id., or when a private actor operates as a "willful participant in joint activity with the State or its agents," *Lugar v. Edmondson Oil Co.,* 457 U.S. 922, 941 (1982). The Supreme Court has also recognized a nominally private entity as a state actor when it has been delegated a public function by the government, *West v. Atkins*, 487 U.S. 42, 56 (1988), when it is "entwined with governmental policies," or when government is "entwined in [its] management or control." *Evans v. Newton*, 382 U.S. 296, 299, 301 (1966).

Based on many of these Supreme Court precedents, a number of scholars have taken the controversial position that "when enforcing federal law, as they are required to do under the Exchange Act, SROs are state actors *** [and] should be subject to the same constitutional limitations as the Commission or any other government agency." Richard L. Stone & Michael A. Perino, Not Just a Private Club: Self Regulatory Organizations as State Actors When Enforcing Federal Law, 1995 Colum. Bus. L. Rev. 453, 455. See also Roberta S. Karmel, Should Securities Industry Self-Regulatory Organizations Be Considered Government Agencies?, 14 Stan. J.L. Bus. & Fin. 151, 197 (2008) (contending that when "SROs are exercising governmental powers, they should be subject to constitutional constraints in their dealings with securities industry personnel and the public [and they] should similarly be bound by the fundamental due process protections contained in the Administrative Procedures Act and similar statutes"). Do you agree?

Even if SROs are not "state actors" *per se*, do SROs engage in state action when they work in concert with the SEC and/or DOJ in investigating and prosecuting conduct by SRO members? Consider the following opinion by a unanimous Commission.

IN THE MATTER OF THE APPLICATION OF WARREN E. TURK FOR REVIEW OF DISCIPLINARY ACTION TAKEN BY NYSE, INC.

OPINION OF THE COMMISSION

Exchange Act Release No. 55942 (June 22, 2007)

***

In order to sustain disciplinary action by a self-regulatory organization ("SRO") such as the NYSE, we must determine whether Turk engaged in the conduct found by the NYSE, whether the conduct violated the NYSE rules he was found to have violated, and whether those rules were applied in a manner consistent with the purposes of the Exchange Act. As discussed below, we have concluded that we are unable to make all of the findings required to sustain the NYSE's action against Turk and have determined, therefore, to remand the case to the NYSE for further proceedings.

Turk acknowledges that he failed to appear for testimony, as alleged and found by the Exchange. Such a failure establishes a *prima facie* violation of NYSE Rules 476 and 477. Turk argues, however, that he could not be forced to testify at the NYSE because he could invoke the Fifth Amendment's right against self-incrimination. Turk argues that the right against self-incrimination applied to the NYSE because the Exchange is a "state actor" generally or, alternatively, because, under the particular circumstances of this case, the Exchange engaged in "state action" in conducting its investigation of Turk.

According to Turk, the NYSE and other SROs are state actors, subject to the right against self-incrimination, because "Congress has effectively required that anyone who wants to work in the securities business must be a member of a self-regulatory organization or must be employed by a member of a self-regulatory organization." Numerous courts and we have repeatedly held, however, that the SROs generally are not state actors, and we see no basis for deviating from that established precedent. [*United States v. Solomon*, 509 F.2d 863, 869 (2d Cir. 1975); *Marchiano v. National Ass'n of Secs. Dealers, Inc.*, 134 F. Supp.2d 90, 95 (D.D.C. 2001); *Vladislav Steven Zubkis*, 53 S.E.C. 794, 797 n.2 (1998)] As the Second Circuit has held in articulating a standard that would apply equally to other SROs, including the Exchange, "The NASD is a private actor, not a state actor. It is a private corporation that receives no federal or state funding. Its creation was not mandated by statute, nor does the government appoint its members or serve on any NASD board or committee." [*D.L. Cromwell Invs., Inc. v. NASD Regulation, Inc.*, 279 F.3d 155, 162 (2d Cir. 2002) (citing *Desiderio v. National Ass'n of Secs. Dealers, Inc.*, 191 F.3d 198, 206 (2d Cir. 1999)]

Alternatively, Turk argues that the NYSE engaged in state action under the circumstances of this specific case because, according to Turk, "NYSE Enforcement has worked in concert with the SEC and the United States Attorney's office in investigating specialists and coordinating the civil and criminal charges brought against them." We recently addressed the question of whether an SRO, although not generally a state actor, can, under certain circumstances, engage in state action such that it becomes subject to the right against self-incrimination. In *Frank P. Quattrone*, [Exchange Act Rel. No. 53547 (Mar. 24, 2006), 87 SEC Docket 2155] where we set aside NASD's action based on procedural deficiencies, we noted that the Fifth Amendment restricts only governmental conduct, and will constrain a private entity only insofar as its actions are found to be "fairly attributable" to the government. A violation of the Fifth Amendment, therefore, requires "state action" on the part of the private entity whose actions are being challenged.

Although SROs are not, as discussed above, generally state actors, under certain limited circumstances, they may engage in state action. As we noted in *Quattrone*, the Supreme Court has held that private parties' actions may constitute state action if there is such a "close nexus between the State and the challenged action" that the seemingly private behavior "may be fairly treated as that of the State itself." [*Brentwood Acad. v. Tennessee Secondary Sch. Ath. Ass'n*, 531 U.S. 288, 295 (2001)] According to the Court, "no one fact can function as a necessary condition across the board for finding state action; nor is any one set of circumstances absolutely sufficient, for there may be some countervailing reason against attributing activity to the government." Id. at 295-296. The Court has identified certain facts "that can bear on the fairness of such an attribution," such as whether a challenged activity "results from the State's exercise of its 'coercive power'"; whether "the State provides 'significant encouragement, either overt or covert'"; or whether "a private actor operates as a 'willful participant in the joint activity with the State or its agents.'" Id. at 296. Some courts have described this last fact pattern as the "joint action" test, and have focused on inquiries such as whether "the state has so far insinuated itself into a position of interdependence with the private entity that it must be recognized as a joint participant in the challenged activity" or whether "the particular actions challenged are inextricably intertwined with those of the government." [See, e.g., *Kirtley v. Rainey*, 326 F.3d 1088, 1092, 1094 (9th Cir. 2003)]

In *D.L. Cromwell Invs., Inc. v. NASD Regulation, Inc.*, the court found that NASD Enforcement issued certain requests for information "as a product of its private investigation" and accepted NASD testimony that "none of the demands [for information] was generated by governmental persuasion or collusion . . . ." [*D.L. Cromwell*, 279 F.3rd at 163] However, the court also observed that, although NASD Enforcement had not acted in concert with government regulators when NASD Enforcement issued its information requests in that case, NASD could nevertheless, in certain circumstances, be deemed a state actor. The court noted that NASD's Criminal Prosecution Assistance Unit, which, at the time, was a self-contained group within NASD Enforcement, "was in fact working with the government, and when it does it may well be a state actor." [Id.]

In another recent decision involving the question of whether NASD can become subject to the right against self-incrimination by engaging in state action, *Justin F. Ficken*, [Exchange Act Rel. No. 54,699 (Nov. 3, 2006), 89 SEC Docket 685] we determined to remand the case to NASD for further development of the evidentiary record where the applicant had been limited in his ability to introduce evidence on that question. [Id. at 696] In remanding that case to NASD, we noted, among other things, that the case had been considered by NASD prior to the issuance of our decision in *Quattrone*.

Turk argues that our decisions in *Quattrone* and *Ficken* support setting aside the Exchange's action against him or, at a minimum, justify remanding the case to the Exchange for further proceedings. The record shows that the parties did not litigate extensively the issue of state action before the Exchange and introduced only limited evidence regarding this issue. Turk notes, however, that the evidentiary hearing in this case occurred before either *Quattrone* or *Ficken* had been decided.

The evidence Turk identifies to support his contention that the Exchange engaged in state action includes: (1) that the Commission and the NYSE requested Turk's testimony concerning his activities as a specialist within one month of each other; (2) that the Commission and the NYSE brought charges in connection with their respective investigations of NYSE specialists on the same day in April 2005 and that the United States Attorney brought criminal charges against other NYSE specialists three days after the Commission and the NYSE brought their proceedings; [The U.S. Attorney has not brought charges against Turk] (3) that press releases issued by the Commission, the NYSE, and the United States Attorney in connection with their investigations indicated that the regulators cooperated with and assisted each other;[22] and (4) that Van der

---

22. The press releases to which Turk refers were issued on April 12, 2005. The Commission's press release, announcing the institution of proceedings against twenty NYSE specialists including Turk, states, in relevant part, "The staff acknowledges the

Moolen told Turk, at the time that Van der Moolen informed Turk that it placed him on administrative leave, thus removing him from the NYSE trading floor, that it was acting upon a request by the United States Attorney's office. Turk has also indicated at various points in the proceeding that he hoped to develop additional unspecified evidence beyond what he has cited on appeal if the proceeding were remanded to the NYSE for further fact-finding.

We have held that the burden of demonstrating joint activities sufficient to render an SRO a state actor is high, and that burden falls on the party asserting state action. [*Ficken,* 89 SEC Docket at 695] The evidence Turk has presented to date does not meet that standard. That evidence by itself indicates that, in investigating Turk, government and NYSE personnel cooperated to some extent. We have observed previously that cooperation and information sharing between the Commission and an SRO will rarely render the SRO a state actor, and the mere fact of such cooperation is generally insufficient, standing alone, to demonstrate state action. [*Quattrone*, 87 SEC Docket at 2165] We also note that the court in *D.L. Cromwell* found no state action where NASD and government regulators "pursued similar evidentiary trails" in their parallel investigations because "their independent investigations were proceeding in the same direction . . . ." [*D.L. Cromwell*, 279 F.3d at 162-63]

Nevertheless, while the evidence Turk identifies is insufficient to establish state action, he should have a further opportunity to develop and present his state action claim. Because the evidence presented to date might be the product of more than cooperation, and because Turk's NYSE evidentiary hearing occurred before the issuance of our decisions in *Quattrone* and *Ficken*, we believe it is appropriate to provide Turk an opportunity to develop a full evidentiary record on the state action question.

On remand, Turk may seek discovery in connection with his efforts to prove that the NYSE engaged in state action. As we noted in *Ficken*, a party must be afforded "a full opportunity to conduct discovery" to obtain the "affirmative evidence" that is "essential to his opposition" to summary judgment, [*Ficken*, 89 SEC Docket at 695 n. 35] but he "may not use the discovery process to go on a fishing expedition in the hopes that some evidence will turn up to support an otherwise unsubstantiated theory." [Id. at 695 n.36] Not every defense of state action deserves discovery and a hearing. A respondent must provide a reasonable and credible basis to conclude that the SRO's relationship with the government in the case suggests such a "close nexus between the State and the challenged action" that the seemingly private behavior "may be fairly treated as that of the State itself." [*Brentwood Acad. v. Tennessee Secondary Sch. Ath. Ass'n,* 531 U.S. 288, 295 (2001)]

Turk will be required on remand to state "the precise manner in which

---

assistance of the U.S. Attorney's office, the FBI, and the NYSE Division of Enforcement." The NYSE press release states, in relevant part, "NYSE Regulation worked cooperatively in this matter with the U.S. Department of Justice and the U.S. Securities and Exchange Commission. The Exchange acknowledges their substantial support and assistance." In its press release announcing the indictments of fifteen NYSE specialists (as noted, not including Turk), the United States Attorney's office thanked the NYSE, "which has been cooperating with the Government in its continuing investigation." ***

[the facts he does possess] support[] his claims," to explain "why he needs additional discovery," to "state with some precision the materials he hope[s] to obtain with further discovery," and to explain "exactly how" the further information would support his claims. [*Ficken*, 89 SEC Docket at 695-96 n. 37] Turk must be able to satisfy these standards to obtain discovery in opposition to a properly supported motion for summary judgment. To the extent that Turk meets this burden, the NYSE will be expected to give due consideration to any requests Turk makes for additional discovery. [See *Ficken*, 89 SEC Docket at 696] We do not intend to suggest any view on the outcome of this remand.

NOTES AND QUESTIONS

1. ***Cooperation Plus What?*** The SEC observed in *Turk* "that cooperation and information sharing between the Commission and an SRO will rarely render the SRO a state actor, and the mere fact of such cooperation is generally insufficient, standing alone, to demonstrate state action." What other facts, in addition to cooperation and information sharing with the SEC or DOJ, might prompt a court to find that actions by an SRO constitute "state" action?

2. ***The PCAOB as Part of the Federal Government.*** Chapter 10.C of this casebook discusses the Public Company Accounting Oversight Board (PCAOB), an independent regulatory entity created by Congress in SOX to regulate the accounting profession, subject to SEC oversight. The SEC appoints the PCAOB's Chairperson and its four other members, approves the PCAOB's budget, approves any rules adopted by the PCAOB, and retains review power over any disciplinary actions taken by the PCAOB. The PCAOB's principal source of funding comes from "accounting support fees" which Congress authorizes the PCAOB to levy on public companies in accordance with a formula based on market capitalization. Although Congress designated the PCAOB as a private entity (by specifying that the PCAOB "shall not be an agency or establishment of the federal government"), litigation quickly ensued over its constitutional status. In *Free Enter. Fund v. Pub. Co. Accounting Oversight Bd.*, 130 S. Ct. 3138 (2010), the Court make clear that SOX's provisions rendered the PCAOB a private-sector entity for statutory purposes only. For constitutional purposes, "the Board is 'part of the Government.'" Id. at 3148 (quoting *Lebron v. Nat'l RR Pass. Corp.*, 513 U.S. 374, 397 (1997)).

The Supreme Court's prior ruling in *Lebron* sheds significant light on why the PCAOB and SROs in the securities industry may have different constitutional statuses notwithstanding their many similarities. As it did in *Free Enterprise Fund,* the Court in *Lebron* confronted the challenged entity's authorizing statute, which declared that Amtrak "will not be an agency or establishment of the United States Government." Id. at 391. Yet the *Lebron* Court held that:

> it is not for Congress to make the final determination of Amtrak's status as a Government entity for purposes of determining the constitutional rights of citizens affected by its actions. If Amtrak is, by its very nature, what the Constitution regards as the Government, congressional pronouncement that it is not such can no more relieve it of its First Amendment restrictions than a similar pronouncement could exempt the Federal Bureau of Investigation from the Fourth Amendment.

Id. at 392. It then set out a three prong test for determining whether an ostensibly private entity is actually part of "Government itself." Id. at 397. Under this test, when (1) "the Government creates a corporation by special law," (2) "for the furtherance of governmental objectives," and (3) "retains for itself permanent authority to appoint a majority of the directors of that corporation," that "corporation is part of the Government," at least for purposes of constitutional law. Id. at 400. Applying *Lebron*'s three prongs to the NYSE and the FINRA, is it likely that those SROs would be found to be part of the federal government for constitutional purposes? How does the *Lebron* "government itself" analysis relate to the question of state action at issue in *Solomon* and *Turk*?

F. PARALLEL PROCEEDINGS

The phrase "parallel proceedings" is frequently used to describe concurrent or successive civil and criminal investigations or prosecutions by the SEC and the DOJ, though the phrase can take on an even broader construct if state officials or SRO officials become involved. Because the federal securities laws specifically provide for both civil and criminal enforcement, and because federal securities laws often have state blue sky analogues, such parallel proceedings are a relatively common occurrence and raise complicated issues for both potential defendants and government prosecutors. The first Subsection focuses on general issues raised by multiple investigations, and the second Subsection explores the issues of multiple sanctions and prosecutions in light of the Double Jeopardy Clause of the Fifth Amendment.

1. Multiple Investigations of the Same Conduct or Activities

SEC v. DRESSER INDUSTRIES, INC.

628 F.2d 1368 (D.C. Cir. 1980) (en banc)

J. SKELLY WRIGHT, CHIEF JUDGE:

Dresser Industries, Inc. (Dresser) appeals from a decision of the District Court requiring obedience to a subpoena *duces tecum* issued by the Securities and Exchange Commission (SEC) on April 21, 1978, and denying Dresser's motion to quash the subpoena. The subpoena was issued in connection with an SEC investigation into Dresser's use of corporate funds to make what are euphemistically called "questionable foreign payments," and into the adequacy of Dresser's disclosures of such payments under the securities laws.

The principal issue facing this *en banc* court is whether Dresser is entitled to special protection against this SEC subpoena because of a parallel investigation into the same questionable foreign payments now being conducted by a federal grand jury under the guidance of the United States Department of Justice (Justice). Dresser argues principally that the SEC subpoena abuses the civil discovery process of the SEC for the purpose of criminal discovery and infringes the role of the grand jury in independently investigating allegations of criminal wrongdoing. On November 19, 1979 a panel of this court issued a decision affirming the District Court but, with Judge Robb dissenting, attaching a condition prohibiting the SEC from providing Justice with the information received from Dresser under this subpoena. Because of the importance of this issue to enforcement of the regulatory laws of the United States, this court voted to vacate the panel opinions and rehear the case *en banc*.

I. BACKGROUND

A. *Origin of the Investigations*

Illegal and questionable corporate payments surfaced as a major public problem in late 1973, when several major scandals implicated prominent American corporations in improper use of corporate funds to influence government officials in the United States and foreign countries. The exposure of these activities disrupted public faith in the integrity of our political system and eroded international trust in the legitimacy of American corporate operations abroad.[3] SEC investigation revealed that many corporate officials were falsifying financial records to shield questionable foreign and domestic payments from exposure to the public and even, in many cases, to corporate directors and accountants. Since the completeness and accuracy of corporate financial reporting is the cornerstone of federal regulation of the securities markets, such falsification became a matter of grave concern to the SEC.

Beginning in the spring of 1974 the SEC brought a series of injunctive actions against certain American corporations. It obtained consent decrees prohibiting future violations of the securities laws and establishing internal corporate procedures for investigation, disclosure, and prevention of illegal corporate payments. However, the problem of questionable foreign payments proved so widespread that the SEC devised a "Voluntary Disclosure Program" to encourage corporations to conduct investigations of their past conduct and make appropriate disclosures without direct SEC coercion. Participation in the Voluntary Disclosure Program would not insulate a corporation from an SEC enforcement action, but the Commission would be less likely to exercise its discretion to initiate enforcement actions against participants. The most important elements of the Voluntary Disclosure Program were (1) an independent committee of the corporation would conduct a thorough investigation into questionable foreign and domestic payments made by the corporation; (2) the committee would disclose the results of this investigation to the board of directors in full; (3) the corporation would disclose the substance of the report to the public and the SEC on Form 8-K; and (4) the corporation would issue a policy statement prohibiting future questionable and illegal payments and maintenance of false or incomplete records in connection with them. Except in "egregious cases" the SEC would not require that public disclosures include specific names, dates, and places. Rather, the disclosures might be "generic" in form. Thus companies participating in the Voluntary Disclosure Program would

---

3. The Senate Committee on Banking, Housing, and Urban Affairs reported in May 1977:

> Recent investigations by the SEC have revealed corrupt foreign payments by over 300 U.S. companies involving hundreds of millions of dollars. These revelations have had severe adverse effects. Foreign governments friendly to the United States in Japan, Italy, and the Netherlands have come under intense pressure from their own people. The image of American democracy abroad has been tarnished. Confidence in the financial integrity of our corporations has been impaired. The efficient functioning of our capital markets has been hampered.

S.Rep.No. 114, 95th Cong., 1st Sess. 3 (1977).

ordinarily be spared the consequences to their employees, property, and business that might result from public disclosure of specific instances of foreign bribery or kickbacks. However, companies participating in the Voluntary Disclosure Program had to agree to grant SEC requests for access to the final report and to the unexpurgated underlying documentations.

B. *The Dresser Investigations*

On January 27, 1976 an attorney and other representatives of Dresser met with members of the SEC staff to discuss a proposed filing. At the meeting Dresser agreed to conduct an internal inquiry into questionable foreign payments, in accordance with the terms of the Voluntary Disclosure Program. The next day Dresser submitted a Form 8-K describing, in generic terms, one questionable foreign payment. On November 11, 1976 Dresser filed a second Form 8-K reporting the results of the internal investigation. On February 10, 1977 the company supplemented this report with a third Form 8-K concerning a questionable payment not reported in the earlier reports. The reports concerned Dresser's foreign activities after November 1, 1973. All disclosures were in generic, not specific, terms.

As part of its general monitoring program the SEC staff requested access to the documents underlying Dresser's report. On July 15, 1977 Dresser refused to grant such access. The company argued that allowing the staff to make notes or copies might subject its documents to public disclosure through the Freedom of Information Act. Dresser stated that such disclosure could endanger certain of its employees working abroad. During the ensuing discussions with the staff Dresser attempted to impose conditions of confidentiality upon any SEC examination of its documents, but the staff did not agree. Instead, it issued a recommendation to the Commission for a formal order of investigation in the Dresser case. This recommendation was predicated on the staff's conclusions that Dresser:

1. may have used corporate funds for non-corporate purposes;
2. may have made false and misleading statements concerning the existence of and circumstances surrounding material obligations of Dresser to certain foreign governments and to other entities; and
3. may have made false entries and caused false entries to be made upon the books and records of Dresser, and its affiliates and subsidiaries with respect to, among other things, payments to foreign government officials.

Moreover, the staff reported that Dresser's proxy soliciting materials, reports, and statements may have been misleading with respect to the potential risks involved in its conduct of business through questionable foreign payments, and may have included false statements in connection with such payments. Dresser vigorously opposed issuance of an order of investigation.

Meanwhile, the Department of Justice had established a task force on transnational payments to investigate possible criminal violations arising from illegal foreign payments. Two SEC attorneys participated in the task force. In the summer of 1977 the Justice task force requested access to SEC files on the approximately 400 companies, including Dresser, that had participated in the Voluntary Disclosure Program. Pursuant to Commission authorization the SEC staff transmitted all such files to the Justice task force in August 1977. After its preliminary investigation of the Form 8-K's submitted by Dresser under the Voluntary Disclosure Program, Justice presented Dresser's case to a grand jury in the District of Columbia on January 25, 1978.

Before any summons or subpoena had issued in either the SEC or the grand jury investigation, Dresser filed suit in the Southern District of Texas against the SEC and Justice to enjoin any further investigation of it by either agency. While Dresser's suit was pending in the Southern District of Texas, the District of Columbia grand jury subpoenaed Dresser's documents on April 21, 1978. At roughly the same time the SEC issued a formal order of private investigation, authorizing the staff to subpoena the documents and to obtain other relevant evidence. Pursuant to that order the staff issued a subpoena *duces tecum*, returnable on May 4, 1978. This subpoena covered substantially the same documents and materials subpoenaed by the grand jury, and more. Dresser did not respond to the subpoena.

On May 1, 1978 the District Court in Houston, Texas dismissed Dresser's suit against Justice without opinion. Three days later, after the period for compliance with its subpoena had lapsed, the SEC applied to the District Court for the District of Columbia for enforcement. In the meantime, Dresser had appealed the adverse judgment in the Texas action to the Fifth Circuit, and sought interim relief. On May 5 Judge Coleman of the Fifth Circuit enjoined further prosecution of the SEC subpoena enforcement action until after the District Court for the Southern District of Texas had ruled on Dresser's action against the SEC. Judge Coleman also obtained a stipulation from Justice that Justice would not require Dresser or its agents to appear before the grand jury until after the Company had filed a motion to quash the grand jury subpoena in the District of Columbia and had received a ruling on such motion.

On May 8, 1978 Dresser filed a motion to quash the grand jury subpoena in the District Court for the District of Columbia. On May 19 the District Court (Parker, J.) denied Dresser's motion to quash, but imposed a protective order requiring strict confidentiality in accordance with Rule 6(e) of the Federal Rules of Criminal Procedure. In imposing the protective order the court stated that the "concern of Dresser and especially its employees is not illusory and should not be lightly considered." This was in reference to Dresser's argument that public disclosures of the names, places, and dates connected with its questionable foreign payments could endanger the lives of its employees in certain turbulent foreign countries. Dresser thereafter complied with this grand jury subpoena.

On May 26, 1978 the Southern District of Texas dismissed Dresser's action against the SEC without reaching the merits. Dresser appealed to the Fifth Circuit and on June 8 obtained an order from the court that:

> Until the appeal in this case shall have been decided in this court, and except for proceedings before the Grand Jury in the District of Columbia, the Securities and Exchange Commission, its officers and employees, are enjoined to preserve inviolate the confidentiality of any information obtained by the subpoena here in issue. This order is not intended to interfere with pending proceedings in the District of Columbia to enforce the SEC subpoenas.

On June 2, 1978 the District Court for the District of Columbia issued an order to Dresser to show cause why it should not be required to appear, give testimony, and produce records in obedience to the SEC subpoena. On June 7 Dresser filed a motion for leave to obtain discovery from the SEC concerning the agency's alleged bad faith and attempted abuse of the judicial process, and on June 13 filed a motion to quash the SEC subpoena.

The District Court (Flannery, J.) denied Dresser's motion to compel discovery on June 16, without opinion. Judge Flannery explained in court that he had carefully examined the papers filed by Dresser, that discovery is rarely necessary in subpoena enforcement cases, and that he did not think this was an appropriate case for it. Then, on June 30, 1978, the District Court (Flannery, J.) issued a memorandum opinion and order rejecting all of Dresser's objections to the SEC subpoena and requiring Dresser to comply with the subpoena within ten days after notice from the SEC. *** This appeal followed.

Meanwhile, the United States Court of Appeals for the Fifth Circuit affirmed the decisions of the District Court for the Southern District of Texas dismissing Dresser's actions against Justice and the SEC in that court, largely on ripeness grounds. *Dresser Industries, Inc. v. United States*, 596 F.2d 1231 (5th Cir. 1979). Accordingly, the interlocutory injunction requiring the SEC to preserve inviolate the confidentiality of Dresser's materials pending a decision on appeal was dissolved.

Having set forth the complicated procedural history of this case, we turn now to the principles that govern parallel administrative and criminal proceedings concerning the same conduct.

II. GENERAL PRINCIPLES

A. *Parallel Investigations*

The civil and regulatory laws of the United States frequently overlap with the criminal laws, creating the possibility of parallel civil and criminal proceedings, either successive or simultaneous. In the absence of substantial prejudice to the rights of the parties involved, such parallel proceedings are unobjectionable under our jurisprudence. As long ago as 1912 the Supreme Court recognized that under one statutory scheme—that of the Sherman Act—a transaction or course of conduct could give rise to both criminal proceedings and civil suits. *Standard Sanitary Manufacturing Co. v. United States*, 226 U.S. 20, 52 (1912). The Court held that the government could initiate such proceedings either "simultaneously or successively," with discretion in the courts to prevent injury in particular cases. Id. It explained:

> The Sherman Act provides for a criminal proceeding to punish violations and suits in equity to restrain such violations, and the suits may be brought simultaneously or successively. The order of their bringing must depend upon the Government; the dependence of their trials cannot be fixed by a hard and fast rule or made imperatively to turn upon the character of the suit. Circumstances may determine and are for the consideration of the court. An imperative rule that the civil suit must await the trial of the criminal action might result in injustice or take from the statute a great deal of its power. ***

Id.

The Supreme Court returned to this theme in *United States v. Kordel*, 397 U.S. 1 (1970). In that case the Food and Drug Administration (FDA) investigated a company and certain of its officers in connection with possible violations of the Federal Food, Drug, and Cosmetic Act, 21 U.S.C.§ 301 et seq. *** Before the company had responded [to interrogatories issued by the FDA in connection with a civil seizure proceeding,] the FDA notified it that the agency was contemplating a criminal proceeding against it in connection with the same alleged violations of the statute. The company therefore moved to stay civil proceedings or, in the alternative, to extend the time for answering the interrogatories until after disposition of the criminal proceedings. The District Court denied this motion. *** After it received the answers, the Department of Health, Education, and Welfare formally recommended criminal prosecution to the Justice Department. Justice obtained an indictment, and subsequently convictions. The case reached the Supreme Court upon appeal of the convictions of several of the company's officers.

The officers in *Kordel* argued that use of the civil discovery process to compel answers to interrogatories that could be used to build the government's case in a parallel criminal proceeding "reflected such unfairness and want of consideration for justice" as to require reversal. 397 U.S. at 11. The Supreme Court did not agree. The Court noted that the government had not brought the civil action "solely to obtain evidence for its criminal prosecution," id. at 11-12, or without notice to the defendants that it contemplated a criminal action, id. at 12. Moreover, the defendant was not unrepresented by counsel, id., and had no reason to fear "prejudice from adverse pretrial publicity or other unfair injury," id. Nor were there any other "special circumstances" suggesting that the parallel proceedings were unconstitutional or improper. Id. In the absence of such "special circumstances" the Court recognized that prompt investigation of both civil and criminal claims can be necessary to the public interest. It said:

> The public interest in protecting consumers throughout the Nation from misbranded drugs requires prompt action by the agency charged with responsibility for administration of the federal food and drug laws. But a rational decision whether to proceed criminally against those responsible for the misbranding may have to await consideration of a fuller record than that before the agency at the time of the civil seizure of the offending products. It would stultify enforcement of federal law to require a governmental agency such as the FDA invariably to choose either to forgo recommendation of a criminal prosecution once it seeks civil relief, or to defer civil proceedings pending the ultimate outcome of a criminal trial.

Id. at 11.

The Constitution, therefore, does not ordinarily require a stay of civil proceedings pending the outcome of criminal proceedings. See *Baxter v. Palmigiano*, 425 U.S. 308 (1976). Nevertheless, a court may decide in its discretion to stay civil proceedings, postpone civil discovery, or impose protective orders and conditions "when the interests of justice seem[ ] to require such action, sometimes at the request of the prosecution, *** sometimes at the request of the defense[.]" *United States v. Kordel*, supra, 397 U.S. at 12 n.27. The court must make such determinations in the light of the particular circumstances of the case.

Other than where there is specific evidence of agency bad faith or malicious governmental tactics, the strongest case for deferring civil proceedings until after completion of criminal proceedings is where a party under indictment for a serious offense is required to defend a civil or administrative action involving the same matter. The noncriminal proceeding, if not deferred, might undermine the party's Fifth Amendment privilege against self-incrimination, expand rights of criminal discovery beyond the limits of Federal Rule of Criminal Procedure 16(b), expose the basis of the defense to the prosecution in advance of criminal trial, or otherwise prejudice the case.[20] If delay of the noncriminal proceeding would not seriously injure the public interest, a court may be justified in deferring it. *** In some such cases, however, the courts may adequately protect the government and the private party by merely deferring civil discovery or entering an appropriate protective order. *Gordon v. FDIC*, 427 F.2d 578, 580-581 (D.C.Cir.1970). The case at bar is a far weaker one for staying the administrative investigation. No indictment has been returned; no Fifth Amendment privilege is threatened; Rule 16(b) has not come into effect; and the SEC subpoena does not require Dresser to reveal the basis for its defense.

B. *SEC Investigations*

The case at bar concerns enforcement of the securities laws of the United States, especially the Securities Act of 1933 and the Securities Exchange Act of 1934. These statutes explicitly empower the SEC to investigate possible infractions of the securities laws with a view to both civil and criminal enforcement, and to transmit the fruits of its investigations to Justice in the event of potential criminal proceedings. The '34 Act provides in relevant part: "The Commission may, in its discretion, make such investigations as it deems necessary to determine whether any person has violated, is violating, or is about to violate any provision of this chapter[.]" Section 21(a) of the '34 Act. This investigative authority includes the power to administer oaths and affirmations, subpoena witnesses, take evidence, and require production of any books, papers, correspondence, memoranda, or other records which the SEC deems relevant or material. Id., Section 21(b). If it determines that a person "is engaged or is about to engage in acts or practices constituting a violation" of the Act, the SEC may bring an action in federal district court to enjoin such acts or practices. Id., Section 21(d). Under the same subsection of the '34 Act the SEC may "transmit such evidence as may be available concerning such acts or practices *** to the Attorney General, who may, in his discretion, institute the necessary criminal proceedings under this chapter." Id. The '33 Act is to similar effect. See Sections 19(b), 20(a), (b) of the '33 Act.

Effective enforcement of the securities laws requires that the SEC and Justice be able to investigate possible violations simultaneously. Dissemination of false or misleading information by companies to members of the investing public may distort the efficient workings of the securities markets and injure investors who rely on the accuracy and completeness of the company's public disclosures. If the SEC suspects that a company has violated the securities laws, it must be able to respond quickly: it must be able to obtain relevant information concerning the alleged violation and to seek prompt judicial redress if necessary. Similarly, Justice must act quickly if it suspects that the laws have been broken.

---

20. In some cases the government seeks postponement of the noncriminal proceeding, to prevent the criminal defendant from broadening his rights of criminal discovery against the government. E.g., *Campbell v. Eastland*, 307 F.2d 478 (5th Cir. 1962).

Grand jury investigations take time, as do criminal prosecutions. If Justice moves too slowly the statute of limitations may run, witnesses may die or move away, memories may fade, or enforcement resources may be diverted. See *United States v. Fields*, 592 F.2d 638, 646 (2d Cir. 1978). The SEC cannot always wait for Justice to complete the criminal proceedings if it is to obtain the necessary prompt civil remedy; neither can Justice always await the conclusion of the civil proceeding without endangering its criminal case. Thus we should not block parallel investigations by these agencies in the absence of "special circumstances" in which the nature of the proceedings demonstrably prejudices substantial rights of the investigated party or of the government. See *United States v. Kordel*, supra, 397 U.S. at 11-13. ***

In essence, Dresser has launched this attack on the parallel SEC and Justice proceedings in order to obtain protection against the bare SEC proceeding, which it fears will result in public disclosure of sensitive corporate documents. The prejudice Dresser claims it will suffer from the parallel nature of the proceedings is speculative and undefined if indeed Dresser would suffer any prejudice from it at all. Any entitlement to confidential treatment of its documents must arise under the laws pertaining to the SEC; the fortuity of a parallel grand jury investigation cannot expand Dresser's rights in this SEC enforcement action. ***

IV. COOPERATION BETWEEN SEC AND JUSTICE

In its initial decision in this case a panel of this court *** affirmed the District Court and ordered enforcement of the SEC subpoena. Out of a concern that the SEC subpoena might somehow "subvert the limitations of criminal discovery," however, the panel, with one judge dissenting, modified the terms of the subpoena enforcement order. It required that "once the Justice Department initiates criminal proceedings by means of a grand jury, the SEC may not provide the Justice Department with the fruits of the Commission's civil discovery gathered after the decision to prosecute." We affirm the judgment of the District Court and reject the panel's modification.

First, we note that no party to this case had suggested or requested a modification such as that imposed by the panel majority, either in the District Court or in this court. In supplemental briefs submitted to the *en banc* court both the SEC and Justice vigorously oppose the modification, while Dresser's support for it is lukewarm at most. Dresser had argued that the SEC investigation is flatly prohibited[.] *** The reactions of the parties, therefore, suggest that the panel's modification might serve more to impede securities law enforcement than to protect the interests of Dresser.

Second, we note that there is no support for the panel's modification in either the relevant statutes or legislative history. Both the '33 Act and the '34 Act—and other statutes related to securities law enforcement as well—expressly authorize the SEC to "transmit such evidence as may be available *** to the Attorney General, who may, in his discretion, institute the necessary criminal proceedings under this subchapter." Section 20(b) of the '33 Act; Section 21(d) of the '34 Act. The statutes impose no limitation on when this transmittal may occur. The parties have not cited any portions of the legislative histories of these Acts relevant to this question, nor have we found any. But the SEC and Justice find considerable support for their interpretation in the legislative history of the Foreign Corrupt Practices Act of 1977.

The Foreign Corrupt Practices Act outlaws corporate bribery of foreign officials and associated inaccurate or misleading financial recordkeeping. In passing the statute Congress recognized the role of the SEC in combatting such practices under the '33 and '34 Acts, and sought to "strengthen the Commission's ability to enforce compliance with the existing requirements [sic] of the securities laws[.]" S.Rep.No. 114, 95th Cong., 1st Sess. 12 (1977). Both the Senate and the House reports on the bill acknowledged the SEC's dual investigative role in preparing cases for civil and criminal enforcement actions. They also recognize the necessity of close cooperation between the SEC and Justice in preparing such cases. ***

Although the legislative history of the Foreign Corrupt Practices Act is not directly probative of congressional intent governing the '33 and '34 Acts, these statements by the 95th Congress are nevertheless entitled to some weight. The remarks in the committee reports concerning the investigative practices of the SEC and Justice were not intended to change, but to reaffirm, past practice. This indicates that Congress understands and approves of the "close working relationship" between the agencies in their investigative capacities. Since such a "close working relationship" will govern the activities of the agencies in enforcing the laws against questionable foreign payments under the new statute, it would be impractical for us to attempt to screen the agencies from each other when they are investigating the same sort of offense under the former statutes.

Congress manifestly did not intend that the SEC be forbidden to share information with Justice at this stage of the investigation. Under the panel majority's theory of the case the SEC would be foreclosed from sharing the fruits of its investigation with Justice as soon as Justice begins its own investigation through a grand jury. Only by waiting until the close of the SEC proceeding before initiating its own grand jury investigation could Justice obtain access to the evidence procured by the SEC. In view of Congress' concern that the agencies share information "at the earliest stage of any investigation in order to insure that the evidence needed for a criminal prosecution does not become stale," S.Rep.No. 114, supra, at 12, and that the agencies avoid "a costly duplication of effort," H.R.Rep.No. 640, supra, at 9, it would be unreasonable to prevent a sharing of information at this point in the investigation.

Third, we note that there is little or no judicial precedent for the panel's modification. The only support adduced by the panel opinion is a District Court opinion in *SEC v. Gilbert*, 79 F.R.D. 683 (S.D.N.Y.1978). In that case, which arose on the defendant's request for a protective order under the discovery rules of the Federal Rules of Civil Procedure—as contrasted to an investigative subpoena enforcement proceeding as in this case—the court ordered the SEC "not to furnish the U.S. Attorney specially with any information procured in the course of discovery in this case." Id. at 687. The court offered no authority for this order nor, indeed, any reason for its application. While we recognize the similarity of *Gilbert* to this case in many respects, its lack of reasoning and its distinguishable procedural posture make it but weak authority.

In fact, the reasoning of the Supreme Court in [*United States v. LaSalle Nat'l Bank*, 437 U.S. 298 (1978)] is contrary to that of the panel in two respects, and should govern this case in lieu of *Gilbert*. The *LaSalle* Court considered, and explicitly rejected, the course adopted by the panel majority: "[I]t is unrealistic to attempt to build a partial information barrier between the two branches of the executive." *United States v. LaSalle Nat'l Bank*, supra, 437 U.S. at 312. More fundamentally, the *LaSalle* Court conceived of the controversy before it as an analysis of the good or bad faith of the IRS investigation. A bad faith investigation, in the Court's conception, is one conducted solely for criminal enforcement purposes. See id. at 307-308, 316, & 316 n.18. Where the agency has a legitimate noncriminal purpose for the investigation, it acts in good faith under the *LaSalle* conception even if it might use the information gained in the investigation for criminal enforcement purposes as well. In the present case the SEC plainly has a legitimate noncriminal purpose for its investigation of Dresser. It follows that the investigation is in good faith, in the absence of complicating factors. There is, therefore, no reason to impose a protective order such as that imposed by the panel majority.

Finally, we note that the panel's modification would serve no compelling purpose, and might interfere with enforcement of the securities laws by the SEC and Justice. As the Second Circuit has said, the procedure permitting the SEC to communicate with Justice during the preliminary stages of an investigation has "significant advantages." *United States v. Fields*, supra, 592 F.2d at 646:

> Allowing early participation in the case by the United States Attorney minimizes statute of limitations problems. The more time a United States Attorney has, the easier it is for him to become familiar with the complex facts of a securities fraud case, to prepare the case, and to present it to a grand jury before expiration of the applicable statute of limitations. Earlier initiation of criminal proceedings moreover is consistent with a defendant's right to a speedy trial. ***

Id. The panel's modification would "interfere with this commendable example of inter-agency cooperation," id., to the detriment of securities law enforcement and in contravention of the will of Congress. On the other side of the balance, the panel's concern for preserving the limitations on criminal discovery is largely irrelevant at this stage of the proceedings, as Dresser agrees. Thus this would be an inappropriate situation to impose a "prophylactic" rule against cooperation between the agencies. We believe the courts can prevent any injustice that may arise in the particular circumstances of parallel investigations in the future. We decline to adopt the position of the panel majority. ***

HARRY T. EDWARDS, CIRCUIT JUDGE, CONCURRING:

I concur in the opinion of the court in this case. I wish to point out, however, that I do not read the court's opinion as expressing any view as to the proper outcome in a case of this sort *once an indictment has issued.* Once an indictment has issued, the policy interest expressed in *United States v. LaSalle National Bank*, 437 U.S. 298, 312 (1978), concerning the impermissibility of broadening the scope of criminal discovery through the summons authority of an agency, may come into play. I express no opinion as to whether or not the summons authority of a government agency may continue once an indictment has been issued or, if it may, whether protective conditions need be placed on the exercise of that power. These issues raise questions which are not presented here. The resolution of these questions, therefore, must await another day.

NOTES AND QUESTIONS

1. ***Horizontal Proceedings vs. Vertical Proceedings.*** The *Dresser* case involved what we may term "horizontal proceedings"—concurrent or successive proceedings initiated by different agencies in the federal government. The phrase "vertical proceedings" can be used to connote multiple layers of investigations/prosecutions by different authorities, such as multiple proceedings brought by the federal government (the SEC and/or the DOJ), state officials (often involving many different states acting under both criminal and civil authority), and SROs (often the FINRA and the NYSE). Coordination is typically easiest among the various agencies of the federal government. As a matter of policy, should coordination be encouraged among all others with regulatory authority? How could such coordination be accomplished?

2. ***Calls for Federal Preemption.*** In the aftermath of several high profile parallel proceedings by the SEC and state attorneys general (most notably, investigations and prosecutions by then-NY Attorney General Eliot Spitzer involving analysts' conflicts and mutual fund trading abuses), Congress considered, but ultimately abandoned, legislation that would have preempted state investigations of a wide range of conduct in connection with nationally traded securities. See Securities Fraud Deterrence and Investor Restitution Act of 2003, H.R. 2179, 108th Cong. Should Congress legislate that only the SEC can investigate certain conduct? If so, which types of conduct? Professor Renee Jones has argued that "vertical competition functions to improve the performance of regulators at both levels of government and increase the public's satisfaction with their representatives." Renee M. Jones, Dynamic Federalism: Competition, Cooperation and Securities Enforcement, 11 Conn. Ins. L.J. 107, 110 (2004-05). Does vertical competition have a substantial downside? See Amanda M. Rose, The Multienforcer Approach to Securities Fraud Deterrence: A Critical Analysis, 158 U. Pa. L. Rev. 2173 (2010) (suggesting that multiple enforcers may not make sense from a deterrence perspective); John C. Coffee, Jr. & Hillary A. Sale, Redesigning the SEC: Does the Treasury Have a Better Idea?, 95 Va. L. Rev. 707, 780 (2009) (favoring "legislation authorizing the SEC to take action *ex post* to invalidate any rule, regulation, or order made by a state securities regulator, or any provision in a settlement between state regulators and defendants, that in the SEC's judgment unreasonably restrained competition, interfered with fair and orderly markets, impeded the national market system, or was otherwise contrary to the public interest or the protection of investors").

3. ***Risks of Agency Capture.*** Might the possibility of state investigations and enforcement actions constitute a useful check on the securities industry's potential "capture" of SEC and SRO regulators? See Jonathan R. Macey, Wall Street in Turmoil: State-Federal Relations Post-Eliot Spitzer, 70 Brook. L. Rev. 117, 118 (2004) (maintaining that the SEC's passivity in areas including analysts' conflicts and mutual fund trading "was likely caused by the agency's capture by the same special interests it was ostensibly regulating"). See also Jonathan R. Macey, Positive Political Theory and Federal Usurpation of the Regulation of Corporate Governance: The Coming Preemption of the Martin Act, 80 Notre Dame L. Rev. 251 (2005). If a capture hypothesis, at least in part, explains the SEC's response to the regulatory problems that prompted these scandals, what other forces may have facilitated that capture?

For the view that the SEC "has made industry-oriented mistakes" at times but that "none of this represents 'capture,'" see Harvey J. Goldschmid, The SEC at 70: Let's Celebrate its Reinvigorated Golden Years, 80 Notre Dame L. Rev. 825, 832 (2005).

4. Cooperation vs. Collusion. The court in *Dresser* expressed the view that "parallel proceedings are unobjectionable under our jurisprudence" absent "substantial prejudice to the rights of the parties involved." What constitutes substantial prejudice? Instructive in this regard is *United States v. Stringer*, 408 F. Supp. 2d 1083 (D. Or. 2006), vacated, 535 F.3d 929 (9th Cir. 2008). The trial court dismissed the government's indictment and suppressed statements made by defendants to the SEC, finding that the SEC and the U.S. Attorneys Office had engaged in improper collusion that violated the defendants' due process and Fifth Amendment rights.

> ***Defendants were given the standard SEC Form 1622, which is given to all testifying witnesses. This form informs witnesses of their right to counsel, their Fifth Amendment rights, and the routine uses of information. The "routine uses" listed included a proviso that the SEC often makes its files available to other governmental agencies, particularly the USAO. Form 1662 also noted that any information given to the SEC may be used in any federal criminal proceeding.***
>
> Defendants argue that the SEC and USAO worked together on a single investigation, with the USAO hiding behind the SEC to sidestep defendants' constitutional rights that they would have otherwise asserted in the criminal proceeding, and build up its criminal case against them.
>
> The prosecution argues that the USAO and the SEC were conducting parallel proceedings, which is an acceptable approach for civil and criminal authorities investigating the same matter. The prosecution also argues that defendants were provided with adequate notice that their statements could be used in a criminal prosecution through Form 1662.
>
> The court concludes that these were not parallel investigations. The USAO identified potential criminal liability and a few targets in the beginning of the investigation, and elected to gather information through the SEC instead of conducting its own investigation. The government was concerned that the presence of a criminal investigation would halt the successful discovery by the SEC, witnesses would be less cooperative and more likely to invoke their constitutional rights, and that the rules of criminal discovery would be invoked. The government was aware that there was no parallel proceeding.
>
> The delay by the USAO was not for the purpose of reviewing evidence gathered by the SEC to make an informed decision as to whether the case warranted prosecution. From the beginning, the USAO consistently held the position that a criminal prosecution was likely. Almost a year after the SEC investigation began and two years before the USAO made its presence known, the USAO reiterated its position that the case would most likely warrant criminal prosecution, yet decided not to conduct a parallel criminal investigation. Moreover, the USAO was actively involved in the SEC investigation: meeting regularly, receiving documents, requesting interviews be conducted in Oregon to establish jurisdiction, advising what information was needed for a successful criminal prosecution, specifically instructing on how best to conduct interviews to gather evidence for false statement cases, intentionally hiding its presence from FLIR's attorneys, and repeatedly planning with the SEC as to when it would be best to surface and conduct an overt criminal investigation.

> The strategy to conceal the criminal investigation from defendants was an abuse of the investigative process. ***

408 F. Supp. 2d. at 1086-88.

The Ninth Circuit, however, saw things differently. Vacating the district court's orders and finding in favor of the government, the appellate court held:

> [I]n a standard form it sent to the defendants, the [SEC] fully disclosed the possibility that information received in the course of the civil investigation could be used for criminal proceedings. There was no deceit; rather, at most, there was a government decision not to conduct the criminal investigation openly, a decision we hold the government was free to make. There is nothing improper about the government undertaking simultaneous criminal and civil investigations, and nothing in the government's actual conduct of those investigations amounted to deceit or an affirmative misrepresentation justifying the rare sanction of dismissal of criminal charges or suppression of evidence received in the course of the investigations.

535 F.3d at 932. The court also emphasized "that the SEC began its civil investigation first and brought in the U.S. Attorney later" and concluded that such timing "tends to negate any likelihood that the government began the civil investigation in bad faith, as, for example, in order to obtain evidence for a criminal prosecution." Id. at 939. How might the Ninth Circuit's holding in *Stringer* affect the decisions made by defense counsel and witnesses in SEC investigations? In addition to a prohibition of outright deceit, what other limits, if any, should be placed on inter-agency cooperation?

5. Enforcement Actions by SROs. Is there reason for concern that the SEC or the DOJ could instruct an SRO to launch an investigation of a broker-dealer or associated person because of the fewer constitutional constraints that would be imposed on SRO officials? In this regard, consider the parallel investigations conducted by the DOJ and the NYSE in the *Solomon* and *Turk* cases set out in the previous Section of this Chapter. Would you feel differently about the outcome of the cases if there were evidence that the DOJ had asked the NYSE to initiate the investigation and to seek testimony from potential targets? Is this simply a variation of the concerns raised in *Stringer?*

6. Administrative Subpoenas Post-Indictment. Note that the *Dresser* court did not consider whether the SEC may issue and enforce a subpoena after the return of a criminal indictment. Yet Judge Edwards wrote separately to express his concern with this possibility. On what was his concern based? In such cases, what, specifically, should be done?

---

2. *Multiple Prosecutions and Sanctions and the Double Jeopardy Clause*

The Double Jeopardy Clause of the Fifth Amendment protects defendants against multiple criminal prosecutions and multiple criminal punishments for the same offense. We have already seen that while Congress has given the SEC the authority to seek in federal court, or impose in administrative proceedings, a wide array of sanctions, the SEC's arsenal of enforcement remedies is entirely a civil one. Does this end the inquiry for purposes of the constitutionality of multiple prosecutions and sanctions by both the SEC and DOJ for the same securities law violations?

In *United States v. Halper*, 490 U.S. 435, 448-49 (1989), the Supreme Court held that "a defendant who already has been punished in a criminal prosecution may not be subjected to an additional civil sanction to the extent that the second sanction may not fairly be characterized as remedial, but only as a deterrent or retribution." *Halper,* which involved first criminal and then civil sanctions brought under the Federal False Claims Act, opened the door to constitutional challenges in cases where the remedy sought by the SEC arguably could be characterized as punitive. The Court's holding in *Halper* also implicated double jeopardy concerns in cases where the SEC obtained a civil monetary penalty against a defendant and the Department of Justice subsequently sought to initiate a criminal prosecution. See, e.g., *United States v. Marcus Schloss & Co.*, 724 F. Supp. 1123, 1126-27 (S.D.N.Y. 1989) (holding that imposition of civil monetary penalty under Exchange Act Section 21A did not preclude, on double jeopardy grounds, criminal prosecution for insider trading where the defendant's consent order entered into with the SEC was agreed to with knowledge of an ongoing grand jury investigation). The court in *Marcus Schloss,* however, did not answer the more difficult question of whether the imposition of an unconsented to civil penalty for insider trading would bar the imposition of a subsequent criminal prosecution and penalty.

Less than a decade after deciding *Halper*, a majority of the Supreme Court found its analysis "unworkable" and "disavow[ed]" its reasoning in *Hudson v. United States*, 522 U.S. 93, 96, 102 (1997). The following case discusses *Hudson.*

SEC v. PALMISANO

135 F.3d 860 (2d Cir. 1998)

AMALYA L. KEARSE, CIRCUIT JUDGE:

Defendant pro se Joseph C. Palmisano appeals from so much of a judgment of the United States District Court for the District of Vermont, Franklin S. Billings, Jr., Judge, as orders him, in this civil enforcement action brought by the Securities and Exchange Commission ("SEC"), to disgorge approximately $9.2 million and to pay an additional civil penalty of $500,000, for violations of the Securities Act of 1933 ("Securities Act"), the Securities Exchange Act of 1934 ("Exchange Act"), and SEC Rule 10b-5. On appeal, Palmisano contends principally that the disgorgement order and the civil penalty violate the Double Jeopardy Clause of the Fifth Amendment because he had been punished for the same conduct in a criminal proceeding. For the reasons set forth below, we modify the judgment in one respect and, as modified, we affirm.

I. BACKGROUND

Prior to 1994, Palmisano was an attorney who specialized in bankruptcy law. From at least December 1987 through November 1992, he operated a fraudulent Ponzi-type scheme in which he induced some 90 persons to invest with him a total of approximately $7.9 million. Palmisano solicited investments from his clients and others for the avowed purpose of purchasing property of bankrupt or distressed companies, which would then be sold at a profit. He represented that the invested funds would be placed in a separate escrow account, and he told some investors that their investments involved "no risk" to principal and would produce tax-free returns of 20-30 percent per year. In fact, there was no reasonable basis for these representations. Palmisano did not invest the money as promised but instead used it for his own personal purposes and used some investors' money to make distributions to other investors in order to perpetuate the scheme.

Palmisano gave his investors various written instruments representing their investments. At the time, there was no registration statement in effect with the SEC.

In July 1994, the United States filed a 40-count indictment charging Palmisano with a variety of criminal conduct in connection with the above scheme. The present civil enforcement action was filed by the SEC on the same day. The civil complaint alleged the sale of unregistered securities, in violation of §§ 5(a) and (c) of the Securities Act, and the sale of securities by means of fraud and misrepresentation, in violation of § 17(a) of the Securities Act, and of § 10(b) of the Exchange Act, and Rule 10b-5. It requested principally that the district court enjoin Palmisano from violating the securities laws, order disgorgement of all gains he derived from his unlawful conduct, and impose a monetary penalty on him pursuant to the remedial provisions added to the Securities Act and the Exchange Act by the Securities Enforcement Remedies and Penny Stock Reform Act of 1990 ("Remedies Act").

In the criminal case, Palmisano pleaded guilty in September 1995 to 44 counts of a 45-count superseding indictment, including counts of mail fraud, wire fraud, money laundering, and securities fraud. The securities fraud counts were based on the same conduct that was alleged in the civil complaint. Following his plea of guilty, Palmisano was sentenced principally to 188 months' imprisonment, to be followed by a five-year term of supervised release, and was ordered to make restitution to his victims in the amount of $3,779,868.49. In addition, property involved in Palmisano's money-laundering violation, to wit, $700,000 and all interest and proceeds traceable thereto, was ordered forfeited to the United States.

In the meantime, the SEC had moved for summary judgment in the present civil action, and its motion had not been decided when Palmisano pleaded guilty in the criminal case. Following the entry of the guilty plea, the SEC argued that it was entitled to summary judgment in this case on the ground of collateral estoppel. The magistrate judge to whom the summary judgment motion was referred recommended granting the motion on that ground. Although Palmisano objected on the basis that the facts of the criminal and civil actions were different, and on other grounds not at issue here, the district court granted the motion on the basis of the collateral estoppel effect of Palmisano's plea of guilty to the securities fraud charges.

Judgment was entered in the present action, enjoining Palmisano from future securities law violations, ordering him to disgorge approximately $9.2 million, comprising $6,169,291.98 in unlawful gains plus $2,989,086.42 in prejudgment interest, and ordering him to pay a $500,000 civil penalty.

II. DISCUSSION

Palmisano has appealed from so much of the judgment as imposes the $9.2 million disgorgement obligation and the $500,000 civil penalty, contending principally that each of those sanctions, in light of the punishment imposed in his criminal case, violates his right to be free from double jeopardy. ***[W]e conclude that [Palmisano's contentions] are without merit.

A. The Possibility of Overlapping Remedies

***[T]here is one aspect of the present judgment that warrants consideration here. The present judgment does not indicate how the disgorgement ordered is to be affected by Palmisano's payment of the restitution ordered in the criminal proceeding, which raises the possibility that the total amount that Palmisano is to pay in disgorgement and restitution could exceed his unlawful gains. The SEC, in its brief on this appeal, has conceded that payments by Palmisano to his victims pursuant to the restitution order in the criminal case should be credited toward the disgorgement ordered here: "Defendant is only required to give back the proceeds of his securities fraud once. Thus, to the extent he pays back the victims of his securities fraud as a result of the criminal restitution order, those payments should be credited towards the disgorgement award." (SEC brief on appeal at 13 n. 11.)

We conclude that that acknowledged limitation should be specified in the present judgment. Accordingly, we modify the judgment to provide that to the extent that Palmisano pays or has paid restitution as ordered in the criminal judgment, such payments will offset his disgorgement obligation under the present judgment.

B. The Principal Double Jeopardy Contentions

Palmisano's principal double jeopardy arguments are that because he was subjected to sanctions in his criminal case, his right to be free from double jeopardy is violated by the requirements in this action for disgorgement and payment of a civil fine. In support of these arguments, he relies primarily on *United States v. Halper,* 490 U.S. 435 (1989), which held that civil penalties constitute punishment within the meaning of the Double Jeopardy Clause if they are "overwhelmingly disproportionate" to the harm suffered by the government. *Id.* at 449. Even assuming that Palmisano's contentions could have been viewed as valid under *Halper*, they are plainly meritless in light of *Hudson v. United States,* [118 S.Ct. 488] (1997), in which the Supreme Court largely "disavow[ed] the method of analysis used in *United States v. Halper*," *Hudson v. United States,* 118 S.Ct. at 491, and reaffirmed the traditional rule that the Double Jeopardy Clause prohibits multiple sanctions for the same offense only if those sanctions are "*criminal* punishments," 118 S.Ct. at 493 (emphasis in original). Under the traditional analysis, there was no double jeopardy here.

In protecting an already-punished person against further punishments, the Double Jeopardy Clause does not prohibit the imposition of all additional sanctions "that could, in common parlance, be described as punishment," 118 S.Ct. at 493; rather it "protects only against the imposition of multiple *criminal* punishments for the same offense" in successive proceedings, id. Whether a particular punishment is criminal or civil is, at least initially, a matter of statutory interpretation. See, e.g., id.; *Helvering v. Mitchell,* 303 U.S. 391, 399 (1938). Thus, the first question the court must ask is "whether the legislature, 'in establishing the penalizing mechanism, indicated either expressly or impliedly a preference for one label or the other.' " *Hudson v. United States,* 118 S.Ct. at 493 (quoting *United States v. Ward,* 448 U.S. 242, 248 (1980)). If the court determines that the legislature has indicated an intention to establish a sanction that is civil, the court must then ask whether the statutory scheme is "so punitive either in purpose or effect," as to "transfor[m] what was clearly intended as a civil remedy into a criminal penalty." *Hudson v. United States,* 118 S.Ct. at 493. Congress's designation of a penalty as civil is entitled to considerable deference. Such a designation will not be overborne unless the statute, considered on its face and without reference to the level of sanction imposed in the particular case, see, e.g., *Hudson v. United States,* 118 S.Ct. at 493; *Kennedy v. Mendoza-Martinez,* 372 U.S. 144, 169 (1963), is clearly so punitive as to "render [it] criminal despite Congress' intent to the contrary," *United States v. Ursery,*116 S.Ct. 2135, 2148 (1996). " '[O]nly the clearest proof' " of its punitive character "will suffice to override legislative intent and transform" a sanction labeled "civil" into one that is criminal. *Hudson v. United States,* 118 S.Ct. at 493 (quoting *United States v. Ward,* 448 U.S. at 249, 100 S.Ct. at 2641).

The test to be used in determining whether a sanction is so punitive in nature as to transform what was intended as a civil remedy into a criminal penalty, and thus subject to the Double Jeopardy Clause's bar on multiple punishments, is the same inquiry that is used in determining whether other criminal proceeding protections apply. See *Hudson v. United States,* 118 S.Ct. at 493 (citing *United States v. Ward,* 448 U.S. at 248 (addressing Fifth Amendment privilege against self-incrimination), and *Kennedy v. Mendoza-Martinez,* 372 U.S. at 167 (addressing Fifth and Sixth Amendment rights to "criminal trial and all its incidents, including indictment, notice, confrontation, jury trial, assistance of counsel, and compulsory process for obtaining witnesses")). Thus, consideration of the seven factors set out in *Kennedy v. Mendoza-Martinez* is appropriate:

> (1) "[w]hether the sanction involves an affirmative disability or restraint"; (2) "whether it has historically been regarded as a punishment"; (3) "whether it comes into play only on a finding of *scienter*"; (4) "whether its operation will promote the traditional aims of punishment—retribution and deterrence"; (5) "whether the behavior to which it applies is already a crime"; (6) "whether an alternative purpose to which it may rationally be connected is assignable for it"; and (7) "whether it appears excessive in relation to the alternative purpose assigned."

Hudson v. United States, 118 S.Ct. at 493 (quoting *Kennedy v. Mendoza-Martinez,* 372 U.S. at 168-69).

This seven-factor list, though not exhaustive, provides "useful guideposts," *Hudson v. United States,* 118 S.Ct. at 493, and no single factor is dispositive, see, e.g., id. at 494. For example, the nature of the sanction cannot turn solely on whether the conduct at issue is also a crime, for it is well established that " 'Congress may impose both a criminal and a civil sanction in respect to the same act or omission,' " *United States v. Ursery,* 116 S.Ct. at 2149. Thus, in *Ursery,* the Court ruled that the property forfeitures authorized in 18

U.S.C. § 981(a)(1)(A) and 21 U.S.C. § 881(a)(6) in order to "require disgorgement of the fruits of illegal conduct," 116 S.Ct. at 2145, are properly classified as civil penalties, not as criminal punishment. See id. at 2149 (the "goal of ensuring that persons do not profit from their illegal acts" is "nonpunitive"). Nor does the nature of the sanction turn solely on whether it has a goal of deterrence. Although deterrence is a traditional purpose of criminal punishment, that purpose "is insufficient to render a sanction criminal, as deterrence 'may serve civil as well as criminal goals.'" *Hudson v. United States,* 118 S.Ct. at 496. In the context of the banking industry, for example, government regulation in the form of monetary sanctions to deter fraud and self-dealing is designed to, *inter alia,* foster public confidence and promote the stability of the banking industry, and the *Hudson* Court noted that "[t]o hold that the mere presence of a deterrent purpose renders such sanctions 'criminal' for double jeopardy purposes would severely undermine the Government's ability to engage in effective regulation." 118 S.Ct. at 496. Thus, the Court concluded that administratively imposed monetary penalties for violation of banking regulations are properly classified as civil, not criminal, sanctions. See id.

Applying these principles to the sanctions imposed in the present case for violations of the securities laws, we note that the threshold matter of Congress's intent clearly favors classifying disgorgement and the fines at issue here as civil. The penalties provided for in the Remedies Act are expressly designated as civil: the subsections authorizing the fines are labeled "[m]oney penalties in civil actions," and within those provisions the fine is referred to as a "civil penalty." [Securities Act Section 20(d); Exchange Act Section 21(d)(3)]. Further, although disgorgement is not specifically provided for in the securities statutes, Congress has expressly endorsed that sanction, see, e.g., H.R. Rep. No. 101-616, at 13 (1990) (Remedies Act authorizes courts "to order the payment of civil money penalties, *in addition to disgorgement*" (emphasis added)). The disgorgement remedy, which has long been upheld as within the general equity powers granted to the district court by § 22(a) of the Securities Act and § 27 of the Exchange Act has not been considered a criminal sanction.

Turning to the seven factors that guide the second step of the double jeopardy inquiry, we conclude that neither disgorgement nor the monetary penalties set out in the Remedies Act are so punitive in purpose or effect as to override Congress's intent to provide for civil penalties. Although disgorgement and the Remedies Act fines apply to conduct that may also be prosecuted under a criminal statute, and they possess some characteristics common to criminal laws, such as requiring scienter and effecting deterrence, see, e.g., H.R. Rep. No. 101-616, at 17 (Remedies Act "would greatly increase deterrence"), neither disgorgement nor money penalties have historically been viewed as punishment. Rather, the "payment of fixed or variable sums of money" is a sanction that has long been recognized as civil. *Hudson v. United States,* 118 S.Ct. at 496. Moreover, such monetary sanctions do not involve an "affirmative disability or restraint," as that term is normally understood, see id.; certainly neither approaches the type of restraint involved in imprisonment.

In addition, these remedies have a clear rational purpose other than punishment. Disgorgement, like the forfeitures discussed in *Ursery,* is designed in part to ensure that the defendant not profit from his illegal acts, a goal that is nonpunitive. Further, the deterrence of securities fraud serves other important nonpunitive goals, such as encouraging investor confidence, increasing the efficiency of financial markets, and promoting the stability of the securities industry. All of these goals are advanced by the structure of the Remedies Act, which establishes three levels of fines; each tier sets maximum dollar amounts (distinguishing between individuals and corporations), with the proviso that a fine may exceed that tier's stated dollar maximum in order to match the defendant's unlawful gains. See [Securities Act Section 20(d)(2); Exchange Act Section 21(d)(3)(B)]. The first tier of fines applies to all securities law violations; the second provides higher maximum fines for violations that involved fraud; and the third provides the highest maximums for violations that involved fraud and "resulted in substantial losses or created a significant risk of substantial losses to other persons." Id. The linkage of the size of the potential fine to the level of the violator's scienter, the risk of loss to others, and the amount of the defendant's unlawful profits minimizes the possibility that a fine will be excessive in relation to Congress's nonpunitive goals.

We conclude that there is little indication, and certainly not the "clearest proof," required under *Hudson*, that disgorgement and the fines provided by the Remedies Act are criminal punishments. The Double Jeopardy Clause is therefore inapplicable. ***

NOTES AND QUESTIONS

1. **Halper *vs.* Hudson**. As *Palmisano* made clear, *Hudson* slammed shut the double jeopardy door that may have been opened by *Halper*. As a matter of constitutional policy, which analysis is superior? Which framework is more workable?

2. **Palmisano *vs.* Johnson.** Can the Second Circuit's decision in *Palmisano* be easily reconciled with the D.C. Circuit's observation in *Johnson v. SEC* (a statutes of limitations case set out in Section D.2 supra) that many SEC sanctions are imposed for punitive, rather than remedial, purposes? What result in *Palmisano* had the defendant been subject to a prior criminal fine in addition to jail time, restitution, and forfeiture? Could a district judge grant the SEC's request to impose a civil penalty?

3. ***The Justifications for Multiple Sanctions.*** Even if multiple criminal and civil sanctions are permissible as a constitutional matter, what policy interests are served by their imposition? SEC officials have suggested at least one possible justification:

> If we have caught someone who has defrauded scores of poor elderly couples and deprived them of millions of dollars in life's savings, even if we have won on the civil side and made him disgorge his profits and enjoined him from ever doing it again—even if we have made him pay severe penalties—it does not mean he should be absolved of the punishment and condemnation due him as a criminal. On the other hand, if we are unable to prove every element on the criminal side, at least we have the civil system as a backstop for correction and deterrence.

Thomas C. Newkirk and Ira L. Brandriss, The Advantages of a Dual System: Parallel Streams of Civil and Criminal Enforcement of the U.S. Securities Laws, Remarks at the 16th International Symposium on Economic Crime (Sept. 19, 1998). Recognizing the important "backstop" role served by civil enforcement, is there nonetheless a compelling justification for parallel civil sanctions *after* a defendant has been prosecuted and convicted in a criminal action?

4. Multiple Sanctions Imposed by an SRO and the SEC. In *Jones v. SEC*, 115 F.3d 1173 (4th Cir. 1997), the Fourth Circuit held that the SEC could affirm sanctions upon a registered representative imposed by the NASD (a censure, a three-day suspension, and a $22,500 fine) and then, with respect to the same misconduct, impose on that representative its own additional sanctions (a permanent injunction, a censure, and a suspension totaling 30 months). The representative had argued that the SEC was precluded from so doing based on the following three points:

> (1) because the SEC has a right to review, modify, and cancel (but not increase) the NASD's sanction and did not do so, it is now bound by its decision not to do so under principles of res judicata; (2) to permit the SEC to increase the NASD's sanction through a separate proceeding violates the Maloney Act which recognizes the NASD as a quasi-public regulatory body whose sanctions the SEC may not increase, see [Exchange Act Section 19(e)]; and (3) the SEC's sanction is a second penalty for the same conduct that violates the Fifth Amendment's Double Jeopardy Clause.

Id. at 1177. Assuming that the court's decision was correct as a matter of law, should the SEC make a practice of affirming SRO sanctions against an individual or entity and then further penalizing that individual or entity by adding its own sanctions for the same misconduct?

Chapter 10

ENFORCEMENT ISSUES INVOLVING ATTORNEYS AND ACCOUNTANTS

This Chapter examines the role of the federal government in regulating attorneys engaged in securities law practice and accountants responsible for the auditing of companies required to file reports with the SEC. The statutory basis for this regulation stems largely from the Sarbanes-Oxley Act of 2002 (SOX), and its lightening rod was, of course, the financial and corporate governance scandals at Enron, WorldCom and many other companies.

Until the SOX was enacted at the end of July 2002, securities attorneys were regulated principally by state bar associations. These bar associations (along with the American Bar Association (ABA)) usually howled in protest in those rare instances when the SEC stated what it believed to be the professional responsibilities of securities lawyers. Congress intervened in 2002 because of the widely-held belief that lawyer malfeasance had played a role in numerous securities fraud scandals, and also because of concerns expressed by academics and others that bar association rules were ambiguous and overly deferential to attorney discretion. Specifically, Section 307 of the SOX mandates that the SEC promulgate rules of professional conduct for securities lawyers, including a rule that would require an attorney for a securities issuer to report securities law violations to the client's board of directors. In January 2003, the SEC fulfilled this requirement by adopting the standards set out in 17 C.F.R. Part 205.

As for accountants, prior to July 2002 they were regulated primarily by private independent organizations such as the American Institute of Certified Public Accountants (AICPA) and the Financial Accounting Standards Board (FASB). The SEC also promulgated rules defining minimum accounting standards and "independence" requirements for auditors of reporting companies. But after the malfeasance of auditors was blamed for the collapses of Enron and WorldCom, as well as for a large number of other earnings restatements in the early 2000s, the SOX established a new independent board to regulate auditors under the supervision of the SEC—the Public Company Accounting Oversight Board (PCAOB). That Act also specified nine types of non-audit services which can no longer be provided contemporaneously by the auditor of a public company, and charged the PCAOB with enforcement of these new independence requirements.

This Chapter is divided into three sections. Section A addresses the SEC's regulation of attorneys and accountants under Rule 102(e) of its Rules of Practice, an SEC rule in existence since 1935, and now codified by the SOX as a new Section 4C of the Exchange Act. Section B focuses on the professional obligations of securities attorneys. After reading the most famous Rule 102(e) proceeding ever brought against attorneys, you will be asked how an attorney faced with those same facts today should respond based on SEC rules promulgated under the SOX. Finally, Section C explores the regulatory regime for auditors of public companies and for broker-dealers registered with the SEC (which is the vast majority of them).

At several points in this Chapter, there will be discussion of the roles played by lawyers and accountants in the financial frauds leading up to the enactment of the SOX in 2002 and as well as in the failures of the financial institutions that began the financial crisis of 2008. As investigations and litigation over the 2008 crisis continue, a nagging question will be whether the SOX accomplished its intended purpose. One also wonders whether the Dodd-Frank Act should have said more about lawyers and accountants than it did.

A. SEC DISCIPLINE OF PROFESSIONALS UNDER RULE 102(e)

As discussed above, codification of the SEC's power to discipline attorneys and accountants was confined until 2002 to the SEC's own Rules of Practice. SEC Rule 102(e) provides, in part, that:

> The Commission may censure a person or deny, temporarily or permanently, the privilege of appearing or practicing before it in any way to any person who is found by the Commission after notice of and opportunity for hearing in the matter:
>
> (i) Not to possess the requisite qualifications to represent others; or
>
> (ii) To be lacking in character or integrity or to have engaged in unethical or improper professional conduct; or
>
> (iii) To have willfully violated, or willfully aided and abetted the violation of any provision of the Federal securities laws, or the rules and regulations thereunder.[a] ***

17 C.F.R. § 201.102(e)(1). Rule 102(f) ensures that Rule 102(e) enforcement has a very broad reach by providing that:

> For the purposes of these Rules of Practice, practicing before the Commission shall include, but shall not be limited to:
>
> (1) Transacting any business with the Commission; and
>
> (2) The preparation of any statement, opinion or other paper by any attorney, accountant, engineer or other professional or expert, filed with the Commission in any registration statement, notification, application, report or other document with the consent of such attorney, accountant, engineer or other professional or expert.

17 C.F.R. § 201.102(f).

Prior to July 2002, Rule 102(e)'s validity was not free from doubt. On the one hand, the SEC argued, and all courts agreed, Rule 102(e) constitutes a proper exercise of the SEC's general authority under the federal securities laws "to make such rules and regulations as may be necessary or appropriate *** for the execution of [its] functions ***." See, e.g., *Touche Ross & Co. v. S.E.C.*, 609

---

a. Ed. Note—In 1995, the SEC renumbered its Rules of Practice, such that former Rule 2(e) became present Rule 102(e).

F.2d 570, 577 (2d Cir. 1979) (quoting Exchange Act Section 23(a) and citing to its analogues in Section 19 of the Securities Act, Section 20 of the Public Utility Holding Company Act, Section 319 of the Trust Indenture Act, Section 38 of the Investment Company Act, and Section 211 of the Investment Advisers Act). In explicitly rejecting the Commission's lack of authority to promulgate Rule 2(e), the *Touche Ross* court stated that:

> Although there is no express statutory provision authorizing the Commission to discipline professionals appearing before it, Rule 2(e), promulgated pursuant to its statutory rulemaking authority, represents an attempt by the Commission to protect the integrity of its own processes. It provides the Commission with the means to ensure that those professionals, on whom the Commission relies heavily in the performance of its statutory duties, perform their tasks diligently and with a reasonable degree of competence. As such the Rule is "reasonably related" to the purposes of the securities laws. *Mourning v. Family Publications Service, Inc.,* [411 U.S. 356 (1973)]. Moreover, we hold that the Rule does not violate, nor is it inconsistent with, any other provision of the securities laws. We therefore sustain the validity of the Rule as a necessary adjunct to the Commission's power to protect the integrity of its administrative procedures and the public in general.

Id. at 582. For additional cases upholding the validity of Rule 102(e), see *Davy v. SEC*, 792 F.2d 1418, 1421-22 (9th Cir. 1986) (concluding that the Commission had statutory authority to adopt Rule 102(e)); *Checkosky v. SEC*, 23 F.3d 452, 456 (D.C. Cir. 1994) (""There can be little doubt that the Commission, like any other institution in which lawyers or other professionals participate, has authority to police the behavior of practitioners before it"") (Silberman, J., quoting *Polydoroff v. ICC*, 773 F.2d 372, 374 (D.C. Cir. 1985)).

Yet others, including a former SEC Commissioner, took the position that Rule 102(e) exceeded the agency's general rulemaking authority. In the case of *In re Keating, Muething & Klekamp*, 47 S.E.C. 95 (1979), then SEC Commissioner (now Professor) Roberta Karmel, wrote a scathing dissent to the Commission's order imposing sanctions on a law firm for its failure to carry out its professional responsibilities with respect to certain SEC filings by a law firm client, stating that:

> in my opinion, it is improper for an independent federal administrative agency to impose sanctions which are not specified by Congress. In addition, the potential corruption of justice when an administrative agency with significant prosecutorial responsibilities has the power to sanction an adversary representing and advising a client persuades me that the Commission should not exercise disciplinary power against attorneys.

Id. at 111. Section 602 of the SOX puts an end to this debate by codifying Rule 102(e) in what is now Section 4C of the Exchange Act.

Over the last few decades, the SEC has applied Rule 102(e) to attorneys and accountants in very different ways. Indeed, as we will see, the SEC traditionally has initiated Rule 102(e) proceedings against attorneys only following a judicial or administrative finding that the attorney has violated the federal securities laws. Yet the SEC has used Rule 102(e) rather routinely to discipline accounting firms and individual accountants for "unethical and improper professional conduct" and to set standards of conduct for the accounting profession. Moreover, although for most of its history the rule was silent as to the requisite state of mind necessary for liability, the SEC had long maintained that negligent conduct could trigger Rule 102(e) discipline of an accountant. Attorneys, however, were traditionally subject to Rule 102(e) discipline only when they acted intentionally.

In 1998, in response to the D.C. Circuit's unambiguous demand for clearer standards regarding state of mind in *Checkosky v. SEC*, 139 F.3d 221 (D.C. Cir. 1998), the SEC amended Rule 102(e) to clarify its operative standard for disciplining members of the accounting profession. To that end, Rule 102(e)(1) now contains a subpart (iv) that provides:

> With respect to persons licensed to practice as accountants, "improper professional conduct" under § 201.102(e)(1)(ii) means:
>
> (A) Intentional or knowing conduct, including reckless conduct, that results in a violation of applicable professional standards; or
>
> (B) Either of the following two types of negligent conduct:
>
>> (1) A single instance of highly unreasonable conduct that results in a violation of applicable professional standards in circumstances in which an accountant knows, or should know, that heightened scrutiny is warranted.
>>
>> (2) Repeated instances of unreasonable conduct, each resulting in a violation of applicable professional standards, that indicate a lack of competence to practice before the Commission.

In new Section 4C(b) of the Exchange Act, Congress adopted this definition of "improper professional conduct" in toto, making it applicable "[w]ith respect to any registered public accounting firm or associated person." (The SOX's new registration requirement for accounting firms is discussed in Section C below).

Significantly, neither Section 4C of the Exchange Act nor Rule 102(e) itself supplies a state of mind for other professionals. Thus, whether the same standard of negligence or a different higher standard shall apply to lawyers and other professionals is left to ad hoc adjudication in an SEC enforcement proceeding or to future SEC rulemaking.

NOTES AND QUESTIONS

1. ***The Impact of Sanctions.*** How would a temporary or permanent suspension under Section 4C/Rule 102(e) impact the professional life of a certified public accountant? A lawyer? How would it impact an accounting firm? A law firm? How do the sanctions available under Section 4C/Rule 102(e) compare with the remedies available in enforcement actions brought against professionals for "causing" or "aiding and abetting" their clients' violations of the securities laws? (For a review of these remedies, see Chapter 9.C supra.)

2. ***Protecting the Integrity of the SEC's Processes.*** In addition to the statutory remedies in the federal securities laws, what other avenues might be available to the SEC to, in the words of the court in *Touche Ross*, "protect the integrity of its own processes?" What are the advantages and disadvantages of the SEC's use of these other avenues?

3. ***"Practice Before the Commission."*** Note the definition in Rule 102(f) of "practice before the Commission." What issues might be raised by its breadth? Would you favor a narrowing of this definition? Why or why not? Note also that neither Rule 102(e) nor Rule 102(f) contains a requirement that

a professional's "unethical or improper professional conduct" necessarily relate to his or her representation of a client before the SEC. Should the SEC nonetheless have to demonstrate such a nexus before imposing disciplinary sanctions under Section 4C / Rule 102(e)?

4. ***State of Mind.*** Do you agree with the SEC's decision to apply to accountants the standard of negligence set forth in Rule 102(e)(1)(iv)? The accounting profession lobbied the SEC vigorously for a scienter standard. Would this have been preferable? SEC Commissioner Norman Johnson clearly thought so, and went as far as to argue that his fellow Commissioners exceeded their rulemaking authority by amending Rule 102(e) to impose a standard of negligence:

> The Standard exceeds the Commission's authority in several ways. It improperly gives the Commission de facto substantive regulatory authority over the accounting profession, and it arrogates to the Commission authority to enforce the securities laws that is reserved to the federal courts. Accountants, like attorneys, are members of "ancient professions," regulated according to rigorous ethical rules enforced by professional societies and state licensing boards. I simply do not believe that we should recast negligent violations of an accounting standard as improper professional conduct under the Commission's Rules of Practice. That is not an appropriate role for the Commission. Difficult ethical and professional responsibility concerns are generally matters most appropriately dealt with by professional organizations or, in certain cases, malpractice litigation. Nor do I believe that mere misjudgments or negligence establishes either professional incompetence warranting Commission disciplinary action or the likelihood of future danger to the Commission's processes.

Amendment to Rule 102(e) of the Commission's Rules of Practice, Securities Act Release No. 7593, 1998 WL 729201 at *28 (Oct. 19, 1998) (Commissioner Johnson, dissenting). Of course, any doubt over the SEC's authority to issue Rule 102(e)(1)(iv)'s standard of negligence for accountants has now been removed through Congress's inclusion of that language in Exchange Act 4C(b).

Should the standard governing "improper professional conduct" for accountants be applied to determinations involving attorneys and other professionals? Why or why not? As we will see from the Commission's opinion in *In Re Carter & Johnson*, set out in this Chapter's next section, the Commission offered the following justification for requiring scienter in order to impose "aiding and abetting" liability on an attorney under Rule 2(e)(1)(iii):

> If a securities lawyer is to bring his best independent judgment to bear on a disclosure problem, he must have the freedom to make innocent—or even, in certain cases, careless—mistakes without fear of legal liability or loss of the ability to practice before the Commission. Concern about his own liability may alter the balance of his judgment in one direction as surely as an unseemly obeisance to the wishes of his client can do so in the other. While one imbalance results in disclosure rather than concealment, neither is, in the end, truly in the public interest. Lawyers who are seen by their clients as being motivated by fears for their personal liability will not be consulted on difficult issues.

In re Carter & Johnson, 47 S.E.C. 471, 504 (1981). And at least until recently, the Commission appeared to adopt the similar view that scienter was required to establish that an attorney had engaged in "improper professional conduct" under Rule 102(e)(1)(ii). Assuming this to have been the standard for securities attorneys in the past, should it continue into the future?

5. Evidentiary Privileges as a Hindrance to Rule 102(e) Proceedings. The initiation of a Rule 102(e) enforcement proceeding against an attorney or an accountant is feasible only if the SEC can obtain the evidence necessary to prosecute. However, communications between lawyers and clients are generally subject to the attorney-client privilege, and lawyers' work papers are often protected from compelled production by the work product privilege. Thus, in order for the SEC to effectively prosecute a lawyer for violating Rule 102(e), the Commission may have to obtain a waiver from the client, perhaps as part of settling an enforcement proceeding against the client.

On the other hand, no evidentiary privilege applies to information disclosed to an accountant from a client. See *Couch v. United States*, 409 U.S. 322, 335 (1973) ("no confidential accountant-client privilege exists under federal law, and no state-created privilege has been recognized in federal cases"). Audit work papers also are not protected by a work product privilege, as the Supreme Court recognized in *United States v. Arthur Young & Co.*, 465 U.S. 805, 817-18 (1984), when it stated that:

> the attorney work-product doctrine was founded upon the private attorney's role as the client's confidential adviser and advocate***. An independent certified public accountant performs a different role.*** To insulate from disclosure a certified public accountant's interpretations of the client's financial statements would be to ignore the significance of the accountant's role as a disinterested analyst charged with public obligations.

As a practical matter, the fact that evidentiary privileges surround the attorney-client relationship but not the accountant-client relationship tends to make it easier for the SEC to bring enforcement proceedings, including Rule 102(e) discipline proceedings, against accountants than against attorneys.

B. ETHICAL AND PROPER CONDUCT FOR SECURITIES ATTORNEYS

1. State Rules Governing Professional Conduct

As discussed above, the professional conduct of lawyers has historically been regulated by state bar associations, which adopt codes similar to the model ethics codes of the American Bar Association (ABA). Most state codes are based on the ABA's Model Rules of Professional Conduct (last revised in 2007), and a minority of states (most notably New York) base their codes on the ABA's earlier Model Code of Professional Responsibility while making selective changes to some provisions.

The ABA Model Rules make it clear that a lawyer may not assist a client in committing a securities law violation or counsel the client to commit such a violation and that the lawyer may not affirmatively make misrepresentations either to the SEC or to investors (for example, in an opinion letter). In this regard, Model Rule 1.2(d) provides that a lawyer shall not knowingly assist a client in, or counsel a client to engage in, a crime or fraud. Model Rule 4.1 further states that, in the course of representing a client a lawyer shall not knowingly "make a false statement of material fact or law to a third person."

In 2003, after years of debate, the ABA opted to revise its Model Rules to clarify the professional responsibilities of a lawyer with knowledge of misrepresentations or other illegal acts by a client or by an agent of a client, particularly when the client is a corporation or other organization. The new rule that speaks to this situation most directly is ABA Model Rule 1.13(b):

> (b) If a lawyer for an organization knows that an officer, employee or other person associated with the organization is engaged in action, intends to act or refuses to act in a matter related to the representation that is a violation of a legal obligation to the organization, or a violation of law that reasonably might be imputed to the organization, and that is likely to result in substantial injury to the organization, then the lawyer shall proceed as is reasonably necessary in the best interest of the organization. Unless the lawyer reasonably believes that it is not necessary in the best interest of the organization to do so, the lawyer shall refer the matter to higher authority in the organization, including, if warranted by the circumstances to the highest authority that can act on behalf of the organization as determined by applicable law.

The "highest authority" referred to in this rule generally would be the board of directors, at least where the organization is a public corporation. Model Rule 1.13(c) goes on to specify that when the highest authority:

> insists upon or fails to address in a timely and appropriate manner an action, or a refusal to act, that is clearly a violation of law, and *** the lawyer reasonably believes that the violation is reasonably certain to result in substantial injury to the organization, then the lawyer may reveal information relating to the representation whether or not Rule 1.6 permits such disclosure, but only if and to the extent the lawyer reasonably believes necessary to prevent substantial injury to the organization.

Model Rule 1.13(d) makes clear that the above paragraph does not apply to information acquired by a lawyer retained to investigate an alleged violation of the law by an organization or one of its agents, or to defend the organization or its agents against such alleged violations.

The year 2003 also brought ABA Model Rule 1.6 (Confidentiality of Information) more in line with the prevailing rule in the vast majority of states. Model Rule 1.6(b) now specifies that a lawyer *may* (but is not required to) disclose client confidences to a third party:

> (2) to prevent the client from committing a crime or fraud that is reasonably certain to result in substantial injury to the financial interests or property of another and in furtherance of which the client has used or is using the lawyer's services;
>
> (3) to prevent, mitigate or rectify substantial injury to the financial interests or property of another that is reasonably certain to result or has resulted from the client's commission of a crime or fraud in furtherance of which the client has used the lawyer's services.

Prior to this revision, Model Rule 1.6 had mandated strict confidentiality, with the client-crime exception limited to disclosures necessary to prevent "reasonably certain death or substantial bodily harm."

As we shall see in Subsection B.3 of this Chapter, the ABA instituted the 2003 changes to its Model Rules only after Congress required the SEC to adopt a stringent "reporting-up" rule, requiring lawyers representing securities issuers to report to the board of directors "evidence of a material violation of securities law or breach of fiduciary duty" by the corporations or its agents. As you read the lengthy and highly detailed requirements in the rules promulgated by the SEC, refer back to the provisions in Model Rules 1.13 and 1.6. How are the provisions similar to the SEC requirements? How do they differ?

NOTES AND QUESTIONS

*1. **Securities Attorneys as Gatekeepers.*** The term "gatekeeper" lends itself to a variety of definitions. Professor Kraakman uses the term broadly to describe "private parties who are able to disrupt misconduct by withholding their cooperation from wrongdoers." Reinier H. Kraakman, Gatekeepers: The Anatomy of a Third-Party Enforcement Strategy, 2 J.L. Econ. & Org. 53, 53 (1986). In his 2006 book, Professor Coffee focuses more specifically on a gatekeeper "as an agent who acts as a reputational intermediary to assure investors as to the quality of the 'signal' by the corporate issuer." He elaborates:

> The reputational intermediary does so by lending or "pledging" its reputational capital to the corporation, thus enabling investors or the market to rely on the corporation's own disclosures or assurances where they otherwise might not. The gatekeeper has such reputational capital because it is a repeat player who has served many clients over many years.

John C. Coffee, Jr., Gatekeepers: The Professions and Corporate Governance 2 (2006). In previous chapters of this Casebook, we have examined the gatekeeping roles of auditors and underwriters. Do securities attorneys function as gatekeepers? How are their roles similar to those of auditors or underwriters? How does the role of an attorney differ?

Professors Fisch and Rosen contrast the vision of an attorney as gatekeeper with the so-called "hired-gun" or total commitment model of lawyering:

> At its core, the hired gun model is based on a strong version of client primacy. The attorney is affirmatively required to assist his or her client to the fullest extent permitted by law. The gatekeeper model incorporates public policy limitations on attorney conduct that may constrain an attorney from following some client instructions even if those instructions are legal. In addition, the model may require the attorney to take affirmative steps to prevent or limit client wrongdoing.

Jill E. Fisch & Kenneth M. Rosen, Is There a Role for Lawyers in Preventing Future Enrons?, 48 Vill. L. Rev. 1097, 1102 (2003). They go on to note that the "hired gun model has been the dominant influence on state ethics rules." Id. at 1103. Does revised Model Rule 1.6 signal that the ABA may have somewhat retreated from the hired gun model? As you read the materials in this Section of the Chapter, consider how effective the SEC has been in communicating its view that securities attorneys serve as gatekeepers.

*2. **Disclosing Client Confidences to Prevent Fraud.*** States vary considerably as to whether a lawyer may disclose to sources outside the corporation that a client is about to engage in conduct that constitutes securities fraud. At one end of the spectrum, there are a few states (including California and Washington, as well as the District of Columbia) that *prohibit* a lawyer from revealing such a fraud. The vast majority of states have adopted a middle position—consistent with revised Model Rule 1.6—that a lawyer *may* disclose such confidential information if necessary to prevent the client from committing a fraud that is reasonably certain to result in substantial financial injury. At the other end of the spectrum, a few states (including New Jersey and Florida) provide that a lawyer *must* disclose client confidences to prevent criminal acts.

For example, New Jersey's Rule of Professional Conduct 1.6(b) specifies that an attorney with confidential information relating to the representation of a client:

> *shall* reveal such information to the proper authorities, as soon as, and to the extent the lawyer reasonably believes necessary, to prevent the client *** from committing a criminal, illegal or fraudulent act that the lawyer reasonably believes is likely to result in substantial bodily harm or substantial injury to the financial interest or property of another.

Of these three possibilities, which is the best rule? Does your answer change depending on whether your role is typically that of a client? A lawyer? An investor? Should it change? Does your answer stem directly from your position on the gatekeeper vs. hired gun debate?

3. ***Noisy Withdrawals.*** Even in the minority of jurisdictions that prohibit lawyers from revealing information necessary to prevent a client's securities fraud, securities lawyers may (and often must) withdraw from representation on account of a client's conduct. May a lawyer inform third parties as to the fact of his or her withdrawal? Are there instances when a lawyer must do so? In this regard, consider ABA Model Rule 4.1(b), which states that a lawyer shall not "fail to disclose a material fact to a third person when disclosure is necessary to avoid assisting a criminal or fraudulent act by a client, unless disclosure is prohibited by Rule 1.6." Comment 3 to this Model Rule 4.1 notes specifically that:

> Ordinarily, a lawyer can avoid assisting a client's crime or fraud by withdrawing from the representation. Sometimes it may be necessary for the lawyer to give notice of the fact of withdrawal and to disaffirm an opinion, document, affirmation or the like. In extreme cases, substantive law may require a lawyer to disclose information relating to the representation to avoid being deemed to have assisted the client's crime or fraud. If the lawyer can avoid assisting a client's crime or fraud only by disclosing this information, then under paragraph (b) the lawyer is required to do so, unless the disclosure is prohibited by Rule 1.6.

How is the "noisy withdrawal" permitted under the comment to Model Rule 4.1 different from outright disclosure? What factors should a lawyer consider in determining whether to make a noisy withdrawal?

---

2. SEC Efforts to Regulate Attorney Conduct Through Rule 102(e) Proceedings

Despite the preeminence of state bar associations in regulating lawyers, the SEC has long claimed a corresponding right to set professional standards for securities lawyers under Rule 102(e) as well as through enforcement actions for aiding and abetting a client's violation of Rule 10b-5. Yet the SEC has rarely exercised that right. One notable exception is *SEC v. National Student Mktg. Corp.*, 457 F. Supp. 682 (D.D.C. 1978). In that case, which the SEC brought under Rule 10b-5, attorneys representing National Student Marketing ("National") had discovered that National's proxy materials had overstated earnings but nonetheless had allowed a merger between National and another company to go forward without resoliciting approval of the merger from the shareholders of both companies based on corrected information. The court held that the attorneys aided and abetted their client's fraud because the attorneys neglected their duty to protest their client's decision to go ahead with the merger. The court emphasized that '[t]heir silence was not only a breach of this duty to speak, but in addition lent the appearance of legitimacy to the closing." Id. at 713. The court, however, failed to comment specifically on what seemed to be the SEC's position: that the lawyers for both corporations had a professional responsibility to alert the SEC to the fraud intended by their clients.

The case below documents another instance where the SEC sought to establish professional standards for securities lawyers, this time in the context of a Rule 2(e) proceeding. As you read the Commission's very lengthy opinion, consider whether it clearly explains what was expected of the securities attorneys or whether it simply raises additional questions.

IN RE CARTER & JOHNSON

47 S.E.C. 471 (1981)

William R. Carter and Charles J. Johnson, Jr., respondents, appeal from the initial decision of the Administrative Law Judge in this proceeding brought under Rule 2(e) of the Commission's Rules of Practice. In an opinion dated March 7, 1979, the Administrative Law Judge found that, in connection with their representation of National Telephone Company, Inc. during the period from May 1974 to May 1975, Carter and Johnson willfully violated and willfully aided and abetted violations of Sections 10(b) and 13(a) of the Securities Exchange Act of 1934 (the "Exchange Act") and Rules 10b-5, 12b-20 and 13a-11 thereunder and that they engaged in unethical and improper professional conduct. In light of these findings, the Administrative Law Judge concluded that Carter and Johnson should be suspended from appearing or practicing before the Commission for periods of one year and nine months, respectively.

For the reasons stated more fully below, we reverse the decision of the Administrative Law Judge with respect to both respondents. We have concluded that the record does not adequately support the Administrative Law Judge's findings of violative conduct by respondents. Moreover, we conclude that certain concepts of proper ethical and professional conduct were not sufficiently developed, at the time of the conduct here at issue, to permit a finding that either respondent breached applicable ethical or professional standards. In addition, we are today giving notice of an interpretation by the Commission of the term "unethical or improper professional conduct," as that term is used in Rule 2(e)(1)(ii). This interpretation will be applicable prospectively in cases of this kind. ***

III.

RESPONDENTS' CONDUCT

A. National Telephone Company. The conduct at issue in these proceedings occurred in connection with respondents' legal representation of National Telephone Company, Inc. ("National") during the period from mid-1974 through mid-1975. National, a Connecticut corporation with its principal offices located in East Hartford, Connecticut, was founded in 1971 to lease sophisticated telephone equipment systems to commercial customers pursuant to long-term (5- to 10-year) leases. National enjoyed an impressive growth rate in its first three years, increasing its total assets from $320,123 to $19,028,613 and its net income from $2,390 to $633,485 during this period. At the same time, the company's backlog grew from $66,000 to $2,610,000 and the value of equipment leases written by it increased from $255,422 to $13,292,549.

The architect of National's meteoric rise was Sheldon L. Hart, one of its founders and, at all times relevant to these proceedings, its controlling stockholder. From its incorporation until his resignation on May 24, 1975, Hart was National's chief executive officer, chairman of the board of directors, president and treasurer. National's chief in-house counsel was Mark I. Lurie who, assisted by Brian Kay, was one of respondents' principal contacts with the company.

In large measure, National was a prisoner of its own success. As is commonly the case with equipment leasing companies, the greater part of National's costs in connection with a new lease, including equipment, marketing and installation expenses, was incurred well before rental payments commenced. Since rental payments were National's only significant source of revenues, the company's cash flow situation worsened with each new lease, and continued growth and operations could only be sustained through external financing. Between 1971 and 1973, National managed to obtain needed capital from an initial public offering of stock under Regulation A, short-term loans from local banks, and an offering of convertible debentures in September of 1973.

National's last successful effort to secure significant outside financing resulted in the execution, in May and June of 1974, of a $15 million credit agreement (the "Credit Agreement") with a group of five banks. Although the Credit Agreement was not closed (in amended form) until December 1974, the banks were willing to advance substantial sums to National under a variety of demand arrangements prior to the closing. *** Unfortunately, funds available under the Credit Agreement, as amended, were not sufficient to finance National's expansion and operations much beyond the closing, and the pressure on National's cash flow continued.

National finally ran out of time in July of 1975, after being unable to secure sufficient external financing after the closing of the Credit Agreement. On July 2, 1975, National was forced to file a petition for an arrangement under Chapter XI of the Bankruptcy Act; in March of 1976 this proceeding was converted into a reorganization under Chapter X of the Bankruptcy Act.

On November 26, 1975, the Commission authorized a formal investigation into the facts and circumstances surrounding National's collapse in order to determine whether any violations of the federal securities laws had occurred. This investigation covered the involvement of respondents, as well as of their law firm.

An injunctive proceeding was initiated by the Commission on January 16, 1978, in the United States District Court for the District of Columbia, against Hart, Lurie, the company's management directors, the company's independent auditors and others, alleging violations of the antifraud and reporting provisions of the Exchange Act, and the rules thereunder. That action has now been settled by all named defendants, without admitting or denying the allegations in the complaint, through issuance of permanent injunctions against future violations of the federal securities laws and the ordering of certain ancillary equitable relief. Also on January 16, 1978, the Commission issued a Report of Investigation, pursuant to §21(a) of the Exchange Act, discussing the conduct of National's outside directors in failing to ensure that the company timely disclosed the matters discussed herein, as well as a release discussing the role of National's independent auditors in the alleged accounting deficiencies.

B. Respondents and Their Law Firm. Carter, an attorney admitted to practice in the State of New York, was born in 1917. He received his law degree from Harvard Law School and has been working for the law firm now known as Brown, Wood, Ivey, Mitchell & Petty ("Brown, Wood") since 1945, having become a partner of the firm in 1954. Carter's principal areas of practice have been securities, general corporate and antitrust law.

Johnson, also admitted to practice as an attorney in the State of New York, as well as in the State of Connecticut, was born in 1932. He received his legal education at Harvard Law School and joined Brown, Wood's predecessor firm in 1956, becoming a partner in 1967. Johnson's principal areas of practice have been corporate and securities law.

Kenneth M. Socha worked with Carter and Johnson on a variety of legal matters affecting National, including all of the matters which are the basis of these proceedings. Socha joined Brown, Wood as an associate in 1970 and continued in that capacity during all periods relevant to these proceedings.[31]

Brown, Wood first came to Hart's attention in April of 1973 when Socha and a Brown, Wood partner who has since left the firm represented an underwriter in a proposed financing by National that was never consummated. After this financing failed to materialize, Hart requested Brown, Wood to represent National as special counsel in the preparation and filing of the Form S-1 registration statement for National's 1973 debenture offering.

During 1974 and 1975, Brown, Wood, principally through Carter, Johnson and Socha, provided a wide range of legal services to National, including the preparation of a Form S-8 registration statement, proxy materials and an annual report for the company's 1974 annual stockholders meeting, other Commission filings, press releases and communications to National's stockholders. Johnson was charged with the overall coordination of Brown, Wood's legal efforts on National's behalf and was generally kept aware of progress on all significant projects. In March of 1974, after another Brown, Wood partner left the firm, Johnson asked Carter to assist Socha in working on the Credit Agreement. Thereafter Carter assumed primary responsibility for that project.

In July of 1974, Johnson was elected secretary of National, agreeing to serve in such capacity at Hart's urging. Although his principal duty as secretary was to attend meetings of the board of directors and prepare appropriate minutes, Johnson testified that he attended a total of only four meetings during this period. *** The National board of directors held at least three additional meetings during Johnson's tenure as secretary at which he was not present. ***

---

31. Socha was not named as a respondent in these proceedings or in any other Commission action relating to National's activities. Given his role in the representation of National during the period here at issue, however, a discussion of Socha's activities is essential to an understanding of the relevant facts; nevertheless, nothing we say today is intended to reflect adversely on Socha's activities in this regard.

C. Chronology of National's Final Year: May 1974 to May 1975. In order fully to appreciate respondents' role in the events at issue here, it is necessary to set forth the following rather lengthy description of the 12 months immediately preceding public disclosure of the circumstances that led to National's bankruptcy. Except as may be noted below, the record contains ample evidence to support the conclusion that both respondents were aware of the facts and circumstances described.

1. May to August 1974: National Executes a $15 Million Credit Agreement; the Annual Report Projections; the Continuing Need for Additional Financing. National's story lies in its unrelenting need to secure ever greater amounts of outside financing. As explained above, given the nature of its leasing business, the more installations the company contracted for, the greater became the gap between internally generated cash flow and the soaring needs of front-end equipment installation costs. As early as 1973, National had begun to explore the availability of longterm debt to supplement its earlier public equity and debt offerings and to replace existing, expensive short-term indebtedness.

In May and June of 1974, negotiations with a consortium of five banks, in which Carter, Johnson and Socha were all participants, culminated in the execution of the Credit Agreement, which was dated as of April 30, 1974. The Credit Agreement provided for an interim revolving loan of up to $15 million, evidenced by rolling 90-day notes, until November 29, 1974, at which time National had the option to convert the principal amount then outstanding into six-year term notes. As discussed below, the Credit Agreement (as amended) was not formally closed until December 20, 1974, in part because National was unable to satisfy the closing conditions relating to its liquidity and debt-to-net-worth ratios. Ultimately the banks agreed to waive these conditions.

Since the Credit Agreement contemplated that the loans thereunder[32] would be secured by substantially all of National's assets, it was necessary for National to transfer these assets to Systems, a transfer which in turn required the approval of National's stockholders. In order to secure this approval, National called its annual stockholders meeting for June 27, 1974, and Brown, Wood was asked to prepare the proxy materials for this meeting. Carter and Johnson also participated in the preparation of National's 1974 Annual Report. These proxy materials, along with National's 1974 Annual Report, were sent to National's stockholders on June 17 and filed with the Commission on June 19.

In urging approval of the asset transfers necessitated by the Credit Agreement, National's proxy statement disclosed that

> [t]he future growth and operations of the Company are dependent upon its ability to obtain financing such as is supplied by the Credit Agreement.

National's 1974 Annual Report contained projections of future lease installations which showed, by each quarter, a doubling of annual installations from

---

32. Since National was prohibited by Connecticut law from obtaining secured loans from banks whose principal offices were located outside the state, it created a New York subsidiary, National Telecommunications Systems, Inc. ("Systems"), to enter into the Credit Agreement with the banks. National agreed to transfer its leases and title to the underlying equipment to Systems to be pledged as security for the Credit Agreement loans, for which National was to act as guarantor.

approximately $13.3 million in fiscal 1974 to approximately $27 million in fiscal 1975. In response to a specific request from Hart, Carter advised National orally and in writing that, in light of Securities Act Release No. 5362 (Feb. 2, 1973), a copy of which Carter sent to Hart, it was permissible to include projections in the Annual Report, but that the assumptions underlying the projections should also be disclosed. Hart ignored this advice and the Annual Report was distributed without assumptions. This incident is the first example in the record of Hart's uncooperative reaction to respondents' advice concerning the disclosure demands of the federal securities laws.

National's management, as well as Carter and Johnson, were well aware that the company would need substantial outside financing in addition to that provided by the Credit Agreement to realize the Annual Report projections. As early as the July 1 meeting of National's board of directors the company had already borrowed $10 million of the $15 million which would be available under the Credit Agreement. At that meeting, which was attended by Johnson in his new capacity as corporate secretary, Hart announced that National needed at least $17 million in new financing to achieve the new lease installation projections in the Annual Report. After Hart reported to the meeting on the various alternatives being explored for additional funds, the directors focused on the importance of this issue to the continuing growth and viability of the company. The minutes of that meeting reflect the board's conclusion that "it [was] essential ... to continue to explore all appropriate means for obtaining financing for the Corporation's operations." ***

It is clear that National did not want for opportunities to disclose to its stockholders the continuing financial squeeze in which it found itself. After the Credit Agreement was signed, the first of these opportunities arose on or about June 18, when Hart sent a one-page letter to the company's stockholders announcing the declaration of a 3% stock dividend, payable in three equal installments of 1% each on August 1, September 3 and October 1, 1974. The record does not specifically reflect whether respondents were aware of or consulted on this letter before it was sent, although it may be inferred that Brown, Wood received a copy at the same time National's stockholders did, by virtue of the fact that the law firm was on National's general mailing list.

As the summer of 1974 wore on, both the severity of and concern for National's financial predicament intensified, fueled in large measure by the deteriorating credit markets. At an August 19 meeting of National's board of directors—the second board meeting attended by Johnson—Hart once again reported on his continuing attempts to raise more capital. ***

2. September to December 1974: National's Growing Cash Crisis; Preparations for the Closing under the Credit Agreement. By early fall of 1974, National's cash needs outstripped its existing financing sources and a severe cash crisis ensued. A meeting between National and its bankers was held on September 11, 1974; neither respondent was present. By that date, National had already received from the bank group more than $13.2 million of the $15 million contemplated by the Credit Agreement, which had yet to be closed. Moreover, in the preceding months, National had borrowed an additional $1.5 million from two of the lending banks, an amount that was not originally contemplated by the pending agreement, thus bringing the total funds already advanced by the banks to something approximating the $15 million provided for under the original agreement.

At the September 11 meeting with the banks, Hart indicated that the projected equity offering had been ruled out by National's investment bankers, due to deteriorating market conditions. He further reported that National's cash flow problems had caused the company voluntarily to institute a "wind-down" program, effective September 1. As he described it, this program, projected to last five months, was a severe retrenchment, designed to protect the banks' existing investment. Under it, National would limit its operations to the conversion of present inventory—approximately $5 million—into installed systems under new leases, phase out further marketing and installation efforts and reduce the company to a "pure maintenance organization." Hart requested an increase in the total amount of the banks' planned loan from $15 to $21 million in order to finance this wind-down program. The banks, however, hesitated, agreeing only that no decision would be made on lending National additional funds until the pending $15 million Credit Agreement was closed.

Hart, in fact, had lied to the banks. No wind-down program had been instituted or, as it turned out, would be until almost eight months later, in May of 1975. There is, however, no evidence in the record that respondents were, or ever became, aware of Hart's September 11, 1974 deception.

Despite the tenor of the September 11 meeting with the banks and the representations Hart had made concerning the wind-down of the company's operations, the day after the meeting Hart once again sent out an optimistic letter to stockholders and others. The letter gave no hint of National's precarious financial situation, stating rather that August had been "an outstanding month." ***

At the October 15, 1974 meeting of National's board of directors, attended by Johnson, there was a further discussion of National's "tight cash position," its inability to secure additional credit despite vigorous efforts, and its continued need for external financing. By that time, National had already increased its borrowings from the bank group from $13.2 million (the September 11 figure) to $14.3 million of the initially planned $15 million loan, with the additional $1.5 million in separate loans from two of the banks still outstanding. Hart stated to the board that he had discussed with the banks a "contingency plan" for the orderly "wind-down" of National's sales activities, but apparently did not disclose to the board or to Johnson who was present that he had falsely represented to the banks that such a program was already being implemented.

The board of directors became increasingly concerned about the company's financial situation recognizing that a curtailment of National's operations and a termination of its sales would soon become necessary unless significant additional financing were obtained, and that one of the major impediments to obtaining such financing was the failure to close the Credit Agreement. The board therefore instructed Hart to take immediate steps to close the Credit Agreement.

Two days later, on October 17, National issued a press release reporting its results for the second fiscal quarter ended September 30, 1974. The release, which respondents did not prepare or review, but which they did receive after the fact, disclosed a substantial increase in lease installations, net income and earnings per share over the corresponding fiscal quarter in 1973, but once again made no mention of the financial crisis then facing the company. Thus the gap between National's public posture and the private realities continued to widen.

The banks' position and the concerned reaction of National's board of directors made closing the Credit Agreement the first order of the day for National. As a result, on October 18, respondents both attended a meeting with various representatives of National and the lending banks to discuss what remained to be done to close the Credit Agreement. The extent of the company's unsecured borrowings, its unsuccessful efforts to obtain other financing and its past due operating expenses were also discussed, along with the steps the company had purportedly taken to curtail operations. Significantly, a wind-down plan—this time characterized as a "contingency" plan—was also discussed, with Hart again asking the banks to increase the Credit Agreement coverage by $6 million to fund such a plan, in order to protect their existing $15 million investment.

In light of his presence at the July 1, August 19 and October 15 board meetings, as well as the October 18 bank meeting, Johnson was well aware of National's cash crisis, its continuing failure to obtain needed financing and its purported "wind-down" program. This, in addition to the well-known depressed state of the credit markets and the fact that National had projected, confirmed and continued to report, without obviously relevant qualifications, rapidly growing sales and earnings, undoubtedly prompted Johnson to instruct Socha to draft a disclosure letter to National's stockholders approximately two days after the October 18 bank meeting.

The proposed stockholders letter, which was reviewed by both Carter and Johnson and sent to the company in early November, was a candid summary of National's financial predicament, noting that National would "in the near future" have to obtain significant financing in addition to the Credit Agreement. It concluded:

> The Company's efforts to obtain additional financing have been adversely affected by tight credit conditions, increased interest costs, a generally unfavorable equity market and certain factors that are peculiar to its business such as the negative cash flow described above. In view of these factors the Company has determined that it would be prudent to curtail its sales operations and, therefore, to emphasize liquidity rather than growth until such time as additional debt or equity financing can be obtained.

Johnson subsequently told Lurie that this was the type of communication "that a company ... interested in keeping its stockholders advised on a regular basis should be making." Despite this advice, National's management declined to issue the letter. Neither respondent elected to pursue the matter.

During this period, Hart continued his efforts to develop further outside sources of financing for National. Carter was informed by Hart and others about negotiations concerning numerous such potential sources for financing that were in various stages of completion.

***[O]n November 26, a draft of an amendment to the Credit Agreement (the "Amendment"), prepared by the banks' counsel, White & Case, but worked on and reviewed by Carter, treated the wind-down plan as an attached exhibit. The November 26 draft of the Amendment also reflected a new total commitment of $21 million—indicating that Hart's $6 million request had been agreed to—but provided that National had to implement the plan to wind-down its operations, and thus terminate sales, if it desired to borrow more than $17 million.[41]

It is important to note, at this point, that both Carter and Johnson must have been aware that, if National were to implement the wind-down plan, the company would have no reasonable opportunity to meet the projections of $27 million in lease installations which were set forth in the 1974 Annual Report and indirectly reconfirmed the company's September 12 letter to its stockholders. The wind-down plan, which Socha summarized in a December 2 memorandum to Johnson, provided that National would not be permitted to enter into any further leases. Obviously, under these circumstances, the company's sales and earnings growth would be halted—short of projected levels.

In early December, Socha received from National a draft of the company's quarterly report to its stockholders for the second fiscal quarter ended September 30, 1974. The report contained a series of graphs, illustrating the successful results of National's operations, but once again made no mention of the dire financial straights in which the company found itself in December. Such an omission was especially significant in light of the disclosure recommendations which Brown, Wood had by then made to National. When Socha inquired whether the use of the graphs had been cleared by Johnson, Lurie informed him that they had. This was not true, as Johnson noted on the copy of the draft report circulated to him by Socha. The quarterly report was mailed as proposed, and neither respondent ever spoke with the company's management about the disclosure problems it presented or about Lurie's misrepresentation to Socha.

It thus appears that, by early December, Carter and Johnson were both fully aware that (1) National was experiencing a cash crisis severe enough to threaten the continued viability of the company if further financing could not be found, (2) when closed, the Credit Agreement, as modified by the Amendment, would not provide the necessary additional financing, (3) National's earlier projections could no longer be achieved if the Credit Agreement's wind-down plan were to be implemented, and (4) National's management was unreceptive when confronted with respondents' advice to disclose the company's financial problems.

With this background, National and respondents moved on to the final preparations for the closing under the Credit Agreement and the Amendment.

3. December 1974 to January 1975: The Lease Maintenance Plan; the Closing; Related Public Disclosure. In the final days leading to the closing, National's "wind-down" plan was renegotiated somewhat and finally emerged with a new name, the lease maintenance plan ("LMP"). All the witnesses speaking to the question agreed that the term "lease maintenance plan" had no generally accepted meaning in the industry and that they had never used or heard this term before. Moreover, the terms "wind-down plan," "contingency

41. Carter wrote a note on his copy of the November 26 draft questioning the amount of new financing that would be available with a limit of $17 million, since over $15 million was already outstanding in bank borrowings. Carter did not follow up on this question.

plan," and "lease maintenance plan," were all intended to refer to the same thing.

The need to revise the original wind-down plan emerged when the consulting firm hired by National to evaluate the plan reported to the banks that, in its original form, the plan was neither feasible nor in the best interests of the banks. Rather, the independent consultants advised that the best course would be to allow National limited continuing growth, financed with additional bank borrowings, and that a wind-down should be implemented only as a last resort and only if the company were unable to obtain additional outside financing.

At a meeting held on December 11, with Carter and representatives of National and the banks present, final details of the Amendment were negotiated. A draft of the Amendment dated December 13, 1974, which was prepared by White & Case, contemplated an arrangement under which the banks would permit Systems to borrow up to $19 million at any time on or before April 30, 1975. These borrowings were to be secured by the telephone leases and equipment transferred to Systems by National and guaranteed by National. If either (1) National and/or Systems attempted to borrow in excess of $19 million from the existing bank group or (2) National failed to meet a specified liquidity test, National and Systems were required to implement the LMP. Their failure to do so in accordance with the provisions of the LMP was an event of default under the Credit Agreement, as modified by the Amendment (the "Amended Credit Agreement"), and resulted in all outstanding indebtedness under that Agreement becoming due and payable upon demand.

The December 13 draft of the Amendment for the first time contained a reference to a "lease maintenance plan" and indicated that the LMP was to be attached as an exhibit to the Amendment. The effect of the implementation of the LMP on National's operations and growth would obviously be both dramatic and devastating. Indeed, as one expert called by respondents testified, the LMP was a "sort of a holding pattern short of bankruptcy or levy by the creditors." The LMP required National to terminate all sales activities, dismiss all sales personnel, and limit its operations to those necessary to service existing leases. In effect, the company would be transformed into a mere service agency, maintaining existing leases, but writing no new ones. Moreover, the final $2 million of the funds to be provided by the banks was only available until June 30, 1975 and could only be used to implement the LMP, principally by financing the installation of equipment already in inventory to complete existing orders. ***

On December 19, the day immediately preceding the closing under the Amended Credit Agreement, at a day-long pre-closing meeting, Hart told Carter that he did not want the terms of the LMP made public or filed with the Commission. Although Carter testified that he could not recall the reason for this request, he speculated that Hart sought not to publicize the LMP because he was concerned that the disclosure of the LMP's effects on the company's business would have a negative impact on the morale of National's sales personnel. After reading the LMP, Carter advised Hart that the LMP would have to be filed with the Commission if it were an exhibit to the Amendment, as originally had been contemplated. However, Carter added that the LMP need not be filed with the Commission or publicized if it were not an exhibit but rather merely referred to in the Amendment. Hart agreed, and the Amendment was modified to delete the LMP as an exhibit.

Also at the December 19 pre-closing conference, Carter reviewed and extensively revised a press release prepared by National announcing the closing of the Amended Credit Agreement. The revised press release was reviewed by all parties at the meeting, including the company's management. No one raised any objections to the revisions proposed by Carter.

On December 20, the Amended Credit Agreement was closed and National immediately borrowed $18 million from the banks. Of this amount, over $16.8 million was used to repay existing demand indebtedness based on advances the banks had made to National since the original Credit Agreement had been signed six months earlier. All or virtually all of the remainder was used to pay various operating expenses which National had already incurred. ***

Immediately after the closing, National issued the press release that Carter had redrafted the day before. The release stated, in its entirety:

> *PRESS RELEASE—FOR IMMEDIATE RELEASE*
> EAST HARTFORD, CONN., DECEMBER 20, 1974
>
> National Telephone Company today announced the execution of a $6,000,000 extension of a $15,000,000 Credit Agreement with a group of banks headed by Bankers Trust Company of New York. Included in the $21 million is a contingency fund of $2 million which is available until June 30, 1975 and which may be utilized by the Company only for the purpose of funding a lease maintenance program in the event additional financing is not otherwise available.
>
> Of the $21 million, the Company has borrowed $18 million pursuant to a seven-year term loan, of which approximately $16,500,000 was used to repay outstanding short-term loans. The balance will be used for general operating expenses. Participating in the loans are Bankers Trust Company of New York, Mellon Bank N.A. of Pittsburgh, Central National Bank of Cleveland, The Connecticut Bank and Trust Company and The Hartford National Bank and Trust Company of Hartford, Connecticut.

The press release did not discuss either of the following matters each of which was then within knowledge of Carter and Johnson.

> (1) The precise nature and effects on National's business of the LMP and the likelihood that National would be required to implement the LMP within a short period of time; and
>
> (2) The substantial limitations placed on National's operations by the Amended Credit Agreement.

It is also apparent from the record that the press release's statement indicating that the balance of the financing remaining after the repayment outstanding bank debt "will be used for general operating expenses" was misleading, in light of the substantial overdue obligations of National then existing.

The second major item of public disclosure concerning the closing was a stockholders' letter mailed, without respondents' knowledge, by National on or about December 23. This letter, which was issued in the face of Socha's advice to National that no further public statements should be issued concerning the

Amended Credit Agreement unless such statements were cleared by Brown, Wood, contained numerous misstatements and omissions, including the following:

(1) The letter indicated that the company "was stronger now than ever before in its history" and that it had "a greater availability of capital, expanding productivity and growing earnings" and was "looking forward to an outstanding year in calendar 1975."

(2) The letter indicated that the entire additional $6 million loan to National could be used for future operating expenses.

(3) The letter made no reference to National's repayment of existing bank loans and other pre-existing debts with the proceeds of the financing, its continuing cash needs and shortages, or the LMP.

Respondents first learned of the letter on December 27, when Brian Kay, who was aware that National had ignored Socha's advice that all public disclosure should be reviewed by them, voluntarily telephoned Socha and dictated the letter to him. Socha thought that the letter's description of the Amended Credit Agreement was "seriously inadequate" and immediately gave a copy of it to Johnson. Carter, too, was consulted. While respondents felt that the letter did not make "adequate disclosure" with respect to the Amended Credit Agreement, they concluded that, when read together with the earlier December 20 press release which Carter had revised, it was not materially false or misleading, and that no corrective action by National was therefore required. Johnson later did, however, orally express his dissatisfaction with the letter to Lurie.

With the close of 1974, the record reveals that respondents were in the uncomfortable position of attempting to provide disclosure advice to an aggressive client whose unreceptive management actively frustrated the giving of advice and ignored what advice managed to get through. It is in the context of this attitude that respondents and National moved into the new year, with the final efforts to save the company and the resulting sharp needs to attend to the company's public disclosure obligations.

4. January to March 1975: National's December 1974 Form 8-K; the Triggering of the LMP; Disclosure Pressures from the Banks. On January 9, 1975, National filed a current report on Form 8-K for the month of December 1974, reporting on the closing under the Amended Credit Agreement. This document was drafted by Carter, who accepted full responsibility for it.

The Amended Credit Agreement, which was attached to the Form 8-K as an exhibit, made frequent reference to the LMP. And the 8-K itself stated that $2 million of National's recent $21 million loan arrangement was "a contingency fund available until June 30, 1975 only for the purpose of financing a lease maintenance program in the event additional financing is not otherwise available." As previously requested by Hart, however, the LMP itself was not included as an exhibit to the Agreement or the filing; nor was the term "lease maintenance plan" specifically defined or the effects which it would have on the company discussed.

Between the January 9, 1975 filing of National's form 8-K and mid-March, National's financial condition deteriorated even further, to a degree requiring the implementation of the LMP. In addition, the gap between

National's public disclosure posture and its private financial condition continued to widen and National's board of directors was becoming increasingly uncomfortable with the situation. ***

On March 17—***over six weeks after the LMP had in fact been triggered—Brown, Wood was informed for the first time, by the *banks'* lawyers, White & Case, that events requiring implementation of the LMP had occurred. The White & Case lawyers had received a telephone call from a vice president of one of the banks informing them of this fact and reporting that no public disclosure had been made by National. The bank vice president also sought White & Case's advice on how to respond to trade creditors of National who were making inquiries to the banks about the company.

During their March 17 conversation, the White & Case lawyers advised Carter that National and its counsel, Brown, Wood, had the responsibility to determine what disclosure, if any, would be appropriate under the circumstances, and they sought assurances that, if proper disclosure were deemed necessary, it would be forthcoming. Carter, who admittedly considered the triggering of the LMP clearly material, assured White & Case that, if what they said were true, Brown, Wood would contact National and "get a statement out." ***

On the following day, March 18, Carter telephoned Lurie and informed him of the call from the White & Case lawyers. Lurie neither confirmed nor denied that the LMP had been triggered. Rather, he dissembled, stating that the situation was "tight," but adding that, "if they were careful, they would be all right." Carter advised Lurie that, if the LMP had indeed been triggered, the fact should be disclosed publicly, although he did not press Lurie for a definite answer on whether the LMP had in fact been triggered, or on whether National's management was in fact implementing the LMP as required by the Amended Credit Agreement.

Carter informed Johnson both of the telephone call from the banks' lawyers and the subsequent conversations with Lurie. While Johnson's first reaction was to find out what the facts were, neither he nor anyone else at Brown, Wood sought to verify the facts by contacting anyone at National. Nor did they seek to contact anyone outside of National, such as the consulting firm, which they knew had been charged by the parties with responsibility for monitoring National's compliance with the terms of the Amended Credit Agreement.

5. April to May 1975: Respondents' Disclosure Advice; National's Board Acts; Hart's Resignation; Public Disclosure. In early April, Carter and Johnson once again discussed the need to disclose National's obligation to implement the LMP. As a result of a conversation with Hart, Johnson had become "morally certain" that National was required to implement the LMP, and that the failure to do so would result in National's being in default under the Amended Credit Agreement, although he did not believe, nor did Carter, that Hart intended to implement the LMP even though it was required.

On April 21, in response to a comment letter from the Commission's staff, National filed an amendment to its current report on Form 8-K for the month of December 1974. Carter participated in the preparation of that amendment, which concerned technical matters not at issue here. As was the case with the original Form 8-K, the nature of the LMP was not described, even though, by this time, both respondents had been told—and, indeed, believed—that National was obligated to implement the LMP, both understood that it had not done so and both knew that the failure to do so in the circumstances was an event of default under the Amended Credit Agreement.

On April 23, 1975 both respondents met with Hart and advised him in no uncertain terms that immediate disclosure was required. In response to Hart's protestations that National would soon obtain additional financing, respondents advised him that these hopes, as well as any negotiations for a waiver of the LMP by the banks, did not serve to excuse National's legal obligation to make prompt disclosure.

Shortly before the April 23 meeting, the vice president of one of the lending banks had written to Hart requesting, among other things, a "written response from your counsel regarding [National's] obligation to make public disclosure regarding significant transactions which may have transpired during the last several months, particularly with regard to the implementing of the lease maintenance plan." Presumably as a result of this request, Hart telephoned Johnson on April 28—only five days after having received the unambiguous and forceful advice that disclosure was required—to request that Johnson issue a legal opinion for the banks to the effect that disclosure of the triggering of the LMP was *not* necessary. Johnson testified that he replied as follows:

> I'm incredulous. I just can't believe this. You sat in my office last week and I told you as clearly and positively and precisely as I could that my advice was that you should disclose that you had gone into the lease maintenance mode.

Ultimately, Hart responded to the bank's request for an opinion of counsel with a letter from National stating that no disclosure had been made because, "in the opinion of the company," none was required.

In late April, after the telephone encounter with Hart described above, Johnson instructed Socha to draft a disclosure document for National to issue, either in its next report to the Commission or in a special letter to the stockholders. In doing so, Johnson specified that the draft should be one that would be "acceptable to a person as emotionally involved as Hart." Both respondents reviewed and approved the draft prepared by Socha and it was forwarded to Hart on or about May 1, with the suggestion that Hart call Carter or Johnson about it.

The proposed document indicated that, under the Amended Credit Agreement, National was required to cease writing new leases when its borrowings exceeded $19 million; that the company was seeking a waiver of this requirement by the banks, as well as new financing; that the company was hopeful that both of these efforts would succeed; and that the company had curtailed its sales operations because it had not obtained essential additional financing. National did not issue this disclosure document in any form and the record does not indicate any response to Brown, Wood's disclosure advice. Neither respondent questioned anyone at the company about management's failure to make the suggested disclosure.

On May 9, Kay called Socha to seek his approval of a draft of the company's proposed current report on Form 8-K for the month of April. Socha reiterated Brown, Wood's earlier advice that disclosure should be made concerning National's present status under the Amended Credit Agreement and of the event of default that resulted from the company's failure to implement the LMP. Although Kay agreed to include the suggested disclosure, the report actually filed with the Commission did not contain any such disclosure, because Lurie would not permit it.

On May 12, *** Socha called Kay and asked for a copy of the company's April Form 8-K. Kay replied that Lurie would not permit him to mail a copy to Brown, Wood or to the Commission. The April Form 8-K was eventually filed with the Commission on May 15, 1975. Socha testified that he was required to obtain a copy of it from the Commission. ***

The internal and external tensions which had been developing around National came to a head on Saturday afternoon, May 24, at [a] special meeting of the board of directors in Hartford, Connecticut. Johnson was there, acting as secretary, having been asked to attend by Hart. Also present at the meeting was independent counsel who had been consulted by the outside directors and asked to attend the meeting in the expectation that Johnson would not be there. It was at this meeting that the outside directors learned for the first time that, for over a month, Brown, Wood had been recommending disclosure and Johnson read a draft of the letter which Brown, Wood had sent to Hart on May 1, disclosing that the LMP had been triggered and its effect on the company. One of the nonmanagement directors testified that he had no prior indication that Brown, Wood had been recommending this disclosure to Hart and that when he heard the letter read by Johnson he "was shocked to the core."

At the May 24 meeting, Hart resigned each of his corporate offices, although he remained a director of the company, Johnson prepared a press release which was unanimously approved by the Board and it was decided that Brown, Wood would continue as company counsel. Johnson, however, resigned as secretary of the company.

The press release prepared by Johnson during the May 24 meeting announced that National would immediately curtail the writing of new leases, and described the management changes and the company's need for outside financing. It also expressed the company's hope that its growth structure could be resumed in the future. The release made no mention of the fact that the company had defaulted under the Amended Credit Agreement. The release was made public on May 27, 1975.

6. May to July 1975: The Events Following Public Disclosure. Following the disclosure contained in the May 27 press release and the company's subsequent current report on Form 8-K for the month of May 1975, the market price for National's common stock declined from the $13 bid, $14 asked range to the $3 bid, $4 asked range and the market for the company's common stock became virtually nonexistent. On July 2, National initiated proceedings for an arrangement under the bankruptcy laws. Among the creditors in the resulting proceeding was Brown, Wood, which submitted a claim for legal fees in excess of $200,000.

IV.

AIDING AND ABETTING[a]

[The Commission next reviewed the ALJ's findings that Carter and Johnson had "aided and abetted" National's violations of Sections 10(b) and 13(a) of the Exchange Act and Rules 10b-5, 12b-20 and 13a-11 thereunder. There were essentially two theories underlying those findings. First, the ALJ found that Carter and Johnson had aided and abetted National's violations by participating in the drafting of the December 20, 1974 press release and the Form 8-K filed with the SEC. Second, the ALJ found that Carter and Johnson had aided and abetted National's continuing fraud by "failing to ensure that the required disclosures were made or to communicate to National's board of directors concerning management's refusal to make such disclosures." In connection with both theories, the Commission observed that "the crucial inquiry in a Rule 2(e) proceeding against a lawyer inevitably tends to focus on the awareness or the intent element of the offense of aiding and abetting." The Commission therefore held explicitly that a "finding of *willful aiding and abetting* within the meaning of Rule 2(e)(1)(iii) requires a showing that respondents were aware or knew that their role was part of an activity that was improper or illegal."

With respect to the ALJs first rationale for the "aiding and abetting" finding, the Commission agreed with the ALJ's determination that "National's failure to disclose the nature of the LMP in the December 20 press release and the December Form 8-K constituted a violation of Sections 10(b) and 13(a) of the Exchange Act and Rules 10b-5, 12b-20 and 13a-11 thereunder." The Commission also agreed that the respondents were "deeply involved" in National's disclosure activities and participated in the drafting of these documents. Yet the Commission reversed the ALJ's finding because the evidence did not show definitively that Carter and Johnson had fully appreciated the materiality of the LMP at the time the December press release and the Form 8-K were prepared. In reaching this conclusion, the Commission reasoned that:

> If a securities lawyer is to bring his best independent judgment to bear on a disclosure problem, he must have the freedom to make innocent—or even, in certain cases, careless—mistakes without fear of legal liability or loss of the ability to practice before the Commission. Concern about his own liability may alter the balance of his judgment in one direction as surely as an unseemly obeisance to the wishes of his client can do so in the other. While one imbalance results in disclosure rather than concealment, neither is, in the end, truly in the public interest. Lawyers who are seen by their clients as being motivated by fears for their personal liability will not be consulted on difficult issues.

The Commission also took issue with respect to the ALJ's second rationale, which focused on Carter and Johnson's repeated instances of silence and inaction subsequent to the press release and SEC filing in December 1974. Although it agreed with the ALJ's conclusion that National had "violated the federal securities laws through its continued failure to make adequate disclosures in public statements and Commission filings regarding its deteriorat-

---

a. Ed. Note—The following discussion summarizes and, where indicated, quotes from Part IV of the Commission's opinion.

ing cash position, its inability to meet earlier growth projections, the triggering of the LMP, and the impact the LMP would have on National," it reversed the ALJ's ultimate finding because it was "unable to infer that respondents intended to aid the violations by not acting." Here the Commission emphasized that:

> Our review of the record, which includes respondents' periodic exhortations to Hart to improve the quality of National's disclosure, leads us to believe that respondents did not intend to assist the violations by their inaction or silence. Rather, they seemed to be at a loss for how to deal with a difficult client.

The Commission concluded that:

> Association of a law firm with a client lends an air of legitimacy and authority to the actions of a client. There are occasions when, but for the law firms's association, a violation could not have occurred. Under those circumstances, if the firm were cognizant of how it was being used and acquiesced, or if it gained some benefit from the violation beyond that normally obtained in a legal relationship, inaction would probably give rise to an inference of intent. This, however, is not such a case, and we find that respondents did not intend to assist the violation by their inaction.]

V.

ETHICAL AND PROFESSIONAL RESPONSIBILITIES

A. The Findings of the Administrative Law Judge. The Administrative Law Judge found that both respondents "failed to carry out their professional responsibilities with respect to appropriate disclosure to all concerned, including stockholders, directors and the investing public ... and thus knowingly engaged in unethical and improper professional conduct, as charged in the Order." In particular, he held that respondents' failure to advise National's board of directors of Hart's refusal to disclose adequately the company's perilous financial condition was itself a violation of ethical and professional standards referred to in Rule 2(e)(1)(ii).

Respondents argue that the Commission has never promulgated standards of professional conduct for lawyers and that the Commission's application in hindsight of new standards would be fundamentally unfair. Moreover, even if it is permissible for the Commission to apply—without specific adoption or notice—generally recognized professional standards, they argue that no such standards applicable to respondents' conduct existed in 1974-75, nor do they exist today.

We agree that, in general, elemental notions of fairness dictate that the Commission should not establish new rules of conduct and impose them retroactively upon professionals who acted at the time without reason to believe that their conduct was unethical or improper. At the same time, however, we perceive no unfairness whatsoever in holding those professionals who practice before us to generally recognized norms of professional conduct, whether or not such norms had previously been explicitly adopted or endorsed by the Commission. To do so upsets no justifiable expectations, since the professional is already subject to those norms.

The ethical and professional responsibilities of lawyers who become aware that their client is engaging in violations of the securities laws have not been so firmly and unambiguously established that we believe all practicing lawyers can be held to an awareness of generally recognized norms. We also recognize that the Commission has never articulated or endorsed any such standards. That being the case, we reverse the Administrative Law Judge's findings under subparagraph (ii) of Rule 2(e)(1) with respect to both respondents. Nevertheless, we believe that respondents' conduct raises serious questions about the obligations of securities lawyers, and the Commission is hereby giving notice of its interpretation of "unethical or improper professional conduct" as that term is used in Rule 2(e)(1)(ii). The Commission intends to issue a release soliciting comment from the public as to whether this interpretation should be expanded or modified.

B. Interpretive Background. Our concern focuses on the professional obligations of the lawyer who gives essentially correct disclosure advice to a client that does not follow that advice and as a result violates the federal securities laws. ***

While precise standards have not yet emerged, it is fair to say that there exists considerable acceptance of the proposition that a lawyer must, in order to discharge his professional responsibilities, make all efforts within reason to persuade his client to avoid or terminate proposed illegal action. Such efforts could include, where appropriate, notification to the board of directors of a corporate client. ***

We are mindful that, when a lawyer represents a corporate client, the client—and the entity to which he owes his allegiance—is the corporation itself and not management or any other individual connected with the corporation. [ABA E.C. 5-18] Moreover, the lawyer should try to "insure that decisions of his client are made only after the client has been informed of relevant considerations." [ABA E.C. 7-8] These unexceptionable principles take on a special coloration when a lawyer becomes aware that one or more specific members of a corporate client's management is deciding not to follow his disclosure advice, especially if he knows that those in control, such as the board of directors, may not have participated in or been aware of that decision. Moreover, it is well established that no lawyer, even in the most zealous pursuit of his client's interests, is privileged to assist his client in conduct the lawyer knows to be illegal. [ABA D.R. 7-102(A)(7)] The application of these recognized principles to the special role of the securities lawyer giving disclosure advice, however, is not a simple task.

The securities lawyer who is an active participant in a company's ongoing disclosure program will ordinarily draft and revise disclosure documents, comment on them and file them with the Commission. He is often involved on an intimate, day-to-day basis in the judgments that determine what will be disclosed and what will be withheld from the public markets. When a lawyer serving in such a capacity concludes that his client's disclosures are not adequate to comply with the law, and so advises his client, he is "aware," in a literal sense, of a continuing violation of the securities laws. On the other hand, the lawyer is only an adviser, and the final judgment—and, indeed, responsibility—as to what course of conduct is to be taken must lie with the client. Moreover, disclosure issues often present difficult choices between multiple shades of gray, and while a lawyer's judgment may be to draw the disclosure obligation more broadly than his client, both parties recognize the degree of uncertainty involved.

The problems of professional conduct that arise in this relationship are well-illustrated by the facts of this case. In rejecting Brown, Wood's advice to include the assumptions underlying its projections in its 1974 Annual Report, in declining to issue two draft stockholders letters offered by respondents and in ignoring the numerous more informal urgings by both respondents and Socha to make disclosure, Hart and Lurie indicated that they were inclined to resist any public pronouncements that were at odds with the rapid growth which had been projected and reported for the company.

If the record ended there, we would be hesitant to suggest that any unprofessional conduct might be involved. Hart and Lurie were, in effect, pressing the company's lawyers hard for the minimum disclosure required by law. That fact alone is not an appropriate basis for a finding that a lawyer must resign or take some extraordinary action. Such a finding would inevitably drive a wedge between reporting companies and their outside lawyers; the more sophisticated members of management would soon realize that there is nothing to gain in consulting outside lawyers.

However, much more was involved in this case. In sending out a patently misleading letter to stockholders on December 23 in contravention of Socha's plain and express advice to clear all such disclosure with Brown, Wood, in deceiving respondents about Johnson's approval of the company's quarterly report to its stockholders in early December and in dissembling in response to respondents' questions about the implementation of the LMP, the company's management erected a wall between National and its outside lawyers—a wall apparently designed to keep out good legal advice in conflict with management's improper disclosure plans.

Any ambiguity in the situation plainly evaporated in late April and early May of 1975 when Hart first asked Johnson for a legal opinion flatly contrary to the express disclosure advice Johnson had given Hart only five days earlier, and when Lurie soon thereafter prohibited Kay from delivering a copy of the company's April 1975 Form 8-K to Brown, Wood.

These actions reveal a conscious desire on the part of National's management no longer to look to Brown, Wood for independent disclosure advice, but rather to embrace the firm within Hart's fraud and use it as a shield to avoid the pressures exerted by the banks toward disclosure. Such a role is a perversion of the normal lawyer-client relationship, and no lawyer may claim that, in these circumstance, he need do no more than stubbornly continue to suggest disclosure when he knows his suggestions are falling on deaf ears.

C. "*Unethical or Improper Professional Conduct.*" The Commission is of the view that a lawyer engages in "unethical or improper professional conduct" under the following circumstances: When a lawyer with significant responsibilities in the effectuation of a company's compliance with the disclosure requirements of the federal securities laws becomes aware that his client is engaged in a substantial and continuing failure to satisfy those disclosure requirements, his continued participation violates professional standards unless he takes prompt steps to end the client's noncompliance. The Commission has determined that this interpretation will be applicable only to conduct occurring after the date of this opinion.

We do not imply that a lawyer is obliged, at the risk of being held to have violated Rule 2(e), to seek to correct every isolated disclosure action or inaction which he believes to be at variance with applicable disclosure standards, although there may be isolated disclosure failures that are so serious that their correction becomes a matter of primary professional concern. It is also clear, however, that a lawyer is not privileged to unthinkingly permit himself to be co-opted into an ongoing fraud and cast as a dupe or a shield for a wrong-doing client.

Initially, counselling accurate disclosure is sufficient, even if his advice is not accepted. But there comes a point at which a reasonable lawyer must conclude that his advice is not being followed, or even sought in good faith, and that his client is involved in a continuing course of violating the securities laws. At this critical juncture, the lawyer must take further, more affirmative steps in order to avoid the inference that he has been co-opted, willingly or unwillingly, into the scheme of non-disclosure.

The lawyer is in the best position to choose his next step. Resignation is one option, although we recognize that other considerations, including the protection of the client against forseeable prejudice, must be taken into account in the case of withdrawal. [See, e.g. ABA D.R. 2-110; ABA E.C. 2-32.] A direct approach to the board of directors or one or more individual directors or officers may be appropriated; or he may choose to try to enlist the aid of other members of the firm's management. What is required, in short, is some prompt action[77] that leads to the conclusion that the lawyer is engaged in efforts to correct the underlying problem, rather than having capitulated to the desires of a strong-willed, but misguided client.

Some have argued that resignation is the only permissible course when a client chooses not to comply with disclosure advice. We do not agree. Premature resignation serves neither the end of an effective lawyer-client relationship nor, in most cases, the effective administration of the securities laws. The lawyer's continued interaction with his client will ordinarily hold the greatest promise of corrective action. So long as a lawyer is acting in good faith and exerting reasonable efforts to prevent violations of the law by his client, his professional obligations have been met. In general, the best result is that which promotes the continued, strong-minded and independent participation by the lawyer.

We recognize, however, that the "best result" is not always obtainable, and that there may occur situations where the lawyer must conclude that the misconduct is so extreme or irretrievable, or the involvement of his client's management and board of directors in the misconduct is so thoroughgoing and pervasive that any action short of resignation would be futile. We would anticipate that cases where a lawyer has no choice but to resign would be rare

---

77. In those cases where resignation is not the only alternative, should a lawyer choose not to resign, we do not believe the action taken *must be successful* to avoid the inference that the lawyer had improperly participated in his client's fraud. Rather, the acceptability of the action must be considered in the light of all relevant surrounding circumstances. Similarly, what is "prompt" in any one case depends on the situation then facing the lawyer.

and of an egregious nature.[78]

D. *Conclusion.*

As noted above, because the Commission has never adopted or endorsed standards of professional conduct which would have applied to respondents' activities during the period here in question, and since generally accepted norms of professional conduct which existed outside the scope of Rule 2(e) did not, during the relevant time period, unambiguously cover the situation in which respondents found themselves in 1974-75, no finding of unethical or unprofessional conduct would be appropriate. That being the case, we reverse the findings of the Administrative Law Judge under Rule 2(e)(1)(ii). In future proceedings of this nature, however, the Commission will apply the interpretation of subparagraph (ii) of Rule 2(e)(1) set forth in this opinion. ***

NOTES AND QUESTIONS

1. ***Affirmative Duty to Halt a Client's Noncompliance.*** Does the Commission's opinion in *Carter & Johnson* effectively impose an affirmative duty on securities lawyers to halt their client's noncompliance with the federal securities laws? Consider the facts as detailed in *Carter & Johnson* and assume that the standards for "ethical and professional" conduct announced in Part V of the opinion had previously been articulated. What should Carter and Johnson have done differently? When in the chronology of events was action advisable? When was action required?

2. ***Independence vs. Interdependence.*** In an article that includes substantial analysis of the facts and issues raised in *Carter & Johnson*, one of your co-authors has contrasted the view that lawyers and their clients are "morally independent" with the view that they are "morally interdependent." Ultimately, he concludes that:

> As monitors of corporate conduct and as dealmakers designing transactions, lawyers often participate in their clients' conduct to an extent that a distinction between the lawyers' acts and those of clients is difficult if not impossible to make. In such cases, the moral independence theory is no longer tenable, and lawyers are morally responsible for at least some of their clients' actions.
>
> Lawyers have important obligations to their clients, but also to others who may be harmed by clients. Although balancing these obligations may be difficult, moral action requires recognizing and making choices, not opting out of choices by denial. Lawyers who acknowledge their moral interdependence with clients may change the way they choose their clients and the type of advice they give. Clients will also be more likely to trust, and follow the advice of, lawyers whose conception of their moral responsibilities corresponds with functions they actually perform.

Richard W. Painter, The Moral Interdependence of Corporate Lawyers and their Clients, 67 S. Cal. L. Rev. 507, 583-84 (1994). Does moral responsibility for client conduct translate into moral responsibility to do something about that

---

78. This case does not involve, nor do we here deal with, the additional question of when a lawyer, aware of his client's intention to commit fraud or an illegal act, has a professional duty to disclose that fact either publicly or to an affected third party. Our interpretation today does not require such action at any point, although other existing standards of professional conduct might be so interpreted. See, e.g., ABA D.R. 7-102(B).

conduct? At what point should a moral responsibility—what the morally righteous attorney would do—translate into a legal responsibility? Who should be charged with making this determination—the SEC, Congress, or state bar associations?

*3. **The SEC's Rule 102(e) Retreat with Respect to Lawyers.*** The SEC's case against Carter and Johnson, brought over 25 years ago, was the last enforcement action brought by the SEC against a lawyer or law firm for "improper professional conduct." After an outcry from the legal profession against the *Carter & Johnson* proceeding, the SEC went so far as to announce that:

> With respect to attorneys, the Commission generally has not sought to develop or apply independent standards of professional conduct. The great majority of Rule 2(e) proceedings against attorneys involve allegations of violations of the law (not of professional standards); thus, the Commission, as a matter of policy, generally refrains from using its administrative forum to conduct de novo determinations of the professional obligation of attorneys.

Disciplinary Proceedings Involving Professionals Appearing or Practicing Before the Commission, Exchange Act Release No. 25893, 41 SEC Docket 465 (July 13, 1988). Why did the SEC retreat from Rule 102(e) proceedings against lawyers but not from similar proceedings against accountants? Are some of the justifications for SEC regulation of accountants lacking when it comes to lawyers? Is it possible that by retreating from Rule 102(e) proceedings against lawyers, the SEC sent the bar a mixed message concerning its view of securities attorneys as gatekeepers?

---

3. The Enron Scandal and Questions of Professional Responsibility

TESTIMONY BY SUSAN P. KONIAK, PROFESSOR OF LAW, BOSTON UNIVERSITY SCHOOL OF LAW, FEBRUARY 6, 2002

U.S. SENATE COMMITTEE ON THE JUDICIARY ACCOUNTABILITY ISSUES: LESSONS LEARNED FROM ENRON'S FALL

***Twelve years ago in a court opinion dealing with some aspects of the Lincoln Savings and Loan fraud, Judge Stanley Sporkin wrote:

> Where ... were the ... accountants and attorneys...? [W]ith all the professional talent involved (both accounting and legal), why [didn't] at least one professional ... [act] to stop the overreaching that took place in this case?

[*Lincoln Sav. & Loan Ass'n v. Wall*, 743 F. Supp. 901, 920 (D.D.C. 1990)]

Now, there is Enron. And we are here asking the same questions, Judge Sporkin and others were asking 12 years ago. To paraphrase Pete Seeger, "When will [we] ever learn?" ***

All too often lawyers act as if they were wearing magic caps—hats that transport them to some alternative reality, a law free zone, in which they are free to do anything and everything for the person or entity paying the lawyers' fees—hats that transport them to a magic land where lawyers need not fear that law will come crashing down on them. "It may hit the client, but it will never hit me." There are no such magic caps. But the scant attention that has thus far been paid to the role of lawyers in this mess suggests that the myth of the magic cap has spread far and wide.***

The mere fact that there are always lawyers around when securities fraud is taking place does not mean that lawyers cause securities fraud nor does it demonstrate that they are always in a position to discover it or stop it from taking place. They aren't. In plain English, fraud, as I tell my students year in and year out, is lying to someone to get them to give you their stuff. Fraud-doers are by definition liars (sneaks, cheats) and many are slick enough at lying to fool a room full of experienced lawyers. On the other hand, not all fraud-doers are quite that slick, and I dare say when it comes to securities fraud being slick enough to keep it from one's lawyers for a significant period of time takes some considerable degree of skill. Don't get me wrong, even a sophisticated and careful lawyer may not be able to detect a complex and well crafted scheme to defraud others in connection with the sale or purchase of securities. But then again many a sophisticated lawyer is not careful, at least, not about detecting securities fraud, and all too many sophisticated lawyers are all too willing to turn a blind eye.***

To make this as simple as possible a lawyer has done wrong and is likely to be in significant legal trouble when three things are true. One, the client is breaking the law. Two, the lawyer has enough facts in front of her to have been able to figure out, with the exercise of reasonable care, that number one is true. And three, with number one and number two in place, the lawyer either acts to help the client to break the law or does nothing to stop the client from breaking the law in those instances (which are not as few as some would like to think) when the lawyer has a duty to intervene.

Using the three part test I have just laid out, we can gauge the universe of lawyers who might be in trouble by asking which clients are we likely, in the end, to discover were breaking the law? [I'm] assuming [that] Enron will be in that category; possibly Arthur Andersen, possibly the partnerships that appear to have been part of what now appears to be a fraudulent scheme, some investors in those partnerships, maybe some investment banks. And while that list may include some innocent parties, it is at least as likely to have left out some individuals and entities who we will later discover were involved in violations of law.

The lawyers for any of the individuals or entities that turn out to be on the "broke the law" list constitute the universe of lawyers who need to start worrying. Vinson & Elkins was Enron's outside counsel, but other law firms may have represented Enron during what may have been its crime spree and might have been in a position to have figured out that Enron was breaking the law and to have helped it to do so. Enron's in-house counsel were certainly in a position to satisfy all three parts of the test I set forth above, as were Andersen's in-house counsel, and any outside law firms who may have advised Andersen on Enron related-questions during the years Andersen was auditing and advising Enron. ***

But as my list of potential law breakers was designed to emphasize, the lawyers who may be in trouble for assisting their clients' unlawful conduct (assuming those clients turn out to have broken the law) does not end with lawyers representing Enron and Andersen.

Now, we move to question two: Did any of the lawyers for clients who were breaking the law have enough facts in front of them to have figured out with the exercise of reasonable care that law breaking was going on? Well, the Powers report[a] strongly suggests that if Enron was breaking the law, its in-house counsel and Vinson & Elkins had enough facts in front of them to have figured it out, had they been exercising reasonable care. I hasten to add that does not make either in-house counsel or outside counsel, guilty of any crime, but it does leave them in legal jeopardy in malpractice actions brought on Enron's behalf by the Trustee in bankruptcy or whomever ultimately emerges as the new management or entity in control of Enron.

To take just one example detailed in the Powers report, knowing that the Board had waived Enron's conflict of interest rules (and possibly having advised that it was a good idea to do so), it does not appear that any lawyer (within or outside) Enron bothered to worry much about the "procedures" that were supposed to prevent bad things from happening to Enron due to the conflicting roles its CFO was not licensed to play. The Powers report says whatever procedures were supposed to be in place, not only failed miserably but were not designed well enough to do anything but fail. It was Enron's lawyers who should have designed better procedures, or at least, monitored whatever procedures were designed to see to it that they had some reasonable chance of working. I do not know whether this was within the scope of Vinson & Elkins retainer, but in-house counsel was apparently not paying all this much mind. Some lawyer or group of lawyers appears to have been hopelessly careless on this matter. Indeed, it seems to me that a reasonably careful lawyer would have strongly advised the board not to waive the conflict rules in the first place, especially not as to the company's CFO.

The fact that agents within Enron, including senior management, may have been actively engaged in fraud does not, in most states, relieve the lawyer from a claim of negligence for having failed to take steps to have saved her client, the corporation, from harm (legal and financial) that these wrongdoing agents may have been causing. Again, if a careful lawyer would not have discerned that agents within the client corporation were acting unlawfully, which includes breaching their duties to the corporation by self-dealing or taking actions that would leave the corporation open to a multitude of civil lawsuits and possibly criminal charges, the lawyer should not be found liable. The liability of the lawyer will turn on how many red flags were in front of him, indicating ongoing fraud. The Powers report suggests there were signs aplenty. A company's lawyers can avoid liability for negligence, but not if they are careless about detecting wrongdoing by the CEO or CFO or other senior management, and only if they take steps to bring any signs of serious wrongdoing to the attention of the board and advise management and the board that the

---

a. Ed. Note—In October 2001, as Enron's corporate scandal was nearing public exposure, the Board of Directors established a Special Investigation Committee, which was chaired by outside director William C. Powers, Jr., Dean of University of Texas School of Law. The Committee's Report of February 1, 2002 has become known as the "Powers Report," and is available at 2002 WL 198018.

wrongdoing must stop. The Powers report suggests that that did not happen, although we have yet to hear from the lawyers involved.

Malpractice, is of course a matter of state law. But extreme negligence amounting to reckless disregard of the fact that corporate actors are engaged in securities fraud has long been a matter of federal law, although that may no longer be the case. Before the mid-1990s, federal securities law, as interpreted by the courts, provided that lawyers could be sued by shareholders in a derivative action and by the SEC for failing to take steps to stop securities fraud that those lawyers had to be deaf, dumb and blind not to have detected (i.e., fraud the lawyers recklessly ignored or to which the lawyers deliberately closed their eyes). This was "aiding and abetting" securities fraud. It should be the law [for private securities fraud actions] today, but for a number of reasons it isn't. That should change.

Before getting to why it should change. Let me explain why it is necessary for federal law to punish lawyer recklessness when state law allows a malpractice action for negligence and thus by definition presumably deters recklessness as well, both by leaving lawyers liable for less serious carelessness (negligence) and by providing punitive damages when that negligence gets out of control and rises to the level of recklessness.

First, there is the fact plain for all to see: the existence of state negligence actions has not proven to be an effective deterrent, possibly because lawyers bet on the fraud-doers staying in control of the corporation through fraud and thus there being no "clean, new" management with an interest in suing them. Possibly because lawyers believe that the wrongdoing of high corporate officials will somehow be attributed to the corporation in such a way as to bar a negligence suit or that even if such a suit may legally proceed, a jury will be loathe to hit the lawyers hard when management was so dirty itself. Perhaps, some state tort law reform, e.g., laws capping damages, have rendered it worthwhile for lawyers to risk a negligence suit when the fees to be reaped are high enough to pay whatever damages may be imposed (discounted by the risk that the negligence may go undiscovered or unprosecuted).

Perhaps it is as simple as lawyers believing (and being trained to act) as if the agents for their clients were their clients, making it much more difficult to internalize the notion that there is a client out there that doesn't know what's going on. Perhaps (and I believe there is something to this) the elimination of private causes of action against lawyers for aiding and abetting liability, the changes to RICO, restrictions on joint and several liability in many actions against lawyers, and other changes in federal law have encouraged lawyers to overlook that something as relatively trivial as negligently failing to take action to stop a fraud could still offend the law at all. ***

Lawyers are notorious for never "knowing" their clients are guilty. That inability is built into the ethos of the bar, which still takes its shape from the paradigm of the lawyer as advocate, And by and large, as to lawyers charged with defending clients in court, that ethos is okay. We do not want lawyers to substitute their judgment of the client's guilt for that of the jury or that of the judge. Although I hasten to add that this "no judging" attitude sometimes leads to abuse in courtrooms too, as when litigators believe they have a license in civil and criminal cases to assist perjury on the ground that they are incapable of "knowing" what the truth of the matter is. That caveat made, in general it is appropriate that the trial lawyer leave "judging" the client to the finder of fact. That's what trials are for.

But none of that applies to the lawyer who is not litigating a matter after the alleged wrong has occurred, but rather one who enters the scene before or during the client's wrongdoing—the lawyer in the role of a facilitator of the client's transactions. Indeed, very few lawyers practice in court compared to the number whose daily work is to facilitate transactions. The transaction or office lawyer, as distinguished from her trial colleagues, must understand what the client is doing and whether that is within or without the law. Otherwise, there is simply no reason for the lawyer being there.

But transaction lawyers share the ethic of trial lawyers that makes it difficult to believe, difficult to "know" that their clients are breaking the law. Complicating that problem is the fact that every good transaction lawyer understands, what every good lawyer knows, the lines of the law are almost always fuzzy at the edges. It is simply not easy to "know for sure" when those lines have been crossed, particularly when clients want to walk on the wild side and expect their lawyers to support that behavior. The lawyer who seems too quick to judge his client is likely to be replaced rapidly with one much more willing to "believe" that his client is right.

Letting lawyers know that there is a price to be paid for failing to "know" what the facts in front of the lawyer plainly suggest—that the client is committing fraud—is absolutely necessary. Without that we create a world in which fraud doers can count on high-priced and savvy lawyers to help them with their schemes, as long as the fraud doer never directly admits to the lawyer precisely what he is up to. This is not a world we should encourage. It is a world our law should try to erase.

In 1964, Judge Friendly said this about the importance of holding lawyers and accountants liable when they recklessly disregarded evidence of their client's securities fraud:

> Congress did not mean that every mistake of law or misstatement of fact should subject an attorney or an accountant to criminal liability simply because more skilled practitioners would not have made them. But Congress equally could not have intended that men holding themselves out as members of these ancient professions should be able to escape criminal liability on a plea of ignorance when they have shut their eyes to what was plainly to be seen or have represented a knowledge they knew they did not possess.

[*United States v. Benjamin*, 328 F.2d 854, 863 (2d Cir. 1964)]

Congress should change the securities laws to make clear once again that such recklessness on the part of lawyers and accountants is enough to subject a lawyer to a private suit for money damages from those the lawyer's recklessness has helped to harm. Such recklessness is rightly thought of as "criminal," given the learning, privileged position, substantial financial rewards and expertise that come with being a securities lawyer. And if it's rightly thought of as criminal when such privileged folks behave recklessly, it should be a civil wrong as well.

Were the lawyers who represented Enron negligent? Were they reckless? Did they actually know, what we now suspect, that Enron through its agents was committing securities fraud? I can tell you this much I am highly doubtful that they "knew," if "knowing" means subjectively believing that Enron was breaking the law. I am sure they convinced themselves that however close to the legal line Enron was, it had not crossed it. I am sure they refused to see and took no steps to actively ferret out, facts that would have burst that bubble—facts that would have made it difficult to maintain their "belief" that nothing was rotten in the state of Denmark. Hard as I am on lawyers, I can hardly blame them. The law as "reformed" by Congress invited them to act that way. If they "knew" I am sure that it was only in the sense that it may have crossed their mind, but any agile legal mind can formulate a doubt about whether something is "illegal" to chase those occasional bogey-men away.

But the facts (as we know them so far) do seem to suggest that at least some of Enron's lawyers and likely some of the lawyers for other actors in this drama went way beyond negligence. According to the Powers report there were not just red flags all over the place but cannons booming and music playing, all with the same message: Enron's financial condition is way different than what it (with its lawyers' help and its accountants' blessings) was leading everyone to believe. A jury need not accept a lawyer's denial of knowledge. It is perfectly free to infer that with so many major clues, some of these lawyers did "know," no matter what they were telling themselves or what they tell the jury under oath. That is, a jury can decide not to believe the lawyer, assuming a court allows the case to get to the jury, something Congress's reforms discourage judges from doing in cases when "actual knowledge" is in doubt.

But whatever happens or doesn't happen to the lawyers in Enron, there is every reason to believe that there will be securities fraud in our future and every reason to believe that its success will depend in part on lawyer's being asleep at the wheel or acting with reckless abandon. Keep in mind that in the past, as will be the case here—assuming lawyers are found to have substantially assisted fraud at Enron—the lawyers who have done wrong were (and will be) members of our finest law firms, not some nobodies from nowhere. The bar can complain all it wants about federal encroachment on self-regulation, but one thing should be abundantly clear by now: Without the discipline that fairly certain and substantial liability brings, the bar will not reform itself. Lawyers need law at least as much, if not more, than everyone else. You do neither the bar nor anyone else a favor by leaving them behind the curtain trusting in their magic caps.***

If Enron was the Emerald City, no matter what individual or groups of individuals end up to have been standing behind the curtain playing the Wizard of Oz (be it Enron's CEO, its CFO, some or all of its board of directors or whomever), I guarantee you one thing: A lawyer was standing beside them making sure the curtain stayed drawn and all the bells and whistles were hooked up and operating to fool Dorothy, the brainless scarecrow and the cowardly lion. ***

NOTES AND QUESTIONS

1. Recognizing Securities Fraud. Do you agree with Professor Koniak's statement that "lawyers are notorious for never 'knowing' that their clients are guilty"? What reforms does she propose in order to give lawyers a greater incentive to more readily recognize fraudulent actions by their clients? Do you agree with Professor Koniak's recommendations?

*2. **Magic Caps.*** Recall the facts set out in the *Carter & Johnson* opinion. Does Professor Koniak's theory of "magic caps" ring true? What examples, if any, might illustrate this phenomenon?

*3. **Professional Independence.*** In their analysis of lawyers' roles in the Enron scandal, Professor Deborah Rhode and Paul Paton draw attention to "the financial incentives created by Vinson & Elkins' dependence on Enron-related work and employment opportunities." They note, in particular, that

> [i]n 2001, Enron was Vinson & Elkins' largest client, accounting for more than seven percent of the law firm's revenues. Both Enron's general counsel and deputy general counsel at the time were former Vinson & Elkins partners; an additional twenty or so Vinson & Elkins attorneys reportedly had taken jobs at Enron since 1991.

Deborah L. Rhode & Paul D. Paton, Lawyers, Ethics, and Enron, 8 Stan. J. of Law, Bus. & Fin. 9, 25 (2002).

As we will see, in the aftermath of Enron and WorldCom, Congress made the independence of auditors a high legislative priority. Should similar attention be paid to the independence of lawyers? Is reliance on general rules of professional responsibility enough? In answering no, Professor Rhode and Mr. Paton maintain:

> Increased competition from within and outside the bar has led to increased pressure on firms to favor responsiveness to client demands over broader societal concerns. Allegiance to management's short-term financial interests may compromise obligations to the broader public, as well as to the entity itself, which is, at least in theory, the lawyer's client.
>
> The challenges of maintaining independent judgment are compounded in a competitive market where powerful clients can shop for expedient rather than ethical advice. Yet while resisting client pressures can carry financial risks, so, too, can satisfying their demands. In the long run, firms' reputational interests are not well served by assisting conduct that cuts ethical corners. ***

Id. at 26. See also John C. Coffee, Jr. ,The Attorney as Gatekeeper: An Agenda for the SEC, 103 Colum. L. Rev. 1293, 1311-12 (2003) (suggesting that the SEC read Section 307 of the SOX "to grant it the authority to define the point at which the attorney is not sufficiently independent of the client to perform certain tasks").

---

4. Section 307 of the SOX and the SEC's Standards for Professional Conduct

In the wake of allegations against lawyers at Enron and other corporations rocked by scandal, the SEC received various recommendations for change. The most publicized proposal came from a group of forty law professors (including your casebook authors) who urged the SEC to add to Rule 102(e) a requirement that lawyers representing securities issuers must report known securities law violations to senior management and then, if necessary, to the issuer's board of directors. The law professors emphasized that their proposed requirement was substantially less demanding than the requirement imposed on accountants by Section 10A of the Exchange Act, which requires the reporting of illegal acts to the client's directors as well as to the SEC if senior management fails to take remedial action. See Letter dated March 7, 2002 from Richard W. Painter, et al. to Harvey Pitt, Chairperson of the Securities and Exchange Commission. The ABA, however, lobbied the SEC against the proposed requirement and the SEC responded by declaring that federal professional responsibility standards for lawyers should be mandated, if at all, by Congress rather than by the SEC. See Letter dated March 28, 2002 from David Becker, General Counsel, Securities and Exchange Commission, to Richard W. Painter.

In the summer of 2002, Senators John Edwards (D N.C.), Mike Enzi (R WY), and John Corzine (D N.J.) responded to Mr. Becker's invitation by sponsoring the provision that became Section 307 of the SOX.

Section 307. Rules of Professional Responsibility for Attorneys

> Not later than 180 days after the date of enactment of this Act, the Commission shall issue rules, in the public interest and for the protection of investors, setting forth minimum standards of professional conduct for attorneys appearing and practicing before the Commission in any way in the representation of issuers, including a rule—
>
> (1) requiring an attorney to report evidence of a material violation of securities law or breach of fiduciary duty or similar violation by the company or any agent thereof, to the chief legal counsel or the chief executive officer of the company (or the equivalent thereof); and
>
> (2) if the counsel or officer does not appropriately respond to the evidence (adopting, as necessary, appropriate remedial measures or sanctions with respect to the violation), requiring the attorney to report the evidence to the audit committee of the board of directors of the issuer or to another committee of the board of directors comprised solely of directors not employed directly or indirectly by the issuer, or to the board of directors.

In response to this directive, on November 21, 2002, the SEC published for comment a proposed rule that generated vigorous debate. Set out below is the significantly modified final rule, which the SEC adopted a little more than two months later. See Final Rule: Implementation of Standards of Professional Conduct for Attorneys, Exchange Act Release No. 47276 (Jan. 29, 2003). As you read through this lengthy rule, consider some of the questions and issues that are bound to be raised as securities attorneys assess their duties and responsibilities under it.

STANDARDS OF PROFESSIONAL CONDUCT FOR ATTORNEYS APPEARING AND PRACTICING BEFORE THE COMMISSION IN THE REPRESENTATION OF AN ISSUER

17 C.F.R. Part 205—Effective date: August 5, 2003

§ 205.1 Purpose and scope

This part sets forth minimum standards of professional conduct for attorneys appearing and practicing before the Commission in the representation of an issuer. These standards supplement applicable standards of any jurisdiction where an attorney is admitted or practices and are not intended to limit the ability of any jurisdiction to impose additional obligations on an attorney not inconsistent with the application of this part. Where the standards of a state or other United States jurisdiction where an attorney is admitted or practices conflict with this part, this part shall govern.

§ 205.2 Definitions

For purposes of this part, the following definitions apply:

(a) *Appearing and practicing* before the Commission:

(1) Means:

(i) Transacting any business with the Commission, including communications in any form;

(ii) Representing an issuer in a Commission administrative proceeding or in connection with any Commission investigation, inquiry, information request, or subpoena;

(iii) Providing advice in respect of the United States securities laws or the Commission's rules or regulations thereunder regarding any document that the attorney has notice will be filed with or submitted to, or incorporated into any document that will be filed with or submitted to, the Commission, including the provision of such advice in the context of preparing, or participating in the preparation of, any such document; or

(iv) Advising an issuer as to whether information or a statement, opinion, or other writing is required under the United States securities laws or the Commission's rules or regulations thereunder to be filed with or submitted to, or incorporated into any document that will be filed with or submitted to, the Commission; but

(2) Does not include an attorney who:

(i) Conducts the activities in paragraphs (a)(1)(i) through (a)(1)(iv) of this section other than in the context of providing legal services to an issuer with whom the attorney has an attorney-client relationship; or

(ii) Is a non-appearing foreign attorney.

(b) *Appropriate response* means a response to an attorney regarding reported evidence of a material violation as a result of which the attorney reasonably believes:

(1) That no material violation, as defined in paragraph (i) of this section, has occurred, is ongoing, or is about to occur;

(2) That the issuer has, as necessary, adopted appropriate remedial measures, including appropriate steps or sanctions to stop any material violations that are ongoing, to prevent any material violation that has yet to occur, and to remedy or otherwise appropriately address any material violation that has already occurred and to minimize the likelihood of its recurrence; or

(3) That the issuer, with the consent of the issuer's board of directors, a committee thereof to whom a report could be made pursuant to §§ 205.3(b)(3), or a qualified legal compliance committee, has retained or directed an attorney

to review the reported evidence of a material violation and either:

(i) Has substantially implemented any remedial recommendations made by such attorney after a reasonable investigation and evaluation of the reported evidence; or

(ii) Has been advised that such attorney may, consistent with his or her professional obligations, assert a colorable defense on behalf of the issuer (or the issuer's officer, director, employee, or agent, as the case may be) in any investigation or judicial or administrative proceeding relating to the reported evidence of a material violation.

(c) *Attorney* means any person who is admitted, licensed, or otherwise qualified to practice law in any jurisdiction, domestic or foreign, or who holds himself or herself out as admitted, licensed, or otherwise qualified to practice law.

(d) *Breach of fiduciary duty* refers to any breach of fiduciary or similar duty to the issuer recognized under an applicable federal or state statute or at common law, including but not limited to misfeasance, nonfeasance, abdication of duty, abuse of trust, and approval of unlawful transactions.

(e) *Evidence of a material violation* means credible evidence, based upon which it would be unreasonable, under the circumstances, for a prudent and competent attorney not to conclude that it is reasonably likely that a material violation has occurred, is ongoing, or is about to occur.

(f) *Foreign government issuer* means a foreign issuer as defined in 17 CFR 230.405 eligible to register securities on Schedule B of the Securities Act of 1933.

(g) *In the representation of an issuer* means providing legal services as an attorney for an issuer, regardless of whether the attorney is employed or retained by the issuer.

(h) *Issuer* means an issuer (as defined in section 3 of the Securities Exchange Act of 1934), the securities of which are registered under section 12 of that Act, or that is required to file reports under section 15(d) of that Act, or that files or has filed a registration statement that has not yet become effective under the Securities Act of 1933, and that it has not withdrawn, but does not include a foreign government issuer. For purposes of paragraphs (a) and (g) of this section, the term "issuer" includes any person controlled by an issuer, where an attorney provides legal services to such person on behalf of, or at the behest, or for the benefit of the issuer, regardless of whether the attorney is employed or retained by the issuer.

(i) *Material violation* means a material violation of an applicable United States federal or state securities law, a material breach of fiduciary duty arising under United States federal or state law, or a similar material violation of any United States federal or state law.

(j) *Non-appearing foreign attorney* means an attorney:

(1) Who is admitted to practice law in a jurisdiction outside the United States;

(2) Who does not hold himself or herself out as practicing, and does not give legal advice regarding, United States federal or state securities or other laws (except as provided in paragraph (j)(3)(ii) of this section); and

(3) Who:

(i) Conducts activities that would constitute appearing and practicing before the Commission only incidentally to, and in the ordinary course of, the practice of law in a jurisdiction outside the United States; or

(ii) Is appearing and practicing before the Commission only in consultation with counsel, other than a non-appearing foreign attorney, admitted or licensed to practice in a state or other United States jurisdiction.

(k) *Qualified legal compliance committee* means a committee of an issuer (which also may be an audit or other committee of the issuer) that:

(1) Consists of at least one member of the issuer's audit committee (or, if the issuer has no audit committee, one member from an equivalent committee of independent directors) and two or more members of the issuer's board of directors who are not employed, directly or indirectly, by the issuer and who are not, in the case of a registered investment company, "interested persons" as defined in section 2(a)(19) of the Investment Company Act of 1940;

(2) Has adopted written procedures for the confidential receipt, retention, and consideration of any report of evidence of a material violation under §§ 205.3;

(3) Has been duly established by the issuer's board of directors, with the authority and responsibility:

(i) To inform the issuer's chief legal officer and chief executive officer (or the equivalents thereof) of any report of evidence of a material violation (except in the circumstances described in §§205.3(b)(4));

(ii) To determine whether an investigation is necessary regarding any report of evidence of a material violation by the issuer, its officers, directors, employees or agents and, if it determines an investigation is necessary or appropriate, to:

(A) Notify the audit committee or the full board of directors;

(B) Initiate an investigation, which may be conducted either by the chief legal officer (or the equivalent thereof) or by outside attorneys; and

(C) Retain such additional expert personnel as the committee deems necessary; and

(iii) At the conclusion of any such investigation, to:

(A) Recommend, by majority vote, that the issuer implement an appropriate response to evidence of a material violation; and

(B) Inform the chief legal officer and the chief executive officer (or the equivalents thereof) and the board of directors of the results of any such investigation under this section and the appropriate remedial measures to be adopted; and

(4) Has the authority and responsibility, acting by majority vote, to take all other appropriate action, including the authority to notify the Commission in the event that the issuer fails in any material respect to implement an appropriate response that the qualified legal compliance committee has recommended the

issuer to take.

(l) *Reasonable* or *reasonably* denotes, with respect to the actions of an attorney, conduct that would not be unreasonable for a prudent and competent attorney.

(m) *Reasonably believes* means that an attorney believes the matter in question and that the circumstances are such that the belief is not unreasonable.

(n) *Report* means to make known to directly, either in person, by telephone, by e-mail, electronically, or in writing.

§ 205.3 Issuer as client

(a) *Representing an issuer.* An attorney appearing and practicing before the Commission in the representation of an issuer owes his or her professional and ethical duties to the issuer as an organization. That the attorney may work with and advise the issuer's officers, directors, or employees in the course of representing the issuer does not make such individuals the attorney's clients.

(b) *Duty to report evidence of a material violation.*

(1) If an attorney, appearing and practicing before the Commission in the representation of an issuer, becomes aware of evidence of a material violation by the issuer or by any officer, director, employee, or agent of the issuer, the attorney shall report such evidence to the issuer's chief legal officer (or the equivalent thereof) or to both the issuer's chief legal officer and its chief executive officer (or the equivalents thereof) forthwith. By communicating such information to the issuer's officers or directors, an attorney does not reveal client confidences or secrets or privileged or otherwise protected information related to the attorney's representation of an issuer.

(2) The chief legal officer (or the equivalent thereof) shall cause such inquiry into the evidence of a material violation as he or she reasonably believes is appropriate to determine whether the material violation described in the report has occurred, is ongoing, or is about to occur. If the chief legal officer (or the equivalent thereof) determines no material violation has occurred, is ongoing, or is about to occur, he or she shall notify the reporting attorney and advise the reporting attorney of the basis for such determination. Unless the chief legal officer (or the equivalent thereof) reasonably believes that no material violation has occurred, is ongoing, or is about to occur, he or she shall take all reasonable steps to cause the issuer to adopt an appropriate response, and shall advise the reporting attorney thereof. In lieu of causing an inquiry under this paragraph (b), a chief legal officer (or the equivalent thereof) may refer a report of evidence of a material violation to a qualified legal compliance committee under paragraph (c)(2) of this section if the issuer has duly established a qualified legal compliance committee prior to the report of evidence of a material violation.

(3) Unless an attorney who has made a report under paragraph (b)(1) of this section reasonably believes that the chief legal officer or the chief executive officer of the issuer (or the equivalent thereof) has provided an appropriate response within a reasonable time, the attorney shall report the evidence of a material violation to:

(i) The audit committee of the issuer's board of directors;

(ii) Another committee of the issuer's board of directors consisting solely of directors who are not employed, directly or indirectly, by the issuer and are not, in the case of a registered investment company, "interested persons" as defined in section 2(a)(19) of the Investment Company Act of 1940 (15 U.S.C. 80a-2(a)(19)) (if the issuer's board of directors has no audit committee); or

(iii) The issuer's board of directors (if the issuer's board of directors has no committee consisting solely of directors who are not employed, directly or indirectly, by the issuer and are not, in the case of a registered investment company, "interested persons" as defined in section 2(a)(19) of the Investment Company Act of 1940 (15 U.S.C. 80a-2(a)(19))).

(4) If an attorney reasonably believes that it would be futile to report evidence of a material violation to the issuer's chief legal officer and chief executive officer (or the equivalents thereof) under paragraph (b)(1) of this section, the attorney may report such evidence as provided under paragraph (b)(3) of this section.

(5) An attorney retained or directed by an issuer to investigate evidence of a material violation reported under paragraph (b)(1), (b)(3), or (b)(4) of this section shall be deemed to be appearing and practicing before the Commission. Directing or retaining an attorney to investigate reported evidence of a material violation does not relieve an officer or director of the issuer to whom such evidence has been reported under paragraph (b)(1), (b)(3), or (b)(4) of this section from a duty to respond to the reporting attorney.

(6) An attorney shall not have any obligation to report evidence of a material violation under this paragraph (b) if:

(i) The attorney was retained or directed by the issuer's chief legal officer (or the equivalent thereof) to investigate such evidence of a material violation and:

(A) The attorney reports the results of such investigation to the chief legal officer (or the equivalent thereof); and

(B) Except where the attorney and the chief legal officer (or the equivalent thereof) each reasonably believes that no material violation has occurred, is ongoing, or is about to occur, the chief legal officer (or the equivalent thereof) reports the results of the investigation to the issuer's board of directors, a committee thereof to whom a report could be made pursuant to paragraph (b)(3) of this section, or a qualified legal compliance committee; or

(ii) The attorney was retained or directed by the chief legal officer (or the equivalent thereof) to assert, consistent with his or her professional obligations, a colorable defense on behalf of the issuer (or the issuer's officer, director, employee, or agent, as the case may be) in any investigation or judicial or administrative proceeding relating to such evidence of a material violation, and the chief legal officer (or the equivalent thereof) provides reasonable and timely reports on the progress and outcome of such proceeding to the issuer's board of directors, a committee thereof to whom a report could be made pursuant to paragraph (b)(3) of this section, or a qualified legal compliance committee.

(7) An attorney shall not have any obligation to report evidence of a material violation under this paragraph (b) if such attorney was retained or directed by a qualified legal compliance committee:

(i) To investigate such evidence of a material violation; or

(ii) To assert, consistent with his or her professional obligations, a colorable defense on behalf of the issuer (or the issuer's officer, director, employee, or agent, as the case may be) in any investigation or judicial or administrative proceeding relating to such evidence of a material violation.

(8) An attorney who receives what he or she reasonably believes is an appropriate and timely response to a report he or she has made pursuant to paragraph (b)(1), (b)(3), or (b)(4) of this section need do nothing more under this section with respect to his or her report.

(9) An attorney who does not reasonably believe that the issuer has made an appropriate response within a reasonable time to the report or reports made pursuant to paragraph (b)(1), (b)(3), or (b)(4) of this section shall explain his or her reasons therefor to the chief legal officer (or the equivalent thereof), the chief executive officer (or the equivalent thereof), and directors to whom the attorney reported the evidence of a material violation pursuant to paragraph (b)(1), (b)(3), or (b)(4) of this section.

(10) An attorney formerly employed or retained by an issuer who has reported evidence of a material violation under this part and reasonably believes that he or she has been discharged for so doing may notify the issuer's board of directors or any committee thereof that he or she believes that he or she has been discharged for reporting evidence of a material violation under this section.

(c) *Alternative reporting procedures for attorneys retained or employed by an issuer that has established a qualified legal compliance committee.*

(1) If an attorney, appearing and practicing before the Commission in the representation of an issuer, becomes aware of evidence of a material violation by the issuer or by any officer, director, employee, or agent of the issuer, the attorney may, as an alternative to the reporting requirements of paragraph (b) of this section, report such evidence to a qualified legal compliance committee, if the issuer has previously formed such a committee. An attorney who reports evidence of a material violation to such a qualified legal compliance committee has satisfied his or her obligation to report such evidence and is not required to assess the issuer's response to the reported evidence of a material violation.

(2) A chief legal officer (or the equivalent thereof) may refer a report of evidence of a material violation to a previously established qualified legal compliance committee in lieu of causing an inquiry to be conducted under paragraph (b)(2) of this section. The chief legal officer (or the equivalent thereof) shall inform the reporting attorney that the report has been referred to a qualified legal compliance committee. Thereafter, pursuant to the requirements under §§ 205.2(k), the qualified legal compliance committee shall be responsible for responding to the evidence of a material violation reported to it under this paragraph (c).

(d) *Issuer confidences.*

(1) Any report under this section (or the contemporaneous record thereof) or any response thereto (or the contemporaneous record thereof) may be used by an attorney in connection with any investigation, proceeding, or litigation in which the attorney's compliance with this part is in issue.

(2) An attorney appearing and practicing before the Commission in the representation of an issuer may reveal to the Commission, without the issuer's consent, confidential information related to the representation to the extent the attorney reasonably believes necessary:

(i) To prevent the issuer from committing a material violation that is likely to cause substantial injury to the financial interest or property of the issuer or investors;

(ii) To prevent the issuer, in a Commission investigation or administrative proceeding from committing perjury, proscribed in 18 U.S.C. 1621; suborning perjury, proscribed in 18 U.S.C. 1622; or committing any act proscribed in 18 U.S.C. 1001 that is likely to perpetrate a fraud upon the Commission; or

(iii) To rectify the consequences of a material violation by the issuer that caused, or may cause, substantial injury to the financial interest or property of the issuer or investors in the furtherance of which the attorney's services were used.

§ 205.4 Responsibilities of supervisory attorneys

(a) An attorney supervising or directing another attorney who is appearing and practicing before the Commission in the representation of an issuer is a supervisory attorney. An issuer's chief legal officer (or the equivalent thereof) is a supervisory attorney under this section.

(b) A supervisory attorney shall make reasonable efforts to ensure that a subordinate attorney, as defined in §§ 205.5(a), that he or she supervises or directs conforms to this part. To the extent a subordinate attorney appears and practices before the Commission in the representation of an issuer, that subordinate attorney's supervisory attorneys also appear and practice before the Commission.

(c) A supervisory attorney is responsible for complying with the reporting requirements in §§ 205.3 when a subordinate attorney has reported to the supervisory attorney evidence of a material violation.

(d) A supervisory attorney who has received a report of evidence of a material violation from a subordinate attorney under §§205.3 may report such evidence to the issuer's qualified legal compliance committee if the issuer has duly formed such a committee.

§ 205.5 Responsibilities of a subordinate attorney

(a) An attorney who appears and practices before the Commission in the representation of an issuer on a matter under the supervision or direction of another attorney (other than under the direct supervision or direction of the issuer's chief legal officer (or the equivalent thereof)) is a subordinate attorney.

(b) A subordinate attorney shall comply with this part notwithstanding that the subordinate attorney acted at the direction of or under the supervision of another person.

(c) A subordinate attorney complies with §§ 205.3 if the subordinate attorney reports to his or her supervising attorney under §§ 205.3(b) evidence of a material violation of which the subordinate attorney has become aware in appearing and practicing before the Commission.

(d) A subordinate attorney may take the steps permitted or required by §§ 205.3(b) or (c) if the subordinate attorney reasonably believes that a supervisory attorney to whom he or she has reported evidence of a material violation under §§ 205.3(b) has failed to comply with §§ 205.3.

§ 205.6 Sanctions and discipline

(a) A violation of this part by any attorney appearing and practicing before the Commission in the representation of an issuer shall subject such attorney to the civil penalties and remedies for a violation of the federal securities laws available to the Commission in an action brought by the Commission thereunder.

(b) An attorney appearing and practicing before the Commission who violates any provision of this part is subject to the disciplinary authority of the Commission, regardless of whether the attorney may also be subject to discipline for the same conduct in a jurisdiction where the attorney is admitted or practices. An administrative disciplinary proceeding initiated by the Commission for violation of this part may result in an attorney being censured, or being temporarily or permanently denied the privilege of appearing or practicing before the Commission.

(c) An attorney who complies in good faith with the provisions of this part shall not be subject to discipline or otherwise liable under inconsistent standards imposed by any state or other United States jurisdiction where the attorney is admitted or practices.

(d) An attorney practicing outside the United States shall not be required to comply with the requirements of this part to the extent that such compliance is prohibited by applicable foreign law.

§ 205.7 No private right of action

(a) Nothing in this part is intended to, or does, create a private right of action against any attorney, law firm, or issuer based upon compliance or noncompliance with its provisions.

(b) Authority to enforce compliance with this part is vested exclusively in the Commission.

NOTES AND QUESTIONS

***1. Applying Part 205 to* Carter & Johnson.** Assume the up-the-ladder reporting rules now required under Part 205 were applicable to the facts of *Carter & Johnson*. How would you answer the following questions:

a. At what point in the representation did Carter and Johnson have "evidence" of a securities law violation requiring them to report to the chief legal officer or (the CLO and the chief executive officer) of National Telephone? Did they satisfy this requirement?

b. At what point should Carter and Johnson have taken their concerns to the audit committee of the board of directors of National Telephone? Is it clear that they did so too late? Would they have clearly violated the rule by waiting as long as they did?

c. What other rules of professional responsibility do you believe the SEC ought to promulgate that would guide lawyers in a similar situation? For example, should Carter and Johnson have been required to resign from the representation at any point? Should they have been required to inform the SEC that they were renouncing any work product that they had done for National Telephone?

*2. **Noisy Withdrawals Revisited.*** There will be instances in which a report to the client's board of directors required by Part 205 will not succeed in persuading the client to respond appropriately to a violation. Under these circumstances, should the lawyer be *required* to make a report outside the board to the SEC, just as auditors are required to do under Section 10A of the Exchange Act? Should the lawyer be *required* to withdraw from the representation, but not to report?

As noted above, the version of Part 205 that the SEC adopted in January 2003 differs in a number of important respects from the rule it had proposed two months earlier. Most significantly, the final version did not require an attorney to make a "noisy withdrawal" in situations where the attorney reasonably believes that the issuer's directors have either made no response or have not made an appropriate response to his or her report of violations. Rather, the SEC opted to go ahead only with the up-the-ladder reporting requirements (as it had to do under Section 307 of the SOX) and to propose for further comment the noisy withdrawal provision. See Final Rule, Exchange Act Release No. 47276, supra. See also Proposed Rule: Implementation of Standards of Professional Conduct for Attorneys, Exchange Act Release No. 47282 (Jan. 29, 2003). The proposed rule would add the following new sub-section to Part 205:

> **Proposed Rule 205.3(d)(1).** *Notice to the Commission where there is no appropriate response within a reasonable time.*
>
> (1) Where an attorney who has reported evidence of a material violation under paragraph 3(b) of this section rather than paragraph 3(c) of this section does not receive an appropriate response, or has not received a response in a reasonable time, to his or her report, and the attorney reasonably believes that a material violation is ongoing or is about to occur and is likely to result in substantial injury to the financial interest or property of the issuer or of investors:
>
> (i) An attorney retained by the issuer shall:
>
> (A) Withdraw forthwith from representing the issuer, indicating that the withdrawal is based on professional considerations;
>
> (B) Within one business day of withdrawing, give written notice to the Commission of the attorney's withdrawal, indicating that the withdrawal was based on professional considerations; and

(C) Promptly disaffirm to the Commission any opinion, document, affirmation, representation, characterization, or the like in a document filed with or submitted to the Commission, or incorporated into such a document, that the attorney has prepared or assisted in preparing and that the attorney reasonably believes is or may be materially false or misleading;

(ii) An attorney employed by the issuer shall:

(A) Within one business day, notify the Commission in writing that he or she intends to disaffirm some opinion, document, affirmation, representation, characterization, or the like in a document filed with or submitted to the Commission, or incorporated into such a document, that the attorney has prepared or assisted in preparing and that the attorney reasonably believes is or may be materially false or misleading; and

(B) Promptly disaffirm to the Commission, in writing, any such opinion, document, affirmation, representation, characterization, or the like; and

(iii) The issuer's chief legal officer (or the equivalent) shall inform any attorney retained or employed to replace the attorney who has withdrawn that the previous attorney's withdrawal was based on professional considerations.

See id. The SEC also proposed a new Rule 205.3(d)(2), which would apply to situations in which the reported material violation has already occurred and is not ongoing. Without specifying any particular time frames, proposed Rule 205.3(d)(2) states that attorneys "may" take the very same steps that would have been required under proposed Rule 205.3(d)(1) if the violation had been ongoing or about to occur. Id.

Should the SEC adopt the above provisions for "noisy withdrawals"? In its January 2003 release, the SEC also proposed for comment an alternative to the noisy withdrawal provision that would require the securities issuer (rather than its attorney) to report to the SEC the attorney's written notice of withdrawal or failure to receive an appropriate response. In connection with this alternative proposal, the SEC proposed to amend Forms 8-K, 20-F, and 40-F to require issuers to disclose to the public an attorney's written notice of withdrawal within two business days of that notice. The alternative proposal would also permit (but would not require) an attorney to inform the SEC of his or her withdrawal in situations where the issuer fails to make the required reports. See id. (proposing alternative Rule 205.3(e) and Rule 205.3(f)). Which would you prefer to see adopted: the proposed rule mandating an attorney's noisy withdrawal or the alternative rule mandating issuer reporting? Does your answer change depending on whether you are usually an attorney? A client? An investor? Should it change?

*3. **SEC Preemption of Inconsistent State Rules.*** Note that Part 205.6(c) provides that the SEC's rules shall govern if state standards conflict with Part 205, and that an attorney who "complies in good faith" with Part 205 "shall not be subject to discipline or otherwise liable under inconsistent standards imposed by any state." This provision, particularly as it relates to the permissive disclosure of client confidences, has been the subject of considerable debate. See Sue Reisinger, Two State Bars Protest SEC Rule Cal., Wash. Dislike "Reporting Out," Nat'l. L.J., Sept. 15, 2003, at 1. See also Thomas G. Bost,

Corporate Lawyers After the Big Quake: The Conceptual Fault Line in the Professional Duty of Confidentiality, 19 Geo. J. of Legal Ethics 1089, 1091 (2006) (noting that California lawyers have been "aggressive and unremitting in pressing before every conceivable forum that the disclosure of client confidences permitted under the Sarbanes-Oxley rules *** will seriously and irreparably erode the attorney-client relationship" and in arguing "that the SEC's asserted preemption of conflicting state laws is not effective, and that, therefore, lawyers disclosing client confidences under the SEC rules face a substantial risk of state bar discipline or liability for breach of fiduciary duty for violating California's strict confidentiality rules)." For arguments supporting the preemptive effect of Part 205.6(c), see Roger C. Cramton et al., Legal and Ethical Duties of Lawyers After Sarbanes-Oxley, 49 Vill. L. Rev. 725, 788-809 (2004). If Part 205.6(c) is challenged in court, how should the judge rule?

4. Multiple Representations and Conflicts of Interest. Recall the discussion of multiple representations in the context of investigations or enforcement proceedings by the SEC. See Chapter 9.B. supra. Could the SEC use its authority under Section 307 of the SOX to regulate conflicts and potential conflicts that may arise when a lawyer simultaneously represents issuers and individual corporate officials?

Multiple representations may raise particularly troubling questions in the context of an IPO where, in many cases, the insider shareholders are for practical purposes also the clients of the lawyer representing the issuer. Full disclosure of the issuer's relationship with its principals is generally required in the issuer's registration statement, yet there may be certain information that the principals do not want publicly disclosed. Also, if there is a secondary offering by the principals as well as, or instead of, a primary offering by the issuer, the principals may have a personal interest in closing the deal despite defects in the issuer's disclosure. Assuming it has the authority to do so, should the SEC adopt rules to address potential conflicts precipitated by multiple representations in the IPO context? Should it do so in other contexts?

5. Compensation of Counsel. Recently, law firms have moved away from hourly billing for securities and transactional work to alternative billing arrangements. These arrangements presumably create added incentives for the lawyers to perform high quality work, conform client payment obligations more closely to client cash flows, and more accurately reflect the value to the client of the legal work. These new methods include taking equity in lieu of fees, contingent fees, and premium billing. See generally Christine Hurt, Counselor, Gatekeeper, Shareholder, Thief: Why Attorneys Who Invest in Their Clients in a Post-Enron World Are "Selling Out," Not "Buying In," 64 Ohio St. L.J. 897 (2003); Donald C. Langevoort, When Lawyers and Law Firms Invest in Their Corporate Clients' Stock, 80 Wash. U. L.Q. 569 (2002). See also Richard W. Painter, Irrationality and Cognitive Bias at a Closing in Arthur Solmssen's *The Comfort Letter*, 69 Fordham L. Rev. 1111 (2000) (criticizing contingent fee arrangements in transactional work, including the $35 million fee that Cravath Swaine and Moore was paid by Time-Warner, contingent on the closing of Time-Warner's merger with AOL). As part of its effort to discern minimum standards of professional responsibility for securities lawyers, should the SEC consider what, if any, effect these various payment methods have on the quality of representation provided to a corporate client?

6. Additional Proposals for SEC Rulemaking Under SOX Section 307. In his essay on attorneys as gatekeepers , Professor Coffee questions what else the SEC can or should do under SOX Section 307 "to make the attorney an effective guardian of the integrity of publicly filed disclosure documents (without imposing obligations that subordinate the attorney's duty of loyalty to the client in this mission)?" Coffee, supra, 103 Colum. L. Rev. at 1310. He offers three proposals: (1) a due diligence requirement in the preparation of disclosure documents; (2) an independence requirement (discussed in the previous sub-section at Note 3); and (3) an attorney certification requirement whereby the attorney principally responsible for the preparation of a disclosure document or report filed with the SEC would certify "(1) that such attorney reasonably believes the statements made in the document or report to be true and correct in all material respects; and (2) that such attorney is not aware of any additional material information whose disclosure is necessary in order to make the statements made, in light of the circumstances under which they were made, not misleading." Id. at 1310-15. Would you support any (or all) of Professor Coffee's proposals? Why or why not? Can you offer a proposal of your own?

PROBLEM 10-1

Cintron, Inc., a Delaware corporation engaged in energy trading, is planning a public offering of common stock. Cintron is an Exchange Act reporting company and does not have a Qualified Legal Compliance Committee (as described in Rule 205.2(k)). Davis, Sullivan & Moore ("DSM"), a New York law firm, represents Cintron in connection with the preparation of a registration statement for the offering. Larry Silver is the partner at DSM in charge of the Cintron stock offering and has been responsible for the firm's representation of Cintron in other securities-related matters over the past five years. Peter Black is a third-year associate at DSM and works for Silver on the Cintron registration statement. The lead underwriter for the stock offering is Gardner, Smith & Co. ("GS"), and the lead underwriter's counsel is another New York law firm, Cromwell & Wardwell ("C&W"). Susan Williams is the C&W partner in charge of representing GS in the Cintron transaction.

Cintron has been engaging in numerous deceitful accounting practices, including disguising substantial losses in off-balance-sheet entities. Up until two weeks before the scheduled closing date for the Cintron stock offering, none of the lawyers involved in the transaction was aware of the problem. Neither were Cintron's auditors at the accounting firm of Batter & Notly.

Two weeks before the Cintron stock offering, however, Sarah Stevens, a junior employee in Cintron's accounting department, sent an e-mail to Peter Black and to Susan Williams, alerting them both to credible evidence of accounting fraud at Cintron. Stevens's allegations, if true, would mean that Cintron's registration statement for the proposed offering, already filed with the SEC and about to become effective, would be materially misleading.

a. What are Peter Black's professional obligations under the SEC's rules of professional responsibility for attorneys?

b. Assume that Peter Black directs Larry Silver's attention to the problem. What are Larry Silver's professional obligations under the SEC's rules of professional responsibility for attorneys?

c. What are Susan Williams's professional obligations under the SEC's rules of professional responsibility for attorneys?

d. Assume that Larry Silver brings this problem to the attention of Cintron's directors but that they refuse to do anything about it and insist on proceeding with the stock offering. What is Larry Silver required to do next? What is he permitted to do?

e. Assume that Susan Williams brings this problem to the attention of GS's directors but that they refuse to do anything about it and insist on proceeding with the Cintron stock offering. What is Susan Williams required to do next? What is she permitted to do?

f. How would the answers to any of the above questions change if Cintron had a Qualified Legal Compliance Committee?

g. With respect to Silver, Black, and DSM, how would your answers to the above questions change if DSM were not a New York law firm, but instead a London law firm? Assume that DSM (i) represented Cintron principally in connection with its compliance with listing requirement for sale of securities under U.K. law and (ii) did not advise Cintron on United States securities laws but did assist Cintron with preparation of documents that Cintron incorporated into securities filings both in the U.S. and in the U.K.

h. How would your answers to the above questions change if Cintron was *not* subject to the reporting requirements of the Exchange Act and was planning a private placement of stock rather than a public offering? Assume that the private placement memorandum that was distributed to investors included several materially misleading statements.

i. If any of the above lawyers fail to meet their professional obligations under the SEC's rules or state rules of professional responsibility, to what extent are they exposed to civil liability? To whom are they possibly liable and under what law?

5. SEC Enforcement Actions Against Attorneys Who Commit, or Cause Their Clients to Commit, Violations of the Federal Securities Laws

In the wake of the scandals at Enron and WorldCom, the SEC initiated an unprecedented number of enforcement actions against attorneys who violated the federal securities laws or who caused their clients to violate such laws. Yet, as we have seen elsewhere in this Casebook, such enforcement actions occurred in the past as well. Recall, for example, cases involving allegedly negligent legal advice involving the securities laws. See, e.g., *In the Matter of Jeffry Feldman*, Securities Act Release No. 7014, 55 SEC Docket 9, 12 (September 20, 1993) (consent order issued under Securities Act Section 8A against lawyer for three Pakistani banks who "caused" violations of the Securities Act's registration provisions by incorrectly advising his client that there was no need to register an offering of rupee-denominated foreign exchange bearer certificates prior to sale in the U.S.), set out in Chapter 9.C.2. Recall also that before the 1990 Remedies Act added "cease and desist" authority to the SEC's arsenal of enforcement weapons, the SEC brought, but eventually dismissed, a high-profile enforcement action under Exchange Act Section 15(c)(4) against an attorney for "causing" a client's violation of the tender offer rules. See *In Re George C. Kern,*

Jr., Exchange Act Release No. 29356, 49 SEC Docket 422 (June 21, 1991) (reversing administrative law judge's order and holding that the Commission lacked the power under Section 15(c)(4) to issue an order of "general compliance"). See Note 7 in Chapter 9 on page 754.

Both before and after Enron and WorldCom, the SEC has initiated enforcement actions against lawyers who allegedly aided and abetted a client's securities law violations. Prior to 2010 and the enactment of Dodd-Frank, Section 20(e) liability often turned on whether the aider and abetter gave "knowing" assistance. See, e.g., *SEC v. Fehn,* 97 F.3d 1276 (9th Cir. 1996) (enjoining attorney for aiding and abetting violations of Rule 10b-5 and other Exchange Act provisions that were committed by the company that retained him, discussed in Note 3 on page 236). In Dodd-Frank, Congress clarified Section 20(e) by specifying that aiding and abetting liability encompasses those who "recklessly" provide substantial assistance as well. (Dodd-Frank also added comparable clarifications to the Securities Act, the Investment Company Act, and the Investment Advisers Act.)

In-house lawyers at brokerage firms—who may often act in the supervisory chain of command—have long faced potential disciplinary sanctions under Exchange Act Section 15(b)(4)(E). See Report Under Exchange Act Section 21(a) in the Matter of John H. Gutfreund, Thomas W. Strauss & John W. Meriwether, Exchange Act Release No. 31554, 52 SEC Docket 2849 (Dec. 3, 1992). Although Salomon Brothers' chief legal officer Donald M. Feuerstein repeatedly advised C.E.O. Gutfreund to report unauthorized U.S. Treasury auction bids by trader Paul Mozer to the Federal Reserve, Gutfreund did not do so. The Commission did not initiate enforcement action against Feuerstein. But in its report on the conduct of other top Salomon officials, the Commission concluded that Feuerstein was Mozer's "supervisor" for purposes of Section 15(b)(4)(E) and as such was obligated to take appropriate steps to deal with Mozer's misconduct. These steps, the SEC suggested, consisted of approaching senior management, but if that failed, they included: (i) approaching the board of directors, (ii) resigning, or (iii) disclosing the misconduct to regulators (within the bounds permitted by the rules of professional responsibility).

Yet in the post-SOX world, the professional conduct of securities attorneys is certain to be subject to even greater scrutiny. Consider these remarks by Stephen Cutler, made in 2004 during his tenure as Director of the SEC's Enforcement Division:

> Consistent with Sarbanes-Oxley's focus on the important role of lawyers as gatekeepers, we have stepped up our scrutiny of the role of lawyers in the corporate frauds we investigate. We have named lawyers as respondents or defendants in more than 30 of our enforcement actions in the past two years.
>
> ***We have seen too many examples of lawyers who twisted themselves into pretzels to accommodate the wishes of company management, and failed in their responsibility to insist that the company comply with the law. These include Warnaco's general counsel, Stanley Silverstein, who recently settled our charges against him for certifying a misleading annual report containing material misstatements that were at the heart of the company's reporting violations; Gemstar-TV Guide's former general counsel Jonathan Orlick, who, we allege, facilitated Gemstar's fraudulent revenue enhancement scheme by providing false certifications to Gemstar's auditors; and Leonard Goldner, the former general counsel of Symbol Technologies, who, we allege,

> manipulated stock option exercise dates to enable certain senior executives of the company, including himself, to profit unfairly at the company's expense.
>
> While all of these are examples of in-house counsel gone astray, I think it's notable that close to half the Commission's actions against lawyers during the past two years involved outside counsel. Last April, for example, we brought an action against counsel to a Pennsylvania school district based on two unqualified legal opinions he issued regarding a note offering. More recently, we sued another bond counsel who, we allege, issued favorable legal opinions on a series of municipal bond underwritings, despite his knowledge that the bond proceeds were being wrongfully commingled and diverted.
>
> We have more to do in this area. Based on our current investigative docket, I think you can expect to see one or more actions against lawyers who, we believe, assisted their clients in engaging in illegal late trading or market timing arrangements that harmed mutual fund investors. We are also considering actions against lawyers, both in-house and outside counsel, who assisted companies or clients in covering up evidence of fraud, or prepared, or signed off on, misleading disclosures regarding the company's condition. One area of particular focus for us is the role of lawyers in internal investigations of their clients or companies. We are concerned that, in some instances, lawyers may have conducted investigations in such a manner as to help hide ongoing fraud, or may have taken actions to actively obstruct such investigations.

Stephen M. Cutler, The Themes of Sarbanes-Oxley as Reflected in the Commission's Enforcement Program, Address at the UCLA School of Law (Sept. 20, 2004). Many scholars and securities practitioners believe that the enforcement actions referenced in Cutler's speech signify a "new era of the SEC as an active and enthusiastic proponent of the attorney's 'gatekeeping' role." Lewis D. Lowenfels et al., Attorneys as Gatekeepers: SEC Actions Against Lawyers in the Age of Sarbanes-Oxley, 37 U. Tol. L. Rev. 877, 878 (2006) (noting that "the intensity of the SEC's actions against lawyers has continued unabated" since the date of Cutler's speech).

The SEC closely examined the role of lawyers in the backdating of stock options, a scandal that has embroiled more than 130 companies in investigations by the SEC and DOJ. As then SEC Chairman Christopher Cox testified to Congress:

> There are many variations on the backdating theme. But here is a typical example of what some companies did: They granted an "in-the-money" option-that is, an option with an exercise price lower than that day's market price. They did this by misrepresenting the date of the option grant, to make it appear that the grant was made on an earlier date when the market value was lower. That, of course, is what is meant by abusive "backdating" in today's parlance.
>
> The purpose of disguising an in-the-money option through backdating is to allow the person who gets the option grant to realize larger potential gains-without the company having to show it as compensation on the financial statements.
>
> Rather obviously, this fact pattern results in a violation of the SEC's disclosure rules, a violation of accounting rules, and also a violation of the tax laws.

Executive Compensation Hearing Before the S. Comm. on Banking, Housing & Urban Affairs , 109th Cong. (2006) (testimony of Christopher Cox, Chairman, SEC).

In 2006-07, for instance, the SEC initiated enforcement actions against six general counsels of public companies due to their involvement in options-backdating scandals. As one SEC official emphasized:

> These scandals [ ] involved some shockingly bad conduct — allegations of secret slush funds; forgery; grants to fictitious employees, former employees and unknown future employees; falsified corporate documents; self-dealing; self-enrichment; attempted cover-ups; and lying to the auditors. In each of these cases we alleged attorneys had actually altered or completely fabricated documents to conceal or advance the scheme.

Linda Chatman Thomsen, SEC Division of Enforcement Director, Remarks Before the Minority Corporate Counsel 2008 CLE Expo, March 27, 2008. In addition, several general counsels were prosecuted not only by the SEC but by the DOJ as well. See, e.g., SEC v. Myron F. Olesnyckyj, Litigation Release No. 20056 (Mar. 27, 2007) (announcing Monster Worldwide former general counsel's settlement of SEC charges and related guilty plea); SEC v. Jacob ("Kobi") Alexander,et al., Litigation Release No. 19964 (Jan. 10, 2007) (announcing Comverse Technology former general counsel's settlement of SEC charges and related guilty plea). But see, Debra Cassens Weiss, Jurors Acquitted Ex-McAfee GC in Backdating Case Because of Intent Issues, ABA Journal--Law News Now (Oct. 6, 2008); SEC v. Roberts, Litigation Release No. 20995 (Apr. 10, 2009) (voluntarily dismissing all claims against former general counsel of McAfee Inc.). Hosts of other in-house lawyers faced civil and criminal charges due to their alleged awareness of, or in some instances participation in, backdating activity. See generally SEC Spotlight on Stock Options Backdating, available at http://www.sec.gov/spotlight/optionsbackdating.htm.

Why did the role of inside counsel draw particular scrutiny in the options backdating scandals? Securities practitioners and academics offer a number of reasons, including:

> [I]nside general counsel are at the epicenter of the legal work and the paper trail which normally accompany a company's grant of stock options. Inside general counsel participate in the drafting of the company's stock option plans. They prepare the minutes of the directors' and compensation committee meetings at which the grants of stock options are authorized and approved. They prepare the periodic reports and the proxy statements which describe the grants and are filed with the SEC. They interface with the company's auditors and are the primary keepers of the company's books and records. They draft the employment contracts for the new hirees. In short, if there are irregularities suspected with respect to the grant of stock options, the initial inquiries would in the normal course be directed to the office of general counsel.
>
> Second, inside general counsel are often in a very vulnerable position as regards option grants. They are under tremendous pressure from management to issue as many options as possible on the most favorable terms possible for management. At the same time they have relatively less clout and less stature than other top executives within the company. ***

Lewis D. Lowenfels & Alan R. Bromberg, 39 Sec. Reg. & L. Rep. 436 (BNA) (Mar. 19, 2007). Clearly, lawyers must never backdate documents and must refuse to do so even if asked. What other lessons can lawyers learn from the backdating scandal?

The SEC has likewise been zealous in pursuing attorneys who breach fiduciary duties owed either to their law firms or their law firms' clients when trading securities on the basis of material nonpublic information. In her 2007 speech cited supra, then-SEC Division of Enforcement Director Linda Thomsen cataloged nine unrelated insider trading actions filed against lawyers during that year, including a settled action against the former managing partner of Katten Muchin Rosenman LLP's Washington, D.C. office who allegedly traded on material nonpublic information that he acquired when he interviewed a lawyer for a position at the firm. More recently, the SEC alleged that the insider trading "ring" surrounding billionaire hedge fund trader Raj Rajaratnam and the Galleon Group included former associates at Ropes & Gray (who also pleaded guilty to criminal securities fraud charges based on illegal tips concerning client M&A activity). See BNA, Lawyer Said to Have Tipped Information In Massive Insider Scheme Pleads Guilty, 43 Sec. Reg. & L. Rep. 142 (Jan. 24, 2011). The SEC and the DOJ are also pursuing civil and criminal securities fraud charges against an attorney for an alleged decade-long pattern of illegal tipping that garnered more than $32 million in illegal profits. See BNA, Middleman in Lawyer/Trader Insider Case Pleads Guilty to Securities Fraud Charges, 43 Sec. Reg. & L. Rep. 832 (Apr. 18, 2011) (quoting Assistant U.S. Attorney's allegations that the attorney, while working as an associate at several prominent law firms, including Cravath, Swain & Moore; Skadden, Arps, Fried, Frank; and Wilson Sonsini,"regularly stole material, nonpublic information regarding anticipated corporate mergers and acquisitions on which his firms were working" and disclosed the information to a "middleman" who passed it on to the trader).

In addition, attorneys must guard against the possibility that a relative or friend might trade securities on the basis of confidential information belonging to their law firm's clients. For two unfortunate examples, see SEC v. Goetz, Litigation Release No. 21990 (June 6, 2011) (announcing settlement of charges that the father of an associate in the L.A. office of a large international law firm, without the knowledge of his daughter, "had misappropriated confidential deal information from her while she worked on the transaction at her parents' house over the holidays in December 2008"); Peter Lattman, Stockbroker Admits to Insider Trading on Info Received From Lawyer Girlfriend, Wall St. J. Law Blog, March 7, 2006 (reporting stockbroker's guilty plea in criminal case as well as the following statement from the Weil Gotshal law firm that "Our former associate brought this matter to our attention when she saw [his] name on a list of individuals who had traded in the stock which had been sent from the NASD as part of its routine market surveillance operations. The Firm and the associate then immediately brought this matter to the attention of the Securities & Exchange Commission").

6. The Financial Crisis of 2008 and the Dodd-Frank Act of 2010

The legal profession also played a significant role in the financial crisis of 2008, first by creating the mortgage-backed securities and other derivative products that in large part caused the crisis and then, in some instances, by assisting financial institutions with concealing their exposure to those investments. One transaction that received much scrutiny involved Lehman Brothers' Repo 105. In that transaction, Lehman's attorneys may have assisted the firm in its efforts to conceal $50 billion in debt on its quarterly balance sheets through temporary sales of the firm's bad assets to other financial institutions in return for cash that the firm used to pay down debt temporarily at the end of each quarter. Despite agreement between Lehman and the counterparty that the transaction would be unwound a few days later, English law apparently allowed it to be treated as a "sale" if the assets were valued at 105% or more of the cash "paid" for them. It did not matter that the parties contemplated that substantially equivalent assets would be transferred back to Lehman and the cash returned a few days later. See Anton R. Valukas, Examiner's Report, In re Lehman Bros. Holdings Inc., No. 08–13555, (Bankr. S.D.N.Y. 2010). Lehman apparently could not find New York lawyers who would agree to characterize the transaction as a sale under U.S. law, but Linklaters in London was willing to opine that the sale coupled with a repurchase agreement constituted a true sale under English law. Linklaters Letter of 31 May 2006 to Lehman Brothers International (Europe), discussed in Valukas, supra. To achieve this end, Lehman had to transfer the securities involved to London, which transfer was no doubt accomplished with the knowledge, if not the assistance, of U.S. lawyers). In London, the transaction was executed through LBIE, Lehman's European broker-dealer in London, which reported to Lehman's auditors in the U.S. that a true sale had occurred under English law (and was thereupon recorded as such on Lehman's consolidated balance sheet for its quarterly report). After the transaction was unwound, it could be repeated at the end of the next quarter and then again in subsequent quarters. Substantial fees were paid to the counterparty each time, all for only one apparent purpose: to prettify Lehman's quarterly balance sheet in order to look better than it actually was.

Even if the opinion letter had been correct in asserting that the transaction was a true sale under English law, should the Linklaters lawyers have told the Lehman board of directors about the transaction and its apparent purpose? Were the Linklaters lawyers "practicing before the Commission" for purposes of the SEC rules adopted under SOX Section 307? Their opinion letter specifically stated that they were not opining on U.S. securities law, but it also stated that Lehman's auditors could rely on the letter and Lehman's status as a reporting company was well known. Did the Linklaters lawyers fall within the exception for foreign attorneys under the SEC rules?

To be sure, the Dodd-Frank Act does not directly address the professional obligations of securities lawyers, as did the SOX. But Dodd-Frank does require the board of directors of financial services firms to have a risk committee, which, in some situations, at least at present, may be the appropriate committee to receive an up-the-ladder report of evidence of illegal conduct in accordance with the SOX.

Furthermore, in-house attorneys responsible for a company's corporate compliance must now consider the ramifications of the new monetary incentives for whistleblowers that were discussed in Chapter 9.B.1. The SEC promulgated the final rules for its congressionally-mandated whistleblower program on May 25, 2011. See Final Rule: Implementation of the Whistleblower Provisions of Section 21F of the Securities Exchange Act of 1934, Exchange Act Release No. 64545; codified at 17 C.F.R. Parts 240.21F *et seq.* Pursuant to these rules, an attorney whistleblower cannot receive a monetary reward if the information she provided to the SEC was derived from a privileged or confidential client communication. Non-attorneys who learn privileged or confidential client information from attorneys are similarly disqualified. However, an attorney is not disqualified if she could have revealed the same information to the SEC pursuant to SEC Rule 205 *et seq.* or under state bar ethics rules (for example, if the disclosure had to be made in order to avoid substantial harm to the corporation from a fraud in which the attorney's services had been used). See Rule 21F-4(b)(4). Do these provisions properly balance the need to protect the attorney-client privilege and the confidential lawyer-client relationship with the need to root out securities fraud?

C. FEDERAL REGULATION OF ACCOUNTANTS

The accounting profession has long been governed by internal standards of professional conduct such as the American Institute of Certified Public Accountants (AICPA), Code of Professional Conduct (1995). Rule 202 of the AICPA Code requires an AICPA member to comply with auditing and other standards "promulgated by bodies designated by [the AICPA council]." Rule 203 states that a member shall not express an opinion or state affirmatively that financial statements are presented in conformity with GAAP (Generally Accepted Accounting Principles, promulgated by the FASB) or claim that he "is not aware of any material modifications that should be made," if such financial statements materially depart from promulgated standards. Rule 301 prohibits a member from disclosing "any confidential client information without the specific consent of the client." However, Rule 301 is not intended to relieve a member of professional obligations under Rules 202 or 203, or to limit the member's duty "to comply with a validly issued and enforceable subpoena or summons." Nor should Rule 301 be interpreted to prevent an AICPA member from exchanging information with a recognized "investigative or disciplinary body." Id., Rule 301. Although the AICPA Code does not ordinarily require the auditor to disclose its findings to persons other than the client itself, such a duty might arise under some circumstances. For example, disclosure to the SEC is required when an issuer reports changes in auditors to the SEC on Form 8-K. Disclosure of confidential client information is also mandatory in response to a successor auditor who makes an inquiry in accordance with applicable rules.

Congress stepped in for the first time to tighten professional standards for accountants in 1995 when it enacted the Private Securities Litigation Reform Act (PSLRA), which added Section 10A to the Exchange Act. Section 10A places an affirmative duty on auditors to report illegal acts first to a client's senior management and then, if the illegal acts are not rectified, directly to the client's board of directors and to the SEC. As pointed out in Chapter 2.G.2, however, the PSLRA introduced a proportionate liability scheme in private litigation for damages under the Exchange Act. This change reduced auditors' exposure to civil liability for accounting fraud and thus may have encouraged them to be less careful.

After auditors were implicated in a large number of accounting frauds in the early 2000s, including the collapses of Enron and WorldCom, Congress once again turned its attention toward the accounting industry and responded with sweeping new regulation under the SOX. Often regarded as the SOX's cornerstone, Title I creates a Public Company Accounting Oversight Board (the "PCAOB" or the "Board") to provide for more effective oversight of the part of the nation's accounting industry that audits public companies. Title II was directed to the issue of auditor independence.

1. *The Public Company Accounting Oversight Board*

The PCAOB's website provides the following description:

> PCAOB is a nonprofit corporation established by Congress to oversee the audits of public companies in order to protect the interests of investors and further the public interest in the preparation of informative, accurate and independent audit reports. The PCAOB also oversees the audits of broker-dealers, including compliance reports filed pursuant to federal securities laws, to promote investor protection.

www.pcaob.org The PCAOB's five members, including a Chairman, are appointed to staggered five-year terms by the SEC, after consultation with the Chairman of the Board of Governors of the Federal Reserve System and the Secretary of the Treasury. The PCAOB's staff includes more than 700 accountants, attorneys, and other employees based in Washington, DC and seven regional offices, with an operational budget of approximately $204 million for fiscal year 2011.

The PCAOB exercises its congressionally-mandated oversight of the accounting profession through four basic functions:

> * **Registration of accounting firms** — No accounting firm may prepare, or substantially contribute to, an audit report for a public company that files financial statements with the SEC, or for a broker-dealer, without first registering with the PCAOB. There are currently 2,431 accounting firms registered with the Board. This includes 906 non-U.S. firms and 522 firms that are registered only because they have broker-dealer audit clients. Registered firms must file annual and other reports that provide the Board and the public with updated information about the firm and its audit practice. Contrary to what some believe, mere registration with the PCAOB does not reflect an examination of the firm's audit quality, which does not happen until we inspect.
>
> * **Inspection of firms and their public company audits** — Since 2003, the PCAOB has conducted more than 1,600 inspections of firms' quality controls and reviewed aspects of more than 7,000 public company audits. The audit engagements the PCAOB reviews are not selected at random. To make the most effective use of its resources, the PCAOB uses a variety of analytical techniques to select high-risk engagements and audit areas that are likely to raise challenging or difficult issues. Throughout this rigorous process, PCAOB inspections have identified numerous audit deficiencies, including failures by the largest U.S. and non-U.S. firms. These findings have led to changes in firm auditing processes, and, in some cases, more audit work performed after the fact or to corrections of client financial statements.
>
> * **Investigation and disciplinary proceedings** — The Board has broad authority to impose sanctions on registered firms and associated persons that have violated applicable laws and standards. The PCAOB has publicly announced the resolution of 37 enforcement proceedings. These proceedings include 29 sanctions on firms, including 19 revocations of firms' registrations, preventing them from auditing public companies in the future, and 40 sanctions on individuals. Sanctions have also included significant monetary penalties. The announced decisions do not, however, reflect the full extent of PCAOB enforcement activity. Under the Sarbanes-Oxley Act, all PCAOB investigations and all contested proceedings (i.e., cases in which the Board files charges and the respondent elects to litigate, rather than settle) are non-public. There are

a significant number of matters under active investigation and an additional number in litigation, which may take years to be resolved.

The Board closely coordinates its enforcement efforts with the SEC. In certain instances, the PCAOB investigates the auditor's conduct and the SEC focuses its investigation on the public company, its management, and other parties. In other cases, the SEC's Division of Enforcement takes responsibility for an auditor investigation and requests that PCAOB defer to that investigation.

* **Establishing auditing, quality control, ethics, independence, and other standards** — The Board is responsible for establishing the auditing and related professional practice standards under which public company audits are performed. Prior to the Sarbanes-Oxley Act, public company audits were performed according to standards set by the profession itself. The PCAOB has an active standard-setting agenda ***

PCAOB Chairman James R. Doty, Testimony Concerning the Role of the Accounting Profession In Preventing Another Financial Crisis Before the Senate Comm. on Banking, Housing and Urban Affairs, Subcomm. on Securities, Insurance, and Investment, April 6, 2011.

The PCAOB's unique design as a congressionally-created regulator in the private sector spawned constitutional controversy from the start. The subjection of the PCAOB to scrutiny as a state actor under the Constitution was itself noteworthy, given the SOX's provisions specifying that "[t]he Board shall not be an agency or establishment of the United States Government" and that "[n]o member or person employed by, or agent for, the Board shall be deemed to be an officer or employee of or agent for the Federal Government by reason of such service." 15 U.S.C. § 7211(b). See Donna M. Nagy, Playing Peekaboo With Constitutional Law: The PCAOB and its Public/Private Status, 80 Notre Dame L. Rev. 975 (2005). But in *Free Enter. Fund v. Pub. Co. Accounting Oversight Bd.,* 130 S. Ct. 3138, 3148 (2010), the Court made clear that these provisions rendered the PCAOB a private-sector entity for statutory purposes only. For constitutional purposes, "the Board is 'part of the Government,' *Lebron v. National Railroad Passenger Corporation,* 513 U.S. 374, 397 (1997), and [ ] its members are "'Officers of the United States'" who "exercis[e] significant authority pursuant to the laws of the United States" (quoting *Buckley v. Valeo,* 424 U.S. 1, 125-126 (1976), quoting U.S. Const., Art. II, § 2, cl. 2).

Against this backdrop, the *Free Enterprise Fund* Court ruled that the PCAOB, as originally constructed in the SOX, violated constitutional principles of separation of powers. The Court, however, chose not to impose the broad injunctive relief requested by the accounting firm and nonprofit organization that had brought the litigation. Instead, Chief Justice John Roberts, joined by four other Justices, opted to sever the SOX provisions that limited the way in which the SEC could remove PCAOB members from office. That is, Congress had specified in the SOX that PCAOB members could be removed only by the SEC and only for willful or unjustifiable transgressions. The Court found that the PCAOB's insulation from SEC control, when coupled with the SEC's insulation from direct presidential control, contravened Article II's vesting of the executive power in the President.

The majority's decision to excise the restrictive removal provisions from the SOX also made possible a quick rejection of petitioners' challenge under the

Appointments Clause. With the SEC now able to remove the five PCAOB members at-will, those members were, in the Court's view, subordinates of the SEC's Commissioners. The Court further found that the PCAOB members were "inferior officers" who, pursuant to the Constitution, may be appointed by the Commissioners acting collectively as the "Head" of the "Department."

Justice Stephen Breyer dissented in an opinion that three other justices joined. The dissenters disagreed with the majority's conclusion regarding the unconstitutionality of the PCAOB as initially structured in the SOX. The dissenters insisted that the SOX's limitations on PCAOB member removal should have been examined from the vantage point of the entire Act, and that, viewed thus, the removal limitations were utterly lacking in practical effect. In particular, the dissent emphasized the SOX provisions specifying that:

> • No Accounting Board rule takes effect unless and until the Commission approves it, § 7217(b)(2);
>
> • The Commission may "abrogat[e], delet[e] or ad[d] to" any rule or any portion of a rule promulgated by the Accounting Board whenever, in the Commission's view, doing so "further[s] the purposes" of the securities and accounting-oversight laws, § 7217(b)(5);
>
> • The Commission may review any sanction the Board imposes and "enhance, modify, cancel, reduce, or require the remission of" that sanction if it finds the Board's action not "appropriate," §§ 7215(e), 7217(c)(3);
>
> • The Commission may promulgate rules restricting or directing the Accounting Board's conduct of all inspections and investigations, §§ 7211(c)(3), 7214(h), 7215(b)(1)-(4);
>
> • The Commission may itself initiate any investigation or promulgate any rule within the Accounting Board's purview, § 7202, and may also remove any Accounting Board member who has unreasonably "failed to enforce compliance with" the relevant "rule[s], or any professional standard," § 7217(d)(3)(C) (emphasis added); [and]
>
> • The Commission may at any time "relieve the Board of any responsibility to enforce compliance with any provision" of the Act, the rules, or professional standards if, in the Commission's view, doing so is in "the public interest," § 7217(d)(1) (emphasis added).

Free Enter. Fund, 130 S.Ct. at 3172-73 (Breyer, J., dissenting). The dissent further emphasized that:

> the Commission has general supervisory powers over the Accounting Board itself: It controls the Board's budget, §§ 7219(b), (d)(1); it can assign to the Board any "duties or functions" that it "determines are necessary or appropriate," § 7211(c)(5); it has full "oversight and enforcement authority over the Board," § 7217(a), including the authority to inspect the Board's activities whenever it believes it "appropriate" to do so, § 7217(d)(2) (emphasis added). And it can censure the Board or its members, as well as remove the members from office, if the members, for example, fail to enforce the Act, violate any

> provisions of the Act, or abuse the authority granted to them under the Act, § 7217(d)(3).

Id. at 3173.

The sum total of these provisions led the dissenters to conclude that the SEC's control over the Board is "virtually absolute." Do you agree? Consider again the PCAOB's four basic functions as summarized by Chairman Doty, supra. Is it arguable that the PCAOB retains substantial discretion and autonomy notwithstanding the SEC's oversight? For analysis by one of your casebook co-authors, see Donna M. Nagy, Is the PCAOB A "Heavily Controlled Component" of the SEC?: An Essential Question in the Constitutional Controversy, 71 U. Pitt. L. Rev. 361 (2010). For an alternative view, see Richard H. Pildes, Separation of Powers, Independent Agencies, and Financial Regulation: The Case of the Sarbanes-Oxley Act, 5 N.Y.U. J. L. & Bus. 485 (2009).

NOTES AND QUESTIONS

1. SEC Attention to the "Numbers Game." Arthur Andersen's role in the collapse of Enron, as well as other high-profile accounting scandals in the early 2000s, brought never before seen public scrutiny to the accounting profession. Yet concerns about accountants' ethics or, even more precisely, the ethics of auditors, were building throughout the 1990s. This momentum is evidenced in part by former SEC Chairperson Arthur Levitt's vow to bring an end to "the numbers game," and by former SEC Enforcement Division Director Richard Walker's pledge to make "combating financial fraud [his] number one priority." See Speech of SEC Chairperson Arthur Levitt, The Numbers Game, (Sept. 28, 1998); SEC Enforcement: Accounting Fraud is Top Priority, Enforcement Officials Tell CPAs, 30 Sec. Reg. & L. Rep. 1757 (BNA) (Dec. 11, 1998). Many of the reforms suggested by Chairperson Levitt, however, were never able to get off the ground. Why might this have been so? Do reforms mandated by Congress send an even more powerful message to the industry? What if the specific reforms are dictated by the PCAOB rather than by Congress or the SEC? Note also that the SOX strengthened the FASB by confirming its authority to establish GAAP (Generally Accepted Accounting Principles), provided the FASB continues to satisfy specified criteria designed to separate it from the accounting profession. See Securities Act Section 19(b). By delegating the formulation of accounting principles to the FASB, is the SEC abdicating an essential regulatory function or is it protecting disclosure accounting by de-politicizing the standard-setting process to the fullest extent possible?

2. Funding Accounting Regulation. Mindful of the problems encountered when the accounting industry funded voluntary self-regulation, Congress determined that both the PCAOB and the FASB must have a guaranteed source of funding to protect their independence. To achieve that end, the SOX requires public companies to pay an "accounting support fee" and directs the PCAOB and the FASB to allocate such fees in accordance with an SEC-approved formula based on (1) their respective budgets and (2) a company's market capitalization. 15 U.S.C. § 7219. The Dodd-Frank Act amended this provision to require nonpublic broker-dealers to contribute to the PCAOB's funding in proportion to net capital. What concerns, if any, are raised by these mechanisms for self-funding?

3. The PCAOB's Strange Design. Then Senator Phil Gramm once described the PCAOB to his colleagues as a "strange of entity," explaining that: "We want it to be private, but we want it to have governmental powers. We have tried to structure it in ways to try to accommodate this." 148 Cong. Rec. 12,122 (2002) (statement of Sen. Gramm). Although the *Free Enterprise Fund* Court put to rest any misconception on the part of Congress that it could have it both ways for constitutional purposes, the Court did nothing to disturb Congress's decision to situate the PCAOB in the private sector for all other purposes. What factors may have contributed to Congress's decision to create the PCAOB as a private entity? What are some of the benefits and costs associated with this decision? As we saw in Chapter 9.E in connection with SRO enforcement in the securities industry, academics and litigants often have challenged the characterization of the FINRA and the NYSE as "private actors." But courts have generally refused to view these SROs as "state actors," at least insofar as the challenge involves a broker's claim of a Fifth Amendment privilege against self-incrimination. What are the similarities between the PCAOB and the FINRA or NYSE? What are the principal differences?

4. Reducing the Incidence of Securities Fraud. Did the scandals at Enron and WorldCom result from the failure of auditing standards? Congress apparently thought so, but others disagree and question whether the PCAOB will be able to modify accounting standards to prevent abuses:

> [O]ne can find few instances of independent auditors colluding with companies to defraud investors. Instead, auditors were usually defrauded in almost all instances. Although imposing more stringent audit standards on auditors might reduce attempts by some to defraud auditors, we must acknowledge that tougher standards will not necessarily prevent fraud. In implementing the goals of [SOX], the PCAOB needs to make certain that individual accountants and their firms are not unduly burdened by and even punished for their clients' acts. Moreover, the Act fails to take into consideration the significant additional costs companies will have to bear to pay for additional internal and external audit services, as well as fees payable to fund the PCAOB. Although discovering financial fraud in early stages is undoubtedly beneficial to all, it is still too early to see whether this effort will actually effectively prevent fraud.

Neil H. Aronson, Preventing Future Enrons: Implementing the Sarbanes-Oxley Act of 2002, 8 Stan. J. L. Bus. & Fin. 127, 135 (2002). Which provisions in the SOX are designed specifically to bolster an auditor's ability to discover fraud in its early stages?

5. Auditors under the Dodd-Frank Act. The Dodd-Frank Act said nothing directly about regulation of lawyers but, as noted above, it did address auditors for broker-dealers. The Act authorizes the PCAOB to establish a program of inspection for auditors of broker-dealers that are registered with the SEC but are not public companies. Substantial discretion has been left to the PCAOB, subject to the approval of the SEC, to determine the details of this program. The PCAOB has promulgated temporary rules and expects to establish a permanent program in 2013.

The Dodd-Frank Act also relaxed one key aspect of regulation under the SOX. Smaller companies – those with less than $75 million of common equity – are now exempt from having to obtain a separate auditor's report on their internal control assurance under Section 404 of the SOX Section 404 had been one of the most controversial provisions of the SOX because of the perception that auditing and reporting on internal controls placed a substantial burden on smaller issuers.

Finally, as discussed in Section B of this Chapter, Section 922 of Dodd-Frank requires the SEC to establish a whistleblower program that pays awards to whistleblowers who voluntarily provide the SEC with information about a violation. This provision should aid auditors with their work to the extent that it encourages persons within a public company to come forward with information about accounting violations. Although a rule proposed, but not thereafter adopted, would have granted the award only for reports to the SEC that had bypassed internal reporting procedures, the final rule creates incentives to submit internal reports prior to reporting evidence of wrongdoing to the SEC. What may have prompted the SEC to alter its position on this issue?

---

2. *Additional Efforts Directed at Enhancing Auditor Independence*

Congress's determination to prevent the re-occurrence of Enron and WorldCom- type scandals did not end with its creation of the PCAOB. In Title II of the SOX, Congress added to Exchange Act Section 10A a host of new provisions designed to enhance the independence of the accounting firms that audit public companies. These provisions are discussed in the Senate Report that follows.

U.S. SENATE REPORT
COMMITTEE ON BANKING, HOUSING, AND URBAN AFFAIRS
TO ACCOMPANY S. 2673, JULY 3, 2002

TITLE II—AUDITOR INDEPENDENCE

***Public confidence in the integrity of financial statements of publicly-traded companies is based on belief in the independence of the auditor from the audit client. As noted above, each of the country's federal securities laws requires comprehensive financial statements that must be prepared, in the words of the Securities Act of 1933, by "an *independent* public or certified accountant."

The statutory independent audit requirement has two sides. It grants a franchise to the nation's public accountants—their services, and only their services, and certification, must be secured before an issuer of securities can go to market, have the securities listed on the nation's stock exchanges, or comply with the reporting requirements of the securities laws. This is a source of significant private benefit to the public accountants.

But the franchise is conditional. It comes in return for the CPA's assumption of a public duty and obligation. As a unanimous Supreme Court noted nearly 20 years ago:

> In certifying the public reports that collectively depict a corporation's financial status, the independent auditor assumes a *public* responsibility. *** [That auditor] owes ultimate allegiance to the corporation's creditors and stockholders, as well as to the investing public. This 'public watchdog' function demands that the accountant maintain total independence from the client at all

times and requires complete fidelity to the public trust.

United States v. *Arthur Young,* 465 U.S. 805, 817–18 (1984) (emphasis added).

*** There is arguably an inherent conflict in the fact that an auditor is paid by the company for which the audit is being performed. That conflict is implicit in the relationship between the auditor and the audit client. In the last 15 years, however, the rapid growth in management consulting services offered by the major accounting firms has created a second, more substantial conflict that has eroded the independence that the auditor must bring to the audit function.

According to the SEC, 55 percent of the average revenue of the big five accounting firms came from accounting and auditing services in 1988. Twenty-two percent of the average revenue came from management consulting services. By 1999, those figures had fallen to 31 percent for accounting and auditing services, and risen to 50 percent for management consulting services. Recent data reported to the SEC showed on average public accounting firms' non-audit fees comprised 73 percent of their total fees, or $2.69 in non-audit fees for every $1.00 in audit fees. At the same time, the frequency of financial restatements by public companies has dramatically increased. From 1990–97, the number of public company financial restatements averaged 49 per year, but jumped to an average of 150 per year in 1999 and 2000.

For these reasons, the bill includes a number of provisions directed to the issue of auditor independence.

A. Services outside the scope of practice of auditors [Section 201, adding Section 10A(g) to the Exchange Act]

A number of the witnesses who testified before the Committee during the course of the hearings, as well as other informed observers, argued that the growth in the non-audit consulting business done by the large accounting firms for their audit clients has so compromised the independence of the audits that a complete prohibition is required on the provision of consulting services by accounting firms to their audit clients. ***

The Committee considered adopting a complete prohibition on non-audit services by accounting firms for their audit clients, but instead decided on a somewhat more flexible approach.***

The bill provides that it shall be unlawful for a public accounting firm registered with the Board which performs an audit for a public company to provide, contemporaneously with the audit, the following non-audit services:

(1) bookkeeping or other services related to the accounting records or financial statements of the audit client;

(2) financial information systems design and implementation;

(3) appraisal or valuation services, fairness opinions, or contribution-in-kind reports;

(4) actuarial services;

(5) internal audit outsourcing services;

(6) management functions or human resources;

(7) broker or dealer, investment adviser, or investment banking services;

(8) legal services and expert services unrelated to the audit; and

(9) any other services that the Board determines, by regulation, is impermissible.

[Section 102(a), Exchange Act Section 10A(g)]

The Board may, on a case-by-case basis, exempt any person, issuer, public accounting firm, or transaction from the prohibition on the provision of non-audit services to the extent that such exemption is necessary or appropriate in the public interest and is consistent with the protection of investors. [Section 201(b)] A registered public accounting firm may engage in any non-audit service, including tax services, that is not on the list for an audit client only if the activity is approved in advance by the audit committee of the issuer. [Section 201(a), Exchange Act Section 10A(h)] No limitations are placed on accounting firms in providing non-audit services to public companies which they do not audit or to any nonpublic companies. ***

In summary, the bill adopts a strong, balanced approach to assure that in return for the significant private benefits conferred on accounting firms by our securities laws, they maintain their independence from the companies they audit and fulfill their "public trust."

B. Audit committee pre-approval of audit and non-audit services [Section 202, Exchange Act Section 10A(i)]

The legislation requires that audit services, as well as non-audit services other than those proscribed by the bill, must be pre-approved by the audit committee of the public company's board of directors. The Committee heard testimony on the role that the audit committee of a public company should play in connection with the engagement of an auditor to provide audit and non-audit services contemporaneously. ***

After studying this issue, the Committee believes the protection of investors warrants a requirement that a public company's audit committee approve in advance the services that the auditor will provide to such company (if those services are not explicitly prohibited under the bill). Accordingly, the bill requires the audit committee of a public company to pre-approve all of the services, both audit and non-audit, provided to that company by a registered public accounting firm. The bill does not require an issuer's audit committee to pre-approve non-audit services provided by an accounting firm that is not auditing the issuer.

C. Audit partner rotation [Section 203, Exchange Act Section 10A(j)]

The Committee heard testimony from numerous witnesses on whether, in order to maintain the objectivity of its audits, an issuer should be required to rotate its audit firm after a number of consecutive years. ***

The Committee determined that the possibility of requiring audit firm rotation merits further study. The bill directs the U.S. General Accounting Office ("GAO") to analyze the merits and potential effects of requiring mandatory rotation of auditors, and to report its analysis to Congress within one year. [Section 207]

While the bill does not require issuers to rotate their accounting firms, the Committee recognizes the strong benefits that accrue for the issuer and its shareholders when a new accountant "with fresh and skeptical eyes" evaluates the issuer periodically. Accordingly, the bill requires a registered public accounting firm to rotate its lead partner and its review partner on audits so that neither role is performed by the same accountant for the same issuer for more than five consecutive years. ***

D. Disclosure of Accounting Issues [Section 204, Exchange Act Section 10A(k)]

The Committee believes that it is important for the audit committee to be aware of key assumptions underlying a company's financial statements and of disagreements that the auditor has with management. The audit committee should be informed in a timely manner of such disagreements, so that it can independently review them and intervene if it chooses to do so in order to assure the integrity of the audit.

Accordingly, the bill requires a registered independent public accounting firm performing an audit for a public company to report in a timely manner to that company's audit committee (1) the critical accounting policies and practices to be used; (2) all alternative treatments of financial information within GAAP (generally accepted accounting principles) that have been discussed with management; (3) any accounting disagreements between the auditor and management; and (4) other material written communications between the auditor and management.

E. Cooling off period [Section 206, Exchange Act Section 10A(*l*)]

The Committee received extensive testimony on whether to impose a cooling off period between an accountant's employment by an auditor and his or her employment by an issuer.***

The Committee considered various options, including imposing a cooling off period of one, two, or three years, and applying a cooling off period to all employees who worked for the auditor, regardless of whether they worked on the audit of a particular issuer and regardless of the position they would take with that issuer, or applying a cooling off period only to certain groups of employees.

The Committee decided to impose a one-year cooling off period that would apply to an employee of the accounting firm who worked on the issuer's audit and subsequently seeks to be employed by that issuer in a senior management capacity. Thus, the bill provides that an accounting firm may not provide audit services for a public company if that company's chief executive officer, controller, chief financial officer, chief accounting officer, or other individual serving in an equivalent position, was employed by the accounting firm during the one year before the start of the audit services. ***

F. The bill does not create state regulatory standards [Section 209]

Titles I and II are designed to apply only to accounting firms that audit public companies. They are not designed to apply to audits of private companies. Nonetheless, some have raised the concern that the bill could lead state regulatory authorities to impose similar requirements for audits of private companies.

The bill indicates clearly that Congress does not intend that state regulatory authorities should find this Act controlling in their regulation of non-registered accountants. The bill states that it is the intention of the Act that, in supervising non-registered accounting firms, state regulatory authorities should make an independent determination of the proper standards, and should not presume the standards applied by the Board under this bill to be applicable to small- and medium-sized non-registered accounting firms. ***

NOTES AND QUESTIONS

1. ***Ancillary Services for Auditing Clients.*** In the 1990s, the SEC sought to increase the independence of accountants by restricting an auditing firm's ability to provide ancillary services such as consulting to auditing clients of the firm. The SEC, however, received heavy pressure from various members of Congress not to restrict these ancillary services. The tide then turned after the Enron collapse, and Section 10A(g) of the Exchange Act now imposes restrictions almost identical to those that the SEC had been considering years before. How likely is it that ancillary services will distort incentives to provide a truly independent audit? Are there ways in which providing ancillary services to an audit client might improve the quality of an audit? What types of ancillary services, if any, are likely to be given PCAOB approval pursuant to the exemptive authority provided by Section 201(b) of the SOX?

2. ***The Reach of the PCAOB's Authority.*** The Senate Report suggested that auditors may have overlooked so many accounting frauds in the late 1990s and early 2000s, in part because of the way that accounting firms compensate their partners for obtaining and keeping large clients. And the audit partner rotation rule in new Exchange Act Section 10A(j) was designed to address this problem. Should the PCAOB also regulate compensation systems in firms that audit public companies? How so? Should audit fees be fixed by the PCAOB rather than by private agreement between auditor and client? Would the Board need additional statutory authorization to regulate such fees? Consider also that some European jurisdictions require public companies to rotate their auditors every few years. Should the Board adopt such a requirement? Does it have the statutory authorization to do so?

3. ***SEC Rules Regarding Auditor Independence.*** Section 208 of the SOX required the Commission, not later than 180 days after the Act's enactment, to "issue final regulations to carry out each of the subsections (g) through (*l*) of Section 10A" of the Exchange Act. In January 2003, the SEC adopted rules consistent with this directive. These rules:

> revise the Commission's regulations related to the non-audit services that, if provided to an audit client, would impair an accounting firm's independence; require that an issuer's audit committee pre-approve all audit and non-audit services provided to the issuer by the auditor of an issuer's financial statements; prohibit certain partners on the audit engagement team from providing audit services to the issuer for more than five or seven consecutive years, depending on the partner's involvement in the audit, except that certain small accounting firms may be exempted from this requirement; prohibit an accounting firm from auditing an issuer's financial statements if certain members of management of that issuer had been members of the accounting firm's audit engagement team within the one-year period preceding the commencement of audit procedures; require that the auditor of an issuer's financial statements report certain

> matters to the issuer's audit committee, including "critical" accounting policies used by the issuer; and require disclosures to investors of information related to audit and non-audit services provided by, and fees paid to, the auditor of the issuer's financial statements. In addition, under the final rules, an accountant would not be independent from an audit client if an audit partner received compensation based on selling engagements to that client for services other than audit, review and attest services.

Final Rule: Strengthening the Commission's Requirements Regarding Auditor Independence, Exchange Act Release No. 47265 (Jan. 28, 2003).

In April 2006, the SEC approved several new auditor independence and ethics rules that had been proposed by the PCAOB. See Exchange Act Release No. 53677 (April 19, 2006). These new rules "include general rules with respect to ethics and independence, restrict certain types of tax services a registered public accounting firm may provide to its audit clients, and prohibit contingent fee arrangements for any services a registered public accounting firm provides to its audit clients, in order to maintain its independence." Id.

4. Too Big (and Too Few) to Fail. The DOJ's 2002 criminal indictment of Arthur Andersen in connection with the Enron scandal reduced the number of large audit firms from five to four. The "Big Four" that remain are: PricewaterhouseCoopers, Ernst & Young, KPMG, and Deloitte & Touche. Professor Cunningham contends that "allowing another firm to fail would produce acute industry concentration," a prospect that may lead the government and the firms to believe that they are "too big too fail." See Lawrence A. Cunningham, Too Big to Fail: Moral Hazard in Auditing and The Need to Restructure the Industry Before it Unravels, 106 Colum. L. Rev. 1698, 1699 (2006). See also Joseph Nocera, Auditors: Too Few to Fail, N.Y. Times, June 25, 2005, at C1.

In 2005, KPMG avoided criminal indictment by entering into a deferred prosecution agreement. Pursuant to this agreement, the firm agreed to pay $456 million in return for the DOJ's promise not to prosecute it for fraud and conspiracy in connection with the creation and sale of illegal tax shelters. KPMG also consented to specific limitations on its tax practice and to retain for three years an independent monitor. In addition, the firm agreed to cooperate with the government by waiving the attorney-client privilege and by providing all requested information, including information about current and former KPMG partners and employees, many of whom were later indicted. Moreover, in contrast to typical settlements with the SEC, KPMG's deferred prosecution agreement contained detailed admissions of wrongdoing. In 2007, the DOJ dismissed the deferred criminal charge against KPMG. See David Reilly & Paul Davies, Deferred Charge Against KPMG Is Dismissed in Tax Shelter Case, Wall St. J., Jan. 4, 2007, at C3.

To what extent does the "too big to fail" doctrine explain a decision to defer and dismiss criminal prosecution, such as the DOJ's decision regarding KPMG? What additional factors may have influenced the government's decisionmaking? What types of moral hazards come about when the Big Four believe that they are "too big to fail"? Were these moral hazards similar to those that took hold in the investment banking industry in the years leading up to 2008 as a result of the belief that some of those institutions were "too big to fail"?

*5. **The Role of Auditors in the Financial Crisis of 2008.*** The financial crisis of 2008 saw the failure of many large financial firms – Lehman Brothers, American International Group (AIG), Bear Stearns, Merrill Lynch and others. Many other gigantic financial firms almost failed and probably would have but for emergency government aid in the fall of 2008 and into 2009. These rescued firms included Citicorp, Bank of America, Goldman Sachs, Morgan Stanley, JP Morgan Chase and others. All of these firms are Exchange Act reporting companies, and all of them had outside accounting firms audit their financial statements. The financial assets of these firms – often mortgage-backed securities or derivatives based on mortgage-backed securities – were worth far less than they were reported on the firms' balance sheets.

It remains to be seen – in civil litigation and perhaps SEC enforcement proceedings – to what extent this failure in financial reporting was the fault of the auditors, or whether the auditors were entitled to rely upon the firms' internal valuations of assets. The Financial Crisis Inquiry Commission made little mention of auditors in its 2010 Report, which instead focused on the failings of government regulators, rating agencies, the banks themselves, their officers and directors, and other culpable parties. Could seemingly stable banks, insurance companies, and other firms have been so close to insolvency, or actually insolvent, without the auditors having come into possession of at least some facts that should have led them to investigate further?

Plaintiffs' lawyers and state attorneys general have not been so forgiving toward the auditing firms. Many securities class action lawsuits that followed the financial crisis took aim at auditing irregularities and named the auditing firms as defendants. Thus, several such lawsuits pending against officers and directors of the defunct Lehman Bros. sued Lehman's auditors, Ernst & Young. Moreover, New York's Attorney General (now Governor) Andrew Cuomo sued Ernst & Young in connection with the Lehman Brothers Repo 105 transaction. As noted earlier in this Chapter, Lehman's lawyers in the U.K. had reported that Repo 105 was a "true sale" under English law, but this may not have been sufficient justification for the auditors to allow Lehman to report the transaction as a sale of the assets on its financial statements without further inquiry. Such inquiry presumably would have revealed that the transaction exchanged billions in bad assets for cash and the transaction was then unwound shortly after the end of the reporting period.

The PCAOB is also conducting investigations into the role of auditors in the 2008 financial crisis. According to PCAOB chairman James R. Doty, these investigations may lead to disciplinary action against accounting firms or individual auditors. See David F. Hilzenrath, Oversight Board Investigates Lack of Warnings by Auditors Before Financial Crisis, Wash. Post, March 16, 2011.

*6. **An In Pari Delicto Defense?*** Given the limited federal securities law remedies against lawyers and accountants as the result of *Central Bank* and its progeny (*Stoneridge* and *Janus*), failed corporations and their creditors may turn to state law actions against lawyers, accountants, and other professionals for breach of duty to the corporation. Many of these actions are brought by bankruptcy trustees, trustees under the Securities Investor Protection Act (SIPA) or other receivers. A nagging question that pervades many of these cases is whether the wrongful acts of the officers and directors purportedly acting on the corporation's behalf can be attributed to the corporation itself (and to the trustee/receiver) and thereby give the defendants a successful *in pari delicto* defense.

New York's answer to this question came as the result of litigation involving the collapse of Refco, which had been a major brokerage and clearing firm for derivatives as well as currency and futures markets. Between 1998 and 2005, Refco's president had orchestrated a series of loans that hid hundreds of millions of dollars in uncollectible debt on its balance sheet. The disclosure of this deception in 2005 prompted a run on customer accounts, forcing Refco into bankrtupcy. The bankruptcy court established the Refco litigation trust on behalf of Refco's unsecured creditors. Kirschner, the trustee of that trust, sued Refco's investment bankers, lawyers and accountants for their role in the debacle, claiming fraud, breach of fiduciary duty and malpractice.

Even though the creditors who stood to benefit from the litigation were among the victims of the fraud, the fact that the action had been brought on the bankruptcy estate's behalf presumably meant that defenses available against Refco had it sued in its own capacity were likewise available against the trustee. The defendants' assertion of the defense of *in pari delicto*, or "unclean hands," prompted the federal court to request an interpretation of New York law by certifying the question to the New York Court of Appeals. That court's answer was that the *in pari delicto* defense remained intact under the facts presented because the corporate officers, while acting wrongly and perhaps with selfish motives, also acted for the purported benefit of Refco. See *Kirschner v. KPMG, LLP* 15 N.Y.3d 457, 925 N.E. 2d 930 (N.Y. 2010). With the *in pari delicto* defense applicable under these circumstances, it has become extraordinarily difficult for a trustee to mount a successful action against investment bankers, accountants and lawyers when New York law applies.

Two neighboring states, New Jersey and Pennsylvania, approach the question differently. See *NCP Litig. Trust v KPMG LLP*, 187 N.J. 353, 901 A.2d 871 (N.J. 2006), *Official Comm. of Unsecured Creditors of Allegheny Health Educ. & Research Found. v Pricewaterhouse Coopers, LLP*, 605 Pa. 269, 989 A.2d 313 (Pa. 2010). These decisions used carve-outs from traditional agency law in corporate fraud situations in order to deny the *in pari delicto* defense to negligent or reckless outside auditors and other professionals.

Chapter 11

CRIMINAL ENFORCEMENT

Criminal enforcement of the federal securities laws rests exclusively with the Department of Justice (DOJ), which operates through U.S. Attorney's Offices across the United States. The DOJ often receives referrals of cases from the SEC that the latter deems worthy of prosecution. But the DOJ also regularly investigates and prosecutes cases not referred by the SEC.

In prosecuting securities cases, the DOJ has a veritable panoply of crimes from which to choose. Some have been on the books for decades: Securities Act and Exchange Act crimes as well as crimes of a more general nature, especially mail fraud, wire fraud, and crimes created by the Racketeer Influenced and Corrupt Organizations Act (RICO). Others have come into being as part of the Sarbanes-Oxley Act of 2002 (SOX), enacted in response to the scandals at Enron, WorldCom, and other large companies. The SOX has further enhanced the DOJ's options by stiffening the penalties for Exchange Act crimes, mail fraud, and wire fraud.

To be sure, the enactment of criminal offenses does not guarantee their utilization. For example, prosecutors have yet to zealously pursue the culprits responsible for the 2008 financial crisis. They refrained from doing so in significant measure because various senior members of the executive branch were fearful of rattling the markets. See Gretchen Morgenson & Louise Story, In Financial Crisis, No Prosecutions of Top Figures, N.Y. Times, April 14, 2011, at A1.

Nor do stiffened penalties assure that courts will impose the maximums. The judicial obligation is simply to calculate the range proscribed by the federal sentencing guidelines and then to depart from that range only when doing so would be "reasonable." *United States v. Booker*, 543 U.S. 220 (2005) (declaring the sentencing guidelines "advisory" in order to avoid clash with sixth amendment right to jury trial).

The enactment of the new SOX crimes raises several intriguing issues. Why did Congress criminalize conduct that largely already fell within the purview of existing crimes? Moreover, why did it bother stiffening penalties given that such penalties are apt to be more theoretical than real? Concerning both of these questions, consider the analysis offered by Professor William J. Stuntz shortly before the SOX's enactment:

> When making criminal law, Congress has the same two incentives as state legislatures--to pay attention to the needs and wants of prosecutors and the police, and to make popular symbolic statements. *** Unsurprisingly, then, federal criminal law is filled with examples of what one might call the

"carjacking strategy"--superfluous statutes that criminalize some outrageous conduct that caught the public eye at some particular time. Also unsurprisingly, since these federal crimes are symbolic, they generate very few federal prosecutions.

The other large part of the federal criminal code, the part that does generate prosecutions, consists mostly of crimes that law enforcers want. *** This part of federal criminal law is likely to be very broad in part because federal prosecutors will want it to be so, in order to help them go after high-profile or otherwise professionally rewarding cases. And federal prosecutors' voice will carry great weight in Congress largely because of public attitudes toward anyone whom prosecutors target--that such people must deserve punishment. ***

*** Criminal statutes are a grant of power to police and prosecutors, who can choose how aggressively and in what cases to exercise that power. Anytime a principal grants power to an agent, there is a risk that the agent will not use the power in the way the principal would like. That risk is plainly present in criminal lawmaking, for prosecutors may charge differently than legislators would wish.***

*** Consider the ways in which prosecutors' charging decisions are likely to diverge from legislative preferences. One obvious possibility is that prosecutors will charge defendants whom legislators would prefer be left alone. ***

The more serious risk is that, from legislators' point of view, prosecutors will simply prosecute too little. Prosecutors, remember, are paid salary, not by the case; while they have good reason to want to satisfy the public's desires, they also have good reason to want to limit their workload. They can do so in either of two ways--by reducing the number of cases they handle, or by reducing the cost of handling each case. Prosecutors may actually prefer the first strategy. Like other litigators, prosecutors enjoy trying cases ***. But legislators would surely prefer the second. Cheaper case processing means a higher volume of criminal convictions; to the extent the public wants more convictions rather than fewer, legislatures are likely to have the same preference.

How can legislators combat the tendency toward under-enforcement, and how can they steer prosecutors toward cheaper case processing and away from smaller dockets? ***

*** The idea is simple: if the risk is that prosecutors will prosecute too little, making prosecution cheaper will tend to reduce the risk. Broadening criminal liability and raising nominal sentences make prosecution cheaper. ***

*** Broader criminal liability rules raise the threat value of trial, by raising both the odds the government will win and the sentence the defendant might receive if he loses. That allows the government to get more guilty pleas. Making guilty pleas easier to obtain in turn lowers the cost of prosecution. And lowering the cost of prosecution is, from legislators' perspective, a useful counter to prosecutors' tendency to prosecute too little.

William J. Stuntz, The Pathological Politics of Criminal Law, 100 Mich. L. Rev. 505, 546, 549-52 (2001).

An additional issue raised by the new SOX crimes involves their likely effectiveness in taming corporate misconduct. Concerns about efficacy are especially pronounced when the prohibited conduct lacks moral turpitude and thereby falls outside the realm of the criminal law as generally conceived. Some scholars believe that to criminalize merely "economic offenses" causes the criminal sanction to lose its stigma. See Sanford H. Kadish, Some Observations on the Use of Criminal Sanctions in Enforcing Economic Regulations, 30 U. Chi. L. Rev. 423, 437 (1963). Other scholars reply that the public regards as criminal whatever society brands as criminal. See Harry V. Ball & Lawrence M. Friedman, The Use of Criminal Sanctions in the Enforcement of Economic Legislation: A Sociological View, 17 Stan. L. Rev. 197, 216 (1965). Might both of these positions be valid simultaneously? See John C. Coffee, Jr., Hush!: The Criminal Status of Confidential Information After *McNally* and *Carpenter* and the Enduring Problem of Overcriminalization, 26 Am. Crim. L. Rev. 121, 149 (1988).

Professors Butler and Ribstein have offered a new slant on the criminalization of economic offenses. Their analysis builds on the concept of "agency costs" – the costs that every corporation incurs in order to insure that its managers work for the benefit of the shareholders (rather than for their own benefit or not at all). Lamenting the "folly of criminalizing" these costs, they focus on the SOX's new certification crime for CEOs and CFOs (which we encounter later in this Chapter):

> SOX *** enable[es] criminal liability even for those who have not themselves engaged in self-aggrandizement, but have certified reports where they had knowledge of internal control lapses or failed to disclose information to auditors and the audit committee. ***
>
> Criminal sanctions for violating SOX may actually increase agency costs. A major concern of agency theory has been that corporate managers were not being diligent enough in pursuing their obligation to maximize the value of the firm. For example, managers could simply be lazy. Under SOX, laziness– failure to take time to evaluate controls before attesting to their adequacy – can result in criminal liability. Although this threat should take care of the laziness part of the agency costs, it might create a larger problem – instead of being lazy, managers might focus too many of the corportioan's resources on ensuring the adequacy of corporate controls in order to avoid personal liability. That is, in order to avoid criminal liability, the managers are likely to use corporate resources to their own benefit, even though they know that it is not in the best interests of the shareholders.

Henry N. Butler & Larry E. Ribstein, The Sarbanes-Oxley Debacle: What We've Learned; How to Fix It 61 (2006). For differing views among the participants, see Roundtable - The Criminalization of Corporate Law, 2 J. of Bus. & Tech. L. 85-127 (2007).

This Chapter is divided into four sections. Section A examines crimes created by the Securities Act and the Exchange Act, while Section B examines crimes created by the SOX. Sections C and D address two other criminal statutes which come into play when securities transactions are at issue—the federal mail and wire fraud statutes (Section C) and RICO (Section D).

As you read this Chapter, ask yourself whether all of the crimes, at least taken together, are apt to reduce the likelihood that debacles such as those at Enron and WorldCom will occur again. In this regard, note that convictions require proof beyond a reasonable doubt. See *In re Winship*, 397 U.S. 358, 361-62 (1970).

A. THE SECURITIES ACT AND THE EXCHANGE ACT

The only criminal provision in the Securities Act is Section 24, which reads as follows:

> Any person who willfully violates any of the provisions of this act, or the rules and regulations promulgated by the Commission under authority thereof, or any person who willfully, in a registration statement filed under this Act, makes any untrue statement of a material fact or omits to state any material fact required to be stated therein or necessary to make the statements therein not misleading, shall upon conviction be fined not more than $10,000 or imprisoned not more than five years, or both.

Observe that Section 24 piggybacks onto the Securities Act's substantive provisions, authorizing criminal liability when one of those provisions is "willfully" violated.

The same piggybacking approach is evident in Section 24's counterpart, Section 32(a) of the Exchange Act. As you read Section 32(a), note its use of both "willfully and knowingly" as well as "willfully" and also its final clause (known as the "no knowledge" clause):

> Any person who willfully violates any provision of this Act (other than section 30A), or any rule or regulation thereunder the violation of which is made unlawful or the observance of which is required under the terms of this Act, or any person who willfully and knowingly makes, or causes to be made, any statement in any application, report, or document required to be filed under this Act or any rule or regulation thereunder or any undertaking contained in a registration statement as provided in subsection (d) of section 15 of this Act or by any self-regulatory organization in connection with an application for membership or participation therein or to become associated with a member thereof, which statement was false or misleading with respect to any material fact, shall upon conviction be fined not more than $5,000,000 or imprisoned not more than 20 years, or both, except that when such person is a person other than a natural person, a fine not exceeding $25,000,000 may be imposed; but no person shall be subject to imprisonment under this section for the violation of any rule or regulation if he proves that he had no knowledge of such rule or regulation.

The penalties set forth in Section 32(a) are the product of an amendment enacted as part of the SOX. Prior to the SOX, Section 32(a) authorized fines for a natural person of not more than $1,000,000 and imprisonment for not more than 10 years; other defendants could be fined no more than $2,500,000. (The SOX left untouched the criminal penalties set forth in Section 24 of the Securities Act).

As Sections 24 and 32(a) make apparent, a defendant can be convicted under the Securities Act or the Exchange Act only if he commits his violation "willfully." We begin with the meaning of "willfully," and then consider the provisions the violation of which can give rise to criminal liability.

1. *The Requirement that the Defendant Act "Willfully"*

Both the Securities Act and the Exchange Act condition criminal liability on proof that the defendant acted "willfully," but neither Act defines that term. The legislative history of each is likewise silent. To be sure, the term "willfully" is commonplace in federal criminal statutes. See Sharon L. Davies, The

Jurisprudence of Willfulness: An Evolving Theory of Excusable Ignorance, 48 Duke L. J. 341, 420-27 (1998) (listing such statutes). But the term has no generally accepted definition that can simply be imported into the Securities Act or the Exchange Act. Cf. *Bryan v. United States,* 524 U.S. 184, 191 (1998) (describing "willfully" as a "word of many meanings" (quoting *Spies v. United States,* 317 U.S. 492, 497 (1943))).

The following decision interprets the term "willfully" in Section 32(a) of the Exchange Act.

UNITED STATES v. TARALLO

380 F.3d 1174 (9th Cir. 2004)

SUSAN P. GRABER, CIRCUIT JUDGE:

Defendant Aldo Tarallo appeals his convictions on six counts of securities fraud*** and four counts of mail fraud ***. We reverse his convictions with respect to three *** counts for lack of evidence. In affirming the remaining seven counts, we hold that a defendant may commit securities fraud "willfully" in violation of § 32(a)[a] and Rule 10b-5 even if the defendant did not know at the time of the acts that the conduct violated the law. We further hold that a defendant may commit securities fraud "willfully" by intentionally acting with reckless disregard for the truth of material misleading statements. ***

FACTUAL AND PROCEDURAL BACKGROUND

Defendant and two co-defendants, David Colvin and John Larson, together participated in a fraudulent telemarketing scheme. Colvin owned several companies used in the scheme, including Intellinet, Inc., and Larson was Intellinet's sales manager. Defendant was hired by Intellinet as a telemarketer, and he participated in the fraud from April 1997 until February 20, 1998. Defendant and others solicited those called to invest in various businesses whose value and operations were fictitious. These purported businesses included Medical Advantage, Inc. ("Medical Advantage"), Lamelli Medical Technology, Inc. ("Lamelli"), and R.A.C. International, Inc. ("R.A.C.").

Defendant and his co-defendants falsely represented to potential investors that Medical Advantage operated independent weight loss clinics around the country and had a projected 1997 revenue of $8.2 million, and that C. Everett Koop and Tom Brokaw supported or were affiliated with the company. Defendant and his co-defendants falsely represented to potential investors that Lamelli had developed a detoxification system that could detoxify a person of all alcohol or drugs in 15 minutes, that the system had won FDA approval, and that $187 million in revenue was expected to be generated by this alleged invention in 1998. Defendant and his co-defendants falsely represented to potential investors that R.A.C. had generated $2.3 million in revenue in 1997 from sales of motor oil, car batteries, and tools, and that the company projected for 1998 revenues of approximately $3.5 million.

---

a. Author's Note: For ease of reading, references to Sections of the Exchange Act and the Securities Act replace those to the U.S. Code and references to Rule 10b-5 replace those to the Code of Federal Regulations.

Defendant and his co-defendants told potential investors that they would be investing by means of promissory notes, which would be held in a "trust" for a fixed term of between 90 and 180 days. In return, the investors would receive 12 percent interest per annum and shares of "restricted stock" in the company. Defendant told investors that the company's Initial Public Offering ("IPO") would occur on or before the date on which the promissory note was to mature, at which point investors could (at their option) either receive back their invested principal or use it to purchase shares offered in the IPO. Instead of holding the invested funds in trust as promised, however, Colvin and others used those funds for the benefit of Colvin, Larson, Defendant, and their associates, and the investors never saw their money again.

After a nine-day trial, a jury convicted Defendant on six counts of securities fraud and four counts of mail fraud. The district court sentenced him to 37 months' imprisonment on each count, with the sentences to run concurrently. Defendant timely appealed.***

C. Jury Instructions

Defendant claims several errors in the jury instructions relating to the fraud counts as to which there was sufficient evidence. ***

2. Instructions equating "willfully" and "knowingly."

Defendant was charged with, and convicted of, securities fraud under §32(a) and under Rule 10b-5, which was promulgated under the authority of §10(b). ***

The district court instructed the jury on "knowingly" and "willfully" as follows:

> Each of the crimes charged in the indictment requires proof beyond a reasonable doubt that the defendant acted knowingly. An act is done knowingly if the defendant is aware of the act and does not act or fail to act through ignorance, mistake, or accident.
>
> The government is not required to prove that the defendant knew that his acts or omissions were unlawful. Thus, for example, to prove a defendant guilty of securities fraud or mail fraud based on making a false or misleading representation, the government must prove beyond a reasonable doubt that the defendant knew the representation was false or was made with reckless indifference to its truth or falsity, but it need not prove that in making the representation the defendant knew he was committing securities fraud, mail fraud, or any other criminal offense.
>
> In these statutes, willfully has the same meaning as knowingly.

Defendant argues that the court erred by instructing that "willfully" and "knowingly" mean the same thing, and by instructing that the government did not have to prove that defendant knew that his conduct was unlawful. He argues that the "willful" instruction runs afoul of *Bryan v. United States*, 524 U.S. 184, 191-92 (1998), in which the Supreme Court stated:

> As a general matter, when used in the criminal context, a "willful" act is one undertaken with a "bad purpose." In other words, in order to establish a "willful" violation of a statute, "the Government must prove that the defendant

> acted with knowledge that his conduct was unlawful." *Ratzlaf v. United States*, 510 U.S. 135, 137 (1994).

Because §32(a) requires a showing of "willfulness," Defendant argues, it was error to instruct the jury that Defendant could be convicted even if the jury found that he did not know that his conduct was unlawful.

As an initial matter, we note that the district court *did* err in this instruction, although not in the way that Defendant claims.[1] As quoted above, the district court instructed that "[e]ach of the crimes charged in the indictment requires proof beyond a reasonable doubt that the defendant acted *knowingly*." (Emphasis added.) However, § 32(a) states that a person who "willfully" violates any provision of the chapter or any rule or regulation promulgated thereunder is subject to criminal penalty. "Knowingly" is not a required element. Id. "Knowingly" *is* an element for the conviction of any individual who "makes, or causes to be made, any statement in any application, report, or document required to be filed under this chapter or any rule or regulation thereunder or any undertaking contained in a registration statement as provided in subsection (d) of Section 15 of this title." Id. As § 32(a) makes clear, such a person must be found to have engaged in the proscribed conduct "willfully and knowingly."

The conduct for which Defendant was indicted, tried, and convicted did not involve the filing of an application, report, or document required by the securities laws. Instead, his conduct was covered by Rule 10b-5. That conduct clearly falls under the first provision of § 32(a), which requires only that the act be done "willfully," but does not require that the act be done "knowingly." Therefore, the district court's instruction that "[e]ach of the crimes charged in the indictment requires proof beyond a reasonable doubt that the defendant acted knowingly" was erroneous.

However, the district court then went on to equate "willfully" with "knowingly." The district court's error in including "knowingly" in the instructions is therefore harmless so long as the definition the court provided for knowingly *and* willfully satisfies the statutory definition of "willfully." We turn now to that question.

The Supreme Court has taken pains to observe that the word "willful" "is a word of many meanings" and that "its construction is often influenced by its context." *Ratzlaf*, 510 U.S. at 141. We must consider, then, the context in which "willfully" is found in the securities fraud statutes. The question is whether the securities fraud statutes' use of the term "willfully" means that a defendant can be convicted of securities fraud only if he or she *knows that the charged conduct is unlawful*, or whether "willfully" simply means what the district court instructed it means: "knowingly" in the sense that the defendant *intends those actions* and that they are not the product of accident or mistake.

Defendant's argument – that willfulness requires that he knew that he was breaking the law at the time he made his false statements – has been previously rejected by this and other courts. In *United States v. Charnay*, 537

---

1. Although Defendant did not point to the error we are about to discuss, we mention it to put into context our discussion of the claim he does raise.

F.2d 341, 351-52 (9th Cir.1976), we cited with approval the Second Circuit's interpretation of § 32 in *United States v. Peltz*, 433 F.2d 48, 54 (2d Cir.1970). The Second Circuit explained there that "[t]he language makes one point entirely clear. A person can willfully violate an SEC rule even if he does not know of its existence. This conclusion follows from the difference between the standard for violation of the statute or a rule or regulation, to wit, 'willfully,' and that for false or misleading statements, namely 'willfully and knowingly.' " Id. at 54. We quoted a law review article cited in *Peltz*, 433 F.2d at 55, which "concluded it was necessary only that the prosecution establishes a realization on the defendant's part that he was doing a wrongful act." *Charnay*, 537 F.2d at 352 (quoting William B. Herlands, Criminal Law Aspects of the Securities Exchange Act of 1934, 21 Va. L.Rev. 139, 149 (1934)). Adopting the reasoning of the Second Circuit, we "accept[ed] this with the qualifications, doubtless intended by the author, that the act be wrongful under the securities laws and that the knowingly wrongful act involve a significant risk of effecting the violation that has occurred." Id.[3]

We also addressed an argument very similar to Defendant's in *United States v. English*, 92 F.3d 909 (9th Cir.1996). In *English*, the defendant was convicted of securities fraud under [§§ 17(a) and 24 of the Securities Act]. "§17(a) makes it illegal to use instruments of interstate commerce to defraud or deceive purchasers of securities. § 24, a general penalty provision covering § 17(a) and other [Securities Act] offenses, provides that '[a]ny person who *willfully* violates' § 17(a) is subject to fines and incarceration. (emphasis added)." Id. at 914. Section 24 is therefore substantively similar to the willfulness provision of § 32(a). In *English*, we rejected the defendant's argument that § 24's willfulness requirement required that the government prove that the defendant knew that his conduct was illegal. We distinguished *Ratzlaf* and explained that "our cases ... support the conclusion that §§ 17(a] and ... 24 do not require proof of knowledge of illegality." Id. at 915.

Even were we not bound by our existing precedent, we would reach the same result. The final clause of § 32(a) provides that "no person shall be subject to imprisonment under this section for the violation of any rule or regulation if he proves that he had no knowledge of such rule or regulation." The opening sentence of subsection (a) explains that "[a]ny person who *willfully* violates any provision of this chapter ... or any rule or regulation thereunder the violation of which is made unlawful or the observance of which is required under the terms of this chapter" commits a crime. Id. (emphasis added). If "willfully" meant "with knowledge that one's conduct violates a rule or regulation," the last clause proscribing imprisonment-but not a fine-in cases where a defendant did *not* know of the rule or regulation would be nonsensical: If willfully meant "with knowledge that one is breaking the law," there would be no need to proscribe imprisonment (but permit imposition of a fine) for someone who acted *without*

3. The Eighth Circuit has expressed its agreement with *Charnay*, explaining that "[c]ourts that have interpreted 'willfully' in § 32 have reached the same conclusion that we reach in this case: 'willfully' simply requires the intentional doing of the wrongful acts-no knowledge of the rule or regulation is required." *United States v. O'Hagan*, 139 F.3d 641, 647 (8th Cir.1998) (citing *Charnay*).

knowing that he or she was violating a rule or regulation. Such a person could not have been convicted in the first place.

Under our jurisprudence, then, "willfully" as it is used in § 32(a) means intentionally undertaking an act that one knows to be wrongful; "willfully" in this context does not require that the actor know specifically that the conduct was unlawful. The district court's instructions correctly informed the jury that it had to find that defendant intentionally undertook such an act:

> [T]o prove a defendant guilty of securities fraud or mail fraud based on making a false or misleading representation, the government must prove beyond a reasonable doubt that the defendant knew the representation was false or was made with reckless indifference to its truth or falsity, but it need not prove that in making the representation the defendant knew he was committing securities fraud, mail fraud, or any other criminal offense.

The district court's instructions thus required the jury to find that Defendant had made statements that he knew at the time were false, or else made them with a reckless disregard for whether they were false. The district court therefore required the jury to find that Defendant undertook acts that he knew at the time to be wrongful, meeting the standard for defining "willfully" in this circuit. The district court's importation of the term "knowingly" into the jury instructions was harmless beyond a reasonable doubt, because the court equated "knowingly" with "willfully," and the court's definition properly explained "willfully."

3. Recklessness standard for securities fraud.

As discussed above, the district court instructed the jury that it could convict Defendant of both mail fraud and securities fraud if it found that he had made a false statement, which was a representation that either "(a) was then known to be untrue by the person making or causing it to be made or (b) was made or caused to be made with reckless indifference as to its truth or falsity." Defendant argues that the recklessness portion of the instruction was error as to the securities fraud counts.

The comment to Ninth Circuit Model Jury Instruction 9.7 (2000) states that reckless disregard for truth or falsity is sufficient to sustain a conviction for securities fraud. The comment cites *United States v. Farris*, 614 F.2d 634, 638 (9th Cir.1979), for this proposition. Defendant argues that the comment incorrectly describes the law to be applied in this case, because *Farris* was not a §§ 10(b) or a 32(a) prosecution, because *Farris* relied on a civil securities fraud case, and because the Supreme Court's decision in *United States v. O'Hagan*, 521 U.S. 642 (1997), stands for the proposition that recklessness is insufficient to sustain a criminal conviction for securities fraud. In *O'Hagan*, the Supreme Court said that, in order to convict a defendant of securities fraud, the government must prove that the defendant "willfully" violated Rule 10b-5. 521 U.S. at 665-66 (citing § 32(a)).[5] Defendant again cites *Bryan*, 524 U.S. at 191-93,

5. On remand from the Supreme Court, the Eighth Circuit in *O'Hagan*, 139 F.3d at 647, interpreted the Supreme Court's *O'Hagan* opinion as "simply explaining that the statute provides that a negligent or reckless violation of the securities law cannot result in criminal liability; instead, the defendant must act willfully." That statement

for the proposition that willfulness requires actual knowledge and argues that recklessness cannot satisfy this requirement.

Defendant's argument fails. *Farris* explicitly holds that recklessness is adequate to support a conviction for securities fraud. Defendant's attempt to distinguish *Farris* on the ground that *Farris* involved a fraud charge under §17(a), and not under § 10(b), is unpersuasive. As we explained above, "willfully" in the context of § 32(a) is best understood to mean "voluntarily and knowingly wrongful," not "with the intent to violate the law." Therefore, its absence in §17(a) does not render *Farris* distinguishable. We find no error in the recklessness instruction. ***

NOTES AND QUESTIONS

1. ***Did Congress Drop the Ball?*** A defendant must commit her violation "willfully" in order to be found criminally liable under either the Securities Act or the Exchange Act. Why did Congress not provide a definition of this critical term?

2. **Tarallo*'s Definition of "Willfully."*** The *Tarallo* court defined "willfully" as "intentionally undertaking an act that one knows to be 'wrongful,'" but not necessarily "unlawful." See *United States v. Kaiser*, 609 F.3d 556, 569 (2d Cir. 2010) (describing support for this distinction in Second Circuit precedent). What types of evidence would tend to show knowledge of wrongfulness?

3. ***Willfully vs. Scienter***. Several major securities provisions have scienter requirements that play a pivotal role in the context of civil enforcement. The provisions include Section 10(b) and Rule 10b-5 (see Chapter 2.D); Section 17(a)(1) of the Securities Act (see Chapter 3.B); and Section 14(e) of the Exchange Act (see Chapter 5.B). When enforcement of these provisions is criminal, is scienter subsumed under "willfully"? Or does scienter have its own independent significance? Cf. *United States v. Chestman*, 903 F.2d 75, 88 (2d Cir. 1990) (Carman, J., concurring in part and dissenting in part) (insisting on the need to instruct the jury on both willfulness and scienter in prosecution under § 14(e) and Rule 14e-3), vac. on other grds, 947 F.2d 551 (2d Cir. 1991).

4. ***Willfully vs. Recklessly.*** Note that *Tarallo* equated the term "willfully" in Section 32(a) with "recklessly." But "recklessly" satisfies the scienter requirement in civil actions under Section 10(b) of the Exchange Act and Rule 10b-5, Section 17(a)(1) of the Securities Act, and Section 14(e) of the Exchange Act. See Chapter 2.D, 3.B, and 5.B. Thus, *Tarallo* seems to conflate the state of mind requirement for criminal actions with that of civil actions. Is

---

might be read as contrary to our holding here. In context, however, the Eighth Circuit's statement is consistent with our holding that the "willful" requirement of § 32 does not preclude a conviction arising out of recklessness. The Eighth Circuit held, as we do, that § 32 "simply requires the intentional doing of the wrongful acts-no knowledge of the rule or regulation is required." Id. Given that definition of "willful," the Eighth Circuit's formulation appears to be consistent with the view that a defendant could "willfully" violate § 32 by willfully acting with reckless indifference to the truth of statements made in the course of the fraud. We therefore do not believe that our continued adherence to *Farris* creates a circuit split on this question.

it important that these requirements be different? Cf. *United States v. Stewart*, 305 F. Supp. 2d 368, 371 (S.D.N.Y. 2004) (deeming it unnecessary to address the government's argument that civil and criminal actions under Rule 10b-5 have identical state of mind requirements).

To be sure, the term "recklessly" could be defined one way in civil actions and another in criminal actions. Cf. *Safeco Ins. Co. of Am. v. Burr*, 551 U.S. 47, 68 n.18 (2007) (noting in dictum in action under the Fair Credit Reporting Act that "[u]nlike civil recklessness, criminal recklessness *** requires subjective knowledge on the part of the offender"). Would there be drawbacks to erecting multiple definitions of "recklessness" in the securities law context? Is there any reason to suppose that the *Tarallo* court contemplated such multiple definitions?

*5. **Willfully vs. Knowingly.*** Some courts have insisted that the terms "willfully" and "knowingly" in Section 32(a) do not mean the same thing. See, e.g., *United States v. Lake*, 472 F.3d 1247, 1266 (10th Cir. 2007) ("Although it may be unclear what a "knowing" requirement adds to the willfulness required by § [32(a)] ***, there is little doubt that Congress has thought it adds something"); *United States v. Dixon*, 536 F.2d 1388, 1396 & n.7 (2d Cir. 1976). On the other hand, the authors of the leading securities law treatise regard "knowingly" as "redundant" of "willfully." 10 Louis Loss & Joel Seligman, Securities Regulation 4807 (3d ed. rev. 2005). Which view do you find more persuasive? Which view (if either) receives support from *Tarallo*?

*6. **Different Definitions For Different Securities Crimes?*** Should courts define "willfully" differently depending upon the nature of the securities crime involved? Consider the relevance of *Ratzlaf v. United States*, 510 U.S. 135 (1994). At issue in *Ratzlaf* was whether to affirm a conviction for "willfully" violating the antistructuring provision of the Currency and Foreign Transactions Reporting Act (CFTRA) without proof that the defendant knew his conduct was illegal. Like the Securities Act and the Exchange Act, CFTRA sets forth a willfulness requirement in one provision (Section 5322) that is a prerequisite to criminal liability for violations of other provisions. To determine how to define "willfully" for purposes of the crime of antistructuring, the Court found relevant judicial definitions of "willfully" that had been used in connection with other CFTRA crimes. See id. at 141-42. The Court explained that "willfully" had to have the same meaning regardless of which crime was involved:

> A term appearing in several places in a statutory text is generally read the same way each time it appears. We have even stronger cause to construe a *single* formulation *** the same way each time it is called into play. See *United States v. Aversa*, 984 F.2d 493, 498 (CA1 1993) (en banc) ("Ascribing various meanings to a single iteration of [§ 5322(a)'s willfulness requirement]—reading the word differently for each code section to which it applies—would open Pandora's jar. If courts can render meaning so malleable, the usefulness of a single penalty provision for a group of related code sections will be eviscerated and ... almost any code section that references a group of other code sections would become susceptible to individuated interpretation.")

Id. at 143. Does *Ratzlaf* preclude different definitions of "willfully" for different securities crimes? Cf. *United States v. Kaiser*, 609 F.3d 556, 569 (2d Cir. 2010) (noting, but taking no position on, the apparent support for "a higher standard for willfulness in insider trading cases" in *United States v. Cassese*, 428 F.3d 92

(2d Cir. 2005)).

*7. **Emasculating the "No Knowledge" Clause.*** Lower courts have long construed Section 32(a)'s "no knowledge" clause in a fashion that blunts its usefulness for criminal defendants. Consider the following explanation for why the clause is inapplicable to defendants convicted of violating Rule 10b-5:

> [The no knowledge clause] was adopted to ensure that no person could be imprisoned for the violation of a standard contained in a rule of which he had no knowledge. It is equally clear, however, that Congress intended to charge every man with knowledge of the standards prescribed in the securities acts themselves. It would frustrate the intent of Congress to permit a person whose conduct is expressly prohibited by statute to attempt to prove no knowledge of a parallel rule provision. Allowing these defendants to invoke the "no knowledge" clause would have precisely this effect. The conduct here admitted by defendants is prohibited by two provisions of the securities acts. Section 17(a) of the Securities Act of 1933 prohibits securities fraud in language almost identical with the language of Rule 10b-5. Moreover, the fraudulent activity to which defendants have pled guilty, price manipulation, is expressly prohibited by § 9(a)(2) of the 1934 Act. ***

United States v. Lilley, 291 F. Supp. 989, 992-93 (S.D. Tex. 1968). Cf. *United States v. Knueppel*, 293 F. Supp. 2d 199, 202-03 & n.1 (E.D.N.Y. 2003) (noting that because "Section 10(b) is virtually tracked in the language of Rule 10b-5," it is "difficult to imagine a case in which the 'no knowledge' provision could be applicable to a criminal Rule 10b-5 violation"). But cf. *United States v. Behrens*, 644 F.3d 754, 757 (8th Cir. 2011) (rejecting *Lilley* and *Knueppel* because of their reliance on legislative history despite the "unambiguous" language of the no knowledge clause and remanding the case to allow the defendant to invoke the clause). Is *Lilley's* analysis persuasive? If not, why do you suppose it has largely carried the day? In this connection, one commentator has observed that courts may resist regarding the "no knowledge" clause "as an expression of an important governmental policy, at least in a system in which the rules are regularly published and available under the Federal Register Act." Joseph E. Murphy, The Duty of the Government to Make the Law Known, 51 Fordham L. Rev. 255, 281 n. 180 (1982).

In *United States v. O'Hagan,* 521 U.S. 642, 665-66 (1997), the Supreme Court described the "no knowledge" clause as a "sturdy safeguard[ ]" for criminal defendants. Was this empty rhetoric or did the Court have an interpretation of the clause in mind different from that endorsed by *Lilley* and *Knueppel*?

*8. **The Exchange Act vs. Securities Act.*** What are the differences between Section 32(a) and its counterpart in the Securities Act, Section 24? Are these differences that make a difference for purposes of defining "willfully" in Section 24? Cf *United States v. Brown,* 578 F.2d 1280, 1284 (9th Cir. 1978) (noting that the absence of a "no knowledge" clause in Section 24 increases the difficulty of interpreting that Section). Can the definition of "willfully" in Section 32(a) simply be imported into Section 24? Does *Tarrallo* shed any light (or heat) on this question?

*9. **Playing Ostrich.*** Sometimes a defendant maintains that he lacked knowledge of the underlying facts that would have been necessary to make his conduct "willful." Under such circumstances, the government is entitled to an "ostrich" instruction instead of, or, if it wishes, in addition to, an "actual knowledge" instruction. See *United States v. Ferguson*__ F.3d __, 2011 WL 3251464 at * 10 (2d Cir. 2011). An ostrich instruction (also known as "willful blindness," "conscious avoidance," or "deliberate ignorance") is one that:

> essentially '"allows the jury to impute knowledge to [the defendant] of what should be obvious to him, if it [finds], beyond a reasonable doubt, a conscious purpose to avoid enlightenment."'*United States v. Barnhart,* 979 F.2d 647, 651 (8th Cir.1992) (quoting *United States v. Zimmerman,* 832 F.2d 454, 458 (8th Cir.1987) (per curiam)). We are cognizant of the risk, however, that a deliberate ignorance instruction might lead the jury to employ a negligence standard and convict a defendant on the impermissible ground that he should have known an illegal act was taking place. *** Thus, *** [w]hile a district court should not give the deliberate ignorance instruction when the evidence points *solely* to the defendant's actual knowledge of the facts in question, the instruction is particularly appropriate when the defendant denies any knowledge of a criminal scheme despite strong evidence to the contrary.

United States v. King, 351 F.3d 859, 866-67 (8th Cir. 2003).

Does the use of the ostrich instruction risk criminalizing conduct that ought to fall outside the purview of the criminal law?

PROBLEM 11-1

Jack has been tried and convicted for violating Rule 10b-5. Consider whether his conviction is likely to be affirmed if it is based on each of the following:

a. Jack intentionally committed the acts constituting the violation of Rule 10b-5.

b. Jack intentionally committed the acts constituting the violation of Rule 10b-5 and knew that his conduct was illegal.

c. Jack intentionally committed the acts constituting the violation of Rule 10b-5 but believed his conduct not to be wrongful. A reasonable person in his position, however, would have known the conduct was wrongful. There is no evidence one way or the other concerning whether he knew that his conduct was illegal.

2. The Violations That Give Rise to Criminal Liability

As noted, the Securities Act and the Exchange Act authorize criminal liability for "willful" violations of their substantive provisions. Because these substantive provisions also give rise to civil liability, much of the jurisprudence in civil actions also applies in criminal actions. See, e.g., *United States v. O'Hagan*, 521 U.S. 642 (1997) (misappropriation theory); *United States v. Berger*, 473 F.3d 1080, 1098-99 (9th Cir. 2007) (materiality standard). Not germane in criminal actions, however, are the standing requirements that private plaintiffs must meet. See, e.g., *United States v. O'Hagan,* supra, 521 U.S. at 664-65 (holding Rule 10b-5's purchaser-seller requirement inapplicable in a criminal action). Likewise not germane in criminal actions is the need for "identification of or reliance by a particular victim." *United States v. Haddy,* 134 F.3d 542, 551 (3d Cir. 1998).

Not infrequently, criminal actions provide the context in which new substantive securities law may be made. See, e.g., *United States v. Chiarella*, 445 U.S. 222 (1980) (government favors broad view of the duty to abstain or disclose to hold "outsider" liable for insider trading); *Carpenter v. United States*, 484 U.S. 19 (1987) (government urges acceptance of the misappropriation theory of insider trading); *United States v. O'Hagan*, 521 U.S. 642 (1997) (same); *United States v. Bingham*, 992 F.2d 975, 976 (9th Cir. 1993) (government supports adoption of two per se rules of materiality);*United States v. Chestman*, 947 F.2d 551, 569 (2d Cir. 1991) (government favors liberal definition of the trust relationship that is key to the misappropriation theory); *United States v. Holtzclaw*, 950 F. Supp. 306, 1313-14 (S.D. W. Va. 1997) (government favors definition of the term "investment contract" as to which the circuits are divided), aff'd in part, vacated in part on other grounds, 131 F.3d 137 (4th Cir. 1997). In such cases, the provision at issue may present an ambiguity that cannot be resolved by recourse to statutory language or legislative history. Should the court simply select the interpretation that best furthers the underlying statutory policies (whether of the Securities Act or Exchange Act in general or the provision in particular)? Or is it necessary to apply strict construction (sometimes called the rule of lenity) in recognition of the prison sentence and opprobrium that the defendant may face if convicted? The Supreme Court has not been altogether consistent in its answer.

In *United States v. Naftalin,* 441 U.S. 768 (1979), the Court came down on the side of strict construction. At issue in *Naftalin* was whether Section 17(a)(1) of the Securities Act prohibits fraud against brokers as well as fraud against investors. After holding the Section to encompass fraud against brokers, the Court announced that it would have applied strict construction had the statutory language been ambiguous:

> This is a criminal case, and we have long held that " 'ambiguity concerning the ambit of criminal statutes should be resolved in favor of lenity,' " *United States v. Culbert,* 435 U.S. 371, 379 (1978), quoting *Rewis v. United States,* 401 U.S. 808, 812 (1971), and that a defendant may not " 'be subjected to a penalty unless the words of the statute plainly impose it.' " *United States v. Campos-Serrano,* 404 U.S., 293, 297 (1971), quoting *Keppel v. Tiffin Savings Bank,* 197 U.S. 356, 362 (1905). In this case, however, the words of the statute do "plainly impose it."

Id. at 778-79. Cf. *United States v. Hunt*, 2006 WL 2613754 at *8 (S.D.N.Y. 2006) (refusing to apply rule of lenity because of lack of statutory ambiguity).

Yet in *United States v. O'Hagan,* 521 U.S. 642 (1997), the Court eschewed strict construction under circumstances in which *Naftalin* would arguably have required it. Recall that in *O'Hagan,* which your read in Chapter 7, the Court concluded that Section 10(b) and Rule 10b-5 embraced the misappropriation theory of insider trading and upheld a conviction premised on this theory. The Court did not claim that the misappropriation theory followed from statutory language or legislative history. Rather, it adopted the theory based on an analysis of the Exchange Act's policies. See id. at 658-59. Justice Scalia dissented because of the Court's failure to apply the rule of lenity and resolve the ambiguity in the defendant's favor. See id. at 679. See generally Richard W. Painter et al., Don't Ask, Just Tell: Insider Trading After *United*

States v. O'Hagan, 84 Va. L. Rev. 153, 196-99 (1998) (arguing that the Court should have applied the rule of lenity).

To cure fair warning problems that might arise from its approach to statutory construction, the *O'Hagan* Court relied on the fact that a defendant must act "willfully" in order to be convicted:

> To establish a criminal violation of Rule 10b-5, the Government must prove that a person "willfully" violated the provision. *** [T]he statute's "requirement of the presence of culpable intent as a necessary element of the offense does much to destroy any force in the argument that application of the [statute]" in circumstances such as O'Hagan's is unjust. *Boyce Motor Lines, Inc. v. United States,* 342 U.S. 337, 342 (1952).

521 U.S. at 665-66. See *United States v. Wenger*, 427 F.3d 840, 851-52 (10th Cir. 2005) (relying on the willfulness requirement to provide fair warning to defendant regarding conduct prohibited by Section 17(b) of the Securities Act).

NOTES AND QUESTIONS

1. ***"Willfully" Revisited.*** The *O'Hagan* Court did not specify the definition of "willfully" that would suffice to cure fair warning problems. According to Professor Anthony Amsterdam, such a definition would require "not only a knowing what is done but a knowing that what is done is unlawful or, at least, so wrong that it is probably unlawful." Anthony G. Amsterdam, Note, The Void for Vagueness Doctrine in the Supreme Court, 109 U. Pa. L. Rev. 67, 87 n. 98 (1960). Is the definition of "willfully" offered by *Tarallo* consistent or inconsistent?

In arriving at the definition of "willfully," does the rule of lenity have a role to play?

2. ***Lenity's Scope.*** If the rule of lenity applies in criminal securities actions, the implications for civil actions are not self-evident. Can a provision interpreted strictly in a criminal action receive a more liberal interpretation in a later civil action? See *United States v. Chestman,* 947 F.2d 551, 567-70 (2d Cir. 1991) (rejecting liberal interpretation of trust relationship under misappropriation theory in a criminal action, but suggesting that such an interpretation might apply in a civil action); *United States v. Rudi,* 927 F. Supp. 686, 688 (S.D.N.Y. 1996) (rejecting liberal interpretation of Municipal Securities Rulemaking Board provision in a criminal action but suggesting that such an interpretation might apply in a civil action).

Alternatively, perhaps the rule of lenity is as applicable in a civil action as it is in a criminal action in order to insure uniformity of interpretation. See *SEC v. Burns,* 614 F. Supp. 1360, 1367 (S.D. Cal. 1985) (suggesting the need to read Rule 10b-6 strictly in a civil action if strict construction would apply in a criminal action), aff'd, 816 F.2d 471 (9th Cir. 1987); *Drasner v. Thomson McKinnon Sec., Inc.*, 433 F. Supp. 485, 499 (S.D.N.Y. 1977) (insisting on the need to read Regulation T of the Exchange Act the same way in civil and criminal actions). For differing views on these questions, see Margaret V. Sachs, Harmonizing Civil and Criminal Enforcement of Federal Regulatory Statutes: The Case of the Securities Exchange Act of 1934, 2001 U. Ill. L. Rev. 1025; Lawrence M. Solan, Statutory Inflation and Institutional Choice, 44 Wm. & Mary L. Rev. 2209 (2003); Jonathan Marx, Note, How to Construe A Hybrid

Statute, 93 Va. L. Rev. 235 (2007).

*3. **Aiding and Abetting and Conspiracy.*** The DOJ has authority to prosecute the aiding and abetting of Securities Act and Exchange Act crimes pursuant to 18 U.S.C. § 2:

> Whoever commits an offense against the United States or aids, abets, counsels, commands, induces or procures its commission, is punishable as a principal.

18 U.S.C. § 2(a). See, e.g., *United States v. Faulkenberry,* 614 F.3d 573, 583-84 (6th Cir. 2010). Moreover, the DOJ can also charge defendants with conspiracy to commit a securities crime pursuant to 18 U.S.C. § 371:

> If two or more persons conspire either to commit any offense against the United States, or to defraud the United States, or any agency thereof in any manner for any purpose, and one or more of such persons do any act to effect the object of the conspiracy, each shall be fined under this title or imprisoned not more than five years, or both. ***

See, e.g., *United States v. Laurienti,* 611 F.3d 530 (9th Cir. 2010). In the next section of this Chapter, we will contrast this provision with the conspiracy provision enacted as part of the SOX.

*4. **Statute of Limitations.*** The Securities Act and the Exchange Act do not contain a special statute of limitations for criminal actions. Therefore, the general five year federal criminal limitations period set forth in 18 U.S.C. § 3282 controls. See, e.g., *United States v. Flood,* 635 F.3d 1255, 1258 (10th Cir. 2011).

PROBLEM 11-2

Recall *United States v. Tarallo,* which you read earlier in this Chapter in connection with the meaning of "willfully." There the defendants were charged with inducing investors to purchase securities in fictitious companies. Assume that the defendants had moved to dismiss the indictment on the ground that Section 10(b) and Rule 10b-5 do not apply to fictional companies. Their argument is that the text of the statute and the Rule do not mention such companies and the legislative history is likewise silent (which is true). Should the court grant the motion? If it does, does the decision constitute binding precedent in a later civil action?

B. THE SARBANES-OXLEY ACT

The SOX creates several new crimes (listed below), the first two of which will occupy our attention:

> *(i) a new crime of securities fraud.* Section 807 of the SOX, enacted as 18 U.S.C. § 1348;
>
> *(ii) a new crime involving false certification of financial reports.* Section 906 of the SOX, enacted as 18 U.S.C. § 1350;
>
> *(iii) several new crimes involving record tampering.* Section 802 of the SOX creates two crimes, one entitled "destruction, alteration, or falsification of records in federal investigations and bankruptcy," enacted as 18 U.S.C. § 1519, and the other entitled "destruction of corporate audit records," enacted as 18 U.S.C. § 1520. In addition,

Section 1102 of the SOX creates a crime entitled "tampering with a record or otherwise impeding an official proceeding," enacted as 18 U.S.C. § 1512(c).

Note also that Section 902 of the SOX provides that "[a]ny person who attempts or conspires to commit any offense under this chapter shall be subject to the same penalties as those prescribed for the offense, the commission of which was the object of the attempt or conspiracy." 18 U.S.C. § 1349. How does this provision compare with 18 U.S.C. § 371, the conspiracy provision set forth in Note 3 just before Problem 11-2. What is the relationship between these two provisions?

1. The New Crime of Securities Fraud

Section 807 of the SOX creates a new fraud crime involving the securities of publicly traded companies. Enacted as 18 U.S.C. § 1348, it reads as follows:

Section 1348. Securities Fraud

Whoever knowingly executes, or attempts to execute, a scheme or artifice—

(1) to defraud any person in connection with any security of an issuer with a class of securities registered under section 12 of the Securities Exchange Act of 1934 or that is required to file reports under section 15(d) of the Securities Exchange Act of 1934; or

(2) to obtain, by means of false or fraudulent pretenses, representations, or promises, any money or property in connection with the purchase or sale of any security of an issuer with a class of securities registered under section 12 of the Securities Exchange Act of 1934 or that is required to file reports under section 15(d) of the Securities Exchange Act of 1934;

shall be fined under this title, or imprisoned not more than 25 years, or both.

18 U.S.C. § 1348.

The next decision involves a defendant's challenge to an indictment under Section 1348.

UNITED STATES v. MAHAFFY

2006 WL 2224518 (E.D.N.Y. 2006)

I. LEO GLASSER, SENIOR DISTRICT JUDGE:

INTRODUCTION

In this prosecution, defendants Kenneth E. Mahaffy, Jr. ("Mahaffy"), Timothy J. O'Connell ("O'Connell"), David G. Ghysels, Jr. ("Ghysels"), Robert F. Malin ("Malin"), Linus Nwaigwe ("Nwaigwe"), Michael A. Picone ("Picone"), and Keevin H. Leonard ("Leonard"), have been charged in an Indictment alleging securities fraud offenses pursuant to 18 U.S.C. §§ 1348 and 1349; and conspiracy to violate and violation of the Travel Act. *** Before the Court are defendants' motions to dismiss for insufficiency of the Indictment and lack of venue.

BACKGROUND ALLEGATIONS

The charges in this case stem from an alleged operation in which day trading defendants made payments to defendant stockbrokers for access to non-public information. The non-public information concerned pending orders, from institutional clients of the brokerage firms, for the purchase or sale of large blocks of securities. The day trading defendants, and others, used that information to purchase or sell the subject securities prior to the brokerage firms' execution of their clients' orders. The Indictment describes this operation as a "front-running" scheme, which:

> harms a brokerage firm's customers because it allows the stock trader to take advantage of limited opportunities to purchase and sell the same securities in which the firm's customers are interested before the customers are able to do so. As a result, the firm's customers may not obtain as favorable a price as they would have absent the front-running. (Id., ¶ 15).

I. The Defendants and Other Relevant Persons

*** The A.B. Watley Group ("Watley"), which operated primarily as a day trading firm, was a broker-dealer of securities registered with the United States Securities and Exchange Commission ("SEC") and the National Association of Securities Dealers ("NASD") ***.

Defendant Robert F. Malin was Vice-Chairman of the Board of Directors and President of Watley. He worked at Watley's principal office, managed Watley's business activities and supervised its day traders. Defendant Linus Nwaigwe was Watley's Director of Compliance, responsible for ensuring that Watley's employees complied with federal securities laws and followed SEC rules and regulations. In December 2002, Defendant Michael Picone was Chief Operating Officer of Watley. In August 2003, Picone entered into a consulting agreement with Watley. Between August 2003 and July 2005, Picone provided various financial and accounting services to Watley pursuant to this agreement. Defendant Keevin Leonard managed, supervised and trained Watley's day traders. He was also licensed by the NASD to act as a stockbroker and a General Securities Principal.

Millennium Brokerage, LLC ("Millennium") was a broker-dealer of securities registered with the SEC and NASD , and maintained its principal office in Woodcliff, New Jersey. *** Millennium was a day trading firm. In March, 2003, a group of former Watley day traders began working at Millennium's Park Avenue branch.

E*Trade Professional Trading, LLC ("E*Trade") was also a registered broker-dealer ***. In October 2003, a group of former Watley traders began day trading on behalf of a hedge fund called Ellis Island Trading ("Ellis Island") ***. In December 2003, the same group of day traders terminated their relationship and became employed at E*Trade's principal office. The day traders continued to be employed at E*Trade until at least February 2004.

*** As stockbrokers at Merrill Lynch, Citigroup and Lehman (collectively, the "Brokerage Firms"), Mahaffy, O'Connell, and Coughlin each owed fiduciary and other duties of trust and confidentiality to their respective Brokerage Firms and the clients of their respective firms.

II. The "Front-Running" Scheme

According to the Indictment, between January 2002 and February 2004, Mahaffy, O'Connell, Ghysels, Malin, Nwaigwe, Picone and Leonard, with others, participated in a fraudulent "front-running" scheme. Stockbrokers Mahaffy, O'Connell and Ghysels, in violation of their fiduciary and other duties of trust and confidence owed to their employers and their Brokerage Firms' clients, provided day traders at Watley, Millennium, Ellis Island and E*Trade (the "Day Traders") with customer order information by permitting the Day Traders to secretly listen to their Brokerage Firms' internal speaker systems known as "squawk boxes." The information broadcast through the squawk boxes included material, non-public information concerning large orders to purchase and sell securities that had been placed with the Brokerage Firms by their institutional clients. The large orders involved quantities of securities that were sufficiently large that the transactions could be expected to influence the market price for the securities in question.

The Day Traders then used the information disseminated through the squawk boxes to purchase and sell those securities prior to the Brokerage Firms' execution of their clients' orders.*** The Watley Day traders engaged in this illegal trading activity at the direction and under the supervision of Malin, Nwaigwe, Picone, and Leonard.

In exchange for access to the Brokerage Firms' squawk boxes, the Day Traders paid bribes in the form of cash, commissions and other things of value to Mahaffy, O'Connell and Ghysels.***

In the fall of 2003, Malin and Picone tried to find new sources of squawk box access for A.B. Watley. Between September 2003 and February 2004, Malin, Picone and others agreed to pay secret bribes to Coughlin in exchange for access to Merrill Lynch's squawk box. During this period, Malin and Picone caused a Watley Day Trader to deliver cash bribes to Coughlin of approximately $1,000 per month. They provided the trader with the cash to make the bribe payments by causing Watley to issue reimbursement checks to the trader for bogus business expenses.***

DISCUSSION

*** Defendants move to dismiss Counts One through Twenty-One of the indictment, for conspiracy to violate and the substantive violation of 18 U.S.C. § 1348, on the basis that the Indictment does not plead facts that, if proven true, would substantiate a finding that the statute has been violated and a crime has been committed. ***

The Court has identified no previous convictions under 18 U.S.C. § 1348. However, because the text and legislative history of 18 U.S.C. § 1348 clearly establish that it was modeled on the mail and wire fraud statutes, it is useful to be guided by the numerous and well-established precedents on those statutes in construing this statute. As a threshold matter, the government clearly need only prove a violation of subsection (1) or subsection (2), but not both, for there to be a violation of Section 1348.

A violation of section 1348(1) requires proof of three elements: (1) fraudulent intent (2) a scheme or artifice to defraud and (3) a nexus with a security.

A. Satisfying the requirement of "in connection" with a security

Defendants argue that the Indictment is insufficient because it fails to allege that the defendants "intended to cause an economic loss *to any holder or putative holder* of the securities at issue ." (Malin Mem. Supp. at 9) (emphasis added). The statute, however, defines no such narrow range of prospective victims; it is sufficient that the Indictment alleges the defendants intended to defraud "*any* person *in connection with* any security." 18 U .S.C. § 1348(1) (emphasis added). It does not restrict, or even contemplate, the status of the victim; rather, it simply requires that the government prove that the scheme to defraud was designed "in connection" with a security. Stated another way, though not with the intention of identifying the outer boundary of the statute's application, the requirement that the scheme be "in connection" with a security is satisfied where as a result of the scheme, the defendants either benefitted, or attempted to benefit, from trading in securities. Cf. *United States v. O'Hagan*, 521 U.S. 642 (1997) (holding defendant had committed fraud "in connection with" a securities transaction when he misappropriated confidential information for trading purposes). This broad construction is consistent with the report of Senator Leahy, the primary author of the statute, that the act "would create a new ... felony for securities fraud-a more general and less technical provision comparable to the bank fraud and health care fraud statutes in Title 18." SAROX-LH 3, 2002 WL 32054437 (A & PSAROX).

A broad interpretation of who might be a victim under the statute is also consistent with precedent interpreting 18 U.S.C. § 1347, the health care fraud statute. In *United States v. Lucien*, 347 F.3d 45 (2d Cir.2003), the Court of Appeals declined to adopt the defendant's narrow construction that the statute was intended to apply only to health care professionals. *** Similarly, the broad language of § 1348 shows that the intent of Congress was not only to protect the holders of securities, but to prohibit all forms of fraudulent conduct associated with securities, regardless of who the conduct affects.

B. Whether a scheme or artifice to defraud has been alleged

The second element of a § 1348(1) violation is a scheme or artifice to defraud. 18 U.S.C. § 1346 provides that "[f]or the purposes of this chapter, the term 'scheme or artifice to defraud' includes a scheme or artifice to deprive another of the intangible right of honest services." Though the Indictment does not specifically allege a deprivation of the intangible right of honest services, it need not for the Court to apply § 1346, because this section only provides a legal definition of criminal activity already encompassed and charged by the language tracking § 1348, that is, "a scheme or artifice to defraud."

The Court of Appeals has held that the deprivation of the intangible right of honest services has occurred, and provides the basis for a mail fraud conviction, where the defendants:

> use the mails or wires to enable an officer or employee of a private entity (or a person in a relationship that gives rise to a duty of loyalty comparable to that owed by employees to employers) purporting to act for and in the interests of his or her employer (or of the person to whom the duty of loyalty is owed) secretly to act in his or her or the defendant's own interests instead, accompanied by a material misrepresentation made or omission of information disclosed to the employer.

United States v. Rybicki, 354 F.3d 124, 127 (2d Cir.2003) (en banc). In *Rybicki*, the defendants, personal injury attorneys, were convicted of conspiracy and a mail and wire fraud in connection with payments to insurance adjusters that were intended to settle personal injury claims on favorable terms to their clients. To apply *Rybicki*'s holding to a charge under 18 U.S.C. § 1348, it is necessary only to substitute "in connection with a security" for "use the mails or wire to."

*** *Rybicki* requires a "material" misrepresentation or omission, a standard that is broader than the "reasonably foreseeable harm" standard adopted in other circuits. "Neither [of the standards]," however, "requires an actual economic loss nor an intent to economically harm the employer." Id. "[T]he reasonably foreseeable harm test is met whenever, at the time of the scheme to defraud, the employee could foresee that the scheme potentially might be detrimental to the employer's economic well-being." *Coffey*, 361 F.Supp.2d at 117. The materiality test only requires that the misrepresentation or omission "would naturally tend to lead or is capable of leading a reasonable employer to change its conduct." *Rybicki*, 354 F.3d at 145. Thus, " 'honest services' fraud is sufficiently pleaded where [the Indictment] alleges a perhaps unquantifiable harm inflicted on the defrauded entities which may, but does not necessarily result in, direct economic harm. Potential harm is the only prerequisite." *Coffey*, 361 F.Supp.2d at 118. This statement of the law is a conservative one, applying the statute only where potential economic harm may result. The materiality test adopted in *Rybicki*, requiring only that the omission would tend to lead a reasonable employer to change its conduct, does not even require that potential economic harm would result, but only that the employer would change its conduct in response. In any event, the alleged conduct in this case satisfies both standards, as the Brokerage Firms' reputations would likely be damaged, thus leading to economic harm, based on the exposure of its brokers' dual-allegiances. ***

The parties have discussed at length whether the allegations in this case meet the formal elements of a traditional "front running" scheme. *** Whether or not a classic "front-running" scheme has been alleged, however, is immaterial, as front-running is but one of the "loopholes in statutes prohibiting specific frauds" that the "mail and wire frauds have often been used to plug." *[[United States v] Dial,* [757 F.2d 163,169 (7th Cir. 1985)]. *** The essential fraud alleged by the Indictment is not a traditional "front-running" scheme *** but the misappropriation of confidential information by the brokers and the failure to disclose to their employers that they were selling access to that information. Thereby, the Brokerage Firms were allegedly defrauded of confidential information, and both the Brokerage Firms and the firms' institutional clients were defrauded of the intangible right of honest services.

C. The requirement of fraudulent intent

Though the text of the statute does not explicitly require the intentional mens rea, precedent compels this Court to read into 18 U .S.C. § 1348 the well-established requirement of fraudulent intent, which is requisite to a conviction under the other federal fraud statutes. In *Chandler*, the Court of Appeals interpreted the identical mens rea language of 18 U.S.C. § 1344. The court held, without noting the absence of an explicit "intent" or "willfulness" requirement from the text of the statute, that to establish a violation, the

Government must prove "the defendant engaged in or attempted to engage in a pattern or course of conduct designed to deceive ... with the *intent to victimize* the institution by exposing it to actual or potential loss." *Chandler*, 98 F.3d at 715 (emphasis in original). The fraudulent intent requirement is also implied in the securities fraud statute, which addresses similar kinds of conduct and offenses. Fraudulent intent typically requires a showing of "intent to deceive and intent to cause actual harm." *United States v. Stavroulakis*, 952 F.2d 686, 694 (2d Cir.1992). However, "when the "necessary result" of the actor's scheme is to injure others, fraudulent intent may be inferred from the scheme itself." *United States v. D'Amato*, 39 F.3d 1249, 1257 (2d Cir.1994). And where the scheme results in the deprivation of honest services, "actual or intended economic or pecuniary harm need not be established ... '[T]he only intent that need be proven ... is the intent to deprive another of the intangible right of honest services.' " *Rybicki*, 354 F.3d at 145 (quoting *United States v. Sancho*, 157 F.3d 918, 921 (2d Cir.1998)).

D. Application of the law

Against this understanding of the statute, the Court holds that the Indictment sufficiently states a crime under 18 U.S.C. § 1348(1). It is indisputable that the alleged scheme was in connection with securities. If the allegations in the Indictment are proven true, a jury could conclude that there existed a scheme either to deprive the brokerage firm and its clients of the intangible right to honest services, or the Brokerage Firms of their confidential information. Tracing the *Rybicki* language, one could conclude that the defendant stockbrokers, purportedly acting in the interest of the Brokerage Firms, secretly acted in their own and the day traders' best interest by surreptitiously selling access to the non-public institutional investors' orders, and made a material omission to their employer by failing to disclose their relationships with the day traders. *** Additionally, a jury could find that the institutional orders were confidential proprietary information of the Brokerage Firms, and the scheme to misappropriate that information fraudulent. As to intent, a jury could conclude that the deprivation of honest services or misappropriation of information was the necessary result of the scheme, and thus infer the requisite mens rea.

Finally, even though the Watley defendants may not have had a duty to the Brokerage Firms or the firms' clients, and thus might not have committed the substantive § 1348(1) offense directly, it is axiomatic "that a defendant who does not directly commit a substantive offense may nevertheless be liable if the commission of the offense by a co-conspirator in furtherance of the conspiracy was reasonably foreseeable to the defendant as a consequence of their criminal agreement." *Cephas v. Nash*, 328 F.3d 98, 101 n. 3 (2d Cir.2003). A jury could conclude that, having entered the conspiracy charged under § 1349, the day traders should reasonably have foreseen the brokers' substantive violation of § 1348(1). ***

Because the Indictment satisfactorily alleges a crime under 18 U.S.C. § 1348(1), and the government need only prove a violation of a single subsection to support a conviction under 18 U.S.C. § 1348, the Defendant's motion to dismiss for insufficiency of the Indictment must be denied.***

CONCLUSION

For the foregoing reasons, the Defendants' motions to dismiss for insufficiency of the Indictment are denied. The motions to dismiss for lack of venue are denied, though Defendants are granted leave to renew the venue motions at the completion of the case.

NOTES AND QUESTIONS

1. ***Publicly Traded Companies Only.*** Why do you suppose that Congress limited the new crime of securities fraud to the securities of issuers with a class of securities registered pursuant to Section 12 or those required to file reports under Section 15(d)? Was this a good idea?

2. ***Another "In Connection With" Requirement.*** How does the "in connection with" requirement of Section 1348 compare with that of Rule 10b-5? Would Rule 10b-5's version of the requirement have posed a problem for the government's prosecution of Mahaffy and his confederates?

3. ***Again the Question of Intent.*** Is Section 1348's intent requirement less demanding than the one imposed by Section 32(a) of the Exchange Act? Commentators sharply disagree with each other on this point. Compare Michael A. Perino, Enron's Legislative Aftermath: Some Reflections on the Deterrence Aspects of the Sarbanes-Oxley Act of 2002, 76 St. John's L. Rev. 671, 682 (2002) (noting that "[t]he real difficulty prosecutors have always had *** is proving criminal intent – something the new securities fraud statute does nothing to change") with Abbe D. Lowell & Kathryn C. Arnold, Corporate Crime After 2000: A New Law Enforcement Challenge or Deja Vu?, 40 Am. Crim. L. Rev. 219, 223 (2003) (noting the absence of the term "willfully" in Section 1348 and observing that this represents "a significant reduction in proof"). What appears to be the view of *Mahaffy* on this question?

4. ***Mails and Wires.*** Notice that in contrast to Section 10(b) and Rule 10b-5, Section 1348 does not have a jurisdictional means requirement. Does this give prosecutors an appreciable advantage? Was it likely to have been an advantage in *Mahaffy* in particular?

PROBLEM 11-3

Imdrone, Inc., is a drug company that had spent years fueling the market's interest in miraclex, a treatment for certain potent cancers. Optimism concerning the effectiveness of miraclex rested largely on a few small clinical trials. In 2001, Imdrone applied to the Food and Drug Administration for permission to market miraclex.

On December 20, 2001, an FDA official told the company that it had made its decision on the application and that the official announcement would come on December 28. On December 21, the Imdrone general counsel issued a company-wide blackout on trading in Imdrone stock.

Overcome by curiosity, Imdrone's president (Watson) telephoned a friend at the FDA on December 22. The friend told Watson that "things looked very bad" for miraclex. Watson thereupon called his broker that same day and directed her to sell his considerable block of Imdrone stock. She refused, citing the blackout on trading.

Can Watson be charged with violating Section 1348?

2. *The New Crime of Failing to Certify Financial Reports*

Section 906 of the SOX requires CEOs and CFOs of reporting companies to certify the periodic financial reports that their companies file with the SEC and in addition criminalizes the making of false certifications. Enacted as 18 U.S.C. § 1350, it reads as follows:

18 U.S.C. § 1350. Failure of corporate officers to certify financial reports

> (a) Certification of periodic financial reports.—Each periodic report containing financial statements filed by an issuer with the Securities Exchange Commission pursuant to section 13(a) or 15(d) of the Securities Exchange Act of 1934 shall be accompanied by a written statement by the chief executive officer and chief financial officer (or equivalent thereof) of the issuer.
>
> (b) Content.—The statement required under subsection (a) shall certify that the periodic report containing the financial statements fully complies with the requirements of section 13(a) or 15(d) of the Securities Exchange Act of 1934 and that information contained in the periodic report fairly presents, in all material respects, the financial condition and results of operations of the issuer.
>
> (c) Criminal penalties.—Whoever—
>
> > (1) certifies any statement as set forth in subsections (a) and (b) of this section knowing that the periodic report accompanying the statement does not comport with all the requirements set forth in this section shall be fined not more than $1,000,000 or imprisoned not more than 10 years, or both; or
> >
> > (2) willfully certifies any statement as set forth in subsections (a) and (b) of this section knowing that the periodic report accompanying the statement does not comport with all the requirements set forth in this section shall be fined not more than $5,000,000, or imprisoned not more than 20 years, or both.

18 U.S.C. § 1350.

The next decision involves a defendant's challenge to an indictment under Section 1350.

UNITED STATES v. SCRUSHY

2004 WL 2713262 (N.D. Ala. 2004)

KARON OWEN BOWDRE, DISTRICT JUDGE:

This cause is before the court on Defendant Scrushy's Motion to Dismiss Counts 27-29 of the Superseding Indictment. This motion challenges the constitutionality of the Sarbanes- Oxley Act of 2002. Neither the validity of the charges made nor the guilt or innocence of the defendant are placed in issue by this motion. Having considered the motion, the written submissions and oral arguments of counsel, and the applicable law, the court finds that this motion is due to be denied.

Defendant Richard M. Scrushy is the former chief executive officer of HealthSouth Corporation, a provider of various healthcare services to the public, doing business nationally and internationally. Mr. Scrushy was initially indicted under an eighty-five count indictment on October 29, 2003 . The Government subsequently filed a fifty-eight count Superseding Indictment on September 29, 2004, alleging various criminal offenses related to alleged wrongful inflation of HealthSouth stock values leading to the wrongful enrichment of Mr. Scrushy and others. The indictment includes three counts (27-29) for false certification under Section 906 of the Sarbanes-Oxley Act of 2002, and seeks penalties under 18 U.S.C.A. § 1350(c)(2).

Defendant's motion raises an issue of first impression: the constitutionality of Section 906 of the Sarbanes-Oxley Act, 18 U.S.C .A. § 1350. This provision establishes the duty of chief executive officers and chief financial officers of companies that issue publicly traded stocks to certify by written statement the accuracy of the company's periodic financial reports required under the Securities Exchange Act of 1934. The statute further defines the content of the certifications in 18 U.S.C.A. § 1350(b) and establishes the criminal penalties for violations in 18 U.S.C.A. § 1350(c). ***

The defendant contends that this section of Sarbanes-Oxley is so vague as to be unconstitutional on its face. The court disagrees for the reasons explained below.

In keeping with well-established law, the court must begin its analysis with a strong presumption in favor of the constitutionality of an act of Congress. *Parker v. Levy*, 417 U.S. 733 (1974); United States v. Harriss, 347 U.S. 612, 618 (1954). The court is ever mindful that the power to define federal crimes lies with Congress, not the courts. *United States v. Lanier*, 520 U.S. 259, 267 n. 6 (1997). ***

The United States Supreme Court has found that to avoid Constitutional infirmities "the void-for-vagueness doctrine requires that a penal statute must define the criminal offense with sufficient definiteness that ordinary people can understand what conduct is prohibited and in a manner that does not encourage arbitrary and discriminatory enforcement." *Kolender v. Lawson*, 461 U.S. 352, 358 (1983).

In addition to his general challenge of the statute for vagueness, the defendant more specifically challenges the terms "*fairly presents, in all material respects*," in subsection 1350(b), and "*willfully certifies*" in § 1350(c)(2). As discussed more fully below, the defendant argues that the terms "*fairly presents*" and "*in all material respects*" lack sufficient clarity of meaning to inform citizens of their responsibility under the law and, therefore, the statute fails to pass Constitutional muster. The defendant further argues that the term "*willfully certifies*" in itself fails to define an illegal act and, therefore, the statute must be stricken as unconstitutional. The court disagrees on both points.

A great deal of accumulated legal meaning and specific case law attach to these concepts. The Supreme Court has found that "where Congress borrows terms of art in which are accumulated the legal tradition and meaning of centuries of practice, it presumably knows and adopts the cluster of ideas that were attached to each borrowed word in the body of learning from which it was taken and the meaning its use will convey to the judicial mind unless otherwise instructed ." *Morissette v. United States*, 342 U.S. 246, 265 (1952).

Materiality and fair presentation are not static concepts that can be defined statutorily in a way that would encompass all possible applicable situations. The meanings of these concepts necessarily flow with the requirements of the particular statute, the conduct sought to be deterred, the circumstances of the defendant's conduct, and the defendant's conduct in relation to these factors. Accordingly, statutes are drawn with words that have legal history and meaning but that, in most instances, do not have quantitative certainty. As the Supreme Court has recognized in securities cases, "the determination [of materiality] requires delicate assessments of the inferences a 'reasonable shareholder' would draw from a given set of facts, and the significance of those inferences to him, and these assessments are peculiarly ones for the trier of facts." *TSC Industries, Inc. v. Northway, Inc.*, 426 U.S. 438, 449 (1976).

For something to be material in a legal sense, whether a word or a deed, it must be of a weight that would affect a reasonable person's decision or action within the relevant context. *TSC Industries*, 426 U.S. 438. Thus, we are all shielded from exposure to liability or criminal penalty for trivial statements or actions that would hold no sway in a reasonable person's decision-making process.***

Just as materiality is a well-established principle, the concept of "fairly presenting" information is not a novel concept in the business world or in the law. Auditors and accountants have long applied this phrase and been held to this principle regarding financial statements.[4]

Congress has used similar phrases in other statutes. For example, Congress has required by law that businesses "fully and fairly present the financial statements" of their ERISA governed pension plans. 29 U.S.C.A. § 1023(b)(1) (2004). In the Investment Company Act of 1940, Congress codified its declaration of policy regarding the national public interest and investor interest as being adversely affected if purchases were made without "explicit information, fairly presented concerning" the securities and the companies selling them. 15 U.S.C.A. § 80a-1(b)(2004).

Like the words *fairly* and *material*, the word *willful* has a long tradition in the law. In *Screws v. United States*, the Supreme Court provided a summary of the concept of criminal willfulness:

> "[W]illful" is a word "of many meanings, its construction often being influenced by its context." *Spies v. United States*, 317 U.S. 492, 497. At times, as the Court held in *United States v. Murdock*, 290 U.S. 389, 394, the word denotes an act which is intentional rather than accidental.. But "when used in a criminal statute it generally means an act done with a bad purpose." Id., p. 394. In that event *something more is required than the doing of the act proscribed by the statute.. An evil motive to accomplish that which the statute condemns becomes*

4. The American Institute of Certified Public Accountants § 312, "Audit Risk and Materiality in Conducting an Audit," as quoted by SEC Staff Accounting Bulletin: No. 99-Materiality (August 12, 1999), states: "The auditor should consider audit risk and materiality both in (a) planning and setting the scope for the audit and (b) evaluating whether the financial statements taken as a whole are fairly presented in all material respects in conformity with generally accepted accounting principles."

> *a constituent element of the crime. United States v. Murdock*, supra, p. 395. And that issue must be submitted to the jury under appropriate instructions. *United States v. Ragen*, 314 U.S. 513, 524.

Screws v. United States, 325 U.S. 91, 101 (1945) (plurality) (emphasis added).

Under 18 U.S.C.A. § 1350, each requirement for compliance and for imposition of criminal penalties for failure to comply is laid out step by step on the face of the statute. Subsection (a) requires a CEO to make a written statement to accompany the company's periodic financial report required by other Securities Exchange Act provisions. Subsection (b) defines the content of the statement, requiring the CEO certify that the report complies with the applicable Securities Exchange Act provisions *and* "fairly presents, in all material respects, the financial condition and results of operations of the issuer [company or corporation]." Subsection (c) provides the criminal penalties for violating the statute and describes the conduct required for conviction.

In the case *sub judice*, the penalty provision in subsection (c)(2) is at issue. Under its terms, a CEO must act willfully and with knowledge in contravention of the statute to be convicted. The CEO must willfully -that is volitionally, intentionally, and not by accident-make a written statement certifying the truth and accuracy of the periodic financial report describing "the financial condition and results of operations of the issuer." 18 U.S.C.A. § 1350(c)(2). This section further requires that, to be convicted of violating this subsection, the CEO must have *knowledge* that the periodic report he or she is willfully certifying does not meet the statute's requirements of fair representation of the company's financial condition and operations in all material respects. Thus, to be convicted, the CEO must *willfully certify* the accuracy of the periodic financial report *while knowing* it does not fairly state, in all material respects, the financial condition of the company, as required by 18 U.S.C.A. § 1350(c)(2). By these terms, the statute gives fair warning and defines the scienter required to be proven for conviction.

By the Government's own words in its brief in opposition to the initial motion and adopted in its present brief in opposition, the defendant's conduct "cannot be deemed criminal unless it meets the stringent scienter requirements of Section 1350(c)(2). He must not only know that the periodic report contains materially false information, he must falsely certify ... that the report is materially accurate, he must do so knowing that such a false certification is forbidden by law, and he must do so with the specific intent to violate the law" (doc. 169, p. 12). The court finds this statement to be a fair summary of the stringent level of proof the law requires and that the court will require the Government to meet at trial to have these counts submitted to the jury. Indeed, the Government acknowledges that it faces a heavy burden of proof on these allegations. Willfulness and knowledge are factual issues for proof at trial and are generally submitted to the jury.

Defendant further argues that *willfully certifies* as used in 18 U.S.C.A. § 1350(c)(2) does not define a criminal act because *willfully* modifies *certifies*, an inherently innocent act, and that the remainder of the statute does not save it from being unconstitutionally vague. *Willfully* does indeed modify *certifies* in this statute, but the defendant's legal conclusion does not follow from this grammatical fact.

Many criminal statutes use *willfully* to modify inherently innocent, even laudable, acts (e.g., aids, assists, counsels), but the phrases taken together with the remaining language in those statutes adequately define criminal acts and establish penalties.[7] Perhaps the most closely analogous statute to the provision of the Sarbanes Oxley Act *sub judice*, both grammatically and in describing the physical act and requisite state of mind, is the IRS fraud and false statement felony provision. It states: "Any person who ... *willfully makes and subscribes* any return, statement, or other document, which contains or is verified by a written declaration that is made under the penalties of perjury, and which he does not believe to be true and correct as to every material matter; or ... *[w]illfully aids or assists in, or procures, counsels, or advises* the preparation or presentation under, or in connection with any matter arising under the internal revenue laws, of a return affidavit, claim, or other document, which is fraudulent or is false as to any material matter...." 26 U.S.C § 7206(1), (2) (emphasis added) (the statute then continues to describe other violations and provide penalties). This IRS statute has stood and been enforced since 1954. Similarly, the use of *willfully* to modify *certifies* in section § 1350 of the Sarbanes Oxley Act in no way puts the provision's constitutionality in jeopardy.

Taking 18 U.S.C.A. § 1350 in its entirety, as the court must, the court finds 18 U.S.C.A. § 1350(c)(2) is both "sufficiently definite as to give a person of ordinary intelligence fair notice that his contemplated conduct is forbidden," and specific enough to prevent arbitrary or discriminatory enforcement under its terms. See *City of Chicago v. Morales*, 527 U.S. 41 (1999). The court further finds 18 U.S.C.A. § 1350(c)(2) imposes punishment "only for an act *knowingly done* with the purpose of doing that which the statute prohibits, [so the defendant] cannot be said to suffer from a lack of warning or knowledge that the act which he [allegedly did was] in violation of law." See, *Screws v. United States*, 325 U.S. 91, 102, (1945) (plurality) (emphasis added).

*** Fairness, materiality, and willfulness are fact intensive questions generally reserved for the jury. Whether the information contained in the periodic reports certified by Mr. Scrushy fairly presented, in all material respects, the financial condition and results of operations of HealthSouth are questions of fact for the jury and part of the Government's burden of proof in this case. If the jury finds that the reports did not fairly present, in all material respects, the financial condition and results of operations of HealthSouth, the jury must then determine whether Mr. Scrushy *willingly certified* these reports *knowing* that the reports did not comport with the statute's accuracy requirements. See, *United States v. Gaudin*, 515 U.S. 506 (1995); see, *TSC Industries*, 426 U.S. 438 (1976).

---

7. E.g., these felony statutes also use *willfully* as an adverb modifying inherently innocent acts: 14 U.S.C.A. § 88, uses willfully communicates in relation to giving a false distress signal; 15 U.S.C.A. § 1681q uses willfully obtains in relation to information gathered under false pretenses in violation of consumer protection laws; and 18 U.S.C.A. § 893 uses willfully advances in relation to financing extortionate credit transactions. These phrases, in and of themselves, removed from their context would not define a crime, but read in the context of their full provisions do define crimes in a way that has met Constitutional muster.

In accordance with this memorandum opinion, the court hereby denies Defendant Scrushy's Motion to Dismiss Counts 27-29 of the Superseding Indictment. ***

NOTES AND QUESTIONS

1. ***The Reemergence of "Willfully."*** Notice the two different crimes in Section 1350 – one for certification in subsection (c)(1) and the other for certification done "willfully" in subsection (c)(2). What is the difference between certifying and "willfully" certifying? Should the definition of "willfully" used in Section 32(a) of the Exchange Act be imported into Section 1350(c)(2)? What is the difference (if any) between "willfully" in Section 1350(c)(2) and "knowingly" in Section 1348?

2. ***"Willfully" and Mr. Schrushy.*** Mr. Schrushy was eventually tried and acquitted at least partly because the jury concluded that he had not acted "willfully." See Dana Hedgpeth & Dean Starkman, From the Start, Acquittal Seemed Right: Some Jurors in Schrushy Trial Say Skepticism of Prosecutor's Case was Constant, Wash. Post (June 30, 2005) at D3.

3. ***Operations vs. Financial Operations.*** Consider the reference in Section 1350(b) to the issuer's "financial condition and results of operations." Does "results of operations" refer to financial operations only? Should the rule of lenity be invoked to resolve it?

4. ***What's in a Title?*** Note that Section 1350 is entitled "failure of corporate officers to certify financial reports." Does this provision cover the CEO or CFO who fails altogether to certify a report?

5. ***Shareholders Beware.*** Recall the argument by Professors Butler and Ribstein, set forth earlier in this Chapter, that Section 1350 is likely to increase agency costs. Do you agree with them?

6. ***Corporate Criminal Liability in the Post-SOX World.*** Corporations are subject to criminal liability under the SOX, as they are under the Securities Act and the Exchange Act. But today corporations are less vulnerable to being indicted under these statutes, whereas corporate managers are more vulnerable. Professor Leonard Orland has described this phenomenon as follows:

> The corporation is now typically seen by the federal government not as the culprit in need of punishment, but as the facilitator/cooperator in the task of indicting and convicting culpable executives. To discharge its newly created law enforcement partnership with the federal government, the corporation routinely abandons attorney-client privilege and agrees not to contradict a detailed statement of culpability that often becomes the blueprint for prosecution of indicted executives.
>
> At the same time, in an era where the penal policy goal of rehabilitation has been abandoned in the prosecution of individuals, rehabilitation has been rehabilitated, sub silento, as a goal in corporate prosecution. The rehabilitated corporation adopts codes of ethics and compliance programs, reports to and may be managed by outside monitors, files detailed reports to the government, and cooperates with the Justice Department in the prosecution of former senior executives. In short, it demonstrates, on pain of prosecution for failure to do so, that it is indeed a "good corporate citizen."

> Whether or not this approach will be an enduring feature of the American criminal justice system remains to be seen.

Leonard Orland, The Transformation of Corporate Criminal Law, 1 Brook. J. Corp. Fin. & Com. L. 45, 84-85 (2006). For further discussion of these developments, see Harry First, Branch Office of the Prosecutor: The New Role of the Corporation in Business Crime Prosecutions, 89 N.C.L. Rev. 23 (2010).

C. THE MAIL AND WIRE FRAUD STATUTES

Enacted in 1872, the mail fraud statute is renowned for its versatility. Indeed, the mail fraud statute was used to prosecute securities violations prior to the enactment of the federal securities laws. See *United States v. Maze,* 414 U.S. 395, 406 (1974) (Burger, C.J., dissenting). In its current form it reads as follows:

> Whoever, having devised or intending to devise any scheme or artifice to defraud, or for obtaining money or property by means of false or fraudulent pretenses, representations, or promises, or to sell, dispose of, loan, exchange, alter, give away, distribute, supply, or furnish or procure for unlawful use any counterfeit or spurious coin, obligation, security, or other article, or anything represented to be or intimated or held out to be such counterfeit or spurious article, for the purpose of executing such scheme or artifice or attempting so to do, places in any post office or authorized depository for mail matter, any matter or thing whatever to be sent or delivered by the Postal Service, or deposits or causes to be deposited any matter or thing whatever to be sent or delivered by any private or commercial interstate carrier, or takes or receives therefrom, any such matter or thing, or knowingly causes to be delivered by mail or such carrier according to the direction thereon, or at the place at which it is directed to be delivered by the person to whom it is addressed, any such matter or thing, shall be fined under this title or imprisoned not more than 20 years, or both. If the violation affects a financial institution, such person shall be fined not more than $1,000,000 or imprisoned not more than 30 years, or both.

18 U.S.C. § 1341. For discussions of the evolution of the mail fraud statute, see John C. Coffee, Jr., The Metastasis of Mail Fraud: The Continuing Story of the Evolution of a White-Collar Crime, 21 Am. Crim. L. Rev. 1 (1983); Jed S. Rakoff, The Federal Mail Fraud Statute (Part I), 18 Duq. L. Rev. 771 (1980).

The wire fraud statute, enacted in 1952, currently reads as follows:

> Whoever, having devised or intending to devise any scheme or artifice to defraud, or for obtaining money or property by means of false or fraudulent pretenses, representations, or promises, transmits or causes to be transmitted by means of wire, radio, or television communication in interstate or foreign commerce, any writings, signs, signals, pictures, or sounds for the purpose of executing such scheme or artifice, shall be fined under this title or imprisoned not more than 20 years, or both. If the violation affects a financial institution, such person shall be fined not more than $1,000,000 or imprisoned not more than 30 years, or both.

18 U.S.C. § 1343. While wire fraud prosecutions were once less numerous than mail fraud prosecutions, the former have been growing substantially in the wake of the Internet.

The prison terms of up to twenty years authorized by the mail and wire fraud statutes result from an amendment to those statutes that was enacted as part of the SOX. Prior to the SOX, the mail and wire fraud statutes authorized imprisonment for up to five years.

The mail and wire fraud statutes are construed in pari materia. *Pasquantino v. United States*, 544 U.S. 349, 355 n.2 (2005). Conviction under either requires proof of three elements: (i) a scheme to defraud; (ii) the defendant's participation in the scheme with the intent to defraud; and (iii) the use of the mails or wires in furtherance of the scheme. See, e.g., *United States v. Faulkenberry,* 614 F.3d 573, 580-81 (6th Cir. 2010); *United States v. Radziszewski*, 474 F.3d 480, 484-85 (7th Cir. 2007). Courts have interpreted these elements liberally.

Thus, in the view of a number of courts, the intent requirement can be satisfied by recklessness. See, e.g., *United States v. Flood,* 501 F.3d 888, 897-98 (8th Cir. 2007); *United States v. Coyle,* 63 F.3d 1239,1243 (3d Cir. 1995). But see *United States v. Rajwani,* 476 F.3d 243, 247 (5th Cir. 2007) (requiring a "conscious knowing intent to defraud "). Does the text of the mail and wire fraud statutes explicitly impose an intent requirement? Even if the answer is no, there is a presumption of an intent requirement when liability is criminal. See *Posters 'N' Things, Ltd. v. United States,* 511 U.S. 513, 522-23 (1994); *United States v. United States Gypsum Co.,* 438 U.S. 422, 436-37 (1978).

Moreover, the use of the mails or wires does not have to be an "essential element" of the scheme but only "incident to an essential part of" it. *Pereira v. United States,* 347 U.S. 1, 8 (1954). See also *Schmuck v. United States,* 489 U.S. 705, 715 (1989) (noting that a mailing need not itself be fraudulent in order to provide a basis for prosecution). Indeed, the defendant need not herself have used the mails or wires so long as she has "knowledge that the use of the mails [or wires] will follow in the ordinary course of business, or where such use can reasonably be foreseen." *Pereira v. United States,* supra, 347 U.S. at 9.

The Supreme Court addressed the "scheme to defraud" element in the two decisions that follow. As you read them, be alert to interfaces with the federal securities laws.

CARPENTER v. UNITED STATES

484 U.S. 19 (1987)

JUSTICE BYRON R. WHITE:

Petitioners Kenneth Felis and R. Foster Winans were convicted of violating § 10(b) of the Securities Exchange Act of 1934 and Rule 10b-5. They were also found guilty of violating the federal mail and wire fraud statutes, 18 U.S.C. §§ 1341, 1343 ***

I

In 1981, Winans became a reporter for the Wall Street Journal (the Journal) and in the summer of 1982 became one of the two writers of a daily column, "Heard on the Street." That column discussed selected stocks or groups of stocks, giving positive and negative information about those stocks and taking "a point of view with respect to investment in the stocks that it reviews." [*United States v. Winans*, 612 F. Supp. 827, 830 (SDNY 1985). Winans regularly interviewed corporate executives to put together interesting perspectives on the stocks that would be highlighted in upcoming columns, but, at least for the columns at issue here, none contained corporate inside information or any "hold for release" information. Id., at 830, n. 2. Because of the "Heard" column's perceived quality and integrity, it had the potential of affecting the price of the stocks which it examined. The District Court concluded on the basis of testimony presented at trial that the "Heard" column "does have an impact on the market, difficult though it may be to quantify in any particular case." Id., at 830.

The official policy and practice at the Journal was that prior to publication, the contents of the column were the Journal's confidential information. Despite the rule, with which Winans was familiar, he entered into a scheme in October 1983 with Peter Brant and petitioner Felis, both connected with the Kidder Peabody brokerage firm in New York City, to give them advance information as to the timing and contents of the "Heard" column. This permitted Brant and Felis and another conspirator, David Clark, a client of Brant, to buy or sell based on the probable impact of the column on the market. Profits were to be shared. The conspirators agreed that the scheme would not affect the journalistic purity of the "Heard" column, and the District Court did not find that the contents of any of the articles were altered to further the profit potential of petitioners' stock-trading scheme. Id., at 832, 834-835. Over a 4-month period, the brokers made prepublication trades on the basis of information given them by Winans about the contents of some 27 "Heard" columns. The net profits from these trades were about $690,000.

In November 1983, correlations between the "Heard" articles and trading in the Clark and Felis accounts were noted at Kidder Peabody and inquiries began. Brant and Felis denied knowing anyone at the Journal and took steps to conceal the trades. Later, the Securities and Exchange Commission began an investigation. Questions were met by denials both by the brokers at Kidder Peabody and by Winans at the Journal. As the investigation progressed, the conspirators quarreled, and on March 29, 1984, Winans and Carpenter went to the SEC and revealed the entire scheme. This indictment and a bench trial followed. Brant, who had pleaded guilty under a plea agreement, was a witness for the Government.

The District Court found, and the Court of Appeals agreed, that Winans had knowingly breached a duty of confidentiality by misappropriating prepublication information regarding the timing and contents of the "Heard" column, information that had been gained in the course of his employment under the understanding that it would not be revealed in advance of publication and that if it were, he would report it to his employer. It was this appropriation of confidential information that underlay both the securities laws and mail and wire fraud counts. ***

In affirming the mail and wire fraud convictions, the Court of Appeals ruled that Winans had fraudulently misappropriated "property" within the meaning of the mail and wire fraud statutes and that its revelation had harmed the Journal. It was held as well that the use of the mail and wire services had a sufficient nexus with the scheme to satisfy §§ 1341 and 1343. ***

The Court is evenly divided with respect to the convictions under the securities laws and for that reason affirms the judgment below on those counts. For the reasons that follow, we also affirm the judgment with respect to the mail and wire fraud convictions.

II

Petitioners assert that their activities were not a scheme to defraud the Journal within the meaning of the mail and wire fraud statutes;[6] and that in any event, they did not obtain any "money or property" from the Journal, which is a necessary element of the crime under our decision last Term in *McNally v. United States,* 483 U.S. 350 (1987). We are unpersuaded by either submission and address the latter first.

We held in *McNally* that the mail fraud statute does not reach "schemes to defraud citizens of their intangible rights to honest and impartial government," id., at 355, and that the statute is "limited in scope to the protection of property rights." Id., at 360. Petitioners argue that the Journal's interest in prepublication confidentiality for the "Heard" columns is no more than an intangible consideration outside the reach of § 1341; nor does that law, it is urged, protect against mere injury to reputation. This is not a case like *McNally,* however. The Journal, as Winans' employer, was defrauded of much more than its contractual right to his honest and faithful service, an interest too ethereal in itself to fall within the protection of the mail fraud statute, which "had its origin in the desire to protect individual property rights." *McNally,* supra, at 359, n. 8. Here, the object of the scheme was to take the Journal's confidential business information—the publication schedule and contents of the "Heard" column—and its intangible nature does not make it any less "property" protected by the mail and wire fraud statutes. *McNally* did not limit the scope of § 1341 to tangible as distinguished from intangible property rights.

Both courts below expressly referred to the Journal's interest in the confidentiality of the contents and timing of the "Heard" column as a property right, and we agree with that conclusion. Confidential business information has long been recognized as property. See *Dirks v. SEC,* 463 U.S. 646, 653, n. 10 (1983); *Board of Trade of Chicago v. Christie Grain & Stock Co.,* 198 U.S. 236, 250- 251 (1905). *** The Journal had a property right in keeping confidential and making exclusive use, prior to publication, of the schedule and contents of the "Heard" column. *Christie Grain,* supra. ***

Petitioners' arguments that they did not interfere with the Journal's use of the information or did not publicize it and deprive the Journal of the first public use of it miss the point. The confidential information was generated from the business, and the business had a right to decide how to use it prior to disclosing it to the public. Petitioners cannot successfully contend *** that a scheme to defraud requires a monetary loss, such as giving the information to

6. The mail and wire fraud statutes share the same language in relevant part, and accordingly we apply the same analysis to both sets of offenses here.

a competitor; it is sufficient that the Journal has been deprived of its right to exclusive use of the information, for exclusivity is an important aspect of confidential business information and most private property for that matter.

We cannot accept petitioners' further argument that Winans' conduct in revealing prepublication information was no more than a violation of workplace rules and did not amount to fraudulent activity that is proscribed by the mail fraud statute. Sections 1341 and 1343 reach any scheme to deprive another of money or property by means of false or fraudulent pretenses, representations, or promises. As we observed last Term in *McNally,* the words "to defraud" in the mail fraud statute have the "common understanding" of " 'wronging one in his property rights by dishonest methods or schemes,' and 'usually signify the deprivation of something of value by trick, deceit, chicane or overreaching.' " 483 U.S., at 358 (quoting *Hammerschmidt v. United States,* 265 U.S. 182, 188 (1924)). The concept of "fraud" includes the act of embezzlement, which is " 'the fraudulent appropriation to one's own use of the money or goods entrusted to one's care by another.' " *Grin v. Shine,* 187 U.S. 181, 189 (1902). ***

We have little trouble in holding that the conspiracy here to trade on the Journal's confidential information is not outside the reach of the mail and wire fraud statutes, provided the other elements of the offenses are satisfied. The Journal's business information that it intended to be kept confidential was its property; the declaration to that effect in the employee manual merely removed any doubts on that score and made the finding of specific intent to defraud that much easier. Winans continued in the employ of the Journal, appropriating its confidential business information for his own use, all the while pretending to perform his duty of safeguarding it. In fact, he told his editors twice about leaks of confidential information not related to the stock-trading scheme, demonstrating both his knowledge that the Journal viewed information concerning the "Heard" column as confidential and his deceit as he played the role of a loyal employee. Furthermore, the District Court's conclusion that each of the petitioners acted with the required specific intent to defraud is strongly supported by the evidence.

Lastly, we reject the submission that using the wires and the mail to print and send the Journal to its customers did not satisfy the requirement that those mediums be used to execute the scheme at issue. The courts below were quite right in observing that circulation of the "Heard" column was not only anticipated but an essential part of the scheme. Had the column not been made available to Journal customers, there would have been no effect on stock prices and no likelihood of profiting from the information leaked by Winans.

The judgment below is affirmed.

NOTES AND QUESTIONS

1. ***Testing the Limits of the Court's Theory.*** Suppose Winans had shared the columns with his friends, expecting them to trade, but the friends became conscience-stricken and did not do so. Could he still have been prosecuted for mail fraud consistent with the Court's opinion? Cf. John C. Coffee, Jr., Hush!: The Criminal Status of Confidential Information After *McNally* and *Carpenter* and the Enduring Problem of Overcriminalization, 26 Am. Crim. L. Rev. 121, 131 (1988).

*2. **Fraud on the Wall Street Journal vs. Fraud on Investors.*** Why did the Court deem the victim of the fraud to be the Wall Street Journal rather than the investors who traded without knowing what Winans and his friends knew? One commentator has argued that the answer lies with certain Supreme Court securities decisions:

> The Court was driven to focus on Winans's mere taking of information, rather than its profitable use, in part because of constraints created by decisions under the securities laws. Since fraud requires deception, there must be a deceived party to establish the mail fraud violation. The investors who sold to or bought from Winans could not play that role. Under *Chiarella* and *Dirks*, Winans owed no duty of disclosure under the securities laws to these shareholders. He had acquired no nonpublic information about their companies through an insider's breach of duty. *** Accordingly, the investors were not the victims of a fraud. But if the investors were not defrauded, then the victim had to be the Journal.

Michael Dreeben, Insider Trading and Intangible Rights: The Redefinition of the Mail Fraud Statute, 26 Am. Crim. L. Rev. 181, 204-05 (1988). Do you agree with this analysis?

*3. **What About Fair Warning?*** Could the *Carpenter* defendants have challenged their convictions on the ground that they lacked fair warning of the wrongfulness of their conduct?

*4. **Nullifying*** **McNally.** By concluding that the mail fraud statute embraced fraudulent deprivations of intangible property rights, the *Carpenter* Court limited *McNally v. United States,* 483 U.S. 350 (1987), which held that the mail fraud statute did not reach fraudulent deprivations of the intangible right to honest government service. See id. at 358-61. Following *Carpenter*, Congress overturned *McNally* entirely by enacting the following supplement to the mail fraud and wire fraud statutes:

> For the purposes of this chapter, the term "scheme or artifice to defraud" includes a scheme or artifice to deprive another of the intangible right of honest services.

18 U.S.C. § 1346. In 2010, the Supreme Court issued three opinions involving Section 1346, the most pivotal of which was *Skilling v. United States*, 130 S.Ct. 2896 (2010). See also *Black v. United States*, 130 S.Ct. 2963 (2010); *Weyhrauch v. United States*, 130 S.Ct. 2971 (2010). The *Skilling* Court limited the statute to bribery and kickback cases on the theory that such cases comprised the "core" of honest services prosecutions prior to *McNally* and the statute's enactment: "Reading the statute to proscribe a wider range of offensive conduct," the Court observed,"would raise the due process concerns underlying the vagueness doctrine." Id. at 2931. For discussion of *Skilling*, see Sara Sun Beale, An Honest Services Debate, 8 Ohio St. J. Crim. L. 251 (2010); Samuel W. Buell, The Court's Fraud Dud, 6 Duke J. Const. L. & Pub. Pol'y 31 (2010).

*5. **The SOX and the New Crime of Securities Fraud.*** Revisit 18 U.S.C. § 1348, the new crime of securities fraud created by the SOX that is set out in Section B.1 of this Chapter. Could the *Carpenter* defendants have been prosecuted under subsection (2) of Section 1348 if it had been on the books at the time? What are the similarities and differences between subsection (2) of Section 1348 and the mail and wire fraud statutes?

In the decision that follows, the Supreme Court addressed whether the mail fraud and wire fraud statutes require proof that the fraud was material in nature.

NEDER v. UNITED STATES

527 U.S. 1 (1999)

CHIEF JUSTICE WILLIAM H. REHNQUIST:

*** In the mid-1980's, petitioner Ellis E. Neder, Jr., an attorney and real estate developer in Jacksonville, Florida, engaged in a number of real estate transactions financed by fraudulently obtained bank loans. ***

Neder was indicted on, among other things, 9 counts of mail fraud, in violation of 18 U.S.C. § 1341; 9 counts of wire fraud, in violation of § 1343; 12 counts of bank fraud, in violation of § 1344; and 2 counts of filing a false income tax return, in violation of 26 U.S.C. § 7206(1). The fraud counts charged Neder with devising and executing various schemes to defraud lenders in connection with the land acquisition and development loans, totaling over $40 million. The tax counts charged Neder with filing false statements of income on his tax returns. ***

In accordance with then-extant Circuit precedent and over Neder's objection, the District Court instructed the jury that, to convict on the tax offenses, it "need not consider" the materiality of any false statements "even though that language is used in the indictment." App. 256. The question of materiality, the court instructed, "is not a question for the jury to decide." Ibid. The court gave a similar instruction on bank fraud, and subsequently found, outside the presence of the jury, that the evidence established the materiality of all the false statements at issue. In instructing the jury on mail fraud and wire fraud, the District Court did not include materiality as an element of either offense. ***

The Court of Appeals for the Eleventh Circuit affirmed the conviction. It held that the District Court erred under our intervening decision in *United States v. Gaudin,* 515 U.S. 506 (1995), in failing to submit the materiality element of the tax offense to the jury. It concluded, however, that the error was subject to harmless-error analysis and, further, that the error was harmless because "materiality was not in dispute," and thus the error " 'did not contribute to the verdict obtained,' " ibid. (quoting *Yates v. Evatt,* 500 U.S. 391, 403 (1991)). The Court of Appeals also held that materiality is not an element of the mail fraud, wire fraud, and bank fraud statutes, and thus the District Court did not err in failing to submit the question of materiality to the jury.

We granted certiorari to resolve a conflict in the Courts of Appeals on two questions: (1) whether, and under what circumstances, the omission of an element from the judge's charge to the jury can be harmless error, and (2) whether materiality is an element of the federal mail fraud, wire fraud, and bank fraud statutes.

II

*** Neder was tried before an impartial judge, under the correct standard of proof and with the assistance of counsel; a fairly selected, impartial jury was instructed to consider all of the evidence and argument in respect to Neder's defense against the tax charges. Of course, the court erroneously failed to charge the jury on the element of materiality, but that error did not render Neder's trial "fundamentally unfair," as that term is used in our cases. ***

*** In *Chapman* v. *California,* 386 U.S. 18 (1967), we set forth the test for determining whether a constitutional error is harmless. That test, we said, is whether it appears "beyond a reasonable doubt that the error complained of did not contribute to the verdict obtained." Id., at 24.

To obtain a conviction on the tax offense at issue, the Government must prove that the defendant filed a tax return "which he does not believe to be true and correct as to every material matter." 26 U.S.C. § 7206(1). In general, a false statement is material if it has "a natural tendency to influence, or [is] capable of influencing, the decision of the decisionmaking body to which it was addressed." *United States v. Gaudin,* 515 U.S., at 509 (quoting *Kungys v. United States,* 485 U.S. 759, 770 (1988)). In a prosecution under § 7206(1), several courts have determined that "any failure to report income is material." *United States v. Holland,* 880 F.2d 1091, 1096 (CA9 1989). Under either of these formulations, no jury could reasonably find that Neder's failure to report substantial amounts of income on his tax returns was not "a material matter."

At trial, the Government introduced evidence that Neder failed to report over $5 million in income from the loans he obtained. The failure to report such substantial income incontrovertibly establishes that Neder's false statements were material to a determination of his income tax liability. *** We think it beyond cavil here that the error "did not contribute to the verdict obtained." *Chapman,* supra, at 24. ***

III

We also granted certiorari in this case to decide whether materiality is an element of a "scheme or artifice to defraud" under the federal mail fraud (18 U.S.C. § 1341), wire fraud (§ 1343), and bank fraud (§ 1344) statutes. The Court of Appeals concluded that the failure to submit materiality to the jury was not error because the fraud statutes do not require that a "scheme to defraud" employ *material* falsehoods. We disagree.

Under the framework set forth in *United States v. Wells,* 519 U.S. 482 (1997), we first look to the text of the statutes at issue to discern whether they require a showing of materiality. In this case, we need not dwell long on the text because, as the parties agree, none of the fraud statutes defines the phrase "scheme or artifice to defraud," or even mentions materiality. Although the mail fraud and wire fraud statutes contain different jurisdictional elements (§ 1341 requires use of the mails while § 1343 requires use of interstate wire facilities), they both prohibit, in pertinent part, "any scheme or artifice to defraud" or to obtain money or property "by means of false or fraudulent pretenses, representations, or promises." The bank fraud statute, which was modeled on the mail and wire fraud statutes, similarly prohibits any "scheme or artifice to defraud a financial institution" or to obtain any property of a financial institution "by false or fraudulent pretenses, representations, or promises." Thus, based solely on a "natural reading of the full text," id., at 490, materiality would not be an element of the fraud statutes.

That does not end our inquiry, however, because in interpreting statutory language there is a necessary second step. It is a well-established rule of construction that " '[w]here Congress uses terms that have accumulated settled meaning under ... the common law, a court must infer, unless the statute otherwise dictates, that Congress means to incorporate the established meaning of these terms.' " *Nationwide Mut. Ins. Co. v. Darden,* 503 U.S. 318, 322 (1992) (quoting *Community for Creative Non-Violence v. Reid,* 490 U.S. 730, 739 (1989)). Neder contends that "defraud" is just such a term, and that Congress implicitly incorporated its common-law meaning, including its requirement of materiality,[5] into the statutes at issue.

The Government does not dispute that both at the time of the mail fraud statute's original enactment in 1872, and later when Congress enacted the wire fraud and bank fraud statutes, actionable "fraud" had a well-settled meaning at common law. Nor does it dispute that the well-settled meaning of "fraud" required a misrepresentation or concealment of *material* fact. Indeed, as the sources we are aware of demonstrate, the common law could not have conceived of "fraud" without proof of materiality. See *BMW of North America, Inc. v. Gore,* 517 U.S. 559, 579 (1996) ("[A]ctionable fraud requires a *material* misrepresentation or omission" (citing Restatement (Second) of Torts § 538 (1977); W. Keeton, D. Dobbs, R. Keeton, & D. Owen, Prosser and Keeton on Law of Torts § 108 (5th ed.1984))). Thus, under the rule that Congress intends to incorporate the well-settled meaning of the common-law terms it uses, we cannot infer from the absence of an express reference to materiality that Congress intended to drop that element from the fraud statutes. On the contrary, we must *presume* that Congress intended to incorporate materiality " 'unless the statute otherwise dictates.' " Nationwide Mut. Ins., supra, at 322.[7]

---

5. The Restatement instructs that a matter is material if:

> (a) a reasonable man would attach importance to its existence or nonexistence in determining his choice of action in the transaction in question; or
>
> (b) the maker of the representation knows or has reason to know that its recipient regards or is likely to regard the matter as important in determining his choice of action, although a reasonable man would not so regard it.

Restatement (Second) of Torts § 538 (1977).

7. The Government argues that because Congress has provided express materiality requirements in other statutes prohibiting fraudulent conduct, the absence of such an express reference in the fraud statutes at issue " 'speaks volumes.' " Brief for United States 35. These later enacted statutes, however, differ from the fraud statutes here in that they prohibit both "false" and "fraudulent" statements or information. Because the term "false statement" does not imply a materiality requirement, *United States v. Wells,* 519 U.S. 482, 491 (1997), the word "material" limits the statutes' scope to material falsehoods. Moreover, these statutes cannot rebut the presumption that Congress intended to incorporate the common-law meaning of the term "fraud" in the mail fraud, wire fraud, and bank fraud statutes. That rebuttal can only come from the text or structure of the fraud statutes themselves.

The Government attempts to rebut this presumption by arguing that the term "defraud" would bear its common-law meaning only if the fraud statutes "indicated that Congress had codified the crime of false pretenses or one of the common-law torts sounding in fraud." Brief for United States 37. Instead, the Government argues, Congress chose to unmoor the mail fraud statute from its common-law analogs by punishing, not the completed fraud, but rather any person "having devised or intending to devise any scheme or artifice to defraud." Read in this light, the Government contends, there is no basis to infer that Congress intended to limit criminal liability to conduct that would constitute "fraud" at common law, and in particular, to *material* misrepresentations or omissions. Rather, criminal liability would exist so long as the defendant *intended* to deceive the victim, even if the particular means chosen turn out to be immaterial, *i.e.,* incapable of influencing the intended victim.

The Government relies heavily on *Durland v. United States,* 161 U.S. 306 (1896), our first decision construing the mail fraud statute, to support its argument that the fraud statutes sweep more broadly than common-law fraud. But *Durland* was different from this case. There, the defendant, who had used the mails to sell bonds he did not intend to honor, argued that he could not be held criminally liable because his conduct did not fall within the scope of the common-law crime of "false pretenses." We rejected the argument that "the statute reaches only such cases as, at common law, would come within the definition of 'false pretenses,' in order to make out which there must be a misrepresentation as to some existing fact and not a mere promise as to the future." Id. at 312. Instead, we construed the statute to "includ[e] everything designed to defraud by representations as to the past or present, or suggestions and promises as to the future." Id. at 313. Although *Durland* held that the mail fraud statute reaches conduct that would not have constituted "false pretenses" at common law, it did not hold, as the Government argues, that the statute encompasses more than common-law fraud.

In one sense, the Government is correct that the fraud statutes did not incorporate *all* the elements of common-law fraud. The common-law requirements of "justifiable reliance" and "damages," for example, plainly have no place in the federal fraud statutes. See, e.g., *United States v. Stewart,* 872 F.2d 957, 960 (CA10 1989) ("[Under the mail fraud statute,] the government does not have to prove actual reliance upon the defendant's misrepresentations"); *United States v. Rowe,* 56 F.2d 747, 749 (CA2 1932) (L. Hand, J.) ("Civilly of course the [mail fraud statute] would fail without proof of damage, but that has no application to criminal liability"). By prohibiting the "scheme to defraud," rather than the completed fraud, the elements of reliance and damage would clearly be inconsistent with the statutes Congress enacted. But while the language of the fraud statutes is incompatible with these requirements, the Government has failed to show that this language is inconsistent with a materiality requirement.

Accordingly, we hold that materiality of falsehood is an element of the federal mail fraud, wire fraud, and bank fraud statutes. Consistent with our normal practice where the court below has not yet passed on the harmlessness of any error, we remand this case to the Court of Appeals for it to consider in the first instance whether the jury-instruction error was harmless. ***

NOTES AND QUESTIONS

1. Seeking a Definition. Does *Neder* define materiality for purposes of the mail and wire fraud statutes? According to some courts, *Neder* adopted the Restatement's definition, including Section (b) thereof, pursuant to which materiality encompasses fraud that fools gullible people, even if it would not fool reasonable people. See *United States v. Svete,* 556 3d 1157, 1164-66 (11th Cir. 2009) (en banc). Cf. *Neder*, supra, at n. 5. According to other courts, *Neder* adopted the definition provided by *United States v. Gaudin,* 515 U.S. 506, 509 (1995)—having "a natural tendency to influence, or [is] capable of influencing, the decision of the decisionmaking body to which it was addressed." See, e.g., *United States v. Gee,* 226 F.3d 885, 891 (7th Cir. 2000).

Still others apparently conclude that *Neder* did not insist upon a specific definition of materiality, thereby giving them leeway to make that choice. Thus, one court applied the following pre-*Neder* definition of materiality: "'To be material, the information withheld either must be of some independent value or must bear on the ultimate value of the transaction.' " *United States v. Autuori,* 212 F.3d 105, 118 (2d Cir. 2000) (quoting *United States v. Mittelstaedt,* 31 F.3d 1208, 1217 (2d Cir. 1994)). The court that originated this definition derived it from the Supreme Court's *Carpenter* decision. See *United States v. Mittelstaedt,* 31 F.3d 1208, 1217 (2d Cir. 1994). Do you agree that *Carpenter* provides such a definition?

Which reading of *Neder* (if any) do you find the most plausible? Consider this question again in connection with Note 2 below.

2. Securities Law to the Rescue? You will recall from previous Chapters that under the Securities Act and the Exchange Act, a fact is material when there is "a substantial likelihood that, under all the circumstances, the omitted fact would have assumed actual significance in the deliberations of the reasonable shareholder." *TSC Indus., Inc. v. Northway, Inc.,* 426 U.S. 438, 449 (1976). See *Basic Inc, v. Levinson,* 485 U.S. 224, 249 (1988) (adopting *Northway* standard for purposes of Rule 10b-5). See generally Chapter 2.B. Is a court entitled to import this definition of materiality into a mail or wire fraud prosecution involving a securities transaction? See *United States v. Ferguson,* __ F.3d __, 2011 WL 3251464 at *7 (2d Cir. 2011) (applying *Northway/Basic* standard to mail fraud). Would the *Northway/Basic* definition be useable (with minor changes such as substituting "reasonable person" for "reasonable shareholder") if a securities transaction were not involved?

As you also know from Chapter 2, materiality jurisprudence under the federal securities laws does not end with the *Northway/Basic* definition. Aspects of that jurisprudence might be useful in the resolution of materiality questions under the mail and wire fraud statutes regardless of whether the *Northway* definition is itself specifically embraced. For example, can a court import into a mail or wire fraud prosecution the probability/magnitude test for contingent information from *Basic*? Can it import the bespeaks caution doctrine (see generally Chapter 2.B.3.b) or the puffery doctrine (see Note 2 of Chapter 2.B.1)? Do the answers to these questions turn on whether the cases involve securities transactions?

*3. **Possible Conservative Tilt.*** Does *Neder* suggest a conservative tilt in the Court's approach to mail and wire fraud? See *Cleveland v. United States,* 531 U.S. 12, 24-25 (2000) (endorsing strict construction of the mail fraud statute partly because mail fraud is a predicate act under RICO). Cf. *Skilling v. United States*, 130 S.Ct. 2896 (2010) (restricting Section 1346 to cases involving bribery and kickbacks). But cf. *Pasquantino v. United States*, 544 U.S. 349 (2005) (on 5-4 vote, holding wire fraud statute applicable to scheme to smuggle liquor into Canada and deprive that country of tax revenue).

*4. **Statute of Limitations.*** There is no statute of limitations specifically applicable to the federal mail and wire fraud statutes. Therefore, the general federal criminal limitations period of five years set forth in 18 U.S.C. § 3282 is applicable. See, e.g., *United States v. Mullins,* 613 F.3d 1273,1278 (10th Cir. 2010); *United States v. Dickerson,* 370 F.3d 1330, 1333 & n.4 (11th Cir. 2004).

PROBLEM 11-4

Joe developed a technique for bilking the elderly out of their retirement savings. In a mass mailing to residents of retirement communities, Joe urged them to bring an end to their financial worries by buying stock in Stupendix, Inc. (which in fact did not exist). The mailing declared: "Become a Stupendix shareholder now and see your money double in two weeks! Triple in three weeks!" A number of recipients of this letter sent Joe cash (or checks), but did not hear from Joe again (much less reap the promised profits). Joe was indicted under the mail fraud statute as well as under the Sarbanes-Oxley Act's new crime of securities fraud set forth in 18 U.S.C. § 1348(2). On what grounds can he challenge his indictment? Is he likely to prevail on his challenge?

Cf. *United States v. Davis,* 226 F.3d 346 (5th Cir. 2000).

PROBLEM 11-5

Clown, Inc., a reporting company under the Exchange Act, is a toy manufacturer and distributor with $100 million in yearly sales. Beginning approximately five years ago, the company's president (Felix) directed his assistant (Jane) to sell Clown merchandise to specified merchants for cash in off-the-books transactions. Over the years, these transactions (which were implemented through the use of e-mail) generated a total of $100,000. The existence of these transactions was disclosed neither to the accountants nor to the shareholders. If Felix were indicted under the wire fraud statute, could he mount a successful challenge? Suppose he were charged instead with violating 18 U.S.C. § 1348(2)?

Cf. *United States v. Siegel,* 717 F.2d 9 (2d Cir. 1983).

D. RACKETEER INFLUENCED AND CORRUPT ORGANIZATIONS ACT

In 1970, Congress enacted RICO in order to combat organized crime. Prevented by the First Amendment of the Constitution from criminalizing mere membership in organized crime, Congress created a complex new set of crimes premised on offenses (including mail, wire, and securities fraud) in which it believed that organized crime frequently engaged. See 18 U.S.C. §§ 1961-1968. RICO authorizes prison terms of up to twenty years (see Section 1963(a)) as well as the freezing of the defendant's assets prior to trial (see id.).

By far the most frequently invoked RICO offense is Section 1962(c), which is our focus. That Section reads as follows:

> It shall be unlawful for any person employed by or associated with any enterprise engaged in, or the activities which affect, interstate or foreign commerce, to conduct or participate, directly or indirectly, in the conduct of such enterprise's affairs through a pattern of racketeering activity or collection of an unlawful debt.

18 U.S.C. § 1962(c). We examine Section 1962(c)'s constituent elements—(1) racketeering activity; (2) pattern; (3) enterprise; and (4) "conduct[ing] or participat[ing] *** in the conduct of " the enterprise. We conclude our study of RICO by looking briefly at the limits on the RICO private action imposed by the Private Securities Litigation Reform Act of 1995.

RICO is a difficult statute to interpret for several reasons. One is its complexity and strangeness. Indeed, note that terms such as "racketeering activity," "pattern," and "enterprise" are hardly common law classics.

A second reason that RICO is difficult to interpret is that it has a liberal construction clause, which reads as follows: "The provisions of this Title shall be liberally construed to effectuate its remedial purposes." Section 904(a) of RICO, 84 Stat. 947. It is not immediately self-evident how to square the liberal construction clause with the rule of lenity (or strict construction) that normally applies in the criminal context. See generally David Kurzweil, Note, Criminal and Civil RICO: Traditional Canons of Statutory Interpretation and the Liberal Construction Clause, 30 Colum. J. L. & Soc. Probs. 41 (1996). Although it is an integral part of the RICO statute enacted by Congress, the liberal construction clause did not make its way into the United States Code. That fact does not affect its status as law, however.

A third reason that RICO is difficult to interpret has to do with the multiple types of RICO actions. Indeed, RICO is enforceable not only through criminal actions but also through civil actions (brought by either the DOJ or private parties). Must care be taken to construe RICO in a manner that is suitable for all enforcement contexts? Or can RICO be interpreted differently depending on the form of enforcement? This question—which you encountered previously in connection with the federal securities laws—has provoked conflicting commentary. Compare Bryan T. Camp, Dual Construction of RICO: The Road Not Taken in *Reves,* 51 Wash. & Lee L. Rev. 61, 95-96 (1994) (arguing that "[t]o deal with RICO's abundant ambiguities, courts should adopt a doctrine of dual construction, resolving the ambiguities according to a different and more restrictive standard in private civil cases than in cases where the government is either plaintiff or prosecutor") with Matthew C. Blickensderfer, Note, Unleashing RICO, 17 Harv. J. L. & Pub. Pol'y 867, 878 n. 66 (1994) (maintaining that RICO must be interpreted uniformly regardless of the form of enforcement). As you proceed with this Chapter, consider the advantages and disadvantages of "dual construction." Is it plausible to favor "dual construction" under RICO but not under the federal securities laws?

1. Racketeering Activity

A critical element of the offense created by Section 1962(c) is "racketeering activity." RICO provides a definition of "racketeering activity" in Section 1961(1). That definition has six sub-parts, denominated A through F. Sub-part D reads as follows:

> any offense involving fraud connected with a case under title 11 (except a case under section 157 of this title), fraud in the sale of securities, or the felonious manufacture, importation, receiving, concealment, buying, selling, or otherwise dealing in a controlled substance or listed chemical (as defined in section 102 of the Controlled Substances Act), punishable under any law of the United States.

18 U.S.C. § 1961(1)(D). The other sub-parts include various state crimes such as murder and kidnaping (sub-part A); an amalgam of federal crimes from Title 18 of the United States Code, including mail fraud and wire fraud (sub-part B); certain crimes involving labor organizations and union funds (sub-part C); crimes under the Currency and Foreign Transactions Reporting Act (sub-part E); and certain crimes under the Immigration and Nationality Act (sub-part F).

NOTES AND QUESTIONS

1. Invitation to Expansiveness? Notice that sub-part D references specific statutory provisions of the United States Code in connection with bankruptcy fraud and drug crimes but contains no such references in connection with "fraud in the sale of securities." By such drafting, did Congress invite expansive interpretations of the phrase "fraud in the sale of securities"?

2. Rule 10b-5 as RICO Securities Fraud. What is the relationship between RICO's "fraud in the sale of securities" and Rule 10b-5's fraud "in connection with the purchase or sale of any security"? Consider whether you agree with the following view:

> Had Congress intended RICO to be coextensive with § 10(b), it certainly knew how to do so. However, "fraud in the sale of securities" is quite limited in comparison to the broader language Congress used in § 10(b), which prohibits fraud "in connection with the purchase or sale of any security." The "in connection with" language *** does not limit liability to defendants who sold or bought from the plaintiffs. Thus, under the "in connection with" requirement, a defendant may be held liable even though he was not a party to a securities transaction. This concept arises directly out of the "in connection with" language. The language *** "fraud in the sale of securities" *** is much less susceptible to such an interpretation ***.
>
> *** The court's conclusion is that the phrase "fraud in the sale of securities" *** must be read to mean *** that only fraud that occurs as part of the actual securities transaction is a predicate act under that provision. In this case, it is not alleged that defendants sold any securities to plaintiffs. Instead, plaintiffs claim that defendants' issuance of misleading statements caused them to buy their shares *on the open market* at artificially inflated prices. Therefore, defendants have not committed "fraud in the sale of securities" *** and plaintiffs have not stated a RICO claim based on defendants' alleged securities fraud.

In re Par Pharm., Inc. Sec. Litig., 733 F. Supp. 668, 683-84 (S.D.N.Y 1990). But see *Pandick, Inc. v. Rooney*, 632 F. Supp. 1430, 1434 (N.D. Ill. 1986) (making no distinction between RICO's "in" language and Rule 10b-5's "in connection with" language). Moreover, does "fraud in the sale of securities" embrace fraud in the *purchase* of securities? Cf. *Pandick,* supra, 632 F. Supp. at 1434 (giving an affirmative answer). To resolve these questions, what role (if any) should be played by RICO's liberal construction clause? By the rule of lenity?

3. ***Other Federal Securities Provisions Involving Omissions and Misrepresentations.*** To what extent (if at all) does "fraud in the sale of securities" embrace violations of Section 17(a) of the Securities Act? What about Section 14(a) and Rule 14a-9 of the Exchange Act or Section 14(e) of that Act? What about 18 U.S.C. § 1348 (the crime of securities fraud created by the Sarbanes-Oxley Act) and 18 U.S.C. § 1350 (the certification crime created by the Sarbanes-Oxley Act)?

4. ***Duties to Register or Report.*** Does RICO's "fraud in the sale of securities" encompass violations of the registration and reporting requirements of the Securities Act and the Exchange Act? Compare *First Pacific Bancorp, Inc. v. Bro,* 847 F.2d 542, 546 (9th Cir. 1988) (finding that failures to file under Sections 13(d) and 14(a) of the Exchange Act do not qualify as RICO securities fraud) with *United States v. Eisenberg,* 773 F. Supp. 662, 725-26 (D.N.J. 1991) (finding that failure to report beneficial ownership in a registration statement qualifies as RICO securities fraud where it was part of "an affirmative scheme to defraud"). Is it arguable that the registration and reporting requirements should be classified as fraud (at least for purposes of RICO) because the ultimate function of these requirements is to prevent fraud on investors?

5. ***State of Mind.*** Proof that a defendant engaged in a particular act of racketeering activity entails proof that she satisfied that activity's required state of mind. See, e.g., *United States v. Blinder,* 10 F.3d 1468, 1477 (9th Cir. 1993). What state of mind requirement is called for by "fraud in the sale of securities *** punishable under any law of the United States"? Consider the comments of Justice O' Connor:

> The embracing words "offense ...punishable under any law of the United States" plainly signify the elements necessary to bring a criminal prosecution. To the extent that RICO's reference to an "offense" involving fraud in the sale of securities" encompasses conduct that violates § 10(b), the relevant predicate is defined not by §10(b) itself, but rather by § 32(a) of the 1934 Act, which authorizes criminal sanctions against any person who willfully violates the Act or rules promulgated thereunder. ***

Holmes v. Securities Investor Protection Corp., 503 U.S. 258, 280 (1992) (O'Connor, J., concurring in part and concurring in the judgment). Recall the lack of consensus regarding how to define "willfully" in Section 32(a) of the Exchange Act. See supra Section A of this Chapter. Therefore, it is not surprising to see uncertainty about the appropriate definition of "willfully" to import into RICO. Compare *Friedlob v. Trs. of Alpine Mut. Fund Trust,* 905 F. Supp. 843, 858 (D. Colo. 1995) (finding that a RICO defendant acts "willfully" where he acts " 'deliberately and intentionally and his acts, statements, or omissions are not the result of innocent mistake, negligence, inadvertence, or other innocent conduct' " (quoting *In re Colonial Ltd. P'ship Litig.*, 854 F. Supp. 64, 106 (D. Conn. 1994))) with *In re Integrated Res. Real Estate Ltd. P'ships Sec. Litig.,* 850 F. Supp. 1105, 1145 n. 56 (S.D.N.Y. 1994) (finding that a RICO defendant acts "willfully" when he acts "knowingly and willfully" and "with actual knowledge of the illegal activities").

6. Giving the Federal Securities Laws Their Due. Courts deciding RICO cases involving "fraud in the sale of securities" may be called upon to construe the federal securities laws. Is it likely that courts will give those laws (and their accompanying policies) short shrift when construing them in the RICO context? Are constructions of the federal securities laws that emerge from the RICO context applicable outside the RICO context?

---

2. *Pattern*

Under Section 1962(c), the "racketeering activity" must constitute a "pattern." RICO says only that a " 'pattern of racketeering activity' requires at least two acts of racketeering activity" within a ten year period. 18 U.S.C. § 1961(5). Consider the gloss that the Supreme Court placed on "pattern" in the following decision.

H.J. INC. v. NORTHWESTERN BELL TELEPHONE CO.

492 U.S. 229 (1989)

JUSTICE WILLIAM J. BRENNAN, JR.:

The Racketeer Influenced and Corrupt Organizations Act (RICO or Act) imposes criminal and civil liability upon those who engage in certain "prohibited activities." Each prohibited activity is defined in 18 U.S.C. § 1962 to include, as one necessary element, proof either of "a pattern of racketeering activity" or of "collection of an unlawful debt." "Racketeering activity" is defined in RICO to mean "any act or threat involving" specified state-law crimes, any "act" indictable under various specified federal statutes, and certain federal "offenses," 18 U.S.C. § 1961(1); but of the term "pattern" the statute says only that it "requires at least two acts of racketeering activity" within a 10-year period, 18 U.S.C. § 1961(5). We are called upon in this civil case to consider what conduct meets RICO's pattern requirement.

I

*** Petitioners, customers of respondent Northwestern Bell Telephone Co., filed this putative class action in 1986 in the District Court *** . Petitioners alleged violations of §§ 1962(a), (b), (c), and (d) by Northwestern Bell and the other respondents—some of the telephone company's officers and employees, various members of the Minnesota Public Utilities Commission (MPUC), and other unnamed individuals and corporations—and sought an injunction and treble damages under RICO's civil liability provisions, §§ 1964(a) and ©).

The MPUC is the state body responsible for determining the rates that Northwestern Bell may charge. Petitioners' five-count complaint alleged that between 1980 and 1986 Northwestern Bell sought to influence members of the MPUC in the performance of their duties—and in fact caused them to approve rates for the company in excess of a fair and reasonable amount—by making cash payments to commissioners, negotiating with them regarding future employment, and paying for parties and meals, for tickets to sporting events and the like, and for airline tickets. Based upon these factual allegations, petitioners alleged in their first count a pendent state-law claim, asserting that Northwestern Bell violated the Minnesota bribery statute, Minn. Stat. § 609.42 (1988), as well as state common law prohibiting bribery. They also raised four separate claims under § 1962 of RICO. Count II alleged that, in violation of § 1962(a), Northwestern Bell derived income from a pattern of racketeering activity involving predicate acts of bribery and used this income to engage in its business as an interstate "enterprise." Count III claimed a violation of § 1962(b), in that, through this same pattern of racketeering activity, respondents acquired an interest in or control of the MPUC, which was also an interstate "enterprise." In Count IV, petitioners asserted that respondents participated in the conduct and affairs of the MPUC through this pattern of racketeering activity, contrary to § 1962(c). Finally, Count V alleged that respondents conspired together to violate §§ 1962(a), (b), and (c), thereby contravening § 1962(d).

The District Court granted respondents' Federal Rule of Civil Procedure 12(b)(6) motion, dismissing the complaint for failure to state a claim upon which relief could be granted. The court found that "[e]ach of the fraudulent acts alleged by [petitioners] was committed in furtherance of a single scheme to influence MPUC commissioners to the detriment of Northwestern Bell's ratepayers." It held that dismissal was therefore mandated by the Court of Appeals for the Eighth Circuit's decision in *Superior Oil Co. v. Fulmer,* 785 F.2d 252 (1986), which the District Court interpreted as adopting an "extremely restrictive" test for a pattern of racketeering activity that required proof of "multiple illegal schemes." The Court of Appeals for the Eighth Circuit affirmed the dismissal of petitioners' complaint, confirming that under Eighth Circuit precedent "[a] single fraudulent effort or scheme is insufficient" to establish a pattern of racketeering activity, and agreeing with the District Court that petitioners' complaint alleged only a single scheme. Two members of the panel suggested in separate concurrences, however, that the Court of Appeals should reconsider its test for a RICO pattern. Most Courts of Appeals have rejected the Eighth Circuit's interpretation of RICO's pattern concept to require an allegation and proof of multiple schemes, and we granted certiorari to resolve this conflict. We now reverse.

II

*** We begin, of course, with RICO's text, in which Congress followed a "pattern [of] utilizing terms and concepts of breadth." *Russello v. United States,* 464 U.S. 16, 21 (1983). As we remarked in *Sedima* [*S.P.R.L. v. Imrex Co.*, 473 U.S. 479, 496 n.14 (1985)] the section of the statute headed "definitions," 18 U.S.C. § 1961, does not so much define a pattern of racketeering activity as state a minimum necessary condition for the existence of such a pattern. Unlike other provisions in § 1961 that tell us what various concepts used in the Act "mean," 18 U.S.C. § 1961(5) says of the phrase "pattern of racketeering activity" only that it "requires at least two acts of racketeering activity, one of which occurred after [October 15, 1970,] and the last of which occurred within ten years (excluding any period of imprisonment) after the commission of a prior act of racketeering activity." It thus places an outer limit on the concept of a pattern of racketeering activity that is broad indeed.

Section 1961(5) does indicate that Congress envisioned circumstances in which no more than two predicates would be necessary to establish a pattern of racketeering—otherwise it would have drawn a narrower boundary to RICO liability, requiring proof of a greater number of predicates. But, at the same time, the statement that a pattern "requires at least" two predicates implies "that while two acts are necessary, they may not be sufficient." *Sedima,* 473 U.S., at 496, n. 14. Section 1961(5) concerns only the minimum *number* of predicates necessary to establish a pattern; and it assumes that there is something to a RICO pattern *beyond* simply the number of predicate acts involved. The legislative history bears out this interpretation, for the principal sponsor of the Senate bill expressly indicated that "proof of two acts of racketeering activity, without more, does not establish a pattern." 116 Cong. Rec. 18940 (1970) (statement of Sen. McClellan). Section § 1961(5) does not identify, though, these additional prerequisites for establishing the existence of a RICO pattern.

In addition to § 1961(5), there is the key phrase "pattern of racketeering activity" itself, from § 1962, and we must "start with the assumption that the legislative purpose is expressed by the ordinary meaning of the words used." *Richards v. United States,* 369 U.S. 1, 9 (1962). In normal usage, the word "pattern" here would be taken to require more than just a multiplicity of racketeering predicates. A "pattern" is an "arrangement or order of things or activity," 11 Oxford English Dictionary 357 (2d ed. 1989), and the mere fact that there are a number of predicates is no guarantee that they fall into any arrangement or order. It is not the number of predicates but the relationship that they bear to each other or to some external organizing principle that renders them "ordered" or "arranged." The text of RICO conspicuously fails anywhere to identify, however, forms of relationship or external principles to be used in determining whether racketeering activity falls into a pattern for purposes of the Act.

It is reasonable to infer, from this absence of any textual identification of sorts of pattern that would satisfy § 1962's requirement, in combination with the very relaxed limits to the pattern concept fixed in § 1961(5), that Congress intended to take a flexible approach, and envisaged that a pattern might be demonstrated by reference to a range of different ordering principles or relationships between predicates, within the expansive bounds set. For any more specific guidance as to the meaning of "pattern," we must look past the text to RICO's legislative history, as we have done in prior cases construing the Act.

The legislative history *** shows that Congress indeed had a fairly flexible concept of a pattern in mind. A pattern is not formed by "sporadic activity," S. Rep. No. 91-617, p. 158 (1969), and a person cannot "be subjected to the sanctions of title IX simply for committing two widely separated and isolated criminal offenses," 116 Cong. Rec. at 18940 (1970) (Sen. McClellan). Instead, "[t]he term 'pattern' itself requires the showing of a relationship" between the predicates, ibid., and of " 'the threat of continuing activity,' " ibid., quoting S. Rep. No. 91-617, supra at 158. "It is this factor of *continuity plus relationship* which combines to produce a pattern." 116 Cong. Rec., at 18940 (emphasis added). RICO's legislative history reveals Congress' intent that to prove a pattern of racketeering activity a plaintiff or prosecutor must show that the racketeering predicates are related, *and* that they amount to or pose a threat of continued criminal activity.

B

For analytic purposes these two constituents of RICO's pattern requirement must be stated separately, though in practice their proof will often overlap. The element of relatedness is the easier to define, for we may take guidance from a provision elsewhere in the Organized Crime Control Act of 1970 (OCCA), of which RICO formed Title IX. OCCA included as Title X the Dangerous Special Offender Sentencing Act, 18 U.S.C. § 3575 *et seq.* (now partially repealed). Title X provided for enhanced sentences where, among other things, the defendant had committed a prior felony as part of a pattern of criminal conduct or in furtherance of a conspiracy to engage in a pattern of criminal conduct. As we noted in *Sedima,* supra, at 496, n. 14, Congress defined Title X's pattern requirement solely in terms of the *relationship* of the defendant's criminal acts one to another: "[C]riminal conduct forms a pattern if it embraces criminal acts that have the same or similar purposes, results, participants, victims, or methods of commission, or otherwise are interrelated by distinguishing characteristics and are not isolated events." § 3575(e). We have no reason to suppose that Congress had in mind for RICO's pattern of racketeering component any more constrained a notion of the relationships between predicates that would suffice.

RICO's legislative history tells us, however, that the relatedness of racketeering activities is not alone enough to satisfy § 1962's pattern element. To establish a RICO pattern it must also be shown that the predicates themselves amount to, or that they otherwise constitute a threat of, *continuing* racketeering activity. As to this continuity requirement, § 3575(e) is of no assistance. It is this aspect of RICO's pattern element that has spawned the "multiple scheme" test adopted by some lower courts, including the Court of Appeals in this case. But although proof that a RICO defendant has been involved in multiple criminal schemes would certainly be highly relevant to the inquiry into the continuity of the defendant's racketeering activity, it is implausible to suppose that Congress thought continuity might be shown *only* by proof of multiple schemes. The Eighth Circuit's test brings a rigidity to the available methods of proving a pattern that simply is not present in the idea of "continuity" itself; and it does so, moreover, by introducing a concept—the "scheme"—that appears nowhere in the language or legislative history of the Act.[3] We adopt a less inflexible approach that seems to us to derive from a commonsense, everyday understanding of RICO's language and Congress' gloss on it. What a plaintiff or prosecutor must prove is continuity of racketeering activity, or its threat, *simpliciter.* This may be done in a variety of ways, thus making it difficult to formulate in the abstract any general test for continuity. We can, however, begin to delineate the requirement.

"Continuity" is both a closed- and open-ended concept, referring either to a closed period of repeated conduct, or to past conduct that by its nature projects into the future with a threat of repetition. See *Barticheck v. Fidelity Union Bank/First National State,* 832 F.2d 36, 39 (CA3 1987). It is, in either

---

3. Nor does the multiple scheme approach to identifying continuing criminal conduct have the advantage of lessening the uncertainty inherent in RICO's pattern component, for " 'scheme' is hardly a self-defining term." *Barticheck v. Fidelity Union Bank/First National State,* 832 F.2d, at 39. A "scheme" is in the eye of the beholder, since whether a scheme exists depends on the level of generality at which criminal activity is viewed. ***

case, centrally a temporal concept—and particularly so in the RICO context, where *what* must be continuous, RICO's predicate acts or offenses, and the *relationship* these predicates must bear one to another, are distinct requirements. A party alleging a RICO violation may demonstrate continuity over a closed period by proving a series of related predicates extending over a substantial period of time. Predicate acts extending over a few weeks or months and threatening no future criminal conduct do not satisfy this requirement: Congress was concerned in RICO with long-term criminal conduct. Often a RICO action will be brought before continuity can be established in this way. In such cases, liability depends on whether the *threat* of continuity is demonstrated. See S. Rep. No. 91-617, at 158.

Whether the predicates proved establish a threat of continued racketeering activity depends on the specific facts of each case. Without making any claim to cover the field of possibilities—preferring to deal with this issue in the context of concrete factual situations presented for decision—we offer some examples of how this element might be satisfied. A RICO pattern may surely be established if the related predicates themselves involve a distinct threat of long-term racketeering activity, either implicit or explicit. Suppose a hoodlum were to sell "insurance" to a neighborhood's storekeepers to cover them against breakage of their windows, telling his victims he would be reappearing each month to collect the "premium" that would continue their "coverage." Though the number of related predicates involved may be small and they may occur close together in time, the racketeering acts themselves include a specific threat of repetition extending indefinitely into the future, and thus supply the requisite threat of continuity. In other cases, the threat of continuity may be established by showing that the predicate acts or offenses are part of an ongoing entity's regular way of doing business. Thus, the threat of continuity is sufficiently established where the predicates can be attributed to a defendant operating as part of a long-term association that exists for criminal purposes. Such associations include, but extend well beyond, those traditionally grouped under the phrase "organized crime." The continuity requirement is likewise satisfied where it is shown that the predicates are a regular way of conducting defendant's ongoing legitimate business (in the sense that it is not a business that exists for criminal purposes), or of conducting or participating in an ongoing and legitimate RICO "enterprise."[4]

The limits of the relationship and continuity concepts that combine to define a RICO pattern, and the precise methods by which relatedness and continuity or its threat may be proved, cannot be fixed in advance with such clarity that it will always be apparent whether in a particular case a "pattern of racketeering activity" exists. The development of these concepts must await

---

4. Insofar as the concurrence seems to suggest that very short periods of criminal activity that do *not* in any way carry a threat of continued criminal activity constitute "obvious racketeer[ing]" to which Congress intended RICO, with its enhanced penalties, to apply, we have concluded that it is mistaken, and that when Congress said predicates must demonstrate "continuity" before they may form a RICO pattern, it expressed an intent that RICO reach activities that amount to or threaten long-term criminal activity.

future cases, absent a decision by Congress to revisit RICO to provide clearer guidance as to the Act's intended scope. ***

IV

We turn now to the application of our analysis of RICO's pattern requirement. Because respondents prevailed on a motion under Federal Rule of Civil Procedure 12(b)(6), we read the facts alleged in the complaint in the light most favorable to petitioners. ***

Petitioners' complaint alleges that at different times over the course of at least a 6-year period the noncommissioner respondents gave five members of the MPUC numerous bribes, in several different forms, with the objective—in which they were allegedly successful—of causing these commissioners to approve unfair and unreasonable rates for Northwestern Bell. RICO defines bribery as a "racketeering activity," 18 U.S.C. § 1961(1), so petitioners have alleged multiple predicate acts.

Under the analysis we have set forth above, and consistent with the allegations in their complaint, petitioners may be able to prove that the multiple predicates alleged constitute "a pattern of racketeering activity," in that they satisfy the requirements of relationship and continuity. The acts of bribery alleged are said to be related by a common purpose, to influence commissioners in carrying out their duties in order to win approval of unfairly and unreasonably high rates for Northwestern Bell. Furthermore, petitioners claim that the racketeering predicates occurred with some frequency over at least a 6-year period, which may be sufficient to satisfy the continuity requirement. Alternatively, a threat of continuity of racketeering activity might be established at trial by showing that the alleged bribes were a regular way of conducting Northwestern Bell's ongoing business, or a regular way of conducting or participating in the conduct of the alleged and ongoing RICO enterprise, the MPUC.

The Court of Appeals thus erred in affirming the District Court's dismissal of petitioners' complaint for failure to plead "a pattern of racketeering activity." The judgment is reversed, and the case is remanded for further proceedings consistent with this opinion.

JUSTICE ANTONIN G. SCALIA, WITH WHOM THE CHIEF JUSTICE, JUSTICE O'CONNOR, AND JUSTICE KENNEDY JOIN, CONCURRING IN THE JUDGMENT.

*** Elevating to the level of statutory text a phrase taken from the legislative history, the Court counsels the lower courts: " 'continuity plus relationship.' " (emphasis deleted). This seems to me about as helpful to the conduct of their affairs as "life is a fountain." Of the two parts of this talismanic phrase, the relatedness requirement is said to be the "easier to define," ibid., yet here is the Court's definition, *in toto:* " '[C]riminal conduct forms a pattern if it embraces criminal acts that have the same or similar purposes, results, participants, victims, or methods of commission, or otherwise are interrelated by distinguishing characteristics and are not isolated events,' " This definition has the feel of being solidly rooted in law, since it is a direct quotation of 18 U.S.C. § 3575(e). Unfortunately, if normal (and sensible) rules of statutory construction were followed, the existence of § 3575(e)—which is the definition contained in another title of the Act that was explicitly *not* rendered applicable to RICO—suggests that *whatever* "pattern" might mean in RICO, it assuredly *does not* mean that. "[W]here Congress includes particular language in one section of a statute but omits it in another section of the same Act, it is generally presumed that Congress acts intentionally and purposely in the disparate inclusion or exclusion." *Russello v. United States,* 464 U.S. 16, 23 (1983). But that does not really matter, since § 3575(e) is utterly uninformative anyway. It hardly closes in on the target to know that "relatedness" refers to acts that are related by "purposes, results, participants, victims, ... methods of commission, *or* [just in case that is not vague enough] *otherwise.*" Is the fact that the victims of both predicate acts were women enough? Or that both acts had the purpose of enriching the defendant? Or that the different coparticipants of the defendant in both acts were his coemployees? I doubt that the lower courts will find the Court's instructions much more helpful than telling them to look for a "pattern"—which is what the statute already says.

The Court finds "continuity" more difficult to define precisely. "Continuity," it says, "is both a closed- and open-ended concept, referring either to a closed period of repeated conduct, or to past conduct that by its nature projects into the future with a threat of repetition." I have no idea what this concept of a "closed period of repeated conduct" means. Virtually all allegations of racketeering activity, in both civil and criminal suits, will relate to past periods that are "closed" (unless one expects plaintiff or the prosecutor to establish that the defendant not only committed the crimes he did, but is still committing them), and all of them *must* relate to conduct that is "repeated," because of RICO's multiple-act requirement. I had thought, initially, that the Court was seeking to draw a distinction between, on the one hand, past repeated conduct (multiple racketeering acts) that is "closed-ended" in the sense that, in its totality, it constitutes only one criminal "scheme" or "episode"—which would not fall within RICO unless in its nature (for one or more of the reasons later described by the Court) it threatened future criminal endeavors as well—and, on the other hand, past repeated conduct (multiple racketeering acts) that constitutes several separate schemes—which is alone enough to invoke RICO. But of course that cannot be what it means, since the Court rejects the "multiple scheme" concept, not merely as the *exclusive* touchstone of RICO liability, but in all its applications, since it "introduc[es] a concept ... that appears nowhere in the language or legislative history of the Act," and is so vague and "amorphous" as to exist only "in the eye of the beholder." Moreover, the Court tells us that predicate acts extending, not over a "substantial period of time," but only over a "few weeks or months and threatening no future criminal conduct" do not satisfy the continuity requirement. Since the Court has rejected the concept of separate criminal "schemes" or "episodes" as a criterion of "threatening future criminal conduct," I think it must be saying that at least a few months of racketeering activity (and who knows how much more?) is generally for free, as far as RICO is concerned. The "closed period" concept is a sort of safe harbor for racketeering activity that does not last *too* long, no matter how many different crimes and different schemes are involved, so long as it does not otherwise "establish a threat of continued racketeering activity," ibid. A gang of hoodlums that commits one act of extortion on Monday in New York, a second in Chicago on Tuesday, a third in San Francisco on Wednesday, and so on through an entire week, and then finally and completely disbands, cannot be reached under RICO.

I am sure that is not what the statute intends, but I cannot imagine what else the Court's murky discussion can possibly mean. ***

It is, however, unfair to be so critical of the Court's effort, because I would be unable to provide an interpretation of RICO that gives significantly more guidance concerning its application. It is clear to me from the prologue of the statute, which describes a relatively narrow focus upon "organized crime," that the word "pattern" in the phrase "pattern of racketeering activity" was meant to import some requirement beyond the mere existence of multiple predicate acts. Thus, when § 1961(5) says that a pattern "requires at least two acts of racketeering activity" it is describing what is needful but not sufficient. (If that were not the case, the concept of "pattern" would have been unnecessary, and the statute could simply have attached liability to "multiple acts of racketeering activity"). But what that something more is, is beyond me. As I have suggested, it is also beyond the Court. Today's opinion has added nothing to improve our prior guidance, which has created a kaleidoscope of Circuit positions, except to clarify that RICO may in addition be violated when there is a "threat of continuity." It seems to me this increases rather than removes the vagueness. There is no reason to believe that the Courts of Appeals will be any more unified in the future, than they have in the past, regarding the content of this law.

That situation is bad enough with respect to any statute, but it is intolerable with respect to RICO. *** RICO, since it has criminal applications as well, must, even in its civil applications, possess the degree of certainty required for criminal laws. No constitutional challenge to this law has been raised in the present case, and so that issue is not before us. That the highest Court in the land has been unable to derive from this statute anything more than today's meager guidance bodes ill for the day when that challenge is presented.

However unhelpful its guidance may be, however, I think the Court is correct in saying that nothing in the statute supports the proposition that predicate acts constituting part of a single scheme (or single episode) can never support a cause of action under RICO. Since the Court of Appeals here rested its decision on the contrary proposition, I concur in the judgment of the Court reversing the decision below.

NOTES AND QUESTIONS

*1. **Closed Period Continuity—How Much Time is Enough?*** The Court held that "[p]redicate acts extending over a few weeks or months and threatening no future criminal conduct" do not constitute closed period continuity. How much longer would be long enough? See, e.g., *United States v. Wilson,* 605 F.3d 985, 1021(D.C. Cir. 2010) (27 months sufficient); *United States v. Pelullo,* 964 F.2d 193, 209 (3d Cir. 1993) (19 months sufficient); *Wade v. Gaither*, 623 F. Supp. 2d 1277, 1286 (D. Utah 2009) ("nearly twelve full months" sufficient). But cf. *Primary Care Investors, Seven, Inc. v. PHP Healthcare Corp.,* 986 F.2d 1208, 1215-16 (8th Cir. 1993) (11 months insufficient) (collecting cases). Is there something magic about a year?

*2. **Closed Period Continuity and the Centrality of Time.*** In determining whether closed period continuity is present, should time be the exclusive consideration? Compare *Fleet Credit Corp. v. Sion,* 893 F.2d 441, 446-47 (1st Cir. 1990) (giving affirmative answer where defendant committed predicate offenses over a "substantial period of time") with *Resolution Trust Corp. v. Stone,* 998 F.2d 1534, 1543 (10th Cir. 1993) (giving a negative answer). Cf. *Kehr Packages, Inc. v. Fidelcor, Inc.,* 926 F.2d 1406, 1421 (3d Cir. 1991) (Alito, J., concurring in part and dissenting in part) (expressing doubt that any consideration truly matters aside from time). Courts that look at other factors typically take into account "the number of victims, the number of racketeering acts, the variety of racketeering acts, whether the injuries caused were distinct, the complexity and size of the scheme, and the nature or character of the enterprise or unlawful activity." Id. at 1543-44. See *First Capital Asset Mgt., Inc. v. Satinwood, Inc.,* 385 F.3d 159, 181 (2d Cir. 2004) (same).

Does *HJ* preclude consideration of some (or all) of these factors in evaluating closed period continuity?

3. ***Assessing Open-Ended Continuity.*** The Court indicated that open-ended continuity can turn on whether "the predicate acts or offenses are part of an ongoing entity's regular way of doing business." Cf. *United States v. Wilson,* 605 F.3d 985, 1021 (D.C. Cir. 2010) (noting the defendant's statement "'Nothing will stop this money train!'"). Are the factors mentioned in Note 2 relevant to open-ended continuity as well? Cf. *Tabas v. Tabas,* 47 F.3d 1280, 1296 n. 21 (3d Cir. 1995) (answering this question in the affirmative).

4. ***The Merits of Separateness.*** Does *H.J.* suggest the need to retain open-ended continuity and closed period continuity as separate categories? Would it be a good idea to maintain their separateness?

5. ***Void for Vagueness?*** In his concurrence, Justice Scalia encouraged defendants to mount vagueness challenges to the pattern requirement. Such challenges have not met with success. See, e.g., *United States v. Glecier,* 923 F.2d 496, 497 n. 1 (7th Cir. 1991). See generally Joseph E. Bauerschmidt, Note, "Mother of Mercy—Is this the End of RICO?"—Justice Scalia Invites Constitutional Void-for-Vagueness Challenges to RICO "Pattern," 65 Notre Dame. L. Rev. 1106 (1990).

---

3. *The Enterprise*

Under Section 1962(c), the defendant must be "employed by or associated with" a RICO "enterprise." RICO defines an "enterprise" as "includ[ing] any individual, partnership, corporation, association, or other legal entity, and any union or group of individuals associated in fact although not a legal entity." § 1961(4). In *United States v. Turkette,* 452 U.S. 576 (1981), the Supreme Court held that this definition "no more excludes criminal enterprises than it does legitimate ones" and therefore encompasses a criminal gang. Id. at 580-81. Moreover, the Court made the following observations concerning the necessary relationship between the RICO enterprise and the pattern of racketeering activity:

> In order to secure a conviction under RICO, the Government must prove both the existence of an "enterprise" and the connected "pattern of racketeering activity." The enterprise is an entity, for present purposes a group of persons associated together for a common purpose of engaging in a course of conduct.

> The pattern of racketeering activity is, on the other hand, a series of criminal acts as defined by the statute. The former is proved by evidence of an ongoing organization, formal or informal, and by evidence that the various associates function as a continuing unit. While the proof used to establish these separate elements may in particular cases coalesce, proof of one does not necessarily establish the other. The "enterprise" is not the "pattern of racketeering activity;" it is an entity separate and apart from the pattern of activity in which it engages. The existence of an enterprise at all times remains a separate element which must be proved by the Government.

Id. at 583.

NOTES AND QUESTIONS

1. ***Establishing an Association-In-Fact-Enterprise.*** When an enterprise is a corporation or other legal entity, it typically has a structure wholly apart from the pattern of racketeering activity in which it engages. Suppose, however, that the enterprise is an association-in-fact, as in *Turkette.* Under these circumstances, must the enterprise have an identifiable structure that is distinct from the pattern of racketeering activity?

The Supreme Court addressed this question in *Boyle v. United States,* 129 S.Ct. 2237 (2009). On the one hand, the Court held that "an association-in-fact enterprise must have at least three structural features: a purpose, relationships among those associated with the enterprise, and longevity sufficient to permit those associates to pursue the enterprise's purpose." Id. at 2244. On the other hand, the word "structure" need not appear in the jury instructions and "the evidence used to prove the pattern of racketeering activity and the evidence establishing an enterprise 'may in particular cases coalesce.'" Id. at 2244-45 (quoting *United States* v. *Turkette,* 452 U.S. 576, 583 (1981)). The *Boyle* Court explained:

> [A]n association-in-fact enterprise is simply a continuing unit that functions with a common purpose. Such a group need not have a hierarchical structure or a "chain of command"; decisions may be made on an ad hoc basis and by any number of methods-by majority vote, consensus, a show of strength, etc. Members of the group need not have fixed roles; different members may perform different roles at different times. The group need not have a name, regular meetings, dues, established rules and regulations, disciplinary procedures, or induction or initiation ceremonies. While the group must function as a continuing unit and remain in existence long enough to pursue a course of conduct, nothing in RICO exempts an enterprise whose associates engage in spurts of activity punctuated by periods of quiescence. Nor is the statute limited to groups whose crimes are sophisticated, diverse, complex, or unique; for example, a group that does nothing but engage in extortion through old-fashioned, unsophisticated, and brutal means may fall squarely within the statute's reach.

129 S.Ct. at 2245-46. The dissent, written by Justice Stevens and joined by Justice Breyer, argued that the majority "renders the enterprise requirement essentially meaningless in association-in-fact cases." Id. at 2250 (Stevens, J., dissenting). Do you agree?

2. ***Differentiating the Enterprise from the "Person."*** Section 1962(c) differentiates between the "enterprise" and the "person" who is the defendant. The Supreme Court has held that the "enterprise" and the "person" are sufficiently distinct when the enterprise is a corporation with a single shareholder and that shareholder is the defendant: "The corporate owner/employee, a natural person, is distinct from the corporation itself, a legally different entity with different rights and responsibilities due to its different legal status." *Cedric Kushner Promotions, Ltd. v. King,* 533 U.S. 158, 163 (2001). Can the enterprise be a sole proprietorship and the defendant the sole proprietor? In a decision prior to *Cedric*, Judge Posner suggested that the answer turns on whether the proprietorship has employees:

> A sole proprietorship is a recognized legal entity, and, provided it has any employees, is in any event a "group of individuals associated in fact." Since *** the enterprises to which the statute refers include criminal enterprises, and not just legitimate enterprises penetrated or looted by criminals, it would be passing strange to exclude proprietorships. After all, we do not suppose that "Murder, Inc." was really a corporation.***
>
> There would be a problem if the sole proprietorship were strictly a 1-man show. *** [Y]ou cannot associate with yourself, any more than you can conspire with yourself, just by giving yourself a *nom de guerre.* *** But Suter had several people working for him; this made his company an enterprise, and not just a one-man-band. ***

McCullough v. Suter, 757 F.2d 142, 143-44 (7th Cir. 1985). See *Wade v. Gaither*, 623 F. Supp. 2d 1277, 1287 (D. Utah 2009) (noting that all federal appeals courts to confront the issue have adopted the reasoning of *McCullough*). Cf. *Guidry v. Bank of LaPlace,* 954 F.2d 278, 283 (5th Cir. 1992) (finding Section 1962(c) inapplicable to a proprietorship with no employees). Are *McCullough* and *Guidry* consistent with *Cedric*? Can the corporation be the "person" and the enterprise be an association of the corporation and its employees?

---

4. *Conducting or Participating in the Conduct of the Enterprise*

Under Section 1962(c), the defendant must "conduct or participate, directly or indirectly, in the conduct of" the RICO enterprise. The Supreme Court construed this language in the decision that follows.

REVES v. ERNST & YOUNG

507 U.S. 170 (1993)

JUSTICE HAROLD A. BLACKMUN:

This case requires us once again to interpret the provisions of the Racketeer Influenced and Corrupt Organizations (RICO) chapter of the Organized Crime Control Act of 1970. Section 1962(c) makes it unlawful "for any person employed by or associated with any enterprise engaged in, or the activities of which affect, interstate or foreign commerce, to conduct or participate, directly or indirectly, in the conduct of such enterprise's affairs through a pattern of racketeering activity...." The question presented is whether one must participate in the operation or management of the enterprise itself to be subject to liability under this provision.

I

The Farmer's Cooperative of Arkansas and Oklahoma, Inc. (Co-Op), began operating in western Arkansas and eastern Oklahoma in 1946. To raise money for operating expenses, the Co-Op sold promissory notes payable to the holder on demand. Each year, Co-Op members were elected to serve on its board. The board met monthly but delegated actual management of the Co-Op to a general manager. In 1952, the board appointed Jack White as general manager.

In January 1980, White began taking loans from the Co-Op to finance the construction of a gasohol plant by his company, White Flame Fuels, Inc. By the end of 1980, White's debts to the Co-Op totaled approximately $4 million. In September of that year, White and Gene Kuykendall, who served as the accountant for both the Co-Op and White Flame, were indicted for federal tax fraud. At a board meeting on November 12, 1980, White proposed that the Co-Op purchase White Flame. The board agreed. One month later, however, the Co-Op filed a declaratory action against White and White Flame in Arkansas state court alleging that White actually had sold White Flame to the Co-Op in February 1980. The complaint was drafted by White's attorneys and led to a consent decree relieving White of his debts and providing that the Co-Op had owned White Flame since February 15, 1980.

White and Kuykendall were convicted of tax fraud in January 1981. Harry Erwin, the managing partner of Russell Brown and Company, an Arkansas accounting firm, testified for White, and shortly thereafter the Co-Op retained Russell Brown to perform its 1981 financial audit. Joe Drozal, a partner in the Brown firm, was put in charge of the audit and Joe Cabaniss was selected to assist him. On January 2, 1982, Russell Brown and Company merged with Arthur Young and Company, which later became respondent Ernst & Young.

One of Drozal's first tasks in the audit was to determine White Flame's fixed-asset value. After consulting with White and reviewing White Flame's books (which Kuykendall had prepared), Drozal concluded that the plant's value at the end of 1980 was $4,393,242.66, the figure Kuykendall had employed. Using this figure as a base, Drozal factored in the 1981 construction costs and capitalized expenses and concluded that White Flame's 1981 fixed-asset value was approximately $4.5 million. Drozal then had to determine how that value should be treated for accounting purposes. If the Co-Op had owned White Flame from the beginning of construction in 1979, White Flame's value for accounting purposes would be its fixed-asset value of $4.5 million. If, however, the Co-Op had purchased White Flame from White, White Flame would have to be given its fair market value at the time of purchase, which was somewhere between $444,000 and $1.5 million. If White Flame were valued at less than $1.5 million, the Co-Op was insolvent. Drozal concluded that the Co-Op had owned White Flame from the start and that the plant should be valued at $4.5 million on its books.

On April 22, 1982, Arthur Young presented its 1981 audit report to the Co-Op's board. In that audit's Note 9, Arthur Young expressed doubt whether the investment in White Flame could ever be recovered. Note 9 also observed that White Flame was sustaining operating losses averaging $100,000 per month. Arthur Young did not tell the board of its conclusion that the Co-Op always had owned White Flame or that without that conclusion the Co-Op was insolvent.

On May 27, the Co-Op held its 1982 annual meeting. At that meeting, the Co-Op, through Harry C. Erwin, a partner in Arthur Young, distributed to the members condensed financial statements. These included White Flame's $4.5 million asset value among its total assets but omitted the information contained in the audit's Note 9. Cabaniss was also present. Erwin saw the condensed financial statement for the first time when he arrived at the meeting. In a 5-minute presentation, he told his audience that the statements were condensed and that copies of the full audit were available at the Co-Op's office. In response to questions, Erwin explained that the Co-Op owned White Flame and that the plant had incurred approximately $1.2 million in losses but he revealed no other information relevant to the Co-Op's true financial health.

The Co-Op hired Arthur Young also to perform its 1982 audit. The 1982 report, presented to the board on March 7, 1983, was similar to the 1981 report and restated (this time in its Note 8) Arthur Young's doubt whether the investment in White Flame was recoverable. The gasohol plant again was valued at approximately $4.5 million and was responsible for the Co-Op's showing a positive net worth. The condensed financial statement distributed at the annual meeting on March 24, 1983, omitted the information in Note 8. This time, Arthur Young reviewed the condensed statement in advance but did not act to remove its name from the statement. Cabaniss, in a 3-minute presentation at the meeting, gave the financial report. He informed the members that the full audit was available at the Co-Op's office but did not tell them about Note 8 or that the Co-Op was in financial difficulty if White Flame were written down to its fair market value.

In February 1984, the Co-Op experienced a slight run on its demand notes. On February 23, when it was unable to secure further financing, the Co-Op filed for bankruptcy. As a result, the demand notes were frozen in the bankruptcy estate and were no longer redeemable at will by the noteholders.

II

On February 14, 1985, the trustee in bankruptcy filed suit against 40 individuals and entities, including Arthur Young, on behalf of the Co-Op and certain noteholders. The District Court certified a class of noteholders, petitioners here, consisting of persons who had purchased demand notes between February 15, 1980, and February 23, 1984. Petitioners settled with all defendants except Arthur Young. The District Court determined before trial that the demand notes were securities under both federal and state law. The court then granted summary judgment in favor of Arthur Young on the RICO claim. The District Court applied the test established by the Eighth Circuit in *Bennett v. Berg,* 710 F.2d 1361, 1364 (en banc) (1983), that § 1962(c) requires "some participation in the operation or management of the enterprise itself." The court ruled: "Plaintiffs have failed to show anything more than that the accountants reviewed a series of completed transactions, and certified the Co-Op's records as fairly portraying its financial status as of a date three or four months preceding the meetings of the directors and the shareholders at which they presented their reports. We do not hesitate to declare that such activities fail to satisfy the degree of management required by *Bennett v. Berg*."

The case went to trial on the state and federal securities fraud claims. The jury found that Arthur Young had committed both state and federal securities fraud and awarded approximately $6.1 million in damages. The Court of Appeals reversed, concluding that the demand notes were not securities under federal or state law. On writ of certiorari, this Court ruled that the notes were securities within the meaning of § 3(a)(10) of the Securities Exchange Act of 1934. *Reves v. Ernst & Young,* 494 U.S. 56, 70 (1990).

On remand, the Court of Appeals affirmed the judgment of the District Court in all major respects except the damages award, which it reversed and remanded for a new trial. The only part of the Court of Appeals' decision that is at issue here is its affirmance of summary judgment in favor of Arthur Young on the RICO claim. Like the District Court, the Court of Appeals applied the "operation or management" test articulated in *Bennett v. Berg* and held that Arthur Young's conduct did not "rise to the level of participation in the management or operation of the Co-Op." ***

III

"In determining the scope of a statute, we look first to its language. If the statutory language is unambiguous, in the absence of 'a clearly expressed legislative intent to the contrary, that language must ordinarily be regarded as conclusive.' " *United States v. Turkette,* 452 U.S. 576, 580 (1981), quoting *Consumer Product Safety Comm'n v. GTE Sylvania, Inc.,* 447 U.S. 102, 108 (1980). Section 1962(c) makes it unlawful "for any person employed by or associated with any enterprise ... to conduct or participate, directly or indirectly, in the conduct of such enterprise's affairs through a pattern of racketeering activity...."

The narrow question in this case is the meaning of the phrase "to conduct or participate, directly or indirectly, in the conduct of such enterprise's affairs." The word "conduct" is used twice, and it seems reasonable to give each use a similar construction. As a verb, "conduct" means to lead, run, manage, or direct. Webster's Third New International Dictionary 474 (1976). Petitioners urge us to read "conduct" as "carry on," so that almost any involvement in the affairs of an enterprise would satisfy the "conduct or participate" requirement. But context is important, and in the context of the phrase "to conduct ... [an] enterprise's affairs," the word indicates some degree of direction.

The dissent agrees that, when "conduct" is used as a verb, "it is plausible to find in it a suggestion of control." The dissent prefers to focus on "conduct" as a noun, as in the phrase "participate, directly or indirectly, in the conduct of [an] enterprise's affairs." But unless one reads "conduct" to include an element of direction when used as a noun in this phrase, the word becomes superfluous. Congress could easily have written "participate, directly or indirectly, in [an] enterprise's affairs," but it chose to repeat the word "conduct." We conclude, therefore, that as both a noun and a verb in this subsection "conduct" requires an element of direction.

The more difficult question is what to make of the word "participate." This Court previously has characterized this word as a "ter [m] ... of breadth."

Russello [*v. United States*, 464 U.S. 16, 21-22 (1983).] Petitioners argue that Congress used "participate" as a synonym for "aid and abet." That would be a term of breadth indeed, for "aid and abet" "comprehends all assistance rendered by words, acts, encouragement, support, or presence." Black's Law Dictionary 68 (6th ed. 1990). But within the context of § 1962(c), "participate" appears to have a narrower meaning. We may mark the limits of what the term might mean by looking again at what Congress did *not* say. On the one hand, "to participate ... in the conduct of ... affairs" must be broader than "to conduct affairs" or the "participate" phrase would be superfluous. On the other hand, as we already have noted, "to participate ... in the conduct of ... affairs" must be narrower than "to participate in affairs" or Congress' repetition of the word "conduct" would serve no purpose. It seems that Congress chose a middle ground, consistent with a common understanding of the word "participate"—"to take part in." Webster's Third New International Dictionary 1646 (1976).

Once we understand the word "conduct" to require some degree of direction and the word "participate" to require some part in that direction, the meaning of § 1962(c) comes into focus. In order to "participate, directly or indirectly, in the conduct of such enterprise's affairs," one must have some part in directing those affairs. Of course, the word "participate" makes clear that RICO liability is not limited to those with primary responsibility for the enterprise's affairs, just as the phrase "directly or indirectly" makes clear that RICO liability is not limited to those with a formal position in the enterprise,[4] but *some* part in directing the enterprise's affairs is required. The "operation or management" test expresses this requirement in a formulation that is easy to apply.

IV

A

This test finds further support in the legislative history of § 1962. ***

In their comments on the floor, Members of Congress consistently referred to subsection (c) as prohibiting the *operation* of an enterprise through a pattern of racketeering activity and to subsections (a) and (b) as prohibiting the *acquisition* of an enterprise. Representative Cellar, who was chairman of the House Judiciary Committee that voted RICO out in 1970, described § 1962(c) as proscribing the "conduct of the affairs of a business by a person acting in a *managerial* capacity, through racketeering activity." 116 Cong. Rec. 35196 (1970) (emphasis added).

Of course, the fact that Members of Congress understood § 1962(c) to prohibit the operation or management of an enterprise through a pattern of racketeering activity does not necessarily mean that they understood § 1962(c) to be limited to the operation or management of an enterprise. It is clear from other remarks, however, that Congress did not intend RICO to extend beyond

4. For these reasons, we disagree with the suggestion of the Court of Appeals for the District of Columbia Circuit that § 1962(c) requires "*significant control* over or within an enterprise." *Yellow Bus Lines, Inc. v. Drivers, Chauffeurs & Helpers Local Union 639,* 913 F.2d 948, 954 (1990) (en banc) (emphasis added).

the acquisition or operation of an enterprise. *** [C]ritics of the bill raised concerns that racketeering activity was defined so broadly that RICO would reach many crimes not necessarily typical of organized crime. See 116 Cong. Rec. 18912-18914, 18939-18940 (1970) (remarks of Sen. McClellan). Senator McClellan reassured the bill's critics that the critical limitation was not to be found in § 1961(1)'s list of predicate crimes but in the statute's other requirements, including those of § 1962:

> The danger that commission of such offenses by other individuals would subject them to proceedings under title IX [RICO] is even smaller than any such danger under title III of the 1968 [Safe Streets] [A]ct, since commission of a crime listed under title IX provides only one element of title IX's prohibitions. Unless an individual not only commits such a crime but engages in a pattern of such violations, and uses that pattern to obtain or operate an interest in an interstate business, he is not made subject to proceedings under title IX.

116 Cong. Rec., at 18940.

Thus, the legislative history confirms what we have already deduced from the language of § 1962(c)—that one is not liable under that provision unless one has participated in the operation or management of the enterprise itself.

B

RICO's "liberal construction" clause does not require rejection of the "operation or management" test. Congress directed, by § 904(a) of Pub.L. 91-452, 84 Stat. 947, that the "provisions of this title shall be liberally construed to effectuate its remedial purposes." This clause obviously seeks to ensure that Congress' intent is not frustrated by an overly narrow reading of the statute, but it is not an invitation to apply RICO to new purposes that Congress never intended. Nor does the clause help us to determine what purposes Congress had in mind. Those must be gleaned from the statute through the normal means of interpretation. The clause " 'only serves as an aid for resolving an ambiguity; it is not to be used to beget one.' " *Sedima, S.P.R.L. v. Imrex Co.,* 473 U.S. 479, 492, n. 10 (1985), quoting *Callanan v. United States,* 364 U.S. 587, 596 (1961). In this case it is clear that Congress did not intend to extend RICO liability under § 1962(c) beyond those who participate in the operation or management of an enterprise through a pattern of racketeering activity.[8]

V

Petitioners argue that the "operation or management" test is flawed because liability under § 1962(c) is not limited to upper management but may extend to "any person employed by or associated with [the] enterprise." We agree that liability under § 1962(c) is not limited to upper management, but we disagree that the "operation or management" test is inconsistent with this proposition. An enterprise is "operated" not just by upper management but also by lower rung participants in the enterprise who are under the direction of

---

8. Because the meaning of the statute is clear from its language and legislative history, we have no occasion to consider the application of the rule of lenity. We note, however, that the rule of lenity would also favor the narrower "operation or management" test that we adopt.

upper management.[9] An enterprise also might be "operated" or "managed" by others "associated with" the enterprise who exert control over it as, for example, by bribery.

The United States also argues that the "operation or management" test is not consistent with § 1962(c) because it limits the liability of "outsiders" who have no official position within the enterprise. The United States correctly points out that RICO's major purpose was to attack the "infiltration of organized crime and racketeering into legitimate organizations," S. Rep. No. 91-617, at 76, but its argument fails on several counts. First, it ignores the fact that § 1962 has four subsections. Infiltration of legitimate organizations by "outsiders" is clearly addressed in subsections (a) and (b), and the "operation or management" test that applies under subsection (c) in no way limits the application of subsections (a) and (b) to "outsiders." Second, § 1962(c) is limited to persons "employed by or associated with" an enterprise, suggesting a more limited reach than subsections (a) and (b), which do not contain such a restriction. Third, § 1962(c) cannot be interpreted to reach complete "outsiders" because liability depends on showing that the defendants conducted or participated in the conduct of the "*enterprise's* affairs," not just their *own* affairs. Of course, "outsiders" may be liable under § 1962(c) if they are "associated with" an enterprise and participate in the conduct of *its* affairs—that is, participate in the operation or management of the enterprise itself—but it would be consistent with neither the language nor the legislative history of § 1962(c) to interpret it as broadly as petitioners and the United States urge.

In sum, we hold that "to conduct or participate, directly or indirectly, in the conduct of such enterprise's affairs," § 1962(c), one must participate in the operation or management of the enterprise itself.

VI

*** In this case, it is undisputed that Arthur Young relied upon existing Co-Op records in preparing the 1981 and 1982 audit reports. The AICPA's professional standards state that an auditor may draft financial statements in whole or in part based on information from management's accounting system. See [1 CCH AICPA Professional Standards, SAS No. 1, § 110.02 (1982)]. It is also undisputed that Arthur Young's audit reports revealed to the Co-Op's board that the value of the gasohol plant had been calculated based on the Co-Op's investment in the plant. Thus, we only could conclude that Arthur Young participated in the operation or management of the Co-Op itself if Arthur Young's failure to tell the Co-Op's board that the plant should have been given its fair market value constituted such participation. We think that Arthur Young's failure in this respect is not sufficient to give rise to liability under § 1962(c).

The judgment of the Court of Appeals is affirmed.

---

9. At oral argument, there was some discussion about whether low-level employees could be considered to have participated in the conduct of an enterprise's affairs. We need not decide in this case how far § 1962(c) extends down the ladder of operation because it is clear that Arthur Young was not acting under the direction of the Co-Op's officers or board.

JUSTICE DAVID H. SOUTER, WITH WHOM JUSTICE WHITE JOINS, DISSENTING:

In the word "conduct," the Court today finds a clear congressional mandate to limit RICO liability under 18 U.S.C. § 1962(c) to participants in the "operation or management" of a RICO enterprise. What strikes the Court as clear, however, looks at the very least hazy to me, and I accordingly find the statute's "liberal construction" provision not irrelevant, but dispositive. But even if I were to assume, with the majority, that the word "conduct" clearly imports some degree of direction or control into § 1962(c), I would have to say that the majority misapplies its own "operation or management" test to the facts presented here. I therefore respectfully dissent.

The word "conduct" occurs twice in § 1962(c), first as a verb, then as a noun.

> It shall be unlawful for any person employed by or associated with any enterprise engaged in, or the activities of which affect, interstate or foreign commerce, to conduct or participate, directly or indirectly, in the conduct of such enterprise's affairs through a pattern of racketeering activity or collection of unlawful debt.

18 U.S.C. § 1962(c).

Although the Court is surely correct that the cognates should receive consistent readings, and correct again that "context is important" in coming to understand the sense of the terms intended by Congress, the majority goes astray in quoting only the verb form of "conduct" in its statement of the context for divining a meaning that must fit the noun usage as well. Thus, the majority reaches its pivotal conclusion that "in the context of the phrase 'to conduct ... [an] enterprise's affairs,' the word indicates some degree of direction." Ibid. To be sure, if the statutory setting is so abbreviated as to limit consideration to the word as a verb, it is plausible to find in it a suggestion of control, as in the phrase "to conduct an orchestra." (Even so, the suggestion is less than emphatic, since even when "conduct" is used as a verb, "[t]he notion of direction or leadership is often obscured or lost; e.g. an investigation is *conducted* by all those who take part in it." 3 Oxford English Dictionary 691 (2d ed. 1989) (emphasis in original).

In any event, the context is not so limited, and several features of the full subsection at issue support a more inclusive construction of "conduct." The term, when used as a noun, is defined by the majority's chosen dictionary as, for example, "carrying forward" or "carrying out," Webster's Third New International Dictionary 473 (1976), phrases without any implication of direction or control. The suggestion of control is diminished further by the fact that § 1962(c) covers not just those "employed by" an enterprise, but those merely "associated with" it, as well. And associates (like employees) are prohibited not merely from conducting the affairs of an enterprise through a pattern of racketeering, not merely from participating directly in such unlawful conduct, but even from indirect participation in the conduct of an enterprise's affairs in such a manner. The very breadth of this prohibition renders the majority's reading of "conduct" rather awkward, for it is hard to imagine how the "operation or management" test would leave the statute with the capacity to reach the indirect participation of someone merely associated with an enterprise. I think, then, that this contextual examination shows "conduct" to have a long arm, unlimited by any requirement to prove that the activity includes an element of direction. But at the very least, the full context is enough to defeat the majority's conviction that the more restrictive interpretation of the word "conduct" is clearly the one intended.[1]

What, then, if we call it a tie on the contextual analysis? The answer is that Congress has given courts faced with uncertain meaning a clear tiebreaker in RICO's "liberal construction" clause, which directs that the "provisions of this title shall be liberally construed to effectuate its remedial purposes." We have relied before on this "express admonition" to read RICO provisions broadly, see *Sedima, S.P.R.L. v. Imrex Co.,* 473 U.S. 479, 497-498 (1985), and in this instance, the "liberal construction" clause plays its intended part, directing us to recognize the more inclusive definition of the word "conduct," free of any restricting element of direction or control.[2] Because the Court of Appeals employed a narrower reading, I would reverse.

Even if I were to adopt the majority's view of § 1962(c), however, I still could not join the judgment, which seems to me unsupportable under the very "operation or management" test the Court announces. If Arthur Young had confined itself in this case to the role traditionally performed by an outside auditor, I could agree with the majority that Arthur Young took no part in the management or operation of the Farmer's Cooperative of Arkansas and Oklahoma, Inc. (Co-Op). But the record on summary judgment, viewed most favorably to Reves, shows that Arthur Young created the very financial statements it was hired, and purported, to audit. Most importantly, Reves adduced evidence that Arthur Young took on management responsibilities by deciding, in the first instance, what value to assign to the Co-Op's most important fixed asset, the White Flame gasohol plant, and Arthur Young itself conceded below that the alleged activity went beyond traditional auditing. Because I find, then, that even under the majority's "operation or management" test the Court of Appeals erroneously affirmed the summary judgment for Arthur Young, I would (again) reverse.

For our purposes, the line between managing and auditing is fairly clear. ***

---

1. The Court attempts to shore up its interpretation with an examination of relevant legislative materials. The legislative history demonstrates only that when Members of Congress needed a shorthand method of referring to § 1962(c), they spoke of prohibiting "the operation" of an enterprise through a pattern of racketeering activity. As Arthur Young points out, "operation" is essentially interchangeable with "conduct"; each term can include a sense of direction, but each is also definable as "carrying on" or "carrying out." There is no indication that the congressional shorthand was meant to attend to the statutory nuance at issue here. As the Court concedes, "[T]he fact that Members of Congress understood§1962(c) to prohibit the operation or management of an enterprise through a pattern of racketeering activity does not necessarily mean that they understood § 1962(c) to be limited to the operation or management of an enterprise."

2. The majority claims that without an element of direction, the word "conduct," when it appears as a noun, becomes superfluous. Given the redundant language Congress has chosen for § 1962(c), however, any consistent reading of "conduct" will tend to make one of its two appearances superfluous.

*** [M]anagement chooses the assertions to appear in financial statements; the auditor "simply expresses an opinion on the client's financial statements." Brief for Respondent 30. These standards leave no doubt that an accountant can in no sense independently audit financial records when he has selected their substance himself. See *In re Thomas P. Reynolds Securities, Ltd.*, Exchange Act Release No. 29689 (Sept. 16, 1991) ("A company may, of course, rely on an outside firm to prepare its books of account and financial statements. However, once an accounting firm performs those functions, it has become identified with management and may not perform an audit").

The evidence on summary judgment, read favorably to Reves, indicates that Arthur Young did indeed step out of its auditing shoes and into those of management, in creating the financial record on which the Co-Op's solvency was erroneously predicated. ***

Arthur Young realized it could not rely on White Flame's 1980 financial statement, which had been prepared by a convicted felon (who also happened to be the Co-Op's former accountant), and an internal memo that appears in the record shows that Arthur Young had a number of serious questions about White Flame's cost figures for the plant. Nonetheless, Arthur Young "essentially invented" a cost figure that matched, to the penny, the phoney figure that Kuykendall, White Flame's convicted accountant, had created. With this "invented" cost figure in hand, Arthur Young then proceeded to decide, again without consulting management, when the Co-Op had acquired White Flame. Although the Co-Op's 1980 financial statement indicated an acquisition of White Flame in February 1980, as did a local court decree, Arthur Young "adopted a blatant fiction—that the Co-Op [had] owned the entire plant at its inception in May, 1979—in order to justify carrying the asset on [the Co-Op's] books at its total cost, as if the Co-Op had built it from scratch." App. 137. Apparently, the idea that the Co-Op had owned the gasohol plant since 1979 was reflected nowhere in the Co-Op's books, and Arthur Young was solely responsible for the Co-Op's decision to treat the transaction in this manner.[5]

---

5. The majority asserts, as an "undisputed" fact, "that Arthur Young relied upon Co-Op records in preparing the 1981 and 1982 audit reports." In fact, however, the District Court found that Reves had presented evidence sufficient to show that Arthur Young "essentially invented" a cost figure for White Flame (after examining White Flame records created by Kuykendall). Since the Co-Op's 1980 financial statement indicated that the Co-Op had advanced White Flame only $4.1 million through the end of 1980, Arthur Young could not have relied on the Co-Op's records in concluding that the plant's value was nearly $4.4 million at the end of 1980. The District Court also found sufficient evidence in the record to support the conclusion that Arthur Young had created the "blatant fiction" that the Co-Op had owned White Flame from its inception, despite overwhelming evidence to the contrary in the Co-Op's records. See App. 137-138; see also 937 F.2d, at 1317 ("In concluding that the Co-Op had always owned White Flame, [Arthur Young] ignored a great deal of information suggesting exactly the opposite"). The evidence indicates that it was creative accounting, not reliance on the Co-Op's books, that led Arthur Young to treat the Co-Op as the plant's owner from the time of its construction in 1979 (a conclusion necessary to support Arthur Young's decision to value the plant at total cost). Not even the decree procured in the friendly lawsuit engineered by White and his lawyers treated the Co-Op as building the plant, or as owning it before February 1980.

Relying on this fiction, the unreality of which it never shared with the Co-Op's board of directors, let alone the membership, Arthur Young prepared the Co-Op's 1981 financial statement and listed a fixed- asset value of more than $4.5 million for the gasohol plant. Arthur Young listed a similar value for White Flame in the Co-Op's financial statement for 1982. By these actions, Arthur Young took on management responsibilities, for it thereby made assertions about the fixed-asset value of White Flame that were derived, not from information or any figure provided by the Co-Op's management, but from its own financial analysis. ***

The evidence petitioners presented in opposing the motion for summary judgment demonstrated Arthur Young's "participation" in this broad sense. By assuming the authority to make key decisions in stating the Co-Op's own valuation of its major fixed asset, and by creating financial statements that were the responsibility of the Co-Op's management, Arthur Young crossed the line separating "outside" auditors from "inside" financial managers. Because the majority, like the Court of Appeals, affirms the grant of summary judgment in spite of this evidence, I believe that it misapplies its own "operation or management" test, and I therefore respectfully dissent.

NOTES AND QUESTIONS

*1. **Plain Language?*** The majority found it "clear" that Section 1962(c) limits liability to participants in the operation or management of the enterprise. Do you agree?

Suppose that a majority of justices had found the statutory language ambiguous. Under these circumstances, would application of the liberal construction clause have been appropriate? Or would it instead have been appropriate to apply strict construction, on the theory that whatever interpretation emerged must be suitable for criminal actions as well as civil actions?

*2. **Applying the Operation or Management Test to Arthur Young.*** Why didn't Arthur Young's involvement in the Co-Op's affairs satisfy the "operation or management test"? Think about whether you agree that the Court would have found the test satisfied "[h]ad the auditors prepared the misleading summaries or had the plaintiffs' claim for relief relied on misleading statements made by a representative of the accounting firm (rather than a failure to disclose information), or had a representative of the accounting firm made misleading statements at the board meeting." Michael Vitiello, More Noise from the Tower of Babel: Making "Sense" Out of *Reves v. Ernst & Young*, 56 Ohio St. L.J. 1363, 1382 (1995).

Would the *Reves* plaintiffs have stood a better chance of success if they had alleged that Arthur Young was the "person" who directed the affairs of an entity comprised of the Co-Op, Arthur Young, and Jack White? Compare Daniel R. Fischel & Alan O. Sykes, Civil RICO After *Reves*: An Economic Commentary, 1993 Sup. Ct. Rev. 157, 194 (raising this question) with *Walter v. Drayson*, 538 F.3d 1244, 1249 (9th Cir. 2008) (holding that "Section 1962(c)'s conduct requirement applies without regard to the nature of the enterprise").

Is the *Reves* Court correct in its assertion that the operation or management test is "easy to apply"?

3. ***The Operation or Management Test and Outsiders.*** When it comes to applying the operation or management test to outsiders of the enterprise, the appellate courts have been very demanding. Consider the following discussion of the test as applied to banks:

> A bank's financial assistance and professional services may assist a customer engaging in racketeering activities, but that alone does not satisfy the stringent "operation and management" test of *Reves*. See *Schmidt v. Fleet Bank*, 16 F.Supp.2d 340, 346-48 (S.D.N.Y.1998), and cases cited. In *Schmidt*, allegations that the bank approved overdrafts on 500 occasions, misrepresented the status of accounts to investors, and helped its customer conceal his fraudulent scheme were held to be insufficient to satisfy this test. Plaintiffs have not cited and we have not found any post- *Reves* case in which a bank or financial services company was held to have conducted the affairs of a RICO enterprise that was an unrelated customer of the bank.

Dahlgren v. First Nat'l Bank, 533 F.3d 681, 690 (8th Cir. 2008). In thinking about the wisdom of this tough stance towards outsiders, contrast it with the very different approach to insiders described in the next Note.

4. ***The Operation or Management Test and Lower Rung Employees.*** The Court acknowledged that liability under Section 1962(c) encompasses not only outsiders and "upper management" but also "lower rung participants in the enterprise who are under the direction of upper management." But it "[l]eft unclear *** whether *** lower rung participants must themselves play some 'direct[ing]' role, or need only be acting under the direction of upper management". *United States v. Allen,* 155 F.3d 35, 42 (2d Cir. 1998). As the First Circuit put it: "Special care is required in translating *Reves'* concern with 'horizontal' connections–focusing on the liability of an outside adviser–into the 'vertical' question of how far RICO liability may extend within the enterprise but down the organizational ladder." *United States v. Oreto*, 37 F.3d 739, 750 (1st Cir. 1994).

The various federal appellate formulations regarding lower rung employees tend to be somewhat amorphous. See, e.g, *United States v. Burden,* 600 F.3d 204, 219 (2d Cir. 2010) (noting that "[i]t is sufficient to be a lower-level participant and still be liable for directing the enterprise's affairs if one 'exercise[s] broad discretion' in carrying out the principal's instructions") (quoting *United States v. Diaz*, 176 F.3d 52, 92 (2d Cir.1999)); *United States v. Brandao*, 539 F.3d 44, 54 (1st Cir. 2008) (noting that "[i]nsiders-those 'who are integral to carrying out the enterprise's racketeering activities'-by definition participate in the conduct of the enterprise") (quoting *United States v. Houlihan*, 92 F.3d 1271, 1299 (1st Cir.1996)); *United States v. Urban*, 404 F.3d 754, 770 (3d Cir. 2005) (focusing on whether the employees "'knowingly further the illegal aims of the enterprise'") (quoting *United States v. Parise*, 159 F.3d 790, 796 (3d Cir. 1998)). Is greater precision possible?

5. ***The Operation or Management Test and RICO Conspiracy.*** RICO's conspiracy provision reads as follows: "It shall be unlawful for any person to conspire to violate any of the provisions of subsections (a),(b), or (c) of this section." 18 U.S.C. § 1962(d). In the view of all of the circuits to confront the issue, the operation or management test does not apply to conspiracy claims. See *United States v. Wilson*, 605 F.3d 985, 1019 (D.C.Cir. 2010) (collecting cases). The reason is that "a conspirator charged with racketeering conspiracy

need not commit or even agree to commit the predicate acts that are elements of a substantive count to be found guilty of racketeering conspiracy," for 'it suffices that he adopt[ed] the goal of furthering or facilitating the criminal endeavor.'" *United States v. Ciccone*, 312 F.3d 535, 542 (2d Cir. 2002) (quoting *Salinas v. United States*, 522 U.S. 52, 65 (1997)).

6. ***Statute of Limitations.*** RICO does not provide a statute of limitations for criminal liability. Accordingly, RICO prosecutions are governed by the general five year statute of limitations for criminal offenses set forth in 18 U.S.C. § 3282. See *Agency Holding Corp. v. Malley Duff & Assocs., Inc.,* 483 U.S. 143, 155-56 (1987). Thus, the limitations period has expired when the defendant has not committed at least one predicate act within five years of the indictment. See *United States v. Bruno,* 383 F.3d 65, 80 n.10 (2d Cir. 2004).

PROBLEM 11-6

Sam did legal work for Plex, Inc. while an associate at a large law firm. After several years at the firm, Sam left to set up his own firm, with Plex as his sole client. After consulting with Sam, Plex's president (Hugh) decided that Plex would make a private offering. In his work on that offering, Sam suggested to Hugh that the private placement memorandum be drafted so as to hide certain highly risky aspects of the business. Hugh accepted this suggestion. Does Sam operate or manage Plex for purposes of RICO? Would it make a difference if Sam were also a member of the Plex board of directors?

PROBLEM 11-7

Lincoln, Inc., a technology firm and reporting company under the Exchange Act, made a $10 million registered offering in January 2001. The announced purpose of the offering was to raise money to expand the business. But the actual intent was to use half the money raised to pay off accumulated debts. This intent was carried out, but the company made no public acknowledgment as to the actual use of the proceeds. Indeed, in consecutive SEC filings from March 2001 through November 2002, Lincoln misrepresented how the proceeds from the offering had been used.

The perpetrators of the scheme to misrepresent the true use of the proceeds were the five inside directors and the outside accountant (Mary). Mary is senior vice president of the accounting firm of Triplecheck, Inc., having served as a vice president of Lincoln from 1999-2000.

Can prosecutors bring a RICO action based on these facts? Who should be the defendant? The enterprise? What difficulties would the prosecution be likely to encounter?

5. ***Private RICO Securities Actions***

Until 1995, private plaintiffs suing for fraud under the Securities Act and the Exchange Act would typically add a RICO allegation to their complaints. In addition to providing for recovery of treble damages and attorneys' fees and costs, civil RICO afforded plaintiffs an attractive vehicle for circumventing many of the limitations embedded in the federal securities laws. For example, RICO allowed them to sidestep the purchaser-seller requirement, see *Holmes v. Securities Investor Protection Corp.,* 503 U.S. 258, 285-86 (1992) (O' Connor, J., concurring in part and concurring in the judgment); the elimination of aiding and abetting liability, see, e.g., *Jaguar Cars, Inc. v. Royal Oaks Motor Car Co.*, 46 F.3d 258, 270 (3d Cir. 1995); and the Exchange Act's requirement of exclusive federal jurisdiction, see *Tafflin v. Levitt*, 493 U.S. 455 (1990). That RICO made possible such circumventions generated widespread dismay, as did the perception that securities defendants were being coerced into settling dubious RICO claims so as to avoid being labeled racketeers.

Congress responded to these concerns in the Private Securities Litigation Reform Act (PSLRA). That Act amended Section 1964(c) of RICO—the provision authorizing private actions—by stating that for such actions (but not for government actions) an act of racketeering activity does not encompass "conduct that would have been actionable as fraud in the purchase or sale of securities." Moreover, the Conference Report accompanying the legislation expressed Congress's desire that plaintiffs be barred from pleading other offenses (wire or mail fraud, for example) as acts of racketeering activity if those offenses embrace conduct prohibited by the federal securities laws. H.R. Conf. Rep. No. 104-369 at 47 (1995). Courts have displayed a willingness to give effect to this statement in the legislative history. See, e.g., *Bald Eagle Area Sch. Dist. v. Keystone Fin.*, 189 F.3d 321, 329 (3d Cir. 1999). See also *MLSMK, Inv. Co. v. J.P. Morgan Chase & Co.*, 651 F.3d 268, 277 (2d Cir. 2011) (holding that the PSLRA "bars civil RICO claims alleging predicate acts of securities fraud, even when a plaintiff cannot itself pursue a securities fraud action against the defendant"); *Swartz v. KPMG, LLP*, 476 F.3d 756, 761 (9th Cir. 2007) (dismissing the plaintiff's argument that the sale of securities was "incidental" to the fraud).

The PSLRA does, however, permit a plaintiff to assert civil RICO claims against a defendant who, in connection with the fraud, has previously been convicted of a criminal securities law violation. See Section 1964(c). Accordingly, a plaintiff's use of civil RICO for a claim predicated on securities fraud is now entirely dependent on a federal prosecutor's ability to convict a defendant of a crime involving securities fraud. But since criminal prosecutions are by no means infrequent, the civil RICO weapon may well continue to serve as a weapon in the private plaintiff's arsenal. See generally J. Scott Colesanti, The Private Securities Litigation Reform Act of 1995: Did the "Rushed Debate" Really Spell the End of Securities Claims and RICO?, 26 Sec. Reg. L. J. 139, 150-51 (1998) (discussing the conviction exception).

Chapter 12

INTERNATIONAL SECURITIES FRAUD

As originally enacted, the federal securities laws did not indicate whether the fraud provisions applied to transactions that cross national boundaries. Congress's silence carried no consequences so long as securities markets were essentially domestic. But beginning in the 1960s, these markets grew increasingly internationalized, infusing federal securities fraud actions with numerous permutations of foreign elements — foreign plaintiffs and defendants, foreign securities, foreign securities exchanges, and negotiations and trades that occurred (wholly or partly) in foreign countries.

The lower courts thus had to decide which (if any) of these actions they were entitled to hear. They developed a jurisprudence focused on where effects were felt and events occurred as well as on the nationality of the injured investors and the issuer. They applied the jurisprudence in largely the same manner regardless of whether the SEC, the DOJ or a private plaintiff brought the action. The principal architect of this jurisprudence was the renowned Judge Friendly of the Second Circuit, whose thinking on this subject in turn drew upon that of Professor Louis Loss of Harvard Law School. See Margaret V. Sachs, Judge Friendly and the Law of Securities Regulation: The Creation of a Judicial Reputation, 50 SMU L. Rev. 777, 794-96, 800-02 (1997).

Two major developments in 2010 radically transformed this landscape: first, the Supreme Court's decision in *Morrison v. National Australia Bank, Ltd.*, 130 S.Ct. 2869 (2010), and shortly thereafter, the enactment of the Dodd-Frank Act. In *Morrison*, the Court categorically rejected the jurisprudence spawned by Judge Friendly and substituted a new approach in its place. In Section 929P(b) of the Dodd-Frank Act, Congress brought the former jurisprudence back to life, but only for actions filed by the SEC and the DOJ.

This Chapter is divided into four sections. Section A examines private international securities fraud actions in the wake of *Morrison*. Section B addresses the analogous actions by the SEC and the DOJ in the wake of the Dodd-Frank Act. Sections C and D discuss matters relevant to private actions only: whether securities purchasers and sellers can by contract specify the forum and substantive law applicable to any subsequent securities litigation between them (Section C); and the forum non conveniens doctrine (Section D).

A. PRIVATE INTERNATIONAL SECURITIES FRAUD ACTIONS

With the landmark decision that follows, the Supreme Court brought forth a new era in international securities fraud litigation.

MORRISON v. NATIONAL AUSTRALIA BANK, LTD.

130 S. Ct. 2869 (2010)

JUSTICE ANTONIN G. SCALIA:

We decide whether § 10(b) of the Securities Exchange Act of 1934 provides a cause of action to foreign plaintiffs suing foreign and American defendants for misconduct in connection with securities traded on foreign exchanges.

I

Respondent National Australia Bank Limited (National) was, during the relevant time, the largest bank in Australia. Its Ordinary Shares-what in America would be called "common stock" are traded on the Australian Stock Exchange Limited and on other foreign securities exchanges, but not on any exchange in the United States. There are listed on the New York Stock Exchange, however, National's American Depositary Receipts (ADRs), which represent the right to receive a specified number of National's Ordinary Shares.

The complaint alleges the following facts, which we accept as true. In February 1998, National bought respondent HomeSide Lending, Inc., a mortgage servicing company headquartered in Florida. ***

From 1998 until 2001, National's annual reports and other public documents touted the success of HomeSide's business, and respondents Frank Cicutto (National's managing director and chief executive officer), Kevin Race (HomeSide's chief operating officer), and Hugh Harris (HomeSide's chief executive officer) did the same in public statements. But on July 5, 2001, National announced that it was writing down the value of HomeSide's assets by $450 million; and then again on September 3, by another $1.75 billion. The prices of both Ordinary Shares and ADRs slumped. After downplaying the July write-down, National explained the September write-down as the result of a failure to anticipate the lowering of prevailing interest rates (lower interest rates lead to more refinancings, *i.e.,* more early repayments of mortgages), other mistaken assumptions in the financial models, and the loss of goodwill. According to the complaint, however, HomeSide, Race, Harris, and another HomeSide senior executive who is also a respondent here had manipulated HomeSide's financial models to make the rates of early repayment unrealistically low in order to cause the mortgage-servicing rights to appear more valuable than they really were. The complaint also alleges that National and Cicutto were aware of this deception by July 2000, but did nothing about it.

As relevant here, petitioners Russell Leslie Owen and Brian and Geraldine Silverlock, all Australians, purchased National's Ordinary Shares in 2000 and 2001, before the write-downs.[1] They sued National, HomeSide, Cicutto, and the three HomeSide executives in the United States District Court for the Southern District of New York for alleged violations of §§ 10(b) and 20(a) of the Securities Exchange Act of 1934, and SEC Rule 10b-5 . They sought to

---

1. Robert Morrison, an American investor in National's ADRs, also brought suit, but his claims were dismissed by the District Court because he failed to allege damages. Petitioners did not appeal that decision, and it is not before us. ***

represent a class of foreign purchasers of National's Ordinary Shares during a specified period up to the September write-down.

Respondents moved to dismiss for lack of subject-matter jurisdiction under Federal Rule of Civil Procedure 12(b)(1) and for failure to state a claim under Rule 12(b)(6). The District Court granted the motion on the former ground, finding no jurisdiction because the acts in this country were, "at most, a link in the chain of an alleged overall securities fraud scheme that culminated abroad." The Court of Appeals for the Second Circuit affirmed on similar grounds. The acts performed in the United States did not "compris[e] the heart of the alleged fraud." We granted certiorari.

II

Before addressing the question presented, we must correct a threshold error in the Second Circuit's analysis. It considered the extraterritorial reach of § 10(b) to raise a question of subject-matter jurisdiction, wherefore it affirmed the District Court's dismissal under Rule 12(b)(1). In this regard it was following Circuit precedent, see *Schoenbaum v. Firstbrook,* 405 F.2d 200, 208, modified on other grounds en banc, 405 F.2d 215 (1968). The Second Circuit is hardly alone in taking this position, see, *e.g., In re CP Ships Ltd. Securities Litigation,* 578 F.3d 1306, 1313 (C.A.11 2009); *Continental Grain (Australia) Pty. Ltd. v. Pacific Oilseeds, Inc.,* 592 F.2d 409, 421 (C.A.8 1979).

But to ask what conduct § 10(b) reaches is to ask what conduct § 10(b) prohibits, which is a merits question. Subject-matter jurisdiction, by contrast, "refers to a tribunal's"'power to hear a case.""" *Union Pacific R. Co. v. Locomotive Engineers and Trainmen Gen. Comm. of Adjustment, Central Region,* 558 U.S. --,-- (2009) (quoting *Arbaugh v. Y & H Corp.,* 546 U.S. 500, 514 (2006), in turn quoting *United States v. Cotton,* 535 U.S. 625, 630 (2002)). It presents an issue quite separate from the question whether the allegations the plaintiff makes entitle him to relief. See *Bell v. Hood,* 327 U.S. 678, 682 (1946).

In view of this error, which the parties do not dispute, petitioners ask us to remand. We think that unnecessary. Since nothing in the analysis of the courts below turned on the mistake, a remand would only require a new Rule 12(b)(6) label for the same Rule 12(b)(1) conclusion. As we have done before in situations like this, we proceed to address whether petitioners' allegations state a claim.

III

A

It is a "longstanding principle of American law 'that legislation of Congress, unless a contrary intent appears,is meant to apply only within the territorial jurisdiction of the United States.'" *EEOC v. Arabian American Oil Co.,* 499 U.S. 244, 248 (1991) *(Aramco)* (quoting *Foley Bros., Inc. v. Filardo,* 336 U.S. 281,285 (1949)). This principle represents a canon of construction, or a presumption about a statute's meaning, rather than a limit upon Congress's power to legislate, see *Blackmer v. United States,* 284 U.S. 421, 437 (1932). It rests on the perception that Congress ordinarily legislates with respect to domestic, not foreign matters. *Smith v. United States,* 507 U.S. 197, 204, n.5 (1993). Thus, "unless there is the affirmative intention of the Congress clearly expressed" to give a statute extraterritorial effect, "we must presume it is primarily concerned with domestic conditions." *Aramco,* supra, at 248. The canon or presumption applies regardless of whether there is a risk of conflict between the American statute and a foreign law, see *Sale v. Haitian Centers Council, Inc.,* 509 U.S. 155, 173-174 (1993). When a statute gives no clear indication of an extraterritorial application, it has none.

Despite this principle of interpretation, long and often recited in our opinions, the Second Circuit believed that, because the Exchange Act is silent as to the extraterritorial application of § 10(b), it was left to the court to "discern" whether Congress would have wanted the statute to apply. This disregard of the presumption against extraterritoriality did not originate with the Court of Appeals panel in this case. It has been repeated over many decades by various courts of appeals in determining the application of the Exchange Act, and § 10(b) in particular, to fraudulent schemes that involve conduct and effects abroad.

Commentators have criticized the unpredictable and inconsistent application of § 10(b) to transnational cases. See, *e.g.,* Choi & Silberman, Transnational Litigation and Global Securities Class-Action Lawsuits, 2009 Wis. L.Rev. 465, 467-468; Langevoort, *Schoenbaum* Revisited: Limiting the Scope of Antifraud Protection in an Internationalized Securities Marketplace, 55 Law & Contemp. Probs. 241, 244-248 (1992). Some have challenged the premise underlying the Courts of Appeals' approach, namely that Congress did not consider the extraterritorial application of § 10(b) (thereby leaving it open to the courts, supposedly, to determine what Congress would have wanted). See, *e.g.,* Sachs, The International Reach of Rule 10b-5: The Myth of Congressional Silence, 28 Colum. J. Transnat'l L. 677 (1990) (arguing that Congress considered, but rejected, applying the Exchange Act to transactions abroad). Others, more fundamentally, have noted that using congressional silence as a justification for judge-made rules violates the traditional principle that silence means no extraterritorial application. See, e.g., Note, Let There Be Fraud (Abroad): A Proposal for A New U.S. Jurisprudence with Regard to the Extraterritorial Application of the Anti-Fraud Provisions of the 1933 and 1934 Securities Acts, 28 Law & Pol'y Int'l Bus. 477, 492-493 (1997).

The criticisms seem to us justified. The results of judicial-speculation-made-law-divining what Congress would have wanted if it had thought of the situation before the court-demonstrate the wisdom of the presumption against extraterritoriality.

B

On its face, § 10(b) contains nothing to suggest it applies abroad. Petitioners and the Solicitor General contend, however, that three things indicate that § 10(b) or the Exchange Act in general has at least some extraterritorial application.

First, they point to the definition of "interstate commerce," a term used in § 10(b), which includes "trade, commerce, transportation, or communication ... between any foreign country and any State." 15 U.S.C. § 78c(a)(17). But "we have repeatedly held that even statutes that contain broad language in their definitions of 'commerce' that expressly refer to '*foreign* commerce' do not apply abroad." *Aramco,* 499 U.S., at 251.

Petitioners and the Solicitor General next point out that Congress, in describing the purposes of the Exchange Act, observed that the "prices established and offered in such transactions are generally disseminated and quoted throughout the United States and foreign countries." 15 U.S.C. § 78b(2). The antecedent of "such transactions," however, is found in the first sentence of the section, which declares that "transactions in securities as commonly conducted upon securities exchanges and over-the-counter markets are affected with a national public interest." § 78b. Nothing suggests that this *national* public interest pertains to transactions conducted upon *foreign* exchanges and markets.

Finally, there is § 30(b) of the Exchange Act, which *does* mention the Act's extraterritorial application. The Solicitor General argues that "[this] exemption would have no function if the Act did not apply in the first instance to securities transactions that occur abroad."

We are not convinced. In the first place, it would be odd for Congress to indicate the extraterritorial application of the whole Exchange Act by means of a provision imposing a condition precedent to its application abroad. And if the whole Act applied abroad, why would the Commission's enabling regulations be limited to those preventing "evasion" of the Act, rather than all those preventing "violation"? ***

The Solicitor General also fails to account for §30(a). *** Subsection 30(a) contains what § 10(b) lacks: a clear statement of extraterritorial effect. Its explicit provision for a specific extraterritorial application would be quite superfluous if the rest of the Exchange Act already applied to transactions on foreign exchanges-and its limitation of that application to securities of domestic issuers would be inoperative. ***

In short, there is no affirmative indication in the Exchange Act that § 10(b) applies extraterritorially, and we therefore conclude that it does not.

IV

A

Petitioners argue that the conclusion that § 10(b) does not apply extraterritorially does not resolve this case. They contend that they seek no more than domestic application anyway, since Florida is where HomeSide and its senior executives engaged in the deceptive conduct of manipulating HomeSide's financial models; their complaint also alleged that Race and Hughes made misleading public statements there. This is less an answer to the presumption against extraterritorial application than it is an assertion-a quite valid assertion-that that presumption here (as often) is not self-evidently dispositive, but its application requires further analysis. For it is a rare case of prohibited extraterritorial application that lacks *all* contact with the territory of the United States. ***

*** [W]e think that the focus of the Exchange Act is not upon the place where the deception originated, but upon purchases and sales of securities in the United States. Section 10(b) does not punish deceptive conduct, but only deceptive conduct "in connection with the purchase or sale of any security registered on a national securities exchange or any security not so registered." See *SEC v. Zandford,* 535 U.S. 813, 820 (2002). Those purchase-and-sale transactions are the objects of the statute's solicitude. *** And it is in our view only transactions in securities listed on domestic exchanges, and domestic transactions in other securities, to which § 10(b) applies.

The primacy of the domestic exchange is suggested by the very prologue of the Exchange Act, which sets forth as its object "[t]o provide for the regulation of securities exchanges ... operating in interstate and foreign commerce and through the mails, to prevent inequitable and unfair practices on such exchanges . . . ." 48 Stat. 881. We know of no one who thought that the Act was intended to "regulat[e]" *foreign* securities exchanges-or indeed who even believed that under established principles of international law Congress had the power to do so. The Act's registration requirements apply only to securities listed on national securities exchanges. 15 U.S.C. § 78*l* (a).

With regard to securities *not* registered on domestic exchanges, the exclusive focus on *domestic* purchases and sales is strongly confirmed by § 30(a) and (b) ***. Under both provisions it is the foreign location of the *transaction* that establishes (or reflects the presumption of) the Act's inapplicability, absent regulations by the Commission. ***

Finally, we reject the notion that the Exchange Act reaches conduct in this country affecting exchanges or transactions abroad for the same reason that *Aramco* rejected overseas application of Title VII to all domestically concluded employment contracts or all employment contracts with American employers: The probability of incompatibility with the applicable laws of other countries is so obvious that if Congress intended such foreign application "it would have addressed the subject of conflicts with foreign laws and procedures." [*Aramco*], 499 U.S., at 256. Like the United States, foreign countries regulate their domestic securities exchanges and securities transactions occurring within their territorial jurisdiction. And the regulation of other countries often differs from ours as to what constitutes fraud, what disclosures must be made, what damages are recoverable, what discovery is available in litigation, what individual actions may be joined in a single suit, what attorney's fees are recoverable, and many other matters. See, e.g., Brief for United Kingdom of Great Britain and Northern Ireland as *Amicus Curiae* 16-21. The Commonwealth of Australia, the United Kingdom of Great Britain and Northern Ireland, and the Republic of France have filed *amicus* briefs in this case. So have (separately or jointly) such international and foreign organizations as the International Chamber of Commerce, the Swiss Bankers Association, the Federation of German Industries, the French Business Confederation, the Institute of International Bankers, the European Banking Federation, the Australian Bankers' Association, and the Association Francaise des Entreprises Privées. They all complain of the interference with foreign securities regulation that application of § 10(b) abroad would produce, and urge the adoption of a clear test that will avoid that consequence. The transactional test we have adopted-whether the purchase or sale is made in the United States, or involves a security listed on a domestic exchange-meets that requirement.

B

The Solicitor General suggests a different test, which petitioners also endorse: "[A] transnational securities fraud violates [§] 10(b) when the fraud involves significant conduct in the United States that is material to the fraud's success." *** The Solicitor General sets forth a number of purposes such a test would serve: achieving a high standard of business ethics in the securities industry, ensuring honest securities markets and thereby promoting investor confidence, and preventing the United States from becoming a "Barbary Coast" for malefactors perpetrating frauds in foreign markets. But it provides no textual support for the last of these purposes, or for the first two as applied to the foreign securities industry and securities markets abroad. ***

If, moreover, one is to be attracted by the desirable consequences of the "significant and material conduct" test, one should also be repulsed by its adverse consequences. While there is no reason to believe that the United States has become the Barbary Coast for those perpetrating frauds on foreign securities markets, some fear that it has become the Shangri-La of class-action litigation for lawyers representing those allegedly cheated in foreign securities markets. See Brief for Infineon Technologies AG as *Amicus Curiae* 1-2, 22-25; Brief for European Aeronautic Defence & Space Co. N.V. et al. as *Amici Curiae* 2-4; Brief for Securities Industry and Financial Markets Association et al. as *Amici Curiae* 10-16; Coffee, Securities Policeman to the World? The Cost of Global Class Actions, N.Y.L.J. 5 (2008); Buxbaum, Multinational Class Actions Under Federal Securities Law: Managing Jurisdictional Conflict, 46 Colum. J. Transnat'l L. 14, 38-41 (2007). ***

Finally, the Solicitor General argues that the Commission has adopted an interpretation similar to the "significant and material conduct" test, and that we should defer to that. In the two adjudications the Solicitor General cites, however, the Commission did not purport to be providing its own interpretation of the statute, but relied on decisions of federal courts-mainly Court of Appeals decisions that in turn relied on the *Schoenbaum* and *Leasco* decisions of the Second Circuit that we discussed earlier. See *In re United Securities Clearing Corp.,* 52 S.E.C. 92,95, n.14, 96, n.16 (1994); *In re Robert F. Lynch,* Exchange Act Release No. 11737, 8 S.E.C. Docket 75, 77, n. 15 (1975). ***

*** Section 10(b) reaches the use of a manipulative or deceptive device or contrivance only in connection with the purchase or sale of a security listed on an American stock exchange, and the purchase or sale of any other security in the United States. This case involves no securities listed on a domestic exchange, and all aspects of the purchases complained of by those petitioners who still have live claims occurred outside the United States. Petitioners have therefore failed to state a claim on which relief can be granted. We affirm the dismissal of petitioners' complaint on this ground. ***

JUSTICE STEPHEN G. BREYER, CONCURRING IN PART AND CONCURRING IN THE JUDGMENT:

Section 10(b) of the Securities Exchange Act of 1934 applies to fraud "in connection with" two categories of transactions: (1) "the purchase or sale of any security registered on a national securities exchange" or (2) "the purchase or sale of ... any security not so registered." 15 U.S.C. § 78j(b). In this case, the purchased securities are listed only on a few foreign exchanges, none of which has registered with the Securities and Exchange Commission as a "national securities exchange." See § 78f. The first category therefore does not apply. Further, the relevant purchases of these unregistered securities took place entirely in Australia and involved only Australian investors. And in accordance with the presumption against extraterritoriality, I do not read the second category to include such transactions. Thus, while state law or other federal fraud statutes, see, e.g., 18 U.S.C. § 1341 (mail fraud), § 1343 (wire fraud), may apply to the fraudulent activity alleged here to have occurred in the United States, I believe that § 10(b) does not. This case does not require us to consider other circumstances.

To the extent the Court's opinion is consistent with these views, I join it.

JUSTICE JOHN PAUL STEVENS, WITH WHOM JUSTICE GINSBURG JOINS, CONCURRING IN THE JUDGMENT.

While I agree that petitioners have failed to state a claim on which relief can be granted, my reasoning differs from the Court's. I would adhere to the general approach that has been the law in the Second Circuit, and most of the rest of the country, for nearly four decades.

I

If one confines one's gaze to the statutory text, the Court's conclusion is a plausible one. But the federal courts have been construing § 10(b) in a different manner for a long time, and the Court's textual analysis is not nearly so compelling, in my view, as to warrant the abandonment of their doctrine.***

The Second Circuit's test became the "north star" of § 10(b) jurisprudence, not just regionally but nationally as well. With minor variations, other courts converged on the same basic approach. Neither Congress nor the Securities Exchange Commission (Commission) acted to change the law. To the contrary, the Commission largely adopted the Second Circuit's position in its own adjudications.

In light of this history, the Court's critique of the decision below for applying "judge-made rules" is quite misplaced. This entire area of law is replete with judge-made rules, which give concrete meaning to Congress' general commands. ***

II

The Court's other main critique of the Second Circuit's approach – apart from what the Court views as its excessive reliance on functional considerations and reconstructed congressional intent – is that the Second Circuit has "disregard[ed]" the presumption against extraterritoriality. It is the Court, however, that misapplies the presumption, in two main respects.

First, the Court seeks to transform the presumption from a flexible rule of thumb into something more like a clear statement rule. We have been here before. In the case on which the Court primarily relies, *EEOC v. Arabian American Oil Co.,* 499 U.S. 244 (1991) *(Aramco),* Chief Justice Rehnquist's majority opinion included a sentence that appeared to make the same move. See id., at 258.

Yet even *Aramco* – surely the most extreme application of the presumption against extraterritoriality in my time on the Court – contained numerous passages suggesting that the presumption may be overcome without a clear directive. See id., at 248-255 (majority opinion) (repeatedly identifying congressional "intent" as the touchstone of the presumption). And our cases both before and after *Aramco* make perfectly clear that the Court continues to give effect to "*all available evidence* about the meaning" of a provision when considering its extraterritorial application, lest we defy Congress' will. *Sale v. Haitian Centers Council, Inc.,* 509 U.S. 155, 177 (1993) (emphasis added) ***

Second, and more fundamentally, the Court errs in suggesting that the presumption against extraterritoriality is fatal to the Second Circuit's test. For even if the presumption really were a clear statement (or "clear indication") rule, it would have only marginal relevance to this case.

Rather, the real question in this case is how much, and what kinds of, *domestic* contacts are sufficient to trigger application of § 10(b).

The question just stated does not admit of an easy answer. The text of the Exchange Act indicates that § 10(b) extends to at least some activities with an international component, but, again, it is not pellucid as to which ones. The Second Circuit draws the line as follows: § 10(b) extends to transnational frauds "only when substantial acts in furtherance of the fraud were committed within the United States," *SEC v. Berger,* 322 F.3d 187, 193 (C.A.2 2003), or when the fraud was "'intended to produce'" and did produce "'detrimental effects within'" the United States, *Schoenbaum,* 405 F.2d, at 206.

This approach is consistent with the understanding shared by most scholars that Congress, in passing the Exchange Act, "expected U.S. securities laws to apply to certain international transactions or conduct." Buxbaum, Multinational Class Actions Under Federal Securities Law: Managing Jurisdictional Conflict, 46 Colum. J. Transnat'l L. 14, 19 (2007). It is also consistent with the traditional understanding, regnant in the 1930's as it is now, that the presumption against extraterritoriality does not apply "when the conduct [at issue] occurs within the United States," and has lesser force when "the failure to extend the scope of the statute to a foreign setting will result in adverse effects within the United States." *Environmental Defense Fund, Inc. v. Massey,* 986 F.2d 528, 531 (C.A.D.C.1993).

I do not take issue with the Court for beginning its inquiry with the statutory text, rather than the doctrine in the Courts of Appeals. I take issue with the Court for beginning *and ending* its inquiry with the statutory text, when the text does not speak with geographic precision, and for dismissing the long pedigree of, and the persuasive account of congressional intent embodied in, the Second Circuit's rule.

Repudiating the Second Circuit's approach in its entirety, the Court establishes a novel rule that will foreclose private parties from bringing § 10(b) actions whenever the relevant securities were purchased or sold abroad and are not listed on a domestic exchange.[12] The real motor of the Court's opinion, it seems, is not the presumption against extraterritoriality but rather the Court's belief that transactions on domestic exchanges are "the focus of the Exchange Act" and "the objects of [its] solicitude." In reality, however, it is the "public interest" and "the interests of investors" that are the objects of the statute's solicitude. *Europe & Overseas Commodity Traders, S.A. v. Banque Paribas London,* 147 F.3d 118, 125 (C.A.2 1998); S.Rep. No. 1455, 73d Cong., 2d Sess., 68 (1934). And while the clarity and simplicity of the Court's test may have some salutary consequences, like all bright-line rules it also has drawbacks.

Imagine, for example, an American investor who buys shares in a company listed only on an overseas exchange. That company has a major American subsidiary with executives based in New York City; and it was in New York City that the executives masterminded and implemented a massive deception which artificially inflated the stock price-and which will, upon its disclosure, cause the price to plummet. Or, imagine that those same executives go knocking on doors in Manhattan and convince an unsophisticated retiree, on the basis of material misrepresentations, to invest her life savings in the company's doomed securities. Both of these investors would, under the Court's new test, be barred from seeking relief under § 10(b).

The oddity of that result should give pause. For in walling off such individuals from § 10(b), the Court narrows the provision's reach to a degree that would surprise and alarm generations of American investors – and, I am convinced, the Congress that passed the Exchange Act. Indeed, the Court's rule turns § 10(b) jurisprudence (and the presumption against extraterritoriality) on its head, by withdrawing the statute's application from cases in which there is *both* substantial wrongful conduct that occurred in the United States *and* a substantial injurious effect on United States markets and citizens.

III

Some cases involving foreign securities transactions have extensive links to, and ramifications for, this country; this case has Australia written all over it. Accordingly, for essentially the reasons stated in the Court of Appeals' opinion, I would affirm its judgment.

I happen to agree with the result the Court reaches in this case. But "I respectfully dissent," once again, "from the Court's continuing campaign to render the private cause of action under § 10(b) toothless." *Stoneridge,* 552 U.S., at 175 (Stevens J., dissenting).

NOTES AND QUESTIONS

1. ***Does the Text Dictate the Test?*** The Court extracted its "transactional test" from the language of Section 10(b). Are you persuaded by the Court's textual analysis? If the text dictates the test, why was it necessary to invoke the presumption against extraterritoriality in the first place? See William S. Dodge, *Morrison*'s Effects Test, 40 Sw. U. L. Rev. 687, 690 (2011) (raising this question).

---

12. The Court's opinion does not, however, foreclose the Commission from bringing enforcement actions in additional circumstances, as no issue concerning the Commission's authority is presented by this case.

2. ADRs vs. Conventional Shares. Why were the *Morrison* plaintiffs unable to satisfy the transactional test based on the fact that others had traded the National Australia Bank ADRs on the New York Stock Exchange?

ADRs are the form in which the shares of most foreign companies trade in US markets. The SEC offers the following comparison between ADRs and conventional shares in its on-line brochure on international investing:

> Each ADR represents one or more shares of a foreign stock or a fraction of a share. If you own an ADR you have the right to obtain the foreign stock it represents, but U.S. investors usually find it more convenient to own the ADR. The price of an ADR corresponds to the price of the foreign stock in its home market, adjusted for the ratio of ADRs to foreign company shares.
>
> *Owning ADRs has some advantages compared to owning foreign shares directly*: [i] When you buy and sell ADRs you are trading in the U.S. market. Your trade will clear and settle in U.S. dollars. [ii] The depositary bank will convert any dividends or other cash payments into U.S. dollars before sending them to you. [iii] The depositary bank may arrange to vote your shares for you as you instruct.
>
> *On the other hand, there are some disadvantages*: [i] It may take a long time for you to receive information from the company because it must pass through an extra pair of hands. You may receive information about shareholder meetings only a few days before the meeting, well past the time when you could vote your shares. [ii] Depositary banks charge fees for their services and will deduct these fees from the dividends and other distributions on your shares. The depositary bank also will incur expenses, such as for converting foreign currency into U.S. dollars, and usually will pass those expenses on to you.

SEC, International Investing, available at www.sec.gov/investor/pubs/ininvest.htm.

ADRs can be of either the sponsored or unsponsored variety:

> A sponsored ADR is established with the active participation of the issuer of the underlying security and often includes an agreement among the issuer, the depositary bank, and the ADR owners. An unsponsored ADR is established by the depositary bank without the participation of the issuer of the underlying security.

In re European Aeronautic Defense & Space Co. Sec. Litig., 703 F. Supp. 2d 348, 352 n.1 (S.D.N.Y. 2010). When determining if Rule 10b-5 applies to transactions in ADRs, should it matter whether the ADRs in question are sponsored or unsponsored?

3. The Future of Domestic Exchanges. The first prong of the transactional test is premised on the existence of domestic exchanges, but these exchanges are widely expected to be replaced by several global exchanges in the near future. See, e.g., Roberta S. Karmel, The Once and Future New York Stock Exchange: The Regulation of Global Exchanges, 1. Brook. J. Corp. Fin. & Comm. L. 355, 356 (2007) (referring to "the inevitable globalization of exchanges"). Once global exchanges come into being, will the transactional test still be viable?

4. Swaps. In 2000, Congress amended Section 10(b) to encompass securities-based swap agreements: contracts in which the parties agree to exchange payments that turn on the price of a referenced security. Suppose the referenced security trades solely abroad but the parties consummate their agreement in the United States. Under these circumstances, does Section 10(b) apply? The one federal district court to consider this question held Section 10(b) inapplicable:

> Here, Plaintiffs' swaps were the functional equivalent of trading the underlying VW shares on a German exchange. Accordingly, the economic reality is that Plaintiffs' swap agreements are essentially "transactions conducted upon foreign exchanges and markets," and not "domestic transactions" that merit the protection of § 10(b). [*Morrison*,] 130 S.Ct. at 2882, 2884.
>
> In light of *Morrison*'s strong pronouncement that U.S. courts ought not interfere with foreign securities regulation without a clear Congressional mandate, I am loathe to create a rule that would make foreign issuers with little relationship to the U.S. subject to suits here simply because a private party in this country entered into a derivatives contract that references the foreign issuer's stock. Such a holding would turn *Morrison*'s presumption against extraterritoriality on its head.

Elliott Assocs. v. Porsche Automobil Holding SE, 759 F. Supp. 2d 469, 476 (S.D.N.Y. 2010). Do you agree? Is an "economic realities" approach consistent with *Morrison*?

Suppose instead that the swap parties consummate their agreement in a foreign country and the referenced security trades solely in the United States. Under these circumstances, can the foreign swap party sue the U.S. issuer under Rule 10b-5?

5. ***Policy Considerations.*** What policy considerations is the transaction test intended to promote? Does the policy of investor protection play any role? Consider the implications of *Morrison* for the Court's future decision-making in the domestic securities context.

6. ***The Merits vs. Jurisdiction.*** Although it excoriated the lower courts for treating extraterritoriality as a jurisdictional question rather than as a merits question, the Court did not mention how the reclassification would affect litigation. The impact is substantial.

When extraterritoriality is jurisdictional, the court must address it first, before turning to any other aspect of the case. *Steel Co. v. Citizens for a Better Env't*, 523 U.S. 83 (1998). The court is "not entitled simply to assume jurisdiction and resolve an easy merits issue." *United Phosphorus, Ltd. v. Angus Chem. Co.*, 322 F.3d 942, 957 (7th Cir. 2003) (Wood, J. dissenting). The jurisdictional inquiry can be wide-ranging and frequently encompasses the resolution of factual disputes. All of the principal lower court cases in this Chapter attest to these features.

On the other hand, when extraterritoriality is merely one of many merits issues, "there is no reason why the court cannot resolve the most straightforward [merits] issue first." Id. Thus, a potentially protracted jurisdictional inquiry can be averted if the case is amenable to dismissal for, say, a lack of materiality or the failure to plead scienter with sufficient particularity.

Suppose that the federal appeals court in *Morrison*, rather than affirming the trial court, had remanded to that court with directions to treat extraterritoriality as a merits issue. If you had represented the defendants on remand, which merits issues would have competed for your attention?

*7. **State Law as a Last Resort?*** One way for plaintiffs to sidestep *Morrison* might be to file common law fraud claims, whether in state court or in federal court under diversity jurisdiction. See, e.g., *Terra Secs. Asa Konkursbo v. Citigroup, Inc.*, 740 F.Supp. 2d 441, 447-55 (S.D.N.Y. 2010) (dismissing federal securities fraud claims on account of *Morrison* but refusing to dismiss diversity-based common law fraud claim "arising out of the same allegedly fraudulent conduct"). Plaintiffs bringing common law fraud claims must avoid those of the class action variety that would invite SLUSA preclusion (discussed in Chapter 6.D). Cf. *Terra*, supra, 740 F. Supp. 2d at 443 (lawsuit brought by eight plaintiffs).

*8. **The Necessity of Personal Jurisdiction.*** Plaintiffs bringing international securities fraud cases must be alert to the challenge of establishing personal jurisdiction over foreign defendants. The personal jurisdiction inquiry, likely familiar to you from your civil procedure course, focuses on whether there is an act through which each defendant "purposefully avails itself of the privilege of conducting activities within" the United States, "thus invoking the benefits and protections of its laws." *J. McIntyre Mach. Ltd. v. Nicastro,* 131 S.Ct. 2780, 2787-88 (2011), quoting *Hanson v. Denkla*, 353 U.S. 235, 253 (1958).

Increasingly, courts must decide whether the defendant established such national contacts by her use of the Internet. Some courts look to whether her web site was passive or interactive. See, e.g., *Zurich Capital Mkts., Inc. v. Coglianese*, 388 F. Supp. 2d 847, 858 & n. 3 (N.D. Ill. 2004). Others ask whether she deliberately precipitated domestic effects through her online conduct. See, e.g., *IM Partners v. Debit Direct Ltd.*, 394 F. Supp. 2d 503, 513-14 (D. Conn. 2005). See generally Allyson W. Haynes, The Short Arm of the Law: Simplifying Personal Jurisdiction Over Virtually Present Defendants, 64 U. Miami L. Rev. 133 (2009); Allan R. Stein, Personal Jurisdiction and the Internet: Seeing Due Process through the Lens of Regulatory Precision, 98 Nw. U. L. Rev. 411 (2004).

PROBLEM 12-1

Consider whether each of the following falls within the ambit of Rule 10b-5's transactional test:

(a) The shares of Company X, a Canadian company, are traded on the New York Stock Exchange and the Toronto Stock Exchange. An American investor living in Canada buys shares of Company X on the Toronto Stock Exchange.

(b) The shares of Company Y, an American company, are traded on the New York Stock Exchange and the London Stock Exchange. A British investor living in Britain directs his broker to buy shares of Company Y. The broker executes the trade on the NYSE through the brokerage firm's US affiliate.

(c) The shares of Company Z, a German company, are traded on the New York Stock Exchange and on a German exchange. A German investor directs her broker to buy shares of Company Z on the NYSE. Disregarding the directive, the broker buys the shares on the German exchange.

(d) A United States investor purchases shares of a foreign security, not traded on a US exchange, while sitting in his living room by using an interactive web site maintained by the issuer outside the United States.

PROBLEM 12-2

Ben, an American citizen who lives in Kentucky, is a representative of Carlisle, Inc., a Bahamian corporation traded only on the Bahamas Stock Exchange (the "BISX"). Ben solicited investments in Carlisle from the residents of three retirement communities in the southeastern United States. He intentionally presented a deceptively rosy picture of the company, which he held out as being headquartered in Kentucky. He instructed the retirees to mail their checks to a Kentucky address. Upon receipt of the funds, he purchased Carlisle shares on the BISX for the retirees' accounts.

The retirees have now discovered the fraudulent nature of much of Ben's information about Carlisle. They would like to bring a Rule 10b-5 lawsuit. How would *Morrison* affect their prospects?

B. SEC AND DOJ ACTIONS INVOLVING INTERNATIONAL SECURITIES FRAUD

The SEC regularly brings judicial and administrative actions involving international securities fraud. Prior to the Supreme Court's decision in *Morrison*, the SEC premised these actions on the judicially-created conduct and effects tests described in Section A supra. See, e.g., *SEC v. Berger,* 322 F.3d 187 (2d Cir. 2003); *SEC v. Banner Fund Int'l,* 211 F.3d 602 (D.C. Cir. 2000); *SEC v. Marimuthu,* 552 F. Supp. 2d 969, 971-72 (D. Neb. 2008); *SEC v. Stroud,,* Litigation Release 17057 (June 29, 2001).

The Supreme Court's *Morrison* decision removed the conduct and effects tests from the repertoires of the SEC and the DOJ as well as that of private plaintiffs. See Section A supra. Close on *Morrison*'s heels, however, came the Dodd-Frank Act, Section 929P(b) of which resuscitated a focus on conduct and effects when the plaintiff is the SEC or the DOJ.

Section 929P(b) reads as follows:

EXTRATERRITORIAL JURISDICTION OF THE ANTIFRAUD PROVISIONS OF THE FEDERAL SECURITIES LAWS –

(1) UNDER THE SECURITIES ACT OF 1933 – Section 22 of the Securities Act of 1933 (15 U.S.C. 77v(a)) is amended by adding at the end the following new subsection:

> c) EXTRATERRITORIAL JURISDICTION – The district courts of the United States and the United States courts of any Territory shall have jurisdiction of an action or proceeding brought or instituted by the Commission or the United States alleging a violation of section 17(a) involving –
>
> (1) conduct within the United States that constitutes significant steps in furtherance of the violation, even if the securities transaction occurs outside the United States and involves only foreign investors; or

(2) conduct occurring outside the United States that has a foreseeable substantial effect within the United States.

(2) UNDER THE SECURITIES EXCHANGE ACT OF 1934 – Section 27 of the Securities Exchange Act of 1934 (15 U.S.C. 78aa) is amended — *** (B) by adding at the end the following new subsection:

(b) EXTRATERRITORIAL JURISDICTION – The district courts of the United States and the Untied States courts of any Territory shall have jurisdiction of an action or proceeding brought or instituted by the Commission or the United States alleging a violation of the antifraud provisions of this title involving –

(1) conduct within the United States that constitutes significant steps in furtherance of the violation, even if the securities transaction occurs outside the United States and involves only foreign investors; or

(2) conduct occurring outside the United States that has a foreseeable substantial effect within the United States.

To appreciate the scope of the conduct and effects tests as they existed prior to *Morrison*, a good place to begin is *Morrison*'s description of them:

The Second Circuit established that application of § 10(b) could be premised upon either some effect on American securities markets or investors *(Schoenbaum)* or significant conduct in the United States *(Leasco)*. It later formalized these two applications into (1) an "effects test," "whether the wrongful conduct had a substantial effect in the United States or upon United States citizens," and (2) a "conduct test," "whether the wrongful conduct occurred in the United States." *SEC v. Berger,* 322 F.3d 187,192-193(C.A.2 2003). These became the north star of the Second Circuit's § 10(b) jurisprudence, pointing the way to what Congress would have wished. Indeed, the Second Circuit declined to keep its two tests distinct on the ground that "an admixture or combination of the two often gives a better picture of whether there is sufficient United States involvement to justify the exercise of jurisdiction by an American court." *Itoba Ltd. v. Lep Group PLC*, 54 F.3d 118, 122 (1995). The Second Circuit never put forward a textual or even extratextual basis for these tests. As early as *Bersch*, it confessed that "if we were asked to point to language in the statutes, or even in the legislative history, that compelled these conclusions, we would be unable to respond," 519 F.2d, at 993.

As they developed, these tests were not easy to administer. The conduct test was held to apply differently depending on whether the harmed investors were Americans or foreigners: When the alleged damages consisted of losses to American investors abroad, it was enough that acts "of material importance" performed in the United States "significantly contributed" to that result; whereas those acts must have "directly caused" the result when losses to foreigners abroad were at issue. See *Bersch,* 519 F.2d, at 993. And "merely preparatory activities in the United States" did not suffice "to trigger application of the securities laws for injury to foreigners located abroad." Id., at 992.

Other Circuits embraced the Second Circuit's approach, though not its precise application. Like the Second Circuit, they described their decisions regarding the extraterritorial application of § 10(b) as essentially resolving

> matters of policy. See, e.g., *SEC v. Kasser*, 548 F.2d 109, 116 (3rd Cir. 1977); *Continental Grain [(Australia)Party, Ltd.*, 592 F.2d, 409], 421–422; *Grunenthal GmbH v. Hotz*, 712 F.2d 421, 424–425 (9th Cir.1983); *Kauthar SDN BHD v. Sternberg*, 149 F.3d 659, 667 (7th Cir. 1998). While applying the same fundamental methodology of balancing interests and arriving at what seemed the best policy, they produced a proliferation of vaguely related variations on the "conduct" and "effects" tests.

Morrison v. National Australia Bank, Ltd.,130 S.Ct. 2869, 2879-80 (2010).

NOTES AND QUESTIONS

*1. **Conduct and Effects Then and Now.*** Did the Dodd-Frank Act simply reinstate the various versions of the conduct and effects tests as they existed prior to *Morrison*? See generally Richard W. Painter, The Dodd-Frank Extraterritorial Jurisdictional Provision: Was It Effective, Needed or Sufficient?, 1 Harv. Bus. L. Rev. 195, 208-12 (2011) (discussing this question).

As the above excerpt from *Morrison* observed, the Second Circuit permitted jurisdiction to be based on a combination of conduct and effects . See *Morrison,* supra, citing *Itoba Ltd. v. Lep Group PLC*, 54 F.3d 118 (1995). See also *Kauthar SDN BHD v. Sternberg,* 149 F3d 659, 664 n.5 (7th Cir. 1998) (accepting the *Itoba* approach). The Dodd-Frank Act, however, connects the conduct and effects jurisdictional bases with an *"or."* Does the "or" phraseology disallow the combination-type jurisdiction permitted by *Itoba* and *Kauthar*?

*2. **The Nature of the Required Effects.*** What type of domestic effects provides the premise for jurisdiction under the Dodd-Frank Act? The Second Circuit addressed this question in *Bersch v. Drexel Firestone, Inc.*, 519 F.2d 974 (2d Cir. 1975), which involved allegations of fraud in public offerings by a Canadian corporation (IOS) whose shares were not listed on a United States exchange. The purchasers consisted largely of non-resident foreign nationals along with a small number of United States citizens. The district court premised jurisdiction on the affidavit of a University of Pennsylvania finance professor, who stated that " '[t]he false and misleading prospectus issued in connection with the Public Offering impaired investors' confidence and trust and contributed to a steep decline in the purchase of United States securities by foreigners' with attendant adverse effects on the balance of payments and the price of American securities generally." Id. at 987-88. Reversing the district court, the Second Circuit held the effects to be insufficient:

> [W]e do not doubt that the collapse of IOS after the offering had an unfortunate financial effect in the United States. Nevertheless we conclude that the generalized effects described by Professor Mendelson would not be sufficient to confer subject matter jurisdiction over a damage suit by a foreigner under the anti-fraud provisions of the securities laws.
>
> This branch of plaintiff's argument goes back to Mr. Justice Holmes' statement in *Strassheim v. Daily*, 221 U.S. 280, 284-85 (1911) ***:
>
> > Acts done outside a jurisdiction, but intended to produce and producing detrimental effects within it, justify a state in punishing the cause of the harm as if he had been present at the effect, if the state should succeed in getting him within its power.
>
> *** This principle *** does not support subject matter jurisdiction if

> there was no intention that the securities should be offered to anyone in the United States, simply because in the long run there was an adverse effect on this country's general economic interests or on American security prices. Moderation is all. *** This means to us that there is subject matter jurisdiction of fraudulent acts relating to securities which are committed abroad only when these result in injury to purchasers or sellers of those securities in whom the United States has an interest, not where acts simply have an adverse effect on the American economy or American investors generally. ***

519 F.2d at 988-89. See *SEC v. Berger*, 322 F.3d 187, 192 (2d Cir 2003) (adding the requirement that the harm to United States investors or markets be *substantial*). Why not allow jurisdiction on the basis of "generalized effects"?

3. Identifying Conduct "Constitut[ing] Significant Steps in Furtherance of the Violation." As *Morrison* noted, the Second Circuit (and others) distinguished between "merely preparatory" conduct and conduct that "directly caused" harm to foreigners. Judge Friendly acknowledged that "the distinction is a fine one" but maintained that "the line has to be drawn somewhere if the securities laws are not to apply in every instance where something has happened in the United States." *IIT v. Vencap, Ltd.,* 519 F.2d 1001, 1017-18 (2d Cir. 1975).

In drawing this line, Judge Friendly maintained, the nationality of the issuer may make a difference. Consider *IIT v. Cornfeld,* 619 F.2d 909 (2d Cir. 1980), a Rule 10b-5 action involving a foreign investment trust which bought debentures issued by the wholly-owned foreign subsidiary of a United States company. Judge Friendly upheld jurisdiction based upon domestic conduct after deeming the security to be "essentially *** American":

> [A] consequence of the KRCC debentures being essentially of an American security is that the activities occurring in the United States, which on their surface may appear similar to those held in *Bersch* to be "merely preparatory" and thus insufficient to have "directly caused" loss to foreigners, assume a different aspect. The fact that the drafting of the final prospectus in *Bersch* was done in Europe was not just "a formal or ultimate act . . . staged in Europe", as the *Bersch* district court found, 389 F.Supp. at 446, 457. The Bersch prospectus was mainly drafted in Europe because that was where IOS' records and principals were. Here the prospectus was wholly drafted in the United States because the offering, for largest part in form and for all in substance, was of securities of an American based corporation. Similarly while there was some domestic accounting work in *Bersch*, 389 F.Supp. at 456, most of the field work was and in the nature of things had to be done abroad. Here all the accounting work was and had to be done in the United States.

Id. at 920.

When assessing whether the particular quantum of conduct suffices, it can be useful to keep in mind the policy rationales underlying the exercise of conduct-based jurisdiction in the first place. One rationale is that "under many circumstances, the country in which the conduct occurs is in a far better position to investigate and enforce the law more effectively or at lower cost than those countries where the harm is felt, especially when the harm is relatively diffused." Donald C. Langevoort, *Schoenbaum* Revisited: Limiting the Scope of Antifraud Protection in an Internationalized Securities Marketplace, 55 Law & Contemp. Probs. 241, 247 (1992).

Other rationales were articulated by the Third Circuit when it upheld jurisdiction over a fraud action in which the only victim was a Canadian corporation wholly-owned by the Canadian Province of Manitoba:

> First, to deny such jurisdiction may embolden those who wish to defraud foreign securities purchasers or sellers to use the United States as a base of operations. *** We are reluctant to conclude that Congress intended to allow the United States to become a "Barbary Coast," as it were, harboring international securities "pirates."
>
> Also, we are concerned that a holding of no jurisdiction might induce reciprocal responses on the part of other nations. Some countries might decline to act against individuals and corporations seeking to transport securities frauds to the United States. Such parties may well be outside the ambit of the power of our courts. For foreign nations to adopt the position that the defendants are urging this Court to take would enable defrauders beyond the reach of our courts to escape with impunity. By finding jurisdiction here, we may encourage other nations to take appropriate steps against parties who seek to perpetuate frauds in the United States. ***
>
> As a final policy justification ***, we register the opinion that the antifraud provisions of the 1933 and 1934 Acts were designed to insure high standards of conduct in securities transactions within this country in addition to protecting domestic markets and investors from the effects of fraud. ***

SEC v. Kasser, 548 F.2d 109, 116 (3d Cir. 1977).

Which (if any) of these rationales do you find persuasive? Do other rationales occur to you as well?

4. The Dodd-Frank Act's Jurisdictional Terminology. As a general proposition, Congress can take what would otherwise be a merits issue and turn it into a jurisdictional issue simply by declaring it to be such. The Supreme Court elaborated on this theme in ***Arbaugh** v. **Y & H Corp.***, 546 U.S. 500 (2006), which addressed how to classify Title VII's so-called "employee numerosity requirement":

> Of course, Congress could make the employee-numerosity requirement "jurisdictional," just as it has made an amount-in-controversy threshold an ingredient of subject-matter jurisdiction in delineating diversity-of-citizenship jurisdiction under 28 U.S.C. § 1332. If the Legislature clearly states that a threshold limitation on a statute's scope shall count as jurisdictional, then courts and litigants will be duly instructed and will not be left to wrestle with the issue. But when Congress does not rank a statutory limitation on coverage as jurisdictional, courts should treat the restriction as non-jurisdictional in character.

Id. at 514-516 (holding the employee-numerosity requirement to be a merits issue).

The jurisdictional language in Section 929P(b) of the Dodd-Frank Act was drafted before the grant of certiorari in *Morrison*, that is, before the materialization of the risk that the Court would reclassify extraterritoriality as a merits issue. But cf. *In re Parmalat Sec. Litig.*, 497 F. Supp. 2d 526, 529 (S.D.N.Y. 2007) (observing, but not deciding, that Rule 10b-5's extraterritorial scope is probably not jurisdictional). Thus, it is perhaps arguable that Section 929P(b)'s jurisdictional language (not to mention the Section's delineation as an amendment to the jurisdictional provisions of the Securities Act and the Exchange Act) merely tracks the pre-*Morrison* case law. Even if so, that language may have morphed into an affirmative choice to preserve the jurisdictional classification on behalf of the SEC (and the DOJ) once the potential for reclassification emerged in the course of the *Morrison* briefing or became actualized in the wake of the opinion itself. Can you think of any reasons why the SEC might prefer the jurisdictional classification?

Some prominent defense attorneys maintain that Section 929P(b) does not reinstate the conduct and effects tests or otherwise address the substantive scope of the cause of action. Instead, these attorneys argue, the only thing that the Section accomplishes is to confer jurisdiction (which, according to *Morrison*, was already present). See Richard W. Painter, The Dodd-Frank Extraterritorial Jurisdictional Provision: Was It Effective, Needed or Sufficient?, 1 Harv. Bus. L. Rev. 195, 205-08 (2011) (discussing this argument). If you were a federal district judge, would you find this argument persuasive?

5. ***The Benefits of Rule-Making.*** In the decades prior to *Morrison*, the SEC did not issue any rules or releases pertaining to international securities fraud. Moreover, when it addressed other international matters, it stressed that what it had to say did not govern the fraud provisions. See, e.g., Statement of the Commission Regarding Use of the Internet Web Sites to Offer Securities, Solicit Securities Transactions, or Advertise Investment Services Off-Shore, Securities Act Release 7516 (March 23, 1998), 66 SEC Docket 1869, 1870 and n. 5 (1998) (noting that "[t]his interpretation does not address the anti-fraud and anti-manipulation provisions of the securities laws"); Regulation S — Rules Governing Offers and Sales Made Outside the United States Without Registration Under the Securities Act of 1933, Preliminary Note 1 (stating that Regulation S does not apply to the federal securities fraud provisions).

Are there currently aspects of international securities fraud litigation and enforcement that would benefit from SEC rule-making?

6. ***The SEC's Private Action Study.*** Section 929Y of the Dodd-Frank Act directs the SEC to conduct a study on extraterritorial private actions, as follows:

> STUDY ON EXTRATERRITORIAL PRIVATE RIGHTS OF ACTION
>
> (a) IN GENERAL – The Securities and Exchange Commission of the United States shall solicit public comment and thereafter conduct a study to determine the extent to which private rights of action under the antifraud provisions of the Securities and Exchange Act of 1934 should be extended to cover:
>
> > (1) conduct within the United States that constitutes significant steps in furtherance of the violation, even if the securities transaction occurs outside the United States and involves only foreign investors; or
> >
> > (2) conduct occurring outside the United States that has a foreseeable substantial effect within the United States.
>
> (b) CONTENTS – The study shall consider and analyze, among other things, --.
>
> > (1) the scope of such a private right of action, including whether it should extend to all private actors or whether it should be more limited to extend just to institutional investors or otherwise;

(2) what implications such a private right of action would have on institutional comity;

(3) the economic costs and benefits of extending a private right of action for transnational securities frauds;

(4) whether a narrower extraterritorial standard should be adopted.

c) REPORT – A report of the study shall be submitted and recommendations made to the Committee on Banking, Housing, and Urban Affairs of the Senate and the Committee on Financial Services of the House not later than 18 months after the date of enactment of this Act.

How should the SEC respond to these queries? Should conduct and effects considerations govern private actions as well as actions brought by the SEC and the DOJ?

7. Collaboration with Other Countries. In addition to its judicial and administrative actions, the SEC combats international securities fraud by collaborating with other countries. See generally James D. Cox, Coping in a Global Marketplace: Survival Strategies for a 75 Year Old SEC, 95 Va. L. Rev. 941 (2009). In 2010, the SEC responded to 457 requests for enforcement assistance from foreign authorities regarding securities investigations and made 605 requests to foreign authorities for enforcement assistance. See SEC, 2010 Performance and Accountability Report 31.

The SEC's collaboration with other countries takes a number of additional forms as well. The SEC is a member of the International Organization of Securities Commissions (IOSCO), the principal organization for cooperation among securities regulators in different countries. See About IOSCO, http://www/ iosco.org.about/ index.cfm?section=background Founded in 1983 and composed of more than 100 members, IOSCO makes recommendations and proposes guidelines on topics ranging from record-keeping to the Internet. Although IOSCO's recommendations are non-binding, the SEC considers its involvement in the organization to be a substantial part of its international securities regulation. For discussion of IOSCO, see Chris Brummer, How International Financial Law Works and How It Doesn't, 99 Geo. L. J. 257 (2011); Roberta S. Karmel & Claire R. Kelly, The Hardening of Soft Law in Securities Regulation, 34 Brook. J. Int'l L. 883 (2009).

Moreover, the SEC benefits from treaties between the United States and other countries that call for mutual legal assistance on crimes, including securities crimes. These Mutual Legal Assistance Treaties (called MLATs) are negotiated through diplomatic channels and require Senate ratification. Virtually all MLATs have a "dual criminality requirement" — each country must recognize the criminality of the violation for which assistance is sought. The SEC's ability to use these treaties stems from the fact that the federal securities laws may be enforced in criminal as well as civil actions. See Michael D. Mann, et al., International Agreements and Understandings for the Production of Information and Other Mutual Assistance, 29 Int'l Law. 780, 781 (1995).

The SEC has also negotiated "Memoranda of Understanding" (or MOUs) with securities regulators in other countries. MOUs are bilateral non-binding agreements that facilitate the exchange of information and cooperation in securities investigations. MOUs do not require Senate ratification, have no dual criminality requirement, and are generally considered to be more flexible than MLATs. MOUs vary widely in terms of the range of securities violations that they embrace. See Edward H. Cadmus, Note, Revisiting the SEC's Memoranda of Understanding: A Fresh Look, 33 Fordham Int'l L. J. 1800 (2010).

Congress has enacted several provisions that facilitate adoption of MOUs and MLATs. Section 21(a)(2) of the Exchange Act authorizes the Commission to investigate violations of foreign law. Moreover, Section 24(d) of that Act creates an exception from the Freedom of Information Act for certain records received by the Commission from foreign securities regulators.

*8. **Obstacles to International Securities Enforcement.*** Principal obstacles to international securities enforcement efforts include bank secrecy laws and blocking statutes. Bank secrecy laws protect the confidentiality of bank customers and are waivable by those customers. See *SEC v. Benger*, 697 F. Supp. 2d 932, 937 (N.D. Ill. 2010) (identifying Switzerland Cyprus as countries "known for strong bank secrecy laws"); Cf. *SEC v. Thorn*, 2001 WL 1678787 at *6 (S.D. Ohio 2001) (noting that the defendant's investments were protected by Swiss bank secrecy laws).

Blocking statutes, on the other hand, impose penalties for providing information to foreign investors. They are intended to protect national interests rather than individual interests and hence individuals cannot waive them. See Marc J. Gottridge & Thomas Rouhette, France Puts Some Muscle Behind Its Blocking Statute, N.Y. L. J., April 29, 2008, at 4; Cf. *SEC v. Elfindepan, SA*, 169 F. Supp.2d 420, 426-27 (M.D.N.C. 2001) (discussing Costa Rican blocking statute). For a discussion of bank secrecy laws and blocking statutes, see Keith Y. Cohan, Note, The Need for A Refined Balancing Approach when American Discovery Orders Demand the Violation of Foreign Law, 87 Tex. L. Rev. 1009 (2009); Caroline A.A. Greene, Note, International Securities Law Enforcement: Recent Advances in Assistance and Cooperation, 27 Vand. J. Transnat'l L. 635, 664-71 (1994).

*9. **Criminal Enforcement Compared.*** Criminal prosecutions of international securities fraud are by no means unknown. See, e.g., *United States v. Cook*, 573 F.2d 281 (5th Cir. 1978); *United States v. Coffman*, 771 F. Supp. 2d 735 (E.D.Ky. 2011). They nonetheless are relatively unusual. Why would this be the case?

PROBLEM 12-3

Most-Best, Inc. is a soft drink manufacturer incorporated in the United States and headquartered in Chicago. Its wholly-owned subsidiary (Bestest, Inc.), incorporated in Canada and headquartered in Toronto, is responsible for the vast majority of Most-Best's profits. Toronto is also the location of Most-Best's main computer (server).

Most-Best stock is traded on the Toronto Stock Exchange as well as the Chicago Stock Exchange. Six percent of its shareholders are United States citizens and the remainder come from Canada.

Eliza, a United States citizen, is a senior vice president of Most-Best who regularly spends large amounts of time in Toronto in connection with Bestest's activities there. While in Toronto last spring, she prepared the first draft of a press release that announced a new upsurge in Bestest's profitability. She finalized the draft upon her return to Chicago and then posted it on Most-Best's web site. The press release (which contained fraud) was downloaded by Canadian investors in Canada, who then purchased Most-Best stock on the Toronto Stock Exchange. Once the fraudulent nature of the press release became publicly known, the price of Most-Best fell sharply on both exchanges on which it was traded.

Would a federal district court have subject matter jurisdiction over an SEC action against Most-Best?

C. CHOICE OF LAW AND CHOICE OF FORUM CLAUSES

Suppose that a United States investor bought securities from a foreign seller under a contract requiring them to litigate all disputes in the seller's country in accordance with that country's laws. Suppose further that the investor filed a federal securities fraud action and the seller moved for dismissal based on the contract. Would the court be obliged to grant the motion (regardless of whether it had subject matter jurisdiction in the absence of the contract)?

Relevant to such a motion are Section 29(a) of the Exchange Act and/or its Securities Act counterpart, Section 14. Section 29(a) provides as follows:

> Any condition, stipulation, or provision binding any person to waive compliance with any provision of this title or of any rule or regulation thereunder, or of any rule of an exchange required thereby shall be void.

See also Section 14 ("Any condition, stipulation, or provision binding any person acquiring any security to waive compliance with any provision of this title or of the rules and regulations of the Commission shall be void"). In the decision that follows, the court held choice of law and choice of forum clauses enforceable, these antiwaiver provisions notwithstanding.

LIPCON v. UNDERWRITERS AT LLOYD'S, LONDON

148 F.3d 1285 (11th Cir. 1998)

PHYLLIS A. KRAVITCH, SENIOR CIRCUIT JUDGE:

In this appeal, we are confronted with the important question of whether the anti-waiver provisions of the United States securities laws preclude enforcement of certain choice-of-law and forum-selection clauses ("choice clauses") in international agreements. Although we recognize that it is a close question, we follow the weight of circuit authority and conclude that the choice clauses are enforceable despite the anti-waiver provisions. In addition, we conclude that the agreements in this case satisfy scrutiny for fundamental fairness and do not contravene public policy. *** Accordingly, we affirm the district court's decision to dismiss the Lipcons' complaint against Lloyd's.

I.

Lloyd's [London (Lloyd's)] is a large insurance market in which more than three hundred Underwriting Agencies compete for underwriting business. Pursuant to the British Lloyd's Acts of 1871 and 1982, Lloyd's oversees and regulates the competition for underwriting business in the insurance market; according to the *amicus curiae* brief of the British Government, Lloyd's "has statutory powers granted by Parliament to regulate the affairs of the international insurance market in London...." Lloyd's itself, however, does not accept premiums or insure risks. Instead, Underwriting Agencies, which act as syndicates, compete for the insurance business. Each Underwriting Agency is controlled by a Managing Agent, who is responsible for the financial status of its agency. The Managing Agent must attract not only underwriting business from brokers but also the capital with which to insure the risks that are underwritten.

Managing Agents recruit "Names" to provide the underwriting capital. A Name becomes a Member of the Society of Lloyd's through a series of agreements, proof of financial means, and the deposit of an irrevocable letter of credit in favor of Lloyd's. By becoming a Member, a Name obtains the right to participate in the Lloyd's Underwriting Agencies. The Names, however, do not deal directly with Lloyd's or with the Managing Agents. Instead, the Names are represented by Members' Agents, who, pursuant to agreement, act as fiduciaries for the Names. Upon becoming a Name, an individual selects the underwriting agencies in which he wishes to participate. The Names generally join more than one underwriting agency in order to spread their risks across different types of insurance. In large part because of the experience of the Members' Agents, Names generally rely on the advice of their Members' Agents in deciding in which syndicates to invest. Selecting well is of the utmost financial importance because a Name is responsible for his share of an agency's losses.

In addition to providing the indicia of financial security mentioned above, to become a Name one must travel to England to acknowledge the attendant risks of participating in a syndicate by signing a standard-form "General Undertaking." The General Undertaking is a two-page document containing the choice clauses that form the basis for this dispute. The choice clauses provide:

> The rights and obligations of the parties arising out of or relating to the Member's membership of, and/or underwriting of insurance business at, Lloyd's and any other matter referred to in this Undertaking shall be governed by and construed in accordance with the laws of England.
>
> Each party hereto irrevocably agrees that the courts of England shall have exclusive jurisdiction to settle any dispute and/or controversy of whatsoever nature arising out of or relating to the Member's membership of, and/or underwriting of insurance business at, Lloyd's and that accordingly any suit, action or proceeding ... arising out of or relating to such matters shall be brought in such courts....

Irmgard and Mitchell Lipcon are Names who entered into underwriting agreements, and Charles and Barbara Lipcon, who signed letters of credit to provide collateral for the Names, are their spouses. Irmgard and Mitchell first became Names in 1983 and 1984, respectively, and in 1986 signed a revised General Undertaking that contains the choice clauses set out above.

After it became clear that the Names would be responsible for massive losses for asbestos and pollution claims, appellants brought suit in United States District Court for the Southern District of Florida alleging that: (1) Lloyd's actively sought investors from the United States to fill an urgent need to build up capital; (2) concealed information regarding the possible consequences of the risks undertaken; and (3) deliberately and disproportionately exposed the Names to massive liabilities for which sufficient underwriting capital or reinsurance was not available. The Lipcons stated claims under the Securities Act of 1933, §§ 5, 12(1), & 15; the Securities Exchange Act of 1934, §§ 10(b) & 20; the Racketeer Influenced and Corrupt Organizations Act ("RICO"); and various provisions of Florida law. The district court granted the motion to dismiss brought by Lloyd's, finding that the choice clauses are enforceable and preclude litigation arising out of the Lipcons' agreement with Lloyd's in United States courts. ***

II.

*** We note at the outset that although this circuit has not yet ruled on the validity of the Lloyd's choice clauses at issue in this case, we do not write on a clean slate. Thus far, the Second, Fourth, Fifth, Sixth, Seventh, Ninth, and Tenth Circuits have addressed the enforceability of the precise choice clauses that we confront today, and although the reasoning of those courts has not been uniform, all seven courts of appeals have concluded that the clauses are valid and enforceable.

B.

Appellants' first argument is that the choice clauses, which make United States law inapplicable to disputes arising between them and Lloyd's, are unenforceable under the anti-waiver provisions of the United States securities laws. The Securities Act of 1933 provides: "Any condition, stipulation, or provision binding any person acquiring any security to waive compliance with any provision of this subchapter or of the rules and regulations of the Commission shall be void." 15 U.S.C. § 77n. The Securities Exchange Act of 1934 contains a similar provision. See 15 U.S.C. § 78cc(a). *** According to the Securities and Exchange Commission ("SEC"), which filed an *amicus curiae* brief, "These provisions are essential to the enforcement of the securities laws in that they prevent persons from avoiding their obligations under those laws through the simple expedient of requiring investors to waive their rights under those laws as a condition to engaging in securities transactions."

The district court rejected appellants' and the SEC's argument that the anti- waiver provisions categorically render unenforceable the choice clauses in the Lipcons' contract. Instead, the district court reviewed the clauses under the framework for evaluating choice provisions in international agreements first announced in *M/S Bremen v. Zapata Off-Shore Co.,* 407 U.S. 1 (1972). In *Bremen,* an admiralty case that did not involve the securities laws, the Court enforced a choice-of-forum clause that required litigation in the courts of London. Because "[w]e cannot have trade and commerce in world markets and international waters exclusively on our terms, governed by our laws, and resolved in our courts," id. at 9, the Court concluded that forum-selection clauses in international agreements "are prima facie valid and should be enforced unless enforcement is shown by the resisting party to be 'unreasonable' under the circumstances," id. at 10. Although the contract at issue in *Bremen* provided for a forum in which to litigate, as opposed to the substantive law that would apply to, any dispute, the Court noted that the choice-of-forum clause likely would have the effect of a choice-of-law clause:

> [I]t is the general rule in English courts that the parties are assumed, absent contrary indications, to have designated the forum with the view that it should apply its own law.... It is therefore reasonable to conclude that the forum choice

> clause was also an effort to obtain certainty as to the applicable substantive law.

Id. at 14 n.15.

In giving content to *Bremen* 's "strong showing" standard for invalidating international choice-of-forum clauses, courts have announced that those provisions will be found "unreasonable under the circumstances," *Bremen,* 407 U.S. at 10, and thus unenforceable only when: (1) their formation was induced by fraud or overreaching; (2) the plaintiff effectively would be deprived of its day in court because of the inconvenience or unfairness of the chosen forum; (3) the fundamental unfairness of the chosen law would deprive the plaintiff of a remedy; or (4) enforcement of the provisions would contravene a strong public policy. See *Carnival Cruise Lines, Inc. v. Shute,* 499 U.S. 585, 594-95 (1991). Applying this test (hereinafter "the *Bremen* test"), the district court concluded that the choice clauses in this case are enforceable.

Appellants and the SEC contend that the *Bremen* test is inapplicable when Congress has spoken directly as to whether it is permissible to waive United States statutory remedies. They argue that to apply the *Bremen* test — which requires courts to assess public policy — is tantamount to treating "the anti-waiver provisions [of the securities laws] as merely reflecting a Congressional direction to the courts to decide whether 'the public policies incorporated into' the securities laws would be undermined." ***

Although appellants' argument finds strong support in the plain language of the anti-waiver provisions, which facially admit of no exceptions, precedent and policy considerations compel us to conclude that *Bremen* 's framework for evaluating choice clauses in international agreements governs this case. We turn first to an examination of Supreme Court precedent.

In *Scherk v. Alberto-Culver Co.,* 417 U.S. 506 (1974), "the Supreme Court explicitly relied on *Bremen* in a case involving a securities transaction." *Richards v. Lloyd's of London,* 135 F.3d 1289, 1293 (9th Cir.1998). *Scherk* involved an international transaction to sell a company, where that transaction was based upon a contract that included arbitration and choice-of-law clauses that provided for the application of Illinois law by an arbitrator in France. When the deal soured, one of the parties challenged the enforceability of the arbitration provision. In enforcing the provisions, the Court relied in large part upon the nature of international agreements:

> [I]n the absence of the arbitration provision considerable uncertainty existed at the time of the agreement, and still exists, concerning the law applicable to the resolution of disputes arising out of the contract. Such uncertainty will almost inevitably exist with respect to any contract touching two or more countries, each with its own substantive laws and conflict-of-laws rules. A contractual provision specifying in advance the forum in which disputes shall be litigated and the law to be applied is, therefore, an almost indispensable precondition to achievement of the orderliness and predictability essential to any international business transaction.

Scherk, 417 U.S. at 516.

We recognize that *Scherk* differed from the case before us in that the choice clause before the Court in *Scherk* provided, by designating Illinois law as the governing law, for the application of United States securities law, see id. at

519 n.13, and thus that the Court in *Scherk* had no opportunity to decide if an international choice-of-law provision is enforceable if it conflicts with the anti-waiver provisions of the United States securities laws. Nevertheless, the Court's statement in *Scherk* that a choice-of-forum clause is "an almost indispensable precondition to achievement of the orderliness and predictability essential to any international business transaction," 417 U.S. at 516, combined with the Court's observation that a forum-selection clause "might also be viewed as implicitly selecting the law of that place to apply to that transaction," id. at 519 n.13, indicates that international agreements — even those that render United States securities law inapplicable — are *sui generis.*[14]

Appellants nevertheless point our attention to a line of Supreme Court cases that they contend indicate the Court's disapproval of choice provisions that waive the substantive protections of United States law. ***

Appellants claim that the Court in *Mitsubishi Motors Corp. v. Soler Chrysler-Plymouth,* 473 U.S. 614 (1985), indicated its unwillingness to permit choice provisions to eliminate United States statutory remedies. In *Mitsubishi,* the Court held that the Sherman Act did not render unenforceable a forum-selection provision in an international agreement, because "[b]y agreeing to arbitrate a statutory claim, a party does not forgo the *substantive* rights afforded by the statute; it only submits to their resolution in an arbitral, rather than a judicial, forum." Id. at 628 (emphasis added). Appellants rely in particular on the Court's statement that "in the event the choice-of-forum and choice-of-law clauses operated in tandem as a prospective waiver of a party's right to pursue the statutory remedy for antitrust violations, we would have little hesitation in condemning the agreement as against public policy." Id. at 637 n.19. In *Mitsubishi,* however, the Court was not confronted with the scope of the anti-waiver provisions of the United States securities laws. More important, the Court in *Mitsubishi* recognized and affirmed *Scherk*'s policy of treating international commercial agreements as *sui generis.* See *Mitsubishi,* 473 U.S. at 629 .

Appellants rely as well upon *Shearson/American Express, Inc., v. McMahon,* 482 U.S. 220 (1987), in which the Court held that the anti-waiver provision of the Securities Exchange Act of 1934 did not render an arbitration agreement unenforceable, because "[b]y its terms, [section 78cc(a)] only prohibits waiver of the *substantive* obligations imposed by the Exchange Act." Id. at 288 (emphasis added). *McMahon,* however, involved the enforceability of an arbitration clause in a *domestic* securities agreement. Although appellants contend that *McMahon* makes clear the Court's categorical unwillingness to permit waiver of the substantive remedies of the securities laws, we do not think that *McMahon* controls the case before us. As stated above, the Court consistently has treated "truly international agreements," *Scherk,* 417 U.S. at

---

14. We think it clear that the agreement in this case is "truly international," *Scherk,* 417 U.S. at 515, as that term was used in *Scherk.* In this case, the parties to the agreement are from different countries, the negotiations leading up to the agreement took place in the United States whereas the closing took place in England, and the subject matter of the transaction concerned investment in an international insurance market.

515, differently than domestic transactions, which indisputably are subject to the anti-waiver provisions of the securities laws, see *McMahon,* 482 U.S. at 230.

Supreme Court precedent thus suggests that the enforceability of choice clauses in international agreements should be determined by a framework designed specifically for the international commercial context. Because the Supreme Court has not ruled on whether the anti-waiver provisions of the United States securities laws categorically render unenforceable choice-of-law clauses in international agreements, however, we turn to policy considerations.

2.

Underlying the Supreme Court's conclusions in *Bremen* and *Scherk* were two main concerns: (1) ensuring "the orderliness and predictability [that are] essential to any international business transaction," *Scherk,* 417 U.S. at 516; and (2) furthering international comity, see *Scherk,* 417 U.S. at 516; *Bremen,* 407 U.S. at 9.

To conclude that the anti-waiver provisions of the United States securities laws categorically preclude sophisticated parties from entering into international agreements — agreements that by definition involve parties and subject matter that would be subject to the laws of more than one nation if the parties did not contract *ex ante* for provisions governing choice of forum and choice of law — would undermine both policies upon which *Bremen* and *Scherk* were based. As the Ninth Circuit has observed, appellants' assertion that the statutory anti-waiver provisions categorically invalidate the choice clauses in the agreement with Lloyd's would, if correct, expand the reach of United States securities law to "any and all such transactions, no matter how remote from the United States." *Richards v. Lloyd's of London,* 135 F.3d 1289, 1293 (9th Cir.1998).

We also find in the content of the *Bremen* test itself support for our conclusion that the anti-waiver provisions of the United States securities laws do not preclude application of the *Bremen* test to determine the validity of the choice clauses. A court will invalidate a choice clause in an international agreement when "enforcement would contravene a strong public policy of the forum in which the suit is brought...." *Bremen,* 407 U.S. at 15. Thus, "[i]n *Bremen* itself, the Supreme Court contemplated that a forum selection clause may conflict with relevant statutes." *Richards,* 135 F.3d at 1293.

Although we do not deny that there is some force to appellants' argument that the anti-waiver provisions preclude application of the *Bremen* test, we believe that to invalidate the choice provisions for that reason in effect would be to conclude that "the reach of the United States securities laws [is] unbounded," *Richards,* 135 F.3d at 1293, and to ignore the Supreme Court's caveat that "[w]e cannot have trade and commerce in world markets and international waters exclusively on our terms, governed by our laws, and resolved in our courts," *Bremen,* 407 U.S. at 9. Because we are unwilling so to conclude, we hold that the anti-waiver provisions of the United States securities laws do not categorically render unenforceable the Lloyd's choice clauses, and we join the seven other courts of appeals that have addressed the issue in holding that the *Bremen* test controls our resolution of the enforceability of the Lloyd's choice clauses.

III.

Appellants contend on appeal that even if the anti-waiver provisions of the United States securities laws do not *per se* invalidate the choice clauses, the district court erred in concluding that the *Bremen* test was satisfied and that the choice clauses in this case are enforceable. We disagree and conclude that the district court correctly applied the *Bremen* test.

As noted supra, section II.B, forum-selection and choice-of-law clauses "are presumptively valid where the underlying transaction is fundamentally international in character." *Roby v. Corporation of Lloyd's,* 996 F.2d 1353, 1362 (2d Cir. 1993). " This presumption of validity may be overcome, however, by a clear showing that the clauses are 'unreasonable under the circumstances.' " *Roby,* 996 F.2d at 1363 (quoting *Bremen,* 407 U.S. at 10). Choice clauses will be found "unreasonable under the circumstances," *Bremen,* 407 U.S. at 10), and thus unenforceable only when: (1) their formation was induced by fraud or overreaching; (2) the plaintiff effectively would be deprived of its day in court because of the inconvenience or unfairness of the chosen forum; (3) the fundamental unfairness of the chosen law would deprive the plaintiff of a remedy; or (4) enforcement of such provisions would contravene a strong public policy. See *Carnival Cruise Lines, Inc. v. Shute,* 499 U.S. 585, 594-95 (1991); *Bremen,* 407 U.S. at 15-18; Appellants contend that the choice clauses in this case are unreasonable under the first, third, and fourth *Bremen* factors.

A.

Appellants first contend that the choice clauses were the product of fraud and overreaching. The only specific allegation in the complaint of fraud is that Lloyd's "tricked and fraudulently induced [the Lipcons] to sign on or about Nov. 5, 1986 a forum selection clause" by making "fraudulent statements" that included the following:

> The purpose, in both instances, is to bring the agreements into line with ... the new Lloyd's legislation.
>
> * * * * * *
>
> The new Premiums Trust Deed will incorporate some new provisions which are mainly of a technical nature, and will not affect you greatly on a day to day basis.

Appellants contend that allegation of these statements is sufficient to invalidate the choice clauses.

In *Scherk,* the Court stated:

> In *The Bremen* we noted that forum-selection clauses "should be given full effect" when "a freely negotiated private international agreement [is] unaffected by fraud...." This qualification *** means that an arbitration or forum-selection clause in a contract is not enforceable if the *inclusion of that clause in the contract* was the product of fraud or coercion.

417 U.S. at 519 n.14 (emphasis in original). By requiring the plaintiff specifically to allege that the choice clause itself was included in the contract due to fraud in order to succeed in a claim that the choice clause is unenforceable, courts may ensure that more general claims of fraud will be litigated *in the chosen forum,* in accordance with the contractual expectations of the parties.

We conclude that the allegations in the Lipcons' complaint are insufficient to satisfy *Scherk* 's rigorous standard for pleading fraud. The first alleged statement by Lloyd's (or, presumably, by an agent of Lloyd's) — that "[t]he purpose, in both instances, is to bring the agreements into line with ... the new Lloyd's legislation"[16] — is in no way fraudulent or misleading. Indeed, the General Undertaking, which the Lipcons signed on the day that Lloyd's allegedly made this statement, specifically provides that "[t]hroughout the period of his membership of Lloyd's the Member shall comply with the provisions of Lloyd's acts 1871-1982 [and] any subordinate legislation made or to be made thereunder...." ***

The second allegedly fraudulent statement — that "[t]he new Premiums Trust Deed will incorporate some new provisions which are mainly of a technical nature, and will not affect you greatly on a day to day basis" — likewise fails to satisfy *Scherk* 's standard. Appellants contend that the insertion of the choice clauses in the General Undertaking was a change of more than simply "a technical nature" and that the statement thus was misleading and fraudulent. *** An allegation that the Lipcons were induced — even fraudulently induced — to make changes in the Premiums Trust Deed is insufficient to support a claim that the choice clauses, which are contained in a *separate* agreement (the General Undertaking), were induced by fraud. ***

B.

Appellants also contend that the remedies provided by English law are inadequate. They argue that no cause of action exists under the laws of England analogous to an action under Section 12(1) of the Securities Act of 1933 for securities registration violations. Appellants also contend that their remedies under English law for misrepresentations made in connection with the sale of a security are inferior to those available under Section 12(2) of the Securities Act of 1933 because Section 14 of the Lloyd's Act of 1982 immunizes Lloyd's from any claims under the English Misrepresentations Act, absent a showing of bad faith. Finally, appellants assert that Lloyd's is immune from liability under England's Financial Services Act of 1986, which provides private remedies for fraud in connection with securities transactions, and that unlike United States securities law, English law does not recognize controlling person liability.

We have little doubt that "the United States securities laws would provide [appellants] with a greater variety of defendants and a greater chance of success due to lighter scienter and causation requirements...." *Roby,* 996 F.2d at 1366. We will not invalidate choice clauses, however, simply because the remedies available in the contractually chosen forum are less favorable than those available in the courts of the United States. Instead, we will declare unenforceable choice clauses only when the remedies available in the chosen forum are so inadequate that enforcement would be fundamentally unfair. See *Carnival Cruise Lines, Inc. v. Shute,* 499 U.S. 585, 595 (1991)*; Roby,* 996 F.2d at

---

16. It is not clear what the phrase "in both instances" refers to, but we assume *arguendo* that the phrase refers at least in part to the General Undertaking, as well as to the choice clauses specifically.

1360-61; *Riley v. Kingsley Underwriting Agencies, Ltd.*, 969 F.2d 953, 958 (10th Cir.1992).

Like the seven other courts of appeals that have addressed this issue, we hold that English law provides remedies adequate to address the complaints of the aggrieved Names. Although Section 14 of the Lloyd's Act of 1982 exempts Lloyd's, its officers, and its employees from liability under the English Misrepresentations Act, no other entities within Lloyd's — such as the Members' Agents and Managing Agents, both of whom owe a fiduciary duty to the Names — are exempt. In addition, even Lloyd's itself is not immune from liability if appellants can make a credible showing of bad faith. We therefore conclude that the contractually chosen law is not fundamentally unfair and thus does not provide a basis upon which to deny enforcement of the choice clauses.

C.

Appellants argue that enforcement of the choice clauses would contravene a strong public policy, namely the policy expressed in the anti-waiver provisions of the United States securities laws that substantive remedies be available for securities violations. We already have rejected appellants' argument that the anti-waiver provisions categorically render invalid the choice clauses. We now must decide whether enforcement of the choice clauses, which would require appellants to litigate in England under English remedies, would undermine the public policies more generally expressed in the United States securities laws. In so doing, we are mindful that at least one commentator has criticized the decisions of some other courts of appeals on the ground that the public policy inquiry "necessitates an exploration of foreign legal regimes about which U.S. courts are likely to know little or nothing" and requires courts to "determine which of two incommensurables is greater." See D. Hall, Note, No Way Out: An Argument Against Permitting Parties to Opt Out of U.S. Securities Laws in International Transactions, 97 Colum. L.Rev. 57, 83 (1997). ***

In *Roby* and *Bonny,* the Second and Seventh Circuits, respectively, concluded that "[t]he framers of the securities laws were concerned principally with reversing the common law rule favoring 'caveat emptor,' " *Roby,* 996 F.2d at 1364, and accordingly that the United States securities laws embody the policies of "insuring full and fair disclosure by issuers and deterring the exploitation of United States investors," *Bonny* [*v. Society of Lloyd's*, 3 F.3d 156, 161 (7th Cir. 1993)]. Appellants and the SEC do not disagree that the securities laws were intended to ensure disclosure and deter exploitation, but they argue that the Second and Seventh Circuits, as well as the district court in this case, ignored the compensatory function of private actions under the securities laws.

We agree with the SEC that private actions under the securities laws "serve as an important means of providing recompense to investors who have been harmed by wrongdoers." We are more confident than the SEC, however, that the compensatory policy underlying United States securities law will be vindicated by litigation in English courts under English law; this is especially so given our conclusion that English law provides adequate remedies to appellants in this case. Because we conclude that "the available remedies and potential damage recoveries suffice to deter deception of American investors[,] to induce the disclosure of material information to investors," *Bonny,* 3 F.3d at

162, and to provide redress to aggrieved Names, we hold that the choice clauses satisfy the public-policy prong of the *Bremen* test. We thus conclude that the district court did not err in finding that the choice clauses are enforceable. ***

The judgment of the district court is affirmed.

NOTES AND QUESTIONS

*1. **Giving the Antiwaiver Provisions Their Due.*** Did the court give appropriate weight to Section 29(a) of the Exchange Act and Section 14 of the Securities Act? Consider whether you agree with the view of a judge dissenting from a decision similar to *Lipcon*:

> Courts should not employ amorphous public policy to emasculate plain statutory language. ***
>
> The majority turns this *** inside out, by holding that underlying antiwaiver public policy eviscerates specific antiwaiver statutory provisions. Disregarding this express prohibition to assess whether enforcement of the choice clauses contravenes the underlying policy against waiver is akin to overlooking the plain language of a statute to consider its legislative history, a clearly disfavored method of statutory interpretation.

Richards v. Lloyd's of London, 135 F.3d 1289, 1298 (9th Cir. 1998) (Thomas, J., dissenting).

*2. **The Adequacy of Foreign Law.*** The court deemed English remedies "adequate," despite their being "less favorable" to the plaintiffs than federal securities law remedies would have been. When would foreign remedies be "so inadequate that enforcement would be found unfair"?

*3. **Watch Out?*** Consider the observation that *Lipcon* and decisions like it "could allow multinational corporations operating in the United States to avoid enforcement of U.S. statutory law by entering into agreements with other American businesses and consumers through foreign subsidiaries, and then contracting for all disputes to be resolved in a foreign forum." James T. Brittain, Jr., Comment, Foreign Forum Selection Clauses in the Federal Courts: All in the Name of International Comity, 23 Hous. J. Int'l L. 305, 347 (2001). Do you agree?

PROBLEM 12-4

Rodney, a 65 year old retiree from New Jersey with no investment experience, became impressed with the prospects of Maxx, Inc., a German firm, upon perusing its web site. With the assistance of a broker, he purchased Maxx ADRs, which traded on the New York Stock Exchange. Rodney did not notice that his contract of purchase contained the following statement: "All litigation involving my purchase of Maxx stock will take place in Germany and be governed by German law."

Thereafter concluding that the web site had misrepresented Maxx's earnings prospects, Rodney filed a Rule 10b-5 action in a federal district court in a circuit with a decision equivalent to *Lipcon*. Maxx moved to dismiss on the ground that Rodney could bring the action only in Germany.

Should the court grant the motion? How (if at all) would your answer change if a backlog of cases in the German courts made it likely that Rodney's case would not be heard for five years?

PROBLEM 12-5

Fred, who has lost money on virtually all of his many previous investments, purchased securities from Lorraine in a transaction that was in all respects domestic. Their contract provided that all disputes resulting from the purchase would be heard in the state courts of Idaho in accordance with Idaho law. Fred thereafter sued Lorraine for securities fraud in a federal district court, whereupon Lorraine moved to dismiss based on the contract. Assume that the circuit in which the action was filed already has on the books a decision equivalent to *Lipcon.* How should the court rule on the motion?

D. THE FORUM NON CONVENIENS DOCTRINE

The common law doctrine of forum non conveniens allows a federal district court to "dismiss an action on the ground that a court abroad is the more appropriate and convenient forum for adjudicating the controversy." *Sinochem Internat'l Co, Ltd. v. Malaysia Internat'l Shopping Corp.*, 549 U.S. 422, 425 (2007). Such a dismissal order is permissible only when the foreign forum has jurisdiction to hear the case, and when trial in the chosen [domestic] forum would 'establish ... oppressiveness and vexation to a defendant ... out of all proportion to plaintiff's convenience,' or when the 'chosen forum [is] inappropriate because of considerations affecting the court's own administrative and legal problems.'" *Piper Aircraft Co. v. Reyno,* 454 U.S. 235, 241 (1981), quoting *Koster v. Lumbermens Mut. Cas. Co.,* 330 U.S. 518, 524 (1947).

To be sure, the likelihood that a United States forum would "oppress" a foreign defendant is much less today than in 1947, when the Supreme Court issued its two seminal decisions on forum non conveniens – *Koster,* supra and *Gulf Oil Corp. v. Gilbert,* 330 U.S. 501 (1947). In 1947, international travel and communication were relatively difficult and multinational corporations were quite unusual. See generally Martin Davies, Time to Change the Federal Forum Non Conveniens Analysis, 77 Tul. L. Rev. 309 (2002). Thus, "one may wonder whether the entire doctrine of *forum non conveniens* should not be reexamined in light of the transportation revolution" and "the use of multinational subsidiaries to conduct international business." *Fitzgerald v. Texaco, Inc.,* 521 F.2d 448, 456 & n.3 (2d Cir. 1975) (Oakes, J., dissenting).

The doctrine has provided the basis for dismissing numerous federal securities fraud actions. See, e.g., *Robinson v. TCI/US West Communications, Inc.,* 117 F.3d 900 (5th Cir. 1997) (affirming dismissal in favor of England); *Howe v. Goldcorp Invs., Ltd.,* 946 F.2d 944 (1st Cir. 1991) (Breyer, J.) (affirming dismissal in favor of Canada); *In re Banco Santander Secs.-Optimal Litig.,* 732 F. Supp. 2d 1305 (S.D. Fla. 2010) (dismissing in favor of Ireland), aff'd, __ F. Appx __, 2011 WL 3823284 (11th Cir 2011); *Warlop v. Lernout,* 473 F. Supp. 2d 260 (D. Mass. 2007) (dismissing in favor of Belgium); *Windt v. Quest Commc'ns Int'l, Inc.,* 2006 WL 2987097 (D.N.J. 2006) (dismissing in favor of the Netherlands); *Adamowicz v. Barclays Private Equity France* SAS, 2006 WL 728394 (S.D.N.Y. 2006) (dismissing in favor of France); *Dragon Capital Partners L.P. v. Merrill Lynch Capital Servs., Inc.,* 949 F. Supp. 1123 (S.D.N.Y. 1997) (dismissing in favor of Hong Kong). Some argue that federal courts are more receptive to alternative fora located in democratic countries. See, e.g., Anne-Marie Slaughter Burley, International Law and International Relations Theory: A Dual Agenda, 87 Am. J. Int'l L. 205, 232 (1993). If so, is that a bad thing? See Christopher A. Whytlock, The Evolving Forum Shopping System, 96 Cornell L. Rev. 481, 519-520 (2011).

Consider the following decision.

ALFADDA v. FENN

159 F.3d 41 (2d Cir. 1998)

JOSEPH M. MCLAUGHLIN, CIRCUIT JUDGE:

Saudi European Investment Corporation ("SEIC") is incorporated in the Netherlands Antilles to invest Saudi Arabian capital in "Western markets." SEIC's stock is not publicly traded. Until 1989, its principal asset was Saudi European Bank ("SE Bank"), a French-licensed bank, headquartered in Paris. Although SEIC maintained an office in New York, and SE Bank had a branch there, SEIC's operations were indisputably based in France; and it dealt almost exclusively with money from Saudi Arabia. Both SEIC and SE Bank were run by the Chairman of SEIC, Jamal Radwan.

Under its Deed of Incorporation, SEIC was authorized at its founding to issue 40,000 voting shares. It initially issued only 20,000 shares, which were sold in its first offering in 1979. Following a 30:1 split in 1983, there were 600,000 issued shares outstanding and 600,000 more authorized, but unissued, shares.

In 1984, SEIC sought to raise $60 million in capital through a private stock offering of its remaining 600,000 authorized shares. These shares were offered pursuant to a Subscription Agreement and Private Placement Memorandum ("PPM"), which made certain representations about SEIC's financial condition and business plan. The PPM represented that the 1984 offering would consist of 600,000 voting shares to be sold for $100 each and that if the offering was oversubscribed, nonvoting shares would then be issued. Finally, the PPM provided that none of the shares would be sold in the United States. The PPM was prepared for SEIC in the United States by Ronald Reilly, the president of a Texas corporation retained by SEIC to help it raise money.

A number of wealthy Saudi businessmen purchased 600,000 shares in SEIC's 1984 private offering. However, after the 1984 offering closed, Radwan converted certain SEIC "capital notes" (which were essentially stock options) into shares of SEIC voting stock. The existence of the capital notes was not disclosed in the PPM.

Radwan owned 600,000 of the capital notes, which he converted into 600,000 shares of SEIC stock by paying SEIC $33 per share. Radwan then sold the shares to Charles Keating's now infamous Lincoln Savings and Loan for $100 per share. The effect, of course, was that SEIC had now sold 1.2 million voting shares, rather than the 600,000 shares originally contemplated. SEIC, however, did not disclose the sale of the extra shares in the PPM. Moreover, Radwan's sale to Keating contradicted the PPM's representation that shares would not be sold in the United States.

Around 1988, SE Bank began to stumble. A number of French banks with ties to the Middle East had failed in the late 1980's; and the French government began to fear that SE Bank would also fail. In 1988 and 1989, the Governor of the Bank of France requested that SEIC shareholders deposit funds into SE Bank to solve its liquidity problems. However, no shareholders responded. In November 1989, the French government ordered Radwan either to sell the bank to new investors or face the involuntary liquidation of SE Bank. Radwan chose to sell the bank.

The Commission Bancaire, France's banking regulatory authority, became an active player in the sale of SE Bank. Prospective purchasers were required to obtain the Commission Bancaire's approval of a plan to stabilize the bank to avoid future liquidity crises. After an audit of the bank's condition, it was sold for approximately $3.4 million. The new owners injected $9.8 million into SE Bank and rechristened it Societe de Banque Privee, S.A. ("SBP"). As a result of the sale, SEIC shareholders lost all equity in SE Bank.

Soon after the sale of SE Bank, the new entity, SBP, became embroiled in several American lawsuits arising out of SEIC's and Radwan's dealings with Charles Keating. SBP was sued in several investor class actions. The United States' Resolution Trust Company also sued SBP as the successor to SE Bank. To insulate SBP from these claims, French banking authorities reorganized SBP and placed SE Bank's former American holdings in an entity called Societe d'Analyses et d'Etudes Bretonneau ("Bretonneau"). Soon after the spin-off, Bretonneau's banking license was revoked by French authorities and its only business then became the liquidation of SE Bank's former American business.

In July 1987, Abdulrahman Sharbatly, a Saudi investor, filed a criminal complaint in the French *Tribunal de Grande Instance* against Radwan and SEIC, alleging that the misrepresentations contained in the PPM constituted fraud under French penal law. He also filed a civil complaint against Radwan and SEIC involving the same transactions. Under the French criminal code, a private party may bring a civil action for damages (*action civile*) based on a criminal offense, and may initiate a criminal prosecution if the state fails to do so.

One year later, Abdulrahman Al-Turki and Abdullatif Alissa, who also invested in SEIC, filed separate criminal complaints against SEIC with the *Tribunal de Grande Instance*. The Saudi investors charged that "unknown persons" associated with SEIC concealed the existence of Radwan's convertible capital notes and misrepresented in the PPM both the number of shares to be sold in the 1984 offering and the financial condition of SEIC in 1984.

The French examining magistrate indicted Radwan for the crime of "swindling" under Article 405 of the French Penal Code. In October 1994, the *Tribunal Correctionnel* in Paris acquitted Radwan of the criminal charges, and the Court of Appeals for Paris later affirmed the acquittal.

In April 1989, while the French actions were proceeding, Al-Turki, Saad Alissa, Abdullatif Alissa, Abdulaziz Alfadda, Abdullah Abbar, Yusif Bin Ahmed Kanoo (a Saudi Arabian partnership), and Ahmed Zainy filed a civil complaint against Radwan and SEIC in the Court of First Instance in Curacao, Netherlands Antilles. The plaintiff-shareholders alleged that they purchased

SEIC shares in 1984 on the basis of the defendants' misrepresentations regarding SEIC's capital structure.

In September 1989, part of the litigation now before us started. Alfadda, Abbar, Abdulla Kanoo, Abdulaziz Kanoo, Yusif Bin Ahmed Kanoo, and Zainy sued Radwan, SEIC, SE Bank, SBP, Bretonneau, Richard Fenn (Vice-Chairman of SEIC), Alef Bank, S.A., and Alef Investment Corporation N.V. in the United States District Court for the Southern District of New York (McKenna, J.) (the "*Alfadda* action"). The investors alleged that the defendants violated Section 10(b) of the Securities Exchange Act of 1934 and the Racketeer Influenced and Corrupt Organizations Act ("RICO") by: (1) misrepresenting SEIC's value at the time of the 1984 offering; (2) diluting SEIC's stock by selling too many shares in 1984; (3) failing to disclose the existence of the capital notes held by Radwan; and (4) misappropriating SEIC funds (the "SEIC claims"). Plaintiffs also alleged New York state common law claims for fraud and breach of fiduciary duty.

In 1990, Judge McKenna dismissed the *Alfadda* action for lack of subject matter jurisdiction because the claims had no connection to the United States. This Court reversed Judge McKenna, finding that the action had a sufficient connection to this country because of the sales to Keating's Lincoln Savings and Loan. *Alfadda v. Fenn,* 935 F.2d 475, 478 (2d Cir.1991).

On July 5, 1990, Al-Turki, Sharbatly, and the Alissas filed yet another complaint against the *Alfadda* defendants in the United States District Court for the Southern District of New York (the "*Al-Turki* action"). The *Al-Turki* plaintiffs alleged that Fenn, Radwan, SEIC, SE Bank, Alef Investment Corporation N.V., and Alef Bank, S.A. violated RICO by manipulating SBP's assets during SBP's restructuring to prevent plaintiffs from obtaining damages on the SEIC claims (the "SBP claims"). The *Al-Turki* and *Alfadda* actions were consolidated before Judge McKenna.

In 1992, after the *Alfadda* action was remanded to Judge McKenna, the defendants moved for dismissal of the consolidated actions on the ground of *forum non conveniens.* Judge McKenna denied the motion, concluding that although France might be a more convenient forum, the balance of interests did not tilt particularly in its favor. The parties then conducted significant discovery for three years under the supervision of Magistrate Judge Katz.

In 1996, defendants again moved to dismiss the consolidated cases on *forum non conveniens* grounds. This time Judge McKenna granted the motion, reasoning that the suit had little connection to the United States and that France would be a more convenient forum. *** Plaintiffs now appeal, arguing, *inter alia,* that Judge McKenna misapplied the doctrine of *forum non conveniens.*

DISCUSSION

I. *Forum Non Conveniens*

Plaintiffs argue that, given the massive discovery and preparation that went into this suit, application of the *forum non conveniens* doctrine was inappropriate. We disagree.

Our review of a *forum non conveniens* dismissal is severely cabined. See *Piper Aircraft Co. v. Reyno,* 454 U.S. 235, 257 (1981). "[T]he decision lies wholly within the broad discretion of the district court and should be reversed only if that discretion has been clearly abused." *Peregrine Myanmar Ltd. v. Segal,* 89 F.3d 41, 46 (2d Cir. 1996) A *forum non conveniens* analysis proceeds in two steps.

First, the court must determine that there is an adequate alternative forum somewhere. See *Piper,* 454 U.S. at 254 n. 22. An alternative forum is adequate if: (1) the defendants are subject to service of process there; and (2) the forum permits "litigation of the subject matter of the dispute." *Piper,* 454 U.S. at 254 n. 22. That the law of the foreign forum differs from American law "should ordinarily not be given conclusive or even substantial weight" in assessing the adequacy of the forum. Id. at 247.

Having concluded that an adequate alternative forum does exist, the court must then weigh the public and private interests identified in *Gulf Oil Corp. v. Gilbert,* 330 U.S. 501, 508-09 (1947), to determine which forum "will be most convenient and will best serve the ends of justice." *Peregrine Myanmar,* 89 F.3d at 46. If a district court focuses on all the *Gilbert* factors before dismissing a case on *forum non conveniens* grounds, we accord its decision "substantial deference." See *Piper,* 454 U.S. at 257.

The public interests include: (1) having local disputes settled locally; (2) avoiding problems of applying foreign law; and (3) avoiding burdening jurors with cases that have no impact on their community.

The private interests include: (1) ease of access to evidence; (2) the cost for witnesses to attend trial; (3) the availability of compulsory process; and (4) other factors that might shorten trial or make it less expensive. See *Piper,* 454 U.S. at 241; *Gilbert,* 330 U.S. at 508.

In assessing convenience, "[t]here is ordinarily a strong presumption in favor of the plaintiff's choice of forum." *Murray v. British Broad. Corp.,* 81 F.3d 287, 290 (2d Cir. 1996); see *Piper,* 454 U.S. at 255 ("strong presumption in favor of the plaintiff's choice of forum"). Thus, dismissal usually is not appropriate unless "the balance of convenience tilts strongly in favor of trial in the foreign forum." *R. Maganlal & Co. v. M.G. Chem. Co.,* 942 F.2d 164, 167 (2d Cir. 1991). However, this presumption is weaker when the plaintiff is foreign. See *Piper,* 454 U.S. at 255-56 ("the presumption applies with less force when the plaintiff or real parties in interest are foreign").

Neither side challenges Judge McKenna's conclusion that France is an adequate alternative forum. The only issue, therefore, is whether Judge McKenna properly weighed the *Gilbert* factors.

A. *Public Interest Factors*

1. Gilbert *Factors*

Judge McKenna properly concluded that the *Gilbert* public interest factors weigh strongly in favor of France as a forum. First, the interest in having local disputes settled locally weighs heavily against the United States as a forum. This case involves a dispute between a Netherlands Antilles corporation and Saudi Arabian shareholders over the conduct of a French bank. Thus, France has a far greater interest in this litigation than the United States.

The complications of applying foreign law do not weigh in favor of either forum. In adjudicating plaintiffs' RICO and securities laws claims, an American court would apply American law. If the case is transferred to France, however, French law would apply and a consideration of American law would be unnecessary. While plaintiffs will not be able to avail themselves of the benefits of United States securities and racketeering laws in the French forum, "*forum non conveniens* dismissal is not trumped simply because the foreign forum will apply different substantive law than an American court." *Capital Currency Exch., N.V. v. National Westminster Bank PLC,* 155 F.3d 603, 609-10 (2d Cir. 1998). Moreover, the difference in applicable substantive law is properly considered when assessing whether an adequate alternative forum exists, an issue that plaintiffs do not challenge on appeal. See *Piper,* 454 U.S. at 254-55.

The interest in protecting jurors from sitting on cases with no relevance to their own community weighs heavily in favor of France. This suit involves not only plaintiffs' investment in a Netherlands Antilles holding company that owned a French-licensed bank, but also a challenge to a bank restructuring ordered and supervised by French banking authorities. Thus, French jurors have a more significant interest in this case than American jurors. See *Scottish Air Int'l, Inc. v. British Caledonian Group, PLC,* 81 F.3d 1224, 1233-34 (2d Cir. 1996) (Great Britain had greater interest in litigation involving inquiry into internal affairs of British corporation).

2. *Interest in Application of Domestic Law*

Plaintiffs argue that the United States has a significant interest in applying RICO and securities laws to international transactions. Plaintiffs assert that in dismissing the action, Judge McKenna should have considered this significant public interest, and that this interest weighs heavily in favor of the United States as a forum. ***

Plaintiffs' initial argument, that *forum non conveniens* dismissal is never appropriate when a plaintiff alleges a federal securities or racketeering cause of action, is clearly wrong. We have specifically held to the contrary. *PT United Can Co. v. Crown Cork & Seal Co.,* 138 F.3d 65, 74 (2d Cir. 1998) (RICO); *Allstate* [*Life Ins. Co. v. Linter Group Ltd.*, 994 F.2d 996, 1001 (2d Cir. 1993)] (securities).

We also reject plaintiffs' alternative contention that the United States' interest in applying its own securities and RICO laws to the international financial transaction at issue made the Southern District a more convenient forum. We recognize that this argument finds some support in our previous decisions, at least in regard to securities actions. In *Allstate,* we noted that "United States courts have an interest in enforcing United States securities laws." *Allstate,* 994 F.2d at 1002; cf. *Alfadda v. Fenn,* 935 F.2d 475, 478 (2d Cir. 1991) (United States had a sufficient interest in seeing its securities and RICO laws applied to justify exercising *subject matter jurisdiction* over plaintiffs' claims).

However, we made clear that this interest is merely one consideration to be weighed in the totality of the *Gilbert* analysis. *Allstate,* 994 F.2d at 1002 ("[T]his [interest] alone does not prohibit [United States courts] from dismissing a securities action on the ground of forum non conveniens."); Because the traditional *Gilbert* public interest factors weigh heavily in favor of France, we do not agree that the United States' interest in applying its securities and RICO laws rendered Judge McKenna's decision to dismiss on the grounds of *forum non conveniens* an abuse of discretion.

B. *Private Interests*

1. *Traditional Private Interest Factors*

Judge McKenna correctly concluded that the private interests involved in this case also strongly favor litigating in France. First, *all* the defendants and *nearly all* the documentary evidence are located in France. See *Blanco v. Banco Industrial de Venezuela S.A.*, 997 F.2d 974, 982-83 (2d Cir. 1993). In addition, the cost for witnesses to attend trial will be significantly lessened if trial is held in France because almost all the entities involved are based there. See *Blanco,* 997 F.2d at 982. Moreover, France is much closer to Saudi Arabia, so it will presumably be easier for the plaintiffs to travel there. See *Schertenleib v. Traum,* 589 F.2d 1156, 1165 (2d Cir. 1978) (Geneva more convenient forum when "[a]ll of the prospective witnesses, apart from [the defendant], either are Swiss or reside in European countries").

Finally, compulsory process is available in France to secure the live testimony of necessary foreign witnesses outside the reach of United States process. See, e.g., *Schertenleib,* 589 F.2d at 1165 (inability to bring witness to United States for live cross-examination before fact-finder "[p]erhaps the most significant problem" making litigation in United States court inappropriate). The ability to secure witness testimony takes on added importance in this action because "where, as here, appellants have alleged fraud, live testimony of key witnesses is necessary so that the trier of fact can assess the witnesses' demeanor." *Allstate,* 994 F.2d at 1001.

2. *Pretrial Discovery*

Plaintiffs' major argument on the *Gilbert* factors is that significant discovery was conducted, and has been completed, in the Southern District of New York. Plaintiffs contend that the extent of completed discovery weighs heavily in favor of the United States as a forum because: (1) Judge McKenna and Magistrate Judge Katz acquired unusual familiarity with this action in the course of resolving approximately 15 discovery disputes; (2) plaintiffs would be forced to recommence discovery in France since Judge McKenna's previous order precluding the use of discovery in the French *action civile* prevents the parties from using the existing discovery material in a subsequent French civil proceeding; and (3) plaintiffs' financial investment in translating documents from French to English and videotaping depositions of witnesses outside the reach of United States process would be wasted. We are not persuaded. ***

*** Although an issue of first impression in this Court, the Third, Fifth, and Tenth Circuits have concluded that the extent of completed discovery in the American forum is a relevant — but not necessarily dispositive — consideration in assessing convenience. See *Lony v. E.I. Du Pont de Nemours & Co.,* 935 F.2d 604, 613-14 (3d Cir. 1991); *Schexnider v. McDermott Int'l, Inc.,* 817 F.2d 1159, 1163 (5th Cir. 1987); *Gates Learjet Corp. v. Jensen,* 743 F.2d 1325, 1335 (9th Cir. 1984).

There appears to be some disagreement, largely of academic interest, as to whether the extent of completed discovery should be considered a public or a private interest under the *Gilbert* analysis. Compare *Schexnider,* 817 F.2d at 1163 (public interest) with *Gates,* 743 F.2d at 1329 (private interest) *and Lony,* 935 F.2d at 613-14 (discovery "goes to both private concerns ... and public ones"). We see little need to address this quibble, or even whether it should be considered at all in the *Gilbert* analysis. Assuming, *arguendo,* that the extent of completed discovery is relevant — whether as a public or private interest — we do not believe that it tips the balance towards an American forum. The traditional public and private interest factors weigh heavily in favor of France. Completing discovery within the Southern District and investing financial resources in order to facilitate trial in the United States does not sufficiently tip the scales of the *Gilbert* balance, especially since plaintiffs are free to use the existing discovery material to whatever extent the French tribunal will permit.

We do not read Judge McKenna's prior order as preventing the parties from using discovery materials in a future civil proceeding. Judge McKenna ordered that "[n]o discovery obtained in the present action is to be used in the litigations pending in France or the Netherlands Antilles." The order barred the use of discovery in any *pending* action. It does not bar the use of such material in a *future* civil litigation.

Finally, none of the plaintiffs are United States citizens and the *Gilbert* factors strongly favor France as a forum. Thus, we apply a weaker presumption in favor of plaintiffs' forum, and that presumption has been overcome. See *Piper,* 454 U.S. at 255-56. ***

CONCLUSION

Balancing the *Gilbert* factors favors France as a forum. Given the deferential standard of review applicable in *forum non conveniens* inquiries, we find no abuse of discretion in dismissing on *forum non conveniens* grounds. ***

NOTES AND QUESTIONS

1. The Adequacy of the Foreign Forum. As *Alfadda* noted, a forum non conveniens dismissal requires an "adequate" alternative forum. But what is that? Consider the following explanation for why Belgium was inadequate as a forum to adjudicate an action brought mainly by United States investors who had purchased shares of a Belgian corporation on the NASDAQ:

> [T]his Court has two concerns with the adequacy of Belgium as a forum for this class action securities action: Belgium's lack of a class action mechanism and its failure to recognize the fraud-on-the-market theory. Increased difficulty in proceeding as a class in a foreign forum does not, without more, render that forum inadequate. See *Howe v. Goldcorp Investments, Ltd.*, 946 F.2d 944, 952 (1st Cir. 1991). The complete lack of a class action mechanism is, however, an important factor to be weighed in determining the adequacy of an alternative forum. See *Bodner v. Banque Paribas*, 114 F. Supp.2d 117, 132 (E.D.N.Y. 2000). The Court has found no cases, and counsel has cited none, where a court has dismissed a securities fraud class action on forum non conveniens grounds where the plaintiff class has purchased stock on the American exchange and no class action remedy was available in the alternative forum.
>
> As for the fraud-on-the-market theory, courts have so far been reluctant to find a forum inadequate based on the lack of a recognized

> fraud-on-the-market doctrine. See *In re CINAR Corp. Sec. Litig.*, 186 F. Supp.2d 279, 298 (E.D.N.Y. 2002). When combined with the lack of a fraud-on-the-market theory, however, the lack of a class action mechanism creates virtually insurmountable concerns regarding the adequacy of the foreign forum. See *Derensis v. Coopers & Lybrand Chartered Accountants*, 930 F. Supp. 1003, 1007-09 (D.N.J. 1996). Dismissal in favor of Belgium would force each of the thousands of the United States purchasers to file separate actions in Belgium and demonstrate individual reliance on the misstatements. This is a remedy "so clearly inadequate or unsatisfactory that it is no remedy at all." *Piper Aircraft* [*v. Reyno*, 545 U.S. 239, 254 (1981)].

In re Lernout & Hauspie Sec. Litig., 208 F. Supp. 2d 74, 91-92 (D. Mass. 2002).

Two years later, the same judge decided a forum non conveniens motion in a related action — one brought (mainly) by European investors who had purchased shares of the same Belgian corporation on NASDAQ's European counterpart (the EASDAQ). See *Warlop v. Lernout*, 473 F. Supp. 2d 260 (D. Mass. 2007). This time, the judge held Belgium to be an *adequate* forum and granted the motion. To be sure, she acknowledged Belgium's failure to offer either a class action mechanism or the fraud-on-the-market theory. But she took the position that "increased difficulty in proceeding as a class in a foreign forum does not, without more, render that forum inadequate." Id. at 264.

What do these two decisions suggest about the nature of the adequacy inquiry? Consider this question further in connection with the next Note.

2. ***Adequacy vs. the Public/Private Factors.*** To appreciate the significance of the different resolutions regarding Belgium described in Note 1, it may be instructive to examine the court's analyses of the public/private factors. In the NASDAQ action, the court found those factors to favor the United States (in the hypothetical circumstance that Belgium was an adequate forum). The court noted that most class members were from the United States, the NASDAQ was located here, and Massachusetts was the base of the company's American operations. These considerations were said to trump those cutting the other way — the ongoing criminal investigation in Belgium and the witnesses and evidence located there. 208 F. Supp. 2d at 92-93. In the EASDAQ action, on the other hand, the court had this to say:

> The fact that these securities were purchased in Europe and that most class members reside there suggests that Belgium would be a more proper forum. If the Court retained the case, it would likely be forced to adjudicate complex issues of European law. *** In addition, it is not clear that Europe would enforce a class action judgment from this District.
>
> There is very little public interest in retaining the litigation here. *** Most significantly, the shares of stock purchased in this case were all obtained on EASDAQ. This Court has already expended significant judicial resources in protecting the rights of American investors on NASDAQ. By contrast, Belgium, which was the headquarters of L & H, possesses significant interest in this case, as illustrated by the ongoing criminal case.***
>
> Second, the civil fraud cases in Belgium have been stayed pending the conclusion of any attendant criminal investigations. Although the Belgian government's long delay in concluding its criminal investigation of the L & H collapse gives this Court some reason to worry that civil relief will be indefinitely delayed while criminal investigators in Belgium decide how to proceed, this Court also recognizes that a foreign government is pursuing this

> important and complex criminal investigation. However, it is worth adding that civil litigants in Belgium will likely receive the benefit of any factual findings from the criminal proceeding, whereas here it is not clear what the effect of a foreign judgment has. Thus, given the strong European presence in this litigation, this Court finds that Belgium has a more compelling stake in the adjudication of the criminal and civil components of this case for European purchases.

473 F. Supp. 2d at 263-64. What do these two decisions suggest about the nature of the inquiry into the public/private factors? About the operation of the forum non conveniens doctrine in general?

*3. **Forum Choice in Class Actions.*** Should less significance be accorded the forum choice of plaintiffs who represent a class? The Second Circuit initially said no. See *DiRienzo v. Philip Serv. Corp.,* 232 F.3d 49, 62-63 (2d Cir. 2000). But upon rehearing, the court had this to say:

> The district court in the case at hand, relying on *Koster v. (American) Lumbermens Mutual Casualty Co.*, 330 U.S. 518 (1947), gave less weight to the plaintiffs' choice of forum because they sued in a representative capacity. In our prior decision the majority disagreed with the district court's interpretation of *Koster*, but we now vacate that portion of the opinion. For even were the district court correct, *Iragorri* posits that defendants' motion to dismiss should also be viewed with greater skepticism.
>
> Affording less deference to representative plaintiffs does not mean they are deprived of all deference in their choice of forum. ***

DiRienzo v. Philip Serv. Corp., 294 F.3d 21, 28 (2d Cir. 2002). What do you understand the court's new position to be? Why is the question seemingly so difficult for the court to answer?

4. The Importance of Motives. In a decision after *Alfadda*, the Second Circuit stressed the importance of examining the plaintiff's motive in choosing the forum as well as the defendant's motive in contesting the forum:

> We *** understand the Supreme Court's teachings on the deference due to plaintiff's forum choice as instructing that we give greater deference to a plaintiff's forum choice to the extent that it was motivated by legitimate reasons, including the plaintiff's convenience and the ability of a U.S. resident plaintiff to obtain jurisdiction over the defendant, and diminishing deference to a plaintiff's forum choice to the extent that it was motivated by tactical advantage. ***
>
> Courts should be mindful that, just as plaintiffs sometimes choose a forum for forum-shopping reasons, defendants also may move for dismissal under the doctrine of *forum non conveniens* not because of genuine concern with convenience but because of similar forum-shopping reasons. District courts should therefore arm themselves with an appropriate degree of skepticism in assessing whether the defendant has demonstrated genuine inconvenience and a clear preferability of the foreign forum. ***

Iragorri v. United Techs. Corp., 274 F.3d 65, 73-75 (2d Cir. 2001). See *Pension Comm. of Univ. of Montreal Pension Plan v. Bank of Am. Secs., LLC,* 446 F. Supp. 2d 163, 177-78 (S.D.N.Y. 2006) (examining the motives of a group of plaintiffs who wished to litigate in New York). What are the pros and cons of focusing on motives?

5. **Morrison *Revisited.*** What is the likely impact of the Supreme Court's *Morrison* decision on the operation of the forum non conveniens doctrine?

PROBLEM 12-6

Aragon AG is a German company with its principal place of business in Frankfurt. It is traded on the Frankfurt Stock Exchange and also on the Chicago Stock Exchange. Joanna, a citizen of both the United States and Germany who lives 6 months a year in each country, bought shares of Aragon on the Chicago Stock Exchange. Thereafter, she filed a Rule 10b-5 action in a federal district court against Aragon and certain of its officers, most of whom live in Germany.

The defendants have moved for dismissal on forum non conveniens grounds, citing their own convenience along with the location of some of the witnesses. In opposing the defendants' motion, Joanna argued that she has recently encountered significant health problems that have depleted her financial resources. As a result, she says that she cannot afford to litigate the action in Germany because contingency fee arrangements would not be available there. Should the court deny the defendants' motion based on Joanna's financial situation?

Cf. *Murray v. British Broad. Corp.,* 81 F.3d 287 (2d Cir. 1996).

Chapter 13

SECURITIES ARBITRATION

Arbitration is the principal means of resolving disputes between investors and their brokers. To open an account with a brokerage firm, an investor signs a contract containing a pre-dispute arbitration agreement (PDAA). The PDAA requires the arbitration of all future disputes between the investor and the firm (or its brokers). PDAAs have become so routine that it would be extremely unusual for an investor-broker contract not to have one.

Mandatory arbitration of investor-broker disputes is a relatively recent phenomenon as well as a highly controversial one. As we will see, turning points occurred in 1987 and in 1989, when the Supreme Court upheld an agreement to arbitrate, first, an Exchange Act claim and then, a Securities Act claim. Both decisions split the Court 5-4, as did a number of others that we will encounter in this Chapter.

The forum for virtually all securities arbitrations today is the Financial Industry Regulatory Authority (the FINRA), a self-regulatory organization (SRO) established in 2007 as the result of the consolidation of the National Association of Securities Dealers (NASD) and the member regulatory, enforcement, and arbitration divisions of the New York Stock Exchange (NYSE). Before the emergence of the FINRA, the NASD served as the forum for about ninety percent of securities arbitrations, with the remainder occurring mainly in the stock exchanges (chiefly the NYSE).

Not surprisingly, the number of securities arbitration cases mirrors the realities of the larger investment universe. Thus, the dot.com bubble precipitated a surge in claims in the 1990s that fell off after 2003. Similarly, the economic crisis of 2008 fueled a rise in arbitration filings in 2009. Consider the following statistics for 1996-2010, made available by the FINRA:

Arbitration Cases Filed

Year	Cases	Year	Cases
1996	5,631	2004	8,201
1997	5,997	2005	6,074
1998	4,938	2006	4,614
1999	5,608	2007	3,238
2000	5,558	2008	4,982
2001	6,915	2009	7,137
2002	7,704	2010	5,680
2003	8,945		

Dispute Resolution Statistics, at www.finra.org/ArbitrationMediation/AboutFINEADR/Statistics/

Supporters of mandatory arbitration maintain that it is fair, efficient, and economical. They also note that it is often recommended by judges as a form of alternative dispute resolution in a wide spectrum of civil cases. Critics, however, contend that investors can be protected only by a trial, conducted by a judge, based on the rules of evidence (not required in arbitration), with a right to appeal (sharply limited in arbitration). Critics further complain that the system has an inherent pro-broker bias, in part because the forum in which securities arbitrations occur – the FINRA – has a membership consisting entirely of brokerage firms.

The debate over mandatory securities arbitration encompasses every aspect of the arbitration process. Who determines the issues subject to arbitration? To what extent are arbitrators bound by substantive securities law? Do arbitration procedures favor brokers? Should arbitrators have the authority to award punitive damages? Is there adequate judicial review of arbitration decisions?

This Chapter explores these questions in four sections. Section A examines the relationship between the Federal Arbitration Act and the federal securities laws. Section B focuses on the process of securities arbitration. Section C addresses the role that courts continue to play in securities arbitration. Section D includes the results of a large survey of securities arbitration participants regarding their views of the fairness of the process.

A. THE RELATIONSHIP BETWEEN THE FEDERAL ARBITRATION ACT AND THE FEDERAL SECURITIES LAWS

For many years, courts struggled with the following question: when an investor agrees to arbitrate disputes with her broker, does she waive the right to sue him for violating the federal securities laws? The answer turns on the relationship between the federal securities laws and the Federal Arbitration Act of 1925 ("Arbitration Act"). That relationship is not self-evident, and the Supreme Court had viewed the relationship differently at different times.

The Arbitration Act declares arbitration agreements "valid, irrevocable, and enforceable, save upon such grounds as exist at law or in equity for the revocation of any contract." 9 U.S.C. § 2. The Act was intended to "revers[e] centuries of judicial hostility to arbitration agreements ***, to allow parties to avoid 'the costliness and delays of litigation,' and to place arbitration agreements 'upon the same footing as other contracts.' " *Scherk v. Alberto-Culver Co.,* 417 U.S. 506, 510-11 (1974) (quoting H.R. Rep. No. 96, 68th Cong., 1st Sess. 1, 2 (1924)).

The Supreme Court first addressed the interface between the Arbitration Act and the federal securities laws in *Wilko v. Swan,* 346 U.S. 427 (1953). The *Wilko* Court held that a PDAA did not prevent an investor from suing his broker for violating what is now Section 12(a)(2) of the Securities Act. That holding was premised on Section 14 of the Securities Act, which declares "void" "[a]ny condition, stipulation or provision binding any person acquiring any security to waive compliance with any provision" of that Act:

> This arrangement to arbitrate is a "stipulation," and we think the right to select the judicial forum is the kind of "provision" that cannot be waived under § 14 of the Securities Act. *** While a buyer and seller of securities, under some circumstances, may deal at arm's length on equal terms, it is clear that the Securities Act was drafted with an eye to the disadvantages under which buyers labor. ***
>
> When the securities buyer, prior to any violation of the Securities Act, waives his right to sue in courts, he gives up more than would a participant in other business transactions. The security buyer has a wider choice of courts and venue. He thus surrenders one of the advantages the Act gives him and surrenders it at a time when he is less able to judge the weight of the handicap the Securities Act places upon his adversary.
>
> Even though the provisions of the Securities Act, advantageous to the buyer, apply, their effectiveness in application is lessened in arbitration as compared to judicial proceedings. *** This case requires subjective findings on the purpose and knowledge of an alleged violator of the Act. They must be not only determined but applied by the arbitrators without judicial instruction on the law. As their award may be made without explanation of their reasons and without a complete record of their proceedings, the arbitrators' conception of the legal meaning of such statutory requirements as "burden of proof," "reasonable care" or "material fact" cannot be examined. Power to vacate an award is limited. *** [T]he interpretations of the law by the arbitrators in contrast to manifest disregard are not subject, in the federal courts, to judicial review for error in interpretation. *** As the protective provisions of the Securities Act require the exercise of judicial direction to fairly assure their effectiveness, it seems to us that Congress must have intended § 14 to apply to waiver of judicial trial and review.

Id. at 434-37. Lower federal courts thereafter likewise refused to order arbitration of claims made under the Exchange Act on the theory that Section 29(a) of that Act and Section 14 of the Securities Act are virtually identical. See, e.g., *Merrill Lynch Pierce Fenner & Smith, Inc. v. Moore,* 590 F.2d 823, 827-29 (10th Cir. 1978).

The Supreme Court abandoned *Wilko* in stages. By a 5-4 vote, the Court required the arbitration of a Rule 10b-5 claim on the ground that the contract containing the PDAA was "truly international." *Scherk v. Alberto-Culver Co.,* 417 U.S. 506, 515 (1974). The Court thereafter mandated arbitration of state securities claims despite their pendency to a Rule 10b-5 claim that would eventually be litigated. See *Dean Witter Reynolds, Inc. v. Byrd,* 470 U.S. 213, 223 (1985). The Court's abandonment of *Wilko* culminated in the following decision, which again split the Court 5-4.

SHEARSON/AMERICAN EXPRESS, INC. v. McMAHON

482 U.S. 220 (1987)

JUSTICE SANDRA DAY O' CONNOR:

This case presents two questions regarding the enforceability of predispute arbitration agreements between brokerage firms and their customers. The first is whether a claim brought under § 10(b) of the Securities Exchange Act of 1934 (Exchange Act) must be sent to arbitration in accordance with the terms of an arbitration agreement. The second is whether a claim brought under the Racketeer Influenced and Corrupt Organizations Act (RICO) must be arbitrated in accordance with the terms of such an agreement.

I

Between 1980 and 1982, respondents Eugene and Julia McMahon, individually and as trustees for various pension and profit-sharing plans, were customers of petitioner Shearson/American Express Inc. (Shearson), a brokerage firm registered with the Securities and Exchange Commission (SEC or Commission). Two customer agreements signed by Julia McMahon provided for arbitration of any controversy relating to the accounts the McMahons maintained with Shearson. The arbitration provision provided in relevant part as follows:

> "Unless unenforceable due to federal or state law, any controversy arising out of or relating to my accounts, to transactions with you for me or to this agreement or the breach thereof, shall be settled by arbitration in accordance with the rules, then in effect, of the National Association of Securities Dealers, Inc. or the Boards of Directors of the New York Stock Exchange, Inc. and/or the American Stock Exchange, Inc. as I may elect." 618 F.Supp. 384, 385 (1985).

In October 1984, the McMahons filed an amended complaint against Shearson and petitioner Mary Ann McNulty, the registered representative who handled their accounts, in the United States District Court for the Southern District of New York. The complaint alleged that McNulty, with Shearson's knowledge, had violated § 10(b) of the Exchange Act and Rule 10b-5, by engaging in fraudulent, excessive trading on respondents' accounts and by making false statements and omitting material facts from the advice given to respondents. The complaint also alleged a RICO claim, and state law claims for fraud and breach of fiduciary duties.

Relying on the customer agreements, petitioners moved to compel arbitration of the McMahons' claims pursuant to § 3 of the Federal Arbitration Act. The District Court granted the motion in part. The court first rejected the McMahons' contention that the arbitration agreements were unenforceable as contracts of adhesion. It then found that the McMahons' § 10(b) claims were arbitrable under the terms of the agreement, concluding that such a result followed from this Court's decision in *Dean Witter Reynolds Inc. v. Byrd,* 470 U.S. 213 (1985), and the "strong national policy favoring the enforcement of arbitration agreements." The District Court also held that the McMahons' state law claims were arbitrable under *Dean Witter Reynolds Inc. v. Byrd,* supra. It concluded, however, that the McMahons' RICO claim was not arbitrable "because of the important federal policies inherent in the enforcement of RICO by the federal courts."

The Court of Appeals affirmed the District Court on the state law and RICO claims, but it reversed on the Exchange Act claims. ***

*** The [C]ourt [of Appeals] *** acknowledged that *Scherk v. Alberto-Culver Co.,* 417 U.S. 506 (1974), and *Dean Witter Reynolds Inc. v. Byrd,* supra, had "cast some doubt on the applicability of *Wilko* to claims under § 10(b)." The Court of Appeals nevertheless concluded that it was bound by the "clear judicial precedent in this Circuit," and held that *Wilko* must be applied to Exchange Act claims.

We granted certiorari to resolve the conflict among the Courts of Appeals regarding the arbitrability of § 10(b) and RICO claims.

II

The Federal Arbitration Act provides the starting point for answering the questions raised in this case. ***

The Arbitration Act *** establishes a "federal policy favoring arbitration," *Moses H. Cone Memorial Hospital v. Mercury Construction Corp.,* 460 U.S. 1, 24 (1983), requiring that "we rigorously enforce agreements to arbitrate." *Dean Witter Reynolds Inc. v. Byrd,* supra, 470 U.S., at 221. This duty to enforce arbitration agreements is not diminished when a party bound by an agreement raises a claim founded on statutory rights. As we observed in *Mitsubishi Motors Corp. v. Soler Chrysler-Plymouth, Inc.,* "we are well past the time when judicial suspicion of the desirability of arbitration and of the competence of arbitral tribunals" should inhibit enforcement of the Act " 'in controversies based on statutes.' " 473 U.S., at 626-627, quoting *Wilko v. Swan,* supra, 346 U.S., at 432. Absent a well-founded claim that an arbitration agreement resulted from the sort of fraud or excessive economic power that "would provide grounds 'for the revocation of any contract,' " 473 U.S. at 627, the Arbitration Act "provides no basis for disfavoring agreements to arbitrate statutory claims by skewing the otherwise hospitable inquiry into arbitrability." Ibid.

The Arbitration Act, standing alone, therefore mandates enforcement of agreements to arbitrate statutory claims. Like any statutory directive, the Arbitration Act's mandate may be overridden by a contrary congressional command. The burden is on the party opposing arbitration, however, to show that Congress intended to preclude a waiver of judicial remedies for the statutory rights at issue. See id., at 628. If Congress did intend to limit or prohibit waiver of a judicial forum for a particular claim, such an intent "will be deducible from [the statute's] text or legislative history," ibid., or from an inherent conflict between arbitration and the statute's underlying purposes. See id., at 632-637.

To defeat application of the Arbitration Act in this case, therefore, the McMahons must demonstrate that Congress intended to make an exception to the Arbitration Act for claims arising under RICO and the Exchange Act, an intention discernible from the text, history, or purposes of the statute. ***

III

When Congress enacted the Exchange Act in 1934, it did not specifically address the question of the arbitrability of § 10(b) claims. The McMahons contend, however, that congressional intent to require a judicial forum for the resolution of § 10(b) claims can be deduced from § 29(a) of the Exchange Act, which declares void "[a]ny condition, stipulation, or provision binding any person to waive compliance with any provision of [the Act]."

First, we reject the McMahons' argument that § 29(a) forbids waiver of § 27 of the Exchange Act. Section 27 provides in relevant part:

> The district courts of the United States ... shall have exclusive jurisdiction of violations of this title or the rules and regulations thereunder, and of all suits

in equity and actions at law brought to enforce any liability or duty created by this title or the rules and regulations thereunder.

The McMahons contend that an agreement to waive this jurisdictional provision is unenforceable because § 29(a) voids the waiver of "any provision" of the Exchange Act. The language of § 29(a), however, does not reach so far. What the antiwaiver provision of § 29(a) forbids is enforcement of agreements to waive "compliance" with the provisions of the statute. But § 27 itself does not impose any duty with which persons trading in securities must "comply." By its terms, § 29(a) only prohibits waiver of the substantive obligations imposed by the Exchange Act. Because § 27 does not impose any statutory duties, its waiver does not constitute a waiver of "compliance with any provision" of the Exchange Act under § 29(a).

We do not read *Wilko v. Swan,* 346 U.S. 427 (1953), as compelling a different result. In *Wilko,* the Court held that a predispute agreement could not be enforced to compel arbitration of a claim arising under § 12(2) of the Securities Act. The basis for the ruling was § 14 of the Securities Act, which, like § 29(a) of the Exchange Act, declares void any stipulation "to waive compliance with any provision" of the statute. At the beginning of its analysis, the *Wilko* Court stated that the Securities Act's jurisdictional provision was "the kind of 'provision' that cannot be waived under § 14 of the Securities Act." This statement, however, can only be understood in the context of the Court's ensuing discussion explaining why arbitration was inadequate as a means of enforcing "the provisions of the Securities Act, advantageous to the buyer." Ibid. The conclusion in *Wilko* was expressly based on the Court's belief that a judicial forum was needed to protect the substantive rights created by the Securities Act: "As the protective provisions of the Securities Act require the exercise of judicial direction to fairly assure their effectiveness, it seems to us that Congress must have intended § 14 ... to apply to waiver of judicial trial and review." *Wilko* must be understood, therefore, as holding that the plaintiff's waiver of the "right to select the judicial forum" was unenforceable only because arbitration was judged inadequate to enforce the statutory rights created by § 12(2). ***

The second argument offered by the McMahons is that the arbitration agreement effects an impermissible waiver of the substantive protections of the Exchange Act. Ordinarily, "[b]y agreeing to arbitrate a statutory claim, a party does not forgo the substantive rights afforded by the statute; it only submits to their resolution in an arbitral, rather than a judicial, forum." *Mitsubishi Motors Corp. v. Soler Chrysler-Plymouth, Inc.,* 473 U.S., at 628. The McMahons argue, however, that § 29(a) compels a different conclusion. Initially, they contend that predispute agreements are void under § 29(a) because they tend to result from broker overreaching. They reason, as do some commentators, that *Wilko* is premised on the belief "that arbitration clauses in securities sales agreements generally are not freely negotiated." See, e.g., Sterk, Enforceability of Agreements to Arbitrate: An Examination of the Public Policy Defense, 2 Cardozo L. Rev. 481, 519 (1981). According to this view, *Wilko* barred enforcement of predispute agreements because of this frequent inequality of bargaining power, reasoning that Congress intended for § 14 generally to ensure that sellers did not "maneuver buyers into a position that might weaken their ability to recover under the Securities Act." The McMahons urge that we should interpret § 29(a) in the same fashion.

We decline to give *Wilko* a reading so far at odds with the plain language of § 14, or to adopt such an unlikely interpretation of § 29(a). The concern that § 29(a) is directed against is evident from the statute's plain language: it is a concern with whether an agreement "waive[s] compliance with [a] provision" of the Exchange Act. The voluntariness of the agreement is irrelevant to this inquiry: if a stipulation waives compliance with a statutory duty, it is void under § 29(a), whether voluntary or not. Thus, a customer cannot negotiate a reduction in commissions in exchange for a waiver of compliance with the requirements of the Exchange Act, even if the customer knowingly and voluntarily agreed to the bargain. Section 29(a) is concerned, not with whether brokers "maneuver[ed customers] into" an agreement, but with whether the agreement "weaken[s] their ability to recover under the [Exchange] Act." 346 U.S., at 432. The former is grounds for revoking the contract under ordinary principles of contract law; the latter is grounds for voiding the agreement under § 29(a).

The other reason advanced by the McMahons for finding a waiver of their § 10(b) rights is that arbitration does "weaken their ability to recover under the [Exchange] Act." Ibid. That is the heart of the Court's decision in *Wilko,* and respondents urge that we should follow its reasoning. *Wilko* listed several grounds why, in the Court's view, the "effectiveness [of the Act's provisions] in application is lessened in arbitration." First, the *Wilko* Court believed that arbitration proceedings were not suited to cases requiring "subjective findings on the purpose and knowledge of an alleged violator." *Wilko* also was concerned that arbitrators must make legal determinations "without judicial instruction on the law," and that an arbitration award "may be made without explanation of [the arbitrator's] reasons and without a complete record of their proceedings." Finally, *Wilko* noted that the "[p]ower to vacate an award is limited," and that "interpretations of the law by the arbitrators in contrast to manifest disregard are not subject, in the federal courts, to judicial review for error in interpretation." *Wilko* concluded that in view of these drawbacks to arbitration, § 12(2) claims "require[d] the exercise of judicial direction to fairly assure their effectiveness."

As Justice Frankfurter noted in his dissent in *Wilko,* the Court's opinion did not rest on any evidence, either "in the record ... [or] in the facts of which [it could] take judicial notice," that "the arbitral system ... would not afford the plaintiff the rights to which he is entitled." Instead, the reasons given in *Wilko* reflect a general suspicion of the desirability of arbitration and the competence of arbitral tribunals — most apply with no greater force to the arbitration of securities disputes than to the arbitration of legal disputes generally. It is difficult to reconcile *Wilko'* s mistrust of the arbitral process with this Court's subsequent decisions involving the Arbitration Act. See, e.g., *Dean Witter Reynolds Inc. v. Byrd,* 470 U.S. 213 (1985)*; Scherk v. Alberto-Culver Co.,* 417 U.S. 506 (1974).

Indeed, most of the reasons given in *Wilko* have been rejected subsequently by the Court as a basis for holding claims to be nonarbitrable. In *Mitsubishi,* for example, we recognized that arbitral tribunals are readily capable of handling the factual and legal complexities of antitrust claims, notwithstanding the absence of judicial instruction and supervision. Likewise, we have concluded that the streamlined procedures of arbitration do not entail any consequential restriction on substantive rights. Id., at 628. Finally, we have indicated that there is no reason to assume at the outset that arbitrators will not follow the law; although judicial scrutiny of arbitration awards necessarily is limited, such review is sufficient to ensure that arbitrators comply with the requirements of the statute. See id., at 636- 637, and n. 19.

The suitability of arbitration as a means of enforcing Exchange Act rights is evident from our decision in *Scherk.* Although the holding in that case was limited to international agreements, the competence of arbitral tribunals to resolve § 10(b) claims is the same in both settings. ***

Thus, the mistrust of arbitration that formed the basis for the *Wilko* opinion in 1953 is difficult to square with the assessment of arbitration that has prevailed since that time. This is especially so in light of the intervening changes in the regulatory structure of the securities laws. Even if *Wilko*'s assumptions regarding arbitration were valid at the time *Wilko* was decided, most certainly they do not hold true today for arbitration procedures subject to the SEC's oversight authority.

In 1953, when *Wilko* was decided, the Commission had only limited authority over the rules governing self-regulatory organizations (SROs) — the national securities exchanges and registered securities associations — and this authority appears not to have included any authority at all over their arbitration rules. See Brief for Securities and Exchange Commission as *Amicus Curiae* 14-15. Since the 1975 amendments to § 19 of the Exchange Act, however, the Commission has had expansive power to ensure the adequacy of the arbitration procedures employed by the SROs. No proposed rule change may take effect unless the SEC finds that the proposed rule is consistent with the requirements of the Exchange Act, 15 U.S.C. § 78s(b)(2); and the Commission has the power, on its own initiative, to "abrogate, add to, and delete from" any SRO rule if it finds such changes necessary or appropriate to further the objectives of the Act, 15 U.S.C. § 78s(c). In short, the Commission has broad authority to oversee and to regulate the rules adopted by the SROs relating to customer disputes, including the power to mandate the adoption of any rules it deems necessary to ensure that arbitration procedures adequately protect statutory rights.

In the exercise of its regulatory authority, the SEC has specifically approved the arbitration procedures of the New York Stock Exchange, the American Stock Exchange, and the NASD, the organizations mentioned in the arbitration agreement at issue in this case. We conclude that where, as in this case, the prescribed procedures are subject to the Commission's § 19 authority, an arbitration agreement does not effect a waiver of the protections of the Act. While *stare decisis* concerns may counsel against upsetting *Wilko*'s contrary conclusion under the Securities Act, we refuse to extend *Wilko*'s reasoning to the Exchange Act in light of these intervening regulatory developments. The McMahons' agreement to submit to arbitration therefore is not tantamount to an impermissible waiver of the McMahons' rights under § 10(b), and the agreement is not void on that basis under § 29(a).

The final argument offered by the McMahons is that even if § 29(a) as enacted does not void predispute arbitration agreements, Congress subsequently has indicated that it desires § 29(a) to be so interpreted. According to the McMahons, Congress expressed this intent when it failed to make more extensive changes to § 28(b), in the 1975 amendments to the Exchange Act. Before its amendment, § 28(b) provided in relevant part:

> Nothing in this chapter shall be construed to modify existing law (1) with regard to the binding effect on any member of any exchange of any action taken by the authorities of such exchange to settle disputes between its members, or (2) with regard to the binding effect of such action on any person who has agreed to be bound thereby, or (3) with regard to the binding effect on any such member of any disciplinary action taken by the authorities of the exchange. 48 Stat. 903.

The chief aim of this provision was to preserve the self-regulatory role of the securities exchanges, by giving the exchanges a means of enforcing their rules against their members. In 1975, Congress made extensive revisions to the Exchange Act intended to "clarify the scope of the self-regulatory responsibilities of national securities exchanges and registered securities associations ... and the manner in which they are to exercise those responsibilities." S. Rep. No. 94-75, p. 22 (1975). In making these changes, the Senate Report observed: "The self-regulatory organizations must exercise governmental-type powers if they are to carry out their responsibilities under the Exchange Act. When a member violates the Act or a self-regulatory organization's rules, the organization must be in a position to impose appropriate penalties or to revoke relevant privileges." Id., at 24.

The amendments to § 28 reflect this objective. Paragraph (3) of § 28(b) was deleted and replaced with new § 28(c), which provided that the validity of any disciplinary action taken by an SRO would not be affected by a subsequent decision by the SEC to stay or modify the sanction. At the same time, § 28(b) was expanded to ensure that all SROs as well as the Municipal Securities Rulemaking Board had the power to enforce their substantive rules against their members. Section 28(b), as amended, provides:

> Nothing in this chapter shall be construed to modify existing law with regard to the binding effect (1) on any member of or participant in any self- regulatory organization of any action taken by the authorities of such organization to settle disputes between its members or participants, (2) on any municipal securities dealer or municipal securities broker of any action taken pursuant to a procedure established by the Municipal Securities Rulemaking Board to settle disputes between municipal securities dealers and municipal securities brokers, or (3) of any action described in paragraph (1) or (2) on any person who has agreed to be bound thereby.

Thus, the amended version of § 28(b), like the original, mentions neither customers nor arbitration. It is directed at an entirely different problem: enhancing the self-regulatory function of the SROs under the Exchange Act.

The McMahons nonetheless argue that we should find it significant that Congress did *not* take this opportunity to address the general question of the arbitrability of Exchange Act claims. Their argument is based entirely on a sentence from the Conference Report, which they contend amounts to a ratification of *Wilko*'s extension to Exchange Act claims. The Conference Report states:

> The Senate bill amended section 28 of the Securities Exchange Act of 1934 with respect to arbitration proceedings between self-regulatory organizations and their participants, members, or persons dealing with members or participants. The House amendment contained no comparable provision. The House receded to the Senate. It was the clear understanding of the conferees that this amendment did not change existing law, as articulated in *Wilko v. Swan,* 346 U.S. 427 (1953), concerning the effect of arbitration proceedings provisions in agreements entered into by persons dealing with members and participants of self-regulatory organizations. H.R. Conf. Rep. No. 94-229, p. 111 (1975).

The McMahons contend that the conferees would not have acknowledged *Wilko* in a revision of the Exchange Act unless they were aware of lower court decisions extending *Wilko* to § 10(b) claims and intended to approve them. We find this argument fraught with difficulties. We cannot see how Congress could extend *Wilko* to the Exchange Act without enacting into law any provision remotely addressing that subject. And even if it could, there is little reason to interpret the Report as the McMahons suggest. At the outset, the committee may well have mentioned *Wilko* for a reason entirely different from the one postulated by the McMahons — lower courts had applied § 28(b) to the Securities Act, and the committee may simply have wished to make clear that the amendment to § 28(b) was not otherwise intended to affect *Wilko*'s construction of the Securities Act. Moreover, even if the committee were referring to the arbitrability of § 10(b) claims, the quoted sentence does not disclose what committee members thought "existing law" provided. The conference members might have had in mind the two Court of Appeals decisions extending *Wilko* to the Exchange Act, as the McMahons contend. See *Greater Continental Corp. v. Schechter,* 422 F.2d 1100 (CA2 1970); *Moran v. Paine, Webber, Jackson & Curtis,* 389 F.2d 242 (CA3 1968). It is equally likely, however, that the committee had in mind this Court's decision the year before expressing doubts as to whether *Wilko* should be extended to § 10(b) claims. See *Scherk v. Alberto-Culver Co.,* 417 U.S., at 513 ("[A] colorable argument could be made that even the semantic reasoning of the *Wilko* opinion does not control [a case based on § 10(b)]"). Finally, even assuming the conferees had an understanding of existing law that all agreed upon, they specifically disclaimed any intent to change it. Hence, the *Wilko* issue was left to the courts: it was unaffected by the amendment to § 28(b). This statement of congressional inaction simply does not support the proposition that the 1975 Congress intended to engraft onto unamended § 29(a) a meaning different from that of the enacting Congress.

We conclude, therefore, that Congress did not intend for § 29(a) to bar enforcement of all predispute arbitration agreements. In this case, where the SEC has sufficient statutory authority to ensure that arbitration is adequate to vindicate Exchange Act rights, enforcement does not effect a waiver of "compliance with any provision" of the Exchange Act under § 29(a). Accordingly, we hold the McMahons' agreements to arbitrate Exchange Act claims "enforce[able] ... in accord with the explicit provisions of the Arbitration Act." *Scherk v. Alberto-Culver Co.,* supra, at 520.

IV

[The Court held that the McMahons' agreement to arbitrate their RICO claim was enforceable.]

JUSTICE HAROLD A. BLACKMUN, WITH WHOM JUSTICE BRENNAN AND JUSTICE MARSHALL JOIN, CONCURRING IN PART AND DISSENTING IN PART:

I concur in the Court's decision to enforce the arbitration agreement with respect to respondents' RICO claims and thus join Parts I, II, and IV of the Court's opinion. I disagree, however, with the Court's conclusion that respondents' § 10(b) claims also are subject to arbitration.

*** In today's decision *** the Court effectively overrules *Wilko* by accepting the Securities and Exchange Commission's newly adopted position that arbitration procedures in the securities industry and the Commission's oversight of the self-regulatory organizations (SROs) have improved greatly since *Wilko* was decided. The Court thus approves the abandonment of the judiciary's role in the resolution of claims under the Exchange Act and leaves such claims to the arbitral forum of the securities industry at a time when the industry's abuses towards investors are more apparent than ever. ***

II

There are essentially two problems with the Court's conclusion that predispute agreements to arbitrate § 10(b) claims may be enforced. First, the Court gives *Wilko* an overly narrow reading so that it can fit into the syllogism offered by the Commission and accepted by the Court, namely, (1) *Wilko* was really a case concerning whether arbitration was adequate for the enforcement of the substantive provisions of the securities laws; (2) all of the *Wilko* Court's doubts as to arbitration's adequacy are outdated; (3) thus *Wilko* is no longer good law. Second, the Court accepts uncritically petitioners' and the Commission's argument that the problems with arbitration, highlighted by the *Wilko* Court, either no longer exist or are not now viewed as problems by the Court. This acceptance primarily is based upon the Court's belief in the Commission's representations that its oversight of the SROs ensures the adequacy of arbitration.

A

*** The Court in *Wilko* recognized the policy of investor protection in the Securities Act. *** In the Court's view, the express language, legislative history, and purposes of the Securities Act all made predispute agreements to arbitrate § 12(2) claims unenforceable despite the presence of the Arbitration Act.[9]

---

9. In discussing the similar nonwaiver provision under the Exchange Act, § 29(a), the Court now suggests that it can be read only to mean that an investor cannot waive security-investment personnel's "compliance" with a duty under the statute. The Court implies that the literal language of § 29(a) does not apply to an investor's waiver of his own action. It appears, however, that in *Wilko* the Court understood the nonwaiver provision *also* to mean that, at least in the predispute context, an investor could not waive *his* compliance with the provision for dispute resolution in the courts. This reading of the antiwaiver provision makes sense in terms of the policy of investor protection. To counteract the inherent superior position of the securities-industry professional, up to and including the time when a dispute might occur between a broker and the investor, Congress intended to place the investor on "a different basis from other purchasers." Construing § 14 not to allow the investor to waive his right to a judicial forum in the predispute setting serves this congressional purpose of maintaining the

Accordingly, the Court seriously errs when it states that the result in *Wilko* turned only on the perceived inadequacy of arbitration for the enforcement of § 12(2) claims. It is true that the *Wilko* Court discussed the inadequacies of this process and that this discussion constituted one ground for the Court's decision. The discussion, however, occurred *after* the Court had concluded that the language, legislative history, and purposes of the Securities Act mandated an exception to the Arbitration Act for these securities claims. ***

In light of a proper reading of *Wilko,* the pertinent question then becomes whether the language, legislative history, and purposes of the Exchange Act call for an exception to the Arbitration Act for § 10(b) claims. The Exchange Act waiver provision is virtually identical to that of the Securities Act. More importantly, the same concern with investor protection that motivated the Securities Act is evident in the Exchange Act, although the latter, in contrast to the former, is aimed at trading in the secondary securities market. See *Ernst & Ernst v. Hochfelder,* 425 U.S. 185, 195 (1976). We have recognized that both Acts were designed with this common purpose in mind. See id., at 206. ***

In sum, the same reasons that led the Court to find an exception to the Arbitration Act for § 12(2) claims exist for § 10(b) claims as well. It is clear that *Wilko,* when properly read, governs the instant case and mandates that a predispute arbitration agreement should not be enforced as to § 10(b) claims.

B

Even if I were to accept the Court's narrow reading of *Wilko,* as a case dealing only with the inadequacies of arbitration in 1953, I do not think that this case should be resolved differently today so long as the policy of investor protection is given proper consideration in the analysis. Despite improvements in the process of arbitration and changes in the judicial attitude towards it, several aspects of arbitration that were seen by the *Wilko* Court to be inimical to the policy of investor protection still remain. Moreover, I have serious reservations about the Commission's contention that its oversight of the SROs' arbitration procedures will ensure that the process is adequate to protect an investor's rights under the securities Acts.

As the Court observes, in *Wilko* the Court was disturbed by several characteristics of arbitration that made such a process inadequate to safeguard the special position in which the Securities Act had placed the investor. ***

The Court today appears to argue that the *Wilko* Court's assessment of arbitration's inadequacy is outdated, first, because arbitration has improved since 1953, and second, because the Court no longer considers the criticisms of arbitration made in *Wilko* to be valid reasons why statutory claims, such as those under § 10(b), should not be sent to arbitration. It is true that arbitration procedures in the securities industry have improved since *Wilko's* day. Of particular importance has been the development of a code of arbitration by the Commission with the assistance of representatives of the securities industry and the public. See Uniform Code of Arbitration, Exh. C, Fifth Report of the

---

investor in a special position. ***

Securities Industry Conference on Arbitration 29 (Apr.1986) (Fifth SICA Report).

Even those who favor the arbitration of securities claims do not contend, however, that arbitration has changed so significantly as to eliminate the essential characteristics noted by the *Wilko* Court. Indeed, proponents of arbitration would not see these characteristics as "problems," because, in their view, the characteristics permit the unique "streamlined" nature of the arbitral process. As at the time of *Wilko,* preparation of a record of arbitration proceedings is not invariably required today. Moreover, arbitrators are not bound by precedent and are actually discouraged by their associations from giving reasons for a decision. See R. Coulson, Business Arbitration — What You Need to Know 29 (3d ed. 1986) ("Written opinions can be dangerous because they identify targets for the losing party to attack"). Judicial review is still substantially limited to the four grounds listed in § 10 of the Arbitration Act and to the concept of "manifest disregard" of the law.

The Court's "mistrust" of arbitration may have given way recently to an acceptance of this process, not only because of the improvements in arbitration, but also because of the Court's present assumption that the distinctive features of arbitration, its more quick and economical resolution of claims, do not render it inherently inadequate for the resolution of statutory claims. See *Mitsubishi Motors Corp. v. Soler Chrysler-Plymouth, Inc.,* 473 U.S., at 633. Such reasoning, however, should prevail only in the absence of the congressional policy that places the statutory claimant in a special position with respect to possible violators of his statutory rights. As even the most ardent supporter of arbitration would recognize, the arbitral process *at best* places the investor on an equal footing with the securities-industry personnel against whom the claims are brought.

Furthermore, there remains the danger that, *at worst,* compelling an investor to arbitrate securities claims puts him in a forum controlled by the securities industry. This result directly contradicts the goal of both securities Acts to free the investor from the control of the market professional. The Uniform Code provides some safeguards but despite them, and indeed because of the background of the arbitrators, the investor has the impression, frequently justified, that his claims are being judged by a forum composed of individuals sympathetic to the securities industry and not drawn from the public. ***

More surprising than the Court's acceptance of the present adequacy of arbitration for the resolution of securities claims is its confidence in the Commission's oversight of the arbitration procedures of the SROs to ensure this adequacy. *** The Court, however, fails to acknowledge that, until it filed an *amicus* brief in this case, the Commission consistently took the position that § 10(b) claims, like those under § 12(2), should not be sent to arbitration, that predispute arbitration agreements, where the investor was not advised of his right to a judicial forum, were misleading, and that the very regulatory oversight upon which the Commission now relies could not alone make securities-industry arbitration adequate. It is most questionable, then, whether the Commission's recently adopted position is entitled to the deference that the Court accords it.

The Court is swayed by the power given to the Commission by the 1975 amendments to the Exchange Act in order to permit the Commission to oversee the rules and procedures of the SROs, including those dealing with arbitration. ***

*** The Commission does not pretend that its oversight consists of anything other than a general review of SRO rules and the ability to require that an SRO adopt or delete a particular rule. It does not contend that its "sweeping authority," Brief 16, includes a review of specific arbitration proceedings. It thus neither polices nor monitors the results of these arbitrations for possible misapplications of securities laws or for indications of how investors fare in these proceedings. Given, in fact, the present constraints on the Commission's resources in this time of market expansion, it is doubtful whether the Commission could undertake to conduct any such review. ***

JUSTICE JOHN PAUL STEVENS, CONCURRING IN PART AND DISSENTING IN PART:

Gaps in the law must, of course, be filled by judicial construction. But after a statute has been construed, either by this Court or by a consistent course of decision by other federal judges and agencies, it acquires a meaning that should be as clear as if the judicial gloss had been drafted by the Congress itself. This position reflects both respect for Congress' role, see *Boys Market, Inc. v. Retail Clerks,* 398 U.S. 235, 257-258 (1970) (Black, J., dissenting), and the compelling need to preserve the courts' limited resources, see B. Cardozo, The Nature of the Judicial Process 149 (1921).

During the 32 years immediately following this Court's decision in *Wilko v. Swan,* 346 U.S. 427 (1953), each of the eight Circuits that addressed the issue concluded that the holding of *Wilko* was fully applicable to claims arising under the Securities Exchange Act of 1934. This longstanding interpretation creates a strong presumption, in my view, that any mistake that the courts may have made in interpreting the statute is best remedied by the Legislative, not the Judicial, Branch. ***

For this reason, I respectfully dissent from the portion of the Court's judgment that holds *Wilko* inapplicable to the 1934 Act. Like Justice Blackmun, however, I join Parts I, II, and IV of the Court's opinion.

NOTES AND QUESTIONS

1. ***The Import of Section 29(a).*** The *McMahon* majority and Justice Blackmun divide, among other things, over whether Section 29(a) prohibits contractual waivers of the right to sue. Which position do you find more persuasive? For a perspective on Justice Blackmun's opinion from the standpoint of his law clerk at the time, see James A. Fanto, Justice Blackmun and Securities Arbitration: *McMahon* Revisited, 71 N.D. L. Rev. 145 (1995).

2. ***Divining Congress's Intent.*** According to the majority, Congress did not endorse *Wilko* in its 1975 Conference Report. Do you agree? If Congress agreed with *Wilko*, what should it have done to make its views known? If, on the other hand, Congress disagreed with *Wilko*, why did it not overturn the decision by amending the federal securities laws and/or the Arbitration Act?

3. The Value of Private Securities Litigation. Did the majority appear to value private securities litigation? Did it seem sympathetic to aggrieved investors? To what extent (if at all) did the majority's views on these matters color the result?

4. The Question of Voluntariness. In what sense does an investor "voluntarily" agree to arbitrate disputes with her broker? To be sure, the contract that the investor signs upon opening her account must now prominently disclose the PDAA and its consequences, including the loss of the right to sue in court. See FINRA Customer Code 2268. But what if the investor does not want a PDAA but cannot find a brokerage firm that will accommodate her? For a discussion of why the market has not responded to this demand, see Barbara Black, Can Behavioral Economics Inform Our Understanding of Securities Arbitration?, 12 Transactions: Tenn. J. Bus. L. 107 (2011).

5. The Better Decisionmaker. Which is better positioned to evaluate the merits and demerits of mandatory securities arbitration — Congress or the courts? Which of these is likely to be more receptive to the preferences and interests of the securities industry? What weight should be given to these preferences and interests?

6. Burying **Wilko.** Two years after *McMahon*, the Supreme Court explicitly reversed *Wilko* in a decision involving the Securities Act. See *Rodriguez v. Shearson/Am. Express, Inc.*, 490 U.S. 477 (1989) (requiring investors to arbitrate claims under what is now Section 12(a)(2) of the Securities Act). Like *McMahon*, *Rodriguez* divided the Court 5-4.

7. The Question of Preemption. Three years before *McMahon*, the Supreme Court held that the Arbitration Act preempted state laws that invalidated PDAAs. See *Southland Corp. v. Keating*, 465 U.S. 1 (1984) (franchise case). The *Keating* decision came into play in the securities arbitration context when a number of states took steps to insulate investors from the effects of *McMahon*. For example, in 1988, Massachusetts adopted regulations prohibiting brokerage firms from turning away those who refused a PDAA and requiring the disclosure of the prohibition to all prospective customers. See *Sec. Indus. Ass'n. v. Connolly*, 883 F.2d 1114, 1117 (1st Cir. 1989). Constrained by *Keating*, the First Circuit held that the Arbitration Act preempted the regulations. See id. at 1123. The court explained:

> The Commonwealth may well be correct that PDAAs [pre-dispute arbitration agreements] ought to be arrived at with greater negotiation and disclosure between broker-dealers and customers than currently takes place. That judgment, however, is not the Commonwealth's to make, at least in its current embodiment, for it singles out arbitration in an impermissible way. The states are forbidden from critical scrutiny expressed in a fashion which might mask historic hostility toward arbitration. Congress sought to avoid having that possibility come to fruition, choosing instead to emphasize and endorse arbitral efficiencies. That value judgment was within the congressional domain — and only Congress, not the states, may create exceptions to it.
>
> That is not to say, of course, that a state must permit broker-dealers to sail as close to the wind as their consciences (or lack thereof) might permit. Massachusetts has a plenitude of lawful weapons in its ethical armamentarium to preserve the integrity of the securities business as conducted in the

> Commonwealth and to protect consumers. But because the Regulations treat standard-form PDAAs in the securities industry more severely than standard-form contracts are generally treated under Massachusetts law, and because the policies underlying the Regulations, and their method of enforcement, conflict with the national policy favoring arbitration, the state scheme is too discommoding to the federal plan. The Regulations are, therefore, preempted.

Id. at 1124. What about state regulations that do not seek to nullify PDAAs as such but merely raise the standards governing the arbitration process? The Ninth Circuit faced this question in connection with whether to apply certain California disclosure regulations to arbitrators in *Credit Suisse First Boston Corp. v. Grunwald*, 400 F.3d 1119 (9th Cir. 2005). The regulations were more burdensome than, but nonetheless not in conflict with, NASD rules, thereby enabling arbitrators to comply with both without violating either. Id. at 1134-35. But persuaded by an SEC amicus brief, the court held the regulations preempted:

> The Commission has reasonably concluded that allowing California to regulate SRO arbitrations would result in a patchwork of inconsistent state arbitration regulations that would interfere with Congress's intent in delegating SRO regulatory authority to the Commission. *** There is also nothing "arbitrary, capricious, or manifestly contrary to statute" about the Commission's fear that the California Ethics Standards' disclosure rules would undermine the Exchange Act's goal of protecting investors and the public interest. See *Brannan v. United Student Aid Funds, Inc.*, 94 F.3d 1260, 1264 (9th Cir.1996). The only study that has examined the effects of applying the California Ethics Standards to NASD arbitrators concluded that California's disclosure rules were unnecessary and would increase the costs of NASD arbitrations. See Perino Report at 48. Because the Commission's determination that the state law conflicts with SRO rules is well-supported by the record, we conclude that the Exchange Act preempts application of the California Ethics Standards' disclosure rules to NASD-appointed neutral arbitrators.

Credit Suisse, supra, 400 F.3d at 1136.

*8. **Full Circle With the Dodd-Frank Act?*** The Dodd-Frank Act authorizes the SEC to "prohibit, or impose conditions or limitations on the use of," PDAAs in connection with claims based on federal securities law or FINRA rules. See Dodd-Frank Act Section 921 (codified at 15 U.S.C. § 78o). If the SEC were to exercise this authority, brokerage firms could continue to enforce PDAAs in connection with state law claims. For the view that the prospect of bifurcating state and federal claims reduces the likelihood that the SEC will act under Section 921, see Barbara Black, Can Behavioral Economics Inform Our Understanding of Securities Arbitration?, 12 Transactions: Tenn. J. Bus. L. 107, 118-19 (2011). See also Jill I. Gross, The End of Mandatory Securities Arbitration?, 30 Pace L. Rev. 1174 (2010) (arguing that the SEC should not utilize its authority under Section 921).

B. THE PROCESS OF SECURITIES ARBITRATION

The following general description of securities arbitration appears in a brochure published by the Pace Law School Investor Rights Clinic, available at http://www.finra.org/web/groups/foundation/@foundation/documents/foundation/p119054.pdf.

As you read the description, consider the ways in which securities arbitration differs from securities litigation.

INVESTOR'S GUIDE TO SECURITIES INDUSTRY DISPUTES RESOLVING DISPUTES: THE ARBITRATION PROCESS

(ed. by Jill Gross, Edward Pekarek & Alice Oshins)

What is Arbitration?

Arbitration is an alternative to going to court or mediating *** in order to resolve a dispute. Arbitration panels composed of one or three arbitrators read the claims filed by the party that initiates the arbitration, weigh the arguments of the parties, consider the evidence, and then decide how the dispute should be resolved. The panel's decision, called an "award," is final and binding on all the parties. All parties must abide by the award, unless it is successfully challenged in court. Arbitration is generally confidential, and documents submitted in arbitration are not publicly-available, unlike court-related filings.

In 2007, FINRA published a "plain English" Code of Arbitration Procedure for Customer Disputes for all customer arbitrations filed on or after April 16, 2007. Anyone can access the rules that apply to customer cases, also known as the "Customer Code," on the FINRA web site at www.finra.org/ArbitrationMediation/Rules/ CodeOfArbitrationProcedure ***

Parties can agree to use arbitration either before or after a dispute arises. *** By agreeing to arbitration, you give up some features of litigating in court. For example, in arbitration, you are limited in the fact-gathering processes that you may use to build your case (called "discovery"). In addition, arbitrators are not bound by rules that govern the admission of evidence in court. In making decisions, arbitrators are guided by principles of equity (fairness) and justice, rather than by a strict application of settled legal rules to the facts. As a result, arbitration is considered by many to be a faster and less expensive method to resolve disputes than litigation.

It is very difficult to challenge an arbitration award. To do so, you must file the papers needed to ask a court to "vacate" (cancel) or "modify" (change) an award. But the circumstances under which courts are permitted to do so are very limited. If you decide to challenge an arbitration decision in federal court, the Federal Arbitration Act requires you to act quickly. You must file a motion to vacate or modify an award *within three months* of the date the arbitrator delivered the decision. Some states may have arbitration statutes that require you to file the motion in even less time.

Why Arbitration?

There are two reasons to use arbitration to resolve your dispute:

You agreed to before the dispute arose. When you opened your brokerage account, you entered into a customer account agreement. It is very likely that thisagreement includes a clause that requires you to use arbitration to resolve all disputes with your broker.

FINRA CUSTOMER CODE 12200

You want to because you prefer arbitration. Even without a pre-dispute arbitration agreement, all brokerage firms that are registered with FINRA and their employees must agree to arbitrate any dispute upon the demand of the customer.

FINRA CUSTOMER CODE 12201

Is there a Deadline to File an Arbitration?

Yes. A claim is *not eligible* for arbitration if "six years have elapsed from the occurrence or event giving rise to the claim." There are rarely any exceptions to this rule, and you can lose the right to recover any losses if you wait too long to file. Additionally, other time limits imposed by state and federal law, called "statutes of limitation," may also apply***.

FINRA CUSTOMER CODE 12206

What Do You File?

To initiate an arbitration proceeding, you must send to FINRA the following items:

Statement of Claim. To begin an arbitration proceeding, the investor, or "claimant," writes and files a Statement of Claim with FINRA, which, unlike a complaint filed in court, has no required format. You can write it as a letter or in a style more similar to a formal legal complaint. No matter what form your Statement of Claim takes, you should state the basic facts of the dispute and the remedies you seek, including the amount of money you seek as damages. You can also attach any documents – such as account statements, prospectuses, or trade confirmations – that may help to prove your claim. Remember to submit the original to FINRA and the appropriate number of signed and dated copies – one for each respondent (the person or entity against whom the claim is brought) and each arbitrator (one or three as determined by Customer Code 12401).

FINRA CUSTOMER CODE 12302

Common legal claims that investors allege in a Statement of Claim include claims that their broker, firm or both:

* Breached the duty to make only suitable recommendations (a "suitability" claim).

* Misrepresented material facts or failed to disclose material facts, whether inadvertent ("negligent") or intentional ("fraudulent").

* Excessively traded the account for commissions ("churning" or "switching").

* Made trades in the account without permission ("unauthorized trading").

* Failed to execute an investor's order.

* Failed to supervise a broker according to industry standards ("negligent supervision"). ***

Uniform Submission Agreement. Along with the Statement of Claim, you must fill out, date, sign and send to FINRA a Uniform Submission Agreement which states that you agree to abide by the procedural rules of the arbitration forum and to be bound by the decision of the arbitrators. You can download the form at www.finra.org/ ArbitrationMediation/ Parties/Overview/P007950

FINRA CUSTOMER CODE 12302

Claim Information Sheet. FINRA asks that you complete this form to help its staff process your case.This form is also available at www.finra.org/arbitration/ufg.

Forum Fees. You must pay an arbitration filing fee as listed in the fee schedule in Customer Code 12900. If you do not include a check for the appropriate amount in your application, FINRA will not process your claim. The Director may defer or waive all or part of the filing fee if you can show financial hardship.

FINRA CUSTOMER CODE 12900(a)

* * *

What happens after a claim is initiated?

Once you have filed the required application materials, FINRA will serve the Statement of Claim on the respondent(s) (the party or parties named in the Statement of Claim). In turn, each respondent must file an Answer within 45 days from the day it receives the Statement of Claim which must specify "the relevant facts and available defenses" to the claim. In other words, it must contain the respondent's version of what happened and the reasons why the respondent believes the claimant is not entitled to the remedies sought.

FINRA CUSTOMER CODE 12303

In addition to the Answer, each respondent must file:

* A signed Uniform Submission Agreement.

* Any additional documents supporting the Answer.

* Any counterclaim(s) against the claimant, cross-claim(s) against other respondents, or third-party claim(s) against new parties, specifying all relevant facts and remedies requested, with all fees required for additional claims.

Parties must file with FINRA all pleadings and any other documents subsequent to the initial Statement of Claim at the same time and in the same manner as they are served on, or delivered to, the other parties. With each filing, parties must include a certificate of service, which is a list stating the names of the parties served, the date and the method of service and the addresses to which service was made.

FINRA CUSTOMER CODE 12300(c)

***

How are arbitration fees determined?

In arbitration, both sides are required to pay fees. Investors must pay a filing fee when filing the Statement of Claim. The filing fee ranges from $50-$1,800 and depends on the amount of damages that you are seeking. FINRA will partially refund this fee if the claim is settled or withdrawn more than ten days before the date of the hearing – less any other fees or costs assessed against you under the Code, including any hearing session fees assessed under Customer Code 12902. However, certain surcharges and processing fees that the brokerage firms are required to pay cannot be assessed against you. In addition to the filing fee, FINRA charges hearing session fees for each hearing session that takes place with the arbitrator(s), whether telephonic or in-person.

For a panel with one arbitrator, the cost of one hearing session ranges from $50-$450, depending on the amount of the claim. For a panel of three arbitrators, that amount is $600-$1,200. The total fee depends on how many hearing sessions are conducted. A typical live hearing day consists of two sessions, because FINRA defines a "hearing session" as a meeting with the arbitrators of no more than four (4) hours. In the award, the panel decides which parties are ultimately responsible for the hearing session fees. FINRA will bill you for any fees you owe after the case is closed. For the most comprehensive and up-to-dateinformation on fees, see Customer Code 12900 and 12902.

FINRA CUSTOMER CODE 12900 and 12902

How many arbitrators serve on an arbitration?

> The number of arbitrators assigned to a case depends on the amount of damages sought.
>
> * If a claimant seeks $25,000 or less in damages, excluding interest and costs, one arbitrator hears the case.
>
> * If a claimant seeks more than $25,000 and up to $100,000, one arbitrator hears the case, unless any party requests a panel of three arbitrators in its initial pleading.
>
> * If a claimant seeks more than $100,000 in damages, or does not specify any amount of damages, three arbitrators hear the case, unless the parties agree in writing to one arbitrator.

FINRA CUSTOMER CODE 12401

***

Optional All-Public Panel Rule

As of January 31, 2011, customer claimants have the option to select a three-person panel made up of only public [that is, non-industry] arbitrators. Under FINRA Rule 12403, in customer cases decided by three arbitrators, a claimant can choose either an arbitration panel with two public arbitrators and one non-public [that is industry] arbitrator (Majority-Public Panel Rule) or a panel of all public arbitrators (Optional All-Public Panel Rule). Customers may designate their panel selection method in their Statement of Claim or accompanying documentation. If the customer does not choose a panel selection method, FINRA will notify the customer in writing that the customer may elect the Optional All-Public Panel Rule for selecting arbitrators up to 35 days from FINRA's service of the Statement of Claim. If the customer declines to elect a panel selection method in writing within 35 days, the Majority-Public Panel Rule for selecting arbitrators will apply.

How are the arbitrators selected?

FINRA's Neutral List Selection System (NLSS) holds the names of approximately 6,500 arbitrators qualified to hear cases. NLSS randomly generates lists of arbitrators for the parties, from which they can select their arbitrators. Along with the lists, FINRA will send the parties Arbitrator Disclosure Reports, which disclose education and employment history, past arbitration awards and other background information for each of the arbitrators on the lists. You should review this information, and research past awards, to confirm that the arbitrator does not have any potential conflicts of interest with the witnesses, issues or products in your case.

Parties select the arbitrators for their panel through a process of striking and ranking the arbitrators on their lists. For a one-arbitrator panel, FINRA will send one list of ten public arbitrators for arbitrator selection.

For a three-arbitrator panel, FINRA will send three lists:

* a list of ten public arbitrators from the Chair-qualified roster;

* a list of ten arbitrators from the non-public (industry) arbitrator roster; and

* a list of ten additional public arbitrators.

Under the Majority-Public Panel Rule, each party to the arbitration can strike up to four of the arbitrators from each list for any reason; at least four names must remain on the list. Under the Optional All-Public Panel Rule, any party may strike up to all of the names on the non-public list. Each party ranks arbitrators who remain on each list in order of preference. Each list must be ranked separately. Parties may strike and rank arbitrators for any reason, including the arbitrators' educational and work experience and any perceived or actual conflicts of interest.

Once FINRA receives the rankings from all parties, it will consolidate the lists and appoint the arbitrator(s) with the highest combined ranking(s) who is also available to accept the appointment. If the number of arbitrators available to serve from the consolidated list(s) is not sufficient to fill an initial panel, FINRA will appoint the required number of arbitrators from names generated randomly by FINRA's arbitrator database.

FINRA CUSTOMER CODE 12402-12404

Once appointed, you can ask an arbitrator to withdraw from the case for good cause. If the arbitrator refuses to withdraw from the case, you can ask the Director of Arbitration before the first hearing session begins to remove the arbitrator for conflict of interest or bias. The Director will grant your request to remove an arbitrator if it is reasonable to infer that the arbitrator is biased, lacks impartiality, or has a direct or indirect interest in the outcome of the arbitration. The Director will grant this request if you make it after the first hearing session begins only if it is based on new information that was required to be disclosed by the arbitrator earlier.

FINRA CUSTOMER CODE 12405-12408

What is Simplified Arbitration?

If a claimant seeks damages of $25,000 or less, excluding interest and expenses, then FINRA's Simplified Arbitration process applies. One public arbitrator will decide the claim and issue an award based on the written submissions of the parties, unless the claimant requests a hearing. The parties can request documents and information from other parties to submit in support of the claim(s) or defense(s).

If the amount in dispute is greater than $25,000, either because you amend the claim to increase the damages request or an opposing party counterclaims for damages, the case will no longer proceed as a Simplified Arbitration.

FINRA CUSTOMER CODE 12800

***

What is the Initial Prehearing Conference?

The Initial Prehearing Conference is the first time when the parties and arbitrators come together to set the schedule for the case. Usually this conference takes place on the telephone. During this telephone conference, the arbitration panel establishes discovery deadlines, schedules any motions and/or briefs that the parties request to file, and sets dates for the arbitration hearing.

FINRA CUSTOMER CODE 12500

What is Discovery?

The discovery process allows both parties to obtain facts and information from other parties in order to support their own case and prepare for the hearing. FINRA has published a series of guidelines to help the parties in the discovery process, called the "Discovery Guide," which is available at www.finra.org/ArbitrationMediation/ Rules/ RuleGuidanceDiscoveryGuide.

The Discovery Guide contains lists of documents that parties should exchange automatically. In addition, each party can request information and documents that are relevant to the case and that may be in the possession of an adverse, or opposing, party. Rules 12505 to 12511 of the Customer Code govern the discovery process, and include provisions for parties' requests for discovery items that are outside of the document production lists, for parties' objections to discovery requests, and for arbitrator authority to issue sanctions against parties for discovery abuses.

You can object to a discovery request (argue that you don't have to respond to it) if it asks you to provide documentation and information that you believe is, for example, overly burdensome, not relevant to the case, or involves confidential or privileged information.

Clearly state in writing the request to which you are objecting and why, and send the written objection to all parties in the case. There are time frames for producing documents, requesting additional discovery items, and responding and objecting to requests. These time frames are contained in Rules 12505 – 12508.

If the parties cannot agree on their own how to resolve any discovery dispute, then the party who still wants more documents or information may make a motion to compel the reluctant party to produce the requested

documents. The requesting party should explain to the arbitrator(s) why the discovery is relevant and necessary to the case and ask the panel to issue an order compelling production. The arbitrator(s) may schedule a hearing before deciding the motion.

If a party fails to produce documents or information required by a discovery order, the arbitrators can issue sanctions against that party. Sanctions could include assessing fees or penalties, including attorneys' fees; prohibiting a party from admitting evidence; drawing an adverse inference against the party; and even dismissing a claim, defense, or even the entire case. The panel may also initiate a disciplinary referral against a registered broker or brokerage firm that is involved in the proceeding. ***

Where does the hearing take place?

The hearing takes place in a conference room either at a regional FINRA office or in an office building arranged by FINRA in the city where the hearing will take place. Generally, the Director of Arbitration decides the city for the hearing based on where the Claimant lived at the time of the challenged transactions. You may seek to change the hearing location by obtaining the other party's agreement or by writing to FINRA and requesting a change in location.

FINRA CUSTOMER CODE 12213

What happens at the hearing?

The law requires that the arbitrators provide each side with a full and fair opportunity to be heard. Thus, in all arbitrations, except for those subject to Simplified Arbitration procedures, and those settled or dismissed before a hearing under FINRA's rules, the arbitrators will conduct a live hearing.

FINRA CUSTOMER CODE 12600

Testimony and Evidence

The arbitration hearing is where a claimant seeks to prove the claims that are alleged in the Statement of Claim, and respondents try to establish any defenses to those claims and seek to prove any counterclaims. Arbitrators usually accept two types of proof: oral testimony by witnesses and documentary evidence.

Customer Code 12514 requires that parties inform the other party of witnesses they intend to call and provide copies of any documents or other materials that they plan to use at the hearing as evidence at least twenty calendar days before the start of the hearing. Also, parties need to arrange for witnesses and all documentary evidence to be available for presentation at the hearing.

At the hearing, all parties will be present in the room with the arbitrators. The arbitrators open the hearing by reading from a script prepared by FINRA to cover administrative matters. Each party then has the option to give an opening statement outlining what it intends to prove during the hearing.

Direct and Cross Examination

Generally, each claimant then calls witnesses to testify on his or her behalf as to facts within the witnesses' personal knowledge. In addition, each claimant can ask expert witnesses who have specialized training or knowledge to testify as to their opinion on a technical matter to help the arbitrators draw conclusions and render a decision. The claimant conducts a direct examination, or asks questions of any witnesses it calls to testify. Each respondent can ask questions of claimant's witnesses, too, during what is known as "cross examination," and the arbitrator(s) can also question these witnesses.

Exhibits

Parties should offer into the record as exhibits (a paper or document produced and shown to an arbitration panel during a hearing) any documents they would like the arbitrators to consider as evidence. Parties can argue that any evidence presented by another party shouldn't be considered in the arbitrators' decision by objecting orally at the hearing. After considering the objecting party's reasons why the evidence should not be allowed, the arbitrators will examine the documents presented to determine if they will be admitted into evidence (considered as part of your case or disregarded) and into the case record. Arbitrators generally will accept any authentic document into the record, as long as it is relevant and necessary to prove your claims, and it is not unfair to another party.

Rebuttal Evidence

Once each claimant has presented his/her case, each respondent has the right to call fact and expert witnesses, too, and offer relevant exhibits. Once all parties have presented all their evidence on any claims and counterclaims, including rebuttal evidence to contradict the other side's arguments or evidence, all parties generally make a closing statement, summing up the evidence and arguing to the panel what they believe they have proven and what they contend the other side has not proven. Claimants should be certain to repeat their request for damages and any other relief, and to provide specific calculations supporting their request for a damages amount, whether with or without expert testimony.

An arbitration hearing in brief

Arbitration hearings generally take place in this order, although the arbitrators have authority to change the order:

* Swearing in of arbitrators, parties and witnesses

* Opening statement from each party (optional)

* Presentation of facts of the case to arbitrators, including documents and live or written testimony – claimant(s)

* Presentation of facts of the case to arbitrators, including documents and live or written testimony – respondent(s)

* Presentation of any counter-claims, cross-claims or third-party claims

* Rebuttal evidence

* Closing statements (claimant can choose to go last)

* Arbitration panel closes the record

After the arbitration panel has heard all testimony and the record is closed, the panel will then deliberate and issue an award.

When do the arbitrators decide the case?

After closing the hearing, the arbitration panel considers all of the evidence, deliberates together, and decides what relief the claimant is entitled to, if any. In a three-arbitrator panel, an award is based on the vote of a majority of the arbitrators; a unanimous decision is not required. Within thirty days of the date the record is closed, FINRA will mail to the parties the award describing the determination of the panel.

FINRA CUSTOMER CODE 12904

What is contained in an arbitration award?

*** Decisions made in FINRA arbitrations are final; even if new evidence surfaces later, arbitrators cannot reconsider their decisions. In the award, the panel must also decide whether to assess any costs and forum fees against any party, and how to allocate those costs and fees among the parties. Past arbitration awards are available online at http://finraawardsonline.finra.org/.

***

FINRA CUSTOMER CODE 12904

How do I collect an award or settlement?

Many arbitration cases end with a settlement between parties, either through direct negotiation or through mediation. Others are withdrawn or closed before the process begins. Roughly one-half of claimants historically have received some type of monetary award in arbitration claims that go to a final decision each year, although that statistic has varied substantially over the years. If you are awarded damages, you can expect to be paid within thirty days of receiving the written award, unless the losing party files a motion to vacate (overturn) or modify the award in court.

If a broker or firm does not pay an award within thirty days after receiving the award, you should notify FINRA. FINRA can suspend or cancel the registration of a brokerage firm or broker if the member does not comply with an arbitration award or settlement related to an arbitration or mediation. As a result, brokerage firms and brokers who remain in the business generally pay arbitration awards or amounts under settlements that they owe. The broker or firm can legitimately delay paying an award, however, if it has filed a motion to vacate or modify the award in court.

Alternatively, if the broker or firm is no longer registered with FINRA, you may have to go to state or federal court to enforce the award or settlement. If your broker or brokerage firm goes out of business or declares bankruptcy, you might not be able to recover your money – even if the arbitrator or a court has ruled in your favor. ***

NOTES AND QUESTIONS

1. ***Arbitration vs. Litigation.*** How does arbitration differ from litigation? What are the pros and cons of using litigation as the model for arbitration?

2. ***Qualifications and Training of Arbitrators.*** To qualify as a FINRA arbitrator, a person needs only five years of "full-time, paid business or professional experience" and "at least two years of college-level credits." See FINRA, Become An Arbitrator, available at www.FINRA.org/ ArbitrationMediation/Neutrals/BecomeAn Arbitrator/. A law degree is not required, nor is any previous familiarity with the substantive issues likely to be encountered. See id. Qualifying as an arbitrator also requires completion of online training courses on arbitration procedures as well as a "live video or onsite training session." See BasicArbitration Training,www.FINRA.org/ ArbitrationMediation/Neutrals/Education/ArbitrationTraining/Mandatory Training/. But there is no instruction in substantive securities law, a state of affairs that creates a conundrum:

> *** Arbitrators are expected to achieve an equitable resolution of the dispute before them but they may not ignore the law. However, without ample training or legal briefing by the parties on each relevant issue, how can arbitrators know what the law is or how to apply it?

Barbara Black and Jill I. Gross, Making it up as They Go Along: The Role of Law in Securities Arbitration, 23 Cardozo L. Rev. 991, 1029-30 (2002). Should arbitrators be required to undergo training in substantive securities law? Why or why not?

Even more fundamentally, why have issues of qualifications and training received so little attention? According to Professor Jennifer J. Johnson:

> The increased quasi-judicial nature of modern securities arbitration suggests the need for arbitrators versed both in procedural aspects of the arbitration process and substantive securities law. In customer disputes against their securities brokers, however, the value of expert decisionmakers has taken a back seat to other values. After *McMahon*, neutrality rather than expertise has become the rallying cry for investors forced to arbitrate securities claims against their brokers. Indeed, by validating arbitration agreements between members of the securities industry and their investors, the Court may have inadvertently sounded the death knell for expert SRO arbitrators.

Jennifer J. Johnson, Wall Street Meets the Wild West: Bringing Law and Order to Securities Arbitration, 84 N.C.L. Rev. 123, 159-160 (2005).

3. ***Decisions With and Without Explanations.*** As a general proposition, the FINRA does not require arbitrators to explain their decisions. See FINRA Customer Code 12904(f) (stating that '[t]he award *may* contain a rationale underlying the award") (emphasis added). An explanation is nonetheless obligatory, however, where the parties jointly request it "no later than the time for the prehearing exchange of documents." See FINRA Customer Code 12904(g) (placing the duty to explain on the Chairperson of the panel). The explanation, which need not include legal authorities or calculation of damages, entitles the Chairperson to an additional $400 honorarium, an amount which the panel allocates between the parties as part of the final award. Id.

Is the added expense worthwhile? See generally Barbara Black & Jill

Gross, The Explained Award of Damocles: Protection or Peril in Securities Arbitration, 34 Sec. Reg. L. J. 17 (2006). Might your answer be affected by the nature of the securities claims that are typically arbitrated? In this regard, take the following chart into account:

Controversies Involved in Arbitration Cases

Types of Controversy*	2007	2008	2009	2010
Margin Calls	45	64	128	83
Churning	133	212	306	270
Unauthorized Trading	174	248	478	397
Failure to Supervise	830	1029	2691	2372
Negligence	891	1602	3405	2698
Omission of Facts	275	1201	2453	1941
Breach of Contract	953	1658	2802	2184
Breach of Fiduciary Duty	1616	2836	4206	3162
Unsuitability	695	1181	2473	1974
Misrepresentation	739	2005	3408	2601
Online Trading**	1	3	0	0

*Each case can be coded to contain up to four controversy types. Therefore the columns in this table cannot be totaled to determine the number of cases served in a year.

FINRA, Dispute Resolution Statistics. available at www.finra.org/ArbitrationMediation/AboutFINRADR/Statistics/.

*4. **Punitive Damages.*** Punitive damages are not available for claims made under the Securities Act or the Exchange Act (as you will recall from previous Chapters). Punitive damages are, however, sometimes available under state securities laws and when that is the case, arbitrators can award them (when the PDAA was signed after September, 1989). See FINRA Customer Code 2268(d)(4) (prohibiting a PDAA from "includ[ing] any condition which *** limits the ability of the arbitrators to make any award").

Moreover, investors seeking punitive damages under state law benefit from *Mastrobuono v. Shearson Lehman Hutton, Inc.*, 514 U.S. 52 (1995). There the brokerage firm argued that the PDAA (which was signed before the above-mentioned Rule became effective) excluded punitive damages, but the Supreme Court disagreed. In so doing, the Court did not rely exclusively on contract law principles: "'[D]ue regard must be given to the federal policy favoring arbitration, and ambiguities as to the scope of the arbitration clause itself resolved in favor of arbitration.'" Id. at 62 (quoting *Volt Info. Sciences, Inc. v. Bd. of Trustees of Leland Stanford Univ.*, 489 U.S. 468, 476 (1989)). How do the sympathies of the *Mastrobuono* Court compare with those of the *McMahon* Court?

The availability of punitive damages has stirred considerable debate. According to former SEC Chairperson David Ruder:

> Arguments for and against punitive damages are forceful. Proponents of punitive damages argue that punitive damages should be available in arbitration if they are available in a judicial forum and that punitive damages provide important curbs on customer abuse by brokerage firms. The firms, on the other hand, argue that punitive damages are inappropriate in an arbitration system that does not provide a right to trial by jury, has no written opinions, and has limited rights to appeal.

David S. Ruder, Elements of a Fair and Efficient Securities Arbitration System, 40 Ariz. L. Rev. 1101, 1107 (1998). Would a cap on punitive damages be a good idea?

Brokerage firms have attacked punitive damage awards on several grounds. One ground — that of due process — has failed for lack of state action. See, e.g., *Davis v. Prudential Secs., Inc.*, 59 F.3d 1186, 1193-1194 (11th Cir. 1995). See generally Charles Smith, The Application of Due Process to Arbitration Awards of Punitive Damages – Where Is the State Action?, 2007 J. Disp. Resol. 417. Another largely unsuccessful ground is that the award is in "manifest disregard of the law." See, e.g., *Lagstein v. Certain Underwriters at Lloyd's, London,* 607 F.3d 634, 641-42 (9th Cir. 2010). The subject of "manifest disregard of the law" as a ground for appeal is addressed in the next section of this Chapter.

5. Class Arbitrations Against Brokers. The FINRA does not allow arbitrations to occur in a class format. See FINRA Customer Code 12204(a) (stating that "class action claims may not be arbitrated under the Code"). This prohibition aside, class arbitration presents an additional problem, namely, the Supreme Court's insinuation that it clashes with the FAA unless there is a "consensual" agreement permitting it. See *AT & T Mobility, LLC v. Concepcion,* 131 S.Ct. 1740, 1751 (2011). Dividing 5-4, the *Concepcion* Court explained:

> First, the switch from bilateral to class arbitration sacrifices the principal advantage of arbitration—its informality—and makes the process slower, more costly, and more likely to generate procedural morass than final judgment.***
>
> Second, class arbitration *requires* procedural formality. *** If procedures are too informal, absent class members would not be bound by the arbitration. For a class-action money judgment to bind absentees in litigation, class representatives must at all times adequately represent absent class members, and absent members must be afforded notice, an opportunity to be heard, and a right to opt out of the class. *Phillips Petroleum Co. v. Shutts*, 472 U.S. 797, 811–812 (1985). At least this amount of process would presumably be required for absent parties to be bound by the results of arbitration.
>
> We find it unlikely that in passing the FAA Congress meant to leave the disposition of these procedural requirements to an arbitrator. Indeed, class arbitration was not even envisioned by Congress when it passed the FAA in 1925 ***. And it is at the very least odd to think that an arbitrator would be entrusted with ensuring that third parties' due process rights are satisfied.
>
> Third, class arbitration greatly increases risks to defendants. *** The absence of multilayered review makes it more likely that errors will go uncorrected. Defendants are willing to accept the costs of these errors in arbitration, since their impact is limited to the size of individual disputes, and

> presumably outweighed by savings from avoiding the courts. But when damages allegedly owed to tens of thousands of potential claimants are aggregated and decided at once, the risk of an error will often become unacceptable. Faced with even a small chance of a devastating loss, defendants will be pressured into settling questionable claims. ***

Id. at 1751-52. The dissent took a very different view:

> The majority compares the complexity of class arbitration with that of bilateral arbitration. And it finds the former more complex. But, if incentives are at issue, the *relevant* comparison is not "arbitration with arbitration" but a comparison between class arbitration and judicial class actions. ***
>
> Why would a typical defendant (say, a business) prefer a judicial class action to class arbitration? *** Data from California courts confirm that class arbitrations can take considerably less time than in-court proceedings in which class certification is sought. ***
>
> *** But class proceedings have countervailing advantages. In general agreements that forbid the consolidation of claims can lead small-dollar claimants to abandon their claims rather than to litigate. ***

Id. at 1759-60 (Breyer, J., dissenting). Which opinion did you find more persuasive?

*6. **The Emerging Possibility of Arbitrating Class Action Claims Against Issuers.*** The Supreme Court's *Concepcion* opinion, discussed in the preceding Note, has been identified by Professor Barbara Black as a possible "game changer" with the potential to thwart securities class actions against issuers. She argues that with its suggestion that a consensual agreement to arbitrate class claims satisfies the FAA, the Court has opened the door for issuers to amend their charters to authorize arbitration of securities class actions against the company. Acknowledging that such a charter provision would face various legal obstacles, she maintains that those obstacles are reduced by *Concepcion*. See Barbara Black, Arbitration of Investors' Claims Against Issuers: An Idea Whose Time Has Come?, 75 Law & Contemp. Probs __ (forthcoming 2012). See also Barbara Black, Eliminating Securities Class Actions Under the Radar, 2009 Colum. Bus. L. Rev. 802.

*7. **Arbitration vs. Mediation.*** The FINRA sponsors mediation services, instituted because of the perception that arbitration had become less efficient (on account of its growing similarity to litigation).

Mediation differs from arbitration in several respects — it is voluntary and non-binding and does not involve a proceeding resembling a trial. If mediation does not resolve the dispute, the parties can submit to arbitration (or to a court in the unlikely event that arbitration of the dispute is not mandatory). Mediation can also be initiated at any stage during the arbitration process and both processes can occur concurrently.

The FINRA mediation process begins with a session in which the mediator and the parties all have the opportunity to make opening statements. The mediator then holds individual meetings with each party that focus on settlement expectations and possible settlement offers. If a mutually acceptable resolution is reached, the parties sign a written settlement agreement. even if mediation does not produce a settlement, the improved lines of communication often result in more efficient arbitration. See Mediation: An Alternate Path, available at www.finra.org/ArbitrationMediation/Parties/ Overview/MediationAnAlternatePath For an evaluation of the advantages and disadvantages of mediation for investors, see Jill I. Gross, Securities Mediation: Dispute Resolution for the Individual Investor, 21 Ohio St. J. on Disp. Resol. 329 (2006).

Compare the following data on arbitration and mediation:

Summary Arbitration Statistics July 2011

Number of Cases Closed through July:

2009	2010	2011
2,442	3,750	3,603

Turnaround Time (in months) through July:

	2009	2010	2011
Overall	11.7	11.6	14.3
Hearing Decisions	14.7	13.5	15.9
Simplified Decisions	6.2	7.1	6.3

Summary Mediation Statistics July 2011
Mediation Cases in Agreement through July:

2009	2010	2011
284	497	395

Mediation Cases Closed through July:

	2009	2010	2011
Cases Closed	383	517	431
Percent Settled	84%	85%	80%

Turnaround Time (in Days) through July:

2009	2010	2011
102	91	104

FINRA, Dispute Resolution Statistics, available at www.finra.org/ArbitrationMediation/AboutFINRADR/Statistics

C. THE REMAINING JUDICIAL ROLE IN ARBITRATION

The fact that PDAAs are enforceable does not take courts out of the picture altogether (class actions aside). First, there is the arbitrability. Second, there is judicial review.

1. *Arbitrability*

An investor must arbitrate only where (i) she signed an agreement containing a PDAA and (ii) the PDAA encompasses the dispute at issue. But who decides whether these requirements (called matters of arbitrability) have been satisfied — the arbitrators or the courts? Does federal or state law control the outcome? Consider the following decision.

FIRST OPTIONS OF CHICAGO, INC. v. KAPLAN
514 U.S. 938 (1995)

JUSTICE STEPHEN G. BREYER:

In this case we consider two questions about how courts should review certain matters under the federal Arbitration Act: (1) how a district court should review an arbitrator's decision that the parties agreed to arbitrate a dispute, and (2) how a court of appeals should review a district court's decision confirming, or refusing to vacate, an arbitration award.

The case concerns several related disputes between, on one side, First Options of Chicago, Inc., a firm that clears stock trades on the Philadelphia Stock Exchange, and, on the other side, three parties: Manuel Kaplan; his wife, Carol Kaplan; and his wholly owned investment company, MK Investments, Inc. (MKI), whose trading account First Options cleared. The disputes center on a "workout" agreement, embodied in four separate documents, which governs the "working out" of debts to First Options that MKI and the Kaplans incurred as a result of the October 1987 stock market crash. In 1989, after entering into the agreement, MKI lost an additional $1.5 million. First Options then took control of, and liquidated, certain MKI assets; demanded immediate payment of the entire MKI debt; and insisted that the Kaplans personally pay any deficiency. When its demands went unsatisfied, First Options sought arbitration by a panel of the Philadelphia Stock Exchange.

MKI, having signed the only workout document (out of four) that contained an arbitration clause, accepted arbitration. The Kaplans, however, who had not personally signed that document, denied that their disagreement with First Options was arbitrable and filed written objections to that effect with the arbitration panel. The arbitrators decided that they had the power to rule on the merits of the parties' dispute, and did so in favor of First Options. The Kaplans then asked the Federal District Court to vacate the arbitration award, and First Options requested its confirmation. The court confirmed the award. Nonetheless, on appeal the Court of Appeals for the Third Circuit agreed with the Kaplans that their dispute was not arbitrable; and it reversed the District Court's confirmation of the award against them. ***

II

The first question — the standard of review applied to an arbitrator's decision about arbitrability — is a narrow one. To understand just how narrow, consider three types of disagreement present in this case. First, the Kaplans and First Options disagree about whether the Kaplans are personally liable for MKI's debt to First Options. That disagreement makes up the *merits* of the dispute. Second, they disagree about whether they agreed to arbitrate the merits. That disagreement is about the *arbitrability* of the dispute. Third, they disagree about *who should have the primary power to decide the second matter*. Does that power belong primarily to the arbitrators (because the court reviews their arbitrability decision deferentially) or to the court (because the court makes up its mind about arbitrability independently)? We consider here only this third question.

Although the question is a narrow one, it has a certain practical importance. That is because a party who has not agreed to arbitrate will normally have a right to a court's decision about the merits of its dispute (say, as here, its obligation under a contract). But, where the party has agreed to arbitrate, he or she, in effect, has relinquished much of that right's practical value. The party still can ask a court to review the arbitrator's decision, but the court will set that decision aside only in very unusual circumstances. See, e.g., 9 U.S.C. § 10 (award procured by corruption, fraud, or undue means; arbitrator exceeded his powers); *Wilko v. Swan,* 346 U.S. 427, 436-437 (1953) (parties bound by arbitrator's decision not in "manifest disregard" of the law), overruled on other grounds, *Rodriguez de Quijas v. Shearson/American Express, Inc.,* 490 U.S. 477 (1989). Hence, who — court or arbitrator — has the primary authority to decide whether a party has agreed to arbitrate can make a critical difference to a party resisting arbitration.

We believe the answer to the "who" question (*i.e.,* the standard-of-review question) is fairly simple. Just as the arbitrability of the merits of a dispute depends upon whether the parties agreed to arbitrate that dispute, see, e.g., *Mastrobuono v. Shearson Lehman Hutton, Inc.,* [514 U.S. 52], 57 (1995); *Mitsubishi Motors Corp. v. Soler Chrysler-Plymouth, Inc.,* 473 U.S. 614, 626 (1985), so the question "who has the primary power to decide arbitrability" turns upon what the parties agreed about *that* matter. Did the parties agree to submit the arbitrability question itself to arbitration? If so, then the court's standard for reviewing the arbitrator's decision about *that* matter should not differ from the standard courts apply when they review any other matter that parties have agreed to arbitrate. See *AT & T Technologies, Inc. v. Communications Workers,* 475 U.S. 643, 649 (1986) (parties may agree to arbitrate arbitrability). That is to say, the court should give considerable leeway to the arbitrator, setting aside his or her decision only in certain narrow circumstances. See, e.g., 9 U.S.C. § 10. If, on the other hand, the parties did *not* agree to submit the arbitrability question itself to arbitration, then the court should decide that question just as it would decide any other question that the parties did not submit to arbitration, namely, independently. These two answers flow inexorably from the fact that arbitration is simply a matter of contract between the parties; it is a way to resolve those disputes — but only those disputes — that the parties have agreed to submit to arbitration.

We agree with First Options, therefore, that a court must defer to an arbitrator's arbitrability decision when the parties submitted that matter to arbitration. Nevertheless, that conclusion does not help First Options win this case. That is because a fair and complete answer to the standard-of-review question requires a word about how a court should decide whether the parties have agreed to submit the arbitrability issue to arbitration. And, that word makes clear that the Kaplans did not agree to arbitrate arbitrability here.

When deciding whether the parties agreed to arbitrate a certain matter (including arbitrability), courts generally (though with a qualification we discuss below) should apply ordinary state-law principles that govern the formation of contracts. See, e.g., *Mastrobuono,* at 62-63, and n. 9; *Volt Information Sciences, Inc. v. Board of Trustees of Leland Stanford Junior Univ.,* 489 U.S. 468, 475-476 (1989); G. Wilner, 1 Domke on Commercial Arbitration § 4:04, p. 15 (rev. ed. Supp.1993) (hereinafter Domke). The relevant state law here, for example, would require the court to see whether the parties objectively revealed an intent to submit the arbitrability issue to arbitration. See, e.g., *Estate of Jesmer v. Rohlev,* 241 Ill.App.3d 798, 803, (1993) (law of the State whose law governs the workout agreement); *Burkett v. Allstate Ins. Co.,* 368 Pa. 600, 608 (1987) (law of the State where the Kaplans objected to arbitrability).

This Court, however, has (as we just said) added an important qualification, applicable when courts decide whether a party has agreed that arbitrators should decide arbitrability: Courts should not assume that the parties agreed to arbitrate arbitrability unless there is "clea[r] and unmistakabl[e]" evidence that they did so. *AT & T Technologies,* supra, at 649. In this manner the law treats silence or ambiguity about the question "*who* (primarily) should decide arbitrability" differently from the way it treats silence or ambiguity about the question "*whether* a particular merits-related dispute is arbitrable because it is within the scope of a valid arbitration agreement" — for in respect to this latter question the law reverses the presumption. See *Mitsubishi Motors,* supra, at 626 ("'[A]ny doubts concerning the scope of arbitrable issues should be resolved in favor of arbitration'") (quoting *Moses H. Cone Memorial Hospital v. Mercury Constr. Corp.,* 460 U.S. 1, 24-25 (1983)).

But, this difference in treatment is understandable. The latter question arises when the parties have a contract that provides for arbitration of some issues. In such circumstances, the parties likely gave at least some thought to the scope of arbitration. And, given the law's permissive policies in respect to arbitration, see, e.g., *Mitsubishi Motors,* supra, at 626, one can understand why the law would insist upon clarity before concluding that the parties did *not* want to arbitrate a related matter. On the other hand, the former question — the "who (primarily) should decide arbitrability" question — is rather arcane. A party often might not focus upon that question or upon the significance of having arbitrators decide the scope of their own powers. Cf. Cox, Reflections Upon Labor Arbitration, 72 Harv. L. Rev. 1482, 1508-1509 (1959). And, given the principle that a party can be forced to arbitrate only those issues it specifically has agreed to submit to arbitration, one can understand why courts might hesitate to interpret silence or ambiguity on the "who should decide arbitrability" point as giving the arbitrators that power, for doing so might too often force unwilling parties to arbitrate a matter they reasonably would have thought a judge, not an arbitrator, would decide. Ibid.

On the record before us, First Options cannot show that the Kaplans clearly agreed to have the arbitrators decide (*i.e.,* to arbitrate) the question of arbitrability. First Options relies on the Kaplans' filing with the arbitrators a written memorandum objecting to the arbitrators' jurisdiction. But merely arguing the arbitrability issue to an arbitrator does not indicate a clear willingness to arbitrate that issue, *i.e.,* a willingness to be effectively bound by the arbitrator's decision on that point. To the contrary, insofar as the Kaplans were forcefully objecting to the arbitrators deciding their dispute with First Options, one naturally would think that they did *not* want the arbitrators to have binding authority over them. This conclusion draws added support from (1) an obvious explanation for the Kaplans' presence before the arbitrators (*i.e.,* that MKI, Mr. Kaplan's wholly owned firm, was arbitrating workout agreement matters); and (2) Third Circuit law that suggested that the Kaplans might argue arbitrability to the arbitrators without losing their right to independent court review, *Teamsters v. Western Pennsylvania Motor Carriers Assn.*, 574 F. 2d 783, 786-788 (1978).

First Options makes several counterarguments: (1) that the Kaplans had other ways to get an independent court decision on the question of arbitrability without arguing the issue to the arbitrators (*e.g.*, by trying to enjoin the arbitration, or by refusing to participate in the arbitration and then defending against a court petition First Options would have brought to compel arbitration); (2) that permitting parties to argue arbitrability to an arbitrator without being bound by the result would cause delay and waste in the resolution of disputes; and (3) that the Arbitration Act therefore requires a presumption that the Kaplans agreed to be bound by the arbitrators' decision, not the contrary. The first of these points, however, while true, simply does not say anything about whether the Kaplans intended to be bound by the arbitrators' decision. The second point, too, is inconclusive, for factual circumstances vary too greatly to permit a confident conclusion about whether allowing the arbitrator to make an initial (but independently reviewable) arbitrability determination would, in general, slow down the dispute resolution process. And, the third point is legally erroneous, for there is no strong arbitration-related policy favoring First Options in respect to its particular argument here. After all, the basic objective in this area is not to resolve disputes in the quickest manner possible, no matter what the parties' wishes, but to ensure that commercial arbitration agreements, like other contracts, "'are enforced according to their terms,'" *Mastrobuono,* at 54 (quoting *Volt Information Sciences,* 489 U.S., at 479), and according to the intentions of the parties, *Mitsubishi Motors,* 473 U.S., at 626. That policy favors the Kaplans, not First Options.

We conclude that, because the Kaplans did not clearly agree to submit the question of arbitrability to arbitration, the Court of Appeals was correct in finding that the arbitrability of the Kaplan/First Options dispute was subject to independent review by the courts.

III

We turn next to the standard a court of appeals should apply when reviewing a district court decision that refuses to vacate or confirms an arbitration award. Although the Third Circuit sometimes used the words "*de novo* " to describe this standard, its opinion makes clear that it simply believes (as do all Circuits but one) that there is no *special* standard governing its review of a district court's decision in these circumstances. Rather, review of, for example, a district court decision confirming an arbitration award on the ground that the parties agreed to submit their dispute to arbitration should proceed like review of any other district court decision finding an agreement between parties, e.g., accepting findings of fact that are not "clearly erroneous" but deciding questions of law *de novo.*

One Court of Appeals, the Eleventh Circuit, has said something different. Because of federal policy favoring arbitration, that court says that it applies a specially lenient "abuse of discretion" standard (even as to questions of law) when reviewing district court decisions that confirm (but not those that set aside) arbitration awards. See, e.g., *Robbins v. Day,* 954 F.2d, at 681-682. First Options asks us to hold that the Eleventh Circuit's view is correct.

We believe, however, that the majority of Circuits is right in saying that courts of appeals should apply ordinary, not special, standards when reviewing district court decisions upholding arbitration awards. For one thing, it is undesirable to make the law more complicated by proliferating review standards without good reasons. More importantly, the reviewing attitude that a court of appeals takes toward a district court decision should depend upon "the respective institutional advantages of trial and appellate courts," not upon what standard of review will more likely produce a particular substantive result. *Salve Regina College v. Russell,* 499 U.S. 225, 231-233 (1991). The law, for example, tells all courts (trial and appellate) to give administrative agencies a degree of legal leeway when they review certain interpretations of the law that those agencies have made. See, e.g., *Chevron U.S.A. Inc. v. Natural Resources Defense Council, Inc.,* 467 U.S. 837, 843-844 (1984). But no one, to our knowledge, has suggested that this policy of giving leeway to agencies means that a court of appeals should give *extra* leeway to a district court decision that upholds an agency. Similarly, courts grant arbitrators considerable leeway when reviewing most arbitration decisions; but that fact does not mean that appellate courts should give *extra* leeway to district courts that uphold arbitrators. ***

We conclude that the Court of Appeals used the proper standards for reviewing the District Court's arbitrability determinations. ***

NOTES AND QUESTIONS

1. Who Decides. *Kaplan* upheld the presumption that courts decide matters of arbitration. What policies support this presumption? What are its disadvantages?

2. State and Federal Law Together. *Kaplan* accorded a role to both federal and state law in resolving questions of arbitrability. What is the role of each? Is there any actual or perceived unfairness in treating investors with identical arbitration agreements differently depending on their states of residence?

3. Procedural Arbitrability Distinguished. A dispute is eligible for arbitration so long as the underlying event occurred no more than six years earlier. FINRA Customer Code 12206. Who should decide whether the six years has expired? In *Howsam v. Dean Witter Reynolds, Inc.,* 537 U.S. 79 (2002), the Supreme Court held that the answer must come from the arbitrators:

> Linguistically speaking, one might call any potentially dispositive gateway question a "question of arbitrability," for its answer will determine whether the underlying controversy will proceed to arbitration on the merits. The Court's case law, however, makes clear that, for purposes of applying the interpretive rule, the phrase "question of arbitrability" has a far more limited scope. See [*First Options of Chicago, Inc. v. Kaplan*], 514 U.S., at 942. The Court has found the phrase applicable in the kind of narrow circumstance where contracting parties would likely have expected a court to have decided the gateway matter, where they are not likely to have thought that they had agreed that an arbitrator would do so, and, consequently, where reference of the gateway dispute to the court avoids the risk of forcing parties to arbitrate a matter that they may well not have agreed to arbitrate.***
>
> Moreover, the NASD arbitrators, comparatively more expert about the meaning of their own rule, are comparatively better able to interpret and to

> apply it. In the absence of any statement to the contrary in the arbitration agreement, it is reasonable to infer that the parties intended the agreement to reflect that understanding. Cf. *First Options* , 514 U.S. at 944-945. And for the law to assume an expectation that aligns (1) decisionmaker with (2) comparative expertise will help better to secure a fair and expeditious resolution of the underlying controversy — a goal of arbitration systems and judicial systems alike.
>
> We consequently conclude that the NASD's time limit rule falls within the class of gateway procedural disputes that do not present what our cases have called "questions of arbitrability." And the strong pro-court presumption as to the parties' likely intent does not apply.

Id. at 83-86. See generally Barbara Black, Securities Arbitration Is Not Supposed To Be So Complicated: Arbitrability, the Eligibility Rule, and Whose Law Decides, 30 Sec. Reg. L. J. 134 (2002). As a general matter, does the *Howsam* decision favor brokers or investors?

4. Severing the Arbitration Clause From the Contract as a Whole. Suppose the investor claims that he was fraudulently induced into contracting with his broker. Who decides the claim of fraudulent inducement – the arbitrators or the courts? The seminal opinion to address this question came in *Prima Paint Corp. v. Flood & Conklin Mfg. Co.*, 388 U.S. 395 (1967), which involved a consulting agreement growing out of the sale of a business. There the Supreme Court distinguished between fraudulent inducement of the contract as a whole and the agreement to arbitrate in particular:

> [I]f the claim is fraud in the inducement of the arbitration clause itself-an issue which goes to the "making" of the agreement to arbitrate-the federal court may proceed to adjudicate it. But the [Arbitration Act's] statutory language does not permit the federal court to consider claims of fraud in the inducement of the contract generally.

Id. at 403-04. See *Downer v. Siegel*, 489 F.3d 623, 627-28 (5th Cir. 2007) (applying *Prima Paint* distinction to investor-broker contract). What is the rationale for this distinction? Who benefits from it?

The Supreme Court reaffirmed *Prima Paint* in *Buckeye Check Cashing, Inc. v. Cardegna*, 546 U.S. 440 (2006), but its opinion in *Buckeye* left open the question of who decides whether the parties ever contracted in the first place: "The issue of the contract's validity is different from the issue whether any agreement *** was ever concluded. Our opinion today addresses only the former ***." Id. at 444 n.1. Thereafter, in *Granite Rock Co. v. Int'l Bhd. of Teamsters*, 130 S.Ct. 2847 (2010), the Court clarified that "contract formation" issues are "generally for courts to decide." Id. at 2855-56. See *Janiga v. Questar Capital Corp.*, 615 F.3d 735, 741-42 (7th Cir. 2010) (deciding contract formation issue in brokerage context in light of *Granite Rock*). Does *Granite Rock* comport with *Kaplan*?

5. Severing the Delegation Provision from the Arbitration Clause. The Supreme Court confronted a fact pattern falling somewhere between *Kaplan* and *Prima Paint* in *Rent-A-Center, West, Inc. v. Jackson*, 130 S.Ct. 2772 (2010). At issue was the unconscionability of an agreement to arbitrate which in turn contained a provision (the "delegation provision") that expressly gave the arbitrators the authority to decide whether the arbitration agreement was "void or voidable." By a vote of 5-4, the Court held that the unconscionability question was for the arbitrators to decide because the delegation provision constituted "clear and unmistakable evidence" of an agreement to that effect. Id. at 2777. Acknowledging that "the underlying contract is itself an arbitration agreement, the Court held that this fact "made no difference." Id. at 2779.

The dissent observed as follows:

> In my view, a general revocation challenge to a standalone arbitration agreement is, invariably, a challenge to the " 'making' " of the arbitration agreement itself, *Prima Paint*, 388 U.S., at 403, and therefore, under *Prima Paint*, must be decided by the court. *** Moreover, because we are dealing in this case with a challenge to an independently executed arbitration agreement-rather than a clause contained in a contract related to another subject matter-any challenge to the contract itself is also, necessarily, a challenge to the arbitration agreement. They are one and the same.
>
> The Court, however, reads the delegation clause as a distinct mini-arbitration agreement divisible from the contract in which it resides-which just so happens also to be an arbitration agreement. Although the Court simply declares that it "makes no difference" that the underlying subject matter of the agreement is itself an arbitration agreement, that proposition does not follow from-rather it is at odds with- *Prima Paint* 's severability rule.

130 S.Ct. at 2786-87 (Stevens, J., dissenting). Do you agree that the majority's holding clashes with *Prima Paint*? Does the majority's holding clash with *Kaplan*? For whom is *Jackson* a victory?

6. ***Waiving the Right to Arbitrate.*** A party can waive its right to arbitrate by proceeding to litigate the dispute at issue. See, e.g.., *Louisiana Stadium & Exploration Dist. v. Merrill Lynch Pierce Fenner & Smith, Inc.*, 626 F.3d 156 (2d Cir. 2010). In *Louisiana Stadium*, the Second Circuit had this to say about the factors that bear on a waiver defense:

> [W]e consider the following three factors: "(1) the time elapsed from when litigation was commenced until the request for arbitration; (2) the amount of litigation to date, including motion practice and discovery; and (3) proof of prejudice." *Louis Dreyfus Negoce S.A. v. Blystad Shipping & Trading Inc.*, 252 F.3d 218, 229 (2d Cir.2001). There is no rigid formula or bright-line rule for identifying when a party has waived its right to arbitration; rather, the above factors must be applied to the specific context of each particular case. That said, "[t]he key to a waiver analysis is prejudice. 'Waiver of the right to compel arbitration due to participation in litigation may be found only when prejudice to the other party is demonstrated.' " *Thyssen [Inc. v. Calypso Shipping Corp., S.A.,]*, 310 F.3d [102], 105 [2d Cir. 2002)] (quoting *Rush v. Oppenheimer & Co.*, 779 F.2d 885, 887 (2d Cir.1985)). We have recognized two types of prejudice: substantive prejudice and prejudice due to excessive cost and time delay.

Louisiana Stadium, supra, 626 F.3d at 159. Some circuit courts do not share the view that the prejudice factor is central. See, e.g., *Kahn v. Parsons Global Servs., Ltd.*, 521 F.3d 421, 425 (D.C. Cir. 2008) (noting that "[a] finding of prejudice is not necessary in order to conclude that a right to compel arbitration has been waived" but it is a germane consideration that a court may choose to take into account).

The Supreme Court expressed interest in the scope of the waiver defense by granting certiorari in *Citibank, N.A. v. Stok & Assocs., P.A.*, 387 F. App'x 921 (11th Cir. 2010). See 131 S.Ct. 1556 (2011). But it later dismissed certiorari because the parties settled the case. See 131 S.Ct. 2955 (2011).

Do you think that a successful waiver defense should turn largely on prejudice to the objecting party?

What (if any) role do the arbitrators play in connection with the waiver defense? See *Ehleiter v. Grapetree Shores, Inc.*, 482 F.3d 207 (3d Cir. 2007).

PROBLEM 13-1

Mary bought securities from Frank, an independent securities broker, who had authority to sell certain securities on behalf of Duncan, Inc., a member of the FINRA. Mary has concluded that Frank defrauded her in connection with her purchase in violation of Rule 10b-5 and she would like to hold Duncan responsible in arbitration. Mary did not enter into an arbitration agreement with Frank and she signed no agreement of any sort with Duncan.

FINRA rules require members to arbitrate "[a]ny dispute, claim, or controversy *** between a customer and a member and/or associated person arising in connection with the business of such member or in connection with the activities of such associated persons *** upon demand of the customer." Those rules define an "associated person" as "a sole proprietor, partner, officer, director or branch manager of a member, or other natural person occupying a similar status or performing similar functions, or a natural person engaged in the investment banking or securities business who is directly or indirectly controlling or controlled by a member."

Can Mary require Duncan to arbitrate her claim? Who decides that question?

Cf. *John Hancock Life Ins. Co. v. Wilson,* 254 F.3d 48 (2d Cir. 2001).

2. *Judicial Review*

The Arbitration Act gives courts authority to vacate arbitration decisions only in four narrow situations:

> (1) where the award was procured by corruption, fraud, or undue means;
>
> (2) where there was evident partiality or corruption in the arbitrators ***;
>
> (3) where the arbitrators were guilty of misconduct or other misbehavior by which the rights of any party have been prejudiced; or
>
> (4) where the arbitrators exceeded their powers.

9 U.S.C. § 10(a)(1-4). For some time, most courts have upheld the existence of an additional (albeit limited) ground for vacating arbitration decisions – "manifest disregard of the law." This ground originated in *Wilko v. Swan,* 346 U.S. 427 (1953), rev'd on other grounds, *Rodriquez de Quijas v. Shearson/Am. Express, Inc.,* 490 U.S. 477 (1989), the pertinent portion of which appears in the excerpt at the beginning of Section A of this Chapter.

Modification or vacation of a decision based on manifest disregard requires the the court to conclude both "that (1) the arbitrators knew of a governing legal principle yet refused to apply it or ignored it altogether, and (2) the law ignored by the arbitrators was well defined, explicit, and clearly applicable to the case." *Lessin v. Merrill Lynch, Pierce, Fenner & Smith, Inc.,* 481 F.3d 813, 821 (D.C. Cir. 2007) (quoting *LaPrade v. Kidder, Peabody & Co.,* 246 F.3d 702, 706 (D.C. Cir. 2001)).

The Supreme Court called into question the continued availability of the manifest disregard ground in *Hall Street Assocs., LLC v. Mattel, Inc.*, 552 U.S. 576 (2008). There the Court held that the grounds for judicial review cannot be expanded by contract. In so holding, the Court addressed whether *Wilko* had legitimated expansion of such grounds by stating that "'the interpretations of the law by the arbitrators in contrast to manifest disregard [of the law] are not subject, in the federal courts, to judicial review for error in interpretation.'" 552 U.S. at 584 (quoting *Wilko*, 346 U.S. at 436-37). The Court had the following to say about the statement in *Wilko*:

> Hall Street reads this statement as recognizing "manifest disregard of the law" as a further ground for vacatur on top of those listed in § 10, and some Circuits have read it the same way. See, e.g., *McCarthy v. Citigroup Global Markets, Inc.*, 463 F.3d 87, 91 (C.A.1 2006); *Hoeft v. MVL Group, Inc.*, 343 F.3d 57, 64 (C.A.2 2003). Hall Street sees this supposed addition to § 10 as the camel's nose: if judges can add grounds to vacate (or modify), so can contracting parties.
>
> But this is too much for *Wilko* to bear. Quite apart from its leap from a supposed judicial expansion by interpretation to a private expansion by contract, Hall Street overlooks the fact that the statement it relies on expressly rejects just what Hall Street asks for here, general review for an arbitrator's legal errors. Then there is the vagueness of *Wilko*'s phrasing. Maybe the term "manifest disregard" was meant to name a new ground for review, but maybe it merely referred to the § 10 grounds collectively, rather than adding to them. See, e.g., *Mitsubishi Motors Corp. v. Soler Chrysler-Plymouth, Inc.*, 473 U.S. 614, 656 (1985) (Stevens, J., dissenting) ("Arbitration awards are only reviewable for manifest disregard of the law, 9 U.S.C. §§ 10, 207"). Or, as some courts have thought, "manifest disregard" may have been shorthand for § 10(a)(3) or § 10(a)(4), the paragraphs authorizing vacatur when the arbitrators were "guilty of misconduct" or "exceeded their powers." See, e.g., *Kyocera*, [342 F.3d] at 997. We, when speaking as a Court, have merely taken the *Wilko* language as we found it, without embellishment, see *First Options of Chicago, Inc. v. Kaplan*, 514 U.S. 938, 942 (1995), and now that its meaning is implicated, we see no reason to accord it the significance that Hall Street urges.

552 U.S. at 584-85. Where does *Hall Street* leave "manifest disregard of the law"? The Supreme Court has acknowledged the mystery of it all: "We do not decide whether 'manifest disregard' survives our decision in *Hall Street* as an independent ground for judicial review or as a judicial gloss in the enumerated grounds for vacatur set forth in 9 U.S.C. § 10." *Stott-Nielsen, S.A. v. Animal Feeds Int'l Corp.*, 130 S.Ct. 1758, 1768 n.3 (2010).

Not surprisingly, the circuit courts are divided regarding the status of manifest disregard in the wake of *Hall Street.* Compare *Johnson v. Wells Fargo Home Mortg., Inc.,* 635 F.3d 401 (9th Cir. 2011) (manifest disregard survives) with *Citigroup Global Markets, Inc. v. Bacon*, 562 F.3d 349 (5th Cir. 2009) (manifest disregard does not survive) with *Raymond James Fin. Servs., Inc. v. Bishop*, 596 F.3d 183, 193 n.13 (4th Cir. 2010) (collecting cases but not deciding the question). What do you think?

NOTES AND QUESTIONS

1. ***Egregious But Unintentional Legal Errors.*** Why shouldn't manifest disregard encompass an egregious legal error that was made unintentionally? Consider the following view:

> If "manifest disregard" means only a legal error, *** then arbitration cannot be final. Every arbitration could be followed by a suit, seeking review of legal errors, serving the same function as an appeal within a unitary judicial system. That would prevent the parties from achieving the principal objectives of arbitration: swift, inexpensive, and conclusive resolution of disputes. If "manifest disregard" means not just any legal error but rather a "clear" error (one about which there is *** "no reasonable debate"), again arbitration could not be final, and the post-arbitration litigation would be even more complex than a search for simple error — for how blatant a legal mistake must be to count as "clear" or "manifest" error lacks any straightforward answer.

George Watts & Son, Inc. v. Tiffany & Co., 248 F.3d 577, 579 (7th Cir. 2001). Do you agree? Does the phraseology "manifest disregard" presuppose a focus on the arbitrators' intent?

2. Predispositions and Pre-existing Views. The Second Circuit's decision in *STMicroelectronics, N.V. v. Credit Suisse Secs. (USA), LLC*, 648 F.3d 68 (2d Cir. 2011) is instructive regarding several aspects of judicial review. Here Credit Suisse urged the court to overturn the panel's decision because one of the arbitrators (Duval) failed to disclose the extent of his service as an expert witness for claimants. While first characterizing its argument as a matter of "evident partiality or corruption of the arbitrators," Credit Suisse reclassified its argument as one involving "other misbehavior by which the rights of any party have been prejudiced." The court observed:

> There is a reason for Credit Suisse's switch: as it now acknowledges, the decisions under § 10(a)(2)'s "evident partiality" provision have "addresse[d] non-disclosure only of facts bearing on partiality—namely, a relationship with a party, a lawyer, or another arbitrator." Credit Suisse's contention, however, is that Duval failed to disclose (and, in fact, affirmatively misrepresented) facts bearing not on partiality but on an alleged *predisposition*. No one alleges that Duval concealed any relationship with one of the parties, whether financial, familial, or otherwise. Rather, Credit Suisse argues that Duval's experience as an expert for claimants either colored his outlook in their favor or demonstrates that his outlook was already so colored and that, either way, Credit Suisse was entitled to know about that experience before selecting him as an arbitrator. ***

STMicroelectronics, supra, 648 F.3d at 74. After rejecting the predisposition argument for lack of evidence, the court had this to say regarding predisposition arguments in general:

> More fundamentally, the major premise of Credit Suisse's attack on Duval's non-disclosure of his prior testimony fails. There is no contention here that Duval had any prior knowledge of, or misconception about, the facts of this case. Credit Suisse's argument, rather, is that his testimony suggests he had pre-existing views about potentially relevant propositions of law. However, "[a] judge's lack of predisposition regarding the relevant legal issues in a case has never been thought a necessary component of equal justice, and with good reason. For one thing, it is virtually impossible to find a judge who does not have preconceptions about the law." *Repub. Party of Minn. v. White*, 536 U.S. 765, 777 (2002). This is all the more true for arbitrators, "[t]he most sought-after" of whom "are those who are prominent and experienced members of the specific business community in which the dispute to be arbitrated arose." *Int'l Produce, Inc. v. A/S Rosshavet*, 638 F.2d 548, 552 (2d Cir.1981). *** It would be strange if such an arbitrator were forced to search the record of all prior testimony for any statement that might—however tangentially—relate to any of the many legal issues that might arise in any given case. A party might

> like to know that information when shopping for arbitrators, but its absence cannot form a ground for vacating an arbitral award. The rule for which Credit Suisse contends finds no support in the text of the FAA or the case law, and we reject it.

648 F.3d at 77. Do you regard the arbitrator-judge analogy to be a sound one?

3. Seeking Clarification. A few courts have remanded the case to the arbitration panel in order to clarify matters pertaining to the alleged grounds for the appeal. See, e.g., *Rich v. Spartis*, 516 F.3d 75, 83-84 (2d Cir. 2008) (remanding for clarification as to whether the arbitrators awarded damages that exceeded their powers); *Atlas One Fin. Group LLC v. Freecharm, Ltd.*, 2011 WL 1869420 at *2 (S.D. Fla. 2011) (remanding for clarification regarding whether the panel possessed the intent that would qualify as manifest disregard of the law). What are the pros and cons of issuing remands for clarification?

4. Decisions With and Without Explanations Revisited. Recall that arbitrators do not have to give reasons for their decisions (unless the parties jointly request it). What is the impact on judicial review?

5. Sufficient or Insufficient. In *McMahon,* you may remember, the Supreme Court asserted that "[judicial] review is sufficient to ensure that arbitrators comply with the requirements of the statute." Do you agree?

PROBLEM 13-2

Decide whether either of the following arbitrators' decisions warrants reversal based on manifest disregard of the law:

a. Following a closing argument by the customer's attorney that misrepresented the law, the arbitrators awarded the customer substantial damages. The arbitrators' decision did not indicate why damages had been awarded. The legal and factual basis for the award was tenuous at best.

b. In her closing argument to the arbitrators, the customer's attorney stated as follows: "You have to choose between following the legal technicalities and doing what is fair. In this case, fairness and the law point in very different directions." The arbitrators quoted this statement in their decision (which awarded the customer substantial damages) but did not indicate whether they found the statement persuasive. The decision did not otherwise refer to the closing arguments or offer an explanation for the award. The legal and factual basis for the award was tenuous at best.

Cf. *Montes v. Shearson Lehman Bros., Inc.*, 128 F.3d 1456 (11th Cir. 1997).

D. SECURITIES ARBITRATION IN PERSPECTIVE

The following excerpt describes the results of a survey of participants in customer-broker arbitrations, commissioned by the Securities Industry Conference on Arbitration and conducted by Professors Barbara Black and Jill Gross. The Article from which the excerpt is taken played a major role in precipitating the adoption of two important recent changes in the FINRA Customer Code about which you have read – Rule 12403 (optional all-public panels) and Rule 12904(g) (explained awards upon joint request).

WHEN PERCEPTION CHANGES REALITY: AN EMPIRICAL STUDY OF INVESTORS' VIEWS OF THE FAIRNESS OF SECURITIES ARBITRATION

By Jill I. Gross & Barbara Black

2008 J. Disp. Resol. 349

*** This survey gathered a wealth of useful data that adds to the current understanding of participants' perceptions of the fairness of securities arbitration. Our analysis of the data indicates that, overall, survey participants' perceptions of securities arbitration are nuanced, complex and resist summary categorization. Individual investors (customers), however, spoke with a clearer voice. As discussed below, customers have more negative views about their most recent securities arbitration experience than all other participants (as a group) in the process.

A. Customers Have a Favorable View of Arbitrators' Attentiveness and Competence

A majority of customers gave positive assessments, based on their experience at their most recent dispute, of the arbitrators' attentiveness at the hearing and their competence, as well as the sufficiency of time at the hearing to argue the merits of the case (although, for each question, customers' responses were less favorable than those of all other participants as a group). Thus:

- 74% of customers agreed with the positive statement that "at the hearing, the arbitration panel listened to the parties, their representatives and their witnesses," while 20% of customers disagreed with the statement. In comparison, 84% of all other participants agreed with the statement, and 10% of all other participants disagreed with it.

- 54.5% of customers agreed with the positive statement that "the arbitration panel appeared competent to resolve the dispute," while 27% of customers disagreed with the statement. In comparison, 70% of all other participants agreed with the agreement, and 20% of all other participants disagreed with it. ***

B. A Significant Percentage of Customers Believe the Arbitration Panel is Biased

The questions that generated the most negative customer reactions asked about perceptions of arbitrator impartiality, based on their most recent experience in arbitration. Thus:

- 41% of customers disagreed with the positive statement that "the arbitration panel was impartial," while 25% of customers agreed with it. In comparison, 31% of all other participants disagreed with the statement, and 48% of all other participants agreed with it.

- 40% of customers disagreed with the positive statement that "the arbitration panel was open-minded," while 28% of customers agreed with it. In comparison, 29% of all other participants disagreed with the statement, and 49% of all other participants agreed with it.

Customers were more equivocal, however, when asked directly to compare the performance of the public and the industry arbitrator *** .

C. Customers are Dissatisfied with the Outcome

Customers expressed strong dissatisfaction with the outcome of their most recent securities arbitration case. An overwhelming 71% of customers disagreed with the positive statement that "I am satisfied with the outcome," and only 22% of customers agreed with that statement. In comparison, the responses of all other participants were about equally divided, with 45% disagreeing with the statement and 46% of all other participants agreeing with it. ***

We cannot, of course, assess the basis for participants' initial expectations or their reasonableness. As expected, upon closer examination, a party's satisfaction rates tended to decrease in direct correlation to that party's degree of success in his/her most recent dispute as measured by his/her response to questions 11 (manner of resolution) and 12b (percentage of damages originally claimed that were actually awarded). Accordingly, it is clear that customers with less successful outcomes were more disappointed with the results. ***

D. Customers Do Not Believe Arbitration Compares Favorably to Litigation

The survey asked participants to compare their experience in arbitration to a comparable litigation experience. Because of the small number of customers who answered these questions, we believe the responses are of limited utility. Moreover, because so few customer-broker disputes have proceeded through the courts in the last twenty years, we doubt that many of those who responded to this question could make a valid comparison. However, from the perspective of those customers who responded, arbitration fared poorly by comparison. ***

Particularly with respect to customers, who are unlikely to have had any comparable litigation experience, these responses may be best explained as a reflection of their dissatisfaction with their arbitration experience - "anything else must be better than this."

E. Customers Lack Knowledge of the Securities Arbitration Process

Perhaps our most consistent—though not surprising—finding was the customers' lack of knowledge about securities arbitration. Individual investors stated that they have less knowledge about the arbitration process more frequently than other participants in the process. Some of this lack of knowledge relates to the composition of the arbitration panel. Thus,

- 47% of customers knew, prior to the filing of the arbitration, that one arbitrator would be an "industry arbitrator," compared with 94% of all other participants.

- 48% of customers knew, at some time during the dispute, which arbitrators were "public" and which arbitrator was "industry," compared with 88% of all other types of survey participants.

Customers also stated they "did not know" in response to questions assessing the arbitrators' performance more frequently than all other participants as a group. Customers may answer "do not know" because they believe they do not have sufficient knowledge of the substantive and procedural law governing arbitration to answer these questions. Thus,

- 33% of customers said they did not know whether "the arbitration panel did not apply the law to decide the dispute," compared to 11% of all other participants.

- 23% of customers said they did not know whether "at the hearing, the arbitration panel understood the legal arguments in the case," compared with 6% of all other participants.

- 21% of customers said they did not know whether "the arbitration panel was impartial," compared with 6% of all other participants.

- 20% of customers said they did not know whether "the arbitration panel was open-minded," compared with 7% of all other participants. ***

Moreover, in their responses to other questions relating to aspects of arbitration other than arbitrators' performance, customers said they "did not know" more frequently than all other participants. This expression of lack of knowledge, again, may reflect less familiarity with the substantive law and arbitration procedure than what all other participants are likely to have. For example, 18% of customers said that they did not know whether "the discovery process enabled me to obtain the information necessary for a hearing," compared with 4% of all other participants. ***

It is certainly not surprising that many customers express less knowledge of the process since, unlike the other participants, few of them are likely to be lawyers with an expertise in this area or members of the securities industry. While customers may believe (rightly or wrongly) that they have a good understanding of at least some aspects of the judicial system - for example, criminal trials which are frequently featured in popular media both in fictionalized and real-life accounts - they are less likely to believe this about a specialized process whose proceedings do not make headlines, are kept confidential, and are not the subject of television shows. While investors' lack of knowledge may color their views of their most recent securities arbitration experience, we have no basis to assume it results in a more negative assessment. It does indicate, however, that the forum and customers' lawyers need to step up their efforts to educate investors about brokerage firms' legal duties to their customers and, in particular, the securities arbitration process.

F. Customers Have Unfavorable Perceptions Overall of the Fairness of Securities Arbitration

Our study found that customers express a consistently negative impression of the overall arbitration process, whether based on their most recent experience or on their general impressions. Thus, 63% of customers did not believe that, overall, the process was fair, 60% of customers did not have a favorable view of arbitration, 52% of customers would not recommend arbitration to others, and 49% of customers said it was too expensive. Moreover, when directed to respond based on their overall impressions of the fairness of the securities arbitration process, customers responded even more negatively than when directed to focus on their most recent arbitration experience. Thus,

• 61% of customers disagreed with the statement that "arbitration was fair for all parties," 25% of customers agreed with the statement, and 14% of customers neither agreed nor disagreed with the statement. In comparison, 44% of all other participants disagreed with the statement, 45% of all other participants agreed with the statement, and 11% of all other participants neither agreed nor disagreed with the statement.

• 49% of customers disagreed with the statement that "arbitration was without bias," 19% of customers agreed with the statement, 19% of customers said they did not know, and 13% of customers neither agreed nor disagreed with the statement. In comparison, 41% of all other participants disagreed with the statement, 40% of all other participants agreed with the statement, 5% of all other participants said they did not know, and 14% of all other participants neither agreed nor disagreed with the statement. ***

G. Explanations for Customers' Negative Perceptions

Because the survey (intentionally) did not ask open-ended questions, we can offer only theories explaining customers' negative perceptions about the fairness of securities arbitration. Our first three theories directly stem from the process itself; our remaining theories stem from more remote factors.

1. Explanations Related to the Process

Securities Arbitration is Unfair. One explanation may be that securities arbitration is unfair. Indeed, certain of our survey data buttresses this conclusion: while 39% of customers had concerns about the fairness of the process before they filed their dispute with the arbitration forum, a disturbing 63% of customers do not agree that, after their most recent arbitration experience, the process was fair. We were particularly struck by the fact that customers' level of discontent increased by more than 20 percentage points after going through a securities arbitration proceeding.

Moreover, all recent studies of outcomes based on published awards show a decline in investors' win rates in recent years, providing some support for this theory. ***

These studies arguably provide some evidence of a decline in substantive justice for investors, although recent FINRA statistics show improved win rates for customers in 2008. The inability to assess the merits of the claims and the absence of comparable statistics for settled cases makes this evidence of limited value. However, we are aware of no study that has measured the substantive fairness of securities arbitration, taking into account both the merits of the claims and the outcomes of settled cases, nor do we think one could be readily accomplished without more transparent awards and a healthy volume of comparable cases in court or an independent arbitration forum.

Appearance of Bias. A second process-related explanation is that the mere appearance of bias from the presence of an industry arbitrator on a three-arbitrator panel fuels customers' negative perceptions, outweighing other hallmarks of procedural fairness contained in FINRA arbitration rules, such as requirements of notice, a right to be heard, fee waivers for demonstrated hardship, automatic discovery and a convenient hearing location. Our findings lend credence to this theory: 33.6% of customers had concerns about arbitrator bias pre-filing, 41% did not believe the arbitration panel was impartial in their most recent arbitration and 49% of customers disagreed with the statement that arbitration was without bias for all parties. ***

To be sure, the problem of biased arbitrators is not confined to the industry arbitrator. Investors' advocates frequently complain that some public arbitrators consistently favor brokerage firms, either by finding against the customer or awarding low damages amounts, because they want brokerage firms to select them for additional cases. One empirical study found that pro-industry arbitrators, as determined based on published awards, are selected more often to panels than pro-investor arbitrators, particularly where a large brokerage firm is a party, the requested compensatory damages are large, and the customer alleges firm misconduct. Moreover, selection on the basis of arbitrator bias increased after FINRA changed to a system where parties, and not the forum, selected the arbitrators. Ironically, the SEC approved the adoption of the Neutral List Selection System ("NLSS") because it believed "that allowing parties greater input into the selection of the arbitrators to hear their cases will help ensure a more fair and neutral arbitration process."

Investor advocates also criticize the definition of public arbitrator as including individuals who nonetheless have connections to the industry. A recent study focused on the role of attorneys as arbitrators and found that panels where the chair was an attorney who represented brokerage firms in other securities arbitrations awarded customers significantly less in compensatory damages. In contrast, the study did not find that attorneys who represented investors, or who represented both investors and firms, in securities arbitrations were more generous in awards. The study also tested for the effect of the adoption of the NLSS and found that greater party involvement in the selection process correlates with a reduction in the size of awards. It found no evidence that the 2004 rule changes that expanded the definition of non-public arbitrator and tightened the definition of public arbitrator had any effect. Both these studies suggest that brokerage firms have more influence over the arbitration forum by reason of their "repeat player" status than do customers' lawyers and that reform to place the arbitrator selection process in the control of the parties has increased firms' dominance. They also provide support for investor advocates' frequent assertion that the industry is successful in selecting public arbitrators who will side with the industry. It remains to be seen whether the SEC's 2007 approval of the revised list selection system, precluding, among other things, the industry arbitrator from serving as chairperson, as well as its 2008 approval of FINRA's tightened definition of a public arbitrator will redress these criticisms going forward.

Lack of Transparency. The absence of an explanation from most awards in customer cases is a third process-related explanation for customers' negative perceptions. While awards must be in writing and include certain identifying information about the case, the Customer Code does not require arbitrators to include reasons, authorities, or explanations in their awards (although they may choose to include them). ***

Yet, 55% of customers who responded to our survey agreed that they would be more satisfied with the outcome in their most recent arbitration if the award included an explanation. This desire for explained outcomes is consistent with procedural justice theorists who value transparency in decision-making.

Depriving participants of this element of procedural justice may very well foster negative views of the process as a whole. ***

Outcome Trumps All. One final process-centered explanation as to why customers believe securities arbitration is unfair despite many procedural protections is that outcome trumps everything. A customer, however fairly treated by objective standards, will not, in the face of an outcome he perceives as unreasonable, accept that he was treated fairly. Moreover, a customer is likely to view as unfavorable an award of damages that is considerably less than the requested amount.***

2. Explanations Unrelated to the Process

A myriad of factors unrelated to the fairness of the arbitration process itself also could contribute to customers' negative perceptions, some of which are necessarily more conjectural than others.

Investors Have Lost Money. One incontrovertible fact is that investors enter the process after a bad investment experience in which they have lost money and/or believe that they have been wronged by the industry. This fact is very likely to color their perceptions in a negative way, even if they achieve an outcome that, viewed objectively, would be considered favorable.

Unrealistic Expectations. Any attorney that represents customers knows that many of them enter the process with unrealistic expectations. Particularly if they relied on their broker's expertise, investors may have difficulty understanding that the broker is not responsible for the loss of value in the portfolio unless he has violated the law or breached a duty owed to the customer. In addition, investors may not realize that the applicable law in most jurisdictions is anti-investor. Claimants' attorneys also may unduly inflate their clients' expectations about their chances of success. Unless investors' attorneys provide them with a realistic assessment of their chances in arbitration, investors may view any outcome less than a full recovery as "unfair" and "biased" and judge the process accordingly.

Dissatisfaction with Attorney. Investors' perceptions of the arbitration process are likely to be bound up with their assessment of the performance of the attorney who represented them. We did not ask investors questions about their attorneys since this was a survey about the SRO forum. However, if the investor perceived that his lawyer acted unprofessionally, we can expect that this would negatively color his experience. Ultimately, this aspect of the arbitration experience is outside the control of the securities arbitration forum.

Contemporaneous Media Coverage. Customers' negative perceptions could be fueled by what they read in the media. Indeed, 39% of customers reported they had concerns about the fairness of the process before their claim was filed. These concerns may stem from a variety of sources including media coverage.

Exploring this hypothesis, we reviewed 51 articles on customers' securities arbitration that were printed in major newspapers between January 1, 2002 and December 31, 2006. We determined that 46% of the articles contained objective, neutral assessments of customer arbitration, 45% of them were critical of customer arbitration, and 8% contained favorable assessments of the process. Thus, contemporaneous media coverage of securities arbitration was far more negative than positive. Whether the media coverage's portrayal of securities arbitration was accurate or not is somewhat inapposite; it may well have colored customers' subjective perceptions.

The Forum Does Not Adequately Educate Investors. One fairly obvious reaction to the survey findings is that the securities arbitration forum does not adequately educate the users of its services, particularly investors, as to the process and recent reforms to increase its fairness. While there can be no doubt that additional education efforts are warranted, previous investor education initiatives in a variety of contexts have not remedied the problems they were designed to address. Thus, we are not optimistic that lack of knowledge is the sole explanation for investors' negative perceptions nor is it the sole target for correction. ***

Index

References are to Pages